# 2017 SBBI Yearbook

## Stocks, Bonds, Bills, and Inflation

U.S. Capital Markets Performance by Asset Class 1926–2016

Duff & Phelps

WILEY

Cover image: Duff & Phelps
Cover design: James Harrington

Published by John Wiley & Sons, Inc., Hoboken, New Jersey.

ISBN 978-1-119-36667-6 (Hardcover)
ISBN 978-1-119-36714-7 (ePDF)

Printed in the United States of America

10 9 8 7 6 5 4 3 2 1

APR 2 4 2017

# About the Data

The information and data presented in the *2017 Stocks, Bonds, Bills, and Inflation*® (*SBBI*®) *Yearbook* ("*2017 SBBI Yearbook*") has been obtained with the greatest of care from sources believed to be reliable, but is not guaranteed to be complete, accurate, or timely. Duff & Phelps, LLC (www.duffandphelps.com) and/or its data providers expressly disclaim any liability, including incidental or consequential damages, arising from the use of the *2017 SBBI Yearbook* or any errors or omissions that may be contained in the *2017 SBBI Yearbook,* or any other product (existing or to be developed) based upon the methodology and/or data published herein. One of the primary sources of raw data used to produce the derived data and information herein is Morningstar, Inc. Use of raw data from Morningstar, Inc. to produce the information herein does not necessarily constitute agreement by Morningstar, Inc. of any investment philosophy or strategy presented in this publication. "Stocks, Bonds, Bills, and Inflation" and "SBBI" are registered trademarks of Morningstar, Inc. All rights reserved. Used with permission.

# About Duff & Phelps

Duff & Phelps is the premier global valuation and corporate finance advisor with expertise in complex valuation, disputes and investigations, M&A, real estate, restructuring, and compliance and regulatory consulting. The firm's more than 2,000 employees serve a diverse range of clients from offices around the world. For more information, visit www.duffandphelps.com.

*M&A advisory, capital raising and secondary market advisory services in the United States are provided by Duff & Phelps Securities, LLC. Member FINRA/SIPC. Pagemill Partners is a Division of Duff & Phelps Securities, LLC. M&A advisory and capital raising advisory services are provided in a number of European countries through Duff & Phelps Securities Ltd, UK, which includes branches in Ireland and Germany. Duff & Phelps Securities Ltd, UK, is regulated by the Financial Conduct Authority.*

# Additional Resources

Duff & Phelps authors *five* books that focus on U.S. and international valuation theory, data, and risk premia (e.g., equity risk premia, risk-free rates, size premia, industry risk premia, betas, industry multiples and other statistics, etc.) for use in valuation models.

Duff & Phelps produces *one* book that focuses on U.S. capital markets performance data (i.e., the history of returns of the capital markets in the U.S. from 1926 to the present). This resource, the *Stocks, Bonds, Bills, and Inflation*® (SBBI®) *Yearbook* (this book), has been published for over 30 years.[i.1] The *SBBI Yearbook* does not provide extensive valuation data or methodology.[i.2]

The six books are:[i.3]

## U.S. and International Valuation Theory and Data

- *Cost of Capital: Applications and Examples (5th edition)*
- *Valuation Handbook – U.S. Guide to Cost of Capital*
- *Valuation Handbook – U.S. Industry Cost of Capital*
- *Valuation Handbook – International Guide to Cost of Capital*
- *Valuation Handbook – International Industry Cost of Capital*

## U.S. Capital Markets Performance Data

- *Stocks, Bonds, Bills, and Inflation (SBBI) Yearbook*

All six Duff & Phelps books are published by John Wiley & Sons (Hoboken, NJ). Each of the six books is summarized in the following sections.

---

[i.1]  "Stocks, Bonds, Bills, and Inflation" and "SBBI" are registered trademarks of Morningstar, Inc. All rights reserved. Used with permission.

[i.2]  Morningstar previously published two "Ibbotson SBBI" yearbooks: (i) The *SBBI "Classic" Yearbook*, which is now produced by Duff & Phelps and published by John Wiley & Sons as the "SBBI Yearbook" starting in 2016 (the word "Classic" was dropped from the title), and (ii) the *SBBI "Valuation" Yearbook*, which was discontinued by Morningstar in 2013. The former *SBBI Valuation Yearbook* was replaced by the *Valuation Handbook – U.S. Guide to Cost of Capital*, also produced by Duff & Phelps and published by John Wiley & Sons, starting in 2014.

[i.3]  In years 2014 through 2016, the four books comprising the Valuation Handbook series were named as follows: *Valuation Handbook – Guide to Cost of Capital*, *Valuation Handbook – Industry Cost of Capital*, *International Valuation Handbook – Guide to Cost of Capital*, and *International Valuation Handbook – Industry Cost of Capital*. Starting with the 2017 Valuation Handbook editions, the names of the four books have been changed to: *Valuation Handbook – U.S. Guide to Cost of Capital*, *Valuation Handbook – U.S. Industry Cost of Capital*, *Valuation Handbook – International Guide to Cost of Capital*, and *Valuation Handbook – International Industry Cost of Capital*, respectively. For simplicity, in all 2017 books, intra-year updates, marketing materials, online tools, etc., the new names are used (even when referring to pre-2017 editions).

**_Cost of Capital: Applications and Examples_ 5th edition**

To learn more about the latest theory and practice in cost of capital estimation, see _Cost of Capital: Applications and Examples_ 5th edition, by Shannon P. Pratt and Roger J. Grabowski (John Wiley & Sons, Inc., 2014).

The _Cost of Capital: Applications and Examples_ 5th Edition is the authoritative, comprehensive overview of valuation theory, best practices, and proper use of data. This book puts an emphasis on practical application.

The _Cost of Capital: Applications and Examples_ 5th edition is a one-stop shop for background and current thinking on the development and uses of rates of return on capital. This book contains expanded materials on estimating the basic building blocks of the cost of equity capital, the risk-free rate, and equity risk premium, plus in-depth discussion of the volatility created by the 2008 financial crisis, the subsequent recession and uncertain recovery, and how those events have fundamentally changed how we need to interpret the inputs to the models we use to develop these estimates.

The _Cost of Capital: Applications and Examples_ 5th edition includes case studies providing comprehensive discussion of cost of capital estimates for valuing a business and damages calculations for small and medium-sized businesses, cross-referenced to the chapters covering the theory and data. This book puts an emphasis on practical application. To that end, this updated edition provides readers with exclusive access to a companion website filled with supplementary materials, allowing you to continue to learn in a hands-on fashion long after closing the book.

The _Cost of Capital: Applications and Examples_ has been published since 1998, and is updated every three to four years. The 6th edition of this book is scheduled to be available in early 2018.

_"Shannon Pratt and Roger Grabowski have produced a remarkably comprehensive review of the subject...it is a work that valuation practitioners, CFOs, and others will find an invaluable reference."_

**– Professor Richard Brealey**, Emeritus Professor of Finance, London Business School (from the Foreword)

_"Estimating the cost of capital is critical in determining the valuation of assets, in evaluating the capital structure of corporations, and in estimating the long-run expected return of investments. Shannon Pratt and Roger Grabowski have the most thorough text on the subject, not only providing various estimation methods, but also numerous ways to use the cost of capital."_

**– Professor Roger G. Ibbotson,** Professor Emeritus of Finance at the Yale School of Management, Chairman and Chief Investment Officer of Zebra Capital LLC, and former Chairman and founder of Ibbotson Associates, now part of Morningstar, Inc.

### Valuation Handbook – U.S. Guide to Cost of Capital

This annual book includes the U.S. cost of capital data inputs (equity risk premia, size premia, industry risk premia, risk premia over the risk-free rate, risk-free rates) that were previously published in the Morningstar/Ibbotson *Stocks, Bonds, Bills, and Inflation* (SBBI) *Valuation Yearbook* and the Duff & Phelps *Risk Premium Report*.

The *Valuation Handbook – U.S. Guide to Cost of Capital* can be used to develop cost of equity capital estimates (using both the build-up method and CAPM) for an individual business, business ownership interest, security, or intangible asset. Includes many examples for using the data properly.

The *Valuation Handbook – U.S. Guide to Cost of Capital* has been published since 2014, and is updated annually with data through December 31 of the previous year (e.g., the *2014 Valuation Handbook – U.S. Guide to Cost of Capital* is "data through" December 31, 2013; the *2015 Valuation Handbook – U.S. Guide to Cost of Capital* is "data through" December 31, 2014, etc.). This book includes three optional intra-year quarterly updates (March, June, and September).

### Valuation Handbook – U.S. Industry Cost of Capital

This annual book provides industry-level cost of capital estimates (cost of equity capital, cost of debt capital, and weighted average cost of capital, or WACC), plus detailed industry-level statistics for sales, market capitalization, capital structure, various levered and unlevered beta estimates (e.g., ordinary-least squares (OLS) beta, sum beta, peer group beta, downside beta, etc.), valuation (trading) multiples, financial and profitability ratios, equity returns, aggregate forward-looking earnings-per share (EPS) growth rates, and more. Over 300 critical industry-level data points are calculated for approximately 180 U.S. industries (depending on data availability). Industries are organized by standard industrial classification (SIC) code.

The *Valuation Handbook – U.S. Industry Cost of Capital* can be used to benchmark, augment, and support the analyst's own custom analysis of the industry in which a subject business, business ownership interest, security, or intangible asset resides.

The *Valuation Handbook – U.S. Industry Cost of Capital* has been published since 2014, and is updated annually with data through March 31 of the current year (e.g., the *2014 Valuation Handbook – U.S. Industry Cost of Capital* is "data through" March 31, 2014; the *2015 Valuation Handbook – U.S. Industry Cost of Capital* is "data through" March 31, 2015, etc.). This book includes three optional intra-year quarterly updates (June, September, and December).

**Valuation Handbook – International Guide to Cost of Capital**

This annual book provides country-level equity risk premia (ERPs), relative volatility (RV) factors, and country risk premia (CRPs).

This book can be used to estimate country-level cost of equity capital globally, for up to 188 countries, from the perspective of investors based in any one of up to 56 countries (depending on data availability).

The *Valuation Handbook – International Guide to Cost of Capital* has been published since 2014, and is updated annually with data through December of the previous year and March of the current year (e.g., the *2014 Valuation Handbook – International Guide to Cost of Capital* is "data through" December 31, 2013 and March 31, 2014; the *2015 Valuation Handbook – International Guide to Cost of Capital* is "data through" December 31, 2014 and March 31, 2015, etc.). This book includes one optional semi-annual update with data through June and September.

*"Measuring the impact of country risk in determining the international cost of capital is one of the most vexing issues in finance. Any company doing international cost of capital estimation must, at minimum, consult the Valuation Handbook – International Guide to Cost of Capital".*

– **Campbell R. Harvey,** Professor of International Business at the Fuqua School of Business, Duke University

**Valuation Handbook – International Industry Cost of Capital**

This annual book provides the same type of rigorous industry-level analysis published in the U.S.-centric *Valuation Handbook – U.S. Industry Cost of Capital*, on a global scale.

This book includes industry-level analyses for four global economic areas: (i) the "World," (ii) the European Union, (iii) the Eurozone, and (iv) the United Kingdom.[i.4] Industries in the book are identified by their Global Industry Classification Standard (GICS) code. Each of the four global economic area's industry analyses are presented in three currencies: (i) the euro (€ or EUR), (ii) the British pound (£ or GBP), and (iii) the U.S. dollar ($ or USD).

This annual book provides industry-level cost of capital estimates (cost of equity capital, cost of debt capital, and weighted average cost of capital, or WACC), plus detailed industry-level statistics for sales, market capitalization, capital structure, various levered and unlevered beta estimates (e.g., ordinary-least squares (OLS) beta, sum beta, peer group beta, downside beta, etc.), valuation (trading) multiples, financial and profitability ratios, equity returns, aggregate forward-looking earnings-per share (EPS) growth rates, and more. Over 300 critical industry-level data points are calculated for each industry (depending on data availability). Industries are organized by global industry classification standard (GICS) code.

---

[i.4] In the *Valuation Handbook – International Industry Cost of Capital*, "World" companies are defined as companies that (i) are components of the MSCI ACWI IMI, and (ii) satisfy the rigorous screening requirements that are employed to define the company sets used therein.

The *Valuation Handbook – International Industry Cost of Capital* can be used to benchmark, augment, and support the analyst's own custom analysis of the industry in which a subject business, business ownership interest, security, or intangible asset resides.

The *Valuation Handbook – International Industry Cost of Capital* has been published since 2015, and is updated annually with data through March 31 of the current year (e.g., the *2015 Valuation Handbook – International Industry Cost of Capital* is "data through" March 31, 2015; the *2016 Valuation Handbook – International Industry Cost of Capital* is "data through" March 31, 2016, etc.). This book includes one optional semi-annual update with data through September.

To learn more about cost of capital issues, and to ensure that you are using the most recent Duff & Phelps Recommended ERP, visit www.duffandphelps.com/CostofCapital.

### Stocks, Bonds, Bills, and Inflation (SBBI) Yearbook (this book)

This annual book has been the definitive annual resource for historical U.S. capital markets performance data for over 30 years.

Starting with the 2016 edition, the *Stocks, Bonds, Bills, and Inflation (SBBI) Yearbook* is now produced by Duff & Phelps and published by John Wiley & Sons. The *SBBI Yearbook* was previously published by Morningstar, Inc. under the name "Ibbotson *Stocks, Bonds, Bills, and Inflation (SBBI) Classic Yearbook*".[i.5]

This book includes returns, index values, and statistical analyses of U.S. large company stocks, small company stocks, long-term corporate bonds, long-term government bonds, intermediate-term government bonds, U.S. Treasury bills, and inflation from January 1926 to present (monthly).

Anyone serious about investments or investing needs an appreciation of capital market history. Such an appreciation, which can be gained from this book, is equally valuable to the individual and institutional investor, practitioners and scholars in finance, economics, and business; portfolio strategists; and security analysts seeking to benchmark their own investment performance. The *SBBI Yearbook* is a thinking person's guide to using historical data to understand the financial markets and make decisions.

---

[i.5]   The *SBBI Yearbook* was published by Morningstar, Inc. from 2007 through 2015, and by Ibbotson Associates in years prior to 2007.

# Purchasing Information

## U.S. and International Valuation Theory and Data

- *Cost of Capital: Applications and Examples (5th edition)*
- *Valuation Handbook – U.S. Guide to Cost of Capital*
- *Valuation Handbook – U.S. Industry Cost of Capital*
- *Valuation Handbook – International Guide to Cost of Capital*
- *Valuation Handbook – International Industry Cost of Capital*

To order Duff & Phelps valuation data resources published by John Wiley & Sons, please visit www.wiley.com/go/ValuationHandbooks, or call:
U.S. (800) 762-2974  International (317) 572-3993 or fax (317) 572-4002.

## U.S. Capital Markets Performance Data

- *Stocks, Bonds, Bills, and Inflation (SBBI) Yearbook*

To order additional copies of the *SBBI Yearbook* (this book), please visit www.wiley.com/go/sbbiyearbook, or call: U.S. (800) 762-2974 International (317) 572-3993 or fax (317) 572-4002.

# Table of Contents

# Acknowledgements

**Author**

Roger G. Ibbotson

Professor Emeritus of Finance at the Yale School of Management, Chairman and Chief Investment Officer of Zebra Capital LLC, and former Chairman and founder of Ibbotson Associates, now part of Morningstar, Inc.

Roger G. Ibbotson and Rex A. Sinquefield, formerly a director of Dimensional Fund Advisors LP, Austin, Texas, (i) wrote the two journal articles and four books upon which the *Stocks Bonds, Bills, and Inflation (SBBI) Yearbook* is based, and (ii) formulated much of the philosophy and methodology.

**Duff & Phelps Contributors**

Roger J. Grabowski, FASA
Managing Director, Duff & Phelps

James P. Harrington
Director, Duff & Phelps

Carla Nunes, CFA
Managing Director, Duff & Phelps

**Thank you**

We thank others who contributed to this book. Rolf W. Banz provided the small stock returns for 1926–1981. Thomas S. Coleman (Executive Director, Center for Economic Policy, Harris School of Public Policy at the University of Chicago), the late Professor Lawrence Fisher (Rutgers University, The State University of New Jersey), and Roger Ibbotson constructed the model used to generate the intermediate-term government bond series for 1926–1933. The pioneering work of professors Fisher and James H. Lorie of the University of Chicago inspired the original monograph. We also wish to acknowledge the invaluable role of Dr. Stan V. Smith, President of Smith Economics Group, Ltd. and former managing director of Ibbotson Associates, who originated the idea of the *Stocks, Bonds, Bills, and Inflation (SBBI) Yearbook*.

The Center for Research in Security Prices (CRSP®) at the University Of Chicago Booth School Of Business contributed the data and methodology for the returns on the NYSE/NYSE MKT/NASDAQ by capitalization decile used in Chapter 7, "Company Size and Return."

Ken French (Roth Family Distinguished Professor of Finance at the Tuck School of Business at

Dartmouth College) and Eugene Fama (2013 Nobel laureate in economic sciences, and the Robert R. McCormick Distinguished Service Professor of Finance at the University of Chicago), contributed the data and methodology for the returns on the growth and value portfolios. Chapter 9, Liquidity Investing, was written by Roger Ibbotson, and Daniel Y.-J. Kim, Research Director of Zebra Capital Management, and Michael Holmgren, of Integrated Time Series Analytics, helped develop the empirical results. William N. Goetzmann (Edwin J. Beinecke Professor of Finance and Management Studies & Director of the International Center for Finance, Yale School of Management), Roger Ibbotson, and Liang Peng (Associate Professor of Risk Management at Penn State University), assembled the NYSE database for the period prior to 1926, while James Licato converted the research into Chapter 11, "Stock Market Returns from 1815–1925." Licato also created Chapter 12, "International Equity Investing"; and contributed to other chapters. Paul D. Kaplan, Ph.D., CFA (director of research for Morningstar Canada), was the main contributor to Chapter 10, "Using Historical Data in Forecasting and Optimization," and more recently created a set of monthly real stock market total returns going back a full 132 years in Chapter 11. Also, in Chapter 10, Kaplan and Sam Savage (a consulting professor of management science and engineering at Stanford University), present research and methodology that they have aptly dubbed "Markowitz 2.0," which promises to take traditional portfolio optimization into a new age. Kaplan and Thomas Idzorek, CPA, CFA (Head of Investment Methodology and Economic Research, Morningstar, Inc.), all continue to provide valuable insights and analysis for the *SBBI Yearbook*. We also want to thank Laurence B. Siegel (Siegel is the Gary P. Brinson director of research at the CFA Institute Research Foundation, senior advisor to OCP Capital LLC; former director director of research at the Ford Foundation (1994 to 2009) and prior to that at Ibbotson Associates).

We also thank Michael Barad (presently Head of Product Capabilities at Morningstar, Inc., and previously Head of Financial Communications at Ibbotson Associates, and then Morningstar, Inc.), and James P. Harrington (presently a Director at Duff & Phelps, co-author of the Duff & Phelps "Valuation Handbook" series, and previously director of valuation research in Morningstar's Financial Communications Business at Morningstar, Inc.) for their many contributions to the *SBBI Yearbook*.

The authors give special thanks to Senior Associate Kevin Madden and Analysts Aaron Russo and Andrew Vey of Duff & Phelps for their assistance in assembling the exhibits presented herein, analysis, editing, and quality control. We thank Executive Assistant Michelle Phillips for production assistance, and Director Kelly Hunter (both of Duff & Phelps) for securing data permissions. We also thank Drew Carter, former *SBBI Yearbook* senior editor at Morningstar Investment Management LLC, who helped transfer publishing rights and production of the yearbook to Duff & Phelps, starting with the 2016 edition.

# Introduction

Starting with last year's 2016 edition, the *Ibbotson® Stocks, Bonds, Bills, and Inflation (SBBI) Classic Yearbook* is now produced by Duff & Phelps, and published by John Wiley & Sons (Hoboken, NJ).[i.6,i.7] The book will have a slightly different name: the *Stocks, Bonds, Bills, and Inflation (SBBI) Yearbook* (or simply, "*SBBI Yearbook*").[i.8]

**The Difference Between the *2017 SBBI Yearbook* (this book) and Other Duff & Phelps Data Resources Published by John Wiley & Sons**

The *2017 SBBI Yearbook* (this book) provides historical "performance" data of U.S. asset classes, while the other Duff & Phelps data resources published by John Wiley & Sons provide "valuation" data.

Specifically, the other Duff & Phelps data resources published by John Wiley & Sons focus on U.S. and international valuation data and risk premia (e.g., equity risk premia, risk-free rates, size premia, industry risk premia, betas, industry multiples and other statistics, etc.) for use in valuation models, while the *2017 SBBI Yearbook* (this book) is (i) a history of the returns of the capital markets in the U.S. (thus the name, "Stocks, Bonds, Bills, and Inflation," or "SBBI") from 1926 to the present, and (ii) an analysis of the relative performance of U.S. asset classes. The *SBBI Yearbook* has been published for over 30 years. The *SBBI Yearbook* does not provide extensive valuation data or methodology.[i.9]

---

i.6    "Ibbotson" is a registered trademark of Morningstar, Inc. All rights reserved.

i.7    The *Ibbotson Stocks Bonds, Bills, and Inflation (SBBI) Classic Yearbook* (as it was previously named when published by Morningstar from 2006 to 2015, and Ibbotson Associates in prior years) has been published for over 30 years.

i.8    Ibbotson Associates, and then Morningstar, Inc. (Morningstar acquired Ibbotson Associates in 2006) previously published two "SBBI" yearbooks: (i) The *SBBI "Classic" Yearbook*, which is now produced by Duff & Phelps and published by John Wiley & Sons as the "SBBI Yearbook" (this book) starting in 2016 (the word "Classic" was dropped from the title), and (ii) the *SBBI "Valuation" Yearbook*, which was discontinued by Morningstar in 2013. The former *SBBI Valuation Yearbook* was replaced by the *Valuation Handbook – U.S. Guide to Cost of Capital*, also produced by Duff & Phelps and published by John Wiley & Sons, starting in 2014.

i.9    To learn more, see the previous section herein entitled "Other Duff & Phelps Valuation Data Resources Published by John Wiley & Sons", or visit www.wiley.com/go/ValuationHandbooks.

**About the *2017 SBBI Yearbook***

### A Definitive History of U.S. Asset Returns

The *2017 SBBI Yearbook* is the definitive annual resource for historical U.S. capital markets data. The *SBBI Yearbook* includes total returns, index values, and statistical analyses of U.S. large company stocks, small company stocks, long-term corporate bonds, long-term government bonds, intermediate-term government bonds, U.S. Treasury bills, and inflation from January 1926 through December 2016 (monthly).

The *SBBI Yearbook* also provides historical returns for the U.S. equity risk premium, the small stock premium, the default premium, and the horizon premium from 1926 through 2016.

### Updated Annually

The *2017 SBBI Yearbook* (this book), like the other Duff & Phelps data resources published by John Wiley & Sons, is updated annually. In the *2017 SBBI Yearbook* the historical data are updated through December 31, 2016.

### The Motivations for Writing (and Updating) the *SBBI Yearbook*

The motivations for writing (and updating) the *SBBI Yearbook* are straightforward:

- To document this history of security market returns.

- To uncover the relationships between the various asset class returns as revealed by the derived series: inflation, real interest rates, risk premiums, and other premiums.

- To encourage deeper understanding of the underlying economic history through the graphic presentation of data.

- To help answer frequently asked questions.

The asset classes analyzed in the *2017 SBBI Yearbook* highlight the differences between targeted segments of the financial markets in the United States. Our intent is to show historical trade-offs between risk and return.

In this book, the equity markets are segmented between (i) large-cap and (ii) small cap stocks. Fixed-income markets are segmented on two dimensions:

"Riskless" U.S. government securities are differentiated by maturity or investment horizon: (i) U.S. Treasury bills with approximately 30 days to maturity are used to describe the short end of the horizon, (ii) U.S. Treasury securities with approximately five years to maturity are used to describe the middle horizon segment, and (iii) U.S. Treasury securities with approximately 20 years to maturity are used to describe the long maturity end of the market.

A corporate bond series with a long maturity is used to describe fixed-income securities that contain risk of default.

Some indexes of the stock and bond markets are broad, capturing most or all of the capitalization of the market. Our indexes are intentionally narrower. The large-cap stock series captures the largest issues (those in the Standard & Poor's 500 Composite Index), while the small-cap stock series is composed of the smallest issues. By studying these polar cases, we identify the small-stock premium (small minus large stock returns) and the premium of large stocks over bonds and bills. Neither series is intended to be representative of the entire stock market.

Likewise, our long-term U.S. government bond and U.S. Treasury bill indexes show the returns for the longest and shortest ends of the yield curve, rather than the return for the entire Treasury float. Readers and investors should understand that our bond indices are not intended to (and do not) describe the experience of the typical bond investor who is diversified *across* maturities; rather, we present returns on carefully focused segments of the market for U.S. Treasury securities.

**Same Primary Data Sources**

The same data sources used to produce the data in previous versions of the *SBBI Yearbook* are used to produce the *2017 SBBI Yearbook*:

- The primary data source used herein is the Stocks, Bonds, Bills, and Inflation (SBBI) Series from Morningstar's *Direct* database. To learn more about Morningstar's *Direct* database, visit www.corporate.morningstar.com.

- The Center for Research in Security Prices (CRSP) market-cap-based NYSE/NYSE MKT/ NASDAQ indices. To learn more about the Center for Research in Security Prices at the University of Chicago Booth School of Business, visit www.crsp.com.

The *SBBI Yearbook* is updated annually with data through December 31 of the previous year (e.g., the *2016 SBBI Yearbook* is "data through" December 31, 2015; the *2017 SBBI Yearbook* (this book) is "data through" December 31, 2016. etc.).

## History of the *SBBI Yearbook*

*The Journal of Business* published Roger G. Ibbotson and Rex A. Sinquefield's two companion papers on security returns in January 1976 and July 1976. In the first paper, the authors collected historical data on the returns from stocks, government and corporate bonds, U.S. Treasury bills, and consumer goods (inflation). To uncover the risk/return and the real/nominal relationship in the historical data, they presented a framework in which the return on an asset class is the sum of two or more elemental parts. These elements, such as real returns (returns in excess of inflation) and risk premiums (for example, the net return from investing in large-capitalization stocks rather than bills), are referred to throughout the book as "derived series."[i.10]

In the second paper, the authors analyzed the time-series behavior of the derived series and the information contained in the U.S. government bond yield curve to obtain inputs for a simulation model of future security price behavior. Using the methods developed in the two papers, they forecast security returns through the year 2000:[i.11]

> *"In May 1974, in the depths of the worst bear market since the 1930s, two young men at a University of Chicago conference made a brash prediction: The Dow Jones industrial average, floundering in the 800s at the time, would hit 9,218 at the end of 1998 and get to 10,000 by November 1999.*
>
> *You probably have a good idea how things turned out: At the end of 1998, the Dow was at 9,181, just 37 points off the forecast. It hit 10,000 in March 1999, seven months early. Those two young men in Chicago in 1974 had made one of the most spectacular market calls in history."*[i.12]

The response to these works showed that historical data are fascinating in their own right. Both total and component historical returns have a wide range of applications in investment management, corporate finance, academic research, and industry regulation. Subsequent work (the 1977, 1979, and 1982 Institute of Chartered Financial Analysts monographs; the 1989 Dow Jones-Irwin Business and Investment Almanac; and the 1983 through 2016 *Ibbotson Stocks, Bonds, Bills, and Inflation Classic Yearbooks*) updated and further developed the historical data and forecasts.

In 1981, Ibbotson and Sinquefield began tracking a new asset class: small-cap stocks. This class consists of issues listed on the New York Stock Exchange that rank in the ninth and 10th (lowest) deciles when sorted by capitalization (price times number of shares outstanding), plus non-NYSE issues of comparable capitalization. This asset class has been of interest to researchers and investors because of its high long-term returns. Intermediate-term (five years to maturity)

---

[i.10]  For a detailed discussion, see Chapter 3, "Description of the Derived Series" herein.

[i.11]  Roger G. Ibbotson, Rex A. Sinquefield, *Stocks, Bonds, Bills and Inflation: The Past (1926–1976) and the Future (1977–2000)*, *The Journal of Finance* Vol. 35, No. 1 (Mar., 1980), pp. 205–209.

[i.12]  Justin Fox, "9% Forever?," *Fortune* magazine "Investor's Guide 2006," December 26, 2005.
http://archive.fortune.com/magazines/fortune/fortune_archive/2005/12/26/8364640/index.htm

government bonds were added in 1988. Monthly and annual total returns, income returns, capital appreciation returns, and yields are presented.

## Who Should Use the *SBBI Yearbook*

The *SBBI Yearbook* is a history of the returns on the capital markets in the United States from 1926 to the present. It is useful to a wide variety of readers. Foremost, anyone serious about investments or investing needs an appreciation of capital market history. Such an appreciation, which can be gained from this book, is equally valuable to the individual and institutional investor. For students at both the graduate and undergraduate levels, this book is both a source of ideas and a reference. Other intended readers include teachers of these students; practitioners and scholars in finance, economics, and business; portfolio strategists; and security analysts.

Chief financial officers and, in some cases, CEOs of corporations will find this book useful. More generally, persons concerned with history may find it valuable to study the detail of economic history as revealed in more than eight decades of capital market returns.

To these diverse readers, we provide two resources. One is the data. The other is a thinking person's guide to using historical data to understand the financial markets and make decisions. This historical record raises many questions. This book represents our way of appreciating the past only one of the many possible ways but one grounded in real theory. We provide a means for the reader to think about the past and the future of financial markets.

## Recent Changes and Additions to the *SBBI Yearbook*

The *Stocks, Bonds, Bills, and Inflation (SBBI) Yearbook* has been published for over 30 years, originally by Ibbotson Associates, and then by Morningstar, Inc.[i.13]

The most significant recent change is that starting in 2016, the *SBBI Yearbook* is now produced by Duff & Phelps, and published by John Wiley & Sons.

To order additional copies of the *2017 Stocks, Bonds, Bills, and Inflation (SBBI) Yearbook* (this book), visit www.wiley.com/go/sbbiyearbook, or call U.S. (800) 762-2974
International (317) 572-3993 or fax (317) 572-4002.

To order Duff & Phelps valuation data resources published by John Wiley & Sons, please visit: www.wiley.com/go/ValuationHandbooks.

---

[i.13] Morningstar acquired Ibbotson Associates in 2006. Morningstar published the *SBBI Yearbook* under the name *SBBI "Classic" Yearbook* from 2007–2015.

# Chapter 1
# Results of U.S. Capital Markets in 2016 and in the Past Decade

**Large-Cap Stocks**

The market for U.S. large-capitalization stocks is represented herein by the S&P 500 Total Return Index ("total return" includes the reinvestment of dividends).

U.S. Large-cap stocks posted a total return of 11.96% in 2016, up from 1.38% in 2015. Nine months of 2016 produced positive returns; March delivered the highest return at 6.78%, while January's -4.96% was the lowest. An index of large-cap stock total returns, started at $1.00 on December 31, 1925, increased to $6,035.12 by the end of 2016, up from $5,390.43 at the end of 2015.

**Small-Cap Stocks**

U.S. small-cap stocks posted a total return of 25.65% in 2016, up from -3.60% in 2015. Nine months of 2016 produced positive returns; November delivered the highest return at 13.19%, while January's -6.80% was the lowest. An index of small-cap stocks total returns, started at $1.00 on December 31, 1925, increased to $33,212.31 by the end of 2016, up from $26,433.35 at the end of 2015.

**Long-term Corporate Bonds**

U.S. long-term corporate bonds posted a total return of 6.70% in 2016, up from -1.02% in 2015. Nine months of 2016 produced positive returns; March delivered the highest return at 4.23%, while November's -5.10% was the lowest. An index of long-term corporate bonds total returns, started at $1.00 on December 31, 1925, increased to $200.40 by the end of 2016, up from $187.82 at the end of 2015.

The bond default premium, or net return from investing in long-term corporate bonds rather than investing in long-term government bonds of equal maturity, was 4.86% in 2016, compared with -0.37% in 2015.

**Long-term Government Bonds**

U.S. long-term government bonds posted a total return of 1.75% in 2016, up from -0.65% in 2015. Five months of 2016 produced positive returns; June delivered the highest return at 5.90%, while November's -5.99% was the lowest. An index of long-term government bonds total returns, started at $1.00 on December 31, 1925, increased to $134.35 by the end of 2016, up from $132.03 at the end of 2015.

## Intermediate-term Government Bonds

U.S. intermediate-term government bonds posted a total return of 1.92% in 2016, up from 1.79% in 2015. Six months of 2016 produced positive returns; January delivered the highest return at 2.33%, while November's -1.89% was the lowest. An index of intermediate-term government bonds total returns, started at $1.00 on December 31, 1925, increased to $95.78 by the end of 2016, up from $93.97 at the end of 2015.

## Treasury Bills

U.S. Treasury bills posted a total return of 0.20% in 2016, up from the 0.02% posted in 2015. All 12 months of 2016 produced positive returns; December delivered the highest return at 0.02534%, while January's 0.00604% was the lowest. An index of Treasury Bills total returns, started at $1.00 on December 31, 1925, increased to $20.63 by the end of 2016, up from $20.59 at the end of 2015.

## Inflation[1.1]

Inflation increased to 2.07% in 2016, compared to 0.73% in 2015. The result is lower than the long-term historical annual average (1926–2016) of 3.0%. Inflation has remained below 5% for 34 of the last 35 years (the exception was the 6.11% rate in 1990). A cumulative inflation index, beginning at $1.00 at year-end 1925, finished 2016 at $13.47, up from $13.20 at year-end 2015. That is, a "basket" of consumer goods and services that cost $1.00 in 1925 would cost $13.47 today. The two baskets are not identical, but are intended to be comparable.

## A Graphic View of the Decade

Exhibit 1.1 shows the market results for the past decade illustrating the growth of $1.00 invested on December 31, 2006, in stocks, bonds, and bills, along with an index of inflation. A review of the major themes of the past decade, as revealed in the capital markets, follows.

---

[1.1] The inflation rate used for the single month of December 2015 in last year's *2016 SBBI Yearbook* (0.00105760) was an estimate in the data provider's database. The value has been revised to -0.00341710, representing a difference of -0.00447470, or -0.4%. We use the revised December 2015 value in all calculations in the *2017 SBBI Yearbook* (this book); this may cause slight differences in year-end 2015 inflation calculations as appeared in the *2016 SBBI Yearbook* when compared to year-end 2015 inflation calculations as appear in the *2017 SBBI Yearbook*. For example, the annual inflation rate reported for calendar year (January–December) 2015 in last year's *2016 SBBI Yearbook* was 1.18% using the *estimated* December 2015 value, but the annual inflation rate reported for calendar year (January–December) 2015 is reported as 0.73% in the *2017 SBBI Yearbook* (this book) using the *revised* December 2015 value. Longer-term statistics are unaffected (e.g., the long-term 1926–2015 average annual inflation rate (2.98%) is identical using both the *estimated* and the *revised* December 2015 monthly value). This issue does not recur in the *2017 SBBI Yearbook* (this book); the inflation rate used for the single month of December 2016 herein is *not* an estimate; it is taken directly from the United States Department of Labor, Bureau of Labor Statistics, Consumer Price Index for All Urban Consumers, or CPI-U, not seasonally adjusted, at https://www.bls.gov/cpi/.

**Exhibit 1.1:** Wealth Indexes of Investments in U.S. Stocks, Bonds, Bills, and Inflation Index Over the Most Recent Decade (2007–2016) (Year-end 2006 = $1.00)

## The Decade in Perspective

The great stock and bond market rise of the 1980s and 1990s was one of the most unusual in the history of the capital markets. In terms of the magnitude of the rise, these decades most closely resembled the 1920s and 1950s. These four decades accounted for a majority of the market's cumulative total return over the past 91 years. While the importance of a long-term view of investing is noted consistently in this book and elsewhere, the counterpart to this observation is this: to achieve high investment returns, one needs to participate only in the few periods of truly outstanding returns. The bull markets of 1922 to mid-1929, 1949–1961 (roughly speaking, the 1950s), mid-1982 to mid-1987, and 1991–1999 were such periods. More recently, in the 8-year period since the 2008 financial crisis and ending December 2016, an investor in large and small stocks would have realized annual compound returns of approximately 14% and 17%, respectively.[1.2]

---

[1.2] An investment of $1.00 (each) at the end of December 2008 in large stocks and small stocks would have grown to $2.94 and $3.48, respectively, by the end of December 2016. This represents a compound annual return of 14.45% for large stocks, and 16.86% for small stocks over this 8-year (96-month) period.

The average annual compound rate of return of the basic SBBI series over the longer 1926–2016 period (91 years) is compared to the average annual compound rate of return of the SBBI series over the most recent 10-year period (2007–2016) in Exhibit 1.2, with the highest return for each time horizon highlighted in red.

**Exhibit 1.2:** Comparison of the Average Annual Compound Rate of Return of the Basic SBBI Series as Measured Over (i) the 1926–2016 Period (91 years) and (ii) the 2007–2016 Period (most recent 10 years)

| SBBI Series | 1926–2016 | 2007–2016 |
|---|---|---|
| Large-Cap Stocks | 10.0% | 6.9% |
| Small-Cap Stocks | 12.1% | 7.6% |
| Long-term Corp Bonds | 6.0% | 6.9% |
| Long-term Gov't Bonds | 5.5% | 6.5% |
| Inter-term Gov't Bonds | 5.1% | 4.0% |
| U.S. Treasury Bills | 3.4% | 0.7% |
| Inflation | 2.9% | 1.8% |

Looking to Exhibit 1.2, large-cap stocks, small-cap stocks, intermediate-term government bonds, and U.S. Treasury bills posted *lower* returns over the most recent 10-year period (2007–2016) than they did over the 1926–2016 period (91 years). Long-term corporate bonds and long-term government bonds, alternatively, posted *higher* returns in the 2007–2016 period than they did over the 1926–2016 period.

The annual rate of U.S. inflation over the 2007–2016 period was also lower than the rate experienced over the longer-term 1926–2016 period.

It is interesting to place the decades of superior performance in historical context. (see Exhibit 1.3) The 1920s were preceded by mediocre returns and high inflation and were followed by the most devastating stock market crash and economic depression in U.S. history. This sequence of events mitigated the impact of the 1920s bull market on investor wealth. Nevertheless, the stock market became a liquid secondary market that decade, rendering it important for reasons other than return. In contrast, the 1950s were preceded and followed by decades with roughly average equity returns. The 1980s were preceded by a decade of "stagflation", where modest stock price gains were seriously eroded by inflation and were followed by a period of stability in the 1990s.

**Exhibit 1.3:** Compound Annual Rates of Return by Decade

| SBBI Series | 1920s* | 1930s | 1940s | 1950s | 1960s | 1970s | 1980s | 1990s | 2000s | 2010s** |
|---|---|---|---|---|---|---|---|---|---|---|
| Large-Cap Stocks | 19.2% | -0.1% | 9.2% | 19.4% | 7.8% | 5.9% | 17.6% | 18.2% | -0.9% | 12.8% |
| Small-Cap Stocks | -4.5% | 1.4% | 20.7% | 16.9% | 15.5% | 11.5% | 15.8% | 15.1% | 6.3% | 15.3% |
| Long-term Corp Bonds | 5.2% | 6.9% | 2.7% | 1.0% | 1.7% | 6.2% | 13.0% | 8.4% | 7.6% | 7.8% |
| Long-term Gov't Bonds | 5.0% | 4.9% | 3.2% | -0.1% | 1.4% | 5.5% | 12.6% | 8.8% | 7.7% | 6.9% |
| Inter-term Gov't Bonds | 4.2% | 4.6% | 1.8% | 1.3% | 3.5% | 7.0% | 11.9% | 7.2% | 6.2% | 2.9% |
| U.S. Treasury Bills | 3.7% | 0.6% | 0.4% | 1.9% | 3.9% | 6.3% | 8.9% | 4.9% | 2.8% | 0.1% |
| Inflation | -1.1% | -2.0% | 5.4% | 2.2% | 2.5% | 7.4% | 5.1% | 2.9% | 2.5% | 1.6% |

*Based on the period 1926–1929. **Based on the period 2010–2016.

The bond market performance of the 1980s and 1990s has no precedent. Bond yields, which had risen consistently since the 1940s, reached unprecedented levels in 1980–1981. (Other countries experiencing massive inflation have had correspondingly high interest rates.) Never before having had so far to fall, bond yields dropped further and faster than at any other time, producing what is indisputably the greatest bond bull market in history. Unfortunately, the boom came to an end in 1994. After falling to 21-year lows one year earlier, bond yields rose in 1994 to their highest level in over three years. Both long-term and intermediate-term government bond yields have generally fallen since 2000.[1.3]

The historical themes of the past decade, as they relate to the capital markets, can be summarized in three observations. First, the 17.5-year period starting in mid-1982 and ending in 1999 was a rare span of time in which investors quickly accumulated wealth.

Second, the postwar aberration of ever-higher inflation rates ended with a dramatic decrease in inflation in the early 1980s. In the 1990s, inflation was at a 2.9% compound annual rate, significantly lower than the 5.1% and 7.4% annual compound rate of the 1980s and 1970s, respectively, and lower than the longer-term compound annual rate at the end of that decade as measured over the 1926–1999 period (3.1%). The trend of relatively low inflation has continued through the 2000s and beyond. For example, the long-term compound annual rate of inflation over the 1926–2016 period (91 years) was 2.9%, but the compound annual rate over the 2000–2009 period, the most recent 10-year period (2007–2016), and the 2010–2016 period were all significantly lower at 2.5%, 1.8%, and 1.6%, respectively.

Finally, participation in the returns of the capital markets since 1982 reached levels not approached in the 1920s, the 1950s, or even in the atypical boom period of 1967–1972. The growth since 1982 in the importance of pension funds and defined contribution pension plans, like the 401(k), as well as the rapidly increasing popularity of stock and bond mutual funds and exchange-traded products as basic savings vehicles, have enabled more individuals to experience the returns of the capital markets than ever before.

---

[1.3] The yield of SBBI long-term (i.e., approximately 20 years maturity) U.S. government bonds at the end of 1999 was 6.82%; at the end of 2016 the yield of SBBI long-term U.S. government bonds had fallen to 2.72%. The yield of SBBI intermediate-term (i.e., approximately 5 years maturity) U.S. government bonds at the end of 1999 was 6.45%; at the end of 2016 the yield of SBBI intermediate-term U.S. government bonds had fallen to 1.85%.

## Market Results for 2007–2016

Exhibit 1.4 (next page) presents (i) annual total returns for 2007–2016, (ii) quarterly and monthly total returns on the six basic asset classes and inflation for 2016, and (iii) cumulative indexes of the returns based on a starting value of $1.00 invested on December 31, 1925.

Exhibit 1.4 provides the Reader with a plethora of information about the more recent performance of the basic SBBI series which can be used to analyze recent trends. For example, large-cap stocks performed reasonably well in the most recent 10-year period (2007–2016), with 2013 providing the greatest annual return of 32.39%. The only negative return was -37.00% in 2008. Small-cap stocks performed better than large-cap stocks did over the most recent decade, even though they had more years of negative returns than large-cap stocks, with 2007, 2008, 2011, and 2015 providing -5.22%, -36.72%, -3.26%, and -3.60%, respectively. In 2013 small-cap stocks posted their largest annual returns of the decade, 45.07%, which did eclipse the 32.39% posted by large-cap stocks that year. In 2016, small-cap stocks performed significantly better than large-cap stocks, posting an annual return of 25.65% compared to the 11.96% annual return posted by large-cap stocks.

**Exhibit 1.4:** Returns and Indices of Returns on Stocks, Bonds, Bills, and Inflation; Annual, Quarterly, and Monthly Market Results, in Percent (%)

**2007–2016 Annual Returns**

| Period | Large-Cap Stocks | Small-Cap Stocks | Long-term Corp Bonds | Long-term Gov't Bonds | Inter-term Gov't Bonds | U.S. Treasury Bills | Inflation |
|---|---|---|---|---|---|---|---|
| 2007 | 5.49 | -5.22 | 2.60 | 9.88 | 10.05 | 4.66 | 4.08 |
| 2008 | -37.00 | -36.72 | 8.78 | 25.87 | 13.11 | 1.60 | 0.09 |
| 2009 | 26.46 | 28.09 | 3.02 | -14.90 | -2.40 | 0.10 | 2.72 |
| 2010 | 15.06 | 31.26 | 12.44 | 10.14 | 7.12 | 0.12 | 1.50 |
| 2011 | 2.11 | -3.26 | 17.95 | 27.10 | 8.81 | 0.04 | 2.96 |
| 2012 | 16.00 | 18.24 | 10.68 | 3.43 | 1.66 | 0.06 | 1.74 |
| 2013 | 32.39 | 45.07 | -7.07 | -12.78 | -3.68 | 0.02 | 1.51 |
| 2014 | 13.69 | 2.92 | 17.28 | 24.71 | 3.00 | 0.02 | 0.76 |
| 2015 | 1.38 | -3.60 | -1.02 | -0.65 | 1.79 | 0.02 | 0.73 |
| 2016 | 11.96 | 25.65 | 6.70 | 1.75 | 1.92 | 0.20 | 2.07 |

**2016 Quarterly Returns**

| Period | Large-Cap Stocks | Small-Cap Stocks | Long-term Corp Bonds | Long-term Gov't Bonds | Inter-term Gov't Bonds | U.S. Treasury Bills | Inflation |
|---|---|---|---|---|---|---|---|
| I-16 | 1.35 | 0.90 | 7.36 | 7.80 | 3.38 | 0.05 | 0.68 |
| II-16 | 2.46 | 1.99 | 5.46 | 6.21 | 1.43 | 0.04 | 1.21 |
| III-16 | 3.85 | 7.46 | 1.39 | -1.85 | -0.34 | 0.06 | 0.17 |
| IV-16 | 3.82 | 13.63 | -7.05 | -9.46 | -2.47 | 0.06 | 0.00 |

**2016 Monthly Returns**

| Period | Large-Cap Stocks | Small-Cap Stocks | Long-term Corp Bonds | Long-term Gov't Bonds | Inter-term Gov't Bonds | U.S. Treasury Bills | Inflation |
|---|---|---|---|---|---|---|---|
| Dec-15 | -1.58 | -4.90 | 0.00 | -0.22 | -0.17 | 0.01 | -0.34 |
| Jan-16 | -4.96 | -6.80 | 0.67 | 4.76 | 2.33 | 0.01 | 0.17 |
| Feb-16 | -0.13 | 1.10 | 2.32 | 2.94 | 0.57 | 0.02 | 0.08 |
| Mar-16 | 6.78 | 7.08 | 4.23 | -0.03 | 0.45 | 0.02 | 0.43 |
| Apr-16 | 0.39 | 1.08 | 1.46 | -0.53 | -0.10 | 0.01 | 0.47 |
| May-16 | 1.80 | 1.07 | 0.16 | 0.82 | -0.21 | 0.01 | 0.40 |
| Jun-16 | 0.26 | -0.17 | 3.77 | 5.90 | 1.75 | 0.02 | 0.33 |
| Jul-16 | 3.69 | 5.02 | 2.45 | 0.81 | 0.04 | 0.02 | -0.16 |
| Aug-16 | 0.14 | 1.59 | 0.16 | -1.40 | -0.64 | 0.02 | 0.09 |
| Sep-16 | 0.02 | 0.72 | -1.19 | -1.24 | 0.27 | 0.02 | 0.24 |
| Oct-16 | -1.82 | -3.53 | -2.63 | -3.14 | -0.52 | 0.02 | 0.12 |
| Nov-16 | 3.70 | 13.19 | -5.10 | -5.99 | -1.89 | 0.01 | -0.16 |
| Dec-16 | 1.98 | 4.06 | 0.59 | -0.57 | -0.07 | 0.03 | 0.03 |

**2007–2016 Annual Indices (Year-end 1925 = $1.00)**

| Period | Large-Cap Stocks | Small-Cap Stocks | Long-term Corp Bonds | Long-term Gov't Bonds | Inter-term Gov't Bonds | U.S. Treasury Bills | Inflation |
|---|---|---|---|---|---|---|---|
| 2007 | 3,252.974 | 15,091.094 | 105.858 | 78.779 | 71.142 | 20.186 | 11.717 |
| 2008 | 2,049.444 | 9,548.943 | 115.154 | 99.161 | 80.466 | 20.509 | 11.728 |
| 2009 | 2,591.819 | 12,230.866 | 118.628 | 84.383 | 78.532 | 20.529 | 12.047 |
| 2010 | 2,982.234 | 16,054.698 | 133.384 | 92.942 | 84.121 | 20.553 | 12.227 |
| 2011 | 3,045.212 | 15,532.068 | 157.324 | 118.130 | 91.533 | 20.562 | 12.589 |
| 2012 | 3,532.552 | 18,364.597 | 174.120 | 122.180 | 93.054 | 20.574 | 12.808 |
| 2013 | 4,676.681 | 26,641.173 | 161.802 | 106.571 | 89.630 | 20.579 | 13.001 |
| 2014 | 5,316.849 | 27,419.318 | 189.762 | 132.900 | 92.316 | 20.583 | 13.100 |
| 2015 | 5,390.425 | 26,433.349 | 187.822 | 132.032 | 93.970 | 20.586 | 13.195 |
| 2016 | 6,035.116 | 33,212.307 | 200.404 | 134.349 | 95.777 | 20.628 | 13.469 |

**2016 Monthly Indices (Year-end 1925 = $1.00)**

| Period | Large-Cap Stocks | Small-Cap Stocks | Long-term Corp Bonds | Long-term Gov't Bonds | Inter-term Gov't Bonds | U.S. Treasury Bills | Inflation |
|---|---|---|---|---|---|---|---|
| Dec-15 | 5,390.425 | 26,433.349 | 187.822 | 132.032 | 93.970 | 20.586 | 13.195 |
| Jan-16 | 5,122.930 | 24,635.881 | 189.073 | 138.310 | 96.162 | 20.588 | 13.217 |
| Feb-16 | 5,116.018 | 24,906.876 | 193.454 | 142.383 | 96.712 | 20.592 | 13.228 |
| Mar-16 | 5,463.079 | 26,670.283 | 201.640 | 142.335 | 97.146 | 20.596 | 13.285 |
| Apr-16 | 5,484.258 | 26,958.322 | 204.581 | 141.583 | 97.049 | 20.598 | 13.348 |
| May-16 | 5,582.745 | 27,246.776 | 204.915 | 142.751 | 96.842 | 20.600 | 13.402 |
| Jun-16 | 5,597.211 | 27,200.456 | 212.640 | 151.175 | 98.534 | 20.604 | 13.446 |
| Jul-16 | 5,803.573 | 28,565.919 | 217.848 | 152.393 | 98.573 | 20.608 | 13.424 |
| Aug-16 | 5,811.721 | 29,020.117 | 218.207 | 150.253 | 97.937 | 20.612 | 13.436 |
| Sep-16 | 5,812.820 | 29,229.062 | 215.605 | 148.383 | 98.199 | 20.616 | 13.469 |
| Oct-16 | 5,706.787 | 28,197.276 | 209.938 | 143.722 | 97.688 | 20.620 | 13.486 |
| Nov-16 | 5,918.137 | 31,916.497 | 199.235 | 135.120 | 95.846 | 20.622 | 13.465 |
| Dec-16 | 6,035.116 | 33,212.307 | 200.404 | 134.349 | 95.777 | 20.628 | 13.469 |

# Chapter 2
# The Long-Run Perspective

A long view of capital market history, illustrated by the 91-year period (1926–2016) examined here, uncovers the basic relationships between risk and return among the different asset classes and between nominal and real (inflation adjusted) returns. The goal of this study of asset returns is to provide a period long enough to include most or all of the major types of events that investors have experienced and may experience in the future. Such events include war and peace, growth and decline, bull and bear markets, inflation and deflation, and other less dramatic events that affect asset returns.

By studying the past, one can make inferences about the future. While the actual events that occurred during 1926–2016 will not be repeated, the event-types of that period can be expected to recur. It is sometimes said that only a few periods had unusual events, such as the stock market crash of 1929–1932 and World War II. This logic is suspicious because events that are deemed unusual happen with a certain regularity.[2.1] Some of the most unusual events of the century – the market crash of 1987, the equally remarkable inflation of the 1970s and early 1980s, the more recent events of September 11, 2001, and most recently, the 2008–2009 financial crisis – took place over the last three decades or so. To the degree that historical event-types tend to repeat themselves, the examination of past capital market returns is likely informative about what may be expected in the future.

## Stocks, Bonds, Bills, and Inflation: Historical Returns

Exhibit 2.1 depicts the growth of $1.00 invested in large-cap stocks, small-cap stocks, long-term government bonds, Treasury bills, and a hypothetical asset returning the inflation rate over the period from the end of 1925 to the end of 2016. All results assume reinvestment of dividends on stocks, or coupons on bonds, and no taxes. Transaction costs are not included, except in the small stock index starting in 1982.

Each of the cumulative index values is initialized at $1.00 at year-end 1925. The graph vividly illustrates that small-cap stocks and large-cap stocks were the big winners over the entire 91-year period: investments of $1.00 in these assets would have grown to $33,212.31 and $6,035.12, respectively, by year-end 2016. This phenomenal growth was earned by taking substantial risk. In contrast, long-term government bonds (with an approximate 20-year maturity), which exposed the holder to much less risk, grew to only $134.35.

---

[2.1] In 2010, Laurence B. Siegel, research director at the Research Foundation of the CFA Institute at the time, famously referred to these events as "black turkeys." The reference was to "black swans," the term author Nassim Nicholas Taleb gave to unfortunate events that aren't easily foreseeable. Siegel explained in a paper, "Black Swan or Black Turkey?" that market events like the global financial crisis are "everywhere in the data—(they) happen all the time" but investors are "willfully blind" to them. See: Laurence B. Siegel, "Black Swan or Black Turkey? The State of Economic Knowledge and the Crash of 2007–2009," *Financial Analysts Journal*, July/August 2010, Volume 66 Issue 4.

The lowest-risk strategy over the past 91 years (for those with short-term time horizons) was to buy U.S. Treasury bills. Because Treasury bills tended to track inflation, the resulting real (i.e., inflation-adjusted) returns were just above zero for the entire 1926–2016 period.

**Exhibit 2.1:** Wealth Indexes of Investments in the U.S. Capital Markets Index 1926–2016
(Year-end 1925 = $1.00)

### Logarithmic Scale Used on the Index Graphs

A logarithmic scale is used on the vertical axis of the index graphs presented in this book.

A logarithmic scale (see Exhibit 2.2a) allows for the direct comparison of the series' behavior at different points in time. Specifically, the use of a logarithmic scale allows the following interpretation of the data: the same vertical distance, no matter where it is measured on the graph, represents the *same* percentage change in the series. For example, on a logarithmic scale, a 50% gain from $10 to $15 occupies the same vertical distance as a 50% gain from $1,000 to $1,500. On a linear scale, the same percentage gains look different (see Exhibit 2.2b).

A logarithmic scale allows the viewer to compare investment performance across different periods; thus the viewer can concentrate on rates of return, without worrying about the number of dollars invested at any given time.

An additional (and practical) benefit of a logarithmic scale is the way the scale spreads the action out over time. It makes the graph easier to see, and makes it easier to more carefully examine the fluctuations of the individual time series in different periods.

**Exhibit 2.2a:** Logarithmic Scale

**Exhibit 2.2b:** Linear Scale

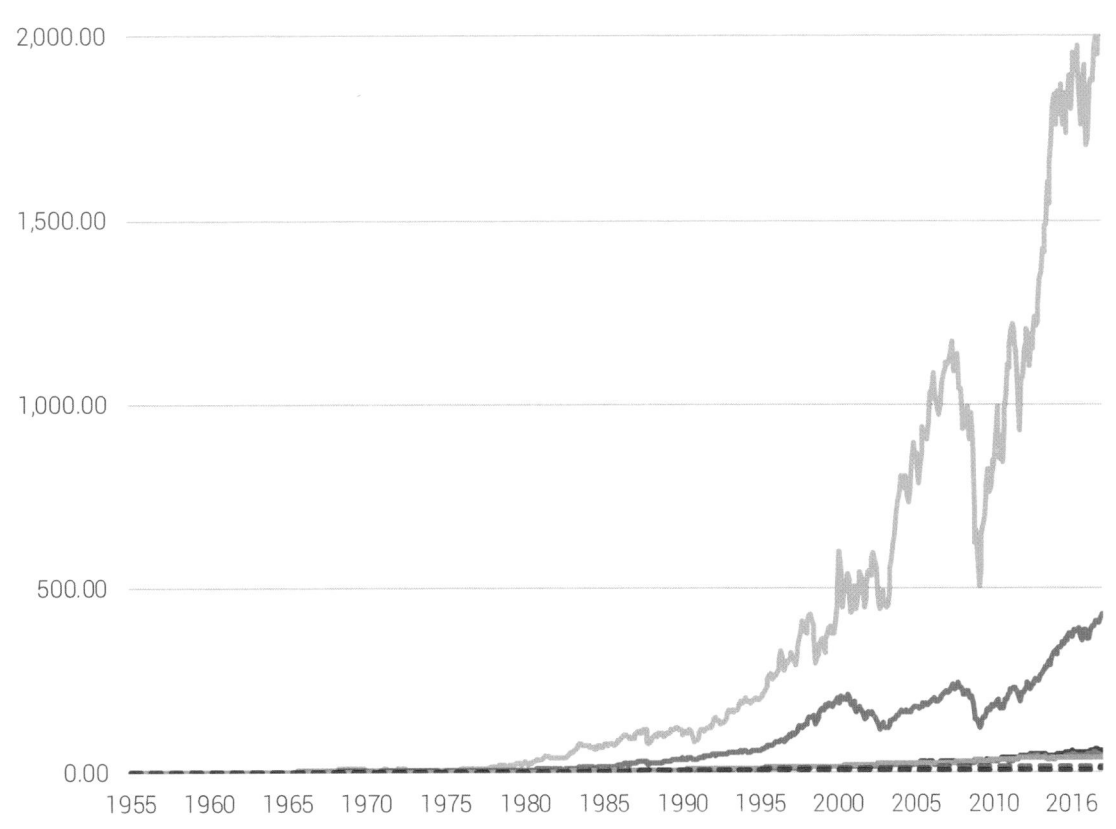

### Large-Cap Stocks

As noted above, an index of S&P 500 total returns initialized on December 31, 1925 at $1.00, closed 2016 at $6,035.12, a compound annual growth rate of 10.0%. The inflation-adjusted S&P 500 total return index closed 2016 at a level of $448.08.

### Small-Cap Stocks

Over the long run, small-capitalization stock returns surpassed the S&P 500, with the small-cap stock total return index ending 2016 at a level of $33,212.31. This represents a compound annual growth rate of 12.1%, the highest rate among the asset classes studied here.

### Long-term Corporate Bonds

Long-term corporate bonds outperformed both types of government bonds over the 1926–2016 period with a compound annual growth rate of 6.0%. This higher return reflected the risk premium that investors require for investing in corporate bonds, which are subject to the risk of default. One dollar invested in the long-term corporate bond index at year-end 1925 was worth $200.40 by the end of 2016.

### Long-term Government Bonds

The long-term government bond total return index, constructed with an approximate 20-year maturity, closed 2016 at a level of $134.35 (based on year-end 1925 equaling $1.00). Looking at capital appreciation component alone, the $1.00 index closed at $1.37, a 0.3% capital gain over the 91-year period. This indicates that the majority of the positive historical returns on long-term government bonds was due to income returns. The compound annual total return for long-term government bonds was 5.5%.

### Intermediate-term Government Bonds

One dollar invested in intermediate-term bonds at the end of 1925 rose to $95.78 by year-end 2016, compared to $93.97 at year-end 2015. The compound annual total return for intermediate-term government bonds over the 1926–2016 period was 5.1%. Capital appreciation caused $1.00 to increase to $1.68 over the 91-year period, representing a compound annual growth rate of 0.6%.

### Treasury Bills

One dollar invested in Treasury bills at the end of 1925 was worth $20.63 by year-end 2016, with a compound annual growth rate of 3.4%. Treasury bill returns followed distinct patterns, described in the next subsection. Moreover, Treasury bills tended to track inflation, so the average annual inflation-adjusted return on Treasury bills (or real riskless rate of return) was only 0.5% over the 91-year period.

## Patterns in Treasury Bill Returns

During the late 1920s and early 1930s, Treasury bill returns were just above zero. (These returns were observed during a largely deflationary period.) Beginning in late 1941, the government kept Treasury bill yields low despite high inflation rates. Treasury bills closely tracked inflation after March 1951, when Treasury bill yields were deregulated in the U.S. Treasury/Federal Reserve Accord. This tracking relationship has weakened since 1973. From 1974 to 1980, Treasury bill returns were generally lower than inflation rates. From 1981 to 2008, real returns on Treasury bills have been positive, with the exception of 2002–2005. Real Treasury bill returns have been negative from 2009 to 2016.

## Federal Reserve Operating Procedure Changes

The disparity between performance and volatility for the periods prior to and after October 1979 can be attributed to the Federal Reserve's new operating procedures. Prior to this date, the Fed used the federal funds rate as an operating target. Subsequently, the Fed de-emphasized this rate as an operating target and, instead, began to focus on the manipulation of the money supply (through non-borrowed reserves). As a result, the federal funds rate underwent much greater volatility, thereby bringing about greater volatility in Treasury returns. In the fall of 1982, however, the Federal Reserve again changed the policy procedures regarding its monetary policy. The Fed abandoned its new monetary controls and returned to a strategy of preventing excessive volatility in interest rates. Volatility in Treasury bill returns from the fall of 1979 through the fall of 1982 was significantly greater than that which has occurred since.

## Inflation

The compound annual inflation rate over 1926–2016 was 2.9%. The inflation index, initiated at $1.00 at year end 1925, grew to $13.47 by year-end 2016. It is interesting to note that the entire increase occurred during the postwar period (specifically, after April 1945).

The years 1926–1933 were generally *deflationary* in nature, and consumer prices did not rise back to their 1926 levels until April 1945. After a brief postwar spurt of inflation (in 1946 and 1947, inflation was 18.2% and 9.0%, respectively), prices rose slowly over most of the 1950s and 1960s. Then, in the 1970s, inflation reached a pace unprecedented in peacetime, peaking at 13.3% in 1979. The 1980s saw a reversion to more moderate, though still substantial, inflation rates averaging about 5% annually. Inflation rates continued to decline in the 1990s with a compound annual rate of 2.9%. Since 2000, inflation has been even milder, with a compound average rate of about 2.1%.

## Summary Statistics of Total Returns

Exhibit 2.3 presents summary statistics of the annual total returns on each asset class over the entire 91-year period of 1926–2016. The data presented in these exhibits are described in detail in Chapters 3 and 6.

**Exhibit 2.3:** Basic Series, Summary Statistics of Annual Total Returns (%)
1926–2016

| Series | Geometric Mean (%) | Arithmetic Mean (%) | Standard Deviation (%) | Distribution (%) |
|---|---|---|---|---|
| Large-Cap Stocks | 10.0 | 12.0 | 19.9 | |
| Small-Cap Stocks* | 12.1 | 16.6 | 31.9 | |
| Long-term Corp Bonds | 6.0 | 6.3 | 8.4 | |
| Long-term Gov't Bonds | 5.5 | 6.0 | 9.9 | |
| Inter-term Gov't Bonds | 5.1 | 5.3 | 5.6 | |
| U.S. Treasury Bills | 3.4 | 3.4 | 3.1 | |
| Inflation | 2.9 | 3.0 | 4.1 | |

*The 1933 small-cap stocks total return was 142.9%, and is not shown here.

-90    0    90

Chapter 2: The Long-Run Perspective

Note that in Exhibit 2.3, the arithmetic mean returns are higher than the geometric mean returns.[2.2] The difference between these two means is related to the standard deviation, or variability, of the series (see Chapter 6).

The "skylines", or histograms, in Exhibit 2.3 show the frequency distribution of returns for each asset class. The height of the skylines shows the number of years in the 1926–2016 period that had a return in that range. The histograms are shown in 5% increments (from -90% to 90%) to fully display the spectrum of returns as seen over the last 90 years, especially in stocks.

Riskier assets, such as large- and small-cap stocks, have spread-out skylines, reflecting the broad distribution of returns from very poor to very good. Less-risky assets, such as bonds, have narrow skylines that resemble a single tall building, indicating the tightness of the distribution around the mean of the series. The histogram for Treasury bills is one-sided, lying almost entirely to the right of the vertical line representing a zero return; that is, Treasury bills almost never experienced negative returns on a yearly basis over the 1926–2016 period (the only negative year was 1938). The inflation skyline shows both positive and negative annual rates. Although a few deflationary months and quarters have occurred recently, the last negative annual inflation rate occurred in 1954.

**Appreciation, Income, and Reinvestment Returns**

Exhibit 2.4 provides further detail on the returns of large-cap stocks, long-term government bonds, and intermediate-term government bonds. Total annual returns are shown as the sum of three components: capital appreciation returns, income returns, and reinvestment returns. The capital appreciation and income components are explained in Chapter 3. The third component, reinvestment return, reflects monthly income reinvested in the total return index in subsequent months in the year. Thus, for a single month the reinvestment return is zero, but over a longer period of time it is nonzero. Because the returns in Exhibit 2.4 are annual, reinvestment return is relevant.

The annual total return formed by compounding the monthly total returns does not equal the sum of the annual capital appreciation and income components; the difference is reinvestment return. A simple example illustrates this point. In 1995, an "up" year on a total return basis, the total annual return on large-cap stocks was 37.58%. The annual capital appreciation was 34.11% and the annual income return was 3.04%, totaling 37.15%. The remaining 0.43% (37.58% minus 37.15%) of the 1995 total return came from the reinvestment of dividends in the market. For more information on calculating annual total and income returns, see Chapter 5.

Monthly income and capital appreciation returns for large-cap stocks are presented at the back of this book in Appendix A-2 and Appendix A-3, respectively. Monthly income and capital appreciation returns are presented for long-term government bonds in Appendix A-7 and Appendix A-8; and for intermediate-term government bonds in Appendix A-11 and Appendix A-12.

---

[2.2]    At the 2-decimal level, Treasury Bills' annual geometric mean and arithmetic mean as measured over the 91-year period 1926–2016 are 3.38% and 3.43%, respectively.

**Exhibit 2.4:** Large-Cap Stocks, Long-term Government Bonds, and Intermediate-term Government Bonds; Annual Total, Income, Capital Appreciation, and Reinvestment Returns, and Long-term Government Bonds and Intermediate-term Government Bonds Year-end Yields (%) 1926–2016

| Year | Large-Cap Stocks Capital Appreciation Return | Income Return | Reinvestment Return | Total Return | Long-term Gov't Bonds Capital Appreciation Return | Income Return | Reinvestment Return | Total Return | Year-end Yield | Intermediate-term Gov't Bonds Capital Appreciation Return | Income Return | Reinvestment Return | Total Return | Year-end Yield |
|---|---|---|---|---|---|---|---|---|---|---|---|---|---|---|
| 1926 | 5.72 | 5.41 | 0.50 | 11.62 | 3.91 | 3.73 | 0.13 | 7.77 | 3.54 | 1.51 | 3.78 | 0.10 | 5.38 | 3.61 |
| 1927 | 30.91 | 5.71 | 0.87 | 37.49 | 5.40 | 3.41 | 0.12 | 8.93 | 3.17 | 0.96 | 3.49 | 0.07 | 4.52 | 3.40 |
| 1928 | 37.88 | 4.81 | 0.91 | 43.61 | -3.12 | 3.22 | 0.01 | 0.10 | 3.40 | -2.73 | 3.64 | 0.01 | 0.92 | 4.01 |
| 1929 | -11.91 | 3.98 | -0.49 | -8.42 | -0.20 | 3.47 | 0.15 | 3.42 | 3.40 | 1.77 | 4.07 | 0.18 | 6.01 | 3.62 |
| 1930 | -28.48 | 4.57 | -0.98 | -24.90 | 1.28 | 3.32 | 0.05 | 4.66 | 3.30 | 3.30 | 3.30 | 0.11 | 6.72 | 2.91 |
| 1931 | -47.07 | 5.35 | -1.62 | -43.34 | -8.46 | 3.33 | -0.17 | -5.31 | 4.07 | -5.40 | 3.16 | -0.08 | -2.32 | 4.12 |
| 1932 | -15.15 | 6.16 | 0.80 | -8.19 | 12.94 | 3.69 | 0.22 | 16.84 | 3.15 | 5.02 | 3.63 | 0.16 | 8.81 | 3.04 |
| 1933 | 46.59 | 6.39 | 1.01 | 53.99 | -3.14 | 3.12 | -0.05 | -0.07 | 3.36 | -0.99 | 2.83 | -0.02 | 1.83 | 3.25 |
| 1934 | -5.94 | 4.46 | 0.04 | -1.44 | 6.76 | 3.18 | 0.09 | 10.03 | 2.93 | 5.97 | 2.93 | 0.09 | 9.00 | 2.49 |
| 1935 | 41.37 | 4.95 | 1.35 | 47.67 | 2.14 | 2.81 | 0.03 | 4.98 | 2.76 | 4.94 | 2.02 | 0.05 | 7.01 | 1.63 |
| 1936 | 27.92 | 5.36 | 0.64 | 33.92 | 4.64 | 2.77 | 0.10 | 7.52 | 2.55 | 1.60 | 1.44 | 0.02 | 3.06 | 1.29 |
| 1937 | -38.59 | 4.66 | -1.09 | -35.03 | -2.48 | 2.66 | 0.05 | 0.23 | 2.73 | 0.05 | 1.48 | 0.03 | 1.56 | 1.14 |
| 1938 | 25.21 | 4.83 | 1.07 | 31.12 | 2.83 | 2.64 | 0.06 | 5.53 | 2.52 | 4.37 | 1.82 | 0.04 | 6.23 | 1.52 |
| 1939 | -5.45 | 4.69 | 0.35 | -0.41 | 3.48 | 2.40 | 0.06 | 5.94 | 2.26 | 3.18 | 1.31 | 0.03 | 4.52 | 0.98 |
| 1940 | -15.29 | 5.36 | 0.14 | -9.78 | 3.77 | 2.23 | 0.09 | 6.09 | 1.94 | 2.04 | 0.90 | 0.02 | 2.96 | 0.57 |
| 1941 | -17.86 | 6.71 | -0.44 | -11.59 | -1.01 | 1.94 | 0.00 | 0.93 | 2.04 | -0.17 | 0.67 | 0.00 | 0.50 | 0.82 |
| 1942 | 12.43 | 6.79 | 1.12 | 20.34 | 0.74 | 2.46 | 0.02 | 3.22 | 2.46 | 1.17 | 0.76 | 0.00 | 1.94 | 0.72 |
| 1943 | 19.45 | 6.24 | 0.21 | 25.90 | -0.37 | 2.44 | 0.02 | 2.08 | 2.48 | 1.23 | 1.56 | 0.02 | 2.81 | 1.45 |
| 1944 | 13.80 | 5.48 | 0.47 | 19.75 | 0.32 | 2.46 | 0.03 | 2.81 | 2.46 | 0.35 | 1.44 | 0.01 | 1.80 | 1.40 |
| 1945 | 30.72 | 4.97 | 0.74 | 36.44 | 8.27 | 2.34 | 0.12 | 10.73 | 1.99 | 1.02 | 1.19 | 0.01 | 2.22 | 1.03 |
| 1946 | -11.87 | 4.09 | -0.29 | -8.07 | -2.15 | 2.04 | 0.01 | -0.10 | 2.12 | -0.08 | 1.08 | 0.00 | 1.00 | 1.12 |
| 1947 | 0.00 | 5.49 | 0.22 | 5.71 | -4.70 | 2.13 | -0.06 | -2.62 | 2.43 | -0.30 | 1.21 | 0.00 | 0.91 | 1.34 |
| 1948 | -0.65 | 6.08 | 0.08 | 5.50 | 0.96 | 2.40 | 0.04 | 3.40 | 2.37 | 0.27 | 1.56 | 0.01 | 1.85 | 1.51 |
| 1949 | 10.26 | 7.50 | 1.03 | 18.79 | 4.15 | 2.25 | 0.06 | 6.45 | 2.09 | 0.95 | 1.36 | 0.01 | 2.32 | 1.23 |
| 1950 | 21.78 | 8.77 | 1.16 | 31.71 | -2.06 | 2.12 | 0.00 | 0.06 | 2.24 | -0.69 | 1.39 | 0.00 | 0.70 | 1.62 |
| 1951 | 16.46 | 6.91 | 0.65 | 24.02 | -6.27 | 2.38 | -0.04 | -3.93 | 2.69 | -1.63 | 1.98 | 0.01 | 0.36 | 2.17 |
| 1952 | 11.78 | 5.93 | 0.66 | 18.37 | -1.48 | 2.66 | -0.02 | 1.16 | 2.79 | -0.57 | 2.19 | 0.01 | 1.63 | 2.35 |
| 1953 | -6.62 | 5.46 | 0.18 | -0.99 | 0.67 | 2.84 | 0.12 | 3.64 | 2.74 | 0.61 | 2.55 | 0.07 | 3.23 | 2.18 |
| 1954 | 45.02 | 6.21 | 1.39 | 52.62 | 4.35 | 2.79 | 0.05 | 7.19 | 2.72 | 1.08 | 1.60 | 0.01 | 2.68 | 1.72 |
| 1955 | 26.40 | 4.56 | 0.60 | 31.56 | -4.07 | 2.75 | 0.03 | -1.29 | 2.95 | -3.10 | 2.45 | 0.00 | -0.65 | 2.80 |
| 1956 | 2.62 | 3.83 | 0.11 | 6.56 | -8.46 | 2.99 | -0.12 | -5.59 | 3.45 | -3.45 | 3.05 | -0.02 | -0.42 | 3.63 |
| 1957 | -14.31 | 3.84 | -0.30 | -10.78 | 3.82 | 3.44 | 0.20 | 7.46 | 3.23 | 4.05 | 3.59 | 0.20 | 7.84 | 2.84 |
| 1958 | 38.06 | 4.38 | 0.93 | 43.36 | -9.23 | 3.27 | -0.14 | -6.09 | 3.82 | -4.17 | 2.93 | -0.05 | -1.29 | 3.81 |
| 1959 | 8.48 | 3.31 | 0.16 | 11.96 | -6.20 | 4.01 | -0.07 | -2.26 | 4.47 | -4.56 | 4.18 | -0.01 | -0.39 | 4.98 |
| 1960 | -2.97 | 3.26 | 0.19 | 0.47 | 9.29 | 4.26 | 0.23 | 13.78 | 3.80 | 7.42 | 4.15 | 0.19 | 11.76 | 3.31 |
| 1961 | 23.13 | 3.48 | 0.28 | 26.89 | -2.86 | 3.83 | 0.00 | 0.97 | 4.15 | -1.72 | 3.54 | 0.03 | 1.85 | 3.84 |
| 1962 | -11.81 | 2.98 | 0.10 | -8.73 | 2.78 | 4.00 | 0.11 | 6.89 | 3.95 | 1.73 | 3.73 | 0.10 | 5.56 | 3.50 |
| 1963 | 18.89 | 3.61 | 0.30 | 22.80 | -2.70 | 3.89 | 0.02 | 1.21 | 4.17 | -2.10 | 3.71 | 0.03 | 1.64 | 4.04 |
| 1964 | 12.97 | 3.33 | 0.18 | 16.48 | -0.72 | 4.15 | 0.07 | 3.51 | 4.23 | -0.03 | 4.00 | 0.07 | 4.04 | 4.03 |
| 1965 | 9.06 | 3.21 | 0.18 | 12.45 | -3.45 | 4.19 | -0.04 | 0.71 | 4.50 | -3.10 | 4.15 | -0.03 | 1.02 | 4.90 |
| 1966 | -13.09 | 3.11 | -0.08 | -10.06 | -1.06 | 4.49 | 0.22 | 3.65 | 4.55 | -0.41 | 4.93 | 0.17 | 4.69 | 4.79 |
| 1967 | 20.09 | 3.64 | 0.25 | 23.98 | -13.55 | 4.59 | -0.23 | -9.18 | 5.56 | -3.85 | 4.88 | -0.02 | 1.01 | 5.77 |
| 1968 | 7.66 | 3.18 | 0.22 | 11.06 | -5.51 | 5.50 | -0.25 | -0.26 | 5.98 | -0.99 | 5.49 | 0.03 | 4.54 | 5.96 |
| 1969 | -11.36 | 2.98 | -0.13 | -8.50 | -10.83 | 5.95 | -0.19 | -5.07 | 6.87 | -7.27 | 6.65 | -0.11 | -0.74 | 8.29 |
| 1970 | 0.10 | 3.33 | 0.43 | 3.86 | 4.84 | 6.74 | 0.52 | 12.11 | 6.48 | 8.71 | 7.49 | 0.66 | 16.86 | 5.90 |

**Exhibit 2.4:** Large-Cap Stocks, Long-term Government Bonds, and Intermediate-term Government Bonds; Annual Total, Income, Capital Appreciation, and Reinvestment Returns, and Long-term Government Bonds, and Intermediate-term Government Bonds Year-end Yields (%) 1926–2016

| | Large-Cap Stocks | | | | Long-term Gov't Bonds | | | | | Intermediate-term Gov't Bonds | | | | |
|---|---|---|---|---|---|---|---|---|---|---|---|---|---|---|
| Year | Capital Appreciation Return | Income Return | Reinvestment Return | Total Return | Capital Appreciation Return | Income Return | Reinvestment Return | Total Return | Year-end Yield | Capital Appreciation Return | Income Return | Reinvestment Return | Total Return | Year-end Yield |
| 1971 | 10.63 | 3.49 | 0.18 | 14.30 | 6.61 | 6.32 | 0.31 | 13.23 | 5.97 | 2.72 | 5.75 | 0.25 | 8.72 | 5.25 |
| 1972 | 15.79 | 2.95 | 0.25 | 18.99 | -0.35 | 5.87 | 0.17 | 5.69 | 5.99 | -0.75 | 5.75 | 0.16 | 5.16 | 5.85 |
| 1973 | -17.37 | 2.86 | -0.19 | -14.69 | -7.70 | 6.51 | 0.08 | -1.11 | 7.26 | -2.19 | 6.58 | 0.22 | 4.61 | 6.79 |
| 1974 | -29.72 | 3.69 | -0.44 | -26.47 | -3.45 | 7.27 | 0.54 | 4.35 | 7.60 | -1.99 | 7.24 | 0.44 | 5.69 | 7.12 |
| 1975 | 31.55 | 5.37 | 0.31 | 37.23 | 0.73 | 7.99 | 0.47 | 9.20 | 8.05 | 0.12 | 7.35 | 0.36 | 7.83 | 7.19 |
| 1976 | 19.15 | 4.49 | 0.29 | 23.93 | 8.07 | 7.89 | 0.80 | 16.75 | 7.21 | 5.25 | 7.10 | 0.51 | 12.87 | 6.00 |
| 1977 | -11.50 | 4.35 | 0.00 | -7.16 | -7.86 | 7.14 | 0.04 | -0.69 | 8.03 | -5.15 | 6.49 | 0.06 | 1.41 | 7.51 |
| 1978 | 1.06 | 5.33 | 0.18 | 6.57 | -9.05 | 7.90 | -0.03 | -1.18 | 8.98 | -4.49 | 7.83 | 0.14 | 3.49 | 8.83 |
| 1979 | 12.31 | 5.89 | 0.41 | 18.61 | -9.84 | 8.86 | -0.25 | -1.23 | 10.12 | -5.07 | 9.04 | 0.12 | 4.09 | 10.33 |
| 1980 | 25.77 | 5.74 | 0.99 | 32.50 | -14.00 | 9.97 | 0.08 | -3.95 | 11.99 | -6.81 | 10.55 | 0.17 | 3.91 | 12.45 |
| 1981 | -9.73 | 4.88 | -0.08 | -4.92 | -10.33 | 11.55 | 0.64 | 1.86 | 13.34 | -4.55 | 12.97 | 1.03 | 9.45 | 13.96 |
| 1982 | 14.76 | 5.61 | 1.18 | 21.55 | 23.95 | 13.50 | 2.91 | 40.36 | 10.95 | 14.23 | 12.81 | 2.06 | 29.10 | 9.90 |
| 1983 | 17.27 | 5.04 | 0.24 | 22.56 | -9.82 | 10.38 | 0.09 | 0.65 | 11.97 | -3.30 | 10.35 | 0.35 | 7.41 | 11.41 |
| 1984 | 1.40 | 4.57 | 0.31 | 6.27 | 2.32 | 11.74 | 1.42 | 15.48 | 11.70 | 1.22 | 11.68 | 1.12 | 14.02 | 11.04 |
| 1985 | 26.33 | 4.72 | 0.67 | 31.73 | 17.84 | 11.25 | 1.88 | 30.97 | 9.56 | 9.01 | 10.29 | 1.04 | 20.33 | 8.55 |
| 1986 | 14.62 | 3.92 | 0.13 | 18.67 | 14.99 | 8.98 | 0.56 | 24.53 | 7.89 | 6.99 | 7.72 | 0.43 | 15.14 | 6.85 |
| 1987 | 2.03 | 3.64 | -0.41 | 5.25 | -10.69 | 7.92 | 0.06 | -2.71 | 9.20 | -4.75 | 7.47 | 0.19 | 2.90 | 8.32 |
| 1988 | 12.40 | 3.99 | 0.22 | 16.61 | 0.36 | 8.97 | 0.34 | 9.67 | 9.19 | -2.26 | 8.24 | 0.13 | 6.10 | 9.17 |
| 1989 | 27.25 | 4.03 | 0.40 | 31.69 | 8.62 | 8.81 | 0.68 | 18.11 | 8.16 | 4.34 | 8.46 | 0.49 | 13.29 | 7.94 |
| 1990 | -6.56 | 3.43 | 0.03 | -3.10 | -2.61 | 8.19 | 0.61 | 6.18 | 8.44 | 1.02 | 8.15 | 0.56 | 9.73 | 7.70 |
| 1991 | 26.31 | 3.76 | 0.40 | 30.47 | 10.10 | 8.22 | 0.98 | 19.30 | 7.30 | 7.36 | 7.43 | 0.67 | 15.46 | 5.97 |
| 1992 | 4.46 | 2.98 | 0.17 | 7.62 | 0.34 | 7.26 | 0.45 | 8.05 | 7.26 | 0.64 | 6.27 | 0.28 | 7.19 | 6.11 |
| 1993 | 7.06 | 2.91 | 0.12 | 10.08 | 10.71 | 7.17 | 0.35 | 18.24 | 6.54 | 5.56 | 5.53 | 0.15 | 11.24 | 5.22 |
| 1994 | -1.54 | 2.83 | 0.03 | 1.32 | -14.29 | 6.59 | -0.08 | -7.77 | 7.99 | -11.14 | 6.07 | -0.08 | -5.14 | 7.80 |
| 1995 | 34.11 | 3.04 | 0.43 | 37.58 | 23.04 | 7.60 | 1.03 | 31.67 | 6.03 | 9.66 | 6.69 | 0.45 | 16.80 | 5.38 |
| 1996 | 20.26 | 2.43 | 0.26 | 22.96 | -7.37 | 6.18 | 0.26 | -0.93 | 6.73 | -3.90 | 5.82 | 0.18 | 2.10 | 6.16 |
| 1997 | 31.01 | 2.10 | 0.25 | 33.36 | 8.51 | 6.64 | 0.71 | 15.85 | 6.02 | 1.95 | 6.14 | 0.30 | 8.38 | 5.73 |
| 1998 | 26.67 | 1.67 | 0.24 | 28.58 | 6.89 | 5.83 | 0.34 | 13.06 | 5.42 | 4.66 | 5.29 | 0.25 | 10.21 | 4.68 |
| 1999 | 19.53 | 1.36 | 0.15 | 21.04 | -14.35 | 5.57 | -0.19 | -8.96 | 6.82 | -7.06 | 5.30 | -0.01 | -1.77 | 6.45 |
| 2000 | -10.14 | 1.11 | -0.07 | -9.10 | 14.36 | 6.50 | 0.62 | 21.48 | 5.58 | 5.94 | 6.19 | 0.46 | 12.59 | 5.07 |
| 2001 | -13.04 | 1.18 | -0.03 | -11.89 | -1.89 | 5.53 | 0.06 | 3.70 | 5.75 | 3.23 | 4.27 | 0.12 | 7.62 | 4.42 |
| 2002 | -23.37 | 1.39 | -0.13 | -22.10 | 11.69 | 5.59 | 0.56 | 17.84 | 4.84 | 8.65 | 3.98 | 0.30 | 12.93 | 2.61 |
| 2003 | 26.38 | 1.99 | 0.31 | 28.68 | -3.36 | 4.80 | 0.01 | 1.45 | 5.11 | -0.48 | 2.85 | 0.03 | 2.40 | 2.97 |
| 2004 | 8.99 | 1.76 | 0.13 | 10.88 | 3.26 | 5.02 | 0.23 | 8.51 | 4.84 | -1.07 | 3.28 | 0.04 | 2.25 | 3.47 |
| 2005 | 3.00 | 1.84 | 0.07 | 4.91 | 3.02 | 4.69 | 0.10 | 7.81 | 4.61 | -2.58 | 3.92 | 0.03 | 1.36 | 4.34 |
| 2006 | 13.62 | 2.01 | 0.17 | 15.79 | -3.64 | 4.68 | 0.15 | 1.19 | 4.91 | -1.51 | 4.54 | 0.11 | 3.14 | 4.65 |
| 2007 | 3.53 | 1.96 | 0.00 | 5.49 | 4.69 | 4.86 | 0.33 | 9.88 | 4.50 | 5.33 | 4.44 | 0.28 | 10.05 | 3.28 |
| 2008 | -38.49 | 1.92 | -0.43 | -37.00 | 20.50 | 4.45 | 0.93 | 25.87 | 3.03 | 9.92 | 2.96 | 0.23 | 13.11 | 1.26 |
| 2009 | 23.45 | 2.48 | 0.53 | 26.46 | -18.25 | 3.47 | -0.12 | -14.90 | 4.58 | -4.42 | 2.01 | 0.00 | -2.40 | 2.42 |
| 2010 | 12.78 | 2.02 | 0.26 | 15.06 | 5.89 | 4.25 | 0.00 | 10.14 | 4.14 | 5.16 | 1.92 | 0.04 | 7.12 | 1.70 |
| 2011 | 0.00 | 2.13 | -0.01 | 2.11 | 22.62 | 3.82 | 0.66 | 27.10 | 2.55 | 7.09 | 1.64 | 0.08 | 8.81 | 0.74 |
| 2012 | 13.41 | 2.50 | 0.10 | 16.00 | 0.95 | 2.46 | 0.03 | 3.43 | 2.46 | 0.93 | 0.73 | 0.01 | 1.66 | 0.61 |
| 2013 | 29.60 | 2.48 | 0.31 | 32.39 | -15.70 | 2.88 | 0.04 | -12.78 | 3.78 | -4.68 | 1.02 | -0.01 | -3.68 | 1.49 |
| 2014 | 11.39 | 2.16 | 0.14 | 13.69 | 20.93 | 3.41 | 0.37 | 24.71 | 2.46 | 1.35 | 1.63 | 0.02 | 3.00 | 1.55 |
| 2015 | -0.73 | 2.10 | 0.01 | 1.38 | -3.11 | 2.47 | -0.02 | -0.65 | 2.68 | 0.29 | 1.51 | 0.00 | 1.79 | 1.69 |
| 2016 | 9.54 | 2.26 | 0.17 | 11.96 | -0.40 | 2.30 | -0.14 | 1.75 | 2.72 | 0.58 | 1.36 | -0.02 | 1.92 | 1.85 |

## Annual Total Returns

Exhibit 2.5 shows annual total returns for the six basic asset classes and inflation for the full 91-year period. This exhibit can be used to compare the performance of each asset class for the same year. Monthly total returns for large-cap stocks, small-cap stocks, long-term corporate bonds, long-term government bonds, intermediate-term government bonds, Treasury bills, and inflation rates are presented in Appendices A-1, A-4, A-5, A-6, A-10, A-14, and A-15, respectively.

## Rolling-Period Returns

Exhibits 2.6, 2.7, and 2.8 show the compound annual total returns of the six basic classes and inflation for five-, 10-, and 20-year holding periods, respectively. Often, these calculations are referred to as rolling period returns because they are obtained by rolling a data window of fixed length along each time series. They are useful for examining the behavior of returns for holding periods similar to those actually experienced by investors and show the effects of time diversification. Holding assets for long periods of time has the effect of lowering the risk of experiencing a loss in asset value.

The highest and lowest returns on the SBBI basic series, expressed as annual rates, are shown for one-, five-, 10-, and 20-year holding periods in Exhibit 2.9. This exhibit also shows the number of times that an asset had a positive return, and the number of times that an asset's return was the highest among all those studied. The number of times positive (or times highest) is compared to the total number of observations – that is, 91 annual, 87 overlapping five-year, 82 overlapping 10-year, and 72 overlapping 20-year holding periods.

## Portfolio Performance

A portfolio is a group of assets, such as stocks and bonds that are held by an investor. Because stocks, bonds, and cash generally do not react identically to the same economic or market stimulus, combining these assets can often produce a better risk-adjusted return. There were plenty of years in which stock returns were up at times when bond returns were down, and vice versa, according to the data in Exhibit 2.4. These offsetting movements can assist in reducing portfolio volatility. Some recent examples include the years 2000 through 2002: Large-cap stocks posted returns of -9.10%, -11.89%, and -22.10%, respectively, while long-term government bonds posted positive returns of 21.48%, 3.70%, and 17.84%, respectively. This illustrates the low correlation of stocks and bonds; that is, they tend (but not always) to move independently of each other. (See Chapter 6 for a more detailed discussion of correlation.)

While bond prices tend to fluctuate less than stock prices, they are still subject to price movement. Investing in a mix of asset classes, such as stocks, bonds, and Treasury bills (cash), may protect a portfolio from major downswings in a single asset class. One of the main advantages of diversification is that it makes investors less dependent on the performance of any single asset class.

## Rolling Period Portfolio Returns

While Exhibit 2.9 displays the performance of single asset classes over various rolling periods, Exhibits 2.10 through 2.14 show the performance of different portfolio allocations over various periods. Once again, Exhibit 2.10 outlines the number of times that each portfolio has a positive return, and the number of times that each portfolio's return was the highest among all those studied. Maximum and minimum returns are also shown. The portfolios presented throughout the analysis are rebalanced so that the allocations remain the same. The exception is Exhibit 2.12, which contains portfolios that were never rebalanced; this is for comparison purposes. The data assumes reinvestment of all income and does not account for taxes or transaction costs.

The one-year holding period results in Exhibit 2.10 make it clear that 1933 was a great year for large-cap stocks, while long-term government bonds shined in 1982. The 30% stock and 70% bond portfolio posted positive returns during all five-year holding periods, while the 70% stock and 30% bond portfolio was never the highest returning portfolio during the five-year holding periods. The 10-year holding period analysis shows that the 100% stock, the 100% bond, and the 90% stock and 10% bond portfolios were the only ones that posted negative 10-year holding period returns. For the 20-year period, there were no negative holding period returns. The effects of time diversification are clearly evident. When portfolios, as well as individual asset classes, are held for longer periods of time, the possibility of losing portfolio value is lowered.

**Exhibit 2.5:** Basic Series
Annual Total Returns (%)
1926–2016

| Year | Large-Cap Stocks | Small-Cap Stocks | Long-term Corp Bonds | Long-term Gov't Bonds | Inter-term Gov't Bonds | U.S. Treasury Bills | Inflation |
|------|------|------|------|------|------|------|------|
| 1926 | 11.62 | 0.28 | 7.37 | 7.77 | 5.38 | 3.27 | -1.49 |
| 1927 | 37.49 | 22.10 | 7.44 | 8.93 | 4.52 | 3.12 | -2.08 |
| 1928 | 43.61 | 39.69 | 2.84 | 0.10 | 0.92 | 3.56 | -0.97 |
| 1929 | -8.42 | -51.36 | 3.27 | 3.42 | 6.01 | 4.75 | 0.20 |
| 1930 | -24.90 | -38.15 | 7.98 | 4.66 | 6.72 | 2.41 | -6.03 |
| 1931 | -43.34 | -49.75 | -1.85 | -5.31 | -2.32 | 1.07 | -9.52 |
| 1932 | -8.19 | -5.39 | 10.82 | 16.84 | 8.81 | 0.96 | -10.30 |
| 1933 | 53.99 | 142.87 | 10.38 | -0.07 | 1.83 | 0.30 | 0.51 |
| 1934 | -1.44 | 24.22 | 13.84 | 10.03 | 9.00 | 0.16 | 2.03 |
| 1935 | 47.67 | 40.19 | 9.61 | 4.98 | 7.01 | 0.17 | 2.99 |
| 1936 | 33.92 | 64.80 | 6.74 | 7.52 | 3.06 | 0.18 | 1.21 |
| 1937 | -35.03 | -58.01 | 2.75 | 0.23 | 1.56 | 0.31 | 3.10 |
| 1938 | 31.12 | 32.80 | 6.13 | 5.53 | 6.23 | -0.02 | -2.78 |
| 1939 | -0.41 | 0.35 | 3.97 | 5.94 | 4.52 | 0.02 | -0.48 |
| 1940 | -9.78 | -5.16 | 3.39 | 6.09 | 2.96 | 0.00 | 0.96 |
| 1941 | -11.59 | -9.00 | 2.73 | 0.93 | 0.50 | 0.06 | 9.72 |
| 1942 | 20.34 | 44.51 | 2.60 | 3.22 | 1.94 | 0.27 | 9.29 |
| 1943 | 25.90 | 88.37 | 2.83 | 2.08 | 2.81 | 0.35 | 3.16 |
| 1944 | 19.75 | 53.72 | 4.73 | 2.81 | 1.80 | 0.33 | 2.11 |
| 1945 | 36.44 | 73.61 | 4.08 | 10.73 | 2.22 | 0.33 | 2.25 |
| 1946 | -8.07 | -11.63 | 1.72 | -0.10 | 1.00 | 0.35 | 18.16 |
| 1947 | 5.71 | 0.92 | -2.34 | -2.62 | 0.91 | 0.50 | 9.01 |
| 1948 | 5.50 | -2.11 | 4.14 | 3.40 | 1.85 | 0.81 | 2.71 |
| 1949 | 18.79 | 19.75 | 3.31 | 6.45 | 2.32 | 1.10 | -1.80 |
| 1950 | 31.71 | 38.75 | 2.12 | 0.06 | 0.70 | 1.20 | 5.79 |
| 1951 | 24.02 | 7.80 | -2.69 | -3.93 | 0.36 | 1.49 | 5.87 |
| 1952 | 18.37 | 3.03 | 3.52 | 1.16 | 1.63 | 1.66 | 0.88 |
| 1953 | -0.99 | -6.49 | 3.41 | 3.64 | 3.23 | 1.82 | 0.62 |
| 1954 | 52.62 | 60.58 | 5.39 | 7.19 | 2.68 | 0.86 | -0.50 |
| 1955 | 31.56 | 20.44 | 0.48 | -1.29 | -0.65 | 1.57 | 0.37 |
| 1956 | 6.56 | 4.28 | -6.81 | -5.59 | -0.42 | 2.46 | 2.86 |
| 1957 | -10.78 | -14.57 | 8.71 | 7.46 | 7.84 | 3.14 | 3.02 |
| 1958 | 43.36 | 64.89 | -2.22 | -6.09 | -1.29 | 1.54 | 1.76 |
| 1959 | 11.96 | 16.40 | -0.97 | -2.26 | -0.39 | 2.95 | 1.50 |
| 1960 | 0.47 | -3.29 | 9.07 | 13.78 | 11.76 | 2.66 | 1.48 |
| 1961 | 26.89 | 32.09 | 4.82 | 0.97 | 1.85 | 2.13 | 0.67 |
| 1962 | -8.73 | -11.90 | 7.95 | 6.89 | 5.56 | 2.73 | 1.22 |
| 1963 | 22.80 | 23.57 | 2.19 | 1.21 | 1.64 | 3.12 | 1.65 |
| 1964 | 16.48 | 23.52 | 4.77 | 3.51 | 4.04 | 3.54 | 1.19 |
| 1965 | 12.45 | 41.75 | -0.46 | 0.71 | 1.02 | 3.93 | 1.92 |
| 1966 | -10.06 | -7.01 | 0.20 | 3.65 | 4.69 | 4.76 | 3.35 |
| 1967 | 23.98 | 83.57 | -4.95 | -9.18 | 1.01 | 4.21 | 3.04 |
| 1968 | 11.06 | 35.97 | 2.57 | -0.26 | 4.54 | 5.21 | 4.72 |
| 1969 | -8.50 | -25.05 | -8.09 | -5.07 | -0.74 | 6.58 | 6.11 |
| 1970 | 3.86 | -17.43 | 18.37 | 12.11 | 16.86 | 6.52 | 5.49 |
| 1971 | 14.30 | 16.50 | 11.01 | 13.23 | 8.72 | 4.39 | 3.36 |
| 1972 | 18.99 | 4.43 | 7.26 | 5.69 | 5.16 | 3.84 | 3.41 |
| 1973 | -14.69 | -30.90 | 1.14 | -1.11 | 4.61 | 6.93 | 8.80 |
| 1974 | -26.47 | -19.95 | -3.06 | 4.35 | 5.69 | 8.00 | 12.20 |
| 1975 | 37.23 | 52.82 | 14.64 | 9.20 | 7.83 | 5.80 | 7.01 |

**Exhibit 2.5:** Basic Series
Annual Total Returns (%)
1926–2016

| Year | Large-Cap Stocks | Small-Cap Stocks | Long-term Corp Bonds | Long-term Gov't Bonds | Inter-term Gov't Bonds | U.S. Treasury Bills | Inflation |
|---|---|---|---|---|---|---|---|
| 1976 | 23.93 | 57.38 | 18.65 | 16.75 | 12.87 | 5.08 | 4.81 |
| 1977 | -7.16 | 25.38 | 1.71 | -0.69 | 1.41 | 5.12 | 6.77 |
| 1978 | 6.57 | 23.46 | -0.07 | -1.18 | 3.49 | 7.18 | 9.03 |
| 1979 | 18.61 | 43.46 | -4.18 | -1.23 | 4.09 | 10.38 | 13.31 |
| 1980 | 32.50 | 39.88 | -2.76 | -3.95 | 3.91 | 11.24 | 12.40 |
| 1981 | -4.92 | 13.88 | -1.24 | 1.86 | 9.45 | 14.71 | 8.94 |
| 1982 | 21.55 | 28.01 | 42.56 | 40.36 | 29.10 | 10.54 | 3.87 |
| 1983 | 22.56 | 39.67 | 6.26 | 0.65 | 7.41 | 8.80 | 3.80 |
| 1984 | 6.27 | -6.67 | 16.86 | 15.48 | 14.02 | 9.85 | 3.95 |
| 1985 | 31.73 | 24.66 | 30.09 | 30.97 | 20.33 | 7.72 | 3.77 |
| 1986 | 18.67 | 6.85 | 19.85 | 24.53 | 15.14 | 6.16 | 1.13 |
| 1987 | 5.25 | -9.30 | -0.27 | -2.71 | 2.90 | 5.47 | 4.41 |
| 1988 | 16.61 | 22.87 | 10.70 | 9.67 | 6.10 | 6.35 | 4.42 |
| 1989 | 31.69 | 10.18 | 16.23 | 18.11 | 13.29 | 8.37 | 4.65 |
| 1990 | -3.10 | -21.56 | 6.78 | 6.18 | 9.73 | 7.81 | 6.11 |
| 1991 | 30.47 | 44.63 | 19.89 | 19.30 | 15.46 | 5.60 | 3.06 |
| 1992 | 7.62 | 23.35 | 9.39 | 8.05 | 7.19 | 3.51 | 2.90 |
| 1993 | 10.08 | 20.98 | 13.19 | 18.24 | 11.24 | 2.90 | 2.75 |
| 1994 | 1.32 | 3.11 | -5.76 | -7.77 | -5.14 | 3.90 | 2.67 |
| 1995 | 37.58 | 34.46 | 27.20 | 31.67 | 16.80 | 5.60 | 2.54 |
| 1996 | 22.96 | 17.62 | 1.40 | -0.93 | 2.10 | 5.21 | 3.32 |
| 1997 | 33.36 | 22.78 | 12.95 | 15.85 | 8.38 | 5.26 | 1.70 |
| 1998 | 28.58 | -7.31 | 10.76 | 13.06 | 10.21 | 4.86 | 1.61 |
| 1999 | 21.04 | 29.79 | -7.45 | -8.96 | -1.77 | 4.68 | 2.68 |
| 2000 | -9.10 | -3.59 | 12.87 | 21.48 | 12.59 | 5.89 | 3.39 |
| 2001 | -11.89 | 22.77 | 10.65 | 3.70 | 7.62 | 3.83 | 1.55 |
| 2002 | -22.10 | -13.28 | 16.33 | 17.84 | 12.93 | 1.65 | 2.38 |
| 2003 | 28.68 | 60.70 | 5.27 | 1.45 | 2.40 | 1.02 | 1.88 |
| 2004 | 10.88 | 18.39 | 8.72 | 8.51 | 2.25 | 1.20 | 3.26 |
| 2005 | 4.91 | 5.69 | 5.87 | 7.81 | 1.36 | 2.98 | 3.42 |
| 2006 | 15.79 | 16.17 | 3.24 | 1.19 | 3.14 | 4.80 | 2.54 |
| 2007 | 5.49 | -5.22 | 2.60 | 9.88 | 10.05 | 4.66 | 4.08 |
| 2008 | -37.00 | -36.72 | 8.78 | 25.87 | 13.11 | 1.60 | 0.09 |
| 2009 | 26.46 | 28.09 | 3.02 | -14.90 | -2.40 | 0.10 | 2.72 |
| 2010 | 15.06 | 31.26 | 12.44 | 10.14 | 7.12 | 0.12 | 1.50 |
| 2011 | 2.11 | -3.26 | 17.95 | 27.10 | 8.81 | 0.04 | 2.96 |
| 2012 | 16.00 | 18.24 | 10.68 | 3.43 | 1.66 | 0.06 | 1.74 |
| 2013 | 32.39 | 45.07 | -7.07 | -12.78 | -3.68 | 0.02 | 1.51 |
| 2014 | 13.69 | 2.92 | 17.28 | 24.71 | 3.00 | 0.02 | 0.76 |
| 2015 | 1.38 | -3.60 | -1.02 | -0.65 | 1.79 | 0.02 | 0.73 |
| 2016 | 11.96 | 25.65 | 6.70 | 1.75 | 1.92 | 0.20 | 2.07 |

**Exhibit 2.6:** Basic Series

Compound Annual Returns for 5-Year Holding Periods (% per annum)

1926–2016

| 5-Year Period | Large-Cap Stocks | Small-Cap Stocks | Long-term Corp Bonds | Long-term Gov't Bonds | Inter-term Gov't Bonds | U.S. Treasury Bills | Inflation |
|---|---|---|---|---|---|---|---|
| 1926–1930 | 8.68 | -12.44 | 5.76 | 4.93 | 4.69 | 3.42 | -2.10 |
| 1927–1931 | -5.10 | -23.74 | 3.87 | 2.25 | 3.11 | 2.98 | -3.75 |
| 1928–1932 | -12.47 | -27.54 | 4.52 | 3.69 | 3.95 | 2.54 | -5.42 |
| 1929–1933 | -11.24 | -19.06 | 6.01 | 3.66 | 4.13 | 1.89 | -5.14 |
| 1930–1934 | -9.93 | -2.37 | 8.09 | 4.95 | 4.71 | 0.98 | -4.80 |
| 1931–1935 | 3.12 | 14.99 | 8.42 | 5.01 | 4.77 | 0.53 | -3.04 |
| 1932–1936 | 22.47 | 45.83 | 10.26 | 7.71 | 5.90 | 0.35 | -0.84 |
| 1933–1937 | 14.29 | 23.96 | 8.60 | 4.46 | 4.45 | 0.22 | 1.96 |
| 1934–1938 | 10.67 | 9.86 | 7.75 | 5.61 | 5.33 | 0.16 | 1.29 |
| 1935–1939 | 10.91 | 5.27 | 5.81 | 4.81 | 4.46 | 0.13 | 0.78 |
| 1936–1940 | 0.50 | -2.64 | 4.59 | 5.03 | 3.65 | 0.10 | 0.38 |
| 1937–1941 | -7.51 | -13.55 | 3.79 | 3.71 | 3.13 | 0.08 | 2.02 |
| 1938–1942 | 4.62 | 10.70 | 3.76 | 4.32 | 3.21 | 0.07 | 3.21 |
| 1939–1943 | 3.77 | 18.71 | 3.10 | 3.63 | 2.54 | 0.14 | 4.44 |
| 1940–1944 | 7.67 | 29.28 | 3.25 | 3.01 | 2.00 | 0.20 | 4.98 |
| 1941–1945 | 16.96 | 45.90 | 3.39 | 3.90 | 1.85 | 0.27 | 5.25 |
| 1942–1946 | 17.87 | 45.05 | 3.19 | 3.69 | 1.95 | 0.33 | 6.82 |
| 1943–1947 | 14.86 | 35.00 | 2.17 | 2.49 | 1.75 | 0.37 | 6.77 |
| 1944–1948 | 10.87 | 18.43 | 2.43 | 2.75 | 1.55 | 0.47 | 6.67 |
| 1945–1949 | 10.69 | 12.66 | 2.15 | 3.46 | 1.66 | 0.62 | 5.84 |
| 1946–1950 | 9.91 | 7.72 | 1.76 | 1.39 | 1.36 | 0.79 | 6.57 |
| 1947–1951 | 16.70 | 12.09 | 0.87 | 0.60 | 1.23 | 1.02 | 4.25 |
| 1948–1952 | 19.37 | 12.55 | 2.05 | 1.37 | 1.37 | 1.25 | 2.65 |
| 1949–1953 | 17.86 | 11.53 | 1.91 | 1.41 | 1.64 | 1.45 | 2.23 |
| 1950–1954 | 23.92 | 18.27 | 2.31 | 1.55 | 1.72 | 1.41 | 2.50 |
| 1951–1955 | 23.89 | 14.97 | 1.98 | 1.28 | 1.44 | 1.48 | 1.43 |
| 1952–1956 | 20.18 | 14.21 | 1.10 | 0.93 | 1.28 | 1.67 | 0.84 |
| 1953–1957 | 13.58 | 10.01 | 2.10 | 2.15 | 2.49 | 1.97 | 1.27 |
| 1954–1958 | 22.31 | 23.22 | 0.96 | 0.16 | 1.58 | 1.91 | 1.49 |
| 1955–1959 | 14.96 | 15.54 | -0.29 | -1.67 | 0.96 | 2.33 | 1.90 |
| 1956–1960 | 8.92 | 10.58 | 1.36 | 1.16 | 3.37 | 2.55 | 2.12 |
| 1957–1961 | 12.79 | 15.93 | 3.77 | 2.53 | 3.83 | 2.48 | 1.68 |
| 1958–1962 | 13.31 | 16.65 | 3.63 | 2.42 | 3.39 | 2.40 | 1.33 |
| 1959–1963 | 9.85 | 10.11 | 4.55 | 3.97 | 4.00 | 2.72 | 1.30 |
| 1960–1964 | 10.73 | 11.43 | 5.73 | 5.17 | 4.91 | 2.83 | 1.24 |
| 1961–1965 | 13.25 | 20.28 | 3.82 | 2.63 | 2.81 | 3.09 | 1.33 |
| 1962–1966 | 5.72 | 12.13 | 2.88 | 3.17 | 3.38 | 3.61 | 1.86 |
| 1963–1967 | 12.39 | 29.86 | 0.30 | -0.14 | 2.47 | 3.91 | 2.23 |
| 1964–1968 | 10.16 | 32.37 | 0.37 | -0.43 | 3.04 | 4.33 | 2.84 |
| 1965–1969 | 4.96 | 19.78 | -2.22 | -2.14 | 2.08 | 4.93 | 3.82 |
| 1966–1970 | 3.31 | 7.51 | 1.23 | -0.02 | 5.10 | 5.45 | 4.54 |
| 1967–1971 | 8.38 | 12.47 | 3.32 | 1.77 | 5.90 | 5.38 | 4.54 |
| 1968–1972 | 7.50 | 0.47 | 5.85 | 4.90 | 6.75 | 5.30 | 4.61 |
| 1969–1973 | 1.97 | -12.25 | 5.55 | 4.72 | 6.77 | 5.65 | 5.41 |
| 1970–1974 | -2.39 | -11.09 | 6.68 | 6.72 | 8.11 | 5.93 | 6.60 |
| 1971–1975 | 3.21 | 0.56 | 6.00 | 6.16 | 6.39 | 5.78 | 6.90 |
| 1972–1976 | 4.89 | 6.80 | 7.42 | 6.82 | 7.19 | 5.92 | 7.20 |
| 1973–1977 | -0.19 | 10.77 | 6.29 | 5.50 | 6.41 | 6.18 | 7.89 |
| 1974–1978 | 4.35 | 24.41 | 6.03 | 5.48 | 6.18 | 6.23 | 7.94 |
| 1975–1979 | 14.82 | 39.80 | 5.78 | 4.33 | 5.86 | 6.69 | 8.15 |

Chapter 2: The Long-Run Perspective

**Exhibit 2.6:** Basic Series
Compound Annual Returns for 5-Year Holding Periods (% per annum)
1926–2016

| 5-Year Period | Large-Cap Stocks | Small-Cap Stocks | Long-term Corp Bonds | Long-term Gov't Bonds | Inter-term Gov't Bonds | U.S. Treasury Bills | Inflation |
|---|---|---|---|---|---|---|---|
| 1976–1980 | 14.02 | 37.35 | 2.36 | 1.68 | 5.08 | 7.77 | 9.21 |
| 1977–1981 | 8.13 | 28.75 | -1.33 | -1.05 | 4.44 | 9.67 | 10.06 |
| 1978–1982 | 14.12 | 29.28 | 5.57 | 6.03 | 9.60 | 10.78 | 9.46 |
| 1979–1983 | 17.35 | 32.51 | 6.87 | 6.42 | 10.42 | 11.12 | 8.39 |
| 1980–1984 | 14.80 | 21.59 | 11.20 | 9.80 | 12.45 | 11.01 | 6.53 |
| 1981–1985 | 14.67 | 18.82 | 17.86 | 16.83 | 15.80 | 10.30 | 4.85 |
| 1982–1986 | 19.87 | 17.32 | 22.51 | 21.62 | 16.98 | 8.60 | 3.30 |
| 1983–1987 | 16.47 | 9.51 | 14.06 | 13.02 | 11.79 | 7.59 | 3.41 |
| 1984–1988 | 15.31 | 6.74 | 15.00 | 14.98 | 11.52 | 7.10 | 3.53 |
| 1985–1989 | 20.36 | 10.34 | 14.88 | 15.50 | 11.38 | 6.81 | 3.67 |
| 1986–1990 | 13.19 | 0.58 | 10.43 | 10.75 | 9.34 | 6.83 | 4.13 |
| 1987–1991 | 15.36 | 6.86 | 10.44 | 9.81 | 9.40 | 6.71 | 4.52 |
| 1988–1992 | 15.88 | 13.63 | 12.50 | 12.14 | 10.30 | 6.31 | 4.22 |
| 1989–1993 | 14.55 | 13.28 | 13.00 | 13.84 | 11.35 | 5.61 | 3.89 |
| 1990–1994 | 8.70 | 11.79 | 8.36 | 8.34 | 7.46 | 4.73 | 3.49 |
| 1991–1995 | 16.59 | 24.51 | 12.22 | 13.10 | 8.81 | 4.29 | 2.79 |
| 1992–1996 | 15.22 | 19.47 | 8.52 | 8.98 | 6.17 | 4.22 | 2.84 |
| 1993–1997 | 20.27 | 19.35 | 9.22 | 10.51 | 6.40 | 4.57 | 2.60 |
| 1994–1998 | 24.06 | 13.16 | 8.74 | 9.52 | 6.20 | 4.96 | 2.37 |
| 1995–1999 | 28.56 | 18.49 | 8.35 | 9.24 | 6.95 | 5.12 | 2.37 |
| 1996–2000 | 18.33 | 10.87 | 5.79 | 7.49 | 6.17 | 5.18 | 2.54 |
| 1997–2001 | 10.70 | 11.82 | 7.66 | 8.48 | 7.29 | 4.90 | 2.18 |
| 1998–2002 | -0.59 | 4.31 | 8.29 | 8.85 | 8.18 | 4.17 | 2.32 |
| 1999–2003 | -0.57 | 16.44 | 7.20 | 6.51 | 6.60 | 3.40 | 2.37 |
| 2000–2004 | -2.30 | 14.32 | 10.70 | 10.32 | 7.46 | 2.70 | 2.49 |
| 2001–2005 | 0.54 | 16.44 | 9.30 | 7.72 | 5.22 | 2.13 | 2.49 |
| 2002–2006 | 6.19 | 15.16 | 7.79 | 7.19 | 4.33 | 2.32 | 2.69 |
| 2003–2007 | 12.83 | 17.23 | 5.12 | 5.70 | 3.79 | 2.92 | 3.03 |
| 2004–2008 | -2.19 | -2.71 | 5.81 | 10.36 | 5.88 | 3.04 | 2.67 |
| 2005–2009 | 0.42 | -1.16 | 4.68 | 5.13 | 4.90 | 2.81 | 2.56 |
| 2006–2010 | 2.29 | 3.21 | 5.94 | 5.58 | 6.06 | 2.23 | 2.18 |
| 2007–2011 | -0.25 | -0.50 | 8.80 | 10.50 | 7.20 | 1.29 | 2.26 |
| 2008–2012 | 1.66 | 4.00 | 10.47 | 9.17 | 5.52 | 0.38 | 1.80 |
| 2009–2013 | 17.94 | 22.78 | 7.04 | 1.45 | 2.18 | 0.07 | 2.08 |
| 2010–2014 | 15.45 | 17.52 | 9.85 | 9.51 | 3.29 | 0.05 | 1.69 |
| 2011–2015 | 12.57 | 10.49 | 7.08 | 7.27 | 2.24 | 0.03 | 1.54 |
| 2012–2016 | 14.66 | 16.42 | 4.96 | 2.61 | 0.91 | 0.06 | 1.36 |

**Exhibit 2.7:** Basic Series
Compound Annual Returns for 10-Year Holding Periods (% per annum)
1926–2016

| 10-Year Period | Large-Cap Stocks | Small-Cap Stocks | Long-term Corp Bonds | Long-term Gov't Bonds | Inter-term Gov't Bonds | U.S. Treasury Bills | Inflation |
|---|---|---|---|---|---|---|---|
| 1926–1935 | 5.86 | 0.34 | 7.08 | 4.97 | 4.73 | 1.97 | -2.57 |
| 1927–1936 | 7.81 | 5.45 | 7.02 | 4.95 | 4.50 | 1.66 | -2.30 |
| 1928–1937 | 0.02 | -5.22 | 6.54 | 4.08 | 4.20 | 1.37 | -1.80 |
| 1929–1938 | -0.89 | -5.70 | 6.88 | 4.63 | 4.73 | 1.02 | -1.98 |
| 1930–1939 | -0.05 | 1.38 | 6.95 | 4.88 | 4.58 | 0.55 | -2.05 |
| 1931–1940 | 1.80 | 5.81 | 6.49 | 5.02 | 4.21 | 0.32 | -1.34 |
| 1932–1941 | 6.43 | 12.28 | 6.97 | 5.69 | 4.51 | 0.21 | 0.58 |
| 1933–1942 | 9.35 | 17.14 | 6.15 | 4.39 | 3.83 | 0.15 | 2.59 |
| 1934–1943 | 7.17 | 14.20 | 5.40 | 4.62 | 3.93 | 0.15 | 2.85 |
| 1935–1944 | 9.28 | 16.66 | 4.53 | 3.91 | 3.22 | 0.17 | 2.86 |
| 1936–1945 | 8.42 | 19.18 | 3.99 | 4.46 | 2.75 | 0.18 | 2.79 |
| 1937–1946 | 4.41 | 11.98 | 3.49 | 3.70 | 2.54 | 0.20 | 4.39 |
| 1938–1947 | 9.62 | 22.24 | 2.96 | 3.40 | 2.48 | 0.22 | 4.97 |
| 1939–1948 | 7.26 | 18.57 | 2.77 | 3.19 | 2.04 | 0.30 | 5.55 |
| 1940–1949 | 9.17 | 20.69 | 2.70 | 3.24 | 1.83 | 0.41 | 5.41 |
| 1941–1950 | 13.38 | 25.37 | 2.57 | 2.64 | 1.60 | 0.53 | 5.91 |
| 1942–1951 | 17.28 | 27.51 | 2.02 | 2.13 | 1.59 | 0.67 | 5.53 |
| 1943–1952 | 17.09 | 23.27 | 2.11 | 1.93 | 1.56 | 0.81 | 4.69 |
| 1944–1953 | 14.31 | 14.93 | 2.17 | 2.08 | 1.60 | 0.96 | 4.43 |
| 1945–1954 | 17.12 | 15.43 | 2.23 | 2.51 | 1.69 | 1.01 | 4.16 |
| 1946–1955 | 16.69 | 11.29 | 1.87 | 1.33 | 1.40 | 1.14 | 3.96 |
| 1947–1956 | 18.43 | 13.14 | 0.98 | 0.76 | 1.25 | 1.35 | 2.53 |
| 1948–1957 | 16.44 | 11.27 | 2.07 | 1.76 | 1.93 | 1.61 | 1.96 |
| 1949–1958 | 20.06 | 17.23 | 1.43 | 0.79 | 1.61 | 1.68 | 1.86 |
| 1950–1959 | 19.35 | 16.90 | 1.00 | -0.07 | 1.34 | 1.87 | 2.20 |
| 1951–1960 | 16.16 | 12.75 | 1.67 | 1.22 | 2.40 | 2.01 | 1.77 |
| 1952–1961 | 16.43 | 15.07 | 2.43 | 1.73 | 2.55 | 2.08 | 1.26 |
| 1953–1962 | 13.44 | 13.28 | 2.86 | 2.29 | 2.94 | 2.19 | 1.30 |
| 1954–1963 | 15.91 | 16.48 | 2.74 | 2.05 | 2.78 | 2.31 | 1.40 |
| 1955–1964 | 12.82 | 13.47 | 2.68 | 1.69 | 2.92 | 2.58 | 1.57 |
| 1956–1965 | 11.06 | 15.33 | 2.58 | 1.89 | 3.09 | 2.82 | 1.73 |
| 1957–1966 | 9.20 | 14.02 | 3.33 | 2.85 | 3.60 | 3.05 | 1.77 |
| 1958–1967 | 12.85 | 23.08 | 1.95 | 1.13 | 2.93 | 3.15 | 1.78 |
| 1959–1968 | 10.00 | 20.73 | 2.44 | 1.75 | 3.52 | 3.52 | 2.07 |
| 1960–1969 | 7.81 | 15.53 | 1.68 | 1.45 | 3.48 | 3.88 | 2.52 |
| 1961–1970 | 8.16 | 13.72 | 2.51 | 1.30 | 3.95 | 4.26 | 2.92 |
| 1962–1971 | 7.04 | 12.30 | 3.10 | 2.47 | 4.63 | 4.49 | 3.19 |
| 1963–1972 | 9.92 | 14.22 | 3.04 | 2.35 | 4.59 | 4.60 | 3.41 |
| 1964–1973 | 5.99 | 7.77 | 2.93 | 2.11 | 4.89 | 4.98 | 4.12 |
| 1965–1974 | 1.22 | 3.20 | 2.13 | 2.20 | 5.05 | 5.43 | 5.20 |
| 1966–1975 | 3.26 | 3.98 | 3.59 | 3.03 | 5.74 | 5.62 | 5.71 |
| 1967–1976 | 6.62 | 9.60 | 5.35 | 4.26 | 6.54 | 5.65 | 5.86 |
| 1968–1977 | 3.58 | 5.50 | 6.07 | 5.20 | 6.58 | 5.74 | 6.24 |
| 1969–1978 | 3.15 | 4.48 | 5.79 | 5.10 | 6.47 | 5.94 | 6.67 |
| 1970–1979 | 5.87 | 11.49 | 6.23 | 5.52 | 6.98 | 6.31 | 7.37 |
| 1971–1980 | 8.48 | 17.53 | 4.16 | 3.90 | 5.73 | 6.77 | 8.05 |
| 1972–1981 | 6.50 | 17.26 | 2.95 | 2.81 | 5.80 | 7.78 | 8.62 |
| 1973–1982 | 6.72 | 19.67 | 5.93 | 5.76 | 8.00 | 8.46 | 8.67 |
| 1974–1983 | 10.66 | 28.40 | 6.45 | 5.95 | 8.28 | 8.65 | 8.16 |
| 1975–1984 | 14.81 | 30.38 | 8.46 | 7.03 | 9.11 | 8.83 | 7.34 |
| 1976–1985 | 14.34 | 27.75 | 9.84 | 8.99 | 10.31 | 9.03 | 7.01 |
| 1977–1986 | 13.85 | 22.90 | 9.95 | 9.70 | 10.53 | 9.14 | 6.63 |

**Exhibit 2.7:** Basic Series
Compound Annual Returns for 10-Year Holding Periods (% per annum)
1926–2016

| 10-Year Period | Large-Cap Stocks | Small-Cap Stocks | Long-term Corp Bonds | Long-term Gov't Bonds | Inter-term Gov't Bonds | U.S. Treasury Bills | Inflation |
|---|---|---|---|---|---|---|---|
| 1978–1987 | 15.29 | 18.99 | 9.73 | 9.47 | 10.69 | 9.17 | 6.39 |
| 1979–1988 | 16.33 | 18.93 | 10.86 | 10.62 | 10.97 | 9.09 | 5.93 |
| 1980–1989 | 17.55 | 15.83 | 13.02 | 12.62 | 11.91 | 8.89 | 5.09 |
| 1981–1990 | 13.93 | 9.32 | 14.09 | 13.75 | 12.52 | 8.55 | 4.49 |
| 1982–1991 | 17.59 | 11.97 | 16.32 | 15.56 | 13.13 | 7.65 | 3.91 |
| 1983–1992 | 16.17 | 11.55 | 13.28 | 12.58 | 11.04 | 6.95 | 3.81 |
| 1984–1993 | 14.93 | 9.96 | 14.00 | 14.41 | 11.43 | 6.35 | 3.71 |
| 1985–1994 | 14.38 | 11.06 | 11.57 | 11.86 | 9.40 | 5.76 | 3.58 |
| 1986–1995 | 14.88 | 11.90 | 11.32 | 11.92 | 9.08 | 5.55 | 3.46 |
| 1987–1996 | 15.29 | 12.98 | 9.48 | 9.39 | 7.77 | 5.46 | 3.68 |
| 1988–1997 | 18.05 | 16.46 | 10.85 | 11.32 | 8.33 | 5.44 | 3.41 |
| 1989–1998 | 19.21 | 13.22 | 10.85 | 11.66 | 8.74 | 5.29 | 3.12 |
| 1990–1999 | 18.21 | 15.09 | 8.36 | 8.79 | 7.20 | 4.92 | 2.93 |
| 1991–2000 | 17.46 | 17.49 | 8.96 | 10.26 | 7.48 | 4.74 | 2.66 |
| 1992–2001 | 12.94 | 15.58 | 8.09 | 8.73 | 6.73 | 4.56 | 2.51 |
| 1993–2002 | 9.34 | 11.58 | 8.75 | 9.67 | 7.29 | 4.37 | 2.46 |
| 1994–2003 | 11.07 | 14.79 | 7.97 | 8.01 | 6.40 | 4.18 | 2.37 |
| 1995–2004 | 12.07 | 16.39 | 9.52 | 9.78 | 7.20 | 3.90 | 2.43 |
| 1996–2005 | 9.07 | 13.62 | 7.53 | 7.60 | 5.69 | 3.64 | 2.52 |
| 1997–2006 | 8.42 | 13.48 | 7.72 | 7.83 | 5.80 | 3.60 | 2.44 |
| 1998–2007 | 5.91 | 10.58 | 6.69 | 7.26 | 5.96 | 3.54 | 2.68 |
| 1999–2008 | -1.38 | 6.44 | 6.50 | 8.42 | 6.24 | 3.22 | 2.52 |
| 2000–2009 | -0.95 | 6.30 | 7.65 | 7.69 | 6.17 | 2.76 | 2.52 |
| 2001–2010 | 1.41 | 9.63 | 7.61 | 6.64 | 5.64 | 2.18 | 2.34 |
| 2002–2011 | 2.92 | 7.05 | 8.30 | 8.83 | 5.76 | 1.80 | 2.48 |
| 2003–2012 | 7.10 | 10.42 | 7.76 | 7.42 | 4.65 | 1.64 | 2.41 |
| 2004–2013 | 7.41 | 9.29 | 6.42 | 5.81 | 4.01 | 1.54 | 2.38 |
| 2005–2014 | 7.67 | 7.77 | 7.23 | 7.30 | 4.09 | 1.42 | 2.12 |
| 2006–2015 | 7.31 | 6.79 | 6.51 | 6.42 | 4.13 | 1.13 | 1.86 |
| 2007–2016 | 6.95 | 7.63 | 6.86 | 6.48 | 4.01 | 0.67 | 1.81 |

**Exhibit 2.8:** Basic Series
Compound Annual Returns for 20-Year Holding Periods (% per annum)
1926–2016

| 20-Year Period | Large-Cap Stocks | Small-Cap Stocks | Long-term Corp Bonds | Long-term Gov't Bonds | Inter-term Gov't Bonds | U.S. Treasury Bills | Inflation |
|---|---|---|---|---|---|---|---|
| 1926–1945 | 7.13 | 9.36 | 5.52 | 4.72 | 3.73 | 1.07 | 0.07 |
| 1927–1946 | 6.10 | 8.67 | 5.24 | 4.32 | 3.51 | 0.93 | 0.99 |
| 1928–1947 | 4.71 | 7.64 | 4.74 | 3.74 | 3.33 | 0.80 | 1.53 |
| 1929–1948 | 3.11 | 5.74 | 4.80 | 3.91 | 3.38 | 0.66 | 1.72 |
| 1930–1949 | 4.46 | 10.61 | 4.80 | 4.06 | 3.20 | 0.48 | 1.61 |
| 1931–1950 | 7.43 | 15.17 | 4.51 | 3.82 | 2.90 | 0.42 | 2.22 |
| 1932–1951 | 11.72 | 19.65 | 4.47 | 3.90 | 3.04 | 0.44 | 3.02 |
| 1933–1952 | 13.15 | 20.16 | 4.11 | 3.15 | 2.69 | 0.48 | 3.63 |
| 1934–1953 | 10.68 | 14.56 | 3.77 | 3.34 | 2.76 | 0.55 | 3.64 |
| 1935–1954 | 13.13 | 16.04 | 3.37 | 3.20 | 2.45 | 0.59 | 3.51 |
| 1936–1955 | 12.48 | 15.17 | 2.92 | 2.89 | 2.07 | 0.66 | 3.37 |
| 1937–1956 | 11.20 | 12.56 | 2.23 | 2.22 | 1.90 | 0.77 | 3.46 |
| 1938–1957 | 12.98 | 16.63 | 2.52 | 2.58 | 2.20 | 0.91 | 3.45 |
| 1939–1958 | 13.48 | 17.90 | 2.10 | 1.98 | 1.83 | 0.99 | 3.69 |
| 1940–1959 | 14.15 | 18.78 | 1.85 | 1.57 | 1.58 | 1.14 | 3.79 |
| 1941–1960 | 14.76 | 18.89 | 2.12 | 1.93 | 2.00 | 1.27 | 3.82 |
| 1942–1961 | 16.86 | 21.13 | 2.22 | 1.93 | 2.07 | 1.37 | 3.37 |
| 1943–1962 | 15.25 | 18.17 | 2.48 | 2.11 | 2.25 | 1.50 | 2.98 |
| 1944–1963 | 15.11 | 15.70 | 2.45 | 2.06 | 2.19 | 1.63 | 2.90 |
| 1945–1964 | 14.95 | 14.44 | 2.45 | 2.10 | 2.30 | 1.79 | 2.86 |
| 1946–1965 | 13.84 | 13.29 | 2.23 | 1.61 | 2.24 | 1.97 | 2.84 |
| 1947–1966 | 13.72 | 13.58 | 2.15 | 1.80 | 2.42 | 2.19 | 2.15 |
| 1948–1967 | 14.63 | 17.03 | 2.01 | 1.45 | 2.43 | 2.38 | 1.87 |
| 1949–1968 | 14.92 | 18.97 | 1.93 | 1.26 | 2.56 | 2.60 | 1.96 |
| 1950–1969 | 13.43 | 16.21 | 1.34 | 0.69 | 2.41 | 2.87 | 2.36 |
| 1951–1970 | 12.09 | 13.23 | 2.09 | 1.26 | 3.17 | 3.13 | 2.35 |
| 1952–1971 | 11.64 | 13.67 | 2.77 | 2.10 | 3.58 | 3.28 | 2.22 |
| 1953–1972 | 11.67 | 13.75 | 2.95 | 2.32 | 3.76 | 3.39 | 2.35 |
| 1954–1973 | 10.84 | 12.04 | 2.83 | 2.08 | 3.83 | 3.64 | 2.75 |
| 1955–1974 | 6.86 | 8.21 | 2.41 | 1.94 | 3.98 | 4.00 | 3.37 |
| 1956–1975 | 7.09 | 9.51 | 3.08 | 2.46 | 4.41 | 4.21 | 3.70 |
| 1957–1976 | 7.90 | 11.78 | 4.34 | 3.55 | 5.06 | 4.34 | 3.80 |
| 1958–1977 | 8.12 | 13.95 | 3.99 | 3.15 | 4.74 | 4.44 | 3.98 |
| 1959–1978 | 6.52 | 12.31 | 4.10 | 3.41 | 4.99 | 4.72 | 4.34 |
| 1960–1979 | 6.83 | 13.49 | 3.93 | 3.46 | 5.22 | 5.09 | 4.92 |
| 1961–1980 | 8.32 | 15.61 | 3.34 | 2.59 | 4.84 | 5.51 | 5.46 |
| 1962–1981 | 6.77 | 14.75 | 3.03 | 2.64 | 5.21 | 6.12 | 5.87 |
| 1963–1982 | 8.31 | 16.92 | 4.47 | 4.04 | 6.28 | 6.51 | 6.01 |
| 1964–1983 | 8.30 | 17.63 | 4.68 | 4.01 | 6.57 | 6.80 | 6.12 |
| 1965–1984 | 7.80 | 16.00 | 5.25 | 4.58 | 7.06 | 7.12 | 6.26 |
| 1966–1985 | 8.66 | 15.25 | 6.67 | 5.97 | 8.00 | 7.31 | 6.36 |
| 1967–1986 | 10.18 | 16.06 | 7.63 | 6.94 | 8.52 | 7.38 | 6.24 |
| 1968–1987 | 9.28 | 12.04 | 7.88 | 7.31 | 8.62 | 7.44 | 6.31 |
| 1969–1988 | 9.54 | 11.47 | 8.30 | 7.82 | 8.70 | 7.50 | 6.30 |
| 1970–1989 | 11.56 | 13.64 | 9.58 | 9.01 | 9.42 | 7.59 | 6.22 |
| 1971–1990 | 11.17 | 13.35 | 9.01 | 8.71 | 9.08 | 7.66 | 6.26 |
| 1972–1991 | 11.91 | 14.58 | 9.43 | 9.00 | 9.40 | 7.72 | 6.24 |
| 1973–1992 | 11.35 | 15.54 | 9.54 | 9.12 | 9.51 | 7.70 | 6.21 |
| 1974–1993 | 12.78 | 18.82 | 10.16 | 10.10 | 9.85 | 7.49 | 5.91 |
| 1975–1994 | 14.60 | 20.33 | 10.00 | 9.42 | 9.25 | 7.29 | 5.44 |
| 1976–1995 | 14.61 | 19.57 | 10.58 | 10.45 | 9.69 | 7.28 | 5.22 |
| 1977–1996 | 14.57 | 17.84 | 9.71 | 9.54 | 9.14 | 7.28 | 5.14 |

Chapter 2: The Long-Run Perspective

**Exhibit 2.8:** Basic Series
Compound Annual Returns for 20-Year Holding Periods (% per annum)
1926–2016

| 20-Year Period | Large-Cap Stocks | Small-Cap Stocks | Long-term Corp Bonds | Long-term Gov't Bonds | Inter-term Gov't Bonds | U.S. Treasury Bills | Inflation |
|---|---|---|---|---|---|---|---|
| 1978–1997 | 16.66 | 17.71 | 10.29 | 10.39 | 9.51 | 7.29 | 4.89 |
| 1979–1998 | 17.76 | 16.04 | 10.86 | 11.14 | 9.85 | 7.17 | 4.52 |
| 1980–1999 | 17.88 | 15.46 | 10.66 | 10.69 | 9.53 | 6.89 | 4.00 |
| 1981–2000 | 15.68 | 13.33 | 11.49 | 11.99 | 9.97 | 6.62 | 3.57 |
| 1982–2001 | 15.24 | 13.76 | 12.13 | 12.09 | 9.88 | 6.09 | 3.21 |
| 1983–2002 | 12.71 | 11.57 | 10.99 | 11.12 | 9.15 | 5.65 | 3.13 |
| 1984–2003 | 12.98 | 12.35 | 10.94 | 11.16 | 8.89 | 5.26 | 3.04 |
| 1985–2004 | 13.22 | 13.69 | 10.54 | 10.82 | 8.30 | 4.83 | 3.00 |
| 1986–2005 | 11.94 | 12.76 | 9.41 | 9.74 | 7.37 | 4.59 | 2.98 |
| 1987–2006 | 11.80 | 13.23 | 8.60 | 8.61 | 6.78 | 4.53 | 3.06 |
| 1988–2007 | 11.82 | 13.48 | 8.75 | 9.27 | 7.14 | 4.49 | 3.04 |
| 1989–2008 | 8.43 | 9.78 | 8.65 | 10.03 | 7.48 | 4.25 | 2.82 |
| 1990–2009 | 8.21 | 10.61 | 8.00 | 8.24 | 6.69 | 3.83 | 2.73 |
| 1991–2010 | 9.14 | 13.49 | 8.28 | 8.44 | 6.56 | 3.45 | 2.50 |
| 1992–2011 | 7.81 | 11.23 | 8.19 | 8.78 | 6.24 | 3.17 | 2.49 |
| 1993–2012 | 8.22 | 11.00 | 8.25 | 8.54 | 5.96 | 3.00 | 2.44 |
| 1994–2013 | 9.22 | 12.01 | 7.19 | 6.90 | 5.20 | 2.85 | 2.37 |
| 1995–2014 | 9.85 | 12.00 | 8.37 | 8.53 | 5.63 | 2.66 | 2.28 |
| 1996–2015 | 8.19 | 10.15 | 7.02 | 7.01 | 4.91 | 2.38 | 2.19 |
| 1997–2016 | 7.68 | 10.52 | 7.29 | 7.16 | 4.90 | 2.13 | 2.12 |

**Exhibit 2.9:** Basic Series

Maximum and Minimum Values of Compound Returns (% per annum) for 1-, 5-, 10-, and 20-Year Holding Periods Using Data From 1926–2016

**Annual Returns**

| Series | Maximum Return | Year | Minimum Return | Year | Times Positive (Out of 91 Years) | Times Highest Returning Asset |
|---|---|---|---|---|---|---|
| Large-Cap Stocks | 53.99 | 1933 | -43.34 | 1931 | 67 | 16 |
| Small-Cap Stocks | 142.87 | 1933 | -58.01 | 1937 | 63 | 41 |
| Long-term Corp Bonds | 42.56 | 1982 | -8.09 | 1969 | 72 | 6 |
| Long-term Gov't Bonds | 40.36 | 1982 | -14.90 | 2009 | 67 | 12 |
| Inter-term Gov't Bonds | 29.10 | 1982 | -5.14 | 1994 | 81 | 4 |
| U.S. Treasury Bills | 14.71 | 1981 | -0.02 | 1938 | 90 | 6 |
| Inflation | 18.16 | 1946 | -10.30 | 1932 | 81 | 6 |

**5-Year Rolling Period Returns**

| Series | Maximum Return | 5-year Period Ending | Minimum Return | 5-year Period Ending | Times Positive (Out of 87 Periods) | Times Highest Returning Asset |
|---|---|---|---|---|---|---|
| Large-Cap Stocks | 28.56 | 1999 | -12.47 | 1932 | 75 | 24 |
| Small-Cap Stocks | 45.90 | 1945 | -27.54 | 1932 | 75 | 46 |
| Long-term Corp Bonds | 22.51 | 1986 | -2.22 | 1969 | 84 | 8 |
| Long-term Gov't Bonds | 21.62 | 1986 | -2.14 | 1969 | 81 | 5 |
| Inter-term Gov't Bonds | 16.98 | 1986 | 0.91 | 2016 | 87 | 3 |
| U.S. Treasury Bills | 11.12 | 1983 | 0.03 | 2015 | 87 | 0 |
| Inflation | 10.06 | 1981 | -5.42 | 1932 | 80 | 1 |

**10-Year Rolling Period Returns**

| Series | Maximum Return | 10-year Period Ending | Minimum Return | 10-year Period Ending | Times Positive (Out of 82 Periods) | Times Highest Returning Asset |
|---|---|---|---|---|---|---|
| Large-Cap Stocks | 20.06 | 1958 | -1.38 | 2008 | 78 | 21 |
| Small-Cap Stocks | 30.38 | 1984 | -5.70 | 1938 | 80 | 48 |
| Long-term Corp Bonds | 16.32 | 1991 | 0.98 | 1956 | 82 | 6 |
| Long-term Gov't Bonds | 15.56 | 1991 | -0.07 | 1959 | 81 | 3 |
| Inter-term Gov't Bonds | 13.13 | 1991 | 1.25 | 1956 | 82 | 2 |
| U.S. Treasury Bills | 9.17 | 1987 | 0.15 | 1942 | 82 | 1 |
| Inflation | 8.67 | 1982 | -2.57 | 1935 | 76 | 1 |

**20-Year Rolling Period Returns**

| Series | Maximum Return | 20-year Period Ending | Minimum Return | 20-year Period Ending | Times Positive (Out of 72 Periods) | Times Highest Returning Asset |
|---|---|---|---|---|---|---|
| Large-Cap Stocks | 17.88 | 1999 | 3.11 | 1948 | 72 | 9 |
| Small-Cap Stocks | 21.13 | 1961 | 5.74 | 1948 | 72 | 62 |
| Long-term Corp Bonds | 12.13 | 2001 | 1.34 | 1969 | 72 | 0 |
| Long-term Gov't Bonds | 12.09 | 2001 | 0.69 | 1969 | 72 | 1 |
| Inter-term Gov't Bonds | 9.97 | 2000 | 1.58 | 1959 | 72 | 0 |
| U.S. Treasury Bills | 7.72 | 1991 | 0.42 | 1950 | 72 | 0 |
| Inflation | 6.36 | 1985 | 0.07 | 1945 | 72 | 0 |

**Exhibit 2.10:** Portfolios

Maximum and Minimum Values of Compound Returns (% per annum) for 1-, 5-, 10-, and 20-Year Holding Periods Using Data From 1926–2016

**Annual Returns**

| Annual Return | Maximum Return | Year | Minimum Return | Year | Arithmetic Annualized Mean | Times Positive (Out of 91 years) | % Positive in 91 years | Times Highest Returning Portfolio |
|---|---|---|---|---|---|---|---|---|
| 100% Large Stocks | 53.99 | 1933 | -43.34 | 1931 | 11.95 | 67 | 74 | 56 |
| 90% Stocks/10% Bonds | 49.03 | 1933 | -39.73 | 1931 | 11.32 | 68 | 75 | 0 |
| 70% Stocks/30% Bonds | 38.68 | 1933 | -32.31 | 1931 | 10.08 | 70 | 77 | 0 |
| 50% Stocks/50% Bonds | 34.71 | 1995 | -24.70 | 1931 | 8.87 | 72 | 79 | 0 |
| 30% Stocks/70% Bonds | 34.72 | 1982 | -16.96 | 1931 | 7.69 | 73 | 80 | 0 |
| 10% Stocks/90% Bonds | 38.48 | 1982 | -11.23 | 2009 | 6.54 | 70 | 77 | 0 |
| 100% LT Gov't Bonds* | 40.36 | 1982 | -14.90 | 2009 | 5.97 | 67 | 74 | 35 |

**5-Year Rolling Period Returns**

| Annual Return | Maximum Return | 5-year Period Ending | Minimum Return | 5-year Period Ending | Arithmetic Annualized Mean | Times Positive (Out of 87 Periods) | % Positive in 87 Periods | Times Highest Returning Portfolio |
|---|---|---|---|---|---|---|---|---|
| 100% Large Stocks | 28.56 | 1999 | -12.47 | 1932 | 10.09 | 75 | 86 | 58 |
| 90% Stocks/10% Bonds | 26.62 | 1999 | -10.31 | 1932 | 9.79 | 79 | 91 | 1 |
| 70% Stocks/30% Bonds | 22.75 | 1999 | -6.31 | 1932 | 9.10 | 82 | 94 | 0 |
| 50% Stocks/50% Bonds | 20.99 | 1986 | -2.77 | 1932 | 8.28 | 82 | 94 | 3 |
| 30% Stocks/70% Bonds | 21.30 | 1986 | 0.12 | 1969 | 7.33 | 87 | 100 | 2 |
| 10% Stocks/90% Bonds | 21.53 | 1986 | -1.38 | 1969 | 6.24 | 84 | 97 | 1 |
| 100% LT Gov't Bonds | 21.62 | 1986 | -2.14 | 1969 | 5.65 | 81 | 93 | 22 |

**10-Year Rolling Period Returns**

| Annual Return | Maximum Return | 10-year Period Ending | Minimum Return | 10-year Period Ending | Arithmetic Annualized Mean | Times Positive (Out of 82 Periods) | % Positive in 82 Periods | Times Highest Returning Portfolio |
|---|---|---|---|---|---|---|---|---|
| 100% Large Stocks | 20.06 | 1958 | -1.38 | 2008 | 10.34 | 78 | 95 | 52 |
| 90% Stocks/10% Bonds | 18.52 | 1998 | -0.25 | 2008 | 10.03 | 81 | 99 | 4 |
| 70% Stocks/30% Bonds | 17.31 | 1991 | 1.74 | 1974 | 9.30 | 82 | 100 | 6 |
| 50% Stocks/50% Bonds | 16.96 | 1991 | 1.98 | 1974 | 8.43 | 82 | 100 | 8 |
| 30% Stocks/70% Bonds | 16.49 | 1991 | 2.13 | 1974 | 7.42 | 82 | 100 | 1 |
| 10% Stocks/90% Bonds | 15.90 | 1991 | 1.81 | 1959 | 6.29 | 82 | 100 | 5 |
| 100% LT Gov't Bonds | 15.56 | 1991 | -0.07 | 1959 | 5.67 | 81 | 99 | 6 |

**20-Year Rolling Period Returns**

| Annual Return | Maximum Return | 20-year Period Ending | Minimum Return | 20-year Period Ending | Arithmetic Annualized Mean | Times Positive (out of 72 Periods) | % Positive in 72 Periods | Times Highest Returning Portfolio |
|---|---|---|---|---|---|---|---|---|
| 100% Large Stocks | 17.88 | 1999 | 3.11 | 1948 | 11.07 | 72 | 100 | 59 |
| 90% Stocks/10% Bonds | 17.28 | 1999 | 3.58 | 1948 | 10.66 | 72 | 100 | 1 |
| 70% Stocks/30% Bonds | 16.04 | 1998 | 4.27 | 1948 | 9.74 | 72 | 100 | 6 |
| 50% Stocks/50% Bonds | 14.75 | 1998 | 4.60 | 1948 | 8.71 | 72 | 100 | 4 |
| 30% Stocks/70% Bonds | 13.38 | 1998 | 3.62 | 1974 | 7.55 | 72 | 100 | 1 |
| 10% Stocks/90% Bonds | 12.53 | 2001 | 1.98 | 1969 | 6.29 | 72 | 100 | 0 |
| 100% LT Gov't Bonds | 12.09 | 2001 | 0.69 | 1969 | 5.61 | 72 | 100 | 1 |

*LT = Long-term

## Summary Statistics of Portfolio Total Returns

Exhibit 2.11 presents summary statistics of the annual total returns on each portfolio over the 1926–2016 period. The summary statistics presented are geometric mean, arithmetic mean, and standard deviation. As more fixed-income is added to the portfolio, the returns – as well as the standard deviation – tend to decrease. Moving from a 100% stock portfolio to a 70% stock and 30% bond portfolio decreases the geometric mean by 0.9% (10.0% – 9.1%), but also decreases the standard deviation by 5.7% (19.9% – 14.2%). This corresponds to the risk/return trade-off: large-cap stocks have a higher level of risk than long-term government bonds, and are rewarded accordingly.

A seemingly counter-intuitive result in Exhibit 2.11 to the risk/return trade-off is when the return and standard deviation of the 100% bond portfolio is compared to the return and standard deviation of (i) the 10% stock/90% bond portfolio, and (ii) the 30% stock/70% bond portfolio. In these cases, *adding* stocks both *increases* return and *decreases* standard deviation, when compared to a portfolio of 100% bonds. This obviously defies the risk/return trade-off, but highlights the benefits of *diversification*.

A portfolio's asset mix can change from its original percentages as a result of differing returns among the various asset classes held in the portfolio. Thus, asset allocation percentages can *change over time without the investor's input*. For example, if a hypothetical investor invests $1.00 in stocks and $1.00 in bonds, the portfolio that he holds is initially 50% stocks and 50% bonds. If the returns of stocks and bonds over the next year are 20% and 5%, respectively, the "stock" portion of his portfolio has now increased to $1.20, and the "bond" portion of his portfolio has now increased to $1.05. The investor's portfolio mix has also changed: it is now approximately 53.3% stocks ($1.20/($1.20 + $1.05)), and 46.7% bonds ($1.05/($1.20 + $1.05)). This concept is illustrated in Exhibit 2.12. For example, the portfolio mix of a portfolio originally comprised of 10% stocks and 90% bonds at the end of 1925 would (if never rebalanced) become a portfolio comprised of 83.3% stocks and 16.7% bonds by the end of 2016.

**Exhibits 2.11, 2.12, 2.13, and 2.14:** Portfolios: Summary Statistics of Annual Returns Always Rebalanced, Never Rebalanced, by Decade, and in the most recent 10-year period (% per annum) (1926−2016)

**Exhibit 2.11:** Portfolio Summary Statistics of Annual Returns (Always Rebalanced) (% per annum)

| Portfolio (Always Rebalanced) | Geometric Mean | Arithmetic Mean | Standard Deviation |
|---|---|---|---|
| 100% Large Stocks | 10.0 | 12.0 | 19.9 |
| 90% Stocks/10% Bonds | 9.8 | 11.3 | 17.9 |
| 70% Stocks/30% Bonds | 9.1 | 10.1 | 14.2 |
| 50% Stocks/50% Bonds | 8.3 | 8.9 | 11.1 |
| 30% Stocks/70% Bonds | 7.3 | 7.7 | 9.2 |
| 10% Stocks/90% Bonds | 6.2 | 6.5 | 9.2 |
| 100% Long-term Gov't Bonds | 5.5 | 6.0 | 9.9 |

**Exhibit 2.12:** Portfolio Summary Statistics of Annual Returns (Never Rebalanced) (% per annum)

| Portfolio (Never Rebalanced) | Ending Portfolio Large-Cap Stocks (% of Portfolio 12/31/2016) | Ending Portfolio Bonds (% of Portfolio 12/31/2016) | Geometric Mean | Arithmetic Mean | Standard Deviation |
|---|---|---|---|---|---|
| 100% Large Stocks | 100.0 | 0.0 | 10.0 | 12.0 | 19.9 |
| 90% Stocks/10% Bonds | 99.8 | 0.2 | 9.9 | 11.7 | 18.9 |
| 70% Stocks/30% Bonds | 99.1 | 0.9 | 9.6 | 11.1 | 17.2 |
| 50% Stocks/50% Bonds | 97.8 | 2.2 | 9.2 | 10.4 | 15.5 |
| 30% Stocks/70% Bonds | 95.1 | 4.9 | 8.7 | 9.6 | 13.8 |
| 10% Stocks/90% Bonds | 83.3 | 16.7 | 7.5 | 8.1 | 10.9 |
| 100% Long-term Gov't Bonds | 0.0 | 100.0 | 5.5 | 6.0 | 9.9 |

**Exhibit 2.13:** Portfolio Summary Statistics of Annual Returns by Decade (Always Rebalanced) (% per annum)

| Portfolio (Always Rebalanced) | 1920s[*] | 1930s | 1940s | 1950s | 1960s | 1970s | 1980s | 1990s | 2000s | 2010s[**] |
|---|---|---|---|---|---|---|---|---|---|---|
| 100% Large Stocks | 19.2 | -0.1 | 9.2 | 19.4 | 7.8 | 5.9 | 17.6 | 18.2 | -0.9 | 12.8 |
| 90% Stocks/10% Bonds | 18.0 | 1.0 | 8.7 | 17.4 | 7.2 | 5.9 | 17.2 | 17.3 | 0.1 | 12.4 |
| 70% Stocks/30% Bonds | 15.3 | 2.8 | 7.6 | 13.4 | 6.1 | 6.0 | 16.5 | 15.5 | 2.1 | 11.5 |
| 50% Stocks/50% Bonds | 12.5 | 4.1 | 6.5 | 9.5 | 4.8 | 6.0 | 15.5 | 13.6 | 3.9 | 10.4 |
| 30% Stocks/70% Bonds | 9.6 | 4.8 | 5.2 | 5.6 | 3.5 | 5.9 | 14.5 | 11.7 | 5.5 | 9.1 |
| 10% Stocks/90% Bonds | 6.6 | 5.0 | 3.9 | 1.8 | 2.1 | 5.7 | 13.3 | 9.8 | 7.0 | 7.7 |
| 100% Long-term Gov't Bonds | 5.0 | 4.9 | 3.2 | -0.1 | 1.4 | 5.5 | 12.6 | 8.8 | 7.7 | 6.9 |

[*]Based on the period 1926–1929     [**]Based on the period 2010–2016

**Exhibit 2.14:** Portfolio Summary Statistics of Annual Returns 2007−2016 (Most Recent Decade) (% per annum)

| Portfolio (Always Rebalanced) | 2007−2016 |
|---|---|
| 100% Large Stocks | 6.9 |
| 90% Stocks/10% Bonds | 7.1 |
| 70% Stocks/30% Bonds | 7.3 |
| 50% Stocks/50% Bonds | 7.4 |
| 30% Stocks/70% Bonds | 7.2 |
| 10% Stocks/90% Bonds | 6.8 |
| 100% Long-term Gov't Bonds | 6.5 |

**Exhibit 2.15:** Portfolio Annual Total Returns (%)
1926–2016

| Year | 100% Large Stocks | 90/10 | 70/30 | 50/50 | 30/70 | 10/90 | 100% Long-term Gov't Bonds |
|---|---|---|---|---|---|---|---|
| 1926 | 11.62 | 11.30 | 10.61 | 9.87 | 9.07 | 8.22 | 7.77 |
| 1927 | 37.49 | 34.45 | 28.49 | 22.69 | 17.06 | 11.60 | 8.93 |
| 1928 | 43.61 | 38.74 | 29.35 | 20.44 | 11.98 | 3.95 | 0.10 |
| 1929 | -8.42 | -6.76 | -3.77 | -1.19 | 0.97 | 2.71 | 3.42 |
| 1930 | -24.90 | -22.08 | -16.33 | -10.46 | -4.48 | 1.59 | 4.66 |
| 1931 | -43.34 | -39.73 | -32.31 | -24.70 | -16.96 | -9.19 | -5.31 |
| 1932 | -8.19 | -4.45 | 2.43 | 8.28 | 12.85 | 15.93 | 16.84 |
| 1933 | 53.99 | 49.03 | 38.68 | 27.89 | 16.80 | 5.56 | -0.07 |
| 1934 | -1.44 | -0.13 | 2.38 | 4.76 | 6.99 | 9.05 | 10.03 |
| 1935 | 47.67 | 42.94 | 33.80 | 25.06 | 16.73 | 8.80 | 4.98 |
| 1936 | 33.92 | 31.15 | 25.69 | 20.35 | 15.12 | 10.02 | 7.52 |
| 1937 | -35.03 | -31.93 | -25.44 | -18.58 | -11.34 | -3.72 | 0.23 |
| 1938 | 31.12 | 29.24 | 24.93 | 19.99 | 14.51 | 8.61 | 5.53 |
| 1939 | -0.41 | 0.65 | 2.51 | 4.00 | 5.09 | 5.77 | 5.94 |
| 1940 | -9.78 | -8.04 | -4.65 | -1.40 | 1.70 | 4.66 | 6.09 |
| 1941 | -11.59 | -10.33 | -7.81 | -5.30 | -2.80 | -0.31 | 0.93 |
| 1942 | 20.34 | 18.62 | 15.18 | 11.75 | 8.32 | 4.91 | 3.22 |
| 1943 | 25.90 | 23.43 | 18.54 | 13.73 | 9.00 | 4.37 | 2.08 |
| 1944 | 19.75 | 17.98 | 14.49 | 11.06 | 7.71 | 4.43 | 2.81 |
| 1945 | 36.44 | 33.72 | 28.39 | 23.18 | 18.11 | 13.16 | 10.73 |
| 1946 | -8.07 | -7.17 | -5.42 | -3.78 | -2.23 | -0.78 | -0.10 |
| 1947 | 5.71 | 4.89 | 3.24 | 1.58 | -0.10 | -1.78 | -2.62 |
| 1948 | 5.50 | 5.46 | 5.26 | 4.91 | 4.41 | 3.77 | 3.40 |
| 1949 | 18.79 | 17.55 | 15.07 | 12.60 | 10.13 | 7.68 | 6.45 |
| 1950 | 31.71 | 28.24 | 21.50 | 15.04 | 8.85 | 2.93 | 0.06 |
| 1951 | 24.02 | 20.97 | 15.05 | 9.36 | 3.88 | -1.38 | -3.93 |
| 1952 | 18.37 | 16.60 | 13.10 | 9.64 | 6.22 | 2.83 | 1.16 |
| 1953 | -0.99 | -0.50 | 0.47 | 1.41 | 2.32 | 3.21 | 3.64 |
| 1954 | 52.62 | 47.50 | 37.65 | 28.33 | 19.51 | 11.18 | 7.19 |
| 1955 | 31.56 | 27.98 | 21.02 | 14.32 | 7.89 | 1.70 | -1.29 |
| 1956 | 6.56 | 5.42 | 3.08 | 0.68 | -1.79 | -4.31 | -5.59 |
| 1957 | -10.78 | -8.99 | -5.39 | -1.75 | 1.92 | 5.61 | 7.46 |
| 1958 | 43.36 | 37.57 | 26.60 | 16.38 | 6.89 | -1.93 | -6.09 |
| 1959 | 11.96 | 10.49 | 7.59 | 4.72 | 1.90 | -0.88 | -2.26 |
| 1960 | 0.47 | 1.83 | 4.53 | 7.21 | 9.86 | 12.48 | 13.78 |
| 1961 | 26.89 | 24.10 | 18.65 | 13.38 | 8.29 | 3.37 | 0.97 |
| 1962 | -8.73 | -7.11 | -3.90 | -0.74 | 2.37 | 5.40 | 6.89 |
| 1963 | 22.80 | 20.52 | 16.03 | 11.66 | 7.40 | 3.25 | 1.21 |
| 1964 | 16.48 | 15.13 | 12.46 | 9.84 | 7.27 | 4.75 | 3.51 |
| 1965 | 12.45 | 11.26 | 8.89 | 6.53 | 4.19 | 1.86 | 0.71 |
| 1966 | -10.06 | -8.72 | -6.02 | -3.29 | -0.53 | 2.25 | 3.65 |
| 1967 | 23.98 | 20.28 | 13.14 | 6.36 | -0.10 | -6.23 | -9.18 |
| 1968 | 11.06 | 9.98 | 7.79 | 5.54 | 3.25 | 0.92 | -0.26 |
| 1969 | -8.50 | -8.08 | -7.28 | -6.56 | -5.91 | -5.33 | -5.07 |
| 1970 | 3.86 | 4.78 | 6.57 | 8.27 | 9.87 | 11.39 | 12.11 |
| 1971 | 14.30 | 14.29 | 14.21 | 14.04 | 13.78 | 13.44 | 13.23 |
| 1972 | 18.99 | 17.62 | 14.90 | 12.22 | 9.57 | 6.97 | 5.69 |
| 1973 | -14.69 | -13.31 | -10.57 | -7.84 | -5.12 | -2.44 | -1.11 |
| 1974 | -26.47 | -23.66 | -17.87 | -11.82 | -5.53 | 1.00 | 4.35 |
| 1975 | 37.23 | 34.30 | 28.51 | 22.84 | 17.29 | 11.86 | 9.20 |

**Exhibit 2.15:** Portfolio Annual Total Returns (%)
1926–2016

| Year | 100% Large Stocks | 90/10 | 70/30 | 50/50 | 30/70 | 10/90 | 100% Long-term Gov't Bonds |
|---|---|---|---|---|---|---|---|
| 1976 | 23.93 | 23.28 | 21.93 | 20.52 | 19.06 | 17.54 | 16.75 |
| 1977 | -7.16 | -6.50 | -5.20 | -3.90 | -2.61 | -1.33 | -0.69 |
| 1978 | 6.57 | 5.86 | 4.40 | 2.88 | 1.30 | -0.34 | -1.18 |
| 1979 | 18.61 | 16.52 | 12.40 | 8.39 | 4.47 | 0.64 | -1.23 |
| 1980 | 32.50 | 28.71 | 21.19 | 13.80 | 6.57 | -0.49 | -3.95 |
| 1981 | -4.92 | -4.16 | -2.69 | -1.30 | 0.02 | 1.27 | 1.86 |
| 1982 | 21.55 | 23.42 | 27.19 | 30.95 | 34.72 | 38.48 | 40.36 |
| 1983 | 22.56 | 20.24 | 15.68 | 11.25 | 6.92 | 2.71 | 0.65 |
| 1984 | 6.27 | 7.26 | 9.18 | 11.05 | 12.87 | 14.62 | 15.48 |
| 1985 | 31.73 | 31.72 | 31.65 | 31.53 | 31.35 | 31.11 | 30.97 |
| 1986 | 18.67 | 19.34 | 20.64 | 21.86 | 23.00 | 24.04 | 24.53 |
| 1987 | 5.25 | 5.07 | 4.24 | 2.83 | 0.93 | -1.40 | -2.71 |
| 1988 | 16.61 | 15.92 | 14.55 | 13.16 | 11.77 | 10.37 | 9.67 |
| 1989 | 31.69 | 30.37 | 27.70 | 25.00 | 22.26 | 19.50 | 18.11 |
| 1990 | -3.10 | -2.15 | -0.26 | 1.61 | 3.46 | 5.28 | 6.18 |
| 1991 | 30.47 | 29.41 | 27.24 | 25.03 | 22.77 | 20.47 | 19.30 |
| 1992 | 7.62 | 7.69 | 7.81 | 7.91 | 7.98 | 8.04 | 8.05 |
| 1993 | 10.08 | 10.90 | 12.53 | 14.16 | 15.80 | 17.43 | 18.24 |
| 1994 | 1.32 | 0.40 | -1.42 | -3.25 | -5.06 | -6.87 | -7.77 |
| 1995 | 37.58 | 37.02 | 35.88 | 34.71 | 33.51 | 32.29 | 31.67 |
| 1996 | 22.96 | 20.41 | 15.41 | 10.56 | 5.85 | 1.29 | -0.93 |
| 1997 | 33.36 | 31.59 | 28.06 | 24.55 | 21.05 | 17.58 | 15.85 |
| 1998 | 28.58 | 27.33 | 24.60 | 21.59 | 18.33 | 14.86 | 13.06 |
| 1999 | 21.04 | 17.75 | 11.36 | 5.23 | -0.63 | -6.25 | -8.96 |
| 2000 | -9.10 | -6.30 | -0.53 | 5.46 | 11.70 | 18.16 | 21.48 |
| 2001 | -11.89 | -10.18 | -6.85 | -3.64 | -0.58 | 2.32 | 3.70 |
| 2002 | -22.10 | -18.45 | -10.90 | -3.04 | 5.12 | 13.54 | 17.84 |
| 2003 | 28.68 | 25.86 | 20.27 | 14.77 | 9.36 | 4.06 | 1.45 |
| 2004 | 10.88 | 10.70 | 10.29 | 9.84 | 9.34 | 8.80 | 8.51 |
| 2005 | 4.91 | 5.28 | 5.96 | 6.58 | 7.12 | 7.60 | 7.81 |
| 2006 | 15.79 | 14.30 | 11.33 | 8.40 | 5.49 | 2.61 | 1.19 |
| 2007 | 5.49 | 6.03 | 7.03 | 7.95 | 8.79 | 9.54 | 9.88 |
| 2008 | -37.00 | -32.14 | -21.55 | -9.72 | 3.43 | 18.02 | 25.87 |
| 2009 | 26.46 | 21.86 | 12.97 | 4.49 | -3.58 | -11.23 | -14.90 |
| 2010 | 15.06 | 14.97 | 14.52 | 13.70 | 12.53 | 11.02 | 10.14 |
| 2011 | 2.11 | 4.69 | 9.81 | 14.88 | 19.85 | 24.72 | 27.10 |
| 2012 | 16.00 | 14.86 | 12.48 | 10.00 | 7.43 | 4.78 | 3.43 |
| 2013 | 32.39 | 27.14 | 17.16 | 7.85 | -0.84 | -8.94 | -12.78 |
| 2014 | 13.69 | 14.80 | 17.03 | 19.24 | 21.44 | 23.62 | 24.71 |
| 2015 | 1.38 | 1.35 | 1.18 | 0.84 | 0.36 | -0.28 | -0.65 |
| 2016 | 11.96 | 11.04 | 9.13 | 7.13 | 5.04 | 2.87 | 1.75 |

## Real Estate Investment Trusts (REITs)[2.3]

Real estate properties can be *directly* owned by individuals (i.e., sole proprietorship), partnerships, corporations (either subchapter C or subchapter S), limited liability company (LLCs) or trusts. An equity investment in real estate can also be made *indirectly* by purchasing shares of an entity holding real property interests. Real estate entities exist substantially for the purpose of holding, directly or indirectly, title to or beneficial interest in real property. The value of a real estate entity includes many components, such as land, buildings, furniture, fixtures and equipment, intangible assets, and often the business operation.

A REIT "is a company dedicated to owning, and in most cases, operating income-producing real estate, such as apartments, shopping centers, offices and warehouses. Some REITs also engage in financing real estate."[2.4] REITs can be classified in three broad categories, (i) equity REITs, (ii) mortgage REITs, and (iii) hybrid REITs.[2.5]

Equity REITs mostly own and operate income-producing real estate. They increasingly have become real estate operating companies engaged in a wide range of real estate activities, including leasing, maintenance and development of real property, and tenant services. One major distinction between equity REITs and other real estate companies is that a REIT must acquire and develop its properties primarily to operate them as part of its own portfolio rather than to resell them once they are developed.

Mortgage REITs mostly lend money directly to real estate owners and operators or extend credit indirectly through the acquisition of loans or mortgage-backed securities. Today's mortgage REITs generally extend mortgage credit only on existing properties. Many mortgage REITs also manage their interest rate and credit risks using securitized mortgage investments, dynamic hedging techniques, and other accepted derivative strategies.

Hybrid REITs generally are companies that use the investment strategies of both equity REITs and mortgage REITs.

---

[2.3]  Data presented throughout this section come from the National Association of Real Estate Investment Trusts® (NAREIT) Equity Index. NAREIT®, the National Association of Real Estate Investment Trusts, is the worldwide representative voice for REITs and publicly traded real estate companies with an interest in U.S. real estate and capital markets. NAREIT's members are REITs and other businesses throughout the world that own, operate, and finance income-producing real estate, as well as those firms and individuals who advise, study, and service those businesses. To learn more, visit: www.reit.com/nareit.

[2.4]  Glossary of REIT Terms, National Association of Real Estate Investment Trusts (NAREIT), available at: https://www.reit.com/investing/reit-basics/reit-faqs/glossary-reit-terms. NAREIT is the worldwide representative voice for REITs and publicly traded real estate companies with an interest in U.S. real estate and capital markets.

[2.5]  Sources: The National Association of Real Estate Investment Trusts® (NAREIT®) website at www.reit.com/nareit; SEC Office of Investor Education and Advocacy "Investor Bulletin: Real Estate Investment Trusts (REITs)," December 2011, available at: http://www.sec.gov/investor/alerts/reits.pdf.

The number of REITs in the U.S. grew dramatically in the last several decades, to over 200 at the end of 2016 from 34 in 1971. This growth enabled a broader group of investors to add real estate to their portfolios and enjoy greater liquidity than they would otherwise be able. Exhibit 2.16 below displays the growth in market cap of U.S. REITs between 1971 and 2016.

**Exhibit 2.16:** All REITs Market Cap ($ Billions)
1971–2016

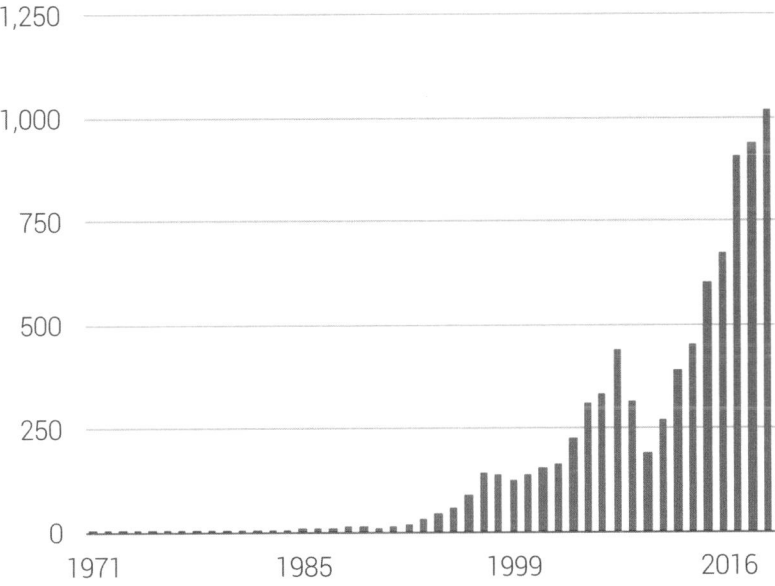

## Historical Returns on Equity REITs

Exhibit 2.17 depicts the growth of $1.00 invested in equity REITs as well as in U.S. small- and large-cap stocks, long-term government bonds, Treasury bills, and a hypothetical asset returning the inflation rate over the period from the end of 1971 to the end of 2016. Of the asset classes shown, small-cap stocks accumulated the highest ending wealth. An investment of $1.00 in small-cap stocks at year-end 1971 would have grown to $273.53 by year-end 2016, a compound return of 13.3%. Notice, however, that the same investment in equity REITs would have returned $159.15, a compound return of 11.9%. Equity REITs outperformed all of the remaining asset classes and inflation during the period.

**Exhibit 2.17:** Wealth Indices of Investments in Equity REITs and Basic Series
Index (Year-end 1971 = $1.00)
1972–2016

## Income Returns on Equity REITs

REITs must pay to shareholders at least 90% of their taxable income each year. As a result, income generated from REITs has proven to be steady and reasonably predictable.

Exhibit 2.18 shows both the income return and capital appreciation return of REITs annually from 1972 to 2016. REITs, similar to equity, can be quite volatile but offer the potential for price appreciation. However, price appreciation is by no means guaranteed (note the large negative price returns of 2007 and 2008). On the other hand, the income produced by REITs has been relatively stable since 1972. Equity REITs posted an average annual income return during that period of 7.3%. The highest annual income return was 18.8% in 1980, while the lowest was 3.7% in 2015.[2.6]

**Exhibit 2.18:** Annual Returns on Equity REITs (%)
1972–2016

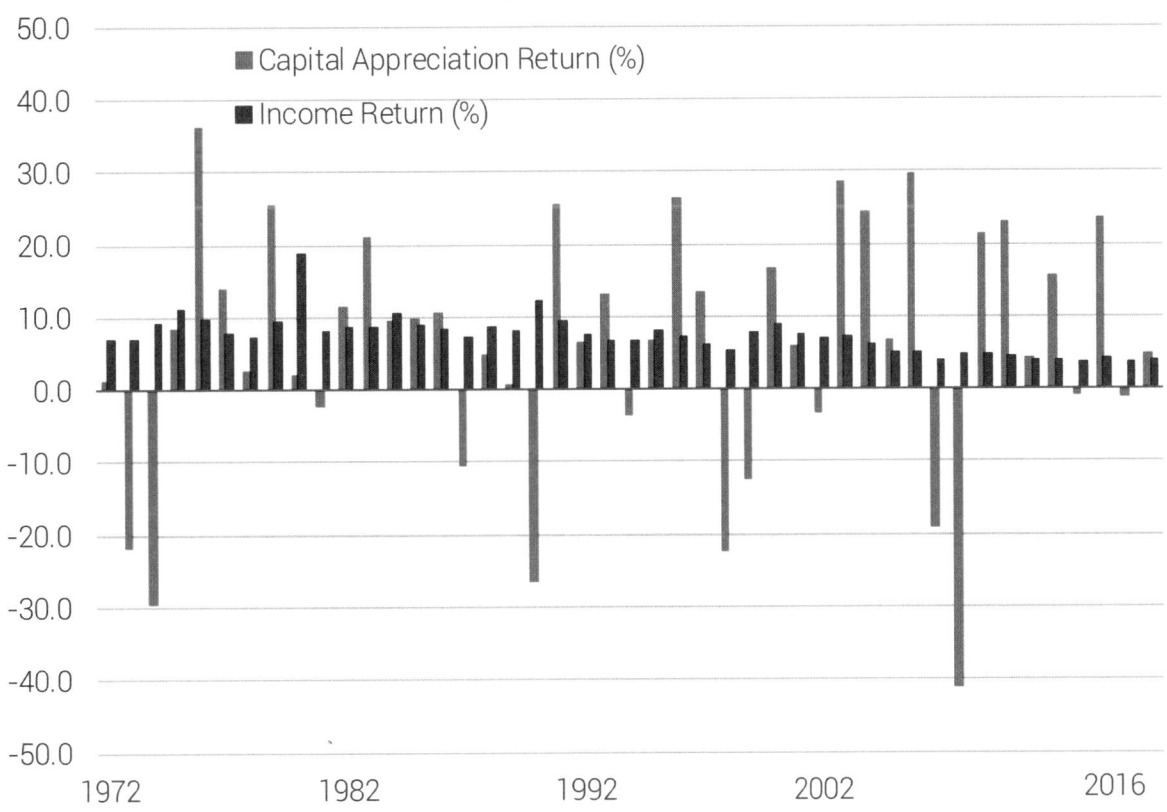

[2.6]    In previous editions of the *SBBI Yearbook*, annualized monthly income returns for the REITs series were calculated slightly differently than we have calculated them in this edition of the book. The annualized monthly income returns in Exhibit 2.18 are calculated in accordance with the methodology outlined on page 5-4. This change in methodology did not change the results of the analysis in Exhibit 2.18 in any significant way.

## Correlation of U.S. REITs Compared to Other U.S. Asset Classes

Diversification is "spreading a portfolio over many investments to avoid excessive exposure to any one source of risk."[2.7] Put simply, diversification is "not putting all your eggs in one basket." Diversification offers the potential of higher returns for the same level of risk, or lower risk for the same level of return.

REITs have been an attractive investment vehicle to investors because they have traditionally had a relatively low and declining correlation to stocks and bonds. Though the reasons are not quite clear, this relationship changed in the early 2000s, when REITs became increasingly correlated with both stocks and bonds, though correlation levels remain fairly low. A low correlation between assets in a portfolio allows for the possibility of an increase in returns without a corresponding increase in risk, or alternatively, a reduction in risk without a corresponding decrease in return. For example, from 1972 to 2016, a portfolio (rebalanced annually) with a mix of 60% stocks and 40% bonds returned 10.0% annually with a standard deviation of 11.7%. Adding a 15% allocation to REITs to the portfolio increases returns to 10.5% annually, and at the same time decreases standard deviation to 11.5%.

In Exhibit 2.19, the correlation of U.S. REITs and (i) U.S. large company stocks and (ii) long-term U.S. government bonds is shown. Correlation is a measure of how alternative investments "move" relative to each other, and is thus a measure of potential diversification benefit. The *higher* the correlation (the more investments "move" together), the *less* potential diversification benefit, whereas the *lower* the correlation (the less investments "move" together), the *greater* the potential diversification benefit. The thinking is that by holding a portfolio of assets that do not have high correlation with each other, as some investments decrease in value, others will increase (and vice versa), and thus potentially mitigate overall portfolio losses.

The correlation of U.S. REITs with both stocks and bonds declined during the 1990s, thus increasing the potential diversification benefit.

In the immediate years leading up to and following the 2008–2009 Financial Crisis, the correlation of U.S. REITs with stocks generally *increased*, decreasing the potential diversification benefit between these two asset classes. This increase in the correlation was likely due, at least in part, to the Federal Reserve's tamping down of interest rates through various market interventions and moral suasion. The publicly-stated intention of these interventions by the Federal Reserve was to boost asset prices (e.g., stocks, housing).

---

[2.7]   Cara Griffith, "Practical Tax Considerations for Working with REITs", State Tax Notes (October 31, 2011): 315–320, quoting Jennifer Weiss: 316. In 2009, the IRS issued guidance that indicates that the distributions may be in the form of cash or stock in certain instances.

**Exhibit 2.19:** Rolling 60-Month Correlations of Equity REITs
1972–2016

In more recent periods (2014 to present), these trends seem to have reversed, with the correlation of U.S. REITs with stocks generally decreasing, and the correlation of U.S. REITs with long-term government bonds generally increasing. This is likely due, at least in part, to the Federal Reserve increasing the federal funds target rate range 0.25% in each of December 2015 and December 2016, and indicating that further rate increases may be on the horizon.[2.8] With the dampening of the exogenous upward pressure on asset prices (e.g., stocks, housing) brought about by the Federal Reserve's tamping down of interest rates, and an outlook that suggests that more rate increases are on the horizon, these correlations seem to be regressing to values more typical of pre-financial-crisis levels.

---

[2.8]   The Federal Reserve maintained a target federal funds range of 0.00%–0.25% through open market operations from December 16, 2008 through December 16, 2015. On December 17, 2015, the Federal Reserve raised the target federal funds range 25 bps to 0.25%–0.50%, and again raised the target range another 25 bps to 0.50%–0.75% on December 15, 2016, and has indicated that further increases may occur in 2017 (see the *Wall Street Journal*, January 15, 2016, "Fed Raises Rates for First Time in 2016, Anticipates 3 Increases in 2017").

## Summary Statistics for Equity REITs and Basic Series

Exhibit 2.20 shows summary statistics of annual total returns for REITs and the SBBI basic series from 1972 to 2016. The summary statistics presented are geometric mean, arithmetic mean, and standard deviation.

While small-cap stocks posted the highest geometric mean over the period analyzed, they also had the highest amount of risk. Equity REITs produced a higher return than large-cap stocks with only slightly higher risk.

**Exhibit 2.20:** Summary Statistics of Annual Returns (%)
1972–2016

|  | Geometric Average | Arithmetic Average | Standard Deviation |
|---|---|---|---|
| Equity REITs | 11.9 | 13.5 | 17.9 |
| Large-Cap Stocks | 10.4 | 11.9 | 17.5 |
| Small-Cap Stocks | 13.3 | 15.6 | 22.7 |
| Long-term Corp Bonds | 8.4 | 8.8 | 10.2 |
| Long-term Gov't Bonds | 8.2 | 8.8 | 12.3 |
| Inter-term Gov't Bonds | 7.0 | 7.2 | 6.6 |
| U.S. Treasury Bills | 4.8 | 4.9 | 3.5 |
| Inflation | 4.0 | 4.1 | 3.1 |

Exhibit 2.21 presents annual serial correlations and cross-correlations from 1972 to 2016 for equity REITs and the six basic SBBI asset classes plus inflation. The serial correlation, or the extent to which the return in one period is related to the return in the next period (discussed in greater detail in Chapter 6) of equity REITs suggests no strong pattern; it can best be interpreted as mostly random or unpredictable.

**Exhibit 2.21:** Serial and Cross-Correlations of Annual Returns
1972–2016

|  | Equity REITs | Large-Cap Stocks | Small-Cap Stocks | Long-term Corp Bonds | Long-term Gov't Bonds | Inter-term Gov't Bonds | U.S. Treasury Bills | Inflation |
|---|---|---|---|---|---|---|---|---|
| Equity REITs | 1.00 |  |  |  |  |  |  |  |
| Large-Cap Stocks | 0.55 | 1.00 |  |  |  |  |  |  |
| Small-Cap Stocks | 0.73 | 0.73 | 1.00 |  |  |  |  |  |
| Long-term Corp Bonds | 0.27 | 0.24 | 0.09 | 1.00 |  |  |  |  |
| Long-term Gov't Bonds | 0.05 | 0.02 | -0.14 | 0.90 | 1.00 |  |  |  |
| Inter-term Gov't Bonds | 0.02 | 0.04 | -0.07 | 0.85 | 0.87 | 1.00 |  |  |
| U.S. Treasury Bills | 0.01 | 0.06 | 0.03 | 0.05 | 0.09 | 0.41 | 1.00 |  |
| Inflation | -0.03 | -0.10 | 0.06 | -0.33 | -0.27 | -0.05 | 0.69 | 1.00 |
| Serial Correlation | 0.11 | 0.00 | 0.00 | -0.10 | -0.29 | 0.06 | 0.89 | 0.75 |

In conclusion, equity REITs have historically offered an attractive risk/return trade-off for investors. They have provided a current income stream along with the potential for long-term capital appreciation. The recent increase in correlation of REIT returns with other investments may lead to a decrease in the overall diversification benefit to investors, but they remain an attractive option.

# Chapter 3
# Description of the Basic Series

This chapter presents the returns for the seven basic SBBI asset classes and describes the construction of these returns. More detail on the construction of some series can be found in the January 1976 *Journal of Business* article, referenced in the Introduction. Annual total returns and capital appreciation returns for each asset class are formed by compounding the monthly returns that appear in Appendix A at the back of this book. Annual income returns are formed by summing the monthly income payments and dividing this sum by the beginning-of-year price. Returns are formed assuming no taxes or transaction costs, except for returns on small capitalization stocks that show the performance of an actual, tax-exempt investment fund including transaction and management costs, starting in 1982.

**Large-Cap Stocks**

One dollar invested in large-capitalization stocks at year-end 1925, with dividends reinvested, grew to $6,035.12 by year-end 2016; this represents a compound annual growth rate of 10.0% (see Exhibit 3.1). Capital appreciation alone caused $1.00 to grow to $175.45 over the 91-year period, a compound annual growth rate of 5.8%. Annual total returns ranged from a high of 54.0% in 1933 to a low of -43.3% in 1931. The 91-year average annual dividend yield was 4.0%.

**Total Returns**

From February 1970 to the present, the large-cap stock total return is provided by S&P Dow Jones Indices, which calculates the total return based on the daily reinvestment of dividends on the ex-dividend date. S&P uses closing pricing from stock exchanges in its calculation. Prior to February 1970, the total return for a given month was calculated by summing the capital appreciation return and the income return as described below.

The large-cap stock total return index is based upon the S&P Composite Index. This index is a readily available, carefully constructed, market-capitalization-weighted benchmark of large-cap stock performance. Market-capitalization-weighted means that the weight of each stock in the index, for a given month, is proportionate to its market capitalization (price times the number of shares outstanding) at the beginning of that month. Currently, the S&P Composite includes 500 of the largest stocks (in terms of stock market value) in the U.S.; prior to March 1957 it consisted of 90 of the largest stocks.

**Capital Appreciation Return**

The capital appreciation component of the large-cap stock total return is the change in the S&P 500 index as reported by S&P Dow Jones Indices from March 1928 to December 2016, and in Standard & Poor's *Trade and Securities Statistics* from January 1926 to February 1928.

## Income Return

From February 1970 to December 2016, the income return was calculated as the difference between the total return and the capital appreciation return. From January 1926 to January 1970, quarterly dividends were extracted from rolling yearly dividends reported quarterly in S&P's *Trade and Securities Statistics*, then allocated to months within each quarter using proportions taken from the 1974 actual distribution of monthly dividends within quarters.

**Exhibit 3.1:** Large Cap Stocks: Total Return and Capital Appreciation Indexes
1926–2016
Index (Year-End 1925 = $1.00)

## Small-Cap Stocks

One dollar invested in small-cap stocks at year-end 1925 grew to $33,212.31 by year-end 2016. This represents a compound annual growth rate of 12.1% over the past 91 years. Total annual returns ranged from a high of 142.9% in 1933 to a low of -58.0% in 1937.

### DFA U.S. Micro Cap Portfolio (April 2001–December 2016)

For April 2001 to December 2016, the small-cap stock return series is the total return achieved by the DFA U.S. Micro Cap Portfolio net of fees and expenses. In April 2001, Dimensional Fund Advisors renamed the DFA U.S. 9–10 Small Company Portfolio (see next page) the DFA U.S. Micro Cap Portfolio and changed some of the criteria. The fund is designed to capture the returns and diversification benefits of a broad cross-section of U.S. small companies on a market-cap weighted basis. The fund's target buy range includes those companies whose market cap falls in the lowest 5% of the market universe defined as the aggregate of the NYSE, NYSE AMEX, and NASDAQ National Market System or companies smaller than the 1,500th largest U.S. company in the same market universe, whichever results in a higher market cap break.

The market universe is examined on a dynamic basis to determine which stocks are eligible for purchase or sale based on market capitalization. To minimize turnover, a hold or buffer range is created for stocks that migrate above the buy range. The upper bound of the hold range is the fifth percentile of the market universe. Stocks that grow above the hold range are eligible for sale and proceeds are reinvested into the portfolio.

At year-end 2016, the DFA U.S. Micro Cap Portfolio contained 1,546 stocks, with a weighted average market cap of $1.128 billion.

### DFA U.S. 9–10 Small Company Portfolio (January 1982–March 2001)

For January 1982 to March 2001, the small-cap stock return series was the total return achieved by the DFA U.S. Small Company 9–10 (for ninth and 10th deciles) Portfolio. The fund's target buy range was a market-cap-weighted universe of the ninth and 10th deciles of the New York Stock Exchange, plus stocks listed on the NYSE Amex (now the NYSE MKT) and NASDAQ National Market with the same or less capitalization as the upper bound of the NYSE ninth decile. Because the lower bound of the 10th decile is near zero, stocks were not purchased if they were smaller than $10 million in market cap (although they were held if they fell below that level).

### NYSE Fifth Quintile Returns (1926–1981)

The equities of smaller companies from 1926 to 1980 are represented by the historical series developed by Professor Rolf W. Banz (see Acknowledgements). This is composed of stocks making up the fifth quintile (i.e., the ninth and 10th deciles) of the New York Stock Exchange (NYSE); the stocks on the NYSE are ranked by capitalization, and each decile contains an equal number of stocks at the beginning of each formation period. The ninth and 10th decile portfolio was first ranked and formed as of December 31, 1925. This portfolio was "held" for five years, with value weighted portfolio returns computed monthly. Every five years the portfolio was rebalanced (i.e., all of the stocks on the NYSE were re-ranked, and a new portfolio of those falling in the ninth and 10th deciles was formed) as of December 31, 1930, and every five years thereafter through December 31, 1980. This method avoided survivorship bias by including the return after the delisting or failure of a stock in constructing the portfolio returns. (Survivorship bias is caused by studying only stocks that have survived events such as bankruptcy and acquisition.)

For 1981, Dimensional Fund Advisors updated the returns using Professor Banz's methods. The data for 1981 are significant to only three decimal places (in decimal form) or one decimal place when returns are expressed in percent.

## Long-term Corporate Bonds

One dollar invested in long-term high-grade corporate bonds at the end of 1925 was worth $200.40 by year-end 2016. The compound annual growth rate over the 91-year period was 6.0%. Total annual returns ranged from a high of 42.6% in 1982 to a low of -8.1% in 1969.

### Total Returns

For 1969 to 2016, corporate bond total returns are represented by the Citigroup Long-Term High-Grade Corporate Bond Index (formerly Salomon Brothers). Because most large corporate bond transactions take place over the counter, a major dealer is the natural source of these data. The index includes nearly all Aaa- and Aa-rated bonds. If a bond is downgraded during a particular month, its return for the month is included in the index before removing the bond from future portfolios.

For 1926 to 1968, total returns were calculated by summing the capital appreciation returns and the income returns. For the period 1946 to 1968, Ibbotson and Sinquefield (1976) backdated the Salomon Brothers index, using Salomon Brothers' monthly yield data; a methodology similar to that used by Salomon was used for 1969 to 2016. Capital appreciation returns were calculated from yields assuming (at the beginning of each monthly holding period) a 20-year maturity, a bond price equal to par, and a coupon equal to the beginning-of-period yield.

For the period 1926 to 1945, Standard & Poor's monthly High Grade Corporate Composite yield data were used, assuming a 4% coupon and a 20-year maturity. The conventional present-value formula for bond price was used for the beginning and end-of-month prices.[3.1] The monthly income return was assumed to be one-twelfth the coupon.

### Long-term Government Bonds

One dollar invested in long-term government bonds at year-end 1925, with coupons reinvested, grew to $134.35 by year end 2016; this represents a compound annual growth rate of 5.5%. Total annual returns ranged from a high of 40.4% in 1982 to a low of -14.9% in 2009 (see Exhibit 3.2). Returns from the capital appreciation component alone caused $1.00 to grow to $1.37 over the 91-year period, representing a compound annual growth rate of 0.3%.

---

[3.1] This formula is presented in Ross, S. A., & Westerfield, R.W. 1988. "Level-Coupon Bonds." P. 97 in *Corporate Finance* (St. Louis: Times Mirror/Mosby).

**Exhibit 3.2:** Long-term Government Bonds: Total Return and Capital Appreciation Indexes 1926–2016

Index (Year-end 1925 = $1.00)

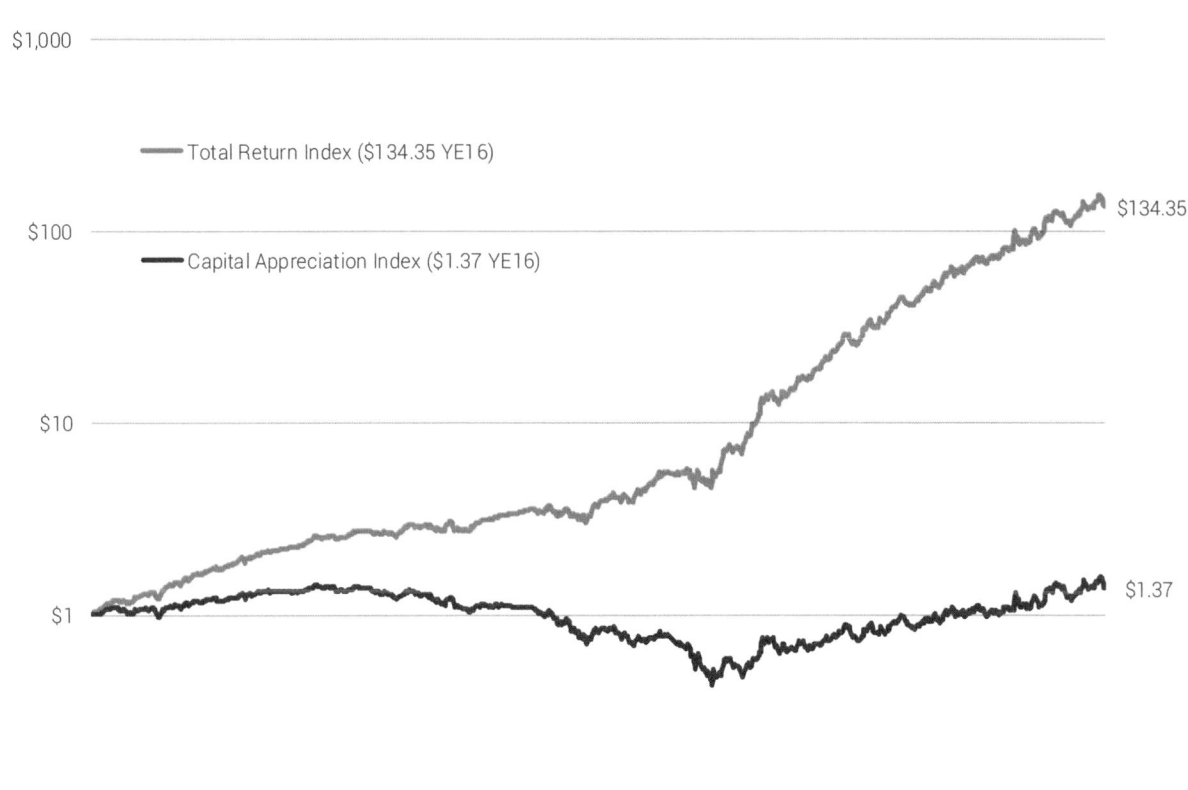

## Total Returns

The total returns on long-term government bonds from 1977 to 2016 are constructed with data from *The Wall Street Journal.* The bond used in 2016 is the 4.5% issue that matures on Feb. 15, 2036. The data for 1926 to 1976 is obtained from the Government Bond File at the Center for Research in Security Prices at the University of Chicago Booth School of Business. The bonds used to construct the index from 1926–2016 are shown in Exhibit 3.4. To the greatest extent possible, a one-bond portfolio with a term of approximately 20 years and a reasonably current coupon – whose returns did not reflect potential tax benefits, impaired negotiability, or special redemption or call privileges – was used each year. Where "flower" bonds (tenderable to the Treasury at par in payment of estate taxes) had to be used, we chose the bond with the smallest potential tax benefit. Where callable bonds had to be used, the term of the bond was assumed to be a simple average of the maturity and first call dates minus the current date. The bond was "held" for the calendar year and returns were computed. The annual total returns for the long-term government bond series from 1926–2016 is illustrated in Exhibit 3.3.

**Exhibit 3.3:** Long-term Government Bonds Annual Total Returns (%)
1926–2016

In October 2001, the U.S. Treasury announced that it would no longer issue 30-year Treasury bonds and the 10-year bond became the longest-term Treasury security offered. This decision was reversed in 2005 and the U.S. Treasury resumed issuing 30-year Treasury bonds in February 2006. The lack of trading long-horizon government bonds in this period may influence yields recorded for 2011 through 2016, for which Ibbotson chooses the Treasury bond with the closest term to 20 years.

Total returns for 1977 to 2016 are calculated as the change in the flat (or and-interest) price.[3.2] The flat price is the average of the bond's bid and ask prices, plus the accrued coupon.[3.3] The accrued coupon is equal to zero on the day a coupon is paid, and increases over time until the next coupon payment according to the formula below.

$$A = fC$$

Where:

| | | |
|---|---|---|
| $A$ | = | Accrued coupon |
| $C$ | = | Semiannual coupon rate |
| $f$ | = | (number of days since last coupon payment)/(number of days from last coupon payment to next coupon payment) |

---

[3.2] "Flat price" is used here to mean the unmodified economic value of the bond, i.e., the and-interest price, or quoted price plus accrued interest. In contrast, some sources use flat price to mean the quoted price.

[3.3] For the purpose of calculating the return in months when a coupon payment is made, the change in the flat price includes the coupon.

## Income Return

For 1977 to 2016, the income return for the long-term government bond series is calculated as the change in flat price plus any coupon actually paid from one period to the next, holding the yield constant over the period. As in the total return series, the exact number of days composing the period is used. For 1926 to 1976, the income return for a given month is calculated as the total return minus the capital appreciation return.

## Capital Appreciation or Return in Excess of Yield

For 1977 to 2016, capital appreciation is taken as the total return minus the income return for each month. For 1926 to 1976, the capital appreciation return (also known as the return in excess of yield) is obtained from the CRSP Government Bond File.

A bond's capital appreciation is defined as the total return minus the income return; that is, the return in excess of yield. This definition omits the capital gain or loss that comes from the movement of a bond's price toward par (in the absence of an interest-rate change) as it matures. Capital appreciation, as defined here, captures changes in bond prices caused by changes in the interest rate.

## Yields

The yield on the long-term government bond series is defined as the internal rate of return that equates the bond's price (the average of bid and ask, plus the accrued coupon) with the stream of cash flows (coupons and principal) promised to the bondholder. The yields reported for 1977 to 2016 were calculated from *The Wall Street Journal* prices for the bonds listed in Exhibit 3.4. For non-callable bonds, the maturity date is shown. For callable bonds, the first call date and the maturity dates are shown as in the following example: 10/15/47–52 refers to a bond that is first callable on Oct. 15, 1947, and matures on Oct. 15, 1952. Dates from 47–99 refer to 1947 to 1999; 00–16 refers to 2000 to 2016. For callable bonds trading below par, the yield to maturity is used; above par, the yield to call is used. The yields for 1926 to 1976 were obtained from the CRSP Government Bond File.

**Exhibit 3.4:** Long-term and Intermediate-term Government Bond Issues

### Long-term Gov't Bonds

| Period Bond Is Held In Index | Coupon (%) | Call/Maturity Date |
|---|---|---|
| 1926–1931 | 4.250 | 10/15/47–52 |
| 1932–1935 | 3.000 | 9/15/51–55 |
| 1936–1941 | 2.875 | 3/15/55–60 |
| 1942–1953 | 2.500 | 9/15/67–72 |
| 1954–1958 | 3.250 | 6/15/78–83 |
| 1959–1960 | 4.000 | 2/15/1980 |
| 1961–1965 | 4.250 | 5/15/75–85 |
| 1966–1972 | 4.250 | 8/15/87–92 |
| 1973–1974 | 6.750 | 2/15/1993 |
| 1975–1976 | 8.500 | 5/15/94–99 |
| 1977–1980 | 7.875 | 2/15/95–00 |
| 1981 | 8.000 | 8/15/96–01 |
| 1982 | 13.375 | 8/15/2001 |
| 1983 | 10.750 | 2/15/2003 |
| 1984 | 11.875 | 11/15/2003 |
| 1985 | 11.750 | 2/15/05–10 |
| 1986–1989 | 10.000 | 5/15/05–10 |
| 1990–1992 | 10.375 | 11/15/07–12 |
| 1993–1996 | 7.250 | 5/15/2016 |
| 1997–1998 | 8.125 | 8/15/2019 |
| 1999–2001 | 8.125 | 8/15/2021 |
| 2002 | 6.250 | 8/15/2023 |
| 2003–2004 | 7.500 | 11/15/2024 |
| 2005 | 6.875 | 8/15/2025 |
| 2006 | 6.750 | 8/15/2026 |
| 2007 | 6.375 | 8/15/2027 |
| 2008 | 5.500 | 8/15/2028 |
| 2009 | 5.250 | 2/15/2029 |
| 2010–2012 | 5.375 | 2/15/2031 |
| 2013 | 4.500 | 2/15/2036 |
| 2014 | 4.500 | 2/15/2036 |
| 2015 | 4.500 | 2/15/2036 |
| 2016 | 4.500 | 2/15/2036 |

### Intermediate-term Gov't Bonds

| Period Bond Is Held In Index | Coupon (%) | Call/Maturity Date |
|---|---|---|
| 1934–1936 | 3.250 | 8/1/1941 |
| 1937 | 3.375 | 3/15/1943 |
| 1938–1940 | 2.500 | 12/15/1945 |
| 1941 | 3.000 | 1/1/1946 |
| 1942 | 3.000 | 1/1/1947 |
| 1943 | 1.750 | 6/15/1948 |
| 1944–1945 | 2.000 | 3/15/1950 |
| 1946 | 2.000 | 6/15/1951 |
| 1947 | 2.000 | 3/15/1952 |
| 1948 | 2.000 | 9/15/1953 |
| 1949 | 2.500 | 3/15/1954 |
| 1950 | 2.250 | 6/15/1955 |
| 1951–1952 | 2.500 | 3/15/1958 |
| 1953 | 2.375 | 6/15/1958 |
| 1954 | 2.375 | 3/15/1959 |
| 1955 | 2.125 | 11/15/1960 |
| 1956 | 2.750 | 9/15/1961 |
| 1957–1958 | 2.500 | 8/15/1963 |
| 1959 | 3.000 | 2/15/1964 |
| 1960 | 2.625 | 2/15/1965 |
| 1961 | 3.750 | 5/15/1966 |
| 1962 | 3.625 | 11/15/1967 |
| 1963 | 3.875 | 5/15/1968 |
| 1964 | 4.000 | 2/15/1969 |
| 1965 | 4.000 | 8/15/1970 |
| 1966 | 4.000 | 8/15/1971 |
| 1967 | 4.000 | 2/15/1972 |
| 1968 | 4.000 | 8/15/1973 |
| 1969 | 5.625 | 8/15/1974 |
| 1970 | 5.750 | 2/15/1975 |
| 1971 | 6.250 | 2/15/1976 |
| 1972 | 1.500 | 10/1/1976 |
| 1973 | 6.250 | 2/15/1978 |
| 1974 | 6.250 | 8/15/1979 |
| 1975 | 6.875 | 5/15/1980 |
| 1976 | 7.000 | 2/15/1981 |
| 1977 | 6.375 | 2/15/1982 |

### Intermediate-term Gov't Bonds (cont.)

| Period Bond Is Held In Index | Coupon (%) | Call/Maturity Date |
|---|---|---|
| 1978 | 8.000 | 2/15/1983 |
| 1979 | 7.250 | 2/15/1984 |
| 1980 | 8.000 | 2/15/1985 |
| 1981 | 13.500 | 2/15/1986 |
| 1982 | 9.000 | 2/15/1987 |
| 1983 | 12.375 | 1/1/1988 |
| 1984 | 14.625 | 1/15/1989 |
| 1985 | 10.500 | 1/15/1990 |
| 1986 | 11.750 | 1/15/1991 |
| 1987 | 11.625 | 1/15/1992 |
| 1988 | 8.750 | 1/15/1993 |
| 1989 | 9.000 | 2/15/1994 |
| 1990 | 8.625 | 10/15/1995 |
| 1991–1992 | 7.875 | 7/15/1996 |
| 1993 | 6.375 | 1/15/1999 |
| 1994 | 5.500 | 4/15/2000 |
| 1995 | 8.500 | 2/15/2000 |
| 1996 | 7.750 | 2/15/2001 |
| 1997 | 6.375 | 8/15/2002 |
| 1998 | 5.750 | 8/15/2003 |
| 1999 | 7.250 | 8/15/2004 |
| 2000 | 6.500 | 8/15/2005 |
| 2001 | 6.500 | 10/15/2006 |
| 2002 | 6.125 | 8/15/2007 |
| 2003 | 5.625 | 5/15/2008 |
| 2004 | 5.500 | 5/15/2009 |
| 2005 | 5.750 | 8/15/2010 |
| 2006 | 5.000 | 8/15/2011 |
| 2007 | 4.875 | 2/15/2012 |
| 2008 | 3.625 | 5/15/2013 |
| 2009 | 4.250 | 8/15/2014 |
| 2010 | 4.125 | 5/15/2015 |
| 2011 | 3.250 | 7/31/2016 |
| 2012 | 2.750 | 5/31/2017 |
| 2013 | 2.375 | 5/31/2018 |
| 2014 | 3.125 | 5/15/2019 |
| 2015 | 3.500 | 5/15/2020 |
| 2016 | 3.125 | 5/15/2021 |

## Intermediate-term Government Bonds

One dollar invested in intermediate-term government bonds at year end 1925, with coupons reinvested, grew to $95.78 by year-end 2016. This represents a 91-year compound annual growth rate of 5.1%. Total annual returns ranged from a high of 29.1% in 1982 to a low of -5.1% in 1994.

Capital appreciation caused $1.00 to increase to $1.68 over the 91-year period, representing a compound annual growth rate of 0.6%. This increase was unexpected: Because yields rose on average over the period, capital appreciation on a hypothetical intermediate-term government bond portfolio with a constant five-year maturity should have been negative. An explanation of the positive average return is given at the end of this chapter.

**Exhibit 3.5:** Intermediate-term Government Bonds: Total Return and Capital Appreciation Indexes 1926–2016

Index (Year-end 1925 = $1.00)

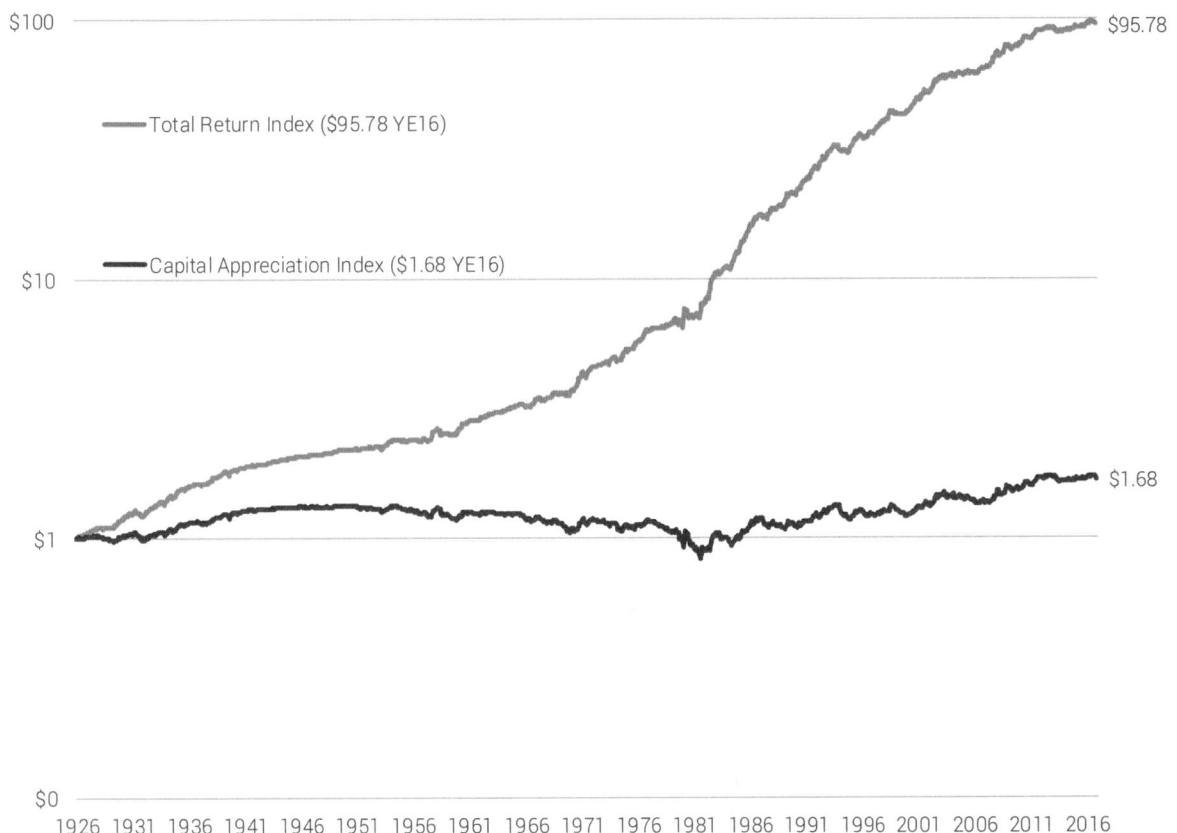

## Total Returns

Total returns of the intermediate-term government bonds for 1987 to 2016 are calculated from *The Wall Street Journal* prices, using the coupon accrual method described above for long-term government bonds (see equation in previous section). The bond used in 2016 is the 3.125% issue maturing on May 15, 2021. Returns for 1934 to 1986 are obtained from the CRSP Government Bond File. The bonds used to construct the index for 1934 to 2016 are shown in Exhibit 3.4.

As with long-term government bonds, one-bond portfolios are used to construct the intermediate-term government bond index. The bond chosen each year is the shortest non-callable bond with a maturity not less than five years, and it is "held" for the calendar year. Monthly returns are computed. (Bonds with impaired negotiability or special redemption privileges are omitted, as are partially or fully tax-exempt bonds starting with 1943.)

For 1934 to 1942, almost all bonds with maturities near five years were partially or fully tax-exempt and selected using the rules described above. Personal tax rates were generally low in that period, so that yields on tax-exempt bonds were similar to yields on taxable bonds.

For 1926 to 1933, there are few bonds suitable for construction of a series with a five year maturity. For this period, five-year bond yield estimates are used. These estimates are obtained from Thomas S. Coleman, Lawrence Fisher, and Roger G. Ibbotson, *Historical U.S. Treasury Yield Curves: 1926–1992 with 1995 update* (Ibbotson Associates, Chicago, 1995). The estimates reflect what a "pure play" five-year Treasury bond, selling at par and with no special redemption or call provisions, would have yielded had one existed. Estimates are for partially tax-exempt bonds for 1926 to 1932 and for fully tax-exempt bonds for 1933. Monthly yields are converted to monthly total returns by calculating the beginning and end-of-month flat prices for the hypothetical bonds. The bond is "bought" at the beginning of the month at par (i.e., the coupon equals the previous month-end yield), assuming a maturity of five years. It is "sold" at the end of the month, with the flat price calculated by discounting the coupons and principal at the end-of-month yield, assuming a maturity of four years and 11 months. The flat price is the price of the bond including coupon accruals, so that the change in flat price represents total return. Monthly income returns are assumed to be equal to the previous end-of month yield, stated in monthly terms. Monthly capital appreciation returns are formed as total returns minus income returns.

## Income Return and Capital Appreciation

For 1987 to 2016, the income return is calculated according to the methodology stated under "Long-term Government Bonds." Monthly capital appreciation (return in excess of yield) over this same period is the difference between total return and income return.

For 1934 to 1986, capital appreciation (return in excess of yield) is taken directly from the CRSP Government Bond File. The income return is calculated as the total return minus the capital appreciation return. Prior to 1934, the income and capital appreciation components of total return are generated from yield estimates as described earlier for total returns.

## Yields

The yield on an intermediate-term government bond is the internal rate of return that equates the bond's price with the stream of cash flows (coupons and principal) promised to the bondholder. The yields reported for 1987 to 2016 are calculated from *The Wall Street Journal* bond prices listed in Exhibit 3.4. For 1934 to 1986, yields were obtained from the CRSP Government Bond File. Yields for 1926 to 1933 are estimates from Coleman, Fisher, and Ibbotson, *Historical U.S. Treasury Yield Curves: 1926–1992 with 1995 update.*

## U.S. Treasury Bills

One dollar invested in U.S. Treasury bills at year-end 1925 grew to $20.63 by year-end 2016; this represents a compound annual growth rate of 3.4%. Total annual returns ranged from a high of 14.7% in 1981 to lows close to zero percent in the years shown in Exhibit 3.6. In Exhibit 3.6, all years in which the annual total return of U.S. Treasury bills was less than 0.5% are shown. The years in which Treasury bills had less than 0.5% annual total return primarily occurred during three periods: (i) the Great Depression (the 1930s), (ii) World War II (the 1940s), and (iii) in the period after the 2008 financial crisis (2009–2016).

**Exhibit 3.6:** Years in which Annual Total Returns of U.S. Treasury Bills Were Less than 0.5% 1926–2016

| Year | Total Return | Year | Total Return |
|------|-------------:|------|-------------:|
| 1933 | 0.3% | 2009 | 0.1% |
| 1934 | 0.2% | 2010 | 0.1% |
| 1935 | 0.2% | 2011 | 0.0% |
| 1936 | 0.2% | 2012 | 0.1% |
| 1937 | 0.3% | 2013 | 0.0% |
| 1938 | 0.0% | 2014 | 0.0% |
| 1939 | 0.0% | 2015 | 0.0% |
| 1940 | 0.0% | 2016 | 0.2% |
| 1941 | 0.1% | | |
| 1942 | 0.3% | | |
| 1943 | 0.3% | | |
| 1944 | 0.3% | | |
| 1945 | 0.3% | | |
| 1946 | 0.4% | | |

## Total Returns

For the U.S. Treasury bill index, data from *The Wall Street Journal* are used for 1977 to 2016; the CRSP U.S. Government Bond File is the source until 1976. Each month a one-bill portfolio containing the shortest-term bill having not less than one month to maturity is constructed. (The bill's original term to maturity is not relevant.) To measure holding-period returns for the one-bill portfolio, the bill is priced as of the last trading day of the previous month end and as of the last trading day of the current month. The price of the bill (*P*) at each time (*t*) is given as:

$$P_t = \left[ 1 - \frac{rd}{360} \right]$$

Where:

| | | |
|---|---|---|
| $P_t$ | = | Price of the bill at time *t* |
| *r* | = | decimal yield (the average of bid and ask quotes) on the bill at time *t* |
| *d* | = | number of days to maturity as of time *t* |

The total return on the bill is the month-end price divided by the previous month-end price, minus one.

## Negative Returns on Treasury Bills

*Monthly* Treasury bill returns (as reported in Appendix A-14) were negative in February 1933, and in 12 months during the 1938 to 1941 period. More recently, since July 2011 monthly Treasury bill returns have been negative in 8 months. Annual total returns have been negative only once, in 1938. Since negative Treasury bill returns seem to contradict logic, an explanation is in order.

Negative yields observed in the data do not imply that investors purchased Treasury bills with a guaranteed negative return. Rather, Treasury bills of that era were exempt from personal property taxes in some states, while cash was not. Further, for a bank to hold U.S. government deposits, Treasury securities were required as collateral. These circumstances created excessive demand for the security, and thus bills were sold at a premium. Given the low interest rates during the period, owners of the bills experienced negative returns.

In 2008, yields on U.S. Treasury bills fell from a little over 3.0% at the beginning of the year to approximately zero percent by the end of the year, but the dynamics were different from those for 1938 to 1941. In the wake of the 2008 financial crisis, investors' behavior could be described as an extreme flight to safety; investors were willing to accept little (if anything) in return for the assurance that they would get their principal back. In other words, the return *of* capital took precedence over the return *on* capital.

From 2009 to 2016, U.S. Treasury bill yields remained near historical lows near zero percent. These low yields can be partially explained by the Federal Funds target rate, which was actually a *range* of zero percent to 0.25% from December 16, 2008 through December 16, 2015. On December 17, 2015, the target "range" was increased to 0.25% to 0.50%, and on December 15, 2016, the target "range" was further increased to 0.50% to 0.75%.[3.4]

## Inflation

A basket of consumer goods purchased for $1.00 at year-end 1925 cost $13.47 by year-end 2016. Of course, the contents of the basket have changed over time. This increase represents a compound annual rate of inflation of 2.9% over the past 91 years. Inflation rates ranged from a high of 18.2% in 1946 to a low of -10.3% in 1932.

## Inflation

The Consumer Price Index for All Urban Consumers, or CPI-U, not seasonally adjusted, is used to measure inflation, which is the rate of change of consumer goods prices. Unfortunately, the CPI is not measured over the same period as the other asset returns. All of the security returns are measured from one month-end to the next month-end. CPI commodity prices are collected during the month. Thus, measured inflation rates lag the other series by about one-half month. Prior to January 1978, the CPI (rather than the CPI-U) was used. For 1978 to 1987, the index uses the year 1967 in determining the items composing the basket of goods. After 1987, a three-year period, 1982 to 1984, was used to determine the items making up the basket of goods. All inflation measures are constructed by the U.S. Department of Labor, Bureau of Labor Statistics, Washington.

### Bond Capital Appreciation Despite Rising Yields

The capital appreciation component of intermediate-term government bond returns caused $1.00 invested at year-end 1925 to grow to $1.68 by the end of 2016, representing a compound annual growth rate of 0.6%. This is surprising because yields, on average, rose over the period.

An investor in a hypothetical five-year constant maturity portfolio, with continuous rebalancing, suffered a capital loss (that is, excluding coupon income) over 1926 to 2016. An investor who rebalanced yearly, choosing bonds according to the method set forth above, fared better. This investor would have earned the 0.6% annualized capital gain recorded here.

This performance relates to the construction of the intermediate-term bond series. For 1926 to 1933, the one-bond portfolio was rebalanced monthly to maintain a constant maturity of five years. For 1934 to 2016, one bond (the shortest bond not less than five years to maturity) was chosen at the beginning of each year and priced monthly. New bonds were not picked each month to maintain a constant maturity intra-year.

There are several possible reasons for the positive capital appreciation return. Chief among these reasons are convexity of the bond portfolio and the substitution of one bond for another at each year-end.

---

[3.4]    Source: Federal Reserve Bank of New York.

**Convexity**

Each year, we "bought" a bond with approximately five years to maturity and held it for one year. During this period, the market yield on the bond fluctuates. Because the duration of the bond shortens (the bond becomes less interest-rate sensitive) as yields rise and the duration lengthens as yields fall, more is gained from a fall in yield than is lost from a rise in yield. This characteristic of a bond is known as convexity.

For example, suppose an 8% coupon bond is bought at par at the beginning of a year; the yield fluctuates (but the portfolio is not rebalanced) during the year; and the bond is sold at par at the end of the year. The price of the bond at both the beginning and end of the year is $100; the change in bond price is zero. However, the fluctuations will have caused the gains during periods of falling yields to exceed the losses during periods of rising yields. Thus the total return for the year exceeds 8%. Because our measure of capital appreciation is the return in excess of yield, rather than the change in bond price, capital appreciation for this bond (as measured) will be greater than zero.

In 1992, the yield for intermediate-term government bonds started the year at 5.97%, rose, fell, and finally rose again to end at 6.11%, slightly higher than the starting point. In the absence of convexity, the capital appreciation return for 1992 would be negative. Because of the fluctuation of yields during the year, however, the capital appreciation return on the intermediate-term government bond index was positive 0.64%.

It should be noted that the return in excess of yield, or capital gain, from convexity is caused by holding, over the year, a bond whose yield at purchase is different from the current market yield. If the portfolio were rebalanced each time the data were sampled (in this case, monthly), by selling the old bond and buying a new five-year bond selling at par, the portfolio would have no convexity. That is, over a period where yields ended where they started, the measured capital appreciation would be zero. However, this is neither a practical way to construct an index of actual bonds nor to manage a bond portfolio.

**Bond Substitution**

Another reason the intermediate term government bond series displays positive capital appreciation even though yields rose is the way in which bonds were removed from the portfolio and replaced with other bonds. In general, it was not possible to replace a bond "sold" by buying one with exactly the same yield. This produces a spurious change in the yield of the series – one that should not be associated with a capital gain or loss.

For example: Suppose a five-year bond yielding 8% is bought at par at the beginning of the year; at that time, four-year bonds yield 7%. Over the year, the yield curve rises in parallel by 1 percentage point so that when it comes time to sell the bond at year-end, it yields 8% and has four years to maturity. Therefore, at both the beginning and end of the year, the price of the bond is $100.

The proceeds from the sale are used to buy a new five-year bond yielding 9%. While the bond price change was zero over the year, the yield of the series has risen from 8% to 9%. Thus it is possible, because of the process of substituting one bond for another, for the yield series to contain a spurious rise that is not, and should not be expected to be, associated with a decline in the price of any particular bond. This phenomenon is likely to be the source of some of the positive capital appreciation in our intermediate-term government bond series.

## Other Issues

Although convexity and bond substitution may explain the anomaly of positive capital appreciation in a bond series with rising yields, there are other incomplete-market problems that may also help explain the capital gain. For example, intermediate-term government bonds were scarce in the 1930s and 1940s. As a result, the bonds chosen for this series occasionally had maturities longer than five years, ranging as high as eight years when bought. The 1930s and the first half of the 1940s were bullish for the bond market. Longer bonds included in this series had higher yields and substantially higher capital gain returns than bonds with exactly five years to maturity might have had if any existed. This upward bias is particularly noticeable in 1934, 1937, and 1938.

In addition, callable and fully or partially tax-exempt bonds were used when necessary to obtain a bond for some years. The conversion of the Treasury bond market from tax-exempt to taxable status produced a one-time upward jump in stated yields, but not a capital loss on any given bond. Therefore, part of the increase in stated yields over 1926 to 2016 was a tax effect that did not cause a capital loss on the intermediate-term bond index. Further, the callable bonds used in the early part of the period may have commanded a return premium for taking this extra risk.

# Chapter 4
# Description of the Derived Series

Historical data suggests that investors are rewarded for taking risks and that returns are related to inflation rates. The risk/return and the real/nominal relationships in the historical data are revealed by looking at the risk-premium and inflation-adjusted series derived from the basic asset series. Annual total returns for the four risk premiums and six inflation-adjusted series are presented in Exhibit 4.9 of this chapter.

### Derived Series Calculated Using Geometric Differences

Derived series are calculated as the geometric differences between two basic asset classes. Returns on basic series A and B and derived series C are related as follows:

$$(1+C) = \left[\frac{1+A}{1+B}\right]$$

where the series returns for A, B, and C are in decimal form (e.g., 5% is indicated by 0.05). Thus C is given by:

$$C = \left[\frac{1+A}{1+B}\right] - 1 \approx A - B$$

As an example, suppose return A equals 15%, or 0.15; and return B is 5%, or 0.05; then C equals (1.15 / 1.05) − 1 = 0.0952, or 9.52%. This result, while slightly different from the simple arithmetic difference of 10%, is conceptually the same.

### Definitions of the Derived Series

From the seven basic asset classes (large-cap stocks, small-cap stocks, long-term corporate bonds, long-term government bonds, intermediate-term government bonds, U.S. Treasury bills, and consumer goods (inflation)), 10 additional series are derived that represent the component or elemental parts of the asset returns.

### Two Categories of Derived Series

The 10 derived series are categorized as (i) risk premiums, or payoffs for taking various types of risk, and (ii) as inflation-adjusted asset returns. The risk premiums are the bond horizon premium, the bond default premium, the equity risk premium, and the small-stock premium. The inflation-adjusted asset return series are constructed by geometrically subtracting inflation from each of the six asset total return series. The 10 derived series are summarized in Exhibit 4.1 (next page).

**Exhibit 4.1:** The Derived Series

| Risk Premia Series | Derivation |
|---|---|
| Equity Risk Premium | $\dfrac{(1 + \textit{Large Stock TR})}{(1 + \textit{Treasury Bill TR})} - 1$ |
| Small-Stock Premium | $\dfrac{(1 + \textit{Small Stock TR})}{(1 + \textit{Large Stock TR})} - 1$ |
| Bond Default Premium | $\dfrac{(1 + \textit{LT Corp Bond TR})}{(1 + \textit{LT Govt Bond})} - 1$ |
| Bond Horizon Premium | $\dfrac{(1 + \textit{LT Govt Bond TR})}{(1 + \textit{Treasury Bill TR})} - 1$ |

| Inflation–Adjusted Series | Derivation |
|---|---|
| Large-Cap Stock Returns | $\dfrac{(1 + \textit{Large Stock TR})}{(1 + \textit{Inflation})} - 1$ |
| Small-Cap Stock Returns | $\dfrac{(1 + \textit{Small Stock TR})}{(1 + \textit{Inflation})} - 1$ |
| Corporate Bond Returns | $\dfrac{(1 + \textit{LT Corp Bond TR})}{(1 + \textit{Inflation})} - 1$ |
| Long-term Government Bond Returns | $\dfrac{(1 + \textit{LT Govt Bond TR})}{(1 + \textit{Inflation})} - 1$ |
| Intermediate-term Government Bond Returns | $\dfrac{(1 + \textit{IT Govt Bond TR})}{(1 + \textit{Inflation})} - 1$ |
| Treasury Bill Returns (Real Riskless Rate of Returns) | $\dfrac{(1 + \textit{Treasury Bill TR})}{(1 + \textit{Inflation})} - 1$ |

## Equity Risk Premium

Large-cap stock returns are composed of inflation, the real riskless rate, and the equity risk premium. The equity risk premium is the geometric difference between large-cap stock total returns and U.S. Treasury bill total returns.

Because large-cap stocks are not strictly comparable with bonds, horizon and default premiums are not used to analyze the components of equity returns (large-cap stocks have characteristics that are analogous to horizon and default risk, but they are not equivalent).

The monthly equity risk premium is given by:

$$\frac{(1 + Large\,Stock\,TR)}{(1 + Treasury\,Bill\,TR)} - 1$$

## Small-Stock Premium

The small-stock premium is the geometric difference between small-cap stock total returns and large-cap stock total returns. The monthly small-stock premium is given by:

$$\frac{(1 + Small\,Stock\,TR)}{(1 + Large\,Stock\,TR)} - 1$$

## Bond Default Premium

The bond default premium is defined as the net return from investing in long-term corporate bonds rather than long-term government bonds of equal maturity. Because there is a possibility of default on a corporate bond, bondholders receive a premium that reflects this possibility, in addition to inflation, the real riskless rate, and the horizon premium.

The monthly bond default premium is given by:

$$\frac{(1 + LT\,Corp\,Bond\,TR)}{(1 + LT\,Govt\,Bond\,TR)} - 1$$

## Components of the Default Premium

Bonds susceptible to default have higher returns (when they do not default) than those of riskless bonds. Default on a bond may be a small loss, such as a late or skipped interest payment, or it may be a larger loss, such as the loss of any or all principal as well as interest. In any case, part of the default premium on a portfolio of bonds is consumed by the losses on those bonds that do default.

The remainder of the default premium (the portion not consumed by defaults) is a pure risk premium, which the investor demands and, over the long run, receives for taking on the risk of default. The expected return on a corporate bond, or portfolio of corporate bonds, is less than the bond's or portfolio's yield. The portion of the yield that is expected to be consumed by defaults must be subtracted. The expected return on a corporate bond is equal to the expected return on a government bond of similar maturity, plus the pure risk premium portion of the bond default premium.

## Callability Risk Is Captured in the Default Premium

Callability risk is the risk that a bond will be redeemed (at or near par) by its issuer before maturity, at a time when market interest rates are lower than the bond's coupon rate. The possibility of redemption is risky because it would prevent the bondholder of the redeemed issue from reinvesting the proceeds at the original (higher) interest rate. The bond default premium, as measured here, also inadvertently captures any premium investors may demand or receive for this risk.

## Bond Horizon Premium

Long-term government bonds behave differently from short-term bills in that their prices (and hence returns) are more sensitive to interest-rate fluctuations. The bond horizon premium is the extra return investors demand for holding long-term bonds instead of U.S. Treasury bills.

The monthly bond horizon premium is given by:

$$\frac{\left(1 + LT\,Govt\,Bond\,TR\right)}{\left(1 + Treasury\,Bill\,TR\right)} - 1$$

Long-term rather than intermediate-term government bonds are used to derive the bond horizon premium so as to capture a "full unit" of price fluctuation risk. Intermediate-term government bonds may display a partial horizon premium, which is smaller than the difference between long-term bonds and short-term bills.

## Determining the Bond Premium: Maturity vs. Duration

Duration is the present-value-weighted average time to receipt of cash flows (coupons and principal) from holding a bond, and can be calculated from the bond's yield, coupon rate, and term to maturity. The duration of a given bond determines the amount of return premium arising from differences in bond life. The bond horizon premium is also referred to as the "maturity premium," based on the observation that bonds with longer maturities command a return premium over shorter-maturity bonds. Duration, not term to maturity, however, is the bond characteristic that determines this return premium.

## Why a "Horizon" Premium?

Investors often strive to match the duration of their bond holdings (cash inflows) with the estimated duration of their obligations (cash outflows). Consequently, investors with short time horizons regard long-duration bonds as risky (due to price fluctuation risk), and short-term bills as riskless. Conversely, investors with long time horizons regard short-term bills as risky (due to the uncertainty about the yield at which bills can be reinvested), and long-duration bonds as riskless or less risky.

Empirically, long-duration bonds bear higher yields and greater returns than short-term bills; that is, the yield curve slopes upward on average over time. This indicates that investors are more averse to the price fluctuation risk of long-duration bonds than to the reinvestment risk of bills.

Bond duration risk is thus in the eye of the beholder, or bondholder. Therefore, rather than identifying the premium as a payoff for long-bond risk (which implies a judgment that short-horizon investors are "right" in their risk perceptions), it is better to go directly to the source of the return differential (the differing time horizons of investors) and use the label "horizon premium."

### Large-Cap Stock Real Returns

Large-cap stock total returns were 10.0% compounded annually over the period 1926 to 2016 in nominal terms. In real (inflation-adjusted) terms, stocks provided a 6.9% compound annual return. Thus, a large-cap stock investor would have experienced a substantial increase in real wealth, or purchasing power, over the 91-year period (i.e., even after adjusting for inflation, large stock investors' wealth increased over the 1926–2016 period).

### Construction

The inflation-adjusted return is a geometric difference and is approximately equal to the arithmetic difference between the large-cap stock total return and the inflation rate. The monthly inflation adjusted large-cap stock return is given by:

$$\frac{\left(1+Large\,Stock\,TR\right)}{\left(1+Inflation\right)}-1$$

The inflation-adjusted large-cap stock return may also be expressed as the geometric sum of the real riskless rate and the equity risk premium:

$$\left[\left(1+Real\,Riskless\,Rate\right)\times\left(1+Equity\,Risk\,Premium\right)\right]-1$$

Exhibit 4.2 depicts (i) what $1.00 invested at the end of December 1925 in large-cap stocks would have grown to by the end of 2016, and (ii) what $1.00 invested at the end of December 1925 in large-cap stocks would have grown to by the end of 2016 if large-cap stock returns were adjusted for inflation.

**Exhibit 4.2:** Large-cap Stocks: Real and Nominal Return Indexes
1926–2016
Index (Year-end 1925 = $1.00)

Chapter 4: Description of the Derived Series

## Small-Cap Stock Real Returns

Small-cap stock total returns were 12.1% compounded annually over the period 1926–2016 in nominal terms. In real terms, small-cap stocks provided a 9.0% compound annual return. Thus, long term a small-cap stock investor would have experienced a substantial increase in real wealth, or purchasing power, over the 91-year period.

## Construction

The inflation-adjusted return is a geometric difference and is approximately equal to the arithmetic difference between the small-cap stock total return and the inflation rate. The monthly inflation-adjusted small-cap stock return is given by:

$$\frac{(1+\text{Small Stock TR})}{(1+\text{Inflation})}-1$$

Exhibit 4.3 depicts (i) what $1.00 invested at the end of December 1925 in small-cap stocks would have grown to by the end of 2016, and (ii) what $1.00 invested at the end of December 1925 in small-cap stocks would have grown to by the end of 2016 if small-cap stock returns were adjusted for inflation.

**Exhibit 4.3:** Small-cap Stocks Real and Nominal Return Indexes
1926–2016
Index (Year-end 1925 = $1.00)

## Long-term Corporate Bond Real Returns

Corporate bonds returned 6.0% compounded annually over the period 1926–2016 in nominal terms, and a 3.0% compound annual return in real (inflation-adjusted) terms. Thus, corporate bonds have outpaced inflation over the past 91 years.

### Construction

The inflation-adjusted return is a geometric difference and is approximately equal to the arithmetic difference between the long-term corporate bond total return and the inflation rate. The monthly inflation-adjusted corporate bond total return is given by:

$$\frac{\left(1 + CorpBondTR\right)}{\left(1 + Inflation\right)} - 1$$

Exhibit 4.4 depicts (i) what $1.00 invested at the end of December 1925 in long-term corporate bonds would have grown to by the end of 2016, and (ii) what $1.00 invested at the end of December 1925 in long-term corporate bonds would have grown to by the end of 2016 if long-term corporate bond returns were adjusted for inflation.

**Exhibit 4.4:** Long-term Corporate Bonds: Real and Nominal Return Indices
1926–2016
Index (Year-end 1925 = $1.00)

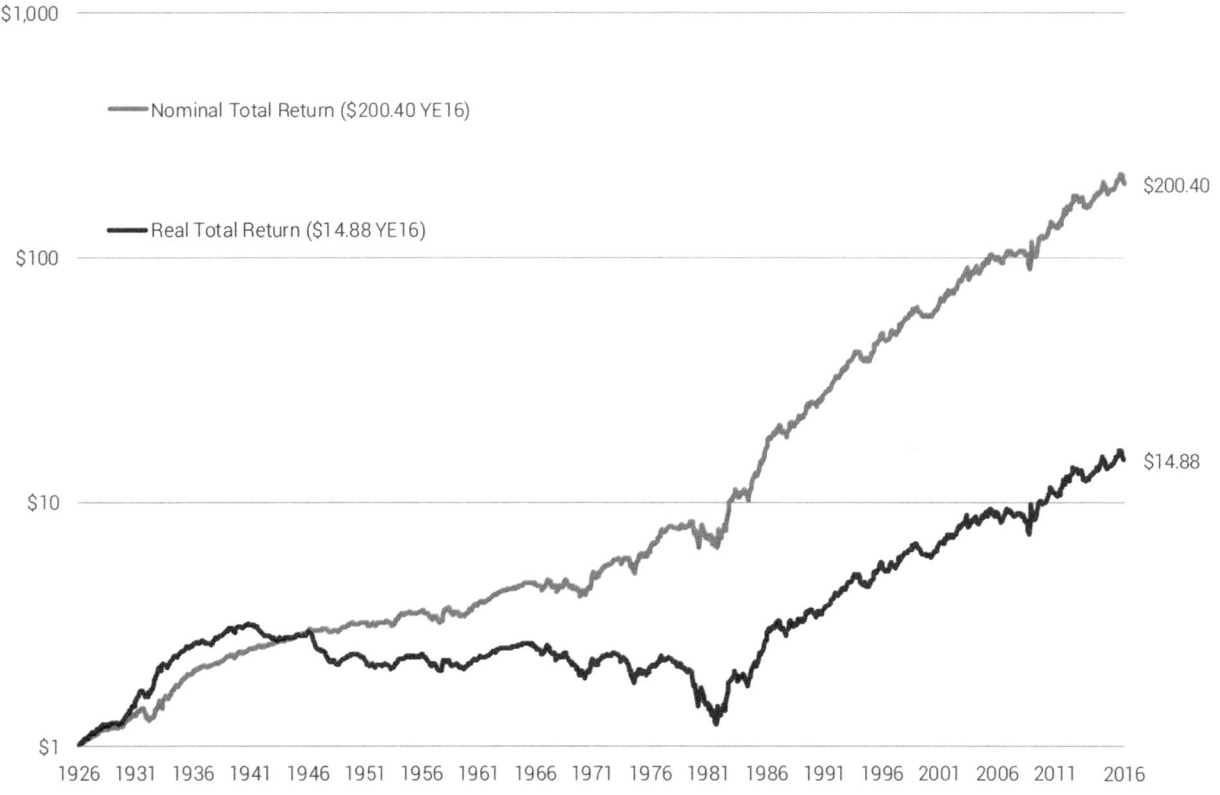

## Long-term Government Bond Real Returns

Long-term government bonds returned 5.5% compounded annually over the period 1926–2016 in nominal terms, and a 2.6% compound annual return in real (inflation-adjusted) terms. Thus, long-term government bonds have outpaced inflation over the past 91 years despite falling bond prices over most of the period.

## Construction

The inflation-adjusted return is a geometric difference and is approximately equal to the arithmetic difference between the long-term government bond total return and the inflation rate. The monthly inflation-adjusted long-term government bond total return is given by:

$$\frac{\left(1 + LT\,Govt\,Bond\,TR\right)}{\left(1 + Inflation\right)} - 1$$

Because government bond returns are composed of inflation, the real riskless rate, and the horizon premium, the inflation-adjusted government bond returns may also be expressed as:

$[(1 + Real\ Riskless\ Rate) \times (1 + Horizon\ Premium)] - 1$

Exhibit 4.5 depicts (i) what $1.00 invested at the end of December 1925 in long-term government bonds would have grown to by the end of 2016, and (ii) what $1.00 invested at the end of December 1925 in long-term government bonds would have grown to by the end of 2016 if long-term government bond returns were adjusted for inflation.

**Exhibit 4.5:** Long-term Government Bonds: Real and Nominal Return Indices
1926–2016
Index (Year-end 1925 = $1.00)

## Intermediate-term Government Bond Real Returns

Intermediate-term government bonds returned 5.1% compounded annually over the period 1926–2016 in nominal terms, and 2.2% in real (inflation-adjusted) terms.

### Construction

The inflation adjusted return is a geometric difference and is approximately equal to the arithmetic difference between the intermediate-term government bond total return and the inflation rate. The monthly inflation-adjusted intermediate-term government bond return is given by:

$$\frac{\left(1 + IT\,Govt\,Bond\,TR\right)}{\left(1 + Inflation\right)} - 1$$

Exhibit 4.6 depicts (i) what $1.00 invested at the end of December 1925 in intermediate-term government bonds would have grown to by the end of 2016, and (ii) what $1.00 invested at the end of December 1925 in intermediate-term government bonds would have grown to by the end of 2016 if intermediate-term government bond returns were adjusted for inflation.

**Exhibit 4.6:** Intermediate-term Government Bonds: Real and Nominal Return Indices 1926–2016

Index (Year-end 1925 = $1.00)

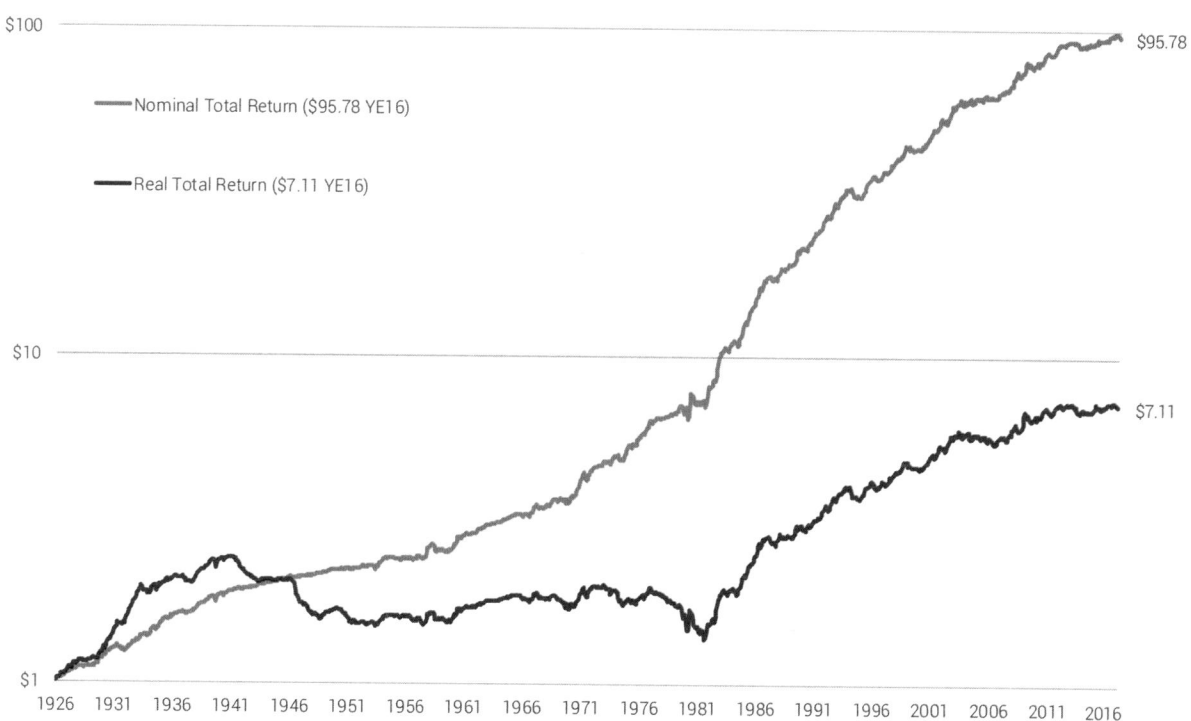

## Real Riskless Rates of Return (U.S. T-Bill Real Returns)

Treasury bills returned 3.4% compounded annually over the 1926–2016 period, in nominal terms, but only a 0.5% compound annual return in real (inflation-adjusted) terms. Thus, an investor in Treasury bills would have barely beaten inflation (or retained purchasing power) over the 91-year period.

### Construction

The real riskless rate of return is the difference in returns between U.S. Treasury bills and inflation. This is given by:

$$\frac{(1+ Treasury\,Bill\,TR)}{(1+Inflation)} -1$$

Exhibit 4.7 depicts (i) what $1.00 invested at the end of December 1925 in U.S. Treasury bills would have grown to by the end of 2016, and (ii) what $1.00 invested at the end of December 1925 in U.S. Treasury bills would have grown to by the end of 2016 if U.S. Treasury bill returns were adjusted for inflation.

**Exhibit 4.7:** U.S. Treasury Bills: Real and Nominal Return Indices
1926–2016
Index (Year-end 1925 = $1.00)

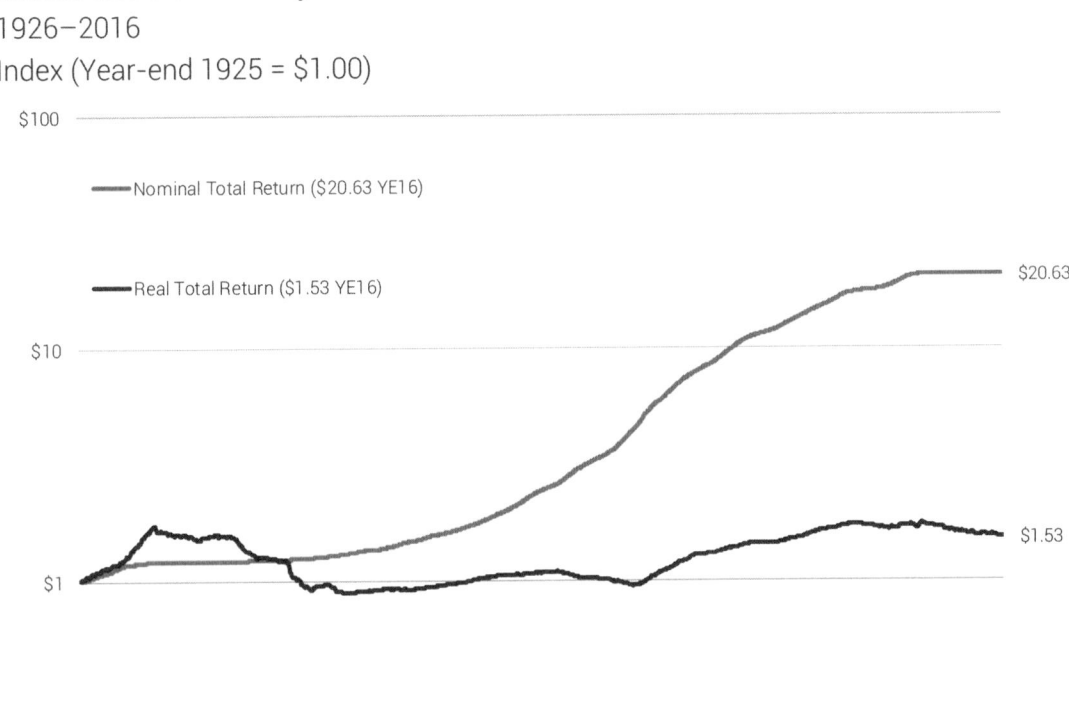

Exhibit 4.8 shows the levels, volatility, and patterns of real interest rates over the last 91 years.

**Exhibit 4.8:** Annual Real Risk-free rates of return (%)
1926–2016

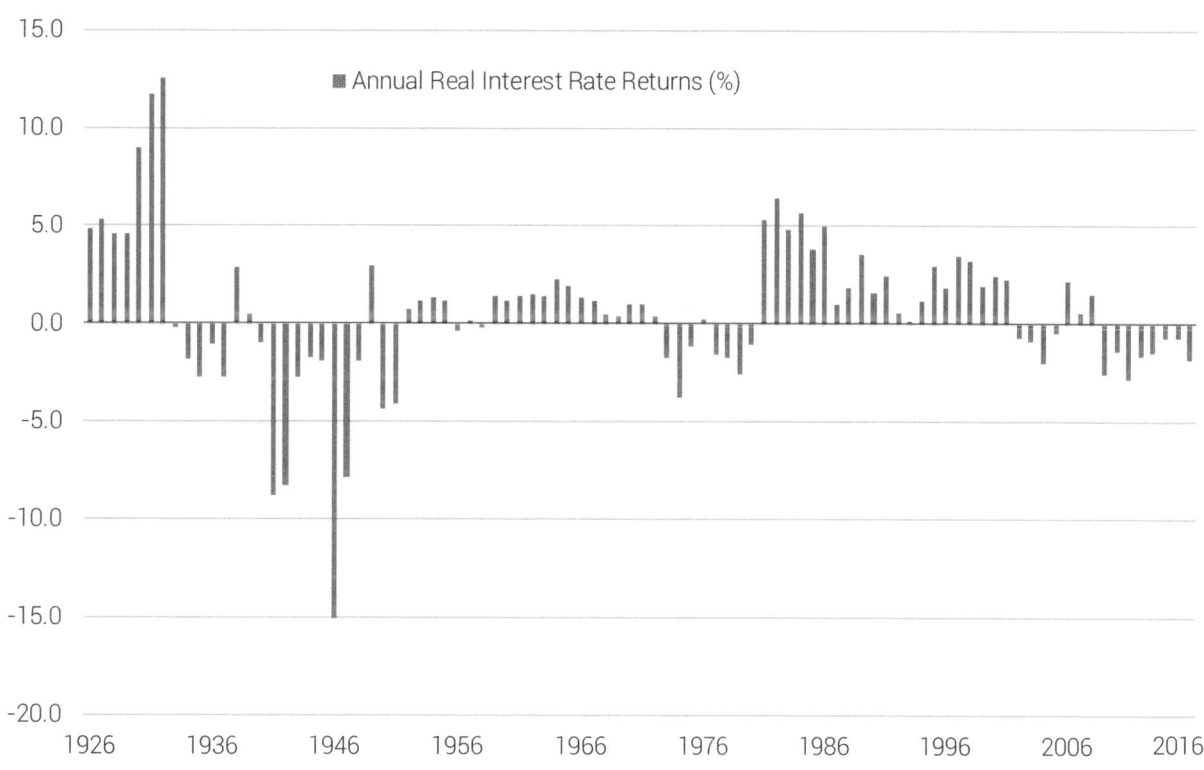

## Returns on the Derived Series

Annual returns for the 10 derived series are calculated from monthly returns in the same manner as the annual basic series. Exhibit 4.9 presents annual returns for each of the 10 derived series. Four of the derived series are risk premiums and six are inflation-adjusted total returns on asset classes.

**Exhibit 4.9:** Annual Return of Derived Series (%)
1926–2016

| | | | | | Inflation-Adjusted | | | | | |
| | Equity Risk Premium | Small Stock Premium | Bond Default Premium | Bond Horizon Premium | Large-Cap Stocks | Small-Cap Stocks | Long-term Corp Bonds | Long-term Gov't Bonds | Inter-term Gov't Bonds | U.S. Treasury Bills |
| Year | | | | | | | | | | |
|---|---|---|---|---|---|---|---|---|---|---|
| Dec-26 | 8.09 | -10.17 | -0.37 | 4.36 | 13.31 | 1.79 | 9.00 | 9.40 | 6.97 | 4.83 |
| Dec-27 | 33.32 | -11.19 | -1.36 | 5.63 | 40.41 | 24.69 | 9.73 | 11.24 | 6.74 | 5.31 |
| Dec-28 | 38.67 | -2.73 | 2.73 | -3.34 | 45.01 | 41.06 | 3.84 | 1.08 | 1.90 | 4.57 |
| Dec-29 | -12.57 | -46.89 | -0.14 | -1.27 | -8.59 | -51.45 | 3.07 | 3.22 | 5.81 | 4.54 |
| Dec-30 | -26.66 | -17.64 | 3.17 | 2.20 | -20.08 | -34.18 | 14.90 | 11.38 | 13.56 | 8.98 |
| Dec-31 | -43.94 | -11.33 | 3.65 | -6.31 | -37.37 | -44.46 | 8.48 | 4.66 | 7.96 | 11.71 |
| Dec-32 | -9.07 | 3.05 | -5.15 | 15.73 | 2.35 | 5.47 | 23.54 | 30.26 | 21.30 | 12.55 |
| Dec-33 | 53.53 | 57.72 | 10.46 | -0.37 | 53.21 | 141.63 | 9.82 | -0.58 | 1.31 | -0.21 |
| Dec-34 | -1.60 | 26.04 | 3.47 | 9.85 | -3.40 | 21.75 | 11.58 | 7.84 | 6.83 | -1.83 |
| Dec-35 | 47.42 | -5.06 | 4.41 | 4.81 | 43.39 | 36.13 | 6.44 | 1.94 | 3.91 | -2.73 |
| Dec-36 | 33.68 | 23.06 | -0.72 | 7.32 | 32.32 | 62.83 | 5.47 | 6.23 | 1.83 | -1.02 |
| Dec-37 | -35.23 | -35.37 | 2.51 | -0.08 | -36.98 | -59.27 | -0.35 | -2.78 | -1.50 | -2.71 |
| Dec-38 | 31.14 | 1.28 | 0.57 | 5.55 | 34.87 | 36.59 | 9.16 | 8.55 | 9.27 | 2.84 |
| Dec-39 | -0.43 | 0.76 | -1.86 | 5.92 | 0.07 | 0.83 | 4.46 | 6.45 | 5.02 | 0.50 |
| Dec-40 | -9.79 | 5.13 | -2.54 | 6.08 | -10.64 | -6.05 | 2.41 | 5.08 | 1.99 | -0.94 |
| Dec-41 | -11.64 | 2.93 | 1.78 | 0.87 | -19.42 | -17.06 | -6.37 | -8.01 | -8.40 | -8.80 |
| Dec-42 | 20.02 | 20.08 | -0.60 | 2.94 | 10.11 | 32.23 | -6.12 | -5.55 | -6.73 | -8.25 |
| Dec-43 | 25.46 | 49.62 | 0.73 | 1.73 | 22.04 | 82.60 | -0.32 | -1.04 | -0.34 | -2.73 |
| Dec-44 | 19.36 | 28.37 | 1.87 | 2.48 | 17.28 | 50.55 | 2.57 | 0.69 | -0.31 | -1.74 |
| Dec-45 | 35.99 | 27.25 | -6.01 | 10.37 | 33.43 | 69.79 | 1.78 | 8.30 | -0.03 | -1.88 |
| Dec-46 | -8.39 | -3.87 | 1.83 | -0.45 | -22.20 | -25.21 | -13.91 | -15.46 | -14.52 | -15.07 |
| Dec-47 | 5.18 | -4.53 | 0.29 | -3.11 | -3.03 | -7.42 | -10.41 | -10.67 | -7.43 | -7.80 |
| Dec-48 | 4.65 | -7.22 | 0.71 | 2.57 | 2.72 | -4.69 | 1.39 | 0.67 | -0.84 | -1.85 |
| Dec-49 | 17.50 | 0.80 | -2.95 | 5.29 | 20.97 | 21.95 | 5.21 | 8.40 | 4.20 | 2.96 |
| Dec-50 | 30.16 | 5.34 | 2.05 | -1.12 | 24.50 | 31.15 | -3.47 | -5.42 | -4.81 | -4.34 |
| Dec-51 | 22.19 | -13.07 | 1.29 | -5.34 | 17.14 | 1.82 | -8.09 | -9.26 | -5.21 | -4.14 |
| Dec-52 | 16.44 | -12.96 | 2.33 | -0.49 | 17.33 | 2.13 | 2.62 | 0.27 | 0.74 | 0.77 |
| Dec-53 | -2.76 | -5.55 | -0.22 | 1.78 | -1.60 | -7.07 | 2.77 | 2.99 | 2.59 | 1.19 |
| Dec-54 | 51.32 | 5.21 | -1.68 | 6.27 | 53.39 | 61.38 | 5.91 | 7.72 | 3.20 | 1.37 |
| Dec-55 | 29.52 | -8.45 | 1.80 | -2.82 | 31.07 | 19.99 | 0.10 | -1.66 | -1.02 | 1.19 |
| Dec-56 | 4.00 | -2.13 | -1.30 | -7.85 | 3.59 | 1.38 | -9.41 | -8.21 | -3.19 | -0.39 |
| Dec-57 | -13.50 | -4.25 | 1.17 | 4.19 | -13.40 | -17.08 | 5.52 | 4.31 | 4.67 | 0.11 |
| Dec-58 | 41.19 | 15.01 | 4.13 | -7.52 | 40.88 | 62.03 | -3.91 | -7.72 | -3.00 | -0.22 |
| Dec-59 | 8.75 | 3.97 | 1.32 | -5.06 | 10.30 | 14.68 | -2.43 | -3.70 | -1.86 | 1.43 |
| Dec-60 | -2.14 | -3.74 | -4.14 | 10.83 | -0.99 | -4.70 | 7.48 | 12.12 | 10.13 | 1.17 |
| Dec-61 | 24.25 | 4.10 | 3.81 | -1.13 | 26.04 | 31.21 | 4.12 | 0.30 | 1.17 | 1.44 |
| Dec-62 | -11.16 | -3.48 | 0.99 | 4.04 | -9.83 | -12.97 | 6.64 | 5.59 | 4.29 | 1.49 |
| Dec-63 | 19.09 | 0.62 | 0.97 | -1.85 | 20.81 | 21.56 | 0.54 | -0.43 | -0.01 | 1.44 |
| Dec-64 | 12.50 | 6.04 | 1.22 | -0.03 | 15.11 | 22.07 | 3.54 | 2.29 | 2.82 | 2.32 |
| Dec-65 | 8.20 | 26.06 | -1.16 | -3.10 | 10.33 | 39.08 | -2.33 | -1.19 | -0.89 | 1.97 |
| Dec-66 | -14.15 | 3.39 | -3.33 | -1.06 | -12.98 | -10.03 | -3.06 | 0.29 | 1.29 | 1.36 |
| Dec-67 | 18.97 | 48.07 | 4.66 | -12.85 | 20.32 | 78.15 | -7.76 | -11.86 | -1.97 | 1.13 |
| Dec-68 | 5.57 | 22.43 | 2.84 | -5.20 | 6.05 | 29.84 | -2.05 | -4.76 | -0.18 | 0.46 |
| Dec-69 | -14.16 | -18.09 | -3.18 | -10.94 | -13.77 | -29.37 | -13.38 | -10.54 | -6.45 | 0.45 |
| Dec-70 | -2.50 | -20.50 | 5.59 | 5.24 | -1.55 | -21.73 | 12.21 | 6.27 | 10.78 | 0.98 |

**Exhibit 4.9:** Annual Return of Derived Series (%)
1926–2016

| | | | | | Inflation-Adjusted | | | | | |
|---|---|---|---|---|---|---|---|---|---|---|
| Year | Equity Risk Premium | Small Stock Premium | Bond Default Premium | Bond Horizon Premium | Large-Cap Stocks | Small-Cap Stocks | Long-term Corp Bonds | Long-term Gov't Bonds | Inter-term Gov't Bonds | U.S. Treasury Bills |
| Dec-71 | 9.50 | 1.92 | -1.96 | 8.47 | 10.59 | 12.71 | 7.41 | 9.55 | 5.19 | 0.99 |
| Dec-72 | 14.59 | -12.24 | 1.49 | 1.78 | 15.07 | 0.99 | 3.72 | 2.20 | 1.69 | 0.41 |
| Dec-73 | -20.22 | -19.01 | 2.27 | -7.52 | -21.59 | -36.49 | -7.04 | -9.10 | -3.85 | -1.72 |
| Dec-74 | -31.92 | 8.87 | -7.11 | -3.38 | -34.46 | -28.65 | -13.60 | -6.99 | -5.80 | -3.74 |
| Dec-75 | 29.70 | 11.36 | 4.99 | 3.21 | 28.23 | 42.80 | 7.13 | 2.04 | 0.76 | -1.13 |
| Dec-76 | 17.93 | 26.99 | 1.62 | 11.11 | 18.24 | 50.15 | 13.20 | 11.40 | 7.69 | 0.26 |
| Dec-77 | -11.68 | 35.04 | 2.41 | -5.53 | -13.04 | 17.43 | -4.74 | -6.99 | -5.02 | -1.55 |
| Dec-78 | -0.57 | 15.85 | 1.12 | -7.80 | -2.25 | 13.24 | -8.34 | -9.36 | -5.08 | -1.69 |
| Dec-79 | 7.46 | 20.96 | -2.98 | -10.52 | 4.68 | 26.62 | -15.43 | -12.83 | -8.13 | -2.59 |
| Dec-80 | 19.12 | 5.56 | 1.24 | -13.65 | 17.89 | 24.45 | -13.48 | -14.54 | -7.55 | -1.03 |
| Dec-81 | -17.11 | 19.78 | -3.04 | -11.20 | -12.73 | 4.53 | -9.34 | -6.50 | 0.47 | 5.30 |
| Dec-82 | 9.95 | 5.31 | 1.57 | 26.97 | 17.02 | 23.23 | 37.25 | 35.13 | 24.28 | 6.42 |
| Dec-83 | 12.64 | 13.96 | 5.57 | -7.49 | 18.07 | 34.56 | 2.37 | -3.03 | 3.48 | 4.82 |
| Dec-84 | -3.26 | -12.18 | 1.20 | 5.12 | 2.23 | -10.22 | 12.42 | 11.08 | 9.68 | 5.67 |
| Dec-85 | 22.28 | -5.36 | -0.67 | 21.58 | 26.94 | 20.13 | 25.36 | 26.21 | 15.96 | 3.81 |
| Dec-86 | 11.78 | -9.96 | -3.76 | 17.30 | 17.34 | 5.66 | 18.51 | 23.14 | 13.85 | 4.98 |
| Dec-87 | -0.20 | -13.82 | 2.51 | -7.76 | 0.81 | -13.13 | -4.48 | -6.82 | -1.44 | 1.01 |
| Dec-88 | 9.65 | 5.37 | 0.94 | 3.13 | 11.67 | 17.67 | 6.02 | 5.03 | 1.61 | 1.85 |
| Dec-89 | 21.51 | -16.33 | -1.59 | 8.99 | 25.84 | 5.29 | 11.07 | 12.87 | 8.26 | 3.56 |
| Dec-90 | -10.13 | -19.05 | 0.57 | -1.51 | -8.68 | -26.08 | 0.64 | 0.07 | 3.42 | 1.61 |
| Dec-91 | 23.55 | 10.86 | 0.49 | 12.98 | 26.59 | 40.33 | 16.32 | 15.75 | 12.03 | 2.46 |
| Dec-92 | 3.97 | 14.62 | 1.24 | 4.39 | 4.59 | 19.87 | 6.31 | 5.01 | 4.17 | 0.59 |
| Dec-93 | 6.98 | 9.90 | -4.28 | 14.91 | 7.13 | 17.74 | 10.16 | 15.08 | 8.26 | 0.14 |
| Dec-94 | -2.49 | 1.76 | 2.18 | -11.24 | -1.32 | 0.42 | -8.22 | -10.17 | -7.62 | 1.20 |
| Dec-95 | 30.29 | -2.27 | -3.39 | 24.69 | 34.17 | 31.13 | 24.06 | 28.41 | 13.91 | 2.98 |
| Dec-96 | 16.87 | -4.34 | 2.35 | -5.83 | 19.01 | 13.84 | -1.86 | -4.12 | -1.18 | 1.82 |
| Dec-97 | 26.70 | -7.94 | -2.51 | 10.07 | 31.13 | 20.72 | 11.06 | 13.91 | 6.57 | 3.49 |
| Dec-98 | 22.62 | -27.91 | -2.04 | 7.83 | 26.54 | -8.78 | 9.00 | 11.27 | 8.46 | 3.19 |
| Dec-99 | 15.63 | 7.23 | 1.67 | -13.04 | 17.88 | 26.39 | -9.87 | -11.34 | -4.34 | 1.95 |
| Dec-00 | -14.16 | 6.06 | -7.09 | 14.72 | -12.08 | -6.75 | 9.17 | 17.50 | 8.90 | 2.42 |
| Dec-01 | -15.13 | 39.33 | 6.70 | -0.13 | -13.23 | 20.89 | 8.96 | 2.11 | 5.97 | 2.24 |
| Dec-02 | -23.36 | 11.33 | -1.28 | 15.93 | -23.91 | -15.29 | 13.63 | 15.10 | 10.31 | -0.71 |
| Dec-03 | 27.38 | 24.88 | 3.76 | 0.42 | 26.31 | 57.74 | 3.32 | -0.42 | 0.51 | -0.84 |
| Dec-04 | 9.56 | 6.77 | 0.19 | 7.22 | 7.39 | 14.66 | 5.29 | 5.09 | -0.97 | -1.99 |
| Dec-05 | 1.88 | 0.74 | -1.80 | 4.69 | 1.45 | 2.20 | 2.37 | 4.25 | -1.99 | -0.42 |
| Dec-06 | 10.49 | 0.32 | 2.03 | -3.45 | 12.93 | 13.29 | 0.69 | -1.32 | 0.59 | 2.20 |
| Dec-07 | 0.79 | -10.16 | -6.63 | 4.99 | 1.36 | -8.94 | -1.43 | 5.57 | 5.74 | 0.56 |
| Dec-08 | -37.99 | 0.43 | -13.58 | 23.89 | -37.06 | -36.78 | 8.68 | 25.76 | 13.00 | 1.51 |
| Dec-09 | 26.34 | 1.28 | 21.06 | -14.99 | 23.11 | 24.69 | 0.29 | -17.16 | -4.99 | -2.56 |
| Dec-10 | 14.92 | 14.08 | 2.08 | 10.01 | 13.37 | 29.33 | 10.78 | 8.52 | 5.54 | -1.35 |
| Dec-11 | 2.07 | -5.26 | -7.20 | 27.05 | -0.83 | -6.04 | 14.55 | 23.44 | 5.68 | -2.84 |
| Dec-12 | 15.93 | 1.93 | 7.01 | 3.37 | 14.02 | 16.21 | 8.78 | 1.66 | -0.08 | -1.65 |
| Dec-13 | 32.36 | 9.58 | 6.54 | -12.80 | 30.42 | 42.91 | -8.45 | -14.07 | -5.11 | -1.46 |
| Dec-14 | 13.67 | -9.47 | -5.95 | 24.69 | 12.83 | 2.15 | 16.40 | 23.77 | 2.22 | -0.73 |
| Dec-15 | 1.36 | -4.91 | -0.37 | -0.67 | 0.65 | -4.29 | -1.74 | -1.37 | 1.05 | -0.71 |
| Dec-16 | 11.74 | 12.22 | 4.86 | 1.55 | 9.68 | 23.09 | 4.53 | -0.31 | -0.15 | -1.84 |

# Chapter 5
# Annual Returns and Indexes

Returns and benchmark indexes are used to measure the rewards investors earn for holding an asset class. Indexes represent levels of wealth or prices, while returns represent changes in levels of wealth. Total returns for specific asset classes can be divided into two primary components: income and capital appreciation. The income return measures the cash stream earned by holding the security, such as coupon interest for bonds or dividend payments for stocks. In contrast, the capital appreciation return results from a change in the price of the security. The method for computing a return varies with the nature of the payment (income or capital appreciation) and the period of measure (monthly or annual). Indexes are computed by establishing a base period and base value and increasing that value by the returns in successive periods. Indexes are used to illustrate the  cumulative growth of wealth from holding an asset class. This chapter describes the computation of the annual returns and indexes.

The first generation of stock indexes was created to assess the market's general direction. One of the oldest and most recognizable market indexes is the Dow Jones Industrial Average, or DJIA, first published on May 26, 1896. When Charles Dow initially calculated the DJIA, which originally consisted of only 12 stocks, the process was simple: Add up the share prices of the stocks in the index and then divide by the number of stocks in the index.[5.1] In this type of index, known as a price-weighted index, higher-priced stocks have a greater influence than lower-priced stocks.

Most modern indexes, however, are market-capitalization weighted, meaning companies with greater overall market capitalization (share price times number of shares outstanding) have a larger influence than companies with lesser market capitalization. Market-cap weighting has a strong theoretical motivation because the capital asset pricing model, or CAPM, implies in its simplest form that every investor should hold every security in proportion to its market capitalization. In contrast, price weighting lacks any theoretical motivation so it is rarely used outside of the Dow Jones Averages (S&P Dow Jones Indices uses market-cap weighting for most of its other indexes).

Market-cap weighting is widely considered to be the central organizing principle of good index construction. Its practical advantage is that the weights adjust automatically as share prices fluctuate, eliminating the need for the frequent and expensive rebalancing that can occur with other weighting schemes. So-called strategic beta or smart beta, or other alternative weighting schemes, seek to outperform market-cap weighted indexes, but deviate from CAPM and are not macroconsistent.

---

[5.1]   Of the original 12 companies listed in the DJIA, General Electric is the only company that remains a component of the average. The total number of companies listed in the DJIA has not changed since 1928, when the number of companies in the index was increased to 30. For more information on the historical makeup of the DJIA, please visit the S&P Dow Jones Indices website at http://www.djaverages.com.

Market-cap weighting is usually implemented with a "float" adjustment that subtracts the number of closely-held and illiquid shares from the number of shares outstanding. A float-adjusted market-cap weighted portfolio is macroconsistent, meaning that if all investors held such a portfolio, all available shares of its constituent stocks would be held, with none left over. Accepting this is an extension of Roll's critique, which states in part that no portfolio can capture shares of all assets (e.g., jewelry, fine wine, automobile collections, etc.) and instruments with market value, so indexes can only approximate a true diversified CAPM portfolio.[5.2] With all other weighting schemes, it is mathematically impossible for all investors to hold the index portfolio.

While there is wide agreement on the general principles of equity index construction, index providers differ in their methodologies that determine which stocks are selected for inclusion, the number of stocks to include, and other details. Exhibit 5.3 summarizes the construction methodologies of the major broad indexes of the U.S. equity market.

### Annual and Monthly Returns

### Returns on the Basic Asset Classes

Summary statistics of annual total returns of the seven basic SBBI asset classes are presented in Exhibit 2.3 in Chapter 2. The monthly total returns on the asset classes and inflation appear in Appendices A-1, A-4, A-5, A-6, A-10, A-14, and A-15.

### Calculating Annual Returns

Annual returns are formed by compounding the 12 monthly returns. Compounding, or linking, monthly returns is multiplying together the return relatives, or one plus the return, then subtracting one from the result. The equation is denoted as the geometric sum as follows:

$$r_{year} = \left[ (1 + r_{Jan}) \times (1 + r_{Feb}) \ldots \times (1 + r_{Dec}) \right] - 1$$

Where:

| | | |
|---|---|---|
| $r_{year}$ | = | The compound total return for the year |
| $r_{Jan}, r_{Feb}, \ldots, r_{Dec}$ | = | The returns for the 12 months of the year |

---

[5.2]  See Roll, R. 1977. "A critique of the asset pricing theory's tests Part I: On past and potential testability of the theory." *Journal of Financial Economics*, Vol. 4, No. 2, P. 129.

The compound return reflects the growth of funds invested in an asset. The following example illustrates the compounding method for a hypothetical year:

| Month | Return (%) | Return (Decimal) | Return Relative |
|---|---|---|---|
| January | 1 | 0.01 | 1.01 |
| February | 6 | 0.06 | 1.06 |
| March | 2 | 0.02 | 1.02 |
| April | 1 | 0.01 | 1.01 |
| May | -3 | -0.03 | 0.97 |
| June | 2 | 0.02 | 1.02 |
| July | -4 | -0.04 | 0.96 |
| August | -2 | -0.02 | 0.98 |
| September | 3 | 0.03 | 1.03 |
| October | -3 | -0.03 | 0.97 |
| November | 2 | 0.02 | 1.02 |
| December | 1 | 0.01 | 1.01 |

The return for this hypothetical year is the geometric sum:

$(1.01 \times 1.06 \times 1.02 \times 1.01 \times 0.97 \times 1.02 \times 0.96 \times 0.98 \times 1.03 \times 0.97 \times 1.02 \times 1.01) - 1 = 1.0567 - 1 = 0.0567$

or a gain of 5.67%. One dollar invested in this hypothetical asset at the beginning of the year would have grown to slightly less than $1.06. Note that this is different from the simple addition result, $(1 + 6 + 2 + 1 - 3 + 2 - 4 - 2 + 3 - 3 + 2 + 1) = 6\%$

## Calculation of Returns From Index Values

Equivalently, annual returns, $r_t$, can be formed by dividing index values according to:

$$r_t = \left[ \frac{V_t}{V_{t-1}} \right] - 1$$

Where:

$r_t$ = The annual return in period $t$

$V_t$ = The index value as of year-end $t$

$V_{t-1}$ = The index value as of the pervious year-end, $t$ -1

The construction of index values is discussed later in this chapter in the section entitled "Calculation of Index Values."

## Calculation of Annual Income Returns

The conversion of monthly income returns to annual income returns is calculated by adding all the cash flows (income payments) for the period, then dividing the sum by the beginning period price:

$$r_I = \frac{(I_{Jan} + I_{Feb} \ldots + I_{Dec})}{P_0}$$

Where:

| | | |
|---|---|---|
| $r_I$ | = | The income return for the year |
| $(I_{Jan}, I_{Feb} \ldots, I_{Dec})$ | = | The income payments for the 12 months of the year |
| $P_0$ | = | The price of the security at the beginning of the year |

The following example illustrates the method for a hypothetical year:

| Month | Beginning of Month Price ($) | Income Return (Decimal) | Income Payment ($) |
|---|---|---|---|
| January | 100 | 0.006 | 0.60 |
| February | 102 | 0.004 | 0.41 |
| March | 105 | 0.002 | 0.21 |
| April | 101 | 0.001 | 0.10 |
| May | 99 | 0.005 | 0.50 |
| June | 103 | 0.004 | 0.41 |
| July | 105 | 0.003 | 0.32 |
| August | 103 | 0.002 | 0.21 |
| September | 105 | 0.003 | 0.32 |
| October | 103 | 0.004 | 0.41 |
| November | 106 | 0.001 | 0.11 |
| December | 105 | 0.002 | 0.21 |

Sum the income payments (not the returns), and divide by the price at the beginning of the year:

(0.60 + 0.41 + 0.21 + 0.10 + 0.50 + 0.41 + 0.32 + 0.21 + 0.32 + 0.41 + 0.11 + 0.21) / 100 = 0.0381

or an annual income return of 3.81%.

Annual income and capital appreciation returns do not sum to the annual total return. The difference may be viewed as a reinvestment return, which is the return from investing income from a given month into the same asset class in subsequent months within the year.

## Index Values

Index values represent the *cumulative* (i.e., compound) effect of investment returns. For example: In 1926 the total return (i.e., with dividends reinvested) of large-cap stocks was approximately 11.6%. A hypothetical investor investing $1.00 as of December 31, 1925, in large-cap stocks would have seen her investment grow to approximately $1.12 ($1.00 x (1+ 0.116)) by the end of 1926. During the following year (1927), the total return of large-cap stocks was approximately 37.5%. The $1.12 our hypothetical investor began 1927 with would have grown to approximately $1.53 ($1.12 x (1 + 0.375)) by the end of 1927. This can also be calculated as:

$1.53 = $1 x (1+ 0.116) x (1 + 0.375)

Of course, the cumulative effect over the entire 1926–2016 period can also be calculated as follows:

$1.00 x (1+ $r_{1926}$) x (1 + $r_{1927}$)... x (1 + $r_{2016}$)

Where "$r_{year}$" is the total return in a given year.

Following this methodology, the $1.00 invested in large-cap stocks at year-end 1925 by our hypothetical investor would have grown to $6,035.12 by the end of 2016. Such growth reveals the power of compounding (reinvesting) one's investment returns.

Year-end index levels (based upon $1.00 invested at the end of 1925) for all six SBBI asset classes plus inflation are displayed in Exhibit 5.1 for the most recent 10 years (2007–2016). Exhibit 5.1 also includes year-end index levels for the capital appreciation ("Capital App") component of total return for large-cap stocks, long-term government bonds, and intermediate-term government bonds.[5.3]

Note that the capital appreciation component of total return is generally a small contributor to total return over the longer term. For example, $1.00 invested at the end of 1925 in large cap stocks would have grown to $6,035.12 by the end of 2016, but capital appreciation contributed only $175.45 to total return, or about 2.9% ($175.45 ÷ $6,035.12). This implies that the other two components of total return (dividend return and reinvestment return) contributed approximately 97.1% to the total return of large-cap stocks over the 1926–2016 period.

---

[5.3] See Appendix B, "Cumulative Wealth Indices of Basic Series," for the full 91-year history (January 1926–December 2016, monthly) of the information found in Exhibit 5.1.

**Exhibit 5.1:** Basic Series

Indexes of the Year-end Cumulative Wealth over Past 10 Years (Year-end 1925 = $1.00)

| Year | Large-Cap Stocks | | Small-Cap Stocks | Long-term Corp Bonds | Long-term Gov't Bonds | | Inter-term Gov't Bonds | | U.S. Treasury Bills | Inflation |
|------|-------|-------|-------|-------|-------|-------|-------|-------|-------|-------|
| | Total Returns | Capital App | Total Returns | Total Returns | Total Returns | Capital App | Total Returns | Capital App | Total Returns | Inflation |
| 2007 | 3,252.97 | 115.08 | 15,091.09 | 105.86 | 78.78 | 1.08 | 71.14 | 1.45 | 20.19 | 11.72 |
| 2008 | 2,049.44 | 70.79 | 9,548.94 | 115.15 | 99.16 | 1.30 | 80.47 | 1.59 | 20.51 | 11.73 |
| 2009 | 2,591.82 | 87.39 | 12,230.87 | 118.63 | 84.38 | 1.06 | 78.53 | 1.52 | 20.53 | 12.05 |
| 2010 | 2,982.23 | 98.56 | 16,054.70 | 133.38 | 92.94 | 1.12 | 84.12 | 1.60 | 20.55 | 12.23 |
| 2011 | 3,045.21 | 98.56 | 15,532.07 | 157.32 | 118.13 | 1.38 | 91.53 | 1.71 | 20.56 | 12.59 |
| 2012 | 3,532.55 | 111.77 | 18,364.60 | 174.12 | 122.18 | 1.39 | 93.05 | 1.73 | 20.57 | 12.81 |
| 2013 | 4,676.68 | 144.85 | 26,641.17 | 161.80 | 106.57 | 1.17 | 89.63 | 1.65 | 20.58 | 13.00 |
| 2014 | 5,316.85 | 161.35 | 27,419.32 | 189.76 | 132.90 | 1.42 | 92.32 | 1.67 | 20.58 | 13.10 |
| 2015 | 5,390.43 | 160.18 | 26,433.35 | 187.82 | 132.03 | 1.37 | 93.97 | 1.67 | 20.59 | 13.20 |
| 2016 | 6,035.12 | 175.45 | 33,212.31 | 200.40 | 134.35 | 1.37 | 95.78 | 1.68 | 20.63 | 13.47 |

## Calculation of Index Values

It is possible to mathematically describe the nature of the indexes in Exhibit 5-1 precisely. These indexes are initialized as of December 31, 1925, at $1.00 (represented by $V_0$ in the equation below). At the end of each month, a cumulative wealth index ($V_n$) for each of the monthly return series is formed. This index is formed for month $n$ by taking the product of one plus the returns each period, in the following manner:

$$V_n = V_0 \left[ \prod_{t=1}^{n} (1 + r_t) \right]$$

Where:

$V_n$       = The index value at end of period $n$

$V_0$       = The initial index value at time 0

$r_t$       = The return in period $t$

## Using Index Values for Performance Measurement

Index values can be used to determine whether an investment portfolio accumulated more wealth over a period than another portfolio would have done, or whether the investment performed as well as an industry benchmark. In the following example, which produced more wealth: the "investor portfolio" or a hypothetical S&P 500 index fund returning exactly the S&P total return?[5.4]

|  | Investor Portfolio (%) | S&P 500 (%) |
|---|---|---|
| January 1990 | -5.35 | -6.71 |
| February 1990 | 0.65 | 1.29 |
| March 1990 | 0.23 | 2.65 |
| Accumulated Wealth of $1.00 | $0.955 | $0.970 |

Taking December 1989 as the base period (i.e., $1.00 invested at the end of 1989) and using the computation method described above, the S&P 500 outperformed the investor portfolio.

## Computing Returns for Non-Calendar Periods

Index values are also useful for computing returns for non-calendar-year periods. For example, using the index values in Appendix B-6 at the back of this book, the capital appreciation return for long-term government bonds from the end of June 1987 through the end of June 1988 can be calculated by dividing the index value in June 1988 (0.661), by the index value in June 1987 (0.683), and subtracting 1.

This yields: (0.661 / 0.683) − 1 = -0.0322, or -3.22%

## Inflation-Adjusted Returns and Indexes[5.5]

Exhibit 5.2 presents the inflation-adjusted year-end index values of the six basic SBBI asset classes over the 1926–2016 period.

Note that the inflation-adjusted year-end index values in Exhibit 5.2 demonstrate that investors in large-cap stocks and small-cap stocks multiplied their real wealth (i.e., purchasing power), over the 1926–2016 period by a factor of 448.08 and 2,465.84, respectively.

---

[5.4]  In this example, each index measures total return and assumes monthly reinvestment of dividends.

[5.5]  The inflation rate used for the single month of December 2015 in last year's *2016 SBBI Yearbook* (0.00105760) was an estimate in the data provider's database. The value has been revised to -0.00341710, representing a difference of -0.00447470, or -0.4%. We use the revised value in all calculations in the *2017 SBBI Yearbook* (this book); this may cause slight differences in year-end 2015 inflation calculations as appeared in the *2016 SBBI Yearbook* when compared to year-end 2015 inflation calculations as appear in the *2017 SBBI Yearbook*. For example, the annual inflation rate reported for calendar year (January–December) 2015 in last year's *2016 SBBI Yearbook* was 1.18% using the *estimated* December 2015 value, but the annual inflation rate reported for calendar year (January–December) 2015 is reported as 0.73% in the *2017 SBBI Yearbook* (this book) using the *revised* December 2015 value. Longer-term statistics are unaffected (e.g., the long-term 1926–2015 average annual inflation rate (2.98%) is identical using both the *estimated* and the *revised* December 2015 monthly value). This issue does not recur in the *2017 SBBI Yearbook* (this book); the inflation rate used for the single month of December 2016 herein is *not* an estimate; it is taken directly from the United States Department of Labor, Bureau of Labor Statistics, Consumer Price Index for All Urban Consumers, or CPI-U, not seasonally adjusted, at https://www.bls.gov/cpi/.

**Exhibit 5.2:** Inflation-Adjusted Series
Indexes of Year-end Cumulative Wealth 1926–2016
(Year-end 1925 = $1.00)

**Inflation-Adjusted**

| Year | Large-Cap Stocks | Small-Cap Stocks | Long-term Corp Bonds | Long-term Gov't Bonds | Inter-term Gov't Bonds | U.S. Treasury Bills |
|------|------------------|------------------|----------------------|-----------------------|------------------------|---------------------|
| Dec-26 | 1.133 | 1.018 | 1.090 | 1.094 | 1.070 | 1.048 |
| Dec-27 | 1.591 | 1.269 | 1.196 | 1.217 | 1.142 | 1.104 |
| Dec-28 | 2.307 | 1.790 | 1.242 | 1.230 | 1.164 | 1.154 |
| Dec-29 | 2.109 | 0.869 | 1.280 | 1.270 | 1.231 | 1.207 |
| Dec-30 | 1.685 | 0.572 | 1.471 | 1.414 | 1.398 | 1.315 |
| Dec-31 | 1.056 | 0.318 | 1.596 | 1.480 | 1.509 | 1.469 |
| Dec-32 | 1.080 | 0.335 | 1.971 | 1.928 | 1.831 | 1.654 |
| Dec-33 | 1.655 | 0.810 | 2.165 | 1.917 | 1.855 | 1.650 |
| Dec-34 | 1.599 | 0.986 | 2.415 | 2.067 | 1.982 | 1.620 |
| Dec-35 | 2.292 | 1.342 | 2.571 | 2.107 | 2.059 | 1.576 |
| Dec-36 | 3.033 | 2.185 | 2.712 | 2.238 | 2.097 | 1.560 |
| Dec-37 | 1.912 | 0.890 | 2.702 | 2.176 | 2.065 | 1.517 |
| Dec-38 | 2.578 | 1.216 | 2.950 | 2.362 | 2.257 | 1.561 |
| Dec-39 | 2.580 | 1.226 | 3.082 | 2.514 | 2.370 | 1.568 |
| Dec-40 | 2.305 | 1.152 | 3.156 | 2.642 | 2.417 | 1.554 |
| Dec-41 | 1.858 | 0.955 | 2.955 | 2.430 | 2.214 | 1.417 |
| Dec-42 | 2.046 | 1.263 | 2.774 | 2.295 | 2.065 | 1.300 |
| Dec-43 | 2.496 | 2.306 | 2.765 | 2.271 | 2.058 | 1.264 |
| Dec-44 | 2.928 | 3.472 | 2.836 | 2.287 | 2.052 | 1.242 |
| Dec-45 | 3.907 | 5.895 | 2.887 | 2.477 | 2.051 | 1.219 |
| Dec-46 | 3.039 | 4.409 | 2.485 | 2.094 | 1.753 | 1.035 |
| Dec-47 | 2.947 | 4.081 | 2.227 | 1.871 | 1.623 | 0.955 |
| Dec-48 | 3.027 | 3.890 | 2.258 | 1.883 | 1.609 | 0.937 |
| Dec-49 | 3.662 | 4.744 | 2.375 | 2.042 | 1.677 | 0.965 |
| Dec-50 | 4.560 | 6.221 | 2.293 | 1.931 | 1.596 | 0.923 |
| Dec-51 | 5.341 | 6.335 | 2.107 | 1.752 | 1.513 | 0.885 |
| Dec-52 | 6.267 | 6.469 | 2.162 | 1.757 | 1.524 | 0.891 |
| Dec-53 | 6.166 | 6.012 | 2.222 | 1.809 | 1.564 | 0.902 |
| Dec-54 | 9.458 | 9.703 | 2.354 | 1.949 | 1.614 | 0.914 |
| Dec-55 | 12.397 | 11.642 | 2.356 | 1.917 | 1.597 | 0.925 |
| Dec-56 | 12.843 | 11.803 | 2.134 | 1.759 | 1.547 | 0.922 |
| Dec-57 | 11.122 | 9.788 | 2.252 | 1.835 | 1.619 | 0.923 |
| Dec-58 | 15.669 | 15.859 | 2.164 | 1.694 | 1.570 | 0.921 |
| Dec-59 | 17.283 | 18.187 | 2.112 | 1.631 | 1.541 | 0.934 |
| Dec-60 | 17.111 | 17.333 | 2.270 | 1.829 | 1.697 | 0.945 |
| Dec-61 | 21.567 | 22.741 | 2.363 | 1.834 | 1.717 | 0.958 |
| Dec-62 | 19.447 | 19.792 | 2.520 | 1.937 | 1.791 | 0.973 |
| Dec-63 | 23.494 | 24.060 | 2.534 | 1.928 | 1.790 | 0.987 |
| Dec-64 | 27.044 | 29.370 | 2.623 | 1.972 | 1.841 | 1.010 |
| Dec-65 | 29.838 | 40.848 | 2.562 | 1.949 | 1.825 | 1.029 |
| Dec-66 | 25.964 | 36.751 | 2.484 | 1.955 | 1.848 | 1.043 |
| Dec-67 | 31.239 | 65.471 | 2.291 | 1.723 | 1.812 | 1.055 |
| Dec-68 | 33.129 | 85.005 | 2.244 | 1.641 | 1.808 | 1.060 |
| Dec-69 | 28.567 | 60.042 | 1.944 | 1.468 | 1.692 | 1.065 |
| Dec-70 | 28.124 | 46.993 | 2.181 | 1.560 | 1.874 | 1.075 |
| Dec-71 | 31.101 | 52.968 | 2.343 | 1.709 | 1.971 | 1.086 |
| Dec-72 | 35.788 | 53.492 | 2.430 | 1.746 | 2.005 | 1.091 |
| Dec-73 | 28.062 | 33.971 | 2.259 | 1.587 | 1.927 | 1.072 |
| Dec-74 | 18.391 | 24.238 | 1.951 | 1.476 | 1.815 | 1.032 |
| Dec-75 | 23.583 | 34.612 | 2.091 | 1.506 | 1.829 | 1.020 |
| Dec-76 | 27.884 | 51.971 | 2.366 | 1.678 | 1.970 | 1.023 |
| Dec-77 | 24.247 | 61.029 | 2.254 | 1.561 | 1.871 | 1.007 |

**Exhibit 5.2:** Inflation-Adjusted Series
Indexes of Year-end Cumulative Wealth 1926–2016
(Year-end 1925 = $1.00)

| Year | **Inflation-Adjusted** | | | | | |
| | Large-Cap Stocks | Small-Cap Stocks | Long-term Corp Bonds | Long-term Gov't Bonds | Inter-term Gov't Bonds | U.S. Treasury Bills |
|---|---|---|---|---|---|---|
| Dec-78 | 23.701 | 69.108 | 2.066 | 1.415 | 1.776 | 0.990 |
| Dec-79 | 24.810 | 87.502 | 1.747 | 1.233 | 1.632 | 0.964 |
| Dec-80 | 29.248 | 108.894 | 1.512 | 1.054 | 1.508 | 0.954 |
| Dec-81 | 25.526 | 113.831 | 1.371 | 0.985 | 1.515 | 1.005 |
| Dec-82 | 29.870 | 140.278 | 1.881 | 1.332 | 1.884 | 1.069 |
| Dec-83 | 35.268 | 188.759 | 1.926 | 1.291 | 1.949 | 1.121 |
| Dec-84 | 36.055 | 169.470 | 2.165 | 1.434 | 2.138 | 1.184 |
| Dec-85 | 45.768 | 203.588 | 2.714 | 1.810 | 2.479 | 1.230 |
| Dec-86 | 53.704 | 215.106 | 3.216 | 2.229 | 2.822 | 1.291 |
| Dec-87 | 54.137 | 186.866 | 3.072 | 2.077 | 2.782 | 1.304 |
| Dec-88 | 60.456 | 219.893 | 3.257 | 2.182 | 2.826 | 1.328 |
| Dec-89 | 76.077 | 231.516 | 3.617 | 2.462 | 3.060 | 1.375 |
| Dec-90 | 69.473 | 171.148 | 3.641 | 2.464 | 3.164 | 1.397 |
| Dec-91 | 87.944 | 240.179 | 4.235 | 2.852 | 3.545 | 1.431 |
| Dec-92 | 91.977 | 287.908 | 4.502 | 2.995 | 3.693 | 1.440 |
| Dec-93 | 98.539 | 338.990 | 4.959 | 3.447 | 3.998 | 1.442 |
| Dec-94 | 97.239 | 340.412 | 4.552 | 3.096 | 3.693 | 1.459 |
| Dec-95 | 130.467 | 446.387 | 5.647 | 3.976 | 4.207 | 1.503 |
| Dec-96 | 155.264 | 508.167 | 5.542 | 3.812 | 4.157 | 1.530 |
| Dec-97 | 203.599 | 613.460 | 6.155 | 4.342 | 4.430 | 1.584 |
| Dec-98 | 257.633 | 559.616 | 6.709 | 4.832 | 4.805 | 1.634 |
| Dec-99 | 303.690 | 707.325 | 6.047 | 4.284 | 4.597 | 1.666 |
| Dec-00 | 266.998 | 659.577 | 6.601 | 5.033 | 5.006 | 1.706 |
| Dec-01 | 231.668 | 797.393 | 7.193 | 5.140 | 5.305 | 1.745 |
| Dec-02 | 176.278 | 675.462 | 8.173 | 5.916 | 5.852 | 1.732 |
| Dec-03 | 222.658 | 1,065.440 | 8.445 | 5.891 | 5.882 | 1.718 |
| Dec-04 | 239.104 | 1,221.614 | 8.892 | 6.191 | 5.824 | 1.683 |
| Dec-05 | 242.563 | 1,248.459 | 9.103 | 6.454 | 5.709 | 1.676 |
| Dec-06 | 273.915 | 1,414.399 | 9.165 | 6.369 | 5.742 | 1.713 |
| Dec-07 | 277.633 | 1,287.985 | 9.035 | 6.724 | 6.072 | 1.723 |
| Dec-08 | 174.755 | 814.233 | 9.819 | 8.455 | 6.861 | 1.749 |
| Dec-09 | 215.148 | 1,015.290 | 9.847 | 7.005 | 6.519 | 1.704 |
| Dec-10 | 243.908 | 1,313.068 | 10.909 | 7.601 | 6.880 | 1.681 |
| Dec-11 | 241.893 | 1,233.774 | 12.497 | 9.384 | 7.271 | 1.633 |
| Dec-12 | 275.803 | 1,433.810 | 13.594 | 9.539 | 7.265 | 1.606 |
| Dec-13 | 359.708 | 2,049.115 | 12.445 | 8.197 | 6.894 | 1.583 |
| Dec-14 | 405.877 | 2,093.132 | 14.486 | 10.145 | 7.047 | 1.571 |
| Dec-15 | 408.513 | 2,003.251 | 14.234 | 10.006 | 7.122 | 1.560 |
| Dec-16 | 448.075 | 2,465.838 | 14.879 | 9.975 | 7.111 | 1.531 |

**Exhibit 5.3:** Major Broad Market U.S. Equity Indexes[*]

| | Index Family Morningstar | MSCI | Russell | S&P Dow Jones |
|---|---|---|---|---|
| **Broad Market Index** | Morningstar U.S. Market Index | MSCI Investable Market | Russell 3000 | S&P Composite 1500[**] |
| **Percent U.S. Market Cap Coverage** | 97% | >99% | 98% | 90% |
| **Total Number of Stocks** | 1,600 | 2500 | 3000 | 1500 |
| **Transparent, Rules-Based Methodology** | Yes | Yes | Yes | No |
| **Eligibility** | Stocks of companies domiciled in the U.S. listed on the NYSE, NYSE MKT, or NASDAQ | Stocks of companies domiciled in the U.S. listed on the NYSE, NYSE MKT, NYSE Arca, or NASDAQ | Stocks of the largest 3000 companies domiciled in the U.S. listed on a U.S. exchange | Stocks of companies domiciled in the U.S. listed on the NYSE, NYSE MKT, NYSE Arca, or NASDAQ chosen for market size, liquidity, and industry group representation by the S&P Index Committee |
| **Exclusion Criteria** | ADRs Limited Partnerships, Investment Trusts (except REITs), Tracking Stocks and Holding Companies | ADRs, Fixed Dividend Shares, Convertible Notes, Warrants, and Rights, Limited Partnerships, Master Limited Partnerships, LLCs, Business Development Companies, Pooled Investment Vehicles, Royalty Trusts and Investment Trusts (except REITs) | ADRs Limited Partnerships, Closed-end Mutual Funds, Price < $1, and Royalty Trusts and LLCs | ADRs Limited Partnerships, Investment Trusts (except REITs), Tracking Stocks and Holding Companies, and Royalty Trusts and LLCs |
| **Market Cap Cutoff Method** | Market Cap Percent | Fixed Number of Stocks | Fixed Number of Stocks | Fixed Number of Stocks |
| **Unique Cap Cutoff Method** | Yes | Yes | Yes | Yes |
| **Unique Style Classification** | Yes | No, stocks may be included in more than one style index | No, stocks may be included in more than one style index | No, stocks may be included in more than one style index |
| **Core Style Index** | Yes | No | No | No |
| **Reconstitution Frequency** | Semiannual | Semiannual | Annual | Ad hoc |

[*]The broad market indices shown in Exhibit 5.3 can be disaggregated into capitalization and style indices. For example, the S&P Composite 1500 can be disaggregated into the S&P 500 (large-cap stocks), S&P 400 (mid-cap stocks), and the S&P 600 (small-cap stocks).

[**]The market for U.S. large-cap stocks is represented by the S&P 500 throughout the Ibbotson® SBBI® Yearbook series.

# Chapter 6
# Statistical Analysis of Returns

Statistical analysis of historical asset returns can reveal the growth rate of wealth invested in an asset or portfolio, the riskiness or volatility of asset classes, the comovement of assets, and the random or cyclical behavior of asset returns. This chapter focuses on arithmetic and geometric mean returns, standard deviations, and serial and cross-correlation coefficients, and discusses the use of each statistic to characterize the various asset classes by growth rate, variability, and safety.

**Calculating Arithmetic Mean Return**

The arithmetic mean of a series is the simple average of the elements in the series. The arithmetic mean return equation is:

$$r_A = \frac{1}{n} \sum_{t=1}^{n} r_t$$

Where:

$r_A$            =   The arithmetic mean return

$r_t$            =   The series return in period $t$, that is, from time $t - 1$ to time $t$

$n$            =   The inclusive number of periods

**Calculating Geometric Mean Return**

The geometric mean of a return series over a period is the compound rate of return over the period. The geometric mean return equation is:

$$r_G = \left[ \prod_{t=1}^{n} (1 + r_t) \right]^{\frac{1}{n}} - 1$$

Where:

$r_G$            =   The geometric mean return

$r_t$            =   The series return in period $t$

$n$            =   The inclusive number of periods

The geometric mean return can be restated using beginning and ending period index values. The equation is:

$$r_G = \left[\frac{V_n}{V_0}\right]^{\frac{1}{n}} - 1$$

Where:

| | | |
|---|---|---|
| $r_G$ | = | The geometric mean return |
| $V_n$ | = | The ending period index value at time $n$ |
| $V_0$ | = | The initial index value at time 0 |
| $n$ | = | The inclusive number of periods |

The annualized geometric mean return over any period of months can also be computed by expressing $n$ as a fraction. For example: starting at the beginning of 2016 to the end of May 2016 is equivalent to five twelfths of a year, or 0.4167. $V_n$ would be the index value at the end of May 2016; $V_0$ would be the index value at the beginning of 2016; and $n$ would be 0.4167.

**Geometric Mean Versus Arithmetic Mean**

A simple example illustrates the difference between geometric and arithmetic means. Suppose $1.00 was invested in a large-cap stock portfolio that experiences successive annual returns of 50% and negative 50%. At the end of the first year, the portfolio is worth $1.50 and at the end of the second year, it is worth $0.75. The annual arithmetic mean is 0.0%, whereas the annual geometric mean is -13.4%. Both are calculated as follows:

$$r_A = \frac{1}{2}(0.50 - 0.50) = 0.00$$

$$r_G = \left[\frac{0.75}{1.00}\right]^{\frac{1}{2}} - 1 = -0.134$$

The geometric mean is backward-looking, measuring the change in wealth over more than one period. On the other hand, the arithmetic mean better represents a typical performance over single periods.

In general, the geometric mean for any period is less than or equal to the arithmetic mean. The two means are equal only for a return series that is constant (i.e., the same return in every period). For a non-constant series, the difference between the two is positively related to the variability or standard deviation of the returns. For example, in Exhibit 6.9, the difference between the arithmetic and geometric mean is much larger for risky large-cap stocks than it is for nearly riskless Treasury bills. This is because the "variability" (as measured by standard deviation) of large-cap stock returns (19.9%) is much greater than the standard deviation of Treasury bill returns (3.1%).

## Calculating Standard Deviation

The standard deviation of a series is a measure of the extent to which observations in the series differ from the arithmetic mean of the series. For a series of asset returns, the standard deviation is a measure of the volatility, or risk, of the asset.

In a normally distributed series, about two-thirds of the observations lie within one standard deviation of the arithmetic mean; about 95% of the observations lie within two standard deviations; and more than 99% lie within three standard deviations.

For example, the standard deviation for large-cap stock returns from 1926 to 2016 was 19.9% with an annual arithmetic mean of 12.0%. Therefore, roughly two-thirds of the observations have annual returns between −7.9% and 31.9% (12.0% plus or minus 19.9%); approximately 95% of the observations are between -27.8% and 51.8% (12.0% plus or minus 39.8%).

The equation for the standard deviation of a series of returns ($\sigma_r$) is:

$$\sigma_r = \sqrt{\frac{1}{n-1}\sum_{t=1}^{n}(r_t - r_A)^2}$$

Where:

$r_t$ = The return in period $t$

$r_A$ = The arithmetic mean of the return series $r$

$n$ = the number of periods

The scaling of the standard deviation depends on the frequency of the data; therefore, a series of monthly returns produces a monthly standard deviation. For example, using the monthly returns for the hypothetical year on page 5-3, a monthly standard deviation of 2.94% calculated as follows:

$$0.0294 = \frac{1}{12-1} \times \left[ \begin{array}{l} (0.01-0.005)^2 + (0.06-0.005)^2 + (0.02-0.005)^2 + \\ (0.01-0.005)^2 + (-0.03-0.005)^2 + (0.02-0.005)^2 + \\ (-0.04-0.005)^2 + (-0.02-0.005)^2 + (0.03-0.005)^2 + \\ (-0.03-0.005)^2 + (0.02-0.005)^2 + (0.01-0.005)^2 \end{array} \right]^{\frac{1}{2}}$$

It is sometimes useful to express the standard deviation of the series in another time scale. To calculate *annualized* monthly standard deviations ($\sigma_n$), one uses the following equation.[6.1]

$$\sigma_n = \sqrt{\left[\sigma_1^2 + (1+\mu_1)^2\right]^n - (1+\mu_1)^{2n}}$$

Where:

| | | |
|---|---|---|
| $n$ | = | The number of periods per year, e.g., 12 for monthly, 4 for quarterly, etc. |
| $\sigma_1$ | = | The monthly standard deviation |
| $\mu_1$ | = | The months arithmetic mean |

Applying this formula to the prior monthly standard deviation of 2.94% results in an annualized monthly standard deviation of 10.78%. The *annualized* monthly standard deviation is calculated as follows:

$$\sqrt{\left[0.0294^2 + (1+0.005)^2\right]^{12} - (1+0.005)^{2(12)}}$$

This equation is the *exact* form of the common *approximation*:

$$\sigma_n \approx \sqrt{n}\sigma_1$$

The "approximation" treats an annual return as if it were the sum of 12 *independent* monthly returns, whereas the "exact form" treats an annual return as the *compound* return of 12 independent monthly returns. While the approximation can be used for "back of the envelope" calculations, the exact formula should be used in applications of quantitative analysis. Forming inputs for mean-variance optimization is one such example. Note that both the exact formula and the approximation assume that there is no monthly autocorrelation.

**Limitations of Standard Deviation[6.2]**

Using the statistical measure of standard deviation of returns is clearly the easiest and most elegant way to mathematically express the concept of risk. However, practitioners and academics alike have noted that standard deviation misses important and essential qualities of risk from the standpoint of an investor of capital.

One limitation of standard deviation as a measure of risk is the tacit assumption that returns can be described by a measure that assumes a normal distribution of returns, while it is empirically acknowledged that many financial market returns exhibit excess kurtosis relative to the normal

---

[6.1] The equation appears in Levy, H. & Gunthorpe, D. 1993. "Optimal Investment Proportions in Senior Securities and Equities Under Alternative Holding Periods." *Journal of Portfolio Management*, Vol. 19, No. 4, P. 33.

[6.2] The Limitations of Standard Deviation, the Semi-Variance and Semi-Standard Deviation, and the Issues Regarding Semi-Variance sections were written by Erik Kobayashi-Solomon and Philip Guziec.

Chapter 6: Statistical Analysis of Returns

(Gaussian) distribution. This characteristic is referred to as a leptokurtic, or "fat-tailed," return distribution. Fat-tailed outcomes reflect market movements far larger than one would reasonably expect from a normal distribution of returns. One of the most extreme examples of a fat-tailed return profile occurred on Oct. 19, 1987, when the Dow Jones Industrial Average declined by 22.68%, or more than 20 standard deviations. The magnitude of the deviation from normal returns can be understood when considering that a normal distribution would predict such a move once in more than 4.5 billion years. More recently, 2008 had 11 days with declines greater than 4 standard deviations, and on May 6, 2010, the Dow Jones Industrial Average declined by 9% in a matter of minutes on an intraday basis, a move that on a daily basis would have been among the top 10 declines in recorded history. Clearly, an awareness of the nature of statistical descriptions of market moves beyond standard deviation is helpful in developing a representative profile of market risk.

## Semivariance and Semistandard Deviation

Given academic and practitioner concerns about variance, various approaches have been suggested to more appropriately measure risk. We take a moment here to briefly discuss investor perception of risk and to review another measure, semivariance.

One criticism of variance and standard deviation is that an investor is less worried about bidirectional variation in value (the essence of the standard deviation measure) than about an ultimately unrecoverable shortfall in investment capital. In considering risk from this point of view, two cases stand out as the most salient: (i) suffering a realized or mark-to-market loss of capital that prevents fulfillment of a goal or mandate over an investment time frame; and (ii) allocating capital in investments that appreciate too little to fulfill a goal or mandate over the investment time frame. The former case involves an excess of variation in an unacceptable direction; the latter case involves a paucity of variation to an acceptable magnitude.

Of these two cases, most academic work has focused on developing a framework to accurately measure and analyze directionally-specific variance. Foremost in this attempt has been the concept of semivariance.

Semivariance characterizes the downside risk of a distribution and focuses on the portion of risk that is below (to the left of) the mean or a specific target. For example, for a 4% target return, the semivariance describes the variance of the data points below (to the left of) the return of 4%. The semivariance below the mean uses the mean return as the target return. The semistandard deviation is simply the square-root of the semivariance. The semivariance (semistandard deviation) is always lower than the total variance (standard deviation) of the distribution.

$$SV_m = \frac{1}{n} \times \sum_{r_t < r_A}^{n} (r_A - r_t)^2$$

$$SV_t = \frac{1}{n} \times \sum_{r_t < r_T}^{n} (r_T - r_t)^2$$

$$SSTD_m = \sqrt{SV_m}$$

$$SSTD_t = \sqrt{SV_t}$$

Where:

| | | |
|---|---|---|
| $SV_m$ | = | The semi-variance below mean |
| $SV_t$ | = | The semi-variance below target |
| $r_A$ | = | The arithmetic mean return |
| $r_t$ | = | The series return in period $t$ |
| $r_T$ | = | The target selection return |
| $n$ | = | The inclusive number of periods |
| $SSTD_m$ | = | The semi-standard deviation below mean |
| $SSTD_t$ | = | The semi-standard deviation below target |

**Issues Regarding Semivariance**

While semivariance seems to intuitively address issues regarding directionality, it does have empirical, theoretical, and practical shortcomings. Empirically, when returns are measured over relatively short time frames, distributions tend to be symmetric. As such, using semivariance for short time frames effectively gives no extra explanatory power (because semivariance simply equates to one half of the variance) and, in fact, limits the data available for analysis (because the calculation of semivariance discards any positive return observations). When returns are measured over relatively longer time frames (on the order of a year or more), asset returns tend to follow a distribution that is positively skewed. As such, for investors with longer time horizons, semivariance has less explanatory power because the data set is limited to the less germane case, while the richer part of the data set is discarded.

From a theoretical standpoint, the assumption implicit in the calculation of semivariance – that investors do not care about positive variance – has repercussions regarding investor utility functions. Namely, ignoring positive variation implies that an investor is indifferent when presented with the choice between making an uncertain but positive return bet and making a bet that is certain to generate the expected payoff. For example, investors would, under the assumptions of semivariance, be agnostic between a 50-50 bet of generating either 5% or 10% and a sure bet paying 7.5%.

Practically speaking, ignoring upside variation means that we ignore the second aspect of risk mentioned above – a paucity of magnitude. In other words, if one attempts to minimize semivariance, without regard to the degree to which an asset or allocation has upside potential, one runs the risk of generating returns which, while low in downside variance, are also low in upside variance. In this case, one has protected oneself from one class of risk by taking on yet another. Given these issues, semivariance has met with limited acceptance among academics and practitioners alike.

## Volatility of the Markets

The volatility of stocks and long-term government bonds is shown by the bar graphs of monthly returns in Exhibit 6.1. The stock market was tremendously volatile in the first few years studied; this period was marked by the 1920s boom, the crash of 1929–1932, and the Great Depression years. The market seemingly settled after World War II and provided more stable returns in the postwar period. In the 1970s and 1980s, stock market volatility increased, but not to the extreme levels of the 1920s and 1930s. In the 1990s and 2000s, volatility was relatively moderate.

Bonds present a mirror image. Long-term government bonds were extremely stable in the 1920s and remained so through the crisis years of the 1930s, providing shelter from the storms of the stock markets. Starting in the late 1960s and early 1970s, however, bond volatility soared; in the 1973–1974 stock market decline, bonds did not provide the shelter they once did. Bond pessimism (i.e., high yields) peaked in 1981 and subsequent returns were sharply positive. While the astronomical interest rates of the 1979–1981 period have passed, the volatility of the bond market remains higher.

**Exhibit 6.1:** Month-by-Month Returns on Stocks and Bonds (%)
1926–2016

## Changes in the Risk of Assets Over Time

Another time series property of great interest is change in volatility or riskiness over time. Such change is indicated by the standard deviation of the series over different subperiods. Exhibit 6.2 shows the annualized monthly standard deviations of the basic data series by decade beginning in 1926 and illustrates differences and changes in return volatility. In this exhibit, the 1920s cover the period 1926–1929 and the 2010s cover the period 2010–2016 (the most recent 10-year period, 2007–2016, is provided in Exhibit 6.3). Equity returns have been the most volatile of the basic series, with volatility peaking in the 1930s due to the instability of the market following the 1929 market crash. The significant bond yield fluctuations of the 1980s caused the fixed-income series' volatility to soar compared to prior decades. Small-cap stocks were the *most* volatile SBBI asset class in all time periods shown in Exhibit 6.2 and 6.3. Treasury bills were the *least* volatile SBBI asset class in all time periods shown in Exhibit 6.2 and 6.3.

Exhibit 6.4 displays the *annualized* standard deviation of the *monthly* returns on each of the basic and derived series from January 1926 to December 2016. The estimates in Exhibit 6.2, Exhibit 6.3, and in Exhibit 6.4 are not strictly comparable to Exhibits 2.3, 6.9, and 6.10, where the 91-year period standard deviation of *annual* returns around the 91-year annual arithmetic mean is reported. The arithmetic mean drifts for a series that does not follow a random pattern. A series with a drifting mean will have much higher deviations around its long-term mean than it has around the mean during a particular calendar year.

**Exhibit 6.2:** Annualized Monthly Standard Deviations by Decade (%)

|  | 1920s* | 1930s | 1940s | 1950s | 1960s | 1970s | 1980s | 1990s | 2000s | 2010s** |
|---|---|---|---|---|---|---|---|---|---|---|
| Large-Cap Stocks | 23.9 | 41.6 | 17.5 | 14.1 | 13.1 | 17.2 | 19.4 | 15.9 | 16.3 | 14.3 |
| Small-Cap Stocks | 24.7 | 78.6 | 34.5 | 14.4 | 21.5 | 30.8 | 22.5 | 20.2 | 26.1 | 20.4 |
| Long-term Corp Bonds | 1.8 | 5.3 | 1.8 | 4.4 | 4.9 | 8.7 | 14.1 | 6.9 | 11.7 | 9.3 |
| Long-term Gov't Bonds | 4.1 | 5.3 | 2.8 | 4.6 | 6.0 | 8.7 | 16.0 | 8.9 | 12.4 | 11.4 |
| Inter-term Gov't Bonds | 1.7 | 3.3 | 1.2 | 2.9 | 3.3 | 5.2 | 8.8 | 4.6 | 5.2 | 3.4 |
| U.S. Treasury Bills | 0.3 | 0.2 | 0.1 | 0.2 | 0.4 | 0.6 | 0.9 | 0.4 | 0.6 | 0.0 |
| Inflation | 2.0 | 2.5 | 3.1 | 1.2 | 0.7 | 1.2 | 1.3 | 0.7 | 1.6 | 1.1 |

*Based on the period 1926–1929   **Based on the period 2010–2016

**Exhibit 6.3:** Annualized Monthly Standard Deviations in the Most Recent 10-year Period (2007–2016) (%)

|  | 2007–2016 |
|---|---|
| Large-Cap Stocks | 16.5 |
| Small-Cap Stocks | 22.7 |
| Long-term Corp Bonds | 11.8 |
| Long-term Gov't Bonds | 12.9 |
| Inter-term Gov't Bonds | 4.2 |
| U.S. Treasury Bills | 0.4 |
| Inflation | 1.5 |

As shown in Exhibit 6.4, large-cap stocks and equity risk premiums have virtually the same annualized monthly standard deviations because there is very little deviation in the U.S. Treasury bill series (the monthly equity risk premium in Exhibit 6.4 is calculated as [(1+ Large Stock total return) ÷ (1+Treasury Bill total return) − 1], as described in Exhibit 4.1). The series with drifting means (U.S. Treasury bills, inflation rates, and inflation-adjusted U.S. Treasury bills) all tend to have very low annualized monthly standard deviations, since these series are quite predictable from month to month. As seen in Exhibits 6.9 and 6.10, however, there is much less predictability for these series over the long term. Because it is difficult to forecast the direction and magnitude of the drift in the long term mean, these series have higher standard deviations over the long term in comparison to their annualized monthly standard deviations.

While equity investors may have the impression that the 2008−2009 global financial crisis was mainly a crisis affecting the equity markets, a careful look at Exhibit 6.4 will show the much greater effect the crisis had on the price fluctuation of bonds in general and long-term corporate bonds in particular. The annualized standard deviation of long-term corporate bonds recorded a historic high value of 25.5% in 2008, a year that saw the collapse of storied investment banks Lehman Brothers and Bear Sterns. The previous record annualized standard deviation for long-term corporate bonds of 20.2% − measured during 1981 − is more than one-fifth lower than the 2008 value, and more than twice the Depression era record of 11.7%, recorded in 1933. In contrast, the peak in large-cap stocks clearly falls early in the series (99.8% in 1933), dwarfing 2009's recorded value of 28.5%. Despite the large number of record-breaking daily equities movements during 2009, this year only represents the eighth-most volatile year for the large-cap stock series. Even removing Depression-era records, 2009 only turns up as the second-most volatile year for large-cap stocks on record, behind 1987 (34.2%) and just ahead of 1998 (27.9%). Another mark of the severity of bond price fluctuations can be seen by noting that the annualized standard deviations for long-term corporate bonds in 2008 were only three percentage points shy of the  annualized standard deviations for the S&P 500 in 2009.

**Exhibit 6.4:** Basic and Derived Series
Annualized Monthly Standard Deviations (%)
1926–2016

| | Basic Series | | | | | | | Derived Series | | | | |
|---|---|---|---|---|---|---|---|---|---|---|---|---|
| Year | Large-Cap Stocks | Small-Cap Stocks | Long-term Corp Bonds | Long-term Gov't Bonds | Inter-term Gov't Bonds | U.S. Treasury Bills | Inflation | Equity Risk Premium | Small Stock Premium | Bond Default Premium | Bond Horizon Premium | Inflation-adjusted T-Bills[*] |
| 1926 | 13.10 | 16.89 | 0.96 | 1.88 | 1.02 | 0.32 | 2.03 | 12.73 | 9.74 | 1.63 | 1.68 | 2.06 |
| 1927 | 17.90 | 21.19 | 1.49 | 2.88 | 1.05 | 0.11 | 2.78 | 17.35 | 11.13 | 2.90 | 2.76 | 3.03 |
| 1928 | 24.62 | 28.68 | 1.87 | 3.21 | 1.27 | 0.32 | 1.72 | 23.65 | 14.48 | 2.74 | 3.06 | 1.84 |
| 1929 | 30.55 | 18.35 | 2.42 | 6.56 | 2.82 | 0.21 | 1.62 | 29.16 | 7.76 | 6.79 | 6.20 | 1.62 |
| 1930 | 21.19 | 25.55 | 2.38 | 2.34 | 2.43 | 0.30 | 2.03 | 20.65 | 11.68 | 2.45 | 2.12 | 2.31 |
| 1931 | 30.04 | 45.35 | 5.91 | 5.24 | 3.72 | 0.16 | 1.35 | 29.72 | 27.44 | 5.25 | 5.18 | 1.75 |
| 1932 | 83.36 | 147.23 | 7.71 | 9.50 | 2.94 | 0.29 | 1.74 | 82.72 | 41.92 | 12.69 | 9.35 | 2.40 |
| 1933 | 99.82 | 286.56 | 11.74 | 5.11 | 3.70 | 0.10 | 4.24 | 99.27 | 72.06 | 7.67 | 5.06 | 4.15 |
| 1934 | 22.64 | 73.85 | 3.10 | 4.50 | 4.07 | 0.04 | 2.03 | 22.59 | 42.03 | 2.52 | 4.46 | 1.94 |
| 1935 | 23.73 | 36.09 | 2.53 | 2.88 | 2.78 | 0.01 | 2.18 | 23.69 | 15.08 | 1.36 | 2.88 | 2.05 |
| 1936 | 19.06 | 66.23 | 1.18 | 2.25 | 1.27 | 0.02 | 1.55 | 19.02 | 37.72 | 1.78 | 2.25 | 1.51 |
| 1937 | 16.33 | 21.81 | 1.99 | 5.04 | 2.44 | 0.05 | 1.74 | 16.28 | 16.46 | 3.93 | 5.01 | 1.63 |
| 1938 | 58.87 | 114.31 | 2.38 | 2.35 | 2.48 | 0.07 | 1.78 | 58.85 | 30.94 | 1.89 | 2.31 | 1.89 |
| 1939 | 31.09 | 95.06 | 5.36 | 8.59 | 5.06 | 0.02 | 2.26 | 31.07 | 43.55 | 8.40 | 8.59 | 2.24 |
| 1940 | 25.56 | 46.88 | 2.02 | 5.20 | 3.25 | 0.02 | 1.09 | 25.55 | 25.68 | 3.92 | 5.19 | 1.07 |
| 1941 | 12.95 | 29.10 | 1.67 | 3.71 | 1.50 | 0.03 | 2.30 | 12.92 | 20.75 | 3.59 | 3.70 | 1.90 |
| 1942 | 17.67 | 37.55 | 0.73 | 1.42 | 0.79 | 0.03 | 1.39 | 17.60 | 25.78 | 1.16 | 1.42 | 1.17 |
| 1943 | 19.59 | 71.56 | 0.90 | 0.65 | 0.51 | 0.01 | 2.35 | 19.53 | 33.94 | 0.58 | 0.65 | 2.21 |
| 1944 | 9.30 | 28.75 | 1.34 | 0.37 | 0.29 | 0.01 | 0.97 | 9.27 | 15.14 | 1.11 | 0.37 | 0.94 |
| 1945 | 17.64 | 37.50 | 1.42 | 2.97 | 0.50 | 0.01 | 1.32 | 17.59 | 16.92 | 1.92 | 2.96 | 1.26 |
| 1946 | 17.72 | 27.25 | 2.15 | 2.73 | 0.94 | 0.00 | 6.65 | 17.65 | 12.20 | 1.74 | 2.72 | 4.66 |
| 1947 | 10.15 | 18.24 | 2.13 | 2.86 | 0.52 | 0.07 | 3.34 | 10.09 | 10.58 | 3.26 | 2.90 | 2.79 |
| 1948 | 21.49 | 24.11 | 2.20 | 1.95 | 0.59 | 0.07 | 2.90 | 21.30 | 6.44 | 1.92 | 1.96 | 2.73 |
| 1949 | 12.02 | 18.75 | 2.17 | 1.83 | 0.47 | 0.02 | 1.63 | 11.89 | 6.72 | 2.44 | 1.80 | 1.71 |
| 1950 | 13.99 | 20.58 | 1.07 | 1.45 | 0.34 | 0.03 | 1.81 | 13.83 | 8.82 | 1.35 | 1.44 | 1.62 |
| 1951 | 15.04 | 16.02 | 3.92 | 3.03 | 1.91 | 0.05 | 1.79 | 14.80 | 6.12 | 2.67 | 2.95 | 1.63 |
| 1952 | 13.32 | 9.66 | 2.85 | 3.24 | 1.32 | 0.08 | 1.15 | 13.11 | 3.78 | 3.82 | 3.23 | 1.14 |
| 1953 | 9.32 | 10.90 | 5.53 | 5.16 | 3.26 | 0.11 | 1.01 | 9.21 | 8.74 | 3.50 | 5.07 | 0.95 |
| 1954 | 19.27 | 20.02 | 2.35 | 3.47 | 1.93 | 0.06 | 0.74 | 19.08 | 10.08 | 2.32 | 3.42 | 0.77 |
| 1955 | 16.11 | 7.70 | 2.17 | 3.60 | 1.65 | 0.14 | 0.67 | 15.91 | 8.83 | 2.36 | 3.47 | 0.71 |
| 1956 | 15.86 | 8.39 | 3.00 | 4.28 | 2.64 | 0.10 | 1.08 | 15.50 | 7.87 | 2.60 | 4.15 | 1.00 |
| 1957 | 11.48 | 10.42 | 9.40 | 8.26 | 5.57 | 0.07 | 0.66 | 11.13 | 9.98 | 5.48 | 8.00 | 0.65 |
| 1958 | 8.74 | 15.44 | 4.56 | 6.29 | 4.50 | 0.27 | 0.90 | 8.47 | 7.99 | 3.73 | 6.16 | 0.88 |
| 1959 | 8.91 | 10.34 | 3.91 | 3.25 | 2.72 | 0.18 | 0.65 | 8.67 | 7.31 | 3.35 | 3.18 | 0.59 |
| 1960 | 13.63 | 13.37 | 3.93 | 6.45 | 4.99 | 0.27 | 0.71 | 13.36 | 7.07 | 3.85 | 6.22 | 0.80 |
| 1961 | 11.16 | 19.02 | 3.63 | 3.55 | 1.57 | 0.07 | 0.51 | 10.94 | 7.72 | 3.93 | 3.51 | 0.50 |
| 1962 | 18.97 | 21.58 | 2.27 | 3.70 | 2.15 | 0.08 | 0.67 | 18.46 | 8.38 | 2.17 | 3.63 | 0.70 |
| 1963 | 11.91 | 13.47 | 1.25 | 0.72 | 0.60 | 0.08 | 0.55 | 11.54 | 7.26 | 1.28 | 0.72 | 0.55 |
| 1964 | 4.63 | 7.05 | 1.46 | 0.91 | 0.78 | 0.06 | 0.41 | 4.47 | 3.78 | 1.84 | 0.87 | 0.38 |
| 1965 | 9.56 | 20.55 | 1.96 | 1.51 | 1.83 | 0.08 | 0.67 | 9.26 | 11.19 | 1.09 | 1.47 | 0.64 |
| 1966 | 9.96 | 17.80 | 4.80 | 8.08 | 4.13 | 0.11 | 0.71 | 9.50 | 13.76 | 5.39 | 7.66 | 0.73 |
| 1967 | 14.89 | 36.96 | 7.33 | 6.58 | 3.81 | 0.16 | 0.44 | 14.24 | 17.30 | 5.14 | 6.27 | 0.54 |
| 1968 | 14.49 | 28.29 | 7.39 | 7.93 | 3.50 | 0.09 | 0.42 | 13.76 | 16.40 | 3.57 | 7.52 | 0.40 |
| 1969 | 12.10 | 18.71 | 6.93 | 9.95 | 5.54 | 0.22 | 0.62 | 11.35 | 9.73 | 7.39 | 9.34 | 0.63 |
| 1970 | 21.43 | 27.68 | 11.28 | 15.07 | 7.05 | 0.22 | 0.44 | 20.17 | 13.26 | 9.22 | 14.11 | 0.47 |
| 1971 | 15.74 | 29.73 | 11.12 | 10.67 | 6.98 | 0.19 | 0.57 | 15.07 | 14.50 | 6.12 | 10.15 | 0.63 |
| 1972 | 7.28 | 16.60 | 3.21 | 5.85 | 1.97 | 0.17 | 0.41 | 7.00 | 11.36 | 3.97 | 5.61 | 0.42 |
| 1973 | 12.53 | 21.94 | 7.57 | 8.38 | 4.99 | 0.37 | 1.53 | 11.62 | 13.88 | 5.12 | 7.71 | 1.34 |
| 1974 | 18.93 | 20.15 | 11.45 | 8.64 | 5.73 | 0.36 | 0.91 | 17.69 | 21.83 | 5.76 | 8.05 | 0.89 |
| 1975 | 24.35 | 46.28 | 11.49 | 9.13 | 5.68 | 0.21 | 0.78 | 22.96 | 19.59 | 4.43 | 8.55 | 0.77 |

**Exhibit 6.4:** Basic and Derived Series
Annualized Monthly Standard Deviations (%)
1926–2016

| | Basic Series | | | | | | | Derived Series | | | | |
|---|---|---|---|---|---|---|---|---|---|---|---|---|
| Year | Large-Cap Stocks | Small-Cap Stocks | Long-term Corp Bonds | Long-term Gov't Bonds | Inter-term Gov't Bonds | U.S. Treasury Bills | Inflation | Equity Risk Premium | Small Stock Premium | Bond Default Premium | Bond Horizon Premium | Inflation-adjusted T-Bills* |
| 1976 | 17.34 | 50.83 | 5.21 | 5.43 | 4.24 | 0.13 | 0.48 | 16.42 | 27.60 | 1.55 | 5.15 | 0.45 |
| 1977 | 8.85 | 17.05 | 4.57 | 5.69 | 2.73 | 0.19 | 0.77 | 8.38 | 13.50 | 1.56 | 5.41 | 0.85 |
| 1978 | 17.92 | 42.56 | 4.45 | 4.45 | 2.07 | 0.36 | 0.67 | 16.73 | 27.21 | 1.66 | 4.21 | 0.78 |
| 1979 | 16.00 | 34.71 | 10.43 | 10.81 | 7.31 | 0.29 | 0.53 | 14.48 | 15.59 | 2.16 | 9.77 | 0.60 |
| 1980 | 23.94 | 39.80 | 20.12 | 21.16 | 16.77 | 0.98 | 1.45 | 22.02 | 14.48 | 4.57 | 18.60 | 1.18 |
| 1981 | 12.33 | 21.37 | 20.21 | 23.25 | 11.84 | 0.51 | 1.15 | 10.75 | 15.65 | 5.23 | 20.23 | 1.00 |
| 1982 | 23.36 | 21.97 | 17.80 | 14.40 | 8.91 | 0.78 | 1.64 | 21.54 | 7.80 | 5.37 | 13.37 | 1.42 |
| 1983 | 12.21 | 21.83 | 10.86 | 11.43 | 5.72 | 0.18 | 0.73 | 11.30 | 14.80 | 3.98 | 10.52 | 0.67 |
| 1984 | 14.99 | 14.57 | 12.97 | 13.34 | 7.17 | 0.34 | 0.61 | 13.62 | 4.41 | 1.92 | 11.97 | 0.61 |
| 1985 | 15.62 | 18.10 | 13.28 | 15.78 | 6.69 | 0.18 | 0.33 | 14.44 | 6.29 | 2.56 | 14.56 | 0.35 |
| 1986 | 21.27 | 15.49 | 9.71 | 21.58 | 6.53 | 0.20 | 1.03 | 20.01 | 6.52 | 9.54 | 20.26 | 1.17 |
| 1987 | 34.17 | 34.45 | 9.67 | 10.09 | 4.93 | 0.23 | 0.68 | 32.50 | 11.31 | 3.03 | 9.49 | 0.64 |
| 1988 | 11.70 | 16.08 | 9.10 | 11.03 | 5.00 | 0.36 | 0.57 | 11.08 | 11.31 | 2.45 | 10.45 | 0.64 |
| 1989 | 16.17 | 11.65 | 7.13 | 9.53 | 6.07 | 0.23 | 0.63 | 14.93 | 6.91 | 2.36 | 8.73 | 0.67 |
| 1990 | 18.28 | 16.85 | 7.55 | 9.89 | 4.75 | 0.18 | 1.16 | 16.95 | 6.80 | 2.67 | 9.18 | 1.16 |
| 1991 | 20.49 | 22.50 | 5.08 | 7.33 | 3.49 | 0.17 | 0.54 | 19.40 | 9.77 | 2.13 | 6.99 | 0.51 |
| 1992 | 7.98 | 21.58 | 5.77 | 7.62 | 5.83 | 0.14 | 0.54 | 7.75 | 19.96 | 2.32 | 7.38 | 0.53 |
| 1993 | 6.65 | 11.43 | 5.53 | 8.38 | 4.44 | 0.05 | 0.57 | 6.48 | 8.29 | 2.38 | 8.15 | 0.57 |
| 1994 | 10.76 | 10.38 | 6.70 | 8.12 | 4.50 | 0.24 | 0.47 | 10.33 | 6.35 | 2.27 | 7.77 | 0.62 |
| 1995 | 6.99 | 12.65 | 7.37 | 9.70 | 3.94 | 0.13 | 0.60 | 6.67 | 8.41 | 1.88 | 9.11 | 0.64 |
| 1996 | 13.25 | 21.06 | 7.62 | 9.33 | 3.89 | 0.09 | 0.61 | 12.63 | 15.18 | 2.14 | 8.87 | 0.62 |
| 1997 | 21.09 | 22.13 | 8.00 | 10.44 | 4.10 | 0.13 | 0.53 | 20.01 | 16.45 | 2.30 | 9.91 | 0.60 |
| 1998 | 27.90 | 25.76 | 5.91 | 7.70 | 4.63 | 0.16 | 0.30 | 26.69 | 6.81 | 4.35 | 7.24 | 0.31 |
| 1999 | 15.78 | 26.31 | 4.57 | 5.25 | 3.45 | 0.10 | 0.77 | 15.02 | 19.21 | 1.90 | 5.00 | 0.77 |
| 2000 | 16.02 | 40.42 | 5.88 | 6.92 | 3.43 | 0.17 | 0.99 | 15.14 | 44.92 | 4.10 | 6.58 | 1.06 |
| 2001 | 18.15 | 34.55 | 8.17 | 9.69 | 5.00 | 0.39 | 1.25 | 17.52 | 21.21 | 6.02 | 9.31 | 0.99 |
| 2002 | 16.90 | 20.14 | 8.82 | 12.36 | 6.77 | 0.04 | 0.83 | 16.64 | 18.02 | 4.50 | 12.15 | 0.79 |
| 2003 | 14.47 | 25.04 | 13.47 | 14.82 | 6.22 | 0.04 | 1.21 | 14.33 | 10.89 | 2.77 | 14.66 | 1.17 |
| 2004 | 8.06 | 18.81 | 9.13 | 9.73 | 4.88 | 0.12 | 1.14 | 7.90 | 10.58 | 1.03 | 9.61 | 1.17 |
| 2005 | 8.31 | 16.11 | 8.56 | 9.66 | 3.76 | 0.19 | 1.96 | 8.03 | 8.78 | 1.38 | 9.39 | 1.97 |
| 2006 | 6.46 | 16.09 | 8.23 | 8.82 | 2.46 | 0.11 | 1.55 | 6.18 | 9.96 | 2.19 | 8.38 | 1.61 |
| 2007 | 10.20 | 11.57 | 5.49 | 7.95 | 5.33 | 0.19 | 1.19 | 9.70 | 6.03 | 4.81 | 7.64 | 1.10 |
| 2008 | 14.20 | 19.83 | 25.50 | 22.57 | 6.94 | 0.23 | 3.20 | 13.96 | 12.23 | 11.16 | 22.44 | 3.07 |
| 2009 | 28.52 | 42.42 | 14.88 | 14.47 | 4.85 | 0.02 | 1.02 | 28.48 | 14.48 | 16.44 | 14.44 | 0.96 |
| 2010 | 22.43 | 32.44 | 9.12 | 13.04 | 4.20 | 0.01 | 0.49 | 22.40 | 9.82 | 7.72 | 13.02 | 0.49 |
| 2011 | 16.51 | 23.35 | 12.24 | 15.43 | 3.41 | 0.01 | 1.34 | 16.51 | 8.54 | 9.31 | 15.42 | 1.26 |
| 2012 | 12.14 | 15.55 | 9.49 | 10.08 | 2.10 | 0.01 | 1.37 | 12.14 | 5.83 | 7.53 | 10.08 | 1.33 |
| 2013 | 11.02 | 16.57 | 8.04 | 8.05 | 3.28 | 0.00 | 0.99 | 11.02 | 7.14 | 3.65 | 8.05 | 0.96 |
| 2014 | 9.33 | 15.73 | 6.62 | 8.34 | 2.50 | 0.00 | 1.34 | 9.33 | 9.62 | 2.62 | 8.34 | 1.32 |
| 2015 | 14.00 | 13.96 | 8.93 | 11.07 | 3.29 | 0.01 | 1.22 | 14.00 | 9.42 | 3.20 | 11.06 | 1.21 |
| 2016 | 11.49 | 22.02 | 9.77 | 11.56 | 3.85 | 0.02 | 0.75 | 11.45 | 11.06 | 7.58 | 11.54 | 0.73 |

*Real Interest Rates

## Correlation Coefficients: Serial and Cross-Correlations

The behavior of an asset return series over time reveals its predictability. For example, a series may be random or unpredictable, or it may be subject to trends, cycles, or other patterns, making the series predictable to some degree. The serial correlation coefficient of a series determines its predictability given knowledge of the last observation. The cross-correlation coefficient (often shortened to "correlation") between two series determines the predictability of one series, conditional on knowledge of the other.

### Serial Correlations

The serial correlation of a return series, also known as the first-order autocorrelation, describes the extent to which the return in one period is related to the return in the next period. A return series with a high (near 1) serial correlation is very predictable from one period to the next, while one with a low (near 0) serial correlation is random and unpredictable.

The serial correlation of a series is closely approximated by the equation for the cross correlation between two series. The data, however, are the series and its "lagged" self. For example, the lagged series is the series of one-period-old returns:

| Year | Return Series | Lagged Return Series |
|------|--------------|---------------------|
| 1 | 0.10 | *undefined* |
| 2 | -0.10 | 0.10 |
| 3 | 0.15 | -0.10 |
| 4 | 0.00 | 0.15 |

### Cross-Correlations

The cross-correlation between two series measures the extent to which they are linearly related.[6.3] The correlation coefficient measures the sensitivity of return on one asset class or portfolio to the return of another. The correlation equation between return series X and Y is:

$$p_{X,Y} = \left[ \frac{Cov(X,Y)}{\sigma_X \sigma_y} \right]$$

Where:

$Cov(X,Y)$ = The covariance of $X$ and $Y$, defined below

$\sigma_X$ = The standard deviation of $X$

$\sigma_y$ = The standard deviation of $Y$

---

[6.3] Two series can be related in a nonlinear way and have a correlation coefficient of zero. An example is the function $y = x^2$, for which $p_{x,y} = 0$.

The covariance equation is:

$$Cov(X,Y) = \frac{1}{n-1}\sum_{t=1}^{n}(r_{X,t} - r_{X,A})(r_{Y,t} - r_{Y,A})$$

Where:

| | | |
|---|---|---|
| $r_{X,t}$ | = | The return for series $X$ in period $t$ |
| $r_{Y,t}$ | = | The return for series $Y$ in period t |
| $r_{X,A}$ | = | The arithmetic mean of series $X$ |
| $r_{Y,A}$ | = | The arithmetic mean of series $Y$ |
| $n$ | = | The number of periods |

**Correlations of the Basic Series**

Exhibit 6.5 presents the annual cross-correlations and serial correlations for the seven basic series. Long-term government bond returns and long-term corporate bond returns are highly correlated with each other, but negatively correlated with inflation. To the degree that inflation is unanticipated, it has a negative effect on fixed-income securities. In addition, U.S. Treasury bills and inflation are reasonably highly correlated, a result of the post-1951 "tracking" described in Chapter 2. Lastly, both the U.S. Treasury bills and inflation series display high serial correlations.

**Exhibit 6.5:** Basic Series: Serial and Cross-Correlations of Historical Annual Returns 1926–2016

| | Large-Cap Stocks | Small-Cap Stocks | Long-term Corp Bonds | Long-term Gov't Bonds | Inter-term Gov't Bonds | U.S. Treasury Bills | Inflation |
|---|---|---|---|---|---|---|---|
| Large-Cap Stocks | 1.00 | | | | | | |
| Small-Cap Stocks | 0.80 | 1.00 | | | | | |
| Long-term Corp Bonds | 0.15 | 0.04 | 1.00 | | | | |
| Long-term Gov't Bonds | 0.00 | -0.10 | 0.89 | 1.00 | | | |
| Inter-term Gov't Bonds | -0.03 | -0.11 | 0.86 | 0.86 | 1.00 | | |
| U.S. Treasury Bills | -0.02 | -0.09 | 0.16 | 0.18 | 0.47 | 1.00 | |
| Inflation | 0.00 | 0.05 | -0.15 | -0.13 | 0.02 | 0.41 | 1.00 |
| Serial Correlation | 0.02 | 0.06 | 0.04 | -0.15 | 0.14 | 0.92 | 0.64 |

## Correlations of the Derived Series

The annual cross-correlations and serial correlations for the four risk premium series and inflation are presented in Exhibit 6.6. Notice that inflation is negatively correlated with the horizon premium. Increasing inflation causes long-term bond yields to rise and prices to fall; therefore, a negative horizon premium is observed in times of rising inflation.

Exhibit 6.7 presents annual cross-correlations and serial correlations for the inflation-adjusted asset return series. It is interesting to observe how the relationship between the asset returns are substantially different when these returns are expressed in inflation-adjusted terms (as compared with nominal terms). In general, the cross-correlations between asset classes are higher when one accounts for inflation (i.e., subtracts inflation from the nominal return).

**Exhibit 6.6:** Risk Premia and Inflation: Serial and Cross-Correlations of Historical Annual Returns 1926–2016

|  | Equity Risk Premium | Small Stock Premium | Bond Default Premium | Bond Horizon Premium | Inflation |
|---|---|---|---|---|---|
| Equity Risk Premium | 1.00 | | | | |
| Small Stock Premium | 0.28 | 1.00 | | | |
| Bond Default Premium | 0.29 | 0.18 | 1.00 | | |
| Bond Horizon Premium | 0.01 | -0.10 | -0.51 | 1.00 | |
| Inflation | -0.07 | 0.11 | 0.00 | -0.26 | 1.00 |
| Serial Correlation | 0.02 | 0.36 | -0.30 | -0.17 | 0.64 |

**Exhibit 6.7:** Inflation-Adjusted Series: Serial and Cross-Correlations of Historical Annual Returns 1926–2016

| Inflation-Adjusted Series | Inflation-Adjusted | | | | | | |
|---|---|---|---|---|---|---|---|
| | Large-Cap Stocks | Small-Cap Stocks | Long-term Corp Bonds | Long-term Gov't Bonds | Inter-term Gov't Bonds | U.S. Treasury Bills[*] | Inflation |
| Large-Cap Stocks | 1.00 | | | | | | |
| Small-Cap Stocks | 0.79 | 1.00 | | | | | |
| Long-term Corp Bonds | 0.21 | 0.07 | 1.00 | | | | |
| Long-term Gov't Bonds | 0.08 | -0.06 | 0.92 | 1.00 | | | |
| Inter-term Gov't Bonds | 0.07 | -0.07 | 0.91 | 0.90 | 1.00 | | |
| U.S. Treasury Bills | 0.09 | -0.07 | 0.53 | 0.50 | 0.70 | 1.00 | |
| Inflation | -0.19 | -0.07 | -0.54 | -0.48 | -0.58 | -0.71 | 1.00 |
| Serial Correlation | 0.01 | 0.03 | 0.15 | -0.06 | 0.21 | 0.67 | 0.64 |

[*]Real Interest Rates

## Is Serial Correlation in the Derived Series Random?

The risk/return relationships in the historical data are represented in the equity risk premium, the small-cap premium, the bond horizon premium, and the bond default premium. The real/nominal historical relationships are represented in the inflation rates and the real interest rates. The objective is to uncover whether each series is random or is subject to any trends, cycles, or other patterns.

The one-year serial correlation coefficients measure the degree of correlation between returns from each year and the previous year for the same series, as seen in Exhibit 6.8. Highly positive (near 1) serial correlations indicate trends, while highly negative (near -1) serial correlations indicate cycles. Looking to exhibit 6.8, the analysis suggests that both inflation rates and real riskless rates follow trends. Serial correlations near zero suggest no patterns (i.e., random behavior), so the analysis suggests that the equity risk premium and the bond horizon premium are random variables.

The small stock premium and the bond default premium, however, fall into a middle range that makes it more difficult to determine whether the small stock premium is a trend (or is random), and whether the bond default premium is a cycle (or is random). In these two cases, one could argue that the small stock premium is a *possible* trend, and the bond default premium is a *possible* cycle.

**Exhibit 6.8:** Interpretation of the Annual Serial Correlations

| Series | Serial Correlation | Interpretation |
| --- | --- | --- |
| Equity Risk Premium | 0.02 | Random |
| Small Stock Premium | 0.36 | Possible Trend |
| Bond Default Premium | -0.30 | Possible Cycle |
| Bond Horizon Premium | -0.17 | Random/Possible Cycle |
| Real Interest Rates | 0.67 | Trend |
| Inflation | 0.64 | Trend |

## Basic Series Summary Statistics

Exhibit 6.9 presents summary statistics of annual total return, and where applicable, income and capital appreciation, for each asset class. The summary statistics presented here are arithmetic mean, geometric mean, standard deviation, and serial correlation. Exhibit 6.10 presents summary statistics for the six inflation-adjusted total return series.

**Exhibit 6.9:** Total Returns, Income Returns, and Capital Appreciation Returns of the SBBI Asset Classes Summary Statistics of Annual Returns (%) 1926–2016

| | Geometric Mean (%) | Arithmetic Mean (%) | Standard Deviation (%) | Serial Correlation |
|---|---|---|---|---|
| **Large-Cap Stocks** | | | | |
| Total Return | 10.0 | 12.0 | 19.9 | 0.02 |
| Income | 4.0 | 4.0 | 1.6 | 0.91 |
| Capital Appreciation | 5.8 | 7.7 | 19.2 | 0.01 |
| **Small-Cap Stocks (TR)** | 12.1 | 16.6 | 31.9 | 0.06 |
| **Long-term Corp Bonds (TR)** | 6.0 | 6.3 | 8.4 | 0.04 |
| **Long-term Gov't Bonds** | | | | |
| Total Return | 5.5 | 6.0 | 9.9 | -0.15 |
| Income | 5.0 | 5.0 | 2.6 | 0.96 |
| Capital Appreciation | 0.3 | 0.7 | 8.9 | -0.26 |
| **Inter-term Gov't Bonds** | | | | |
| Total Return | 5.1 | 5.3 | 5.6 | 0.14 |
| Income | 4.4 | 4.4 | 2.9 | 0.96 |
| Capital Appreciation | 0.6 | 0.7 | 4.5 | -0.17 |
| **U.S. Treasury Bills (TR)** | 3.4 | 3.4 | 3.1 | 0.92 |
| **Inflation** | 2.9 | 3.0 | 4.1 | 0.64 |

Exhibit 6.9 shows that over 1926–2016 small-cap stocks were the riskiest asset class with a standard deviation of 31.9%, but provided the greatest rewards to long-term investors, with an arithmetic mean annual return of 16.6%. The geometric mean of the small-cap series is 12.1%. Large-cap stocks, long-term government bonds, long-term corporate bonds, and intermediate-term government bonds are progressively less risky, and have lower average returns. Treasury bills were nearly riskless and had the lowest return. In general, risk is rewarded by a higher return over the long term.

## Inflation-Adjusted Series Summary Statistics

Inflation-adjusted basic series summary statistics are presented in Exhibit 6.10. Note that the real rate of interest is close to zero (0.5%) on average. For the 91-year period, the geometric and arithmetic means are lower by the amount of inflation than those of the nominal series.

The standard deviations of large-cap and small-cap stock returns remain approximately the same, and a little *lower*, respectively, after adjusting for inflation, while inflation-adjusted returns of long-term corporate bonds, long-term government bonds, intermediate-term government bonds, and Treasury bills are more volatile (i.e., have *higher* standard deviations).

**Exhibit 6.10:** Inflation-Adjusted Series Summary Statistics of Annual Returns (%)
1926–2016

|  | Geometric Mean (%) | Arithmetic Mean (%) | Standard Deviation (%) | Serial Correlation |
|---|---|---|---|---|
| Large-Cap Stocks | 6.9 | 8.9 | 19.9 | 0.01 |
| Small-Cap Stocks | 9.0 | 13.3 | 31.2 | 0.03 |
| Long-term Corp Bonds | 3.0 | 3.4 | 9.5 | 0.15 |
| Long-term Gov't Bonds | 2.6 | 3.1 | 10.9 | -0.06 |
| Inter-term Gov't Bonds | 2.2 | 2.4 | 6.7 | 0.21 |
| U.S. Treasury Bills | 0.5 | 0.5 | 3.8 | 0.67 |

## Rolling-Period Standard Deviations

Rolling-period standard deviations are obtained by rolling a window of fixed length along each time series and computing the standard deviation for the asset class for each window of time. They are useful for examining the volatility or riskiness of returns for holding periods similar to those actually experienced by investors. Exhibits 6.11 and 6.12 graphically depict this volatility. Monthly data are used to maximize the number of data points included in the standard deviation computation. The first 60-month (i.e., 5-year) rolling period covered is January 1926–December 1930, so each of the graphs start at 1930.

Exhibit 6.11 examines the 60-month rolling standard deviation for large-cap stocks, small-cap stocks, and long-term government bonds. It is interesting to see the relatively high standard deviation for small- and large-cap stocks in the 1930s, with an apparent lessening of volatility for 60-month holding periods during the 1980s. Note also how the standard deviation for long-term government bonds reaches the level of both stock asset classes during part of the 1980s. Exhibit 6.12 examines the 60-month rolling standard deviation for long-term and intermediate-term government bonds and Treasury bills. Note that the vertical scale (from 0.0% to 25.0%) of Exhibit 6.11 is different than the vertical scale (from 0.0% to 5.0%) of Exhibit 6.12.

**Exhibit 6.11:** Rolling 60-month Standard Deviations: Large-cap Stocks, Small-cap Stocks and Long-term Government Bonds (%)
1926–2016

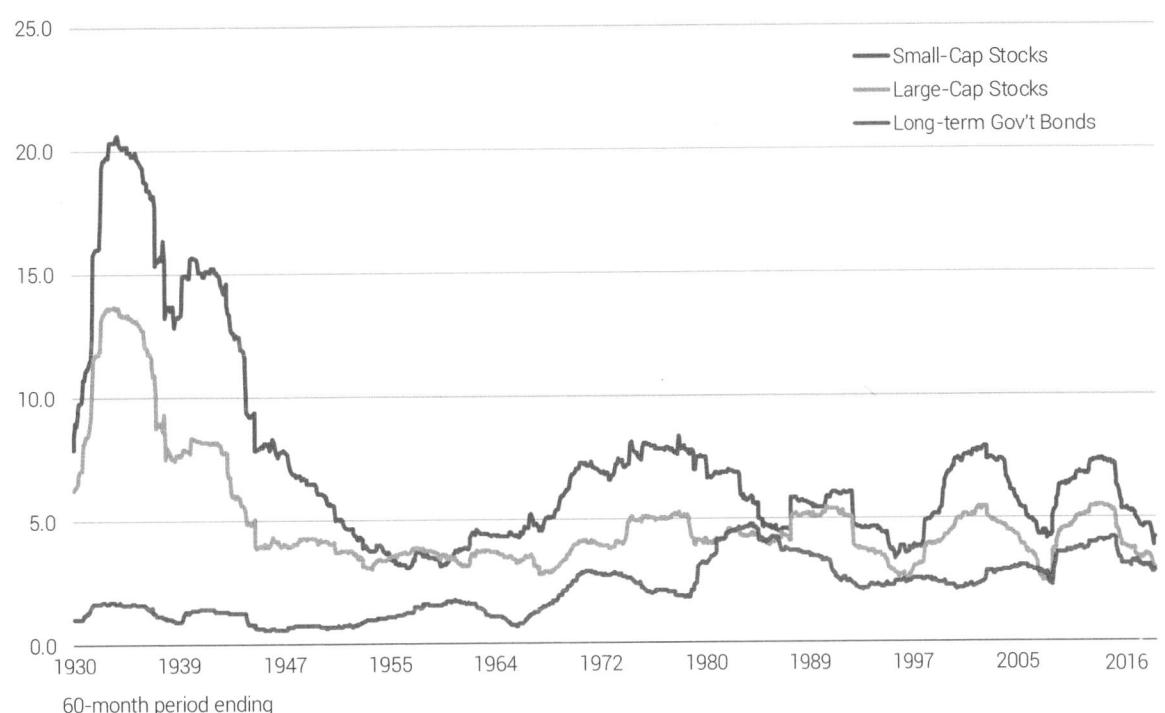

60-month period ending

**Exhibit 6.12:** Rolling 60-month Standard Deviations: Long-term Government Bonds, Intermediate-term Government Bonds, and Treasury Bills (%)
1926–2016

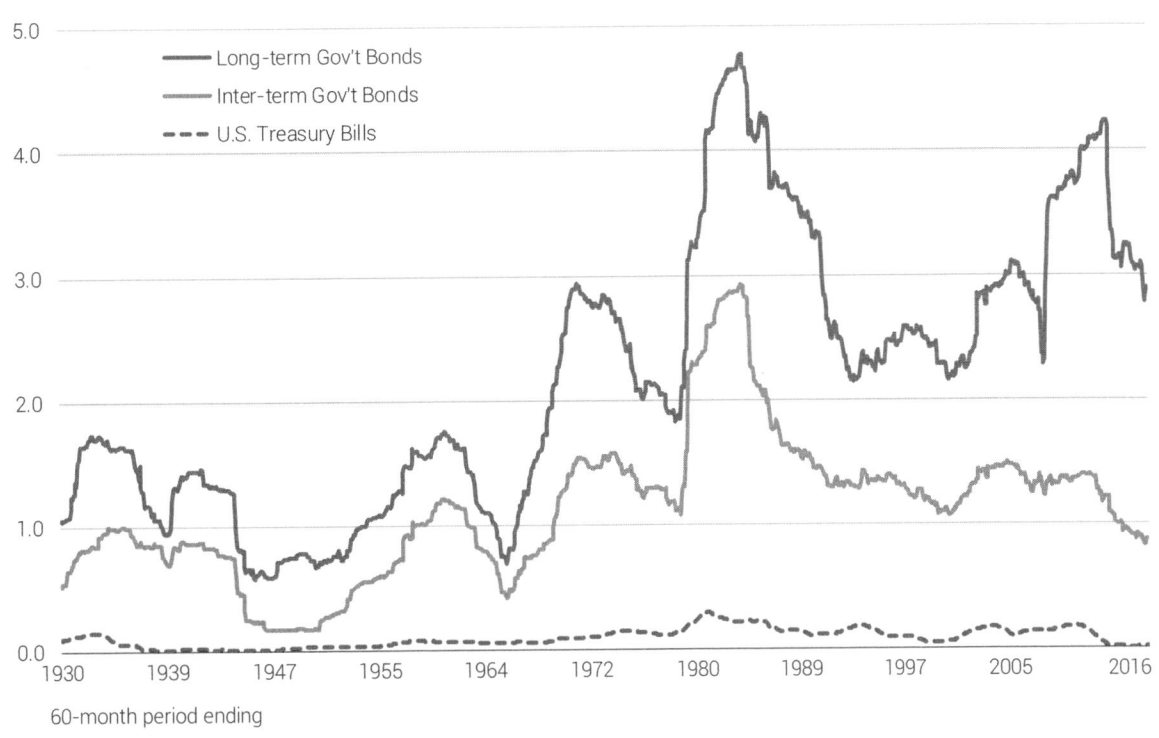

60-month period ending

## Rolling-Period Correlations

Rolling-period correlations are obtained by moving a window of fixed length along time series for two asset classes and computing the cross-correlation between the two asset classes for each window of time. They are useful for examining how asset class returns vary together for holding periods similar to those actually experienced by investors. Exhibits 6.13 and 6.14 graphically depict cross-correlation. Monthly data are used to maximize the number of data points included in the correlation computation. The first 60-month (i.e., 5-year) rolling period covered is January 1926–December 1930, so each of the graphs start at 1930.

Exhibits 6.13 and 6.14 show cross-correlations between two asset classes for 60-month holding periods. Exhibit 6.13 shows the volatility of the correlations between large-cap stocks and long-term government bonds. There are wide fluctuations between strong positive and strong negative correlations over the past 91 years. Exhibit 6.14 shows the correlation between Treasury bills and inflation. These asset classes also show wide fluctuations in correlation over the past 91 years.

**Exhibit 6.13:** Rolling 60-month Correlation: Large-cap Stocks and Long-term Government Bonds 1926–2016

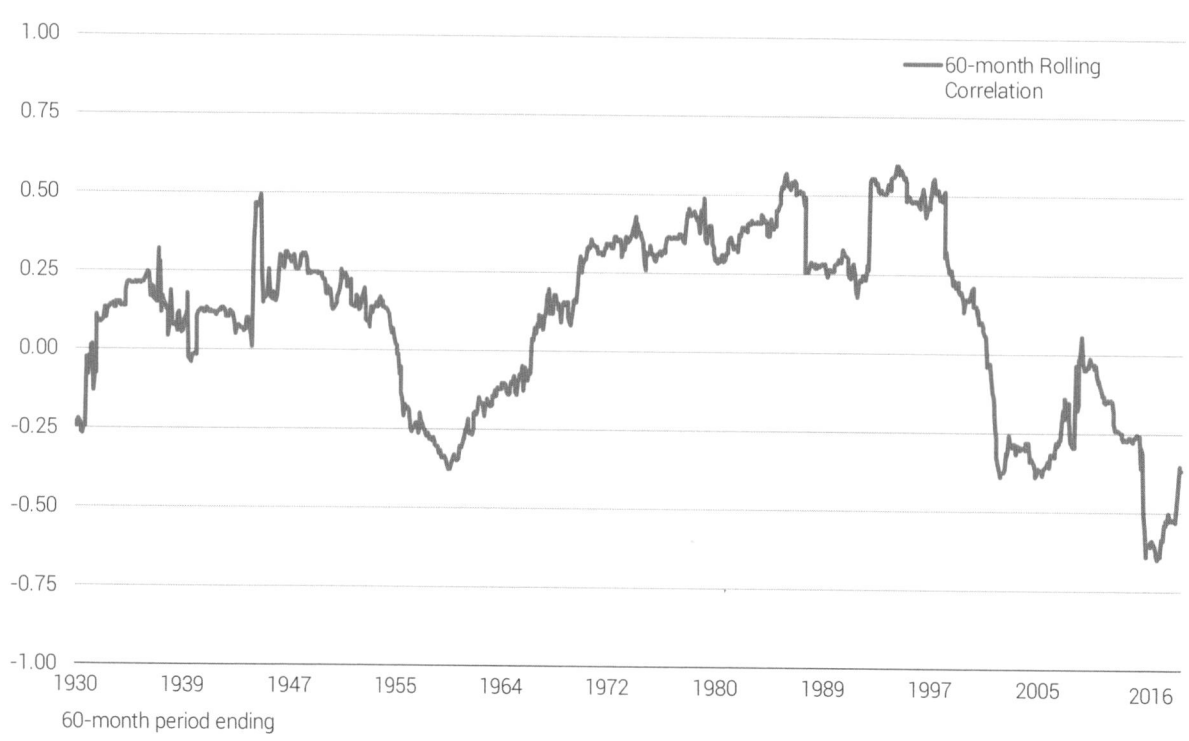

**Exhibit 6.14:** Rolling 60-month Correlation: Treasury Bills and Inflation
1926–2016

60-month period ending

## The True Impact of Asset Allocation on Return

The importance of asset allocation has been the subject of considerable debate and misunderstanding for decades. A May 2010 article pinpoints one of the primary sources of confusion surrounding the importance of asset allocation: How much of a portfolio's level of return comes from a fund's asset-allocation policy?[6.4]

*Note: This section was written by Thomas Idzorek, head of investment methodology and economic research at Morningstar.*

## The Debate

The seminal work on the importance of asset allocation, the catalyst of a 25-year debate, and unfortunately the source of what is arguably the most prolific misunderstanding among investment professionals, is the 1986 article, "Determinants of Portfolio Performance," by Gary Brinson, Randolph Hood, and Gilbert Beebower (BHB).[6.5] BHB regressed the time series returns of each fund on a weighted combination of indexes reflecting each fund's asset-allocation policy. In one of the many analyses that BHB carried out (and probably one of the least important ones), they found that the policy mix explained 93.6% of the average fund's return variation over time (as measured by the R-squared of the regression) — the key word being "variation."

---

[6.4]   Idzorek, T. M. "Asset Allocation is King." *Morningstar Advisor*, April/May, 2010, P. 28.

[6.5]   Brinson, G.P., Hood, L.R., & Beebower, G.L. 1986. " Determinants of Portfolio Performance." *Financial Analysts Journal*, Vol. 42, No. 4, P. 39.

Unfortunately, this 93.6% has been widely misinterpreted. Many practitioners incorrectly believe the number means that 93.6% of a portfolio's return level (for example, a fund's 10-year annualized return) comes from a fund's asset-allocation policy. This is not true. The truth is that, in aggregate, 100% of portfolio return levels comes from asset-allocation policy.

## Return 'Levels' Versus Return 'Variations'

It is imperative to distinguish between return levels and return variations. In the big picture, investors care far more about return levels than they do return variation. The often-cited 93.6% says nothing about return levels, even though that is what so many practitioners mistakenly believe. It is possible to have a high R-squared, indicating that the return variations in the asset class factors did a good job of explaining the return variations of the fund in question, yet see the weighted-average composite asset-allocation policy benchmark produce a significantly different return level from the fund in question. This is the case in BHB's study. Despite the high average 93.6% R-squared of their 91 separate time-series regressions, the average geometric annualized return of the 91 funds in their sample was 9.01% versus 10.11% for the corresponding policy portfolios.

So even though 93.6% is the number that seems to be stuck in everyone's mind, 112% (10.11% divided by 9.01%) of return levels in the study's sample came from asset-allocation policy. To put it bluntly, when it comes to return levels, asset allocation is king. In aggregate, 100% of return levels come from asset allocation before fees and somewhat more after fees. This is a mathematical truth that stems from the concept of an all-inclusive market portfolio and the fact that active management is a zero-sum game. This fundamental truth is somewhat boring; therefore, it is often lost.

# Chapter 7
# Company Size and Return[7.1]

One of the most remarkable discoveries of modern finance is the finding of a relationship between company size and return, generally referred to as the "size effect." The size effect is based on the empirical observation that companies of smaller size tend to have higher returns than do larger companies.

In 1981, study by Rolf Banz examined the returns of New York Stock Exchange (NYSE) small-cap companies compared to the returns of NYSE large-cap companies over the period 1926–1975.[7.2] What Banz found was that the returns of small-cap companies were *greater* than the returns for large-cap companies. Banz's 1981 study is often cited as the first comprehensive study of the size effect. There is a significant (negative) relationship between size and historical equity returns as size decreases, returns tend to increase, and vice versa.

The size effect is not without controversy, nor is this controversy something new. Traditionally, small companies are believed to have greater required rates of return than large companies because small companies are inherently riskier.[7.3] It is not clear, however, whether this is due to size itself, or to other factors closely related to or correlated with size, and thus the qualification that Banz noted in his 1981 article remains pertinent today:[7.4, 7.5]

"It is not known whether size [as measured by market capitalization] per se is responsible for the effect or whether size is just a proxy for one or more true unknown factors correlated with size."

---

[7.1]   This chapter is an overview of the relationship between size and return that is limited to analyzing the relative historical performance of "large-cap stocks" and "small-cap stocks," and does *not* include the much expanded analyses of the "size effect" as it relates to the development of cost of equity capital found in the *2017 Valuation Handbook – U.S. Guide to Cost of Capital* (also published by John Wiley & Sons). The *2017 Valuation Handbook – U.S. Guide to Cost of Capital* includes the data previously published in the Morningstar/Ibbotson® *Stocks, Bonds, Bills, and Inflation*® (SBBI®) *Valuation Yearbook* and the Duff & Phelps *Risk Premium Report*. The *Valuation Handbook – U.S. Guide to Cost of Capital* includes the size premia data, the industry risk premia data, the equity risk premia data, and the methodology that can be used to develop cost of equity capital estimates for an individual business, business ownership interest, security, or intangible asset. For more information about the *2017 Valuation Handbook – U.S. Guide to Cost of Capital* and other Duff & Phelps valuation data resources published by John Wiley & Sons, please go to: www.wiley.com/go/ValuationHandbooks.

[7.2]   Rolf W. Banz, "The Relationship between Return and Market Value of Common Stocks," *Journal of Financial Economics* (March 1981): 3–18. This paper is often cited as the first comprehensive study of the size effect.

[7.3]   Typically cited as possible reasons for the greater risks of smaller companies include (not an exhaustive list): Large firms may have greater ability to enter the market of the small firm and take market share. Large companies likely have more resources to "weather the storm" in economic downturns. Large firms can generally spend more on R&D, advertising, and typically even have greater ability to hire the "best and brightest." Larger firms may have greater access to capital, broader management depth, and less dependency on just a few customers. A larger number of analysts typically follow large firms relative to small firms, so there is probably more information available about large firms, etc.

[7.4]   Even after controlling for size, research suggests that liquidity is still a systematic factor and a predictor of returns. See Roger G. Ibbotson, Zhiwu Chen, Daniel Y.-J. Kim, and Wendy Y. Hu, "Liquidity as an Investment Style" (2013), *Financial Analysts Journal*, vol. 69, no. 3(May/June), p. 30–44. A free download of this article and a 2016 update to this article are available at: www.zebracapm.com.

[7.5]   "Liquidity" is discussed in detail in Chapter 9, "Liquidity Investing."

---

## Construction of the CRSP Size Decile Portfolios

The portfolios used in this chapter are those created by the Center for Research in Security Prices, or CRSP, at the University of Chicago's Booth School of Business. CRSP has refined the methodology of creating size-based portfolios and has applied this methodology to the entire universe of NYSE/NYSE MKT/NASDAQ-listed securities going back to 1926.[7.6] The universe of companies excludes:

- Closed-end mutual funds

- Preferred stocks

- Real estate investment trusts

- Foreign stocks

- American Depositary Receipts

- Unit investment trusts

- Americus Trusts

All companies on the NYSE are ranked by the combined market capitalization of their eligible equity securities. The companies are then split into 10 equally populated groups, or deciles. Eligible companies traded on the NYSE MKT (the former AMEX) and the Nasdaq National Market (NASDAQ) are then assigned to the appropriate deciles according to their capitalization in relation to the NYSE breakpoints.

The portfolios are rebalanced quarterly, using closing prices for the last trading day of March, June, September, and December. Securities added during the quarter are assigned to the appropriate portfolio when two consecutive month-end prices are available. If the final NYSE price of a security that becomes delisted is a month-end price, then that month's return is included in the quarterly return of the security's portfolio. When a month-end NYSE price is missing, the month-end value of the security is derived from merger terms, quotations on regional exchanges, and other sources. If a month-end value still is not determined, the last available daily price is used. Base security returns are monthly holding period returns. All distributions are added to the month-end prices, and

---

[7.6] In October, 2008, NYSE Euronext acquired the American Stock Exchange (AMEX). The "NYSE MKT" is the former American Stock Exchange, or AMEX. The CRSP standard market-cap-based NYSE/AMEX/NASDAQ indices are therefore called the NYSE/NYSE MKT/ NASDAQ indices herein.

appropriate price adjustments are made to account for stock splits and dividends. The return on a portfolio for one month is calculated as the weighted average of the returns for its individual stocks. Annual portfolio returns are calculated by compounding the monthly portfolio returns.[7.7]

## Size of the Deciles

Exhibit 7.1 provides an overview of the CRSP deciles and size groupings in terms of relative size (by aggregate market capitalization) and number of companies as of December 31, 2016.

Decile 1 has 191 companies in it, and accounts for nearly two-thirds of aggregate market cap (66.12%). Decile 10 has 790 companies in it, and accounts for less than 1% of aggregate market cap (0.40%).

**Exhibit 7.1:** Aggregate Market Capitalization and Company Counts of the CRSP (NYSE/NYSE MKT/ NASDAQ) Deciles and Size Groupings
December 31, 2016

| Decile | Historic Average Percentage of Total Capitalization | Recent Number of Companies | Recent Decile Market Capitalization (in $thousands) | Recent Percentage of Total Capitalization |
|---|---|---|---|---|
| 1-Largest | 63.13% | 191 | 15,290,475,300 | 66.12% |
| 2 | 13.95% | 200 | 3,010,671,018 | 13.02% |
| 3 | 7.55% | 202 | 1,609,575,618 | 6.96% |
| 4 | 4.73% | 221 | 1,010,851,810 | 4.37% |
| 5 | 3.26% | 227 | 677,120,067 | 2.93% |
| 6 | 2.41% | 259 | 541,037,999 | 2.34% |
| 7 | 1.79% | 283 | 384,129,198 | 1.66% |
| 8 | 1.33% | 361 | 297,164,943 | 1.28% |
| 9 | 1.03% | 487 | 212,609,644 | 0.92% |
| 10-Smallest | 0.82% | 790 | 92,882,169 | 0.40% |
| Mid-Cap 3-5 | 15.54% | 650 | 3,297,547,494 | 14.26% |
| Low-Cap 6-8 | 5.53% | 903 | 1,222,332,139 | 5.29% |
| Micro-Cap 9-10 | 1.85% | 1,277 | 305,491,813 | 1.32% |

**Source of underlying data:** Calculated (or derived) based on data from CRSP ©2017 Center for Research in Security Prices (CRSP®), The University of Chicago Booth School of Business (2017). Calculations by Duff & Phelps, LLC.

---

[7.7] According to CRSP, in 2016 CRSP "performed a comprehensive check and found changes to index levels back to 1977. Almost all of the changes are due to CRSP adding factor[s] to adjust price values for distribution codes 5663 & 5773. These edits were made in the 201612 iteration...". These edits are detailed in the CRSP document "STOCK & INDEX RELEASE NOTES, December 2016 Annual UPDATE" (available at: http://www.crsp.com/files/images/release_notes/mdaz_201612_annual.pdf). This review of the database caused small changes in the returns over the 1926–2015 period (calculated using the December 31, 2015 data cut) compared to the returns over the 1926–2015 period (calculated using the December 31, 2016 data cut). These changes were not material: the largest/smallest change to the geometric mean return of CRSP standard market-cap-weighted deciles 1–10 over this period was 0.0044%/-0.0146%; the average/median change was -0.0007%/0.0003%.

In Exhibit 7.2, the largest company in each of the CRSP (NYSE/NYSE MKT/NASDAQ) deciles and size groupings (by market capitalization) are listed as of September 30, 2016.

**Exhibit 7.2:** Largest Company (by market capitalization) in CRSP (NYSE/NYSE MKT/NASDAQ) Deciles and Size Groupings as of September 30, 2016

| Decile | Company Name | Recent Market Capitalization (in $thousands) |
|---|---|---|
| 1-Largest | Apple Inc. | 609,163,498 |
| 2 | Apache Corp. | 24,233,747 |
| 3 | Textron Inc. | 10,711,194 |
| 4 | C F Industries Holdings Inc. | 5,676,716 |
| 5 | Ellie Mae Inc. | 3,512,913 |
| 6 | Generac Holdings Inc. | 2,390,899 |
| 7 | Flagstar Bancorp Inc. | 1,569,984 |
| 8 | SEACOR Holdings Inc. | 1,030,426 |
| 9 | Kadant Inc. | 567,843 |
| 10-Smallest | Pioneer Energy Services Corp. | 262,891 |

**Source of underlying data:** CRSP databases ©2017 Center for Research in Security Prices (CRSP®), The University of Chicago Booth School of Business (2017).

The CRSP deciles are re-constituted and rebalanced at the end of each calendar quarter (March, June, September, and December). These quarter-end portfolios are then followed for the subsequent three months. For example, the breakpoints in Exhibit 7.2 were a key input in defining the companies placed in each decile at the end of September 2016; these portfolio compositions were then used to calculate the October, November, and December 2016 returns associated with each decile.[7.8]

---

[7.8] According to the *2017 Valuation Handbook – U.S. Guide to Cost of Capital*, large-capitalization companies (those in CRSP deciles 1–2) have equity capitalizations greater than $10,711.194 million; mid-capitalization companies (those in CRSP deciles 3–5) have equity capitalizations between $2,392.689 million and $10,711.194 million (inclusive), low-capitalization companies (those in CRSP deciles 6–8) have equity capitalizations between $569.279 million and $2,390.899 million (inclusive), and micro-capitalization companies (those in CRSP deciles 9–10) have equity capitalizations of equal to or less than $567.843 million.

**Presentation of the Decile Data**

Exhibit 7.3 is a year-by-year history of the annual returns for the ten CRSP deciles over the 1926–2016 time horizon.

Exhibit 7.4 provides the year-by-year growth of $1.00 over the 1926–2016 time horizon. These are year-end index levels, assuming an investment of $1.00 at year-end 1925.

Exhibit 7.5 is a year-by-year history of the annual *returns*, and the year-by-year *growth* of $1.00 (i.e., year-end index levels; assuming an investment of $1.00 at year-end 1925) over the 1926–2016 time horizon for (i) mid-cap stocks (a portfolio comprised of CRSP deciles 3, 4, and 5), (ii) low-cap stocks (a portfolio comprised of CRSP deciles 6, 7, and 8), (iii) micro-cap stocks (a portfolio comprised of CRSP deciles 9 and 10), and (iv) the "market" (a portfolio comprised of CRSP deciles 1–10).

**Exhibit 7.3:** Size Decile Portfolios of the NYSE/AMEX/NASDAQ
Annual Returns (decimal format)
1926–2016

| Year | Decile 1 | Decile 2 | Decile 3 | Decile 4 | Decile 5 | Decile 6 | Decile 7 | Decile 8 | Decile 9 | Decile 10 |
|------|----------|----------|----------|----------|----------|----------|----------|----------|----------|-----------|
| 1926 | 0.1415 | 0.0710 | 0.0320 | 0.0080 | -0.0216 | 0.0398 | -0.0265 | -0.0619 | -0.0952 | -0.0676 |
| 1927 | 0.3362 | 0.2925 | 0.3218 | 0.3839 | 0.3657 | 0.2216 | 0.3665 | 0.2548 | 0.2992 | 0.2620 |
| 1928 | 0.4011 | 0.3530 | 0.3751 | 0.3383 | 0.5627 | 0.3583 | 0.3341 | 0.2688 | 0.3701 | 0.6634 |
| 1929 | -0.1083 | -0.0677 | -0.2471 | -0.3206 | -0.2577 | -0.3892 | -0.3790 | -0.3925 | -0.4924 | -0.5131 |
| 1930 | -0.2481 | -0.3648 | -0.3737 | -0.3590 | -0.3417 | -0.3799 | -0.3690 | -0.4762 | -0.4616 | -0.4473 |
| 1931 | -0.4195 | -0.5032 | -0.4748 | -0.4655 | -0.4521 | -0.5218 | -0.4784 | -0.4980 | -0.4994 | -0.4750 |
| 1932 | -0.1048 | 0.0105 | 0.0035 | -0.1173 | -0.1287 | -0.0035 | -0.0852 | 0.0109 | -0.0149 | 0.4054 |
| 1933 | 0.4607 | 0.7273 | 0.9892 | 1.1528 | 1.0142 | 1.0245 | 1.0630 | 1.7050 | 2.0659 | 1.9698 |
| 1934 | 0.0052 | 0.0588 | 0.0733 | 0.1596 | 0.1355 | 0.2030 | 0.1897 | 0.1949 | 0.3098 | 0.3214 |
| 1935 | 0.4266 | 0.5307 | 0.4033 | 0.4216 | 0.5600 | 0.5756 | 0.6717 | 0.5890 | 0.5750 | 0.8195 |
| 1936 | 0.3010 | 0.3410 | 0.2900 | 0.3931 | 0.4980 | 0.5091 | 0.5700 | 0.5231 | 0.7158 | 0.8638 |
| 1937 | -0.3164 | -0.3713 | -0.3723 | -0.4466 | -0.4891 | -0.4548 | -0.5083 | -0.5424 | -0.5177 | -0.5394 |
| 1938 | 0.2509 | 0.3438 | 0.3674 | 0.3536 | 0.4511 | 0.4368 | 0.4021 | 0.4714 | 0.2659 | 0.0912 |
| 1939 | 0.0482 | -0.0481 | -0.0236 | -0.0305 | 0.0327 | 0.0637 | 0.0209 | 0.0443 | -0.0616 | 0.1829 |
| 1940 | -0.0703 | -0.0986 | -0.0594 | -0.0561 | -0.0231 | -0.0494 | -0.0575 | -0.0512 | -0.0727 | -0.2836 |
| 1941 | -0.1119 | -0.0818 | -0.0726 | -0.0734 | -0.1164 | -0.1039 | -0.1134 | -0.0801 | -0.1512 | -0.1117 |
| 1942 | 0.1369 | 0.2393 | 0.2085 | 0.2080 | 0.2275 | 0.2137 | 0.3015 | 0.3271 | 0.4377 | 0.6913 |
| 1943 | 0.2325 | 0.3475 | 0.3324 | 0.3892 | 0.4910 | 0.4408 | 0.7466 | 0.6446 | 0.8818 | 1.4050 |
| 1944 | 0.1680 | 0.2542 | 0.2528 | 0.3066 | 0.4195 | 0.4174 | 0.4011 | 0.4436 | 0.5668 | 0.7905 |
| 1945 | 0.3040 | 0.4548 | 0.5459 | 0.6334 | 0.5116 | 0.6112 | 0.6521 | 0.7092 | 0.7956 | 0.9086 |
| 1946 | -0.0531 | -0.0549 | -0.0614 | -0.1138 | -0.0948 | -0.0873 | -0.1211 | -0.1444 | -0.1112 | -0.1773 |
| 1947 | 0.0541 | 0.0098 | -0.0040 | 0.0208 | 0.0342 | -0.0309 | -0.0341 | -0.0178 | -0.0403 | -0.0037 |
| 1948 | 0.0337 | 0.0026 | 0.0263 | -0.0225 | -0.0192 | -0.0408 | -0.0283 | -0.0701 | -0.0800 | -0.0390 |
| 1949 | 0.1852 | 0.2538 | 0.2597 | 0.1983 | 0.1822 | 0.2342 | 0.2189 | 0.1594 | 0.1984 | 0.2509 |
| 1950 | 0.2952 | 0.2875 | 0.2685 | 0.3186 | 0.3615 | 0.3406 | 0.3799 | 0.4002 | 0.4034 | 0.5643 |
| 1951 | 0.2164 | 0.2263 | 0.2117 | 0.1660 | 0.1483 | 0.1311 | 0.1845 | 0.1517 | 0.1072 | 0.0735 |
| 1952 | 0.1433 | 0.1301 | 0.1218 | 0.1190 | 0.1117 | 0.0997 | 0.1031 | 0.0795 | 0.0813 | 0.0259 |
| 1953 | 0.0124 | 0.0153 | 0.0030 | -0.0137 | -0.0288 | -0.0096 | -0.0253 | -0.0772 | -0.0434 | -0.0825 |
| 1954 | 0.4888 | 0.4731 | 0.5887 | 0.5081 | 0.5726 | 0.5956 | 0.5750 | 0.5278 | 0.6148 | 0.6869 |
| 1955 | 0.2875 | 0.1806 | 0.1859 | 0.1932 | 0.1771 | 0.2295 | 0.1839 | 0.1976 | 0.2080 | 0.2574 |
| 1956 | 0.0811 | 0.1138 | 0.0701 | 0.0885 | 0.0794 | 0.0606 | 0.0724 | 0.0642 | 0.0483 | -0.0100 |
| 1957 | -0.0923 | -0.0864 | -0.1315 | -0.1080 | -0.1409 | -0.1833 | -0.1631 | -0.1869 | -0.1446 | -0.1694 |
| 1958 | 0.4070 | 0.4943 | 0.5458 | 0.5893 | 0.5619 | 0.5636 | 0.6832 | 0.6490 | 0.7154 | 0.6834 |
| 1959 | 0.1242 | 0.1001 | 0.1305 | 0.1555 | 0.1939 | 0.1537 | 0.2012 | 0.1784 | 0.2041 | 0.1351 |
| 1960 | 0.0037 | 0.0612 | 0.0468 | 0.0075 | -0.0168 | -0.0064 | -0.0569 | -0.0512 | -0.0382 | -0.0787 |
| 1961 | 0.2627 | 0.2739 | 0.2869 | 0.2914 | 0.2916 | 0.2642 | 0.3104 | 0.3253 | 0.3030 | 0.3235 |
| 1962 | -0.0878 | -0.0959 | -0.1190 | -0.1272 | -0.1681 | -0.1771 | -0.1629 | -0.1489 | -0.1701 | -0.1498 |
| 1963 | 0.2249 | 0.2141 | 0.1647 | 0.1712 | 0.1273 | 0.1853 | 0.1782 | 0.1997 | 0.1280 | 0.1117 |
| 1964 | 0.1599 | 0.1428 | 0.1997 | 0.1625 | 0.1623 | 0.1666 | 0.1597 | 0.1714 | 0.1532 | 0.2094 |
| 1965 | 0.0893 | 0.1925 | 0.2483 | 0.2425 | 0.3217 | 0.3776 | 0.3374 | 0.3190 | 0.3193 | 0.4315 |
| 1966 | -0.1027 | -0.0574 | -0.0507 | -0.0623 | -0.0721 | -0.0452 | -0.0955 | -0.0864 | -0.0589 | -0.1008 |
| 1967 | 0.2197 | 0.2079 | 0.3169 | 0.4564 | 0.5145 | 0.5343 | 0.6472 | 0.8133 | 0.9064 | 1.1416 |
| 1968 | 0.0753 | 0.1654 | 0.1979 | 0.1829 | 0.2759 | 0.3047 | 0.2673 | 0.4047 | 0.3711 | 0.6136 |
| 1969 | -0.0584 | -0.1295 | -0.1172 | -0.1662 | -0.1808 | -0.1871 | -0.2445 | -0.2471 | -0.3158 | -0.3290 |
| 1970 | 0.0231 | 0.0182 | 0.0330 | -0.0699 | -0.0601 | -0.0593 | -0.0973 | -0.1614 | -0.1526 | -0.1785 |

**Source:** CRSP databases ©2017 Center for Research in Security Prices (CRSP®), The University of Chicago Booth School of Business (2017).

**Exhibit 7.3:** Size Decile Portfolios of the NYSE/AMEX/NASDAQ
Annual Returns (decimal format)
1926–2016

| Year | Decile 1 | Decile 2 | Decile 3 | Decile 4 | Decile 5 | Decile 6 | Decile 7 | Decile 8 | Decile 9 | Decile 10 |
|------|----------|----------|----------|----------|----------|----------|----------|----------|----------|-----------|
| 1971 | 0.1484 | 0.1328 | 0.2011 | 0.2472 | 0.1890 | 0.2244 | 0.2018 | 0.1735 | 0.1647 | 0.1853 |
| 1972 | 0.2212 | 0.1278 | 0.0938 | 0.0881 | 0.0863 | 0.0695 | 0.0632 | 0.0205 | -0.0229 | -0.0057 |
| 1973 | -0.1274 | -0.2266 | -0.2278 | -0.2680 | -0.3217 | -0.3191 | -0.3702 | -0.3534 | -0.3897 | -0.4203 |
| 1974 | -0.2803 | -0.2441 | -0.2458 | -0.2834 | -0.2167 | -0.2694 | -0.2558 | -0.2423 | -0.2635 | -0.2715 |
| 1975 | 0.3169 | 0.4573 | 0.5363 | 0.6168 | 0.5966 | 0.5675 | 0.6326 | 0.6579 | 0.6649 | 0.7579 |
| 1976 | 0.2073 | 0.3045 | 0.3811 | 0.4008 | 0.4363 | 0.4808 | 0.5018 | 0.5690 | 0.5101 | 0.5516 |
| 1977 | -0.0884 | -0.0367 | 0.0109 | 0.0376 | 0.1126 | 0.1413 | 0.1754 | 0.2261 | 0.2022 | 0.2310 |
| 1978 | 0.0637 | 0.0229 | 0.1084 | 0.0974 | 0.1207 | 0.1637 | 0.1705 | 0.1632 | 0.1605 | 0.2815 |
| 1979 | 0.1519 | 0.2871 | 0.3061 | 0.3516 | 0.3557 | 0.4889 | 0.4206 | 0.4638 | 0.4594 | 0.4158 |
| 1980 | 0.3275 | 0.3442 | 0.3186 | 0.3043 | 0.3193 | 0.3141 | 0.3623 | 0.3233 | 0.3823 | 0.3071 |
| 1981 | -0.0833 | 0.0059 | 0.0372 | 0.0403 | 0.0484 | 0.0677 | -0.0040 | 0.0055 | 0.0802 | 0.0856 |
| 1982 | 0.1964 | 0.1749 | 0.2081 | 0.2566 | 0.3076 | 0.2940 | 0.2919 | 0.2955 | 0.2608 | 0.2855 |
| 1983 | 0.2057 | 0.1686 | 0.2662 | 0.2633 | 0.2626 | 0.2589 | 0.2725 | 0.3721 | 0.3130 | 0.3690 |
| 1984 | 0.0840 | 0.0770 | 0.0253 | -0.0458 | -0.0269 | 0.0248 | -0.0426 | -0.0745 | -0.0896 | -0.1952 |
| 1985 | 0.3137 | 0.3770 | 0.2910 | 0.3390 | 0.3115 | 0.3097 | 0.3255 | 0.3651 | 0.3077 | 0.2582 |
| 1986 | 0.1801 | 0.1816 | 0.1628 | 0.1732 | 0.1512 | 0.0873 | 0.1248 | 0.0387 | 0.0570 | 0.0041 |
| 1987 | 0.0504 | 0.0037 | 0.0393 | 0.0170 | -0.0382 | -0.0509 | -0.0861 | -0.0808 | -0.1262 | -0.1492 |
| 1988 | 0.1486 | 0.1982 | 0.2126 | 0.2239 | 0.2138 | 0.2339 | 0.2394 | 0.2854 | 0.2285 | 0.2105 |
| 1989 | 0.3295 | 0.3008 | 0.2629 | 0.2308 | 0.2423 | 0.2107 | 0.1784 | 0.1788 | 0.1058 | 0.0550 |
| 1990 | -0.0088 | -0.0853 | -0.1015 | -0.0877 | -0.1410 | -0.1849 | -0.1531 | -0.1979 | -0.2460 | -0.3128 |
| 1991 | 0.3039 | 0.3463 | 0.4140 | 0.3887 | 0.4810 | 0.5326 | 0.4421 | 0.4723 | 0.5065 | 0.4807 |
| 1992 | 0.0474 | 0.1579 | 0.1387 | 0.1249 | 0.2613 | 0.1878 | 0.1920 | 0.1287 | 0.2502 | 0.3398 |
| 1993 | 0.0732 | 0.1319 | 0.1614 | 0.1562 | 0.1695 | 0.1740 | 0.1901 | 0.1853 | 0.1658 | 0.2558 |
| 1994 | 0.0174 | -0.0174 | -0.0423 | -0.0098 | -0.0166 | 0.0037 | -0.0256 | -0.0308 | -0.0310 | -0.0298 |
| 1995 | 0.3942 | 0.3527 | 0.3536 | 0.3271 | 0.3327 | 0.2674 | 0.3303 | 0.2912 | 0.3502 | 0.3047 |
| 1996 | 0.2377 | 0.1956 | 0.1714 | 0.1905 | 0.1318 | 0.1756 | 0.1960 | 0.1709 | 0.2073 | 0.1716 |
| 1997 | 0.3486 | 0.3004 | 0.2509 | 0.2609 | 0.1574 | 0.2838 | 0.2999 | 0.2560 | 0.2524 | 0.2245 |
| 1998 | 0.3515 | 0.1293 | 0.0730 | 0.0723 | 0.0058 | 0.0125 | -0.0066 | 0.0063 | -0.0490 | -0.1159 |
| 1999 | 0.2451 | 0.2013 | 0.3312 | 0.2997 | 0.2580 | 0.3526 | 0.2496 | 0.3943 | 0.3414 | 0.2786 |
| 2000 | -0.1358 | -0.0119 | -0.0645 | -0.0997 | -0.0794 | -0.1052 | -0.1049 | -0.1297 | -0.1345 | -0.1339 |
| 2001 | -0.1531 | -0.0869 | -0.0413 | -0.0050 | -0.0252 | 0.0941 | 0.1170 | 0.2161 | 0.3143 | 0.3641 |
| 2002 | -0.2238 | -0.1767 | -0.1938 | -0.1794 | -0.1750 | -0.2144 | -0.2283 | -0.2001 | -0.1867 | -0.0555 |
| 2003 | 0.2568 | 0.3750 | 0.3990 | 0.4473 | 0.4081 | 0.4769 | 0.5108 | 0.5821 | 0.6859 | 0.9212 |
| 2004 | 0.0789 | 0.2033 | 0.1809 | 0.1873 | 0.1752 | 0.2216 | 0.1894 | 0.2186 | 0.1483 | 0.1886 |
| 2005 | 0.0370 | 0.1255 | 0.1153 | 0.1101 | 0.0996 | 0.0302 | 0.1054 | 0.0757 | 0.0228 | 0.0576 |
| 2006 | 0.1561 | 0.1577 | 0.1453 | 0.1157 | 0.1585 | 0.1496 | 0.1613 | 0.1793 | 0.1676 | 0.1968 |
| 2007 | 0.0712 | 0.0733 | 0.0400 | 0.0440 | 0.0765 | 0.0520 | -0.0141 | -0.0562 | -0.0635 | -0.0996 |
| 2008 | -0.3508 | -0.4191 | -0.4015 | -0.3665 | -0.3521 | -0.4010 | -0.3606 | -0.3564 | -0.3691 | -0.4792 |
| 2009 | 0.2256 | 0.3827 | 0.3783 | 0.4564 | 0.4420 | 0.4122 | 0.4231 | 0.4904 | 0.5029 | 0.8174 |
| 2010 | 0.1312 | 0.2201 | 0.3023 | 0.2121 | 0.2967 | 0.2758 | 0.3147 | 0.3295 | 0.2901 | 0.2930 |
| 2011 | 0.0221 | -0.0011 | -0.0187 | 0.0078 | -0.0049 | -0.0150 | -0.0505 | -0.0591 | -0.0766 | -0.1411 |
| 2012 | 0.1591 | 0.1606 | 0.1656 | 0.1637 | 0.1542 | 0.1845 | 0.1834 | 0.1829 | 0.1472 | 0.2145 |
| 2013 | 0.3254 | 0.3761 | 0.3662 | 0.4185 | 0.4107 | 0.4309 | 0.4188 | 0.4599 | 0.5030 | 0.4908 |
| 2014 | 0.1228 | 0.1603 | 0.1024 | 0.0745 | 0.0566 | 0.0415 | 0.0688 | 0.0159 | 0.0207 | 0.0286 |
| 2015 | 0.0174 | -0.0369 | -0.0277 | -0.0477 | -0.0734 | -0.0730 | -0.0588 | -0.0780 | -0.1135 | -0.1170 |
| 2016 | 0.1163 | 0.1697 | 0.1683 | 0.1349 | 0.1695 | 0.1879 | 0.2523 | 0.2158 | 0.3092 | 0.2162 |

**Source:** CRSP databases ©2017 Center for Research in Security Prices (CRSP®), The University of Chicago Booth School of Business (2017).

**Exhibit 7.4:** Size Decile Portfolios of the NYSE/AMEX/NASDAQ
Year-end Index Values (Year-end 1925 = $1.00)
1926–2016

| Year | Decile 1 | Decile 2 | Decile 3 | Decile 4 | Decile 5 | Decile 6 | Decile 7 | Decile 8 | Decile 9 | Decile 10 |
|------|----------|----------|----------|----------|----------|----------|----------|----------|----------|-----------|
| 1925 | 1.000 | 1.000 | 1.000 | 1.000 | 1.000 | 1.000 | 1.000 | 1.000 | 1.000 | 1.000 |
| 1926 | 1.142 | 1.071 | 1.032 | 1.008 | 0.978 | 1.040 | 0.974 | 0.938 | 0.905 | 0.932 |
| 1927 | 1.525 | 1.384 | 1.364 | 1.395 | 1.336 | 1.270 | 1.330 | 1.177 | 1.175 | 1.177 |
| 1928 | 2.137 | 1.873 | 1.876 | 1.867 | 2.088 | 1.725 | 1.775 | 1.494 | 1.610 | 1.957 |
| 1929 | 1.906 | 1.746 | 1.412 | 1.268 | 1.550 | 1.054 | 1.102 | 0.907 | 0.817 | 0.953 |
| 1930 | 1.433 | 1.109 | 0.884 | 0.813 | 1.020 | 0.653 | 0.696 | 0.475 | 0.440 | 0.527 |
| 1931 | 0.832 | 0.551 | 0.465 | 0.435 | 0.559 | 0.312 | 0.363 | 0.239 | 0.220 | 0.277 |
| 1932 | 0.745 | 0.557 | 0.466 | 0.384 | 0.487 | 0.311 | 0.332 | 0.241 | 0.217 | 0.389 |
| 1933 | 1.088 | 0.962 | 0.927 | 0.826 | 0.981 | 0.630 | 0.685 | 0.652 | 0.665 | 1.154 |
| 1934 | 1.093 | 1.018 | 0.995 | 0.958 | 1.114 | 0.758 | 0.814 | 0.780 | 0.871 | 1.525 |
| 1935 | 1.559 | 1.559 | 1.397 | 1.361 | 1.738 | 1.195 | 1.362 | 1.239 | 1.373 | 2.775 |
| 1936 | 2.029 | 2.090 | 1.802 | 1.897 | 2.603 | 1.803 | 2.138 | 1.887 | 2.355 | 5.172 |
| 1937 | 1.387 | 1.314 | 1.131 | 1.050 | 1.330 | 0.983 | 1.051 | 0.863 | 1.136 | 2.382 |
| 1938 | 1.735 | 1.766 | 1.546 | 1.421 | 1.930 | 1.412 | 1.474 | 1.270 | 1.438 | 2.600 |
| 1939 | 1.819 | 1.681 | 1.510 | 1.377 | 1.993 | 1.502 | 1.504 | 1.326 | 1.349 | 3.075 |
| 1940 | 1.691 | 1.516 | 1.420 | 1.300 | 1.947 | 1.428 | 1.418 | 1.258 | 1.251 | 2.203 |
| 1941 | 1.502 | 1.392 | 1.317 | 1.205 | 1.720 | 1.280 | 1.257 | 1.158 | 1.062 | 1.957 |
| 1942 | 1.707 | 1.725 | 1.591 | 1.455 | 2.111 | 1.553 | 1.636 | 1.536 | 1.527 | 3.310 |
| 1943 | 2.104 | 2.324 | 2.120 | 2.021 | 3.148 | 2.238 | 2.858 | 2.527 | 2.873 | 7.961 |
| 1944 | 2.458 | 2.914 | 2.656 | 2.641 | 4.469 | 3.172 | 4.004 | 3.647 | 4.501 | 14.254 |
| 1945 | 3.205 | 4.240 | 4.107 | 4.314 | 6.755 | 5.111 | 6.615 | 6.234 | 8.083 | 27.204 |
| 1946 | 3.035 | 4.007 | 3.855 | 3.823 | 6.115 | 4.665 | 5.814 | 5.334 | 7.184 | 22.380 |
| 1947 | 3.199 | 4.047 | 3.839 | 3.903 | 6.324 | 4.520 | 5.616 | 5.239 | 6.895 | 22.297 |
| 1948 | 3.307 | 4.057 | 3.940 | 3.815 | 6.202 | 4.336 | 5.457 | 4.872 | 6.343 | 21.427 |
| 1949 | 3.919 | 5.087 | 4.964 | 4.572 | 7.332 | 5.352 | 6.652 | 5.648 | 7.601 | 26.803 |
| 1950 | 5.076 | 6.550 | 6.296 | 6.028 | 9.983 | 7.175 | 9.178 | 7.908 | 10.668 | 41.928 |
| 1951 | 6.175 | 8.032 | 7.629 | 7.029 | 11.464 | 8.116 | 10.872 | 9.107 | 11.811 | 45.011 |
| 1952 | 7.060 | 9.077 | 8.558 | 7.866 | 12.745 | 8.925 | 11.992 | 9.831 | 12.771 | 46.174 |
| 1953 | 7.148 | 9.215 | 8.583 | 7.758 | 12.378 | 8.839 | 11.689 | 9.072 | 12.217 | 42.366 |
| 1954 | 10.641 | 13.575 | 13.637 | 11.699 | 19.466 | 14.104 | 18.410 | 13.859 | 19.728 | 71.467 |
| 1955 | 13.701 | 16.027 | 16.172 | 13.960 | 22.914 | 17.341 | 21.795 | 16.599 | 23.831 | 89.860 |
| 1956 | 14.812 | 17.851 | 17.306 | 15.196 | 24.733 | 18.393 | 23.373 | 17.664 | 24.982 | 88.963 |
| 1957 | 13.445 | 16.310 | 15.029 | 13.555 | 21.247 | 15.021 | 19.560 | 14.364 | 21.369 | 73.892 |
| 1958 | 18.917 | 24.372 | 23.231 | 21.543 | 33.186 | 23.487 | 32.924 | 23.686 | 36.657 | 124.389 |
| 1959 | 21.267 | 26.812 | 26.264 | 24.893 | 39.621 | 27.097 | 39.548 | 27.911 | 44.137 | 141.200 |
| 1960 | 21.346 | 28.453 | 27.492 | 25.081 | 38.954 | 26.923 | 37.297 | 26.483 | 42.451 | 130.086 |
| 1961 | 26.954 | 36.245 | 35.380 | 32.389 | 50.315 | 34.035 | 48.875 | 35.098 | 55.315 | 172.171 |
| 1962 | 24.587 | 32.769 | 31.171 | 28.270 | 41.859 | 28.008 | 40.914 | 29.873 | 45.904 | 146.373 |
| 1963 | 30.115 | 39.784 | 36.306 | 33.109 | 47.188 | 33.198 | 48.204 | 35.837 | 51.777 | 162.718 |
| 1964 | 34.930 | 45.465 | 43.557 | 38.491 | 54.849 | 38.730 | 55.902 | 41.978 | 59.710 | 196.786 |
| 1965 | 38.048 | 54.219 | 54.370 | 47.825 | 72.494 | 53.353 | 74.761 | 55.368 | 78.777 | 281.695 |
| 1966 | 34.140 | 51.105 | 51.611 | 44.848 | 67.270 | 50.942 | 67.618 | 50.586 | 74.134 | 253.306 |
| 1967 | 41.639 | 61.731 | 67.966 | 65.315 | 101.882 | 78.158 | 111.382 | 91.730 | 141.333 | 542.472 |
| 1968 | 44.775 | 71.943 | 81.414 | 77.258 | 129.986 | 101.971 | 141.159 | 128.849 | 193.786 | 875.330 |
| 1969 | 42.159 | 62.626 | 71.873 | 64.422 | 106.490 | 82.896 | 106.641 | 97.009 | 132.594 | 587.329 |

**Source of underlying data:** CRSP databases ©2017 Center for Research in Security Prices (CRSP®), The University of Chicago Booth School of Business (2017). Index values calculated by Duff & Phelps, LLC. Used with permission.

Chapter 7: Company Size and Return

**Exhibit 7.4:** Size Decile Portfolios of the NYSE/AMEX/NASDAQ
Year-end Index Values (Year-end 1925 = $1.00)
1926–2016

| Year | Decile 1 | Decile 2 | Decile 3 | Decile 4 | Decile 5 | Decile 6 | Decile 7 | Decile 8 | Decile 9 | Decile 10 |
|---|---|---|---|---|---|---|---|---|---|---|
| 1970 | 43.134 | 63.763 | 74.248 | 59.919 | 100.094 | 77.980 | 96.265 | 81.354 | 112.359 | 482.513 |
| 1971 | 49.536 | 72.233 | 89.180 | 74.731 | 119.014 | 95.482 | 115.692 | 95.466 | 130.859 | 571.944 |
| 1972 | 60.493 | 81.466 | 97.548 | 81.314 | 129.283 | 102.115 | 123.006 | 97.425 | 127.858 | 568.682 |
| 1973 | 52.789 | 63.003 | 75.327 | 59.518 | 87.689 | 69.528 | 77.473 | 62.994 | 78.029 | 329.654 |
| 1974 | 37.991 | 47.625 | 56.810 | 42.649 | 68.685 | 50.799 | 57.657 | 47.730 | 57.472 | 240.141 |
| 1975 | 50.028 | 69.403 | 87.276 | 68.955 | 109.662 | 79.628 | 94.130 | 79.130 | 95.685 | 422.140 |
| 1976 | 60.401 | 90.538 | 120.537 | 96.593 | 157.511 | 117.912 | 141.366 | 124.153 | 144.496 | 655.008 |
| 1977 | 55.063 | 87.218 | 121.847 | 100.226 | 175.245 | 134.577 | 166.162 | 152.229 | 173.714 | 806.332 |
| 1978 | 58.569 | 89.216 | 135.060 | 109.989 | 196.400 | 156.601 | 194.492 | 177.073 | 201.595 | 1,033.302 |
| 1979 | 67.467 | 114.834 | 176.403 | 148.662 | 266.258 | 233.156 | 276.298 | 259.193 | 294.217 | 1,462.920 |
| 1980 | 89.559 | 154.358 | 232.607 | 193.896 | 351.286 | 306.379 | 376.400 | 342.979 | 406.692 | 1,912.218 |
| 1981 | 82.095 | 155.272 | 241.258 | 201.719 | 368.291 | 327.128 | 374.897 | 344.860 | 439.291 | 2,075.872 |
| 1982 | 98.218 | 182.435 | 291.463 | 253.483 | 481.587 | 423.291 | 484.337 | 446.771 | 553.846 | 2,668.435 |
| 1983 | 118.426 | 213.192 | 369.054 | 320.232 | 608.059 | 532.889 | 616.308 | 613.019 | 727.225 | 3,653.201 |
| 1984 | 128.377 | 229.615 | 378.375 | 305.560 | 591.726 | 546.112 | 590.072 | 567.330 | 662.101 | 2,940.264 |
| 1985 | 168.643 | 316.171 | 488.481 | 409.139 | 776.057 | 715.250 | 782.160 | 774.468 | 865.819 | 3,699.483 |
| 1986 | 199.018 | 373.577 | 568.028 | 480.014 | 893.409 | 777.678 | 879.771 | 804.416 | 915.197 | 3,714.641 |
| 1987 | 209.043 | 374.954 | 590.329 | 488.167 | 859.267 | 738.133 | 803.999 | 739.410 | 799.704 | 3,160.400 |
| 1988 | 240.099 | 449.270 | 715.821 | 597.476 | 1,042.988 | 910.802 | 996.503 | 950.460 | 982.429 | 3,825.620 |
| 1989 | 319.220 | 584.402 | 903.981 | 735.368 | 1,295.700 | 1,102.721 | 1,174.327 | 1,120.376 | 1,086.389 | 4,035.988 |
| 1990 | 316.402 | 534.544 | 812.196 | 670.887 | 1,112.969 | 898.777 | 994.483 | 898.600 | 819.158 | 2,773.407 |
| 1991 | 412.556 | 719.633 | 1,148.477 | 931.692 | 1,648.347 | 1,377.503 | 1,434.171 | 1,322.983 | 1,234.072 | 4,106.537 |
| 1992 | 432.126 | 833.269 | 1,307.725 | 1,048.068 | 2,078.991 | 1,636.255 | 1,709.577 | 1,493.203 | 1,542.801 | 5,502.114 |
| 1993 | 463.770 | 943.157 | 1,518.825 | 1,211.726 | 2,431.413 | 1,921.010 | 2,034.483 | 1,769.962 | 1,798.669 | 6,909.791 |
| 1994 | 471.842 | 926.761 | 1,454.647 | 1,199.798 | 2,391.062 | 1,928.200 | 1,982.487 | 1,715.426 | 1,742.850 | 6,704.019 |
| 1995 | 657.863 | 1,253.621 | 1,969.000 | 1,592.258 | 3,186.643 | 2,443.865 | 2,637.226 | 2,214.965 | 2,353.127 | 8,746.829 |
| 1996 | 814.218 | 1,498.870 | 2,306.537 | 1,895.550 | 3,606.775 | 2,873.033 | 3,154.014 | 2,593.541 | 2,841.010 | 10,247.839 |
| 1997 | 1,098.050 | 1,949.133 | 2,885.136 | 2,390.193 | 4,174.586 | 3,688.292 | 4,099.885 | 3,257.526 | 3,557.962 | 12,548.848 |
| 1998 | 1,483.993 | 2,201.083 | 3,095.766 | 2,563.110 | 4,198.882 | 3,734.480 | 4,072.633 | 3,278.134 | 3,383.472 | 11,094.727 |
| 1999 | 1,847.647 | 2,644.133 | 4,121.155 | 3,331.309 | 5,282.364 | 5,051.194 | 5,089.003 | 4,570.813 | 4,538.532 | 14,185.208 |
| 2000 | 1,596.686 | 2,612.658 | 3,855.327 | 2,999.341 | 4,862.729 | 4,519.558 | 4,555.379 | 3,978.168 | 3,928.140 | 12,285.150 |
| 2001 | 1,352.282 | 2,385.565 | 3,696.088 | 2,984.390 | 4,740.160 | 4,944.666 | 5,088.307 | 4,837.821 | 5,162.618 | 16,757.588 |
| 2002 | 1,049.590 | 1,964.136 | 2,979.917 | 2,448.847 | 3,910.426 | 3,884.366 | 3,926.435 | 3,869.980 | 4,198.590 | 15,827.601 |
| 2003 | 1,319.097 | 2,700.648 | 4,168.910 | 3,544.154 | 5,506.232 | 5,736.636 | 5,932.024 | 6,122.845 | 7,078.575 | 30,407.326 |
| 2004 | 1,423.137 | 3,249.657 | 4,922.953 | 4,207.973 | 6,470.934 | 7,008.080 | 7,055.291 | 7,461.075 | 8,128.059 | 36,141.060 |
| 2005 | 1,475.747 | 3,657.329 | 5,490.771 | 4,671.129 | 7,115.350 | 7,219.514 | 7,799.104 | 8,025.581 | 8,313.642 | 38,221.780 |
| 2006 | 1,706.086 | 4,233.931 | 6,288.669 | 5,211.643 | 8,243.395 | 8,299.368 | 9,057.031 | 9,464.739 | 9,706.608 | 45,742.280 |
| 2007 | 1,827.632 | 4,544.198 | 6,539.947 | 5,440.962 | 8,874.041 | 8,731.143 | 8,929.335 | 8,933.096 | 9,090.511 | 41,187.016 |
| 2008 | 1,186.475 | 2,639.583 | 3,914.070 | 3,446.745 | 5,749.117 | 5,230.105 | 5,709.278 | 5,749.351 | 5,735.386 | 21,450.924 |
| 2009 | 1,454.121 | 3,649.640 | 5,394.817 | 5,019.898 | 8,290.259 | 7,385.717 | 8,124.969 | 8,568.680 | 8,619.500 | 38,985.613 |
| 2010 | 1,644.853 | 4,452.867 | 7,025.587 | 6,084.612 | 10,749.729 | 9,422.776 | 10,681.768 | 11,392.011 | 11,120.059 | 50,409.310 |
| 2011 | 1,681.265 | 4,447.932 | 6,894.532 | 6,132.360 | 10,696.864 | 9,281.415 | 10,142.843 | 10,718.555 | 10,268.606 | 43,295.223 |
| 2012 | 1,948.712 | 5,162.312 | 8,036.155 | 7,136.011 | 12,346.738 | 10,993.659 | 12,003.254 | 12,678.461 | 11,780.502 | 52,580.837 |
| 2013 | 2,582.914 | 7,103.832 | 10,978.840 | 10,122.723 | 17,416.955 | 15,730.437 | 17,029.786 | 18,509.470 | 17,705.616 | 78,385.987 |
| 2014 | 2,900.012 | 8,242.443 | 12,102.987 | 10,876.754 | 18,402.488 | 16,382.715 | 18,201.037 | 18,802.942 | 18,071.732 | 80,631.301 |
| 2015 | 2,950.389 | 7,937.963 | 11,767.615 | 10,358.001 | 17,052.487 | 15,186.080 | 17,131.062 | 17,335.376 | 16,021.248 | 71,195.864 |
| 2016 | 3,293.428 | 9,285.001 | 13,747.526 | 11,755.255 | 19,942.769 | 18,039.183 | 21,453.995 | 21,077.194 | 20,974.852 | 86,589.990 |

**Source of underlying data:** CRSP databases ©2017 Center for Research in Security Prices (CRSP®), The University of Chicago Booth School of Business (2017). Index values calculated by Duff & Phelps, LLC. Used with permission.

**Exhibit 7.5:** Size-Decile Portfolios of the NYSE/AMEX/NASDAQ
Mid-, Low-, Micro-, and Total Capitalization Returns and Index Values
1926–2016

| | Total Return (decimal format) | | | | Index Value (Year-end 1925 = $1.00) | | | |
|---|---|---|---|---|---|---|---|---|
| Year | Mid-Cap | Low-Cap | Micro-Cap | The "Market" (Deciles 1-10) | Mid-Cap | Low-Cap | Micro-Cap | The "Market" (Deciles 1-10) |
| 1925 | – | – | – | – | 1.000 | 1.000 | 1.000 | 1.000 |
| 1926 | 0.0146 | -0.0044 | -0.0868 | 0.0965 | 1.015 | 0.996 | 0.913 | 1.097 |
| 1927 | 0.3483 | 0.2757 | 0.2900 | 0.3281 | 1.368 | 1.270 | 1.178 | 1.456 |
| 1928 | 0.3996 | 0.3332 | 0.4407 | 0.3898 | 1.915 | 1.693 | 1.697 | 2.024 |
| 1929 | -0.2701 | -0.3858 | -0.4967 | -0.1463 | 1.397 | 1.040 | 0.854 | 1.728 |
| 1930 | -0.3631 | -0.3961 | -0.4575 | -0.2874 | 0.890 | 0.628 | 0.463 | 1.231 |
| 1931 | -0.4678 | -0.5041 | -0.4939 | -0.4391 | 0.474 | 0.311 | 0.235 | 0.691 |
| 1932 | -0.0542 | -0.0259 | 0.0854 | -0.0825 | 0.448 | 0.303 | 0.255 | 0.634 |
| 1933 | 1.0388 | 1.1581 | 2.0426 | 0.5698 | 0.913 | 0.655 | 0.774 | 0.995 |
| 1934 | 0.1095 | 0.1980 | 0.3138 | 0.0318 | 1.013 | 0.784 | 1.018 | 1.026 |
| 1935 | 0.4375 | 0.6094 | 0.6399 | 0.4486 | 1.457 | 1.262 | 1.669 | 1.487 |
| 1936 | 0.3616 | 0.5318 | 0.7584 | 0.3249 | 1.984 | 1.934 | 2.934 | 1.970 |
| 1937 | -0.4196 | -0.4900 | -0.5234 | -0.3464 | 1.151 | 0.986 | 1.398 | 1.288 |
| 1938 | 0.3792 | 0.4322 | 0.2203 | 0.2840 | 1.588 | 1.412 | 1.706 | 1.653 |
| 1939 | -0.0147 | 0.0457 | 0.0005 | 0.0268 | 1.564 | 1.477 | 1.707 | 1.697 |
| 1940 | -0.0511 | -0.0522 | -0.1296 | -0.0714 | 1.484 | 1.400 | 1.486 | 1.576 |
| 1941 | -0.0816 | -0.1024 | -0.1419 | -0.1044 | 1.363 | 1.256 | 1.275 | 1.412 |
| 1942 | 0.2122 | 0.2644 | 0.4976 | 0.1648 | 1.653 | 1.589 | 1.910 | 1.644 |
| 1943 | 0.3795 | 0.5815 | 1.0172 | 0.2830 | 2.280 | 2.512 | 3.852 | 2.110 |
| 1944 | 0.3037 | 0.4177 | 0.6323 | 0.2131 | 2.972 | 3.562 | 6.288 | 2.559 |
| 1945 | 0.5650 | 0.6474 | 0.8317 | 0.3869 | 4.652 | 5.868 | 11.517 | 3.549 |
| 1946 | -0.0851 | -0.1123 | -0.1336 | -0.0639 | 4.256 | 5.209 | 9.978 | 3.323 |
| 1947 | 0.0119 | -0.0290 | -0.0281 | 0.0349 | 4.307 | 5.058 | 9.698 | 3.439 |
| 1948 | 0.0012 | -0.0435 | -0.0659 | 0.0190 | 4.312 | 4.838 | 9.059 | 3.504 |
| 1949 | 0.2245 | 0.2123 | 0.2160 | 0.2023 | 5.280 | 5.865 | 11.016 | 4.213 |
| 1950 | 0.3030 | 0.3670 | 0.4570 | 0.3007 | 6.880 | 8.017 | 16.050 | 5.479 |
| 1951 | 0.1839 | 0.1530 | 0.0957 | 0.2080 | 8.146 | 9.244 | 17.586 | 6.619 |
| 1952 | 0.1189 | 0.0964 | 0.0627 | 0.1346 | 9.114 | 10.135 | 18.689 | 7.510 |
| 1953 | -0.0085 | -0.0294 | -0.0562 | 0.0071 | 9.037 | 9.837 | 17.639 | 7.563 |
| 1954 | 0.5612 | 0.5748 | 0.6373 | 0.5022 | 14.109 | 15.491 | 28.880 | 11.361 |
| 1955 | 0.1862 | 0.2081 | 0.2240 | 0.2533 | 16.736 | 18.715 | 35.348 | 14.238 |
| 1956 | 0.0776 | 0.0651 | 0.0294 | 0.0837 | 18.034 | 19.933 | 36.387 | 15.430 |
| 1957 | -0.1262 | -0.1777 | -0.1526 | -0.1002 | 15.758 | 16.390 | 30.835 | 13.884 |
| 1958 | 0.5623 | 0.6187 | 0.7053 | 0.4496 | 24.618 | 26.531 | 52.582 | 20.126 |
| 1959 | 0.1506 | 0.1740 | 0.1825 | 0.1272 | 28.326 | 31.147 | 62.179 | 22.686 |
| 1960 | 0.0219 | -0.0323 | -0.0503 | 0.0121 | 28.947 | 30.141 | 59.053 | 22.961 |
| 1961 | 0.2891 | 0.2916 | 0.3094 | 0.2696 | 37.317 | 38.931 | 77.324 | 29.151 |
| 1962 | -0.1314 | -0.1672 | -0.1661 | -0.1017 | 32.412 | 32.424 | 64.479 | 26.187 |
| 1963 | 0.1593 | 0.1867 | 0.1193 | 0.2098 | 37.577 | 38.475 | 72.173 | 31.680 |
| 1964 | 0.1813 | 0.1652 | 0.1835 | 0.1613 | 44.392 | 44.833 | 85.413 | 36.789 |
| 1965 | 0.2608 | 0.3499 | 0.3798 | 0.1446 | 55.968 | 60.521 | 117.852 | 42.110 |
| 1966 | -0.0586 | -0.0710 | -0.0826 | -0.0874 | 52.689 | 56.224 | 108.123 | 38.429 |
| 1967 | 0.3994 | 0.6388 | 1.0344 | 0.2874 | 73.731 | 92.138 | 219.963 | 49.473 |
| 1968 | 0.2108 | 0.3182 | 0.5015 | 0.1414 | 89.273 | 121.452 | 330.275 | 56.469 |
| 1969 | -0.1469 | -0.2216 | -0.3236 | -0.1091 | 76.161 | 94.537 | 223.386 | 50.306 |
| 1970 | -0.0201 | -0.0987 | -0.1681 | 0.0000 | 74.628 | 85.209 | 185.829 | 50.307 |
| 1971 | 0.2123 | 0.2032 | 0.1767 | 0.1615 | 90.475 | 102.524 | 218.660 | 58.430 |
| 1972 | 0.0906 | 0.0558 | -0.0138 | 0.1684 | 98.674 | 108.248 | 215.642 | 68.268 |
| 1973 | -0.2594 | -0.3435 | -0.4078 | -0.1806 | 73.079 | 71.067 | 127.697 | 55.935 |
| 1974 | -0.2513 | -0.2587 | -0.2676 | -0.2704 | 54.715 | 52.684 | 93.523 | 40.812 |
| 1975 | 0.5709 | 0.6092 | 0.7150 | 0.3875 | 85.952 | 84.780 | 160.389 | 56.628 |
| 1976 | 0.3979 | 0.5074 | 0.5335 | 0.2676 | 120.154 | 127.800 | 245.965 | 71.783 |
| 1977 | 0.0385 | 0.1710 | 0.2177 | -0.0426 | 124.784 | 149.655 | 299.506 | 68.726 |

**Source of underlying data:** CRSP databases ©2017 Center for Research in Security Prices (CRSP®), The University of Chicago Booth School of Business (2017). Index values calculated by Duff & Phelps, LLC. Used with permission.

**Exhibit 7.5:** Size-Decile Portfolios of the NYSE/AMEX/NASDAQ
Mid-, Low-, Micro-, and Total Capitalization Returns and Index Values
1926–2016

| | Total Return (decimal format) | | | | Index Value (Year-end 1925 = $1.00) | | | |
|---|---|---|---|---|---|---|---|---|
| Year | Mid-Cap | Low-Cap | Micro-Cap | The "Market" (Deciles 1-10) | Mid-Cap | Low-Cap | Micro-Cap | The "Market" (Deciles 1-10) |
| 1978 | 0.1075 | 0.1663 | 0.2245 | 0.0749 | 138.195 | 174.537 | 366.734 | 73.871 |
| 1979 | 0.3298 | 0.4626 | 0.4369 | 0.2262 | 183.772 | 255.277 | 526.961 | 90.584 |
| 1980 | 0.3144 | 0.3310 | 0.3464 | 0.3281 | 241.547 | 339.764 | 709.515 | 120.308 |
| 1981 | 0.0409 | 0.0305 | 0.0818 | -0.0365 | 251.427 | 350.125 | 767.527 | 115.918 |
| 1982 | 0.2443 | 0.2939 | 0.2723 | 0.2100 | 312.848 | 453.020 | 976.548 | 140.262 |
| 1983 | 0.2644 | 0.2881 | 0.3410 | 0.2198 | 395.563 | 583.549 | 1,309.560 | 171.085 |
| 1984 | -0.0103 | -0.0224 | -0.1404 | 0.0451 | 391.485 | 570.502 | 1,125.757 | 178.803 |
| 1985 | 0.3115 | 0.3283 | 0.2833 | 0.3217 | 513.415 | 757.823 | 1,444.639 | 236.320 |
| 1986 | 0.1637 | 0.0876 | 0.0320 | 0.1619 | 597.446 | 824.226 | 1,490.934 | 274.581 |
| 1987 | 0.0130 | -0.0689 | -0.1381 | 0.0167 | 605.227 | 767.421 | 1,284.962 | 279.167 |
| 1988 | 0.2168 | 0.2476 | 0.2192 | 0.1803 | 736.413 | 957.414 | 1,566.622 | 329.498 |
| 1989 | 0.2479 | 0.1923 | 0.0815 | 0.2886 | 918.937 | 1,141.478 | 1,694.354 | 424.600 |
| 1990 | -0.1054 | -0.1779 | -0.2745 | -0.0596 | 822.065 | 938.455 | 1,229.323 | 399.294 |
| 1991 | 0.4192 | 0.4869 | 0.5005 | 0.3467 | 1,166.690 | 1,395.373 | 1,844.559 | 537.738 |
| 1992 | 0.1611 | 0.1738 | 0.2817 | 0.0980 | 1,354.653 | 1,637.941 | 2,364.235 | 590.437 |
| 1993 | 0.1627 | 0.1830 | 0.2010 | 0.1114 | 1,575.033 | 1,937.642 | 2,839.527 | 656.226 |
| 1994 | -0.0263 | -0.0152 | -0.0314 | -0.0006 | 1,533.681 | 1,908.153 | 2,750.348 | 655.828 |
| 1995 | 0.3405 | 0.2943 | 0.3320 | 0.3681 | 2,055.896 | 2,469.759 | 3,663.587 | 897.221 |
| 1996 | 0.1683 | 0.1806 | 0.1930 | 0.2136 | 2,401.943 | 2,915.794 | 4,370.639 | 1,088.828 |
| 1997 | 0.2327 | 0.2799 | 0.2402 | 0.3138 | 2,960.813 | 3,731.979 | 5,420.355 | 1,430.547 |
| 1998 | 0.0578 | 0.0052 | -0.0812 | 0.2430 | 3,131.963 | 3,751.452 | 4,980.270 | 1,778.170 |
| 1999 | 0.3068 | 0.3291 | 0.3145 | 0.2522 | 4,092.826 | 4,986.177 | 6,546.706 | 2,226.625 |
| 2000 | -0.0783 | -0.1106 | -0.1331 | -0.1154 | 3,772.517 | 4,434.471 | 5,675.173 | 1,969.647 |
| 2001 | -0.0277 | 0.1313 | 0.3372 | -0.1116 | 3,668.071 | 5,016.553 | 7,589.012 | 1,749.921 |
| 2002 | -0.1853 | -0.2164 | -0.1386 | -0.2114 | 2,988.515 | 3,930.951 | 6,537.363 | 1,379.964 |
| 2003 | 0.4150 | 0.5155 | 0.7832 | 0.3162 | 4,228.646 | 5,957.465 | 11,657.369 | 1,816.276 |
| 2004 | 0.1817 | 0.2109 | 0.1661 | 0.1197 | 4,996.833 | 7,213.835 | 13,594.060 | 2,033.629 |
| 2005 | 0.1104 | 0.0677 | 0.0366 | 0.0615 | 5,548.332 | 7,702.213 | 14,091.889 | 2,158.766 |
| 2006 | 0.1391 | 0.1619 | 0.1798 | 0.1549 | 6,320.011 | 8,949.181 | 16,625.078 | 2,493.121 |
| 2007 | 0.0489 | 0.0002 | -0.0789 | 0.0580 | 6,628.836 | 8,950.995 | 15,312.969 | 2,637.762 |
| 2008 | -0.3796 | -0.3756 | -0.4172 | -0.3667 | 4,112.722 | 5,588.653 | 8,924.590 | 1,670.399 |
| 2009 | 0.4181 | 0.4366 | 0.6124 | 0.2880 | 5,832.103 | 8,028.544 | 14,389.968 | 2,151.468 |
| 2010 | 0.2746 | 0.3034 | 0.2901 | 0.1772 | 7,433.590 | 10,464.496 | 18,563.835 | 2,532.813 |
| 2011 | -0.0078 | -0.0388 | -0.1050 | 0.0074 | 7,375.598 | 10,058.960 | 16,614.806 | 2,551.473 |
| 2012 | 0.1627 | 0.1836 | 0.1741 | 0.1615 | 8,575.958 | 11,906.136 | 19,508.251 | 2,963.534 |
| 2013 | 0.3920 | 0.4337 | 0.4971 | 0.3515 | 11,937.701 | 17,070.187 | 29,205.664 | 4,005.271 |
| 2014 | 0.0834 | 0.0432 | 0.0241 | 0.1158 | 12,933.547 | 17,807.946 | 29,910.426 | 4,469.133 |
| 2015 | -0.0433 | -0.0690 | -0.1138 | -0.0051 | 12,373.084 | 16,579.594 | 26,505.241 | 4,446.236 |
| 2016 | 0.1578 | 0.2145 | 0.2790 | 0.1359 | 14,325.246 | 20,136.252 | 33,899.801 | 5,050.522 |

**Source of underlying data:** CRSP databases ©2017 Center for Research in Security Prices (CRSP®), The University of Chicago Booth School of Business (2017). Index values calculated by Duff & Phelps, LLC. Used with permission.

## Aspects of the Company Size Effect

The company size phenomenon is remarkable in several ways. First, the greater risk of small-cap does not, in the context of the capital asset pricing model, fully account for their higher returns over the long term. In the CAPM only systematic, or beta risk, is rewarded; small-cap stock returns have exceeded those implied by their betas.

Second, the calendar annual return differences between small- and large-cap companies are serially correlated. This suggests that past annual returns may be of some value in predicting future annual returns. Such serial correlation, or autocorrelation, is practically unknown in the market for large-cap stocks and in most other equity markets but is evident in the size premium series.

Third, the size effect is seasonal. For example, small-cap stocks outperformed large-cap stocks in January in a large majority of the years. Such predictability is surprising and suspicious in light of modern capital market theory. These three aspects of the size effect – long-term returns in excess of systematic risk, serial correlation, and seasonality – will be discussed in the following sections.

### The Size Effect: Empirical Evidence

Summary statistics over the 1926–2016 period for CRSP NYSE/NYSE MKT/NASDAQ deciles 1–10 are shown in Exhibit 7.6. As size (in this case, as measured by market cap) *decreases*, return tends to *increase*.[7.9]

For example, the annual arithmetic mean return of decile 1 (the largest-cap companies) was 11.1% over the 1926–2016 period, while the annual arithmetic mean return of decile 10 (the smallest-cap companies) was 20.3%. Note that this increased return comes at a price: risk (as measured by standard deviation) increases from 18.9% for decile 1 to 42.5% for decile 10. The relationship between risk and return is a fundamental principle of finance.

### Do Small-Cap Stocks Always Outperform Large-Cap Stocks?

No. For example, large-cap stocks (defined here as deciles 1-2 of NYSE/NYSE MKT/NASDAQ) have outperformed small-cap stocks (defined here as deciles 9-10) in nearly *half* of the years since 1926. More recently, in five of the last 10 years, large-cap stocks have *outperformed* small-cap stocks. While this might lead some market observers to speculate that there is no size premium, statistical evidence suggests that periods of smaller stocks' underperformance should be expected.

---

[7.9] Traditionally, researchers have used market value of equity (market capitalization, or simply "market cap") as a measure of size in conducting historical rate of return studies. However, market cap is not the only measure of size that can be used to predict return, nor is it necessarily the best measure of size to use. In the *2017 Valuation Handbook – U.S. Guide to Cost of Capital*, which includes the data previously published in the Morningstar/Ibbotson® *Stocks, Bonds, Bills, and Inflation*® (SBBI®) *Valuation Yearbook* and the Duff & Phelps *Risk Premium Report*, the *size effect* is examined in relation to *eight* measures of company size (including market cap): (i) market capitalization, (ii) book value of equity, (iii) 5-year average net income, (iv) market value of invested capital (MVIC), (v) total assets, (vi) 5-year average EBITDA, (vii) sales, and (viii) number of employees. For more information about the *2017 Valuation Handbook – U.S. Guide to Cost of Capital* and other Duff & Phelps valuation data resources published by John Wiley & Sons, please go to: www.wiley.com/go/ValuationHandbooks.

History tells us that small companies are riskier than large companies. Exhibit 7.6 shows the standard deviation (a measure of risk) for each decile of the NYSE/ NYSE AMEX/NASDAQ. As one moves from CRSP decile 1 (comprised of the largest companies) to CRSP decile 10 (comprised of the smallest companies), the standard deviation of return grows. Investors are compensated for taking on this additional risk by the higher returns provided by small companies.

The increased risk faced by investors in small stocks is quite real. It is important to note, however, that the risk/return profile is over the *long-term*. The long-term expected return for any asset class is quite different from short-term expected returns. Investors in small-cap stocks should expect losses and periods of underperformance relative to large-cap stocks, however, the longer small-cap companies are given to "race" against large-cap companies, the greater the chance that small-cap companies outpace their larger counterparts.

**Exhibit 7.6:** Summary Statistics of Annual Returns (CRSP NYSE/NYSE MKT/NASDAQ Deciles) (%) 1926–2016

| Decile | Geometric Mean | Arithmetic Mean | Standard Deviation | Serial Correlation |
|---|---|---|---|---|
| 1 - Largest | 9.3 | 11.1 | 18.9 | 0.07 |
| 2 | 10.6 | 12.8 | 21.5 | 0.01 |
| 3 | 11.0 | 13.6 | 23.3 | -0.03 |
| 4 | 10.8 | 13.8 | 25.6 | -0.03 |
| 5 | 11.5 | 14.6 | 26.2 | -0.03 |
| 6 | 11.4 | 14.8 | 27.1 | 0.01 |
| 7 | 11.6 | 15.4 | 29.0 | 0.01 |
| 8 | 11.6 | 16.1 | 33.0 | 0.00 |
| 9 | 11.6 | 17.0 | 37.2 | 0.06 |
| 10 | 13.3 | 20.3 | 42.5 | 0.14 |
| Mid-Cap | 11.1 | 13.8 | 24.4 | -0.03 |
| Low-Cap | 11.5 | 15.3 | 28.7 | 0.01 |
| Micro-Cap | 12.1 | 18.0 | 38.8 | 0.08 |
| The "Market" (Deciles 1-10) | 9.8 | 11.8 | 20.0 | 0.01 |

**Source of underlying data:** Calculated (or derived) based on data from CRSP US Stock Database and CRSP US Indices Database ©2017 Center for Research in Security Prices (CRSP®), The University of Chicago Booth School of Business. Used with permission. All calculations performed by Duff & Phelps, LLC.

Exhibit 7.7 is a graphical depiction of the year-end index levels presented in Exhibit 7.5 for mid-cap stocks (a portfolio comprised of CRSP deciles 3, 4, and 5), low-cap stocks (a portfolio comprised of CRSP deciles 6, 7, and 8), micro-cap stocks (a portfolio comprised of CRSP deciles 9 and 10), and the "market" (a portfolio comprised of CRSP deciles 1–10).

**Exhibit 7.7:** Size-Decile Portfolios: Size Grouping Return Indexes
1926–2016
Index (Year-end 1925 = $1.00)

## Long-term Returns in Excess of Systematic Risk

The capital asset pricing model, or CAPM, does not fully account for the higher returns of small-cap stocks. Exhibit 7.8 shows the returns in excess of the riskless rate over the past 91 years for each decile of the NYSE/NYSE MKT/NASDAQ. The CAPM can be expressed as follows:

$$k_e = R_f + \beta \times (RP_m)$$

Where:

| | | |
|---|---|---|
| $k_e$ | = | Cost of equity capital |
| $R_f$ | = | Risk-free rate |
| $\beta$ | = | Beta |
| $RP_m$ | = | Equity risk premium (also referred as ERP) |

Exhibit 7.8 uses the CAPM to estimate the return in excess of the riskless rate and compares this estimate to historical performance. According to the CAPM, the expected return on a security should consist of the riskless rate plus an additional return to compensate for the systematic risk of the security. The return in excess of the riskless rate is estimated in the context of the CAPM by multiplying the equity risk premium by beta. The equity risk premium is the return that compensates investors for taking on risk equal to the risk of the market as a whole (systematic risk). Beta measures the extent to which a security or portfolio is exposed to systematic risk. The beta of each decile indicates the degree to which the decile's return moves with that of the overall market.

A beta greater than one indicates that the security or portfolio has greater systematic risk than the market; according to the CAPM equation, investors are compensated for taking on this additional risk. Yet, Exhibit 7.8 illustrates that the smaller deciles have had returns that are not fully explained by their higher betas. This return in excess of that predicted by CAPM increases as one moves from the largest companies in decile 1 to the smallest companies in decile 10. This size-related phenomenon prompted a revision to the CAPM to include a size premium.

This phenomenon can also be viewed graphically, as depicted in the Exhibit 7.9. The security market line is based on the pure CAPM without adjusting for the size premium. Based on the risk (or beta) of a security, the expected return should fluctuate along the security market line. However, the expected returns for the smaller deciles of the NYSE/NYSE MKT/NASDAQ lie *above* the line, indicating that these deciles have had returns in excess of those appropriate for their systematic risk.

**Exhibit 7.8:** Size-Decile Portfolios of the NYSE/NYSE MKT/NASDAQ Long-Term Returns in Excess of CAPM

1926–2016

| Size Grouping | OLS Beta | Arithmetic Mean | Return in Excess of Risk-free Rate (actual) | Return in Excess of Risk-free Rate (as predicted by CAPM) | Size Premium |
|---|---|---|---|---|---|
| Mid-Cap (3–5) | 1.12 | 13.82% | 8.80% | 7.79% | 1.02% |
| Low-Cap (6–8) | 1.22 | 15.26% | 10.24% | 8.49% | 1.75% |
| Micro-Cap (9–10) | 1.35 | 18.04% | 13.02% | 9.35% | 3.67% |
| Breakdown of Deciles 1–10 | | | | | |
| 1-Largest | 0.92 | 11.05% | 6.04% | 6.38% | -0.35% |
| 2 | 1.04 | 12.82% | 7.81% | 7.19% | 0.61% |
| 3 | 1.11 | 13.57% | 8.55% | 7.66% | 0.89% |
| 4 | 1.13 | 13.80% | 8.78% | 7.80% | 0.98% |
| 5 | 1.17 | 14.62% | 9.60% | 8.09% | 1.51% |
| 6 | 1.17 | 14.81% | 9.79% | 8.14% | 1.66% |
| 7 | 1.25 | 15.41% | 10.39% | 8.67% | 1.72% |
| 8 | 1.30 | 16.14% | 11.12% | 9.04% | 2.08% |
| 9 | 1.34 | 16.97% | 11.96% | 9.28% | 2.68% |
| 10-Smallest | 1.39 | 20.27% | 15.25% | 9.66% | 5.59% |

Betas are estimated from monthly returns in excess of the 30-day U.S. Treasury bill total return, January 1926–December 2016. Historical riskless rate measured by the 91-year arithmetic mean income return component of 20-year government bonds (5.02%). Calculated in the context of the CAPM by multiplying the equity risk premium by beta. The equity risk premium is estimated by the arithmetic mean total return of the S&P 500 (11.95%) minus the arithmetic mean income return component of 20-year government bonds (5.02%) from 1926–2016. Source: Morningstar *Direct* and CRSP. Calculated based on data from CRSP US Stock Database and CRSP US Indices Database ©2017 Center for Research. Used with permission. All calculations performed by Duff & Phelps, LLC.

**Exhibit 7.9:** Security Market Line Versus Size-Decile Portfolios of the NYSE/NYSE MKT/NADAQ

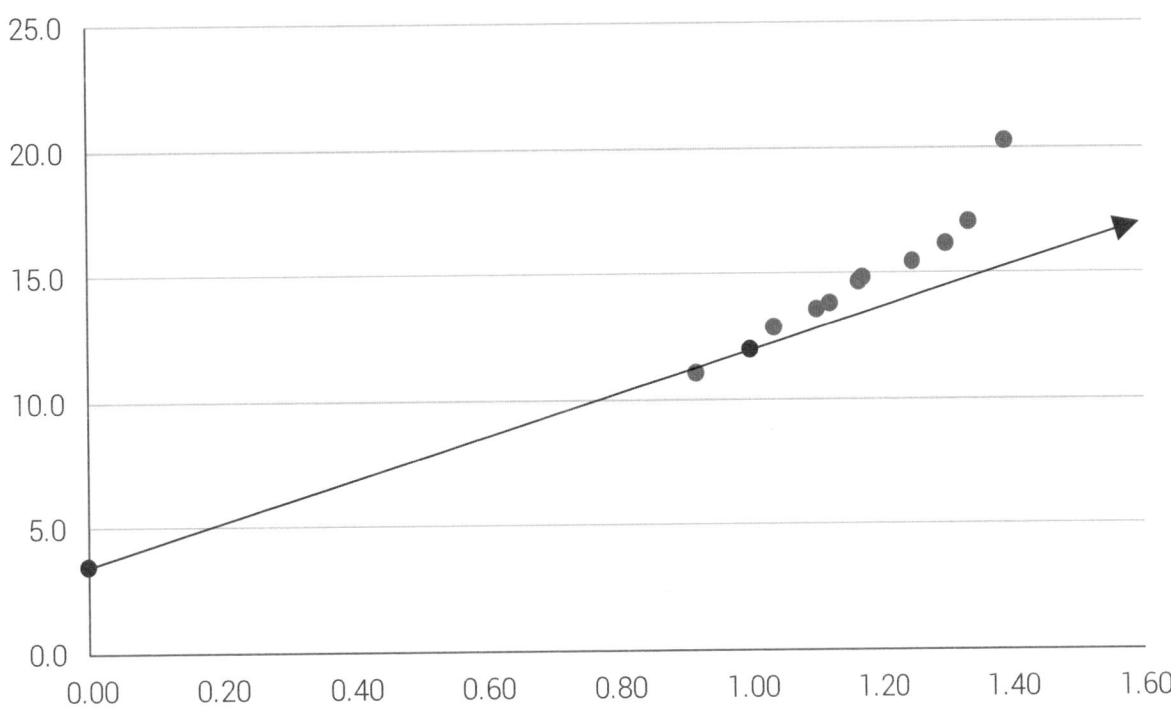

## Serial Correlation in Small-Cap Stock Returns

Serial correlation, or first-order autocorrelation, measures the degree to which the return of a given series is related from period to period. Serial correlation, like cross-correlation, ranges from 1.0 to negative 1.0. A positive serial correlation can be an indicator of a trend in a return series. A serial correlation of 1.0 indicates that returns from one period have a perfectly positive relationship to the returns of the next period; returns are therefore perfectly predictable from one period to the next. A negative serial correlation can be an indicator of a cycle in a return series. A serial correlation of negative 1.0 indicates that returns from one period have a perfectly negative relationship to the next period. A serial correlation near zero indicates that returns are random or unpredictable.

If stock returns have a positive or a negative serial correlation, one can gain some information about future performance based on prior period returns. The serial correlation of returns on large-cap stocks is near zero (see Exhibit 7.6). For the smallest deciles of stocks, the serial correlation tends to be higher. This observation bears further examination.

**Exhibit 7.10:** Size-Decile Portfolios of the NYSE/NYSE MKT/NASDAQ Serial Correlations of Annual Returns in Excess of Decile 1 Returns
1926–2016

| Decile | Serial Correlation of Annual Returns in Excess of Decile 1 Returns |
|---|---|
| Decile 2 | 0.21 |
| Decile 3 | 0.31 |
| Decile 4 | 0.25 |
| Decile 5 | 0.27 |
| Decile 6 | 0.32 |
| Decile 7 | 0.29 |
| Decile 8 | 0.29 |
| Decile 9 | 0.32 |
| Decile 10 | 0.40 |

**Source of underlying data:** Morningstar *Direct* and CRSP. Calculated (or Derived) based on data from CRSP US Stock Database and CRSP US Indices Database ©2017 Center for Research in Security Prices (CRSP®), The University of Chicago Booth School of Business. Used with permission. All calculations performed by Duff & Phelps, LLC.

To remove the randomizing effect of the market as a whole, the returns for decile 1 are geometrically subtracted from the returns for each other decile, two through 10. The result illustrates that these series in excess of decile 1 exhibit greater serial correlation than the individual decile series themselves.

Exhibit 7.10 presents the serial correlations of the excess returns for deciles 2-10. These serial correlations suggest some predictability of smaller company excess returns; however, caution is necessary. The serial correlation of small company excess returns for non-calendar years (e.g., February through January) do not always confirm the results shown here for calendar years (January through December). Therefore, predicting small-company excess returns may not be easy.

The size premiums developed in this chapter also remove the randomizing effect of the market as a whole and appear to be serially correlated. Exhibit 7.11 shows the size premiums for rolling five-year periods for each of the three size groups: mid-cap, low-cap, and micro-cap (a five-year period is used to calculate the beta for each portfolio, which is then used to calculate the size premium). There are periods in which the size premium is positive and periods in which it is negative. However, none of these periods appears to continue for an extended time. Basing a long-term estimate of the size premium on the most recent periods would therefore be inappropriate.

The logic behind using a long history to estimate the size premium is similar to the argument for using a long history in estimating the equity risk premium. Longer historical periods provide more stable estimates of the size premium because unique events are not weighted heavily, and the probability of such events occurring is better represented by an average that covers a long period of time.

**Exhibit 7.11:** Five-Year Rolling-Period Size Premiums for Portfolios of the NYSE/NYSE MKT/ NASDAQ (%)

1926–2016

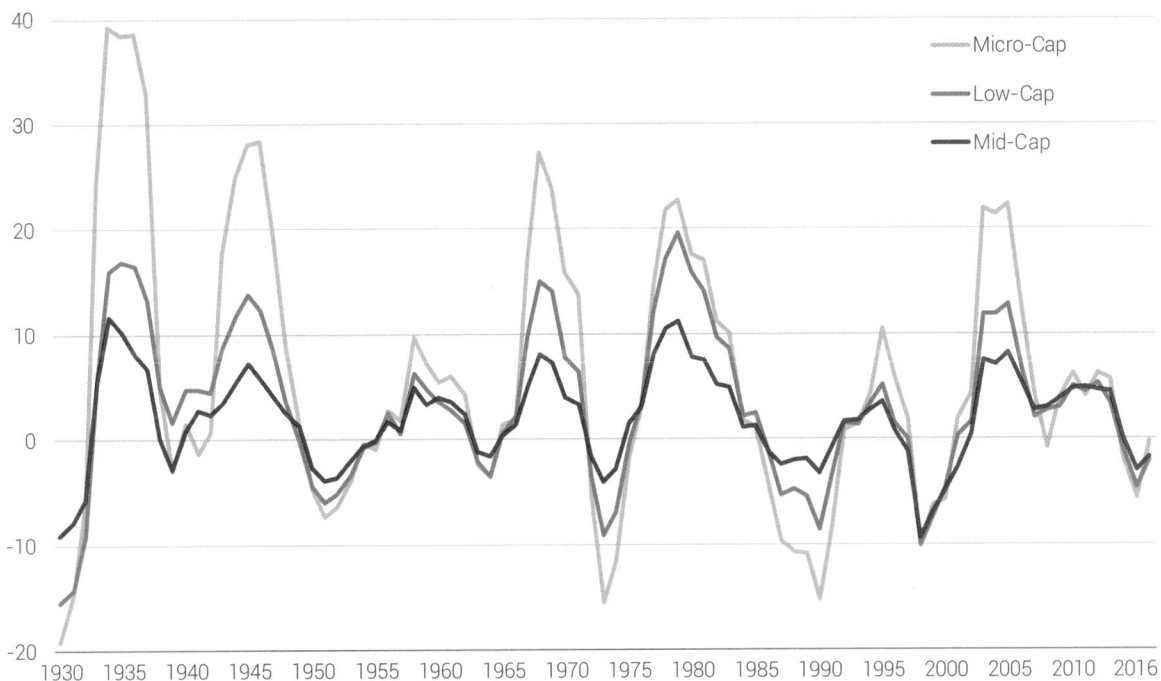

**Source of underlying data:** Morningstar *Direct* and CRSP. Calculated (or Derived) based on data from CRSP US Stock Database and CRSP US Indices Database ©2017 Center for Research in Security Prices (CRSP®), The University of Chicago Booth School of Business. Used with permission. All calculations performed by Duff & Phelps, LLC.

Exhibit 7.12 demonstrates the calculation of the size premium using different starting dates. It shows the realized size premium for a series of periods through 2016. In other words, the left-most values on the graph represents the average realized size premium over the period 1926 to 2016. The next value on the graph represents the average realized size premium over the period 1927 to 2016, and so on, with the last value representing the average over the most recent five years, 2012 to 2016. One notices that the realized size premium, when measured over *longer* periods of time, tends to be relatively stable (the left side of the graph), and the realized size premium, when measured over *shorter* periods of time, can be relatively volatile (the right side of the graph).

**Exhibit 7.12:** Size Premiums for Decile Portfolios of NYSE/NYSE MKT/NASDAQ Calculated with Different Starting Dates (%)
1926–2016

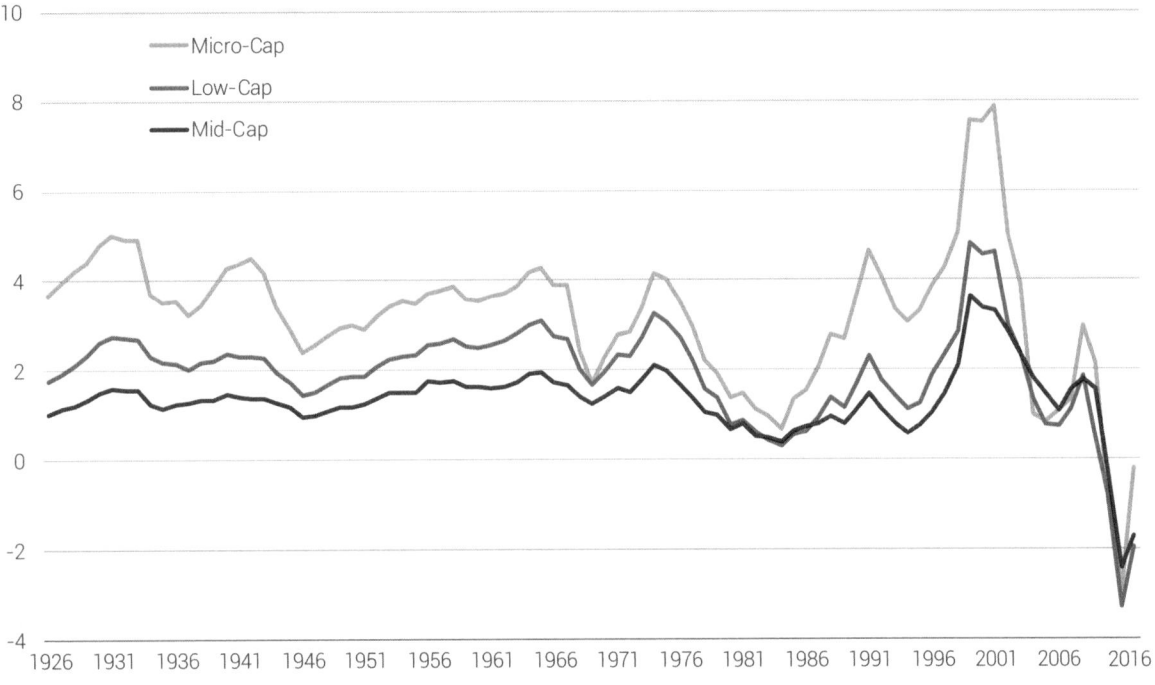

**Source of underlying data:** Morningstar *Direct* and CRSP. Calculated (or Derived) based on data from CRSP US Stock Database and CRSP US Indices Database ©2017 Center for Research in Security Prices (CRSP®), The University of Chicago Booth School of Business. Used with permission. All calculations performed by Duff & Phelps, LLC.

## Seasonality

Unlike the returns on large-cap stocks, the returns on small-cap stocks appear to be seasonal. The January effect denotes the empirical regularity with which rates of return for small stocks have historically been higher in January than in the other months of the year. Small-cap stocks' outperformance has been far greater in January than in any other month.

Exhibit 7.13 shows the returns of capitalization deciles 2-10 in excess of the return on decile 1; the excess returns are segregated into months. For each decile and for each month, the exhibit shows both the average excess return and the number of times the excess return was positive. These two statistics measure the seasonality of the excess return in different ways — the average excess return illustrates the size of the seasonality effect, while the number of positive excess returns shows its reliability.

Virtually all of the small-cap effect occurs in January, as the excess outcomes for small-company stocks are mostly negative in the other months of the year. Excess returns in January relate to size in a precisely rank-ordered fashion, and the January effect seems to pervade all size groups. Yet, simply demonstrating that the size effect is largely produced by the January effect does not refute the existence of the size premium.

**Exhibit 7.13:** Size-Decile Portfolios of the NYSE/NYSE MKT/NASDAQ Returns in Excess of Decile 1 (%)
1926–2016

| Decile | Jan | Feb | Mar | Apr | May | Jun | Jul | Aug | Sep | Oct | Nov | Dec | Total (Jan–Dec) |
|---|---|---|---|---|---|---|---|---|---|---|---|---|---|
| 2 | 0.82 | 0.51 | -0.03 | -0.17 | 0.09 | -0.09 | -0.17 | 0.25 | 0.00 | -0.33 | 0.13 | 0.34 | 1.38 |
|   | 69 | 60 | 44 | 35 | 47 | 44 | 41 | 50 | 44 | 39 | 51 | 50 | |
| 3 | 1.14 | 0.44 | 0.11 | -0.02 | -0.17 | -0.15 | -0.14 | 0.44 | -0.16 | -0.36 | 0.47 | 0.30 | 1.94 |
|   | 65 | 61 | 44 | 34 | 40 | 40 | 44 | 57 | 43 | 38 | 51 | 54 | |
| 4 | 1.34 | 0.59 | 0.02 | -0.23 | 0.12 | -0.07 | -0.21 | 0.24 | -0.01 | -0.82 | 0.38 | 0.51 | 1.94 |
|   | 67 | 59 | 46 | 39 | 45 | 45 | 40 | 53 | 44 | 30 | 51 | 52 | |
| 5 | 2.03 | 0.65 | -0.05 | -0.09 | -0.13 | 0.04 | -0.20 | 0.39 | 0.04 | -0.73 | 0.33 | 0.31 | 2.67 |
|   | 67 | 58 | 41 | 42 | 41 | 44 | 44 | 53 | 45 | 37 | 51 | 49 | |
| 6 | 2.25 | 0.52 | 0.01 | -0.12 | 0.33 | -0.10 | -0.27 | 0.41 | 0.08 | -1.11 | 0.31 | 0.28 | 2.74 |
|   | 67 | 58 | 50 | 38 | 44 | 41 | 44 | 53 | 48 | 36 | 47 | 49 | |
| 7 | 2.89 | 0.60 | 0.04 | -0.11 | 0.12 | -0.23 | -0.16 | 0.30 | 0.20 | -1.04 | 0.31 | 0.15 | 3.10 |
|   | 67 | 59 | 48 | 38 | 40 | 39 | 42 | 45 | 50 | 35 | 48 | 47 | |
| 8 | 3.80 | 0.61 | -0.14 | -0.26 | 0.29 | -0.23 | -0.10 | 0.20 | 0.03 | -1.01 | 0.25 | -0.10 | 3.60 |
|   | 67 | 53 | 43 | 35 | 36 | 41 | 45 | 44 | 46 | 35 | 41 | 41 | |
| 9 | 5.03 | 0.82 | -0.08 | -0.14 | 0.21 | -0.26 | -0.17 | 0.10 | -0.04 | -1.23 | 0.15 | -0.61 | 4.15 |
|   | 66 | 49 | 45 | 35 | 38 | 38 | 41 | 45 | 44 | 36 | 40 | 42 | |
| 10 | 8.15 | 0.94 | -0.52 | 0.06 | 0.56 | -0.38 | 0.36 | -0.12 | 0.63 | -1.46 | -0.60 | -1.33 | 6.93 |
|   | 78 | 48 | 44 | 39 | 39 | 41 | 43 | 37 | 47 | 33 | 33 | 37 | |

First Row: Average excess return in percent (%)
Second Row: Number of times excess return was positive (in 91 years)

**Source of underlying data:** Morningstar *Direct* and CRSP. Calculated (or Derived) based on data from CRSP US Stock Database and CRSP US Indices Database ©2017 Center for Research in Security Prices (CRSP®), The University of Chicago Booth School of Business. Used with permission. All calculations performed by Duff & Phelps, LLC.

# Chapter 8
# Growth and Value Investing

Investment style can be defined broadly as an overarching description of groups of stocks or portfolios based on shared characteristics. Probably the first discussion and consideration of style concerned large-company versus small-company investing, and even this distinction was not prominent until the 1960s. Styles of investing are now broken down into more detail and used for performance measurement, asset allocation, and other purposes. Mutual funds and other investment portfolios are often measured against broad growth or value benchmarks. In some cases, investment-manager-specific style benchmarks are constructed to separate pure stock-selection ability from style effects.

Most investors agree on the broad definitions of growth and value, but when it comes to specifics, definitions can vary widely. In general, growth stocks have high relative growth rates in regard to earnings, sales, or return on equity. Growth stocks usually have relatively high price-to-earnings and price-to-book ratios. Value stocks will generally have lower price-to-earnings and price-to-book values and often have higher dividend yields. Value stocks are often turnaround opportunities, companies that have had disappointing news, or companies with low growth prospects. Value investors generally believe that a value stock has been unfairly beaten down by the market, leading the stock to sell below its "intrinsic" value. Therefore, they buy the stock with the hope that the market will realize the stock's full value and eventually bid the price up to its fair value.

### Fama-French Growth and Value Series

The following commentary and corresponding data make use of the Fama-French growth and value data series.[8.1,8.2]

### Fama-French Index Construction Methodology

Fama-French use all stocks traded on the NYSE to set both growth/value and small/large breakpoints. They then apply these breakpoints to all stocks traded on NYSE, NYSE MKT, and NASDAQ to construct each index.

---

[8.1] Source of Fama-French growth and value return series data used in this chapter: Monthly Historical Benchmark Returns from the Fama-French data library. To learn more visit: http://mba.tuck.dartmouth.edu/pages/faculty/ken.french/data_library.html. All calculations performed by Duff & Phelps, LLC.

[8.2] Eugene Fama, the 2013 Nobel laureate in economic sciences, is the Robert R. McCormick Distinguished Service Professor of Finance and chairman of the Center for Research in Security Prices (CRSP) at the University of Chicago Booth School of Business. Ken French is the Roth Family Distinguished Professor of Finance at the Tuck School of Business at Dartmouth College. Fama and French are prolific researchers and authors who have contributed greatly to the field of modern finance. Fama and French's paper "The Cross-Section of Expected Stock Returns" was the winner of the 1992 Smith Breeden Prize for the best paper in *The Journal of Finance*. See Eugene Fama and Kenneth French, "The Cross-Section of Expected Stock Returns," *Journal of Finance* (June 1992): 427–486. Also see Eugene F. Fama and Kenneth R. French, "A five-factor asset pricing model," *The Journal of Financial Economics* 116 (2015): 1–22.

The market capitalization breakpoint between small-cap and large-cap stocks is set as the median market capitalization of NYSE stocks. This breakpoint is then applied to all stocks traded on NYSE, NYSE MKT, and NASDAQ.

To define value and growth, Fama-French use the book value of equity divided by market capitalization, which is the inverse of how much investors are willing to pay for a dollar of book value. Value companies will have a high book-to-market ratio, while growth companies will have a low book-to-market ratio. Fama-French used *Compustat* as their data source to calculate book value from 1963 forward, and hand-collected data for 1928 to 1962.

Book value was calculated as follows:

$$BV = SE + DT + ITC - PS$$

Where:

| | | |
|---|---|---|
| BV | = | Fama-French book value |
| SE | = | Book value of stockholders' equity |
| DT | = | Balance sheet deferred taxes |
| ITC | = | Investment tax credit (if available) |
| PS | = | Book value of preferred stock. Depending on availability, either redemption, liquidation, or par value (in that order) is used to estimate book value of preferred stock |

Stocks are put into three groups based on book-to-market: low, medium, or high. The definition of low, medium, and high is based on the breakpoints for the bottom 30%, middle 40%, and top 30% of the value of book-to-market for NYSE stocks. These breakpoints are then applied to all stocks traded on the NYSE, NYSE MKT, and NASDAQ. For the growth/value analysis shown in this chapter, only the low and high portfolios are used. The medium portfolios, which are blends of growth and value, are not shown.

Firms with negative book values are not used when calculating the book-to-market breakpoints or when calculating size-specific book-to-market breakpoints. Also, only firms with ordinary common equity (as classified by the Center for Research in Security Prices at the University of Chicago Booth School of Business) are included in the portfolios. This excludes American Depositary Receipts, real estate investment trusts, and unit trusts.

The four size-specific style indices used in this chapter are small-value, small-growth, large-value, and large-growth. These portfolios are defined as the intersections of the two size groups and the low and high book-to-market groups.

## Historical Returns of the Fama-French Series

Using the Fama-French series ("F-F"), Exhibit 8.1 depicts the growth of $1.00 invested in F-F small-growth, F-F small-value, F-F large-growth, and F-F large-value stocks from the end of 1927 to the end of 2016. All results assume reinvestment of dividends and exclude transaction costs. The top two performers during this time period were small-value and large-value stocks, followed by small-growth and large-growth stocks. Over the period from 1928 to 2016 (89 years), small-value stocks outperformed all other stock series in the graph. One dollar invested in small-value stocks at the end of 1927 grew to $115,618.66 by the end of 2016, increasing from $81,430.52 at the end of 2015.

**Exhibit 8.1:** F-F Small-Value Stocks, F-F Small-Growth Stocks, F-F Large-Value Stocks, and F-F Large-Growth Stocks Index (Year-End 1927 = $1.00)
1928–2016

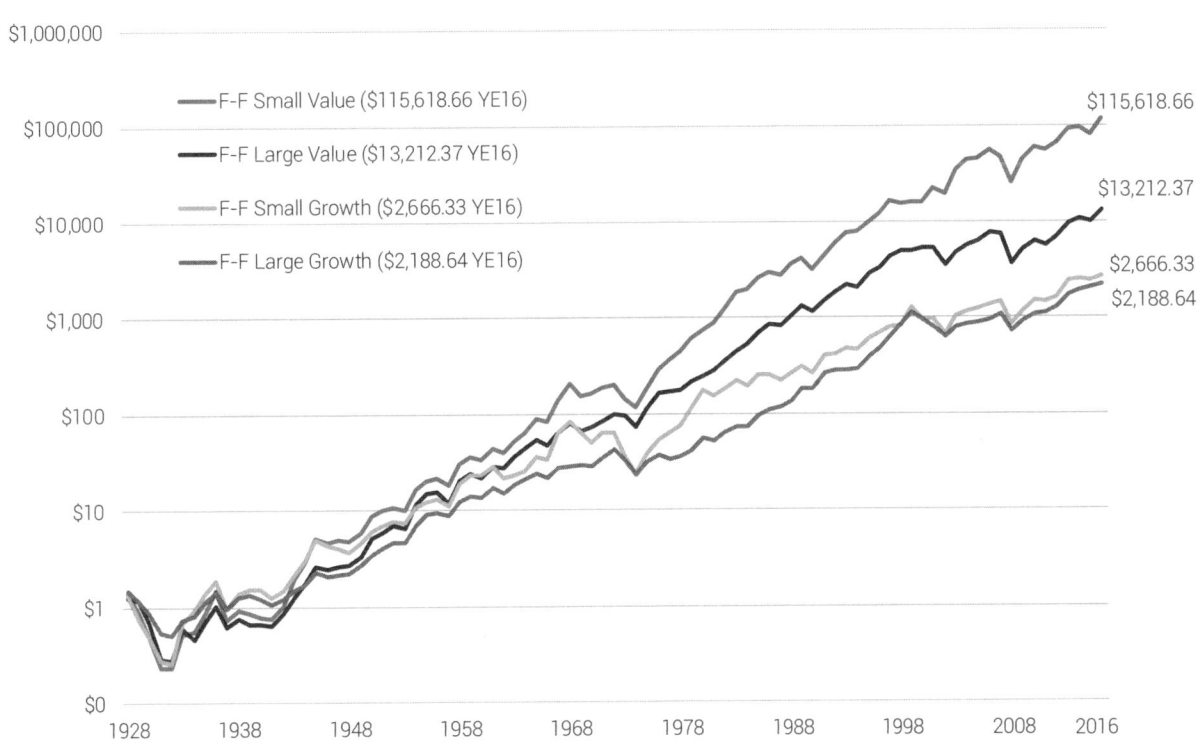

## Summary Statistics for the Fama-French Series

Exhibit 8.2 shows summary statistics of annual total returns for the Fama-French growth and value series from 1928 to 2016. The summary statistics presented are geometric mean, arithmetic mean, and standard deviation.

Value significantly outperformed growth across the market capitalization spectrum. In the large-cap arena, the extra return of value over growth was at the expense of increased risk, as the standard deviation of large-value was 27.3 percentage points versus 19.8 percentage points for large-growth. In the small-cap series, small-value significantly outperformed small-growth and did so with lower volatility (32.2 percentage points versus 32.5 percentage points).

**Exhibit 8.2:** F-F Growth and Value Series Summary Statistics of Annual Returns (%) 1928–2016

|  | Geometric Mean | Arithmetic Mean | Standard Deviation |
|---|---|---|---|
| F-F Large Growth | 9.0 | 10.9 | 19.8 |
| F-F Large Value | 11.3 | 14.7 | 27.3 |
| F-F Small Growth | 9.3 | 13.8 | 32.5 |
| F-F Small Value | 14.0 | 18.6 | 32.2 |

## Returns by Decade for Fama-French Series

Exhibit 8.3 shows the compound returns by decade for the Fama-French growth and value series. Small-value stocks beat small-growth stocks in all decades except the 1930s and the 1990s. It is also interesting to note that small-value stocks were never the worst performing among all four stock series in any decade.

**Exhibit 8.3:** Fama-French Growth and Value Series Compound Annual Rates of Return by Decade (%) 1928–2016

|  | 1920s[*] | 1930s | 1940s | 1950s | 1960s | 1970s | 1980s | 1990s | 2000s | 2010s[**] |
|---|---|---|---|---|---|---|---|---|---|---|
| F-F Large Growth | 8.1 | 1.5 | 7.3 | 17.6 | 7.9 | 3.4 | 15.8 | 19.9 | -1.8 | 13.0 |
| F-F Large Value | 9.0 | -5.5 | 17.2 | 22.2 | 10.7 | 12.2 | 20.2 | 13.9 | 0.3 | 14.4 |
| F-F Small Growth | -13.3 | 7.4 | 11.6 | 17.7 | 10.7 | 5.8 | 10.8 | 15.0 | -1.1 | 12.7 |
| F-F Small Value | -4.8 | -0.3 | 21.0 | 20.0 | 15.4 | 15.0 | 21.1 | 14.5 | 10.6 | 14.7 |

[*]Based on the period 1928–1929   [**]Based on the period 2010–2016

**Exhibit 8.4:** Fama-French Growth and Value Series Compound Annual Rates of Return Over the Most Recent 10 Years (%)
2007–2016

|  | **2007–2016** |
| --- | --- |
| F-F Large Growth | 8.6 |
| F-F Large Value | 5.5 |
| F-F Small Growth | 6.9 |
| F-F Small Value | 7.7 |

## Correlation of Fama-French Series

Exhibit 8.5 presents the annual cross-correlations and serial correlations for the Fama-French growth and value series.

**Exhibit 8.5:** Fama-French Growth and Value Series Serial and Cross-Correlations of Historical Annual Returns
1928–2016

|  | **F-F Large Growth** | **F-F Large Value** | **F-F Small Growth** | **F-F Small Value** | **U.S. Treasury Bills** | **Inflation** |
| --- | --- | --- | --- | --- | --- | --- |
| F-F Large Growth | 1.00 |  |  |  |  |  |
| F-F Large Value | 0.80 | 1.00 |  |  |  |  |
| F-F Small Growth | 0.82 | 0.81 | 1.00 |  |  |  |
| F-F Small Value | 0.73 | 0.90 | 0.86 | 1.00 |  |  |
| U.S. Treasury Bills | -0.02 | -0.04 | -0.10 | -0.08 | 1.00 |  |
| Inflation | -0.02 | 0.06 | 0.00 | 0.05 | 0.42 | 1.00 |
| Serial Correlation | -0.01 | -0.08 | 0.01 | 0.02 | 0.92 | 0.63 |

## Presentation of Annual Fama-French Returns

Exhibit 8.6 shows year-by-year total annual returns for the Fama-French growth and value series from 1928 to 2016. This exhibit compares the performance of large-growth, large-value, small-growth, and small-value.

## Conclusion

What can explain this value effect? Readers of Benjamin Graham and David L. Dodd's "Security Analysis,"[8.3] first published in 1934, would say that the outperformance of value stocks is due to the market coming to realize the full value of a company's securities that were once undervalued. The Graham and Dodd approach to security analysis is to do an independent valuation of a company using accounting data and common market multiples, then look at the stock price to see if the stock is under- or overvalued. Several academic studies have shown that the market overreacts to bad news and underreacts to good news. This would lead us to conclude that there is more room for value stocks (which are more likely to have reported bad news) to improve and outperform growth stocks, which already have high expectations built into them.

[8.3] The sixth edition of this book was published in 2008. See also Cottle, S., Murray, R.F., & Block, F.E. 1988. Graham and Dodd's *Security Analysis*, 5th ed. (New York: McGraw-Hill).

**Exhibit 8.6:** Fama-French Growth and Value Series: Annual Total Returns (decimal format) 1928–2016

| Year | F-F Large Growth | F-F Large Value | F-F Small Growth | F-F Small Value |
|------|------------------|-----------------|------------------|-----------------|
| 1928 | 0.4805 | 0.2363 | 0.3486 | 0.4096 |
| 1929 | -0.2107 | -0.0393 | -0.4423 | -0.3577 |
| 1930 | -0.2644 | -0.4316 | -0.3585 | -0.4638 |
| 1931 | -0.3696 | -0.5824 | -0.4270 | -0.5187 |
| 1932 | -0.0793 | -0.0326 | -0.0525 | 0.0135 |
| 1933 | 0.4465 | 1.1691 | 1.5941 | 1.1869 |
| 1934 | 0.1106 | -0.2151 | 0.3589 | 0.0851 |
| 1935 | 0.4222 | 0.5114 | 0.4834 | 0.5316 |
| 1936 | 0.2646 | 0.4812 | 0.3710 | 0.7319 |
| 1937 | -0.3412 | -0.4107 | -0.4864 | -0.5147 |
| 1938 | 0.3320 | 0.2520 | 0.4381 | 0.2621 |
| 1939 | 0.0773 | -0.1251 | 0.1072 | -0.0355 |
| 1940 | -0.0981 | -0.0262 | 0.0057 | -0.0983 |
| 1941 | -0.1267 | -0.0088 | -0.1734 | -0.0482 |
| 1942 | 0.1317 | 0.3371 | 0.1676 | 0.3500 |
| 1943 | 0.2204 | 0.4402 | 0.4508 | 0.9182 |
| 1944 | 0.1611 | 0.4198 | 0.4123 | 0.4971 |
| 1945 | 0.3195 | 0.4906 | 0.6428 | 0.7461 |
| 1946 | -0.0829 | -0.0829 | -0.1240 | -0.0736 |
| 1947 | 0.0410 | 0.0866 | -0.0838 | 0.0534 |
| 1948 | 0.0335 | 0.0509 | -0.0716 | -0.0230 |
| 1949 | 0.2331 | 0.1871 | 0.2352 | 0.2104 |
| 1950 | 0.2311 | 0.5522 | 0.3101 | 0.5216 |
| 1951 | 0.2005 | 0.1436 | 0.1626 | 0.1227 |
| 1952 | 0.1338 | 0.1954 | 0.0855 | 0.0859 |
| 1953 | 0.0229 | -0.0704 | -0.0068 | -0.0692 |
| 1954 | 0.4779 | 0.7732 | 0.4320 | 0.6343 |
| 1955 | 0.2850 | 0.2978 | 0.1395 | 0.2347 |
| 1956 | 0.0652 | 0.0337 | 0.0765 | 0.0598 |
| 1957 | -0.0914 | -0.2272 | -0.1699 | -0.1590 |
| 1958 | 0.4162 | 0.7230 | 0.7522 | 0.6967 |
| 1959 | 0.1315 | 0.1882 | 0.2142 | 0.1742 |
| 1960 | -0.0236 | -0.0856 | -0.0178 | -0.0602 |
| 1961 | 0.2643 | 0.2889 | 0.2220 | 0.3085 |
| 1962 | -0.1089 | -0.0309 | -0.2233 | -0.0947 |
| 1963 | 0.2188 | 0.3235 | 0.0798 | 0.2834 |
| 1964 | 0.1448 | 0.1916 | 0.0813 | 0.2290 |
| 1965 | 0.1336 | 0.2242 | 0.3999 | 0.4250 |
| 1966 | -0.1077 | -0.1021 | -0.0532 | -0.0776 |
| 1967 | 0.2917 | 0.3174 | 0.8842 | 0.6755 |
| 1968 | 0.0403 | 0.2708 | 0.3273 | 0.4581 |
| 1969 | 0.0288 | -0.1639 | -0.2368 | -0.2584 |
| 1970 | -0.0565 | 0.1063 | -0.2025 | 0.0662 |
| 1971 | 0.2394 | 0.1255 | 0.2586 | 0.1447 |
| 1972 | 0.2132 | 0.1862 | 0.0039 | 0.0728 |
| 1973 | -0.2179 | -0.0367 | -0.4507 | -0.2723 |

**Exhibit 8.6:** Fama-French Growth and Value Series: Annual Total Returns (decimal format) 1928–2016

| Year | F-F Large Growth | F-F Large Value | F-F Small Growth | F-F Small Value |
|------|------------------|-----------------|------------------|-----------------|
| 1974 | -0.2924 | -0.2340 | -0.3190 | -0.1902 |
| 1975 | 0.3444 | 0.5590 | 0.6132 | 0.5712 |
| 1976 | 0.1754 | 0.4462 | 0.3820 | 0.5913 |
| 1977 | -0.0946 | 0.0164 | 0.1935 | 0.2382 |
| 1978 | 0.0700 | 0.0348 | 0.1765 | 0.2212 |
| 1979 | 0.1659 | 0.2267 | 0.4884 | 0.3833 |
| 1980 | 0.3520 | 0.1645 | 0.5266 | 0.2228 |
| 1981 | -0.0713 | 0.1280 | -0.1153 | 0.1768 |
| 1982 | 0.2148 | 0.2767 | 0.1972 | 0.3986 |
| 1983 | 0.1467 | 0.2692 | 0.2212 | 0.4758 |
| 1984 | -0.0072 | 0.1617 | -0.1284 | 0.0752 |
| 1985 | 0.3264 | 0.3175 | 0.2891 | 0.3212 |
| 1986 | 0.1438 | 0.2182 | 0.0195 | 0.1450 |
| 1987 | 0.0743 | -0.0276 | -0.1224 | -0.0712 |
| 1988 | 0.1253 | 0.2596 | 0.1663 | 0.3076 |
| 1989 | 0.3611 | 0.2970 | 0.2058 | 0.1570 |
| 1990 | 0.0106 | -0.1275 | -0.1774 | -0.2513 |
| 1991 | 0.4333 | 0.2735 | 0.5473 | 0.4056 |
| 1992 | 0.0641 | 0.2357 | 0.0582 | 0.3476 |
| 1993 | 0.0238 | 0.1951 | 0.1264 | 0.2941 |
| 1994 | 0.0195 | -0.0578 | -0.0436 | 0.0321 |
| 1995 | 0.3716 | 0.3768 | 0.3513 | 0.2769 |
| 1996 | 0.2125 | 0.1335 | 0.1236 | 0.2071 |
| 1997 | 0.3161 | 0.3188 | 0.1529 | 0.3729 |
| 1998 | 0.3464 | 0.1623 | 0.0304 | -0.0863 |
| 1999 | 0.2943 | -0.0022 | 0.5475 | 0.0559 |
| 2000 | -0.1363 | 0.0580 | -0.2415 | -0.0080 |
| 2001 | -0.1559 | -0.0118 | 0.0016 | 0.4024 |
| 2002 | -0.2150 | -0.3253 | -0.3087 | -0.1241 |
| 2003 | 0.2629 | 0.3507 | 0.5320 | 0.7469 |
| 2004 | 0.0653 | 0.1891 | 0.1254 | 0.2659 |
| 2005 | 0.0282 | 0.1217 | 0.0545 | 0.0353 |
| 2006 | 0.0888 | 0.2261 | 0.1167 | 0.2176 |
| 2007 | 0.1408 | -0.0645 | 0.0736 | -0.1521 |
| 2008 | -0.3371 | -0.4903 | -0.4156 | -0.4439 |
| 2009 | 0.2792 | 0.3915 | 0.3445 | 0.7054 |
| 2010 | 0.1587 | 0.2161 | 0.3066 | 0.3354 |
| 2011 | 0.0414 | -0.0904 | -0.0432 | -0.0704 |
| 2012 | 0.1541 | 0.2299 | 0.1222 | 0.2007 |
| 2013 | 0.3428 | 0.4020 | 0.4899 | 0.3940 |
| 2014 | 0.1132 | 0.0978 | 0.0572 | 0.0255 |
| 2015 | 0.0631 | -0.0754 | -0.0440 | -0.1353 |
| 2016 | 0.0628 | 0.3255 | 0.0910 | 0.4198 |

# Chapter 9
# Liquidity Investing

## What Is Liquidity?[9.1]

Liquidity has many different, but similar meanings. In every case it is related to the ease of movement. Even within the context of financial markets, liquidity has several different meanings. In the banking system, liquidity measures the degree to which loans are made. In the securities markets, liquidity is the ease with which transactions can be made. In valuation, this liquidity impacts value, so that the more liquidity an asset has the more value it has, all other things being equal. The absence of liquidity lowers the value of the asset by the amount of a liquidity discount.

In this chapter, we focus on liquidity as the ease of trading securities in general, especially equities. We focus on liquidity's impact on valuation and in particular its impact on security returns. We will demonstrate that less-liquid securities have higher expected returns.

## Valuation as Present Value of Cash Flows

In equilibrium, an asset has a value that equals its present value, or the discounted sum of its expected cash flows. These future cash flows are unobservable, except for risk-free assets. For stocks, there is great disagreement as to what these expected cash flows might be. This disagreement is the primary reason that stocks are traded. A secondary reason is that they are bought or sold to meet liquidity needs.

The other component of a present value calculation is the discount rate. Similar to the expected cash flows, these discount rates are unobservable. We can usually observe the riskless discount rates from a term structure of riskless bonds, which we unravel from U.S. government discount bonds. But there are usually other premiums that we would add to the riskless term structure. The most common one is an equity risk premium, which is often modified by a beta in the CAPM framework. We might also add a premium for size and another one for value (or distress). We argue here that another premium should be added for lack of liquidity.

The difference of opinion that investors have about expected cash flows leads to the additional risk of a security. The risk of the security reflects not only the changing economy and company cash-flow expectations, but also the divergence of opinion that changes from moment to moment. This risk reduces the value of a security. Ironically though, this divergence of opinion also leads to most of the trading of a security, thereby making the security more liquid for trades, whether they be active or liquidity traders. The higher liquidity increases the security's value.

[9.1] This chapter was written by Roger G. Ibbotson, Professor Emeritus of Finance at the Yale School of Management, Chairman and Chief Investment Officer of Zebra Capital LLC, and former Chairman and founder of Ibbotson Associates, now part of Morningstar, Inc.; and Daniel Y.-J. Kim, Research Director of Zebra Capital Management.

We do not mean to imply that most investors actually make these present-value calculations. Instead, investors rely on simple metrics, such as the price/earnings ratio, or PE ratio, trying to buy stocks with relatively high but unspecified cash flow projections, at relatively low PE ratios. Or they may simply feel that a stock's price is too low or high relative to its estimated value, leading them to buy or sell a security.

**The Liquidity Premium**

Most conventional present-value calculations ignore the liquidity premium. These calculations usually implicitly assume that securities are perfectly liquid. If they are somewhat liquid, a liquidity discount is often made to the present value, at the end of the calculation. Thus, a liquid stock is priced at the present value of the expected cash flows, discounted by the riskless rate and various other risk premiums, such as a beta-adjusted equity risk premium, a size premium, and a value premium. The final present value is then reduced by some percentage due to its lack of liquidity.

The other way to calculate a present value is to add a liquidity premium into the discount rate. Less-liquid securities would then have their cash flows discounted at higher rates. The benefit of this approach is that this liquidity premium can be thought of as causing a higher discount rate. These discount rates are equivalent, under certain conditions, to the expected return that an investor receives for investing in less-liquid securities.

The liquidity premium is the extra return an investor would demand to hold a security that cannot costlessly be traded. This premium is not exactly a risk premium, since it more reflects a transaction cost. We can think of the premium as related to risk, however, because it is the risk of having to buy or sell a security quickly. The less liquid and more hurried the transaction, the higher the cost.

The liquidity premium is potentially interesting to investors who can afford to hold a security over time, instead of continuously trading it. For investors with longer-term horizons, the trading costs become trivial because they happen so infrequently. The liquidity premium is a benefit to the longer-term investor. It means that the less-liquid securities will have higher returns and these higher returns are not likely to be affected by trading costs.

It is sometimes argued that part of the expected return that is demanded from real estate, private equity, or venture capital comes from their relative liquidity.[9.2] In addition to any of their return for other risk characteristics, investors want an extra return for holding an illiquid asset. Thus, investors would want to invest in alternative illiquid assets only if they thought they would receive extra compensation for their lack of liquidity.

The liquidity premium also is substantial within publicly traded securities. There is a difference in the return of the more highly traded securities versus the less traded securities, even though most all public securities can be readily traded. We now examine the relative impact of liquidity across

---

[9.2]   Ibbotson, Roger, Siegel, Laurence B., and Diermeier, Jeffrey, "The Demand for Capital Market Returns," *Financial Analysts Journal*, January/February 1984.

publicly traded stocks on the New York Stock Exchange (NYSE), the NYSE MKT (formerly the NYSE Amex), and the NASDAQ Stock Market.

## Liquidity and Stock Returns

In the U.S. stock market, liquidity has substantial impact on stock returns. We examine the monthly data for the largest 3,500 U.S. stocks by capitalization over the period 1972 through 2016. These stocks are traded on either the NYSE, the NYSE MKT, or the NASDAQ. All are publicly traded and relatively liquid, but of course some are more liquid than others.

We separate the stocks into four quartiles separated from the prior year by the turnover rate. The turnover rate is the number of shares traded during the year divided by the number of shares outstanding for the stock . The stocks with the highest turnover rates are the most liquid, and the stocks with the lowest turnover rates the least liquid. The return, share volume, and capitalization data are from the Center for Research in Security Prices at the University of Chicago Booth School of Business.

Exhibit 9.1 summarizes the results for the four liquidity quartiles. The exhibit illustrates the historical magnitude of the liquidity premium over the period from 1972–2016. Note that there is a substantial difference in the returns of the least-liquid quartile versus the most-liquid quartile, as well as a continual progression of higher returns as we move to less-liquid quartiles. The less-liquid stocks are not necessarily more risky. Measured by the standard deviation, risk seems to increase with liquidity.

**Exhibit 9.1:** Liquidity Quartiles of the NYSE/MKT/NASDAQ, Annualized Returns (%) 1972–2016

| Quartile | Geometric Mean | Arithmetic Mean | Standard Deviation |
|---|---|---|---|
| 1-Less Liquid | 15.14 | 16.92 | 19.82 |
| 2 | 14.15 | 16.13 | 21.06 |
| 3 | 12.30 | 14.61 | 22.46 |
| 4-More Liquid | 7.47 | 11.01 | 27.47 |

Source: Ibbotson, Roger G., and Daniel Y.-J Kim, "Liquidity as an Investment Style: 2017 Update," available at research.zebracapital.com. Updated version of: Ibbotson, Roger G., Chen, Zhiwu, Kim, Daniel Y.-J., and Hu, Wendy Y. "Liquidity as an Investment Style," *Financial Analysts Journal*, May/June 2013, updated with 1972–2016 data.

Exhibit 9.2 shows the same four quartiles of liquidity, but here presented as indexes of cumulative wealth. The quartiles consist of equally weighted portfolios with all dividends reinvested. The least-liquid quartile of stocks is at the top of the graph, and $1.00 invested at the end of 1971 grows to $570.16 by the end of 2016. One dollar invested in the second-least-liquid quartile grows to $385.49 over the period. One dollar invested in the third-least-liquid quartile (the second-most-liquid-quartile) grows to $184.88 over the period. One dollar invested at year-end 1971 into the most-liquid quartile grows to only $25.58 over the period. These large differences in terminal wealth reflect investments at different share turnover rates, but include most types of companies in each liquidity quartile.

**Exhibit 9.2:** Wealth Indices of Investments in Low to High Quartiles of Liquidity in NYSE/AMEX/NASDAQ Stocks, Cumulative Total Returns: Index (Year-End 1971 = $1.00) 1972–2016

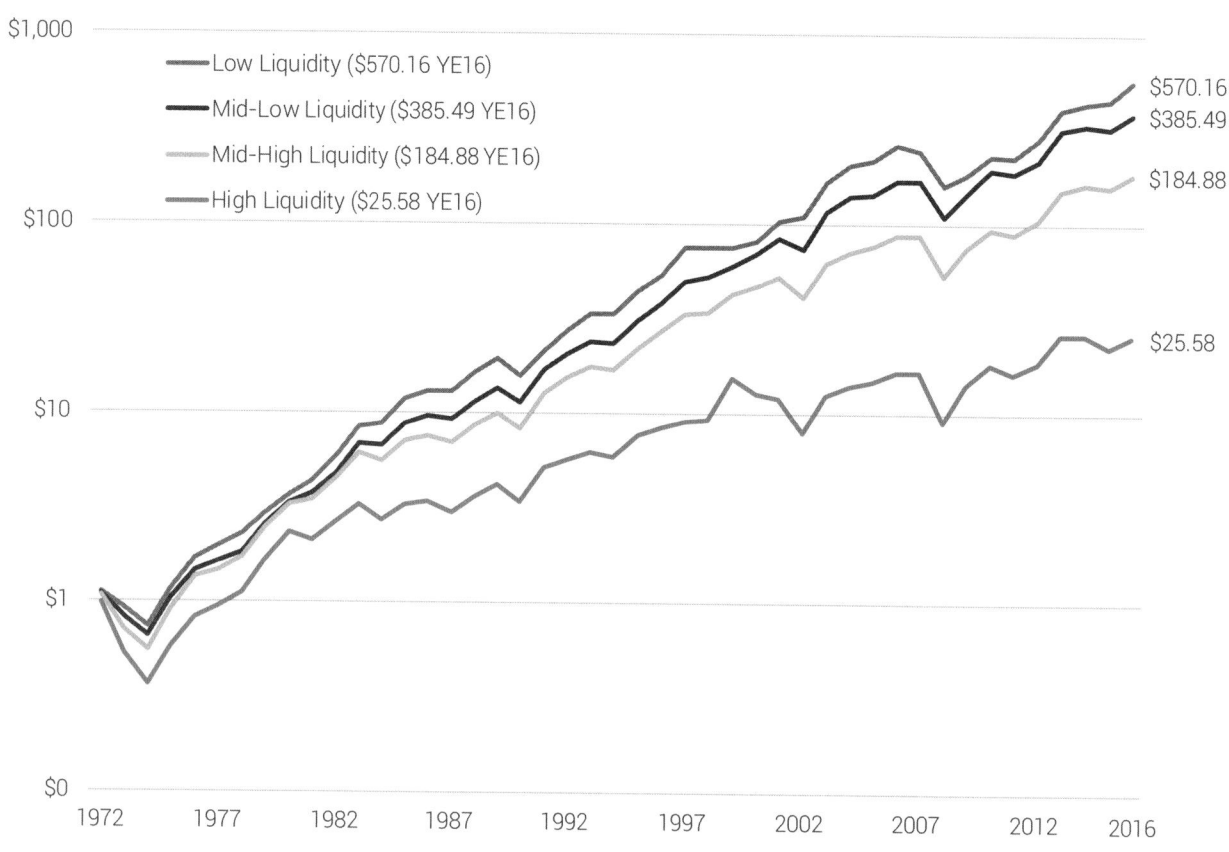

## Liquidity as an Investment Style[9.3]

Similar to small-versus-large or value-versus-growth, liquid-versus-illiquid can be viewed as an investment style. Returns are on average higher for small, value, or illiquid stocks. In this way, liquidity can be thought of as another risk factor, with a risk premium. There are some years in which each style outperforms, as well as some years of underperformance. But each style has a *long-run* positive payoff for investing in it.

Returns on stocks typically are greater than the returns on riskless (or default-free) bonds. This extra expected return is called the equity risk premium. The styles of investing can also add or detract from the investor's return. In fact, styles explain about half of the cross-sectional variation in equity mutual funds, with stock selection, market timing, and fees explaining the other half. Styles seem to explain more of the variation in mutual fund portfolio returns than do industry sectors.[9.4]

---

[9.3]  Ibbotson, Roger G., and Daniel Y.-J Kim, "Liquidity as an Investment Style: 2017 Update," available at research.zebracapital.com. Updated version of: Ibbotson, Roger G., Chen, Zhiwu, Kim, Daniel Y.-J., and Hu, Wendy Y. "Liquidity as an Investment Style," *Financial Analysts Journal*, May/June 2013.

[9.4]  Xiong, James X., Roger G. Ibbotson, Thomas M. Idzorek, and Peng Chen., "The Equal Importance of Asset Allocation and Active Management," *Financial Analysts Journal,* March/April 2010.

The premiums in the equity market are as follows:

- **Equity Risk Premium:** The excess return of stocks relative to risk-free (default-free) government bonds. This premium can be measured over various bond horizons, and the bonds may themselves contain a horizon premium.

- **Size Premium:** The excess return on small stocks versus the return on larger stocks.

- **Value Premium:** The excess return on value stocks versus growth stocks.

- **Liquidity Premium:** The excess return on less-liquid stocks versus more-liquid stocks.

## Liquidity Versus Size

It is natural to think that liquidity and size would be related. The total number of shares of a company that are traded in a given period (say a year) are the number of shares outstanding times the turnover rate. Turnover is a measure of liquidity, adjusted for the number of shares outstanding.

Exhibit 9.3 breaks the universe of stocks into four turnover quartiles and four size-capitalization quartiles, each independently sorted. The numbers in the exhibit are the compound annual (geometric mean) rate of returns for each category. Note that small stocks tend to outperform large stocks in general, but not for the most-liquid stocks. In fact, for the most-liquid stocks shown in column four, the pattern is reversed. The poorest performing category is the highly liquid stocks that are the smallest in size (i.e., that upper-right quartile with a return of -0.29% per year).

The best-performing category is column one, which represents the least-liquid stocks. The worst-performing category is column four, the most-liquid stocks. There is a clear pattern of decreasing returns as the liquidity of the stocks increase. The best-performing category is the small, relatively less liquid stocks, with a 16.03% return.

As shown in the low-minus-high liquidity column, the impact of liquidity is strongest for the smallest companies and weakest for the largest companies. However, the impact of liquidity is strong and consistent across all categories. Liquidity appears to be a much better predictor of returns than does size. Note the mixed results for size shown in the bottom small-minus-large row.

**Exhibit 9.3:** Size and Liquidity Quartile Portfolios, Independently Sorted Each Year
Compound Annual Returns (%)
1972–2016

| | Low Liquidity | Mid-Low Liquidity | Mid-High Liquidity | High Liquidity | Liquidity Effect (%) |
|---|---|---|---|---|---|
| **Micro-Cap** | | | | | |
| Geometric Mean (%) | 16.03 | 15.66 | 9.65 | -0.29 | **16.32** |
| **Small-Cap** | | | | | |
| Geometric Mean (%) | 15.68 | 14.35 | 12.20 | 5.77 | **9.91** |
| **Mid-Cap** | | | | | |
| Geometric Mean (%) | 14.19 | 13.90 | 12.67 | 8.15 | **6.04** |
| **Large-Cap** | | | | | |
| Geometric Mean (%) | 11.20 | 12.05 | 11.75 | 8.89 | **2.31** |
| **Size Effect (%)** | **4.83** | **3.61** | **-2.10** | **-9.18** | |

Compound annual returns (%) from 1972–2016. Source: Ibbotson, Roger G., and Daniel Y.-J Kim, "Liquidity as an Investment Style: 2017 Update," available at research.zebracapital.com. Updated version of: Ibbotson, Roger G., Chen, Zhiwu, Kim, Daniel Y.-J., and Hu, Wendy Y. "Liquidity as an Investment Style," *Financial Analysts Journal*, May/June 2013, updated with 2012–2016 data.

## Liquidity Versus Value/Growth

As noted in Chapter 8, value tends to outperform growth over time. In this chapter, less-liquid stocks are shown to outperform more-liquid stocks. In this section, we examine how liquidity and value/growth interact.

The stocks are ranked by turnover rates and separated into quartiles. Similarly, the stocks are ranked by the earnings-to-price ratios and separated into quartiles. The high-earnings-to-price companies are considered value companies, while the low-earnings-to-price companies are growth companies. The inverse, of course, is the PE ratio, with the growth companies having high PE ratios, and the value companies having low PE ratios.

The earnings used are the trailing reported earnings. The earnings data is from *Compustat*, owned by Standard & Poor's. The portfolios are rebalanced once per year with the earnings lagged by two months to reflect delays in compiling the accounting earnings.

Exhibit 9.4 presents the quartile results for the different levels of liquidity and value/growth. Note that both liquidity and value/growth have a strong impact on stock market returns across all categories. The results appear to be additive. There is an excess return for investing in either low-liquidity or value stocks, and the best return of all was earned by investing in the upper-left category: high-value, low-liquidity stocks, which have a realized return of 19.11%. The worst category is the lower-right corner, high-liquidity growth stocks, which have a return of 2.61%.

**Exhibit 9.4:** Summary Statistics of Value vs. Growth and Liquidity Quartile Portfolios, Independently Sorted Each Year; Compound Annual Returns (%) 1972–2016

| | Low Liquidity | Mid-Low Liquidity | Mid-High Liquidity | High Liquidity | Liquidity Effect (%) |
|---|---|---|---|---|---|
| **High-Value** | | | | | |
| Geometric Mean (%) | 19.11 | 16.79 | 16.14 | 10.11 | **9.00** |
| **Mid-Value** | | | | | |
| Geometric Mean (%) | 15.55 | 14.70 | 12.95 | 11.95 | **3.60** |
| **Mid-Growth** | | | | | |
| Geometric Mean (%) | 13.15 | 12.46 | 10.53 | 6.87 | **6.27[*]** |
| **High-Growth** | | | | | |
| Geometric Mean (%) | 10.37 | 12.22 | 9.00 | 2.61 | **7.77[*]** |
| **Size Effect (%)** | **8.74** | **4.57** | **7.14** | **7.50** | |

[*]Difference due to rounding.

Compound annual returns (%) from 1972–2016. Source: Ibbotson, Roger G., and Daniel Y.-J Kim, "Liquidity as an Investment Style: 2017 Update," available at research.zebracapital.com. Updated version of: Ibbotson, Roger G., Chen, Zhiwu, Kim, Daniel Y.-J., and Hu, Wendy Y. "Liquidity as an Investment Style," *Financial Analysts Journal*, May/June 2013, updated with 2012–2016 data.

## Conclusion

The results confirm that liquidity impacts returns across styles and locations. Investing in less liquid securities generates higher returns. Liquidity seems to be an investment style that is different from size or value. This result seems to hold up in almost any equity market subset and in any location.

## What's Next?

For many years, academics have sought to explain and understand asset prices, with a strong emphasis on market premiums and market anomalies. These premiums and anomalies can be explained by social or behavioral phenomenon in many settings. In a 2014 article, Roger Ibbotson and Tom Idzorek said, "Most of the best-known market premiums and anomalies can be explained by an intuitive and naturally occurring (social or behavioral) phenomenon observed in countless settings: popularity."[9.5]

## Popularity

Popularity is often defined as a social phenomenon associated with being admired, sought after, well known, and/or accepted...can we apply the concept of popularity to the relative performance of different asset classes and different securities? Asset pricing theories have long recognized that expected returns should not be the same for the various instruments in the marketplace. The primary explanation for these differences has been differences in risk. Of course, risk is unpopular – investors do not like risk and want to be compensated for it.

---

[9.5] Ibbotson, R.G., Idzorek, T.H. "Dimensions of Popularity," *Journal of Portfolio Management*, Vol. 40 No. 5, (Special 40th Anniversary Issue 2014), P. 68–74.

Stated simply and broadly, if an asset has characteristics that investors really like, its price will be higher. If the asset has characteristics that investors do not like, its price will be lower, all other things being equal. Thus the asset with more desirable characteristics should have lower expected relative returns, whereas the asset with less desirable characteristics should have higher expected relative returns.

From an equilibrium perspective, the expected return is not only for risk but *anything* the investor finds unattractive or unpopular (e.g., less liquid, high taxability, difficult to diversify, bad management, and so on). Therefore, various assets and individual securities will have different returns in equilibrium. From a behavioral finance perspective, mispricing can occur when stocks are highly traded, are "in the news," or there is much excitement about them. In all cases, the movement from the unpopular dimension to the popular dimension corresponds to relative price increases. Mispricing impacts shorter-term returns but not necessarily long-term returns, since the market recognizes the biases and these will eventually get corrected. Popularity is a key concept that helps to explain valuation as well as long- and short-run returns.

Although risk is clearly unpopular, it is only one dimension of popularity. Popularity can include all sorts of other characteristics that do not fit well into the risk and return paradigm. In many ways, the joint awarding of the 2013 Nobel Prize in Economic Sciences to Eugene Fama (an efficient markets advocate) and to Robert Shiller (a behavioral economist) endorses the merit of both approaches. The merit of both approaches and the link to popularity (voting) was recognized more than 80 years ago in *Security Analysis*, when Ben Graham and David Dodd [1934] wrote:

> *"...the market is not a weighing machine, in which the value of each issue is registered by an exact and impersonal mechanism, in accordance with its specific qualities. Rather we should say that the market is a voting machine, whereon countless individuals register choices which are partly the product of reason and partly the product of emotion."*

# Chapter 10

# Using Historical Data in Wealth Forecasting and Portfolio Optimization

When forecasting the return on an asset or a portfolio, investors are (or should be) interested in the entire probability distribution of future outcomes, not just the mean or "point estimate." An example of a point estimate forecast is that large-cap stocks will have a return of 13% in 2017. It is more helpful to know the uncertainty surrounding this point estimate than to know the point estimate itself. One measure of uncertainty is standard deviation. The large-cap stock return forecast can be expressed as 13% representing the mean and 20% representing the standard deviation.

If the returns on large-cap stocks are normally distributed, the mean (expected return) and the standard deviation provide enough information to forecast the likelihood of any return. Suppose one wants to ascertain the likelihood that large-cap stocks will have a return of -25% or lower in 2017. Given the above example, a return of -25% is [13 - (-25)] / 20 = 1.9 standard deviations below the mean. The likelihood of an observation of 1.9 or more standard deviations below the mean is 2.9%. This can be looked up in any statistics textbook, in the table showing values of the cumulative probability function for a normal distribution. Thus, the likelihood that the stock market will fall by 25% or more in 2017 is 2.9%. This is valuable information, both to the investor who believes that stocks are a sure thing and to the investor who is certain that they will crash tomorrow.

However, historical stock returns are not exactly normally distributed, and a slightly different method needs to be used to make accurate probabilistic forecasts. A description of the model used to forecast the distribution of stock returns appears later in this chapter.

**Probabilistic Forecasts**

Probabilistic forecasts might seem to be too wide to be useful – the most widely quoted forecasters, after all, make very specific predictions. However, the forecast of a probability distribution actually reveals much more than the point estimate. The point estimate reflects what statisticians call an "expected value," but the actual return will likely be higher or lower than the point estimate. By knowing the extent to which actual returns are likely to deviate from the point estimate, the investor can assess the risk of every asset, and thus compare investment opportunities in terms of their risks as well as their expected returns. As Harry Markowitz showed nearly a half-century ago in his Nobel Prize-winning work on portfolio theory, investors care about avoiding risk as well as seeking return. Probabilistic forecasts enable investors to quantify these concepts.

## The Lognormal Distribution

In the lognormal model, the natural logarithms of asset return relatives are assumed to be normally distributed. A return relative is one plus the return. That is, if an asset has a return of 15% in a given period, its return relative is 1.15 (1 + 0.15).

The lognormal distribution is skewed to the right. This means that the expected value, or mean, is greater than the median. Furthermore, if return relatives are lognormally distributed, returns cannot fall below negative 100%. These properties of the lognormal distribution make it a more accurate characterization of the behavior of market returns than does the normal distribution.

In all normal distributions, moreover, the probability of an observation falling one standard deviation below the mean equals the probability of falling one standard deviation above the mean; each has a probability of about 34%. In a lognormal distribution, these probabilities differ and depend on the parameters of the distribution.

### Forecasting Wealth Values and Rates of Return

Using the lognormal model, it is fairly simple to form probabilistic forecasts of both compound rates of return and ending period wealth values. Wealth at time $n$ (assuming reinvestment of all income and no taxes) is:

$$W_n = W_0(1+r_1)(1+r_2)...(1+r_n)$$

Where:

| | | |
|---|---|---|
| $W_n$ | = | The wealth value at time $n$ |
| $W_0$ | = | The initial investment at time 0 |
| $r_1, r_2$, etc. | = | The total returns on the portfolio for the rebalancing ending at times 1, 2, and so forth |

The compound rate of return or geometric mean return over the same period, $r_G$, is:

$$r_G = \left(\frac{W_n}{W_0}\right)^{\frac{1}{n}} - 1$$

Where:

| | | |
|---|---|---|
| $r_G$ | = | The geometric mean return |
| $W_n$ | = | The ending period wealth value at time $n$ |
| $W_0$ | = | The initial wealth value at time 0 |
| $n$ | = | The inclusive number of periods |

By assuming that all $(1+r_n)$ values are lognormally distributed with the same expected value and standard deviation and are all statistically independent of each other, it follows that $W_n$ and $(1+r_G)$ are lognormally distributed. In fact, even if the $(1+r_n)$ values are not themselves lognormally distributed but are independent and identically distributed, $W_n$ and $(1+r_G)$ are approximately lognormal for large enough values of $n$. This "central-limit theorem" means that the lognormal model can be useful in long-term forecasting even if short-term returns are not well described by a lognormal distribution.

## Calculating Parameters of the Lognormal Model

To use the lognormal model, we must first calculate the expected value and standard deviation of the natural logarithm of the return relative of the portfolio. These parameters, denoted $m$ and $s$ respectively, can be calculated from the expected return ($m$) and standard deviation ($s$) of the portfolio as follows:

$$m = \ln(1+\mu) - \left(\frac{s^2}{2}\right)$$

$$s = \sqrt{\ln\left[1+\left(\frac{\sigma}{1+\mu}\right)^2\right]}$$

Where:

ln    =  The natural logarithm function

To calculate a particular percentile of wealth or return for a given time horizon, the only remaining parameter needed is the z-score of the percentile. The z-score of a percentile ranking is that percentile ranking expressed as the number of standard deviations that it is above or below the mean of a normal distribution. For example, the z-score of the 95th percentile is 1.645 because in a normal distribution, the 95th percentile is 1.645 standard deviations above the 50th percentile or median, which is also the mean. Z-scores can be obtained from a table of cumulative values of the standard normal distribution or from software that produces such values.

Given the logarithmic parameters of a portfolio ($m$ and $s$), a time horizon ($n$), and the z-score of a percentile ($z$), the percentile in question in terms of cumulative wealth at the end of the time horizon ($W_n$) is:

$$e^{\left(mn+zs\sqrt{n}\right)}$$

Similarly, the percentile in question in terms of the compound rate of return for the period ($r_G$) is:

$$e^{\left(m+z\frac{s}{\sqrt{n}}\right)} - 1$$

## Mean-Variance Optimization

One important application of the probability forecasts of asset returns is mean-variance optimization. Optimization is the process of identifying portfolios that have the highest possible expected return for a given level of risk, or the lowest possible risk for a given expected return. Such a portfolio is considered "efficient," and the locus of all efficient portfolios is called the efficient frontier. A simple two-asset efficient frontier constructed from large-cap stocks and U.S. Treasury bills is shown in Exhibit 10.1. All investors should hold portfolios that are efficient with respect to the assets in their opportunity set.

**Exhibit 10.1:** Efficient Frontier; Large-cap Stocks and U.S. Treasury Bills
1926–2016

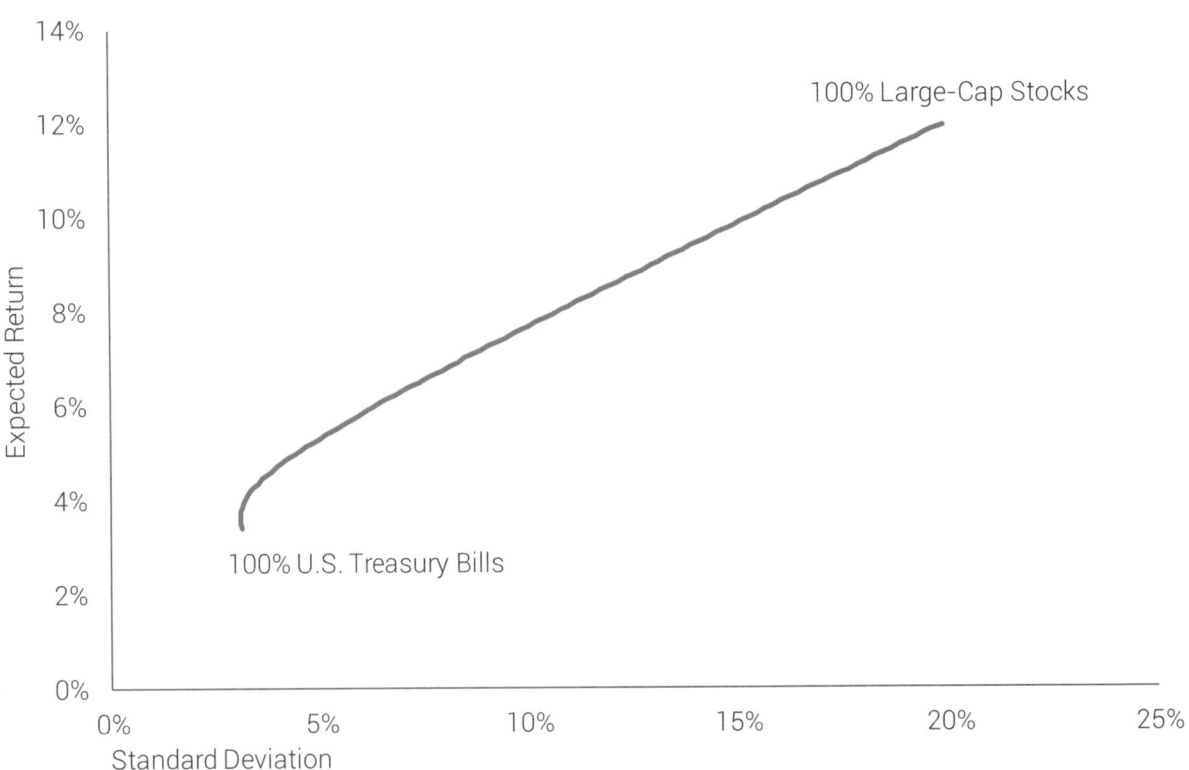

The most widely accepted framework for optimization is Markowitz, or mean-variance, optimization (MVO), which makes the following assumptions: (i) The forecast mean, or expected return, describes the attribute that investors consider to be desirable about an asset; (ii) The risk of the asset is measured by its expected standard deviation of returns; and (iii) The interaction between one asset and another is captured by the expected correlation coefficient of the two assets' returns. MVO thus requires forecasts of the return and standard deviation of each asset, and the correlation of each asset with every other asset.[10.1]

---

[10.1]   The standard deviation is the square root of the variance; hence the term "mean-variance" in describing this form of the optimization problem.

In the 1950s, Harry Markowitz developed both the concept of the efficient frontier and the mathematical means of constructing it (mean-variance optimization).[10.2]

## Estimating Returns, Risks, and Correlations

To simulate future probability distributions of asset and portfolio returns, one typically estimates parameters of the historical return data. The parameters that are required to simulate returns on an asset are its mean and standard deviation. To simulate returns on portfolios of assets, one must also estimate the correlation of each asset in the portfolio with every other asset. Thus, the parameters required to conduct a simulation are the same as those required as inputs into a mean-variance optimization.[10.3]

To illustrate how to estimate the parameters of asset class returns relevant to optimization and forecasting, we construct an example using large-cap stocks, long-term government bonds, and Treasury bills. The techniques used to estimate these parameters are described below.

### Means, or Expected Returns

The mean return (forecast mean, or expected return) on an asset is the probability-weighted average of all possible returns on the asset over a future period. Estimates of expected returns are based on models of asset returns. While many models of asset returns incorporate estimates of gross national product, the money supply, and other macroeconomic variables, the model employed in this chapter does not. This is because we assume (for the present purpose) that asset markets are informationally efficient, with all relevant and available information fully incorporated in asset prices. If this assumption holds, investor expectations (forecasts) can be discerned from market-observable data. Such forecasts are not attempts to outguess, or beat, the market. They are attempts to discern the market's expectations, i.e., to read what the market itself is forecasting.

For some assets, expected returns can be estimated using current market data alone. For example, the yield on a riskless bond is an estimate of its expected return. For other assets, current data are not sufficient. Stocks, for example, have no exact analogue to the yield on a bond. In such cases, we use the statistical time series properties of historical data in forming the estimates.

To know which data to use when estimating expected returns, we need to know the rebalancing frequency of the portfolios and the investment horizon. In our example, we will assume an annual rebalancing frequency and a 20-year planning horizon. The rebalancing frequency gives the time units in which returns are measured.

---

[10.2] Markowitz, H.M. 1959. *Portfolio Selection: Efficient Diversification of Investments* (New York: John Wiley & Sons).

[10.3] It is also possible to conduct a simulation using entire data sets, that is, without estimating the statistical parameters of the data sets. Typically, in such a nonparametric simulation, the frequency of an event occurring in the simulated history is equal to the frequency of the event occurring in the actual history used to construct the data set.

With a 20-year horizon, the relevant riskless rate is the yield on a 20-year coupon bond. This riskless rate is the baseline from which the expected return on every other asset class is derived by adding or subtracting risk premiums.

**Large-Cap Stocks**

The expected return on large-cap stocks is the riskless rate, plus the expected risk premium of large-cap stocks over bonds that are riskless over the investment horizon. With a 20-year horizon, this risk premium is 6.94%, shown as the long-horizon expected equity risk premium in Exhibit 10.2. Hence, the expected return on large-cap stocks is 2.72% (the long-term riskless rate) plus 6.94% (the long-term equity risk premium), or 9.66%.

**Bonds and Bills**

For default-free bonds with a maturity equal to the planning horizon, the expected return is the yield on the bond; that is, the expected return is the long-term riskless rate of 2.72%. For bonds with other maturities, the expected bond horizon premium should be added to the riskless rate (for longer maturities) or subtracted from the riskless rate (for shorter maturities). Because expected capital gains on a bond are zero, the expected horizon premium is estimated by the historical average difference of the income returns on the bonds.[10.4]

For Treasury bills, the expected return over a given time horizon equals the expected return on a Treasury bond of a similar horizon, less the expected horizon premium of bonds over bills. The long-term horizon premium is estimated by the historical average of the difference of the income return on bonds and the return on bills. From Exhibit 10.2, this is 1.83%. Subtracting this from the riskless rate (2.72%) gives us an expected return on bills of 0.89%. Of course, this forecast typically differs from the current yield on a Treasury bill because a portfolio of Treasury bills is rolled over (the proceeds of maturing bills are invested in new bills, at yields not yet known) during the time horizon described.

---

[10.4] The expected capital gain on a par bond is self-evidently zero. For a zero coupon (or other discount) bond, investors expect the price to rise as the bond ages, but the expected portion of this price increase should not be considered a capital gain. It is a form of income return.

**Exhibit 10.2:** Building Blocks for Expected Return Construction

| Yields (Riskless Rates)* | Value (%) |
|---|---|
| Long-term (20-year) U.S. Treasury Coupon Bond Yield | 2.72 |
| Intermediate-term (5-year) U.S. Treasury Coupon Note Yield | 1.85 |
| Short-term (30-day) U.S. Treasury Bill Yield | 0.44 |

| Fixed Income Risk Premiums** | |
|---|---|
| Expected default premium: long-term corporate bond total returns minus long-term government bond total returns | 0.07 |
| Expected long-term horizon premium: long-term government bond income returns minus U.S. Treasury bill total returns* | 1.83 |
| Expected intermediate-term horizon premium: intermediate-term government bond income returns minus U.S. Treasury bill total returns* | 1.11 |

| Equity Risk Premiums*** | |
|---|---|
| Long-horizon expected equity risk premium: large-cap stock total returns minus long-term government bond income returns | 6.94 |
| Intermediate-horizon expected equity risk premium: large-cap stock total returns minus intermediate-term government bond income returns | 7.51 |
| Short-horizon expected equity risk premium: large-cap stock total returns minus U.S. Treasury bill total returns**** | 8.52 |
| Small-cap premium: small-cap stock total return minus large-cap stock total return | 4.62 |

\*  As of December 31, 2016. Maturities are approximate. Source: (i) SBBI Long-term Government Bond series (20-year maturity yield), (ii) SBBI Intermediate-term Government Bond series (5-year maturity yield), (iii) Treasury constant maturities/1-month/Business day (30-day Treasury Bill yield), Board of Governors of the Federal Reserve website at https://www.federalreserve.gov/datadownload/Choose.aspx?rel=H15. SBBI series retrieved from Morningstar *Direct* database.

\*\*  Expected risk premiums for fixed income are based on the differences of historical arithmetic mean returns from 1970–2016. Source: (i) SBBI Long-term Corporate Bond total return series (20-year maturity), (ii) SBBI Long-term Government Bond total return series (20-year maturity), (iii) SBBI Long-term Government Bond income return series (20-year maturity), (iv) SBBI Intermediate-term Government Bond income return series (5-year maturity), and (v) SBBI 30-Day T-Bill total return series. SBBI series retrieved from Morningstar *Direct* database.

\*\*\*  Expected risk premiums for equities are based on the differences of historical arithmetic mean returns from 1926–2016. Source: (i) SBBI Large-cap Stocks total return series (essentially the S&P 500 Index), (ii) SBBI Long-term Government Bond income return series (20-year maturity), (iii) SBBI Intermediate-term Government Bond income return series (5-year maturity), (iv) SBBI 30-Day T-Bill total return series, and (v) SBBI Small-cap stock total return series. SBBI series retrieved from Morningstar *Direct* database.

\*\*\*\*  For U.S. Treasury bills, the income return and total return are the same.

## Standard Deviations

Standard deviations are estimated from historical data as described in Chapter 6. There is no evidence of a major change in the variability of returns on large-cap stocks, so we use the entire period 1926 to 2016 to estimate the standard deviation of these asset classes. For long-term government bonds and Treasury bills, we use the period 1970 to 2016 to estimate these inputs (see Exhibit 10.4). This is because the departure from the Bretton Woods fixed-rate currency exchange agreement in the early 1970s caused a structural shift in the U.S. interest-rate environment. Bond volatility spiked as a result, and has remained well above levels experienced before the regime shift, rendering pre-1970 risk comparisons inappropriate.

## Correlations

Correlations between the asset classes are estimated from historical data as described in Chapter 6. Correlations between major asset classes change over time. Exhibit 10.3 shows the historical correlation of annual returns on large-cap stocks and long-term bonds over 20-year rolling periods from 1926–1945 through 1997–2016.

**Exhibit 10.3:** 20-Year Rolling-Period Correlations of Annual Returns of Large-Cap Stocks and Long-term Government Bonds
1926–2016

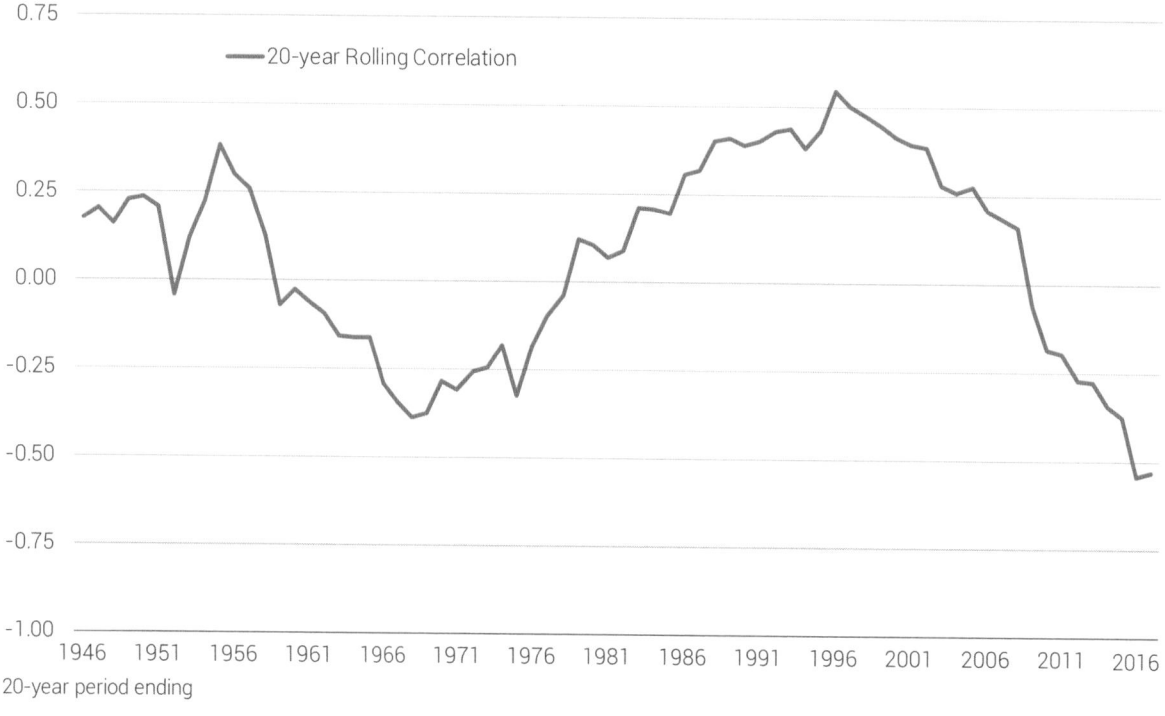

In Exhibit 10.4, a correlation matrix is provided that can be used in conjunction with the information provided in Exhibit 10.2 as inputs in forming portfolios.

**Exhibit 10.4:** Optimization Inputs: Year-end 2016 Large-Cap Stocks, Long-term Government Bonds, and U.S. Treasury Bills (%)

| | Expected Return (%) | Standard Deviation (%) | Correlation | | |
|---|---|---|---|---|---|
| | | | Stocks | Bonds | Bills |
| Stocks | 9.7 | 19.9 | 1.00 | | |
| Bonds | 2.7 | 12.1 | 0.00 | 1.00 | |
| Bills | 0.4 | 3.4 | -0.02 | 0.18 | 1.00 |

**Using Inputs to Form Other Portfolios**

Given a complete set of inputs, the expected return and standard deviation of any portfolio (efficient or other) of the asset classes can be calculated. The expected return of a portfolio is the weighted average of the expected returns of the asset classes:

$$r_p = \sum_{i=1}^{n} x_i r_i$$

Where:

$r_p$     =   The expected return of the portflio $p$

$n$     =   The number of asset classes

$x_i$     =   The portfolio weight of asset class $i$, scaled such that:

$$\sum_{i=1}^{n} x_i = 1$$

Where:

$r_i$     =   The expected return of asset class $i$

For example, referring to the inputs in Exhibit 10.4 (the expected returns and standard deviations shown in Exhibit 10.4 are the equivalent values from Exhibit 10.2, rounded to one decimal), a portfolio comprised of large-cap stocks only would have an expected return of 9.7% and a standard deviation of 19.9%. If the portfolio mix is changed to, say, 60.0% large-cap stocks, 35.0% long-term government bonds, and 5.0% Treasury bills, the expected return of this new portfolio mix can be calculated by applying the above formula (again, using the inputs in Exhibit 10.4):

6.8% = (60.0% x 9.7%) + (35.0% x 2.7%) + (5.0% x 0.4%)

The standard deviation of the portfolio depends not only on the standard deviations of the asset classes, but also on all of the correlations. It is given by:

$$\sigma_p = \sqrt{\sum_{i=1}^{n} \sum_{i=1}^{n} x_i x_j \sigma_i \sigma_j p_{ij}}$$

Where:

| | | |
|---|---|---|
| $\sigma_p$ | = | The standard deviation of the portfolio |
| $x_i$ and $x_j$ | = | The portfolio weights of asset classes $i$ and $j$ |
| $\sigma_i$ and $\sigma_j$ | = | The standard deviations of returns on asset classes $i$ and $j$ |
| $p_{ij}$ | = | The correlation between returns on asset classes $i$ and $j$ (note that $r_{ii}$ equals one and that $r_{ij}$ is equal to $r_{ji}$). |

The standard deviation of the new portfolio (60.0% large-cap stocks, 35.0% long-term government bonds, and 5.0% Treasury bills) can be calculated using the inputs from Exhibit 10.2 and 10.4 as shown in Exhibit 10.5:

**Exhibit 10.5:** Calculation of Example Portfolio Comprised of 60.0% Large-cap stocks, 35.0% Long-term Government Bonds, and 5.0% Treasury Bills

| Stocks (asset class 1) | Bonds (asset class 2) | Bills (asset class 3) |
|---|---|---|
| Stocks & Stocks | Stocks & Bonds | Stocks & Bills |
| $x_1^2 \sigma_1^2 p_{1,1} =$ | $x_1 x_2 \sigma_1 \sigma_2 p_{1,2} =$ | $x_1 x_3 \sigma_1 \sigma_3 p_{1,3} =$ |
| $0.60^2 \times 0.199^2 \times 1.00 =$ | $0.60 \times 0.35 \times 0.199 \times 0.121 \times -0.002 =$ | $0.60 \times 0.05 \times 0.199 \times 0.034 \times -0.017 =$ |
| $= 0.014229$ | $= -0.000010$ | $= -0.000004$ |
| Bonds & Stocks | Bonds & Bonds | Bonds & Bills |
| $x_1 x_2 \sigma_1 \sigma_2 p_{1,2} =$ | $x_2^2 \sigma_2^2 p_{2,2} =$ | $x_2 x_3 \sigma_2 \sigma_3 p_{2,3} =$ |
| $0.35 \times 0.60 \times 0.121 \times 0.199 \times -0.002 =$ | $0.35^2 \times 0.121^2 \times 1.00 =$ | $0.35 \times 0.05 \times 0.121 \times 0.034 \times 0.182 =$ |
| $= -0.000010$ | $= 0.001792$ | $= 0.000013$ |
| Bills & Stocks | Bills & Bonds | Bills & Bills |
| $x_1 x_3 \sigma_1 \sigma_3 p_{1,3} =$ | $x_2 x_3 \sigma_2 \sigma_3 p_{2,3} =$ | $x_3^2 \sigma_3^2 p_{3,3} =$ |
| $0.05 \times 0.60 \times 0.034 \times 0.199 \times -0.017 =$ | $0.05 \times 0.35 \times 0.034 \times 0.121 \times 0.182 =$ | $0.05^2 \times 0.034^2 \times 1.00 =$ |
| $= -0.000004$ | $= 0.000013$ | $= 0.000003$ |

By summing these terms and taking the square root of the total, the result is a standard deviation of 12.7%.

$$\sqrt{\begin{array}{l} 0.014229 + -0.000010 + -0.000004 + \\ -0.000010 + 0.001792 + 0.000013 + \\ -0.000004 + 0.000013 + 0.000003 \end{array}} = 12.7\%$$

## Enhancements to Mean-Variance Optimization

Ibbotson Associates was an early adopter of mean-variance optimization to develop asset class model guidelines and continues to assist the industry in the development of enhancements to the traditional mean-variance approach as well as the state-of-the-art techniques described later in the chapter. Over the last half century, the Markowitz mean-variance optimization (MVO) framework has become the textbook approach for creating these optimal asset allocations, but the approach has several shortcomings.

## Shortcomings of Traditional Optimization Techniques

One notable shortcoming is that the output (optimal asset allocation weights) is very sensitive to the inputs (expected returns, standard deviations, and correlations). Input sensitivity often leads to highly concentrated allocations in only a small number of the available asset classes. For example, if a typical optimization starts with an opportunity set of about 10 asset classes, just a few of these asset choices might end up in the resulting optimal allocation, with the remaining asset choices not even getting a mention.

Mean-variance optimization is a powerful tool, but it needs to be used with caution. For instance, basing mean-variance optimization inputs on shorter periods can contribute to the extreme results. Basing the mean-variance optimization inputs on longer periods, such as those presented elsewhere in this book, can help mitigate the extreme asset allocations mixes. Also, there is usually a more consistent ratio of return to risk amongst the different asset classes when using longer periods.

Placing maximum and minimum allocation constraints on each asset is the most common solution to the problem of highly concentrated asset allocations. For instance, we could specify a minimum allocation of 5% and a maximum allocation of 15% for each of the nine asset choices. This would ensure that each asset gets represented in the final allocation and also that no single asset completely dominates in the final allocation mix. Unfortunately, these artificial minimums and maximums are arbitrary, and usually end up limiting the ability of the optimizer to properly act on the information contained in the inputs.

## Black-Litterman and Resampling Techniques

Two popular enhancements to traditional optimization techniques have emerged in recent years that can help overcome these difficulties. While both of these methods can help develop well diversified asset allocations, they approach the problem in very different ways. The first of these, the Black-Litterman model, attempts to create better inputs. The second, resampled mean-variance optimization, attempts to build a better optimizer.

The Black-Litterman model was created by Fischer Black and Robert Litterman in the late 1980s. The Black-Litterman model combines investors' views regarding expected returns and the expected returns predicted by the capital asset pricing model to form a single blended estimate of expected returns. When this new combined estimate is used as an input within a traditional mean-variance optimization framework, it produces well-diversified portfolios that include not only market-based asset allocations but also allocations in assets that received favorable views.

The second approach, resampled mean-variance optimization, grew out of the work of a number of authors, but is most closely associated with the work of Richard Michaud. While traditional mean-variance optimization treats the capital market assumptions as if they were known with complete certainty, resampled mean-variance optimization recognizes that the capital market assumptions are forecasts, and are therefore not known with complete certainty.

Conceptually, resampled mean-variance optimization is a combination of Monte Carlo simulation[10.5] and the more traditional Markowitz mean-variance optimization approach. The simulation randomly resamples possible returns from a forecasted return distribution or randomly resamples possible returns from a historical distribution. The simulated returns lead to a simulated set of capital market assumptions that are used in a traditional mean-variance optimizer, and the asset allocations are recorded. After combining the asset allocations from the numerous intermediate optimizations, the resulting asset allocations are those that, on average, are predicted to perform best over the range of potential outcomes implied by the capital market assumptions. Research has shown that asset allocations selected from a resampled efficient frontier may outperform those from a traditional efficient frontier.[10.6]

In addition to the problem of getting results that are highly concentrated in just a few of the assets available, there are two more criticisms of the traditional mean-variance optimization framework.

First, the traditional approach focuses on a subset of the total portfolio. Traditionally, the focus is on finding a mix of asset classes that maximizes the expected return, subject to a risk constraint. However, because the purpose of most asset portfolios is to fund a specified future cash-flow stream – a liability – the true risk for the portfolio is not the standard deviation of the assets or the performance of the assets relative to that of peers, but not being able to fund the future liability.

---

[10.5] Monte Carlo simulation is a problem-solving technique utilized to approximate the probability of certain outcomes by performing multiple trial runs, called simulations, using random variables. The probability distribution of the results is calculated and analyzed in order to infer which outcomes are most likely to be produced.

[10.6] See Markowitz, H. & Usmen, N. 2003. "Resampled Frontiers vs. Diffuse Bayes: An Experiment." *Journal of Investment Management*, Vol. 1, No. 4.

An asset allocation approach that takes the future liability into account is called liability-relative optimization (or surplus optimization). The usual method employed to accomplish this is to constrain the optimizer to hold short an asset class representing the liability.

Second, the traditional mean-variance optimization framework assumes that the returns of the assets in the optimization are normally distributed. As illustrated in Exhibit 2.3, the return distributions of different asset classes do not always follow a standard, symmetrical bell-shaped curve. Some assets have distributions that are skewed to the left or right, while others have distributions that are skinnier or fatter than others. These more complicated characteristics are called skewness and kurtosis, respectively. The next wave of enhancements to the traditional mean-variance optimization are frameworks that incorporate these additional types of non-normalities into the optimization.

**Markowitz 1.0**

In 1952, Harry Markowitz, invented portfolio optimization. His genius was based on three principles; risk, reward and the correlation of assets in a portfolio. Over the years, technologies advanced, markets crashed, but the portfolio optimization models used by many investors did not evolve to compensate. This is surprising in light of the fact that Markowitz was a pioneer of technological advancement in the field of computational computer science. Furthermore, he did not stand by idly in the area of portfolio modeling, but continued to make improvements in his own models and to influence the models of others. Few of these improvements, however, were picked up broadly in practice.

Because Markowitz's first effort was so simple and powerful, it attracted a great number of followers. The greater the following became, the fewer questioners debated its merits. Markowitz's original work is synonymous with modern portfolio theory and has been taught in business schools for generations and, not surprisingly, is still widely used today.

Then came the crash of 2008, and people started to ask questions. The confluence of the economic trauma and the technological advances of recent decades made the postcrash environment the perfect moment to upgrade to a new model built around Markowitz's fundamental principles of risk, reward and correlation. We dub our updated model "Markowitz 2.0." This section is an adaptation of a 2009 article, "The New Efficient Frontier," by Paul D. Kaplan, Morningstar Canada's director of research, and Sam L. Savage, consulting professor at Stanford University.

## The Flaw of Averages

The 1952 mean-variance model of Harry Markowitz was the first systematic attempt to cure what Savage (2009) called the "flaw of averages." In general, the flaw of averages is a set of systematic errors that occur when people use single numbers (usually averages) to describe uncertain future quantities. For example, if you plan to rob a bank of $10 million and have one chance in 100 of getting away with it, your average take is $100,000. If you described your activity beforehand as "making $100,000" you would be correct on average. But this is a terrible characterization of a bank heist. Yet as Savage discussed, this very "flaw of averages" is made all the time in business practice, and helps explain why everything is behind schedule, beyond budget, and below projection. This phenomenon was an accessory to the global financial crisis that culminated in 2008.

Markowitz's mean-variance model distinguished between different investments that had the same average (expected) return but different risks, measured as variance or its square root (standard deviation). This breakthrough systematic attempt to cure the flaw of averages ultimately garnered a Nobel Prize for its inventor. However, the use of standard deviation and covariance introduces a higher order version of the flaw of averages in that these concepts are themselves a version of averages.

## Making a Great Idea Better

By taking advantage of the very latest in economic thought and computer technology, we can, in effect, add more thrust to the original framework of the Markowitz portfolio optimization model. The result is a dramatically more powerful model that is more aligned with 21st century investor concerns, markets, and financial instruments, such as options.

Our discussion here will focus on five practical enhancements to traditional portfolio optimization that can be made with current technology:

1. First, we use a scenario-based approach to allow for fat-tailed distributions. "Fat-tailed" return distributions are not possible within the context of traditional mean-variance optimization, where return distributions are assumed to be adequately described by mean and variance.

2. Second, we replace the single-period expected return with the long-term forward-looking geometric mean, as this takes into account accumulation of wealth.

3. Third, we substitute conditional value at risk, or CVaR, which focuses on tail risk, for standard deviation, which looks at average variation.

4. Fourth, the original Markowitz model used a covariance matrix to model the distribution of returns on asset classes; we replace this with a scenario-based model that can be generated with Monte Carlo simulation, and can incorporate any number of distributions.

5. Finally, we exploit new statistical technologies pioneered by Savage in the field of probability management. Savage invented an astonishing new technology called the Distribution String, or DIST, which encapsulates thousands of trials as a single data element or spreadsheet cell, thus eliminating the main disadvantage of the scenario-based approach – the need to store and process large amounts of data.

## The Scenario Approach vs. Lognormal Distributions

One of the limitations of the traditional mean-variance optimization framework assumes that the distribution of returns of the assets in the optimization can be adequately described simply by mean and variance alone. The most common depiction of this assumption is to draw the distribution of each asset class as a symmetrical bell-shaped curve; but asset class returns do not always fall into normal distributions.

Over the years, various alternatives have been put forth to replace mean-variance optimization with an optimization framework that takes into account the non-normal features of return distributions. Some researchers have proposed using distribution curves that exhibit skewness and kurtosis (i.e., have fat tails) while others have proposed using large numbers of scenarios based on historical data, or Monte Carlo simulation.

The scenario-based approach has two main advantages over a distribution curve approach: (i) It is highly flexible; for example, nonlinear instruments such as options can be modeled in a straightforward manner; and (ii) it is mathematically manageable; for example, portfolio returns under the scenarios are simply weighted averages of asset class returns within the scenarios. In this way, the distribution of a portfolio can be derived from the distributions of the assets classes without working complicated equations that might lack analytical solutions; only straightforward portfolio arithmetic is needed.

In standard scenario analysis, there is no precise graphical representation of return distributions. Histograms serve as approximations, such as those shown in Exhibit 2.3. We augment the scenario approach by employing a smoothing technique so that smooth curves represent return distributions. For example, Exhibit 10.6 shows the distribution curve of annual returns of large-cap stocks under our scenario-based approach. Comparing Exhibit 10.6 with the large-cap stock histogram in Exhibit 2.3, we can see that the smooth distribution curve retains the properties of the historical distribution making it more esthetically pleasing and precise. Further, our model can bring all of the power of continuous mathematics to the scenario approach. This was previously enjoyed only by models based on continuous distributions.

In Exhibit 10.6, the solid gray line represents the distribution of annual returns of large-cap stocks when our smoothed scenario-based approach is used and the red line represents the distribution curve of annual returns of large-cap stocks when traditional mean-variance analysis is used and we assume that returns follow a lognormal distribution.

**Exhibit 10.6:** Distribution of Annual Returns: Large-cap Stocks (%)
Lognormal Distribution vs. Scenario-Based Model

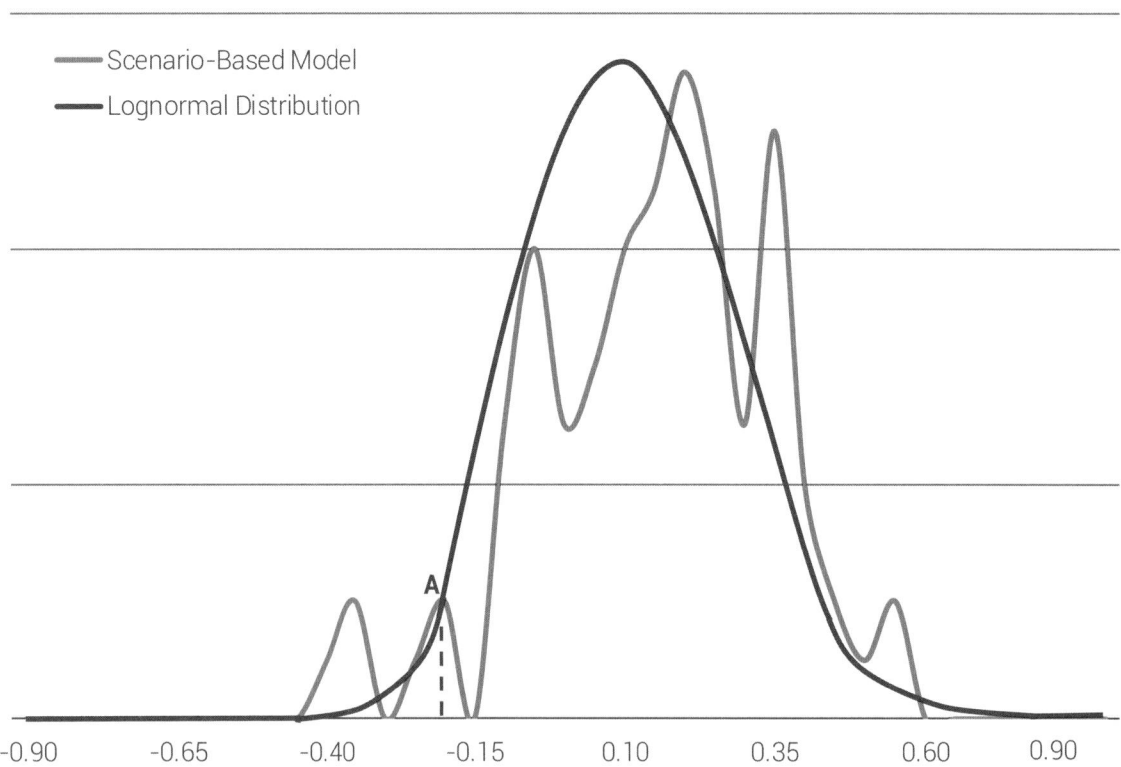

If we extend a vertical line from Point A down to the x-axis, the area to the left (and underneath) each of the curves represents the occurrences of annual returns equal to or less than, in this case, negative 26%. Because these are cumulative distributions, we can calculate the probability that the annual returns of large-cap stocks will be less than or equal to negative 26% by dividing the area underneath each of the smaller curves (to the left of Point A) by the total area underneath each of the entire curves.

For example, looking to the scenario-based model, the area to the left of the vertical line under the scenario-based distribution represents 5% of the total area underneath this entire distribution line. This implies that the probability of large-cap stocks having a loss of 26% or more is 5%. Correspondingly, the area to the left of the vertical line for the lognormal distribution represents 1.6% of the total area under the entire lognormal distribution line. This implies that the probability of large-cap stocks returning negative 26% or less using the traditional mean-variance model is 1.6%.

As Kaplan et al. (2009) discuss, "tail events" have occurred often throughout the history of capital markets all over the world, but the probabilities associated with them may be systematically underestimated within the context of traditional mean-variance analysis, where return distributions are assumed to be lognormal. The scenario-based model proposed by Kaplan and Savage is a real step forward as it better models the nontrivial probabilities associated with tail events. For a more detailed discussion of tail events and their nontriviality, see Chapter 11, where Kaplan introduces a new set of monthly real stock market total returns going back a full 132 years. Using these new returns, we demonstrate that the severity of the financial crisis of 2008 was not unique, but was merely the latest chapter in a long history of market meltdowns.

## Geometric Mean vs. Single-Period Expected Return

In mean-variance optimization, reward is measured by expected return, which is a forecast of arithmetic mean. However, over long periods, investors are not concerned with simple averages of return, rather they are concerned with the accumulation of wealth. We use forecasted long-term geometric mean as the measure of reward because investors who plan on repeatedly reinvesting in the same strategy over an indefinite period would seek the highest rate of growth for the portfolios as measured by geometric mean.[10.7]

## Conditional Value at Risk vs. Standard Deviation

As for risk, much has been written about how investors are not concerned merely with the degree of dispersion of returns (as measured by standard deviation), but rather with how much wealth they could lose. A number of downside risk measures, including value at risk, conditional value at risk, and maximum drawdown, have been proposed to replace standard deviation as the measure of risk in strategic asset allocation. While any one of these could be used, our preference is to use conditional value at risk.

CVaR is related to value at risk. VaR describes the left tail in terms of how much capital can be lost over a given period of time. For example, a 5% VaR answers a question of the form: Having invested $10,000 there is a 5% chance of losing $X or more in 12 months. (The "or more" implications of VaR are sometimes overlooked by investors with serious implications.) Applying this idea to returns, the 5% VaR is the negative of the 5th percentile of the return distribution. CVaR is the expected or average loss of capital should VaR be breached. Therefore CVaR is always greater than VaR.

## Scenarios vs. Correlation

In mean-variance analysis, the covariation of the returns of each pair of asset classes is represented by a single number, the correlation coefficient. This is mathematically equivalent to assuming that a simple linear regression model is an adequate description of how the returns on the two asset classes are related. In fact, the R-squared statistic of a simple linear regression model for two series of returns is equal to the square of the correlation coefficient.

However, for many pairs of asset classes, a linear model misses the most important features of the relationship. For example, during normal times, non-U.S. equities are considered to be good diversifiers for U.S. equity investors. But during global crises, all major equity markets move down together.

---

[10.7]  Ranking investment strategies by forecasted geometric mean is sometimes described as applying the Kelly Criterion, an idea promoted by William Poundstone in his 2005 book, *Fortune's Formula*.

Furthermore, suppose that the returns on two asset class indices were highly correlated, but instead of including direct exposures to both in the model, one was replaced with an option on itself. Instead of having a linear relationship, we now have a nonlinear relationship which cannot be captured by a correlation coefficient.

Fortunately, these sorts of nonlinear relationships between returns on different investments can be handled in a scenario-based model. For example, in scenarios that represent normal times, returns on different equity markets could be modeled as moving somewhat apart from each other; while scenarios that represent global crises could model the markets as moving downward together.

## Probability Management Enables Scenario Analysis

Because it may take thousands of scenarios to adequately model return distributions, until recently, a disadvantage of the scenario-based approach has been that it requires large amounts of data to be stored and processed. Even with the advances in computer hardware, the conventional approach of representing scenarios with large tables of explicit numbers remained problematic.

The phenomenal speed of computers has given rise to the field of probability management, an extension of data management to probability distributions, rather than numbers. The key component of probability management is the Distribution String, or DIST, that can encapsulate thousands of trials as a single data element. The use of DISTs greatly saves on storage and speeds up processing time, so that a Monte Carlo simulation consisting of thousands of trials can be performed on a personal computer in an instant. Monte Carlo simulations that use DISTs are also very adaptable, allowing for almost any return distribution or underlying probability model, rather than being contained by parameters. While not all asset management organizations are prepared to create the DISTs needed to drive geometric mean-CVaR optimization, some outside vendors, such as Morningstar/Ibbotson, can fulfill this role.

Another facet of probability management is interactive simulation technology, which can run thousands of scenarios through a model before the sound of your finger leaving the <Enter> key reaches your ear. These supersonic models allow much deeper intuition into the sensitivities of portfolios, and encourage the user to interactively explore different portfolios, distributional assumptions, and potential black swans. A sample of such an interactive model is available for download from http://www.ProbabilityManagement.org.

## Finale: The New Efficient Frontier

Putting it all together, we form an efficient frontier of forecasted geometric mean and conditional value at risk as shown in Exhibit 10.7,[10.8] incorporating our scenario approach to covariance and new statistical technology. We believe that this efficient frontier is more relevant to investors than

---

[10.8] Other researchers have also proposed using GM and CVaR as the measures or reward and risk in an efficient frontier. See, for example: Sheikh, A.Z. & Qiao, H. 2009. "Non-Normality of Market Returns: A Framework for Asset Allocation Decision Making". Whitepaper, J.P. Morgan Asset Management.

the traditional expected return versus standard deviation frontier of MVO because it shows the trade-off between reward and risk that is meaningful to investors; namely, long-term potential growth versus short-term potential loss.

**Exhibit 10.7:** Geometric Mean – Conditional Value at Risk Efficient Frontier (%)

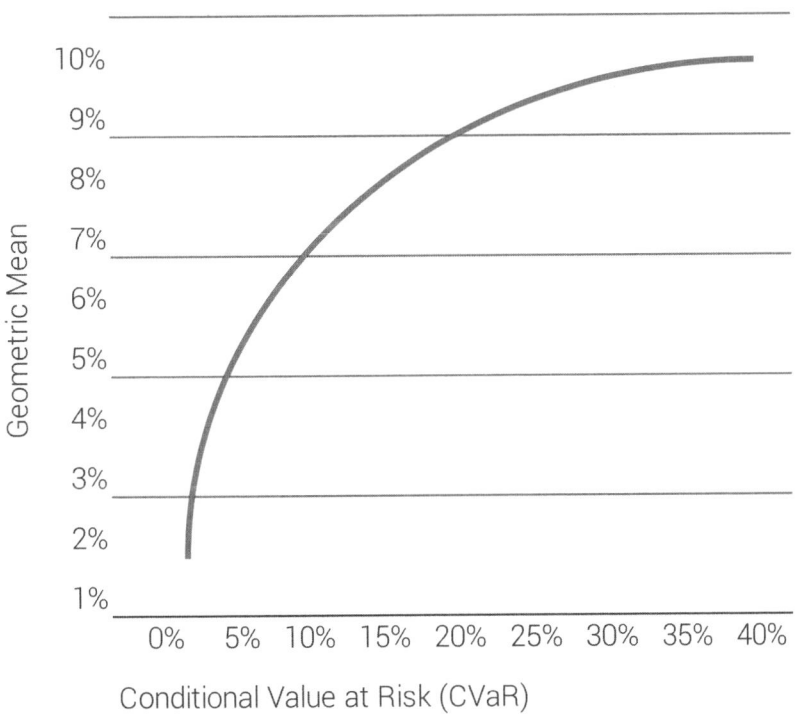

**Approaches to Calculating the Equity Risk Premium**

Researchers have estimated the expected outperformance of stocks over risk-free bonds – the equity risk premium using many approaches. Such studies can be categorized into four groups based on the approaches they have taken, using:

- Historical returns between stocks and bonds;

- Fundamental information such as earnings, dividends, or overall productivity (supply-side models);

- Payoffs demanded by equity investors for bearing the additional risk (demand-side models); and

- Broad surveys of opinions of financial professionals.

The rest of this chapter will focus on the historical and supply-side methods.

## The Historical Equity Risk Premium

The expected equity risk premium can be defined as the additional return an investor expects to receive to compensate for the additional risk associated with investing in equities as opposed to investing in riskless assets.

Unfortunately, the expected equity risk premium is unobservable in the market and therefore must be estimated. Typically, this estimation is arrived at through the use of historical data. The historical equity risk premium can be calculated by subtracting the long-term average of the income return on the riskless asset (Treasuries) from the long-term average stock market return (measured over the same period as that of the riskless asset).

In using a historical measure of the equity risk premium, one assumes that what has happened in the past is representative of what might be expected in the future. In other words, the assumption one makes when using historical data to measure the expected equity risk premium is that the relationship between the returns of the risky asset (equities) and the riskless asset (Treasuries) is stable.

## The Stock Market Benchmark

The stock market benchmark chosen should be a broad index that reflects the behavior of the market as a whole. Commonly used indexes include the S&P 500 and the Russell 3000. Although the Dow Jones Industrial Average is a popular index, it would be inappropriate for calculating the equity risk premium because it is too narrow.

We use the total return of our large-cap stock index (currently represented by the S&P 500) as our market benchmark when calculating the equity risk premium. The S&P 500 was selected as the appropriate market benchmark because it is representative of a large sample of companies across a large number of industries. The S&P 500 is also one of the most widely accepted market benchmarks and is a good measure of the equity market as a whole.

Exhibit 10.8 illustrates the equity risk premium calculation using three different market indexes (the S&P 500, a portfolio comprised of CRSP NYSE/NYSE MKT/NASDAQ deciles 1–10, and a portfolio comprised of CRSP NYSE/NYSE MKT/NASDAQ deciles 1–2) and the income return on three government bonds of different horizons.

**Exhibit 10.8:** Equity Risk Premium with Different Market Indexes (%)
1926–2016

|  | Long-horizon | Intermediate-horizon | Short-horizon |
|---|---|---|---|
| S&P 500 | 6.94 | 7.51 | 8.52 |
| CRSP NYSE/NYSE MKT/NASDAQ Deciles 1-10 | 6.75 | 7.33 | 8.34 |
| CRSP NYSE/NYSE MKT/NASDAQ Deciles 1-2 | 6.30 | 6.88 | 7.89 |

The equity risk premium is calculated by subtracting the arithmetic mean of the government bond income return from the arithmetic mean of the stock market total return. Exhibit 10.9 demonstrates this calculation for the long-horizon equity risk premium.

**Exhibit 10.9:** Long-Horizon Equity Risk Premium Calculation (%)
1926–2016

| | Arithmetic Mean | | |
| --- | --- | --- | --- |
| | **Market Total Return** | **Risk-free Rate** | **Equity Risk Premium** |
| S&P 500 | 11.95 | 5.02 = | 6.94 |
| CRSP NYSE/NYSE MKT/NASDAQ Deciles 1-10 | 11.77 | 5.02 = | 6.75 |
| CRSP NYSE/NYSE MKT/NASDAQ Deciles 1-2 | 11.31 | 5.02 = | 6.30* |

* difference due to rounding

**Source of underlying data in both Exhibit 10.8 and 10.9:** (i) "IA SBBI US Large Stock TR USD Ext" series retrieved from the Morningstar *Direct* database. The "IA SBBI US Large Stock TR USD Ext" return series is essentially the S&P 500 index. The long-term, intermediate-term, and short-term risk-free series used are the "IA SBBI US LT Govt IR USD" series, the "IA SBBI US IT Govt IR USD" series, and the "IA SBBI US 30 Day TBill TR USD" series, respectively. All rights reserved. Used with permission. (ii) CRSP U.S. Stock Database and CRSP U.S. Indices Database © 2017 Center for Research in Security Prices (CRSP®), University of Chicago Booth School of Business. Used with permission. All rights reserved. Calculations performed by Duff & Phelps, LLC.

## The Market Benchmark and Firm Size

Although not restricted to the 500 largest companies, the S&P 500 is considered a large-cap index. The returns of the S&P 500 are cap-weighted. The larger companies in the index therefore receive the majority of the weight. The use of the "NYSE/NYSE MKT/NASDAQ Deciles 1–2" series results in an even purer large-cap index. However, if using a large-cap index to calculate the equity risk premium, an adjustment is usually needed to account for the different risk and return characteristics of small stocks. This was discussed further in Chapter 7 on the size premium.

## The Risk-Free Asset

The equity risk premium can be calculated for a variety of time horizons when given the choice of risk-free asset to be used in the calculation. Chapter 3 provides equity risk premium calculations for short-, intermediate-, and long-term horizons. The short-, intermediate-, and long-horizon equity risk premiums are calculated using the income return from a 30-day Treasury bill, a 5-year Treasury bond, and a 20-year Treasury bond, respectively.

## 20-Year vs. 30-Year Treasuries

Our methodology for estimating the long-horizon equity risk premium makes use of the income return on a 20-year Treasury bond; however, the Treasury stopped issuing 20-year bonds in 1986. The 30-year bond that the Treasury returned to issuing in 2006 is theoretically more correct when dealing with the long-term nature of business valuation, yet Ibbotson Associates instead creates a series of returns using bonds on the market with approximately 20 years to maturity. The reason for the use of a 20-year maturity bond is that 30-year Treasury securities have only been issued over the relatively recent past, starting in February of 1977, and were suspended from 2002 to 2006.

The same reason applies to why we do not use the 10-year Treasury bond – a long history of market data is not available for 10-year bonds. We have persisted in using a 20-year bond to keep the basis of the time series consistent.

## Income Return

Another point to keep in mind when calculating the equity risk premium is that the income return on the appropriate-horizon Treasury security, rather than the total return, is used in the calculation.

The total return comprises three return components: the income return, the capital appreciation return, and the reinvestment return. The income return is defined as the portion of the total return that results from a periodic cash flow or, in this case, the bond coupon payment. The capital appreciation return results from the price change of a bond over a specific period. Bond prices generally change in reaction to unexpected fluctuations in yields. Reinvestment return is the return on a given month's investment income when reinvested into the same asset class in the subsequent months of the year. The income return is thus used in the estimation of the equity risk premium because it represents the truly riskless portion of the return.

## Arithmetic vs. Geometric Mean

The equity risk premium data presented in this book are arithmetic average risk premiums as opposed to geometric average risk premiums. The arithmetic average equity risk premium can be demonstrated to be most appropriate when discounting future cash flows. For use as the expected equity risk premium in either the CAPM or the building-block approach, the arithmetic mean or the simple difference of the arithmetic means of stock market returns and riskless rates is the relevant number. This is because both the CAPM and the building-block approach are additive models, in which the cost of capital is the sum of its parts. The geometric average is more appropriate for reporting past performance because it represents the compound average return.

## Appropriate Historical Period

The equity risk premium can be estimated using any historical time period. For the U.S., market data exist at least as far back as the late 1800s. Therefore, it is possible to estimate the equity risk premium using data that covers roughly the past 125 years.

Our equity risk premium covers 1926 to the present. The original data source for the time series comprising the equity risk premium is the Center for Research in Security Prices. CRSP chose to begin its analysis of market returns with 1926 for two main reasons. CRSP determined that 1926 was approximately when quality financial data became available. They also made a conscious effort to include the period of extreme market volatility from the late 1920s and early 1930s; 1926 was chosen because it includes one full business cycle of data before the market crash of 1929.

Implicit in using history to forecast the future is the assumption that investors' expectations for future outcomes conform to past results. This method assumes that the price of taking on risk changes only slowly, if at all, over time. This "future equals the past" assumption is most applicable to a random time-series variable. A time-series variable is random if its value in one period is independent of its value in other periods.

## Choosing an Appropriate Historical Period

The estimate of the equity risk premium depends on the length of the data series studied. A proper estimate of the equity risk premium requires a data series long enough to give a reliable average without being unduly influenced by very good and very poor short-term returns. When calculated using a long data series, the historical equity risk premium is relatively stable. Furthermore, because an average of the realized equity risk premium is quite volatile when calculated using a short history, using a long series makes it less likely that the analyst can justify any number he or she wants. The magnitude of how shorter periods can affect the result will be explored later in this chapter.

Some analysts estimate the expected equity risk premium using a shorter, more recent period on the basis that recent events are more likely to be repeated in the near future; furthermore, they believe that the 1920s, 1930s, and 1940s contain too many unusual events. This view is suspect because all periods contain unusual events. Some of the most unusual events of the last 100 years took place quite recently, including the inflation of the late 1970s and early 1980s, the October 1987 stock market crash, the collapse of the high-yield bond market, the major contraction and consolidation of the thrift industry, the collapse of the Soviet Union, the development of the European Economic Community, the attacks of Sept. 11, 2001, and the more recent global financial crisis of 2008–2009.

It is even difficult for economists to predict the economic environment of the future. For example, if one were analyzing the stock market in 1987 before the crash, it would be statistically improbable to predict the impending short-term volatility without considering the stock market crash and market volatility of the 1929–1931 period.

Without an appreciation of the 1920s and 1930s, no one would believe that such events could happen. The 91-year period starting with 1926 represents what can happen: It includes high and low returns, volatile and quiet markets, war and peace, inflation and deflation, and prosperity and depression. Restricting attention to a shorter historical period underestimates the amount of change that could occur in a long future period. Finally, because historical event-types (not specific events) tend to repeat themselves, long-run capital market return studies can reveal a great deal about the future. Investors probably expect unusual events to occur from time to time, and their return expectations reflect this.

## A Look at the Historical Results

It is interesting to look at the realized returns and realized equity risk premium in the context of the above discussion. Exhibit 10.10 shows the average stock market return and the average (arithmetic mean) realized long-horizon equity risk premium over various historical periods. The exhibit shows that using a longer historical period provides a more stable estimate of the equity risk premium. The reason is that any unique period will not be weighted heavily in an average covering a longer historical period. It better represents the probability of these unique events occurring over a long period of time.

**Exhibit 10.10:** Stock Market Return and Equity Risk Premium Over Time (%)

| Length | Period Dates | Large-Cap Arithmetic Mean (%) | Long-horizon Equity Risk Premium (%) |
|--------|--------------|------------------------------|--------------------------------------|
| 91 | 1926–2016 | 11.95 | 6.94 |
| 90 | 1927–2016 | 11.96 | 6.92 |
| 80 | 1937–2016 | 11.82 | 6.56 |
| 70 | 1947–2016 | 12.53 | 6.86 |
| 60 | 1957–2016 | 11.38 | 5.19 |
| 50 | 1967–2016 | 11.56 | 4.92 |
| 40 | 1977–2016 | 12.36 | 5.68 |
| 30 | 1987–2016 | 11.61 | 6.07 |
| 20 | 1997–2016 | 9.39 | 4.92 |
| 15 | 2002–2016 | 8.38 | 4.44 |
| 10 | 2007–2016 | 8.76 | 5.32 |
| 5 | 2012–2016 | 15.08 | 12.38 |

Looking carefully at Exhibit 10.11 will clarify this point. The graph shows the realized equity risk premium for a series of periods through 2016, starting with 1926. In other words, the first value on the graph represents the average realized equity risk premium over the period 1926–2016. The next value on the graph represents the average realized equity risk premium over the period 1927–2016, and so on, with the last value representing the average over the most recent five years, 2012–2016.

**Exhibit 10.11:** Equity Risk Premium Using Different Starting Dates
Average Equity Risk Premium (%)
1926–2016

Concentrating on the left side of Exhibit 10.11, one notices that the realized equity risk premium, when measured over long periods, is relatively stable. In viewing the graph from left to right, moving from longer to shorter historical periods, one sees that the value of the realized equity risk premium begins to decline significantly. Why does this occur? The reason is that the severe bear market of 1973–1974 is receiving proportionately more weight in the shorter, more recent average. If you continue to follow the line to the right, however, you will also notice that when 1973 and 1974 fall out of the recent average, the realized equity risk premium jumps up by nearly 1.2 percentage points.

Additionally, use of recent historical periods for estimation purposes can lead to illogical conclusions. As seen in Exhibit 10.10, the bear market in the early 2000s and in 2008 has caused the realized equity risk premium in the shorter historical periods to be lower than the long-term average.

The impact of adding one additional year of data to a historical average is lessened the greater the initial period of measurement. Short-term averages can be affected considerably by one or more unique observations. On the other hand, long-term averages produce more stable results.

Some practitioners argue for a shorter historical period, such as 30 years, as a basis for the equity risk premium estimation. The logic for the use of a shorter period is that historical events and economic scenarios present before this time are unlikely to be repeated. Exhibit 10.12 shows the equity risk premium measured over rolling 30-year periods, and it appears from the graph that the premium has been trending downwards. The 30-year equity risk premium remained close to 4 percentage points for several years in the 1980s and 1990s. However, it has fallen and then risen in the most recent 30-year periods.

**Exhibit 10.12:** Equity Risk Premium Over Rolling 30-year Periods
Average Equity Risk Premium (%)
1926–2016

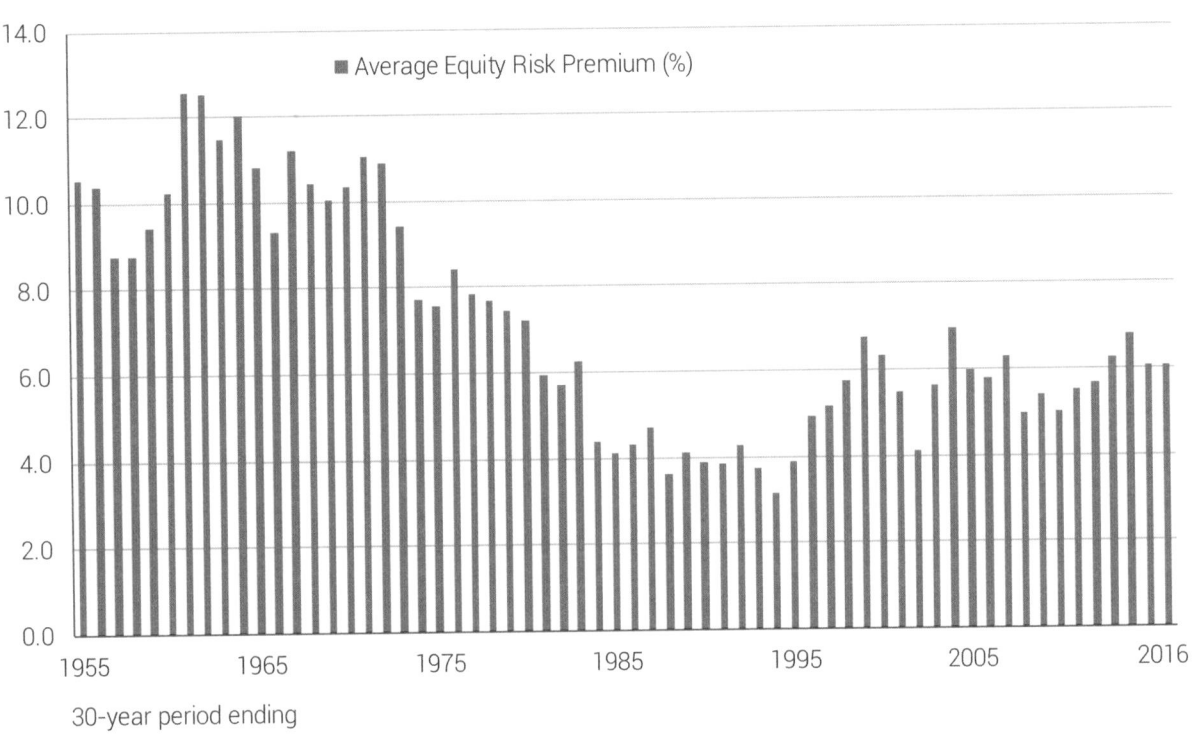

30-year period ending

The key to understanding this result lies again in the years 1973 and 1974. The oil embargo during this period had a tremendous effect on the market. The equity risk premium for these years alone was -21% and -34%, respectively. Periods that include the years 1973 and 1974 result in average equity risk premiums as low as 3.2 percentage points. The 2000s have also had an enormous effect on the equity risk premium.

It is difficult to justify such a large divergence in estimates of return over such a short period. This does not suggest, however, that the years 1973 and 1974 should be excluded from any estimate of the equity risk premium; rather, it emphasizes the importance of using a long historical period when measuring the equity risk premium in order to obtain a reliable average that is not overly influenced by short-term returns. The same holds true when analyzing the poor performance of the early 2000s and 2008.

## The Supply-Side Model

This section is based on the work by Roger G. Ibbotson and Peng Chen, who combined the first and second approaches to arrive at their forecast of the equity risk premium.[10.9] By proposing a new supply-side methodology, the Ibbotson-Chen study challenges current arguments that future returns on stocks over bonds will be negative or close to zero. The results affirm the relationship between the stock market and the overall economy.

Long-term expected equity returns can be forecasted by the use of supply-side models. The supply of stock market returns is generated by the productivity of the corporations in the real economy. Investors should not expect a much higher or lower return than that produced by the companies in the real economy. Thus, over the long run, equity returns should be close to the long-run supply estimate.

Earnings, dividends, and capital gains are supplied by corporate productivity. Exhibit 10.13 illustrates that earnings and dividends have historically grown in tandem with the overall economy (GDP per capita). However, GDP per capita did not outpace the stock market. This is primarily because the P/E ratio increased 2.20 times during the same period. So, assuming that the economy will continue to grow, all three should continue to grow as well.

**Exhibit 10.13:** Capital Gains, GDP Per Capita, Earnings, and Dividends
Index (Year-end 1925 = $1.00)
1926–2016

[10.9] Ibbotson, R.G., & Chen, P. 2003. "Long-Run Stock Returns: Participating in the Real Economy". *Financial Analysts Journal*, Vol. 59, No. 1, P. 88.

## Forward-Looking Earnings Model

Ibbotson and Chen forecast the equity risk premium through a supply-side model using historical data. They used an earnings model as the basis for their supply-side estimate. The earnings model breaks the historical equity return into four pieces, with only three historically being supplied by companies: inflation, income return, and growth in real earnings per share. The growth in the P/E ratio, the fourth piece, is a reflection of investors' changing prediction of future earnings growth. The past supply of corporate growth is forecasted to continue; however, a change in investors' predictions is not. P/E rose dramatically from 1980 through 2001 because people believed that corporate earnings were going to grow faster in the future. This growth in P/E drove a small portion of the rise in equity returns over the same period.

Exhibit 10.14 illustrates the price-to-earnings ratio from 1926 to 2016. The P/E ratio, using one year average earnings, was 10.23 at the beginning of 1926 and ended the year 2016 at 22.56, an average increase of 0.87% per year. The highest P/E was 136.69 recorded in 1932, while the lowest was 7.08 recorded in 1948. Ibbotson Associates revised the calculation of the P/E ratio from a one-year to a three-year average earnings for use in equity forecasting.

**Exhibit 10.14:** Large-cap Stocks P/E Ratio
1926–2016

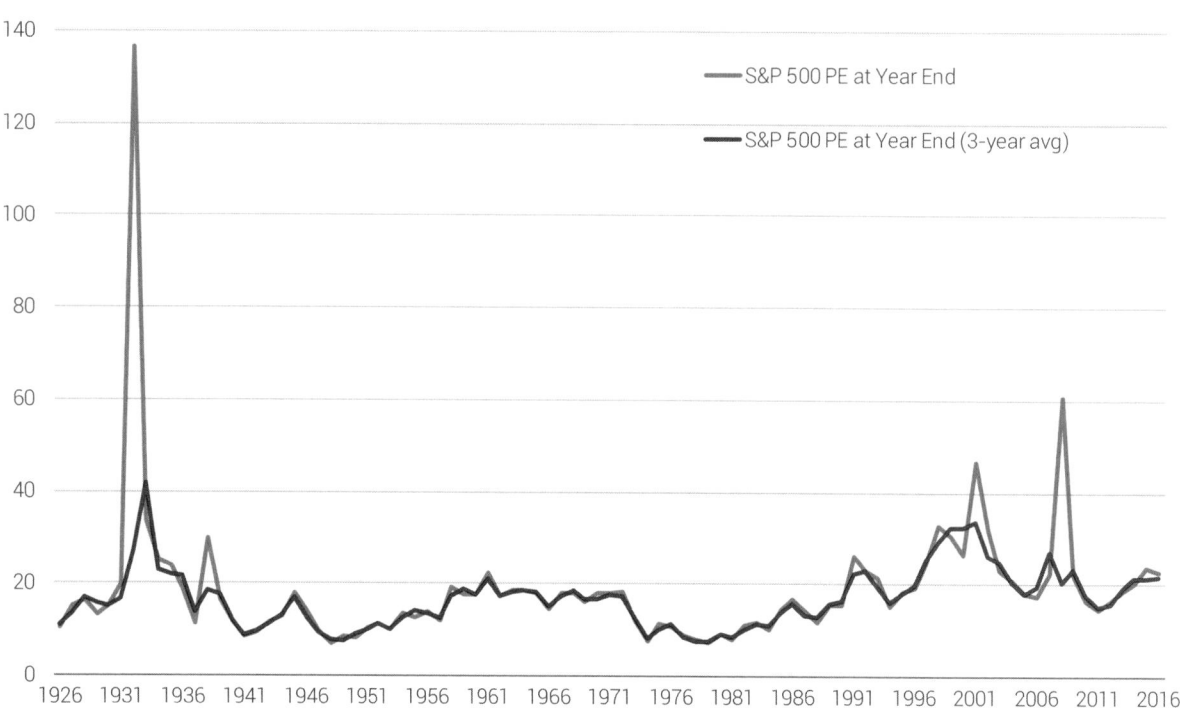

This is because reported earnings are affected not only by the long-term productivity, but also by one-time items that do not necessarily have the same consistent impact year after year. The three year average is more reflective of the long-term trend than the year-by-year numbers. The P/E ratio calculated using the three-year average of earnings had an increase of 0.79% per year.

The historical P/E growth factor, using three-year earnings, of 0.79% per year is subtracted from the equity forecast because it is not believed that P/E will continue to increase in the future. The market serves as the cue. The current P/E ratio is the market's best guess for the future of corporate earnings and there is no reason to believe, at this time, that the market will change its mind. Using this top-down approach, the geometric supply-side equity risk premium is 3.99%, which equates to an arithmetic supply-side equity risk premium of 5.97%.

Another approach in calculating the premium would be to add up the components that constitute the supply of equity return, excluding the P/E component. Thus, the supply of equity return only includes inflation, the growth in real earnings per share, and income return. This forward-looking earnings model calculates the long-term supply of U.S. equity returns to be 9.21%:

$$SR = \left[ (1 + CPI) \times (1 + g_{REPS}) - Inc + Rinv \right]$$

$$9.21\%^* = \left[ (1 + 2.90\%) \times (1 + 2.05\%) - 1 \right] + 3.98\% + 0.21\%$$

*difference due to rounding

Where:

| | | |
|---|---|---|
| $SR$ | = | The supply of the equity return |
| $CPI$ | = | Consumer Price Index (inflation) |
| $g_{REPS}$ | = | The growth in real earning per share |
| $Inc$ | = | The income return |
| $Rinv$ | = | The reinvestment return |

The equity risk premium, based on the supply-side earnings model, is calculated to be 3.99% on a geometric basis:

$$SERP = \frac{(1 + SR)}{(1 + CPI) \times (1 + RRf)} - 1$$

$$3.99\%^* = \frac{1 + 9.21\%}{(1 + 2.90\%) \times (1 + 2.03\%)} - 1$$

*difference due to rounding

Where:

| | | |
|---|---|---|
| $SERP$ | = | The supply-side equity risk premium |
| $SR$ | = | The supply of the equity return |
| $CPI$ | = | Consumer Price Index (inflation) |
| $RRf$ | = | The real risk-free rate |

Converting the geometric average into an arithmetic average results in an equity risk premium of 5.97%:[10.10]

$$R_A = R_G + \frac{\sigma^2}{2}$$

$$5.97\%^* = 3.99\% + \frac{19.88\%^2}{2}$$

$^*$ difference due to rounding

Where:

| | | |
|---|---|---|
| $R_A$ | = | The arithmetic average |
| $R_G$ | = | The geometric average |
| $\sigma$ | = | The standard deviation of equity returns |

Exhibit 10.15 presents the supply-side equity risk premium, on an arithmetic basis, beginning in 1926 and ending in each of the years from 2003 through 2016.[10.11]

---

[10.10] The 1926–2016 supply-side equity risk premia estimate (5.97%) is calculated by Duff & Phelps for the *2017 SBBI Yearbook* using (i) the same methodologies and (ii) the same data sources as were used in previous editions of this book.

[10.11] In last year's *2016 SBBI Yearbook*, Exhibit 10.15 included supply-side ERP estimates for the most recent 25 years, estimated using *refreshed* data inputs over the entire 1926–2015 time horizon. Starting with the *2017 SBBI Yearbook* (this book), this exhibit will only include the years for which supply-side ERP values were actually published in a hardcover book (instead of the most recent 25 years). As such, this exhibit will be made to match (i) the "as published" supply-side ERP values from the *2004–2013 SBBI Valuation Yearbooks* (see "Appendix C-1" in those books), and (ii) the "as published" values from the 2014 (and subsequent years) *Valuation Handbook – U.S. Guide to Cost of Capital* (see "Appendix 3" in those books).

**Exhibit 10.15:** Supply-side Equity Risk Premia over Time, as Published in (i) the *2004–2013 SBBI Valuation Yearbooks* and (ii) the 2014 (and subsequent years) *Valuation Handbook – U.S. Guide to Cost of Capital*

| Period Length (Years) | Period Dates | Source of Revised Values | Supply-Side Equity Risk Premia |
|---|---|---|---|
| 91 | 1926–2016 | *2017 Valuation Handbook – U.S. Guide to Cost of Capital* | 5.97 |
| 90 | 1926–2015 | *2016 Valuation Handbook – U.S. Guide to Cost of Capital* | 6.03 |
| 89 | 1926–2014 | *2015 Valuation Handbook – U.S. Guide to Cost of Capital* | 6.21 |
| 88 | 1926–2013 | *2014 Valuation Handbook – U.S. Guide to Cost of Capital* | 6.18 |
| 87 | 1926–2012 | *2013 SBBI Valuation Yearbook* | 6.11 |
| 86 | 1926–2011 | *2012 SBBI Valuation Yearbook* | 6.14 |
| 85 | 1926–2010 | *2011 SBBI Valuation Yearbook* | 5.99 |
| 84 | 1926–2009 | *2010 SBBI Valuation Yearbook* | 5.18 |
| 83 | 1926–2008 | *2009 SBBI Valuation Yearbook* | 5.73 |
| 82 | 1926–2007 | *2008 SBBI Valuation Yearbook* | 6.23 |
| 81 | 1926–2006 | *2007 SBBI Valuation Yearbook* | 6.35 |
| 80 | 1926–2005 | *2006 SBBI Valuation Yearbook* | 6.28 |
| 79 | 1926–2004 | *2005 SBBI Valuation Yearbook* | 6.14 |
| 78 | 1926–2003 | *2004 SBBI Valuation Yearbook* | 5.93 |

## Long-Term Market Predictions

The supply-side model estimates that stocks will continue to provide significant returns over the long run, averaging around 9.21% per year, assuming historical inflation rates. The equity risk premium, based on the top-down supply-side earnings model, is calculated to be 3.99% on a geometric basis and 5.97% on an arithmetic basis.

Ibbotson and Chen predict future increased earnings growth that will offset lower dividend yields. The fact that earnings will grow as dividend payouts shrink is in line with the Modigliani-Miller theorem, which here refers to the irrelevance over whether a firm pays a dividend or reinvests its returns.

The forecasts for the market are in line with both the historical supply measures of public corporations (i.e., earnings) and overall economic productivity (GDP per capita).

# Chapter 11
# Stock Market Returns From 1815–2016

Studies on the long-horizon predictability of stock returns, by necessity, require a database of return information that dates as far back as possible. Since the late 1970s, Ibbotson Associates has produced a broad set of historical returns on asset classes dating back to 1926. Researchers interested in the dynamics of the U.S. capital markets prior to 1926 had to rely on indexes of uneven quality. In 2000, Roger G. Ibbotson and William N. Goetzmann, professors of finance, and Liang Peng, then a Ph.D. candidate in finance, all at Yale School of Management, assembled a New York Stock Exchange database of annual returns for the periods prior to 1926. The first part of this chapter covers the sources and construction of this annual return database extending back to 1815.

The second part of this chapter introduces a new set of monthly real stock market total returns developed by Paul Kaplan, now director of research at Morningstar Canada. Kaplan used these new returns to demonstrate that the severity of the financial crisis of 2008 was not unique, but was merely the latest chapter in a long history of market meltdowns.

While we firmly believe that a 1926 starting date was approximately when quality financial data came into existence, our hope is that the continuing development of these data sets will allow modern researchers of pre-1926 stock returns, along with future researchers, to test a broad range of hypotheses about the U.S. capital markets as well as open up new areas for more accurate analysis.

## 1815–1925 Data Series Sources and Collection Methods

### Share Price Collection

End-of-month equity prices for companies listed on the New York Stock Exchange were hand-collected from three sources published January 1815 to December 1870. For the period 1871 through 1925, end-of-month NYSE stock prices were collected from the major New York newspapers. *The New York Shipping List,* later called *The New York Shipping and Commercial,* served as the "official" source for NYSE share price collection up until the early 1850s. In the mid-1850s, *The New York Shipping List* reported prices for fewer and fewer stocks. This led to the collection of price quotes from *The New York Herald* and *The New York Times.* While neither claimed to be the official list for the NYSE, the number of securities quoted by each far exceeded the number quoted by *The New York Shipping List.*

It is important to note that in instances where no transaction took place in December, the latest bid and ask prices were averaged to obtain a year-end price. In total, at least two prices from 664 companies were collected. From a low number of eight firms in 1815, the number of firms in the index reached a high point in May of 1883 with 114 listed firms.

Share prices for much of the period of analysis remained around $100. Exhibit 11.1 illustrates this point. The graph shows that the most common price of a share of stock was around $100. The distribution of stock prices is significantly skewed to the left with only a few trading above $200. Such a distribution suggests that management maintained a ceiling on stock prices by paying out most earnings as dividends. No reports of stock splits over the period of data were discovered.

**Exhibit 11.1:** Distribution of Raw Stock Prices 1815–1925

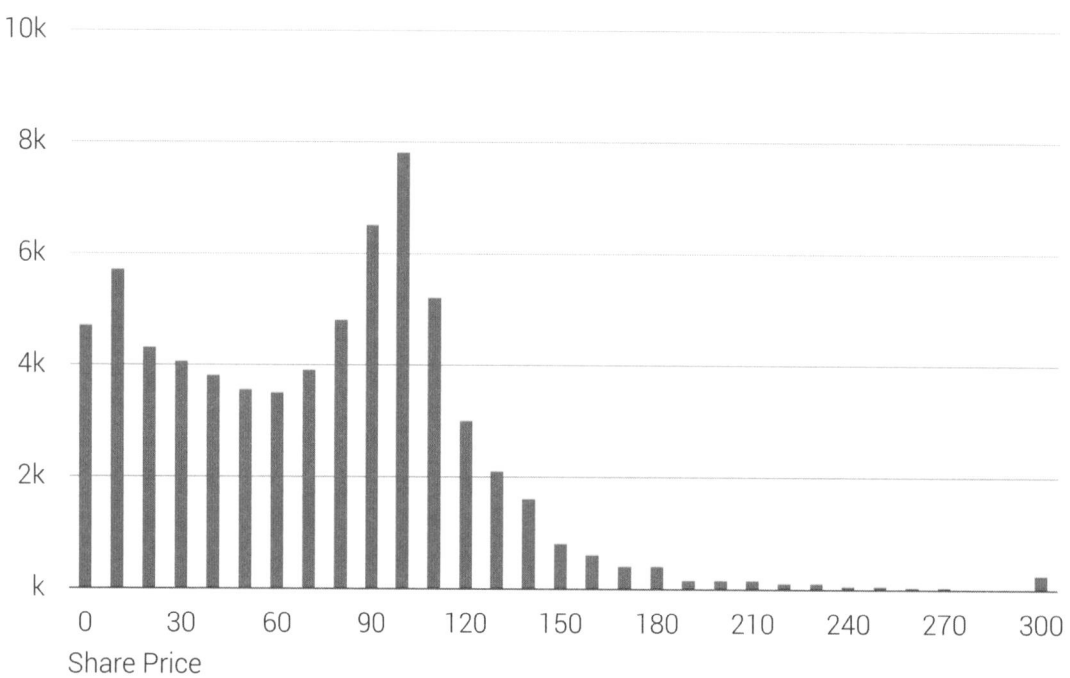

Share Price

### Dividend Collection

Dividend data was collected for the period 1825 to 1870 by identifying the semiannual dividend announcements for equity securities as reported in *The New York Shipping and Commercial*, *The Banker's Magazine*, *The New York Times*, and *The New York Herald*. From 1871 to 1925, aggregate dividend data from the Alfred Cowles[11.1] series was used. Whether the above publications reported dividends for all NYSE stocks is unknown. As a result, there is no way of knowing whether missing dividends meant that they were not paid or possibly not reported. Dividend records were collected for more than 500 stocks in the sample, and most stocks paid dividends semiannually.

Two approaches were used to estimate the income return for each year. The first approach, the low-dividend return estimate, consisted of the summation of all of the dividends paid in a given year by firms whose prices were observed in the preceding year. This number is then divided by the sum of the last available preceding year prices for those firms. The second approach, the high-dividend return estimate, focused solely on firms that paid regular dividends and for which price data was collected. The sample is restricted to firms that have two years of dividend payments (four

---

[11.1] Cowles, A. 1939. *Common Stock Indices* (Bloomington, Ind.: Principia Press).

semiannual dividends) and for which there was a price observation. Using the second approach, dividend yields tend to be quite high by modern standards.

It is important to note that when both a high- and a low-income return series were present, the average was computed. This holds true for the summary statistics table in this chapter as well as the graphs/tables presented throughout. Also, due to missing income return data for 1868, an average of the previous 43 years was computed.

## Price Index Estimation

### Index Calculation Concerns

When attempting to construct an index without having market capitalization data readily available, one is left with one of two options: an equal-weighted index or a price-weighted index. One key concern with an equal weighted index is the effect of a bid-ask bounce. Take for example an illiquid stock that trades at either $1.00 or $2.00 per share. When it rises in price from $1.00 to $2.00, it goes up by 100%. When it decreases in price from $2.00 to $1.00, it drops by 50%. Equally weighting these returns can produce a substantial upward bias. This led us to the construction of a price-weighted index.

### Calculation of the Price-Weighted Index

The procedure used for calculating the price-weighted index is rather simple. For each month, returns are calculated for all stocks that trade in two consecutive periods. These returns are weighted by the price at the beginning of the two periods.

The return of the price-weighted index closely approximates the return to a "buy-and-hold" portfolio over the period. Buy-and-hold portfolios are not sensitive to bid-ask bounce bias. We believe that the price-weighted index does a fairly good job of avoiding such an upward bias.

Companies were rather concentrated into specific industries. In 1815, the index was about evenly split between banks and insurance companies. Banks, transportation firms (primarily canals and railroads), and insurance companies made up the index by the 1850s. By the end of the sample period, the index was dominated by transport companies and other industrials.

## A Look at the Historical Results

It is important to note that there are a few missing months of data that create gaps in the analysis. The NYSE was closed from July 1914 to December 1914 due to World War I. This is obviously an institutional gap. There are additional gaps. We are missing returns for 1822, part of 1848 and 1849, parts of 1866, all of 1867 and January 1868. We do not know whether the records missing from the late 1860s are due to the Civil War, but the NYSE was certainly open at that time — among other things, it was the era of heated speculation and stock price manipulation by legendary financiers Gould, Fisk, and Drew. The number of available security records was quite lower after 1871. A change in the range of coverage by the financial press is the likely culprit for this. Further data collection efforts hopefully will allow these missing records to be filled in.

Exhibit 11.2 illustrates summary statistics of annual returns of large-cap stocks for three periods: (i) the pre-1926 data, (ii) the familiar 1926 to 2016 period, and (iii) a combination of the two.

## Price Return

It is interesting to note that the price-weighted index in Exhibit 11.2 has an annual geometric capital appreciation return from 1825 through 1925 of 1.3%. This number is significantly lower when compared to the 5.8% annual capital appreciation return experienced by large-cap stocks from 1926 to 2016. This once again alludes to the suggestion that dividend policies have evolved over the past two centuries, and that managers of old companies most likely paid out earnings to keep their stock prices lower. In today's financial world, capital appreciation is accepted as a substitute for dividend payments.

The rise in capital appreciation returns over the years is more evident when viewing returns on a 20-year rolling period basis, as Exhibit 11.3 demonstrates. In Exhibit 11.3, the annual geometric (i.e., compound) capital appreciation return is calculated for all 20-year periods ending 1844 through 2016. For example, the leftmost bar in Exhibit 11.3 represents the annual compound rate of return over the period 1825–1844, and the rightmost bar in Exhibit 11.3 represents the annual compound rate of return over the period 1997–2016.

## Income Return

Exhibit 11.2 also illustrates the summary statistics for the annual income return series. The higher income return of 5.9% in the earlier period (1825–1925), and the fact the many stocks traded near par, once again suggest that most companies paid out a large share of their profits rather than retaining them.

Exhibit 11.4 shows annual income returns for 1825 to 2016. In fact, when looking at the time distribution of dividend changes over the new period, dividend decreases were only slightly less common than increases, suggesting that managers may have been less averse to cutting dividends than they are today. Perhaps in the pre-income tax environment of the 19th century, investors had a preference for income return as opposed to capital appreciation.

**Exhibit 11.2:** Large-Cap Stocks: Summary Statistics of Annual Returns (%)
1825–2016

| 1825–1925 | Geometric Mean | Arithmetic Mean | Standard Deviation |
|---|---|---|---|
| Total Return | 7.3 | 8.4 | 16.3 |
| Income Return | 5.9 | 5.9 | 1.9 |
| Capital Appreciation | 1.3 | 2.5 | 16.1 |
| **1926–2016** | | | |
| Total Return | 10.0 | 12.0 | 19.9 |
| Income Return | 4.0 | 4.0 | 1.6 |
| Capital Appreciation | 5.8 | 7.7 | 19.2 |
| **1825–2016** | | | |
| Total Return | 8.6 | 10.1 | 18.1 |
| Income Return | 5.0 | 5.0 | 2.0 |
| Capital Appreciation | 3.4 | 5.0 | 17.8 |

**Exhibit 11.3:** Large-Cap Stocks: 20-year Rolling Annual Geometric Capital Appreciation Returns (%)
1825–2016

20-year period ending

**Exhibit 11.4:** Large-Cap Stocks Annual Income Returns (%)
1825–2016

## Total Return

Looking once again at the summary statistics in Exhibit 11.2, it is interesting to notice that the annual geometric total return for large-cap stocks from 1825 to 1925 was 7.3%. This is quite low when compared to the 10.0% annual geometric total return of the commonly used 1926 to 2016 period. For the entire period, the total return falls somewhere in between. The standard deviation of total return is also slightly lower for 1825 to 1925 (16.3%) versus 1926 to 2016 (19.9%).

Exhibit 11.5 shows year-by-year capital appreciation, average income, and total return from 1815 to 1925 of large-cap stocks. Exhibit 11.6 shows the growth of a dollar invested in large-cap stocks from the end of 1824 to the end of 2016.

**Exhibit 11.5:** Large-Cap Stock Annual Capital Appreciation, Income, and Total Returns (%) 1815–1925

| Year | Capital App | Avg. Income Return | Total Return | Year | Capital App | Avg. Income Return | Total Return |
|---|---|---|---|---|---|---|---|
| 1815 | -6.65 | – | – | 1871 | 3.34 | 5.86 | 9.2 |
| 1816 | -1.93 | – | – | 1872 | 0.5 | 6.33 | 6.83 |
| 1817 | 19.43 | – | – | 1873 | -17.7 | 6.51 | -11.19 |
| 1818 | -3.76 | – | – | 1874 | -5.77 | 7.47 | 1.7 |
| 1819 | -8.82 | – | – | 1875 | -4.72 | 6.61 | 1.89 |
| 1820 | 9.59 | – | – | 1876 | -13.31 | 6.86 | -6.45 |
| 1821 | 3.34 | – | – | 1877 | 1.74 | 5.31 | 7.05 |
| 1822 | -12.85 | – | – | 1878 | 10.5 | 5.54 | 16.04 |
| 1823 | 5.29 | – | – | 1879 | 51.31 | 5.8 | 57.1 |
| 1824 | 3.7 | – | – | 1880 | 19.83 | 5.28 | 25.12 |
| 1825 | -12.99 | 3.81 | -9.18 | 1881 | 1.88 | 5.48 | 7.36 |
| 1826 | -1.22 | 3.48 | 2.27 | 1882 | -9.54 | 5.32 | -4.22 |
| 1827 | -6.24 | 4.57 | -1.67 | 1883 | -15.04 | 5.65 | -9.39 |
| 1828 | -17.95 | 4.34 | -13.61 | 1884 | -24.28 | 5.81 | -18.47 |
| 1829 | 10.33 | 5.1 | 15.43 | 1885 | 45.32 | 5.53 | 50.85 |
| 1830 | 27.31 | 4.2 | 31.51 | 1886 | 12.46 | 4.23 | 16.69 |
| 1831 | -17.05 | 3.07 | -13.98 | 1887 | -12.13 | 4.43 | -7.7 |
| 1832 | 8.6 | 4.48 | 13.08 | 1888 | 2.09 | 4.36 | 6.45 |
| 1833 | -6.09 | 4.24 | -1.85 | 1889 | 4.49 | 4.28 | 8.77 |
| 1834 | 8.84 | 4.4 | 13.24 | 1890 | -10.72 | 4.14 | -6.59 |
| 1835 | -6.74 | 4.38 | -2.36 | 1891 | 2.95 | 4.78 | 7.74 |
| 1836 | 4.33 | 7.76 | 12.09 | 1892 | 10.35 | 4.44 | 14.79 |
| 1837 | -18.02 | 4.6 | -13.43 | 1893 | -16.86 | 4.54 | -12.33 |
| 1838 | 12.2 | 8.99 | 21.19 | 1894 | -2.82 | 4.76 | 1.94 |
| 1839 | -26.62 | 7.64 | -18.97 | 1895 | 2.14 | 4.42 | 6.56 |
| 1840 | 3.01 | 6.03 | 9.04 | 1896 | 0.69 | 4.17 | 4.86 |
| 1841 | -23.52 | 7.46 | -16.06 | 1897 | 14.15 | 4.27 | 18.41 |
| 1842 | 2.34 | 8.71 | 11.05 | 1898 | 12.17 | 4.21 | 16.38 |
| 1843 | 39.16 | 16.4 | 55.56 | 1899 | 4.17 | 3.72 | 7.89 |
| 1844 | 2.81 | 9.29 | 12.11 | 1900 | 17.99 | 4.98 | 22.97 |
| 1845 | -11.61 | 5.56 | -6.05 | 1901 | 24.6 | 4.66 | 29.26 |
| 1846 | 23.21 | 5.7 | 28.91 | 1902 | 5.29 | 4.15 | 9.44 |
| 1847 | 7.65 | 8.48 | 16.13 | 1903 | -12.88 | 4.35 | -8.53 |
| 1848 | 5.28 | 7.45 | 12.72 | 1904 | 14.94 | 4.72 | 19.66 |
| 1849 | 7.8 | 10.64 | 18.44 | 1905 | 6.67 | 4 | 10.67 |
| 1850 | 10.48 | 6.57 | 17.05 | 1906 | -1.09 | 4.19 | 3.1 |
| 1851 | -5.78 | 7.74 | 1.95 | 1907 | -26.26 | 4.47 | -21.79 |
| 1852 | 18.07 | 7.3 | 25.38 | 1908 | 28.47 | 6.09 | 34.56 |
| 1853 | -8.15 | 6.94 | -1.2 | 1909 | 18.12 | 4.87 | 22.99 |
| 1854 | -20.34 | 9.71 | -10.63 | 1910 | -15.5 | 4.56 | -10.94 |
| 1855 | 16.26 | 5.6 | 21.86 | 1911 | 2.17 | 5.19 | 7.37 |
| 1856 | 2.49 | 6.28 | 8.77 | 1912 | 0.03 | 5.27 | 5.3 |
| 1857 | -24.22 | 10.99 | -13.23 | 1913 | -14.44 | 5.12 | -9.32 |
| 1858 | 10.38 | 6.68 | 17.07 | 1914 | -8.47 | 5.22 | -3.25 |
| 1859 | -0.62 | 7.56 | 6.94 | 1915 | 15.88 | 5.85 | 21.73 |
| 1860 | -3.93 | 3.88 | -0.06 | 1916 | 1.29 | 5.91 | 7.19 |
| 1861 | -3.73 | 5.27 | 1.54 | 1917 | -23.48 | 7.04 | -16.44 |
| 1862 | 49.15 | 5.85 | 55 | 1918 | 2.88 | 8.38 | 11.27 |
| 1863 | 40.95 | 5.46 | 46.41 | 1919 | 9.38 | 6.71 | 16.09 |
| 1864 | 10.53 | 6.07 | 16.61 | 1920 | -20.74 | 5.72 | -15.02 |
| 1865 | -1.33 | 6.08 | 4.75 | 1921 | 4.26 | 6.75 | 11.02 |
| 1866 | 0.46 | 6.85 | 7.31 | 1922 | 19.74 | 6.98 | 26.72 |
| 1867 | -2.61 | 6.48 | 3.87 | 1923 | -2.13 | 6.04 | 3.9 |
| 1868 | 1.52 | 6.56 | 8.08 | 1924 | 19.34 | 6.43 | 25.77 |
| 1869 | -2.85 | 6.53 | 3.67 | 1925 | 23.22 | 5.91 | 29.12 |
| 1870 | -1.44 | 6.66 | 5.22 | | | | |

**Exhibit 11.6:** Large-Cap Stocks
Annual Capital Appreciation and Total Return Index Values (Year-end 1824 = $1.00)
1825–2016

| Year | Capital App | Total Return | Year | Capital App | Total Return | Year | Capital App | Total Return | Year | Capital App | Total Return | Year | Capital App | Total Return |
|---|---|---|---|---|---|---|---|---|---|---|---|---|---|---|
| 1824 | 1.00 | 1.00 | 1864 | 1.65 | 20.48 | 1904 | 3.32 | 322.65 | 1944 | 3.98 | 3,475.00 | 1984 | 50.07 | 253,307.97 |
| 1825 | 0.87 | 0.91 | 1865 | 1.63 | 21.45 | 1905 | 3.54 | 357.07 | 1945 | 5.20 | 4,741.16 | 1985 | 63.25 | 333,674.52 |
| 1826 | 0.86 | 0.93 | 1866 | 1.64 | 23.02 | 1906 | 3.51 | 368.14 | 1946 | 4.58 | 4,358.48 | 1986 | 72.50 | 395,955.17 |
| 1827 | 0.81 | 0.91 | 1867 | 1.59 | 23.91 | 1907 | 2.58 | 287.92 | 1947 | 4.58 | 4,607.26 | 1987 | 73.97 | 416,745.26 |
| 1828 | 0.66 | 0.79 | 1868 | 1.62 | 25.84 | 1908 | 3.32 | 387.42 | 1948 | 4.55 | 4,860.72 | 1988 | 83.14 | 485,959.49 |
| 1829 | 0.73 | 0.91 | 1869 | 1.57 | 26.79 | 1909 | 3.92 | 476.49 | 1949 | 5.02 | 5,774.17 | 1989 | 105.80 | 639,941.57 |
| 1830 | 0.93 | 1.20 | 1870 | 1.55 | 28.19 | 1910 | 3.31 | 424.37 | 1950 | 6.11 | 7,605.32 | 1990 | 98.86 | 620,076.25 |
| 1831 | 0.77 | 1.03 | 1871 | 1.60 | 30.78 | 1911 | 3.39 | 455.63 | 1951 | 7.12 | 9,431.85 | 1991 | 124.87 | 808,987.42 |
| 1832 | 0.84 | 1.16 | 1872 | 1.61 | 32.89 | 1912 | 3.39 | 479.76 | 1952 | 7.95 | 11,164.24 | 1992 | 130.44 | 870,627.40 |
| 1833 | 0.79 | 1.14 | 1873 | 1.32 | 29.21 | 1913 | 2.90 | 435.04 | 1953 | 7.43 | 11,053.81 | 1993 | 139.64 | 958,375.23 |
| 1834 | 0.86 | 1.29 | 1874 | 1.25 | 29.70 | 1914 | 2.65 | 420.90 | 1954 | 10.77 | 16,870.72 | 1994 | 137.49 | 971,030.23 |
| 1835 | 0.80 | 1.26 | 1875 | 1.19 | 30.26 | 1915 | 3.07 | 512.38 | 1955 | 13.62 | 22,195.57 | 1995 | 184.39 | 1,335,922.09 |
| 1836 | 0.83 | 1.42 | 1876 | 1.03 | 28.31 | 1916 | 3.11 | 549.24 | 1956 | 13.97 | 23,650.70 | 1996 | 221.76 | 1,642,651.99 |
| 1837 | 0.68 | 1.23 | 1877 | 1.05 | 30.31 | 1917 | 2.38 | 458.96 | 1957 | 11.97 | 21,100.58 | 1997 | 290.52 | 2,190,696.19 |
| 1838 | 0.77 | 1.49 | 1878 | 1.16 | 35.17 | 1918 | 2.45 | 510.66 | 1958 | 16.53 | 30,250.56 | 1998 | 368.00 | 2,816,766.01 |
| 1839 | 0.56 | 1.20 | 1879 | 1.75 | 55.25 | 1919 | 2.68 | 592.84 | 1959 | 17.93 | 33,867.05 | 1999 | 439.86 | 3,409,456.41 |
| 1840 | 0.58 | 1.31 | 1880 | 2.10 | 69.13 | 1920 | 2.13 | 503.78 | 1960 | 17.40 | 34,026.09 | 2000 | 395.26 | 3,099,046.19 |
| 1841 | 0.44 | 1.10 | 1881 | 2.14 | 74.22 | 1921 | 2.22 | 559.27 | 1961 | 21.42 | 43,175.19 | 2001 | 343.71 | 2,730,698.66 |
| 1842 | 0.45 | 1.22 | 1882 | 1.93 | 71.09 | 1922 | 2.65 | 708.68 | 1962 | 18.89 | 39,406.64 | 2002 | 263.40 | 2,127,200.44 |
| 1843 | 0.63 | 1.90 | 1883 | 1.64 | 64.41 | 1923 | 2.60 | 736.34 | 1963 | 22.46 | 48,391.83 | 2003 | 332.88 | 2,737,377.48 |
| 1844 | 0.65 | 2.14 | 1884 | 1.24 | 52.51 | 1924 | 3.10 | 926.09 | 1964 | 25.37 | 56,368.11 | 2004 | 362.82 | 3,035,260.01 |
| 1845 | 0.57 | 2.01 | 1885 | 1.81 | 79.21 | 1925 | 3.82 | 1,195.79 | 1965 | 27.67 | 63,386.53 | 2005 | 373.71 | 3,184,350.34 |
| 1846 | 0.71 | 2.59 | 1886 | 2.03 | 92.44 | 1926 | 4.04 | 1,334.79 | 1966 | 24.05 | 57,007.77 | 2006 | 424.60 | 3,687,295.26 |
| 1847 | 0.76 | 3.00 | 1887 | 1.79 | 85.32 | 1927 | 5.29 | 1,835.18 | 1967 | 28.88 | 70,675.76 | 2007 | 439.59 | 3,889,873.98 |
| 1848 | 0.80 | 3.39 | 1888 | 1.82 | 90.83 | 1928 | 7.29 | 2,635.47 | 1968 | 31.09 | 78,493.50 | 2008 | 270.41 | 2,450,704.90 |
| 1849 | 0.86 | 4.01 | 1889 | 1.91 | 98.79 | 1929 | 6.42 | 2,413.69 | 1969 | 27.56 | 71,817.97 | 2009 | 333.83 | 3,099,270.93 |
| 1850 | 0.95 | 4.69 | 1890 | 1.70 | 92.28 | 1930 | 4.59 | 1,812.75 | 1970 | 27.59 | 74,587.91 | 2010 | 376.50 | 3,566,125.53 |
| 1851 | 0.90 | 4.78 | 1891 | 1.75 | 99.42 | 1931 | 2.43 | 1,027.17 | 1971 | 30.52 | 85,254.24 | 2011 | 376.49 | 3,641,434.19 |
| 1852 | 1.06 | 6.00 | 1892 | 1.93 | 114.12 | 1932 | 2.06 | 943.02 | 1972 | 35.34 | 101,448.22 | 2012 | 426.96 | 4,224,190.76 |
| 1853 | 0.97 | 5.93 | 1893 | 1.61 | 100.06 | 1933 | 3.02 | 1,452.15 | 1973 | 29.20 | 86,546.70 | 2013 | 553.34 | 5,592,327.94 |
| 1854 | 0.78 | 5.30 | 1894 | 1.56 | 102.00 | 1934 | 2.84 | 1,431.20 | 1974 | 20.53 | 63,640.17 | 2014 | 616.37 | 6,357,834.47 |
| 1855 | 0.90 | 6.45 | 1895 | 1.60 | 108.69 | 1935 | 4.02 | 2,113.44 | 1975 | 27.00 | 87,332.47 | 2015 | 611.89 | 6,445,816.40 |
| 1856 | 0.92 | 7.02 | 1896 | 1.61 | 113.97 | 1936 | 5.14 | 2,830.34 | 1976 | 32.17 | 108,228.58 | 2016 | 670.23 | 7,216,731.07 |
| 1857 | 0.70 | 6.09 | 1897 | 1.83 | 134.96 | 1937 | 3.16 | 1,838.97 | 1977 | 28.47 | 100,481.60 | | | |
| 1858 | 0.77 | 7.13 | 1898 | 2.06 | 157.07 | 1938 | 3.95 | 2,411.29 | 1978 | 28.77 | 107,084.26 | | | |
| 1859 | 0.77 | 7.63 | 1899 | 2.14 | 169.45 | 1939 | 3.74 | 2,401.38 | 1979 | 32.31 | 127,012.20 | | | |
| 1860 | 0.74 | 7.62 | 1900 | 2.53 | 208.38 | 1940 | 3.17 | 2,166.42 | 1980 | 40.64 | 168,296.17 | | | |
| 1861 | 0.71 | 7.74 | 1901 | 3.15 | 269.34 | 1941 | 2.60 | 1,915.29 | 1981 | 36.69 | 160,010.53 | | | |
| 1862 | 1.06 | 12.00 | 1902 | 3.32 | 294.77 | 1942 | 2.92 | 2,304.86 | 1982 | 42.10 | 194,486.86 | | | |
| 1863 | 1.49 | 17.56 | 1903 | 2.89 | 269.63 | 1943 | 3.49 | 2,901.82 | 1983 | 49.38 | 238,354.20 | | | |

Those familiar with the history of U.S. capital markets as documented in this book may have found former Federal Reserve Chairman Alan Greenspan's characterization of the financial crisis of 2008 as a "once-in-a-century credit tsunami" quite surprising. A more appropriate statement may have been the one made by Leslie Rahl (founder of Capital Market Risk Advisors) more than a year before the crisis when she said, "We seem to have a once-in-a-lifetime crisis every three or four years."[11.2]

The contrast between Mr. Greenspan and Ms. Rahl's perspectives was the inspiration for an article in Morningstar magazine on the history of market meltdowns titled, "Déja Vu All Over Again."[11.3,11.4] In that article, Paul Kaplan (Ph.D., CFA, Director of Research, Morningstar Canada) illustrated the frequency and severity of the major drawdowns for various countries using time series of stock market total returns. For the U.S., Kaplan naturally used the SBBI large-cap stock index (the SBBI large-cap stock index is essentially the S&P 500 index). The results of the study clearly demonstrate that the severity of the financial crisis of 2008 was not unique, but was merely the latest chapter in a long history of market meltdowns.

In 2009, a team of researchers at Morningstar expanded the analysis into a complete study on global equity market history as a contribution to the CFA Institute's book on the global history of market crashes.[11.5] In this study, the research team used monthly *real* total returns that go back into history as far as was possible with reasonably reliable data.[11.6] The benefit of using real returns is to make meaningful return comparisons, as our study spans such a long period. The benefit of going further back in history is, of course, to give a longer-term and more robust historical perspective on market crashes, in terms of frequency, length, and magnitude.

To complete the study, the research team needed to find monthly data from before 1925 on both stock returns and inflation, and calculate real returns. Because there was no such return series in existence, they had to create one out of readable available data.

---

[11.2]   Wright, C. 2007. "Tail Tales." *CFA Institute Magazine*, March/April.

[11.3]   Morningstar magazine is a publication for financial advisors and institutional investors. For more information about Morningstar magazine, call 312-384-4000 or visit us online: global.morningstar.com/MorningstarMagazine.

[11.4]   Kaplan, P.D. 2009. "Déjà Vu All Over Again." *Morningstar Advisor magazine*, February/March, P. 28.

[11.5]   Kaplan, P.D., Idzorek, T., Gambera, M., et al. 2009. "The History and Economics of Stock Market Crashes." In *Insights into the Global Financial Crisis*. Edited by Laurence B. Siegel (Charlottesville, Va.: *CFA Institute*).

[11.6]   That is, returns that include the reinvestment of dividends and are adjusted for inflation.

Robert J. Shiller, 2013 Nobel laureate in economic sciences and the Sterling professor of economics at Yale University, posts monthly U.S. stock market returns and inflation data on his website that go back to 1871. Unfortunately, Shiller's stock data is based on monthly average prices rather than month-end prices. So the research team could use his inflation data, but not his stock market data. Separately, Roger Ibbotson and some colleagues created an annual price and total return series for the NYSE that goes back to 1815 (as previously discussed in this chapter).[11.7] However, annual returns are at too low a frequency to measure the largest drawdowns of the period, such as the large drop in the stock market during the panic of 1907. Fortunately, there is a book that contains daily price data on the Dow Jones Averages going back to 1885.[11.8] The team estimated the monthly price returns in the broader NYSE price index from the monthly price returns on the Dow Jones Averages and then interpolated the total returns by assuming that the dividend levels remained constant during each year.

The Morningstar team produced a time series of U.S. stock market real total returns from 1871 to 2016. The first 15 years of this history (1871–1885) is *annual* real total returns, and the remaining 131 years (1886–2016) is *monthly* total real returns, for a total of 146 years.[11.9]

**Truth in Numbers**

The significance of this data is in the lessons that we can learn from it. Over the entire 146-year period, the Real U.S. Stock Market Index grew from $1.00 to $13,234.01 in 1870 dollars. This is a compound annual real total return of 6.7%, almost the same as the post-1925 compound annual real total return of 6.9%. However, as Exhibit 11.7 shows, it was a very bumpy ride with a number of major drawdowns, some of which can be linked with specific economic and political events.

Exhibit 11.7 shows the growth of $1.00 invested in the U.S. stock market at the end of 1870 through December 2016 in real terms, along with a line that shows the highest level that the index had achieved as of that date (shown in gray).[11.10] Whenever this line is above the cumulative value line (shown in red), the index was below its most recent peak. The bigger the gap, the more severe the decline; the wider the gap, the longer the time until the index returned to its peak. Wherever this line coincides with the index line, the index was climbing to a new peak.

---

[11.7] Goetzmann, W.N., Ibbotson, R.G., & Peng, L. 2000. "A New Historical Database for the NYSE 1815 to 1925: Performance and Predictability." *Journal of Financial Markets*, Vol. 4, No. 1, P. 1.

[11.8] Pierce, P., ed. 1982. *The Dow Jones Averages 1885-1980* (Homewood, Ill.: Dow Jones-Irwin).

[11.9] The number of years and time horizon of the original Morningstar study was reported incorrectly in last year's *2016 SBBI Yearbook*. The description of the Morningstar study was described as "...a time series of U.S. stock market real total returns from 1870 to 2015. The first 15 years of this history (1870–1884) is *annual* real total returns, and the remaining 131 years (1875–2015) is *monthly* total real returns, for a total of 146 years." This should have read, "...a time series of U.S. stock market real total returns from 1871 to 2015. The first 15 years of this history (1871–1885) is *annual* real total returns, and the remaining 130 years (1886–2015) is *monthly* total real returns, for a total of 145 years."

[11.10] We have changed Exhibit 11.7 slightly in the *2017 SBBI Yearbook* (this book) compared to previous editions. The information in Exhibit 11.7 first appeared in the *2010 SBBI Yearbook*. In the 2010 through 2016 *SBBI Yearbooks*, the graph shown in Exhibit 11.7 included both *annual* returns (for years 1871–1885) and *monthly* data (for years 1886–present), which distorted the graph slightly. The 2017 version of Exhibit 11.7 includes only *monthly* data points over the entire 146-year time horizon (1871–2016). For each of the first 15 years of the graph (1871–1885), the annual returns were converted to "monthly" returns by calculating the single monthly return that could be applied to each standard 12-month period (January through December) that would result in an annual geometric annual return matching the original study. For example, for year 1871 the original Morningstar study reported an annual return of 7.56%. The single value calculated for the imputed "monthly" returns for January 1871 through December 1871 was therefore 0.609% $(1+7.56\%)^{(1/12)}$.

**Exhibit 11.7:** Large-cap Stocks: Real Return Index
1870–2016

Exhibit 11.8 lists all of the drawdowns that exceeded 20%. There were 17 such declines, including the most recent one that ended in May 2013. Not surprisingly, the largest of all market declines started just before the Crash of 1929 and did not recover until toward the end of 1936. The U.S. stock market lost 79% of its real value in less than three years, and took more than five years to recover. The most recent drawdown, the global financial crisis, was the second greatest decline, and it lasted nearly a decade. The combined effect of the crash of the Internet bubble in 2000 and the global financial crisis of 2008 caused the U.S. stock market to lose 54% of its real value from August of 2000 to February 2009.

The history of stock market drawdowns presented here shows that investing in stocks can be very risky, and that the most recent crisis was hardly a "once-in-a-century" event. We should use this long-run data to better gauge the potential risks and long-term rewards of investing in risky assets such as stocks.

**Exhibit 11.8:** Largest Declines in U.S. Stock Market History, in Real Total Return Terms 1870–2016

| Peak | Trough | Decline (%) | Recovery | Event(s) |
|------|--------|-------------|----------|----------|
| Aug. 1929 | May 1932 | 79.00 | Nov. 1936 | Crash of 1929, 1st part of Great Depression |
| Aug. 2000 | Feb. 2009 | 54.00 | May 2013 | Dot-com bubble burst (00-02), Crash 07-09 |
| Dec.1972 | Sep. 1974 | 51.86 | Dec, 1984 | Inflationary Bear Market, Vietnam, Watergate |
| Jun.1911 | Dec. 1920 | 50.96 | Dec. 1924 | WWI, Post-war Auto Bubble Burst |
| Feb.1937 | Mar. 1938 | 49.93 | Feb. 1945 | 2nd part of Great Depression, WWII |
| May 1946 | Feb. 1948 | 37.18 | Oct. 1950 | Post-war Bear Market |
| Nov.1968 | Jun. 1970 | 35.46 | Nov. 1972 | Start of Inflationary Bear Market |
| Jan.1906 | Oct. 1907 | 34.22 | Aug. 1908 | Panic of 1907 |
| Apr.1899 | Jun. 1900 | 30.41 | Mar. 1901 | Cornering of Northern Pacific Stock |
| Aug.1987 | Nov. 1987 | 30.16 | Jul. 1989 | Black Monday |
| Oct.1892 | Jul. 1893 | 27.32 | Mar. 1894 | Silver Agitation |
| Dec.1961 | Jun. 1962 | 22.80 | Apr. 1963 | Height of the Cold War, Cuban Missile Crisis |
| Nov.1886 | Mar. 1888 | 22.04 | May 1889 | Depression, Railroad Strikes |
| Apr.1903 | Sep. 1903 | 21.67 | Nov. 1904 | Rich Man's Panic |
| Aug.1897 | Mar. 1898 | 21.13 | Aug. 1898 | Outbreak of Boer War |
| Sep.1909 | Jul. 1910 | 20.55 | Feb. 1911 | Enforcement of the Sherman Anti-Trust Act |
| May1890 | Jul. 1891 | 20.11 | Feb. 1892 | Baring Brothers Crisis |

Traditional measures of risk, such as standard deviation, can underestimate the risk of drawdowns that are many standard deviations away from the mean (i.e., on the left tail of a distribution). We suggest that these traditional measures of risk be supplemented with measures that better capture the "fat-tailed" nature of the historical returns and drawdowns as presented here. A complete discussion of incorporating fat-tailed distributions into risk measures is found in Chapter 10.

## Reaching Back Beyond 1926

Collection efforts have yielded a comprehensive database of NYSE security prices for nearly the entire history of the exchange. The goal of these studies is to assemble a NYSE database for the period prior to 1926. The 1926 starting date was approximately when high-quality financial data came into existence. However, with a pre-1926 database assembled, researchers can expand their analyses back to the early 1800s. It is our hope that the long time series outlined in this chapter will lead to a better understanding of how the U.S. stock market evolved from an emerging market at the turn of the 18th century to the largest capital market in the world today.

## The Origin of Market Bubbles

As we've seen so far in this chapter, we have witnessed many asset-price bubbles. In each case, the story seems to be the same: Positive feedback and herding among speculative investors produce runaway prices until the deviation from equilibrium is so large that the market becomes unstable, creating a high probability (or an inevitability) of a crash. This raises the question, Do asset-price bubbles typically share the same characteristics and do all bubbles originate in the same manner? If yes, can we identify these factors beforehand and predict when a bubble will burst? James Xiong, head of quantitative research at Morningstar Investment Management, addressed these questions in an article in Morningstar magazine, "The Chinese Art Market and the Origin of Bubbles."[11.11] The rest of this section has been written by Xiong and adapted from his article.

## Herd Behavior and Market Bubbles

A number of studies have considered herd behavior as a possible explanation for the excessive volatility observed in financial markets.[11.12] The thinking behind this approach is simple: Interaction of market participants through herding can lead to large fluctuations in aggregate demand, leading to heavy tails in the distribution of returns. In the popular literature, "crowd effects" often have been associated with large fluctuations in market prices of financial assets.

Robert Shiller provides evidence to support his argument that "irrational exuberance" played a role in producing the ups and downs of the stock and real estate markets.[11.13] He listed 12 precipitating factors that gave rise to the booms in the stock markets and housing markets. These factors are amplified via feedback loops and naturally occurring Ponzi schemes, aided by the media, and can ultimately lead to market crashes.

Shiller also demonstrates that psychological factors, such as herd behavior and epidemics, are exerting important effects. For example, the influence of authority over people can be enormous; people are ready to believe authorities even when they plainly contradict matter-of-fact judgment.

---

[11.11]   Xiong, J. 2012. "The Chinese Art Market and the Origin of Bubbles." *Morningstar magazine*, August/September, P. 64.

[11.12]   See three references: Bannerjee, A.V. 1992. "A Simple Model of Herd Behavior," *Quarterly Journal of Economics*, Vol. 107, P. 797. Topol R. 1991. "Bubbles and Volatility of Stock Prices: Effect of Mimetic Contagion," *The Economic Journal*, Vol. 101, P. 786. Shiller, R.J. 1989. *Market Volatility* (Cambridge, Mass.: MIT Press).

[11.13]   Shiller, R.J. 2005. *Irrational Exuberance*, 2nd ed. (Princeton, N.J: Princeton University Press).

He cites many other factors, including that people tend to follow other people and choose not to exercise their own judgment about the market; also, most people purchase stocks based on direct interpersonal communication instead of independent research.

Rama Cont and Jean-Philippe Bouchaud[11.14] provide a mathematical model to link two well-known market phenomena: the heavy tails observed in the distribution of stock market returns on one hand and herding behavior in financial markets on the other hand.

### Predicting Crashes

In the 1990s, two groups of researchers[11.15] independently discovered an apparent tendency of stock prices to exhibit log-periodic power laws (LPPL) before a crash. The fundamental hypothesis of the model is that financial crashes are macroscopic examples of critical phenomena. A critical phenomenon indicates a highly correlated unstable market. In other words, as some traders say, "In a market crisis, all correlations jump to one."

Collective behaviors in people emerge through the forces of imitation, which leads to herding. Herding behavior of investors can result in a significant deviation of financial prices from their fundamental values. A speculative bubble, which is caused by a positive feedback investing style, also leads to a faster-than exponential power law growth of prices.[11.16] The competition between such nonlinear positive feedbacks and negative feedbacks contributes to nonlinear oscillations. For example, technical investors who have a positive view of the market bid up prices at the expense of fundamental investors, who view the market as ridiculously overpriced. The result is that a log-periodic modulation of the price accelerates up to the crash point. Exhibit 11.9 shows an example of what smooth log-periodic oscillations look like. Notice how the oscillations and the index value increase at an increasing rate as the date gets closer to the crash date.

Like any other models, the LPPL model has been debated and challenged, and we will not attempt to discuss that here. Major stock market crashes around the world, however, can be quantitatively explained by this model. These crashes include the 1929 crash, the 1987 crash, the crash of the Russian market in 1998, the 1990 Japanese Nikkei Index crash, several Hong Kong crashes in the 1990s, the Internet bubble crash in 2000, the financial crisis of 2008–2009, and more than 20 emerging-markets crashes. All of these market bubbles appeared to show the similar LPPL before they crashed.

---

[11.14] Cont, R. & Bouchaud, J.-P. 2000. "Herd Behavior and Aggregate Fluctuations in Financial Markets," *Journal of Macroeconomic Dynamics*, Vol. 4, P. 170.

[11.15] See two references: Sornette, D., Johansen, A. & Bouchaud, J.-P. 1996. "Stock Market Crashes, Precursors and Replicas," *J. Phys. I.* (France), Vol. 6, P. 167. Feigenbaum, J. & Freund, P.G.O. 1996. "Discrete Scale Invariance in Stock Markets Before Crashes," *International Journal of Modern Physics B*, Vol. 10, P. 3737.

[11.16] Sornette, D. 2003. *Why Stock Markets Crash: Critical Events in Complex Financial Systems* (Princeton, N.J.: Princeton University Press).

**Exhibit 11.9:** Example of Log-Periodic Oscillations

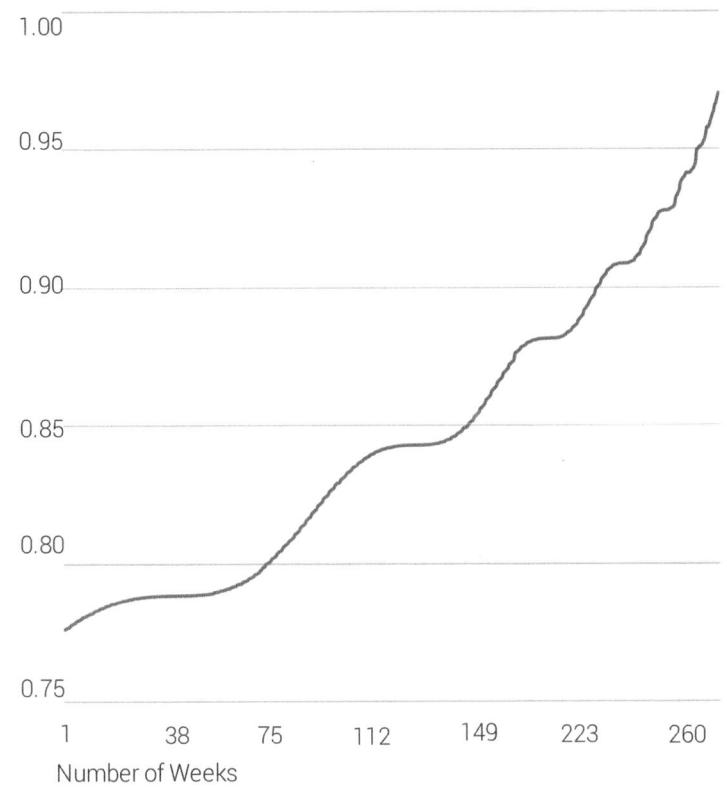

## Chinese Stock Market Crash of 2007

Greed and fear are rooted in human nature, so it is unlikely that people will change anytime soon. Greediness and fear also drive herding and positive feedbacks, so investors should expect these factors to remain in markets. The latest herding example occurred not too long ago, in 2007. In particular, we'll look at the Chinese stock market crash.

We use the Shanghai Stock Exchange Composite Index to represent the Chinese stock market. The Chinese stock market is dominated by individual investors, unlike equity markets in developed countries where a form of polarization exists between individual and institutional investors. Millions of new Chinese small investors flooded into the booming Chinese stock market from 2005 to 2007, indicating a strong herd behavior. The bubble burst in October 2007. A year after the crash, the Shanghai Composite had lost about 64% of its value, a classic example of herd behavior leading to a market crash in an emerging market.

Using the LPPL model, Exhibit 11.10 shows that the Chinese stock market crash in 2007 was predictable. The red line charts the price of the index. The gray line is the calculated curve based on the LPPL model. The out-of-sample test was made Sept. 25, 2007. The model predicted a crash date of Sept. 5, 2007. The actual crash started Oct. 17, 2007, 42 days later than predicted. The time-series price index is reasonably fitted by the log periodic power law model; we can see the precursors of log-periodic oscillations before the crash occurred.

**Exhibit 11.10:** Chinese Stock Market Crash Predicted by LPPL Model

## NASDAQ Crash of 2000

History provides many examples of bubbles driven by unrealistic expectations of future earnings. These types of bubbles do not just occur in developing markets. An example is the NASDAQ crash of 2000.

The NASDAQ Composite Index consists mainly of technology stocks, such as Internet, e-commerce, software, computer hardware, and telecommunications names. When the NASDAQ closed at a high of 5,049 on March 10, 2000, many stocks were trading at four-digit price/earnings (P/E) ratios.[11.17] Brocade Communications Systems, for example, had a P/E of 6,185; Trend Micro ADR had a P/E of 4,350; and SeaChange International traded at a P/E of 3,765. Investors in these companies seemed to be focusing on high future earnings, and seemingly did not focus on other economic fundamentals.

Exhibit 11.11 shows the bubble phase of the NASDAQ. The red line stands for the price of the index.

---

[11.17] The March 10, 2000 closing level (5,049) was an all-time high close for the NASDAQ at the time. The NASDAQ did not close above this price until over 14 years later, April 23, 2014, when the index closed at 5,056.06.

The gray line is based on the LPPL model. Again, the model clearly picked up the signals of an impending crash and almost perfectly predicted it.

**Exhibit 11.11:** NASDAQ Market Crash Predicted by LPPL Model

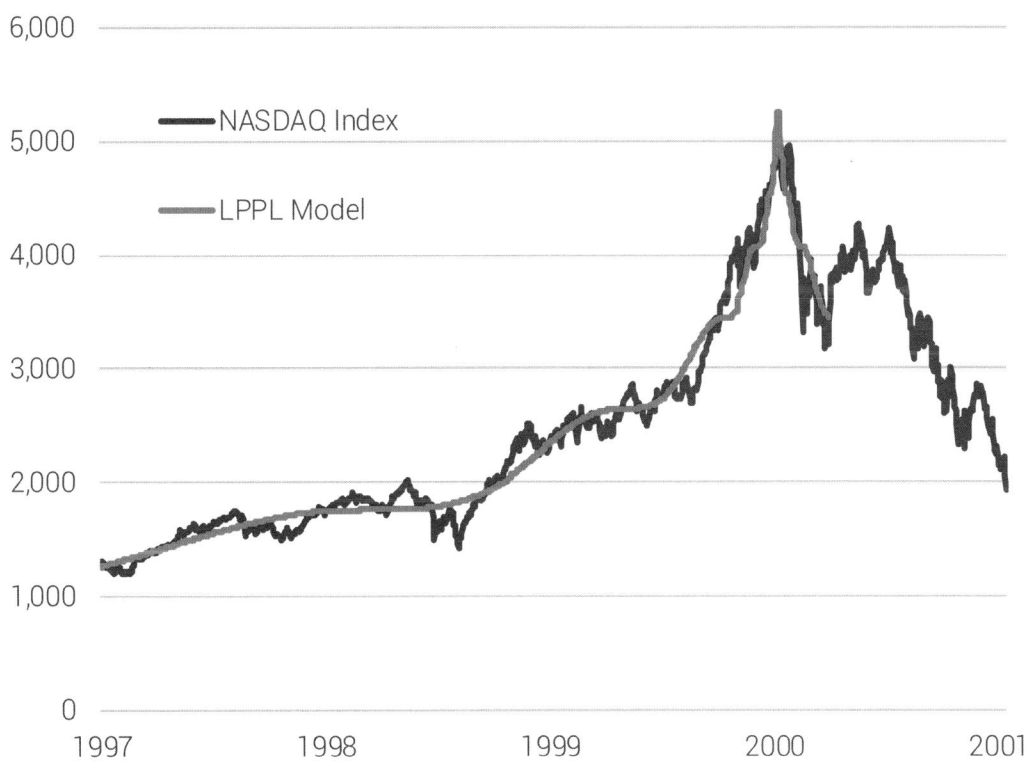

### The LPPL Model

The log-periodic power law can be quantified as:[11.18]

$$\ln\left[p(t)\right] = A - B\tau^m + C\tau^m \cos\left[\omega\ln(\tau) - \varphi\right]$$

Where:

| | | |
|---|---|---|
| $p(t)$ | = | price |
| $A$ | = | The peak value of $\ln(p(t))$ |
| $B$ | = | Base for the slope of the logarithmic curve |
| $\tau$ | = | $t_c - t$; which is the distance to the end of the bubble |
| $m$ | = | Growth accelerator; must be $0 < m < 1$ |
| $C$ | = | Base for the oscillations; must be $> 0$ |
| $\omega$ | = | Angular log-frequency |
| $\varphi$ | = | Arbitrary phase determining the unit of time |

---

[11.18] Sornette, D. 2003. *Why Stock Markets Crash: Critical Events in Complex Financial Systems* (Princeton, N.J.: Princeton University Press).

A geometric description for LPPL Model is that a log-periodic modulation of the ln(price) accelerates up to the crash point. The combination of $B$ with a value greater than 0 and $m$ with a value between 0 and 1 accelerates the slope so that it is faster than a typical exponential acceleration. The combination of $C$ and the cosine segment determines the amplitude and frequency of the log-periodic oscillations.

We used the Levenberg-Marquardt algorithm to predict the crash for the two bubbles (Exhibits 11.10 and 11.11 ). The fitted parameters are exhibited in Exhibit 11.12.

**Exhibit 11.12:** Best Fitted Parameters for the Shanghai Composite Index and the NASDAQ Index

| Stock | $t_c$ | $m$ | $w$ | $\phi$ | $A$ | $B$ | $C$ |
|---|---|---|---|---|---|---|---|
| Shanghai Index | September 2007 | 0.64 | 10.90 | 4.91 | 2.17 | 0.15 | -0.01 |
| NASDAQ Index | March 2000 | 0.45 | 6.45 | 5.26 | 8.61 | 0.88 | 0.06 |

## Power of the Model

We showed that two recent market bubbles displayed the same LPPL signature before they crashed. Our analyses indicate that all the bubbles have the same origins and similarly move toward a crash.

Positive feedback and herding produce runaway prices until the deviation from equilibrium is so large that the market is unstable and has a high probability to crash. When the stock price accelerates at a much faster rate than the exponential growth rate, the skyrocketing return will always come with an increased crash hazard rate.

Financial markets are complex systems. In such systems, a speculative bubble can easily be created through positive feedback. What is more challenging is that, as complex systems grow, two things happen.[11.19] These systems require exponentially greater amounts of energy to keep operating, and they become vastly more risky and prone to catastrophic failure.

---

[11.19] Rickards, J. 2011. *Currency Wars: The Making of the Next Global Crisis* (New York: Portfolio/Penguin).

# Chapter 12
# International Equity Investing[12.1]

International investment opportunities are growing rapidly, encouraged by open markets and the accelerating economies of many nations. The evidence in favor of taking a global approach to investing is plentiful, as are the possible rewards an investor can reap.

However, significant risks are present as well – risks that apply strictly to the international marketplace. In this chapter, we consider both the rewards and the risks associated with international investments.

### Construction of the International Indexes

Our analysis of international investing uses the indexes created by Morgan Stanley Capital International, Inc. The MSCI® indexes are designed to measure the performance of the developed and emerging stock markets, reflecting the performance of the entire range of stocks available to investors in each local market.[12.2]

---

[12.1] This chapter is an overview of international equity investing that is limited to analyzing the relative historical performance of international (versus U.S.) equities, and does not include the much-expanded analyses of (i) country-level risks and (ii) industry-level risks (on a global scale) that are the subject of the *Valuation Handbook – International Guide to Cost of Capital* and *Valuation Handbook – International Industry Cost of Capital*, respectively. These two resources are also authored by Duff & Phelps, and published by John Wiley & Sons, and are summarized as follows:

*Valuation Handbook – International Guide to Cost of Capital:* This annual book provides country-level equity risk premia (ERPs), relative volatility (RV) factors, and country risk premia (CRPs). This book can be used to estimate country-level cost of equity capital globally, for up to 188 countries, from the perspective of investors based in any one of up to 56 countries (depending on data availability). The *Valuation Handbook – International Guide to Cost of Capital* has been published since 2014, and is updated annually with data through December of the previous year and March of the current year. This book includes one optional semi-annual update with data through June and September.

*Valuation Handbook – International Industry Cost of Capital:* This annual book provides industry-level analyses for four global economic areas: (i) the "World," (ii) the European Union, (iii) the Eurozone, and (iv) the United Kingdom, each in three currencies: (i) the euro (€ or EUR), (ii) the British pound (£ or GBP), and (iii) the U.S. dollar ($ or USD). Industries in the book are identified by their Global Industry Classification Standard (GICS) code. This annual book includes industry level cost of capital estimates (cost of equity capital, cost of debt capital, and weighted average cost of capital, or WACC), plus detailed industry-level statistics for sales, market capitalization, capital structure, various levered and unlevered beta estimates (e.g., ordinary-least squares (OLS) beta, sum beta, peer group beta, downside beta, etc.), valuation (trading) multiples, financial and profitability ratios, equity returns, aggregate forward-looking earnings-per share (EPS) growth rates, etc. (depending on data availability). The *Valuation Handbook – International Industry Cost of Capital* has been published since 2015, and is updated annually with data through March 31 of the current year. This book includes one optional semi-annual update with data through September.

To learn more about cost of capital issues, and to ensure that you are using the most recent Duff & Phelps Recommended ERP, visit www.duffandphelps.com/CostofCapital. To purchase Duff & Phelps valuation data resources published by John Wiley & Sons, please go to: www.wiley.com/go/ValuationHandbooks.

[12.2] The international stock series presented throughout this chapter is represented by the MSCI EAFE® equities index. The MSCI EAFE Index is an equity index which captures large- and mid-cap representation across Developed Markets countries around the world, excluding the US and Canada. With 930 constituents, the index covers approximately 85% of the free float-adjusted market capitalization in each country. MSCI's line of products and services includes indexes, analytical models, data, real estate benchmarks and ESG research. MSCI serves 98 of the top 100 largest money managers, according to the most recent P&I ranking. For more information, visit us at www.msci.com.

From January 1970 to October 2001, inclusion in the MSCI indexes was based upon market capitalization. Stocks chosen for the indexes were required to have a target market representation of 60% of total market capitalization.

MSCI has enhanced its index construction methodology by free-float-adjusting constituents' index weights and increasing the target market representation. Target market representation is increased from 60% of total market capitalization to 85% of free-float-adjusted market cap within each industry group, within each country. MSCI defines the free float of a security as the proportion of shares outstanding that is deemed to be available for purchase in the public equity markets by international investors.

### Benefits of Investing Internationally

The arguments for investing internationally can be powerful. Examples may include (i) participation in the more than half of the world's investable assets that exist outside the U.S., (ii) growth potential, (iii) diversification, and (iv) potential improvement of the risk/reward trade-off.

### Investment Opportunities

An investor who chooses to ignore investment opportunities outside of the U.S. is missing out on a significant percentage of the investable developed stock market opportunities in the world. Exhibit 12.1 presents the relative size of international and domestic developed markets as of December 31, 2016. In 2016, the total developed world stock market capitalization was $33.7 trillion, with $13.4 trillion representing international stock market capitalization.[12.3]

**Exhibit 12.1:** MSCI World Stock Market Capitalization: $33.7 Trillion
December 31, 2016

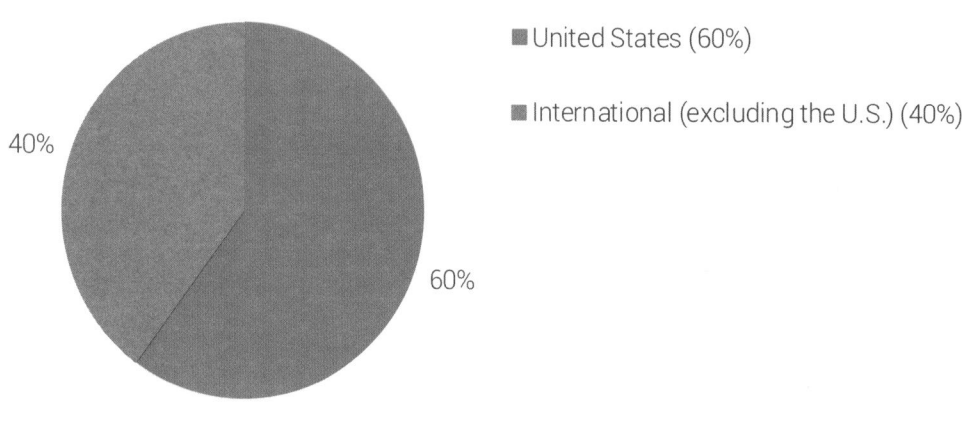

United States (60%)

International (excluding the U.S.) (40%)

40%

60%

---

[12.3]  Source: MSCI World Index Equity Fact Sheet. For more information, visit: MSCI.com.

## Growth Potential

Exhibit 12.2 depicts the growth of $1.00 invested in international stocks (as represented by the MSCI EAFE index), and U.S. large-cap stocks (i.e., the S&P 500 total return index), long-term government bonds, Treasury bills, and a hypothetical asset returning the inflation rate over the period from the end of 1969 to the end of 2016.[124] Of the asset classes shown in Exhibit 12.2, the $1.00 invested at year-end 1969 in U.S. large-cap stocks grew the most by year-end 2016 ($100.49), followed by International Stocks ($64.76).

In the time horizon over which this analysis is performed (1970–2016), international stocks generally outperformed U.S. large-cap stocks from 1970 through the late 1990s, but in more recent years U.S. large-cap stocks have generally outperformed international stocks.

To illustrate this seeming reversal of relative performance in more recent years, consider that a $1.00 investment at year-end 1969 in U.S. large-cap stocks would have grown to $18.60 by end of 1995, but the same dollar invested in international stocks would have grown to $24.83. However, a $1.00 investment at year-end 1995 in U.S. large-cap stocks would have grown to $5.40 by the end of 2016 (21 years), but the same dollar invested in international stocks would have grown to only $2.61.

**Exhibit 12.2:** Global Investing
Index (Year-end 1969 = $1.00)
1970–2016

---

[124]  In this chapter, the "U.S." series used are the same "SBBI" series used throughout the rest of this book. "U.S." is added to these series' names in this chapter only to differentiate them from the MSCI EAFE equities index, which is used to represent "international" equities in this chapter.

The effects of the 2008 financial crisis are apparent in Exhibit 12.2. In 2008, U.S. large-cap stocks fell 37.0% and international stocks fell 43.1%. In the eight-year period after 2008, both U.S. large-cap stocks and international stocks have recovered, with U.S. large-cap stocks producing a 14.5% annual return, significantly outperforming international stocks, which produced an annual return of 7.4%.

An additional perspective of the relative returns of U.S. large-cap stocks and international stocks is provided in Exhibit 12.3, which shows the performance of international and U.S. large-cap stocks over rolling 10-year holding periods ending 1979 through 2016.

International stocks outperformed in each of the 10-year periods ending 1979 through 1994, but U.S. large-cap stocks outperformed International stocks in 16 out of the 22 10-year periods ending 1995 through 2016, sometimes quite significantly.

**Exhibit 12.3:** U.S. Large-Cap Stocks and International Stocks, 10-Year Holding Period Annual Total Returns (%)
1970–2016

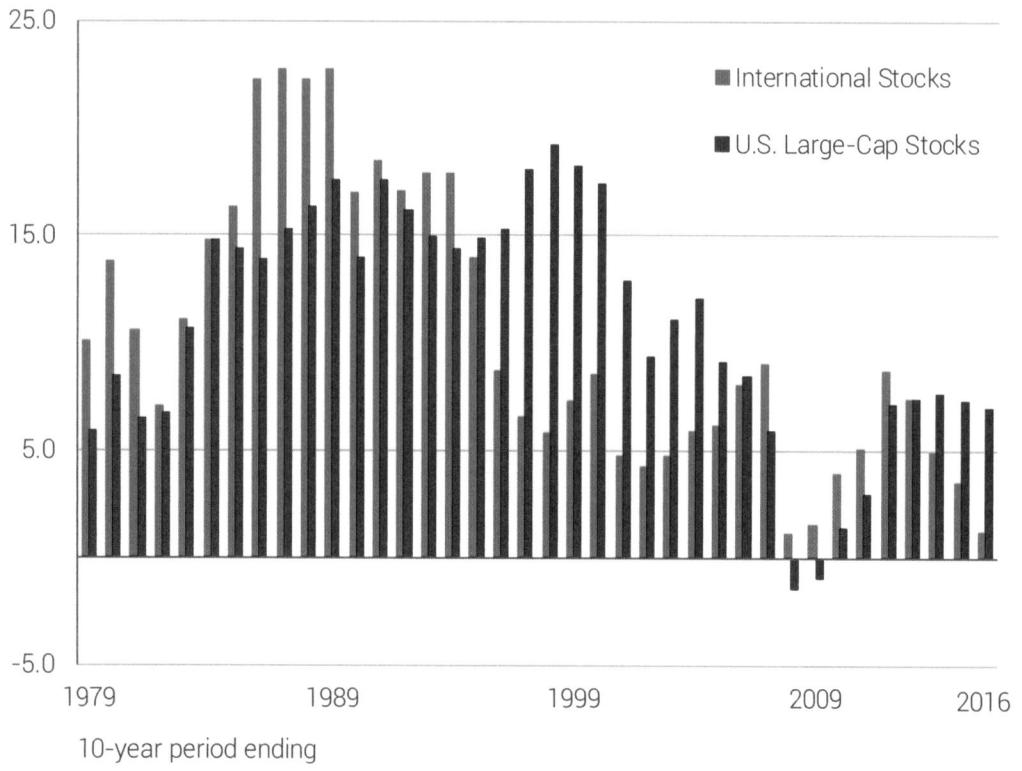

Just as U.S. stock prices fluctuate from one period to the next, prices of international stocks are subject to significant gains and declines. However, past returns from international stocks have fluctuated even more so than the returns of U.S. stocks. Annual ranges of returns provide an indication of the historical volatility (risk) experienced by investments in various markets.

Exhibit 12.4 illustrates the range of annual returns for U.S. large-cap stocks and international stocks, as well as European and Pacific regional equity composites, over the period 1970 through 2016. Although all of the composites have similar compound returns over the period, the three international composites exhibit greater volatility than the U.S. composite. All investments have the potential of dramatic ups and downs; however, a long-term approach to investing may help reduce the pain of volatility.

**Exhibit 12.4:** Global Stock Market Returns: Annual Ranges of Returns (%)
1970–2016

### Diversification

Diversification can be another important benefit of international investing. By spreading risks among foreign and U.S. stocks, investors can potentially lower overall investment risk and/or improve investment returns. Fluctuations may occur at different times for different markets, and if growth is slow in one country, global investing provides a means of possibly participating in stronger market returns elsewhere. Investing abroad may help an investor balance such fluctuations. Because it is almost impossible to forecast which markets will be top performers in any given year, it can be very valuable to be invested in a portfolio diversified across several countries.

Exhibit 12.5 depicts the growth of $1.00 invested at year-end 1969 in U.S. large-cap stocks, European, and Pacific stocks as well as a "global diversification portfolio" that is comprised of an equally weighted mix of the U.S. large-cap stocks, European, and Pacific stocks. Notice that the U.S. large-cap stocks index was the top performer, followed (in order of performance) by the global diversification portfolio, Europe, and Pacific indexes at the end of the 47-year period.

**Exhibit 12.5:** Benefits of Global Diversification
Index (Year-end 1969 = $1.00)
1970–2016

Large-Cap Stocks ($100.49 YE16)

Global Diversification Portfolio ($96.25 YE16)

European Stocks ($79.76 YE16)

Pacific Stocks ($60.89 YE16)

The cross-correlation coefficient between two series, covered in Chapter 6, measures the extent to which they are linearly related. The correlation coefficient measures the sensitivity of returns on one asset class or portfolio to the returns of another.

Exhibit 12.6 examines the 60-month rolling period correlation between international and U.S. large-cap stocks. Exhibit 12.6 illustrates the recent rise in cross-correlation between the two, suggesting that the benefit of diversification has suffered in recent years. The maximum benefit to an investor would have come in the 60-month period ending July 1987, where the cross-correlation was 0.26. The least amount of diversification benefit would have come in the 60-month period ending February 2013, where the cross-correlation was 0.93. The monthly average over the entire period was 0.63.

**Exhibit 12.6:** Rolling 60-Month Correlations: U.S. Large-Cap Stocks and International Stocks 1970–2016

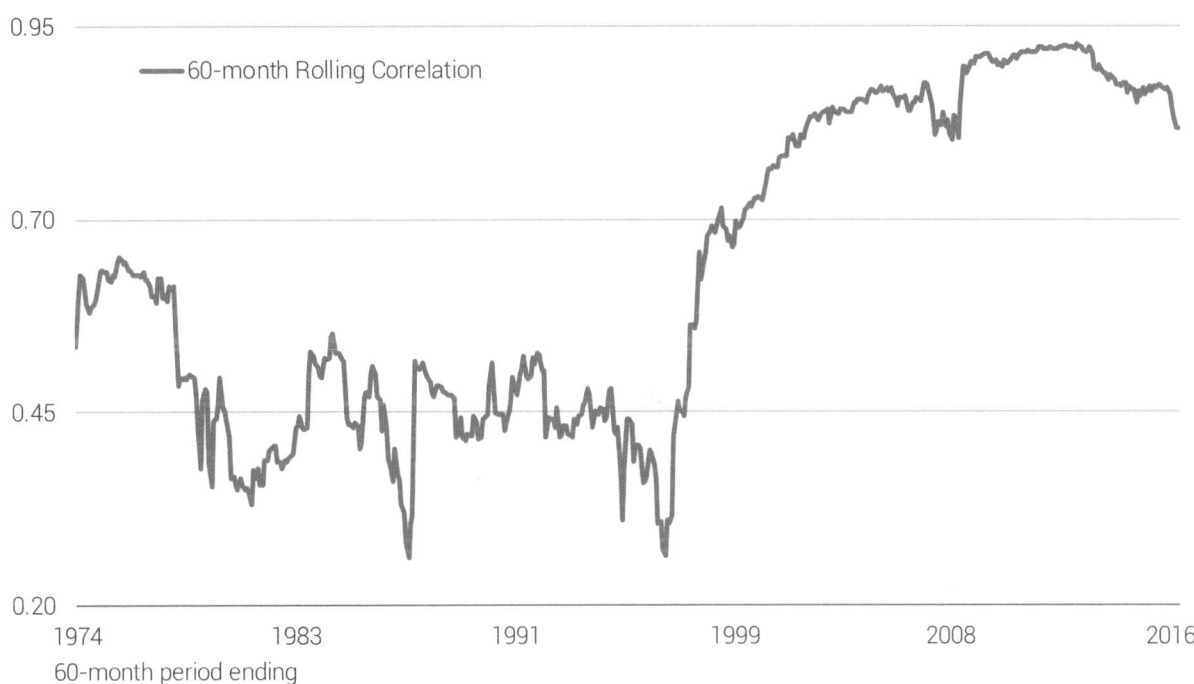

60-month period ending

As discussed previously in regard to REITs (see Chapter 2), diversification is "spreading a portfolio over many investments to avoid excessive exposure to any one source of risk."[12.5] Put simply, diversification is "not putting all your eggs in one basket." Diversification offers the potential of higher returns for the same level of risk, or lower risk for the same level of return.

A low correlation between assets in a portfolio allows for the possibility of an increase in returns without a corresponding increase in risk, or alternatively, a reduction in risk without a corresponding decrease in return.

---

[12.5]  Cara Griffith, "Practical Tax Considerations for Working with REITs," State Tax Notes (October 31, 2011): 315–320, quoting Jennifer Weiss: 316. In 2009, the IRS issued guidance that indicates that the distributions may be in the form of cash or stock in certain instances.

## Risks Typically Associated With International Investment[12.6]

The risks associated with international investing can largely be characterized as *financial, economic,* or *political.* Many of these are the types of risks associated with investing in general – the possibility of loan default, the possibility of delayed payments of suppliers' credits, the possibility of inefficiencies brought about by the work of complying with unfamiliar (or burdensome) regulation, unexpected increases in taxes and transaction fees, differences in information availability, and liquidity issues, to name just a few. Some risks, however, are typically associated more with global investing – currency risk, lack of good accounting information, poorly developed legal systems, and even expropriation, government instability, or war.

### Financial Risks

Financial risks typically entail an issue that is specifically money-centric (e.g., loan default, inability to easily repatriate profits to the home country, etc.). Among these types of risks, currency risk is probably the most familiar. Currency risk is the *financial* risk that exchange rates (the value of one currency versus another) will change unexpectedly.

For example, when a French investor invests in Brazil, he or she must first convert Euros into the local currency, in this case the Brazilian Real (BRL). The returns that the French investor experiences in local currency terms are identical to the returns that a Brazilian investor would experience, but the French investor faces an additional risk in the form of currency risk when returns are "brought home" and must be converted back to Euros.[12.7]

Expected changes in exchange rates can often be hedged. However, even when currency hedging is used, exchange rate risk often remains. To the extent the Euro unexpectedly *increases* in value versus the Real (i.e., the Euro appreciates against the Real), the French investor is able to purchase fewer Euros for each Real he realized in the Brazilian investment when returns from the investment are repatriated, and his return is thus *diminished.*[12.8,12.9]

Conversely, to the extent the Euro unexpectedly *decreases* in value versus the Real (i.e., the Euro depreciates against the Real), the French investor is able to purchase more Euros for each Real he realized in the Brazilian investment when returns from the investment are repatriated, and his return is thus *enhanced.*

---

[12.6]  The following section is largely excerpted from the *2016 Valuation Handbook – International Guide to Cost of Capital*, Chapter 1, "International Cost of Capital – Overview." To purchase Duff & Phelps valuation International and U.S. data resources published by John Wiley & Sons, please go to: www.wiley.com/go/ValuationHandbooks.

[12.7]  For this example, we assume that the French and local investor are both subject to the same regulations, taxes, and local risks when investing in the same local asset.

[12.8]  We say "unexpectedly" for a reason. If the investor had been able to predict (at the time of investing) the precise exchange rate at which he/she would be repatriating his/her returns, these "expected" changes to the exchange rate would have been reflected in the expected cash flows of the investment at inception.

[12.9]  For example, say the French investor had achieved a 10% return in local (Brazilian) terms on his investment in a given year, but the Euro had unexpectedly appreciated by 3% in value relative to the Real over the same period. When the returns are repatriated, the French investor's overall return is diminished to approximately 6.7% [(1+10%)*(1-3%)-1] in Euro terms. Conversely, had the Euro depreciated in value versus the Real by 3%, the repatriated returns would be enhanced to approximately 13.3% [(1+10%)*(1+3%)-1] in Euro terms.

For example, in 2007 Brazilian equities returned an astonishing 50% return in local terms (see Exhibit 12.7). Because the Euro *depreciated* against the Real in 2007, French-based investors in Brazilian stocks experienced an even *higher* return (62%) when they repatriated their returns and converted them to Euros. Similarly, in 2009 the Euro *depreciated* relative to the South African Rand (ZAR), and French-based investors realized higher returns in Euros once again versus the local South African investors. In a more recent example, U.S.-based investors investing in U.S. equities realized an approximate return of just 1.0% in 2015, but French investors making a similar investment in the U.S. realized an approximate 13% return when they repatriated their returns and converted them to Euros (the Euro *depreciated* against the U.S. Dollar in 2015, so the French investors could purchase *more* Euros with their Dollars when they repatriated their returns).

It is important to note that currency conversion effects can also work to *diminish* realized returns. For example, in 2015 Brazilian equities returned -12% in local terms. Because the Euro *appreciated* against the Real in 2015, French-based investors in Brazilian stocks experienced an even *lower* return (-34%) when they repatriated their returns and converted them to Euros.

**Exhibit 12.7:** Currency Conversion Effects

|  |  | Return in Local Terms | Return to French Investors (EUR) | Currency Conversion Effect |
|---|---|---|---|---|
| 2007 | Brazil (BRL) | 50% | 62% | 12% |
| 2009 | South Africa (ZAR) | 26% | 53% | 27% |
| 2015 | Japan (JPY) | 10% | 22% | 12% |
| 2015 | Switzerland (CHF) | 2% | 13% | 11% |
| 2015 | Brazil (BRL) | -12% | -34% | -22% |
| 2015 | Argentina (ARS) | 52% | 11% | -41% |
| 2015 | United States (USD) | 1% | 13% | 12% |

**Source of underlying data:** Morgan Stanley Capital International (MSCI) Brazil, South Africa, Japan, Switzerland, Brazil, and Argentina, gross return (GR) equity indices. For more information about MSCI, visit www.msci.com. The S&P 500 Index was used as the proxy for the United States equity market. For more information about S&P indices, visit http://us.spindices.com/indices/equity/sp-500. All data accessed through the Morningstar *Direct* database. For more information about Morningstar *Direct*, visit http://corporate.morningstar.com/.

A common misstep we often encounter is companies constructing forward-looking budgets or projection analyses in local currencies, and then converting these projections to the currency of the parent company using the spot rate.

This mistakenly assumes that the exchange rate will not change in the future. Projections, which are inherently forward-looking, need to embody expected currency conversion rates. We are interested in currency risks over the period of the projected net cash flows, not just in the spot market. Even then, these are merely estimates of future currency exchange rates and the actual exchange rate can vary from these estimates.

Does currency risk affect the cost of capital? One team of researchers found that emerging market exchange risks have a significant impact on risk premiums and are time varying (for countries in the sample). They found that exchange risks affect risk premiums as a separate risk factor and represent more than 50% of total risk premiums for investments in emerging market equities. The exchange risk from investments in emerging markets was found to even affect the risk premiums for investments in developed market equities.[12.10]

While exchange rate volatility appears to be partly systematic, researchers have found that despite not being a constant, the currency risk premium is small and seems to fluctuate around zero.[12.11] A recently published academic paper set out to study whether corporate managers should include foreign exchange risk premia in cost of equity estimations. The authors empirically estimated the differences between the cost of equity estimates of several risk-return models, including some models that have an explicit currency risk premia and others that do not. They found that adjusting for currency risk makes little difference, on average, in the cost of equity estimates, even for small firms and for firms with extreme currency exposure estimates. The authors concluded that, at a minimum, these results applied to U.S. companies, but future research would still have to be conducted for other countries.[12.12]

Rather than attempting to quantify and add a currency risk premium to the discount rate, using expected or forward exchange rates to translate projected cash flows into the home currency will inherently capture the currency risk, if any, priced by market participants.[12.13]

**Economic Risks**

Global investors may also be exposed to *economic* risks associated with international investing. These risks may include the volatility of a country's economy as reflected in the current (and expected) inflation rate, the current account balance as a percentage of goods and services, burdensome regulation, and labor rules, among others. In the current environment, an economic risk that has come to the forefront is the sovereign debt crisis. The recent economic and financial crisis in Greece, for example, has prompted many governments around the world to re-think their own fiscal policies, as it becomes evident that current debt loads are likely unsustainable in many of these countries.

---

[12.10] Francesca Carrieri, Vihang Errunza, and Basma Majerbi, "Does Emerging Market Exchange Risk Affect Global Equity Prices?" *Journal of Financial Quantitative Analysis* (September 2006): 511–540.

[12.11] Sercu, Piet (2009), *International Finance: Theory into Practice*, Princeton, NJ: Princeton University Press, Chapter 19.

[12.12] Krapl, A. and O'Brien, T. J. (2016), "Estimating Cost of Equity: Do You Need to Adjust for Foreign Exchange Risk?," *Journal of International Financial Management & Accounting*, 27: 5–25.

[12.13] This assumes that the valuation is being conducted in the home currency, by discounting projected cash flows denominated in the home currency, with a discount rate also denominated in home currency. Alternatively, the analyst can conduct the entire valuation in foreign currency terms (projected cash flows and discount rate are both in foreign currency terms), in which case the estimated value would be translated into the home currency using a spot exchange rate.

In Exhibit 12.8a, the 20 countries with the *overall* highest estimated government debt-to-GDP ratios are shown (regardless of the size of their economies), as of calendar year 2015. For example, the United States has a debt-to-GDP ratio of 106% (i.e., the United States' government debt is 6% *larger* than the United States' annual GDP), and Jordan has a debt-to-GDP ratio of 92% (i.e., Jordan's government debt is 8% *less* than Jordan's annual GDP)

In Exhibit 12.8b, the estimated government debt-to-GDP ratios for the 20 countries with the *largest* economies (as measured by GDP) are shown, also as of calendar year 2015. The rank of GDP size is shown in parentheses after each country's name. Saudi Arabia (with a ranking of "20") is the smallest GDP, and the United States (with a ranking of "1") is the largest GDP.

**Exhibit 12.8a:** 2015 Government Debt-to-GDP (in percent)

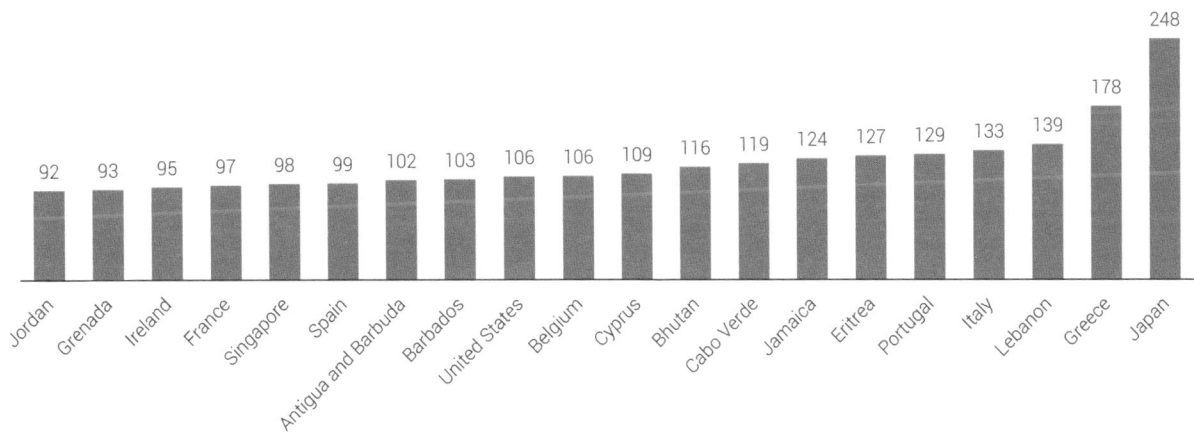

**Exhibit 12.8b:** 2015 Government Debt-to-GDP (in percent), 20 countries with largest GDP

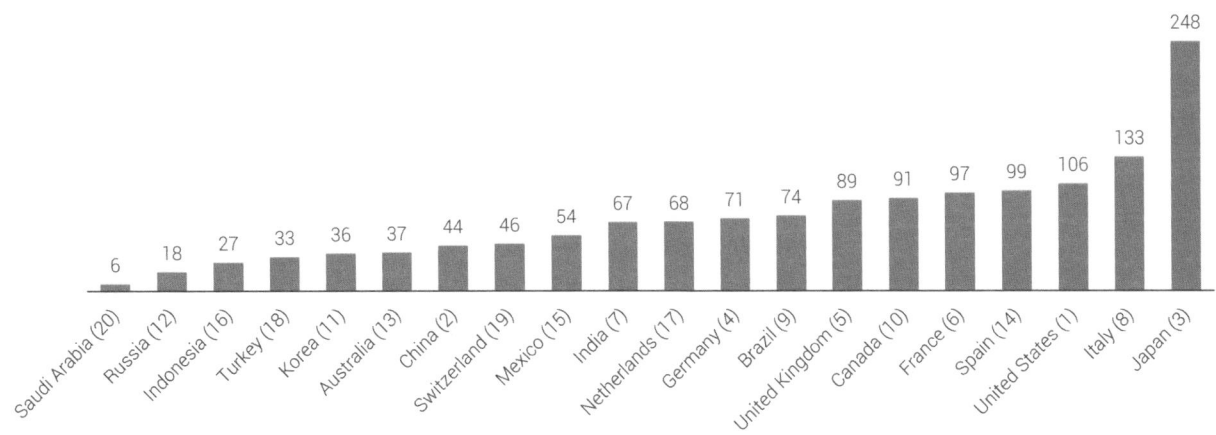

**Source of underlying data for Exhibit 12.8a and Exhibit 12.8b:** World Economic Outlook Database from the International Monetary Fund (IMF). For additional information, please visit: http://www.imf.org/external/pubs/ft/weo/2016/01/weodata/download.aspx.

There are costs that tend to go hand-in-hand with what might be considered unsustainable debt levels by governments. Lenders may demand a higher expected return to compensate them for additional default risk when investing not only in the country's sovereign debt, but also in businesses operating in those countries.

Governments may decide to increase the money supply in an effort to inflate their way out of debt. Ultimately, some governments may decide on outright currency devaluation or even a repudiation of debt (i.e., defaulting on their debt obligations). These risks are not entirely limited to less developed countries, but less developed countries may be more willing to resort to these extreme measures than developed countries.

## Political Risks

*Political* risks can include government instability, expropriation, bureaucratic inefficiency, corruption, and even war. A relatively recent example of the effects of political risk is Venezuela's expropriation of various foreign-owned oil, gas, and mining interests. These actions tend to reduce Venezuela's attractiveness to foreign investors, who will likely demand a significantly higher expected return in exchange for future investment in the country – in effect raising their cost of capital estimates for projects located in Venezuela.

Exhibit 12.9 summarizes some of the risks that investors may view as unique or country-specific.

**Exhibit 12.9:** Reasons Typically Cited for Adding a Country Risk Premium Adjustment

## Political Risks

- Repudiation of contracts by governments
- Expropriation of private investments in total or part through change in taxation
- Economic planning failures
- Political leadership and frequency of change
- External conflict
- Corruption in government
- Military in politics
- Organized religion in politics
- Lack of law-and-order tradition
- Racial and national tensions
- Civil war
- Poor quality of the bureaucracy
- Poorly developed legal system
- Political terrorism

## Financial Risks

- Currency volatility plus the inability to convert, hedge, or repatriate profits
- Loan default or unfavorable loan restructuring
- Delayed payment of suppliers' credits
- Losses from exchange controls
- Foreign trade collection experience

## Economic Risks

- Volatility of the economy
- Inflation: current and future expected
- Debt service as a percentage of exports of goods and services
- Current account balance of the country in which the subject company operates as a percentage of goods and services
- Parallel foreign exchange rate market indicators
- Labor issues

## International and Domestic Series Summary Data

Exhibit 12.10 shows summary statistics of annual total returns for various international regions and composites. The summary statistics presented are geometric mean, arithmetic mean, and standard deviation. From 1970 to 2016, the Pacific regional composite was the riskiest, with a standard deviation of 29.5 percentage points. The geometric mean of the Pacific regional composite was 9.1%, below that of EAFE and the World composite, which were considerably less risky.

**Exhibit 12.10:** Summary Statistics of Annual Returns (%) 1970–2016

| Series | Geometric Mean | Arithemtic Mean | Standard Deviation |
|--------|---------|---------|---------|
| EAFE | 9.3 | 11.5 | 21.9 |
| Pacific | 9.1 | 12.7 | 29.5 |
| Europe | 9.8 | 11.9 | 21.6 |
| World | 9.4 | 11.0 | 17.6 |
| Canada | 9.3 | 11.5 | 21.7 |
| U.S. | 10.3 | 11.7 | 17.1 |

Exhibit 12.11 shows the compound returns by decade for the various international regions and composites. The Pacific regional composite provided the highest compound annual rate of return in the first two decades but performed rather poorly in the 1990s as well as in the last two periods. The 1990s were a good time to be a domestic U.S. investor, with a compound annual rate of return of 18.2%.

**Exhibit 12.11:** Compound Annual Rates of Return by Decade, and the Most Recent 10 Years (%)

| Series | 1970s | 1980s | 1990s | 2000s | 2010s[*] | 2007–2016 |
|--------|-------|-------|-------|-------|-------|-----------|
| EAFE | 10.1 | 22.8 | 7.3 | 1.6 | 4.3 | 1.2 |
| Pacific | 14.8 | 26.4 | 0.5 | -0.3 | 5.3 | 1.8 |
| Europe | 8.6 | 18.5 | 14.5 | 2.4 | 3.9 | 1.0 |
| World | 7.0 | 19.9 | 12.0 | 0.2 | 8.8 | 4.4 |
| Canada | 11.0 | 11.7 | 9.8 | 9.2 | 2.9 | 3.2 |
| U.S. | 5.9 | 17.6 | 18.2 | -0.9 | 12.8 | 6.9 |

[*]Based on the period 2010–2016

Exhibit 12.12 shows the annualized monthly standard deviations by decade for the various international regions and composites. The World composite was the least risky in the 1970s, 1980s, and the 1990s. The Canadian index was the riskiest in the 2000s as well as the most recent decade. The domestic U.S. portfolio was the least risky in the most recent decade.

**Exhibit 12.12:** Annualized Monthly Standard Deviation by Decade (%)

| Series | 1970s | 1980s | 1990s | 2000s | 2010s* | 2007–2016 |
|--------|-------|-------|-------|-------|--------|-----------|
| EAFE   | 17.4  | 21.6  | 18.7  | 18.5  | 16.8   | 19.3      |
| Pacific | 22.1 | 26.6  | 24.8  | 18.2  | 15.2   | 17.4      |
| Europe | 18.6  | 21.5  | 16.8  | 20.4  | 18.9   | 21.2      |
| World  | 15.1  | 17.6  | 15.7  | 16.9  | 15.0   | 17.5      |
| Canada | 20.6  | 24.8  | 18.6  | 25.9  | 17.0   | 23.0      |
| U.S.   | 17.2  | 19.4  | 15.9  | 16.3  | 14.3   | 16.5      |

*Based on the period 2010–2016

Exhibit 12.13 presents annual cross-correlations and serial correlations from 1970 to 2016 for the six basic SBBI series and inflation as well as international stocks, as defined by the MSCI EAFE Index. International stocks, when compared to U.S. large-cap stocks, provided a higher cross-correlation than when compared to U.S. small-cap stocks. The serial correlation of international stocks suggests no pattern, and the return from period to period can best be interpreted as random or unpredictable.

**Exhibit 12.13:** Basic Series and International Stocks: Serial and Cross-Correlations of Historical Annual Returns
1970–2016

|  | International Stocks | Large-Cap Stocks | Small-Cap Stocks | Long-term Corp Bonds | Long-term Gov't Bonds | Inter-term Gov't Bonds | U.S. Treasury Bills | Inflation |
|---|---|---|---|---|---|---|---|---|
| International Stocks | 1.00 | | | | | | | |
| Large-Cap Stocks | 0.66 | 1.00 | | | | | | |
| Small-Cap Stocks | 0.50 | 0.72 | 1.00 | | | | | |
| Long-term Corp Bonds | 0.02 | 0.23 | 0.06 | 1.00 | | | | |
| Long-term Gov't Bonds | -0.13 | 0.02 | -0.15 | 0.89 | 1.00 | | | |
| Inter-term Gov't Bonds | -0.12 | 0.03 | -0.11 | 0.85 | 0.85 | 1.00 | | |
| U.S. Treasury Bills | 0.03 | 0.06 | 0.01 | 0.06 | 0.09 | 0.42 | 1.00 | |
| Inflation | -0.06 | -0.11 | 0.04 | -0.32 | -0.27 | -0.04 | 0.69 | 1.00 |
| Serial Correlation | 0.08 | 0.00 | 0.00 | -0.09 | -0.29 | 0.07 | 0.88 | 0.75 |

## Conclusion

Country risk is generally described as financial, economic, or political in nature. These rules may create incremental complexities when developing cost of capital estimates for a business, business ownership interest, security, or an intangible asset based outside of a mature market such as the United States.

International investments are no different from any other investment when it comes to information gathering. Investors interested in or already taking part in the international marketplace should learn as much as possible about the corresponding significant rewards and risks. International investments are not for everyone, and the most appropriate mix for an individual investor depends on his or her risk tolerance, investment goals, time horizon, and financial resources.[12.14]

---

[12.14] This chapter is an overview of international equity investing that is limited to analyzing the relative historical performance of international (versus U.S.) equities, and does not include the much-expanded analyses of (i) country-level risks and (ii) industry-level risks (on a global scale) that are the subject of the *Valuation Handbook – International Guide to Cost of Capital* and *Valuation Handbook – International Industry Cost of Capital*, respectively. These two resources are also written by Duff & Phelps, updated annually (optional intra-year updates are available) and published by John Wiley & Sons. For more information about other Duff & Phelps valuation data resources published by John Wiley & Sons, please go to: www.wiley.com/go/ValuationHandbooks.

# Appendix A
# Monthly and Annual Returns of Basic Series

**Basic Series**

**Real Riskless Rates of Return**

## Appendix A-1

Large-Capitalization Stocks: Total Return
From 1926 to 2016

| Year | Jan | Feb | Mar | Apr | May | Jun | Jul | Aug | Sep | Oct | Nov | Dec | Jan–Dec* |
|---|---|---|---|---|---|---|---|---|---|---|---|---|---|
| 1926 | 0.0000 | -0.0385 | -0.0575 | 0.0253 | 0.0179 | 0.0457 | 0.0479 | 0.0248 | 0.0252 | -0.0284 | 0.0347 | 0.0196 | 0.1162 |
| 1927 | -0.0193 | 0.0537 | 0.0087 | 0.0201 | 0.0607 | -0.0067 | 0.0670 | 0.0515 | 0.0450 | -0.0502 | 0.0721 | 0.0279 | 0.3749 |
| 1928 | -0.0040 | -0.0125 | 0.1101 | 0.0345 | 0.0197 | -0.0385 | 0.0141 | 0.0803 | 0.0259 | 0.0168 | 0.1292 | 0.0049 | 0.4361 |
| 1929 | 0.0583 | -0.0019 | -0.0012 | 0.0176 | -0.0362 | 0.1140 | 0.0471 | 0.1028 | -0.0476 | -0.1973 | -0.1246 | 0.0282 | -0.0842 |
| 1930 | 0.0639 | 0.0259 | 0.0812 | -0.0080 | -0.0096 | -0.1625 | 0.0386 | 0.0141 | -0.1282 | -0.0855 | -0.0089 | -0.0706 | -0.2490 |
| 1931 | 0.0502 | 0.1193 | -0.0675 | -0.0935 | -0.1279 | 0.1421 | -0.0722 | 0.0182 | -0.2973 | 0.0896 | -0.0798 | -0.1400 | -0.4334 |
| 1932 | -0.0271 | 0.0570 | -0.1158 | -0.1997 | -0.2196 | -0.0022 | 0.3815 | 0.3869 | -0.0346 | -0.1349 | -0.0417 | 0.0565 | -0.0819 |
| 1933 | 0.0087 | -0.1772 | 0.0353 | 0.4256 | 0.1683 | 0.1338 | -0.0862 | 0.1206 | -0.1118 | -0.0855 | 0.1127 | 0.0253 | 0.5399 |
| 1934 | 0.1069 | -0.0322 | 0.0000 | -0.0251 | -0.0736 | 0.0229 | -0.1132 | 0.0611 | -0.0033 | -0.0286 | 0.0942 | -0.0010 | -0.0144 |
| 1935 | -0.0411 | -0.0341 | -0.0286 | 0.0980 | 0.0409 | 0.0699 | 0.0850 | 0.0280 | 0.0256 | 0.0777 | 0.0474 | 0.0394 | 0.4767 |
| 1936 | 0.0670 | 0.0224 | 0.0268 | -0.0751 | 0.0545 | 0.0333 | 0.0701 | 0.0151 | 0.0031 | 0.0775 | 0.0134 | -0.0029 | 0.3392 |
| 1937 | 0.0390 | 0.0191 | -0.0077 | -0.0809 | -0.0024 | -0.0504 | 0.1045 | -0.0483 | -0.1403 | -0.0981 | -0.0866 | -0.0459 | -0.3503 |
| 1938 | 0.0152 | 0.0674 | -0.2487 | 0.1447 | -0.0330 | 0.2503 | 0.0744 | -0.0226 | 0.0166 | 0.0776 | -0.0273 | 0.0401 | 0.3112 |
| 1939 | -0.0674 | 0.0390 | -0.1339 | -0.0027 | 0.0733 | -0.0612 | 0.1105 | -0.0648 | 0.1673 | -0.0123 | -0.0398 | 0.0270 | -0.0041 |
| 1940 | -0.0336 | 0.0133 | 0.0124 | -0.0024 | -0.2289 | 0.0809 | 0.0341 | 0.0350 | 0.0123 | 0.0422 | -0.0316 | 0.0009 | -0.0978 |
| 1941 | -0.0463 | -0.0060 | 0.0071 | -0.0612 | 0.0183 | 0.0578 | 0.0579 | 0.0010 | -0.0068 | -0.0657 | -0.0284 | -0.0407 | -0.1159 |
| 1942 | 0.0161 | -0.0159 | -0.0652 | -0.0400 | 0.0796 | 0.0221 | 0.0337 | 0.0164 | 0.0290 | 0.0678 | -0.0021 | 0.0549 | 0.2034 |
| 1943 | 0.0737 | 0.0583 | 0.0545 | 0.0035 | 0.0552 | 0.0223 | -0.0526 | 0.0171 | 0.0263 | -0.0108 | -0.0654 | 0.0617 | 0.2590 |
| 1944 | 0.0171 | 0.0042 | 0.0195 | -0.0100 | 0.0505 | 0.0543 | -0.0193 | 0.0157 | -0.0008 | 0.0023 | 0.0133 | 0.0374 | 0.1975 |
| 1945 | 0.0158 | 0.0683 | -0.0441 | 0.0902 | 0.0195 | -0.0007 | -0.0180 | 0.0641 | 0.0438 | 0.0322 | 0.0396 | 0.0116 | 0.3644 |
| 1946 | 0.0714 | -0.0641 | 0.0480 | 0.0393 | 0.0288 | -0.0370 | -0.0239 | -0.0674 | -0.0997 | -0.0060 | -0.0027 | 0.0457 | -0.0807 |
| 1947 | 0.0255 | -0.0077 | -0.0149 | -0.0363 | 0.0014 | 0.0554 | 0.0381 | -0.0203 | -0.0111 | 0.0238 | -0.0175 | 0.0233 | 0.0571 |
| 1948 | -0.0379 | -0.0388 | 0.0793 | 0.0292 | 0.0879 | 0.0054 | -0.0508 | 0.0158 | -0.0276 | 0.0710 | -0.0961 | 0.0346 | 0.0550 |
| 1949 | 0.0039 | -0.0296 | 0.0328 | -0.0179 | -0.0258 | 0.0014 | 0.0650 | 0.0219 | 0.0263 | 0.0340 | 0.0175 | 0.0486 | 0.1879 |
| 1950 | 0.0197 | 0.0199 | 0.0070 | 0.0486 | 0.0509 | -0.0548 | 0.0119 | 0.0443 | 0.0592 | 0.0093 | 0.0169 | 0.0513 | 0.3171 |
| 1951 | 0.0637 | 0.0157 | -0.0156 | 0.0509 | -0.0299 | -0.0228 | 0.0711 | 0.0478 | 0.0013 | -0.0103 | 0.0096 | 0.0424 | 0.2402 |
| 1952 | 0.0181 | -0.0282 | 0.0503 | -0.0402 | 0.0343 | 0.0490 | 0.0196 | -0.0071 | -0.0176 | 0.0020 | 0.0571 | 0.0382 | 0.1837 |
| 1953 | -0.0049 | -0.0106 | -0.0212 | -0.0237 | 0.0077 | -0.0134 | 0.0273 | -0.0501 | 0.0034 | 0.0540 | 0.0204 | 0.0053 | -0.0099 |
| 1954 | 0.0536 | 0.0111 | 0.0325 | 0.0516 | 0.0418 | 0.0031 | 0.0589 | -0.0275 | 0.0851 | -0.0167 | 0.0909 | 0.0534 | 0.5262 |
| 1955 | 0.0197 | 0.0098 | -0.0030 | 0.0396 | 0.0055 | 0.0841 | 0.0622 | -0.0025 | 0.0130 | -0.0284 | 0.0827 | 0.0015 | 0.3156 |

*Compound annual return

# Appendix A-1

Large-Capitalization Stocks: Total Return
From 1926 to 2016

| Year | Jan | Feb | Mar | Apr | May | Jun | Jul | Aug | Sep | Oct | Nov | Dec | Year | Jan–Dec* |
|---|---|---|---|---|---|---|---|---|---|---|---|---|---|---|
| 1956 | -0.0347 | 0.0413 | 0.0710 | -0.0004 | -0.0593 | 0.0409 | 0.0530 | -0.0328 | -0.0440 | 0.0066 | -0.0050 | 0.0370 | 1956 | 0.0656 |
| 1957 | -0.0401 | -0.0264 | 0.0215 | 0.0388 | 0.0437 | 0.0004 | 0.0131 | -0.0505 | -0.0602 | -0.0302 | 0.0231 | -0.0395 | 1957 | -0.1078 |
| 1958 | 0.0445 | -0.0141 | 0.0328 | 0.0337 | 0.0212 | 0.0279 | 0.0449 | 0.0176 | 0.0501 | 0.0270 | 0.0284 | 0.0535 | 1958 | 0.4336 |
| 1959 | 0.0053 | 0.0049 | 0.0020 | 0.0402 | 0.0240 | -0.0022 | 0.0363 | -0.0102 | -0.0443 | 0.0128 | 0.0186 | 0.0292 | 1959 | 0.1196 |
| 1960 | -0.0700 | 0.0147 | -0.0123 | -0.0161 | 0.0326 | 0.0211 | -0.0234 | 0.0317 | -0.0590 | -0.0007 | 0.0465 | 0.0479 | 1960 | 0.0047 |
| 1961 | 0.0645 | 0.0319 | 0.0270 | 0.0051 | 0.0239 | -0.0275 | 0.0342 | 0.0243 | -0.0184 | 0.0298 | 0.0447 | 0.0046 | 1961 | 0.2689 |
| 1962 | -0.0366 | 0.0209 | -0.0046 | -0.0607 | -0.0811 | -0.0803 | 0.0652 | 0.0208 | -0.0465 | 0.0064 | 0.1086 | 0.0153 | 1962 | -0.0873 |
| 1963 | 0.0506 | -0.0239 | 0.0370 | 0.0500 | 0.0193 | -0.0188 | -0.0022 | 0.0535 | -0.0097 | 0.0339 | -0.0046 | 0.0262 | 1963 | 0.2280 |
| 1964 | 0.0283 | 0.0147 | 0.0165 | 0.0075 | 0.0162 | 0.0178 | 0.0195 | -0.0118 | 0.0301 | 0.0096 | 0.0005 | 0.0056 | 1964 | 0.1648 |
| 1965 | 0.0345 | 0.0031 | -0.0133 | 0.0356 | -0.0030 | -0.0473 | 0.0147 | 0.0272 | 0.0334 | 0.0289 | -0.0031 | 0.0106 | 1965 | 0.1245 |
| 1966 | 0.0062 | -0.0131 | -0.0205 | 0.0220 | -0.0492 | -0.0146 | -0.0120 | -0.0725 | -0.0053 | 0.0494 | 0.0095 | 0.0002 | 1966 | -0.1006 |
| 1967 | 0.0798 | 0.0072 | 0.0409 | 0.0437 | -0.0477 | 0.0190 | 0.0468 | -0.0070 | 0.0342 | -0.0276 | 0.0065 | 0.0278 | 1967 | 0.2398 |
| 1968 | -0.0425 | -0.0261 | 0.0110 | 0.0834 | 0.0161 | 0.0105 | -0.0172 | 0.0164 | 0.0400 | 0.0087 | 0.0531 | -0.0402 | 1968 | 0.1106 |
| 1969 | -0.0068 | -0.0426 | 0.0359 | 0.0229 | 0.0026 | -0.0542 | -0.0587 | 0.0454 | -0.0236 | 0.0459 | -0.0297 | -0.0177 | 1969 | -0.0850 |
| 1970 | -0.0743 | 0.0557 | 0.0044 | -0.0875 | -0.0578 | -0.0466 | 0.0769 | 0.0478 | 0.0362 | -0.0083 | 0.0506 | 0.0598 | 1970 | 0.0386 |
| 1971 | 0.0432 | 0.0117 | 0.0394 | 0.0389 | -0.0391 | 0.0033 | -0.0387 | 0.0388 | -0.0044 | -0.0391 | 0.0002 | 0.0888 | 1971 | 0.1430 |
| 1972 | 0.0206 | 0.0277 | 0.0083 | 0.0068 | 0.0197 | -0.0194 | 0.0048 | 0.0369 | -0.0025 | 0.0119 | 0.0481 | 0.0142 | 1972 | 0.1899 |
| 1973 | -0.0149 | -0.0352 | 0.0008 | -0.0383 | -0.0163 | -0.0040 | 0.0407 | -0.0341 | 0.0427 | 0.0017 | -0.1109 | 0.0198 | 1973 | -0.1469 |
| 1974 | -0.0072 | -0.0007 | -0.0205 | -0.0359 | -0.0302 | -0.0114 | -0.0742 | -0.0864 | -0.1152 | 0.1681 | -0.0489 | -0.0156 | 1974 | -0.2647 |
| 1975 | 0.1272 | 0.0638 | 0.0254 | 0.0510 | 0.0476 | 0.0477 | -0.0644 | -0.0176 | -0.0312 | 0.0653 | 0.0282 | -0.0081 | 1975 | 0.3723 |
| 1976 | 0.1217 | -0.0084 | 0.0337 | -0.0078 | -0.0111 | 0.0443 | -0.0048 | -0.0018 | 0.0258 | -0.0186 | -0.0041 | 0.0561 | 1976 | 0.2393 |
| 1977 | -0.0473 | -0.0182 | -0.0105 | 0.0042 | -0.0196 | 0.0494 | -0.0124 | -0.0172 | 0.0015 | -0.0389 | 0.0316 | 0.0075 | 1977 | -0.0716 |
| 1978 | -0.0574 | -0.0203 | 0.0294 | 0.0902 | 0.0092 | -0.0138 | 0.0583 | 0.0301 | -0.0032 | -0.0872 | 0.0215 | 0.0196 | 1978 | 0.0657 |
| 1979 | 0.0443 | -0.0321 | 0.0596 | 0.0094 | -0.0247 | 0.0435 | 0.0134 | 0.0577 | 0.0043 | -0.0640 | 0.0475 | 0.0214 | 1979 | 0.1861 |
| 1980 | 0.0622 | -0.0001 | -0.0972 | 0.0462 | 0.0515 | 0.0316 | 0.0696 | 0.0101 | 0.0294 | 0.0202 | 0.1065 | -0.0302 | 1980 | 0.3250 |
| 1981 | -0.0418 | 0.0174 | 0.0400 | -0.0193 | 0.0026 | -0.0063 | 0.0021 | -0.0577 | -0.0493 | 0.0540 | 0.0413 | -0.0256 | 1981 | -0.0492 |
| 1982 | -0.0131 | -0.0559 | -0.0052 | 0.0452 | -0.0341 | -0.0150 | -0.0178 | 0.1214 | 0.0125 | 0.1151 | 0.0404 | 0.0193 | 1982 | 0.2155 |
| 1983 | 0.0372 | 0.0229 | 0.0369 | 0.0788 | -0.0087 | 0.0389 | -0.0295 | 0.0150 | 0.0138 | -0.0116 | 0.0211 | -0.0052 | 1983 | 0.2256 |
| 1984 | -0.0056 | -0.0352 | 0.0173 | 0.0095 | -0.0554 | 0.0217 | -0.0124 | 0.1104 | 0.0002 | 0.0039 | -0.0112 | 0.0263 | 1984 | 0.0627 |
| 1985 | 0.0779 | 0.0122 | 0.0007 | -0.0009 | 0.0578 | 0.0157 | -0.0015 | -0.0085 | -0.0313 | 0.0462 | 0.0686 | 0.0484 | 1985 | 0.3173 |

*Compound annual return

## Appendix A-1

Large-Capitalization Stocks: Total Return
From 1926 to 2016

| Year | Jan | Feb | Mar | Apr | May | Jun | Jul | Aug | Sep | Oct | Nov | Dec | Year | Jan–Dec* |
|---|---|---|---|---|---|---|---|---|---|---|---|---|---|---|
| 1986 | 0.0056 | 0.0747 | 0.0558 | -0.0113 | 0.0532 | 0.0169 | -0.0559 | 0.0742 | -0.0827 | 0.0577 | 0.0243 | -0.0255 | 1986 | 0.1867 |
| 1987 | 0.1347 | 0.0395 | 0.0289 | -0.0089 | 0.0087 | 0.0505 | 0.0507 | 0.0373 | -0.0219 | -0.2154 | -0.0824 | 0.0761 | 1987 | 0.0525 |
| 1988 | 0.0421 | 0.0466 | -0.0309 | 0.0111 | 0.0086 | 0.0459 | -0.0038 | -0.0339 | 0.0426 | 0.0278 | -0.0143 | 0.0174 | 1988 | 0.1661 |
| 1989 | 0.0732 | -0.0249 | 0.0233 | 0.0519 | 0.0405 | -0.0057 | 0.0903 | 0.0195 | -0.0041 | -0.0232 | 0.0204 | 0.0240 | 1989 | 0.3169 |
| 1990 | -0.0671 | 0.0129 | 0.0265 | -0.0249 | 0.0975 | -0.0067 | -0.0032 | -0.0904 | -0.0487 | -0.0043 | 0.0646 | 0.0279 | 1990 | -0.0310 |
| 1991 | 0.0436 | 0.0715 | 0.0242 | 0.0024 | 0.0431 | -0.0458 | 0.0466 | 0.0237 | -0.0167 | 0.0134 | -0.0403 | 0.1144 | 1991 | 0.3047 |
| 1992 | -0.0186 | 0.0130 | -0.0194 | 0.0294 | 0.0049 | -0.0149 | 0.0409 | -0.0205 | 0.0118 | 0.0035 | 0.0341 | 0.0123 | 1992 | 0.0762 |
| 1993 | 0.0084 | 0.0136 | 0.0211 | -0.0242 | 0.0268 | 0.0029 | -0.0040 | 0.0379 | -0.0077 | 0.0207 | -0.0095 | 0.0121 | 1993 | 0.1008 |
| 1994 | 0.0340 | -0.0271 | -0.0436 | 0.0128 | 0.0164 | -0.0245 | 0.0328 | 0.0410 | -0.0245 | 0.0225 | -0.0364 | 0.0148 | 1994 | 0.0132 |
| 1995 | 0.0259 | 0.0390 | 0.0295 | 0.0294 | 0.0400 | 0.0232 | 0.0332 | 0.0025 | 0.0422 | -0.0036 | 0.0439 | 0.0193 | 1995 | 0.3758 |
| 1996 | 0.0340 | 0.0093 | 0.0096 | 0.0147 | 0.0258 | 0.0038 | -0.0442 | 0.0211 | 0.0563 | 0.0276 | 0.0756 | -0.0198 | 1996 | 0.2296 |
| 1997 | 0.0625 | 0.0078 | -0.0411 | 0.0597 | 0.0609 | 0.0448 | 0.0796 | -0.0560 | 0.0548 | -0.0334 | 0.0463 | 0.0172 | 1997 | 0.3336 |
| 1998 | 0.0111 | 0.0721 | 0.0512 | 0.0101 | -0.0172 | 0.0406 | -0.0106 | -0.1446 | 0.0641 | 0.0813 | 0.0606 | 0.0576 | 1998 | 0.2858 |
| 1999 | 0.0418 | -0.0311 | 0.0400 | 0.0387 | -0.0236 | 0.0555 | -0.0312 | -0.0049 | -0.0274 | 0.0633 | 0.0203 | 0.0589 | 1999 | 0.2104 |
| 2000 | -0.0502 | -0.0189 | 0.0978 | -0.0301 | -0.0205 | 0.0247 | -0.0156 | 0.0621 | -0.0528 | -0.0042 | -0.0788 | 0.0049 | 2000 | -0.0910 |
| 2001 | 0.0355 | -0.0912 | -0.0634 | 0.0777 | 0.0067 | -0.0243 | -0.0098 | -0.0626 | -0.0808 | 0.0191 | 0.0767 | 0.0088 | 2001 | -0.1189 |
| 2002 | -0.0146 | -0.0193 | 0.0376 | -0.0606 | -0.0074 | -0.0712 | -0.0780 | 0.0066 | -0.1087 | 0.0880 | 0.0589 | -0.0587 | 2002 | -0.2210 |
| 2003 | -0.0262 | -0.0150 | 0.0097 | 0.0824 | 0.0527 | 0.0128 | 0.0176 | 0.0195 | -0.0106 | 0.0566 | 0.0088 | 0.0524 | 2003 | 0.2868 |
| 2004 | 0.0184 | 0.0139 | -0.0151 | -0.0157 | 0.0137 | 0.0194 | -0.0331 | 0.0040 | 0.0108 | 0.0153 | 0.0405 | 0.0340 | 2004 | 0.1088 |
| 2005 | -0.0244 | 0.0210 | -0.0177 | -0.0190 | 0.0318 | 0.0014 | 0.0372 | -0.0091 | 0.0081 | -0.0167 | 0.0378 | 0.0003 | 2005 | 0.0491 |
| 2006 | 0.0265 | 0.0027 | 0.0124 | 0.0134 | -0.0288 | 0.0014 | 0.0062 | 0.0238 | 0.0258 | 0.0326 | 0.0190 | 0.0140 | 2006 | 0.1579 |
| 2007 | 0.0151 | -0.0196 | 0.0112 | 0.0443 | 0.0349 | -0.0166 | -0.0310 | 0.0150 | 0.0374 | 0.0159 | -0.0418 | -0.0069 | 2007 | 0.0549 |
| 2008 | -0.0600 | -0.0325 | -0.0043 | 0.0487 | 0.0130 | -0.0843 | -0.0084 | 0.0145 | -0.0891 | -0.1679 | -0.0718 | 0.0106 | 2008 | -0.3700 |
| 2009 | -0.0843 | -0.1065 | 0.0876 | 0.0957 | 0.0559 | 0.0020 | 0.0756 | 0.0361 | 0.0373 | -0.0186 | 0.0600 | 0.0193 | 2009 | 0.2646 |
| 2010 | -0.0360 | 0.0310 | 0.0603 | 0.0158 | -0.0799 | -0.0523 | 0.0701 | -0.0451 | 0.0892 | 0.0380 | 0.0001 | 0.0668 | 2010 | 0.1506 |
| 2011 | 0.0237 | 0.0343 | 0.0004 | 0.0296 | -0.0113 | -0.0167 | -0.0203 | -0.0543 | -0.0703 | 0.1093 | -0.0022 | 0.0102 | 2011 | 0.0211 |
| 2012 | 0.0448 | 0.0432 | 0.0329 | -0.0063 | -0.0601 | 0.0412 | 0.0139 | 0.0225 | 0.0258 | -0.0185 | 0.0058 | 0.0091 | 2012 | 0.1600 |
| 2013 | 0.0518 | 0.0136 | 0.0375 | 0.0193 | 0.0234 | -0.0134 | 0.0509 | -0.0290 | 0.0314 | 0.0460 | 0.0305 | 0.0253 | 2013 | 0.3239 |
| 2014 | -0.0346 | 0.0457 | 0.0084 | 0.0074 | 0.0235 | 0.0207 | -0.0138 | 0.0400 | -0.0140 | 0.0244 | 0.0269 | -0.0025 | 2014 | 0.1369 |
| 2015 | -0.0300 | 0.0575 | -0.0158 | 0.0096 | 0.0129 | -0.0194 | 0.0210 | -0.0603 | -0.0247 | 0.0844 | 0.0030 | -0.0158 | 2015 | 0.0138 |
| 2016 | -0.0496 | -0.0013 | 0.0678 | 0.0039 | 0.0180 | 0.0026 | 0.0369 | 0.0014 | 0.0002 | -0.0182 | 0.0370 | 0.0198 | 2016 | 0.1196 |

*Compound annual return

## Appendix A-2

Large-Capitalization Stocks: Income Returns
From 1926 to 2016

| Year | Jan | Feb | Mar | Apr | May | Jun | Jul | Aug | Sep | Oct | Nov | Dec | Year | Jan–Dec* |
|------|------|------|------|------|------|------|------|------|------|------|------|------|------|------|
| 1926 | 0.0016 | 0.0055 | 0.0016 | 0.0026 | 0.0102 | 0.0025 | 0.0024 | 0.0078 | 0.0023 | 0.0030 | 0.0123 | 0.0030 | 1926 | 0.0541 |
| 1927 | 0.0015 | 0.0061 | 0.0022 | 0.0029 | 0.0085 | 0.0027 | 0.0020 | 0.0070 | 0.0018 | 0.0029 | 0.0105 | 0.0029 | 1927 | 0.0571 |
| 1928 | 0.0011 | 0.0051 | 0.0017 | 0.0021 | 0.0071 | 0.0020 | 0.0016 | 0.0062 | 0.0019 | 0.0023 | 0.0092 | 0.0021 | 1928 | 0.0481 |
| 1929 | 0.0012 | 0.0039 | 0.0012 | 0.0016 | 0.0066 | 0.0016 | 0.0014 | 0.0048 | 0.0013 | 0.0020 | 0.0091 | 0.0029 | 1929 | 0.0398 |
| 1930 | 0.0014 | 0.0044 | 0.0013 | 0.0016 | 0.0068 | 0.0020 | 0.0020 | 0.0066 | 0.0019 | 0.0032 | 0.0130 | 0.0036 | 1930 | 0.0457 |
| 1931 | 0.0013 | 0.0050 | 0.0017 | 0.0024 | 0.0093 | 0.0031 | 0.0020 | 0.0087 | 0.0022 | 0.0051 | 0.0180 | 0.0053 | 1931 | 0.0535 |
| 1932 | 0.0012 | 0.0063 | 0.0024 | 0.0027 | 0.0137 | 0.0067 | 0.0045 | 0.0115 | 0.0024 | 0.0037 | 0.0172 | 0.0046 | 1932 | 0.0616 |
| 1933 | 0.0015 | 0.0072 | 0.0018 | 0.0034 | 0.0096 | 0.0021 | 0.0018 | 0.0060 | 0.0018 | 0.0031 | 0.0100 | 0.0030 | 1933 | 0.0639 |
| 1934 | 0.0010 | 0.0045 | 0.0009 | 0.0019 | 0.0076 | 0.0021 | 0.0020 | 0.0069 | 0.0022 | 0.0033 | 0.0114 | 0.0031 | 1934 | 0.0446 |
| 1935 | 0.0011 | 0.0055 | 0.0023 | 0.0024 | 0.0086 | 0.0021 | 0.0020 | 0.0063 | 0.0018 | 0.0026 | 0.0080 | 0.0023 | 1935 | 0.0495 |
| 1936 | 0.0015 | 0.0056 | 0.0014 | 0.0020 | 0.0087 | 0.0028 | 0.0020 | 0.0063 | 0.0019 | 0.0025 | 0.0093 | 0.0029 | 1936 | 0.0536 |
| 1937 | 0.0012 | 0.0045 | 0.0017 | 0.0022 | 0.0079 | 0.0025 | 0.0019 | 0.0071 | 0.0019 | 0.0036 | 0.0146 | 0.0045 | 1937 | 0.0466 |
| 1938 | 0.0019 | 0.0065 | 0.0018 | 0.0035 | 0.0113 | 0.0032 | 0.0017 | 0.0048 | 0.0017 | 0.0016 | 0.0061 | 0.0024 | 1938 | 0.0483 |
| 1939 | 0.0015 | 0.0065 | 0.0016 | 0.0027 | 0.0110 | 0.0026 | 0.0018 | 0.0066 | 0.0027 | 0.0023 | 0.0094 | 0.0033 | 1939 | 0.0469 |
| 1940 | 0.0016 | 0.0066 | 0.0025 | 0.0024 | 0.0107 | 0.0043 | 0.0030 | 0.0087 | 0.0028 | 0.0028 | 0.0108 | 0.0038 | 1940 | 0.0536 |
| 1941 | 0.0019 | 0.0089 | 0.0030 | 0.0040 | 0.0140 | 0.0043 | 0.0030 | 0.0096 | 0.0029 | 0.0029 | 0.0137 | 0.0044 | 1941 | 0.0671 |
| 1942 | 0.0023 | 0.0091 | 0.0023 | 0.0037 | 0.0157 | 0.0037 | 0.0024 | 0.0093 | 0.0023 | 0.0034 | 0.0117 | 0.0032 | 1942 | 0.0679 |
| 1943 | 0.0020 | 0.0076 | 0.0018 | 0.0026 | 0.0104 | 0.0025 | 0.0016 | 0.0068 | 0.0025 | 0.0025 | 0.0101 | 0.0027 | 1943 | 0.0624 |
| 1944 | 0.0017 | 0.0068 | 0.0025 | 0.0025 | 0.0101 | 0.0032 | 0.0015 | 0.0071 | 0.0023 | 0.0023 | 0.0094 | 0.0023 | 1944 | 0.0548 |
| 1945 | 0.0015 | 0.0067 | 0.0021 | 0.0022 | 0.0081 | 0.0027 | 0.0020 | 0.0061 | 0.0019 | 0.0019 | 0.0072 | 0.0017 | 1945 | 0.0497 |
| 1946 | 0.0017 | 0.0054 | 0.0017 | 0.0017 | 0.0064 | 0.0021 | 0.0016 | 0.0056 | 0.0018 | 0.0020 | 0.0088 | 0.0027 | 1946 | 0.0409 |
| 1947 | 0.0020 | 0.0070 | 0.0019 | 0.0026 | 0.0103 | 0.0028 | 0.0020 | 0.0076 | 0.0026 | 0.0026 | 0.0110 | 0.0027 | 1947 | 0.0549 |
| 1948 | 0.0020 | 0.0082 | 0.0021 | 0.0027 | 0.0097 | 0.0024 | 0.0024 | 0.0082 | 0.0025 | 0.0032 | 0.0121 | 0.0041 | 1948 | 0.0608 |
| 1949 | 0.0026 | 0.0099 | 0.0027 | 0.0033 | 0.0115 | 0.0035 | 0.0028 | 0.0100 | 0.0026 | 0.0045 | 0.0162 | 0.0050 | 1949 | 0.0750 |
| 1950 | 0.0024 | 0.0100 | 0.0029 | 0.0035 | 0.0116 | 0.0032 | 0.0034 | 0.0118 | 0.0033 | 0.0051 | 0.0179 | 0.0051 | 1950 | 0.0877 |
| 1951 | 0.0024 | 0.0092 | 0.0028 | 0.0028 | 0.0107 | 0.0033 | 0.0024 | 0.0085 | 0.0021 | 0.0034 | 0.0122 | 0.0035 | 1951 | 0.0691 |
| 1952 | 0.0025 | 0.0083 | 0.0026 | 0.0029 | 0.0111 | 0.0029 | 0.0020 | 0.0075 | 0.0020 | 0.0029 | 0.0106 | 0.0027 | 1952 | 0.0593 |
| 1953 | 0.0023 | 0.0076 | 0.0023 | 0.0028 | 0.0110 | 0.0029 | 0.0021 | 0.0077 | 0.0021 | 0.0030 | 0.0114 | 0.0032 | 1953 | 0.0546 |
| 1954 | 0.0024 | 0.0084 | 0.0023 | 0.0026 | 0.0088 | 0.0024 | 0.0017 | 0.0065 | 0.0020 | 0.0028 | 0.0101 | 0.0026 | 1954 | 0.0621 |
| 1955 | 0.0017 | 0.0063 | 0.0019 | 0.0019 | 0.0068 | 0.0018 | 0.0015 | 0.0053 | 0.0016 | 0.0021 | 0.0078 | 0.0022 | 1955 | 0.0456 |

*Compound annual return

## Appendix A-2

Large-Capitalization Stocks: Income Returns
From 1926 to 2016

| Year | Jan | Feb | Mar | Apr | May | Jun | Jul | Aug | Sep | Oct | Nov | Dec | Year | Jan–Dec* |
|---|---|---|---|---|---|---|---|---|---|---|---|---|---|---|
| 1956 | 0.0018 | 0.0066 | 0.0018 | 0.0016 | 0.0064 | 0.0018 | 0.0015 | 0.0053 | 0.0015 | 0.0015 | 0.0059 | 0.0018 | 1956 | 0.0383 |
| 1957 | 0.0017 | 0.0063 | 0.0018 | 0.0018 | 0.0068 | 0.0017 | 0.0017 | 0.0056 | 0.0018 | 0.0019 | 0.0071 | 0.0019 | 1957 | 0.0384 |
| 1958 | 0.0018 | 0.0065 | 0.0020 | 0.0019 | 0.0062 | 0.0018 | 0.0018 | 0.0057 | 0.0017 | 0.0016 | 0.0060 | 0.0015 | 1958 | 0.0438 |
| 1959 | 0.0014 | 0.0051 | 0.0014 | 0.0014 | 0.0050 | 0.0014 | 0.0014 | 0.0048 | 0.0013 | 0.0016 | 0.0054 | 0.0015 | 1959 | 0.0331 |
| 1960 | 0.0015 | 0.0056 | 0.0016 | 0.0014 | 0.0057 | 0.0016 | 0.0014 | 0.0056 | 0.0014 | 0.0017 | 0.0062 | 0.0016 | 1960 | 0.0326 |
| 1961 | 0.0014 | 0.0050 | 0.0014 | 0.0012 | 0.0047 | 0.0014 | 0.0014 | 0.0046 | 0.0013 | 0.0015 | 0.0054 | 0.0014 | 1961 | 0.0348 |
| 1962 | 0.0013 | 0.0046 | 0.0013 | 0.0013 | 0.0049 | 0.0015 | 0.0016 | 0.0055 | 0.0017 | 0.0020 | 0.0071 | 0.0018 | 1962 | 0.0298 |
| 1963 | 0.0014 | 0.0050 | 0.0016 | 0.0015 | 0.0050 | 0.0014 | 0.0013 | 0.0048 | 0.0014 | 0.0017 | 0.0059 | 0.0018 | 1963 | 0.0361 |
| 1964 | 0.0013 | 0.0048 | 0.0013 | 0.0014 | 0.0048 | 0.0014 | 0.0012 | 0.0044 | 0.0013 | 0.0015 | 0.0057 | 0.0017 | 1964 | 0.0333 |
| 1965 | 0.0013 | 0.0046 | 0.0013 | 0.0014 | 0.0047 | 0.0014 | 0.0013 | 0.0047 | 0.0014 | 0.0016 | 0.0056 | 0.0016 | 1965 | 0.0321 |
| 1966 | 0.0013 | 0.0047 | 0.0013 | 0.0015 | 0.0049 | 0.0015 | 0.0014 | 0.0053 | 0.0017 | 0.0018 | 0.0064 | 0.0017 | 1966 | 0.0311 |
| 1967 | 0.0016 | 0.0052 | 0.0015 | 0.0014 | 0.0048 | 0.0015 | 0.0014 | 0.0047 | 0.0014 | 0.0014 | 0.0054 | 0.0015 | 1967 | 0.0364 |
| 1968 | 0.0013 | 0.0051 | 0.0016 | 0.0014 | 0.0049 | 0.0015 | 0.0013 | 0.0049 | 0.0014 | 0.0015 | 0.0051 | 0.0014 | 1968 | 0.0318 |
| 1969 | 0.0013 | 0.0048 | 0.0014 | 0.0014 | 0.0048 | 0.0014 | 0.0014 | 0.0053 | 0.0015 | 0.0016 | 0.0056 | 0.0010 | 1969 | 0.0298 |
| 1970 | 0.0021 | 0.0031 | 0.0029 | 0.0030 | 0.0032 | 0.0034 | 0.0036 | 0.0033 | 0.0032 | 0.0031 | 0.0031 | 0.0030 | 1970 | 0.0333 |
| 1971 | 0.0032 | 0.0022 | 0.0026 | 0.0035 | 0.0017 | 0.0026 | 0.0024 | 0.0029 | 0.0025 | 0.0041 | 0.0013 | 0.0041 | 1971 | 0.0349 |
| 1972 | 0.0011 | 0.0024 | 0.0023 | 0.0024 | 0.0041 | 0.0008 | 0.0024 | 0.0024 | 0.0023 | 0.0025 | 0.0025 | 0.0024 | 1972 | 0.0295 |
| 1973 | 0.0022 | 0.0022 | 0.0022 | 0.0025 | 0.0026 | 0.0026 | 0.0027 | 0.0026 | 0.0041 | 0.0015 | 0.0030 | 0.0032 | 1973 | 0.0286 |
| 1974 | 0.0029 | 0.0029 | 0.0028 | 0.0032 | 0.0033 | 0.0033 | 0.0036 | 0.0039 | 0.0042 | 0.0050 | 0.0043 | 0.0046 | 1974 | 0.0369 |
| 1975 | 0.0044 | 0.0039 | 0.0037 | 0.0037 | 0.0035 | 0.0034 | 0.0033 | 0.0035 | 0.0035 | 0.0037 | 0.0035 | 0.0034 | 1975 | 0.0537 |
| 1976 | 0.0034 | 0.0030 | 0.0030 | 0.0032 | 0.0032 | 0.0034 | 0.0033 | 0.0033 | 0.0032 | 0.0036 | 0.0037 | 0.0036 | 1976 | 0.0449 |
| 1977 | 0.0033 | 0.0034 | 0.0035 | 0.0040 | 0.0040 | 0.0041 | 0.0038 | 0.0038 | 0.0040 | 0.0045 | 0.0047 | 0.0046 | 1977 | 0.0435 |
| 1978 | 0.0041 | 0.0045 | 0.0045 | 0.0048 | 0.0044 | 0.0043 | 0.0044 | 0.0042 | 0.0041 | 0.0044 | 0.0048 | 0.0048 | 1978 | 0.0533 |
| 1979 | 0.0046 | 0.0044 | 0.0045 | 0.0077 | 0.0017 | 0.0048 | 0.0047 | 0.0046 | 0.0043 | 0.0046 | 0.0049 | 0.0046 | 1979 | 0.0589 |
| 1980 | 0.0045 | 0.0043 | 0.0046 | 0.0051 | 0.0049 | 0.0047 | 0.0046 | 0.0043 | 0.0043 | 0.0042 | 0.0042 | 0.0037 | 1980 | 0.0574 |
| 1981 | 0.0039 | 0.0041 | 0.0040 | 0.0041 | 0.0042 | 0.0041 | 0.0043 | 0.0044 | 0.0046 | 0.0048 | 0.0047 | 0.0044 | 1981 | 0.0488 |
| 1982 | 0.0045 | 0.0047 | 0.0049 | 0.0055 | 0.0047 | 0.0054 | 0.0051 | 0.0054 | 0.0049 | 0.0047 | 0.0043 | 0.0041 | 1982 | 0.0561 |
| 1983 | 0.0041 | 0.0039 | 0.0038 | 0.0040 | 0.0035 | 0.0037 | 0.0035 | 0.0037 | 0.0041 | 0.0032 | 0.0037 | 0.0036 | 1983 | 0.0504 |
| 1984 | 0.0036 | 0.0037 | 0.0038 | 0.0040 | 0.0040 | 0.0043 | 0.0040 | 0.0041 | 0.0037 | 0.0039 | 0.0039 | 0.0040 | 1984 | 0.0457 |
| 1985 | 0.0038 | 0.0036 | 0.0035 | 0.0037 | 0.0037 | 0.0035 | 0.0034 | 0.0035 | 0.0036 | 0.0036 | 0.0035 | 0.0033 | 1985 | 0.0472 |

*Compound annual return

## Appendix A-2

Large-Capitalization Stocks: Income Returns
From 1926 to 2016

| Year | Jan | Feb | Mar | Apr | May | Jun | Jul | Aug | Sep | Oct | Nov | Dec | Year | Jan–Dec* |
|------|------|------|------|------|------|------|------|------|------|------|------|------|------|----------|
| 1986 | 0.0032 | 0.0033 | 0.0030 | 0.0029 | 0.0030 | 0.0028 | 0.0028 | 0.0030 | 0.0028 | 0.0030 | 0.0027 | 0.0028 | 1986 | 0.0392 |
| 1987 | 0.0029 | 0.0026 | 0.0025 | 0.0026 | 0.0026 | 0.0026 | 0.0024 | 0.0024 | 0.0022 | 0.0023 | 0.0030 | 0.0032 | 1987 | 0.0364 |
| 1988 | 0.0016 | 0.0048 | 0.0025 | 0.0016 | 0.0055 | 0.0026 | 0.0016 | 0.0047 | 0.0029 | 0.0019 | 0.0046 | 0.0028 | 1988 | 0.0399 |
| 1989 | 0.0021 | 0.0040 | 0.0025 | 0.0018 | 0.0053 | 0.0023 | 0.0019 | 0.0040 | 0.0025 | 0.0020 | 0.0039 | 0.0026 | 1989 | 0.0403 |
| 1990 | 0.0017 | 0.0043 | 0.0022 | 0.0019 | 0.0055 | 0.0021 | 0.0020 | 0.0039 | 0.0025 | 0.0024 | 0.0047 | 0.0030 | 1990 | 0.0343 |
| 1991 | 0.0020 | 0.0042 | 0.0020 | 0.0020 | 0.0046 | 0.0021 | 0.0017 | 0.0040 | 0.0024 | 0.0016 | 0.0036 | 0.0028 | 1991 | 0.0376 |
| 1992 | 0.0013 | 0.0034 | 0.0024 | 0.0015 | 0.0039 | 0.0025 | 0.0015 | 0.0035 | 0.0026 | 0.0013 | 0.0038 | 0.0022 | 1992 | 0.0298 |
| 1993 | 0.0013 | 0.0031 | 0.0024 | 0.0012 | 0.0040 | 0.0022 | 0.0013 | 0.0035 | 0.0023 | 0.0013 | 0.0034 | 0.0020 | 1993 | 0.0291 |
| 1994 | 0.0015 | 0.0029 | 0.0021 | 0.0013 | 0.0040 | 0.0023 | 0.0013 | 0.0034 | 0.0025 | 0.0016 | 0.0031 | 0.0025 | 1994 | 0.0283 |
| 1995 | 0.0017 | 0.0029 | 0.0022 | 0.0015 | 0.0036 | 0.0020 | 0.0014 | 0.0028 | 0.0021 | 0.0014 | 0.0028 | 0.0018 | 1995 | 0.0304 |
| 1996 | 0.0014 | 0.0023 | 0.0017 | 0.0013 | 0.0029 | 0.0016 | 0.0016 | 0.0023 | 0.0021 | 0.0014 | 0.0022 | 0.0017 | 1996 | 0.0243 |
| 1997 | 0.0012 | 0.0019 | 0.0015 | 0.0013 | 0.0023 | 0.0013 | 0.0014 | 0.0014 | 0.0016 | 0.0011 | 0.0017 | 0.0014 | 1997 | 0.0210 |
| 1998 | 0.0009 | 0.0017 | 0.0013 | 0.0010 | 0.0016 | 0.0012 | 0.0010 | 0.0012 | 0.0017 | 0.0010 | 0.0015 | 0.0012 | 1998 | 0.0167 |
| 1999 | 0.0008 | 0.0012 | 0.0012 | 0.0008 | 0.0014 | 0.0011 | 0.0008 | 0.0013 | 0.0011 | 0.0007 | 0.0013 | 0.0011 | 1999 | 0.0136 |
| 2000 | 0.0007 | 0.0012 | 0.0011 | 0.0007 | 0.0014 | 0.0007 | 0.0007 | 0.0014 | 0.0007 | 0.0007 | 0.0012 | 0.0008 | 2000 | 0.0111 |
| 2001 | 0.0008 | 0.0011 | 0.0009 | 0.0009 | 0.0016 | 0.0007 | 0.0009 | 0.0015 | 0.0010 | 0.0010 | 0.0015 | 0.0012 | 2001 | 0.0118 |
| 2002 | 0.0010 | 0.0015 | 0.0009 | 0.0008 | 0.0017 | 0.0012 | 0.0010 | 0.0017 | 0.0013 | 0.0016 | 0.0018 | 0.0016 | 2002 | 0.0139 |
| 2003 | 0.0012 | 0.0020 | 0.0014 | 0.0013 | 0.0018 | 0.0014 | 0.0014 | 0.0016 | 0.0013 | 0.0016 | 0.0017 | 0.0017 | 2003 | 0.0199 |
| 2004 | 0.0011 | 0.0017 | 0.0013 | 0.0011 | 0.0016 | 0.0015 | 0.0012 | 0.0018 | 0.0015 | 0.0013 | 0.0019 | 0.0016 | 2004 | 0.0176 |
| 2005 | 0.0009 | 0.0021 | 0.0014 | 0.0011 | 0.0019 | 0.0016 | 0.0012 | 0.0021 | 0.0012 | 0.0011 | 0.0026 | 0.0013 | 2005 | 0.0184 |
| 2006 | 0.0010 | 0.0023 | 0.0014 | 0.0012 | 0.0021 | 0.0013 | 0.0012 | 0.0025 | 0.0012 | 0.0011 | 0.0025 | 0.0014 | 2006 | 0.0201 |
| 2007 | 0.0011 | 0.0023 | 0.0012 | 0.0010 | 0.0023 | 0.0012 | 0.0010 | 0.0021 | 0.0016 | 0.0011 | 0.0022 | 0.0017 | 2007 | 0.0196 |
| 2008 | 0.0012 | 0.0023 | 0.0016 | 0.0012 | 0.0023 | 0.0017 | 0.0015 | 0.0023 | 0.0017 | 0.0015 | 0.0031 | 0.0028 | 2008 | 0.0192 |
| 2009 | 0.0014 | 0.0035 | 0.0022 | 0.0018 | 0.0028 | 0.0018 | 0.0015 | 0.0025 | 0.0016 | 0.0012 | 0.0026 | 0.0015 | 2009 | 0.0248 |
| 2010 | 0.0010 | 0.0025 | 0.0016 | 0.0010 | 0.0021 | 0.0015 | 0.0013 | 0.0023 | 0.0017 | 0.0012 | 0.0024 | 0.0015 | 2010 | 0.0202 |
| 2011 | 0.0011 | 0.0023 | 0.0015 | 0.0011 | 0.0022 | 0.0016 | 0.0011 | 0.0028 | 0.0015 | 0.0016 | 0.0028 | 0.0017 | 2011 | 0.0213 |
| 2012 | 0.0012 | 0.0027 | 0.0016 | 0.0012 | 0.0026 | 0.0016 | 0.0013 | 0.0028 | 0.0016 | 0.0013 | 0.0030 | 0.0020 | 2012 | 0.0250 |
| 2013 | 0.0014 | 0.0025 | 0.0015 | 0.0012 | 0.0026 | 0.0016 | 0.0014 | 0.0023 | 0.0016 | 0.0014 | 0.0024 | 0.0018 | 2013 | 0.0248 |
| 2014 | 0.0010 | 0.0026 | 0.0015 | 0.0012 | 0.0024 | 0.0016 | 0.0013 | 0.0023 | 0.0015 | 0.0012 | 0.0024 | 0.0017 | 2014 | 0.0216 |
| 2015 | 0.0010 | 0.0026 | 0.0016 | 0.0011 | 0.0024 | 0.0017 | 0.0012 | 0.0022 | 0.0017 | 0.0014 | 0.0025 | 0.0018 | 2015 | 0.0210 |
| 2016 | 0.0011 | 0.0028 | 0.0018 | 0.0012 | 0.0026 | 0.0017 | 0.0013 | 0.0026 | 0.0014 | 0.0012 | 0.0029 | 0.0016 | 2016 | 0.0226 |

*Compound annual return

## Appendix A-3

Large-Capitalization Stocks: Capital Appreciation Returns
From 1926 to 2016

| Year | Jan | Feb | Mar | Apr | May | Jun | Jul | Aug | Sep | Oct | Nov | Dec | Year | Jan–Dec* |
|---|---|---|---|---|---|---|---|---|---|---|---|---|---|---|
| 1926 | -0.0016 | -0.0440 | -0.0591 | 0.0227 | 0.0077 | 0.0432 | 0.0455 | 0.0171 | 0.0229 | -0.0313 | 0.0223 | 0.0166 | 1926 | 0.0572 |
| 1927 | -0.0208 | 0.0477 | 0.0065 | 0.0172 | 0.0522 | -0.0094 | 0.0650 | 0.0445 | 0.0432 | -0.0531 | 0.0616 | 0.0250 | 1927 | 0.3091 |
| 1928 | -0.0051 | -0.0176 | 0.1083 | 0.0324 | 0.0127 | -0.0405 | 0.0125 | 0.0741 | 0.0240 | 0.0145 | 0.1199 | 0.0029 | 1928 | 0.3788 |
| 1929 | 0.0571 | -0.0058 | -0.0023 | 0.0161 | -0.0428 | 0.1124 | 0.0456 | 0.0980 | -0.0489 | -0.1993 | -0.1337 | 0.0253 | 1929 | -0.1191 |
| 1930 | 0.0625 | 0.0215 | 0.0799 | -0.0095 | -0.0165 | -0.1646 | 0.0367 | 0.0075 | -0.1301 | -0.0888 | -0.0218 | -0.0742 | 1930 | -0.2848 |
| 1931 | 0.0489 | 0.1144 | -0.0692 | -0.0959 | -0.1372 | 0.1390 | -0.0742 | 0.0095 | -0.2994 | 0.0844 | -0.0978 | -0.1453 | 1931 | -0.4707 |
| 1932 | -0.0283 | 0.0507 | -0.1182 | -0.2025 | -0.2333 | -0.0089 | 0.3770 | 0.3754 | -0.0369 | -0.1386 | -0.0589 | 0.0519 | 1932 | -0.1515 |
| 1933 | 0.0073 | -0.1844 | 0.0336 | 0.4222 | 0.1587 | 0.1317 | -0.0880 | 0.1146 | -0.1136 | -0.0885 | 0.1027 | 0.0223 | 1933 | 0.4659 |
| 1934 | 0.1059 | -0.0367 | -0.0009 | -0.0270 | -0.0813 | 0.0208 | -0.1152 | 0.0541 | -0.0055 | -0.0319 | 0.0829 | -0.0042 | 1934 | -0.0594 |
| 1935 | -0.0421 | -0.0396 | -0.0309 | 0.0956 | 0.0323 | 0.0678 | 0.0831 | 0.0217 | 0.0239 | 0.0751 | 0.0393 | 0.0371 | 1935 | 0.4137 |
| 1936 | 0.0655 | 0.0168 | 0.0254 | -0.0771 | 0.0458 | 0.0306 | 0.0681 | 0.0088 | 0.0013 | 0.0750 | 0.0041 | -0.0058 | 1936 | 0.2792 |
| 1937 | 0.0378 | 0.0146 | -0.0094 | -0.0831 | -0.0103 | -0.0529 | 0.1026 | -0.0554 | -0.1421 | -0.1017 | -0.1011 | -0.0504 | 1937 | -0.3859 |
| 1938 | 0.0133 | 0.0608 | -0.2504 | 0.1412 | -0.0443 | 0.2470 | 0.0727 | -0.0274 | 0.0149 | 0.0760 | -0.0334 | 0.0377 | 1938 | 0.2521 |
| 1939 | -0.0689 | 0.0325 | -0.1354 | -0.0055 | 0.0623 | -0.0638 | 0.1087 | -0.0714 | 0.1646 | -0.0146 | -0.0491 | 0.0238 | 1939 | -0.0545 |
| 1940 | -0.0352 | 0.0066 | 0.0099 | -0.0049 | -0.2395 | 0.0766 | 0.0311 | 0.0262 | 0.0095 | 0.0394 | -0.0424 | -0.0028 | 1940 | -0.1529 |
| 1941 | -0.0482 | -0.0149 | 0.0040 | -0.0653 | 0.0043 | 0.0535 | 0.0548 | -0.0087 | -0.0097 | -0.0686 | -0.0421 | -0.0451 | 1941 | -0.1786 |
| 1942 | 0.0138 | -0.0250 | -0.0675 | -0.0437 | 0.0640 | 0.0184 | 0.0313 | 0.0070 | 0.0267 | 0.0644 | -0.0138 | 0.0517 | 1942 | 0.1243 |
| 1943 | 0.0716 | 0.0506 | 0.0527 | 0.0009 | 0.0449 | 0.0198 | -0.0543 | 0.0103 | 0.0237 | -0.0132 | -0.0755 | 0.0590 | 1943 | 0.1945 |
| 1944 | 0.0154 | -0.0025 | 0.0169 | -0.0125 | 0.0404 | 0.0510 | -0.0208 | 0.0087 | -0.0031 | 0.0000 | 0.0039 | 0.0351 | 1944 | 0.1380 |
| 1945 | 0.0143 | 0.0616 | -0.0462 | 0.0880 | 0.0115 | -0.0033 | -0.0201 | 0.0580 | 0.0419 | 0.0303 | 0.0324 | 0.0099 | 1945 | 0.3072 |
| 1946 | 0.0697 | -0.0695 | 0.0463 | 0.0376 | 0.0224 | -0.0391 | -0.0255 | -0.0729 | -0.1015 | -0.0080 | -0.0115 | 0.0429 | 1946 | -0.1187 |
| 1947 | 0.0235 | -0.0147 | -0.0169 | -0.0389 | -0.0089 | 0.0526 | 0.0362 | -0.0279 | -0.0137 | 0.0212 | -0.0285 | 0.0207 | 1947 | 0.0000 |
| 1948 | -0.0399 | -0.0470 | 0.0771 | 0.0265 | 0.0782 | 0.0030 | -0.0532 | 0.0076 | -0.0301 | 0.0678 | -0.1082 | 0.0305 | 1948 | -0.0065 |
| 1949 | 0.0013 | -0.0394 | 0.0301 | -0.0212 | -0.0373 | -0.0021 | 0.0621 | 0.0120 | 0.0237 | 0.0295 | 0.0012 | 0.0436 | 1949 | 0.1026 |
| 1950 | 0.0173 | 0.0100 | 0.0041 | 0.0451 | 0.0393 | -0.0580 | 0.0085 | 0.0325 | 0.0559 | 0.0041 | -0.0010 | 0.0461 | 1950 | 0.2178 |
| 1951 | 0.0612 | 0.0065 | -0.0183 | 0.0481 | -0.0406 | -0.0260 | 0.0687 | 0.0393 | -0.0009 | -0.0138 | -0.0026 | 0.0389 | 1951 | 0.1646 |
| 1952 | 0.0156 | -0.0365 | 0.0477 | -0.0431 | 0.0232 | 0.0461 | 0.0176 | -0.0146 | -0.0196 | -0.0008 | 0.0465 | 0.0355 | 1952 | 0.1178 |
| 1953 | -0.0072 | -0.0182 | -0.0236 | -0.0265 | -0.0032 | -0.0163 | 0.0253 | -0.0578 | 0.0013 | 0.0510 | 0.0090 | 0.0020 | 1953 | -0.0662 |
| 1954 | 0.0512 | 0.0027 | 0.0302 | 0.0490 | 0.0329 | 0.0007 | 0.0572 | -0.0340 | 0.0831 | -0.0195 | 0.0808 | 0.0508 | 1954 | 0.4502 |
| 1955 | 0.0181 | 0.0035 | -0.0049 | 0.0377 | -0.0013 | 0.0823 | 0.0607 | -0.0078 | 0.0113 | -0.0305 | 0.0749 | -0.0007 | 1955 | 0.2640 |

*Compound annual return

# Appendix A-3

Large-Capitalization Stocks: Capital Appreciation Returns
From 1926 to 2016

| Year | Jan | Feb | Mar | Apr | May | Jun | Jul | Aug | Sep | Oct | Nov | Dec | Year | Jan–Dec* |
|---|---|---|---|---|---|---|---|---|---|---|---|---|---|---|
| 1956 | -0.0365 | 0.0347 | 0.0693 | -0.0021 | -0.0657 | 0.0392 | 0.0515 | -0.0381 | -0.0455 | 0.0051 | -0.0110 | 0.0353 | 1956 | 0.0262 |
| 1957 | -0.0418 | -0.0326 | 0.0196 | 0.0370 | 0.0369 | -0.0013 | 0.0114 | -0.0561 | -0.0619 | -0.0321 | 0.0161 | -0.0415 | 1957 | -0.1431 |
| 1958 | 0.0428 | -0.0206 | 0.0309 | 0.0318 | 0.0150 | 0.0261 | 0.0431 | 0.0119 | 0.0484 | 0.0254 | 0.0224 | 0.0520 | 1958 | 0.3806 |
| 1959 | 0.0038 | -0.0002 | 0.0005 | 0.0388 | 0.0189 | -0.0036 | 0.0349 | -0.0150 | -0.0456 | 0.0113 | 0.0132 | 0.0276 | 1959 | 0.0848 |
| 1960 | -0.0715 | 0.0092 | -0.0139 | -0.0175 | 0.0269 | 0.0195 | -0.0248 | 0.0261 | -0.0604 | -0.0024 | 0.0403 | 0.0463 | 1960 | -0.0297 |
| 1961 | 0.0632 | 0.0269 | 0.0255 | 0.0038 | 0.0191 | -0.0288 | 0.0328 | 0.0196 | -0.0197 | 0.0283 | 0.0393 | 0.0032 | 1961 | 0.2313 |
| 1962 | -0.0379 | 0.0163 | -0.0059 | -0.0620 | -0.0860 | -0.0818 | 0.0636 | 0.0153 | -0.0482 | 0.0044 | 0.1016 | 0.0135 | 1962 | -0.1181 |
| 1963 | 0.0491 | -0.0289 | 0.0355 | 0.0485 | 0.0143 | -0.0202 | -0.0035 | 0.0487 | -0.0110 | 0.0322 | -0.0105 | 0.0244 | 1963 | 0.1889 |
| 1964 | 0.0269 | 0.0099 | 0.0152 | 0.0061 | 0.0115 | 0.0164 | 0.0182 | -0.0162 | 0.0287 | 0.0081 | -0.0052 | 0.0039 | 1964 | 0.1297 |
| 1965 | 0.0332 | -0.0015 | -0.0145 | 0.0342 | -0.0077 | -0.0486 | 0.0134 | 0.0225 | 0.0320 | 0.0273 | -0.0088 | 0.0090 | 1965 | 0.0906 |
| 1966 | 0.0049 | -0.0179 | -0.0218 | 0.0205 | -0.0541 | -0.0161 | -0.0135 | -0.0778 | -0.0070 | 0.0475 | 0.0031 | -0.0015 | 1966 | -0.1309 |
| 1967 | 0.0782 | 0.0020 | 0.0394 | 0.0422 | -0.0524 | 0.0175 | 0.0453 | -0.0117 | 0.0328 | -0.0291 | 0.0011 | 0.0263 | 1967 | 0.2009 |
| 1968 | -0.0438 | -0.0312 | 0.0094 | 0.0819 | 0.0112 | 0.0091 | -0.0185 | 0.0115 | 0.0385 | 0.0072 | 0.0480 | -0.0416 | 1968 | 0.0766 |
| 1969 | -0.0082 | -0.0474 | 0.0344 | 0.0215 | -0.0022 | -0.0556 | -0.0602 | 0.0401 | -0.0250 | 0.0442 | -0.0353 | -0.0187 | 1969 | -0.1136 |
| 1970 | -0.0765 | 0.0527 | 0.0015 | -0.0905 | -0.0610 | -0.0500 | 0.0733 | 0.0445 | 0.0330 | -0.0114 | 0.0474 | 0.0568 | 1970 | 0.0010 |
| 1971 | 0.0400 | 0.0095 | 0.0368 | 0.0354 | -0.0407 | 0.0007 | -0.0411 | 0.0359 | -0.0070 | -0.0432 | -0.0011 | 0.0847 | 1971 | 0.1063 |
| 1972 | 0.0195 | 0.0253 | 0.0059 | 0.0044 | 0.0156 | -0.0202 | 0.0023 | 0.0345 | -0.0049 | 0.0093 | 0.0456 | 0.0118 | 1972 | 0.1579 |
| 1973 | -0.0171 | -0.0375 | -0.0014 | -0.0408 | -0.0189 | -0.0066 | 0.0380 | -0.0367 | 0.0401 | -0.0013 | -0.1139 | 0.0166 | 1973 | -0.1737 |
| 1974 | -0.0100 | -0.0036 | -0.0233 | -0.0391 | -0.0336 | -0.0147 | -0.0778 | -0.0903 | -0.1193 | 0.1630 | -0.0532 | -0.0202 | 1974 | -0.2972 |
| 1975 | 0.1228 | 0.0599 | 0.0217 | 0.0473 | 0.0441 | 0.0443 | -0.0677 | -0.0211 | -0.0346 | 0.0616 | 0.0247 | -0.0115 | 1975 | 0.3155 |
| 1976 | 0.1183 | -0.0114 | 0.0307 | -0.0110 | -0.0144 | 0.0409 | -0.0081 | -0.0051 | 0.0226 | -0.0222 | -0.0078 | 0.0525 | 1976 | 0.1915 |
| 1977 | -0.0505 | -0.0217 | -0.0140 | 0.0002 | -0.0236 | 0.0454 | -0.0162 | -0.0210 | -0.0025 | -0.0434 | 0.0270 | 0.0028 | 1977 | -0.1150 |
| 1978 | -0.0615 | -0.0248 | 0.0249 | 0.0854 | 0.0048 | -0.0181 | 0.0539 | 0.0259 | -0.0073 | -0.0916 | 0.0166 | 0.0149 | 1978 | 0.0106 |
| 1979 | 0.0397 | -0.0365 | 0.0552 | 0.0017 | -0.0263 | 0.0387 | 0.0087 | 0.0531 | 0.0000 | -0.0686 | 0.0426 | 0.0168 | 1979 | 0.1231 |
| 1980 | 0.0576 | -0.0044 | -0.1018 | 0.0411 | 0.0466 | 0.0270 | 0.0650 | 0.0058 | 0.0252 | 0.0160 | 0.1024 | -0.0339 | 1980 | 0.2577 |
| 1981 | -0.0457 | 0.0133 | 0.0360 | -0.0235 | -0.0017 | -0.0104 | -0.0022 | -0.0621 | -0.0538 | 0.0491 | 0.0366 | -0.0301 | 1981 | -0.0973 |
| 1982 | -0.0175 | -0.0606 | -0.0101 | 0.0397 | -0.0388 | -0.0204 | -0.0229 | 0.1160 | 0.0076 | 0.1104 | 0.0361 | 0.0152 | 1982 | 0.1476 |
| 1983 | 0.0331 | 0.0190 | 0.0331 | 0.0748 | -0.0122 | 0.0352 | -0.0330 | 0.0113 | 0.0097 | -0.0148 | 0.0174 | -0.0088 | 1983 | 0.1727 |
| 1984 | -0.0092 | -0.0389 | 0.0135 | 0.0055 | -0.0594 | 0.0175 | -0.0165 | 0.1063 | -0.0035 | -0.0001 | -0.0151 | 0.0224 | 1984 | 0.0140 |
| 1985 | 0.0741 | 0.0086 | -0.0029 | -0.0046 | 0.0541 | 0.0121 | -0.0048 | -0.0120 | -0.0348 | 0.0426 | 0.0651 | 0.0451 | 1985 | 0.2633 |

*Compound annual return

## Appendix A-3

Large-Capitalization Stocks: Capital Appreciation Returns
From 1926 to 2016

| Year | Jan | Feb | Mar | Apr | May | Jun | Jul | Aug | Sep | Oct | Nov | Dec | Year | Jan–Dec* |
|---|---|---|---|---|---|---|---|---|---|---|---|---|---|---|
| 1986 | 0.0024 | 0.0715 | 0.0528 | -0.0141 | 0.0502 | 0.0141 | -0.0587 | 0.0712 | -0.0854 | 0.0546 | 0.0216 | -0.0283 | 1986 | 0.1462 |
| 1987 | 0.1318 | 0.0369 | 0.0264 | -0.0115 | 0.0060 | 0.0479 | 0.0482 | 0.0350 | -0.0242 | -0.2176 | -0.0853 | 0.0729 | 1987 | 0.0203 |
| 1988 | 0.0404 | 0.0418 | -0.0333 | 0.0094 | 0.0032 | 0.0433 | -0.0054 | -0.0386 | 0.0397 | 0.0260 | -0.0189 | 0.0147 | 1988 | 0.1240 |
| 1989 | 0.0711 | -0.0289 | 0.0208 | 0.0501 | 0.0351 | -0.0079 | 0.0884 | 0.0155 | -0.0065 | -0.0252 | 0.0165 | 0.0214 | 1989 | 0.2725 |
| 1990 | -0.0688 | 0.0085 | 0.0243 | -0.0269 | 0.0920 | -0.0089 | -0.0052 | -0.0943 | -0.0512 | -0.0067 | 0.0599 | 0.0248 | 1990 | -0.0656 |
| 1991 | 0.0415 | 0.0673 | 0.0222 | 0.0003 | 0.0386 | -0.0479 | 0.0449 | 0.0196 | -0.0191 | 0.0118 | -0.0439 | 0.1116 | 1991 | 0.2631 |
| 1992 | -0.0199 | 0.0096 | -0.0218 | 0.0279 | 0.0010 | -0.0174 | 0.0394 | -0.0240 | 0.0091 | 0.0021 | 0.0303 | 0.0101 | 1992 | 0.0446 |
| 1993 | 0.0070 | 0.0105 | 0.0187 | -0.0254 | 0.0227 | 0.0008 | -0.0053 | 0.0344 | -0.0100 | 0.0194 | -0.0129 | 0.0101 | 1993 | 0.0706 |
| 1994 | 0.0325 | -0.0300 | -0.0457 | 0.0115 | 0.0124 | -0.0268 | 0.0315 | 0.0376 | -0.0269 | 0.0209 | -0.0395 | 0.0123 | 1994 | -0.0154 |
| 1995 | 0.0243 | 0.0361 | 0.0273 | 0.0280 | 0.0363 | 0.0213 | 0.0318 | -0.0003 | 0.0401 | -0.0050 | 0.0410 | 0.0174 | 1995 | 0.3411 |
| 1996 | 0.0326 | 0.0069 | 0.0079 | 0.0134 | 0.0229 | 0.0023 | -0.0457 | 0.0188 | 0.0542 | 0.0261 | 0.0734 | -0.0215 | 1996 | 0.2026 |
| 1997 | 0.0613 | 0.0059 | -0.0426 | 0.0584 | 0.0586 | 0.0435 | 0.0781 | -0.0574 | 0.0532 | -0.0345 | 0.0446 | 0.0157 | 1997 | 0.3101 |
| 1998 | 0.0102 | 0.0704 | 0.0499 | 0.0091 | -0.0188 | 0.0394 | -0.0116 | -0.1458 | 0.0624 | 0.0803 | 0.0591 | 0.0564 | 1998 | 0.2667 |
| 1999 | 0.0410 | -0.0323 | 0.0388 | 0.0379 | -0.0250 | 0.0544 | -0.0320 | -0.0063 | -0.0286 | 0.0625 | 0.0191 | 0.0578 | 1999 | 0.1953 |
| 2000 | -0.0509 | -0.0201 | 0.0967 | -0.0308 | -0.0219 | 0.0239 | -0.0163 | 0.0607 | -0.0535 | -0.0049 | -0.0801 | 0.0041 | 2000 | -0.1014 |
| 2001 | 0.0346 | -0.0923 | -0.0642 | 0.0768 | 0.0051 | -0.0250 | -0.0108 | -0.0641 | -0.0817 | 0.0181 | 0.0752 | 0.0076 | 2001 | -0.1304 |
| 2002 | -0.0156 | -0.0208 | 0.0367 | -0.0614 | -0.0091 | -0.0725 | -0.0790 | 0.0049 | -0.1100 | 0.0864 | 0.0571 | -0.0603 | 2002 | -0.2337 |
| 2003 | -0.0274 | -0.0170 | 0.0084 | 0.0810 | 0.0509 | 0.0113 | 0.0162 | 0.0179 | -0.0119 | 0.0550 | 0.0071 | 0.0508 | 2003 | 0.2638 |
| 2004 | 0.0173 | 0.0122 | -0.0164 | -0.0168 | 0.0121 | 0.0180 | -0.0343 | 0.0023 | 0.0094 | 0.0140 | 0.0386 | 0.0325 | 2004 | 0.0899 |
| 2005 | -0.0253 | 0.0189 | -0.0191 | -0.0201 | 0.0300 | -0.0001 | 0.0360 | -0.0112 | 0.0069 | -0.0177 | 0.0352 | -0.0009 | 2005 | 0.0300 |
| 2006 | 0.0255 | 0.0005 | 0.0111 | 0.0122 | -0.0309 | 0.0001 | 0.0051 | 0.0213 | 0.0246 | 0.0315 | 0.0165 | 0.0126 | 2006 | 0.1362 |
| 2007 | 0.0141 | -0.0218 | 0.0100 | 0.0433 | 0.0326 | -0.0178 | -0.0320 | 0.0129 | 0.0358 | 0.0148 | -0.0440 | -0.0086 | 2007 | 0.0353 |
| 2008 | -0.0612 | -0.0348 | -0.0060 | 0.0475 | 0.0107 | -0.0860 | -0.0099 | 0.0122 | -0.0908 | -0.1694 | -0.0749 | 0.0078 | 2008 | -0.3849 |
| 2009 | -0.0857 | -0.1099 | 0.0854 | 0.0939 | 0.0531 | 0.0002 | 0.0741 | 0.0336 | 0.0357 | -0.0198 | 0.0574 | 0.0178 | 2009 | 0.2345 |
| 2010 | -0.0370 | 0.0285 | 0.0588 | 0.0148 | -0.0820 | -0.0539 | 0.0688 | -0.0475 | 0.0876 | 0.0369 | -0.0023 | 0.0653 | 2010 | 0.1278 |
| 2011 | 0.0226 | 0.0320 | -0.0011 | 0.0285 | -0.0135 | -0.0183 | -0.0215 | -0.0568 | -0.0718 | 0.1077 | -0.0051 | 0.0085 | 2011 | 0.0000 |
| 2012 | 0.0436 | 0.0406 | 0.0313 | -0.0075 | -0.0627 | 0.0396 | 0.0126 | 0.0198 | 0.0242 | -0.0198 | 0.0028 | 0.0071 | 2012 | 0.1341 |
| 2013 | 0.0504 | 0.0111 | 0.0360 | 0.0181 | 0.0208 | -0.0150 | 0.0495 | -0.0313 | 0.0297 | 0.0446 | 0.0280 | 0.0236 | 2013 | 0.2960 |
| 2014 | -0.0356 | 0.0431 | 0.0069 | 0.0062 | 0.0210 | 0.0191 | -0.0151 | 0.0377 | -0.0155 | 0.0232 | 0.0245 | -0.0042 | 2014 | 0.1139 |
| 2015 | -0.0310 | 0.0549 | -0.0174 | 0.0085 | 0.0105 | -0.0210 | 0.0197 | -0.0626 | -0.0264 | 0.0830 | 0.0005 | -0.0175 | 2015 | -0.0073 |
| 2016 | -0.0507 | -0.0041 | 0.0660 | 0.0027 | 0.0153 | 0.0009 | 0.0356 | -0.0012 | -0.0012 | -0.0194 | 0.0342 | 0.0182 | 2016 | 0.0954 |

*Compound annual return

# Appendix A-4

Small-Capitalization Stocks: Total Returns
From 1926 to 2016

| Year | Jan | Feb | Mar | Apr | May | Jun | Jul | Aug | Sep | Oct | Nov | Dec | Year | Jan–Dec* |
|---|---|---|---|---|---|---|---|---|---|---|---|---|---|---|
| 1926 | 0.0699 | -0.0639 | -0.1073 | 0.0179 | -0.0066 | 0.0378 | 0.0112 | 0.0256 | -0.0001 | -0.0227 | 0.0207 | 0.0332 | 1926 | 0.0028 |
| 1927 | 0.0296 | 0.0547 | -0.0548 | 0.0573 | 0.0734 | -0.0303 | 0.0516 | -0.0178 | 0.0047 | -0.0659 | 0.0808 | 0.0316 | 1927 | 0.2210 |
| 1928 | 0.0482 | -0.0236 | 0.0531 | 0.0910 | 0.0438 | -0.0842 | 0.0059 | 0.0442 | 0.0890 | 0.0276 | 0.1147 | -0.0513 | 1928 | 0.3969 |
| 1929 | 0.0035 | -0.0026 | -0.0200 | 0.0306 | -0.1336 | 0.0533 | 0.0114 | -0.0164 | -0.0922 | -0.2768 | -0.1500 | -0.0501 | 1929 | -0.5136 |
| 1930 | 0.1293 | 0.0643 | 0.1007 | -0.0698 | -0.0542 | -0.2168 | 0.0301 | -0.0166 | -0.1459 | -0.1097 | -0.0028 | -0.1166 | 1930 | -0.3815 |
| 1931 | 0.2103 | 0.2566 | -0.0708 | -0.2164 | -0.1379 | 0.1819 | -0.0557 | -0.0763 | -0.3246 | 0.0770 | -0.1008 | -0.2195 | 1931 | -0.4975 |
| 1932 | 0.1019 | 0.0291 | -0.1311 | -0.2220 | -0.1193 | 0.0033 | 0.3523 | 0.7346 | -0.1320 | -0.1775 | -0.1227 | -0.0492 | 1932 | -0.0539 |
| 1933 | -0.0083 | -0.1278 | 0.1118 | 0.5038 | 0.6339 | 0.2617 | -0.0550 | 0.0924 | -0.1595 | -0.1236 | 0.0654 | 0.0055 | 1933 | 1.4287 |
| 1934 | 0.3891 | 0.0166 | -0.0012 | 0.0240 | -0.1275 | -0.0024 | -0.2259 | 0.1546 | -0.0167 | 0.0097 | 0.0948 | 0.0172 | 1934 | 0.2422 |
| 1935 | -0.0328 | -0.0592 | -0.1189 | 0.0791 | -0.0024 | 0.0305 | 0.0855 | 0.0545 | 0.0357 | 0.0994 | 0.1412 | 0.0598 | 1935 | 0.4019 |
| 1936 | 0.3009 | 0.0602 | 0.0066 | -0.1795 | 0.0272 | -0.0231 | 0.0873 | 0.0210 | 0.0542 | 0.0635 | 0.1400 | 0.0160 | 1936 | 0.6480 |
| 1937 | 0.1267 | 0.0658 | 0.0120 | -0.1679 | -0.0408 | -0.1183 | 0.1235 | -0.0736 | -0.2539 | -0.1093 | -0.1453 | -0.1694 | 1937 | -0.5801 |
| 1938 | 0.0534 | 0.0343 | -0.3600 | 0.2776 | -0.0849 | 0.3498 | 0.1499 | -0.1001 | -0.0157 | 0.2136 | -0.0689 | 0.0487 | 1938 | 0.3280 |
| 1939 | -0.0848 | 0.0107 | -0.2466 | 0.0142 | 0.1088 | -0.1042 | 0.2535 | -0.1590 | 0.5145 | -0.0397 | -0.1053 | 0.0422 | 1939 | 0.0035 |
| 1940 | 0.0009 | 0.0821 | 0.0632 | 0.0654 | -0.3674 | 0.1051 | 0.0231 | 0.0255 | 0.0213 | 0.0545 | 0.0245 | -0.0447 | 1940 | -0.0516 |
| 1941 | 0.0025 | -0.0288 | 0.0319 | -0.0669 | 0.0045 | 0.0753 | 0.2165 | -0.0060 | -0.0469 | -0.0672 | -0.0495 | -0.1204 | 1941 | -0.0900 |
| 1942 | 0.1894 | -0.0073 | -0.0709 | -0.0353 | -0.0032 | 0.0336 | 0.0737 | 0.0325 | 0.0912 | 0.1087 | -0.0511 | 0.0413 | 1942 | 0.4451 |
| 1943 | 0.2132 | 0.1931 | 0.1445 | 0.0933 | 0.1156 | -0.0083 | -0.1083 | -0.0002 | 0.0428 | 0.0123 | -0.1113 | 0.1241 | 1943 | 0.8837 |
| 1944 | 0.0641 | 0.0295 | 0.0749 | -0.0532 | 0.0740 | 0.1384 | -0.0299 | 0.0318 | -0.0020 | -0.0108 | 0.0499 | 0.0869 | 1944 | 0.5372 |
| 1945 | 0.0482 | 0.1009 | -0.0861 | 0.1157 | 0.0500 | 0.0855 | -0.0556 | 0.0557 | 0.0679 | 0.0701 | 0.1172 | 0.0171 | 1945 | 0.7361 |
| 1946 | 0.1562 | -0.0637 | 0.0273 | 0.0696 | 0.0591 | -0.0462 | -0.0530 | -0.0849 | -0.1603 | -0.0118 | -0.0141 | 0.0373 | 1946 | -0.1163 |
| 1947 | 0.0421 | -0.0041 | -0.0336 | -0.1031 | -0.0534 | 0.0552 | 0.0789 | -0.0037 | 0.0115 | 0.0282 | -0.0303 | 0.0359 | 1947 | 0.0092 |
| 1948 | -0.0154 | -0.0783 | 0.0986 | 0.0368 | 0.1059 | 0.0048 | -0.0578 | 0.0006 | -0.0526 | 0.0647 | -0.1116 | 0.0088 | 1948 | -0.0211 |
| 1949 | 0.0182 | -0.0481 | 0.0629 | -0.0336 | -0.0564 | -0.0096 | 0.0671 | 0.0256 | 0.0489 | 0.0472 | 0.0016 | 0.0690 | 1949 | 0.1975 |
| 1950 | 0.0492 | 0.0221 | -0.0037 | 0.0411 | 0.0255 | -0.0777 | 0.0591 | 0.0530 | 0.0521 | -0.0059 | 0.0322 | 0.0953 | 1950 | 0.3875 |
| 1951 | 0.0830 | 0.0061 | -0.0477 | 0.0367 | -0.0331 | -0.0529 | 0.0373 | 0.0605 | 0.0215 | -0.0222 | -0.0083 | 0.0044 | 1951 | 0.0780 |
| 1952 | 0.0191 | -0.0300 | 0.0175 | -0.0519 | 0.0032 | 0.0272 | 0.0112 | -0.0006 | -0.0161 | -0.0103 | 0.0485 | 0.0160 | 1952 | 0.0303 |
| 1953 | 0.0409 | 0.0269 | -0.0067 | -0.0287 | 0.0141 | -0.0486 | 0.0152 | -0.0628 | -0.0262 | 0.0292 | 0.0126 | -0.0266 | 1953 | -0.0649 |
| 1954 | 0.0756 | 0.0094 | 0.0183 | 0.0140 | 0.0451 | 0.0086 | 0.0808 | 0.0014 | 0.0410 | 0.0068 | 0.0779 | 0.1112 | 1954 | 0.6058 |
| 1955 | 0.0201 | 0.0479 | 0.0085 | 0.0150 | 0.0078 | 0.0293 | 0.0064 | -0.0028 | 0.0109 | -0.0170 | 0.0468 | 0.0163 | 1955 | 0.2044 |

*Compound annual return

Appendix A-4 (10)

## Appendix A-4

Small-Capitalization Stocks: Total Returns
From 1926 to 2016

| Year | Jan | Feb | Mar | Apr | May | Jun | Jul | Aug | Sep | Oct | Nov | Dec | Year | Jan–Dec* |
|------|-----|-----|-----|-----|-----|-----|-----|-----|-----|-----|-----|-----|------|----------|
| 1956 | -0.0047 | 0.0278 | 0.0431 | 0.0047 | -0.0398 | 0.0056 | 0.0283 | -0.0134 | -0.0260 | 0.0104 | 0.0053 | 0.0038 | 1956 | 0.0428 |
| 1957 | 0.0236 | -0.0200 | 0.0167 | 0.0248 | 0.0075 | 0.0073 | -0.0060 | -0.0386 | -0.0452 | -0.0832 | 0.0113 | -0.0481 | 1957 | -0.1457 |
| 1958 | 0.1105 | -0.0170 | 0.0471 | 0.0376 | 0.0387 | 0.0324 | 0.0492 | 0.0428 | 0.0518 | 0.0407 | 0.0496 | 0.0313 | 1958 | 0.6489 |
| 1959 | 0.0575 | 0.0295 | 0.0027 | 0.0117 | 0.0014 | -0.0042 | 0.0327 | -0.0088 | -0.0431 | 0.0227 | 0.0222 | 0.0322 | 1959 | 0.1640 |
| 1960 | -0.0306 | 0.0050 | -0.0315 | -0.0187 | 0.0205 | 0.0340 | -0.0189 | 0.0525 | -0.0738 | -0.0401 | 0.0437 | 0.0332 | 1960 | -0.0329 |
| 1961 | 0.0915 | 0.0589 | 0.0619 | 0.0127 | 0.0427 | -0.0543 | 0.0031 | 0.0130 | -0.0339 | 0.0262 | 0.0613 | 0.0079 | 1961 | 0.3209 |
| 1962 | 0.0136 | 0.0187 | 0.0057 | -0.0777 | -0.1009 | -0.0785 | 0.0763 | 0.0289 | -0.0659 | -0.0373 | 0.1248 | -0.0089 | 1962 | -0.1190 |
| 1963 | 0.0906 | 0.0034 | 0.0149 | 0.0312 | 0.0436 | -0.0118 | 0.0033 | 0.0517 | -0.0163 | 0.0236 | -0.0106 | -0.0048 | 1963 | 0.2357 |
| 1964 | 0.0274 | 0.0365 | 0.0219 | 0.0093 | 0.0157 | 0.0163 | 0.0398 | -0.0029 | 0.0402 | 0.0205 | 0.0011 | -0.0112 | 1964 | 0.2352 |
| 1965 | 0.0529 | 0.0390 | 0.0238 | 0.0509 | -0.0078 | -0.0901 | 0.0449 | 0.0595 | 0.0347 | 0.0572 | 0.0371 | 0.0622 | 1965 | 0.4175 |
| 1966 | 0.0756 | 0.0311 | -0.0192 | 0.0343 | -0.0961 | -0.0012 | -0.0012 | -0.1080 | -0.0164 | -0.0107 | 0.0491 | 0.0065 | 1966 | -0.0701 |
| 1967 | 0.1838 | 0.0450 | 0.0615 | 0.0271 | -0.0085 | 0.1017 | 0.0951 | 0.0020 | 0.0565 | -0.0311 | 0.0117 | 0.0965 | 1967 | 0.8357 |
| 1968 | 0.0154 | -0.0709 | -0.0109 | 0.1461 | 0.0999 | 0.0030 | -0.0345 | 0.0367 | 0.0599 | 0.0030 | 0.0764 | 0.0062 | 1968 | 0.3597 |
| 1969 | -0.0166 | -0.0990 | 0.0396 | 0.0395 | 0.0173 | -0.1165 | -0.1070 | 0.0732 | -0.0261 | 0.0610 | -0.0557 | -0.0687 | 1969 | -0.2505 |
| 1970 | -0.0608 | 0.0387 | -0.0285 | -0.1728 | -0.1031 | -0.0929 | 0.0554 | 0.0949 | 0.1086 | -0.0706 | 0.0137 | 0.0726 | 1970 | -0.1743 |
| 1971 | 0.1592 | 0.0317 | 0.0564 | 0.0247 | -0.0605 | -0.0319 | -0.0563 | 0.0583 | -0.0226 | -0.0551 | -0.0373 | 0.1144 | 1971 | 0.1650 |
| 1972 | 0.1130 | 0.0296 | -0.0143 | 0.0129 | -0.0191 | -0.0305 | -0.0413 | 0.0186 | -0.0349 | -0.0175 | 0.0592 | -0.0214 | 1972 | 0.0443 |
| 1973 | -0.0432 | -0.0799 | -0.0208 | -0.0621 | -0.0811 | -0.0290 | 0.1194 | -0.0445 | 0.1064 | 0.0084 | -0.1962 | -0.0014 | 1973 | -0.3090 |
| 1974 | 0.1326 | -0.0085 | -0.0074 | -0.0464 | -0.0793 | -0.0147 | -0.0219 | -0.0681 | -0.0653 | 0.1063 | -0.0438 | -0.0788 | 1974 | -0.1995 |
| 1975 | 0.2767 | 0.0285 | 0.0618 | 0.0531 | 0.0663 | 0.0750 | -0.0254 | -0.0574 | -0.0182 | -0.0050 | 0.0320 | -0.0197 | 1975 | 0.5282 |
| 1976 | 0.2684 | 0.1390 | -0.0015 | -0.0359 | -0.0361 | 0.0459 | 0.0045 | -0.0290 | 0.0104 | -0.0209 | 0.0404 | 0.1180 | 1976 | 0.5738 |
| 1977 | 0.0450 | -0.0039 | 0.0131 | 0.0228 | -0.0028 | 0.0772 | 0.0030 | -0.0107 | 0.0092 | -0.0330 | 0.1086 | 0.0081 | 1977 | 0.2538 |
| 1978 | -0.0189 | 0.0347 | 0.1032 | 0.0788 | 0.0820 | -0.0189 | 0.0684 | 0.0939 | -0.0032 | -0.2427 | 0.0732 | 0.0168 | 1978 | 0.2346 |
| 1979 | 0.1321 | -0.0282 | 0.1120 | 0.0387 | 0.0035 | 0.0472 | 0.0171 | 0.0756 | -0.0344 | -0.1154 | 0.0858 | 0.0588 | 1979 | 0.4346 |
| 1980 | 0.0836 | -0.0284 | -0.1778 | 0.0694 | 0.0750 | 0.0452 | 0.1323 | 0.0604 | 0.0418 | 0.0333 | 0.0766 | -0.0338 | 1980 | 0.3988 |
| 1981 | 0.0207 | 0.0094 | 0.0943 | 0.0657 | 0.0422 | 0.0076 | -0.0316 | -0.0684 | -0.0733 | 0.0742 | 0.0276 | -0.0220 | 1981 | 0.1388 |
| 1982 | -0.0196 | -0.0296 | -0.0086 | 0.0383 | -0.0248 | -0.0159 | -0.0015 | 0.0698 | 0.0327 | 0.1305 | 0.0779 | 0.0132 | 1982 | 0.2801 |
| 1983 | 0.0628 | 0.0712 | 0.0525 | 0.0767 | 0.0870 | 0.0348 | -0.0088 | -0.0197 | 0.0133 | -0.0568 | 0.0516 | -0.0145 | 1983 | 0.3967 |
| 1984 | -0.0008 | -0.0645 | 0.0174 | -0.0085 | -0.0521 | 0.0300 | -0.0420 | 0.0998 | 0.0027 | -0.0217 | -0.0336 | 0.0150 | 1984 | -0.0667 |
| 1985 | 0.1059 | 0.0272 | -0.0214 | -0.0174 | 0.0276 | 0.0106 | 0.0260 | -0.0072 | -0.0544 | 0.0261 | 0.0620 | 0.0470 | 1985 | 0.2466 |

*Compound annual return

## Appendix A-4

Small-Capitalization Stocks: Total Returns
From 1926 to 2016

| Year | Jan | Feb | Mar | Apr | May | Jun | Jul | Aug | Sep | Oct | Nov | Dec | Year | Jan–Dec* |
|---|---|---|---|---|---|---|---|---|---|---|---|---|---|---|
| 1986 | 0.0112 | 0.0719 | 0.0477 | 0.0064 | 0.0360 | 0.0026 | -0.0710 | 0.0218 | -0.0559 | 0.0346 | -0.0031 | -0.0262 | 1986 | 0.0685 |
| 1987 | 0.0943 | 0.0809 | 0.0233 | -0.0313 | -0.0039 | 0.0266 | 0.0364 | 0.0287 | -0.0081 | -0.2919 | -0.0397 | 0.0520 | 1987 | -0.0930 |
| 1988 | 0.0556 | 0.0760 | 0.0408 | 0.0209 | -0.0179 | 0.0612 | -0.0025 | -0.0246 | 0.0227 | -0.0123 | -0.0437 | 0.0394 | 1988 | 0.2287 |
| 1989 | 0.0404 | 0.0083 | 0.0358 | 0.0279 | 0.0362 | -0.0201 | 0.0407 | 0.0122 | 0.0000 | -0.0604 | -0.0051 | -0.0134 | 1989 | 0.1018 |
| 1990 | -0.0764 | 0.0187 | 0.0368 | -0.0266 | 0.0561 | 0.0144 | -0.0382 | -0.1296 | -0.0829 | -0.0572 | 0.0450 | 0.0194 | 1990 | -0.2156 |
| 1991 | 0.0841 | 0.1113 | 0.0680 | 0.0034 | 0.0334 | -0.0485 | 0.0407 | 0.0261 | 0.0032 | 0.0317 | -0.0276 | 0.0601 | 1991 | 0.4463 |
| 1992 | 0.1128 | 0.0452 | -0.0249 | -0.0403 | -0.0014 | -0.0519 | 0.0370 | -0.0228 | 0.0131 | 0.0259 | 0.0885 | 0.0441 | 1992 | 0.2335 |
| 1993 | 0.0543 | -0.0180 | 0.0289 | -0.0306 | 0.0342 | -0.0038 | 0.0166 | 0.0339 | 0.0316 | 0.0471 | -0.0175 | 0.0194 | 1993 | 0.2098 |
| 1994 | 0.0618 | -0.0023 | -0.0446 | 0.0060 | -0.0012 | -0.0262 | 0.0184 | 0.0337 | 0.0105 | 0.0115 | -0.0326 | 0.0002 | 1994 | 0.0311 |
| 1995 | 0.0283 | 0.0252 | 0.0145 | 0.0352 | 0.0298 | 0.0568 | 0.0645 | 0.0358 | 0.0195 | -0.0487 | 0.0192 | 0.0239 | 1995 | 0.3446 |
| 1996 | 0.0028 | 0.0369 | 0.0228 | 0.0848 | 0.0749 | -0.0582 | -0.0943 | 0.0476 | 0.0291 | -0.0175 | 0.0288 | 0.0204 | 1996 | 0.1762 |
| 1997 | 0.0420 | -0.0206 | -0.0490 | -0.0276 | 0.1022 | 0.0498 | 0.0605 | 0.0509 | 0.0844 | -0.0386 | -0.0155 | -0.0171 | 1997 | 0.2278 |
| 1998 | -0.0059 | 0.0649 | 0.0481 | 0.0168 | -0.0497 | -0.0206 | -0.0671 | -0.2010 | 0.0369 | 0.0356 | 0.0758 | 0.0252 | 1998 | -0.0731 |
| 1999 | 0.0279 | -0.0687 | -0.0379 | 0.0949 | 0.0387 | 0.0568 | 0.0092 | -0.0191 | -0.0221 | -0.0087 | 0.0971 | 0.1137 | 1999 | 0.2979 |
| 2000 | 0.0595 | 0.2358 | -0.0751 | -0.1251 | -0.0808 | 0.1368 | -0.0322 | 0.0925 | -0.0217 | -0.0706 | -0.1110 | 0.0189 | 2000 | -0.0359 |
| 2001 | 0.1380 | -0.0702 | -0.0480 | 0.0731 | 0.0960 | 0.0359 | -0.0254 | -0.0295 | -0.1278 | 0.0645 | 0.0674 | 0.0672 | 2001 | 0.2277 |
| 2002 | 0.0110 | -0.0277 | 0.0884 | 0.0243 | -0.0273 | -0.0356 | -0.1448 | -0.0057 | -0.0674 | 0.0257 | 0.0836 | -0.0429 | 2002 | -0.1328 |
| 2003 | -0.0223 | -0.0288 | 0.0111 | 0.0928 | 0.1162 | 0.0440 | 0.0738 | 0.0473 | 0.0009 | 0.0894 | 0.0430 | 0.0277 | 2003 | 0.6070 |
| 2004 | 0.0578 | 0.0050 | 0.0014 | -0.0409 | 0.0000 | 0.0441 | -0.0747 | -0.0152 | 0.0501 | 0.0184 | 0.0897 | 0.0458 | 2004 | 0.1839 |
| 2005 | -0.0410 | 0.0083 | -0.0323 | -0.0622 | 0.0603 | 0.0452 | 0.0763 | -0.0139 | 0.0061 | -0.0281 | 0.0453 | 0.0018 | 2005 | 0.0569 |
| 2006 | 0.0914 | 0.0025 | 0.0455 | -0.0041 | -0.0589 | -0.0089 | -0.0345 | 0.0278 | 0.0056 | 0.0545 | 0.0225 | 0.0161 | 2006 | 0.1617 |
| 2007 | 0.0115 | -0.0050 | 0.0102 | 0.0150 | 0.0315 | -0.0033 | -0.0651 | 0.0116 | 0.0148 | 0.0170 | -0.0842 | -0.0006 | 2007 | -0.0522 |
| 2008 | -0.0765 | -0.0314 | 0.0031 | 0.0207 | 0.0398 | -0.0905 | 0.0448 | 0.0338 | -0.0737 | -0.2071 | -0.1284 | 0.0566 | 2008 | -0.3672 |
| 2009 | -0.1191 | -0.1311 | 0.0958 | 0.1739 | 0.0343 | 0.0276 | 0.0982 | 0.0273 | 0.0576 | -0.0727 | 0.0178 | 0.0869 | 2009 | 0.2809 |
| 2010 | -0.0294 | 0.0439 | 0.0808 | 0.0727 | -0.0742 | -0.0724 | 0.0714 | -0.0798 | 0.1216 | 0.0434 | 0.0424 | 0.0819 | 2010 | 0.3126 |
| 2011 | -0.0109 | 0.0587 | 0.0325 | 0.0168 | -0.0192 | -0.0216 | -0.0269 | -0.0893 | -0.1058 | 0.1543 | -0.0060 | 0.0086 | 2011 | -0.0326 |
| 2012 | 0.0696 | 0.0191 | 0.0298 | -0.0142 | -0.0697 | 0.0512 | -0.0091 | 0.0312 | 0.0419 | -0.0205 | 0.0094 | 0.0380 | 2012 | 0.1824 |
| 2013 | 0.0568 | 0.0110 | 0.0487 | -0.0079 | 0.0518 | 0.0046 | 0.0741 | -0.0348 | 0.0705 | 0.0348 | 0.0555 | 0.0189 | 2013 | 0.4507 |
| 2014 | -0.0443 | 0.0421 | 0.0097 | -0.0341 | 0.0010 | 0.0434 | -0.0584 | 0.0454 | -0.0569 | 0.0652 | -0.0075 | 0.0337 | 2014 | 0.0292 |
| 2015 | -0.0490 | 0.0603 | 0.0229 | -0.0195 | 0.0138 | 0.0163 | -0.0244 | -0.0443 | -0.0431 | 0.0603 | 0.0284 | -0.0490 | 2015 | -0.0360 |
| 2016 | -0.0680 | 0.0110 | 0.0708 | 0.0108 | 0.0107 | -0.0017 | 0.0502 | 0.0159 | 0.0072 | -0.0353 | 0.1319 | 0.0406 | 2016 | 0.2565 |

*Compound annual return

## Appendix A-5

Long-term Corporate Bonds: Total Returns
From 1926 to 2016

| Year | Jan | Feb | Mar | Apr | May | Jun | Jul | Aug | Sep | Oct | Nov | Dec | Year | Jan–Dec* |
|------|-----|-----|-----|-----|-----|-----|-----|-----|-----|-----|-----|-----|------|----------|
| 1926 | 0.0072 | 0.0045 | 0.0084 | 0.0097 | 0.0044 | 0.0004 | 0.0057 | 0.0044 | 0.0057 | 0.0097 | 0.0057 | 0.0056 | 1926 | 0.0737 |
| 1927 | 0.0056 | 0.0069 | 0.0083 | 0.0055 | -0.0011 | 0.0043 | 0.0003 | 0.0083 | 0.0149 | 0.0055 | 0.0068 | 0.0068 | 1927 | 0.0744 |
| 1928 | 0.0027 | 0.0068 | 0.0041 | 0.0014 | -0.0078 | -0.0024 | -0.0010 | 0.0083 | 0.0030 | 0.0083 | -0.0036 | 0.0084 | 1928 | 0.0284 |
| 1929 | 0.0043 | 0.0030 | -0.0087 | 0.0019 | 0.0045 | -0.0046 | 0.0020 | 0.0020 | 0.0034 | 0.0073 | -0.0018 | 0.0192 | 1929 | 0.0327 |
| 1930 | 0.0059 | 0.0072 | 0.0138 | 0.0084 | 0.0057 | 0.0110 | 0.0056 | 0.0136 | 0.0108 | 0.0054 | -0.0012 | -0.0090 | 1930 | 0.0798 |
| 1931 | 0.0203 | 0.0068 | 0.0094 | 0.0067 | 0.0134 | 0.0052 | 0.0052 | 0.0012 | -0.0014 | -0.0363 | -0.0189 | -0.0286 | 1931 | -0.0185 |
| 1932 | -0.0052 | -0.0238 | 0.0356 | -0.0176 | 0.0107 | -0.0009 | 0.0043 | 0.0436 | 0.0301 | 0.0074 | 0.0073 | 0.0139 | 1932 | 0.1082 |
| 1933 | 0.0547 | -0.0523 | 0.0047 | -0.0095 | 0.0588 | 0.0190 | 0.0161 | 0.0093 | -0.0014 | 0.0040 | -0.0248 | 0.0257 | 1933 | 0.1038 |
| 1934 | 0.0257 | 0.0146 | 0.0187 | 0.0104 | 0.0090 | 0.0158 | 0.0047 | 0.0047 | -0.0061 | 0.0102 | 0.0129 | 0.0101 | 1934 | 0.1384 |
| 1935 | 0.0211 | 0.0141 | 0.0043 | 0.0112 | 0.0042 | 0.0112 | 0.0111 | -0.0042 | 0.0000 | 0.0042 | 0.0069 | 0.0083 | 1935 | 0.0961 |
| 1936 | 0.0082 | 0.0054 | 0.0082 | 0.0026 | 0.0040 | 0.0082 | 0.0011 | 0.0067 | 0.0067 | 0.0025 | 0.0109 | 0.0010 | 1936 | 0.0674 |
| 1937 | 0.0024 | -0.0046 | -0.0114 | 0.0068 | 0.0040 | 0.0053 | 0.0039 | -0.0017 | 0.0025 | 0.0067 | 0.0067 | 0.0067 | 1937 | 0.0275 |
| 1938 | 0.0038 | 0.0010 | -0.0087 | 0.0138 | 0.0010 | 0.0095 | 0.0066 | -0.0019 | 0.0109 | 0.0080 | 0.0037 | 0.0122 | 1938 | 0.0613 |
| 1939 | 0.0022 | 0.0064 | 0.0022 | 0.0064 | 0.0049 | 0.0035 | -0.0007 | -0.0392 | 0.0151 | 0.0237 | 0.0079 | 0.0078 | 1939 | 0.0397 |
| 1940 | 0.0049 | 0.0021 | 0.0049 | -0.0092 | -0.0021 | 0.0121 | 0.0021 | 0.0007 | 0.0092 | 0.0049 | 0.0063 | -0.0023 | 1940 | 0.0339 |
| 1941 | 0.0006 | 0.0006 | -0.0022 | 0.0078 | 0.0049 | 0.0063 | 0.0063 | 0.0034 | 0.0048 | 0.0034 | -0.0094 | 0.0006 | 1941 | 0.0273 |
| 1942 | 0.0006 | -0.0008 | 0.0063 | 0.0006 | 0.0020 | 0.0034 | 0.0020 | 0.0035 | 0.0020 | 0.0006 | -0.0023 | 0.0049 | 1942 | 0.0260 |
| 1943 | 0.0049 | 0.0006 | 0.0020 | 0.0049 | 0.0048 | 0.0048 | 0.0019 | 0.0019 | 0.0005 | -0.0009 | -0.0023 | 0.0049 | 1943 | 0.0283 |
| 1944 | 0.0020 | 0.0034 | 0.0048 | 0.0034 | 0.0005 | 0.0020 | 0.0034 | 0.0034 | 0.0019 | 0.0019 | 0.0048 | 0.0149 | 1944 | 0.0473 |
| 1945 | 0.0076 | 0.0046 | 0.0018 | 0.0018 | -0.0011 | 0.0032 | -0.0011 | 0.0004 | 0.0032 | 0.0032 | 0.0032 | 0.0133 | 1945 | 0.0408 |
| 1946 | 0.0128 | 0.0034 | 0.0034 | -0.0043 | 0.0019 | 0.0019 | -0.0012 | -0.0088 | -0.0026 | 0.0020 | -0.0025 | 0.0113 | 1946 | 0.0172 |
| 1947 | 0.0005 | 0.0005 | 0.0067 | 0.0020 | 0.0020 | 0.0004 | 0.0020 | -0.0071 | -0.0131 | -0.0099 | -0.0098 | 0.0024 | 1947 | -0.0234 |
| 1948 | 0.0024 | 0.0039 | 0.0115 | 0.0038 | 0.0008 | -0.0083 | -0.0052 | 0.0055 | 0.0024 | 0.0024 | 0.0085 | 0.0131 | 1948 | 0.0414 |
| 1949 | 0.0038 | 0.0038 | 0.0007 | 0.0023 | 0.0038 | 0.0084 | 0.0099 | 0.0037 | 0.0021 | 0.0067 | 0.0021 | -0.0145 | 1949 | 0.0331 |
| 1950 | 0.0037 | 0.0007 | 0.0022 | -0.0008 | -0.0008 | 0.0023 | 0.0069 | 0.0038 | -0.0039 | -0.0008 | 0.0054 | 0.0023 | 1950 | 0.0212 |
| 1951 | 0.0019 | -0.0044 | -0.0237 | -0.0009 | -0.0015 | -0.0093 | 0.0205 | 0.0114 | -0.0057 | -0.0145 | -0.0061 | 0.0058 | 1951 | -0.0269 |
| 1952 | 0.0199 | -0.0085 | 0.0076 | -0.0004 | 0.0031 | 0.0016 | 0.0016 | 0.0063 | -0.0018 | 0.0039 | 0.0108 | -0.0091 | 1952 | 0.0352 |
| 1953 | -0.0080 | -0.0040 | -0.0033 | -0.0248 | -0.0030 | 0.0109 | 0.0177 | -0.0085 | 0.0253 | 0.0227 | -0.0073 | 0.0172 | 1953 | 0.0341 |
| 1954 | 0.0124 | 0.0198 | 0.0039 | -0.0034 | -0.0042 | 0.0063 | 0.0040 | 0.0018 | 0.0040 | 0.0040 | 0.0025 | 0.0017 | 1954 | 0.0539 |
| 1955 | -0.0097 | -0.0063 | 0.0092 | -0.0001 | -0.0018 | 0.0029 | -0.0041 | -0.0038 | 0.0076 | 0.0078 | -0.0030 | 0.0063 | 1955 | 0.0048 |

*Compound annual return

## Appendix A-5

Long-term Corporate Bonds: Total Returns
From 1926 to 2016

| Year | Jan | Feb | Mar | Apr | May | Jun | Jul | Aug | Sep | Oct | Nov | Dec | Year | Jan–Dec* |
|------|-----|-----|-----|-----|-----|-----|-----|-----|-----|-----|-----|-----|------|----------|
| 1956 | 0.0104 | 0.0026 | -0.0146 | -0.0115 | 0.0052 | -0.0018 | -0.0093 | -0.0208 | 0.0012 | -0.0105 | -0.0126 | -0.0082 | 1956 | -0.0681 |
| 1957 | 0.0197 | 0.0093 | 0.0050 | -0.0066 | -0.0075 | -0.0322 | -0.0110 | -0.0009 | 0.0095 | 0.0023 | 0.0311 | 0.0685 | 1957 | 0.0871 |
| 1958 | 0.0099 | -0.0008 | -0.0046 | 0.0163 | 0.0031 | -0.0038 | -0.0153 | -0.0320 | -0.0096 | 0.0107 | 0.0105 | -0.0058 | 1958 | -0.0222 |
| 1959 | -0.0028 | 0.0126 | -0.0083 | -0.0172 | -0.0114 | 0.0044 | 0.0089 | -0.0068 | -0.0088 | 0.0165 | 0.0135 | -0.0096 | 1959 | -0.0097 |
| 1960 | 0.0107 | 0.0128 | 0.0191 | -0.0022 | -0.0021 | 0.0141 | 0.0257 | 0.0117 | -0.0063 | 0.0008 | -0.0070 | 0.0104 | 1960 | 0.0907 |
| 1961 | 0.0148 | 0.0210 | -0.0029 | -0.0116 | 0.0049 | -0.0080 | 0.0040 | -0.0018 | 0.0144 | 0.0127 | 0.0028 | -0.0026 | 1961 | 0.0482 |
| 1962 | 0.0080 | 0.0052 | 0.0151 | 0.0142 | 0.0000 | -0.0026 | -0.0015 | 0.0143 | 0.0089 | 0.0068 | 0.0062 | 0.0023 | 1962 | 0.0795 |
| 1963 | 0.0059 | 0.0023 | 0.0026 | -0.0051 | 0.0048 | 0.0043 | 0.0028 | 0.0035 | -0.0023 | 0.0049 | 0.0015 | -0.0034 | 1963 | 0.0219 |
| 1964 | 0.0087 | 0.0054 | -0.0062 | 0.0040 | 0.0057 | 0.0048 | 0.0052 | 0.0037 | 0.0021 | 0.0050 | -0.0004 | 0.0088 | 1964 | 0.0477 |
| 1965 | 0.0081 | 0.0009 | 0.0012 | 0.0021 | -0.0008 | 0.0003 | 0.0019 | -0.0006 | -0.0015 | 0.0046 | -0.0057 | -0.0149 | 1965 | -0.0046 |
| 1966 | 0.0022 | -0.0113 | -0.0059 | 0.0013 | -0.0026 | 0.0030 | -0.0098 | -0.0259 | 0.0078 | 0.0261 | -0.0020 | 0.0201 | 1966 | 0.0020 |
| 1967 | 0.0450 | -0.0201 | 0.0117 | -0.0071 | -0.0254 | -0.0223 | 0.0041 | -0.0007 | 0.0094 | -0.0281 | -0.0272 | 0.0127 | 1967 | -0.0495 |
| 1968 | 0.0361 | 0.0037 | -0.0197 | 0.0048 | 0.0032 | 0.0122 | 0.0341 | 0.0206 | -0.0053 | -0.0160 | -0.0226 | -0.0233 | 1968 | 0.0257 |
| 1969 | 0.0139 | -0.0160 | -0.0200 | 0.0335 | -0.0227 | 0.0035 | 0.0005 | -0.0020 | -0.0244 | 0.0127 | -0.0471 | -0.0134 | 1969 | -0.0809 |
| 1970 | 0.0141 | 0.0401 | -0.0045 | -0.0250 | -0.0163 | 0.0001 | 0.0556 | 0.0100 | 0.0139 | -0.0096 | 0.0584 | 0.0372 | 1970 | 0.1837 |
| 1971 | 0.0532 | -0.0366 | 0.0258 | -0.0236 | -0.0161 | 0.0107 | -0.0025 | 0.0554 | -0.0102 | 0.0282 | 0.0029 | 0.0223 | 1971 | 0.1101 |
| 1972 | -0.0033 | 0.0107 | 0.0024 | 0.0035 | 0.0163 | -0.0068 | 0.0030 | 0.0072 | 0.0031 | 0.0101 | 0.0249 | -0.0004 | 1972 | 0.0726 |
| 1973 | -0.0054 | 0.0023 | 0.0045 | 0.0061 | -0.0039 | -0.0056 | -0.0476 | 0.0356 | 0.0356 | -0.0066 | 0.0078 | -0.0089 | 1973 | 0.0114 |
| 1974 | -0.0053 | 0.0009 | -0.0307 | -0.0341 | 0.0105 | -0.0285 | -0.0211 | -0.0268 | 0.0174 | 0.0885 | 0.0117 | -0.0075 | 1974 | -0.0306 |
| 1975 | 0.0596 | 0.0137 | -0.0247 | -0.0052 | 0.0106 | 0.0304 | -0.0030 | -0.0175 | -0.0126 | 0.0553 | -0.0088 | 0.0442 | 1975 | 0.1464 |
| 1976 | 0.0188 | 0.0061 | 0.0167 | -0.0015 | -0.0103 | 0.0150 | 0.0149 | 0.0231 | 0.0167 | 0.0070 | 0.0319 | 0.0347 | 1976 | 0.1865 |
| 1977 | -0.0303 | -0.0020 | 0.0094 | 0.0100 | 0.0106 | 0.0175 | -0.0005 | 0.0136 | -0.0022 | -0.0038 | 0.0061 | -0.0105 | 1977 | 0.0171 |
| 1978 | -0.0089 | 0.0051 | 0.0042 | -0.0023 | -0.0108 | 0.0023 | 0.0101 | 0.0257 | -0.0048 | -0.0205 | 0.0134 | -0.0133 | 1978 | -0.0007 |
| 1979 | 0.0184 | -0.0128 | 0.0107 | -0.0052 | 0.0228 | 0.0269 | -0.0031 | 0.0006 | -0.0179 | -0.0890 | 0.0222 | -0.0108 | 1979 | -0.0418 |
| 1980 | -0.0645 | -0.0665 | -0.0062 | 0.1376 | 0.0560 | 0.0341 | -0.0429 | -0.0445 | -0.0237 | -0.0159 | 0.0017 | 0.0248 | 1980 | -0.0276 |
| 1981 | -0.0130 | -0.0269 | 0.0311 | -0.0769 | 0.0595 | 0.0023 | -0.0372 | -0.0345 | -0.0199 | 0.0521 | 0.1267 | -0.0580 | 1981 | -0.0124 |
| 1982 | -0.0129 | 0.0312 | 0.0306 | 0.0338 | 0.0245 | -0.0468 | 0.0540 | 0.0837 | 0.0623 | 0.0759 | 0.0201 | 0.0108 | 1982 | 0.4256 |
| 1983 | -0.0094 | 0.0428 | 0.0072 | 0.0548 | -0.0324 | -0.0046 | -0.0455 | 0.0051 | 0.0392 | -0.0025 | 0.0142 | -0.0033 | 1983 | 0.0626 |
| 1984 | 0.0270 | -0.0172 | -0.0235 | -0.0073 | -0.0483 | 0.0199 | 0.0586 | 0.0307 | 0.0314 | 0.0572 | 0.0212 | 0.0128 | 1984 | 0.1686 |
| 1985 | 0.0325 | -0.0373 | 0.0179 | 0.0296 | 0.0820 | 0.0083 | -0.0121 | 0.0260 | 0.0071 | 0.0329 | 0.0370 | 0.0469 | 1985 | 0.3009 |

*Compound annual return

## Appendix A-5

Long-term Corporate Bonds: Total Returns
From 1926 to 2016

| Year | Jan | Feb | Mar | Apr | May | Jun | Jul | Aug | Sep | Oct | Nov | Dec | Year | Jan–Dec* |
|---|---|---|---|---|---|---|---|---|---|---|---|---|---|---|
| 1986 | 0.0045 | 0.0752 | 0.0256 | 0.0016 | -0.0164 | 0.0218 | 0.0031 | 0.0275 | -0.0114 | 0.0189 | 0.0233 | 0.0117 | 1986 | 0.1985 |
| 1987 | 0.0216 | 0.0058 | -0.0087 | -0.0502 | -0.0052 | 0.0155 | -0.0119 | -0.0075 | -0.0422 | 0.0507 | 0.0125 | 0.0212 | 1987 | -0.0027 |
| 1988 | 0.0517 | 0.0138 | -0.0188 | -0.0149 | -0.0057 | 0.0379 | -0.0111 | 0.0054 | 0.0326 | 0.0273 | -0.0169 | 0.0039 | 1988 | 0.1070 |
| 1989 | 0.0202 | -0.0129 | 0.0064 | 0.0213 | 0.0379 | 0.0395 | 0.0178 | -0.0163 | 0.0040 | 0.0276 | 0.0070 | 0.0006 | 1989 | 0.1623 |
| 1990 | -0.0191 | -0.0012 | -0.0011 | -0.0191 | 0.0385 | 0.0216 | 0.0102 | -0.0292 | 0.0091 | 0.0132 | 0.0285 | 0.0167 | 1990 | 0.0678 |
| 1991 | 0.0150 | 0.0121 | 0.0108 | 0.0138 | 0.0039 | -0.0018 | 0.0167 | 0.0275 | 0.0271 | 0.0043 | 0.0106 | 0.0436 | 1991 | 0.1989 |
| 1992 | -0.0173 | 0.0096 | -0.0073 | 0.0016 | 0.0254 | 0.0156 | 0.0308 | 0.0090 | 0.0099 | -0.0156 | 0.0069 | 0.0228 | 1992 | 0.0939 |
| 1993 | 0.0250 | 0.0256 | 0.0025 | 0.0052 | 0.0020 | 0.0293 | 0.0100 | 0.0287 | 0.0043 | 0.0051 | -0.0188 | 0.0067 | 1993 | 0.1319 |
| 1994 | 0.0202 | -0.0286 | -0.0383 | -0.0097 | -0.0062 | -0.0081 | 0.0309 | -0.0031 | -0.0265 | -0.0050 | 0.0018 | 0.0157 | 1994 | -0.0576 |
| 1995 | 0.0256 | 0.0289 | 0.0095 | 0.0175 | 0.0631 | 0.0079 | -0.0101 | 0.0214 | 0.0153 | 0.0185 | 0.0242 | 0.0228 | 1995 | 0.2720 |
| 1996 | 0.0014 | -0.0373 | -0.0130 | -0.0160 | 0.0005 | 0.0172 | 0.0010 | -0.0070 | 0.0259 | 0.0361 | 0.0263 | -0.0186 | 1996 | 0.0140 |
| 1997 | -0.0028 | 0.0028 | -0.0221 | 0.0184 | 0.0128 | 0.0187 | 0.0528 | -0.0240 | 0.0226 | 0.0191 | 0.0101 | 0.0163 | 1997 | 0.1295 |
| 1998 | 0.0137 | -0.0007 | 0.0038 | 0.0053 | 0.0167 | 0.0115 | -0.0056 | 0.0089 | 0.0413 | -0.0190 | 0.0270 | 0.0010 | 1998 | 0.1076 |
| 1999 | 0.0123 | -0.0401 | 0.0002 | -0.0024 | -0.0176 | -0.0160 | -0.0113 | -0.0026 | 0.0093 | 0.0047 | -0.0024 | -0.0102 | 1999 | -0.0745 |
| 2000 | -0.0021 | 0.0092 | 0.0169 | -0.0115 | -0.0161 | 0.0326 | 0.0179 | 0.0135 | 0.0046 | 0.0045 | 0.0263 | 0.0270 | 2000 | 0.1287 |
| 2001 | 0.0359 | 0.0127 | -0.0029 | -0.0128 | 0.0132 | 0.0055 | 0.0361 | 0.0157 | -0.0152 | 0.0437 | -0.0188 | -0.0090 | 2001 | 0.1065 |
| 2002 | 0.0175 | 0.0130 | -0.0295 | 0.0253 | 0.0113 | 0.0073 | 0.0094 | 0.0452 | 0.0330 | -0.0240 | 0.0103 | 0.0361 | 2002 | 0.1633 |
| 2003 | 0.0021 | 0.0264 | -0.0080 | 0.0229 | 0.0471 | -0.0143 | -0.0881 | 0.0219 | 0.0503 | -0.0203 | 0.0052 | 0.0139 | 2003 | 0.0527 |
| 2004 | 0.0187 | 0.0178 | 0.0118 | -0.0534 | -0.0071 | 0.0093 | 0.0184 | 0.0395 | 0.0101 | 0.0164 | -0.0200 | 0.0257 | 2004 | 0.0872 |
| 2005 | 0.0277 | -0.0112 | -0.0125 | 0.0327 | 0.0295 | 0.0141 | -0.0244 | 0.0233 | -0.0310 | -0.0204 | 0.0099 | 0.0225 | 2005 | 0.0587 |
| 2006 | -0.0093 | 0.0128 | -0.0404 | -0.0224 | -0.0020 | 0.0039 | 0.0237 | 0.0361 | 0.0183 | 0.0127 | 0.0246 | -0.0232 | 2006 | 0.0324 |
| 2007 | -0.0051 | 0.0287 | -0.0231 | 0.0140 | -0.0178 | -0.0148 | -0.0032 | 0.0152 | 0.0135 | 0.0088 | 0.0079 | 0.0028 | 2007 | 0.0260 |
| 2008 | 0.0017 | -0.0071 | -0.0059 | 0.0091 | -0.0277 | -0.0061 | -0.0109 | 0.0121 | -0.0863 | -0.0450 | 0.1174 | 0.1560 | 2008 | 0.0878 |
| 2009 | -0.0949 | -0.0308 | -0.0018 | -0.0030 | 0.0489 | 0.0350 | 0.0565 | 0.0235 | 0.0273 | 0.0016 | 0.0044 | -0.0275 | 2009 | 0.0302 |
| 2010 | 0.0096 | 0.0039 | 0.0045 | 0.0357 | -0.0051 | 0.0519 | 0.0170 | 0.0473 | -0.0144 | -0.0203 | -0.0057 | -0.0036 | 2010 | 0.1244 |
| 2011 | -0.0198 | 0.0157 | -0.0072 | 0.0239 | 0.0257 | -0.0210 | 0.0473 | 0.0240 | 0.0575 | 0.0094 | -0.0356 | 0.0512 | 2011 | 0.1795 |
| 2012 | 0.0194 | 0.0057 | -0.0303 | 0.0251 | 0.0344 | 0.0064 | 0.0612 | -0.0093 | -0.0126 | 0.0206 | -0.0092 | -0.0062 | 2012 | 0.1068 |
| 2013 | -0.0313 | 0.0093 | -0.0018 | 0.0349 | -0.0536 | -0.0371 | 0.0031 | -0.0074 | 0.0014 | 0.0211 | -0.0086 | 0.0002 | 2013 | -0.0707 |
| 2014 | 0.0331 | 0.0168 | 0.0062 | 0.0160 | 0.0188 | 0.0020 | 0.0024 | 0.0356 | -0.0271 | 0.0225 | 0.0173 | 0.0183 | 2014 | 0.1728 |
| 2015 | 0.0599 | -0.0320 | 0.0058 | -0.0223 | -0.0204 | -0.0320 | 0.0239 | -0.0067 | 0.0133 | 0.0020 | 0.0020 | 0.0000 | 2015 | -0.0102 |
| 2016 | 0.0067 | 0.0232 | 0.0423 | 0.0146 | 0.0016 | 0.0377 | 0.0245 | 0.0016 | -0.0119 | -0.0263 | -0.0510 | 0.0059 | 2016 | 0.0670 |

*Compound annual return

## Appendix A-6

Long-term Government Bonds: Total Returns
From 1926 to 2016

| Year | Jan | Feb | Mar | Apr | May | Jun | Jul | Aug | Sep | Oct | Nov | Dec | Year | Jan–Dec* |
|---|---|---|---|---|---|---|---|---|---|---|---|---|---|---|
| 1926 | 0.0138 | 0.0063 | 0.0041 | 0.0076 | 0.0014 | 0.0038 | 0.0004 | 0.0000 | 0.0038 | 0.0102 | 0.0160 | 0.0078 | 1926 | 0.0777 |
| 1927 | 0.0075 | 0.0088 | 0.0253 | -0.0005 | 0.0109 | -0.0069 | 0.0050 | 0.0076 | 0.0018 | 0.0099 | 0.0097 | 0.0072 | 1927 | 0.0893 |
| 1928 | -0.0036 | 0.0061 | 0.0045 | -0.0004 | -0.0077 | 0.0041 | -0.0217 | 0.0076 | -0.0041 | 0.0158 | 0.0003 | 0.0004 | 1928 | 0.0010 |
| 1929 | -0.0090 | -0.0157 | -0.0144 | 0.0275 | -0.0162 | 0.0110 | 0.0000 | -0.0034 | 0.0028 | 0.0382 | 0.0236 | -0.0089 | 1929 | 0.0342 |
| 1930 | -0.0057 | 0.0129 | 0.0083 | -0.0016 | 0.0140 | 0.0051 | 0.0034 | 0.0013 | 0.0074 | 0.0035 | 0.0042 | -0.0070 | 1930 | 0.0466 |
| 1931 | -0.0121 | 0.0085 | 0.0104 | 0.0086 | 0.0145 | 0.0004 | -0.0042 | 0.0012 | -0.0281 | -0.0330 | 0.0027 | -0.0220 | 1931 | -0.0531 |
| 1932 | 0.0034 | 0.0413 | -0.0018 | 0.0604 | -0.0188 | 0.0065 | 0.0481 | 0.0003 | 0.0057 | -0.0017 | 0.0032 | 0.0131 | 1932 | 0.1684 |
| 1933 | 0.0148 | -0.0258 | 0.0097 | -0.0032 | 0.0303 | 0.0050 | -0.0017 | 0.0044 | 0.0023 | -0.0091 | -0.0149 | -0.0113 | 1933 | -0.0007 |
| 1934 | 0.0257 | 0.0081 | 0.0197 | 0.0126 | 0.0131 | 0.0067 | 0.0040 | -0.0118 | -0.0146 | 0.0182 | 0.0037 | 0.0112 | 1934 | 0.1003 |
| 1935 | 0.0182 | 0.0092 | 0.0041 | 0.0079 | -0.0057 | 0.0092 | 0.0046 | -0.0133 | 0.0009 | 0.0061 | 0.0010 | 0.0070 | 1935 | 0.0498 |
| 1936 | 0.0055 | 0.0081 | 0.0106 | 0.0035 | 0.0040 | 0.0021 | 0.0060 | 0.0111 | -0.0031 | 0.0006 | 0.0205 | 0.0038 | 1936 | 0.0752 |
| 1937 | -0.0013 | 0.0086 | -0.0412 | 0.0039 | 0.0053 | -0.0018 | 0.0138 | -0.0104 | 0.0045 | 0.0042 | 0.0096 | 0.0082 | 1937 | 0.0023 |
| 1938 | 0.0057 | 0.0052 | -0.0037 | 0.0210 | 0.0044 | 0.0004 | 0.0043 | 0.0000 | 0.0022 | 0.0087 | -0.0022 | 0.0080 | 1938 | 0.0553 |
| 1939 | 0.0059 | 0.0080 | 0.0125 | 0.0118 | 0.0171 | -0.0027 | 0.0113 | -0.0201 | -0.0545 | 0.0410 | 0.0162 | 0.0145 | 1939 | 0.0594 |
| 1940 | -0.0017 | 0.0027 | 0.0177 | -0.0035 | -0.0299 | 0.0258 | 0.0052 | 0.0028 | 0.0110 | 0.0031 | 0.0205 | 0.0067 | 1940 | 0.0609 |
| 1941 | -0.0201 | 0.0020 | 0.0096 | 0.0129 | 0.0027 | 0.0066 | 0.0022 | 0.0018 | -0.0012 | 0.0140 | -0.0029 | -0.0177 | 1941 | 0.0093 |
| 1942 | 0.0069 | 0.0011 | 0.0092 | -0.0029 | 0.0075 | 0.0003 | 0.0018 | 0.0038 | 0.0003 | 0.0024 | -0.0035 | 0.0049 | 1942 | 0.0322 |
| 1943 | 0.0033 | -0.0006 | 0.0009 | 0.0048 | 0.0050 | 0.0018 | -0.0001 | 0.0021 | 0.0011 | 0.0005 | -0.0001 | 0.0018 | 1943 | 0.0208 |
| 1944 | 0.0021 | 0.0032 | 0.0021 | 0.0013 | 0.0028 | 0.0008 | 0.0036 | 0.0027 | 0.0014 | 0.0012 | 0.0024 | 0.0042 | 1944 | 0.0281 |
| 1945 | 0.0127 | 0.0077 | 0.0021 | 0.0160 | 0.0056 | 0.0169 | -0.0086 | 0.0026 | 0.0054 | 0.0104 | 0.0125 | 0.0194 | 1945 | 0.1073 |
| 1946 | 0.0025 | 0.0032 | 0.0010 | -0.0135 | -0.0012 | 0.0070 | -0.0040 | -0.0112 | -0.0009 | 0.0074 | -0.0054 | 0.0145 | 1946 | -0.0010 |
| 1947 | -0.0006 | 0.0021 | 0.0020 | -0.0037 | 0.0033 | 0.0010 | 0.0063 | 0.0081 | -0.0044 | -0.0037 | -0.0174 | -0.0192 | 1947 | -0.0262 |
| 1948 | 0.0020 | 0.0046 | 0.0034 | 0.0045 | 0.0141 | -0.0084 | -0.0021 | 0.0001 | 0.0014 | 0.0007 | 0.0076 | 0.0056 | 1948 | 0.0340 |
| 1949 | 0.0082 | 0.0049 | 0.0074 | 0.0011 | 0.0019 | 0.0167 | 0.0033 | 0.0111 | -0.0011 | 0.0019 | 0.0021 | 0.0052 | 1949 | 0.0645 |
| 1950 | -0.0061 | 0.0021 | 0.0008 | 0.0030 | 0.0033 | -0.0025 | 0.0055 | 0.0014 | -0.0072 | -0.0048 | 0.0035 | 0.0016 | 1950 | 0.0006 |
| 1951 | 0.0058 | -0.0074 | -0.0157 | -0.0063 | -0.0069 | -0.0062 | 0.0138 | 0.0099 | -0.0080 | 0.0010 | -0.0136 | -0.0061 | 1951 | -0.0393 |
| 1952 | 0.0028 | 0.0014 | 0.0111 | 0.0171 | -0.0034 | 0.0003 | -0.0020 | -0.0070 | -0.0130 | 0.0148 | -0.0015 | -0.0086 | 1952 | 0.0116 |
| 1953 | 0.0012 | -0.0087 | -0.0088 | -0.0105 | -0.0148 | 0.0223 | 0.0039 | -0.0008 | 0.0299 | 0.0074 | -0.0049 | 0.0206 | 1953 | 0.0364 |
| 1954 | 0.0089 | 0.0240 | 0.0058 | 0.0104 | -0.0087 | 0.0163 | 0.0134 | -0.0036 | -0.0010 | 0.0006 | -0.0025 | 0.0064 | 1954 | 0.0719 |
| 1955 | -0.0241 | -0.0078 | 0.0087 | 0.0001 | 0.0073 | -0.0076 | -0.0102 | 0.0004 | 0.0073 | 0.0144 | -0.0045 | 0.0037 | 1955 | -0.0129 |

*Compound annual return

## Appendix A-6

Long-term Government Bonds: Total Returns
From 1926 to 2016

| Year | Jan | Feb | Mar | Apr | May | Jun | Jul | Aug | Sep | Oct | Nov | Dec | Year | Jan–Dec* |
|------|------|------|------|------|------|------|------|------|------|------|------|------|------|----------|
| 1956 | 0.0083 | -0.0002 | -0.0149 | -0.0113 | 0.0225 | 0.0027 | -0.0209 | -0.0187 | 0.0050 | -0.0054 | -0.0057 | -0.0179 | 1956 | -0.0559 |
| 1957 | 0.0346 | 0.0025 | -0.0024 | -0.0222 | -0.0023 | -0.0180 | -0.0041 | 0.0002 | 0.0076 | -0.0050 | 0.0533 | 0.0307 | 1957 | 0.0746 |
| 1958 | -0.0084 | 0.0100 | 0.0102 | 0.0186 | 0.0001 | -0.0160 | -0.0278 | -0.0436 | -0.0117 | 0.0139 | 0.0120 | -0.0181 | 1958 | -0.0609 |
| 1959 | -0.0080 | 0.0117 | 0.0017 | -0.0117 | -0.0006 | 0.0010 | 0.0060 | -0.0041 | -0.0057 | 0.0150 | -0.0119 | -0.0159 | 1959 | -0.0226 |
| 1960 | 0.0112 | 0.0204 | 0.0282 | -0.0170 | 0.0152 | 0.0173 | 0.0368 | -0.0067 | 0.0075 | -0.0028 | -0.0066 | 0.0279 | 1960 | 0.1378 |
| 1961 | -0.0107 | 0.0200 | -0.0038 | 0.0115 | -0.0046 | -0.0075 | 0.0035 | -0.0038 | 0.0129 | 0.0071 | -0.0020 | -0.0125 | 1961 | 0.0097 |
| 1962 | -0.0014 | 0.0103 | 0.0253 | 0.0082 | 0.0046 | -0.0076 | -0.0109 | 0.0187 | 0.0061 | 0.0084 | 0.0021 | 0.0035 | 1962 | 0.0689 |
| 1963 | -0.0001 | 0.0008 | 0.0009 | -0.0012 | 0.0023 | 0.0019 | 0.0031 | 0.0021 | 0.0004 | -0.0026 | 0.0051 | -0.0006 | 1963 | 0.0121 |
| 1964 | -0.0014 | -0.0011 | 0.0037 | 0.0047 | 0.0050 | 0.0069 | 0.0008 | 0.0020 | 0.0050 | 0.0043 | 0.0017 | 0.0030 | 1964 | 0.0351 |
| 1965 | 0.0040 | 0.0014 | 0.0054 | 0.0036 | 0.0018 | 0.0047 | 0.0022 | -0.0013 | -0.0034 | 0.0027 | -0.0062 | -0.0078 | 1965 | 0.0071 |
| 1966 | -0.0104 | -0.0250 | 0.0296 | -0.0063 | -0.0059 | -0.0016 | -0.0037 | -0.0206 | 0.0332 | 0.0228 | -0.0149 | 0.0413 | 1966 | 0.0365 |
| 1967 | 0.0154 | -0.0221 | 0.0198 | -0.0291 | -0.0039 | -0.0312 | 0.0068 | -0.0084 | -0.0005 | -0.0400 | -0.0197 | 0.0192 | 1967 | -0.0918 |
| 1968 | 0.0328 | -0.0033 | -0.0212 | 0.0227 | 0.0043 | 0.0230 | 0.0289 | -0.0003 | -0.0102 | -0.0132 | -0.0269 | -0.0363 | 1968 | -0.0026 |
| 1969 | -0.0206 | 0.0042 | 0.0010 | 0.0427 | -0.0490 | 0.0214 | 0.0079 | -0.0069 | -0.0531 | 0.0365 | -0.0243 | -0.0068 | 1969 | -0.0507 |
| 1970 | -0.0021 | 0.0587 | -0.0068 | -0.0413 | -0.0468 | 0.0486 | 0.0319 | -0.0019 | 0.0228 | -0.0109 | 0.0791 | -0.0084 | 1970 | 0.1211 |
| 1971 | 0.0506 | -0.0163 | 0.0526 | -0.0283 | -0.0006 | -0.0159 | 0.0030 | 0.0471 | 0.0204 | 0.0167 | -0.0047 | 0.0044 | 1971 | 0.1323 |
| 1972 | -0.0064 | 0.0088 | -0.0082 | 0.0027 | 0.0270 | -0.0065 | 0.0216 | 0.0029 | -0.0083 | 0.0234 | 0.0226 | -0.0229 | 1972 | 0.0569 |
| 1973 | -0.0321 | 0.0014 | 0.0082 | 0.0046 | -0.0105 | -0.0021 | -0.0433 | 0.0391 | 0.0318 | 0.0215 | -0.0183 | -0.0082 | 1973 | -0.0111 |
| 1974 | -0.0083 | -0.0024 | -0.0292 | -0.0253 | 0.0123 | 0.0045 | -0.0029 | -0.0232 | 0.0247 | 0.0489 | 0.0296 | 0.0171 | 1974 | 0.0435 |
| 1975 | 0.0225 | 0.0131 | -0.0267 | -0.0182 | 0.0212 | 0.0292 | -0.0087 | -0.0068 | -0.0098 | 0.0475 | -0.0109 | 0.0390 | 1975 | 0.0920 |
| 1976 | 0.0090 | 0.0062 | 0.0166 | 0.0018 | -0.0158 | 0.0208 | 0.0078 | 0.0211 | 0.0145 | 0.0084 | 0.0339 | 0.0327 | 1976 | 0.1675 |
| 1977 | -0.0388 | -0.0049 | 0.0091 | 0.0071 | 0.0125 | 0.0164 | -0.0070 | 0.0198 | -0.0029 | -0.0093 | 0.0093 | -0.0168 | 1977 | -0.0069 |
| 1978 | -0.0080 | 0.0004 | -0.0021 | -0.0005 | -0.0058 | -0.0062 | 0.0143 | 0.0218 | -0.0106 | -0.0200 | 0.0189 | -0.0130 | 1978 | -0.0118 |
| 1979 | 0.0191 | -0.0135 | 0.0129 | -0.0112 | 0.0261 | 0.0311 | -0.0085 | -0.0035 | -0.0122 | -0.0841 | 0.0311 | 0.0057 | 1979 | -0.0123 |
| 1980 | -0.0741 | -0.0467 | -0.0315 | 0.1523 | 0.0419 | 0.0359 | -0.0476 | -0.0432 | -0.0262 | -0.0263 | 0.0100 | 0.0352 | 1980 | -0.0395 |
| 1981 | -0.0115 | -0.0436 | 0.0384 | -0.0518 | 0.0622 | -0.0179 | -0.0353 | -0.0386 | -0.0145 | 0.0829 | 0.1410 | -0.0713 | 1981 | 0.0186 |
| 1982 | 0.0046 | 0.0182 | 0.0231 | 0.0373 | 0.0034 | -0.0223 | 0.0501 | 0.0781 | 0.0618 | 0.0634 | -0.0002 | 0.0312 | 1982 | 0.4036 |
| 1983 | -0.0309 | 0.0492 | -0.0094 | 0.0350 | -0.0386 | 0.0039 | -0.0486 | 0.0020 | 0.0505 | -0.0132 | 0.0183 | -0.0059 | 1983 | 0.0065 |
| 1984 | 0.0244 | -0.0178 | -0.0156 | -0.0106 | -0.0516 | 0.0150 | 0.0693 | 0.0266 | 0.0343 | 0.0561 | 0.0118 | 0.0091 | 1984 | 0.1548 |
| 1985 | 0.0364 | -0.0493 | 0.0307 | 0.0242 | 0.0896 | 0.0142 | -0.0180 | 0.0259 | -0.0021 | 0.0338 | 0.0401 | 0.0541 | 1985 | 0.3097 |

*Compound annual return

## Appendix A-6

Long-term Government Bonds: Total Returns
From 1926 to 2016

| Year | Jan | Feb | Mar | Apr | May | Jun | Jul | Aug | Sep | Oct | Nov | Dec | Year | Jan–Dec* |
|---|---|---|---|---|---|---|---|---|---|---|---|---|---|---|
| 1986 | -0.0025 | 0.1145 | 0.0770 | -0.0080 | -0.0505 | 0.0613 | -0.0108 | 0.0499 | -0.0500 | 0.0289 | 0.0267 | -0.0018 | 1986 | 0.2453 |
| 1987 | 0.0161 | 0.0202 | -0.0223 | -0.0473 | -0.0105 | 0.0098 | -0.0178 | -0.0165 | -0.0369 | 0.0623 | 0.0037 | 0.0165 | 1987 | -0.0271 |
| 1988 | 0.0666 | 0.0052 | -0.0307 | -0.0160 | -0.0102 | 0.0368 | -0.0170 | 0.0058 | 0.0345 | 0.0308 | -0.0196 | 0.0110 | 1988 | 0.0967 |
| 1989 | 0.0203 | -0.0179 | 0.0122 | 0.0159 | 0.0401 | 0.0550 | 0.0238 | -0.0259 | 0.0019 | 0.0379 | 0.0078 | -0.0006 | 1989 | 0.1811 |
| 1990 | -0.0343 | -0.0025 | -0.0044 | -0.0202 | 0.0415 | 0.0230 | 0.0107 | -0.0419 | 0.0117 | 0.0215 | 0.0402 | 0.0187 | 1990 | 0.0618 |
| 1991 | 0.0130 | 0.0030 | 0.0038 | 0.0140 | 0.0000 | -0.0063 | 0.0157 | 0.0340 | 0.0303 | 0.0054 | 0.0082 | 0.0581 | 1991 | 0.1930 |
| 1992 | -0.0324 | 0.0051 | -0.0094 | 0.0016 | 0.0243 | 0.0200 | 0.0398 | 0.0067 | 0.0185 | -0.0198 | 0.0010 | 0.0246 | 1992 | 0.0805 |
| 1993 | 0.0280 | 0.0354 | 0.0021 | 0.0072 | 0.0047 | 0.0449 | 0.0191 | 0.0434 | 0.0005 | 0.0096 | -0.0259 | 0.0020 | 1993 | 0.1824 |
| 1994 | 0.0257 | -0.0450 | -0.0395 | -0.0150 | -0.0082 | -0.0100 | 0.0363 | -0.0086 | -0.0331 | -0.0025 | 0.0066 | 0.0161 | 1994 | -0.0777 |
| 1995 | 0.0273 | 0.0287 | 0.0091 | 0.0169 | 0.0790 | 0.0139 | -0.0168 | 0.0236 | 0.0175 | 0.0294 | 0.0249 | 0.0272 | 1995 | 0.3167 |
| 1996 | -0.0011 | -0.0483 | -0.0210 | -0.0165 | -0.0054 | 0.0203 | 0.0018 | -0.0139 | 0.0290 | 0.0404 | 0.0351 | -0.0256 | 1996 | -0.0093 |
| 1997 | -0.0079 | 0.0005 | -0.0252 | 0.0255 | 0.0095 | 0.0197 | 0.0626 | -0.0317 | 0.0316 | 0.0341 | 0.0148 | 0.0184 | 1997 | 0.1585 |
| 1998 | 0.0200 | -0.0072 | 0.0025 | 0.0026 | 0.0182 | 0.0228 | -0.0040 | 0.0465 | 0.0395 | -0.0218 | 0.0097 | -0.0032 | 1998 | 0.1306 |
| 1999 | 0.0121 | -0.0520 | -0.0008 | 0.0021 | -0.0185 | -0.0078 | -0.0079 | -0.0051 | 0.0084 | -0.0012 | -0.0061 | -0.0155 | 1999 | -0.0896 |
| 2000 | 0.0228 | 0.0264 | 0.0367 | -0.0076 | -0.0054 | 0.0244 | 0.0173 | 0.0240 | -0.0157 | 0.0187 | 0.0319 | 0.0243 | 2000 | 0.2148 |
| 2001 | 0.0005 | 0.0191 | -0.0074 | -0.0313 | 0.0037 | 0.0085 | 0.0376 | 0.0206 | 0.0081 | 0.0464 | -0.0471 | -0.0183 | 2001 | 0.0370 |
| 2002 | 0.0138 | 0.0115 | -0.0436 | 0.0410 | 0.0015 | 0.0187 | 0.0303 | 0.0464 | 0.0417 | -0.0294 | -0.0122 | 0.0507 | 2002 | 0.1784 |
| 2003 | -0.0106 | 0.0329 | -0.0135 | 0.0102 | 0.0592 | -0.0154 | -0.0982 | 0.0166 | 0.0546 | -0.0283 | 0.0027 | 0.0139 | 2003 | 0.0145 |
| 2004 | 0.0187 | 0.0230 | 0.0141 | -0.0588 | -0.0051 | 0.0121 | 0.0155 | 0.0395 | 0.0096 | 0.0154 | -0.0234 | 0.0250 | 2004 | 0.0851 |
| 2005 | 0.0300 | -0.0128 | -0.0072 | 0.0373 | 0.0297 | 0.0167 | -0.0288 | 0.0333 | -0.0338 | -0.0196 | 0.0076 | 0.0267 | 2005 | 0.0781 |
| 2006 | -0.0118 | 0.0238 | -0.0539 | -0.0247 | 0.0010 | 0.0092 | 0.0199 | 0.0299 | 0.0170 | 0.0077 | 0.0207 | -0.0236 | 2006 | 0.0119 |
| 2007 | -0.0102 | 0.0335 | -0.0145 | 0.0085 | -0.0200 | -0.0091 | 0.0284 | 0.0199 | 0.0012 | 0.0155 | 0.0468 | -0.0029 | 2007 | 0.0988 |
| 2008 | 0.0213 | 0.0018 | 0.0106 | -0.0288 | -0.0164 | 0.0220 | -0.0025 | 0.0242 | 0.0112 | -0.0383 | 0.1443 | 0.0967 | 2008 | 0.2587 |
| 2009 | -0.1124 | -0.0056 | 0.0641 | -0.0649 | -0.0248 | 0.0083 | 0.0019 | 0.0231 | 0.0176 | -0.0171 | 0.0208 | -0.0584 | 2009 | -0.1490 |
| 2010 | 0.0264 | 0.0032 | -0.0179 | 0.0304 | 0.0437 | 0.0446 | 0.0024 | 0.0702 | -0.0153 | -0.0317 | -0.0137 | -0.0388 | 2010 | 0.1014 |
| 2011 | -0.0196 | 0.0113 | -0.0006 | 0.0199 | 0.0355 | -0.0179 | 0.0422 | 0.0862 | 0.0704 | -0.0306 | 0.0251 | 0.0270 | 2011 | 0.2710 |
| 2012 | 0.0002 | -0.0196 | -0.0302 | 0.0409 | 0.0643 | -0.0136 | 0.0247 | -0.0068 | -0.0146 | -0.0014 | 0.0144 | -0.0202 | 2012 | 0.0343 |
| 2013 | -0.0332 | 0.0114 | -0.0062 | 0.0378 | -0.0629 | -0.0285 | -0.0173 | -0.0079 | 0.0061 | 0.0128 | -0.0236 | -0.0207 | 2013 | -0.1278 |
| 2014 | 0.0548 | 0.0074 | 0.0063 | 0.0181 | 0.0279 | -0.0025 | 0.0057 | 0.0369 | -0.0170 | 0.0300 | 0.0286 | 0.0290 | 2014 | 0.2471 |
| 2015 | 0.0709 | -0.0523 | 0.0137 | -0.0250 | -0.0159 | -0.0298 | 0.0329 | 0.0012 | 0.0174 | -0.0053 | -0.0065 | -0.0022 | 2015 | -0.0065 |
| 2016 | 0.0476 | 0.0294 | -0.0003 | -0.0053 | 0.0082 | 0.0590 | 0.0081 | -0.0140 | -0.0124 | -0.0314 | -0.0599 | -0.0057 | 2016 | 0.0175 |

*Compound annual return

## Appendix A-7

Long-term Government Bonds: Income Returns
From 1926 to 2016

| Year | Jan | Feb | Mar | Apr | May | Jun | Jul | Aug | Sep | Oct | Nov | Dec | Year | Jan–Dec* |
|------|------|------|------|------|------|------|------|------|------|------|------|------|------|----------|
| 1926 | 0.0031 | 0.0028 | 0.0032 | 0.0030 | 0.0028 | 0.0033 | 0.0031 | 0.0031 | 0.0030 | 0.0030 | 0.0031 | 0.0030 | 1926 | 0.0373 |
| 1927 | 0.0030 | 0.0027 | 0.0029 | 0.0027 | 0.0028 | 0.0027 | 0.0027 | 0.0029 | 0.0027 | 0.0028 | 0.0027 | 0.0027 | 1927 | 0.0341 |
| 1928 | 0.0027 | 0.0025 | 0.0027 | 0.0026 | 0.0027 | 0.0027 | 0.0027 | 0.0029 | 0.0027 | 0.0030 | 0.0027 | 0.0029 | 1928 | 0.0322 |
| 1929 | 0.0029 | 0.0027 | 0.0028 | 0.0034 | 0.0030 | 0.0029 | 0.0032 | 0.0030 | 0.0032 | 0.0031 | 0.0026 | 0.0031 | 1929 | 0.0347 |
| 1930 | 0.0029 | 0.0026 | 0.0029 | 0.0027 | 0.0027 | 0.0029 | 0.0028 | 0.0026 | 0.0029 | 0.0027 | 0.0026 | 0.0028 | 1930 | 0.0332 |
| 1931 | 0.0028 | 0.0026 | 0.0029 | 0.0027 | 0.0026 | 0.0028 | 0.0027 | 0.0027 | 0.0027 | 0.0029 | 0.0031 | 0.0032 | 1931 | 0.0333 |
| 1932 | 0.0032 | 0.0032 | 0.0031 | 0.0030 | 0.0028 | 0.0028 | 0.0028 | 0.0028 | 0.0026 | 0.0027 | 0.0026 | 0.0027 | 1932 | 0.0369 |
| 1933 | 0.0027 | 0.0023 | 0.0027 | 0.0025 | 0.0028 | 0.0025 | 0.0026 | 0.0026 | 0.0025 | 0.0027 | 0.0025 | 0.0028 | 1933 | 0.0312 |
| 1934 | 0.0029 | 0.0024 | 0.0027 | 0.0025 | 0.0025 | 0.0024 | 0.0024 | 0.0024 | 0.0023 | 0.0026 | 0.0025 | 0.0025 | 1934 | 0.0318 |
| 1935 | 0.0025 | 0.0021 | 0.0022 | 0.0023 | 0.0023 | 0.0022 | 0.0024 | 0.0023 | 0.0023 | 0.0023 | 0.0024 | 0.0024 | 1935 | 0.0281 |
| 1936 | 0.0024 | 0.0023 | 0.0024 | 0.0022 | 0.0022 | 0.0024 | 0.0023 | 0.0023 | 0.0021 | 0.0023 | 0.0022 | 0.0022 | 1936 | 0.0277 |
| 1937 | 0.0021 | 0.0020 | 0.0022 | 0.0023 | 0.0022 | 0.0025 | 0.0024 | 0.0023 | 0.0023 | 0.0023 | 0.0024 | 0.0023 | 1937 | 0.0266 |
| 1938 | 0.0023 | 0.0021 | 0.0023 | 0.0022 | 0.0022 | 0.0021 | 0.0021 | 0.0022 | 0.0021 | 0.0022 | 0.0021 | 0.0022 | 1938 | 0.0264 |
| 1939 | 0.0021 | 0.0019 | 0.0021 | 0.0019 | 0.0020 | 0.0018 | 0.0019 | 0.0018 | 0.0019 | 0.0023 | 0.0020 | 0.0019 | 1939 | 0.0240 |
| 1940 | 0.0020 | 0.0018 | 0.0019 | 0.0018 | 0.0019 | 0.0019 | 0.0020 | 0.0019 | 0.0018 | 0.0018 | 0.0018 | 0.0017 | 1940 | 0.0223 |
| 1941 | 0.0016 | 0.0016 | 0.0018 | 0.0017 | 0.0017 | 0.0016 | 0.0016 | 0.0016 | 0.0016 | 0.0016 | 0.0014 | 0.0016 | 1941 | 0.0194 |
| 1942 | 0.0021 | 0.0019 | 0.0021 | 0.0020 | 0.0019 | 0.0021 | 0.0021 | 0.0021 | 0.0020 | 0.0021 | 0.0020 | 0.0021 | 1942 | 0.0246 |
| 1943 | 0.0020 | 0.0019 | 0.0021 | 0.0020 | 0.0019 | 0.0021 | 0.0021 | 0.0021 | 0.0020 | 0.0020 | 0.0021 | 0.0021 | 1943 | 0.0244 |
| 1944 | 0.0021 | 0.0020 | 0.0021 | 0.0020 | 0.0022 | 0.0020 | 0.0021 | 0.0021 | 0.0020 | 0.0021 | 0.0020 | 0.0020 | 1944 | 0.0246 |
| 1945 | 0.0021 | 0.0018 | 0.0020 | 0.0019 | 0.0019 | 0.0019 | 0.0018 | 0.0019 | 0.0018 | 0.0019 | 0.0018 | 0.0018 | 1945 | 0.0234 |
| 1946 | 0.0017 | 0.0015 | 0.0016 | 0.0017 | 0.0018 | 0.0016 | 0.0019 | 0.0017 | 0.0018 | 0.0019 | 0.0018 | 0.0019 | 1946 | 0.0204 |
| 1947 | 0.0018 | 0.0016 | 0.0018 | 0.0017 | 0.0017 | 0.0019 | 0.0018 | 0.0017 | 0.0018 | 0.0018 | 0.0017 | 0.0021 | 1947 | 0.0213 |
| 1948 | 0.0020 | 0.0019 | 0.0022 | 0.0020 | 0.0018 | 0.0021 | 0.0019 | 0.0021 | 0.0020 | 0.0019 | 0.0021 | 0.0020 | 1948 | 0.0240 |
| 1949 | 0.0020 | 0.0018 | 0.0019 | 0.0018 | 0.0020 | 0.0019 | 0.0017 | 0.0019 | 0.0017 | 0.0018 | 0.0017 | 0.0017 | 1949 | 0.0225 |
| 1950 | 0.0018 | 0.0016 | 0.0018 | 0.0016 | 0.0019 | 0.0017 | 0.0018 | 0.0018 | 0.0017 | 0.0019 | 0.0018 | 0.0018 | 1950 | 0.0212 |
| 1951 | 0.0020 | 0.0017 | 0.0019 | 0.0020 | 0.0021 | 0.0020 | 0.0023 | 0.0021 | 0.0019 | 0.0023 | 0.0021 | 0.0022 | 1951 | 0.0238 |
| 1952 | 0.0023 | 0.0021 | 0.0023 | 0.0022 | 0.0020 | 0.0022 | 0.0022 | 0.0021 | 0.0023 | 0.0023 | 0.0021 | 0.0024 | 1952 | 0.0266 |
| 1953 | 0.0023 | 0.0021 | 0.0025 | 0.0024 | 0.0024 | 0.0027 | 0.0025 | 0.0025 | 0.0025 | 0.0023 | 0.0024 | 0.0024 | 1953 | 0.0284 |
| 1954 | 0.0023 | 0.0022 | 0.0025 | 0.0022 | 0.0020 | 0.0025 | 0.0022 | 0.0023 | 0.0022 | 0.0021 | 0.0023 | 0.0023 | 1954 | 0.0279 |
| 1955 | 0.0022 | 0.0022 | 0.0024 | 0.0022 | 0.0025 | 0.0023 | 0.0023 | 0.0027 | 0.0024 | 0.0025 | 0.0024 | 0.0024 | 1955 | 0.0275 |

*Compound annual return

# Appendix A-7

Long-term Government Bonds: Income Returns
From 1926 to 2016

| Year | Jan | Feb | Mar | Apr | May | Jun | Jul | Aug | Sep | Oct | Nov | Dec | Year | Jan–Dec* |
|------|-----|-----|-----|-----|-----|-----|-----|-----|-----|-----|-----|-----|------|----------|
| 1956 | 0.0025 | 0.0023 | 0.0023 | 0.0026 | 0.0026 | 0.0023 | 0.0026 | 0.0026 | 0.0025 | 0.0029 | 0.0027 | 0.0028 | 1956 | 0.0299 |
| 1957 | 0.0029 | 0.0025 | 0.0026 | 0.0029 | 0.0029 | 0.0025 | 0.0033 | 0.0030 | 0.0031 | 0.0031 | 0.0029 | 0.0029 | 1957 | 0.0344 |
| 1958 | 0.0027 | 0.0025 | 0.0027 | 0.0026 | 0.0024 | 0.0027 | 0.0027 | 0.0027 | 0.0032 | 0.0032 | 0.0028 | 0.0033 | 1958 | 0.0327 |
| 1959 | 0.0031 | 0.0031 | 0.0035 | 0.0033 | 0.0033 | 0.0036 | 0.0035 | 0.0035 | 0.0034 | 0.0035 | 0.0035 | 0.0036 | 1959 | 0.0401 |
| 1960 | 0.0035 | 0.0037 | 0.0036 | 0.0032 | 0.0037 | 0.0034 | 0.0032 | 0.0034 | 0.0032 | 0.0033 | 0.0032 | 0.0033 | 1960 | 0.0426 |
| 1961 | 0.0033 | 0.0030 | 0.0031 | 0.0031 | 0.0034 | 0.0032 | 0.0033 | 0.0033 | 0.0032 | 0.0034 | 0.0032 | 0.0031 | 1961 | 0.0383 |
| 1962 | 0.0037 | 0.0032 | 0.0033 | 0.0033 | 0.0032 | 0.0030 | 0.0034 | 0.0034 | 0.0030 | 0.0035 | 0.0031 | 0.0032 | 1962 | 0.0400 |
| 1963 | 0.0032 | 0.0029 | 0.0031 | 0.0034 | 0.0033 | 0.0030 | 0.0036 | 0.0033 | 0.0034 | 0.0034 | 0.0032 | 0.0036 | 1963 | 0.0389 |
| 1964 | 0.0035 | 0.0032 | 0.0037 | 0.0035 | 0.0032 | 0.0038 | 0.0035 | 0.0035 | 0.0034 | 0.0034 | 0.0035 | 0.0035 | 1964 | 0.0415 |
| 1965 | 0.0033 | 0.0032 | 0.0038 | 0.0033 | 0.0033 | 0.0038 | 0.0034 | 0.0037 | 0.0035 | 0.0034 | 0.0037 | 0.0037 | 1965 | 0.0419 |
| 1966 | 0.0038 | 0.0034 | 0.0040 | 0.0036 | 0.0041 | 0.0039 | 0.0038 | 0.0043 | 0.0041 | 0.0040 | 0.0038 | 0.0039 | 1966 | 0.0449 |
| 1967 | 0.0040 | 0.0034 | 0.0039 | 0.0035 | 0.0043 | 0.0039 | 0.0043 | 0.0042 | 0.0040 | 0.0045 | 0.0045 | 0.0044 | 1967 | 0.0459 |
| 1968 | 0.0050 | 0.0042 | 0.0043 | 0.0049 | 0.0046 | 0.0042 | 0.0048 | 0.0042 | 0.0044 | 0.0045 | 0.0043 | 0.0049 | 1968 | 0.0550 |
| 1969 | 0.0050 | 0.0046 | 0.0047 | 0.0055 | 0.0047 | 0.0055 | 0.0052 | 0.0048 | 0.0055 | 0.0057 | 0.0049 | 0.0060 | 1969 | 0.0595 |
| 1970 | 0.0056 | 0.0052 | 0.0056 | 0.0054 | 0.0055 | 0.0064 | 0.0059 | 0.0057 | 0.0056 | 0.0055 | 0.0058 | 0.0053 | 1970 | 0.0674 |
| 1971 | 0.0051 | 0.0046 | 0.0056 | 0.0048 | 0.0047 | 0.0056 | 0.0052 | 0.0055 | 0.0050 | 0.0047 | 0.0051 | 0.0050 | 1971 | 0.0632 |
| 1972 | 0.0050 | 0.0047 | 0.0049 | 0.0048 | 0.0055 | 0.0049 | 0.0051 | 0.0049 | 0.0047 | 0.0052 | 0.0048 | 0.0045 | 1972 | 0.0587 |
| 1973 | 0.0054 | 0.0051 | 0.0056 | 0.0057 | 0.0058 | 0.0055 | 0.0061 | 0.0062 | 0.0055 | 0.0063 | 0.0056 | 0.0060 | 1973 | 0.0651 |
| 1974 | 0.0061 | 0.0055 | 0.0059 | 0.0068 | 0.0068 | 0.0061 | 0.0072 | 0.0065 | 0.0071 | 0.0070 | 0.0062 | 0.0067 | 1974 | 0.0727 |
| 1975 | 0.0068 | 0.0060 | 0.0066 | 0.0067 | 0.0067 | 0.0070 | 0.0068 | 0.0069 | 0.0073 | 0.0072 | 0.0061 | 0.0075 | 1975 | 0.0799 |
| 1976 | 0.0065 | 0.0061 | 0.0071 | 0.0064 | 0.0059 | 0.0073 | 0.0065 | 0.0065 | 0.0064 | 0.0061 | 0.0066 | 0.0063 | 1976 | 0.0789 |
| 1977 | 0.0059 | 0.0057 | 0.0065 | 0.0061 | 0.0067 | 0.0062 | 0.0059 | 0.0067 | 0.0061 | 0.0063 | 0.0063 | 0.0062 | 1977 | 0.0714 |
| 1978 | 0.0069 | 0.0060 | 0.0069 | 0.0063 | 0.0075 | 0.0069 | 0.0073 | 0.0070 | 0.0065 | 0.0073 | 0.0071 | 0.0068 | 1978 | 0.0790 |
| 1979 | 0.0079 | 0.0065 | 0.0074 | 0.0076 | 0.0077 | 0.0071 | 0.0076 | 0.0073 | 0.0068 | 0.0082 | 0.0083 | 0.0083 | 1979 | 0.0886 |
| 1980 | 0.0083 | 0.0084 | 0.0099 | 0.0100 | 0.0087 | 0.0086 | 0.0084 | 0.0081 | 0.0097 | 0.0097 | 0.0091 | 0.0108 | 1980 | 0.0997 |
| 1981 | 0.0094 | 0.0088 | 0.0111 | 0.0101 | 0.0104 | 0.0109 | 0.0109 | 0.0110 | 0.0114 | 0.0117 | 0.0113 | 0.0100 | 1981 | 0.1155 |
| 1982 | 0.0108 | 0.0103 | 0.0124 | 0.0112 | 0.0101 | 0.0120 | 0.0114 | 0.0112 | 0.0100 | 0.0091 | 0.0095 | 0.0093 | 1982 | 0.1350 |
| 1983 | 0.0087 | 0.0081 | 0.0089 | 0.0085 | 0.0091 | 0.0090 | 0.0088 | 0.0103 | 0.0096 | 0.0095 | 0.0094 | 0.0094 | 1983 | 0.1038 |
| 1984 | 0.0103 | 0.0092 | 0.0098 | 0.0104 | 0.0103 | 0.0106 | 0.0116 | 0.0106 | 0.0094 | 0.0108 | 0.0091 | 0.0098 | 1984 | 0.1174 |
| 1985 | 0.0096 | 0.0082 | 0.0094 | 0.0102 | 0.0097 | 0.0080 | 0.0094 | 0.0085 | 0.0088 | 0.0089 | 0.0081 | 0.0086 | 1985 | 0.1125 |

*Compound annual return

## Appendix A-7

Long-term Government Bonds: Income Returns
From 1926 to 2016

| Year | Jan | Feb | Mar | Apr | May | Jun | Jul | Aug | Sep | Oct | Nov | Dec | Year | Jan–Dec* |
|------|------|------|------|------|------|------|------|------|------|------|------|------|------|----------|
| 1986 | 0.0079 | 0.0073 | 0.0071 | 0.0063 | 0.0062 | 0.0070 | 0.0066 | 0.0063 | 0.0065 | 0.0069 | 0.0059 | 0.0070 | 1986 | 0.0898 |
| 1987 | 0.0064 | 0.0059 | 0.0066 | 0.0065 | 0.0066 | 0.0075 | 0.0073 | 0.0075 | 0.0075 | 0.0079 | 0.0075 | 0.0078 | 1987 | 0.0792 |
| 1988 | 0.0072 | 0.0071 | 0.0072 | 0.0070 | 0.0078 | 0.0076 | 0.0071 | 0.0083 | 0.0076 | 0.0076 | 0.0070 | 0.0075 | 1988 | 0.0897 |
| 1989 | 0.0080 | 0.0069 | 0.0079 | 0.0070 | 0.0080 | 0.0070 | 0.0068 | 0.0066 | 0.0065 | 0.0072 | 0.0064 | 0.0064 | 1989 | 0.0881 |
| 1990 | 0.0073 | 0.0066 | 0.0071 | 0.0075 | 0.0075 | 0.0068 | 0.0074 | 0.0071 | 0.0069 | 0.0081 | 0.0071 | 0.0072 | 1990 | 0.0819 |
| 1991 | 0.0071 | 0.0064 | 0.0064 | 0.0076 | 0.0068 | 0.0063 | 0.0076 | 0.0068 | 0.0068 | 0.0065 | 0.0060 | 0.0068 | 1991 | 0.0822 |
| 1992 | 0.0061 | 0.0059 | 0.0067 | 0.0065 | 0.0061 | 0.0067 | 0.0063 | 0.0060 | 0.0058 | 0.0057 | 0.0061 | 0.0063 | 1992 | 0.0726 |
| 1993 | 0.0059 | 0.0055 | 0.0063 | 0.0057 | 0.0052 | 0.0062 | 0.0054 | 0.0056 | 0.0050 | 0.0049 | 0.0053 | 0.0055 | 1993 | 0.0717 |
| 1994 | 0.0055 | 0.0049 | 0.0058 | 0.0057 | 0.0063 | 0.0061 | 0.0060 | 0.0066 | 0.0061 | 0.0066 | 0.0064 | 0.0066 | 1994 | 0.0659 |
| 1995 | 0.0070 | 0.0059 | 0.0064 | 0.0058 | 0.0065 | 0.0054 | 0.0056 | 0.0057 | 0.0052 | 0.0057 | 0.0051 | 0.0049 | 1995 | 0.0760 |
| 1996 | 0.0054 | 0.0048 | 0.0052 | 0.0059 | 0.0058 | 0.0054 | 0.0062 | 0.0057 | 0.0060 | 0.0058 | 0.0052 | 0.0056 | 1996 | 0.0618 |
| 1997 | 0.0056 | 0.0051 | 0.0059 | 0.0059 | 0.0058 | 0.0059 | 0.0058 | 0.0049 | 0.0058 | 0.0054 | 0.0047 | 0.0054 | 1997 | 0.0664 |
| 1998 | 0.0048 | 0.0044 | 0.0052 | 0.0049 | 0.0048 | 0.0052 | 0.0049 | 0.0048 | 0.0044 | 0.0042 | 0.0045 | 0.0045 | 1998 | 0.0583 |
| 1999 | 0.0042 | 0.0040 | 0.0053 | 0.0048 | 0.0045 | 0.0055 | 0.0051 | 0.0054 | 0.0052 | 0.0050 | 0.0056 | 0.0055 | 1999 | 0.0557 |
| 2000 | 0.0057 | 0.0051 | 0.0054 | 0.0047 | 0.0056 | 0.0052 | 0.0052 | 0.0050 | 0.0046 | 0.0053 | 0.0048 | 0.0045 | 2000 | 0.0650 |
| 2001 | 0.0049 | 0.0042 | 0.0045 | 0.0047 | 0.0050 | 0.0047 | 0.0052 | 0.0046 | 0.0041 | 0.0048 | 0.0041 | 0.0046 | 2001 | 0.0553 |
| 2002 | 0.0048 | 0.0043 | 0.0043 | 0.0054 | 0.0049 | 0.0044 | 0.0051 | 0.0044 | 0.0042 | 0.0040 | 0.0040 | 0.0045 | 2002 | 0.0559 |
| 2003 | 0.0041 | 0.0038 | 0.0040 | 0.0040 | 0.0039 | 0.0036 | 0.0038 | 0.0042 | 0.0046 | 0.0041 | 0.0039 | 0.0047 | 2003 | 0.0480 |
| 2004 | 0.0042 | 0.0038 | 0.0043 | 0.0039 | 0.0040 | 0.0048 | 0.0043 | 0.0045 | 0.0040 | 0.0038 | 0.0041 | 0.0043 | 2004 | 0.0502 |
| 2005 | 0.0041 | 0.0035 | 0.0041 | 0.0039 | 0.0040 | 0.0036 | 0.0034 | 0.0040 | 0.0035 | 0.0039 | 0.0039 | 0.0039 | 2005 | 0.0469 |
| 2006 | 0.0040 | 0.0036 | 0.0039 | 0.0039 | 0.0048 | 0.0044 | 0.0045 | 0.0043 | 0.0039 | 0.0042 | 0.0039 | 0.0036 | 2006 | 0.0468 |
| 2007 | 0.0043 | 0.0038 | 0.0039 | 0.0042 | 0.0041 | 0.0040 | 0.0046 | 0.0042 | 0.0037 | 0.0043 | 0.0039 | 0.0037 | 2007 | 0.0486 |
| 2008 | 0.0040 | 0.0034 | 0.0037 | 0.0035 | 0.0037 | 0.0040 | 0.0039 | 0.0036 | 0.0039 | 0.0037 | 0.0036 | 0.0033 | 2008 | 0.0445 |
| 2009 | 0.0024 | 0.0030 | 0.0035 | 0.0029 | 0.0033 | 0.0038 | 0.0036 | 0.0036 | 0.0034 | 0.0033 | 0.0035 | 0.0034 | 2009 | 0.0347 |
| 2010 | 0.0036 | 0.0033 | 0.0040 | 0.0038 | 0.0034 | 0.0037 | 0.0031 | 0.0032 | 0.0026 | 0.0027 | 0.0032 | 0.0032 | 2010 | 0.0425 |
| 2011 | 0.0035 | 0.0032 | 0.0036 | 0.0034 | 0.0036 | 0.0032 | 0.0032 | 0.0034 | 0.0026 | 0.0022 | 0.0024 | 0.0022 | 2011 | 0.0382 |
| 2012 | 0.0021 | 0.0020 | 0.0022 | 0.0025 | 0.0023 | 0.0018 | 0.0020 | 0.0018 | 0.0017 | 0.0021 | 0.0019 | 0.0019 | 2012 | 0.0246 |
| 2013 | 0.0022 | 0.0022 | 0.0021 | 0.0026 | 0.0023 | 0.0024 | 0.0030 | 0.0028 | 0.0029 | 0.0029 | 0.0027 | 0.0031 | 2013 | 0.0288 |
| 2014 | 0.0032 | 0.0026 | 0.0029 | 0.0028 | 0.0028 | 0.0025 | 0.0027 | 0.0026 | 0.0023 | 0.0025 | 0.0023 | 0.0022 | 2014 | 0.0341 |
| 2015 | 0.0020 | 0.0015 | 0.0021 | 0.0019 | 0.0020 | 0.0023 | 0.0024 | 0.0022 | 0.0021 | 0.0021 | 0.0022 | 0.0022 | 2015 | 0.0247 |
| 2016 | 0.0021 | 0.0020 | 0.0018 | 0.0017 | 0.0020 | 0.0018 | 0.0014 | 0.0016 | 0.0015 | 0.0016 | 0.0018 | 0.0022 | 2016 | 0.0230 |

*Compound annual return

## Appendix A-8

Long-term Government Bonds: Capital Appreciation Returns
From 1926 to 2016

| Year | Jan | Feb | Mar | Apr | May | Jun | Jul | Aug | Sep | Oct | Nov | Dec | Year | Jan–Dec* |
|---|---|---|---|---|---|---|---|---|---|---|---|---|---|---|
| 1926 | 0.0106 | 0.0035 | 0.0009 | 0.0046 | -0.0014 | 0.0005 | -0.0027 | -0.0031 | 0.0007 | 0.0072 | 0.0129 | 0.0048 | 1926 | 0.0391 |
| 1927 | 0.0045 | 0.0061 | 0.0224 | -0.0032 | 0.0081 | -0.0096 | 0.0022 | 0.0047 | -0.0009 | 0.0071 | 0.0071 | 0.0045 | 1927 | 0.0540 |
| 1928 | -0.0063 | 0.0036 | 0.0019 | -0.0029 | -0.0104 | 0.0015 | -0.0245 | 0.0047 | -0.0067 | 0.0128 | -0.0024 | -0.0024 | 1928 | -0.0312 |
| 1929 | -0.0119 | -0.0184 | -0.0171 | 0.0242 | -0.0192 | 0.0081 | -0.0032 | -0.0064 | -0.0004 | 0.0351 | 0.0211 | -0.0120 | 1929 | -0.0020 |
| 1930 | -0.0086 | 0.0102 | 0.0055 | -0.0043 | 0.0113 | 0.0022 | 0.0007 | -0.0013 | 0.0045 | 0.0008 | 0.0017 | -0.0098 | 1930 | 0.0128 |
| 1931 | -0.0149 | 0.0059 | 0.0076 | 0.0059 | 0.0119 | -0.0024 | -0.0069 | -0.0015 | -0.0307 | -0.0360 | -0.0004 | -0.0252 | 1931 | -0.0846 |
| 1932 | 0.0002 | 0.0382 | -0.0049 | 0.0574 | -0.0216 | 0.0037 | 0.0453 | -0.0025 | 0.0031 | -0.0044 | 0.0006 | 0.0104 | 1932 | 0.1294 |
| 1933 | 0.0122 | -0.0282 | 0.0070 | -0.0057 | 0.0274 | 0.0025 | -0.0043 | 0.0018 | -0.0002 | -0.0117 | -0.0174 | -0.0140 | 1933 | -0.0314 |
| 1934 | 0.0228 | 0.0057 | 0.0170 | 0.0101 | 0.0106 | 0.0043 | 0.0016 | -0.0143 | -0.0169 | 0.0155 | 0.0013 | 0.0087 | 1934 | 0.0676 |
| 1935 | 0.0157 | 0.0070 | 0.0019 | 0.0056 | -0.0079 | 0.0070 | 0.0022 | -0.0156 | -0.0014 | 0.0038 | -0.0014 | 0.0047 | 1935 | 0.0214 |
| 1936 | 0.0031 | 0.0059 | 0.0083 | 0.0013 | 0.0019 | -0.0003 | 0.0037 | 0.0088 | -0.0053 | -0.0017 | 0.0183 | 0.0017 | 1936 | 0.0464 |
| 1937 | -0.0034 | 0.0067 | -0.0434 | 0.0016 | 0.0031 | -0.0043 | 0.0114 | -0.0128 | 0.0022 | 0.0019 | 0.0072 | 0.0059 | 1937 | -0.0248 |
| 1938 | 0.0034 | 0.0031 | -0.0059 | 0.0187 | 0.0022 | -0.0017 | 0.0022 | -0.0022 | 0.0001 | 0.0065 | -0.0043 | 0.0059 | 1938 | 0.0283 |
| 1939 | 0.0038 | 0.0061 | 0.0105 | 0.0099 | 0.0151 | -0.0045 | 0.0095 | -0.0219 | -0.0564 | 0.0386 | 0.0142 | 0.0125 | 1939 | 0.0348 |
| 1940 | -0.0037 | 0.0009 | 0.0158 | -0.0053 | -0.0318 | 0.0239 | 0.0032 | 0.0009 | 0.0092 | 0.0013 | 0.0187 | 0.0050 | 1940 | 0.0377 |
| 1941 | -0.0217 | 0.0004 | 0.0078 | 0.0112 | 0.0011 | 0.0050 | 0.0005 | 0.0002 | -0.0028 | 0.0124 | -0.0044 | -0.0194 | 1941 | -0.0101 |
| 1942 | 0.0048 | -0.0008 | 0.0071 | -0.0049 | 0.0056 | -0.0018 | -0.0003 | 0.0017 | -0.0017 | 0.0004 | -0.0055 | 0.0028 | 1942 | 0.0074 |
| 1943 | 0.0013 | -0.0024 | -0.0012 | 0.0028 | 0.0031 | -0.0003 | -0.0021 | 0.0000 | -0.0009 | -0.0015 | -0.0021 | -0.0003 | 1943 | -0.0037 |
| 1944 | 0.0000 | 0.0012 | 0.0000 | -0.0006 | 0.0006 | -0.0012 | 0.0015 | 0.0006 | -0.0006 | -0.0009 | 0.0003 | 0.0022 | 1944 | 0.0032 |
| 1945 | 0.0105 | 0.0058 | 0.0001 | 0.0141 | 0.0037 | 0.0150 | -0.0104 | 0.0007 | 0.0037 | 0.0085 | 0.0108 | 0.0177 | 1945 | 0.0827 |
| 1946 | 0.0008 | 0.0017 | -0.0006 | -0.0152 | -0.0030 | 0.0054 | -0.0058 | -0.0129 | -0.0028 | 0.0055 | -0.0072 | 0.0126 | 1946 | -0.0215 |
| 1947 | -0.0024 | 0.0005 | 0.0002 | -0.0054 | 0.0016 | -0.0009 | 0.0044 | 0.0064 | -0.0062 | -0.0055 | -0.0191 | -0.0213 | 1947 | -0.0470 |
| 1948 | 0.0000 | 0.0028 | 0.0013 | 0.0025 | 0.0123 | -0.0105 | -0.0041 | -0.0020 | -0.0006 | -0.0012 | 0.0055 | 0.0036 | 1948 | 0.0096 |
| 1949 | 0.0062 | 0.0031 | 0.0055 | -0.0006 | 0.0000 | 0.0148 | 0.0016 | 0.0092 | -0.0029 | 0.0001 | 0.0004 | 0.0035 | 1949 | 0.0415 |
| 1950 | -0.0080 | 0.0005 | -0.0010 | 0.0014 | 0.0014 | -0.0042 | 0.0037 | -0.0004 | -0.0089 | -0.0067 | 0.0017 | -0.0001 | 1950 | -0.0206 |
| 1951 | 0.0038 | -0.0091 | -0.0176 | -0.0083 | -0.0090 | -0.0082 | 0.0116 | 0.0077 | -0.0098 | -0.0013 | -0.0157 | -0.0083 | 1951 | -0.0627 |
| 1952 | 0.0005 | -0.0007 | 0.0088 | 0.0149 | -0.0054 | -0.0019 | -0.0042 | -0.0091 | -0.0153 | 0.0124 | -0.0036 | -0.0110 | 1952 | -0.0148 |
| 1953 | -0.0011 | -0.0108 | -0.0113 | -0.0129 | -0.0171 | 0.0195 | 0.0014 | -0.0033 | 0.0275 | 0.0051 | -0.0073 | 0.0182 | 1953 | 0.0067 |
| 1954 | 0.0066 | 0.0218 | 0.0034 | 0.0081 | -0.0107 | 0.0138 | 0.0113 | -0.0059 | -0.0031 | -0.0015 | -0.0048 | 0.0042 | 1954 | 0.0435 |
| 1955 | -0.0264 | -0.0100 | 0.0063 | -0.0022 | 0.0048 | -0.0099 | -0.0125 | -0.0023 | 0.0049 | 0.0119 | -0.0069 | 0.0013 | 1955 | -0.0407 |

*Compound annual return

## Appendix A-8

Long-term Government Bonds: Capital Appreciation Returns
From 1926 to 2016

| Year | Jan | Feb | Mar | Apr | May | Jun | Jul | Aug | Sep | Oct | Nov | Dec | Year | Jan–Dec* |
|---|---|---|---|---|---|---|---|---|---|---|---|---|---|---|
| 1956 | 0.0058 | -0.0025 | -0.0172 | -0.0139 | 0.0199 | 0.0004 | -0.0234 | -0.0213 | 0.0025 | -0.0084 | -0.0084 | -0.0207 | 1956 | -0.0846 |
| 1957 | 0.0317 | 0.0000 | -0.0050 | -0.0250 | -0.0052 | -0.0206 | -0.0074 | -0.0028 | 0.0045 | -0.0081 | 0.0504 | 0.0277 | 1957 | 0.0382 |
| 1958 | -0.0112 | 0.0075 | 0.0075 | 0.0160 | -0.0024 | -0.0187 | -0.0306 | -0.0463 | -0.0149 | 0.0106 | 0.0092 | -0.0213 | 1958 | -0.0923 |
| 1959 | -0.0111 | 0.0087 | -0.0018 | -0.0150 | -0.0038 | -0.0026 | 0.0025 | -0.0076 | -0.0091 | 0.0115 | -0.0154 | -0.0195 | 1959 | -0.0620 |
| 1960 | 0.0077 | 0.0167 | 0.0246 | -0.0202 | 0.0115 | 0.0139 | 0.0335 | -0.0101 | 0.0043 | -0.0061 | -0.0098 | 0.0247 | 1960 | 0.0929 |
| 1961 | -0.0140 | 0.0170 | -0.0069 | 0.0085 | -0.0080 | -0.0106 | 0.0001 | -0.0071 | 0.0097 | 0.0037 | -0.0052 | -0.0156 | 1961 | -0.0286 |
| 1962 | -0.0051 | 0.0071 | 0.0220 | 0.0049 | 0.0014 | -0.0106 | -0.0143 | 0.0153 | 0.0031 | 0.0049 | -0.0010 | 0.0003 | 1962 | 0.0278 |
| 1963 | -0.0033 | -0.0022 | -0.0022 | -0.0046 | -0.0011 | -0.0011 | -0.0005 | -0.0011 | -0.0029 | -0.0060 | 0.0019 | -0.0042 | 1963 | -0.0270 |
| 1964 | -0.0048 | -0.0043 | 0.0000 | 0.0012 | 0.0018 | 0.0031 | -0.0028 | -0.0015 | 0.0015 | 0.0009 | -0.0018 | -0.0005 | 1964 | -0.0072 |
| 1965 | 0.0007 | -0.0018 | 0.0016 | 0.0003 | -0.0015 | 0.0009 | -0.0012 | -0.0050 | -0.0069 | -0.0007 | -0.0100 | -0.0115 | 1965 | -0.0345 |
| 1966 | -0.0142 | -0.0284 | 0.0256 | -0.0099 | -0.0100 | -0.0054 | -0.0074 | -0.0249 | 0.0292 | 0.0188 | -0.0187 | 0.0374 | 1966 | -0.0106 |
| 1967 | 0.0115 | -0.0255 | 0.0159 | -0.0326 | -0.0082 | -0.0351 | 0.0026 | -0.0126 | -0.0045 | -0.0445 | -0.0241 | 0.0148 | 1967 | -0.1355 |
| 1968 | 0.0278 | -0.0075 | -0.0254 | 0.0178 | -0.0003 | 0.0188 | 0.0241 | -0.0045 | -0.0146 | -0.0177 | -0.0312 | -0.0412 | 1968 | -0.0551 |
| 1969 | -0.0256 | -0.0005 | -0.0036 | 0.0371 | -0.0537 | 0.0159 | 0.0027 | -0.0117 | -0.0586 | 0.0309 | -0.0293 | -0.0129 | 1969 | -0.1083 |
| 1970 | -0.0077 | 0.0535 | -0.0124 | -0.0467 | -0.0523 | 0.0422 | 0.0260 | -0.0076 | 0.0172 | -0.0164 | 0.0733 | -0.0137 | 1970 | 0.0484 |
| 1971 | 0.0455 | -0.0209 | 0.0470 | -0.0331 | -0.0053 | -0.0214 | -0.0022 | 0.0416 | 0.0154 | 0.0120 | -0.0098 | -0.0006 | 1971 | 0.0661 |
| 1972 | -0.0114 | 0.0041 | -0.0131 | -0.0021 | 0.0215 | -0.0113 | 0.0165 | -0.0021 | -0.0129 | 0.0182 | 0.0178 | -0.0275 | 1972 | -0.0035 |
| 1973 | -0.0375 | -0.0037 | 0.0026 | -0.0012 | -0.0162 | -0.0076 | -0.0495 | 0.0329 | 0.0263 | 0.0153 | -0.0238 | -0.0142 | 1973 | -0.0770 |
| 1974 | -0.0144 | -0.0079 | -0.0350 | -0.0320 | 0.0055 | -0.0016 | -0.0101 | -0.0298 | 0.0176 | 0.0419 | 0.0233 | 0.0105 | 1974 | -0.0345 |
| 1975 | 0.0157 | 0.0071 | -0.0333 | -0.0249 | 0.0145 | 0.0222 | -0.0155 | -0.0133 | -0.0171 | 0.0403 | -0.0170 | 0.0316 | 1975 | 0.0073 |
| 1976 | 0.0025 | 0.0001 | 0.0094 | -0.0046 | -0.0217 | 0.0135 | 0.0013 | 0.0142 | 0.0081 | 0.0023 | 0.0273 | 0.0265 | 1976 | 0.0807 |
| 1977 | -0.0447 | -0.0106 | 0.0026 | 0.0010 | 0.0058 | 0.0102 | -0.0130 | 0.0131 | -0.0089 | -0.0156 | 0.0031 | -0.0230 | 1977 | -0.0786 |
| 1978 | -0.0149 | -0.0056 | -0.0090 | -0.0068 | -0.0133 | -0.0132 | 0.0070 | 0.0148 | -0.0171 | -0.0273 | 0.0117 | -0.0198 | 1978 | -0.0905 |
| 1979 | 0.0112 | -0.0200 | 0.0056 | -0.0188 | 0.0184 | 0.0240 | -0.0161 | -0.0108 | -0.0190 | -0.0922 | 0.0229 | -0.0026 | 1979 | -0.0984 |
| 1980 | -0.0824 | -0.0551 | -0.0413 | 0.1424 | 0.0332 | 0.0272 | -0.0560 | -0.0513 | -0.0359 | -0.0360 | 0.0009 | 0.0244 | 1980 | -0.1400 |
| 1981 | -0.0209 | -0.0524 | 0.0274 | -0.0618 | 0.0518 | -0.0288 | -0.0462 | -0.0496 | -0.0259 | 0.0712 | 0.1297 | -0.0813 | 1981 | -0.1033 |
| 1982 | -0.0062 | 0.0079 | 0.0107 | 0.0262 | -0.0067 | -0.0343 | 0.0387 | 0.0669 | 0.0519 | 0.0543 | -0.0097 | 0.0219 | 1982 | 0.2395 |
| 1983 | -0.0396 | 0.0410 | -0.0183 | 0.0265 | -0.0477 | -0.0051 | -0.0574 | -0.0083 | 0.0408 | -0.0227 | 0.0089 | -0.0152 | 1983 | -0.0982 |
| 1984 | 0.0141 | -0.0270 | -0.0254 | -0.0210 | -0.0619 | 0.0044 | 0.0577 | 0.0160 | 0.0248 | 0.0453 | 0.0027 | -0.0007 | 1984 | 0.0232 |
| 1985 | 0.0268 | -0.0575 | 0.0212 | 0.0140 | 0.0798 | 0.0061 | -0.0274 | 0.0174 | -0.0109 | 0.0248 | 0.0320 | 0.0455 | 1985 | 0.1784 |

*Compound annual return

## Appendix A-8

Long-term Government Bonds: Capital Appreciation Returns
From 1926 to 2016

| Year | Jan | Feb | Mar | Apr | May | Jun | Jul | Aug | Sep | Oct | Nov | Dec | Year | Jan–Dec* |
|------|------|------|------|------|------|------|------|------|------|------|------|------|------|---------|
| 1986 | -0.0105 | 0.1073 | 0.0699 | -0.0142 | -0.0567 | 0.0543 | -0.0174 | 0.0437 | -0.0565 | 0.0220 | 0.0208 | -0.0087 | 1986 | 0.1499 |
| 1987 | 0.0096 | 0.0143 | -0.0289 | -0.0538 | -0.0171 | 0.0023 | -0.0251 | -0.0240 | -0.0444 | 0.0544 | -0.0038 | 0.0088 | 1987 | -0.1069 |
| 1988 | 0.0595 | -0.0019 | -0.0378 | -0.0230 | -0.0180 | 0.0292 | -0.0241 | -0.0025 | 0.0269 | 0.0232 | -0.0266 | 0.0035 | 1988 | 0.0036 |
| 1989 | 0.0124 | -0.0248 | 0.0044 | 0.0088 | 0.0321 | 0.0480 | 0.0170 | -0.0325 | -0.0046 | 0.0307 | 0.0014 | -0.0070 | 1989 | 0.0862 |
| 1990 | -0.0416 | -0.0090 | -0.0115 | -0.0277 | 0.0340 | 0.0162 | 0.0033 | -0.0490 | 0.0048 | 0.0135 | 0.0331 | 0.0114 | 1990 | -0.0261 |
| 1991 | 0.0059 | -0.0033 | -0.0026 | 0.0065 | -0.0068 | -0.0126 | 0.0082 | 0.0272 | 0.0236 | -0.0011 | 0.0022 | 0.0513 | 1991 | 0.1010 |
| 1992 | -0.0385 | -0.0008 | -0.0161 | -0.0049 | 0.0181 | 0.0133 | 0.0334 | 0.0007 | 0.0127 | -0.0255 | -0.0051 | 0.0183 | 1992 | 0.0034 |
| 1993 | 0.0222 | 0.0299 | -0.0042 | 0.0015 | -0.0006 | 0.0387 | 0.0138 | 0.0378 | -0.0045 | 0.0048 | -0.0312 | -0.0035 | 1993 | 0.1071 |
| 1994 | 0.0202 | -0.0498 | -0.0453 | -0.0208 | -0.0146 | -0.0161 | 0.0303 | -0.0152 | -0.0392 | -0.0091 | 0.0002 | 0.0095 | 1994 | -0.1429 |
| 1995 | 0.0203 | 0.0227 | 0.0028 | 0.0112 | 0.0725 | 0.0084 | -0.0223 | 0.0179 | 0.0122 | 0.0237 | 0.0198 | 0.0223 | 1995 | 0.2304 |
| 1996 | -0.0065 | -0.0530 | -0.0262 | -0.0224 | -0.0112 | 0.0149 | -0.0045 | -0.0196 | 0.0230 | 0.0345 | 0.0299 | -0.0312 | 1996 | -0.0737 |
| 1997 | -0.0135 | -0.0046 | -0.0311 | 0.0196 | 0.0037 | 0.0138 | 0.0567 | -0.0367 | 0.0258 | 0.0287 | 0.0101 | 0.0130 | 1997 | 0.0851 |
| 1998 | 0.0152 | -0.0116 | -0.0028 | -0.0023 | 0.0135 | 0.0176 | -0.0088 | 0.0416 | 0.0350 | -0.0260 | 0.0052 | -0.0077 | 1998 | 0.0689 |
| 1999 | 0.0079 | -0.0560 | -0.0061 | -0.0028 | -0.0230 | -0.0133 | -0.0130 | -0.0105 | 0.0032 | -0.0062 | -0.0117 | -0.0210 | 1999 | -0.1435 |
| 2000 | 0.0171 | 0.0213 | 0.0312 | -0.0123 | -0.0111 | 0.0192 | 0.0120 | 0.0190 | -0.0203 | 0.0135 | 0.0270 | 0.0198 | 2000 | 0.1436 |
| 2001 | -0.0044 | 0.0149 | -0.0119 | -0.0360 | -0.0013 | 0.0038 | 0.0324 | 0.0159 | 0.0040 | 0.0416 | -0.0512 | -0.0229 | 2001 | -0.0189 |
| 2002 | 0.0090 | 0.0072 | -0.0479 | 0.0355 | -0.0034 | 0.0143 | 0.0252 | 0.0420 | 0.0374 | -0.0334 | -0.0161 | 0.0462 | 2002 | 0.1169 |
| 2003 | -0.0147 | 0.0291 | -0.0175 | 0.0062 | 0.0553 | -0.0190 | -0.1020 | 0.0124 | 0.0501 | -0.0324 | -0.0012 | 0.0093 | 2003 | -0.0336 |
| 2004 | 0.0146 | 0.0192 | 0.0098 | -0.0627 | -0.0090 | 0.0074 | 0.0113 | 0.0350 | 0.0057 | 0.0115 | -0.0275 | 0.0207 | 2004 | 0.0326 |
| 2005 | 0.0260 | -0.0163 | -0.0112 | 0.0334 | 0.0256 | 0.0131 | -0.0322 | 0.0292 | -0.0373 | -0.0235 | 0.0037 | 0.0228 | 2005 | 0.0302 |
| 2006 | -0.0157 | 0.0203 | -0.0578 | -0.0285 | -0.0038 | 0.0048 | 0.0154 | 0.0256 | 0.0132 | 0.0035 | 0.0169 | -0.0272 | 2006 | -0.0364 |
| 2007 | -0.0146 | 0.0297 | -0.0184 | 0.0043 | -0.0242 | -0.0131 | 0.0238 | 0.0157 | -0.0025 | 0.0112 | 0.0429 | -0.0066 | 2007 | 0.0469 |
| 2008 | 0.0173 | -0.0015 | 0.0069 | -0.0324 | -0.0202 | 0.0180 | -0.0064 | 0.0206 | 0.0074 | -0.0420 | 0.1407 | 0.0934 | 2008 | 0.2050 |
| 2009 | -0.1149 | -0.0086 | 0.0606 | -0.0679 | -0.0281 | 0.0046 | -0.0018 | 0.0195 | 0.0142 | -0.0203 | 0.0173 | -0.0618 | 2009 | -0.1825 |
| 2010 | 0.0228 | -0.0002 | -0.0219 | 0.0266 | 0.0403 | 0.0409 | -0.0007 | 0.0670 | -0.0180 | -0.0344 | -0.0169 | -0.0420 | 2010 | 0.0589 |
| 2011 | -0.0231 | 0.0081 | -0.0042 | 0.0165 | 0.0318 | -0.0212 | 0.0389 | 0.0829 | 0.0679 | -0.0328 | 0.0228 | 0.0248 | 2011 | 0.2262 |
| 2012 | -0.0020 | -0.0216 | -0.0324 | 0.0384 | 0.0620 | -0.0153 | 0.0227 | -0.0087 | -0.0163 | -0.0035 | 0.0124 | -0.0221 | 2012 | 0.0095 |
| 2013 | -0.0354 | 0.0092 | -0.0083 | 0.0352 | -0.0651 | -0.0309 | -0.0203 | -0.0107 | 0.0032 | 0.0099 | -0.0262 | -0.0262 | 2013 | -0.1570 |
| 2014 | 0.0516 | 0.0048 | 0.0034 | 0.0154 | 0.0251 | -0.0051 | 0.0030 | 0.0343 | -0.0194 | 0.0274 | 0.0263 | 0.0268 | 2014 | 0.2093 |
| 2015 | 0.0689 | -0.0538 | 0.0116 | -0.0269 | -0.0179 | -0.0321 | 0.0305 | -0.0010 | 0.0153 | -0.0074 | -0.0086 | -0.0044 | 2015 | -0.0311 |
| 2016 | 0.0455 | 0.0275 | -0.0022 | -0.0070 | 0.0063 | 0.0572 | 0.0066 | -0.0156 | -0.0140 | -0.0331 | -0.0616 | -0.0079 | 2016 | -0.0040 |

*Compound annual return

## Appendix A-9

Long-term Government Bonds: Yields
From 1926 to 2016

| Year | Jan | Feb | Mar | Apr | May | Jun | Jul | Aug | Sep | Oct | Nov | Dec | Year | Jan–Dec* |
|---|---|---|---|---|---|---|---|---|---|---|---|---|---|---|
| 1926 | 0.0374 | 0.0372 | 0.0371 | 0.0368 | 0.0369 | 0.0368 | 0.0370 | 0.0373 | 0.0372 | 0.0367 | 0.0358 | 0.0354 | 1926 | 0.0354 |
| 1927 | 0.0351 | 0.0347 | 0.0331 | 0.0333 | 0.0327 | 0.0334 | 0.0333 | 0.0329 | 0.0330 | 0.0325 | 0.0320 | 0.0317 | 1927 | 0.0317 |
| 1928 | 0.0321 | 0.0318 | 0.0317 | 0.0319 | 0.0327 | 0.0326 | 0.0344 | 0.0341 | 0.0346 | 0.0336 | 0.0338 | 0.0340 | 1928 | 0.0340 |
| 1929 | 0.0349 | 0.0363 | 0.0377 | 0.0358 | 0.0373 | 0.0367 | 0.0369 | 0.0375 | 0.0375 | 0.0347 | 0.0331 | 0.0340 | 1929 | 0.0340 |
| 1930 | 0.0347 | 0.0339 | 0.0335 | 0.0338 | 0.0329 | 0.0328 | 0.0327 | 0.0328 | 0.0324 | 0.0324 | 0.0322 | 0.0330 | 1930 | 0.0330 |
| 1931 | 0.0343 | 0.0338 | 0.0332 | 0.0327 | 0.0317 | 0.0319 | 0.0325 | 0.0326 | 0.0353 | 0.0385 | 0.0385 | 0.0407 | 1931 | 0.0407 |
| 1932 | 0.0390 | 0.0367 | 0.0370 | 0.0336 | 0.0349 | 0.0347 | 0.0320 | 0.0321 | 0.0319 | 0.0322 | 0.0322 | 0.0315 | 1932 | 0.0315 |
| 1933 | 0.0308 | 0.0326 | 0.0321 | 0.0325 | 0.0308 | 0.0306 | 0.0309 | 0.0308 | 0.0308 | 0.0315 | 0.0327 | 0.0336 | 1933 | 0.0336 |
| 1934 | 0.0321 | 0.0317 | 0.0307 | 0.0300 | 0.0292 | 0.0289 | 0.0288 | 0.0299 | 0.0310 | 0.0300 | 0.0299 | 0.0293 | 1934 | 0.0293 |
| 1935 | 0.0281 | 0.0275 | 0.0274 | 0.0269 | 0.0276 | 0.0270 | 0.0268 | 0.0281 | 0.0282 | 0.0279 | 0.0280 | 0.0276 | 1935 | 0.0276 |
| 1936 | 0.0285 | 0.0281 | 0.0275 | 0.0274 | 0.0273 | 0.0273 | 0.0271 | 0.0264 | 0.0268 | 0.0269 | 0.0257 | 0.0255 | 1936 | 0.0255 |
| 1937 | 0.0258 | 0.0253 | 0.0285 | 0.0284 | 0.0282 | 0.0285 | 0.0277 | 0.0286 | 0.0284 | 0.0283 | 0.0278 | 0.0273 | 1937 | 0.0273 |
| 1938 | 0.0271 | 0.0268 | 0.0273 | 0.0259 | 0.0257 | 0.0259 | 0.0257 | 0.0259 | 0.0259 | 0.0254 | 0.0257 | 0.0252 | 1938 | 0.0252 |
| 1939 | 0.0249 | 0.0245 | 0.0237 | 0.0229 | 0.0217 | 0.0221 | 0.0213 | 0.0231 | 0.0278 | 0.0247 | 0.0236 | 0.0226 | 1939 | 0.0226 |
| 1940 | 0.0229 | 0.0228 | 0.0215 | 0.0220 | 0.0246 | 0.0227 | 0.0224 | 0.0223 | 0.0215 | 0.0214 | 0.0199 | 0.0194 | 1940 | 0.0194 |
| 1941 | 0.0213 | 0.0213 | 0.0206 | 0.0196 | 0.0195 | 0.0191 | 0.0191 | 0.0190 | 0.0193 | 0.0182 | 0.0186 | 0.0204 | 1941 | 0.0204 |
| 1942 | 0.0247 | 0.0247 | 0.0244 | 0.0246 | 0.0243 | 0.0244 | 0.0244 | 0.0244 | 0.0244 | 0.0244 | 0.0247 | 0.0246 | 1942 | 0.0246 |
| 1943 | 0.0245 | 0.0246 | 0.0247 | 0.0246 | 0.0244 | 0.0244 | 0.0245 | 0.0245 | 0.0246 | 0.0247 | 0.0248 | 0.0248 | 1943 | 0.0248 |
| 1944 | 0.0248 | 0.0247 | 0.0247 | 0.0248 | 0.0247 | 0.0248 | 0.0247 | 0.0247 | 0.0247 | 0.0247 | 0.0247 | 0.0246 | 1944 | 0.0246 |
| 1945 | 0.0240 | 0.0237 | 0.0236 | 0.0228 | 0.0226 | 0.0217 | 0.0224 | 0.0223 | 0.0221 | 0.0216 | 0.0210 | 0.0199 | 1945 | 0.0199 |
| 1946 | 0.0199 | 0.0198 | 0.0198 | 0.0207 | 0.0209 | 0.0206 | 0.0209 | 0.0217 | 0.0219 | 0.0216 | 0.0220 | 0.0212 | 1946 | 0.0212 |
| 1947 | 0.0214 | 0.0214 | 0.0213 | 0.0217 | 0.0216 | 0.0216 | 0.0214 | 0.0210 | 0.0213 | 0.0217 | 0.0229 | 0.0243 | 1947 | 0.0243 |
| 1948 | 0.0243 | 0.0241 | 0.0241 | 0.0239 | 0.0231 | 0.0238 | 0.0241 | 0.0242 | 0.0242 | 0.0243 | 0.0239 | 0.0237 | 1948 | 0.0237 |
| 1949 | 0.0233 | 0.0231 | 0.0227 | 0.0227 | 0.0227 | 0.0217 | 0.0216 | 0.0210 | 0.0212 | 0.0212 | 0.0212 | 0.0209 | 1949 | 0.0209 |
| 1950 | 0.0215 | 0.0214 | 0.0215 | 0.0214 | 0.0213 | 0.0216 | 0.0214 | 0.0214 | 0.0220 | 0.0225 | 0.0224 | 0.0224 | 1950 | 0.0224 |
| 1951 | 0.0221 | 0.0228 | 0.0241 | 0.0248 | 0.0254 | 0.0259 | 0.0252 | 0.0246 | 0.0253 | 0.0254 | 0.0264 | 0.0269 | 1951 | 0.0269 |
| 1952 | 0.0268 | 0.0269 | 0.0263 | 0.0254 | 0.0257 | 0.0259 | 0.0261 | 0.0267 | 0.0277 | 0.0269 | 0.0272 | 0.0279 | 1952 | 0.0279 |
| 1953 | 0.0279 | 0.0287 | 0.0294 | 0.0303 | 0.0314 | 0.0301 | 0.0301 | 0.0303 | 0.0284 | 0.0281 | 0.0286 | 0.0274 | 1953 | 0.0274 |
| 1954 | 0.0291 | 0.0279 | 0.0278 | 0.0273 | 0.0279 | 0.0272 | 0.0266 | 0.0269 | 0.0271 | 0.0272 | 0.0274 | 0.0272 | 1954 | 0.0272 |
| 1955 | 0.0286 | 0.0292 | 0.0288 | 0.0290 | 0.0287 | 0.0293 | 0.0300 | 0.0301 | 0.0298 | 0.0292 | 0.0295 | 0.0295 | 1955 | 0.0295 |

*Compound annual return

## Appendix A-9

Long-term Government Bonds: Yields
From 1926 to 2016

| Year | Jan | Feb | Mar | Apr | May | Jun | Jul | Aug | Sep | Oct | Nov | Dec | Year | Jan–Dec* |
|------|-----|-----|-----|-----|-----|-----|-----|-----|-----|-----|-----|-----|------|----------|
| 1956 | 0.0292 | 0.0293 | 0.0303 | 0.0311 | 0.0299 | 0.0299 | 0.0313 | 0.0325 | 0.0324 | 0.0329 | 0.0333 | 0.0345 | 1956 | 0.0345 |
| 1957 | 0.0328 | 0.0328 | 0.0331 | 0.0345 | 0.0348 | 0.0361 | 0.0365 | 0.0367 | 0.0364 | 0.0369 | 0.0340 | 0.0323 | 1957 | 0.0323 |
| 1958 | 0.0330 | 0.0326 | 0.0321 | 0.0311 | 0.0313 | 0.0324 | 0.0343 | 0.0371 | 0.0380 | 0.0374 | 0.0368 | 0.0382 | 1958 | 0.0382 |
| 1959 | 0.0408 | 0.0402 | 0.0403 | 0.0414 | 0.0417 | 0.0419 | 0.0417 | 0.0423 | 0.0429 | 0.0421 | 0.0432 | 0.0447 | 1959 | 0.0447 |
| 1960 | 0.0441 | 0.0429 | 0.0411 | 0.0426 | 0.0417 | 0.0407 | 0.0382 | 0.0390 | 0.0387 | 0.0391 | 0.0399 | 0.0380 | 1960 | 0.0380 |
| 1961 | 0.0404 | 0.0392 | 0.0397 | 0.0391 | 0.0397 | 0.0404 | 0.0404 | 0.0410 | 0.0403 | 0.0400 | 0.0404 | 0.0415 | 1961 | 0.0415 |
| 1962 | 0.0419 | 0.0414 | 0.0398 | 0.0394 | 0.0393 | 0.0401 | 0.0412 | 0.0401 | 0.0398 | 0.0395 | 0.0396 | 0.0395 | 1962 | 0.0395 |
| 1963 | 0.0398 | 0.0400 | 0.0401 | 0.0405 | 0.0406 | 0.0407 | 0.0407 | 0.0408 | 0.0410 | 0.0415 | 0.0414 | 0.0417 | 1963 | 0.0417 |
| 1964 | 0.0421 | 0.0424 | 0.0424 | 0.0423 | 0.0422 | 0.0419 | 0.0421 | 0.0423 | 0.0421 | 0.0421 | 0.0422 | 0.0423 | 1964 | 0.0423 |
| 1965 | 0.0422 | 0.0424 | 0.0422 | 0.0422 | 0.0423 | 0.0423 | 0.0424 | 0.0428 | 0.0433 | 0.0433 | 0.0441 | 0.0450 | 1965 | 0.0450 |
| 1966 | 0.0458 | 0.0477 | 0.0460 | 0.0467 | 0.0473 | 0.0477 | 0.0482 | 0.0499 | 0.0480 | 0.0467 | 0.0480 | 0.0455 | 1966 | 0.0455 |
| 1967 | 0.0448 | 0.0465 | 0.0455 | 0.0477 | 0.0482 | 0.0507 | 0.0505 | 0.0514 | 0.0517 | 0.0549 | 0.0567 | 0.0556 | 1967 | 0.0556 |
| 1968 | 0.0536 | 0.0542 | 0.0560 | 0.0547 | 0.0548 | 0.0534 | 0.0517 | 0.0520 | 0.0531 | 0.0543 | 0.0566 | 0.0598 | 1968 | 0.0598 |
| 1969 | 0.0617 | 0.0618 | 0.0620 | 0.0593 | 0.0635 | 0.0623 | 0.0621 | 0.0630 | 0.0677 | 0.0653 | 0.0676 | 0.0687 | 1969 | 0.0687 |
| 1970 | 0.0693 | 0.0651 | 0.0661 | 0.0699 | 0.0743 | 0.0709 | 0.0687 | 0.0694 | 0.0680 | 0.0693 | 0.0637 | 0.0648 | 1970 | 0.0648 |
| 1971 | 0.0612 | 0.0629 | 0.0593 | 0.0619 | 0.0624 | 0.0641 | 0.0643 | 0.0610 | 0.0598 | 0.0588 | 0.0596 | 0.0597 | 1971 | 0.0597 |
| 1972 | 0.0606 | 0.0602 | 0.0613 | 0.0615 | 0.0597 | 0.0607 | 0.0593 | 0.0595 | 0.0606 | 0.0591 | 0.0577 | 0.0599 | 1972 | 0.0599 |
| 1973 | 0.0685 | 0.0688 | 0.0686 | 0.0687 | 0.0703 | 0.0710 | 0.0760 | 0.0728 | 0.0703 | 0.0689 | 0.0712 | 0.0726 | 1973 | 0.0726 |
| 1974 | 0.0740 | 0.0748 | 0.0783 | 0.0816 | 0.0810 | 0.0812 | 0.0823 | 0.0855 | 0.0837 | 0.0795 | 0.0771 | 0.0760 | 1974 | 0.0760 |
| 1975 | 0.0796 | 0.0788 | 0.0824 | 0.0852 | 0.0836 | 0.0813 | 0.0829 | 0.0844 | 0.0862 | 0.0819 | 0.0838 | 0.0805 | 1975 | 0.0805 |
| 1976 | 0.0802 | 0.0802 | 0.0792 | 0.0797 | 0.0821 | 0.0807 | 0.0805 | 0.0790 | 0.0781 | 0.0779 | 0.0749 | 0.0721 | 1976 | 0.0721 |
| 1977 | 0.0764 | 0.0775 | 0.0772 | 0.0771 | 0.0765 | 0.0754 | 0.0768 | 0.0754 | 0.0764 | 0.0781 | 0.0777 | 0.0803 | 1977 | 0.0803 |
| 1978 | 0.0816 | 0.0822 | 0.0831 | 0.0838 | 0.0852 | 0.0865 | 0.0858 | 0.0843 | 0.0860 | 0.0889 | 0.0877 | 0.0898 | 1978 | 0.0898 |
| 1979 | 0.0886 | 0.0908 | 0.0902 | 0.0922 | 0.0903 | 0.0877 | 0.0895 | 0.0907 | 0.0927 | 0.1034 | 0.1009 | 0.1012 | 1979 | 0.1012 |
| 1980 | 0.1114 | 0.1186 | 0.1239 | 0.1076 | 0.1037 | 0.1006 | 0.1074 | 0.1140 | 0.1185 | 0.1231 | 0.1230 | 0.1199 | 1980 | 0.1199 |
| 1981 | 0.1211 | 0.1283 | 0.1248 | 0.1332 | 0.1265 | 0.1304 | 0.1370 | 0.1445 | 0.1482 | 0.1384 | 0.1220 | 0.1334 | 1981 | 0.1334 |
| 1982 | 0.1415 | 0.1402 | 0.1387 | 0.1348 | 0.1358 | 0.1412 | 0.1352 | 0.1254 | 0.1183 | 0.1112 | 0.1125 | 0.1095 | 1982 | 0.1095 |
| 1983 | 0.1113 | 0.1060 | 0.1083 | 0.1051 | 0.1112 | 0.1119 | 0.1198 | 0.1210 | 0.1157 | 0.1188 | 0.1176 | 0.1197 | 1983 | 0.1197 |
| 1984 | 0.1180 | 0.1217 | 0.1253 | 0.1284 | 0.1381 | 0.1374 | 0.1293 | 0.1270 | 0.1235 | 0.1173 | 0.1169 | 0.1170 | 1984 | 0.1170 |
| 1985 | 0.1127 | 0.1209 | 0.1181 | 0.1162 | 0.1062 | 0.1055 | 0.1091 | 0.1068 | 0.1082 | 0.1051 | 0.1011 | 0.0956 | 1985 | 0.0956 |

*Compound annual return

## Appendix A-9

Long-term Government Bonds: Yields
From 1926 to 2016

| Year | Jan | Feb | Mar | Apr | May | Jun | Jul | Aug | Sep | Oct | Nov | Dec | Year | Jan–Dec* |
|------|------|------|------|------|------|------|------|------|------|------|------|------|------|------|
| 1986 | 0.0958 | 0.0841 | 0.0766 | 0.0782 | 0.0848 | 0.0790 | 0.0809 | 0.0763 | 0.0827 | 0.0803 | 0.0779 | 0.0789 | 1986 | 0.0789 |
| 1987 | 0.0778 | 0.0763 | 0.0795 | 0.0859 | 0.0880 | 0.0877 | 0.0907 | 0.0936 | 0.0992 | 0.0926 | 0.0931 | 0.0920 | 1987 | 0.0920 |
| 1988 | 0.0852 | 0.0854 | 0.0901 | 0.0929 | 0.0952 | 0.0917 | 0.0947 | 0.0950 | 0.0917 | 0.0889 | 0.0923 | 0.0919 | 1988 | 0.0919 |
| 1989 | 0.0903 | 0.0935 | 0.0929 | 0.0918 | 0.0878 | 0.0822 | 0.0801 | 0.0841 | 0.0847 | 0.0810 | 0.0808 | 0.0816 | 1989 | 0.0816 |
| 1990 | 0.0865 | 0.0876 | 0.0889 | 0.0924 | 0.0883 | 0.0864 | 0.0860 | 0.0920 | 0.0914 | 0.0898 | 0.0858 | 0.0844 | 1990 | 0.0844 |
| 1991 | 0.0837 | 0.0841 | 0.0844 | 0.0837 | 0.0845 | 0.0860 | 0.0850 | 0.0818 | 0.0790 | 0.0791 | 0.0789 | 0.0730 | 1991 | 0.0730 |
| 1992 | 0.0776 | 0.0777 | 0.0797 | 0.0803 | 0.0781 | 0.0765 | 0.0726 | 0.0725 | 0.0710 | 0.0741 | 0.0748 | 0.0726 | 1992 | 0.0726 |
| 1993 | 0.0725 | 0.0698 | 0.0702 | 0.0701 | 0.0701 | 0.0668 | 0.0656 | 0.0623 | 0.0627 | 0.0623 | 0.0651 | 0.0654 | 1993 | 0.0654 |
| 1994 | 0.0637 | 0.0682 | 0.0725 | 0.0745 | 0.0759 | 0.0774 | 0.0746 | 0.0761 | 0.0800 | 0.0809 | 0.0808 | 0.0799 | 1994 | 0.0799 |
| 1995 | 0.0780 | 0.0758 | 0.0755 | 0.0745 | 0.0677 | 0.0670 | 0.0691 | 0.0674 | 0.0663 | 0.0641 | 0.0623 | 0.0603 | 1995 | 0.0603 |
| 1996 | 0.0609 | 0.0659 | 0.0684 | 0.0706 | 0.0717 | 0.0703 | 0.0707 | 0.0726 | 0.0704 | 0.0671 | 0.0643 | 0.0673 | 1996 | 0.0673 |
| 1997 | 0.0689 | 0.0694 | 0.0723 | 0.0705 | 0.0701 | 0.0688 | 0.0637 | 0.0672 | 0.0649 | 0.0623 | 0.0614 | 0.0602 | 1997 | 0.0602 |
| 1998 | 0.0589 | 0.0599 | 0.0602 | 0.0604 | 0.0592 | 0.0576 | 0.0584 | 0.0547 | 0.0517 | 0.0540 | 0.0535 | 0.0542 | 1998 | 0.0542 |
| 1999 | 0.0536 | 0.0587 | 0.0592 | 0.0594 | 0.0615 | 0.0627 | 0.0639 | 0.0649 | 0.0646 | 0.0651 | 0.0662 | 0.0682 | 1999 | 0.0682 |
| 2000 | 0.0666 | 0.0646 | 0.0618 | 0.0630 | 0.0640 | 0.0622 | 0.0611 | 0.0594 | 0.0612 | 0.0600 | 0.0576 | 0.0558 | 2000 | 0.0558 |
| 2001 | 0.0562 | 0.0549 | 0.0559 | 0.0593 | 0.0594 | 0.0590 | 0.0561 | 0.0546 | 0.0542 | 0.0506 | 0.0553 | 0.0575 | 2001 | 0.0575 |
| 2002 | 0.0569 | 0.0563 | 0.0604 | 0.0575 | 0.0578 | 0.0566 | 0.0544 | 0.0510 | 0.0480 | 0.0508 | 0.0521 | 0.0484 | 2002 | 0.0484 |
| 2003 | 0.0495 | 0.0472 | 0.0486 | 0.0481 | 0.0436 | 0.0452 | 0.0542 | 0.0532 | 0.0490 | 0.0518 | 0.0519 | 0.0511 | 2003 | 0.0511 |
| 2004 | 0.0499 | 0.0483 | 0.0474 | 0.0531 | 0.0539 | 0.0532 | 0.0523 | 0.0493 | 0.0488 | 0.0478 | 0.0502 | 0.0484 | 2004 | 0.0484 |
| 2005 | 0.0465 | 0.0479 | 0.0488 | 0.0461 | 0.0440 | 0.0429 | 0.0456 | 0.0432 | 0.0464 | 0.0484 | 0.0481 | 0.0461 | 2005 | 0.0461 |
| 2006 | 0.0474 | 0.0457 | 0.0507 | 0.0532 | 0.0535 | 0.0531 | 0.0518 | 0.0496 | 0.0484 | 0.0481 | 0.0467 | 0.0491 | 2006 | 0.0491 |
| 2007 | 0.0502 | 0.0477 | 0.0493 | 0.0489 | 0.0510 | 0.0521 | 0.0501 | 0.0487 | 0.0489 | 0.0480 | 0.0445 | 0.0450 | 2007 | 0.0450 |
| 2008 | 0.0436 | 0.0438 | 0.0432 | 0.0458 | 0.0475 | 0.0460 | 0.0465 | 0.0449 | 0.0443 | 0.0478 | 0.0372 | 0.0303 | 2008 | 0.0303 |
| 2009 | 0.0394 | 0.0401 | 0.0355 | 0.0410 | 0.0432 | 0.0429 | 0.0430 | 0.0415 | 0.0403 | 0.0420 | 0.0406 | 0.0458 | 2009 | 0.0458 |
| 2010 | 0.0441 | 0.0441 | 0.0458 | 0.0437 | 0.0407 | 0.0376 | 0.0377 | 0.0327 | 0.0341 | 0.0367 | 0.0380 | 0.0414 | 2010 | 0.0414 |
| 2011 | 0.0432 | 0.0426 | 0.0429 | 0.0416 | 0.0391 | 0.0409 | 0.0378 | 0.0315 | 0.0265 | 0.0291 | 0.0273 | 0.0255 | 2011 | 0.0255 |
| 2012 | 0.0249 | 0.0272 | 0.0297 | 0.0268 | 0.0221 | 0.0233 | 0.0216 | 0.0223 | 0.0235 | 0.0238 | 0.0228 | 0.0246 | 2012 | 0.0246 |
| 2013 | 0.0291 | 0.0285 | 0.0287 | 0.0264 | 0.0309 | 0.0330 | 0.0344 | 0.0351 | 0.0349 | 0.0342 | 0.0361 | 0.0378 | 2013 | 0.0378 |
| 2014 | 0.0342 | 0.0339 | 0.0337 | 0.0326 | 0.0309 | 0.0313 | 0.0310 | 0.0287 | 0.0300 | 0.0282 | 0.0264 | 0.0246 | 2014 | 0.0246 |
| 2015 | 0.0200 | 0.0238 | 0.0230 | 0.0249 | 0.0262 | 0.0285 | 0.0263 | 0.0264 | 0.0253 | 0.0259 | 0.0265 | 0.0268 | 2015 | 0.0268 |
| 2016 | 0.0236 | 0.0217 | 0.0218 | 0.0223 | 0.0219 | 0.0179 | 0.0175 | 0.0186 | 0.0196 | 0.0220 | 0.0267 | 0.0272 | 2016 | 0.0272 |

*Compound annual return

# Appendix A-10

Intermediate-term Government Bonds: Total Returns

From 1926 to 2016

| Year | Jan | Feb | Mar | Apr | May | Jun | Jul | Aug | Sep | Oct | Nov | Dec | Year | Jan–Dec* |
|------|------|------|------|------|------|------|------|------|------|------|------|------|------|------|
| 1926 | 0.0068 | 0.0032 | 0.0041 | 0.0090 | 0.0008 | 0.0027 | 0.0013 | 0.0009 | 0.0050 | 0.0054 | 0.0045 | 0.0089 | 1926 | 0.0538 |
| 1927 | 0.0057 | 0.0038 | 0.0038 | 0.0016 | 0.0020 | 0.0029 | 0.0043 | 0.0056 | 0.0060 | -0.0035 | 0.0083 | 0.0037 | 1927 | 0.0452 |
| 1928 | 0.0046 | -0.0004 | 0.0010 | -0.0003 | -0.0006 | 0.0017 | -0.0090 | 0.0050 | 0.0028 | 0.0032 | 0.0019 | -0.0007 | 1928 | 0.0092 |
| 1929 | -0.0029 | -0.0018 | 0.0005 | 0.0089 | -0.0061 | 0.0107 | 0.0066 | 0.0052 | -0.0014 | 0.0168 | 0.0180 | 0.0044 | 1929 | 0.0601 |
| 1930 | -0.0041 | 0.0094 | 0.0161 | -0.0071 | 0.0061 | 0.0142 | 0.0054 | 0.0022 | 0.0063 | 0.0076 | 0.0070 | 0.0024 | 1930 | 0.0672 |
| 1931 | -0.0071 | 0.0099 | 0.0052 | 0.0083 | 0.0119 | -0.0214 | 0.0016 | 0.0017 | -0.0113 | -0.0105 | 0.0049 | -0.0159 | 1931 | -0.0232 |
| 1932 | -0.0032 | 0.0128 | 0.0078 | 0.0194 | -0.0090 | 0.0108 | 0.0120 | 0.0124 | 0.0027 | 0.0045 | 0.0031 | 0.0118 | 1932 | 0.0881 |
| 1933 | -0.0016 | -0.0001 | 0.0099 | 0.0057 | 0.0199 | 0.0008 | -0.0006 | 0.0073 | 0.0026 | -0.0025 | 0.0027 | -0.0253 | 1933 | 0.0183 |
| 1934 | 0.0130 | 0.0052 | 0.0189 | 0.0182 | 0.0120 | 0.0091 | -0.0024 | -0.0092 | -0.0138 | 0.0190 | 0.0046 | 0.0125 | 1934 | 0.0900 |
| 1935 | 0.0114 | 0.0105 | 0.0125 | 0.0107 | -0.0035 | 0.0113 | 0.0038 | -0.0071 | -0.0057 | 0.0109 | 0.0014 | 0.0120 | 1935 | 0.0701 |
| 1936 | -0.0004 | 0.0069 | 0.0031 | 0.0024 | 0.0038 | 0.0012 | 0.0022 | 0.0050 | 0.0010 | 0.0025 | 0.0081 | -0.0057 | 1936 | 0.0306 |
| 1937 | -0.0031 | 0.0007 | -0.0164 | 0.0047 | 0.0080 | -0.0013 | 0.0059 | -0.0043 | 0.0081 | 0.0032 | 0.0042 | 0.0062 | 1937 | 0.0156 |
| 1938 | 0.0085 | 0.0052 | -0.0013 | 0.0230 | 0.0023 | 0.0075 | 0.0010 | 0.0015 | -0.0013 | 0.0093 | -0.0001 | 0.0052 | 1938 | 0.0623 |
| 1939 | 0.0029 | 0.0082 | 0.0081 | 0.0038 | 0.0095 | 0.0002 | 0.0040 | -0.0147 | -0.0263 | 0.0315 | 0.0074 | 0.0108 | 1939 | 0.0452 |
| 1940 | -0.0014 | 0.0035 | 0.0088 | 0.0002 | -0.0214 | 0.0187 | 0.0003 | 0.0043 | 0.0047 | 0.0036 | 0.0056 | 0.0028 | 1940 | 0.0296 |
| 1941 | 0.0001 | -0.0047 | 0.0069 | 0.0033 | 0.0012 | 0.0056 | 0.0000 | 0.0011 | 0.0000 | 0.0023 | -0.0092 | -0.0016 | 1941 | 0.0050 |
| 1942 | 0.0074 | 0.0015 | 0.0023 | 0.0022 | 0.0016 | 0.0013 | 0.0000 | 0.0017 | -0.0023 | 0.0017 | 0.0017 | 0.0000 | 1942 | 0.0194 |
| 1943 | 0.0039 | 0.0013 | 0.0021 | 0.0024 | 0.0057 | 0.0033 | 0.0021 | 0.0002 | 0.0014 | 0.0017 | 0.0015 | 0.0021 | 1943 | 0.0281 |
| 1944 | 0.0011 | 0.0016 | 0.0020 | 0.0028 | 0.0005 | 0.0007 | 0.0029 | 0.0024 | 0.0011 | 0.0011 | 0.0009 | 0.0010 | 1944 | 0.0180 |
| 1945 | 0.0052 | 0.0038 | 0.0004 | 0.0014 | 0.0012 | 0.0019 | 0.0000 | 0.0016 | 0.0017 | 0.0016 | 0.0010 | 0.0021 | 1945 | 0.0222 |
| 1946 | 0.0039 | 0.0048 | -0.0038 | -0.0020 | 0.0006 | 0.0033 | -0.0010 | 0.0004 | -0.0011 | 0.0026 | -0.0008 | 0.0032 | 1946 | 0.0100 |
| 1947 | 0.0023 | 0.0006 | 0.0024 | -0.0013 | 0.0008 | 0.0008 | 0.0006 | 0.0026 | 0.0000 | -0.0023 | 0.0006 | 0.0021 | 1947 | 0.0091 |
| 1948 | 0.0015 | 0.0018 | 0.0018 | 0.0019 | 0.0053 | -0.0008 | -0.0002 | -0.0004 | 0.0010 | 0.0013 | 0.0021 | 0.0032 | 1948 | 0.0185 |
| 1949 | 0.0028 | 0.0011 | 0.0025 | 0.0015 | 0.0023 | 0.0050 | 0.0020 | 0.0031 | 0.0008 | 0.0006 | 0.0002 | 0.0012 | 1949 | 0.0232 |
| 1950 | -0.0005 | 0.0008 | 0.0000 | 0.0008 | 0.0020 | 0.0003 | 0.0020 | -0.0007 | -0.0004 | 0.0001 | 0.0018 | 0.0008 | 1950 | 0.0070 |
| 1951 | 0.0022 | 0.0007 | -0.0127 | 0.0057 | -0.0040 | 0.0050 | 0.0058 | 0.0036 | -0.0057 | 0.0016 | 0.0032 | -0.0016 | 1951 | 0.0036 |
| 1952 | 0.0038 | -0.0020 | 0.0067 | 0.0054 | 0.0019 | -0.0035 | -0.0034 | -0.0024 | 0.0019 | 0.0066 | -0.0006 | 0.0019 | 1952 | 0.0163 |
| 1953 | -0.0002 | 0.0003 | -0.0017 | -0.0096 | -0.0117 | 0.0155 | 0.0056 | -0.0008 | 0.0194 | 0.0038 | 0.0014 | 0.0103 | 1953 | 0.0323 |
| 1954 | 0.0065 | 0.0100 | 0.0027 | 0.0043 | -0.0073 | 0.0125 | -0.0005 | 0.0011 | -0.0020 | -0.0009 | -0.0001 | 0.0005 | 1954 | 0.0268 |
| 1955 | -0.0032 | -0.0052 | 0.0024 | 0.0004 | 0.0001 | -0.0036 | -0.0071 | 0.0007 | 0.0082 | 0.0072 | -0.0053 | -0.0011 | 1955 | -0.0065 |

*Compound annual return

## Appendix A-10

Intermediate-term Government Bonds: Total Returns
From 1926 to 2016

| Year | Jan | Feb | Mar | Apr | May | Jun | Jul | Aug | Sep | Oct | Nov | Dec | Year | Jan–Dec* |
|---|---|---|---|---|---|---|---|---|---|---|---|---|---|---|
| 1956 | 0.0105 | 0.0003 | -0.0100 | -0.0001 | 0.0112 | 0.0003 | -0.0095 | -0.0103 | 0.0092 | -0.0019 | -0.0047 | 0.0011 | 1956 | -0.0042 |
| 1957 | 0.0237 | -0.0013 | 0.0018 | -0.0101 | -0.0017 | -0.0106 | -0.0015 | 0.0109 | 0.0002 | 0.0043 | 0.0396 | 0.0216 | 1957 | 0.0784 |
| 1958 | 0.0034 | 0.0139 | 0.0053 | 0.0052 | 0.0060 | -0.0068 | -0.0091 | -0.0356 | -0.0017 | 0.0002 | 0.0132 | -0.0061 | 1958 | -0.0129 |
| 1959 | -0.0013 | 0.0107 | -0.0037 | -0.0052 | -0.0001 | -0.0077 | 0.0034 | -0.0078 | 0.0020 | 0.0174 | -0.0092 | -0.0020 | 1959 | -0.0039 |
| 1960 | 0.0154 | 0.0072 | 0.0292 | -0.0064 | 0.0031 | 0.0217 | 0.0267 | -0.0005 | 0.0029 | 0.0016 | -0.0094 | 0.0210 | 1960 | 0.1176 |
| 1961 | -0.0059 | 0.0090 | 0.0037 | 0.0054 | -0.0028 | -0.0025 | 0.0007 | 0.0019 | 0.0079 | 0.0014 | -0.0019 | 0.0018 | 1961 | 0.0185 |
| 1962 | -0.0045 | 0.0155 | 0.0089 | 0.0025 | 0.0049 | -0.0028 | -0.0012 | 0.0125 | 0.0021 | 0.0051 | 0.0060 | 0.0056 | 1962 | 0.0556 |
| 1963 | -0.0029 | 0.0017 | 0.0027 | 0.0030 | 0.0014 | 0.0014 | 0.0003 | 0.0019 | 0.0014 | 0.0011 | 0.0040 | 0.0003 | 1963 | 0.0164 |
| 1964 | 0.0033 | 0.0012 | 0.0016 | 0.0033 | 0.0081 | 0.0036 | 0.0027 | 0.0027 | 0.0045 | 0.0032 | -0.0004 | 0.0058 | 1964 | 0.0404 |
| 1965 | 0.0042 | 0.0018 | 0.0043 | 0.0026 | 0.0035 | 0.0049 | 0.0017 | 0.0019 | -0.0005 | 0.0000 | 0.0007 | -0.0149 | 1965 | 0.0102 |
| 1966 | 0.0003 | -0.0084 | 0.0187 | -0.0019 | 0.0011 | -0.0024 | -0.0025 | -0.0125 | 0.0216 | 0.0075 | 0.0028 | 0.0223 | 1966 | 0.0469 |
| 1967 | 0.0118 | -0.0013 | 0.0183 | -0.0089 | 0.0044 | -0.0227 | 0.0133 | -0.0036 | 0.0007 | -0.0049 | 0.0028 | 0.0007 | 1967 | 0.0101 |
| 1968 | 0.0145 | 0.0040 | -0.0026 | -0.0016 | 0.0064 | 0.0167 | 0.0176 | 0.0021 | 0.0055 | 0.0009 | -0.0013 | -0.0173 | 1968 | 0.0454 |
| 1969 | 0.0086 | -0.0013 | 0.0097 | 0.0079 | -0.0082 | -0.0084 | 0.0082 | -0.0018 | -0.0300 | 0.0333 | -0.0047 | -0.0193 | 1969 | -0.0074 |
| 1970 | 0.0030 | 0.0439 | 0.0087 | -0.0207 | 0.0110 | 0.0061 | 0.0152 | 0.0116 | 0.0196 | 0.0095 | 0.0451 | 0.0054 | 1970 | 0.1686 |
| 1971 | 0.0168 | 0.0224 | 0.0186 | -0.0327 | 0.0011 | -0.0187 | 0.0027 | 0.0350 | 0.0026 | 0.0220 | 0.0052 | 0.0110 | 1971 | 0.0872 |
| 1972 | 0.0106 | 0.0014 | 0.0015 | 0.0014 | 0.0016 | 0.0045 | 0.0015 | 0.0015 | 0.0014 | 0.0016 | 0.0045 | 0.0192 | 1972 | 0.0516 |
| 1973 | -0.0006 | -0.0075 | 0.0046 | 0.0064 | 0.0057 | -0.0006 | -0.0276 | 0.0254 | 0.0250 | 0.0050 | 0.0064 | 0.0040 | 1973 | 0.0461 |
| 1974 | 0.0009 | 0.0035 | -0.0212 | -0.0152 | 0.0130 | -0.0087 | 0.0007 | -0.0012 | 0.0319 | 0.0109 | 0.0236 | 0.0185 | 1974 | 0.0569 |
| 1975 | 0.0053 | 0.0148 | -0.0059 | -0.0186 | 0.0260 | 0.0027 | -0.0030 | -0.0009 | 0.0010 | 0.0366 | -0.0010 | 0.0198 | 1975 | 0.0783 |
| 1976 | 0.0057 | 0.0084 | 0.0075 | 0.0116 | -0.0145 | 0.0159 | 0.0119 | 0.0189 | 0.0076 | 0.0147 | 0.0321 | 0.0026 | 1976 | 0.1287 |
| 1977 | -0.0190 | 0.0048 | 0.0055 | 0.0051 | 0.0056 | 0.0102 | 0.0001 | 0.0008 | 0.0015 | -0.0060 | 0.0079 | -0.0023 | 1977 | 0.0141 |
| 1978 | 0.0013 | 0.0017 | 0.0037 | 0.0024 | -0.0002 | -0.0021 | 0.0098 | 0.0079 | 0.0057 | -0.0112 | 0.0092 | 0.0063 | 1978 | 0.0349 |
| 1979 | 0.0055 | -0.0059 | 0.0112 | 0.0033 | 0.0193 | 0.0205 | -0.0011 | -0.0091 | 0.0006 | -0.0468 | 0.0363 | 0.0087 | 1979 | 0.0409 |
| 1980 | -0.0135 | -0.0641 | 0.0143 | 0.1198 | 0.0490 | -0.0077 | -0.0106 | -0.0387 | -0.0038 | -0.0152 | 0.0029 | 0.0171 | 1980 | 0.0391 |
| 1981 | 0.0032 | -0.0235 | 0.0263 | -0.0216 | 0.0245 | 0.0060 | -0.0270 | -0.0178 | 0.0164 | 0.0611 | 0.0624 | -0.0142 | 1981 | 0.0945 |
| 1982 | 0.0050 | 0.0148 | 0.0042 | 0.0299 | 0.0146 | -0.0135 | 0.0464 | 0.0469 | 0.0325 | 0.0531 | 0.0080 | 0.0185 | 1982 | 0.2910 |
| 1983 | 0.0007 | 0.0252 | -0.0049 | 0.0259 | -0.0122 | 0.0016 | -0.0198 | 0.0081 | 0.0315 | 0.0019 | 0.0103 | 0.0047 | 1983 | 0.0741 |
| 1984 | 0.0177 | -0.0064 | -0.0035 | -0.0003 | -0.0250 | 0.0099 | 0.0393 | 0.0101 | 0.0202 | 0.0383 | 0.0192 | 0.0143 | 1984 | 0.1402 |
| 1985 | 0.0206 | -0.0179 | 0.0166 | 0.0264 | 0.0485 | 0.0108 | -0.0045 | 0.0148 | 0.0113 | 0.0162 | 0.0195 | 0.0257 | 1985 | 0.2033 |

*Compound annual return

# Appendix A-10

Intermediate-term Government Bonds: Total Returns
From 1926 to 2016

| Year | Jan | Feb | Mar | Apr | May | Jun | Jul | Aug | Sep | Oct | Nov | Dec | Year | Jan–Dec* |
|---|---|---|---|---|---|---|---|---|---|---|---|---|---|---|
| 1986 | 0.0082 | 0.0275 | 0.0338 | 0.0081 | -0.0215 | 0.0276 | 0.0157 | 0.0266 | -0.0110 | 0.0162 | 0.0113 | 0.0007 | 1986 | 0.1514 |
| 1987 | 0.0107 | 0.0059 | -0.0031 | -0.0244 | -0.0038 | 0.0122 | 0.0025 | -0.0038 | -0.0141 | 0.0299 | 0.0083 | 0.0093 | 1987 | 0.0290 |
| 1988 | 0.0316 | 0.0123 | -0.0086 | -0.0044 | -0.0049 | 0.0181 | -0.0047 | -0.0009 | 0.0196 | 0.0148 | -0.0115 | -0.0010 | 1988 | 0.0610 |
| 1989 | 0.0121 | -0.0051 | 0.0049 | 0.0220 | 0.0212 | 0.0324 | 0.0235 | -0.0246 | 0.0069 | 0.0237 | 0.0084 | 0.0012 | 1989 | 0.1329 |
| 1990 | -0.0105 | 0.0007 | 0.0002 | -0.0077 | 0.0261 | 0.0151 | 0.0174 | -0.0092 | 0.0094 | 0.0171 | 0.0193 | 0.0161 | 1990 | 0.0973 |
| 1991 | 0.0107 | 0.0048 | 0.0023 | 0.0117 | 0.0059 | -0.0023 | 0.0129 | 0.0247 | 0.0216 | 0.0134 | 0.0128 | 0.0265 | 1991 | 0.1546 |
| 1992 | -0.0195 | 0.0022 | -0.0079 | 0.0098 | 0.0222 | 0.0177 | 0.0242 | 0.0150 | 0.0194 | -0.0182 | -0.0084 | 0.0146 | 1992 | 0.0719 |
| 1993 | 0.0270 | 0.0243 | 0.0043 | 0.0088 | -0.0009 | 0.0201 | 0.0005 | 0.0223 | 0.0056 | 0.0018 | -0.0093 | 0.0032 | 1993 | 0.1124 |
| 1994 | 0.0138 | -0.0258 | -0.0257 | -0.0105 | -0.0002 | -0.0028 | 0.0169 | 0.0026 | -0.0158 | -0.0023 | -0.0070 | 0.0053 | 1994 | -0.0514 |
| 1995 | 0.0182 | 0.0234 | 0.0063 | 0.0143 | 0.0369 | 0.0079 | -0.0016 | 0.0086 | 0.0064 | 0.0121 | 0.0149 | 0.0095 | 1995 | 0.1680 |
| 1996 | 0.0006 | -0.0138 | -0.0118 | -0.0050 | -0.0032 | 0.0117 | 0.0025 | -0.0005 | 0.0155 | 0.0183 | 0.0149 | -0.0078 | 1996 | 0.0210 |
| 1997 | 0.0025 | 0.0002 | -0.0114 | 0.0148 | 0.0077 | 0.0103 | 0.0264 | -0.0098 | 0.0151 | 0.0150 | -0.0001 | 0.0106 | 1997 | 0.0838 |
| 1998 | 0.0180 | -0.0039 | 0.0026 | 0.0061 | 0.0070 | 0.0079 | 0.0027 | 0.0271 | 0.0330 | 0.0041 | -0.0098 | 0.0037 | 1998 | 0.1021 |
| 1999 | 0.0055 | -0.0262 | 0.0086 | 0.0021 | -0.0147 | 0.0032 | -0.0005 | 0.0015 | 0.0097 | -0.0008 | -0.0008 | -0.0048 | 1999 | -0.0177 |
| 2000 | -0.0053 | 0.0078 | 0.0203 | -0.0043 | 0.0052 | 0.0191 | 0.0072 | 0.0134 | 0.0096 | 0.0079 | 0.0174 | 0.0214 | 2000 | 0.1259 |
| 2001 | 0.0098 | 0.0105 | 0.0076 | -0.0114 | -0.0007 | 0.0066 | 0.0247 | 0.0095 | 0.0253 | 0.0180 | -0.0171 | -0.0082 | 2001 | 0.0762 |
| 2002 | 0.0036 | 0.0108 | -0.0242 | 0.0239 | 0.0118 | 0.0169 | 0.0272 | 0.0167 | 0.0288 | -0.0024 | -0.0169 | 0.0279 | 2002 | 0.1293 |
| 2003 | -0.0089 | 0.0179 | -0.0007 | 0.0013 | 0.0273 | -0.0035 | -0.0319 | -0.0027 | 0.0307 | -0.0136 | -0.0014 | 0.0109 | 2003 | 0.0240 |
| 2004 | 0.0052 | 0.0124 | 0.0100 | -0.0334 | -0.0049 | 0.0049 | 0.0082 | 0.0195 | 0.0012 | 0.0064 | -0.0127 | 0.0067 | 2004 | 0.0225 |
| 2005 | 0.0026 | -0.0111 | -0.0038 | 0.0167 | 0.0103 | 0.0043 | -0.0144 | 0.0161 | -0.0124 | -0.0063 | 0.0059 | 0.0061 | 2005 | 0.0136 |
| 2006 | -0.0036 | -0.0017 | -0.0056 | -0.0008 | -0.0004 | 0.0022 | 0.0125 | 0.0135 | 0.0079 | 0.0052 | 0.0088 | -0.0067 | 2006 | 0.0314 |
| 2007 | -0.0020 | 0.0170 | 0.0024 | 0.0047 | -0.0102 | 0.0011 | 0.0175 | 0.0185 | 0.0057 | -0.0048 | 0.0425 | 0.0048 | 2007 | 0.1005 |
| 2008 | 0.0263 | 0.0234 | 0.0073 | -0.0293 | -0.0084 | 0.0075 | 0.0064 | 0.0104 | 0.0085 | 0.0146 | 0.0430 | 0.0160 | 2008 | 0.1311 |
| 2009 | -0.0163 | -0.0082 | 0.0186 | -0.0166 | -0.0132 | -0.0076 | 0.0056 | 0.0097 | 0.0075 | 0.0030 | 0.0184 | -0.0241 | 2009 | -0.0240 |
| 2010 | 0.0194 | 0.0071 | -0.0088 | 0.0094 | 0.0151 | 0.0129 | 0.0158 | 0.0128 | 0.0049 | 0.0064 | -0.0082 | -0.0171 | 2010 | 0.0712 |
| 2011 | 0.0062 | -0.0053 | -0.0005 | 0.0154 | 0.0179 | -0.0001 | 0.0202 | 0.0210 | 0.0008 | 0.0009 | 0.0036 | 0.0049 | 2011 | 0.0881 |
| 2012 | 0.0008 | -0.0052 | -0.0070 | 0.0129 | 0.0083 | -0.0020 | 0.0077 | 0.0015 | 0.0004 | -0.0024 | 0.0048 | -0.0031 | 2012 | 0.0166 |
| 2013 | -0.0061 | 0.0064 | -0.0143 | 0.0060 | -0.0165 | -0.0139 | 0.0026 | -0.0074 | 0.0121 | 0.0051 | 0.0011 | -0.0122 | 2013 | -0.0368 |
| 2014 | 0.0131 | 0.0024 | -0.0068 | 0.0048 | 0.0094 | -0.0017 | -0.0047 | 0.0075 | -0.0049 | 0.0089 | 0.0078 | -0.0060 | 2014 | 0.0300 |
| 2015 | 0.0241 | -0.0123 | 0.0074 | -0.0014 | 0.0005 | -0.0053 | 0.0051 | 0.0011 | 0.0099 | -0.0052 | -0.0040 | -0.0017 | 2015 | 0.0179 |
| 2016 | 0.0233 | 0.0057 | 0.0045 | -0.0010 | -0.0021 | 0.0175 | 0.0004 | -0.0064 | 0.0027 | -0.0052 | -0.0189 | -0.0007 | 2016 | 0.0192 |

*Compound annual return

## Appendix A-11

Intermediate-term Government Bonds: Income Returns

From 1926 to 2016

| Year | Jan | Feb | Mar | Apr | May | Jun | Jul | Aug | Sep | Oct | Nov | Dec | Year | Jan–Dec* |
|------|-----|-----|-----|-----|-----|-----|-----|-----|-----|-----|-----|-----|------|----------|
| 1926 | 0.0032 | 0.0032 | 0.0032 | 0.0031 | 0.0031 | 0.0031 | 0.0032 | 0.0032 | 0.0032 | 0.0031 | 0.0031 | 0.0030 | 1926 | 0.0378 |
| 1927 | 0.0029 | 0.0029 | 0.0029 | 0.0029 | 0.0029 | 0.0029 | 0.0029 | 0.0029 | 0.0028 | 0.0029 | 0.0028 | 0.0028 | 1927 | 0.0349 |
| 1928 | 0.0028 | 0.0028 | 0.0029 | 0.0029 | 0.0030 | 0.0030 | 0.0032 | 0.0032 | 0.0032 | 0.0032 | 0.0032 | 0.0033 | 1928 | 0.0364 |
| 1929 | 0.0034 | 0.0035 | 0.0036 | 0.0035 | 0.0037 | 0.0035 | 0.0035 | 0.0034 | 0.0035 | 0.0033 | 0.0030 | 0.0030 | 1929 | 0.0407 |
| 1930 | 0.0031 | 0.0030 | 0.0028 | 0.0030 | 0.0029 | 0.0027 | 0.0026 | 0.0026 | 0.0026 | 0.0025 | 0.0024 | 0.0024 | 1930 | 0.0330 |
| 1931 | 0.0026 | 0.0025 | 0.0024 | 0.0023 | 0.0021 | 0.0026 | 0.0026 | 0.0026 | 0.0028 | 0.0031 | 0.0031 | 0.0034 | 1931 | 0.0316 |
| 1932 | 0.0035 | 0.0034 | 0.0033 | 0.0030 | 0.0032 | 0.0031 | 0.0029 | 0.0027 | 0.0027 | 0.0027 | 0.0027 | 0.0025 | 1932 | 0.0363 |
| 1933 | 0.0026 | 0.0026 | 0.0025 | 0.0025 | 0.0021 | 0.0022 | 0.0022 | 0.0021 | 0.0021 | 0.0022 | 0.0022 | 0.0027 | 1933 | 0.0283 |
| 1934 | 0.0030 | 0.0024 | 0.0027 | 0.0024 | 0.0023 | 0.0021 | 0.0021 | 0.0021 | 0.0021 | 0.0026 | 0.0022 | 0.0023 | 1934 | 0.0293 |
| 1935 | 0.0021 | 0.0018 | 0.0018 | 0.0017 | 0.0016 | 0.0015 | 0.0015 | 0.0014 | 0.0015 | 0.0016 | 0.0015 | 0.0016 | 1935 | 0.0202 |
| 1936 | 0.0014 | 0.0013 | 0.0013 | 0.0012 | 0.0012 | 0.0013 | 0.0012 | 0.0012 | 0.0011 | 0.0011 | 0.0011 | 0.0010 | 1936 | 0.0144 |
| 1937 | 0.0010 | 0.0010 | 0.0012 | 0.0015 | 0.0013 | 0.0014 | 0.0014 | 0.0013 | 0.0014 | 0.0012 | 0.0012 | 0.0011 | 1937 | 0.0148 |
| 1938 | 0.0018 | 0.0016 | 0.0017 | 0.0017 | 0.0015 | 0.0014 | 0.0013 | 0.0014 | 0.0013 | 0.0014 | 0.0013 | 0.0013 | 1938 | 0.0182 |
| 1939 | 0.0013 | 0.0011 | 0.0012 | 0.0010 | 0.0011 | 0.0009 | 0.0009 | 0.0009 | 0.0011 | 0.0015 | 0.0010 | 0.0009 | 1939 | 0.0131 |
| 1940 | 0.0009 | 0.0008 | 0.0008 | 0.0007 | 0.0007 | 0.0010 | 0.0008 | 0.0008 | 0.0007 | 0.0007 | 0.0006 | 0.0005 | 1940 | 0.0090 |
| 1941 | 0.0006 | 0.0006 | 0.0008 | 0.0006 | 0.0006 | 0.0006 | 0.0005 | 0.0005 | 0.0005 | 0.0005 | 0.0004 | 0.0007 | 1941 | 0.0067 |
| 1942 | 0.0008 | 0.0006 | 0.0007 | 0.0006 | 0.0006 | 0.0006 | 0.0006 | 0.0006 | 0.0006 | 0.0006 | 0.0006 | 0.0006 | 1942 | 0.0076 |
| 1943 | 0.0014 | 0.0013 | 0.0014 | 0.0013 | 0.0013 | 0.0013 | 0.0013 | 0.0012 | 0.0012 | 0.0012 | 0.0012 | 0.0012 | 1943 | 0.0156 |
| 1944 | 0.0013 | 0.0012 | 0.0013 | 0.0012 | 0.0013 | 0.0012 | 0.0012 | 0.0012 | 0.0011 | 0.0012 | 0.0011 | 0.0011 | 1944 | 0.0144 |
| 1945 | 0.0012 | 0.0010 | 0.0010 | 0.0010 | 0.0010 | 0.0010 | 0.0010 | 0.0010 | 0.0009 | 0.0010 | 0.0009 | 0.0009 | 1945 | 0.0119 |
| 1946 | 0.0009 | 0.0008 | 0.0007 | 0.0009 | 0.0009 | 0.0009 | 0.0009 | 0.0009 | 0.0010 | 0.0010 | 0.0009 | 0.0010 | 1946 | 0.0108 |
| 1947 | 0.0010 | 0.0009 | 0.0010 | 0.0009 | 0.0010 | 0.0011 | 0.0010 | 0.0010 | 0.0010 | 0.0010 | 0.0010 | 0.0012 | 1947 | 0.0121 |
| 1948 | 0.0013 | 0.0012 | 0.0014 | 0.0013 | 0.0012 | 0.0013 | 0.0012 | 0.0013 | 0.0013 | 0.0013 | 0.0014 | 0.0013 | 1948 | 0.0156 |
| 1949 | 0.0013 | 0.0012 | 0.0013 | 0.0012 | 0.0013 | 0.0012 | 0.0010 | 0.0011 | 0.0010 | 0.0010 | 0.0010 | 0.0010 | 1949 | 0.0136 |
| 1950 | 0.0011 | 0.0010 | 0.0011 | 0.0010 | 0.0012 | 0.0011 | 0.0012 | 0.0011 | 0.0011 | 0.0013 | 0.0013 | 0.0013 | 1950 | 0.0139 |
| 1951 | 0.0016 | 0.0014 | 0.0015 | 0.0018 | 0.0017 | 0.0017 | 0.0018 | 0.0017 | 0.0015 | 0.0019 | 0.0017 | 0.0018 | 1951 | 0.0198 |
| 1952 | 0.0018 | 0.0017 | 0.0019 | 0.0017 | 0.0016 | 0.0017 | 0.0018 | 0.0018 | 0.0021 | 0.0020 | 0.0017 | 0.0021 | 1952 | 0.0219 |
| 1953 | 0.0019 | 0.0018 | 0.0021 | 0.0021 | 0.0022 | 0.0027 | 0.0024 | 0.0023 | 0.0023 | 0.0020 | 0.0020 | 0.0020 | 1953 | 0.0255 |
| 1954 | 0.0016 | 0.0014 | 0.0014 | 0.0013 | 0.0011 | 0.0016 | 0.0011 | 0.0012 | 0.0011 | 0.0012 | 0.0014 | 0.0014 | 1954 | 0.0160 |
| 1955 | 0.0018 | 0.0017 | 0.0020 | 0.0019 | 0.0021 | 0.0020 | 0.0020 | 0.0025 | 0.0023 | 0.0023 | 0.0021 | 0.0022 | 1955 | 0.0245 |

*Compound annual return

# Appendix A-11

Intermediate-term Government Bonds: Income Returns

From 1926 to 2016

| Year | Jan | Feb | Mar | Apr | May | Jun | Jul | Aug | Sep | Oct | Nov | Dec | Year | Jan–Dec* |
|---|---|---|---|---|---|---|---|---|---|---|---|---|---|---|
| 1956 | 0.0025 | 0.0021 | 0.0022 | 0.0026 | 0.0026 | 0.0023 | 0.0025 | 0.0027 | 0.0026 | 0.0030 | 0.0028 | 0.0030 | 1956 | 0.0305 |
| 1957 | 0.0030 | 0.0025 | 0.0026 | 0.0029 | 0.0030 | 0.0027 | 0.0036 | 0.0032 | 0.0032 | 0.0033 | 0.0031 | 0.0028 | 1957 | 0.0359 |
| 1958 | 0.0024 | 0.0021 | 0.0022 | 0.0021 | 0.0019 | 0.0021 | 0.0021 | 0.0022 | 0.0032 | 0.0032 | 0.0029 | 0.0032 | 1958 | 0.0293 |
| 1959 | 0.0031 | 0.0030 | 0.0033 | 0.0032 | 0.0033 | 0.0037 | 0.0038 | 0.0037 | 0.0039 | 0.0039 | 0.0038 | 0.0041 | 1959 | 0.0418 |
| 1960 | 0.0039 | 0.0039 | 0.0039 | 0.0032 | 0.0037 | 0.0035 | 0.0031 | 0.0030 | 0.0028 | 0.0029 | 0.0028 | 0.0031 | 1960 | 0.0415 |
| 1961 | 0.0030 | 0.0028 | 0.0029 | 0.0027 | 0.0030 | 0.0029 | 0.0031 | 0.0031 | 0.0030 | 0.0032 | 0.0030 | 0.0030 | 1961 | 0.0354 |
| 1962 | 0.0035 | 0.0031 | 0.0031 | 0.0031 | 0.0031 | 0.0029 | 0.0033 | 0.0032 | 0.0028 | 0.0033 | 0.0029 | 0.0030 | 1962 | 0.0373 |
| 1963 | 0.0030 | 0.0028 | 0.0029 | 0.0032 | 0.0031 | 0.0036 | 0.0034 | 0.0031 | 0.0033 | 0.0033 | 0.0031 | 0.0034 | 1963 | 0.0371 |
| 1964 | 0.0034 | 0.0030 | 0.0035 | 0.0033 | 0.0031 | 0.0037 | 0.0034 | 0.0033 | 0.0033 | 0.0034 | 0.0034 | 0.0034 | 1964 | 0.0400 |
| 1965 | 0.0033 | 0.0031 | 0.0037 | 0.0033 | 0.0033 | 0.0040 | 0.0040 | 0.0036 | 0.0034 | 0.0044 | 0.0038 | 0.0037 | 1965 | 0.0415 |
| 1966 | 0.0040 | 0.0036 | 0.0043 | 0.0038 | 0.0042 | 0.0038 | 0.0045 | 0.0047 | 0.0046 | 0.0047 | 0.0042 | 0.0042 | 1966 | 0.0493 |
| 1967 | 0.0041 | 0.0035 | 0.0040 | 0.0033 | 0.0042 | 0.0043 | 0.0049 | 0.0042 | 0.0042 | 0.0044 | 0.0046 | 0.0044 | 1967 | 0.0488 |
| 1968 | 0.0051 | 0.0043 | 0.0043 | 0.0049 | 0.0048 | 0.0058 | 0.0059 | 0.0042 | 0.0044 | 0.0044 | 0.0042 | 0.0047 | 1968 | 0.0549 |
| 1969 | 0.0054 | 0.0048 | 0.0049 | 0.0057 | 0.0050 | 0.0067 | 0.0065 | 0.0054 | 0.0061 | 0.0067 | 0.0056 | 0.0068 | 1969 | 0.0665 |
| 1970 | 0.0066 | 0.0061 | 0.0063 | 0.0059 | 0.0062 | 0.0053 | 0.0053 | 0.0062 | 0.0060 | 0.0057 | 0.0058 | 0.0050 | 1970 | 0.0749 |
| 1971 | 0.0047 | 0.0043 | 0.0047 | 0.0040 | 0.0044 | 0.0048 | 0.0049 | 0.0056 | 0.0048 | 0.0046 | 0.0047 | 0.0046 | 1971 | 0.0575 |
| 1972 | 0.0048 | 0.0044 | 0.0046 | 0.0044 | 0.0052 | 0.0053 | 0.0059 | 0.0050 | 0.0047 | 0.0053 | 0.0051 | 0.0049 | 1972 | 0.0575 |
| 1973 | 0.0056 | 0.0048 | 0.0054 | 0.0056 | 0.0056 | 0.0059 | 0.0073 | 0.0064 | 0.0055 | 0.0060 | 0.0055 | 0.0056 | 1973 | 0.0658 |
| 1974 | 0.0057 | 0.0051 | 0.0054 | 0.0065 | 0.0067 | 0.0063 | 0.0063 | 0.0067 | 0.0072 | 0.0067 | 0.0061 | 0.0064 | 1974 | 0.0724 |
| 1975 | 0.0061 | 0.0055 | 0.0059 | 0.0060 | 0.0063 | 0.0069 | 0.0060 | 0.0061 | 0.0069 | 0.0068 | 0.0055 | 0.0067 | 1975 | 0.0735 |
| 1976 | 0.0060 | 0.0055 | 0.0066 | 0.0059 | 0.0054 | 0.0055 | 0.0052 | 0.0062 | 0.0056 | 0.0054 | 0.0058 | 0.0050 | 1976 | 0.0710 |
| 1977 | 0.0051 | 0.0050 | 0.0056 | 0.0053 | 0.0058 | 0.0066 | 0.0070 | 0.0059 | 0.0056 | 0.0059 | 0.0059 | 0.0059 | 1977 | 0.0649 |
| 1978 | 0.0066 | 0.0057 | 0.0066 | 0.0060 | 0.0071 | 0.0070 | 0.0074 | 0.0068 | 0.0065 | 0.0072 | 0.0072 | 0.0069 | 1978 | 0.0783 |
| 1979 | 0.0079 | 0.0066 | 0.0075 | 0.0077 | 0.0077 | 0.0075 | 0.0079 | 0.0073 | 0.0070 | 0.0084 | 0.0089 | 0.0086 | 1979 | 0.0904 |
| 1980 | 0.0086 | 0.0083 | 0.0107 | 0.0103 | 0.0081 | 0.0079 | 0.0079 | 0.0076 | 0.0097 | 0.0094 | 0.0096 | 0.0111 | 1980 | 0.1055 |
| 1981 | 0.0101 | 0.0095 | 0.0117 | 0.0106 | 0.0110 | 0.0118 | 0.0116 | 0.0120 | 0.0130 | 0.0129 | 0.0121 | 0.0108 | 1981 | 0.1297 |
| 1982 | 0.0107 | 0.0102 | 0.0122 | 0.0112 | 0.0101 | 0.0118 | 0.0113 | 0.0109 | 0.0097 | 0.0089 | 0.0087 | 0.0085 | 1982 | 0.1281 |
| 1983 | 0.0084 | 0.0079 | 0.0084 | 0.0081 | 0.0086 | 0.0085 | 0.0082 | 0.0103 | 0.0094 | 0.0092 | 0.0091 | 0.0091 | 1983 | 0.1035 |
| 1984 | 0.0096 | 0.0088 | 0.0095 | 0.0101 | 0.0104 | 0.0105 | 0.0113 | 0.0105 | 0.0095 | 0.0110 | 0.0093 | 0.0093 | 1984 | 0.1168 |
| 1985 | 0.0090 | 0.0081 | 0.0089 | 0.0097 | 0.0090 | 0.0073 | 0.0083 | 0.0081 | 0.0082 | 0.0081 | 0.0074 | 0.0078 | 1985 | 0.1029 |

*Compound annual return

## Appendix A-11

Intermediate-term Government Bonds: Income Returns

From 1926 to 2016

| Year | Jan | Feb | Mar | Apr | May | Jun | Jul | Aug | Sep | Oct | Nov | Dec | Year | Jan–Dec* |
|------|------|------|------|------|------|------|------|------|------|------|------|------|------|----------|
| 1986 | 0.0071 | 0.0066 | 0.0068 | 0.0060 | 0.0060 | 0.0068 | 0.0062 | 0.0057 | 0.0058 | 0.0060 | 0.0052 | 0.0060 | 1986 | 0.0772 |
| 1987 | 0.0055 | 0.0052 | 0.0060 | 0.0058 | 0.0062 | 0.0071 | 0.0066 | 0.0068 | 0.0068 | 0.0073 | 0.0070 | 0.0070 | 1987 | 0.0747 |
| 1988 | 0.0065 | 0.0066 | 0.0064 | 0.0063 | 0.0072 | 0.0070 | 0.0064 | 0.0077 | 0.0072 | 0.0071 | 0.0067 | 0.0071 | 1988 | 0.0824 |
| 1989 | 0.0077 | 0.0066 | 0.0078 | 0.0071 | 0.0080 | 0.0070 | 0.0067 | 0.0061 | 0.0065 | 0.0071 | 0.0063 | 0.0060 | 1989 | 0.0846 |
| 1990 | 0.0071 | 0.0064 | 0.0069 | 0.0071 | 0.0075 | 0.0067 | 0.0072 | 0.0068 | 0.0065 | 0.0074 | 0.0067 | 0.0067 | 1990 | 0.0815 |
| 1991 | 0.0064 | 0.0059 | 0.0059 | 0.0070 | 0.0065 | 0.0059 | 0.0069 | 0.0062 | 0.0061 | 0.0058 | 0.0052 | 0.0056 | 1991 | 0.0743 |
| 1992 | 0.0052 | 0.0052 | 0.0060 | 0.0058 | 0.0056 | 0.0058 | 0.0053 | 0.0050 | 0.0047 | 0.0044 | 0.0050 | 0.0053 | 1992 | 0.0627 |
| 1993 | 0.0049 | 0.0045 | 0.0049 | 0.0045 | 0.0041 | 0.0050 | 0.0041 | 0.0044 | 0.0041 | 0.0038 | 0.0042 | 0.0043 | 1993 | 0.0553 |
| 1994 | 0.0045 | 0.0039 | 0.0048 | 0.0049 | 0.0058 | 0.0055 | 0.0055 | 0.0060 | 0.0055 | 0.0060 | 0.0061 | 0.0063 | 1994 | 0.0607 |
| 1995 | 0.0067 | 0.0056 | 0.0060 | 0.0054 | 0.0062 | 0.0050 | 0.0051 | 0.0051 | 0.0047 | 0.0052 | 0.0047 | 0.0043 | 1995 | 0.0669 |
| 1996 | 0.0046 | 0.0041 | 0.0045 | 0.0053 | 0.0054 | 0.0050 | 0.0058 | 0.0052 | 0.0056 | 0.0053 | 0.0043 | 0.0050 | 1996 | 0.0582 |
| 1997 | 0.0052 | 0.0047 | 0.0054 | 0.0055 | 0.0054 | 0.0055 | 0.0054 | 0.0046 | 0.0054 | 0.0050 | 0.0043 | 0.0052 | 1997 | 0.0614 |
| 1998 | 0.0046 | 0.0041 | 0.0049 | 0.0046 | 0.0045 | 0.0049 | 0.0047 | 0.0046 | 0.0041 | 0.0035 | 0.0036 | 0.0039 | 1998 | 0.0529 |
| 1999 | 0.0037 | 0.0035 | 0.0048 | 0.0043 | 0.0041 | 0.0052 | 0.0048 | 0.0051 | 0.0048 | 0.0046 | 0.0052 | 0.0052 | 1999 | 0.0530 |
| 2000 | 0.0054 | 0.0052 | 0.0056 | 0.0048 | 0.0059 | 0.0054 | 0.0053 | 0.0051 | 0.0047 | 0.0051 | 0.0047 | 0.0043 | 2000 | 0.0619 |
| 2001 | 0.0032 | 0.0026 | 0.0027 | 0.0033 | 0.0042 | 0.0040 | 0.0044 | 0.0039 | 0.0034 | 0.0035 | 0.0030 | 0.0035 | 2001 | 0.0427 |
| 2002 | 0.0038 | 0.0034 | 0.0034 | 0.0045 | 0.0039 | 0.0034 | 0.0037 | 0.0029 | 0.0027 | 0.0022 | 0.0022 | 0.0028 | 2002 | 0.0398 |
| 2003 | 0.0024 | 0.0024 | 0.0024 | 0.0023 | 0.0023 | 0.0019 | 0.0020 | 0.0025 | 0.0029 | 0.0022 | 0.0023 | 0.0029 | 2003 | 0.0285 |
| 2004 | 0.0026 | 0.0024 | 0.0026 | 0.0023 | 0.0027 | 0.0034 | 0.0030 | 0.0031 | 0.0026 | 0.0026 | 0.0027 | 0.0030 | 2004 | 0.0328 |
| 2005 | 0.0031 | 0.0028 | 0.0034 | 0.0033 | 0.0034 | 0.0031 | 0.0030 | 0.0037 | 0.0031 | 0.0035 | 0.0036 | 0.0036 | 2005 | 0.0392 |
| 2006 | 0.0037 | 0.0034 | 0.0039 | 0.0037 | 0.0044 | 0.0041 | 0.0043 | 0.0040 | 0.0036 | 0.0039 | 0.0036 | 0.0034 | 2006 | 0.0454 |
| 2007 | 0.0041 | 0.0036 | 0.0037 | 0.0038 | 0.0038 | 0.0038 | 0.0043 | 0.0038 | 0.0032 | 0.0037 | 0.0035 | 0.0028 | 2007 | 0.0444 |
| 2008 | 0.0031 | 0.0024 | 0.0022 | 0.0020 | 0.0025 | 0.0028 | 0.0028 | 0.0025 | 0.0026 | 0.0024 | 0.0020 | 0.0015 | 2008 | 0.0296 |
| 2009 | 0.0012 | 0.0014 | 0.0018 | 0.0014 | 0.0016 | 0.0021 | 0.0022 | 0.0021 | 0.0019 | 0.0018 | 0.0018 | 0.0015 | 2009 | 0.0201 |
| 2010 | 0.0022 | 0.0019 | 0.0021 | 0.0019 | 0.0018 | 0.0019 | 0.0015 | 0.0013 | 0.0010 | 0.0009 | 0.0009 | 0.0011 | 2010 | 0.0192 |
| 2011 | 0.0019 | 0.0017 | 0.0019 | 0.0019 | 0.0018 | 0.0014 | 0.0014 | 0.0012 | 0.0007 | 0.0008 | 0.0007 | 0.0007 | 2011 | 0.0164 |
| 2012 | 0.0007 | 0.0006 | 0.0008 | 0.0009 | 0.0007 | 0.0005 | 0.0006 | 0.0005 | 0.0004 | 0.0005 | 0.0005 | 0.0004 | 2012 | 0.0073 |
| 2013 | 0.0007 | 0.0007 | 0.0004 | 0.0007 | 0.0006 | 0.0008 | 0.0012 | 0.0011 | 0.0013 | 0.0011 | 0.0009 | 0.0010 | 2013 | 0.0102 |
| 2014 | 0.0016 | 0.0012 | 0.0013 | 0.0014 | 0.0014 | 0.0012 | 0.0013 | 0.0013 | 0.0014 | 0.0014 | 0.0012 | 0.0012 | 2014 | 0.0163 |
| 2015 | 0.0014 | 0.0010 | 0.0014 | 0.0012 | 0.0011 | 0.0013 | 0.0014 | 0.0013 | 0.0013 | 0.0011 | 0.0012 | 0.0014 | 2015 | 0.0151 |
| 2016 | 0.0015 | 0.0012 | 0.0011 | 0.0010 | 0.0011 | 0.0011 | 0.0008 | 0.0009 | 0.0010 | 0.0010 | 0.0011 | 0.0015 | 2016 | 0.0136 |

*Compound annual return

## Appendix A-12

Intermediate-term Government Bonds: Capital Appreciation Returns

From 1926 to 2016

| Year | Jan | Feb | Mar | Apr | May | Jun | Jul | Aug | Sep | Oct | Nov | Dec | Year | Jan–Dec* |
|---|---|---|---|---|---|---|---|---|---|---|---|---|---|---|
| 1926 | 0.0036 | 0.0000 | 0.0009 | 0.0059 | -0.0023 | -0.0005 | -0.0018 | -0.0023 | 0.0018 | 0.0023 | 0.0014 | 0.0059 | 1926 | 0.0151 |
| 1927 | 0.0027 | 0.0009 | 0.0009 | -0.0014 | -0.0009 | 0.0000 | 0.0014 | 0.0027 | 0.0032 | -0.0064 | 0.0055 | 0.0009 | 1927 | 0.0096 |
| 1928 | 0.0018 | -0.0032 | -0.0018 | -0.0032 | -0.0036 | -0.0014 | -0.0122 | 0.0018 | -0.0005 | 0.0000 | -0.0014 | -0.0041 | 1928 | -0.0273 |
| 1929 | -0.0063 | -0.0054 | -0.0031 | 0.0054 | -0.0098 | 0.0072 | 0.0031 | 0.0018 | -0.0049 | 0.0135 | 0.0150 | 0.0014 | 1929 | 0.0177 |
| 1930 | -0.0073 | 0.0064 | 0.0133 | -0.0100 | 0.0032 | 0.0115 | 0.0028 | -0.0005 | 0.0037 | 0.0051 | 0.0046 | 0.0000 | 1930 | 0.0330 |
| 1931 | -0.0097 | 0.0074 | 0.0028 | 0.0060 | 0.0098 | -0.0240 | -0.0009 | -0.0009 | -0.0142 | -0.0136 | 0.0018 | -0.0193 | 1931 | -0.0540 |
| 1932 | -0.0067 | 0.0094 | 0.0045 | 0.0164 | -0.0122 | 0.0077 | 0.0091 | 0.0096 | 0.0000 | 0.0018 | 0.0005 | 0.0092 | 1932 | 0.0502 |
| 1933 | -0.0041 | -0.0028 | 0.0074 | 0.0032 | 0.0178 | -0.0014 | -0.0028 | 0.0051 | 0.0005 | -0.0047 | 0.0005 | -0.0280 | 1933 | -0.0099 |
| 1934 | 0.0100 | 0.0028 | 0.0162 | 0.0158 | 0.0097 | 0.0070 | -0.0045 | -0.0113 | -0.0160 | 0.0164 | 0.0024 | 0.0102 | 1934 | 0.0597 |
| 1935 | 0.0093 | 0.0088 | 0.0107 | 0.0090 | -0.0050 | 0.0098 | 0.0022 | -0.0086 | -0.0072 | 0.0093 | -0.0002 | 0.0105 | 1935 | 0.0494 |
| 1936 | -0.0017 | 0.0056 | 0.0018 | 0.0012 | 0.0026 | -0.0001 | 0.0010 | 0.0038 | -0.0001 | 0.0014 | 0.0070 | -0.0067 | 1936 | 0.0160 |
| 1937 | -0.0042 | -0.0004 | -0.0176 | 0.0032 | 0.0067 | -0.0027 | 0.0045 | -0.0056 | 0.0068 | 0.0020 | 0.0030 | 0.0051 | 1937 | 0.0005 |
| 1938 | 0.0067 | 0.0036 | -0.0030 | 0.0214 | 0.0008 | 0.0061 | -0.0003 | 0.0000 | -0.0026 | 0.0079 | -0.0014 | 0.0039 | 1938 | 0.0437 |
| 1939 | 0.0016 | 0.0071 | 0.0069 | 0.0028 | 0.0084 | -0.0007 | 0.0030 | -0.0155 | -0.0273 | 0.0300 | 0.0063 | 0.0098 | 1939 | 0.0318 |
| 1940 | -0.0023 | 0.0027 | 0.0080 | -0.0005 | -0.0221 | 0.0177 | -0.0005 | 0.0035 | 0.0040 | 0.0030 | 0.0050 | 0.0023 | 1940 | 0.0204 |
| 1941 | -0.0006 | -0.0052 | 0.0061 | 0.0027 | 0.0006 | 0.0051 | -0.0004 | 0.0006 | -0.0004 | 0.0018 | -0.0096 | -0.0023 | 1941 | -0.0017 |
| 1942 | 0.0066 | 0.0009 | 0.0016 | 0.0016 | 0.0010 | 0.0006 | -0.0006 | 0.0011 | -0.0029 | 0.0011 | 0.0011 | -0.0006 | 1942 | 0.0117 |
| 1943 | 0.0025 | 0.0001 | 0.0007 | 0.0010 | 0.0044 | 0.0020 | 0.0008 | -0.0010 | 0.0002 | 0.0005 | 0.0002 | 0.0008 | 1943 | 0.0123 |
| 1944 | -0.0002 | 0.0004 | 0.0007 | 0.0016 | -0.0008 | -0.0005 | 0.0016 | 0.0012 | 0.0000 | -0.0001 | -0.0003 | -0.0001 | 1944 | 0.0035 |
| 1945 | 0.0040 | 0.0028 | 0.0005 | 0.0005 | 0.0002 | 0.0009 | -0.0010 | 0.0006 | 0.0008 | 0.0006 | 0.0001 | 0.0012 | 1945 | 0.0102 |
| 1946 | 0.0030 | 0.0040 | -0.0006 | -0.0028 | -0.0003 | 0.0024 | -0.0019 | -0.0005 | -0.0020 | 0.0015 | -0.0018 | 0.0022 | 1946 | -0.0008 |
| 1947 | 0.0012 | -0.0003 | 0.0014 | -0.0022 | -0.0002 | -0.0003 | -0.0005 | 0.0016 | -0.0010 | -0.0033 | -0.0004 | 0.0008 | 1947 | -0.0030 |
| 1948 | 0.0002 | 0.0006 | 0.0003 | 0.0006 | 0.0042 | -0.0021 | -0.0015 | -0.0018 | -0.0003 | 0.0000 | 0.0006 | 0.0019 | 1948 | 0.0027 |
| 1949 | 0.0015 | -0.0001 | 0.0012 | 0.0003 | 0.0010 | 0.0038 | 0.0010 | 0.0019 | -0.0002 | -0.0004 | -0.0008 | 0.0002 | 1949 | 0.0095 |
| 1950 | -0.0016 | -0.0002 | -0.0011 | -0.0003 | 0.0007 | -0.0008 | 0.0009 | -0.0019 | -0.0015 | -0.0013 | 0.0005 | -0.0004 | 1950 | -0.0069 |
| 1951 | 0.0006 | -0.0007 | -0.0142 | 0.0040 | -0.0058 | 0.0033 | 0.0040 | 0.0019 | -0.0072 | -0.0003 | 0.0015 | -0.0034 | 1951 | -0.0163 |
| 1952 | 0.0019 | -0.0037 | 0.0048 | 0.0037 | 0.0004 | -0.0053 | -0.0052 | -0.0042 | -0.0002 | 0.0046 | -0.0023 | -0.0002 | 1952 | -0.0057 |
| 1953 | -0.0022 | -0.0016 | -0.0038 | -0.0117 | -0.0139 | 0.0129 | 0.0032 | -0.0031 | 0.0171 | 0.0018 | -0.0006 | 0.0083 | 1953 | 0.0061 |
| 1954 | 0.0049 | 0.0086 | 0.0013 | 0.0031 | -0.0084 | 0.0109 | -0.0016 | -0.0001 | -0.0032 | -0.0021 | -0.0015 | -0.0010 | 1954 | 0.0108 |
| 1955 | -0.0050 | -0.0070 | 0.0004 | -0.0015 | -0.0020 | -0.0057 | -0.0091 | -0.0018 | 0.0059 | 0.0050 | -0.0074 | -0.0033 | 1955 | -0.0310 |

*Compound annual return

## Appendix A-12

Intermediate-term Government Bonds: Capital Appreciation Returns
From 1926 to 2016

| Year | Jan | Feb | Mar | Apr | May | Jun | Jul | Aug | Sep | Oct | Nov | Dec | Year | Jan–Dec* |
|---|---|---|---|---|---|---|---|---|---|---|---|---|---|---|
| 1956 | 0.0080 | -0.0018 | -0.0122 | -0.0027 | 0.0086 | -0.0020 | -0.0120 | -0.0130 | 0.0066 | -0.0049 | -0.0075 | -0.0019 | 1956 | -0.0345 |
| 1957 | 0.0207 | -0.0037 | -0.0009 | -0.0130 | -0.0047 | -0.0133 | -0.0051 | 0.0077 | -0.0030 | 0.0010 | 0.0365 | 0.0188 | 1957 | 0.0405 |
| 1958 | 0.0010 | 0.0117 | 0.0031 | 0.0031 | 0.0041 | -0.0088 | -0.0112 | -0.0378 | -0.0048 | -0.0029 | 0.0103 | -0.0093 | 1958 | -0.0417 |
| 1959 | -0.0045 | 0.0078 | -0.0070 | -0.0084 | -0.0034 | -0.0113 | -0.0004 | -0.0116 | -0.0019 | 0.0134 | -0.0130 | -0.0060 | 1959 | -0.0456 |
| 1960 | 0.0115 | 0.0032 | 0.0253 | -0.0096 | -0.0006 | 0.0182 | 0.0236 | -0.0034 | 0.0001 | -0.0013 | -0.0122 | 0.0180 | 1960 | 0.0742 |
| 1961 | -0.0089 | 0.0063 | 0.0008 | 0.0026 | -0.0058 | -0.0054 | -0.0024 | -0.0013 | 0.0049 | -0.0018 | -0.0049 | -0.0012 | 1961 | -0.0172 |
| 1962 | -0.0080 | 0.0124 | 0.0058 | -0.0006 | 0.0018 | -0.0056 | -0.0045 | 0.0092 | -0.0007 | 0.0018 | 0.0031 | 0.0026 | 1962 | 0.0173 |
| 1963 | -0.0059 | -0.0011 | -0.0002 | -0.0002 | -0.0017 | -0.0015 | -0.0030 | -0.0012 | -0.0019 | -0.0022 | 0.0008 | -0.0032 | 1963 | -0.0210 |
| 1964 | -0.0001 | -0.0019 | 0.0006 | -0.0001 | 0.0049 | 0.0000 | -0.0006 | -0.0006 | 0.0012 | 0.0000 | -0.0037 | 0.0024 | 1964 | -0.0003 |
| 1965 | 0.0009 | -0.0013 | 0.0145 | -0.0007 | 0.0002 | 0.0012 | -0.0016 | -0.0017 | -0.0039 | -0.0034 | -0.0031 | -0.0186 | 1965 | -0.0310 |
| 1966 | -0.0037 | -0.0120 | 0.0144 | -0.0056 | -0.0032 | -0.0064 | -0.0065 | -0.0171 | 0.0170 | 0.0031 | -0.0015 | 0.0180 | 1966 | -0.0041 |
| 1967 | 0.0077 | -0.0048 | 0.0144 | -0.0122 | 0.0002 | -0.0265 | 0.0089 | -0.0078 | -0.0035 | -0.0095 | -0.0018 | -0.0038 | 1967 | -0.0385 |
| 1968 | 0.0095 | -0.0003 | -0.0069 | -0.0065 | 0.0015 | 0.0123 | 0.0128 | -0.0021 | 0.0011 | -0.0035 | -0.0054 | -0.0220 | 1968 | -0.0099 |
| 1969 | 0.0032 | -0.0061 | 0.0048 | 0.0021 | -0.0131 | -0.0142 | 0.0024 | -0.0072 | -0.0361 | 0.0266 | -0.0103 | -0.0260 | 1969 | -0.0727 |
| 1970 | -0.0035 | 0.0378 | 0.0024 | -0.0266 | 0.0049 | -0.0006 | 0.0087 | 0.0054 | 0.0136 | 0.0037 | 0.0393 | 0.0005 | 1970 | 0.0871 |
| 1971 | 0.0121 | 0.0181 | 0.0139 | -0.0367 | -0.0034 | -0.0240 | -0.0027 | 0.0294 | -0.0022 | 0.0173 | 0.0005 | 0.0064 | 1971 | 0.0272 |
| 1972 | 0.0058 | -0.0030 | -0.0031 | -0.0030 | -0.0035 | -0.0003 | -0.0034 | -0.0035 | -0.0033 | -0.0037 | -0.0006 | 0.0143 | 1972 | -0.0075 |
| 1973 | -0.0062 | -0.0123 | -0.0008 | 0.0007 | 0.0001 | -0.0059 | -0.0336 | 0.0190 | 0.0195 | -0.0010 | 0.0009 | -0.0016 | 1973 | -0.0219 |
| 1974 | -0.0048 | -0.0016 | -0.0266 | -0.0217 | 0.0063 | -0.0147 | -0.0066 | -0.0078 | 0.0247 | 0.0043 | 0.0175 | 0.0120 | 1974 | -0.0199 |
| 1975 | -0.0008 | 0.0092 | -0.0119 | -0.0246 | 0.0197 | -0.0035 | -0.0094 | -0.0070 | -0.0059 | 0.0298 | -0.0065 | 0.0131 | 1975 | 0.0012 |
| 1976 | -0.0003 | 0.0028 | 0.0010 | 0.0057 | -0.0200 | 0.0090 | 0.0059 | 0.0127 | 0.0019 | 0.0093 | 0.0264 | -0.0024 | 1976 | 0.0525 |
| 1977 | -0.0241 | -0.0002 | -0.0001 | -0.0001 | -0.0002 | 0.0048 | -0.0051 | -0.0052 | -0.0041 | -0.0118 | 0.0019 | -0.0082 | 1977 | -0.0515 |
| 1978 | -0.0053 | -0.0041 | -0.0029 | -0.0036 | -0.0073 | -0.0087 | 0.0028 | 0.0010 | -0.0008 | -0.0184 | 0.0020 | -0.0005 | 1978 | -0.0449 |
| 1979 | -0.0024 | -0.0125 | 0.0038 | -0.0044 | 0.0116 | 0.0135 | -0.0086 | -0.0163 | -0.0065 | -0.0553 | 0.0274 | 0.0001 | 1979 | -0.0507 |
| 1980 | -0.0221 | -0.0724 | 0.0036 | 0.1095 | 0.0409 | -0.0152 | -0.0185 | -0.0463 | -0.0135 | -0.0246 | -0.0067 | 0.0060 | 1980 | -0.0681 |
| 1981 | -0.0069 | -0.0331 | 0.0146 | -0.0322 | 0.0135 | -0.0059 | -0.0386 | -0.0298 | 0.0034 | 0.0482 | 0.0502 | -0.0250 | 1981 | -0.0455 |
| 1982 | -0.0057 | 0.0046 | -0.0080 | 0.0186 | 0.0045 | -0.0253 | 0.0351 | 0.0359 | 0.0228 | 0.0442 | -0.0007 | 0.0100 | 1982 | 0.1423 |
| 1983 | -0.0076 | 0.0173 | -0.0133 | 0.0177 | -0.0208 | -0.0069 | -0.0280 | -0.0023 | 0.0220 | -0.0073 | 0.0012 | -0.0043 | 1983 | -0.0330 |
| 1984 | 0.0081 | -0.0153 | -0.0129 | -0.0104 | -0.0353 | -0.0007 | 0.0280 | -0.0005 | 0.0106 | 0.0274 | 0.0099 | 0.0050 | 1984 | 0.0122 |
| 1985 | 0.0116 | -0.0261 | 0.0077 | 0.0167 | 0.0395 | 0.0035 | -0.0129 | 0.0067 | 0.0031 | 0.0081 | 0.0121 | 0.0178 | 1985 | 0.0901 |

*Compound annual return

# Appendix A-12

Intermediate-term Government Bonds: Capital Appreciation Returns

From 1926 to 2016

| Year | Jan | Feb | Mar | Apr | May | Jun | Jul | Aug | Sep | Oct | Nov | Dec | Year | Jan–Dec* |
|------|-----|-----|-----|-----|-----|-----|-----|-----|-----|-----|-----|-----|------|----------|
| 1986 | 0.0011 | 0.0210 | 0.0270 | 0.0021 | -0.0274 | 0.0208 | 0.0095 | 0.0209 | -0.0168 | 0.0102 | 0.0061 | -0.0053 | 1986 | 0.0699 |
| 1987 | 0.0051 | 0.0007 | -0.0091 | -0.0302 | -0.0100 | 0.0051 | -0.0040 | -0.0106 | -0.0209 | 0.0226 | 0.0013 | 0.0023 | 1987 | -0.0475 |
| 1988 | 0.0251 | 0.0057 | -0.0151 | -0.0107 | -0.0122 | 0.0111 | -0.0111 | -0.0086 | 0.0124 | 0.0077 | -0.0182 | -0.0081 | 1988 | -0.0226 |
| 1989 | 0.0044 | -0.0117 | -0.0029 | 0.0149 | 0.0132 | 0.0254 | 0.0168 | -0.0307 | 0.0004 | 0.0166 | 0.0021 | -0.0048 | 1989 | 0.0434 |
| 1990 | -0.0176 | -0.0057 | -0.0067 | -0.0148 | 0.0186 | 0.0084 | 0.0102 | -0.0160 | 0.0030 | 0.0096 | 0.0126 | 0.0095 | 1990 | 0.0102 |
| 1991 | 0.0042 | -0.0011 | -0.0036 | 0.0046 | -0.0006 | -0.0081 | 0.0060 | 0.0184 | 0.0155 | 0.0077 | 0.0076 | 0.0209 | 1991 | 0.0736 |
| 1992 | -0.0247 | -0.0030 | -0.0139 | 0.0039 | 0.0166 | 0.0118 | 0.0189 | 0.0100 | 0.0147 | -0.0226 | -0.0134 | 0.0093 | 1992 | 0.0064 |
| 1993 | 0.0221 | 0.0198 | -0.0006 | 0.0043 | -0.0051 | 0.0152 | -0.0036 | 0.0179 | 0.0015 | -0.0020 | -0.0135 | -0.0011 | 1993 | 0.0556 |
| 1994 | 0.0093 | -0.0297 | -0.0306 | -0.0154 | -0.0060 | -0.0084 | 0.0115 | -0.0034 | -0.0213 | -0.0084 | -0.0131 | -0.0010 | 1994 | -0.1114 |
| 1995 | 0.0115 | 0.0178 | 0.0003 | 0.0090 | 0.0307 | 0.0030 | -0.0066 | 0.0035 | 0.0017 | 0.0069 | 0.0102 | 0.0052 | 1995 | 0.0966 |
| 1996 | -0.0040 | -0.0178 | -0.0164 | -0.0103 | -0.0086 | 0.0067 | -0.0033 | -0.0057 | 0.0100 | 0.0129 | 0.0102 | -0.0128 | 1996 | -0.0390 |
| 1997 | -0.0027 | -0.0045 | -0.0168 | 0.0093 | 0.0024 | 0.0048 | 0.0210 | -0.0143 | 0.0098 | 0.0100 | -0.0045 | 0.0054 | 1997 | 0.0195 |
| 1998 | 0.0134 | -0.0080 | -0.0024 | 0.0015 | 0.0025 | 0.0030 | -0.0020 | 0.0225 | 0.0289 | 0.0006 | -0.0134 | -0.0002 | 1998 | 0.0466 |
| 1999 | 0.0018 | -0.0297 | 0.0038 | -0.0023 | -0.0188 | -0.0020 | -0.0053 | -0.0035 | 0.0049 | -0.0054 | -0.0060 | -0.0100 | 1999 | -0.0706 |
| 2000 | -0.0107 | 0.0026 | 0.0147 | -0.0091 | -0.0007 | 0.0138 | 0.0019 | 0.0083 | 0.0049 | 0.0028 | 0.0127 | 0.0171 | 2000 | 0.0594 |
| 2001 | 0.0066 | 0.0079 | 0.0049 | -0.0146 | -0.0049 | 0.0025 | 0.0203 | 0.0056 | 0.0219 | 0.0145 | -0.0201 | -0.0117 | 2001 | 0.0323 |
| 2002 | -0.0003 | 0.0073 | -0.0276 | 0.0193 | 0.0079 | 0.0135 | 0.0234 | 0.0138 | 0.0261 | -0.0046 | -0.0191 | 0.0251 | 2002 | 0.0865 |
| 2003 | -0.0113 | 0.0155 | -0.0031 | -0.0010 | 0.0250 | -0.0054 | -0.0339 | -0.0053 | 0.0279 | -0.0158 | -0.0038 | 0.0080 | 2003 | -0.0048 |
| 2004 | 0.0025 | 0.0100 | 0.0074 | -0.0357 | -0.0076 | 0.0015 | 0.0051 | 0.0164 | -0.0014 | 0.0039 | -0.0154 | 0.0036 | 2004 | -0.0107 |
| 2005 | -0.0005 | -0.0139 | -0.0073 | 0.0134 | 0.0069 | 0.0012 | -0.0173 | 0.0124 | -0.0155 | -0.0098 | 0.0023 | 0.0026 | 2005 | -0.0258 |
| 2006 | -0.0073 | -0.0051 | -0.0095 | -0.0045 | -0.0049 | -0.0019 | 0.0082 | 0.0095 | 0.0042 | 0.0012 | 0.0052 | -0.0102 | 2006 | -0.0151 |
| 2007 | -0.0061 | 0.0134 | -0.0012 | 0.0009 | -0.0141 | -0.0028 | 0.0132 | 0.0147 | 0.0026 | -0.0085 | 0.0390 | 0.0021 | 2007 | 0.0533 |
| 2008 | 0.0231 | 0.0210 | 0.0051 | -0.0314 | -0.0110 | 0.0047 | 0.0036 | 0.0079 | 0.0058 | 0.0122 | 0.0410 | 0.0145 | 2008 | 0.0992 |
| 2009 | -0.0175 | -0.0096 | 0.0168 | -0.0179 | -0.0148 | -0.0097 | 0.0034 | 0.0076 | 0.0056 | 0.0012 | 0.0166 | -0.0256 | 2009 | -0.0442 |
| 2010 | 0.0172 | 0.0052 | -0.0109 | 0.0073 | 0.0133 | 0.0111 | 0.0143 | 0.0115 | 0.0039 | 0.0055 | -0.0091 | -0.0182 | 2010 | 0.0516 |
| 2011 | 0.0044 | -0.0070 | -0.0024 | 0.0136 | 0.0161 | -0.0015 | 0.0188 | 0.0198 | 0.0001 | 0.0002 | 0.0028 | 0.0043 | 2011 | 0.0709 |
| 2012 | 0.0002 | -0.0059 | -0.0078 | 0.0120 | 0.0075 | -0.0025 | 0.0071 | 0.0010 | 0.0000 | -0.0029 | 0.0043 | -0.0036 | 2012 | 0.0093 |
| 2013 | -0.0068 | 0.0057 | -0.0146 | 0.0053 | -0.0170 | -0.0147 | 0.0014 | -0.0084 | 0.0108 | 0.0040 | 0.0002 | -0.0132 | 2013 | -0.0468 |
| 2014 | 0.0115 | 0.0011 | -0.0082 | 0.0033 | 0.0080 | -0.0030 | -0.0060 | 0.0061 | -0.0062 | 0.0075 | 0.0066 | -0.0072 | 2014 | 0.0135 |
| 2015 | 0.0227 | -0.0132 | 0.0061 | -0.0025 | -0.0007 | -0.0065 | 0.0037 | -0.0002 | 0.0087 | -0.0063 | -0.0053 | -0.0031 | 2015 | 0.0029 |
| 2016 | 0.0218 | 0.0045 | 0.0034 | -0.0020 | -0.0033 | 0.0164 | -0.0004 | -0.0074 | 0.0017 | -0.0062 | -0.0199 | -0.0022 | 2016 | 0.0058 |

*Compound annual return

## Appendix A-13

Intermediate-term Government Bonds: Yields
From 1926 to 2016

| Year | Jan | Feb | Mar | Apr | May | Jun | Jul | Aug | Sep | Oct | Nov | Dec | Year | Jan–Dec* |
|---|---|---|---|---|---|---|---|---|---|---|---|---|---|---|
| 1926 | 0.0386 | 0.0386 | 0.0384 | 0.0371 | 0.0376 | 0.0377 | 0.0381 | 0.0386 | 0.0382 | 0.0377 | 0.0374 | 0.0361 | 1926 | 0.0361 |
| 1927 | 0.0355 | 0.0353 | 0.0351 | 0.0354 | 0.0356 | 0.0356 | 0.0353 | 0.0347 | 0.0340 | 0.0354 | 0.0342 | 0.0340 | 1927 | 0.0340 |
| 1928 | 0.0336 | 0.0343 | 0.0347 | 0.0354 | 0.0362 | 0.0365 | 0.0392 | 0.0388 | 0.0389 | 0.0389 | 0.0392 | 0.0401 | 1928 | 0.0401 |
| 1929 | 0.0415 | 0.0427 | 0.0434 | 0.0422 | 0.0444 | 0.0428 | 0.0421 | 0.0417 | 0.0428 | 0.0398 | 0.0365 | 0.0362 | 1929 | 0.0362 |
| 1930 | 0.0378 | 0.0364 | 0.0335 | 0.0357 | 0.0350 | 0.0325 | 0.0319 | 0.0320 | 0.0312 | 0.0301 | 0.0291 | 0.0291 | 1930 | 0.0291 |
| 1931 | 0.0312 | 0.0296 | 0.0290 | 0.0277 | 0.0256 | 0.0308 | 0.0310 | 0.0312 | 0.0343 | 0.0373 | 0.0369 | 0.0412 | 1931 | 0.0412 |
| 1932 | 0.0427 | 0.0406 | 0.0396 | 0.0360 | 0.0387 | 0.0370 | 0.0350 | 0.0329 | 0.0329 | 0.0325 | 0.0324 | 0.0304 | 1932 | 0.0304 |
| 1933 | 0.0313 | 0.0319 | 0.0303 | 0.0296 | 0.0258 | 0.0261 | 0.0267 | 0.0256 | 0.0255 | 0.0265 | 0.0264 | 0.0325 | 1933 | 0.0325 |
| 1934 | 0.0325 | 0.0321 | 0.0296 | 0.0272 | 0.0257 | 0.0246 | 0.0253 | 0.0271 | 0.0298 | 0.0271 | 0.0267 | 0.0249 | 1934 | 0.0249 |
| 1935 | 0.0233 | 0.0218 | 0.0199 | 0.0184 | 0.0193 | 0.0175 | 0.0171 | 0.0187 | 0.0201 | 0.0183 | 0.0183 | 0.0163 | 1935 | 0.0163 |
| 1936 | 0.0166 | 0.0155 | 0.0151 | 0.0149 | 0.0143 | 0.0143 | 0.0141 | 0.0133 | 0.0133 | 0.0130 | 0.0114 | 0.0129 | 1936 | 0.0129 |
| 1937 | 0.0134 | 0.0135 | 0.0184 | 0.0175 | 0.0156 | 0.0164 | 0.0151 | 0.0168 | 0.0147 | 0.0141 | 0.0131 | 0.0114 | 1937 | 0.0114 |
| 1938 | 0.0205 | 0.0200 | 0.0204 | 0.0174 | 0.0173 | 0.0164 | 0.0164 | 0.0164 | 0.0168 | 0.0156 | 0.0158 | 0.0152 | 1938 | 0.0152 |
| 1939 | 0.0149 | 0.0138 | 0.0127 | 0.0122 | 0.0108 | 0.0110 | 0.0105 | 0.0131 | 0.0180 | 0.0127 | 0.0116 | 0.0098 | 1939 | 0.0098 |
| 1940 | 0.0103 | 0.0098 | 0.0083 | 0.0084 | 0.0127 | 0.0092 | 0.0093 | 0.0086 | 0.0078 | 0.0072 | 0.0061 | 0.0057 | 1940 | 0.0057 |
| 1941 | 0.0077 | 0.0089 | 0.0075 | 0.0069 | 0.0067 | 0.0055 | 0.0056 | 0.0055 | 0.0056 | 0.0051 | 0.0076 | 0.0082 | 1941 | 0.0082 |
| 1942 | 0.0083 | 0.0081 | 0.0077 | 0.0074 | 0.0071 | 0.0070 | 0.0071 | 0.0069 | 0.0076 | 0.0073 | 0.0070 | 0.0072 | 1942 | 0.0072 |
| 1943 | 0.0166 | 0.0166 | 0.0164 | 0.0162 | 0.0153 | 0.0149 | 0.0147 | 0.0149 | 0.0149 | 0.0147 | 0.0147 | 0.0145 | 1943 | 0.0145 |
| 1944 | 0.0150 | 0.0150 | 0.0148 | 0.0143 | 0.0146 | 0.0147 | 0.0142 | 0.0139 | 0.0139 | 0.0139 | 0.0140 | 0.0140 | 1944 | 0.0140 |
| 1945 | 0.0127 | 0.0118 | 0.0120 | 0.0118 | 0.0117 | 0.0114 | 0.0118 | 0.0115 | 0.0112 | 0.0109 | 0.0109 | 0.0103 | 1945 | 0.0103 |
| 1946 | 0.0099 | 0.0087 | 0.0101 | 0.0111 | 0.0112 | 0.0103 | 0.0110 | 0.0112 | 0.0120 | 0.0114 | 0.0121 | 0.0112 | 1946 | 0.0112 |
| 1947 | 0.0116 | 0.0117 | 0.0112 | 0.0120 | 0.0121 | 0.0122 | 0.0124 | 0.0117 | 0.0121 | 0.0136 | 0.0138 | 0.0134 | 1947 | 0.0134 |
| 1948 | 0.0160 | 0.0158 | 0.0157 | 0.0155 | 0.0142 | 0.0149 | 0.0154 | 0.0160 | 0.0161 | 0.0161 | 0.0158 | 0.0151 | 1948 | 0.0151 |
| 1949 | 0.0153 | 0.0153 | 0.0148 | 0.0147 | 0.0144 | 0.0129 | 0.0125 | 0.0117 | 0.0118 | 0.0120 | 0.0124 | 0.0123 | 1949 | 0.0123 |
| 1950 | 0.0131 | 0.0132 | 0.0137 | 0.0138 | 0.0134 | 0.0139 | 0.0134 | 0.0145 | 0.0154 | 0.0162 | 0.0159 | 0.0162 | 1950 | 0.0162 |
| 1951 | 0.0179 | 0.0180 | 0.0211 | 0.0202 | 0.0215 | 0.0208 | 0.0199 | 0.0194 | 0.0212 | 0.0212 | 0.0209 | 0.0217 | 1951 | 0.0217 |
| 1952 | 0.0212 | 0.0222 | 0.0209 | 0.0199 | 0.0198 | 0.0213 | 0.0228 | 0.0241 | 0.0242 | 0.0227 | 0.0235 | 0.0235 | 1952 | 0.0235 |
| 1953 | 0.0242 | 0.0245 | 0.0253 | 0.0277 | 0.0307 | 0.0279 | 0.0272 | 0.0279 | 0.0241 | 0.0237 | 0.0238 | 0.0218 | 1953 | 0.0218 |
| 1954 | 0.0187 | 0.0157 | 0.0153 | 0.0142 | 0.0173 | 0.0131 | 0.0138 | 0.0138 | 0.0152 | 0.0161 | 0.0168 | 0.0172 | 1954 | 0.0172 |
| 1955 | 0.0227 | 0.0240 | 0.0240 | 0.0242 | 0.0246 | 0.0257 | 0.0276 | 0.0280 | 0.0267 | 0.0257 | 0.0273 | 0.0280 | 1955 | 0.0280 |

*Compound annual return

## Appendix A-13

Intermediate-term Government Bonds: Yields

From 1926 to 2016

| Year | Jan | Feb | Mar | Apr | May | Jun | Jul | Aug | Sep | Oct | Nov | Dec | Year | Jan–Dec* |
|------|-----|-----|-----|-----|-----|-----|-----|-----|-----|-----|-----|-----|------|----------|
| 1956 | 0.0271 | 0.0275 | 0.0300 | 0.0305 | 0.0287 | 0.0292 | 0.0317 | 0.0346 | 0.0331 | 0.0342 | 0.0359 | 0.0363 | 1956 | 0.0363 |
| 1957 | 0.0326 | 0.0333 | 0.0334 | 0.0357 | 0.0366 | 0.0390 | 0.0399 | 0.0385 | 0.0390 | 0.0388 | 0.0320 | 0.0284 | 1957 | 0.0284 |
| 1958 | 0.0282 | 0.0259 | 0.0253 | 0.0246 | 0.0238 | 0.0250 | 0.0281 | 0.0365 | 0.0376 | 0.0382 | 0.0359 | 0.0381 | 1958 | 0.0381 |
| 1959 | 0.0395 | 0.0378 | 0.0393 | 0.0413 | 0.0420 | 0.0447 | 0.0448 | 0.0477 | 0.0482 | 0.0448 | 0.0482 | 0.0498 | 1959 | 0.0498 |
| 1960 | 0.0471 | 0.0464 | 0.0409 | 0.0431 | 0.0432 | 0.0390 | 0.0334 | 0.0343 | 0.0343 | 0.0346 | 0.0377 | 0.0331 | 1960 | 0.0331 |
| 1961 | 0.0363 | 0.0350 | 0.0348 | 0.0342 | 0.0355 | 0.0368 | 0.0373 | 0.0376 | 0.0365 | 0.0369 | 0.0381 | 0.0384 | 1961 | 0.0384 |
| 1962 | 0.0402 | 0.0377 | 0.0366 | 0.0367 | 0.0363 | 0.0375 | 0.0384 | 0.0365 | 0.0366 | 0.0362 | 0.0355 | 0.0350 | 1962 | 0.0350 |
| 1963 | 0.0368 | 0.0370 | 0.0370 | 0.0371 | 0.0374 | 0.0378 | 0.0385 | 0.0388 | 0.0392 | 0.0398 | 0.0396 | 0.0404 | 1963 | 0.0404 |
| 1964 | 0.0402 | 0.0407 | 0.0411 | 0.0411 | 0.0399 | 0.0399 | 0.0401 | 0.0402 | 0.0399 | 0.0399 | 0.0409 | 0.0403 | 1964 | 0.0403 |
| 1965 | 0.0413 | 0.0416 | 0.0414 | 0.0416 | 0.0415 | 0.0413 | 0.0416 | 0.0420 | 0.0429 | 0.0437 | 0.0444 | 0.0490 | 1965 | 0.0490 |
| 1966 | 0.0482 | 0.0507 | 0.0477 | 0.0489 | 0.0496 | 0.0510 | 0.0525 | 0.0565 | 0.0526 | 0.0519 | 0.0522 | 0.0479 | 1966 | 0.0479 |
| 1967 | 0.0459 | 0.0470 | 0.0437 | 0.0466 | 0.0465 | 0.0530 | 0.0508 | 0.0528 | 0.0537 | 0.0562 | 0.0566 | 0.0577 | 1967 | 0.0577 |
| 1968 | 0.0548 | 0.0549 | 0.0563 | 0.0577 | 0.0574 | 0.0547 | 0.0518 | 0.0523 | 0.0520 | 0.0528 | 0.0541 | 0.0596 | 1968 | 0.0596 |
| 1969 | 0.0637 | 0.0651 | 0.0640 | 0.0636 | 0.0666 | 0.0699 | 0.0693 | 0.0711 | 0.0799 | 0.0735 | 0.0761 | 0.0829 | 1969 | 0.0829 |
| 1970 | 0.0820 | 0.0730 | 0.0724 | 0.0790 | 0.0778 | 0.0780 | 0.0757 | 0.0743 | 0.0707 | 0.0697 | 0.0591 | 0.0590 | 1970 | 0.0590 |
| 1971 | 0.0570 | 0.0526 | 0.0493 | 0.0585 | 0.0593 | 0.0656 | 0.0663 | 0.0585 | 0.0591 | 0.0545 | 0.0543 | 0.0525 | 1971 | 0.0525 |
| 1972 | 0.0556 | 0.0563 | 0.0570 | 0.0577 | 0.0586 | 0.0587 | 0.0595 | 0.0604 | 0.0613 | 0.0623 | 0.0625 | 0.0585 | 1972 | 0.0585 |
| 1973 | 0.0641 | 0.0671 | 0.0673 | 0.0671 | 0.0671 | 0.0686 | 0.0776 | 0.0725 | 0.0674 | 0.0677 | 0.0674 | 0.0679 | 1973 | 0.0679 |
| 1974 | 0.0687 | 0.0691 | 0.0751 | 0.0801 | 0.0786 | 0.0822 | 0.0838 | 0.0857 | 0.0797 | 0.0787 | 0.0743 | 0.0712 | 1974 | 0.0712 |
| 1975 | 0.0730 | 0.0709 | 0.0737 | 0.0798 | 0.0749 | 0.0758 | 0.0782 | 0.0800 | 0.0815 | 0.0736 | 0.0754 | 0.0719 | 1975 | 0.0719 |
| 1976 | 0.0743 | 0.0736 | 0.0733 | 0.0719 | 0.0771 | 0.0747 | 0.0732 | 0.0697 | 0.0692 | 0.0667 | 0.0594 | 0.0600 | 1976 | 0.0600 |
| 1977 | 0.0673 | 0.0673 | 0.0673 | 0.0674 | 0.0674 | 0.0662 | 0.0675 | 0.0689 | 0.0700 | 0.0733 | 0.0727 | 0.0751 | 1977 | 0.0751 |
| 1978 | 0.0773 | 0.0784 | 0.0791 | 0.0800 | 0.0820 | 0.0843 | 0.0836 | 0.0833 | 0.0835 | 0.0887 | 0.0882 | 0.0883 | 1978 | 0.0883 |
| 1979 | 0.0895 | 0.0928 | 0.0918 | 0.0929 | 0.0899 | 0.0864 | 0.0887 | 0.0933 | 0.0951 | 0.1112 | 0.1033 | 0.1033 | 1979 | 0.1033 |
| 1980 | 0.1093 | 0.1294 | 0.1285 | 0.1009 | 0.0903 | 0.0944 | 0.0996 | 0.1133 | 0.1171 | 0.1244 | 0.1264 | 0.1245 | 1980 | 0.1245 |
| 1981 | 0.1275 | 0.1371 | 0.1328 | 0.1427 | 0.1385 | 0.1404 | 0.1533 | 0.1636 | 0.1625 | 0.1472 | 0.1311 | 0.1396 | 1981 | 0.1396 |
| 1982 | 0.1397 | 0.1385 | 0.1406 | 0.1355 | 0.1343 | 0.1417 | 0.1315 | 0.1209 | 0.1144 | 0.1018 | 0.1020 | 0.0990 | 1982 | 0.0990 |
| 1983 | 0.1057 | 0.1010 | 0.1048 | 0.0997 | 0.1059 | 0.1080 | 0.1168 | 0.1175 | 0.1108 | 0.1131 | 0.1127 | 0.1141 | 1983 | 0.1141 |
| 1984 | 0.1137 | 0.1181 | 0.1219 | 0.1251 | 0.1363 | 0.1365 | 0.1274 | 0.1276 | 0.1242 | 0.1154 | 0.1121 | 0.1104 | 1984 | 0.1104 |
| 1985 | 0.1081 | 0.1152 | 0.1131 | 0.1084 | 0.0974 | 0.0964 | 0.1002 | 0.0982 | 0.0973 | 0.0949 | 0.0911 | 0.0855 | 1985 | 0.0855 |

*Compound annual return

## Appendix A-13

Intermediate-term Government Bonds: Yields
From 1926 to 2016

| Year | Jan | Feb | Mar | Apr | May | Jun | Jul | Aug | Sep | Oct | Nov | Dec | Year | Jan–Dec* |
|------|-----|-----|-----|-----|-----|-----|-----|-----|-----|-----|-----|-----|------|----------|
| 1986 | 0.0870 | 0.0815 | 0.0743 | 0.0737 | 0.0816 | 0.0756 | 0.0728 | 0.0668 | 0.0718 | 0.0687 | 0.0669 | 0.0685 | 1986 | 0.0685 |
| 1987 | 0.0685 | 0.0683 | 0.0708 | 0.0793 | 0.0821 | 0.0806 | 0.0818 | 0.0849 | 0.0912 | 0.0844 | 0.0840 | 0.0832 | 1987 | 0.0832 |
| 1988 | 0.0782 | 0.0768 | 0.0807 | 0.0836 | 0.0870 | 0.0839 | 0.0871 | 0.0895 | 0.0859 | 0.0837 | 0.0892 | 0.0917 | 1988 | 0.0917 |
| 1989 | 0.0896 | 0.0927 | 0.0934 | 0.0895 | 0.0860 | 0.0791 | 0.0745 | 0.0834 | 0.0833 | 0.0786 | 0.0779 | 0.0794 | 1989 | 0.0794 |
| 1990 | 0.0842 | 0.0855 | 0.0871 | 0.0907 | 0.0864 | 0.0843 | 0.0819 | 0.0859 | 0.0851 | 0.0826 | 0.0795 | 0.0770 | 1990 | 0.0770 |
| 1991 | 0.0772 | 0.0774 | 0.0783 | 0.0772 | 0.0773 | 0.0793 | 0.0778 | 0.0732 | 0.0693 | 0.0673 | 0.0653 | 0.0597 | 1991 | 0.0597 |
| 1992 | 0.0683 | 0.0690 | 0.0720 | 0.0711 | 0.0674 | 0.0647 | 0.0604 | 0.0581 | 0.0547 | 0.0601 | 0.0634 | 0.0611 | 1992 | 0.0611 |
| 1993 | 0.0588 | 0.0547 | 0.0549 | 0.0540 | 0.0551 | 0.0517 | 0.0526 | 0.0486 | 0.0483 | 0.0488 | 0.0519 | 0.0522 | 1993 | 0.0522 |
| 1994 | 0.0515 | 0.0575 | 0.0638 | 0.0670 | 0.0682 | 0.0699 | 0.0675 | 0.0683 | 0.0730 | 0.0749 | 0.0778 | 0.0780 | 1994 | 0.0780 |
| 1995 | 0.0754 | 0.0708 | 0.0707 | 0.0685 | 0.0606 | 0.0598 | 0.0616 | 0.0606 | 0.0601 | 0.0582 | 0.0553 | 0.0538 | 1995 | 0.0538 |
| 1996 | 0.0528 | 0.0573 | 0.0614 | 0.0640 | 0.0663 | 0.0645 | 0.0654 | 0.0670 | 0.0643 | 0.0607 | 0.0578 | 0.0616 | 1996 | 0.0616 |
| 1997 | 0.0629 | 0.0639 | 0.0677 | 0.0656 | 0.0650 | 0.0639 | 0.0589 | 0.0624 | 0.0601 | 0.0576 | 0.0587 | 0.0573 | 1997 | 0.0573 |
| 1998 | 0.0545 | 0.0562 | 0.0567 | 0.0564 | 0.0558 | 0.0551 | 0.0556 | 0.0503 | 0.0435 | 0.0434 | 0.0467 | 0.0468 | 1998 | 0.0468 |
| 1999 | 0.0467 | 0.0535 | 0.0526 | 0.0532 | 0.0576 | 0.0581 | 0.0594 | 0.0602 | 0.0590 | 0.0604 | 0.0619 | 0.0645 | 1999 | 0.0645 |
| 2000 | 0.0675 | 0.0669 | 0.0636 | 0.0657 | 0.0658 | 0.0626 | 0.0621 | 0.0601 | 0.0589 | 0.0582 | 0.0551 | 0.0507 | 2000 | 0.0507 |
| 2001 | 0.0499 | 0.0482 | 0.0471 | 0.0504 | 0.0515 | 0.0510 | 0.0464 | 0.0450 | 0.0399 | 0.0365 | 0.0413 | 0.0442 | 2001 | 0.0442 |
| 2002 | 0.0459 | 0.0442 | 0.0504 | 0.0461 | 0.0443 | 0.0412 | 0.0358 | 0.0325 | 0.0265 | 0.0276 | 0.0323 | 0.0261 | 2002 | 0.0261 |
| 2003 | 0.0310 | 0.0276 | 0.0283 | 0.0285 | 0.0228 | 0.0240 | 0.0322 | 0.0335 | 0.0267 | 0.0307 | 0.0317 | 0.0297 | 2003 | 0.0297 |
| 2004 | 0.0315 | 0.0293 | 0.0276 | 0.0360 | 0.0378 | 0.0374 | 0.0362 | 0.0322 | 0.0326 | 0.0316 | 0.0356 | 0.0347 | 2004 | 0.0347 |
| 2005 | 0.0375 | 0.0405 | 0.0421 | 0.0392 | 0.0377 | 0.0374 | 0.0415 | 0.0385 | 0.0422 | 0.0446 | 0.0440 | 0.0434 | 2005 | 0.0434 |
| 2006 | 0.0449 | 0.0460 | 0.0481 | 0.0491 | 0.0502 | 0.0506 | 0.0487 | 0.0465 | 0.0455 | 0.0452 | 0.0439 | 0.0465 | 2006 | 0.0465 |
| 2007 | 0.0479 | 0.0448 | 0.0451 | 0.0449 | 0.0483 | 0.0490 | 0.0457 | 0.0420 | 0.0413 | 0.0435 | 0.0333 | 0.0328 | 2007 | 0.0328 |
| 2008 | 0.0301 | 0.0256 | 0.0245 | 0.0316 | 0.0340 | 0.0330 | 0.0322 | 0.0303 | 0.0289 | 0.0260 | 0.0161 | 0.0126 | 2008 | 0.0126 |
| 2009 | 0.0180 | 0.0202 | 0.0168 | 0.0206 | 0.0238 | 0.0259 | 0.0251 | 0.0234 | 0.0222 | 0.0219 | 0.0180 | 0.0242 | 2009 | 0.0242 |
| 2010 | 0.0242 | 0.0231 | 0.0254 | 0.0238 | 0.0208 | 0.0184 | 0.0151 | 0.0124 | 0.0115 | 0.0102 | 0.0124 | 0.0170 | 2010 | 0.0170 |
| 2011 | 0.0215 | 0.0229 | 0.0234 | 0.0206 | 0.0172 | 0.0175 | 0.0134 | 0.0091 | 0.0090 | 0.0090 | 0.0084 | 0.0074 | 2011 | 0.0074 |
| 2012 | 0.0078 | 0.0093 | 0.0109 | 0.0084 | 0.0068 | 0.0074 | 0.0058 | 0.0056 | 0.0056 | 0.0062 | 0.0052 | 0.0061 | 2012 | 0.0061 |
| 2013 | 0.0094 | 0.0083 | 0.0079 | 0.0067 | 0.0104 | 0.0136 | 0.0133 | 0.0152 | 0.0127 | 0.0118 | 0.0117 | 0.0149 | 2013 | 0.0149 |
| 2014 | 0.0160 | 0.0158 | 0.0175 | 0.0168 | 0.0150 | 0.0157 | 0.0171 | 0.0157 | 0.0171 | 0.0153 | 0.0137 | 0.0155 | 2014 | 0.0155 |
| 2015 | 0.0125 | 0.0153 | 0.0140 | 0.0146 | 0.0147 | 0.0162 | 0.0154 | 0.0154 | 0.0134 | 0.0149 | 0.0162 | 0.0169 | 2015 | 0.0169 |
| 2016 | 0.0142 | 0.0133 | 0.0126 | 0.0130 | 0.0137 | 0.0102 | 0.0103 | 0.0120 | 0.0116 | 0.0130 | 0.0179 | 0.0185 | 2016 | 0.0185 |

*Compound annual return

## Appendix A-14

U.S. Treasury Bills: Total Returns
From 1926 to 2016

| Year | Jan | Feb | Mar | Apr | May | Jun | Jul | Aug | Sep | Oct | Nov | Dec | Year | Jan–Dec* |
|------|------|------|------|------|------|------|------|------|------|------|------|------|------|------|
| 1926 | 0.0034 | 0.0027 | 0.0030 | 0.0034 | 0.0001 | 0.0035 | 0.0022 | 0.0025 | 0.0023 | 0.0032 | 0.0031 | 0.0028 | 1926 | 0.0327 |
| 1927 | 0.0025 | 0.0026 | 0.0030 | 0.0025 | 0.0030 | 0.0026 | 0.0030 | 0.0028 | 0.0021 | 0.0025 | 0.0021 | 0.0022 | 1927 | 0.0312 |
| 1928 | 0.0025 | 0.0033 | 0.0029 | 0.0022 | 0.0032 | 0.0031 | 0.0032 | 0.0032 | 0.0027 | 0.0041 | 0.0038 | 0.0006 | 1928 | 0.0356 |
| 1929 | 0.0034 | 0.0036 | 0.0034 | 0.0036 | 0.0044 | 0.0052 | 0.0033 | 0.0040 | 0.0035 | 0.0046 | 0.0037 | 0.0037 | 1929 | 0.0475 |
| 1930 | 0.0014 | 0.0030 | 0.0035 | 0.0021 | 0.0026 | 0.0027 | 0.0020 | 0.0009 | 0.0022 | 0.0009 | 0.0013 | 0.0014 | 1930 | 0.0241 |
| 1931 | 0.0015 | 0.0004 | 0.0013 | 0.0008 | 0.0009 | 0.0008 | 0.0006 | 0.0003 | 0.0003 | 0.0010 | 0.0017 | 0.0012 | 1931 | 0.0107 |
| 1932 | 0.0023 | 0.0023 | 0.0016 | 0.0011 | 0.0006 | 0.0002 | 0.0003 | 0.0003 | 0.0003 | 0.0002 | 0.0002 | 0.0001 | 1932 | 0.0096 |
| 1933 | 0.0001 | -0.0003 | 0.0004 | 0.0010 | 0.0004 | 0.0002 | 0.0002 | 0.0003 | 0.0002 | 0.0001 | 0.0002 | 0.0002 | 1933 | 0.0030 |
| 1934 | 0.0005 | 0.0002 | 0.0002 | 0.0001 | 0.0001 | 0.0001 | 0.0001 | 0.0001 | 0.0001 | 0.0001 | 0.0001 | 0.0001 | 1934 | 0.0016 |
| 1935 | 0.0001 | 0.0002 | 0.0001 | 0.0001 | 0.0001 | 0.0001 | 0.0001 | 0.0001 | 0.0001 | 0.0001 | 0.0002 | 0.0001 | 1935 | 0.0017 |
| 1936 | 0.0001 | 0.0001 | 0.0002 | 0.0002 | 0.0002 | 0.0003 | 0.0001 | 0.0002 | 0.0001 | 0.0002 | 0.0001 | 0.0000 | 1936 | 0.0018 |
| 1937 | 0.0001 | 0.0002 | 0.0001 | 0.0003 | 0.0006 | 0.0003 | 0.0003 | 0.0002 | 0.0004 | 0.0002 | 0.0002 | 0.0000 | 1937 | 0.0031 |
| 1938 | 0.0000 | 0.0000 | -0.0001 | 0.0001 | 0.0000 | 0.0000 | -0.0001 | 0.0000 | 0.0002 | 0.0001 | -0.0006 | 0.0000 | 1938 | -0.0002 |
| 1939 | -0.0001 | 0.0001 | -0.0001 | 0.0000 | 0.0001 | 0.0001 | 0.0000 | -0.0001 | 0.0001 | 0.0000 | 0.0000 | 0.0000 | 1939 | 0.0002 |
| 1940 | 0.0000 | 0.0000 | 0.0000 | 0.0000 | -0.0002 | 0.0000 | 0.0001 | -0.0001 | 0.0000 | 0.0000 | 0.0000 | 0.0000 | 1940 | 0.0000 |
| 1941 | -0.0001 | -0.0001 | 0.0001 | -0.0001 | 0.0000 | 0.0000 | 0.0003 | 0.0001 | 0.0001 | 0.0000 | 0.0000 | 0.0001 | 1941 | 0.0006 |
| 1942 | 0.0002 | 0.0001 | 0.0001 | 0.0001 | 0.0003 | 0.0002 | 0.0003 | 0.0003 | 0.0003 | 0.0003 | 0.0003 | 0.0003 | 1942 | 0.0027 |
| 1943 | 0.0003 | 0.0003 | 0.0003 | 0.0003 | 0.0003 | 0.0003 | 0.0003 | 0.0003 | 0.0003 | 0.0003 | 0.0003 | 0.0003 | 1943 | 0.0035 |
| 1944 | 0.0003 | 0.0003 | 0.0002 | 0.0003 | 0.0003 | 0.0003 | 0.0003 | 0.0003 | 0.0002 | 0.0003 | 0.0003 | 0.0002 | 1944 | 0.0033 |
| 1945 | 0.0003 | 0.0002 | 0.0002 | 0.0003 | 0.0003 | 0.0002 | 0.0003 | 0.0003 | 0.0003 | 0.0003 | 0.0002 | 0.0003 | 1945 | 0.0033 |
| 1946 | 0.0003 | 0.0003 | 0.0003 | 0.0003 | 0.0003 | 0.0003 | 0.0003 | 0.0003 | 0.0003 | 0.0003 | 0.0003 | 0.0003 | 1946 | 0.0035 |
| 1947 | 0.0003 | 0.0003 | 0.0003 | 0.0003 | 0.0003 | 0.0003 | 0.0003 | 0.0003 | 0.0006 | 0.0006 | 0.0006 | 0.0008 | 1947 | 0.0050 |
| 1948 | 0.0007 | 0.0007 | 0.0009 | 0.0008 | 0.0008 | 0.0009 | 0.0008 | 0.0009 | 0.0004 | 0.0004 | 0.0004 | 0.0004 | 1948 | 0.0081 |
| 1949 | 0.0010 | 0.0009 | 0.0010 | 0.0009 | 0.0010 | 0.0010 | 0.0009 | 0.0009 | 0.0009 | 0.0009 | 0.0008 | 0.0009 | 1949 | 0.0110 |
| 1950 | 0.0009 | 0.0009 | 0.0010 | 0.0009 | 0.0010 | 0.0010 | 0.0010 | 0.0010 | 0.0010 | 0.0012 | 0.0011 | 0.0011 | 1950 | 0.0120 |
| 1951 | 0.0013 | 0.0010 | 0.0011 | 0.0013 | 0.0012 | 0.0012 | 0.0013 | 0.0013 | 0.0012 | 0.0016 | 0.0011 | 0.0012 | 1951 | 0.0149 |
| 1952 | 0.0015 | 0.0012 | 0.0011 | 0.0012 | 0.0013 | 0.0015 | 0.0015 | 0.0015 | 0.0016 | 0.0014 | 0.0010 | 0.0016 | 1952 | 0.0166 |
| 1953 | 0.0016 | 0.0014 | 0.0018 | 0.0016 | 0.0017 | 0.0018 | 0.0015 | 0.0017 | 0.0016 | 0.0013 | 0.0008 | 0.0013 | 1953 | 0.0182 |
| 1954 | 0.0011 | 0.0007 | 0.0008 | 0.0009 | 0.0005 | 0.0006 | 0.0005 | 0.0005 | 0.0009 | 0.0007 | 0.0006 | 0.0008 | 1954 | 0.0086 |
| 1955 | 0.0008 | 0.0009 | 0.0010 | 0.0010 | 0.0014 | 0.0010 | 0.0010 | 0.0016 | 0.0016 | 0.0018 | 0.0017 | 0.0018 | 1955 | 0.0157 |

*Compound annual return

## Appendix A-14

U.S. Treasury Bills: Total Returns
From 1926 to 2016

| Year | Jan | Feb | Mar | Apr | May | Jun | Jul | Aug | Sep | Oct | Nov | Dec | Year | Jan–Dec* |
|------|------|------|------|------|------|------|------|------|------|------|------|------|------|----------|
| 1956 | 0.0022 | 0.0019 | 0.0015 | 0.0019 | 0.0023 | 0.0020 | 0.0022 | 0.0017 | 0.0018 | 0.0025 | 0.0020 | 0.0024 | 1956 | 0.0246 |
| 1957 | 0.0027 | 0.0024 | 0.0023 | 0.0025 | 0.0026 | 0.0024 | 0.0030 | 0.0025 | 0.0026 | 0.0029 | 0.0028 | 0.0024 | 1957 | 0.0314 |
| 1958 | 0.0028 | 0.0012 | 0.0009 | 0.0008 | 0.0011 | 0.0003 | 0.0007 | 0.0004 | 0.0019 | 0.0018 | 0.0011 | 0.0022 | 1958 | 0.0154 |
| 1959 | 0.0021 | 0.0019 | 0.0022 | 0.0020 | 0.0022 | 0.0025 | 0.0025 | 0.0019 | 0.0031 | 0.0030 | 0.0026 | 0.0034 | 1959 | 0.0295 |
| 1960 | 0.0033 | 0.0029 | 0.0035 | 0.0019 | 0.0027 | 0.0024 | 0.0013 | 0.0017 | 0.0016 | 0.0022 | 0.0013 | 0.0016 | 1960 | 0.0266 |
| 1961 | 0.0019 | 0.0014 | 0.0020 | 0.0017 | 0.0018 | 0.0020 | 0.0018 | 0.0014 | 0.0017 | 0.0019 | 0.0015 | 0.0019 | 1961 | 0.0213 |
| 1962 | 0.0024 | 0.0020 | 0.0020 | 0.0022 | 0.0024 | 0.0020 | 0.0027 | 0.0023 | 0.0021 | 0.0026 | 0.0020 | 0.0023 | 1962 | 0.0273 |
| 1963 | 0.0025 | 0.0023 | 0.0023 | 0.0025 | 0.0024 | 0.0023 | 0.0027 | 0.0025 | 0.0027 | 0.0029 | 0.0027 | 0.0029 | 1963 | 0.0312 |
| 1964 | 0.0030 | 0.0026 | 0.0031 | 0.0029 | 0.0026 | 0.0030 | 0.0030 | 0.0028 | 0.0028 | 0.0029 | 0.0029 | 0.0031 | 1964 | 0.0354 |
| 1965 | 0.0028 | 0.0030 | 0.0036 | 0.0031 | 0.0031 | 0.0035 | 0.0031 | 0.0033 | 0.0031 | 0.0031 | 0.0035 | 0.0033 | 1965 | 0.0393 |
| 1966 | 0.0038 | 0.0035 | 0.0038 | 0.0034 | 0.0041 | 0.0038 | 0.0035 | 0.0041 | 0.0040 | 0.0045 | 0.0040 | 0.0040 | 1966 | 0.0476 |
| 1967 | 0.0043 | 0.0036 | 0.0039 | 0.0032 | 0.0033 | 0.0027 | 0.0032 | 0.0031 | 0.0032 | 0.0039 | 0.0036 | 0.0033 | 1967 | 0.0421 |
| 1968 | 0.0040 | 0.0039 | 0.0038 | 0.0043 | 0.0045 | 0.0043 | 0.0048 | 0.0042 | 0.0043 | 0.0044 | 0.0042 | 0.0043 | 1968 | 0.0521 |
| 1969 | 0.0053 | 0.0046 | 0.0046 | 0.0053 | 0.0048 | 0.0051 | 0.0053 | 0.0050 | 0.0062 | 0.0060 | 0.0052 | 0.0064 | 1969 | 0.0658 |
| 1970 | 0.0060 | 0.0062 | 0.0057 | 0.0050 | 0.0053 | 0.0058 | 0.0052 | 0.0053 | 0.0054 | 0.0046 | 0.0046 | 0.0042 | 1970 | 0.0652 |
| 1971 | 0.0038 | 0.0033 | 0.0030 | 0.0028 | 0.0029 | 0.0037 | 0.0040 | 0.0047 | 0.0037 | 0.0037 | 0.0037 | 0.0037 | 1971 | 0.0439 |
| 1972 | 0.0029 | 0.0025 | 0.0027 | 0.0029 | 0.0030 | 0.0029 | 0.0031 | 0.0029 | 0.0034 | 0.0040 | 0.0037 | 0.0037 | 1972 | 0.0384 |
| 1973 | 0.0044 | 0.0042 | 0.0046 | 0.0052 | 0.0051 | 0.0051 | 0.0064 | 0.0070 | 0.0068 | 0.0065 | 0.0056 | 0.0064 | 1973 | 0.0693 |
| 1974 | 0.0063 | 0.0058 | 0.0056 | 0.0075 | 0.0075 | 0.0060 | 0.0070 | 0.0060 | 0.0081 | 0.0051 | 0.0054 | 0.0070 | 1974 | 0.0800 |
| 1975 | 0.0058 | 0.0043 | 0.0041 | 0.0044 | 0.0044 | 0.0041 | 0.0048 | 0.0048 | 0.0053 | 0.0056 | 0.0041 | 0.0048 | 1975 | 0.0580 |
| 1976 | 0.0047 | 0.0034 | 0.0040 | 0.0042 | 0.0037 | 0.0043 | 0.0047 | 0.0042 | 0.0044 | 0.0041 | 0.0040 | 0.0040 | 1976 | 0.0508 |
| 1977 | 0.0036 | 0.0035 | 0.0038 | 0.0038 | 0.0037 | 0.0040 | 0.0042 | 0.0044 | 0.0043 | 0.0049 | 0.0050 | 0.0049 | 1977 | 0.0512 |
| 1978 | 0.0049 | 0.0046 | 0.0053 | 0.0054 | 0.0051 | 0.0054 | 0.0056 | 0.0056 | 0.0062 | 0.0068 | 0.0070 | 0.0078 | 1978 | 0.0718 |
| 1979 | 0.0077 | 0.0073 | 0.0081 | 0.0080 | 0.0082 | 0.0081 | 0.0077 | 0.0077 | 0.0083 | 0.0087 | 0.0099 | 0.0095 | 1979 | 0.1038 |
| 1980 | 0.0080 | 0.0089 | 0.0121 | 0.0126 | 0.0081 | 0.0061 | 0.0053 | 0.0064 | 0.0075 | 0.0095 | 0.0096 | 0.0131 | 1980 | 0.1124 |
| 1981 | 0.0104 | 0.0107 | 0.0121 | 0.0108 | 0.0115 | 0.0135 | 0.0124 | 0.0128 | 0.0124 | 0.0121 | 0.0107 | 0.0087 | 1981 | 0.1471 |
| 1982 | 0.0080 | 0.0092 | 0.0098 | 0.0113 | 0.0106 | 0.0096 | 0.0105 | 0.0076 | 0.0051 | 0.0059 | 0.0063 | 0.0067 | 1982 | 0.1054 |
| 1983 | 0.0069 | 0.0062 | 0.0063 | 0.0071 | 0.0069 | 0.0067 | 0.0074 | 0.0076 | 0.0076 | 0.0076 | 0.0070 | 0.0073 | 1983 | 0.0880 |
| 1984 | 0.0076 | 0.0071 | 0.0073 | 0.0081 | 0.0078 | 0.0075 | 0.0082 | 0.0083 | 0.0086 | 0.0100 | 0.0073 | 0.0064 | 1984 | 0.0985 |
| 1985 | 0.0065 | 0.0058 | 0.0062 | 0.0072 | 0.0066 | 0.0055 | 0.0062 | 0.0055 | 0.0060 | 0.0065 | 0.0061 | 0.0065 | 1985 | 0.0772 |

*Compound annual return

## Appendix A-14

U.S. Treasury Bills: Total Returns
From 1926 to 2016

| Year | Jan | Feb | Mar | Apr | May | Jun | Jul | Aug | Sep | Oct | Nov | Dec | Year | Jan–Dec* |
|---|---|---|---|---|---|---|---|---|---|---|---|---|---|---|
| 1986 | 0.0056 | 0.0053 | 0.0060 | 0.0052 | 0.0049 | 0.0052 | 0.0052 | 0.0046 | 0.0045 | 0.0046 | 0.0039 | 0.0049 | 1986 | 0.0616 |
| 1987 | 0.0042 | 0.0043 | 0.0047 | 0.0044 | 0.0038 | 0.0048 | 0.0046 | 0.0047 | 0.0045 | 0.0060 | 0.0035 | 0.0039 | 1987 | 0.0547 |
| 1988 | 0.0029 | 0.0046 | 0.0044 | 0.0046 | 0.0051 | 0.0049 | 0.0051 | 0.0059 | 0.0062 | 0.0061 | 0.0057 | 0.0063 | 1988 | 0.0635 |
| 1989 | 0.0055 | 0.0061 | 0.0067 | 0.0067 | 0.0079 | 0.0071 | 0.0070 | 0.0074 | 0.0065 | 0.0068 | 0.0069 | 0.0061 | 1989 | 0.0837 |
| 1990 | 0.0057 | 0.0057 | 0.0064 | 0.0069 | 0.0068 | 0.0063 | 0.0068 | 0.0066 | 0.0060 | 0.0068 | 0.0057 | 0.0060 | 1990 | 0.0781 |
| 1991 | 0.0052 | 0.0048 | 0.0044 | 0.0053 | 0.0047 | 0.0042 | 0.0049 | 0.0046 | 0.0046 | 0.0042 | 0.0039 | 0.0038 | 1991 | 0.0560 |
| 1992 | 0.0034 | 0.0028 | 0.0034 | 0.0032 | 0.0028 | 0.0032 | 0.0031 | 0.0026 | 0.0026 | 0.0023 | 0.0023 | 0.0028 | 1992 | 0.0351 |
| 1993 | 0.0023 | 0.0022 | 0.0025 | 0.0024 | 0.0022 | 0.0025 | 0.0024 | 0.0025 | 0.0026 | 0.0022 | 0.0025 | 0.0023 | 1993 | 0.0290 |
| 1994 | 0.0025 | 0.0021 | 0.0027 | 0.0027 | 0.0032 | 0.0031 | 0.0028 | 0.0037 | 0.0037 | 0.0038 | 0.0037 | 0.0044 | 1994 | 0.0390 |
| 1995 | 0.0042 | 0.0040 | 0.0046 | 0.0045 | 0.0054 | 0.0047 | 0.0045 | 0.0047 | 0.0043 | 0.0047 | 0.0042 | 0.0049 | 1995 | 0.0560 |
| 1996 | 0.0043 | 0.0039 | 0.0039 | 0.0046 | 0.0042 | 0.0040 | 0.0045 | 0.0041 | 0.0044 | 0.0042 | 0.0041 | 0.0046 | 1996 | 0.0521 |
| 1997 | 0.0045 | 0.0039 | 0.0043 | 0.0043 | 0.0049 | 0.0037 | 0.0043 | 0.0041 | 0.0044 | 0.0042 | 0.0039 | 0.0048 | 1997 | 0.0526 |
| 1998 | 0.0043 | 0.0039 | 0.0039 | 0.0043 | 0.0040 | 0.0041 | 0.0040 | 0.0043 | 0.0046 | 0.0032 | 0.0031 | 0.0038 | 1998 | 0.0486 |
| 1999 | 0.0035 | 0.0035 | 0.0043 | 0.0037 | 0.0034 | 0.0040 | 0.0038 | 0.0039 | 0.0039 | 0.0039 | 0.0036 | 0.0044 | 1999 | 0.0468 |
| 2000 | 0.0041 | 0.0043 | 0.0047 | 0.0046 | 0.0050 | 0.0040 | 0.0048 | 0.0050 | 0.0051 | 0.0056 | 0.0051 | 0.0050 | 2000 | 0.0589 |
| 2001 | 0.0054 | 0.0038 | 0.0042 | 0.0039 | 0.0032 | 0.0028 | 0.0030 | 0.0031 | 0.0028 | 0.0022 | 0.0017 | 0.0015 | 2001 | 0.0383 |
| 2002 | 0.0014 | 0.0013 | 0.0013 | 0.0015 | 0.0014 | 0.0013 | 0.0015 | 0.0014 | 0.0014 | 0.0014 | 0.0012 | 0.0011 | 2002 | 0.0165 |
| 2003 | 0.0010 | 0.0009 | 0.0010 | 0.0010 | 0.0009 | 0.0010 | 0.0007 | 0.0007 | 0.0008 | 0.0007 | 0.0007 | 0.0008 | 2003 | 0.0102 |
| 2004 | 0.0007 | 0.0006 | 0.0009 | 0.0008 | 0.0006 | 0.0008 | 0.0010 | 0.0011 | 0.0011 | 0.0011 | 0.0015 | 0.0016 | 2004 | 0.0120 |
| 2005 | 0.0016 | 0.0016 | 0.0021 | 0.0021 | 0.0024 | 0.0023 | 0.0024 | 0.0030 | 0.0029 | 0.0027 | 0.0031 | 0.0032 | 2005 | 0.0298 |
| 2006 | 0.0035 | 0.0034 | 0.0037 | 0.0036 | 0.0043 | 0.0040 | 0.0040 | 0.0042 | 0.0041 | 0.0041 | 0.0042 | 0.0040 | 2006 | 0.0480 |
| 2007 | 0.0044 | 0.0038 | 0.0043 | 0.0044 | 0.0041 | 0.0040 | 0.0040 | 0.0042 | 0.0032 | 0.0032 | 0.0034 | 0.0027 | 2007 | 0.0466 |
| 2008 | 0.0021 | 0.0013 | 0.0017 | 0.0018 | 0.0018 | 0.0017 | 0.0015 | 0.0013 | 0.0015 | 0.0008 | 0.0003 | 0.0000 | 2008 | 0.0160 |
| 2009 | 0.0000 | 0.0001 | 0.0002 | 0.0001 | 0.0000 | 0.0001 | 0.0001 | 0.0001 | 0.0001 | 0.0000 | 0.0000 | 0.0001 | 2009 | 0.0010 |
| 2010 | 0.0000 | 0.0000 | 0.0001 | 0.0001 | 0.0001 | 0.0001 | 0.0001 | 0.0001 | 0.0001 | 0.0001 | 0.0001 | 0.0001 | 2010 | 0.0012 |
| 2011 | 0.0001 | 0.0001 | 0.0000 | 0.0000 | 0.0000 | 0.0000 | 0.0000 | 0.0001 | 0.0000 | 0.0000 | 0.0000 | 0.0000 | 2011 | 0.0004 |
| 2012 | 0.0000 | 0.0000 | 0.0000 | 0.0000 | 0.0001 | 0.0000 | 0.0000 | 0.0001 | 0.0001 | 0.0001 | 0.0001 | 0.0001 | 2012 | 0.0006 |
| 2013 | 0.0000 | 0.0000 | 0.0000 | 0.0000 | 0.0000 | 0.0000 | 0.0000 | 0.0000 | 0.0000 | 0.0000 | 0.0000 | 0.0000 | 2013 | 0.0002 |
| 2014 | 0.0000 | 0.0000 | 0.0000 | 0.0000 | 0.0000 | 0.0000 | 0.0000 | 0.0000 | 0.0000 | 0.0000 | 0.0000 | 0.0000 | 2014 | 0.0002 |
| 2015 | 0.0000 | 0.0000 | 0.0000 | 0.0000 | 0.0000 | 0.0000 | 0.0000 | 0.0000 | 0.0000 | 0.0000 | 0.0000 | 0.0001 | 2015 | 0.0002 |
| 2016 | 0.0001 | 0.0002 | 0.0002 | 0.0001 | 0.0001 | 0.0002 | 0.0002 | 0.0002 | 0.0002 | 0.0002 | 0.0001 | 0.0003 | 2016 | 0.0020 |

*Compound annual return

## Appendix A-15

Inflation
From 1926 to 2016

| Year | Jan | Feb | Mar | Apr | May | Jun | Jul | Aug | Sep | Oct | Nov | Dec | Year | Jan–Dec* |
|---|---|---|---|---|---|---|---|---|---|---|---|---|---|---|
| 1926 | 0.0000 | -0.0037 | -0.0056 | 0.0094 | -0.0056 | -0.0075 | -0.0094 | -0.0057 | 0.0057 | 0.0038 | 0.0038 | 0.0000 | 1926 | -0.0149 |
| 1927 | -0.0076 | -0.0076 | -0.0058 | 0.0000 | 0.0077 | 0.0096 | -0.0190 | -0.0058 | 0.0058 | 0.0058 | -0.0019 | -0.0019 | 1927 | -0.0208 |
| 1928 | -0.0019 | -0.0097 | 0.0000 | 0.0020 | 0.0058 | -0.0078 | 0.0000 | 0.0020 | 0.0078 | -0.0019 | -0.0019 | -0.0039 | 1928 | -0.0097 |
| 1929 | -0.0019 | -0.0020 | -0.0039 | -0.0039 | 0.0059 | 0.0039 | 0.0098 | 0.0039 | -0.0019 | 0.0000 | -0.0019 | -0.0058 | 1929 | 0.0020 |
| 1930 | -0.0039 | -0.0039 | -0.0059 | 0.0059 | -0.0059 | -0.0059 | -0.0139 | -0.0060 | 0.0061 | -0.0060 | -0.0081 | -0.0143 | 1930 | -0.0603 |
| 1931 | -0.0145 | -0.0147 | -0.0064 | -0.0064 | -0.0108 | -0.0109 | -0.0022 | -0.0022 | -0.0044 | -0.0067 | -0.0112 | -0.0091 | 1931 | -0.0952 |
| 1932 | -0.0206 | -0.0140 | -0.0047 | -0.0071 | -0.0144 | -0.0073 | 0.0000 | -0.0123 | -0.0050 | -0.0075 | -0.0050 | -0.0101 | 1932 | -0.1030 |
| 1933 | -0.0153 | -0.0155 | -0.0079 | -0.0027 | 0.0027 | 0.0106 | 0.0289 | 0.0102 | -0.0050 | 0.0000 | 0.0000 | -0.0051 | 1933 | 0.0051 |
| 1934 | 0.0051 | 0.0076 | 0.0000 | -0.0025 | 0.0025 | 0.0025 | 0.0000 | 0.0025 | 0.0150 | -0.0074 | -0.0025 | -0.0025 | 1934 | 0.0203 |
| 1935 | 0.0149 | 0.0074 | -0.0024 | 0.0098 | -0.0048 | -0.0024 | -0.0049 | 0.0000 | 0.0049 | 0.0000 | 0.0049 | 0.0024 | 1935 | 0.0299 |
| 1936 | 0.0000 | -0.0048 | -0.0049 | 0.0000 | 0.0000 | 0.0098 | 0.0048 | 0.0072 | 0.0024 | -0.0024 | 0.0000 | 0.0000 | 1936 | 0.0121 |
| 1937 | 0.0072 | 0.0024 | 0.0071 | 0.0047 | 0.0047 | 0.0023 | 0.0046 | 0.0023 | 0.0092 | -0.0046 | -0.0069 | -0.0023 | 1937 | 0.0310 |
| 1938 | -0.0139 | -0.0094 | 0.0000 | 0.0047 | -0.0047 | 0.0000 | 0.0024 | -0.0024 | 0.0000 | -0.0047 | -0.0024 | 0.0024 | 1938 | -0.0278 |
| 1939 | -0.0048 | -0.0048 | -0.0024 | -0.0024 | 0.0000 | 0.0000 | 0.0000 | 0.0000 | 0.0193 | -0.0047 | 0.0000 | -0.0048 | 1939 | -0.0048 |
| 1940 | -0.0024 | 0.0072 | -0.0024 | 0.0000 | 0.0024 | 0.0024 | -0.0024 | -0.0024 | 0.0024 | 0.0000 | 0.0000 | 0.0048 | 1940 | 0.0096 |
| 1941 | 0.0000 | 0.0000 | 0.0047 | 0.0094 | 0.0070 | 0.0186 | 0.0046 | 0.0091 | 0.0180 | 0.0110 | 0.0087 | 0.0022 | 1941 | 0.0972 |
| 1942 | 0.0130 | 0.0085 | 0.0127 | 0.0063 | 0.0104 | 0.0021 | 0.0041 | 0.0061 | 0.0020 | 0.0101 | 0.0060 | 0.0080 | 1942 | 0.0929 |
| 1943 | 0.0000 | 0.0020 | 0.0158 | 0.0117 | 0.0077 | -0.0019 | -0.0076 | -0.0038 | 0.0039 | 0.0038 | -0.0019 | 0.0019 | 1943 | 0.0316 |
| 1944 | -0.0019 | -0.0019 | 0.0000 | 0.0058 | 0.0038 | 0.0019 | 0.0057 | 0.0038 | 0.0000 | 0.0000 | 0.0000 | 0.0038 | 1944 | 0.0211 |
| 1945 | 0.0000 | -0.0019 | 0.0000 | 0.0019 | 0.0075 | 0.0093 | 0.0018 | 0.0000 | -0.0037 | 0.0000 | 0.0037 | 0.0037 | 1945 | 0.0225 |
| 1946 | 0.0000 | -0.0037 | 0.0074 | 0.0055 | 0.0055 | 0.0109 | 0.0590 | 0.0220 | 0.0116 | 0.0196 | 0.0240 | 0.0078 | 1946 | 0.1816 |
| 1947 | 0.0000 | -0.0016 | 0.0218 | 0.0000 | -0.0030 | 0.0076 | 0.0091 | 0.0105 | 0.0238 | 0.0000 | 0.0058 | 0.0130 | 1947 | 0.0901 |
| 1948 | 0.0114 | -0.0085 | -0.0028 | 0.0142 | 0.0070 | 0.0070 | 0.0125 | 0.0041 | 0.0000 | -0.0041 | -0.0068 | -0.0069 | 1948 | 0.0271 |
| 1949 | -0.0014 | -0.0111 | 0.0028 | 0.0014 | -0.0014 | 0.0014 | -0.0070 | 0.0028 | 0.0042 | -0.0056 | 0.0014 | -0.0056 | 1949 | -0.0180 |
| 1950 | -0.0042 | -0.0028 | 0.0043 | 0.0014 | 0.0042 | 0.0056 | 0.0098 | 0.0083 | 0.0069 | 0.0055 | 0.0041 | 0.0135 | 1950 | 0.0579 |
| 1951 | 0.0160 | 0.0118 | 0.0039 | 0.0013 | 0.0039 | -0.0013 | 0.0013 | 0.0000 | 0.0064 | 0.0051 | 0.0051 | 0.0038 | 1951 | 0.0587 |
| 1952 | 0.0000 | -0.0063 | 0.0000 | 0.0038 | 0.0013 | 0.0025 | 0.0076 | 0.0013 | -0.0012 | 0.0013 | 0.0000 | -0.0012 | 1952 | 0.0088 |
| 1953 | -0.0025 | -0.0050 | 0.0025 | 0.0013 | 0.0025 | 0.0038 | 0.0025 | 0.0025 | 0.0012 | 0.0025 | -0.0037 | -0.0012 | 1953 | 0.0062 |
| 1954 | 0.0025 | -0.0012 | -0.0012 | -0.0025 | 0.0037 | 0.0012 | 0.0000 | -0.0012 | -0.0025 | -0.0025 | 0.0012 | -0.0025 | 1954 | -0.0050 |
| 1955 | 0.0000 | 0.0000 | 0.0000 | 0.0000 | 0.0000 | 0.0000 | 0.0037 | -0.0025 | 0.0037 | 0.0000 | 0.0012 | -0.0025 | 1955 | 0.0037 |

*Compound annual return

# Appendix A-15

Inflation
From 1926 to 2016

| Year | Jan | Feb | Mar | Apr | May | Jun | Jul | Aug | Sep | Oct | Nov | Dec | Year | Jan–Dec* |
|---|---|---|---|---|---|---|---|---|---|---|---|---|---|---|
| 1956 | -0.0012 | 0.0000 | 0.0012 | 0.0012 | 0.0050 | 0.0062 | 0.0074 | -0.0012 | 0.0012 | 0.0061 | 0.0000 | 0.0024 | 1956 | 0.0286 |
| 1957 | 0.0012 | 0.0036 | 0.0024 | 0.0036 | 0.0024 | 0.0060 | 0.0047 | 0.0012 | 0.0012 | 0.0000 | 0.0035 | 0.0000 | 1957 | 0.0302 |
| 1958 | 0.0059 | 0.0012 | 0.0070 | 0.0023 | 0.0000 | 0.0012 | 0.0012 | -0.0012 | 0.0000 | 0.0000 | 0.0012 | -0.0012 | 1958 | 0.0176 |
| 1959 | 0.0012 | -0.0012 | 0.0000 | 0.0012 | 0.0012 | 0.0046 | 0.0023 | -0.0011 | 0.0034 | 0.0034 | 0.0000 | 0.0000 | 1959 | 0.0150 |
| 1960 | -0.0011 | 0.0011 | 0.0000 | 0.0057 | 0.0000 | 0.0023 | 0.0000 | 0.0000 | 0.0011 | 0.0045 | 0.0011 | 0.0000 | 1960 | 0.0148 |
| 1961 | 0.0000 | 0.0000 | 0.0000 | 0.0000 | 0.0000 | 0.0011 | 0.0045 | -0.0011 | 0.0022 | 0.0000 | 0.0000 | 0.0000 | 1961 | 0.0067 |
| 1962 | 0.0000 | 0.0022 | 0.0022 | 0.0022 | 0.0000 | 0.0000 | 0.0022 | 0.0000 | 0.0055 | -0.0011 | 0.0011 | -0.0011 | 1962 | 0.0122 |
| 1963 | 0.0011 | 0.0011 | 0.0011 | 0.0000 | 0.0000 | 0.0044 | 0.0044 | 0.0000 | 0.0000 | 0.0011 | 0.0021 | 0.0022 | 1963 | 0.0165 |
| 1964 | 0.0011 | -0.0011 | 0.0011 | 0.0011 | 0.0000 | 0.0022 | 0.0022 | -0.0011 | 0.0022 | 0.0011 | 0.0021 | 0.0011 | 1964 | 0.0119 |
| 1965 | 0.0000 | 0.0000 | 0.0011 | 0.0032 | 0.0021 | 0.0053 | 0.0011 | -0.0021 | 0.0021 | 0.0011 | 0.0000 | 0.0032 | 1965 | 0.0192 |
| 1966 | 0.0000 | 0.0063 | 0.0031 | 0.0042 | 0.0010 | 0.0031 | 0.0031 | 0.0051 | 0.0020 | 0.0041 | 0.0030 | 0.0010 | 1966 | 0.0335 |
| 1967 | 0.0000 | 0.0010 | 0.0020 | 0.0020 | 0.0030 | 0.0030 | 0.0050 | 0.0030 | 0.0020 | 0.0030 | 0.0038 | 0.0030 | 1967 | 0.0304 |
| 1968 | 0.0039 | 0.0029 | 0.0049 | 0.0029 | 0.0029 | 0.0058 | 0.0048 | 0.0029 | 0.0029 | 0.0057 | 0.0054 | 0.0028 | 1968 | 0.0472 |
| 1969 | 0.0028 | 0.0037 | 0.0084 | 0.0065 | 0.0028 | 0.0064 | 0.0046 | 0.0045 | 0.0045 | 0.0036 | 0.0034 | 0.0062 | 1969 | 0.0611 |
| 1970 | 0.0035 | 0.0053 | 0.0053 | 0.0061 | 0.0043 | 0.0052 | 0.0034 | 0.0017 | 0.0051 | 0.0051 | 0.0016 | 0.0051 | 1970 | 0.0549 |
| 1971 | 0.0008 | 0.0017 | 0.0034 | 0.0033 | 0.0050 | 0.0058 | 0.0025 | 0.0025 | 0.0008 | 0.0016 | 0.0024 | 0.0041 | 1971 | 0.0336 |
| 1972 | 0.0008 | 0.0049 | 0.0016 | 0.0024 | 0.0032 | 0.0024 | 0.0040 | 0.0016 | 0.0040 | 0.0032 | 0.0073 | 0.0032 | 1972 | 0.0341 |
| 1973 | 0.0031 | 0.0070 | 0.0093 | 0.0069 | 0.0061 | 0.0068 | 0.0023 | 0.0181 | 0.0030 | 0.0081 | 0.0085 | 0.0065 | 1973 | 0.0880 |
| 1974 | 0.0087 | 0.0129 | 0.0113 | 0.0056 | 0.0111 | 0.0096 | 0.0075 | 0.0128 | 0.0120 | 0.0086 | 0.0061 | 0.0071 | 1974 | 0.1220 |
| 1975 | 0.0045 | 0.0070 | 0.0038 | 0.0051 | 0.0044 | 0.0082 | 0.0106 | 0.0031 | 0.0049 | 0.0061 | 0.0029 | 0.0042 | 1975 | 0.0701 |
| 1976 | 0.0024 | 0.0024 | 0.0024 | 0.0042 | 0.0059 | 0.0053 | 0.0059 | 0.0047 | 0.0041 | 0.0041 | 0.0029 | 0.0029 | 1976 | 0.0481 |
| 1977 | 0.0057 | 0.0103 | 0.0062 | 0.0079 | 0.0056 | 0.0066 | 0.0044 | 0.0038 | 0.0038 | 0.0027 | 0.0049 | 0.0038 | 1977 | 0.0677 |
| 1978 | 0.0054 | 0.0069 | 0.0069 | 0.0090 | 0.0099 | 0.0103 | 0.0072 | 0.0051 | 0.0071 | 0.0080 | 0.0055 | 0.0055 | 1978 | 0.0903 |
| 1979 | 0.0089 | 0.0117 | 0.0097 | 0.0115 | 0.0123 | 0.0093 | 0.0130 | 0.0101 | 0.0104 | 0.0090 | 0.0093 | 0.0105 | 1979 | 0.1331 |
| 1980 | 0.0144 | 0.0137 | 0.0144 | 0.0113 | 0.0099 | 0.0110 | 0.0008 | 0.0065 | 0.0092 | 0.0087 | 0.0091 | 0.0086 | 1980 | 0.1240 |
| 1981 | 0.0081 | 0.0104 | 0.0072 | 0.0064 | 0.0082 | 0.0086 | 0.0114 | 0.0077 | 0.0101 | 0.0021 | 0.0029 | 0.0029 | 1981 | 0.0894 |
| 1982 | 0.0036 | 0.0032 | -0.0011 | 0.0042 | 0.0098 | 0.0122 | 0.0055 | 0.0021 | 0.0017 | 0.0027 | -0.0017 | -0.0041 | 1982 | 0.0387 |
| 1983 | 0.0024 | 0.0003 | 0.0007 | 0.0072 | 0.0054 | 0.0034 | 0.0040 | 0.0033 | 0.0050 | 0.0027 | 0.0017 | 0.0013 | 1983 | 0.0380 |
| 1984 | 0.0056 | 0.0046 | 0.0023 | 0.0049 | 0.0029 | 0.0032 | 0.0032 | 0.0042 | 0.0048 | 0.0025 | 0.0000 | 0.0006 | 1984 | 0.0395 |
| 1985 | 0.0019 | 0.0041 | 0.0044 | 0.0041 | 0.0037 | 0.0031 | 0.0016 | 0.0022 | 0.0031 | 0.0031 | 0.0034 | 0.0025 | 1985 | 0.0377 |

*Compound annual return

## Appendix A-15

Inflation
From 1926 to 2016

| Year | Jan | Feb | Mar | Apr | May | Jun | Jul | Aug | Sep | Oct | Nov | Dec | Year | Jan–Dec* |
|------|------|------|------|------|------|------|------|------|------|------|------|------|------|----------|
| 1986 | 0.0031 | -0.0027 | -0.0046 | -0.0021 | 0.0031 | 0.0049 | 0.0003 | 0.0018 | 0.0049 | 0.0009 | 0.0009 | 0.0009 | 1986 | 0.0113 |
| 1987 | 0.0060 | 0.0039 | 0.0045 | 0.0054 | 0.0030 | 0.0041 | 0.0021 | 0.0056 | 0.0050 | 0.0026 | 0.0014 | -0.0003 | 1987 | 0.0441 |
| 1988 | 0.0026 | 0.0026 | 0.0043 | 0.0052 | 0.0034 | 0.0043 | 0.0042 | 0.0042 | 0.0067 | 0.0033 | 0.0008 | 0.0017 | 1988 | 0.0442 |
| 1989 | 0.0050 | 0.0041 | 0.0058 | 0.0065 | 0.0057 | 0.0024 | 0.0024 | 0.0016 | 0.0032 | 0.0048 | 0.0024 | 0.0016 | 1989 | 0.0465 |
| 1990 | 0.0103 | 0.0047 | 0.0055 | 0.0016 | 0.0023 | 0.0054 | 0.0038 | 0.0092 | 0.0084 | 0.0060 | 0.0022 | 0.0000 | 1990 | 0.0611 |
| 1991 | 0.0060 | 0.0015 | 0.0015 | 0.0015 | 0.0030 | 0.0029 | 0.0015 | 0.0029 | 0.0044 | 0.0015 | 0.0029 | 0.0007 | 1991 | 0.0306 |
| 1992 | 0.0015 | 0.0036 | 0.0051 | 0.0014 | 0.0014 | 0.0036 | 0.0021 | 0.0028 | 0.0028 | 0.0035 | 0.0014 | -0.0007 | 1992 | 0.0290 |
| 1993 | 0.0049 | 0.0035 | 0.0035 | 0.0028 | 0.0014 | 0.0014 | 0.0000 | 0.0028 | 0.0021 | 0.0041 | 0.0007 | 0.0000 | 1993 | 0.0275 |
| 1994 | 0.0027 | 0.0034 | 0.0034 | 0.0014 | 0.0007 | 0.0034 | 0.0027 | 0.0040 | 0.0027 | 0.0007 | 0.0013 | 0.0000 | 1994 | 0.0267 |
| 1995 | 0.0040 | 0.0040 | 0.0033 | 0.0033 | 0.0020 | 0.0020 | 0.0000 | 0.0026 | 0.0020 | 0.0033 | -0.0007 | -0.0007 | 1995 | 0.0254 |
| 1996 | 0.0059 | 0.0032 | 0.0052 | 0.0039 | 0.0019 | 0.0006 | 0.0019 | 0.0019 | 0.0032 | 0.0032 | 0.0019 | 0.0000 | 1996 | 0.0332 |
| 1997 | 0.0032 | 0.0031 | 0.0025 | 0.0013 | -0.0006 | 0.0012 | 0.0012 | 0.0019 | 0.0025 | 0.0025 | -0.0006 | -0.0012 | 1997 | 0.0170 |
| 1998 | 0.0019 | 0.0019 | 0.0019 | 0.0018 | 0.0018 | 0.0012 | 0.0012 | 0.0012 | 0.0012 | 0.0024 | 0.0000 | -0.0006 | 1998 | 0.0161 |
| 1999 | 0.0024 | 0.0012 | 0.0030 | 0.0073 | 0.0000 | 0.0000 | 0.0030 | 0.0024 | 0.0048 | 0.0018 | 0.0006 | 0.0000 | 1999 | 0.0268 |
| 2000 | 0.0030 | 0.0059 | 0.0082 | 0.0006 | 0.0012 | 0.0052 | 0.0023 | 0.0000 | 0.0052 | 0.0017 | 0.0006 | -0.0006 | 2000 | 0.0339 |
| 2001 | 0.0063 | 0.0040 | 0.0023 | 0.0040 | 0.0045 | 0.0017 | -0.0028 | 0.0000 | 0.0045 | -0.0034 | -0.0017 | -0.0039 | 2001 | 0.0155 |
| 2002 | 0.0023 | 0.0040 | 0.0056 | 0.0056 | 0.0000 | 0.0006 | 0.0011 | 0.0033 | 0.0017 | 0.0017 | 0.0000 | -0.0022 | 2002 | 0.0238 |
| 2003 | 0.0044 | 0.0077 | 0.0060 | -0.0022 | -0.0016 | 0.0011 | 0.0011 | 0.0038 | 0.0033 | -0.0011 | -0.0027 | -0.0011 | 2003 | 0.0188 |
| 2004 | 0.0049 | 0.0054 | 0.0064 | 0.0032 | 0.0059 | 0.0032 | -0.0016 | 0.0005 | 0.0021 | 0.0053 | 0.0005 | -0.0037 | 2004 | 0.0326 |
| 2005 | 0.0021 | 0.0058 | 0.0078 | 0.0067 | -0.0010 | 0.0005 | 0.0046 | 0.0051 | 0.0122 | 0.0020 | -0.0080 | -0.0040 | 2005 | 0.0342 |
| 2006 | 0.0076 | 0.0020 | 0.0055 | 0.0085 | 0.0050 | 0.0020 | 0.0030 | 0.0020 | -0.0049 | -0.0054 | -0.0015 | 0.0015 | 2006 | 0.0254 |
| 2007 | 0.0031 | 0.0054 | 0.0091 | 0.0065 | 0.0061 | 0.0019 | -0.0003 | -0.0018 | 0.0028 | 0.0021 | 0.0059 | -0.0007 | 2007 | 0.0408 |
| 2008 | 0.0050 | 0.0029 | 0.0087 | 0.0061 | 0.0084 | 0.0101 | 0.0053 | -0.0040 | -0.0014 | -0.0101 | -0.0192 | -0.0103 | 2008 | 0.0009 |
| 2009 | 0.0044 | 0.0050 | 0.0024 | 0.0025 | 0.0029 | 0.0086 | -0.0016 | 0.0022 | 0.0006 | 0.0010 | 0.0007 | -0.0018 | 2009 | 0.0272 |
| 2010 | 0.0034 | 0.0002 | 0.0041 | 0.0017 | 0.0008 | -0.0010 | 0.0002 | 0.0014 | 0.0006 | 0.0012 | 0.0004 | 0.0017 | 2010 | 0.0150 |
| 2011 | 0.0048 | 0.0049 | 0.0098 | 0.0064 | 0.0047 | -0.0011 | 0.0009 | 0.0028 | 0.0015 | -0.0021 | -0.0008 | -0.0025 | 2011 | 0.0296 |
| 2012 | 0.0044 | 0.0044 | 0.0076 | 0.0030 | -0.0012 | -0.0015 | -0.0016 | 0.0056 | 0.0045 | -0.0004 | -0.0047 | -0.0027 | 2012 | 0.0174 |
| 2013 | 0.0030 | 0.0082 | 0.0026 | -0.0010 | 0.0018 | 0.0024 | 0.0004 | 0.0012 | 0.0012 | -0.0026 | -0.0020 | -0.0001 | 2013 | 0.0151 |
| 2014 | 0.0037 | 0.0037 | 0.0064 | 0.0033 | 0.0035 | 0.0019 | -0.0004 | -0.0017 | 0.0008 | -0.0025 | -0.0054 | -0.0057 | 2014 | 0.0076 |
| 2015 | -0.0047 | 0.0043 | 0.0060 | 0.0020 | 0.0051 | 0.0035 | 0.0001 | -0.0014 | -0.0016 | -0.0004 | -0.0021 | -0.0034 | 2015 | 0.0073 |
| 2016 | 0.0017 | 0.0008 | 0.0043 | 0.0047 | 0.0040 | 0.0033 | -0.0016 | 0.0009 | 0.0024 | 0.0012 | -0.0016 | 0.0003 | 2016 | 0.0207 |

*Compound annual return

## Appendix A-16

U.S. Treasury Bills: Inflation-Adjusted Total Returns
From 1926 to 2016

| Year | Jan | Feb | Mar | Apr | May | Jun | Jul | Aug | Sep | Oct | Nov | Dec | Year | Jan–Dec[*] |
|------|-----|-----|-----|-----|-----|-----|-----|-----|-----|-----|-----|-----|------|------------|
| 1926 | 0.0034 | 0.0064 | 0.0086 | -0.0059 | 0.0057 | 0.0110 | 0.0118 | 0.0083 | -0.0035 | -0.0006 | -0.0007 | 0.0028 | 1926 | 0.0483 |
| 1927 | 0.0101 | 0.0103 | 0.0088 | 0.0025 | -0.0047 | -0.0069 | 0.0224 | 0.0086 | -0.0037 | -0.0033 | 0.0040 | 0.0042 | 1927 | 0.0531 |
| 1928 | 0.0045 | 0.0131 | 0.0029 | 0.0003 | -0.0026 | 0.0110 | 0.0032 | 0.0013 | -0.0051 | 0.0060 | 0.0058 | 0.0045 | 1928 | 0.0457 |
| 1929 | 0.0054 | 0.0055 | 0.0074 | 0.0075 | -0.0015 | 0.0013 | -0.0064 | 0.0002 | 0.0055 | 0.0046 | 0.0057 | 0.0095 | 1929 | 0.0454 |
| 1930 | 0.0053 | 0.0069 | 0.0094 | -0.0038 | 0.0085 | 0.0087 | 0.0161 | 0.0070 | -0.0039 | 0.0069 | 0.0095 | 0.0159 | 1930 | 0.0898 |
| 1931 | 0.0162 | 0.0153 | 0.0077 | 0.0072 | 0.0118 | 0.0118 | 0.0028 | 0.0026 | 0.0047 | 0.0078 | 0.0130 | 0.0104 | 1931 | 0.1171 |
| 1932 | 0.0234 | 0.0166 | 0.0064 | 0.0083 | 0.0152 | 0.0076 | 0.0003 | 0.0127 | 0.0053 | 0.0077 | 0.0052 | 0.0103 | 1932 | 0.1255 |
| 1933 | 0.0157 | 0.0155 | 0.0084 | 0.0036 | -0.0022 | -0.0103 | -0.0279 | -0.0098 | 0.0002 | 0.0001 | 0.0002 | 0.0053 | 1933 | -0.0021 |
| 1934 | -0.0046 | -0.0073 | 0.0002 | 0.0026 | -0.0024 | -0.0024 | 0.0001 | -0.0024 | -0.0147 | 0.0075 | 0.0026 | 0.0026 | 1934 | -0.0183 |
| 1935 | -0.0146 | -0.0071 | 0.0026 | -0.0095 | 0.0050 | 0.0026 | 0.0050 | 0.0001 | -0.0047 | 0.0001 | -0.0046 | -0.0023 | 1935 | -0.0273 |
| 1936 | 0.0001 | 0.0050 | 0.0051 | 0.0002 | 0.0002 | -0.0094 | -0.0047 | -0.0070 | -0.0023 | 0.0026 | 0.0001 | 0.0000 | 1936 | -0.0102 |
| 1937 | -0.0070 | -0.0022 | -0.0069 | -0.0043 | -0.0040 | -0.0020 | -0.0043 | -0.0021 | -0.0088 | 0.0048 | 0.0071 | 0.0024 | 1937 | -0.0271 |
| 1938 | 0.0141 | 0.0095 | -0.0001 | -0.0046 | 0.0048 | 0.0000 | -0.0024 | 0.0024 | 0.0002 | 0.0049 | 0.0018 | -0.0024 | 1938 | 0.0284 |
| 1939 | 0.0047 | 0.0049 | 0.0023 | 0.0024 | 0.0001 | 0.0001 | 0.0000 | -0.0001 | -0.0189 | 0.0048 | 0.0000 | 0.0048 | 1939 | 0.0050 |
| 1940 | 0.0024 | -0.0071 | 0.0024 | 0.0000 | -0.0025 | -0.0023 | 0.0025 | 0.0023 | -0.0024 | 0.0000 | 0.0000 | -0.0047 | 1940 | -0.0094 |
| 1941 | -0.0001 | -0.0001 | -0.0046 | -0.0094 | -0.0069 | -0.0182 | -0.0042 | -0.0089 | -0.0176 | -0.0109 | -0.0086 | -0.0021 | 1941 | -0.0880 |
| 1942 | -0.0126 | -0.0083 | -0.0124 | -0.0062 | -0.0100 | -0.0018 | -0.0038 | -0.0058 | -0.0017 | -0.0097 | -0.0057 | -0.0076 | 1942 | -0.0825 |
| 1943 | 0.0003 | -0.0017 | -0.0152 | -0.0112 | -0.0074 | 0.0022 | 0.0080 | 0.0042 | -0.0036 | -0.0035 | 0.0022 | -0.0016 | 1943 | -0.0273 |
| 1944 | 0.0022 | 0.0022 | 0.0002 | -0.0055 | -0.0036 | -0.0016 | -0.0054 | -0.0035 | 0.0002 | 0.0003 | 0.0003 | -0.0035 | 1944 | -0.0174 |
| 1945 | 0.0003 | 0.0021 | 0.0002 | -0.0016 | -0.0072 | -0.0090 | -0.0015 | -0.0003 | 0.0040 | 0.0003 | -0.0034 | -0.0034 | 1945 | -0.0188 |
| 1946 | 0.0003 | 0.0040 | -0.0070 | -0.0052 | -0.0051 | -0.0105 | -0.0554 | -0.0212 | -0.0111 | -0.0189 | -0.0232 | -0.0075 | 1946 | -0.1507 |
| 1947 | 0.0003 | 0.0018 | -0.0210 | 0.0003 | 0.0033 | -0.0073 | -0.0087 | -0.0101 | -0.0226 | 0.0006 | -0.0052 | -0.0120 | 1947 | -0.0780 |
| 1948 | -0.0105 | 0.0093 | 0.0037 | -0.0132 | -0.0062 | -0.0060 | -0.0115 | -0.0032 | 0.0004 | 0.0045 | 0.0073 | 0.0074 | 1948 | -0.0185 |
| 1949 | 0.0023 | 0.0121 | -0.0018 | -0.0005 | 0.0024 | -0.0004 | 0.0079 | -0.0019 | -0.0033 | 0.0065 | -0.0006 | 0.0065 | 1949 | 0.0296 |
| 1950 | 0.0052 | 0.0037 | -0.0033 | -0.0006 | -0.0032 | -0.0046 | -0.0087 | -0.0073 | -0.0058 | -0.0043 | -0.0030 | -0.0123 | 1950 | -0.0434 |
| 1951 | -0.0145 | -0.0107 | -0.0028 | 0.0000 | -0.0026 | 0.0025 | 0.0001 | 0.0013 | -0.0052 | -0.0035 | -0.0040 | -0.0026 | 1951 | -0.0414 |
| 1952 | 0.0015 | 0.0075 | 0.0011 | -0.0026 | 0.0000 | -0.0010 | -0.0060 | 0.0002 | 0.0029 | 0.0001 | 0.0010 | 0.0029 | 1952 | 0.0077 |
| 1953 | 0.0041 | 0.0064 | -0.0007 | 0.0004 | -0.0008 | -0.0019 | -0.0010 | -0.0008 | 0.0004 | -0.0012 | 0.0045 | 0.0025 | 1953 | 0.0119 |
| 1954 | -0.0014 | 0.0019 | 0.0020 | 0.0034 | -0.0032 | -0.0007 | 0.0005 | 0.0017 | 0.0034 | 0.0032 | -0.0006 | 0.0033 | 1954 | 0.0137 |
| 1955 | 0.0008 | 0.0009 | 0.0010 | 0.0010 | 0.0014 | 0.0010 | -0.0027 | 0.0041 | -0.0021 | 0.0018 | 0.0005 | 0.0043 | 1955 | 0.0119 |

[*]Compound annual return

## Appendix A-16

U.S. Treasury Bills: Inflation-Adjusted Total Returns
From 1926 to 2016

| Year | Jan | Feb | Mar | Apr | May | Jun | Jul | Aug | Sep | Oct | Nov | Dec | Year | Jan–Dec* |
|---|---|---|---|---|---|---|---|---|---|---|---|---|---|---|
| 1956 | 0.0035 | 0.0019 | 0.0003 | 0.0006 | -0.0027 | -0.0042 | -0.0052 | 0.0029 | 0.0006 | -0.0036 | 0.0020 | 0.0000 | 1956 | -0.0039 |
| 1957 | 0.0015 | -0.0012 | -0.0001 | -0.0011 | 0.0002 | -0.0035 | -0.0018 | 0.0013 | 0.0014 | 0.0029 | -0.0008 | 0.0024 | 1957 | 0.0011 |
| 1958 | -0.0031 | 0.0000 | -0.0060 | -0.0015 | 0.0011 | -0.0009 | -0.0005 | 0.0016 | 0.0019 | 0.0018 | -0.0001 | 0.0034 | 1958 | -0.0022 |
| 1959 | 0.0009 | 0.0030 | 0.0022 | 0.0008 | 0.0010 | -0.0021 | 0.0002 | 0.0030 | -0.0003 | -0.0004 | 0.0026 | 0.0034 | 1959 | 0.0143 |
| 1960 | 0.0045 | 0.0017 | 0.0035 | -0.0037 | 0.0027 | 0.0001 | 0.0013 | 0.0017 | 0.0005 | -0.0023 | 0.0002 | 0.0016 | 1960 | 0.0117 |
| 1961 | 0.0019 | 0.0014 | 0.0020 | 0.0017 | 0.0018 | 0.0009 | -0.0026 | 0.0025 | -0.0006 | 0.0019 | 0.0015 | 0.0019 | 1961 | 0.0144 |
| 1962 | 0.0024 | -0.0002 | -0.0002 | 0.0000 | 0.0024 | 0.0020 | 0.0005 | 0.0023 | -0.0034 | 0.0037 | 0.0020 | 0.0034 | 1962 | 0.0149 |
| 1963 | 0.0014 | 0.0012 | 0.0012 | 0.0025 | 0.0024 | -0.0021 | -0.0017 | 0.0025 | 0.0027 | 0.0018 | 0.0016 | 0.0008 | 1963 | 0.0144 |
| 1964 | 0.0019 | 0.0037 | 0.0020 | 0.0018 | 0.0026 | 0.0009 | 0.0008 | 0.0039 | 0.0006 | 0.0019 | 0.0008 | 0.0020 | 1964 | 0.0232 |
| 1965 | 0.0028 | 0.0030 | 0.0025 | -0.0001 | 0.0010 | -0.0018 | 0.0020 | 0.0054 | 0.0010 | 0.0021 | 0.0014 | 0.0002 | 1965 | 0.0197 |
| 1966 | 0.0038 | -0.0028 | 0.0007 | -0.0007 | 0.0031 | 0.0007 | 0.0005 | -0.0010 | 0.0020 | 0.0005 | 0.0040 | 0.0030 | 1966 | 0.0136 |
| 1967 | 0.0043 | 0.0026 | 0.0019 | 0.0012 | 0.0003 | -0.0004 | -0.0019 | 0.0001 | 0.0012 | 0.0010 | 0.0006 | 0.0004 | 1967 | 0.0113 |
| 1968 | 0.0001 | 0.0009 | -0.0011 | 0.0014 | 0.0015 | -0.0015 | 0.0000 | 0.0013 | 0.0014 | -0.0013 | 0.0005 | 0.0014 | 1968 | 0.0046 |
| 1969 | 0.0024 | 0.0009 | -0.0037 | -0.0011 | 0.0021 | -0.0013 | 0.0008 | 0.0005 | 0.0017 | 0.0024 | -0.0002 | 0.0002 | 1969 | 0.0045 |
| 1970 | 0.0025 | 0.0009 | 0.0004 | -0.0011 | 0.0009 | 0.0006 | 0.0018 | 0.0036 | 0.0002 | -0.0005 | 0.0012 | -0.0008 | 1970 | 0.0098 |
| 1971 | 0.0030 | 0.0016 | -0.0004 | -0.0006 | -0.0020 | -0.0020 | 0.0015 | 0.0022 | 0.0029 | 0.0020 | 0.0021 | -0.0004 | 1971 | 0.0099 |
| 1972 | 0.0021 | -0.0024 | 0.0011 | 0.0005 | -0.0002 | 0.0005 | -0.0009 | 0.0013 | -0.0006 | 0.0008 | 0.0013 | 0.0006 | 1972 | 0.0041 |
| 1973 | 0.0012 | -0.0029 | -0.0047 | -0.0017 | -0.0010 | -0.0017 | 0.0041 | -0.0109 | 0.0038 | -0.0016 | -0.0017 | -0.0002 | 1973 | -0.0172 |
| 1974 | -0.0024 | -0.0070 | -0.0057 | 0.0019 | -0.0035 | -0.0036 | -0.0004 | -0.0068 | -0.0039 | -0.0035 | -0.0031 | -0.0002 | 1974 | -0.0374 |
| 1975 | 0.0013 | -0.0027 | 0.0003 | -0.0007 | -0.0001 | -0.0040 | -0.0057 | 0.0017 | 0.0004 | -0.0006 | -0.0020 | 0.0006 | 1975 | -0.0113 |
| 1976 | 0.0023 | 0.0010 | 0.0016 | 0.0000 | -0.0022 | -0.0010 | -0.0012 | -0.0005 | 0.0003 | 0.0000 | 0.0011 | 0.0012 | 1976 | 0.0026 |
| 1977 | -0.0021 | -0.0067 | -0.0024 | -0.0041 | -0.0018 | -0.0026 | -0.0002 | 0.0006 | 0.0005 | 0.0022 | 0.0001 | 0.0011 | 1977 | -0.0155 |
| 1978 | -0.0005 | -0.0023 | -0.0016 | -0.0036 | -0.0048 | -0.0049 | -0.0016 | 0.0005 | -0.0009 | -0.0012 | 0.0015 | 0.0024 | 1978 | -0.0169 |
| 1979 | -0.0011 | -0.0043 | -0.0015 | -0.0035 | -0.0041 | -0.0012 | -0.0052 | -0.0024 | -0.0021 | -0.0002 | 0.0005 | -0.0010 | 1979 | -0.0259 |
| 1980 | -0.0063 | -0.0048 | -0.0023 | 0.0013 | -0.0018 | -0.0049 | 0.0045 | -0.0001 | -0.0017 | 0.0008 | 0.0005 | 0.0044 | 1980 | -0.0103 |
| 1981 | 0.0022 | 0.0003 | 0.0048 | 0.0043 | 0.0033 | 0.0049 | 0.0010 | 0.0051 | 0.0023 | 0.0099 | 0.0078 | 0.0059 | 1981 | 0.0530 |
| 1982 | 0.0044 | 0.0060 | 0.0109 | 0.0070 | 0.0007 | -0.0026 | 0.0050 | 0.0056 | 0.0034 | 0.0032 | 0.0081 | 0.0109 | 1982 | 0.0642 |
| 1983 | 0.0045 | 0.0058 | 0.0056 | 0.0000 | 0.0015 | 0.0033 | 0.0034 | 0.0043 | 0.0026 | 0.0049 | 0.0054 | 0.0059 | 1983 | 0.0482 |
| 1984 | 0.0020 | 0.0025 | 0.0050 | 0.0032 | 0.0049 | 0.0043 | 0.0050 | 0.0041 | 0.0038 | 0.0074 | 0.0073 | 0.0058 | 1984 | 0.0567 |
| 1985 | 0.0046 | 0.0017 | 0.0017 | 0.0031 | 0.0029 | 0.0024 | 0.0047 | 0.0033 | 0.0029 | 0.0034 | 0.0027 | 0.0040 | 1985 | 0.0381 |

*Compound annual return

# Appendix A-16

U.S. Treasury Bills: Inflation-Adjusted Total Returns
From 1926 to 2016

| Year | Jan | Feb | Mar | Apr | May | Jun | Jul | Aug | Sep | Oct | Nov | Dec | Year | Jan–Dec* |
|------|------|------|------|------|------|------|------|------|------|------|------|------|------|------|
| 1986 | 0.0025 | 0.0081 | 0.0106 | 0.0074 | 0.0019 | 0.0003 | 0.0049 | 0.0028 | -0.0004 | 0.0037 | 0.0030 | 0.0040 | 1986 | 0.0498 |
| 1987 | -0.0019 | 0.0004 | 0.0002 | -0.0009 | 0.0008 | 0.0007 | 0.0025 | -0.0009 | -0.0004 | 0.0034 | 0.0020 | 0.0042 | 1987 | 0.0101 |
| 1988 | 0.0003 | 0.0020 | 0.0001 | -0.0005 | 0.0016 | 0.0006 | 0.0008 | 0.0017 | -0.0006 | 0.0028 | 0.0048 | 0.0047 | 1988 | 0.0185 |
| 1989 | 0.0005 | 0.0020 | 0.0009 | 0.0002 | 0.0022 | 0.0047 | 0.0045 | 0.0058 | 0.0033 | 0.0020 | 0.0045 | 0.0045 | 1989 | 0.0356 |
| 1990 | -0.0046 | 0.0010 | 0.0010 | 0.0053 | 0.0044 | 0.0008 | 0.0029 | -0.0026 | -0.0024 | 0.0008 | 0.0034 | 0.0060 | 1990 | 0.0161 |
| 1991 | -0.0008 | 0.0033 | 0.0029 | 0.0038 | 0.0018 | 0.0012 | 0.0034 | 0.0017 | 0.0002 | 0.0028 | 0.0010 | 0.0031 | 1991 | 0.0246 |
| 1992 | 0.0019 | -0.0008 | -0.0017 | 0.0018 | 0.0013 | -0.0004 | 0.0009 | -0.0002 | -0.0003 | -0.0012 | 0.0009 | 0.0035 | 1992 | 0.0059 |
| 1993 | -0.0026 | -0.0013 | -0.0010 | -0.0004 | 0.0008 | 0.0011 | 0.0024 | -0.0003 | 0.0005 | -0.0019 | 0.0018 | 0.0023 | 1993 | 0.0014 |
| 1994 | -0.0002 | -0.0013 | -0.0007 | 0.0014 | 0.0025 | -0.0003 | 0.0000 | -0.0004 | 0.0010 | 0.0032 | 0.0023 | 0.0044 | 1994 | 0.0120 |
| 1995 | 0.0001 | 0.0000 | 0.0013 | 0.0011 | 0.0034 | 0.0027 | 0.0045 | 0.0020 | 0.0023 | 0.0014 | 0.0049 | 0.0055 | 1995 | 0.0298 |
| 1996 | -0.0016 | 0.0007 | -0.0012 | 0.0007 | 0.0023 | 0.0034 | 0.0026 | 0.0022 | 0.0012 | 0.0011 | 0.0022 | 0.0046 | 1996 | 0.0182 |
| 1997 | 0.0013 | 0.0007 | 0.0018 | 0.0031 | 0.0056 | 0.0024 | 0.0030 | 0.0022 | 0.0019 | 0.0017 | 0.0045 | 0.0060 | 1997 | 0.0349 |
| 1998 | 0.0024 | 0.0020 | 0.0021 | 0.0024 | 0.0022 | 0.0029 | 0.0028 | 0.0031 | 0.0033 | 0.0008 | 0.0031 | 0.0044 | 1998 | 0.0319 |
| 1999 | 0.0011 | 0.0023 | 0.0012 | -0.0035 | 0.0034 | 0.0040 | 0.0008 | 0.0015 | -0.0009 | 0.0021 | 0.0030 | 0.0044 | 1999 | 0.0195 |
| 2000 | 0.0012 | -0.0016 | -0.0035 | 0.0040 | 0.0039 | -0.0013 | 0.0025 | 0.0050 | -0.0001 | 0.0039 | 0.0045 | 0.0056 | 2000 | 0.0242 |
| 2001 | -0.0009 | -0.0002 | 0.0019 | 0.0000 | -0.0013 | 0.0011 | 0.0058 | 0.0031 | -0.0017 | 0.0056 | 0.0034 | 0.0054 | 2001 | 0.0224 |
| 2002 | -0.0009 | -0.0026 | -0.0043 | -0.0040 | 0.0014 | 0.0007 | 0.0004 | -0.0019 | -0.0002 | -0.0003 | 0.0012 | 0.0033 | 2002 | -0.0071 |
| 2003 | -0.0034 | -0.0068 | -0.0050 | 0.0032 | 0.0025 | -0.0001 | -0.0004 | -0.0031 | -0.0024 | 0.0018 | 0.0034 | 0.0019 | 2003 | -0.0084 |
| 2004 | -0.0042 | -0.0048 | -0.0055 | -0.0024 | -0.0052 | -0.0023 | 0.0026 | 0.0006 | -0.0010 | -0.0041 | 0.0010 | 0.0053 | 2004 | -0.0199 |
| 2005 | -0.0005 | -0.0041 | -0.0057 | -0.0046 | 0.0034 | 0.0018 | -0.0022 | -0.0021 | -0.0093 | 0.0007 | 0.0113 | 0.0072 | 2005 | -0.0042 |
| 2006 | -0.0041 | 0.0013 | -0.0019 | -0.0049 | -0.0006 | 0.0020 | 0.0010 | 0.0023 | 0.0090 | 0.0095 | 0.0057 | 0.0025 | 2006 | 0.0220 |
| 2007 | 0.0014 | -0.0015 | -0.0048 | -0.0021 | -0.0020 | 0.0020 | 0.0042 | 0.0060 | 0.0005 | 0.0011 | -0.0025 | 0.0034 | 2007 | 0.0056 |
| 2008 | -0.0028 | -0.0016 | -0.0069 | -0.0043 | -0.0066 | -0.0083 | -0.0037 | 0.0053 | 0.0029 | 0.0110 | 0.0198 | 0.0105 | 2008 | 0.0151 |
| 2009 | -0.0043 | -0.0048 | -0.0023 | -0.0024 | -0.0029 | -0.0084 | 0.0017 | -0.0021 | -0.0005 | -0.0009 | -0.0007 | 0.0018 | 2009 | -0.0256 |
| 2010 | -0.0034 | -0.0002 | -0.0040 | -0.0016 | -0.0007 | 0.0011 | -0.0001 | -0.0013 | -0.0005 | -0.0011 | -0.0003 | -0.0016 | 2010 | -0.0135 |
| 2011 | -0.0047 | -0.0048 | -0.0096 | -0.0064 | -0.0047 | 0.0011 | -0.0009 | -0.0027 | -0.0015 | 0.0021 | 0.0008 | 0.0025 | 2011 | -0.0284 |
| 2012 | -0.0044 | -0.0044 | -0.0075 | -0.0030 | 0.0012 | 0.0015 | 0.0017 | -0.0055 | -0.0044 | 0.0005 | 0.0048 | 0.0028 | 2012 | -0.0165 |
| 2013 | -0.0029 | -0.0081 | -0.0026 | 0.0011 | -0.0018 | -0.0024 | -0.0004 | -0.0012 | -0.0012 | 0.0026 | 0.0020 | 0.0001 | 2013 | -0.0146 |
| 2014 | -0.0037 | -0.0036 | -0.0064 | -0.0033 | -0.0035 | -0.0018 | 0.0004 | 0.0017 | -0.0007 | 0.0025 | 0.0054 | 0.0057 | 2014 | -0.0073 |
| 2015 | 0.0047 | -0.0043 | -0.0059 | -0.0020 | -0.0051 | -0.0035 | -0.0001 | 0.0015 | 0.0016 | 0.0004 | 0.0021 | 0.0035 | 2015 | -0.0071 |
| 2016 | -0.0016 | -0.0006 | -0.0041 | -0.0046 | -0.0039 | -0.0031 | 0.0018 | -0.0007 | -0.0022 | -0.0011 | 0.0017 | -0.0001 | 2016 | -0.0184 |

*Compound annual return

# Appendix B
# Cumulative Wealth Indexes of Basic Series

**Basic Series**

Appendix B-1: Large-Capitalization Stocks: Total Return Index

Appendix B-2: Large-Capitalization Stocks: Capital Appreciation Index

Appendix B-3: Small-Capitalization Stocks: Total Return Index

Appendix B-4: Long-term Corporate Bonds: Total Return Index

Appendix B-5: Long-term Government Bonds: Total Return Index

Appendix B-6: Long-term Government Bonds: Capital Appreciation Index

Appendix B-7: Intermediate-term Government Bonds: Total Return Index

Appendix B-8: Intermediate-term Government Bonds: Capital Appreciation Index

Appendix B-9: U.S. Treasury Bills: Total Return Index

Appendix B-10: Inflation Index

# Appendix B-1

Large-Capitalization Stocks: Total Return Index
From 1926 to 2016

| Year | Jan | Feb | Mar | Apr | May | Jun | Jul | Aug | Sep | Oct | Nov | Dec | Yr End | Index |
|---|---|---|---|---|---|---|---|---|---|---|---|---|---|---|
| 1925 | | | | | | | | | | | | 1.000 | 1925 | 1.000 |
| 1926 | 1.000 | 0.962 | 0.906 | 0.929 | 0.946 | 0.989 | 1.036 | 1.062 | 1.089 | 1.058 | 1.095 | 1.116 | 1926 | 1.116 |
| 1927 | 1.095 | 1.154 | 1.164 | 1.187 | 1.259 | 1.251 | 1.334 | 1.403 | 1.466 | 1.393 | 1.493 | 1.535 | 1927 | 1.535 |
| 1928 | 1.529 | 1.509 | 1.676 | 1.733 | 1.768 | 1.700 | 1.724 | 1.862 | 1.910 | 1.942 | 2.193 | 2.204 | 1928 | 2.204 |
| 1929 | 2.332 | 2.328 | 2.325 | 2.366 | 2.280 | 2.540 | 2.660 | 2.933 | 2.794 | 2.243 | 1.963 | 2.018 | 1929 | 2.018 |
| 1930 | 2.147 | 2.203 | 2.382 | 2.363 | 2.340 | 1.960 | 2.035 | 2.064 | 1.800 | 1.646 | 1.631 | 1.516 | 1930 | 1.516 |
| 1931 | 1.592 | 1.782 | 1.662 | 1.506 | 1.314 | 1.500 | 1.392 | 1.418 | 0.996 | 1.085 | 0.999 | 0.859 | 1931 | 0.859 |
| 1932 | 0.836 | 0.883 | 0.781 | 0.625 | 0.488 | 0.487 | 0.672 | 0.933 | 0.900 | 0.779 | 0.746 | 0.789 | 1932 | 0.789 |
| 1933 | 0.795 | 0.654 | 0.678 | 0.966 | 1.129 | 1.280 | 1.169 | 1.310 | 1.164 | 1.064 | 1.184 | 1.214 | 1933 | 1.214 |
| 1934 | 1.344 | 1.301 | 1.301 | 1.268 | 1.175 | 1.202 | 1.066 | 1.131 | 1.127 | 1.095 | 1.198 | 1.197 | 1934 | 1.197 |
| 1935 | 1.148 | 1.109 | 1.077 | 1.182 | 1.231 | 1.317 | 1.429 | 1.469 | 1.507 | 1.624 | 1.700 | 1.767 | 1935 | 1.767 |
| 1936 | 1.886 | 1.928 | 1.980 | 1.831 | 1.931 | 1.995 | 2.135 | 2.167 | 2.174 | 2.342 | 2.374 | 2.367 | 1936 | 2.367 |
| 1937 | 2.459 | 2.506 | 2.487 | 2.286 | 2.280 | 2.165 | 2.391 | 2.276 | 1.957 | 1.765 | 1.612 | 1.538 | 1937 | 1.538 |
| 1938 | 1.561 | 1.666 | 1.252 | 1.433 | 1.386 | 1.733 | 1.862 | 1.820 | 1.850 | 1.993 | 1.939 | 2.016 | 1938 | 2.016 |
| 1939 | 1.881 | 1.954 | 1.692 | 1.688 | 1.811 | 1.701 | 1.889 | 1.766 | 2.062 | 2.036 | 1.955 | 2.008 | 1939 | 2.008 |
| 1940 | 1.941 | 1.966 | 1.991 | 1.986 | 1.531 | 1.655 | 1.712 | 1.772 | 1.793 | 1.869 | 1.810 | 1.812 | 1940 | 1.812 |
| 1941 | 1.728 | 1.718 | 1.730 | 1.624 | 1.653 | 1.749 | 1.850 | 1.852 | 1.839 | 1.718 | 1.670 | 1.602 | 1941 | 1.602 |
| 1942 | 1.627 | 1.602 | 1.497 | 1.437 | 1.552 | 1.586 | 1.640 | 1.666 | 1.715 | 1.831 | 1.827 | 1.927 | 1942 | 1.927 |
| 1943 | 2.070 | 2.190 | 2.310 | 2.318 | 2.446 | 2.500 | 2.368 | 2.409 | 2.472 | 2.446 | 2.286 | 2.427 | 1943 | 2.427 |
| 1944 | 2.468 | 2.479 | 2.527 | 2.502 | 2.628 | 2.771 | 2.717 | 2.760 | 2.758 | 2.764 | 2.801 | 2.906 | 1944 | 2.906 |
| 1945 | 2.952 | 3.154 | 3.015 | 3.287 | 3.351 | 3.349 | 3.288 | 3.499 | 3.652 | 3.770 | 3.919 | 3.965 | 1945 | 3.965 |
| 1946 | 4.248 | 3.976 | 4.167 | 4.330 | 4.455 | 4.290 | 4.188 | 3.906 | 3.516 | 3.495 | 3.486 | 3.645 | 1946 | 3.645 |
| 1947 | 3.738 | 3.709 | 3.654 | 3.521 | 3.526 | 3.721 | 3.863 | 3.785 | 3.743 | 3.832 | 3.765 | 3.853 | 1947 | 3.853 |
| 1948 | 3.707 | 3.563 | 3.846 | 3.958 | 4.305 | 4.329 | 4.109 | 4.174 | 4.059 | 4.347 | 3.929 | 4.065 | 1948 | 4.065 |
| 1949 | 4.081 | 3.960 | 4.090 | 4.017 | 3.913 | 3.919 | 4.174 | 4.265 | 4.377 | 4.526 | 4.605 | 4.829 | 1949 | 4.829 |
| 1950 | 4.924 | 5.022 | 5.057 | 5.303 | 5.573 | 5.267 | 5.330 | 5.566 | 5.895 | 5.949 | 6.050 | 6.360 | 1950 | 6.360 |
| 1951 | 6.765 | 6.871 | 6.764 | 7.109 | 6.896 | 6.739 | 7.218 | 7.563 | 7.573 | 7.495 | 7.567 | 7.888 | 1951 | 7.888 |
| 1952 | 8.030 | 7.804 | 8.197 | 7.867 | 8.137 | 8.536 | 8.703 | 8.642 | 8.490 | 8.507 | 8.993 | 9.336 | 1952 | 9.336 |
| 1953 | 9.291 | 9.192 | 8.997 | 8.783 | 8.851 | 8.732 | 8.971 | 8.521 | 8.551 | 9.012 | 9.196 | 9.244 | 1953 | 9.244 |
| 1954 | 9.739 | 9.848 | 10.168 | 10.693 | 11.139 | 11.173 | 11.831 | 11.506 | 12.485 | 12.277 | 13.393 | 14.108 | 1954 | 14.108 |
| 1955 | 14.387 | 14.528 | 14.485 | 15.059 | 15.142 | 16.416 | 17.437 | 17.393 | 17.618 | 17.118 | 18.533 | 18.561 | 1955 | 18.561 |

# Appendix B-1

Large-Capitalization Stocks: Total Return Index
From 1926 to 2016

| Year | Jan | Feb | Mar | Apr | May | Jun | Jul | Aug | Sep | Oct | Nov | Dec | Yr End | Index |
|------|-----|-----|-----|-----|-----|-----|-----|-----|-----|-----|-----|-----|--------|-------|
| 1956 | 17.917 | 18.657 | 19.982 | 19.973 | 18.788 | 19.557 | 20.594 | 19.919 | 19.043 | 19.169 | 19.072 | 19.778 | 1956 | 19.778 |
| 1957 | 18.986 | 18.485 | 18.882 | 19.614 | 20.472 | 20.481 | 20.749 | 19.701 | 18.516 | 17.957 | 18.372 | 17.646 | 1957 | 17.646 |
| 1958 | 18.431 | 18.170 | 18.767 | 19.400 | 19.810 | 20.363 | 21.277 | 21.651 | 22.735 | 23.348 | 24.012 | 25.298 | 1958 | 25.298 |
| 1959 | 25.430 | 25.554 | 25.605 | 26.635 | 27.273 | 27.213 | 28.199 | 27.911 | 26.674 | 27.017 | 27.519 | 28.322 | 1959 | 28.322 |
| 1960 | 26.340 | 26.729 | 26.400 | 25.976 | 26.821 | 27.388 | 26.748 | 27.596 | 25.968 | 25.949 | 27.154 | 28.455 | 1960 | 28.455 |
| 1961 | 30.291 | 31.257 | 32.100 | 32.262 | 33.033 | 32.125 | 33.223 | 34.029 | 33.404 | 34.401 | 35.940 | 36.106 | 1961 | 36.106 |
| 1962 | 34.784 | 35.511 | 35.349 | 33.204 | 30.512 | 28.061 | 29.891 | 30.512 | 29.092 | 29.279 | 32.459 | 32.954 | 1962 | 32.954 |
| 1963 | 34.620 | 33.794 | 35.045 | 36.798 | 37.510 | 36.805 | 36.726 | 38.692 | 38.318 | 39.617 | 39.435 | 40.469 | 1963 | 40.469 |
| 1964 | 41.612 | 42.222 | 42.917 | 43.238 | 43.940 | 44.721 | 45.592 | 45.055 | 46.409 | 46.856 | 46.878 | 47.139 | 1964 | 47.139 |
| 1965 | 48.763 | 48.913 | 48.264 | 49.984 | 49.833 | 47.477 | 48.177 | 49.488 | 51.140 | 52.618 | 52.453 | 53.008 | 1965 | 53.008 |
| 1966 | 53.335 | 52.634 | 51.555 | 52.688 | 50.096 | 49.363 | 48.769 | 45.234 | 44.993 | 47.214 | 47.662 | 47.674 | 1966 | 47.674 |
| 1967 | 51.478 | 51.846 | 53.967 | 56.325 | 53.641 | 54.658 | 57.215 | 56.817 | 58.758 | 57.136 | 57.507 | 59.104 | 1967 | 59.104 |
| 1968 | 56.592 | 55.113 | 55.718 | 60.363 | 61.334 | 61.980 | 60.916 | 61.913 | 64.387 | 64.945 | 68.393 | 65.642 | 1968 | 65.642 |
| 1969 | 65.193 | 62.414 | 64.653 | 66.131 | 66.303 | 62.708 | 59.024 | 61.705 | 60.251 | 63.014 | 61.141 | 60.059 | 1969 | 60.059 |
| 1970 | 55.594 | 58.693 | 58.949 | 53.793 | 50.685 | 48.321 | 52.035 | 54.522 | 56.495 | 56.025 | 58.858 | 62.375 | 1970 | 62.375 |
| 1971 | 65.070 | 65.830 | 68.422 | 71.082 | 68.306 | 68.532 | 65.879 | 68.436 | 68.132 | 65.465 | 65.478 | 71.295 | 1971 | 71.295 |
| 1972 | 72.762 | 74.778 | 75.396 | 75.909 | 77.404 | 75.898 | 76.260 | 79.072 | 78.872 | 79.807 | 83.648 | 84.838 | 1972 | 84.838 |
| 1973 | 83.573 | 80.627 | 80.692 | 77.602 | 76.340 | 76.035 | 79.127 | 76.429 | 79.692 | 79.823 | 70.971 | 72.376 | 1973 | 72.376 |
| 1974 | 71.857 | 71.804 | 70.334 | 67.812 | 65.763 | 65.016 | 60.193 | 54.994 | 48.660 | 56.840 | 54.062 | 53.220 | 1974 | 53.220 |
| 1975 | 59.989 | 63.815 | 65.435 | 68.771 | 72.048 | 75.486 | 70.625 | 69.384 | 67.220 | 71.612 | 73.630 | 73.033 | 1975 | 73.033 |
| 1976 | 81.925 | 81.234 | 83.971 | 83.318 | 82.391 | 86.043 | 85.631 | 85.473 | 87.683 | 86.050 | 85.698 | 90.508 | 1976 | 90.508 |
| 1977 | 86.229 | 84.657 | 83.767 | 84.116 | 82.466 | 86.542 | 85.465 | 83.996 | 84.125 | 80.849 | 83.406 | 84.029 | 1977 | 84.029 |
| 1978 | 79.205 | 77.599 | 79.881 | 87.089 | 87.890 | 86.679 | 91.734 | 94.494 | 94.193 | 85.980 | 87.826 | 89.551 | 1978 | 89.551 |
| 1979 | 93.520 | 90.517 | 95.913 | 96.811 | 94.421 | 98.528 | 99.850 | 105.611 | 106.065 | 99.273 | 103.993 | 106.216 | 1979 | 106.216 |
| 1980 | 112.819 | 112.809 | 101.842 | 106.550 | 112.034 | 115.579 | 123.622 | 124.871 | 128.545 | 131.147 | 145.119 | 140.741 | 1980 | 140.741 |
| 1981 | 134.852 | 137.194 | 142.681 | 139.922 | 140.280 | 139.402 | 139.688 | 131.622 | 125.137 | 131.890 | 137.333 | 133.812 | 1981 | 133.812 |
| 1982 | 132.064 | 124.682 | 124.032 | 129.638 | 125.218 | 123.338 | 121.143 | 135.849 | 137.543 | 153.374 | 159.568 | 162.643 | 1982 | 162.643 |
| 1983 | 168.691 | 172.558 | 178.933 | 193.029 | 191.350 | 198.797 | 192.931 | 195.827 | 198.531 | 196.236 | 200.375 | 199.328 | 1983 | 199.328 |
| 1984 | 198.216 | 191.241 | 194.553 | 196.399 | 185.527 | 189.557 | 187.205 | 207.881 | 207.932 | 208.733 | 206.395 | 211.833 | 1984 | 211.833 |
| 1985 | 228.337 | 231.134 | 231.287 | 231.069 | 244.420 | 248.249 | 247.888 | 245.771 | 238.084 | 249.081 | 266.165 | 279.041 | 1985 | 279.041 |

## Appendix B-1

Large-Capitalization Stocks: Total Return Index
From 1926 to 2016

| Year | Jan | Feb | Mar | Apr | May | Jun | Jul | Aug | Sep | Oct | Nov | Dec | Yr End | Index |
|------|-----|-----|-----|-----|-----|-----|-----|-----|-----|-----|-----|-----|--------|-------|
| 1986 | 280.599 | 301.573 | 318.399 | 314.813 | 331.562 | 337.165 | 318.307 | 341.911 | 313.645 | 331.733 | 339.795 | 331.124 | 1986 | 331.124 |
| 1987 | 375.712 | 390.558 | 401.827 | 398.259 | 401.712 | 421.998 | 443.376 | 459.920 | 449.837 | 352.959 | 323.879 | 348.510 | 1987 | 348.510 |
| 1988 | 363.169 | 380.098 | 368.356 | 372.430 | 375.651 | 392.890 | 391.400 | 378.113 | 394.222 | 405.199 | 399.424 | 406.392 | 1988 | 406.392 |
| 1989 | 436.151 | 425.282 | 435.203 | 457.799 | 476.321 | 473.619 | 516.383 | 526.478 | 524.342 | 512.167 | 522.612 | 535.162 | 1989 | 535.162 |
| 1990 | 499.233 | 505.664 | 519.063 | 506.113 | 555.462 | 551.715 | 549.946 | 500.236 | 475.891 | 473.865 | 504.496 | 518.549 | 1990 | 518.549 |
| 1991 | 541.132 | 579.832 | 593.873 | 595.278 | 620.959 | 592.510 | 620.127 | 634.819 | 624.195 | 632.587 | 607.099 | 676.530 | 1991 | 676.530 |
| 1992 | 663.923 | 672.521 | 659.441 | 678.803 | 682.131 | 671.983 | 699.435 | 685.120 | 693.171 | 695.566 | 719.250 | 728.077 | 1992 | 728.077 |
| 1993 | 734.164 | 744.170 | 759.871 | 741.505 | 761.340 | 763.570 | 760.498 | 789.355 | 783.301 | 799.504 | 791.883 | 801.458 | 1993 | 801.458 |
| 1994 | 828.705 | 806.212 | 771.064 | 780.952 | 793.768 | 774.311 | 799.737 | 832.526 | 812.168 | 830.414 | 800.172 | 812.041 | 1994 | 812.041 |
| 1995 | 833.100 | 865.567 | 891.107 | 917.348 | 954.012 | 976.171 | 1,008.543 | 1,011.079 | 1,053.749 | 1,049.983 | 1,096.075 | 1,117.188 | 1995 | 1,117.188 |
| 1996 | 1,155.212 | 1,165.923 | 1,177.145 | 1,194.501 | 1,225.306 | 1,229.980 | 1,175.640 | 1,200.439 | 1,268.005 | 1,302.978 | 1,401.466 | 1,373.696 | 1996 | 1,373.696 |
| 1997 | 1,459.519 | 1,470.958 | 1,410.518 | 1,494.724 | 1,585.729 | 1,656.772 | 1,788.598 | 1,688.397 | 1,780.865 | 1,721.388 | 1,801.076 | 1,832.007 | 1997 | 1,832.007 |
| 1998 | 1,852.271 | 1,985.866 | 2,087.559 | 2,108.561 | 2,072.320 | 2,156.496 | 2,133.532 | 1,825.071 | 1,941.987 | 2,099.951 | 2,227.225 | 2,355.569 | 1998 | 2,355.569 |
| 1999 | 2,454.070 | 2,377.800 | 2,472.933 | 2,568.698 | 2,508.042 | 2,647.232 | 2,564.573 | 2,551.885 | 2,481.928 | 2,638.986 | 2,692.631 | 2,851.217 | 1999 | 2,851.217 |
| 2000 | 2,707.964 | 2,656.704 | 2,916.606 | 2,828.858 | 2,770.818 | 2,839.127 | 2,794.740 | 2,968.334 | 2,811.626 | 2,799.739 | 2,579.009 | 2,591.631 | 2000 | 2,591.631 |
| 2001 | 2,683.580 | 2,438.886 | 2,284.382 | 2,461.903 | 2,478.396 | 2,418.076 | 2,394.272 | 2,244.386 | 2,063.147 | 2,102.489 | 2,263.763 | 2,283.594 | 2001 | 2,283.594 |
| 2002 | 2,250.269 | 2,206.872 | 2,289.871 | 2,151.041 | 2,135.194 | 1,983.104 | 1,828.513 | 1,840.518 | 1,640.492 | 1,784.881 | 1,889.937 | 1,778.908 | 2002 | 1,778.908 |
| 2003 | 1,732.307 | 1,706.315 | 1,722.883 | 1,864.797 | 1,963.048 | 1,988.090 | 2,023.143 | 2,062.598 | 2,040.695 | 2,156.136 | 2,175.106 | 2,289.179 | 2003 | 2,289.179 |
| 2004 | 2,331.197 | 2,363.599 | 2,327.941 | 2,291.397 | 2,322.841 | 2,368.008 | 2,289.635 | 2,298.897 | 2,323.795 | 2,359.295 | 2,454.757 | 2,538.289 | 2004 | 2,538.289 |
| 2005 | 2,476.418 | 2,528.532 | 2,483.757 | 2,436.651 | 2,514.181 | 2,517.750 | 2,611.382 | 2,587.555 | 2,608.512 | 2,565.027 | 2,662.041 | 2,662.968 | 2005 | 2,662.968 |
| 2006 | 2,733.478 | 2,740.894 | 2,775.012 | 2,812.274 | 2,731.333 | 2,735.036 | 2,751.907 | 2,817.383 | 2,889.987 | 2,984.160 | 3,040.907 | 3,083.564 | 2006 | 3,083.564 |
| 2007 | 3,130.198 | 3,068.975 | 3,103.301 | 3,240.763 | 3,353.849 | 3,298.131 | 3,195.872 | 3,243.779 | 3,365.092 | 3,418.621 | 3,275.700 | 3,252.974 | 2007 | 3,252.974 |
| 2008 | 3,057.856 | 2,958.519 | 2,945.744 | 3,089.211 | 3,129.224 | 2,865.419 | 2,841.332 | 2,882.431 | 2,625.585 | 2,184.624 | 2,027.867 | 2,049.444 | 2008 | 2,049.444 |
| 2009 | 1,876.704 | 1,676.877 | 1,823.763 | 1,998.314 | 2,110.086 | 2,114.271 | 2,274.189 | 2,356.297 | 2,444.222 | 2,398.816 | 2,542.705 | 2,591.819 | 2009 | 2,591.819 |
| 2010 | 2,498.581 | 2,575.980 | 2,731.428 | 2,774.551 | 2,553.001 | 2,419.356 | 2,588.863 | 2,471.991 | 2,692.603 | 2,795.054 | 2,795.413 | 2,982.234 | 2010 | 2,982.234 |
| 2011 | 3,052.918 | 3,157.508 | 3,158.764 | 3,252.312 | 3,215.497 | 3,161.897 | 3,097.601 | 2,929.334 | 2,723.405 | 3,021.054 | 3,014.378 | 3,045.212 | 2011 | 3,045.212 |
| 2012 | 3,181.685 | 3,319.267 | 3,428.502 | 3,406.981 | 3,202.219 | 3,334.157 | 3,380.466 | 3,456.603 | 3,545.928 | 3,480.455 | 3,500.645 | 3,532.552 | 2012 | 3,532.552 |
| 2013 | 3,715.521 | 3,765.959 | 3,907.195 | 3,982.473 | 4,075.631 | 4,020.900 | 4,225.500 | 4,103.123 | 4,231.795 | 4,426.321 | 4,561.209 | 4,676.681 | 2013 | 4,676.681 |
| 2014 | 4,514.989 | 4,721.521 | 4,761.209 | 4,796.404 | 4,908.995 | 5,010.403 | 4,941.305 | 5,138.982 | 5,066.915 | 5,190.675 | 5,330.276 | 5,316.849 | 2014 | 5,316.849 |
| 2015 | 5,157.241 | 5,453.636 | 5,367.389 | 5,418.879 | 5,488.562 | 5,382.314 | 5,495.080 | 5,163.541 | 5,035.777 | 5,460.566 | 5,476.805 | 5,390.425 | 2015 | 5,390.425 |
| 2016 | 5,122.930 | 5,116.018 | 5,463.079 | 5,484.258 | 5,582.745 | 5,597.211 | 5,803.573 | 5,811.721 | 5,812.820 | 5,706.787 | 5,918.137 | 6,035.116 | 2016 | 6,035.116 |

## Appendix B-2

Large-Capitalization Stocks: Capital Appreciation Index
From 1926 to 2016

| Year | Jan | Feb | Mar | Apr | May | Jun | Jul | Aug | Sep | Oct | Nov | Dec | Yr End | Index |
|------|------|------|------|------|------|------|------|------|------|------|------|------|--------|-------|
| 1925 | | | | | | | | | | | | 1.000 | 1925 | 1.000 |
| 1926 | 0.998 | 0.955 | 0.898 | 0.918 | 0.926 | 0.966 | 1.009 | 1.027 | 1.050 | 1.017 | 1.040 | 1.057 | 1926 | 1.057 |
| 1927 | 1.035 | 1.085 | 1.092 | 1.111 | 1.168 | 1.158 | 1.233 | 1.288 | 1.343 | 1.272 | 1.350 | 1.384 | 1927 | 1.384 |
| 1928 | 1.377 | 1.353 | 1.499 | 1.548 | 1.567 | 1.504 | 1.523 | 1.636 | 1.675 | 1.699 | 1.903 | 1.908 | 1928 | 1.908 |
| 1929 | 2.017 | 2.005 | 2.001 | 2.033 | 1.946 | 2.165 | 2.263 | 2.485 | 2.364 | 1.893 | 1.640 | 1.681 | 1929 | 1.681 |
| 1930 | 1.786 | 1.824 | 1.970 | 1.951 | 1.919 | 1.603 | 1.662 | 1.675 | 1.457 | 1.328 | 1.299 | 1.202 | 1930 | 1.202 |
| 1931 | 1.261 | 1.405 | 1.308 | 1.183 | 1.020 | 1.162 | 1.076 | 1.086 | 0.761 | 0.825 | 0.745 | 0.636 | 1931 | 0.636 |
| 1932 | 0.618 | 0.650 | 0.573 | 0.457 | 0.350 | 0.347 | 0.478 | 0.658 | 0.633 | 0.545 | 0.513 | 0.540 | 1932 | 0.540 |
| 1933 | 0.544 | 0.444 | 0.458 | 0.652 | 0.755 | 0.855 | 0.780 | 0.869 | 0.770 | 0.702 | 0.774 | 0.792 | 1933 | 0.792 |
| 1934 | 0.875 | 0.843 | 0.842 | 0.820 | 0.753 | 0.769 | 0.680 | 0.717 | 0.713 | 0.690 | 0.748 | 0.745 | 1934 | 0.745 |
| 1935 | 0.713 | 0.685 | 0.664 | 0.727 | 0.751 | 0.802 | 0.868 | 0.887 | 0.908 | 0.976 | 1.015 | 1.053 | 1935 | 1.053 |
| 1936 | 1.121 | 1.140 | 1.169 | 1.079 | 1.129 | 1.163 | 1.242 | 1.253 | 1.255 | 1.349 | 1.354 | 1.346 | 1936 | 1.346 |
| 1937 | 1.397 | 1.418 | 1.404 | 1.288 | 1.274 | 1.207 | 1.331 | 1.257 | 1.078 | 0.969 | 0.871 | 0.827 | 1937 | 0.827 |
| 1938 | 0.838 | 0.889 | 0.666 | 0.760 | 0.726 | 0.906 | 0.972 | 0.945 | 0.959 | 1.032 | 0.998 | 1.035 | 1938 | 1.035 |
| 1939 | 0.964 | 0.995 | 0.861 | 0.856 | 0.909 | 0.851 | 0.944 | 0.876 | 1.020 | 1.005 | 0.956 | 0.979 | 1939 | 0.979 |
| 1940 | 0.944 | 0.951 | 0.960 | 0.955 | 0.726 | 0.782 | 0.806 | 0.828 | 0.835 | 0.868 | 0.832 | 0.829 | 1940 | 0.829 |
| 1941 | 0.789 | 0.777 | 0.781 | 0.730 | 0.733 | 0.772 | 0.814 | 0.807 | 0.799 | 0.745 | 0.713 | 0.681 | 1941 | 0.681 |
| 1942 | 0.690 | 0.673 | 0.628 | 0.600 | 0.639 | 0.650 | 0.671 | 0.676 | 0.694 | 0.738 | 0.728 | 0.766 | 1942 | 0.766 |
| 1943 | 0.821 | 0.862 | 0.908 | 0.908 | 0.949 | 0.968 | 0.915 | 0.925 | 0.947 | 0.934 | 0.864 | 0.915 | 1943 | 0.915 |
| 1944 | 0.929 | 0.926 | 0.942 | 0.930 | 0.968 | 1.017 | 0.996 | 1.005 | 1.002 | 1.002 | 1.005 | 1.041 | 1944 | 1.041 |
| 1945 | 1.056 | 1.121 | 1.069 | 1.163 | 1.176 | 1.172 | 1.149 | 1.216 | 1.266 | 1.305 | 1.347 | 1.361 | 1945 | 1.361 |
| 1946 | 1.455 | 1.354 | 1.417 | 1.470 | 1.503 | 1.444 | 1.408 | 1.305 | 1.172 | 1.163 | 1.150 | 1.199 | 1946 | 1.199 |
| 1947 | 1.227 | 1.209 | 1.189 | 1.143 | 1.132 | 1.192 | 1.235 | 1.201 | 1.184 | 1.209 | 1.175 | 1.199 | 1947 | 1.199 |
| 1948 | 1.151 | 1.097 | 1.182 | 1.213 | 1.308 | 1.312 | 1.242 | 1.252 | 1.214 | 1.296 | 1.156 | 1.191 | 1948 | 1.191 |
| 1949 | 1.193 | 1.146 | 1.180 | 1.155 | 1.112 | 1.110 | 1.179 | 1.193 | 1.221 | 1.257 | 1.259 | 1.313 | 1949 | 1.313 |
| 1950 | 1.336 | 1.350 | 1.355 | 1.416 | 1.472 | 1.386 | 1.398 | 1.444 | 1.524 | 1.531 | 1.529 | 1.600 | 1950 | 1.600 |
| 1951 | 1.697 | 1.708 | 1.677 | 1.758 | 1.687 | 1.643 | 1.755 | 1.824 | 1.823 | 1.798 | 1.793 | 1.863 | 1951 | 1.863 |
| 1952 | 1.892 | 1.823 | 1.910 | 1.828 | 1.870 | 1.956 | 1.991 | 1.962 | 1.923 | 1.922 | 2.011 | 2.082 | 1952 | 2.082 |
| 1953 | 2.067 | 2.030 | 1.982 | 1.929 | 1.923 | 1.892 | 1.940 | 1.828 | 1.830 | 1.923 | 1.940 | 1.944 | 1953 | 1.944 |
| 1954 | 2.044 | 2.049 | 2.111 | 2.215 | 2.288 | 2.289 | 2.420 | 2.338 | 2.532 | 2.483 | 2.683 | 2.820 | 1954 | 2.820 |
| 1955 | 2.871 | 2.881 | 2.867 | 2.975 | 2.971 | 3.216 | 3.411 | 3.384 | 3.422 | 3.318 | 3.567 | 3.564 | 1955 | 3.564 |

## Appendix B-2

Large-Capitalization Stocks: Capital Appreciation Index
From 1926 to 2016

| Year | Jan | Feb | Mar | Apr | May | Jun | Jul | Aug | Sep | Oct | Nov | Dec | Yr End | Index |
|------|------|------|------|------|------|------|------|------|------|------|------|------|--------|--------|
| 1956 | 3.434 | 3.553 | 3.799 | 3.792 | 3.542 | 3.681 | 3.871 | 3.723 | 3.554 | 3.572 | 3.533 | 3.658 | 1956 | 3.658 |
| 1957 | 3.505 | 3.390 | 3.457 | 3.585 | 3.717 | 3.712 | 3.755 | 3.544 | 3.324 | 3.218 | 3.270 | 3.134 | 1957 | 3.134 |
| 1958 | 3.268 | 3.201 | 3.299 | 3.404 | 3.455 | 3.545 | 3.698 | 3.742 | 3.923 | 4.023 | 4.113 | 4.327 | 1958 | 4.327 |
| 1959 | 4.343 | 4.342 | 4.345 | 4.513 | 4.599 | 4.582 | 4.742 | 4.671 | 4.458 | 4.508 | 4.567 | 4.694 | 1959 | 4.694 |
| 1960 | 4.358 | 4.398 | 4.337 | 4.261 | 4.375 | 4.461 | 4.350 | 4.464 | 4.194 | 4.184 | 4.353 | 4.554 | 1960 | 4.554 |
| 1961 | 4.842 | 4.972 | 5.099 | 5.118 | 5.216 | 5.066 | 5.232 | 5.335 | 5.230 | 5.378 | 5.589 | 5.607 | 1961 | 5.607 |
| 1962 | 5.395 | 5.483 | 5.451 | 5.113 | 4.673 | 4.291 | 4.563 | 4.633 | 4.410 | 4.429 | 4.879 | 4.945 | 1962 | 4.945 |
| 1963 | 5.188 | 5.038 | 5.217 | 5.470 | 5.549 | 5.437 | 5.418 | 5.682 | 5.619 | 5.800 | 5.739 | 5.879 | 1963 | 5.879 |
| 1964 | 6.038 | 6.097 | 6.190 | 6.227 | 6.299 | 6.402 | 6.519 | 6.413 | 6.597 | 6.650 | 6.616 | 6.642 | 1964 | 6.642 |
| 1965 | 6.862 | 6.852 | 6.752 | 6.984 | 6.929 | 6.592 | 6.681 | 6.832 | 7.050 | 7.243 | 7.179 | 7.244 | 1965 | 7.244 |
| 1966 | 7.279 | 7.149 | 6.993 | 7.136 | 6.750 | 6.641 | 6.552 | 6.042 | 6.000 | 6.285 | 6.305 | 6.295 | 1966 | 6.295 |
| 1967 | 6.788 | 6.801 | 7.069 | 7.368 | 6.981 | 7.103 | 7.426 | 7.339 | 7.579 | 7.359 | 7.367 | 7.560 | 1967 | 7.560 |
| 1968 | 7.229 | 7.003 | 7.069 | 7.648 | 7.734 | 7.804 | 7.660 | 7.748 | 8.046 | 8.104 | 8.493 | 8.140 | 1968 | 8.140 |
| 1969 | 8.073 | 7.690 | 7.955 | 8.126 | 8.108 | 7.658 | 7.197 | 7.485 | 7.298 | 7.621 | 7.352 | 7.215 | 1969 | 7.215 |
| 1970 | 6.663 | 7.014 | 7.024 | 6.389 | 5.999 | 5.699 | 6.117 | 6.389 | 6.600 | 6.524 | 6.834 | 7.222 | 1970 | 7.222 |
| 1971 | 7.511 | 7.582 | 7.861 | 8.140 | 7.808 | 7.814 | 7.492 | 7.761 | 7.707 | 7.374 | 7.366 | 7.990 | 1971 | 7.990 |
| 1972 | 8.146 | 8.352 | 8.401 | 8.438 | 8.570 | 8.397 | 8.416 | 8.706 | 8.664 | 8.745 | 9.143 | 9.252 | 1972 | 9.252 |
| 1973 | 9.093 | 8.752 | 8.740 | 8.383 | 8.225 | 8.171 | 8.481 | 8.170 | 8.498 | 8.487 | 7.520 | 7.645 | 1973 | 7.645 |
| 1974 | 7.568 | 7.541 | 7.365 | 7.078 | 6.840 | 6.740 | 6.216 | 5.654 | 4.980 | 5.792 | 5.484 | 5.373 | 1974 | 5.373 |
| 1975 | 6.033 | 6.394 | 6.533 | 6.842 | 7.143 | 7.460 | 6.955 | 6.809 | 6.573 | 6.978 | 7.150 | 7.068 | 1975 | 7.068 |
| 1976 | 7.904 | 7.814 | 8.054 | 7.966 | 7.851 | 8.172 | 8.107 | 8.065 | 8.248 | 8.064 | 8.002 | 8.422 | 1976 | 8.422 |
| 1977 | 7.996 | 7.823 | 7.713 | 7.715 | 7.533 | 7.875 | 7.747 | 7.584 | 7.565 | 7.237 | 7.432 | 7.453 | 1977 | 7.453 |
| 1978 | 6.995 | 6.821 | 6.991 | 7.589 | 7.625 | 7.487 | 7.890 | 8.095 | 8.036 | 7.300 | 7.422 | 7.532 | 1978 | 7.532 |
| 1979 | 7.832 | 7.545 | 7.962 | 7.975 | 7.765 | 8.065 | 8.136 | 8.567 | 8.567 | 7.980 | 8.320 | 8.459 | 1979 | 8.459 |
| 1980 | 8.947 | 8.908 | 8.001 | 8.330 | 8.718 | 8.953 | 9.535 | 9.591 | 9.832 | 9.990 | 11.013 | 10.640 | 1980 | 10.640 |
| 1981 | 10.153 | 10.288 | 10.658 | 10.408 | 10.391 | 10.283 | 10.260 | 9.623 | 9.105 | 9.553 | 9.902 | 9.604 | 1981 | 9.604 |
| 1982 | 9.436 | 8.864 | 8.774 | 9.122 | 8.768 | 8.589 | 8.393 | 9.366 | 9.437 | 10.479 | 10.857 | 11.022 | 1982 | 11.022 |
| 1983 | 11.387 | 11.603 | 11.988 | 12.884 | 12.727 | 13.175 | 12.740 | 12.884 | 13.009 | 12.817 | 13.041 | 12.926 | 1983 | 12.926 |
| 1984 | 12.806 | 12.309 | 12.475 | 12.543 | 11.799 | 12.005 | 11.807 | 13.063 | 13.017 | 13.017 | 12.820 | 13.107 | 1984 | 13.107 |
| 1985 | 14.078 | 14.199 | 14.158 | 14.093 | 14.855 | 15.035 | 14.962 | 14.783 | 14.268 | 14.876 | 15.844 | 16.558 | 1985 | 16.558 |

# Appendix B-2

Large-Capitalization Stocks: Capital Appreciation Index
From 1926 to 2016

| Year | Jan | Feb | Mar | Apr | May | Jun | Jul | Aug | Sep | Oct | Nov | Dec | Yr End | Index |
|---|---|---|---|---|---|---|---|---|---|---|---|---|---|---|
| 1986 | 16.597 | 17.784 | 18.723 | 18.458 | 19.385 | 19.658 | 18.505 | 19.822 | 18.129 | 19.119 | 19.531 | 18.979 | 1986 | 18.979 |
| 1987 | 21.480 | 22.273 | 22.861 | 22.599 | 22.735 | 23.825 | 24.973 | 25.846 | 25.222 | 19.733 | 18.049 | 19.364 | 1987 | 19.364 |
| 1988 | 20.147 | 20.989 | 20.289 | 20.480 | 20.546 | 21.434 | 21.318 | 20.495 | 21.310 | 21.863 | 21.450 | 21.765 | 1988 | 21.765 |
| 1989 | 23.313 | 22.638 | 23.109 | 24.267 | 25.119 | 24.920 | 27.122 | 27.543 | 27.363 | 26.674 | 27.115 | 27.696 | 1989 | 27.696 |
| 1990 | 25.790 | 26.010 | 26.641 | 25.925 | 28.310 | 28.058 | 27.912 | 25.279 | 23.985 | 23.825 | 25.252 | 25.879 | 1990 | 25.879 |
| 1991 | 26.954 | 28.767 | 29.406 | 29.416 | 30.551 | 29.088 | 30.393 | 30.990 | 30.397 | 30.756 | 29.406 | 32.687 | 1991 | 32.687 |
| 1992 | 32.036 | 32.343 | 31.637 | 32.520 | 32.551 | 31.986 | 33.245 | 32.448 | 32.743 | 32.812 | 33.805 | 34.147 | 1992 | 34.147 |
| 1993 | 34.387 | 34.748 | 35.397 | 34.498 | 35.281 | 35.308 | 35.120 | 36.329 | 35.966 | 36.664 | 36.191 | 36.556 | 1993 | 36.556 |
| 1994 | 37.744 | 36.610 | 34.935 | 35.338 | 35.776 | 34.818 | 35.914 | 37.264 | 36.261 | 37.018 | 35.556 | 35.993 | 1994 | 35.993 |
| 1995 | 36.867 | 38.197 | 39.241 | 40.338 | 41.803 | 42.692 | 44.049 | 44.035 | 45.800 | 45.572 | 47.443 | 48.271 | 1995 | 48.271 |
| 1996 | 49.845 | 50.191 | 50.588 | 51.267 | 52.439 | 52.557 | 50.153 | 51.097 | 53.865 | 55.272 | 59.328 | 58.052 | 1996 | 58.052 |
| 1997 | 61.611 | 61.977 | 59.336 | 62.801 | 66.480 | 69.369 | 74.788 | 70.492 | 74.238 | 71.679 | 74.875 | 76.053 | 1997 | 76.053 |
| 1998 | 76.825 | 82.237 | 86.344 | 87.128 | 85.488 | 88.859 | 87.827 | 75.022 | 79.703 | 86.103 | 91.194 | 96.335 | 1998 | 96.335 |
| 1999 | 100.286 | 97.048 | 100.813 | 104.638 | 102.025 | 107.580 | 104.132 | 103.481 | 100.526 | 106.813 | 108.849 | 115.145 | 1999 | 115.145 |
| 2000 | 109.284 | 107.087 | 117.444 | 113.827 | 111.333 | 113.997 | 112.134 | 118.941 | 112.580 | 112.022 | 103.053 | 103.471 | 2000 | 103.471 |
| 2001 | 107.054 | 97.174 | 90.935 | 97.920 | 98.419 | 95.958 | 94.924 | 88.839 | 81.579 | 83.055 | 89.299 | 89.975 | 2001 | 89.975 |
| 2002 | 88.574 | 86.735 | 89.921 | 84.398 | 83.632 | 77.572 | 71.444 | 71.793 | 63.894 | 69.417 | 73.379 | 68.952 | 2002 | 68.952 |
| 2003 | 67.061 | 65.921 | 66.472 | 71.859 | 75.517 | 76.372 | 77.611 | 78.998 | 78.054 | 82.344 | 82.931 | 87.141 | 2003 | 87.141 |
| 2004 | 88.647 | 89.729 | 88.261 | 86.779 | 87.828 | 89.408 | 86.342 | 86.539 | 87.350 | 88.574 | 91.992 | 94.978 | 2004 | 94.978 |
| 2005 | 92.576 | 94.326 | 92.523 | 90.663 | 93.378 | 93.365 | 96.723 | 95.638 | 96.302 | 94.593 | 97.922 | 97.829 | 2005 | 97.829 |
| 2006 | 100.320 | 100.366 | 101.476 | 102.713 | 99.537 | 99.546 | 100.052 | 102.180 | 104.691 | 107.990 | 109.768 | 111.152 | 2006 | 111.152 |
| 2007 | 112.715 | 110.253 | 111.353 | 116.173 | 119.955 | 117.818 | 114.050 | 115.517 | 119.651 | 121.425 | 116.077 | 115.076 | 2007 | 115.076 |
| 2008 | 108.037 | 104.282 | 103.660 | 108.589 | 109.748 | 100.314 | 99.325 | 100.535 | 91.408 | 75.921 | 70.238 | 70.788 | 2008 | 70.788 |
| 2009 | 64.724 | 57.609 | 62.529 | 68.402 | 72.033 | 72.048 | 77.389 | 79.987 | 82.843 | 81.206 | 85.863 | 87.390 | 2009 | 87.390 |
| 2010 | 84.158 | 86.558 | 91.647 | 93.000 | 85.376 | 80.776 | 86.331 | 82.235 | 89.435 | 92.731 | 92.519 | 98.560 | 2010 | 98.560 |
| 2011 | 100.792 | 104.013 | 103.904 | 106.865 | 105.422 | 103.497 | 101.275 | 95.524 | 88.668 | 98.220 | 97.723 | 98.557 | 2011 | 98.557 |
| 2012 | 102.852 | 107.027 | 110.380 | 109.553 | 102.689 | 106.751 | 108.096 | 110.232 | 112.904 | 110.670 | 110.985 | 111.769 | 2012 | 111.769 |
| 2013 | 117.406 | 118.704 | 122.976 | 125.200 | 127.800 | 125.883 | 132.109 | 127.975 | 131.781 | 137.659 | 141.513 | 144.853 | 2013 | 144.853 |
| 2014 | 139.699 | 145.722 | 146.732 | 147.642 | 150.747 | 153.620 | 151.303 | 157.001 | 154.565 | 158.151 | 162.031 | 161.353 | 2014 | 161.353 |
| 2015 | 156.344 | 164.926 | 162.057 | 163.438 | 165.153 | 161.683 | 164.874 | 154.557 | 150.469 | 162.956 | 163.038 | 160.180 | 2015 | 160.180 |
| 2016 | 152.053 | 151.425 | 161.419 | 161.854 | 164.336 | 164.484 | 170.342 | 170.134 | 169.924 | 166.623 | 172.317 | 175.453 | 2016 | 175.453 |

## Appendix B-3

Small-Capitalization Stocks: Total Return Index
From 1926 to 2016

| Year | Jan | Feb | Mar | Apr | May | Jun | Jul | Aug | Sep | Oct | Nov | Dec | Yr End | Index |
|------|------|------|------|------|------|------|------|------|------|------|------|------|--------|-------|
| 1925 | | | | | | | | | | | | 1.000 | 1925 | 1.000 |
| 1926 | 1.070 | 1.001 | 0.894 | 0.910 | 0.904 | 0.938 | 0.949 | 0.973 | 0.973 | 0.951 | 0.971 | 1.003 | 1926 | 1.003 |
| 1927 | 1.032 | 1.089 | 1.029 | 1.088 | 1.168 | 1.133 | 1.191 | 1.170 | 1.176 | 1.098 | 1.187 | 1.224 | 1927 | 1.224 |
| 1928 | 1.283 | 1.253 | 1.319 | 1.440 | 1.503 | 1.376 | 1.384 | 1.445 | 1.574 | 1.617 | 1.803 | 1.710 | 1928 | 1.710 |
| 1929 | 1.716 | 1.712 | 1.677 | 1.729 | 1.498 | 1.578 | 1.596 | 1.569 | 1.425 | 1.030 | 0.876 | 0.832 | 1929 | 0.832 |
| 1930 | 0.939 | 1.000 | 1.101 | 1.024 | 0.968 | 0.758 | 0.781 | 0.768 | 0.656 | 0.584 | 0.583 | 0.515 | 1930 | 0.515 |
| 1931 | 0.623 | 0.783 | 0.727 | 0.570 | 0.491 | 0.581 | 0.548 | 0.507 | 0.342 | 0.368 | 0.331 | 0.259 | 1931 | 0.259 |
| 1932 | 0.285 | 0.293 | 0.255 | 0.198 | 0.175 | 0.175 | 0.237 | 0.411 | 0.357 | 0.293 | 0.257 | 0.245 | 1932 | 0.245 |
| 1933 | 0.243 | 0.212 | 0.235 | 0.354 | 0.578 | 0.729 | 0.689 | 0.753 | 0.633 | 0.555 | 0.591 | 0.594 | 1933 | 0.594 |
| 1934 | 0.825 | 0.839 | 0.838 | 0.858 | 0.749 | 0.747 | 0.578 | 0.667 | 0.656 | 0.663 | 0.726 | 0.738 | 1934 | 0.738 |
| 1935 | 0.714 | 0.672 | 0.592 | 0.639 | 0.637 | 0.656 | 0.713 | 0.751 | 0.778 | 0.855 | 0.976 | 1.035 | 1935 | 1.035 |
| 1936 | 1.346 | 1.427 | 1.436 | 1.179 | 1.211 | 1.183 | 1.286 | 1.313 | 1.384 | 1.472 | 1.678 | 1.705 | 1936 | 1.705 |
| 1937 | 1.921 | 2.047 | 2.072 | 1.724 | 1.654 | 1.458 | 1.638 | 1.517 | 1.132 | 1.008 | 0.862 | 0.716 | 1937 | 0.716 |
| 1938 | 0.754 | 0.780 | 0.499 | 0.638 | 0.584 | 0.788 | 0.906 | 0.815 | 0.802 | 0.974 | 0.907 | 0.951 | 1938 | 0.951 |
| 1939 | 0.870 | 0.879 | 0.663 | 0.672 | 0.745 | 0.667 | 0.837 | 0.704 | 1.066 | 1.023 | 0.915 | 0.954 | 1939 | 0.954 |
| 1940 | 0.955 | 1.033 | 1.099 | 1.171 | 0.741 | 0.818 | 0.837 | 0.859 | 0.877 | 0.925 | 0.947 | 0.905 | 1940 | 0.905 |
| 1941 | 0.907 | 0.881 | 0.909 | 0.848 | 0.852 | 0.916 | 1.115 | 1.108 | 1.056 | 0.985 | 0.936 | 0.823 | 1941 | 0.823 |
| 1942 | 0.979 | 0.972 | 0.903 | 0.872 | 0.869 | 0.898 | 0.964 | 0.995 | 1.086 | 1.204 | 1.143 | 1.190 | 1942 | 1.190 |
| 1943 | 1.444 | 1.723 | 1.971 | 2.155 | 2.404 | 2.384 | 2.126 | 2.126 | 2.217 | 2.244 | 1.994 | 2.242 | 1943 | 2.242 |
| 1944 | 2.385 | 2.456 | 2.640 | 2.499 | 2.684 | 3.055 | 2.964 | 3.059 | 3.053 | 3.020 | 3.170 | 3.446 | 1944 | 3.446 |
| 1945 | 3.612 | 3.977 | 3.634 | 4.055 | 4.257 | 4.621 | 4.364 | 4.607 | 4.920 | 5.265 | 5.882 | 5.983 | 1945 | 5.983 |
| 1946 | 6.917 | 6.476 | 6.653 | 7.117 | 7.537 | 7.189 | 6.808 | 6.230 | 5.232 | 5.170 | 5.097 | 5.287 | 1946 | 5.287 |
| 1947 | 5.509 | 5.487 | 5.303 | 4.756 | 4.502 | 4.750 | 5.125 | 5.106 | 5.165 | 5.311 | 5.150 | 5.335 | 1947 | 5.335 |
| 1948 | 5.254 | 4.842 | 5.320 | 5.515 | 6.099 | 6.128 | 5.774 | 5.778 | 5.474 | 5.828 | 5.177 | 5.223 | 1948 | 5.223 |
| 1949 | 5.318 | 5.062 | 5.380 | 5.199 | 4.906 | 4.859 | 5.185 | 5.318 | 5.578 | 5.841 | 5.851 | 6.254 | 1949 | 6.254 |
| 1950 | 6.562 | 6.706 | 6.682 | 6.956 | 7.134 | 6.580 | 6.969 | 7.338 | 7.720 | 7.675 | 7.922 | 8.677 | 1950 | 8.677 |
| 1951 | 9.398 | 9.455 | 9.004 | 9.334 | 9.026 | 8.548 | 8.867 | 9.403 | 9.606 | 9.392 | 9.314 | 9.355 | 1951 | 9.355 |
| 1952 | 9.533 | 9.248 | 9.410 | 8.922 | 8.950 | 9.193 | 9.296 | 9.291 | 9.142 | 9.047 | 9.486 | 9.638 | 1952 | 9.638 |
| 1953 | 10.032 | 10.302 | 10.233 | 9.939 | 10.079 | 9.589 | 9.735 | 9.123 | 8.884 | 9.143 | 9.258 | 9.013 | 1953 | 9.013 |
| 1954 | 9.694 | 9.786 | 9.965 | 10.104 | 10.561 | 10.651 | 11.512 | 11.528 | 12.000 | 12.082 | 13.024 | 14.473 | 1954 | 14.473 |
| 1955 | 14.764 | 15.471 | 15.602 | 15.837 | 15.960 | 16.428 | 16.533 | 16.487 | 16.667 | 16.384 | 17.152 | 17.431 | 1955 | 17.431 |

# Appendix B-3

Small-Capitalization Stocks: Total Return Index
From 1926 to 2016

| Year | Jan | Feb | Mar | Apr | May | Jun | Jul | Aug | Sep | Oct | Nov | Dec | Yr End | Index |
|---|---|---|---|---|---|---|---|---|---|---|---|---|---|---|
| 1956 | 17.348 | 17.830 | 18.598 | 18.685 | 17.942 | 18.042 | 18.552 | 18.303 | 17.827 | 18.013 | 18.108 | 18.177 | 1956 | 18.177 |
| 1957 | 18.607 | 18.234 | 18.540 | 19.000 | 19.143 | 19.283 | 19.167 | 18.427 | 17.595 | 16.131 | 16.314 | 15.529 | 1957 | 15.529 |
| 1958 | 17.245 | 16.952 | 17.750 | 18.418 | 19.131 | 19.752 | 20.722 | 21.610 | 22.730 | 23.655 | 24.828 | 25.605 | 1958 | 25.605 |
| 1959 | 27.076 | 27.875 | 27.951 | 28.277 | 28.315 | 28.196 | 29.118 | 28.863 | 27.619 | 28.245 | 28.873 | 29.804 | 1959 | 29.804 |
| 1960 | 28.891 | 29.034 | 28.120 | 27.594 | 28.158 | 29.116 | 28.565 | 30.064 | 27.844 | 26.728 | 27.896 | 28.823 | 1960 | 28.823 |
| 1961 | 31.460 | 33.314 | 35.376 | 35.825 | 37.355 | 35.326 | 35.436 | 35.898 | 34.682 | 35.590 | 37.772 | 38.072 | 1961 | 38.072 |
| 1962 | 38.591 | 39.314 | 39.537 | 36.464 | 32.786 | 30.213 | 32.518 | 33.458 | 31.254 | 30.087 | 33.842 | 33.540 | 1962 | 33.540 |
| 1963 | 36.580 | 36.705 | 37.251 | 38.412 | 40.088 | 39.613 | 39.744 | 41.799 | 41.118 | 42.090 | 41.642 | 41.444 | 1963 | 41.444 |
| 1964 | 42.581 | 44.134 | 45.099 | 45.520 | 46.234 | 46.985 | 48.857 | 48.715 | 50.676 | 51.716 | 51.772 | 51.193 | 1964 | 51.193 |
| 1965 | 53.902 | 56.003 | 57.335 | 60.252 | 59.782 | 54.397 | 56.837 | 60.220 | 62.310 | 65.876 | 68.319 | 72.567 | 1965 | 72.567 |
| 1966 | 78.051 | 80.479 | 78.935 | 81.645 | 73.797 | 73.709 | 73.617 | 65.669 | 64.595 | 63.902 | 67.041 | 67.479 | 1966 | 67.479 |
| 1967 | 79.884 | 83.475 | 88.606 | 91.003 | 90.232 | 99.411 | 108.862 | 109.085 | 115.244 | 111.662 | 112.964 | 123.870 | 1967 | 123.870 |
| 1968 | 125.779 | 116.861 | 115.586 | 132.468 | 145.698 | 146.137 | 141.088 | 146.266 | 155.034 | 155.505 | 167.388 | 168.429 | 1968 | 168.429 |
| 1969 | 165.634 | 149.238 | 155.142 | 161.265 | 164.063 | 144.954 | 129.449 | 138.925 | 135.301 | 143.552 | 135.552 | 126.233 | 1969 | 126.233 |
| 1970 | 118.554 | 123.145 | 119.641 | 98.970 | 88.762 | 80.519 | 84.975 | 93.037 | 103.140 | 95.856 | 97.170 | 104.226 | 1970 | 104.226 |
| 1971 | 120.820 | 124.647 | 131.675 | 134.923 | 126.760 | 122.710 | 115.802 | 122.555 | 119.780 | 113.180 | 108.954 | 121.423 | 1971 | 121.423 |
| 1972 | 135.142 | 139.141 | 137.144 | 138.912 | 136.257 | 132.099 | 126.645 | 129.005 | 124.506 | 122.329 | 129.576 | 126.807 | 1972 | 126.807 |
| 1973 | 121.329 | 111.635 | 109.318 | 102.527 | 94.211 | 91.476 | 102.398 | 97.837 | 108.242 | 109.155 | 87.737 | 87.618 | 1973 | 87.618 |
| 1974 | 99.238 | 98.393 | 97.661 | 93.129 | 85.745 | 84.485 | 82.637 | 77.009 | 71.978 | 79.629 | 76.143 | 70.142 | 1974 | 70.142 |
| 1975 | 89.551 | 92.105 | 97.799 | 102.990 | 109.821 | 118.053 | 115.056 | 108.456 | 106.488 | 105.954 | 109.341 | 107.189 | 1975 | 107.189 |
| 1976 | 135.960 | 154.854 | 154.626 | 149.081 | 143.698 | 150.298 | 150.976 | 146.592 | 148.123 | 145.028 | 150.881 | 168.691 | 1976 | 168.691 |
| 1977 | 176.275 | 175.587 | 177.880 | 181.941 | 181.434 | 195.445 | 196.028 | 193.924 | 195.715 | 189.249 | 209.804 | 211.500 | 1977 | 211.500 |
| 1978 | 207.502 | 214.707 | 236.868 | 255.528 | 276.484 | 271.254 | 289.807 | 317.010 | 316.002 | 239.303 | 256.811 | 261.120 | 1978 | 261.120 |
| 1979 | 295.623 | 287.279 | 319.448 | 331.805 | 332.955 | 348.676 | 354.642 | 381.457 | 368.351 | 325.827 | 353.796 | 374.614 | 1979 | 374.614 |
| 1980 | 405.926 | 394.411 | 324.303 | 346.795 | 372.814 | 389.666 | 441.224 | 467.894 | 487.473 | 503.725 | 542.326 | 523.992 | 1980 | 523.992 |
| 1981 | 534.839 | 539.866 | 590.776 | 629.590 | 656.158 | 661.145 | 640.253 | 596.460 | 552.739 | 593.752 | 610.140 | 596.717 | 1981 | 596.717 |
| 1982 | 585.021 | 567.705 | 562.822 | 584.378 | 569.886 | 560.825 | 559.983 | 599.070 | 618.660 | 699.395 | 753.878 | 763.829 | 1982 | 763.829 |
| 1983 | 811.793 | 869.617 | 915.267 | 985.448 | 1,071.150 | 1,108.462 | 1,098.662 | 1,077.054 | 1,091.418 | 1,029.455 | 1,082.532 | 1,066.828 | 1983 | 1,066.828 |
| 1984 | 1,065.974 | 997.219 | 1,014.571 | 1,005.947 | 953.537 | 982.143 | 940.893 | 1,034.794 | 1,037.588 | 1,015.072 | 980.966 | 995.680 | 1984 | 995.680 |
| 1985 | 1,101.123 | 1,131.073 | 1,106.869 | 1,087.609 | 1,117.627 | 1,129.474 | 1,158.840 | 1,150.497 | 1,087.910 | 1,116.304 | 1,185.515 | 1,241.234 | 1985 | 1,241.234 |

## Appendix B-3

Small-Capitalization Stocks: Total Return Index
From 1926 to 2016

| Year | Jan | Feb | Mar | Apr | May | Jun | Jul | Aug | Sep | Oct | Nov | Dec | Yr End | Index |
|---|---|---|---|---|---|---|---|---|---|---|---|---|---|---|
| 1986 | 1,255.136 | 1,345.380 | 1,409.555 | 1,418.576 | 1,469.645 | 1,473.466 | 1,368.850 | 1,398.691 | 1,320.504 | 1,366.193 | 1,361.958 | 1,326.275 | 1986 | 1,326.275 |
| 1987 | 1,451.342 | 1,568.756 | 1,605.308 | 1,555.062 | 1,548.997 | 1,590.200 | 1,648.084 | 1,695.384 | 1,681.651 | 1,190.777 | 1,143.503 | 1,202.965 | 1987 | 1,202.965 |
| 1988 | 1,269.850 | 1,366.359 | 1,422.106 | 1,451.828 | 1,425.841 | 1,513.102 | 1,509.319 | 1,472.190 | 1,505.609 | 1,487.090 | 1,422.104 | 1,478.135 | 1988 | 1,478.135 |
| 1989 | 1,537.852 | 1,550.616 | 1,606.128 | 1,650.939 | 1,710.703 | 1,676.318 | 1,744.544 | 1,765.827 | 1,765.609 | 1,659.171 | 1,650.709 | 1,628.590 | 1989 | 1,628.590 |
| 1990 | 1,504.166 | 1,532.294 | 1,588.682 | 1,546.423 | 1,633.177 | 1,656.695 | 1,593.409 | 1,386.904 | 1,271.929 | 1,199.175 | 1,253.138 | 1,277.449 | 1990 | 1,277.449 |
| 1991 | 1,384.882 | 1,539.019 | 1,643.673 | 1,649.261 | 1,704.347 | 1,621.686 | 1,687.688 | 1,731.737 | 1,737.279 | 1,792.350 | 1,742.881 | 1,847.629 | 1991 | 1,847.629 |
| 1992 | 2,056.041 | 2,148.974 | 2,095.465 | 2,011.018 | 2,008.202 | 1,903.976 | 1,974.424 | 1,929.407 | 1,954.682 | 2,005.308 | 2,182.778 | 2,279.038 | 1992 | 2,279.038 |
| 1993 | 2,402.790 | 2,359.540 | 2,427.731 | 2,353.442 | 2,433.930 | 2,424.681 | 2,464.931 | 2,548.492 | 2,629.024 | 2,752.851 | 2,704.676 | 2,757.147 | 1993 | 2,757.147 |
| 1994 | 2,927.539 | 2,920.805 | 2,790.537 | 2,807.281 | 2,803.912 | 2,730.449 | 2,780.690 | 2,874.399 | 2,904.580 | 2,937.983 | 2,842.205 | 2,842.773 | 1994 | 2,842.773 |
| 1995 | 2,923.223 | 2,996.889 | 3,040.344 | 3,147.364 | 3,241.155 | 3,425.253 | 3,646.182 | 3,776.715 | 3,850.361 | 3,662.848 | 3,733.175 | 3,822.398 | 1995 | 3,822.398 |
| 1996 | 3,833.100 | 3,974.542 | 4,065.161 | 4,409.887 | 4,740.188 | 4,464.309 | 4,043.324 | 4,235.787 | 4,359.048 | 4,282.765 | 4,406.108 | 4,495.993 | 1996 | 4,495.993 |
| 1997 | 4,684.825 | 4,588.317 | 4,363.490 | 4,243.057 | 4,676.698 | 4,909.597 | 5,206.628 | 5,471.645 | 5,933.452 | 5,704.421 | 5,616.003 | 5,519.969 | 1997 | 5,519.969 |
| 1998 | 5,487.401 | 5,843.533 | 6,124.607 | 6,227.501 | 5,917.994 | 5,796.083 | 5,407.166 | 4,320.326 | 4,479.746 | 4,639.225 | 4,990.878 | 5,116.648 | 1998 | 5,116.648 |
| 1999 | 5,259.403 | 4,898.082 | 4,712.444 | 5,159.655 | 5,359.334 | 5,663.744 | 5,715.850 | 5,606.678 | 5,482.770 | 5,435.070 | 5,962.815 | 6,640.787 | 1999 | 6,640.787 |
| 2000 | 7,035.914 | 8,694.983 | 8,041.990 | 7,035.937 | 6,467.433 | 7,352.178 | 7,115.438 | 7,773.616 | 7,604.928 | 7,068.020 | 6,283.470 | 6,402.228 | 2000 | 6,402.228 |
| 2001 | 7,285.735 | 6,774.277 | 6,449.111 | 6,920.541 | 7,584.913 | 7,857.212 | 7,657.638 | 7,431.738 | 6,481.962 | 6,900.049 | 7,365.112 | 7,860.047 | 2001 | 7,860.047 |
| 2002 | 7,946.508 | 7,726.390 | 8,409.402 | 8,613.751 | 8,378.596 | 8,080.318 | 6,910.288 | 6,870.899 | 6,407.800 | 6,572.481 | 7,121.940 | 6,816.409 | 2002 | 6,816.409 |
| 2003 | 6,664.403 | 6,472.468 | 6,544.313 | 7,151.625 | 7,982.644 | 8,333.880 | 8,948.920 | 9,372.204 | 9,380.639 | 10,219.268 | 10,658.697 | 10,953.943 | 2003 | 10,953.943 |
| 2004 | 11,587.081 | 11,645.016 | 11,661.319 | 11,184.371 | 11,184.371 | 11,677.602 | 10,805.285 | 10,641.045 | 11,174.161 | 11,379.766 | 12,400.531 | 12,968.475 | 2004 | 12,968.475 |
| 2005 | 12,436.767 | 12,539.993 | 12,134.951 | 11,380.157 | 12,066.380 | 12,611.781 | 13,574.060 | 13,385.380 | 13,467.031 | 13,088.607 | 13,681.521 | 13,706.148 | 2005 | 13,706.148 |
| 2006 | 14,958.890 | 14,996.287 | 15,678.618 | 15,614.336 | 14,694.652 | 14,563.869 | 14,061.416 | 14,452.323 | 14,533.256 | 15,325.319 | 15,670.138 | 15,922.427 | 2006 | 15,922.427 |
| 2007 | 16,105.535 | 16,025.008 | 16,188.463 | 16,431.290 | 16,948.875 | 16,892.944 | 15,793.213 | 15,976.415 | 16,212.866 | 16,488.484 | 15,100.154 | 15,091.094 | 2007 | 15,091.094 |
| 2008 | 13,936.625 | 13,499.015 | 13,540.862 | 13,821.158 | 14,371.240 | 13,070.643 | 13,656.208 | 14,117.787 | 13,077.306 | 10,368.996 | 9,037.613 | 9,548.943 | 2008 | 9,548.943 |
| 2009 | 8,411.664 | 7,308.895 | 8,009.087 | 9,401.867 | 9,724.351 | 9,992.743 | 10,974.031 | 11,273.622 | 11,922.982 | 11,056.182 | 11,252.982 | 12,230.866 | 2009 | 12,230.866 |
| 2010 | 11,871.278 | 12,392.427 | 13,393.735 | 14,367.460 | 13,301.395 | 12,338.374 | 13,219.333 | 12,164.431 | 13,643.625 | 14,235.759 | 14,839.355 | 16,054.698 | 2010 | 16,054.698 |
| 2011 | 15,879.702 | 16,811.840 | 17,358.225 | 17,649.843 | 17,310.966 | 16,937.049 | 16,481.443 | 15,009.650 | 13,421.629 | 15,492.586 | 15,399.631 | 15,532.068 | 2011 | 15,532.068 |
| 2012 | 16,613.100 | 16,930.410 | 17,434.936 | 17,187.360 | 15,989.401 | 16,808.058 | 16,655.105 | 17,174.744 | 17,894.366 | 17,527.532 | 17,692.290 | 18,364.597 | 2012 | 18,364.597 |
| 2013 | 19,407.706 | 19,621.191 | 20,576.743 | 20,414.187 | 21,471.642 | 21,570.411 | 23,168.779 | 22,362.505 | 23,939.062 | 24,772.141 | 26,146.995 | 26,641.173 | 2013 | 26,641.173 |
| 2014 | 25,460.969 | 26,532.876 | 26,790.245 | 25,876.698 | 25,902.575 | 27,026.746 | 25,448.384 | 26,603.741 | 25,089.988 | 26,725.855 | 26,525.411 | 27,419.318 | 2014 | 27,419.318 |
| 2015 | 26,075.771 | 27,648.140 | 28,281.283 | 27,729.798 | 28,112.469 | 28,570.702 | 27,873.577 | 26,638.777 | 25,490.646 | 27,027.732 | 27,795.320 | 26,433.349 | 2015 | 26,433.349 |
| 2016 | 24,635.881 | 24,906.876 | 26,670.283 | 26,958.322 | 27,246.776 | 27,200.456 | 28,565.919 | 29,020.117 | 29,229.062 | 28,197.276 | 31,916.497 | 33,212.307 | 2016 | 33,212.307 |

# Appendix B-4

Long-term Corporate Bonds: Total Return Index
From 1926 to 2016

| Year | Jan | Feb | Mar | Apr | May | Jun | Jul | Aug | Sep | Oct | Nov | Dec | Yr End | Index |
|------|-----|-----|-----|-----|-----|-----|-----|-----|-----|-----|-----|-----|--------|-------|
| 1925 | | | | | | | | | | | | 1.000 | 1925 | 1.000 |
| 1926 | 1.007 | 1.012 | 1.020 | 1.030 | 1.035 | 1.035 | 1.041 | 1.046 | 1.052 | 1.062 | 1.068 | 1.074 | 1926 | 1.074 |
| 1927 | 1.080 | 1.087 | 1.096 | 1.102 | 1.101 | 1.106 | 1.106 | 1.115 | 1.132 | 1.138 | 1.146 | 1.154 | 1927 | 1.154 |
| 1928 | 1.157 | 1.165 | 1.169 | 1.171 | 1.162 | 1.159 | 1.158 | 1.168 | 1.171 | 1.181 | 1.177 | 1.186 | 1928 | 1.186 |
| 1929 | 1.192 | 1.195 | 1.185 | 1.187 | 1.192 | 1.187 | 1.189 | 1.192 | 1.196 | 1.204 | 1.202 | 1.225 | 1929 | 1.225 |
| 1930 | 1.233 | 1.241 | 1.259 | 1.269 | 1.276 | 1.290 | 1.298 | 1.315 | 1.329 | 1.337 | 1.335 | 1.323 | 1930 | 1.323 |
| 1931 | 1.350 | 1.359 | 1.372 | 1.381 | 1.400 | 1.407 | 1.414 | 1.416 | 1.414 | 1.362 | 1.337 | 1.299 | 1931 | 1.299 |
| 1932 | 1.292 | 1.261 | 1.306 | 1.283 | 1.297 | 1.295 | 1.301 | 1.358 | 1.399 | 1.409 | 1.419 | 1.439 | 1932 | 1.439 |
| 1933 | 1.518 | 1.438 | 1.445 | 1.431 | 1.516 | 1.544 | 1.569 | 1.584 | 1.582 | 1.588 | 1.549 | 1.588 | 1933 | 1.588 |
| 1934 | 1.629 | 1.653 | 1.684 | 1.701 | 1.717 | 1.744 | 1.752 | 1.760 | 1.749 | 1.767 | 1.790 | 1.808 | 1934 | 1.808 |
| 1935 | 1.846 | 1.872 | 1.880 | 1.901 | 1.909 | 1.931 | 1.952 | 1.944 | 1.944 | 1.952 | 1.966 | 1.982 | 1935 | 1.982 |
| 1936 | 1.998 | 2.009 | 2.026 | 2.031 | 2.039 | 2.056 | 2.058 | 2.072 | 2.086 | 2.091 | 2.114 | 2.116 | 1936 | 2.116 |
| 1937 | 2.121 | 2.111 | 2.087 | 2.101 | 2.110 | 2.121 | 2.129 | 2.125 | 2.131 | 2.145 | 2.159 | 2.174 | 1937 | 2.174 |
| 1938 | 2.182 | 2.184 | 2.165 | 2.195 | 2.197 | 2.218 | 2.233 | 2.229 | 2.253 | 2.271 | 2.279 | 2.307 | 1938 | 2.307 |
| 1939 | 2.312 | 2.327 | 2.332 | 2.347 | 2.359 | 2.367 | 2.365 | 2.272 | 2.307 | 2.361 | 2.380 | 2.399 | 1939 | 2.399 |
| 1940 | 2.410 | 2.415 | 2.427 | 2.405 | 2.400 | 2.429 | 2.434 | 2.436 | 2.458 | 2.470 | 2.486 | 2.480 | 1940 | 2.480 |
| 1941 | 2.482 | 2.483 | 2.478 | 2.497 | 2.509 | 2.525 | 2.541 | 2.550 | 2.562 | 2.570 | 2.546 | 2.548 | 1941 | 2.548 |
| 1942 | 2.549 | 2.547 | 2.563 | 2.565 | 2.570 | 2.579 | 2.584 | 2.593 | 2.598 | 2.600 | 2.601 | 2.614 | 1942 | 2.614 |
| 1943 | 2.627 | 2.628 | 2.634 | 2.647 | 2.659 | 2.672 | 2.677 | 2.682 | 2.684 | 2.681 | 2.675 | 2.688 | 1943 | 2.688 |
| 1944 | 2.693 | 2.703 | 2.716 | 2.725 | 2.726 | 2.732 | 2.741 | 2.750 | 2.755 | 2.761 | 2.774 | 2.815 | 1944 | 2.815 |
| 1945 | 2.837 | 2.850 | 2.855 | 2.860 | 2.857 | 2.866 | 2.863 | 2.864 | 2.873 | 2.882 | 2.892 | 2.930 | 1945 | 2.930 |
| 1946 | 2.968 | 2.978 | 2.988 | 2.975 | 2.981 | 2.986 | 2.983 | 2.956 | 2.949 | 2.955 | 2.947 | 2.980 | 1946 | 2.980 |
| 1947 | 2.982 | 2.983 | 3.003 | 3.009 | 3.015 | 3.017 | 3.023 | 3.001 | 2.962 | 2.933 | 2.904 | 2.911 | 1947 | 2.911 |
| 1948 | 2.918 | 2.929 | 2.963 | 2.974 | 2.977 | 2.952 | 2.936 | 2.953 | 2.960 | 2.967 | 2.992 | 3.031 | 1948 | 3.031 |
| 1949 | 3.043 | 3.054 | 3.056 | 3.063 | 3.075 | 3.101 | 3.132 | 3.143 | 3.150 | 3.171 | 3.178 | 3.132 | 1949 | 3.132 |
| 1950 | 3.143 | 3.145 | 3.152 | 3.150 | 3.147 | 3.154 | 3.176 | 3.188 | 3.176 | 3.173 | 3.190 | 3.198 | 1950 | 3.198 |
| 1951 | 3.204 | 3.190 | 3.114 | 3.111 | 3.107 | 3.078 | 3.141 | 3.177 | 3.159 | 3.113 | 3.094 | 3.112 | 1951 | 3.112 |
| 1952 | 3.174 | 3.147 | 3.171 | 3.169 | 3.179 | 3.184 | 3.189 | 3.209 | 3.204 | 3.216 | 3.251 | 3.221 | 1952 | 3.221 |
| 1953 | 3.196 | 3.183 | 3.172 | 3.094 | 3.084 | 3.118 | 3.173 | 3.146 | 3.226 | 3.299 | 3.275 | 3.331 | 1953 | 3.331 |
| 1954 | 3.373 | 3.439 | 3.453 | 3.441 | 3.427 | 3.448 | 3.462 | 3.468 | 3.482 | 3.496 | 3.505 | 3.511 | 1954 | 3.511 |
| 1955 | 3.477 | 3.455 | 3.486 | 3.486 | 3.480 | 3.490 | 3.476 | 3.462 | 3.489 | 3.516 | 3.505 | 3.527 | 1955 | 3.527 |

## Appendix B-4

Long-term Corporate Bonds: Total Return Index
From 1926 to 2016

| Year | Jan | Feb | Mar | Apr | May | Jun | Jul | Aug | Sep | Oct | Nov | Dec | Yr End | Index |
|------|-----|-----|-----|-----|-----|-----|-----|-----|-----|-----|-----|-----|--------|-------|
| 1956 | 3.564 | 3.573 | 3.521 | 3.481 | 3.499 | 3.493 | 3.460 | 3.388 | 3.392 | 3.357 | 3.314 | 3.287 | 1956 | 3.287 |
| 1957 | 3.352 | 3.383 | 3.400 | 3.377 | 3.352 | 3.244 | 3.209 | 3.206 | 3.236 | 3.244 | 3.344 | 3.573 | 1957 | 3.573 |
| 1958 | 3.609 | 3.606 | 3.589 | 3.648 | 3.659 | 3.645 | 3.590 | 3.475 | 3.441 | 3.478 | 3.515 | 3.494 | 1958 | 3.494 |
| 1959 | 3.484 | 3.528 | 3.499 | 3.439 | 3.400 | 3.415 | 3.445 | 3.422 | 3.392 | 3.447 | 3.494 | 3.460 | 1959 | 3.460 |
| 1960 | 3.498 | 3.542 | 3.610 | 3.602 | 3.594 | 3.645 | 3.739 | 3.783 | 3.759 | 3.762 | 3.735 | 3.774 | 1960 | 3.774 |
| 1961 | 3.830 | 3.911 | 3.899 | 3.854 | 3.873 | 3.842 | 3.857 | 3.850 | 3.906 | 3.955 | 3.966 | 3.956 | 1961 | 3.956 |
| 1962 | 3.988 | 4.008 | 4.069 | 4.127 | 4.127 | 4.116 | 4.110 | 4.169 | 4.206 | 4.234 | 4.261 | 4.270 | 1962 | 4.270 |
| 1963 | 4.296 | 4.305 | 4.317 | 4.295 | 4.315 | 4.334 | 4.346 | 4.361 | 4.351 | 4.372 | 4.379 | 4.364 | 1963 | 4.364 |
| 1964 | 4.402 | 4.426 | 4.398 | 4.416 | 4.441 | 4.463 | 4.486 | 4.502 | 4.512 | 4.534 | 4.533 | 4.572 | 1964 | 4.572 |
| 1965 | 4.609 | 4.614 | 4.619 | 4.629 | 4.625 | 4.627 | 4.635 | 4.633 | 4.626 | 4.647 | 4.620 | 4.552 | 1965 | 4.552 |
| 1966 | 4.562 | 4.510 | 4.483 | 4.489 | 4.478 | 4.491 | 4.447 | 4.332 | 4.366 | 4.480 | 4.471 | 4.560 | 1966 | 4.560 |
| 1967 | 4.766 | 4.670 | 4.724 | 4.691 | 4.572 | 4.470 | 4.488 | 4.485 | 4.527 | 4.400 | 4.280 | 4.335 | 1967 | 4.335 |
| 1968 | 4.491 | 4.508 | 4.419 | 4.440 | 4.454 | 4.509 | 4.662 | 4.758 | 4.733 | 4.658 | 4.552 | 4.446 | 1968 | 4.446 |
| 1969 | 4.508 | 4.436 | 4.347 | 4.493 | 4.391 | 4.406 | 4.408 | 4.400 | 4.292 | 4.347 | 4.142 | 4.086 | 1969 | 4.086 |
| 1970 | 4.144 | 4.310 | 4.291 | 4.184 | 4.115 | 4.116 | 4.345 | 4.388 | 4.449 | 4.406 | 4.664 | 4.837 | 1970 | 4.837 |
| 1971 | 5.095 | 4.908 | 5.035 | 4.916 | 4.837 | 4.889 | 4.876 | 5.146 | 5.094 | 5.238 | 5.253 | 5.370 | 1971 | 5.370 |
| 1972 | 5.352 | 5.409 | 5.422 | 5.441 | 5.530 | 5.493 | 5.509 | 5.549 | 5.566 | 5.622 | 5.762 | 5.760 | 1972 | 5.760 |
| 1973 | 5.729 | 5.742 | 5.768 | 5.803 | 5.780 | 5.748 | 5.474 | 5.669 | 5.871 | 5.832 | 5.878 | 5.825 | 1973 | 5.825 |
| 1974 | 5.795 | 5.800 | 5.622 | 5.430 | 5.487 | 5.331 | 5.218 | 5.078 | 5.167 | 5.624 | 5.690 | 5.647 | 1974 | 5.647 |
| 1975 | 5.984 | 6.066 | 5.916 | 5.885 | 5.947 | 6.128 | 6.110 | 6.003 | 5.927 | 6.255 | 6.200 | 6.474 | 1975 | 6.474 |
| 1976 | 6.596 | 6.636 | 6.747 | 6.737 | 6.667 | 6.767 | 6.868 | 7.027 | 7.144 | 7.194 | 7.424 | 7.681 | 1976 | 7.681 |
| 1977 | 7.448 | 7.434 | 7.503 | 7.579 | 7.659 | 7.793 | 7.789 | 7.895 | 7.878 | 7.848 | 7.895 | 7.813 | 1977 | 7.813 |
| 1978 | 7.743 | 7.783 | 7.815 | 7.797 | 7.713 | 7.731 | 7.809 | 8.010 | 7.971 | 7.808 | 7.912 | 7.807 | 1978 | 7.807 |
| 1979 | 7.951 | 7.849 | 7.932 | 7.892 | 8.072 | 8.289 | 8.263 | 8.269 | 8.121 | 7.398 | 7.563 | 7.481 | 1979 | 7.481 |
| 1980 | 6.998 | 6.533 | 6.492 | 7.386 | 7.799 | 8.065 | 7.719 | 7.376 | 7.201 | 7.086 | 7.098 | 7.274 | 1980 | 7.274 |
| 1981 | 7.180 | 6.987 | 7.204 | 6.650 | 7.046 | 7.062 | 6.799 | 6.565 | 6.434 | 6.769 | 7.627 | 7.185 | 1981 | 7.185 |
| 1982 | 7.092 | 7.313 | 7.537 | 7.792 | 7.983 | 7.609 | 8.020 | 8.691 | 9.233 | 9.933 | 10.133 | 10.242 | 1982 | 10.242 |
| 1983 | 10.146 | 10.580 | 10.657 | 11.241 | 10.876 | 10.826 | 10.334 | 10.386 | 10.794 | 10.767 | 10.920 | 10.883 | 1983 | 10.883 |
| 1984 | 11.177 | 10.985 | 10.727 | 10.649 | 10.134 | 10.336 | 10.942 | 11.278 | 11.632 | 12.297 | 12.558 | 12.718 | 1984 | 12.718 |
| 1985 | 13.132 | 12.642 | 12.868 | 13.249 | 14.336 | 14.455 | 14.280 | 14.651 | 14.755 | 15.240 | 15.804 | 16.546 | 1985 | 16.546 |

## Appendix B-4

Long-term Corporate Bonds: Total Return Index
From 1926 to 2016

| Year | Jan | Feb | Mar | Apr | May | Jun | Jul | Aug | Sep | Oct | Nov | Dec | Yr End | Index |
|------|-----|-----|-----|-----|-----|-----|-----|-----|-----|-----|-----|-----|--------|-------|
| 1986 | 16.620 | 17.870 | 18.327 | 18.357 | 18.056 | 18.449 | 18.506 | 19.015 | 18.799 | 19.154 | 19.600 | 19.829 | 1986 | 19.829 |
| 1987 | 20.258 | 20.375 | 20.198 | 19.184 | 19.084 | 19.380 | 19.149 | 19.006 | 18.204 | 19.127 | 19.366 | 19.776 | 1987 | 19.776 |
| 1988 | 20.799 | 21.086 | 20.689 | 20.381 | 20.265 | 21.033 | 20.800 | 20.912 | 21.594 | 22.183 | 21.808 | 21.893 | 1988 | 21.893 |
| 1989 | 22.335 | 22.047 | 22.188 | 22.661 | 23.520 | 24.449 | 24.884 | 24.479 | 24.576 | 25.255 | 25.432 | 25.447 | 1989 | 25.447 |
| 1990 | 24.961 | 24.931 | 24.903 | 24.428 | 25.368 | 25.916 | 26.181 | 25.416 | 25.647 | 25.986 | 26.726 | 27.173 | 1990 | 27.173 |
| 1991 | 27.580 | 27.914 | 28.216 | 28.605 | 28.717 | 28.665 | 29.144 | 29.945 | 30.757 | 30.889 | 31.216 | 32.577 | 1991 | 32.577 |
| 1992 | 32.014 | 32.321 | 32.085 | 32.136 | 32.953 | 33.467 | 34.497 | 34.808 | 35.153 | 34.604 | 34.843 | 35.637 | 1992 | 35.637 |
| 1993 | 36.528 | 37.463 | 37.557 | 37.752 | 37.828 | 38.936 | 39.326 | 40.454 | 40.628 | 40.835 | 40.068 | 40.336 | 1993 | 40.336 |
| 1994 | 41.151 | 39.974 | 38.443 | 38.070 | 37.834 | 37.528 | 38.687 | 38.567 | 37.545 | 37.358 | 37.425 | 38.012 | 1994 | 38.012 |
| 1995 | 38.985 | 40.112 | 40.493 | 41.202 | 43.802 | 44.148 | 43.702 | 44.637 | 45.320 | 46.158 | 47.275 | 48.353 | 1995 | 48.353 |
| 1996 | 48.421 | 46.615 | 46.009 | 45.273 | 45.295 | 46.074 | 46.121 | 45.798 | 46.984 | 48.680 | 49.960 | 49.031 | 1996 | 49.031 |
| 1997 | 48.894 | 49.031 | 47.947 | 48.829 | 49.454 | 50.379 | 53.039 | 51.766 | 52.936 | 53.947 | 54.492 | 55.380 | 1997 | 55.380 |
| 1998 | 56.139 | 56.100 | 56.313 | 56.611 | 57.557 | 58.219 | 57.893 | 58.408 | 60.820 | 59.664 | 61.275 | 61.339 | 1998 | 61.339 |
| 1999 | 62.091 | 59.603 | 59.617 | 59.473 | 58.427 | 57.493 | 56.843 | 56.693 | 57.221 | 57.492 | 57.356 | 56.772 | 1999 | 56.772 |
| 2000 | 56.652 | 57.174 | 58.142 | 57.476 | 56.552 | 58.396 | 59.442 | 60.245 | 60.525 | 60.797 | 62.394 | 64.077 | 2000 | 64.077 |
| 2001 | 66.377 | 67.222 | 67.026 | 66.166 | 67.041 | 67.412 | 69.844 | 70.937 | 69.858 | 72.913 | 71.542 | 70.900 | 2001 | 70.900 |
| 2002 | 72.139 | 73.080 | 70.925 | 72.720 | 73.542 | 74.079 | 74.772 | 78.152 | 80.729 | 78.794 | 79.605 | 82.480 | 2002 | 82.480 |
| 2003 | 82.651 | 84.830 | 84.152 | 86.083 | 90.135 | 88.845 | 81.016 | 82.788 | 86.954 | 85.192 | 85.634 | 86.824 | 2003 | 86.824 |
| 2004 | 88.445 | 90.023 | 91.081 | 86.215 | 85.600 | 86.400 | 87.993 | 91.468 | 92.391 | 93.905 | 92.028 | 94.396 | 2004 | 94.396 |
| 2005 | 97.007 | 95.924 | 94.730 | 97.824 | 100.711 | 102.132 | 99.640 | 101.959 | 98.794 | 96.778 | 97.734 | 99.937 | 2005 | 99.937 |
| 2006 | 99.012 | 100.277 | 96.223 | 94.068 | 93.877 | 94.242 | 96.478 | 99.958 | 101.791 | 103.085 | 105.625 | 103.178 | 2006 | 103.178 |
| 2007 | 102.652 | 105.602 | 103.167 | 104.616 | 102.756 | 101.231 | 100.905 | 102.437 | 103.825 | 104.735 | 105.559 | 105.858 | 2007 | 105.858 |
| 2008 | 106.037 | 105.284 | 104.664 | 105.617 | 102.688 | 102.064 | 100.949 | 102.173 | 93.351 | 89.151 | 99.616 | 115.154 | 2008 | 115.154 |
| 2009 | 104.231 | 101.025 | 100.847 | 100.543 | 105.464 | 109.157 | 115.322 | 118.032 | 121.259 | 121.450 | 121.987 | 118.628 | 2009 | 118.628 |
| 2010 | 119.762 | 120.226 | 120.768 | 125.085 | 124.446 | 130.911 | 133.133 | 139.433 | 137.426 | 134.640 | 133.869 | 133.384 | 2010 | 133.384 |
| 2011 | 130.742 | 132.801 | 131.846 | 134.997 | 138.468 | 135.566 | 141.976 | 145.378 | 153.736 | 155.178 | 149.657 | 157.324 | 2011 | 157.324 |
| 2012 | 160.381 | 161.290 | 156.402 | 160.328 | 165.848 | 166.912 | 177.119 | 175.479 | 173.267 | 176.836 | 175.211 | 174.120 | 2012 | 174.120 |
| 2013 | 168.667 | 170.233 | 169.933 | 175.865 | 166.437 | 160.269 | 160.772 | 159.582 | 159.806 | 163.171 | 161.770 | 161.802 | 2013 | 161.802 |
| 2014 | 167.162 | 169.977 | 171.035 | 173.771 | 177.034 | 177.389 | 177.820 | 184.154 | 179.172 | 183.199 | 186.359 | 189.762 | 2014 | 189.762 |
| 2015 | 201.120 | 194.678 | 195.807 | 191.443 | 187.541 | 181.545 | 185.882 | 184.631 | 187.084 | 187.455 | 187.821 | 187.822 | 2015 | 187.822 |
| 2016 | 189.073 | 193.454 | 201.640 | 204.581 | 204.915 | 212.640 | 217.848 | 218.207 | 215.605 | 209.938 | 199.235 | 200.404 | 2016 | 200.404 |

# Appendix B-5

Long-term Government Bonds: Total Return Index
From 1926 to 2016

| Year | Jan | Feb | Mar | Apr | May | Jun | Jul | Aug | Sep | Oct | Nov | Dec | Yr End | Index |
|------|-----|-----|-----|-----|-----|-----|-----|-----|-----|-----|-----|-----|--------|-------|
| 1925 | | | | | | | | | | | | 1.000 | 1925 | 1.000 |
| 1926 | 1.014 | 1.020 | 1.024 | 1.032 | 1.034 | 1.038 | 1.038 | 1.038 | 1.042 | 1.053 | 1.069 | 1.078 | 1926 | 1.078 |
| 1927 | 1.086 | 1.095 | 1.123 | 1.122 | 1.135 | 1.127 | 1.132 | 1.141 | 1.143 | 1.154 | 1.166 | 1.174 | 1927 | 1.174 |
| 1928 | 1.170 | 1.177 | 1.182 | 1.182 | 1.173 | 1.178 | 1.152 | 1.161 | 1.156 | 1.174 | 1.175 | 1.175 | 1928 | 1.175 |
| 1929 | 1.165 | 1.146 | 1.130 | 1.161 | 1.142 | 1.155 | 1.155 | 1.151 | 1.154 | 1.198 | 1.226 | 1.215 | 1929 | 1.215 |
| 1930 | 1.208 | 1.224 | 1.234 | 1.232 | 1.249 | 1.256 | 1.260 | 1.262 | 1.271 | 1.276 | 1.281 | 1.272 | 1930 | 1.272 |
| 1931 | 1.257 | 1.267 | 1.280 | 1.291 | 1.310 | 1.311 | 1.305 | 1.307 | 1.270 | 1.228 | 1.231 | 1.204 | 1931 | 1.204 |
| 1932 | 1.208 | 1.258 | 1.256 | 1.332 | 1.307 | 1.315 | 1.379 | 1.379 | 1.387 | 1.385 | 1.389 | 1.407 | 1932 | 1.407 |
| 1933 | 1.428 | 1.391 | 1.405 | 1.400 | 1.443 | 1.450 | 1.447 | 1.454 | 1.457 | 1.444 | 1.422 | 1.406 | 1933 | 1.406 |
| 1934 | 1.442 | 1.454 | 1.483 | 1.501 | 1.521 | 1.531 | 1.537 | 1.519 | 1.497 | 1.524 | 1.530 | 1.547 | 1934 | 1.547 |
| 1935 | 1.575 | 1.590 | 1.596 | 1.609 | 1.600 | 1.615 | 1.622 | 1.600 | 1.602 | 1.611 | 1.613 | 1.624 | 1935 | 1.624 |
| 1936 | 1.633 | 1.647 | 1.664 | 1.670 | 1.677 | 1.680 | 1.690 | 1.709 | 1.704 | 1.705 | 1.740 | 1.746 | 1936 | 1.746 |
| 1937 | 1.744 | 1.759 | 1.687 | 1.693 | 1.702 | 1.699 | 1.723 | 1.705 | 1.712 | 1.720 | 1.736 | 1.750 | 1937 | 1.750 |
| 1938 | 1.760 | 1.770 | 1.763 | 1.800 | 1.808 | 1.809 | 1.817 | 1.817 | 1.821 | 1.837 | 1.833 | 1.847 | 1938 | 1.847 |
| 1939 | 1.858 | 1.873 | 1.896 | 1.919 | 1.951 | 1.946 | 1.968 | 1.929 | 1.824 | 1.898 | 1.929 | 1.957 | 1939 | 1.957 |
| 1940 | 1.954 | 1.959 | 1.994 | 1.987 | 1.927 | 1.977 | 1.987 | 1.993 | 2.015 | 2.021 | 2.062 | 2.076 | 1940 | 2.076 |
| 1941 | 2.034 | 2.039 | 2.058 | 2.085 | 2.090 | 2.104 | 2.109 | 2.113 | 2.110 | 2.140 | 2.133 | 2.096 | 1941 | 2.096 |
| 1942 | 2.110 | 2.112 | 2.132 | 2.126 | 2.142 | 2.142 | 2.146 | 2.154 | 2.155 | 2.160 | 2.152 | 2.163 | 1942 | 2.163 |
| 1943 | 2.170 | 2.169 | 2.171 | 2.181 | 2.192 | 2.196 | 2.196 | 2.201 | 2.203 | 2.204 | 2.204 | 2.208 | 1943 | 2.208 |
| 1944 | 2.213 | 2.220 | 2.224 | 2.227 | 2.234 | 2.235 | 2.243 | 2.249 | 2.253 | 2.255 | 2.261 | 2.270 | 1944 | 2.270 |
| 1945 | 2.299 | 2.317 | 2.321 | 2.358 | 2.372 | 2.412 | 2.391 | 2.397 | 2.410 | 2.435 | 2.466 | 2.514 | 1945 | 2.514 |
| 1946 | 2.520 | 2.528 | 2.531 | 2.497 | 2.493 | 2.511 | 2.501 | 2.473 | 2.471 | 2.489 | 2.475 | 2.511 | 1946 | 2.511 |
| 1947 | 2.510 | 2.515 | 2.520 | 2.511 | 2.519 | 2.522 | 2.537 | 2.558 | 2.547 | 2.537 | 2.493 | 2.445 | 1947 | 2.445 |
| 1948 | 2.450 | 2.462 | 2.470 | 2.481 | 2.516 | 2.495 | 2.490 | 2.490 | 2.494 | 2.496 | 2.514 | 2.529 | 1948 | 2.529 |
| 1949 | 2.549 | 2.562 | 2.581 | 2.584 | 2.589 | 2.632 | 2.641 | 2.670 | 2.667 | 2.672 | 2.678 | 2.692 | 1949 | 2.692 |
| 1950 | 2.675 | 2.681 | 2.683 | 2.691 | 2.700 | 2.693 | 2.708 | 2.712 | 2.692 | 2.679 | 2.689 | 2.693 | 1950 | 2.693 |
| 1951 | 2.709 | 2.689 | 2.646 | 2.630 | 2.612 | 2.596 | 2.632 | 2.657 | 2.636 | 2.639 | 2.603 | 2.587 | 1951 | 2.587 |
| 1952 | 2.595 | 2.598 | 2.627 | 2.672 | 2.663 | 2.664 | 2.658 | 2.640 | 2.606 | 2.644 | 2.640 | 2.617 | 1952 | 2.617 |
| 1953 | 2.620 | 2.598 | 2.575 | 2.548 | 2.510 | 2.566 | 2.576 | 2.574 | 2.651 | 2.671 | 2.658 | 2.713 | 1953 | 2.713 |
| 1954 | 2.737 | 2.802 | 2.819 | 2.848 | 2.823 | 2.869 | 2.908 | 2.897 | 2.894 | 2.896 | 2.889 | 2.907 | 1954 | 2.907 |
| 1955 | 2.837 | 2.815 | 2.840 | 2.840 | 2.861 | 2.839 | 2.810 | 2.811 | 2.832 | 2.872 | 2.859 | 2.870 | 1955 | 2.870 |

# Appendix B-5

Long-term Government Bonds: Total Return Index
From 1926 to 2016

| Year | Jan | Feb | Mar | Apr | May | Jun | Jul | Aug | Sep | Oct | Nov | Dec | Yr End | Index |
|------|-----|-----|-----|-----|-----|-----|-----|-----|-----|-----|-----|-----|--------|-------|
| 1956 | 2.894 | 2.893 | 2.850 | 2.818 | 2.881 | 2.889 | 2.829 | 2.776 | 2.790 | 2.775 | 2.759 | 2.710 | 1956 | 2.710 |
| 1957 | 2.803 | 2.810 | 2.804 | 2.741 | 2.735 | 2.686 | 2.675 | 2.675 | 2.696 | 2.682 | 2.825 | 2.912 | 1957 | 2.912 |
| 1958 | 2.887 | 2.916 | 2.946 | 3.001 | 3.001 | 2.953 | 2.871 | 2.746 | 2.714 | 2.751 | 2.785 | 2.734 | 1958 | 2.734 |
| 1959 | 2.712 | 2.744 | 2.749 | 2.717 | 2.715 | 2.718 | 2.734 | 2.723 | 2.708 | 2.748 | 2.716 | 2.673 | 1959 | 2.673 |
| 1960 | 2.702 | 2.757 | 2.835 | 2.787 | 2.829 | 2.878 | 2.984 | 2.964 | 2.986 | 2.978 | 2.958 | 3.041 | 1960 | 3.041 |
| 1961 | 3.008 | 3.068 | 3.057 | 3.092 | 3.078 | 3.055 | 3.065 | 3.054 | 3.093 | 3.115 | 3.109 | 3.070 | 1961 | 3.070 |
| 1962 | 3.066 | 3.098 | 3.176 | 3.202 | 3.217 | 3.192 | 3.158 | 3.217 | 3.236 | 3.263 | 3.270 | 3.282 | 1962 | 3.282 |
| 1963 | 3.281 | 3.284 | 3.287 | 3.283 | 3.290 | 3.297 | 3.307 | 3.314 | 3.315 | 3.307 | 3.324 | 3.322 | 1963 | 3.322 |
| 1964 | 3.317 | 3.313 | 3.326 | 3.341 | 3.358 | 3.381 | 3.384 | 3.390 | 3.407 | 3.422 | 3.428 | 3.438 | 1964 | 3.438 |
| 1965 | 3.452 | 3.457 | 3.475 | 3.488 | 3.494 | 3.511 | 3.518 | 3.514 | 3.502 | 3.511 | 3.490 | 3.462 | 1965 | 3.462 |
| 1966 | 3.427 | 3.341 | 3.440 | 3.418 | 3.398 | 3.393 | 3.380 | 3.310 | 3.420 | 3.498 | 3.447 | 3.589 | 1966 | 3.589 |
| 1967 | 3.644 | 3.564 | 3.634 | 3.528 | 3.515 | 3.405 | 3.428 | 3.399 | 3.398 | 3.262 | 3.198 | 3.259 | 1967 | 3.259 |
| 1968 | 3.366 | 3.355 | 3.284 | 3.359 | 3.373 | 3.451 | 3.550 | 3.549 | 3.513 | 3.466 | 3.373 | 3.251 | 1968 | 3.251 |
| 1969 | 3.184 | 3.197 | 3.201 | 3.337 | 3.174 | 3.242 | 3.267 | 3.245 | 3.073 | 3.185 | 3.107 | 3.086 | 1969 | 3.086 |
| 1970 | 3.079 | 3.260 | 3.238 | 3.104 | 2.959 | 3.103 | 3.202 | 3.196 | 3.269 | 3.233 | 3.489 | 3.460 | 1970 | 3.460 |
| 1971 | 3.634 | 3.575 | 3.763 | 3.657 | 3.655 | 3.597 | 3.607 | 3.777 | 3.854 | 3.918 | 3.900 | 3.917 | 1971 | 3.917 |
| 1972 | 3.892 | 3.927 | 3.895 | 3.905 | 4.011 | 3.985 | 4.071 | 4.082 | 4.049 | 4.143 | 4.237 | 4.140 | 1972 | 4.140 |
| 1973 | 4.007 | 4.013 | 4.046 | 4.064 | 4.021 | 4.013 | 3.839 | 3.989 | 4.116 | 4.205 | 4.128 | 4.094 | 1973 | 4.094 |
| 1974 | 4.060 | 4.050 | 3.932 | 3.833 | 3.880 | 3.897 | 3.886 | 3.796 | 3.890 | 4.080 | 4.200 | 4.272 | 1974 | 4.272 |
| 1975 | 4.368 | 4.426 | 4.308 | 4.229 | 4.319 | 4.445 | 4.407 | 4.377 | 4.334 | 4.539 | 4.490 | 4.665 | 1975 | 4.665 |
| 1976 | 4.707 | 4.736 | 4.815 | 4.824 | 4.747 | 4.846 | 4.884 | 4.987 | 5.059 | 5.102 | 5.274 | 5.447 | 1976 | 5.447 |
| 1977 | 5.236 | 5.210 | 5.257 | 5.295 | 5.361 | 5.449 | 5.411 | 5.518 | 5.502 | 5.451 | 5.502 | 5.410 | 1977 | 5.410 |
| 1978 | 5.366 | 5.368 | 5.357 | 5.355 | 5.323 | 5.290 | 5.366 | 5.483 | 5.425 | 5.316 | 5.416 | 5.346 | 1978 | 5.346 |
| 1979 | 5.448 | 5.375 | 5.444 | 5.383 | 5.524 | 5.696 | 5.647 | 5.627 | 5.559 | 5.091 | 5.250 | 5.280 | 1979 | 5.280 |
| 1980 | 4.889 | 4.660 | 4.514 | 5.201 | 5.419 | 5.613 | 5.346 | 5.115 | 4.982 | 4.851 | 4.899 | 5.071 | 1980 | 5.071 |
| 1981 | 5.013 | 4.795 | 4.979 | 4.721 | 5.015 | 4.925 | 4.751 | 4.568 | 4.502 | 4.875 | 5.562 | 5.166 | 1981 | 5.166 |
| 1982 | 5.189 | 5.284 | 5.406 | 5.608 | 5.627 | 5.501 | 5.777 | 6.228 | 6.613 | 7.033 | 7.031 | 7.251 | 1982 | 7.251 |
| 1983 | 7.027 | 7.372 | 7.303 | 7.558 | 7.267 | 7.295 | 6.940 | 6.954 | 7.305 | 7.209 | 7.341 | 7.298 | 1983 | 7.298 |
| 1984 | 7.476 | 7.343 | 7.228 | 7.152 | 6.782 | 6.884 | 7.361 | 7.557 | 7.816 | 8.254 | 8.352 | 8.427 | 1984 | 8.427 |
| 1985 | 8.734 | 8.304 | 8.558 | 8.766 | 9.551 | 9.686 | 9.512 | 9.759 | 9.738 | 10.067 | 10.471 | 11.037 | 1985 | 11.037 |

## Appendix B-5

Long-term Government Bonds: Total Return Index
From 1926 to 2016

| Year | Jan | Feb | Mar | Apr | May | Jun | Jul | Aug | Sep | Oct | Nov | Dec | Yr End | Index |
|---|---|---|---|---|---|---|---|---|---|---|---|---|---|---|
| 1986 | 11.009 | 12.270 | 13.215 | 13.109 | 12.447 | 13.210 | 13.068 | 13.720 | 13.034 | 13.410 | 13.769 | 13.745 | 1986 | 13.745 |
| 1987 | 13.966 | 14.247 | 13.930 | 13.271 | 13.132 | 13.260 | 13.024 | 12.810 | 12.337 | 13.106 | 13.154 | 13.372 | 1987 | 13.372 |
| 1988 | 14.263 | 14.337 | 13.897 | 13.675 | 13.536 | 14.035 | 13.797 | 13.876 | 14.355 | 14.796 | 14.506 | 14.665 | 1988 | 14.665 |
| 1989 | 14.963 | 14.695 | 14.875 | 15.111 | 15.717 | 16.582 | 16.977 | 16.537 | 16.569 | 17.198 | 17.332 | 17.322 | 1989 | 17.322 |
| 1990 | 16.728 | 16.686 | 16.613 | 16.278 | 16.954 | 17.344 | 17.530 | 16.796 | 16.992 | 17.358 | 18.056 | 18.392 | 1990 | 18.392 |
| 1991 | 18.632 | 18.689 | 18.760 | 19.023 | 19.024 | 18.904 | 19.202 | 19.855 | 20.458 | 20.569 | 20.738 | 21.942 | 1991 | 21.942 |
| 1992 | 21.231 | 21.339 | 21.140 | 21.173 | 21.687 | 22.121 | 23.001 | 23.155 | 23.584 | 23.117 | 23.140 | 23.709 | 1992 | 23.709 |
| 1993 | 24.374 | 25.237 | 25.290 | 25.472 | 25.591 | 26.739 | 27.251 | 28.433 | 28.448 | 28.722 | 27.979 | 28.034 | 1993 | 28.034 |
| 1994 | 28.755 | 27.462 | 26.378 | 25.981 | 25.767 | 25.508 | 26.435 | 26.209 | 25.342 | 25.280 | 25.447 | 25.856 | 1994 | 25.856 |
| 1995 | 26.561 | 27.322 | 27.572 | 28.039 | 30.255 | 30.675 | 30.161 | 30.873 | 31.413 | 32.337 | 33.143 | 34.044 | 1995 | 34.044 |
| 1996 | 34.007 | 32.366 | 31.687 | 31.163 | 30.994 | 31.622 | 31.678 | 31.237 | 32.142 | 33.440 | 34.612 | 33.727 | 1996 | 33.727 |
| 1997 | 33.459 | 33.476 | 32.633 | 33.465 | 33.783 | 34.448 | 36.603 | 35.441 | 36.560 | 37.807 | 38.366 | 39.074 | 1997 | 39.074 |
| 1998 | 39.856 | 39.570 | 39.668 | 39.771 | 40.497 | 41.421 | 41.256 | 43.173 | 44.876 | 43.896 | 44.320 | 44.178 | 1998 | 44.178 |
| 1999 | 44.713 | 42.390 | 42.355 | 42.444 | 41.660 | 41.337 | 41.012 | 40.803 | 41.147 | 41.099 | 40.849 | 40.218 | 1999 | 40.218 |
| 2000 | 41.135 | 42.220 | 43.768 | 43.437 | 43.200 | 44.254 | 45.018 | 46.100 | 45.376 | 46.227 | 47.699 | 48.856 | 2000 | 48.856 |
| 2001 | 48.882 | 49.816 | 49.447 | 47.899 | 48.079 | 48.488 | 50.309 | 51.343 | 51.758 | 54.160 | 51.607 | 50.662 | 2001 | 50.662 |
| 2002 | 51.361 | 51.951 | 49.686 | 51.721 | 51.798 | 52.769 | 54.368 | 56.888 | 59.258 | 57.517 | 56.817 | 59.699 | 2002 | 59.699 |
| 2003 | 59.065 | 61.011 | 60.186 | 60.798 | 64.397 | 63.406 | 57.178 | 58.129 | 61.306 | 59.573 | 59.732 | 60.564 | 2003 | 60.564 |
| 2004 | 61.699 | 63.117 | 64.007 | 60.244 | 59.939 | 60.666 | 61.609 | 64.040 | 64.657 | 65.649 | 64.115 | 65.717 | 2004 | 65.717 |
| 2005 | 67.691 | 66.826 | 66.348 | 68.820 | 70.862 | 72.047 | 69.973 | 72.302 | 69.860 | 68.489 | 69.010 | 70.852 | 2005 | 70.852 |
| 2006 | 70.018 | 71.687 | 67.821 | 66.148 | 66.213 | 66.819 | 68.148 | 70.186 | 71.383 | 71.932 | 73.425 | 71.694 | 2006 | 71.694 |
| 2007 | 70.961 | 73.335 | 72.272 | 72.887 | 71.428 | 70.782 | 72.790 | 74.235 | 74.323 | 75.476 | 79.009 | 78.779 | 2007 | 78.779 |
| 2008 | 80.460 | 80.608 | 81.460 | 79.111 | 77.812 | 79.526 | 79.330 | 81.251 | 82.164 | 79.016 | 90.416 | 99.161 | 2008 | 99.161 |
| 2009 | 88.012 | 87.518 | 93.129 | 87.081 | 84.921 | 85.629 | 85.790 | 87.769 | 89.314 | 87.790 | 89.620 | 84.383 | 2009 | 84.383 |
| 2010 | 86.608 | 86.881 | 85.328 | 87.921 | 91.762 | 95.851 | 96.085 | 102.831 | 101.255 | 98.041 | 96.696 | 92.942 | 2010 | 92.942 |
| 2011 | 91.121 | 92.152 | 92.095 | 93.929 | 97.261 | 95.516 | 99.545 | 108.129 | 115.743 | 112.200 | 115.022 | 118.130 | 2011 | 118.130 |
| 2012 | 118.153 | 115.832 | 112.337 | 116.937 | 124.452 | 122.763 | 125.797 | 124.936 | 123.107 | 122.933 | 124.699 | 122.180 | 2012 | 122.180 |
| 2013 | 118.128 | 119.478 | 118.739 | 123.222 | 115.477 | 112.184 | 110.242 | 109.373 | 110.043 | 111.454 | 108.829 | 106.571 | 2013 | 106.571 |
| 2014 | 112.409 | 113.239 | 113.951 | 116.016 | 119.248 | 118.944 | 119.618 | 124.031 | 121.919 | 125.570 | 129.157 | 132.900 | 2014 | 132.900 |
| 2015 | 142.323 | 134.875 | 136.717 | 133.295 | 131.172 | 127.260 | 131.448 | 131.603 | 133.898 | 133.183 | 132.321 | 132.032 | 2015 | 132.032 |
| 2016 | 138.310 | 142.383 | 142.335 | 141.583 | 142.751 | 151.175 | 152.393 | 150.253 | 148.383 | 143.722 | 135.120 | 134.349 | 2016 | 134.349 |

## Appendix B-6

Long-term Government Bonds: Capital Appreciation Index
From 1926 to 2016

| Year | Jan | Feb | Mar | Apr | May | Jun | Jul | Aug | Sep | Oct | Nov | Dec | Yr End | Index |
|---|---|---|---|---|---|---|---|---|---|---|---|---|---|---|
| 1925 | | | | | | | | | | | | 1.000 | 1925 | 1.000 |
| 1926 | 1.011 | 1.014 | 1.015 | 1.020 | 1.018 | 1.019 | 1.016 | 1.013 | 1.014 | 1.021 | 1.034 | 1.039 | 1926 | 1.039 |
| 1927 | 1.044 | 1.050 | 1.074 | 1.070 | 1.079 | 1.069 | 1.071 | 1.076 | 1.075 | 1.083 | 1.090 | 1.095 | 1927 | 1.095 |
| 1928 | 1.088 | 1.092 | 1.094 | 1.091 | 1.080 | 1.081 | 1.055 | 1.060 | 1.053 | 1.066 | 1.064 | 1.061 | 1928 | 1.061 |
| 1929 | 1.048 | 1.029 | 1.011 | 1.036 | 1.016 | 1.024 | 1.021 | 1.014 | 1.014 | 1.050 | 1.072 | 1.059 | 1929 | 1.059 |
| 1930 | 1.050 | 1.061 | 1.066 | 1.062 | 1.074 | 1.076 | 1.077 | 1.075 | 1.080 | 1.081 | 1.083 | 1.072 | 1930 | 1.072 |
| 1931 | 1.056 | 1.063 | 1.071 | 1.077 | 1.090 | 1.087 | 1.080 | 1.078 | 1.045 | 1.007 | 1.007 | 0.982 | 1931 | 0.982 |
| 1932 | 0.982 | 1.019 | 1.014 | 1.072 | 1.049 | 1.053 | 1.101 | 1.098 | 1.101 | 1.097 | 1.097 | 1.109 | 1932 | 1.109 |
| 1933 | 1.122 | 1.091 | 1.098 | 1.092 | 1.122 | 1.124 | 1.120 | 1.122 | 1.122 | 1.108 | 1.089 | 1.074 | 1933 | 1.074 |
| 1934 | 1.098 | 1.105 | 1.123 | 1.135 | 1.147 | 1.152 | 1.153 | 1.137 | 1.118 | 1.135 | 1.137 | 1.146 | 1934 | 1.146 |
| 1935 | 1.164 | 1.173 | 1.175 | 1.181 | 1.172 | 1.180 | 1.183 | 1.164 | 1.163 | 1.167 | 1.166 | 1.171 | 1935 | 1.171 |
| 1936 | 1.175 | 1.182 | 1.191 | 1.193 | 1.195 | 1.195 | 1.199 | 1.210 | 1.203 | 1.201 | 1.223 | 1.225 | 1936 | 1.225 |
| 1937 | 1.221 | 1.229 | 1.176 | 1.178 | 1.182 | 1.176 | 1.190 | 1.175 | 1.177 | 1.180 | 1.188 | 1.195 | 1937 | 1.195 |
| 1938 | 1.199 | 1.203 | 1.196 | 1.218 | 1.221 | 1.219 | 1.222 | 1.219 | 1.219 | 1.227 | 1.222 | 1.229 | 1938 | 1.229 |
| 1939 | 1.233 | 1.241 | 1.254 | 1.266 | 1.285 | 1.280 | 1.292 | 1.263 | 1.192 | 1.238 | 1.256 | 1.272 | 1939 | 1.272 |
| 1940 | 1.267 | 1.268 | 1.288 | 1.281 | 1.241 | 1.270 | 1.274 | 1.275 | 1.287 | 1.289 | 1.313 | 1.319 | 1940 | 1.319 |
| 1941 | 1.291 | 1.291 | 1.301 | 1.316 | 1.317 | 1.324 | 1.325 | 1.325 | 1.321 | 1.338 | 1.332 | 1.306 | 1941 | 1.306 |
| 1942 | 1.312 | 1.311 | 1.321 | 1.314 | 1.322 | 1.319 | 1.319 | 1.321 | 1.319 | 1.319 | 1.312 | 1.316 | 1942 | 1.316 |
| 1943 | 1.317 | 1.314 | 1.313 | 1.316 | 1.320 | 1.320 | 1.317 | 1.317 | 1.316 | 1.314 | 1.311 | 1.311 | 1943 | 1.311 |
| 1944 | 1.311 | 1.312 | 1.312 | 1.312 | 1.312 | 1.311 | 1.313 | 1.314 | 1.313 | 1.312 | 1.312 | 1.315 | 1944 | 1.315 |
| 1945 | 1.329 | 1.337 | 1.337 | 1.356 | 1.361 | 1.381 | 1.367 | 1.368 | 1.373 | 1.384 | 1.399 | 1.424 | 1945 | 1.424 |
| 1946 | 1.425 | 1.427 | 1.427 | 1.405 | 1.401 | 1.408 | 1.400 | 1.382 | 1.378 | 1.386 | 1.376 | 1.393 | 1946 | 1.393 |
| 1947 | 1.390 | 1.390 | 1.391 | 1.383 | 1.385 | 1.384 | 1.390 | 1.399 | 1.391 | 1.383 | 1.357 | 1.328 | 1947 | 1.328 |
| 1948 | 1.328 | 1.332 | 1.333 | 1.337 | 1.353 | 1.339 | 1.333 | 1.331 | 1.330 | 1.328 | 1.336 | 1.341 | 1948 | 1.341 |
| 1949 | 1.349 | 1.353 | 1.360 | 1.360 | 1.360 | 1.380 | 1.382 | 1.395 | 1.391 | 1.391 | 1.391 | 1.396 | 1949 | 1.396 |
| 1950 | 1.385 | 1.386 | 1.384 | 1.386 | 1.388 | 1.382 | 1.387 | 1.387 | 1.374 | 1.365 | 1.367 | 1.367 | 1950 | 1.367 |
| 1951 | 1.372 | 1.360 | 1.336 | 1.325 | 1.313 | 1.302 | 1.317 | 1.328 | 1.315 | 1.313 | 1.292 | 1.282 | 1951 | 1.282 |
| 1952 | 1.282 | 1.281 | 1.293 | 1.312 | 1.305 | 1.302 | 1.297 | 1.285 | 1.266 | 1.281 | 1.277 | 1.263 | 1952 | 1.263 |
| 1953 | 1.261 | 1.248 | 1.233 | 1.218 | 1.197 | 1.220 | 1.222 | 1.218 | 1.251 | 1.258 | 1.248 | 1.271 | 1953 | 1.271 |
| 1954 | 1.280 | 1.307 | 1.312 | 1.322 | 1.308 | 1.326 | 1.341 | 1.333 | 1.329 | 1.327 | 1.321 | 1.326 | 1954 | 1.326 |
| 1955 | 1.291 | 1.279 | 1.287 | 1.284 | 1.290 | 1.277 | 1.261 | 1.258 | 1.265 | 1.280 | 1.271 | 1.272 | 1955 | 1.272 |

## Appendix B-6

Long-term Government Bonds: Capital Appreciation Index
From 1926 to 2016

| Year | Jan | Feb | Mar | Apr | May | Jun | Jul | Aug | Sep | Oct | Nov | Dec | Yr End | Index |
|------|------|------|------|------|------|------|------|------|------|------|------|------|------|------|
| 1956 | 1.280 | 1.277 | 1.255 | 1.237 | 1.262 | 1.262 | 1.233 | 1.207 | 1.210 | 1.200 | 1.189 | 1.165 | 1956 | 1.165 |
| 1957 | 1.202 | 1.202 | 1.196 | 1.166 | 1.160 | 1.136 | 1.127 | 1.124 | 1.129 | 1.120 | 1.177 | 1.209 | 1957 | 1.209 |
| 1958 | 1.196 | 1.205 | 1.214 | 1.233 | 1.230 | 1.207 | 1.170 | 1.116 | 1.100 | 1.111 | 1.122 | 1.098 | 1958 | 1.098 |
| 1959 | 1.085 | 1.095 | 1.093 | 1.076 | 1.072 | 1.070 | 1.072 | 1.064 | 1.054 | 1.067 | 1.050 | 1.030 | 1959 | 1.030 |
| 1960 | 1.038 | 1.055 | 1.081 | 1.059 | 1.071 | 1.086 | 1.122 | 1.111 | 1.116 | 1.109 | 1.098 | 1.125 | 1960 | 1.125 |
| 1961 | 1.109 | 1.128 | 1.121 | 1.130 | 1.121 | 1.109 | 1.109 | 1.101 | 1.112 | 1.116 | 1.110 | 1.093 | 1961 | 1.093 |
| 1962 | 1.088 | 1.095 | 1.119 | 1.125 | 1.126 | 1.115 | 1.099 | 1.115 | 1.119 | 1.124 | 1.123 | 1.124 | 1962 | 1.124 |
| 1963 | 1.120 | 1.117 | 1.115 | 1.110 | 1.109 | 1.107 | 1.107 | 1.106 | 1.102 | 1.096 | 1.098 | 1.093 | 1963 | 1.093 |
| 1964 | 1.088 | 1.083 | 1.083 | 1.085 | 1.087 | 1.090 | 1.087 | 1.085 | 1.087 | 1.088 | 1.086 | 1.085 | 1964 | 1.085 |
| 1965 | 1.086 | 1.084 | 1.086 | 1.086 | 1.085 | 1.086 | 1.084 | 1.079 | 1.072 | 1.071 | 1.060 | 1.048 | 1965 | 1.048 |
| 1966 | 1.033 | 1.004 | 1.030 | 1.019 | 1.009 | 1.004 | 0.996 | 0.971 | 1.000 | 1.019 | 1.000 | 1.037 | 1966 | 1.037 |
| 1967 | 1.049 | 1.022 | 1.038 | 1.005 | 0.996 | 0.961 | 0.964 | 0.952 | 0.947 | 0.905 | 0.883 | 0.896 | 1967 | 0.896 |
| 1968 | 0.921 | 0.914 | 0.891 | 0.907 | 0.907 | 0.924 | 0.946 | 0.942 | 0.928 | 0.912 | 0.883 | 0.847 | 1968 | 0.847 |
| 1969 | 0.825 | 0.825 | 0.822 | 0.853 | 0.807 | 0.820 | 0.822 | 0.812 | 0.765 | 0.788 | 0.765 | 0.755 | 1969 | 0.755 |
| 1970 | 0.750 | 0.790 | 0.780 | 0.743 | 0.705 | 0.734 | 0.753 | 0.748 | 0.761 | 0.748 | 0.803 | 0.792 | 1970 | 0.792 |
| 1971 | 0.828 | 0.811 | 0.849 | 0.821 | 0.816 | 0.799 | 0.797 | 0.830 | 0.843 | 0.853 | 0.845 | 0.844 | 1971 | 0.844 |
| 1972 | 0.835 | 0.838 | 0.827 | 0.825 | 0.843 | 0.834 | 0.847 | 0.846 | 0.835 | 0.850 | 0.865 | 0.841 | 1972 | 0.841 |
| 1973 | 0.810 | 0.807 | 0.809 | 0.808 | 0.795 | 0.789 | 0.750 | 0.774 | 0.795 | 0.807 | 0.788 | 0.777 | 1973 | 0.777 |
| 1974 | 0.765 | 0.759 | 0.733 | 0.709 | 0.713 | 0.712 | 0.705 | 0.684 | 0.696 | 0.725 | 0.742 | 0.750 | 1974 | 0.750 |
| 1975 | 0.761 | 0.767 | 0.741 | 0.723 | 0.733 | 0.750 | 0.738 | 0.728 | 0.716 | 0.745 | 0.732 | 0.755 | 1975 | 0.755 |
| 1976 | 0.757 | 0.757 | 0.764 | 0.761 | 0.744 | 0.754 | 0.755 | 0.766 | 0.772 | 0.774 | 0.795 | 0.816 | 1976 | 0.816 |
| 1977 | 0.780 | 0.771 | 0.773 | 0.774 | 0.779 | 0.787 | 0.776 | 0.787 | 0.780 | 0.767 | 0.770 | 0.752 | 1977 | 0.752 |
| 1978 | 0.741 | 0.737 | 0.730 | 0.725 | 0.715 | 0.706 | 0.711 | 0.721 | 0.709 | 0.690 | 0.698 | 0.684 | 1978 | 0.684 |
| 1979 | 0.692 | 0.678 | 0.682 | 0.669 | 0.681 | 0.697 | 0.686 | 0.679 | 0.666 | 0.604 | 0.618 | 0.617 | 1979 | 0.617 |
| 1980 | 0.566 | 0.535 | 0.512 | 0.585 | 0.605 | 0.621 | 0.587 | 0.556 | 0.537 | 0.517 | 0.518 | 0.530 | 1980 | 0.530 |
| 1981 | 0.519 | 0.492 | 0.505 | 0.474 | 0.499 | 0.484 | 0.462 | 0.439 | 0.428 | 0.458 | 0.518 | 0.476 | 1981 | 0.476 |
| 1982 | 0.473 | 0.476 | 0.481 | 0.494 | 0.491 | 0.474 | 0.492 | 0.525 | 0.552 | 0.582 | 0.577 | 0.589 | 1982 | 0.589 |
| 1983 | 0.566 | 0.589 | 0.578 | 0.594 | 0.565 | 0.563 | 0.530 | 0.526 | 0.547 | 0.535 | 0.540 | 0.532 | 1983 | 0.532 |
| 1984 | 0.539 | 0.524 | 0.511 | 0.500 | 0.469 | 0.472 | 0.499 | 0.507 | 0.519 | 0.543 | 0.544 | 0.544 | 1984 | 0.544 |
| 1985 | 0.558 | 0.526 | 0.538 | 0.545 | 0.589 | 0.592 | 0.576 | 0.586 | 0.580 | 0.594 | 0.613 | 0.641 | 1985 | 0.641 |

# Appendix B-6

Long-term Government Bonds: Capital Appreciation Index
From 1926 to 2016

| Year | Jan | Feb | Mar | Apr | May | Jun | Jul | Aug | Sep | Oct | Nov | Dec | Yr End | Index |
|------|------|------|------|------|------|------|------|------|------|------|------|------|--------|-------|
| 1986 | 0.634 | 0.702 | 0.751 | 0.741 | 0.699 | 0.737 | 0.724 | 0.755 | 0.713 | 0.728 | 0.743 | 0.737 | 1986 | 0.737 |
| 1987 | 0.744 | 0.755 | 0.733 | 0.693 | 0.682 | 0.683 | 0.666 | 0.650 | 0.621 | 0.655 | 0.652 | 0.658 | 1987 | 0.658 |
| 1988 | 0.697 | 0.696 | 0.670 | 0.654 | 0.642 | 0.661 | 0.645 | 0.644 | 0.661 | 0.676 | 0.658 | 0.661 | 1988 | 0.661 |
| 1989 | 0.669 | 0.652 | 0.655 | 0.661 | 0.682 | 0.715 | 0.727 | 0.703 | 0.700 | 0.722 | 0.723 | 0.718 | 1989 | 0.718 |
| 1990 | 0.688 | 0.681 | 0.674 | 0.655 | 0.677 | 0.688 | 0.691 | 0.657 | 0.660 | 0.669 | 0.691 | 0.699 | 1990 | 0.699 |
| 1991 | 0.703 | 0.701 | 0.699 | 0.703 | 0.699 | 0.690 | 0.695 | 0.714 | 0.731 | 0.730 | 0.732 | 0.769 | 1991 | 0.769 |
| 1992 | 0.740 | 0.739 | 0.727 | 0.724 | 0.737 | 0.747 | 0.772 | 0.772 | 0.782 | 0.762 | 0.758 | 0.772 | 1992 | 0.772 |
| 1993 | 0.789 | 0.813 | 0.809 | 0.811 | 0.810 | 0.841 | 0.853 | 0.885 | 0.881 | 0.885 | 0.858 | 0.855 | 1993 | 0.855 |
| 1994 | 0.872 | 0.829 | 0.791 | 0.775 | 0.763 | 0.751 | 0.774 | 0.762 | 0.732 | 0.726 | 0.726 | 0.733 | 1994 | 0.733 |
| 1995 | 0.748 | 0.765 | 0.767 | 0.775 | 0.831 | 0.838 | 0.820 | 0.834 | 0.845 | 0.865 | 0.882 | 0.901 | 1995 | 0.901 |
| 1996 | 0.896 | 0.848 | 0.826 | 0.807 | 0.798 | 0.810 | 0.807 | 0.791 | 0.809 | 0.837 | 0.862 | 0.835 | 1996 | 0.835 |
| 1997 | 0.824 | 0.820 | 0.794 | 0.810 | 0.813 | 0.824 | 0.871 | 0.839 | 0.861 | 0.885 | 0.894 | 0.906 | 1997 | 0.906 |
| 1998 | 0.920 | 0.909 | 0.907 | 0.904 | 0.917 | 0.933 | 0.925 | 0.963 | 0.997 | 0.971 | 0.976 | 0.968 | 1998 | 0.968 |
| 1999 | 0.976 | 0.921 | 0.916 | 0.913 | 0.892 | 0.880 | 0.869 | 0.860 | 0.863 | 0.857 | 0.847 | 0.829 | 1999 | 0.829 |
| 2000 | 0.844 | 0.862 | 0.889 | 0.878 | 0.868 | 0.885 | 0.895 | 0.912 | 0.894 | 0.906 | 0.930 | 0.949 | 2000 | 0.949 |
| 2001 | 0.944 | 0.958 | 0.947 | 0.913 | 0.912 | 0.915 | 0.945 | 0.960 | 0.964 | 1.004 | 0.952 | 0.931 | 2001 | 0.931 |
| 2002 | 0.939 | 0.946 | 0.900 | 0.932 | 0.929 | 0.943 | 0.966 | 1.007 | 1.045 | 1.010 | 0.993 | 1.039 | 2002 | 1.039 |
| 2003 | 1.024 | 1.054 | 1.036 | 1.042 | 1.100 | 1.079 | 0.969 | 0.981 | 1.030 | 0.996 | 0.995 | 1.004 | 2003 | 1.004 |
| 2004 | 1.019 | 1.039 | 1.049 | 0.983 | 0.974 | 0.981 | 0.992 | 1.027 | 1.033 | 1.045 | 1.016 | 1.037 | 2004 | 1.037 |
| 2005 | 1.064 | 1.047 | 1.035 | 1.070 | 1.097 | 1.111 | 1.076 | 1.107 | 1.066 | 1.041 | 1.045 | 1.069 | 2005 | 1.069 |
| 2006 | 1.052 | 1.073 | 1.011 | 0.982 | 0.978 | 0.983 | 0.998 | 1.024 | 1.037 | 1.041 | 1.058 | 1.030 | 2006 | 1.030 |
| 2007 | 1.015 | 1.045 | 1.026 | 1.030 | 1.005 | 0.992 | 1.016 | 1.032 | 1.029 | 1.040 | 1.085 | 1.078 | 2007 | 1.078 |
| 2008 | 1.097 | 1.095 | 1.102 | 1.067 | 1.045 | 1.064 | 1.057 | 1.079 | 1.087 | 1.041 | 1.188 | 1.299 | 2008 | 1.299 |
| 2009 | 1.150 | 1.140 | 1.209 | 1.127 | 1.095 | 1.100 | 1.098 | 1.120 | 1.136 | 1.113 | 1.132 | 1.062 | 2009 | 1.062 |
| 2010 | 1.086 | 1.086 | 1.062 | 1.090 | 1.134 | 1.181 | 1.180 | 1.259 | 1.236 | 1.194 | 1.174 | 1.124 | 2010 | 1.124 |
| 2011 | 1.099 | 1.107 | 1.103 | 1.121 | 1.157 | 1.132 | 1.176 | 1.274 | 1.360 | 1.315 | 1.345 | 1.379 | 2011 | 1.379 |
| 2012 | 1.376 | 1.346 | 1.303 | 1.353 | 1.437 | 1.415 | 1.447 | 1.434 | 1.411 | 1.406 | 1.423 | 1.392 | 2012 | 1.392 |
| 2013 | 1.343 | 1.355 | 1.344 | 1.391 | 1.300 | 1.260 | 1.235 | 1.221 | 1.225 | 1.237 | 1.205 | 1.173 | 2013 | 1.173 |
| 2014 | 1.234 | 1.240 | 1.244 | 1.263 | 1.295 | 1.288 | 1.292 | 1.336 | 1.311 | 1.347 | 1.382 | 1.419 | 2014 | 1.419 |
| 2015 | 1.517 | 1.435 | 1.452 | 1.413 | 1.387 | 1.343 | 1.384 | 1.382 | 1.403 | 1.393 | 1.381 | 1.375 | 2015 | 1.375 |
| 2016 | 1.437 | 1.477 | 1.474 | 1.463 | 1.472 | 1.557 | 1.567 | 1.543 | 1.521 | 1.471 | 1.380 | 1.369 | 2016 | 1.369 |

## Appendix B-7

Intermediate-term Government Bonds: Total Return Index

From 1926 to 2016

| Year | Jan | Feb | Mar | Apr | May | Jun | Jul | Aug | Sep | Oct | Nov | Dec | Yr End | Index |
|------|------|------|------|------|------|------|------|------|------|------|------|------|--------|-------|
| 1925 | | | | | | | | | | | | 1.000 | 1925 | 1.000 |
| 1926 | 1.007 | 1.010 | 1.014 | 1.023 | 1.024 | 1.027 | 1.028 | 1.029 | 1.034 | 1.040 | 1.044 | 1.054 | 1926 | 1.054 |
| 1927 | 1.060 | 1.064 | 1.068 | 1.070 | 1.072 | 1.075 | 1.079 | 1.086 | 1.092 | 1.088 | 1.097 | 1.101 | 1927 | 1.101 |
| 1928 | 1.107 | 1.106 | 1.107 | 1.107 | 1.106 | 1.108 | 1.098 | 1.104 | 1.107 | 1.110 | 1.112 | 1.112 | 1928 | 1.112 |
| 1929 | 1.108 | 1.106 | 1.107 | 1.117 | 1.110 | 1.122 | 1.129 | 1.135 | 1.133 | 1.153 | 1.173 | 1.178 | 1929 | 1.178 |
| 1930 | 1.174 | 1.185 | 1.204 | 1.195 | 1.202 | 1.219 | 1.226 | 1.229 | 1.236 | 1.246 | 1.255 | 1.258 | 1930 | 1.258 |
| 1931 | 1.249 | 1.261 | 1.267 | 1.278 | 1.293 | 1.266 | 1.268 | 1.270 | 1.255 | 1.242 | 1.248 | 1.228 | 1931 | 1.228 |
| 1932 | 1.224 | 1.240 | 1.250 | 1.274 | 1.263 | 1.276 | 1.292 | 1.307 | 1.311 | 1.317 | 1.321 | 1.337 | 1932 | 1.337 |
| 1933 | 1.335 | 1.334 | 1.348 | 1.355 | 1.382 | 1.383 | 1.382 | 1.393 | 1.396 | 1.393 | 1.396 | 1.361 | 1933 | 1.361 |
| 1934 | 1.379 | 1.386 | 1.412 | 1.438 | 1.455 | 1.468 | 1.465 | 1.451 | 1.431 | 1.458 | 1.465 | 1.483 | 1934 | 1.483 |
| 1935 | 1.500 | 1.516 | 1.535 | 1.552 | 1.546 | 1.564 | 1.570 | 1.558 | 1.550 | 1.566 | 1.569 | 1.587 | 1935 | 1.587 |
| 1936 | 1.587 | 1.598 | 1.603 | 1.607 | 1.613 | 1.615 | 1.618 | 1.626 | 1.628 | 1.632 | 1.645 | 1.636 | 1936 | 1.636 |
| 1937 | 1.631 | 1.632 | 1.605 | 1.613 | 1.625 | 1.623 | 1.633 | 1.626 | 1.639 | 1.644 | 1.651 | 1.661 | 1937 | 1.661 |
| 1938 | 1.676 | 1.684 | 1.682 | 1.721 | 1.725 | 1.738 | 1.740 | 1.742 | 1.740 | 1.756 | 1.756 | 1.765 | 1938 | 1.765 |
| 1939 | 1.770 | 1.785 | 1.799 | 1.806 | 1.823 | 1.823 | 1.831 | 1.804 | 1.756 | 1.812 | 1.825 | 1.845 | 1939 | 1.845 |
| 1940 | 1.842 | 1.849 | 1.865 | 1.865 | 1.825 | 1.860 | 1.860 | 1.868 | 1.877 | 1.884 | 1.894 | 1.899 | 1940 | 1.899 |
| 1941 | 1.900 | 1.891 | 1.904 | 1.910 | 1.912 | 1.923 | 1.923 | 1.925 | 1.925 | 1.930 | 1.912 | 1.909 | 1941 | 1.909 |
| 1942 | 1.923 | 1.926 | 1.930 | 1.935 | 1.938 | 1.940 | 1.940 | 1.944 | 1.939 | 1.943 | 1.946 | 1.946 | 1942 | 1.946 |
| 1943 | 1.953 | 1.956 | 1.960 | 1.965 | 1.976 | 1.983 | 1.987 | 1.987 | 1.990 | 1.993 | 1.996 | 2.000 | 1943 | 2.000 |
| 1944 | 2.003 | 2.006 | 2.010 | 2.015 | 2.016 | 2.017 | 2.023 | 2.028 | 2.030 | 2.033 | 2.034 | 2.036 | 1944 | 2.036 |
| 1945 | 2.047 | 2.055 | 2.056 | 2.059 | 2.061 | 2.065 | 2.065 | 2.068 | 2.072 | 2.075 | 2.077 | 2.082 | 1945 | 2.082 |
| 1946 | 2.090 | 2.100 | 2.092 | 2.088 | 2.089 | 2.096 | 2.094 | 2.094 | 2.092 | 2.098 | 2.096 | 2.102 | 1946 | 2.102 |
| 1947 | 2.107 | 2.109 | 2.114 | 2.111 | 2.112 | 2.114 | 2.115 | 2.121 | 2.121 | 2.116 | 2.117 | 2.122 | 1947 | 2.122 |
| 1948 | 2.125 | 2.129 | 2.132 | 2.136 | 2.148 | 2.146 | 2.146 | 2.145 | 2.147 | 2.149 | 2.154 | 2.161 | 1948 | 2.161 |
| 1949 | 2.167 | 2.169 | 2.175 | 2.178 | 2.183 | 2.194 | 2.198 | 2.205 | 2.207 | 2.208 | 2.208 | 2.211 | 1949 | 2.211 |
| 1950 | 2.210 | 2.212 | 2.212 | 2.213 | 2.218 | 2.218 | 2.223 | 2.221 | 2.220 | 2.221 | 2.225 | 2.227 | 1950 | 2.227 |
| 1951 | 2.231 | 2.233 | 2.205 | 2.217 | 2.208 | 2.219 | 2.232 | 2.240 | 2.227 | 2.231 | 2.238 | 2.235 | 1951 | 2.235 |
| 1952 | 2.243 | 2.239 | 2.253 | 2.266 | 2.270 | 2.262 | 2.254 | 2.249 | 2.253 | 2.268 | 2.267 | 2.271 | 1952 | 2.271 |
| 1953 | 2.271 | 2.271 | 2.267 | 2.246 | 2.219 | 2.254 | 2.266 | 2.265 | 2.309 | 2.317 | 2.321 | 2.345 | 1953 | 2.345 |
| 1954 | 2.360 | 2.383 | 2.390 | 2.400 | 2.382 | 2.412 | 2.411 | 2.414 | 2.409 | 2.406 | 2.406 | 2.407 | 1954 | 2.407 |
| 1955 | 2.400 | 2.387 | 2.393 | 2.394 | 2.394 | 2.386 | 2.369 | 2.370 | 2.390 | 2.407 | 2.394 | 2.392 | 1955 | 2.392 |

Intermediate-term Government Bonds: Total Return Index

From 1926 to 2016

| Year | Jan | Feb | Mar | Apr | May | Jun | Jul | Aug | Sep | Oct | Nov | Dec | Yr End | Index |
|------|-----|-----|-----|-----|-----|-----|-----|-----|-----|-----|-----|-----|--------|-------|
| 1956 | 2.417 | 2.418 | 2.393 | 2.393 | 2.420 | 2.421 | 2.398 | 2.373 | 2.395 | 2.390 | 2.379 | 2.382 | 1956 | 2.382 |
| 1957 | 2.438 | 2.435 | 2.439 | 2.415 | 2.411 | 2.385 | 2.382 | 2.408 | 2.408 | 2.418 | 2.514 | 2.568 | 1957 | 2.568 |
| 1958 | 2.577 | 2.613 | 2.627 | 2.640 | 2.656 | 2.638 | 2.614 | 2.521 | 2.517 | 2.518 | 2.551 | 2.535 | 1958 | 2.535 |
| 1959 | 2.532 | 2.559 | 2.550 | 2.536 | 2.536 | 2.517 | 2.525 | 2.505 | 2.510 | 2.554 | 2.530 | 2.525 | 1959 | 2.525 |
| 1960 | 2.564 | 2.583 | 2.658 | 2.641 | 2.649 | 2.707 | 2.779 | 2.778 | 2.786 | 2.790 | 2.764 | 2.822 | 1960 | 2.822 |
| 1961 | 2.805 | 2.831 | 2.841 | 2.856 | 2.848 | 2.841 | 2.843 | 2.848 | 2.871 | 2.875 | 2.869 | 2.874 | 1961 | 2.874 |
| 1962 | 2.861 | 2.906 | 2.932 | 2.939 | 2.953 | 2.945 | 2.941 | 2.978 | 2.984 | 3.000 | 3.018 | 3.034 | 1962 | 3.034 |
| 1963 | 3.026 | 3.031 | 3.039 | 3.048 | 3.053 | 3.057 | 3.058 | 3.064 | 3.068 | 3.071 | 3.083 | 3.084 | 1963 | 3.084 |
| 1964 | 3.094 | 3.098 | 3.103 | 3.113 | 3.138 | 3.150 | 3.158 | 3.167 | 3.181 | 3.191 | 3.190 | 3.209 | 1964 | 3.209 |
| 1965 | 3.222 | 3.228 | 3.242 | 3.250 | 3.262 | 3.278 | 3.283 | 3.290 | 3.288 | 3.288 | 3.290 | 3.242 | 1965 | 3.242 |
| 1966 | 3.242 | 3.215 | 3.275 | 3.269 | 3.273 | 3.265 | 3.257 | 3.216 | 3.286 | 3.311 | 3.320 | 3.394 | 1966 | 3.394 |
| 1967 | 3.434 | 3.429 | 3.492 | 3.461 | 3.476 | 3.397 | 3.443 | 3.430 | 3.433 | 3.416 | 3.425 | 3.428 | 1967 | 3.428 |
| 1968 | 3.478 | 3.491 | 3.482 | 3.477 | 3.499 | 3.557 | 3.620 | 3.628 | 3.648 | 3.651 | 3.646 | 3.583 | 1968 | 3.583 |
| 1969 | 3.614 | 3.609 | 3.644 | 3.673 | 3.643 | 3.613 | 3.642 | 3.636 | 3.527 | 3.644 | 3.627 | 3.557 | 1969 | 3.557 |
| 1970 | 3.568 | 3.724 | 3.757 | 3.679 | 3.720 | 3.742 | 3.799 | 3.843 | 3.919 | 3.956 | 4.134 | 4.156 | 1970 | 4.156 |
| 1971 | 4.226 | 4.321 | 4.401 | 4.257 | 4.262 | 4.182 | 4.193 | 4.340 | 4.351 | 4.447 | 4.470 | 4.519 | 1971 | 4.519 |
| 1972 | 4.567 | 4.573 | 4.580 | 4.586 | 4.594 | 4.614 | 4.621 | 4.628 | 4.635 | 4.642 | 4.662 | 4.752 | 1972 | 4.752 |
| 1973 | 4.749 | 4.713 | 4.735 | 4.765 | 4.792 | 4.790 | 4.657 | 4.776 | 4.895 | 4.920 | 4.951 | 4.971 | 1973 | 4.971 |
| 1974 | 4.975 | 4.993 | 4.887 | 4.813 | 4.876 | 4.833 | 4.837 | 4.831 | 4.985 | 5.040 | 5.159 | 5.254 | 1974 | 5.254 |
| 1975 | 5.282 | 5.360 | 5.328 | 5.229 | 5.365 | 5.380 | 5.363 | 5.359 | 5.364 | 5.561 | 5.555 | 5.665 | 1975 | 5.665 |
| 1976 | 5.697 | 5.745 | 5.788 | 5.855 | 5.770 | 5.862 | 5.932 | 6.044 | 6.089 | 6.179 | 6.378 | 6.394 | 1976 | 6.394 |
| 1977 | 6.273 | 6.303 | 6.338 | 6.371 | 6.407 | 6.472 | 6.473 | 6.478 | 6.487 | 6.449 | 6.499 | 6.484 | 1977 | 6.484 |
| 1978 | 6.492 | 6.503 | 6.527 | 6.543 | 6.542 | 6.528 | 6.592 | 6.644 | 6.682 | 6.608 | 6.668 | 6.710 | 1978 | 6.710 |
| 1979 | 6.747 | 6.707 | 6.783 | 6.805 | 6.936 | 7.079 | 7.071 | 7.006 | 7.010 | 6.682 | 6.925 | 6.985 | 1979 | 6.985 |
| 1980 | 6.891 | 6.449 | 6.542 | 7.325 | 7.684 | 7.625 | 7.544 | 7.252 | 7.225 | 7.115 | 7.136 | 7.258 | 1980 | 7.258 |
| 1981 | 7.281 | 7.110 | 7.297 | 7.140 | 7.315 | 7.358 | 7.160 | 7.033 | 7.148 | 7.585 | 8.058 | 7.944 | 1981 | 7.944 |
| 1982 | 7.984 | 8.102 | 8.137 | 8.379 | 8.502 | 8.387 | 8.776 | 9.188 | 9.486 | 9.990 | 10.070 | 10.256 | 1982 | 10.256 |
| 1983 | 10.263 | 10.522 | 10.471 | 10.742 | 10.611 | 10.628 | 10.417 | 10.501 | 10.832 | 10.852 | 10.964 | 11.015 | 1983 | 11.015 |
| 1984 | 11.211 | 11.139 | 11.100 | 11.097 | 10.819 | 10.926 | 11.355 | 11.469 | 11.701 | 12.149 | 12.382 | 12.560 | 1984 | 12.560 |
| 1985 | 12.818 | 12.588 | 12.798 | 13.136 | 13.772 | 13.922 | 13.859 | 14.064 | 14.222 | 14.453 | 14.735 | 15.113 | 1985 | 15.113 |

## Appendix B-7

Intermediate-term Government Bonds: Total Return Index
From 1926 to 2016

| Year | Jan | Feb | Mar | Apr | May | Jun | Jul | Aug | Sep | Oct | Nov | Dec | Yr End | Index |
|------|-----|-----|-----|-----|-----|-----|-----|-----|-----|-----|-----|-----|--------|-------|
| 1986 | 15.238 | 15.657 | 16.186 | 16.318 | 15.968 | 16.409 | 16.667 | 17.109 | 16.921 | 17.195 | 17.389 | 17.401 | 1986 | 17.401 |
| 1987 | 17.587 | 17.691 | 17.636 | 17.205 | 17.140 | 17.350 | 17.394 | 17.328 | 17.085 | 17.596 | 17.741 | 17.906 | 1987 | 17.906 |
| 1988 | 18.472 | 18.698 | 18.537 | 18.455 | 18.364 | 18.698 | 18.610 | 18.593 | 18.957 | 19.238 | 19.017 | 18.999 | 1988 | 18.999 |
| 1989 | 19.230 | 19.133 | 19.227 | 19.650 | 20.067 | 20.717 | 21.203 | 20.682 | 20.824 | 21.318 | 21.497 | 21.524 | 1989 | 21.524 |
| 1990 | 21.299 | 21.313 | 21.318 | 21.154 | 21.707 | 22.035 | 22.418 | 22.213 | 22.422 | 22.804 | 23.243 | 23.618 | 1990 | 23.618 |
| 1991 | 23.870 | 23.984 | 24.039 | 24.320 | 24.464 | 24.409 | 24.725 | 25.335 | 25.881 | 26.228 | 26.565 | 27.270 | 1991 | 27.270 |
| 1992 | 26.737 | 26.796 | 26.583 | 26.843 | 27.438 | 27.923 | 28.600 | 29.029 | 29.592 | 29.054 | 28.810 | 29.230 | 1992 | 29.230 |
| 1993 | 30.021 | 30.749 | 30.883 | 31.156 | 31.126 | 31.753 | 31.769 | 32.476 | 32.657 | 32.714 | 32.411 | 32.516 | 1993 | 32.516 |
| 1994 | 32.964 | 32.113 | 31.286 | 30.957 | 30.951 | 30.863 | 31.385 | 31.466 | 30.968 | 30.896 | 30.680 | 30.843 | 1994 | 30.843 |
| 1995 | 31.404 | 32.140 | 32.341 | 32.805 | 34.014 | 34.284 | 34.230 | 34.525 | 34.745 | 35.164 | 35.687 | 36.025 | 1995 | 36.025 |
| 1996 | 36.048 | 35.551 | 35.131 | 34.955 | 34.844 | 35.253 | 35.340 | 35.323 | 35.872 | 36.527 | 37.072 | 36.782 | 1996 | 36.782 |
| 1997 | 36.873 | 36.880 | 36.460 | 37.000 | 37.286 | 37.671 | 38.666 | 38.289 | 38.867 | 39.451 | 39.445 | 39.864 | 1997 | 39.864 |
| 1998 | 40.583 | 40.426 | 40.530 | 40.777 | 41.062 | 41.385 | 41.495 | 42.619 | 44.023 | 44.203 | 43.772 | 43.933 | 1998 | 43.933 |
| 1999 | 44.175 | 43.015 | 43.387 | 43.476 | 42.834 | 42.972 | 42.950 | 43.016 | 43.435 | 43.401 | 43.365 | 43.155 | 1999 | 43.155 |
| 2000 | 42.925 | 43.260 | 44.140 | 43.950 | 44.179 | 45.024 | 45.347 | 45.953 | 46.394 | 46.760 | 47.573 | 48.589 | 2000 | 48.589 |
| 2001 | 49.066 | 49.583 | 49.958 | 49.390 | 49.356 | 49.680 | 50.907 | 51.391 | 52.694 | 53.642 | 52.725 | 52.291 | 2001 | 52.291 |
| 2002 | 52.477 | 53.043 | 51.761 | 52.997 | 53.621 | 54.526 | 56.007 | 56.942 | 58.583 | 58.442 | 57.451 | 59.054 | 2002 | 59.054 |
| 2003 | 58.529 | 59.576 | 59.534 | 59.613 | 61.239 | 61.027 | 59.080 | 58.918 | 60.730 | 59.906 | 59.820 | 60.469 | 2003 | 60.469 |
| 2004 | 60.781 | 61.533 | 62.148 | 60.072 | 59.777 | 60.067 | 60.558 | 61.740 | 61.815 | 62.211 | 61.422 | 61.832 | 2004 | 61.832 |
| 2005 | 61.995 | 61.308 | 61.075 | 62.095 | 62.735 | 63.005 | 62.099 | 63.100 | 62.320 | 61.930 | 62.293 | 62.674 | 2005 | 62.674 |
| 2006 | 62.448 | 62.342 | 61.992 | 61.942 | 61.915 | 62.054 | 62.831 | 63.682 | 64.183 | 64.513 | 65.081 | 64.643 | 2006 | 64.643 |
| 2007 | 64.515 | 65.615 | 65.775 | 66.084 | 65.407 | 65.477 | 66.620 | 67.852 | 68.241 | 67.911 | 70.799 | 71.142 | 2007 | 71.142 |
| 2008 | 73.011 | 74.721 | 75.268 | 73.059 | 72.444 | 72.987 | 73.452 | 74.216 | 74.845 | 75.936 | 79.202 | 80.466 | 2008 | 80.466 |
| 2009 | 79.152 | 78.504 | 79.966 | 78.642 | 77.607 | 77.014 | 77.446 | 78.194 | 78.778 | 79.016 | 80.471 | 78.532 | 2009 | 78.532 |
| 2010 | 80.056 | 80.621 | 79.913 | 80.667 | 81.883 | 82.940 | 84.252 | 85.331 | 85.750 | 86.296 | 85.586 | 84.121 | 2010 | 84.121 |
| 2011 | 84.645 | 84.196 | 84.156 | 85.453 | 86.984 | 86.975 | 88.735 | 90.601 | 90.677 | 90.760 | 91.083 | 91.533 | 2011 | 91.533 |
| 2012 | 91.610 | 91.130 | 90.488 | 91.656 | 92.412 | 92.231 | 92.944 | 93.083 | 93.122 | 92.901 | 93.346 | 93.054 | 2012 | 93.054 |
| 2013 | 92.483 | 93.076 | 91.748 | 92.302 | 90.782 | 89.519 | 89.755 | 89.095 | 90.172 | 90.633 | 90.737 | 89.630 | 2013 | 89.630 |
| 2014 | 90.804 | 91.020 | 90.399 | 90.833 | 91.690 | 91.531 | 91.101 | 91.782 | 91.335 | 92.150 | 92.874 | 92.316 | 2014 | 92.316 |
| 2015 | 94.542 | 93.381 | 94.076 | 93.945 | 93.989 | 93.493 | 93.967 | 94.072 | 95.005 | 94.513 | 94.132 | 93.970 | 2015 | 93.970 |
| 2016 | 96.162 | 96.712 | 97.146 | 97.049 | 96.842 | 98.534 | 98.573 | 97.937 | 98.199 | 97.688 | 95.846 | 95.777 | 2016 | 95.777 |

# Appendix B-8

Intermediate-term Government Bonds: Capital Appreciation Index

From 1926 to 2016

| Year | Jan | Feb | Mar | Apr | May | Jun | Jul | Aug | Sep | Oct | Nov | Dec | Yr End | Index |
|------|-----|-----|-----|-----|-----|-----|-----|-----|-----|-----|-----|-----|--------|-------|
| 1925 | | | | | | | | | | | | 1.000 | 1925 | 1.000 |
| 1926 | 1.004 | 1.004 | 1.005 | 1.010 | 1.008 | 1.008 | 1.006 | 1.004 | 1.005 | 1.008 | 1.009 | 1.015 | 1926 | 1.015 |
| 1927 | 1.018 | 1.019 | 1.020 | 1.018 | 1.017 | 1.017 | 1.019 | 1.022 | 1.025 | 1.018 | 1.024 | 1.025 | 1927 | 1.025 |
| 1928 | 1.027 | 1.023 | 1.022 | 1.018 | 1.015 | 1.013 | 1.001 | 1.003 | 1.002 | 1.002 | 1.001 | 0.997 | 1928 | 0.997 |
| 1929 | 0.991 | 0.985 | 0.982 | 0.987 | 0.978 | 0.985 | 0.988 | 0.990 | 0.985 | 0.998 | 1.013 | 1.014 | 1929 | 1.014 |
| 1930 | 1.007 | 1.013 | 1.027 | 1.017 | 1.020 | 1.032 | 1.034 | 1.034 | 1.038 | 1.043 | 1.048 | 1.048 | 1930 | 1.048 |
| 1931 | 1.038 | 1.045 | 1.048 | 1.055 | 1.065 | 1.040 | 1.039 | 1.038 | 1.023 | 1.009 | 1.011 | 0.991 | 1931 | 0.991 |
| 1932 | 0.985 | 0.994 | 0.998 | 1.015 | 1.002 | 1.010 | 1.019 | 1.029 | 1.029 | 1.031 | 1.032 | 1.041 | 1932 | 1.041 |
| 1933 | 1.037 | 1.034 | 1.042 | 1.045 | 1.063 | 1.062 | 1.059 | 1.064 | 1.065 | 1.060 | 1.061 | 1.031 | 1933 | 1.031 |
| 1934 | 1.041 | 1.044 | 1.061 | 1.078 | 1.088 | 1.096 | 1.091 | 1.079 | 1.061 | 1.079 | 1.081 | 1.092 | 1934 | 1.092 |
| 1935 | 1.103 | 1.112 | 1.124 | 1.134 | 1.129 | 1.140 | 1.142 | 1.132 | 1.124 | 1.135 | 1.134 | 1.146 | 1935 | 1.146 |
| 1936 | 1.144 | 1.151 | 1.153 | 1.154 | 1.157 | 1.157 | 1.158 | 1.163 | 1.163 | 1.164 | 1.172 | 1.165 | 1936 | 1.165 |
| 1937 | 1.160 | 1.159 | 1.139 | 1.143 | 1.150 | 1.147 | 1.152 | 1.146 | 1.154 | 1.156 | 1.159 | 1.165 | 1937 | 1.165 |
| 1938 | 1.173 | 1.177 | 1.174 | 1.199 | 1.200 | 1.207 | 1.207 | 1.207 | 1.204 | 1.213 | 1.211 | 1.216 | 1938 | 1.216 |
| 1939 | 1.218 | 1.227 | 1.235 | 1.239 | 1.249 | 1.248 | 1.252 | 1.232 | 1.199 | 1.235 | 1.243 | 1.255 | 1939 | 1.255 |
| 1940 | 1.252 | 1.255 | 1.265 | 1.265 | 1.237 | 1.259 | 1.258 | 1.262 | 1.267 | 1.271 | 1.278 | 1.280 | 1940 | 1.280 |
| 1941 | 1.280 | 1.273 | 1.281 | 1.284 | 1.285 | 1.292 | 1.291 | 1.292 | 1.291 | 1.294 | 1.281 | 1.278 | 1941 | 1.278 |
| 1942 | 1.287 | 1.288 | 1.290 | 1.292 | 1.293 | 1.294 | 1.293 | 1.295 | 1.291 | 1.293 | 1.294 | 1.293 | 1942 | 1.293 |
| 1943 | 1.296 | 1.297 | 1.297 | 1.299 | 1.304 | 1.307 | 1.308 | 1.307 | 1.307 | 1.308 | 1.308 | 1.309 | 1943 | 1.309 |
| 1944 | 1.309 | 1.309 | 1.310 | 1.312 | 1.311 | 1.311 | 1.313 | 1.314 | 1.314 | 1.314 | 1.314 | 1.314 | 1944 | 1.314 |
| 1945 | 1.319 | 1.323 | 1.322 | 1.323 | 1.323 | 1.324 | 1.323 | 1.324 | 1.325 | 1.325 | 1.326 | 1.327 | 1945 | 1.327 |
| 1946 | 1.331 | 1.336 | 1.330 | 1.327 | 1.326 | 1.329 | 1.327 | 1.326 | 1.324 | 1.326 | 1.323 | 1.326 | 1946 | 1.326 |
| 1947 | 1.328 | 1.327 | 1.329 | 1.326 | 1.326 | 1.326 | 1.325 | 1.327 | 1.326 | 1.322 | 1.321 | 1.322 | 1947 | 1.322 |
| 1948 | 1.322 | 1.323 | 1.323 | 1.324 | 1.330 | 1.327 | 1.325 | 1.323 | 1.322 | 1.322 | 1.323 | 1.326 | 1948 | 1.326 |
| 1949 | 1.328 | 1.328 | 1.329 | 1.330 | 1.331 | 1.336 | 1.337 | 1.340 | 1.340 | 1.339 | 1.338 | 1.338 | 1949 | 1.338 |
| 1950 | 1.336 | 1.336 | 1.334 | 1.334 | 1.335 | 1.334 | 1.335 | 1.333 | 1.331 | 1.329 | 1.330 | 1.329 | 1950 | 1.329 |
| 1951 | 1.330 | 1.329 | 1.310 | 1.315 | 1.308 | 1.312 | 1.317 | 1.320 | 1.310 | 1.310 | 1.312 | 1.307 | 1951 | 1.307 |
| 1952 | 1.310 | 1.305 | 1.311 | 1.316 | 1.317 | 1.310 | 1.303 | 1.297 | 1.297 | 1.303 | 1.300 | 1.300 | 1952 | 1.300 |
| 1953 | 1.297 | 1.295 | 1.290 | 1.275 | 1.257 | 1.274 | 1.278 | 1.274 | 1.295 | 1.298 | 1.297 | 1.308 | 1953 | 1.308 |
| 1954 | 1.314 | 1.326 | 1.327 | 1.331 | 1.320 | 1.334 | 1.332 | 1.332 | 1.328 | 1.325 | 1.323 | 1.322 | 1954 | 1.322 |
| 1955 | 1.315 | 1.306 | 1.307 | 1.305 | 1.302 | 1.295 | 1.283 | 1.281 | 1.288 | 1.295 | 1.285 | 1.281 | 1955 | 1.281 |

# Appendix B-8

Intermediate-term Government Bonds: Capital Appreciation Index
From 1926 to 2016

| Year | Jan | Feb | Mar | Apr | May | Jun | Jul | Aug | Sep | Oct | Nov | Dec | Yr End | Index |
|------|-----|-----|-----|-----|-----|-----|-----|-----|-----|-----|-----|-----|--------|-------|
| 1956 | 1.291 | 1.289 | 1.273 | 1.270 | 1.281 | 1.278 | 1.263 | 1.246 | 1.255 | 1.248 | 1.239 | 1.237 | 1956 | 1.237 |
| 1957 | 1.262 | 1.258 | 1.257 | 1.240 | 1.234 | 1.218 | 1.212 | 1.221 | 1.217 | 1.219 | 1.263 | 1.287 | 1957 | 1.287 |
| 1958 | 1.288 | 1.303 | 1.307 | 1.311 | 1.317 | 1.305 | 1.290 | 1.242 | 1.236 | 1.232 | 1.245 | 1.233 | 1958 | 1.233 |
| 1959 | 1.228 | 1.237 | 1.228 | 1.218 | 1.214 | 1.200 | 1.200 | 1.186 | 1.184 | 1.200 | 1.184 | 1.177 | 1959 | 1.177 |
| 1960 | 1.190 | 1.194 | 1.224 | 1.213 | 1.212 | 1.234 | 1.263 | 1.259 | 1.259 | 1.257 | 1.242 | 1.264 | 1960 | 1.264 |
| 1961 | 1.253 | 1.261 | 1.262 | 1.265 | 1.258 | 1.251 | 1.248 | 1.246 | 1.252 | 1.250 | 1.244 | 1.243 | 1961 | 1.243 |
| 1962 | 1.233 | 1.248 | 1.255 | 1.254 | 1.257 | 1.250 | 1.244 | 1.255 | 1.255 | 1.257 | 1.261 | 1.264 | 1962 | 1.264 |
| 1963 | 1.257 | 1.255 | 1.255 | 1.255 | 1.253 | 1.251 | 1.247 | 1.246 | 1.243 | 1.240 | 1.241 | 1.237 | 1963 | 1.237 |
| 1964 | 1.237 | 1.235 | 1.233 | 1.233 | 1.239 | 1.239 | 1.238 | 1.237 | 1.239 | 1.239 | 1.234 | 1.237 | 1964 | 1.237 |
| 1965 | 1.238 | 1.237 | 1.237 | 1.236 | 1.237 | 1.238 | 1.236 | 1.234 | 1.229 | 1.225 | 1.221 | 1.199 | 1965 | 1.199 |
| 1966 | 1.194 | 1.180 | 1.197 | 1.190 | 1.186 | 1.179 | 1.171 | 1.151 | 1.171 | 1.174 | 1.173 | 1.194 | 1966 | 1.194 |
| 1967 | 1.203 | 1.197 | 1.214 | 1.200 | 1.200 | 1.168 | 1.178 | 1.169 | 1.165 | 1.154 | 1.152 | 1.148 | 1967 | 1.148 |
| 1968 | 1.159 | 1.158 | 1.150 | 1.143 | 1.145 | 1.159 | 1.173 | 1.171 | 1.172 | 1.168 | 1.162 | 1.136 | 1968 | 1.136 |
| 1969 | 1.140 | 1.133 | 1.139 | 1.141 | 1.126 | 1.110 | 1.113 | 1.105 | 1.065 | 1.093 | 1.082 | 1.054 | 1969 | 1.054 |
| 1970 | 1.050 | 1.090 | 1.092 | 1.063 | 1.068 | 1.068 | 1.077 | 1.083 | 1.098 | 1.102 | 1.145 | 1.145 | 1970 | 1.145 |
| 1971 | 1.159 | 1.180 | 1.197 | 1.153 | 1.149 | 1.121 | 1.118 | 1.151 | 1.149 | 1.169 | 1.169 | 1.177 | 1971 | 1.177 |
| 1972 | 1.183 | 1.180 | 1.176 | 1.173 | 1.169 | 1.168 | 1.164 | 1.160 | 1.156 | 1.152 | 1.151 | 1.168 | 1972 | 1.168 |
| 1973 | 1.161 | 1.146 | 1.145 | 1.146 | 1.146 | 1.140 | 1.101 | 1.122 | 1.144 | 1.143 | 1.144 | 1.142 | 1973 | 1.142 |
| 1974 | 1.137 | 1.135 | 1.105 | 1.081 | 1.088 | 1.072 | 1.065 | 1.056 | 1.083 | 1.087 | 1.106 | 1.120 | 1974 | 1.120 |
| 1975 | 1.119 | 1.129 | 1.116 | 1.088 | 1.110 | 1.106 | 1.095 | 1.088 | 1.081 | 1.114 | 1.106 | 1.121 | 1975 | 1.121 |
| 1976 | 1.121 | 1.124 | 1.125 | 1.131 | 1.109 | 1.119 | 1.125 | 1.139 | 1.142 | 1.152 | 1.183 | 1.180 | 1976 | 1.180 |
| 1977 | 1.151 | 1.151 | 1.151 | 1.151 | 1.151 | 1.156 | 1.150 | 1.144 | 1.140 | 1.126 | 1.128 | 1.119 | 1977 | 1.119 |
| 1978 | 1.113 | 1.109 | 1.105 | 1.101 | 1.093 | 1.084 | 1.087 | 1.088 | 1.087 | 1.067 | 1.069 | 1.069 | 1978 | 1.069 |
| 1979 | 1.066 | 1.053 | 1.057 | 1.052 | 1.064 | 1.079 | 1.069 | 1.052 | 1.045 | 0.987 | 1.015 | 1.015 | 1979 | 1.015 |
| 1980 | 0.992 | 0.920 | 0.924 | 1.025 | 1.067 | 1.051 | 1.031 | 0.983 | 0.970 | 0.946 | 0.940 | 0.946 | 1980 | 0.946 |
| 1981 | 0.939 | 0.908 | 0.921 | 0.892 | 0.904 | 0.898 | 0.864 | 0.838 | 0.841 | 0.881 | 0.926 | 0.903 | 1981 | 0.903 |
| 1982 | 0.897 | 0.902 | 0.894 | 0.911 | 0.915 | 0.892 | 0.923 | 0.956 | 0.978 | 1.021 | 1.021 | 1.031 | 1982 | 1.031 |
| 1983 | 1.023 | 1.041 | 1.027 | 1.045 | 1.023 | 1.016 | 0.988 | 0.986 | 1.007 | 1.000 | 1.001 | 0.997 | 1983 | 0.997 |
| 1984 | 1.005 | 0.990 | 0.977 | 0.967 | 0.933 | 0.932 | 0.958 | 0.958 | 0.968 | 0.994 | 1.004 | 1.009 | 1984 | 1.009 |
| 1985 | 1.021 | 0.994 | 1.002 | 1.019 | 1.059 | 1.063 | 1.049 | 1.056 | 1.059 | 1.068 | 1.081 | 1.100 | 1985 | 1.100 |

## Appendix B-8

Intermediate-term Government Bonds: Capital Appreciation Index
From 1926 to 2016

| Year | Jan | Feb | Mar | Apr | May | Jun | Jul | Aug | Sep | Oct | Nov | Dec | Yr End | Index |
|---|---|---|---|---|---|---|---|---|---|---|---|---|---|---|
| 1986 | 1.101 | 1.124 | 1.155 | 1.157 | 1.125 | 1.149 | 1.160 | 1.184 | 1.164 | 1.176 | 1.183 | 1.177 | 1986 | 1.177 |
| 1987 | 1.183 | 1.184 | 1.173 | 1.138 | 1.126 | 1.132 | 1.127 | 1.116 | 1.092 | 1.117 | 1.118 | 1.121 | 1987 | 1.121 |
| 1988 | 1.149 | 1.156 | 1.138 | 1.126 | 1.112 | 1.125 | 1.112 | 1.103 | 1.116 | 1.125 | 1.105 | 1.096 | 1988 | 1.096 |
| 1989 | 1.100 | 1.088 | 1.085 | 1.101 | 1.115 | 1.144 | 1.163 | 1.127 | 1.128 | 1.146 | 1.149 | 1.143 | 1989 | 1.143 |
| 1990 | 1.123 | 1.117 | 1.109 | 1.093 | 1.113 | 1.122 | 1.134 | 1.116 | 1.119 | 1.130 | 1.144 | 1.155 | 1990 | 1.155 |
| 1991 | 1.160 | 1.158 | 1.154 | 1.160 | 1.159 | 1.150 | 1.156 | 1.178 | 1.196 | 1.205 | 1.214 | 1.240 | 1991 | 1.240 |
| 1992 | 1.209 | 1.206 | 1.189 | 1.193 | 1.213 | 1.228 | 1.251 | 1.263 | 1.282 | 1.253 | 1.236 | 1.248 | 1992 | 1.248 |
| 1993 | 1.275 | 1.301 | 1.300 | 1.305 | 1.299 | 1.318 | 1.314 | 1.337 | 1.339 | 1.336 | 1.318 | 1.317 | 1993 | 1.317 |
| 1994 | 1.329 | 1.290 | 1.250 | 1.231 | 1.224 | 1.213 | 1.227 | 1.223 | 1.197 | 1.187 | 1.171 | 1.170 | 1994 | 1.170 |
| 1995 | 1.184 | 1.205 | 1.205 | 1.216 | 1.253 | 1.257 | 1.249 | 1.253 | 1.255 | 1.264 | 1.277 | 1.283 | 1995 | 1.283 |
| 1996 | 1.278 | 1.255 | 1.235 | 1.222 | 1.212 | 1.220 | 1.216 | 1.209 | 1.221 | 1.237 | 1.249 | 1.233 | 1996 | 1.233 |
| 1997 | 1.230 | 1.225 | 1.204 | 1.215 | 1.218 | 1.224 | 1.250 | 1.232 | 1.244 | 1.256 | 1.251 | 1.257 | 1997 | 1.257 |
| 1998 | 1.274 | 1.264 | 1.261 | 1.263 | 1.266 | 1.270 | 1.267 | 1.296 | 1.333 | 1.334 | 1.316 | 1.316 | 1998 | 1.316 |
| 1999 | 1.318 | 1.279 | 1.284 | 1.281 | 1.257 | 1.255 | 1.248 | 1.244 | 1.250 | 1.243 | 1.235 | 1.223 | 1999 | 1.223 |
| 2000 | 1.210 | 1.213 | 1.231 | 1.220 | 1.219 | 1.236 | 1.238 | 1.248 | 1.254 | 1.258 | 1.274 | 1.296 | 2000 | 1.296 |
| 2001 | 1.304 | 1.315 | 1.321 | 1.302 | 1.295 | 1.298 | 1.325 | 1.332 | 1.361 | 1.381 | 1.353 | 1.338 | 2001 | 1.338 |
| 2002 | 1.337 | 1.347 | 1.310 | 1.335 | 1.346 | 1.364 | 1.396 | 1.415 | 1.452 | 1.445 | 1.418 | 1.453 | 2002 | 1.453 |
| 2003 | 1.437 | 1.459 | 1.455 | 1.453 | 1.489 | 1.481 | 1.431 | 1.424 | 1.463 | 1.440 | 1.435 | 1.446 | 2003 | 1.446 |
| 2004 | 1.450 | 1.464 | 1.475 | 1.423 | 1.412 | 1.414 | 1.421 | 1.444 | 1.442 | 1.448 | 1.426 | 1.431 | 2004 | 1.431 |
| 2005 | 1.430 | 1.410 | 1.400 | 1.419 | 1.429 | 1.430 | 1.405 | 1.423 | 1.401 | 1.387 | 1.390 | 1.394 | 2005 | 1.394 |
| 2006 | 1.384 | 1.377 | 1.364 | 1.357 | 1.351 | 1.348 | 1.359 | 1.372 | 1.378 | 1.380 | 1.387 | 1.373 | 2006 | 1.373 |
| 2007 | 1.364 | 1.383 | 1.381 | 1.382 | 1.363 | 1.359 | 1.377 | 1.397 | 1.401 | 1.389 | 1.443 | 1.446 | 2007 | 1.446 |
| 2008 | 1.479 | 1.511 | 1.518 | 1.471 | 1.455 | 1.461 | 1.467 | 1.478 | 1.487 | 1.505 | 1.567 | 1.589 | 2008 | 1.589 |
| 2009 | 1.562 | 1.547 | 1.573 | 1.545 | 1.522 | 1.507 | 1.512 | 1.523 | 1.532 | 1.534 | 1.559 | 1.519 | 2009 | 1.519 |
| 2010 | 1.545 | 1.553 | 1.537 | 1.548 | 1.568 | 1.586 | 1.608 | 1.627 | 1.633 | 1.642 | 1.627 | 1.598 | 2010 | 1.598 |
| 2011 | 1.605 | 1.593 | 1.590 | 1.611 | 1.637 | 1.635 | 1.665 | 1.698 | 1.699 | 1.699 | 1.704 | 1.711 | 2011 | 1.711 |
| 2012 | 1.711 | 1.701 | 1.688 | 1.708 | 1.721 | 1.717 | 1.729 | 1.730 | 1.730 | 1.726 | 1.733 | 1.727 | 2012 | 1.727 |
| 2013 | 1.715 | 1.725 | 1.699 | 1.708 | 1.679 | 1.655 | 1.657 | 1.643 | 1.661 | 1.668 | 1.668 | 1.646 | 2013 | 1.646 |
| 2014 | 1.665 | 1.667 | 1.653 | 1.659 | 1.672 | 1.667 | 1.657 | 1.667 | 1.657 | 1.669 | 1.680 | 1.668 | 2014 | 1.668 |
| 2015 | 1.706 | 1.683 | 1.694 | 1.689 | 1.688 | 1.677 | 1.683 | 1.683 | 1.698 | 1.687 | 1.678 | 1.673 | 2015 | 1.673 |
| 2016 | 1.709 | 1.717 | 1.723 | 1.719 | 1.714 | 1.742 | 1.741 | 1.728 | 1.731 | 1.721 | 1.686 | 1.683 | 2016 | 1.683 |

## Appendix B-9

U.S. Treasury Bills: Total Return Index
From 1926 to 2016

| Year | Jan | Feb | Mar | Apr | May | Jun | Jul | Aug | Sep | Oct | Nov | Dec | Yr End | Index |
|------|-----|-----|-----|-----|-----|-----|-----|-----|-----|-----|-----|-----|--------|-------|
| 1925 |     |     |     |     |     |     |     |     |     |     |     | 1.000 | 1925 | 1.000 |
| 1926 | 1.003 | 1.006 | 1.009 | 1.013 | 1.013 | 1.016 | 1.018 | 1.021 | 1.023 | 1.027 | 1.030 | 1.033 | 1926 | 1.033 |
| 1927 | 1.035 | 1.038 | 1.041 | 1.044 | 1.047 | 1.049 | 1.053 | 1.055 | 1.058 | 1.060 | 1.063 | 1.065 | 1927 | 1.065 |
| 1928 | 1.068 | 1.071 | 1.074 | 1.077 | 1.080 | 1.084 | 1.087 | 1.091 | 1.093 | 1.098 | 1.102 | 1.103 | 1928 | 1.103 |
| 1929 | 1.107 | 1.111 | 1.114 | 1.118 | 1.123 | 1.129 | 1.133 | 1.137 | 1.141 | 1.147 | 1.151 | 1.155 | 1929 | 1.155 |
| 1930 | 1.157 | 1.160 | 1.164 | 1.167 | 1.170 | 1.173 | 1.175 | 1.176 | 1.179 | 1.180 | 1.181 | 1.183 | 1930 | 1.183 |
| 1931 | 1.185 | 1.185 | 1.187 | 1.188 | 1.189 | 1.190 | 1.190 | 1.191 | 1.191 | 1.192 | 1.194 | 1.196 | 1931 | 1.196 |
| 1932 | 1.198 | 1.201 | 1.203 | 1.205 | 1.205 | 1.206 | 1.206 | 1.206 | 1.207 | 1.207 | 1.207 | 1.207 | 1932 | 1.207 |
| 1933 | 1.207 | 1.207 | 1.208 | 1.209 | 1.209 | 1.210 | 1.210 | 1.210 | 1.210 | 1.210 | 1.211 | 1.211 | 1933 | 1.211 |
| 1934 | 1.211 | 1.212 | 1.212 | 1.212 | 1.214 | 1.212 | 1.212 | 1.212 | 1.212 | 1.213 | 1.213 | 1.213 | 1934 | 1.213 |
| 1935 | 1.213 | 1.213 | 1.213 | 1.213 | 1.214 | 1.214 | 1.214 | 1.214 | 1.214 | 1.214 | 1.215 | 1.215 | 1935 | 1.215 |
| 1936 | 1.215 | 1.215 | 1.215 | 1.216 | 1.216 | 1.216 | 1.216 | 1.216 | 1.217 | 1.217 | 1.217 | 1.217 | 1936 | 1.217 |
| 1937 | 1.217 | 1.217 | 1.218 | 1.218 | 1.219 | 1.219 | 1.219 | 1.220 | 1.220 | 1.220 | 1.221 | 1.221 | 1937 | 1.221 |
| 1938 | 1.221 | 1.221 | 1.221 | 1.221 | 1.221 | 1.221 | 1.221 | 1.221 | 1.221 | 1.221 | 1.221 | 1.221 | 1938 | 1.221 |
| 1939 | 1.220 | 1.221 | 1.220 | 1.220 | 1.220 | 1.221 | 1.221 | 1.221 | 1.221 | 1.221 | 1.221 | 1.221 | 1939 | 1.221 |
| 1940 | 1.221 | 1.221 | 1.221 | 1.221 | 1.221 | 1.221 | 1.221 | 1.221 | 1.221 | 1.221 | 1.221 | 1.221 | 1940 | 1.221 |
| 1941 | 1.221 | 1.221 | 1.221 | 1.221 | 1.221 | 1.221 | 1.221 | 1.221 | 1.221 | 1.221 | 1.221 | 1.222 | 1941 | 1.222 |
| 1942 | 1.222 | 1.222 | 1.222 | 1.222 | 1.222 | 1.223 | 1.223 | 1.223 | 1.224 | 1.224 | 1.225 | 1.225 | 1942 | 1.225 |
| 1943 | 1.225 | 1.226 | 1.226 | 1.226 | 1.227 | 1.227 | 1.227 | 1.228 | 1.228 | 1.228 | 1.229 | 1.229 | 1943 | 1.229 |
| 1944 | 1.229 | 1.230 | 1.230 | 1.230 | 1.231 | 1.231 | 1.231 | 1.232 | 1.232 | 1.233 | 1.233 | 1.233 | 1944 | 1.233 |
| 1945 | 1.233 | 1.234 | 1.234 | 1.234 | 1.235 | 1.235 | 1.235 | 1.236 | 1.236 | 1.237 | 1.237 | 1.237 | 1945 | 1.237 |
| 1946 | 1.238 | 1.238 | 1.238 | 1.239 | 1.239 | 1.239 | 1.240 | 1.240 | 1.240 | 1.241 | 1.241 | 1.242 | 1946 | 1.242 |
| 1947 | 1.242 | 1.242 | 1.243 | 1.243 | 1.243 | 1.244 | 1.244 | 1.244 | 1.245 | 1.246 | 1.247 | 1.248 | 1947 | 1.248 |
| 1948 | 1.249 | 1.250 | 1.251 | 1.252 | 1.253 | 1.254 | 1.255 | 1.256 | 1.256 | 1.257 | 1.257 | 1.258 | 1948 | 1.258 |
| 1949 | 1.259 | 1.260 | 1.262 | 1.263 | 1.264 | 1.265 | 1.266 | 1.267 | 1.269 | 1.270 | 1.271 | 1.272 | 1949 | 1.272 |
| 1950 | 1.273 | 1.274 | 1.275 | 1.276 | 1.278 | 1.279 | 1.280 | 1.281 | 1.283 | 1.284 | 1.286 | 1.287 | 1950 | 1.287 |
| 1951 | 1.289 | 1.290 | 1.291 | 1.293 | 1.295 | 1.296 | 1.298 | 1.300 | 1.301 | 1.303 | 1.305 | 1.306 | 1951 | 1.306 |
| 1952 | 1.308 | 1.310 | 1.311 | 1.313 | 1.314 | 1.316 | 1.318 | 1.320 | 1.322 | 1.324 | 1.326 | 1.328 | 1952 | 1.328 |
| 1953 | 1.330 | 1.332 | 1.334 | 1.337 | 1.339 | 1.341 | 1.343 | 1.345 | 1.348 | 1.349 | 1.350 | 1.352 | 1953 | 1.352 |
| 1954 | 1.354 | 1.355 | 1.356 | 1.357 | 1.357 | 1.358 | 1.359 | 1.360 | 1.361 | 1.362 | 1.363 | 1.364 | 1954 | 1.364 |
| 1955 | 1.365 | 1.366 | 1.367 | 1.369 | 1.371 | 1.372 | 1.373 | 1.376 | 1.378 | 1.380 | 1.383 | 1.385 | 1955 | 1.385 |

## Appendix B-9

U.S. Treasury Bills: Total Return Index
From 1926 to 2016

| Year | Jan | Feb | Mar | Apr | May | Jun | Jul | Aug | Sep | Oct | Nov | Dec | Yr End | Index |
|------|------|------|------|------|------|------|------|------|------|------|------|------|--------|-------|
| 1956 | 1.388 | 1.391 | 1.393 | 1.396 | 1.399 | 1.402 | 1.405 | 1.407 | 1.410 | 1.413 | 1.416 | 1.419 | 1956 | 1.419 |
| 1957 | 1.423 | 1.426 | 1.430 | 1.433 | 1.437 | 1.441 | 1.445 | 1.448 | 1.452 | 1.456 | 1.460 | 1.464 | 1957 | 1.464 |
| 1958 | 1.468 | 1.470 | 1.471 | 1.472 | 1.474 | 1.474 | 1.475 | 1.476 | 1.479 | 1.481 | 1.483 | 1.486 | 1958 | 1.486 |
| 1959 | 1.489 | 1.492 | 1.496 | 1.499 | 1.502 | 1.505 | 1.509 | 1.512 | 1.517 | 1.521 | 1.525 | 1.530 | 1959 | 1.530 |
| 1960 | 1.535 | 1.540 | 1.545 | 1.548 | 1.552 | 1.556 | 1.558 | 1.561 | 1.563 | 1.567 | 1.569 | 1.571 | 1960 | 1.571 |
| 1961 | 1.574 | 1.576 | 1.579 | 1.582 | 1.585 | 1.588 | 1.591 | 1.593 | 1.596 | 1.599 | 1.601 | 1.604 | 1961 | 1.604 |
| 1962 | 1.608 | 1.612 | 1.615 | 1.618 | 1.622 | 1.626 | 1.630 | 1.634 | 1.637 | 1.641 | 1.645 | 1.648 | 1962 | 1.648 |
| 1963 | 1.652 | 1.656 | 1.660 | 1.664 | 1.668 | 1.672 | 1.677 | 1.681 | 1.685 | 1.690 | 1.695 | 1.700 | 1963 | 1.700 |
| 1964 | 1.705 | 1.709 | 1.715 | 1.720 | 1.724 | 1.729 | 1.734 | 1.739 | 1.744 | 1.749 | 1.754 | 1.760 | 1964 | 1.760 |
| 1965 | 1.765 | 1.770 | 1.776 | 1.782 | 1.787 | 1.794 | 1.799 | 1.805 | 1.811 | 1.817 | 1.823 | 1.829 | 1965 | 1.829 |
| 1966 | 1.836 | 1.842 | 1.849 | 1.856 | 1.863 | 1.870 | 1.877 | 1.885 | 1.892 | 1.901 | 1.908 | 1.916 | 1966 | 1.916 |
| 1967 | 1.924 | 1.931 | 1.939 | 1.945 | 1.951 | 1.957 | 1.963 | 1.969 | 1.975 | 1.983 | 1.990 | 1.997 | 1967 | 1.997 |
| 1968 | 2.005 | 2.012 | 2.020 | 2.029 | 2.038 | 2.046 | 2.056 | 2.065 | 2.074 | 2.083 | 2.092 | 2.101 | 1968 | 2.101 |
| 1969 | 2.112 | 2.121 | 2.131 | 2.143 | 2.153 | 2.164 | 2.175 | 2.186 | 2.200 | 2.213 | 2.225 | 2.239 | 1969 | 2.239 |
| 1970 | 2.252 | 2.266 | 2.279 | 2.291 | 2.303 | 2.316 | 2.328 | 2.341 | 2.353 | 2.364 | 2.375 | 2.385 | 1970 | 2.385 |
| 1971 | 2.394 | 2.402 | 2.409 | 2.416 | 2.423 | 2.432 | 2.442 | 2.453 | 2.462 | 2.471 | 2.480 | 2.490 | 1971 | 2.490 |
| 1972 | 2.497 | 2.503 | 2.510 | 2.517 | 2.525 | 2.532 | 2.540 | 2.547 | 2.556 | 2.566 | 2.575 | 2.585 | 1972 | 2.585 |
| 1973 | 2.596 | 2.607 | 2.619 | 2.633 | 2.646 | 2.660 | 2.677 | 2.695 | 2.714 | 2.732 | 2.747 | 2.764 | 1973 | 2.764 |
| 1974 | 2.782 | 2.798 | 2.813 | 2.835 | 2.856 | 2.873 | 2.893 | 2.911 | 2.934 | 2.949 | 2.965 | 2.986 | 1974 | 2.986 |
| 1975 | 3.003 | 3.016 | 3.028 | 3.042 | 3.055 | 3.067 | 3.082 | 3.097 | 3.113 | 3.131 | 3.144 | 3.159 | 1975 | 3.159 |
| 1976 | 3.174 | 3.184 | 3.197 | 3.210 | 3.222 | 3.237 | 3.252 | 3.265 | 3.280 | 3.293 | 3.306 | 3.319 | 1976 | 3.319 |
| 1977 | 3.331 | 3.343 | 3.356 | 3.368 | 3.381 | 3.394 | 3.408 | 3.423 | 3.438 | 3.455 | 3.472 | 3.489 | 1977 | 3.489 |
| 1978 | 3.506 | 3.522 | 3.541 | 3.560 | 3.578 | 3.597 | 3.618 | 3.638 | 3.660 | 3.685 | 3.711 | 3.740 | 1978 | 3.740 |
| 1979 | 3.769 | 3.796 | 3.827 | 3.858 | 3.889 | 3.921 | 3.951 | 3.981 | 4.014 | 4.049 | 4.089 | 4.128 | 1979 | 4.128 |
| 1980 | 4.161 | 4.198 | 4.248 | 4.302 | 4.336 | 4.363 | 4.386 | 4.414 | 4.447 | 4.489 | 4.532 | 4.592 | 1980 | 4.592 |
| 1981 | 4.639 | 4.689 | 4.746 | 4.797 | 4.852 | 4.917 | 4.978 | 5.042 | 5.105 | 5.166 | 5.221 | 5.267 | 1981 | 5.267 |
| 1982 | 5.309 | 5.358 | 5.411 | 5.472 | 5.530 | 5.583 | 5.641 | 5.684 | 5.713 | 5.747 | 5.783 | 5.822 | 1982 | 5.822 |
| 1983 | 5.862 | 5.899 | 5.936 | 5.978 | 6.020 | 6.060 | 6.105 | 6.151 | 6.198 | 6.245 | 6.289 | 6.335 | 1983 | 6.335 |
| 1984 | 6.383 | 6.428 | 6.475 | 6.528 | 6.579 | 6.629 | 6.683 | 6.738 | 6.796 | 6.864 | 6.914 | 6.959 | 1984 | 6.959 |
| 1985 | 7.004 | 7.044 | 7.088 | 7.138 | 7.186 | 7.225 | 7.271 | 7.311 | 7.355 | 7.403 | 7.448 | 7.496 | 1985 | 7.496 |

## Appendix B-9

U.S. Treasury Bills: Total Return Index
From 1926 to 2016

| Year | Jan | Feb | Mar | Apr | May | Jun | Jul | Aug | Sep | Oct | Nov | Dec | Yr End | Index |
|------|-----|-----|-----|-----|-----|-----|-----|-----|-----|-----|-----|-----|--------|-------|
| 1986 | 7.538 | 7.578 | 7.623 | 7.663 | 7.700 | 7.741 | 7.781 | 7.817 | 7.852 | 7.889 | 7.919 | 7.958 | 1986 | 7.958 |
| 1987 | 7.991 | 8.025 | 8.063 | 8.099 | 8.129 | 8.169 | 8.206 | 8.245 | 8.282 | 8.331 | 8.360 | 8.393 | 1987 | 8.393 |
| 1988 | 8.418 | 8.456 | 8.493 | 8.532 | 8.576 | 8.617 | 8.661 | 8.712 | 8.766 | 8.819 | 8.869 | 8.926 | 1988 | 8.926 |
| 1989 | 8.975 | 9.030 | 9.090 | 9.152 | 9.224 | 9.289 | 9.354 | 9.423 | 9.485 | 9.549 | 9.614 | 9.673 | 1989 | 9.673 |
| 1990 | 9.728 | 9.783 | 9.846 | 9.914 | 9.981 | 10.043 | 10.111 | 10.178 | 10.238 | 10.308 | 10.366 | 10.429 | 1990 | 10.429 |
| 1991 | 10.483 | 10.533 | 10.579 | 10.635 | 10.685 | 10.730 | 10.782 | 10.832 | 10.881 | 10.928 | 10.970 | 11.012 | 1991 | 11.012 |
| 1992 | 11.049 | 11.081 | 11.118 | 11.154 | 11.185 | 11.221 | 11.255 | 11.285 | 11.314 | 11.340 | 11.366 | 11.398 | 1992 | 11.398 |
| 1993 | 11.425 | 11.450 | 11.479 | 11.506 | 11.531 | 11.561 | 11.588 | 11.617 | 11.647 | 11.673 | 11.702 | 11.728 | 1993 | 11.728 |
| 1994 | 11.758 | 11.783 | 11.814 | 11.846 | 11.884 | 11.921 | 11.954 | 11.998 | 12.042 | 12.088 | 12.132 | 12.186 | 1994 | 12.186 |
| 1995 | 12.237 | 12.286 | 12.342 | 12.397 | 12.464 | 12.522 | 12.579 | 12.638 | 12.692 | 12.752 | 12.806 | 12.868 | 1995 | 12.868 |
| 1996 | 12.923 | 12.974 | 13.025 | 13.084 | 13.140 | 13.192 | 13.252 | 13.306 | 13.365 | 13.421 | 13.476 | 13.538 | 1996 | 13.538 |
| 1997 | 13.599 | 13.652 | 13.710 | 13.769 | 13.837 | 13.888 | 13.948 | 14.005 | 14.067 | 14.127 | 14.182 | 14.250 | 1997 | 14.250 |
| 1998 | 14.311 | 14.367 | 14.423 | 14.485 | 14.544 | 14.603 | 14.662 | 14.725 | 14.792 | 14.840 | 14.886 | 14.942 | 1998 | 14.942 |
| 1999 | 14.994 | 15.048 | 15.112 | 15.168 | 15.219 | 15.280 | 15.338 | 15.397 | 15.457 | 15.517 | 15.573 | 15.641 | 1999 | 15.641 |
| 2000 | 15.706 | 15.774 | 15.848 | 15.920 | 16.001 | 16.064 | 16.141 | 16.223 | 16.305 | 16.397 | 16.480 | 16.563 | 2000 | 16.563 |
| 2001 | 16.652 | 16.715 | 16.784 | 16.850 | 16.905 | 16.952 | 17.004 | 17.056 | 17.103 | 17.142 | 17.172 | 17.197 | 2001 | 17.197 |
| 2002 | 17.221 | 17.243 | 17.266 | 17.293 | 17.318 | 17.340 | 17.367 | 17.391 | 17.416 | 17.440 | 17.460 | 17.480 | 2002 | 17.480 |
| 2003 | 17.497 | 17.512 | 17.530 | 17.547 | 17.563 | 17.580 | 17.592 | 17.604 | 17.619 | 17.631 | 17.644 | 17.659 | 2003 | 17.659 |
| 2004 | 17.671 | 17.682 | 17.697 | 17.711 | 17.722 | 17.737 | 17.754 | 17.774 | 17.794 | 17.814 | 17.842 | 17.871 | 2004 | 17.871 |
| 2005 | 17.900 | 17.930 | 17.968 | 18.005 | 18.048 | 18.089 | 18.132 | 18.186 | 18.238 | 18.288 | 18.345 | 18.403 | 2005 | 18.403 |
| 2006 | 18.468 | 18.530 | 18.598 | 18.664 | 18.745 | 18.819 | 18.894 | 18.974 | 19.051 | 19.128 | 19.209 | 19.287 | 2006 | 19.287 |
| 2007 | 19.372 | 19.447 | 19.529 | 19.615 | 19.694 | 19.773 | 19.851 | 19.934 | 19.998 | 20.063 | 20.131 | 20.186 | 2007 | 20.186 |
| 2008 | 20.229 | 20.256 | 20.291 | 20.326 | 20.363 | 20.398 | 20.429 | 20.455 | 20.486 | 20.503 | 20.509 | 20.509 | 2008 | 20.509 |
| 2009 | 20.509 | 20.512 | 20.515 | 20.518 | 20.518 | 20.520 | 20.522 | 20.525 | 20.527 | 20.527 | 20.527 | 20.529 | 2009 | 20.529 |
| 2010 | 20.529 | 20.529 | 20.531 | 20.533 | 20.535 | 20.538 | 20.541 | 20.544 | 20.546 | 20.549 | 20.551 | 20.553 | 2010 | 20.553 |
| 2011 | 20.555 | 20.557 | 20.559 | 20.560 | 20.560 | 20.561 | 20.560 | 20.562 | 20.562 | 20.562 | 20.562 | 20.562 | 2011 | 20.562 |
| 2012 | 20.562 | 20.563 | 20.564 | 20.564 | 20.565 | 20.566 | 20.567 | 20.568 | 20.569 | 20.571 | 20.572 | 20.574 | 2012 | 20.574 |
| 2013 | 20.575 | 20.575 | 20.576 | 20.577 | 20.577 | 20.577 | 20.577 | 20.578 | 20.578 | 20.578 | 20.579 | 20.579 | 2013 | 20.579 |
| 2014 | 20.580 | 20.581 | 20.581 | 20.581 | 20.582 | 20.582 | 20.582 | 20.582 | 20.582 | 20.583 | 20.582 | 20.583 | 2014 | 20.583 |
| 2015 | 20.583 | 20.583 | 20.583 | 20.584 | 20.584 | 20.584 | 20.583 | 20.584 | 20.584 | 20.584 | 20.584 | 20.586 | 2015 | 20.586 |
| 2016 | 20.588 | 20.592 | 20.596 | 20.598 | 20.600 | 20.604 | 20.608 | 20.612 | 20.616 | 20.620 | 20.622 | 20.628 | 2016 | 20.628 |

# Appendix B-10

Inflation Index
From 1926 to 2016

| Year | Jan | Feb | Mar | Apr | May | Jun | Jul | Aug | Sep | Oct | Nov | Dec | Yr End | Index |
|------|-----|-----|-----|-----|-----|-----|-----|-----|-----|-----|-----|-----|--------|-------|
| 1925 |     |     |     |     |     |     |     |     |     |     |     | 1.000 | 1925 | 1.000 |
| 1926 | 1.000 | 0.996 | 0.991 | 1.000 | 0.994 | 0.987 | 0.978 | 0.972 | 0.978 | 0.981 | 0.985 | 0.985 | 1926 | 0.985 |
| 1927 | 0.978 | 0.970 | 0.965 | 0.965 | 0.972 | 0.981 | 0.963 | 0.957 | 0.963 | 0.968 | 0.966 | 0.965 | 1927 | 0.965 |
| 1928 | 0.963 | 0.953 | 0.953 | 0.955 | 0.961 | 0.953 | 0.953 | 0.955 | 0.963 | 0.961 | 0.959 | 0.955 | 1928 | 0.955 |
| 1929 | 0.953 | 0.952 | 0.948 | 0.944 | 0.950 | 0.953 | 0.963 | 0.966 | 0.965 | 0.965 | 0.963 | 0.957 | 1929 | 0.957 |
| 1930 | 0.953 | 0.950 | 0.944 | 0.950 | 0.944 | 0.939 | 0.926 | 0.920 | 0.926 | 0.920 | 0.912 | 0.899 | 1930 | 0.899 |
| 1931 | 0.886 | 0.873 | 0.868 | 0.862 | 0.853 | 0.844 | 0.842 | 0.840 | 0.836 | 0.831 | 0.821 | 0.814 | 1931 | 0.814 |
| 1932 | 0.797 | 0.786 | 0.782 | 0.777 | 0.765 | 0.760 | 0.760 | 0.750 | 0.747 | 0.741 | 0.737 | 0.730 | 1932 | 0.730 |
| 1933 | 0.719 | 0.708 | 0.702 | 0.700 | 0.702 | 0.709 | 0.730 | 0.737 | 0.737 | 0.737 | 0.737 | 0.734 | 1933 | 0.734 |
| 1934 | 0.737 | 0.743 | 0.743 | 0.741 | 0.743 | 0.745 | 0.745 | 0.747 | 0.758 | 0.752 | 0.750 | 0.749 | 1934 | 0.749 |
| 1935 | 0.760 | 0.765 | 0.764 | 0.771 | 0.767 | 0.765 | 0.762 | 0.762 | 0.765 | 0.765 | 0.769 | 0.771 | 1935 | 0.771 |
| 1936 | 0.771 | 0.767 | 0.764 | 0.764 | 0.764 | 0.771 | 0.775 | 0.780 | 0.782 | 0.780 | 0.780 | 0.780 | 1936 | 0.780 |
| 1937 | 0.786 | 0.788 | 0.793 | 0.797 | 0.801 | 0.803 | 0.806 | 0.808 | 0.816 | 0.812 | 0.806 | 0.804 | 1937 | 0.804 |
| 1938 | 0.793 | 0.786 | 0.786 | 0.790 | 0.786 | 0.786 | 0.788 | 0.786 | 0.786 | 0.782 | 0.780 | 0.782 | 1938 | 0.782 |
| 1939 | 0.778 | 0.775 | 0.773 | 0.771 | 0.771 | 0.771 | 0.771 | 0.771 | 0.786 | 0.782 | 0.782 | 0.778 | 1939 | 0.778 |
| 1940 | 0.777 | 0.782 | 0.780 | 0.780 | 0.782 | 0.784 | 0.782 | 0.780 | 0.782 | 0.782 | 0.782 | 0.786 | 1940 | 0.786 |
| 1941 | 0.786 | 0.786 | 0.790 | 0.797 | 0.803 | 0.818 | 0.821 | 0.829 | 0.844 | 0.853 | 0.860 | 0.862 | 1941 | 0.862 |
| 1942 | 0.873 | 0.881 | 0.892 | 0.898 | 0.907 | 0.909 | 0.912 | 0.918 | 0.920 | 0.929 | 0.935 | 0.942 | 1942 | 0.942 |
| 1943 | 0.942 | 0.944 | 0.959 | 0.970 | 0.978 | 0.976 | 0.968 | 0.965 | 0.968 | 0.972 | 0.970 | 0.972 | 1943 | 0.972 |
| 1944 | 0.970 | 0.968 | 0.968 | 0.974 | 0.978 | 0.980 | 0.985 | 0.989 | 0.989 | 0.989 | 0.989 | 0.993 | 1944 | 0.993 |
| 1945 | 0.993 | 0.991 | 0.991 | 0.993 | 1.000 | 1.009 | 1.011 | 1.011 | 1.007 | 1.007 | 1.011 | 1.015 | 1945 | 1.015 |
| 1946 | 1.015 | 1.011 | 1.019 | 1.024 | 1.030 | 1.041 | 1.102 | 1.127 | 1.140 | 1.162 | 1.190 | 1.199 | 1946 | 1.199 |
| 1947 | 1.199 | 1.197 | 1.223 | 1.223 | 1.220 | 1.229 | 1.240 | 1.253 | 1.283 | 1.283 | 1.291 | 1.307 | 1947 | 1.307 |
| 1948 | 1.322 | 1.311 | 1.307 | 1.326 | 1.335 | 1.345 | 1.361 | 1.367 | 1.367 | 1.361 | 1.352 | 1.343 | 1948 | 1.343 |
| 1949 | 1.341 | 1.326 | 1.330 | 1.331 | 1.330 | 1.331 | 1.322 | 1.326 | 1.331 | 1.324 | 1.326 | 1.318 | 1949 | 1.318 |
| 1950 | 1.313 | 1.309 | 1.315 | 1.317 | 1.322 | 1.330 | 1.343 | 1.354 | 1.363 | 1.371 | 1.376 | 1.395 | 1950 | 1.395 |
| 1951 | 1.417 | 1.434 | 1.439 | 1.441 | 1.447 | 1.445 | 1.447 | 1.447 | 1.456 | 1.464 | 1.471 | 1.477 | 1951 | 1.477 |
| 1952 | 1.477 | 1.467 | 1.467 | 1.473 | 1.475 | 1.479 | 1.490 | 1.492 | 1.490 | 1.492 | 1.492 | 1.490 | 1952 | 1.490 |
| 1953 | 1.486 | 1.479 | 1.482 | 1.484 | 1.488 | 1.493 | 1.497 | 1.501 | 1.503 | 1.507 | 1.501 | 1.499 | 1953 | 1.499 |
| 1954 | 1.503 | 1.501 | 1.499 | 1.495 | 1.501 | 1.503 | 1.503 | 1.501 | 1.497 | 1.493 | 1.495 | 1.492 | 1954 | 1.492 |
| 1955 | 1.492 | 1.492 | 1.492 | 1.492 | 1.492 | 1.492 | 1.497 | 1.493 | 1.499 | 1.499 | 1.501 | 1.497 | 1955 | 1.497 |

## Appendix B-10

Inflation Index
From 1926 to 2016

| Year | Jan | Feb | Mar | Apr | May | Jun | Jul | Aug | Sep | Oct | Nov | Dec | Yr End | Index |
|------|-----|-----|-----|-----|-----|-----|-----|-----|-----|-----|-----|-----|--------|-------|
| 1956 | 1.495 | 1.495 | 1.497 | 1.499 | 1.507 | 1.516 | 1.527 | 1.525 | 1.527 | 1.536 | 1.536 | 1.540 | 1956 | 1.540 |
| 1957 | 1.542 | 1.547 | 1.551 | 1.557 | 1.561 | 1.570 | 1.577 | 1.579 | 1.581 | 1.581 | 1.587 | 1.587 | 1957 | 1.587 |
| 1958 | 1.596 | 1.598 | 1.609 | 1.613 | 1.613 | 1.615 | 1.616 | 1.615 | 1.615 | 1.615 | 1.616 | 1.615 | 1958 | 1.615 |
| 1959 | 1.616 | 1.615 | 1.615 | 1.616 | 1.618 | 1.626 | 1.629 | 1.628 | 1.633 | 1.639 | 1.639 | 1.639 | 1959 | 1.639 |
| 1960 | 1.637 | 1.639 | 1.639 | 1.648 | 1.648 | 1.652 | 1.652 | 1.652 | 1.654 | 1.661 | 1.663 | 1.663 | 1960 | 1.663 |
| 1961 | 1.663 | 1.663 | 1.663 | 1.663 | 1.663 | 1.665 | 1.672 | 1.670 | 1.674 | 1.674 | 1.674 | 1.674 | 1961 | 1.674 |
| 1962 | 1.674 | 1.678 | 1.682 | 1.685 | 1.685 | 1.685 | 1.689 | 1.689 | 1.698 | 1.696 | 1.696 | 1.695 | 1962 | 1.695 |
| 1963 | 1.696 | 1.698 | 1.700 | 1.700 | 1.700 | 1.708 | 1.715 | 1.715 | 1.715 | 1.717 | 1.719 | 1.723 | 1963 | 1.723 |
| 1964 | 1.724 | 1.723 | 1.724 | 1.726 | 1.726 | 1.730 | 1.734 | 1.732 | 1.736 | 1.737 | 1.741 | 1.743 | 1964 | 1.743 |
| 1965 | 1.743 | 1.743 | 1.745 | 1.750 | 1.754 | 1.764 | 1.765 | 1.762 | 1.765 | 1.767 | 1.771 | 1.777 | 1965 | 1.777 |
| 1966 | 1.777 | 1.788 | 1.793 | 1.801 | 1.803 | 1.808 | 1.814 | 1.823 | 1.827 | 1.834 | 1.834 | 1.836 | 1966 | 1.836 |
| 1967 | 1.836 | 1.838 | 1.842 | 1.845 | 1.851 | 1.857 | 1.866 | 1.872 | 1.875 | 1.881 | 1.886 | 1.892 | 1967 | 1.892 |
| 1968 | 1.899 | 1.905 | 1.914 | 1.920 | 1.926 | 1.937 | 1.946 | 1.952 | 1.957 | 1.968 | 1.976 | 1.981 | 1968 | 1.981 |
| 1969 | 1.987 | 1.994 | 2.011 | 2.024 | 2.030 | 2.043 | 2.052 | 2.061 | 2.071 | 2.078 | 2.089 | 2.102 | 1969 | 2.102 |
| 1970 | 2.110 | 2.121 | 2.132 | 2.145 | 2.155 | 2.166 | 2.173 | 2.177 | 2.188 | 2.199 | 2.207 | 2.218 | 1970 | 2.218 |
| 1971 | 2.220 | 2.223 | 2.231 | 2.238 | 2.250 | 2.263 | 2.268 | 2.274 | 2.276 | 2.279 | 2.283 | 2.292 | 1971 | 2.292 |
| 1972 | 2.294 | 2.305 | 2.309 | 2.315 | 2.322 | 2.328 | 2.337 | 2.341 | 2.350 | 2.358 | 2.363 | 2.371 | 1972 | 2.371 |
| 1973 | 2.378 | 2.395 | 2.417 | 2.434 | 2.449 | 2.466 | 2.471 | 2.516 | 2.523 | 2.544 | 2.562 | 2.579 | 1973 | 2.579 |
| 1974 | 2.602 | 2.635 | 2.665 | 2.680 | 2.710 | 2.736 | 2.756 | 2.791 | 2.825 | 2.849 | 2.873 | 2.894 | 1974 | 2.894 |
| 1975 | 2.907 | 2.927 | 2.939 | 2.953 | 2.967 | 2.991 | 3.022 | 3.032 | 3.047 | 3.065 | 3.084 | 3.097 | 1975 | 3.097 |
| 1976 | 3.104 | 3.112 | 3.119 | 3.132 | 3.151 | 3.168 | 3.186 | 3.201 | 3.214 | 3.227 | 3.237 | 3.246 | 1976 | 3.246 |
| 1977 | 3.264 | 3.298 | 3.318 | 3.345 | 3.363 | 3.386 | 3.400 | 3.413 | 3.426 | 3.436 | 3.453 | 3.466 | 1977 | 3.466 |
| 1978 | 3.484 | 3.508 | 3.533 | 3.564 | 3.600 | 3.637 | 3.663 | 3.682 | 3.708 | 3.737 | 3.758 | 3.778 | 1978 | 3.778 |
| 1979 | 3.812 | 3.857 | 3.894 | 3.939 | 3.987 | 4.024 | 4.076 | 4.117 | 4.160 | 4.197 | 4.237 | 4.281 | 1979 | 4.281 |
| 1980 | 4.343 | 4.402 | 4.466 | 4.516 | 4.561 | 4.611 | 4.615 | 4.644 | 4.687 | 4.728 | 4.771 | 4.812 | 1980 | 4.812 |
| 1981 | 4.851 | 4.901 | 4.937 | 4.968 | 5.009 | 5.052 | 5.110 | 5.149 | 5.201 | 5.212 | 5.227 | 5.242 | 1981 | 5.242 |
| 1982 | 5.261 | 5.278 | 5.272 | 5.294 | 5.346 | 5.412 | 5.441 | 5.453 | 5.462 | 5.477 | 5.467 | 5.445 | 1982 | 5.445 |
| 1983 | 5.458 | 5.460 | 5.464 | 5.503 | 5.533 | 5.551 | 5.574 | 5.592 | 5.620 | 5.635 | 5.644 | 5.652 | 1983 | 5.652 |
| 1984 | 5.683 | 5.710 | 5.723 | 5.750 | 5.767 | 5.786 | 5.805 | 5.829 | 5.857 | 5.872 | 5.872 | 5.875 | 1984 | 5.875 |
| 1985 | 5.886 | 5.911 | 5.937 | 5.961 | 5.983 | 6.002 | 6.011 | 6.024 | 6.043 | 6.061 | 6.082 | 6.097 | 1985 | 6.097 |

# Appendix B-10

Inflation Index
From 1926 to 2016

| Year | Jan | Feb | Mar | Apr | May | Jun | Jul | Aug | Sep | Oct | Nov | Dec | Yr End | Index |
|---|---|---|---|---|---|---|---|---|---|---|---|---|---|---|
| 1986 | 6.115 | 6.099 | 6.071 | 6.058 | 6.076 | 6.106 | 6.108 | 6.119 | 6.149 | 6.155 | 6.160 | 6.166 | 1986 | 6.166 |
| 1987 | 6.203 | 6.227 | 6.255 | 6.289 | 6.307 | 6.333 | 6.346 | 6.382 | 6.413 | 6.430 | 6.439 | 6.438 | 1987 | 6.438 |
| 1988 | 6.454 | 6.471 | 6.499 | 6.532 | 6.555 | 6.583 | 6.610 | 6.638 | 6.683 | 6.705 | 6.711 | 6.722 | 1988 | 6.722 |
| 1989 | 6.756 | 6.783 | 6.822 | 6.867 | 6.906 | 6.923 | 6.940 | 6.951 | 6.973 | 7.007 | 7.023 | 7.034 | 1989 | 7.034 |
| 1990 | 7.107 | 7.140 | 7.180 | 7.191 | 7.207 | 7.246 | 7.274 | 7.341 | 7.403 | 7.447 | 7.464 | 7.464 | 1990 | 7.464 |
| 1991 | 7.509 | 7.520 | 7.531 | 7.542 | 7.564 | 7.587 | 7.598 | 7.620 | 7.654 | 7.665 | 7.687 | 7.693 | 1991 | 7.693 |
| 1992 | 7.704 | 7.732 | 7.771 | 7.782 | 7.793 | 7.821 | 7.838 | 7.860 | 7.882 | 7.910 | 7.921 | 7.916 | 1992 | 7.916 |
| 1993 | 7.955 | 7.983 | 8.011 | 8.033 | 8.044 | 8.055 | 8.055 | 8.078 | 8.094 | 8.128 | 8.133 | 8.133 | 1993 | 8.133 |
| 1994 | 8.156 | 8.184 | 8.212 | 8.223 | 8.228 | 8.256 | 8.278 | 8.312 | 8.334 | 8.340 | 8.351 | 8.351 | 1994 | 8.351 |
| 1995 | 8.384 | 8.418 | 8.446 | 8.474 | 8.490 | 8.507 | 8.507 | 8.530 | 8.546 | 8.574 | 8.569 | 8.563 | 1995 | 8.563 |
| 1996 | 8.613 | 8.641 | 8.686 | 8.719 | 8.736 | 8.741 | 8.758 | 8.775 | 8.803 | 8.831 | 8.847 | 8.847 | 1996 | 8.847 |
| 1997 | 8.875 | 8.903 | 8.926 | 8.937 | 8.931 | 8.942 | 8.953 | 8.970 | 8.993 | 9.015 | 9.009 | 8.998 | 1997 | 8.998 |
| 1998 | 9.015 | 9.032 | 9.048 | 9.065 | 9.082 | 9.093 | 9.104 | 9.115 | 9.126 | 9.149 | 9.149 | 9.143 | 1998 | 9.143 |
| 1999 | 9.165 | 9.177 | 9.204 | 9.271 | 9.271 | 9.271 | 9.299 | 9.322 | 9.366 | 9.383 | 9.389 | 9.389 | 1999 | 9.389 |
| 2000 | 9.416 | 9.472 | 9.550 | 9.556 | 9.567 | 9.617 | 9.640 | 9.640 | 9.690 | 9.707 | 9.712 | 9.707 | 2000 | 9.707 |
| 2001 | 9.768 | 9.807 | 9.829 | 9.868 | 9.913 | 9.930 | 9.902 | 9.902 | 9.946 | 9.913 | 9.896 | 9.857 | 2001 | 9.857 |
| 2002 | 9.879 | 9.919 | 9.974 | 10.030 | 10.030 | 10.036 | 10.047 | 10.080 | 10.097 | 10.114 | 10.114 | 10.091 | 2002 | 10.091 |
| 2003 | 10.136 | 10.214 | 10.276 | 10.253 | 10.237 | 10.248 | 10.259 | 10.298 | 10.331 | 10.320 | 10.292 | 10.281 | 2003 | 10.281 |
| 2004 | 10.331 | 10.387 | 10.454 | 10.488 | 10.549 | 10.582 | 10.566 | 10.571 | 10.594 | 10.649 | 10.655 | 10.616 | 2004 | 10.616 |
| 2005 | 10.638 | 10.700 | 10.783 | 10.856 | 10.845 | 10.850 | 10.900 | 10.956 | 11.090 | 11.112 | 11.023 | 10.978 | 2005 | 10.978 |
| 2006 | 11.062 | 11.084 | 11.146 | 11.241 | 11.296 | 11.319 | 11.352 | 11.375 | 11.319 | 11.257 | 11.241 | 11.257 | 2006 | 11.257 |
| 2007 | 11.292 | 11.352 | 11.456 | 11.530 | 11.600 | 11.623 | 11.620 | 11.599 | 11.631 | 11.655 | 11.725 | 11.717 | 2007 | 11.717 |
| 2008 | 11.775 | 11.809 | 11.912 | 11.984 | 12.085 | 12.207 | 12.271 | 12.222 | 12.205 | 12.081 | 11.850 | 11.728 | 2008 | 11.728 |
| 2009 | 11.779 | 11.837 | 11.866 | 11.896 | 11.930 | 12.032 | 12.013 | 12.040 | 12.048 | 12.059 | 12.068 | 12.047 | 2009 | 12.047 |
| 2010 | 12.088 | 12.091 | 12.141 | 12.162 | 12.171 | 12.159 | 12.162 | 12.178 | 12.186 | 12.201 | 12.206 | 12.227 | 2010 | 12.227 |
| 2011 | 12.285 | 12.346 | 12.466 | 12.546 | 12.605 | 12.592 | 12.603 | 12.638 | 12.657 | 12.631 | 12.620 | 12.589 | 2011 | 12.589 |
| 2012 | 12.644 | 12.700 | 12.797 | 12.835 | 12.820 | 12.801 | 12.781 | 12.852 | 12.909 | 12.904 | 12.843 | 12.808 | 2012 | 12.808 |
| 2013 | 12.846 | 12.951 | 12.985 | 12.972 | 12.995 | 13.026 | 13.031 | 13.047 | 13.062 | 13.028 | 13.002 | 13.001 | 2013 | 13.001 |
| 2014 | 13.050 | 13.098 | 13.182 | 13.226 | 13.272 | 13.297 | 13.291 | 13.269 | 13.279 | 13.246 | 13.174 | 13.100 | 2014 | 13.100 |
| 2015 | 13.038 | 13.095 | 13.173 | 13.199 | 13.267 | 13.313 | 13.314 | 13.295 | 13.274 | 13.268 | 13.240 | 13.195 | 2015 | 13.195 |
| 2016 | 13.217 | 13.228 | 13.285 | 13.348 | 13.402 | 13.446 | 13.424 | 13.436 | 13.469 | 13.486 | 13.465 | 13.469 | 2016 | 13.469 |

# Appendix C
# Rates of Return for All Yearly Holding Periods 1926–2016

**Basic Series: Total Rates of Return for All Holdings Periods**

## Appendix C-1

Large-Capitalization Stocks: Percent per annum total returns for all historical periods

From 1926 to 2016

| End Date | Start Date 1926 | 1927 | 1928 | 1929 | 1930 | 1931 | 1932 | 1933 | 1934 | 1935 | 1936 | 1937 | 1938 | 1939 | 1940 | 1941 | 1942 | 1943 | 1944 | 1945 |
|---|---|---|---|---|---|---|---|---|---|---|---|---|---|---|---|---|---|---|---|---|
| 1926 | 11.6 | | | | | | | | | | | | | | | | | | | |
| 1927 | 23.9 | 37.5 | | | | | | | | | | | | | | | | | | |
| 1928 | 30.1 | 40.5 | 43.6 | | | | | | | | | | | | | | | | | |
| 1929 | 19.2 | 21.8 | 14.7 | -8.4 | | | | | | | | | | | | | | | | |
| 1930 | 8.7 | 8.0 | -0.4 | -17.1 | -24.9 | | | | | | | | | | | | | | | |
| 1931 | -2.5 | -5.1 | -13.5 | -27.0 | -34.8 | -43.3 | | | | | | | | | | | | | | |
| 1932 | -3.3 | -5.6 | -12.5 | -22.7 | -26.9 | -27.9 | -8.2 | | | | | | | | | | | | | |
| 1933 | 2.5 | 1.2 | -3.8 | -11.2 | -11.9 | -7.1 | 18.9 | 54.0 | | | | | | | | | | | | |
| 1934 | 2.0 | 0.9 | -3.5 | -9.7 | -9.9 | -5.7 | 11.7 | 23.2 | -1.4 | | | | | | | | | | | |
| 1935 | 5.9 | 5.2 | 1.8 | -3.1 | -2.2 | 3.1 | 19.8 | 30.9 | 20.6 | 47.7 | | | | | | | | | | |
| 1936 | 8.1 | 7.8 | 4.9 | 0.9 | 2.3 | 7.7 | 22.5 | 31.6 | 24.9 | 40.6 | 33.9 | | | | | | | | | |
| 1937 | 3.7 | 3.0 | 0.0 | -3.9 | -3.3 | 0.2 | 10.2 | 14.3 | 6.1 | 8.7 | -6.7 | -35.0 | | | | | | | | |
| 1938 | 5.5 | 5.1 | 2.5 | -0.9 | 0.0 | 3.6 | 13.0 | 16.9 | 10.7 | 13.9 | 4.5 | -7.7 | 31.1 | | | | | | | |
| 1939 | 5.1 | 4.6 | 2.3 | -0.8 | -0.1 | 3.2 | 11.2 | 14.3 | 8.7 | 10.9 | 3.2 | -5.3 | 14.3 | -0.4 | | | | | | |
| 1940 | 4.0 | 3.5 | 1.3 | -1.6 | -1.0 | 1.8 | 8.6 | 11.0 | 5.9 | 7.2 | 0.5 | -6.5 | 5.6 | -5.2 | -9.8 | | | | | |
| 1941 | 3.0 | 2.4 | 0.3 | -2.4 | -1.9 | 0.5 | 6.4 | 8.2 | 3.5 | 4.3 | -1.6 | -7.5 | 1.0 | -7.4 | -10.7 | -11.6 | | | | |
| 1942 | 3.9 | 3.5 | 1.5 | -1.0 | -0.4 | 2.0 | 7.6 | 9.3 | 5.3 | 6.1 | 1.2 | -3.4 | 4.6 | -1.1 | -1.4 | 3.1 | 20.3 | | | |
| 1943 | 5.0 | 4.7 | 2.9 | 0.6 | 1.3 | 3.7 | 9.0 | 10.8 | 7.2 | 8.2 | 4.0 | 0.4 | 7.9 | 3.8 | 4.8 | 10.2 | 23.1 | 25.9 | | |
| 1944 | 5.8 | 5.5 | 3.8 | 1.7 | 2.5 | 4.8 | 9.8 | 11.5 | 8.3 | 9.3 | 5.7 | 2.6 | 9.5 | 6.3 | 7.7 | 12.5 | 22.0 | 22.8 | 19.8 | |
| 1945 | 7.1 | 6.9 | 5.4 | 3.5 | 4.3 | 6.6 | 11.5 | 13.2 | 10.4 | 11.5 | 8.4 | 5.9 | 12.6 | 10.1 | 12.0 | 17.0 | 25.4 | 27.2 | 27.8 | 36.4 |
| 1946 | 6.4 | 6.1 | 4.7 | 2.8 | 3.5 | 5.6 | 10.1 | 11.6 | 8.8 | 9.7 | 6.8 | 4.4 | 10.1 | 7.7 | 8.9 | 12.4 | 17.9 | 17.3 | 14.5 | 12.0 |
| 1947 | 6.3 | 6.1 | 4.7 | 3.0 | 3.7 | 5.6 | 9.8 | 11.2 | 8.6 | 9.4 | 6.7 | 4.5 | 9.6 | 7.5 | 8.5 | 11.4 | 15.8 | 14.9 | 12.3 | 9.9 |
| 1948 | 6.3 | 6.1 | 4.7 | 3.1 | 3.8 | 5.6 | 9.6 | 10.8 | 8.4 | 9.1 | 6.6 | 4.6 | 9.2 | 7.3 | 8.2 | 10.6 | 14.2 | 13.2 | 10.9 | 8.8 |
| 1949 | 6.8 | 6.6 | 5.3 | 3.8 | 4.5 | 6.3 | 10.1 | 11.2 | 9.0 | 9.7 | 7.4 | 5.6 | 10.0 | 8.3 | 9.2 | 11.5 | 14.8 | 14.0 | 12.2 | 10.7 |
| 1950 | 7.7 | 7.5 | 6.4 | 4.9 | 5.6 | 7.4 | 11.1 | 12.3 | 10.2 | 11.0 | 8.9 | 7.3 | 11.5 | 10.0 | 11.0 | 13.4 | 16.6 | 16.1 | 14.8 | 13.9 |
| 1951 | 8.3 | 8.1 | 7.1 | 5.7 | 6.4 | 8.2 | 11.7 | 12.9 | 11.0 | 11.7 | 9.8 | 8.4 | 12.4 | 11.1 | 12.1 | 14.3 | 17.3 | 16.9 | 15.9 | 15.3 |
| 1952 | 8.6 | 8.5 | 7.5 | 6.2 | 6.9 | 8.6 | 12.0 | 13.2 | 11.3 | 12.1 | 10.3 | 9.0 | 12.8 | 11.6 | 12.5 | 14.6 | 17.4 | 17.1 | 16.1 | 15.7 |
| 1953 | 8.3 | 8.1 | 7.2 | 5.9 | 6.5 | 8.2 | 11.4 | 12.4 | 10.7 | 11.4 | 9.6 | 8.3 | 11.9 | 10.7 | 11.5 | 13.4 | 15.7 | 15.3 | 14.3 | 13.7 |
| 1954 | 9.6 | 9.5 | 8.6 | 7.4 | 8.1 | 9.7 | 12.9 | 14.0 | 12.4 | 13.1 | 11.6 | 10.4 | 13.9 | 12.9 | 13.9 | 15.8 | 18.2 | 18.0 | 17.4 | 17.1 |
| 1955 | 10.2 | 10.2 | 9.3 | 8.2 | 8.9 | 10.5 | 13.7 | 14.7 | 13.2 | 13.9 | 12.5 | 11.4 | 14.8 | 13.9 | 14.9 | 16.8 | 19.1 | 19.0 | 18.5 | 18.4 |
| 1956 | 10.1 | 10.1 | 9.2 | 8.2 | 8.8 | 10.4 | 13.4 | 14.4 | 12.9 | 13.6 | 12.2 | 11.2 | 14.4 | 13.5 | 14.4 | 16.1 | 18.2 | 18.1 | 17.5 | 17.3 |
| 1957 | 9.4 | 9.3 | 8.5 | 7.4 | 8.1 | 9.5 | 12.3 | 13.2 | 11.8 | 12.4 | 11.0 | 10.0 | 13.0 | 12.1 | 12.8 | 14.3 | 16.2 | 15.9 | 15.2 | 14.9 |
| 1958 | 10.3 | 10.2 | 9.5 | 8.5 | 9.1 | 10.6 | 13.3 | 14.3 | 12.9 | 13.6 | 12.3 | 11.4 | 14.3 | 13.5 | 14.3 | 15.8 | 17.6 | 17.5 | 16.9 | 16.7 |
| 1959 | 10.3 | 10.3 | 9.5 | 8.6 | 9.2 | 10.6 | 13.3 | 14.2 | 12.9 | 13.5 | 12.3 | 11.4 | 14.2 | 13.4 | 14.1 | 15.6 | 17.3 | 17.1 | 16.6 | 16.4 |
| 1960 | 10.0 | 10.0 | 9.3 | 8.3 | 8.9 | 10.3 | 12.8 | 13.7 | 12.4 | 13.0 | 11.8 | 10.9 | 13.5 | 12.8 | 13.5 | 14.8 | 16.4 | 16.1 | 15.6 | 15.3 |
| 1961 | 10.5 | 10.4 | 9.7 | 8.8 | 9.4 | 10.8 | 13.3 | 14.1 | 12.9 | 13.4 | 12.3 | 11.5 | 14.1 | 13.4 | 14.0 | 15.3 | 16.9 | 16.7 | 16.2 | 16.0 |
| 1962 | 9.9 | 9.9 | 9.2 | 8.3 | 8.8 | 10.1 | 12.5 | 13.2 | 12.1 | 12.6 | 11.4 | 10.7 | 13.0 | 12.3 | 12.9 | 14.1 | 15.5 | 15.3 | 14.7 | 14.4 |
| 1963 | 10.2 | 10.2 | 9.5 | 8.7 | 9.2 | 10.5 | 12.8 | 13.5 | 12.4 | 12.9 | 11.8 | 11.1 | 13.4 | 12.7 | 13.3 | 14.5 | 15.8 | 15.6 | 15.1 | 14.9 |
| 1964 | 10.4 | 10.4 | 9.7 | 8.9 | 9.4 | 10.6 | 12.9 | 13.6 | 12.5 | 13.0 | 12.0 | 11.3 | 13.5 | 12.9 | 13.5 | 14.5 | 15.8 | 15.6 | 15.2 | 14.9 |
| 1965 | 10.4 | 10.4 | 9.8 | 9.0 | 9.5 | 10.7 | 12.9 | 13.6 | 12.5 | 13.0 | 12.0 | 11.3 | 13.5 | 12.9 | 13.4 | 14.5 | 15.7 | 15.5 | 15.0 | 14.8 |
| 1966 | 9.9 | 9.8 | 9.2 | 8.4 | 8.9 | 10.1 | 12.2 | 12.8 | 11.8 | 12.2 | 11.2 | 10.5 | 12.6 | 12.0 | 12.4 | 13.4 | 14.5 | 14.3 | 13.8 | 13.6 |
| 1967 | 10.2 | 10.2 | 9.6 | 8.8 | 9.3 | 10.4 | 12.5 | 13.1 | 12.1 | 12.5 | 11.6 | 10.9 | 12.9 | 12.4 | 12.8 | 13.8 | 14.9 | 14.7 | 14.2 | 14.0 |
| 1968 | 10.2 | 10.2 | 9.6 | 8.9 | 9.3 | 10.4 | 12.4 | 13.1 | 12.1 | 12.5 | 11.6 | 10.9 | 12.9 | 12.3 | 12.8 | 13.7 | 14.7 | 14.5 | 14.1 | 13.9 |
| 1969 | 9.8 | 9.7 | 9.1 | 8.4 | 8.9 | 9.9 | 11.8 | 12.4 | 11.4 | 11.8 | 10.9 | 10.3 | 12.1 | 11.6 | 12.0 | 12.8 | 13.8 | 13.6 | 13.1 | 12.9 |
| 1970 | 9.6 | 9.6 | 9.0 | 8.3 | 8.7 | 9.7 | 11.6 | 12.2 | 11.2 | 11.6 | 10.7 | 10.1 | 11.9 | 11.3 | 11.7 | 12.5 | 13.5 | 13.2 | 12.8 | 12.5 |

# Appendix C-1

Large-Capitalization Stocks: Percent per annum total returns for all historical periods

From 1926 to 2016

| End Date | Start Date 1926 | 1927 | 1928 | 1929 | 1930 | 1931 | 1932 | 1933 | 1934 | 1935 | 1936 | 1937 | 1938 | 1939 | 1940 | 1941 | 1942 | 1943 | 1944 | 1945 |
|---|---|---|---|---|---|---|---|---|---|---|---|---|---|---|---|---|---|---|---|---|
| 1971 | 9.7 | 9.7 | 9.1 | 8.4 | 8.9 | 9.8 | 11.7 | 12.2 | 11.3 | 11.7 | 10.8 | 10.2 | 11.9 | 11.4 | 11.8 | 12.6 | 13.5 | 13.3 | 12.8 | 12.6 |
| 1972 | 9.9 | 9.9 | 9.3 | 8.7 | 9.1 | 10.1 | 11.9 | 12.4 | 11.5 | 11.9 | 11.0 | 10.5 | 12.1 | 11.6 | 12.0 | 12.8 | 13.7 | 13.4 | 13.0 | 12.8 |
| 1973 | 9.3 | 9.3 | 8.7 | 8.1 | 8.5 | 9.4 | 11.1 | 11.7 | 10.8 | 11.1 | 10.3 | 9.7 | 11.3 | 10.8 | 11.1 | 11.8 | 12.6 | 12.4 | 12.0 | 11.7 |
| 1974 | 8.4 | 8.4 | 7.8 | 7.2 | 7.5 | 8.4 | 10.1 | 10.5 | 9.7 | 10.0 | 9.1 | 8.5 | 10.1 | 9.5 | 9.8 | 10.5 | 11.2 | 10.9 | 10.5 | 10.2 |
| 1975 | 9.0 | 8.9 | 8.4 | 7.7 | 8.1 | 9.0 | 10.6 | 11.1 | 10.2 | 10.5 | 9.8 | 9.2 | 10.7 | 10.2 | 10.5 | 11.1 | 11.9 | 11.6 | 11.2 | 11.0 |
| 1976 | 9.2 | 9.2 | 8.7 | 8.0 | 8.4 | 9.3 | 10.9 | 11.4 | 10.5 | 10.8 | 10.1 | 9.5 | 11.0 | 10.5 | 10.8 | 11.5 | 12.2 | 12.0 | 11.6 | 11.3 |
| 1977 | 8.9 | 8.8 | 8.3 | 7.7 | 8.1 | 8.9 | 10.5 | 10.9 | 10.1 | 10.4 | 9.6 | 9.1 | 10.5 | 10.0 | 10.3 | 10.9 | 11.6 | 11.4 | 11.0 | 10.7 |
| 1978 | 8.9 | 8.8 | 8.3 | 7.7 | 8.0 | 8.9 | 10.4 | 10.8 | 10.0 | 10.3 | 9.6 | 9.0 | 10.4 | 9.9 | 10.2 | 10.8 | 11.5 | 11.3 | 10.9 | 10.6 |
| 1979 | 9.0 | 9.0 | 8.5 | 7.9 | 8.2 | 9.1 | 10.6 | 11.0 | 10.2 | 10.5 | 9.8 | 9.2 | 10.6 | 10.2 | 10.4 | 11.0 | 11.7 | 11.4 | 11.1 | 10.8 |
| 1980 | 9.4 | 9.4 | 8.9 | 8.3 | 8.7 | 9.5 | 11.0 | 11.4 | 10.6 | 10.9 | 10.2 | 9.7 | 11.1 | 10.6 | 10.9 | 11.5 | 12.2 | 12.0 | 11.6 | 11.4 |
| 1981 | 9.1 | 9.1 | 8.6 | 8.1 | 8.4 | 9.2 | 10.6 | 11.0 | 10.3 | 10.6 | 9.9 | 9.4 | 10.7 | 10.2 | 10.5 | 11.1 | 11.7 | 11.5 | 11.1 | 10.9 |
| 1982 | 9.3 | 9.3 | 8.8 | 8.3 | 8.6 | 9.4 | 10.8 | 11.2 | 10.5 | 10.8 | 10.1 | 9.6 | 10.9 | 10.5 | 10.8 | 11.3 | 11.9 | 11.7 | 11.4 | 11.2 |
| 1983 | 9.6 | 9.5 | 9.1 | 8.5 | 8.9 | 9.6 | 11.0 | 11.5 | 10.7 | 11.0 | 10.3 | 9.9 | 11.2 | 10.7 | 11.0 | 11.6 | 12.2 | 12.0 | 11.7 | 11.5 |
| 1984 | 9.5 | 9.5 | 9.0 | 8.5 | 8.8 | 9.6 | 11.0 | 11.4 | 10.7 | 10.9 | 10.3 | 9.8 | 11.0 | 10.6 | 10.9 | 11.4 | 12.0 | 11.8 | 11.5 | 11.3 |
| 1985 | 9.8 | 9.8 | 9.4 | 8.9 | 9.2 | 9.9 | 11.3 | 11.7 | 11.0 | 11.3 | 10.7 | 10.2 | 11.4 | 11.1 | 11.3 | 11.8 | 12.4 | 12.3 | 12.0 | 11.8 |
| 1986 | 10.0 | 10.0 | 9.5 | 9.0 | 9.4 | 10.1 | 11.4 | 11.8 | 11.2 | 11.4 | 10.8 | 10.4 | 11.6 | 11.2 | 11.5 | 12.0 | 12.6 | 12.4 | 12.1 | 11.9 |
| 1987 | 9.9 | 9.9 | 9.5 | 9.0 | 9.3 | 10.0 | 11.3 | 11.7 | 11.0 | 11.3 | 10.7 | 10.3 | 11.5 | 11.1 | 11.3 | 11.8 | 12.4 | 12.2 | 12.0 | 11.8 |
| 1988 | 10.0 | 10.0 | 9.6 | 9.1 | 9.4 | 10.1 | 11.4 | 11.8 | 11.1 | 11.4 | 10.8 | 10.4 | 11.6 | 11.2 | 11.4 | 11.9 | 12.5 | 12.3 | 12.1 | 11.9 |
| 1989 | 10.3 | 10.3 | 9.9 | 9.4 | 9.7 | 10.5 | 11.7 | 12.1 | 11.5 | 11.7 | 11.2 | 10.8 | 11.9 | 11.6 | 11.8 | 12.3 | 12.9 | 12.7 | 12.4 | 12.3 |
| 1990 | 10.1 | 10.1 | 9.7 | 9.2 | 9.5 | 10.2 | 11.5 | 11.8 | 11.2 | 11.5 | 10.9 | 10.5 | 11.6 | 11.3 | 11.5 | 12.0 | 12.5 | 12.4 | 12.1 | 11.9 |
| 1991 | 10.4 | 10.4 | 10.0 | 9.5 | 9.8 | 10.5 | 11.8 | 12.1 | 11.5 | 11.8 | 11.2 | 10.8 | 11.9 | 11.6 | 11.8 | 12.3 | 12.9 | 12.7 | 12.4 | 12.3 |
| 1992 | 10.3 | 10.3 | 9.9 | 9.5 | 9.8 | 10.5 | 11.7 | 12.1 | 11.5 | 11.7 | 11.1 | 10.8 | 11.9 | 11.5 | 11.8 | 12.2 | 12.7 | 12.6 | 12.3 | 12.2 |
| 1993 | 10.3 | 10.3 | 9.9 | 9.5 | 9.8 | 10.5 | 11.7 | 12.0 | 11.4 | 11.7 | 11.1 | 10.8 | 11.8 | 11.5 | 11.7 | 12.2 | 12.7 | 12.6 | 12.3 | 12.2 |
| 1994 | 10.2 | 10.2 | 9.8 | 9.4 | 9.7 | 10.3 | 11.5 | 11.8 | 11.3 | 11.5 | 10.9 | 10.6 | 11.6 | 11.3 | 11.5 | 12.0 | 12.5 | 12.3 | 12.1 | 11.9 |
| 1995 | 10.5 | 10.5 | 10.2 | 9.7 | 10.0 | 10.7 | 11.9 | 12.2 | 11.6 | 11.9 | 11.3 | 11.0 | 12.0 | 11.7 | 11.9 | 12.4 | 12.9 | 12.8 | 12.5 | 12.4 |
| 1996 | 10.7 | 10.7 | 10.4 | 9.9 | 10.2 | 10.9 | 12.0 | 12.4 | 11.8 | 12.0 | 11.5 | 11.2 | 12.2 | 11.9 | 12.1 | 12.6 | 13.1 | 12.9 | 12.7 | 12.6 |
| 1997 | 11.0 | 11.0 | 10.7 | 10.2 | 10.5 | 11.2 | 12.3 | 12.7 | 12.1 | 12.3 | 11.9 | 11.5 | 12.5 | 12.2 | 12.5 | 12.9 | 13.4 | 13.3 | 13.1 | 12.9 |
| 1998 | 11.2 | 11.2 | 10.9 | 10.5 | 10.8 | 11.4 | 12.5 | 12.9 | 12.4 | 12.6 | 12.1 | 11.8 | 12.8 | 12.5 | 12.7 | 13.2 | 13.7 | 13.5 | 13.3 | 13.2 |
| 1999 | 11.3 | 11.3 | 11.0 | 10.6 | 10.9 | 11.5 | 12.7 | 13.0 | 12.5 | 12.7 | 12.2 | 11.9 | 12.9 | 12.6 | 12.9 | 13.3 | 13.8 | 13.7 | 13.5 | 13.3 |
| 2000 | 11.0 | 11.0 | 10.7 | 10.3 | 10.6 | 11.2 | 12.3 | 12.6 | 12.1 | 12.3 | 11.9 | 11.6 | 12.5 | 12.2 | 12.5 | 12.9 | 13.3 | 13.2 | 13.0 | 12.9 |
| 2001 | 10.7 | 10.7 | 10.4 | 10.0 | 10.3 | 10.9 | 11.9 | 12.2 | 11.7 | 11.9 | 11.5 | 11.2 | 12.1 | 11.8 | 12.0 | 12.4 | 12.9 | 12.7 | 12.5 | 12.4 |
| 2002 | 10.2 | 10.2 | 9.9 | 9.5 | 9.7 | 10.3 | 11.4 | 11.7 | 11.1 | 11.3 | 10.9 | 10.6 | 11.5 | 11.2 | 11.4 | 11.8 | 12.2 | 12.1 | 11.8 | 11.7 |
| 2003 | 10.4 | 10.4 | 10.1 | 9.7 | 10.0 | 10.5 | 11.6 | 11.9 | 11.4 | 11.6 | 11.1 | 10.8 | 11.7 | 11.4 | 11.6 | 12.0 | 12.4 | 12.3 | 12.1 | 12.0 |
| 2004 | 10.4 | 10.4 | 10.1 | 9.7 | 10.0 | 10.6 | 11.6 | 11.9 | 11.4 | 11.6 | 11.1 | 10.8 | 11.7 | 11.4 | 11.6 | 12.0 | 12.4 | 12.3 | 12.1 | 11.9 |
| 2005 | 10.4 | 10.3 | 10.0 | 9.7 | 9.9 | 10.5 | 11.5 | 11.8 | 11.3 | 11.5 | 11.0 | 10.7 | 11.6 | 11.3 | 11.5 | 11.9 | 12.3 | 12.2 | 12.0 | 11.8 |
| 2006 | 10.4 | 10.4 | 10.1 | 9.7 | 10.0 | 10.5 | 11.5 | 11.8 | 11.3 | 11.5 | 11.1 | 10.8 | 11.6 | 11.4 | 11.6 | 11.9 | 12.3 | 12.2 | 12.0 | 11.9 |
| 2007 | 10.4 | 10.3 | 10.0 | 9.7 | 9.9 | 10.5 | 11.5 | 11.7 | 11.3 | 11.4 | 11.0 | 10.7 | 11.6 | 11.3 | 11.5 | 11.8 | 12.2 | 12.1 | 11.9 | 11.8 |
| 2008 | 9.6 | 9.6 | 9.3 | 8.9 | 9.2 | 9.7 | 10.6 | 10.9 | 10.4 | 10.6 | 10.1 | 9.8 | 10.7 | 10.4 | 10.6 | 10.9 | 11.3 | 11.1 | 10.9 | 10.8 |
| 2009 | 9.8 | 9.8 | 9.5 | 9.1 | 9.4 | 9.9 | 10.8 | 11.1 | 10.6 | 10.8 | 10.4 | 10.1 | 10.9 | 10.6 | 10.8 | 11.1 | 11.5 | 11.4 | 11.1 | 11.0 |
| 2010 | 9.9 | 9.8 | 9.6 | 9.2 | 9.4 | 9.9 | 10.9 | 11.1 | 10.7 | 10.8 | 10.4 | 10.1 | 10.9 | 10.7 | 10.8 | 11.2 | 11.5 | 11.4 | 11.2 | 11.1 |
| 2011 | 9.8 | 9.8 | 9.5 | 9.1 | 9.3 | 9.8 | 10.8 | 11.0 | 10.6 | 10.7 | 10.3 | 10.0 | 10.8 | 10.5 | 10.7 | 11.0 | 11.4 | 11.3 | 11.1 | 10.9 |
| 2012 | 9.8 | 9.8 | 9.5 | 9.2 | 9.4 | 9.9 | 10.8 | 11.0 | 10.6 | 10.8 | 10.4 | 10.1 | 10.9 | 10.6 | 10.8 | 11.1 | 11.5 | 11.3 | 11.1 | 11.0 |
| 2013 | 10.1 | 10.1 | 9.8 | 9.4 | 9.7 | 10.2 | 11.1 | 11.3 | 10.9 | 11.0 | 10.6 | 10.4 | 11.1 | 10.9 | 11.0 | 11.4 | 11.7 | 11.6 | 11.4 | 11.3 |
| 2014 | 10.1 | 10.1 | 9.8 | 9.5 | 9.7 | 10.2 | 11.1 | 11.4 | 10.9 | 11.1 | 10.7 | 10.4 | 11.2 | 10.9 | 11.1 | 11.4 | 11.7 | 11.6 | 11.4 | 11.3 |
| 2015 | 10.0 | 10.0 | 9.7 | 9.4 | 9.6 | 10.1 | 11.0 | 11.2 | 10.8 | 10.9 | 10.5 | 10.3 | 11.0 | 10.8 | 10.9 | 11.3 | 11.6 | 11.5 | 11.3 | 11.2 |
| 2016 | 10.0 | 10.0 | 9.7 | 9.4 | 9.6 | 10.1 | 11.0 | 11.2 | 10.8 | 11.0 | 10.6 | 10.3 | 11.0 | 10.8 | 11.0 | 11.3 | 11.6 | 11.5 | 11.3 | 11.2 |

## Appendix C-1

Large-Capitalization Stocks: Percent per annum total returns for all historical periods

From 1926 to 2016

| End Date | Start Date 1946 | 1947 | 1948 | 1949 | 1950 | 1951 | 1952 | 1953 | 1954 | 1955 | 1956 | 1957 | 1958 | 1959 | 1960 | 1961 | 1962 | 1963 | 1964 | 1965 |
|---|---|---|---|---|---|---|---|---|---|---|---|---|---|---|---|---|---|---|---|---|
| 1926 | | | | | | | | | | | | | | | | | | | | |
| 1927 | | | | | | | | | | | | | | | | | | | | |
| 1928 | | | | | | | | | | | | | | | | | | | | |
| 1929 | | | | | | | | | | | | | | | | | | | | |
| 1930 | | | | | | | | | | | | | | | | | | | | |
| 1931 | | | | | | | | | | | | | | | | | | | | |
| 1932 | | | | | | | | | | | | | | | | | | | | |
| 1933 | | | | | | | | | | | | | | | | | | | | |
| 1934 | | | | | | | | | | | | | | | | | | | | |
| 1935 | | | | | | | | | | | | | | | | | | | | |
| 1936 | | | | | | | | | | | | | | | | | | | | |
| 1937 | | | | | | | | | | | | | | | | | | | | |
| 1938 | | | | | | | | | | | | | | | | | | | | |
| 1939 | | | | | | | | | | | | | | | | | | | | |
| 1940 | | | | | | | | | | | | | | | | | | | | |
| 1941 | | | | | | | | | | | | | | | | | | | | |
| 1942 | | | | | | | | | | | | | | | | | | | | |
| 1943 | | | | | | | | | | | | | | | | | | | | |
| 1944 | | | | | | | | | | | | | | | | | | | | |
| 1945 | | | | | | | | | | | | | | | | | | | | |
| 1946 | -8.1 | | | | | | | | | | | | | | | | | | | |
| 1947 | -1.4 | 5.7 | | | | | | | | | | | | | | | | | | |
| 1948 | 0.8 | 5.6 | 5.5 | | | | | | | | | | | | | | | | | |
| 1949 | 5.1 | 9.8 | 11.9 | 18.8 | | | | | | | | | | | | | | | | |
| 1950 | 9.9 | 14.9 | 18.2 | 25.1 | 31.7 | | | | | | | | | | | | | | | |
| 1951 | 12.1 | 16.7 | 19.6 | 24.7 | 27.8 | 24.0 | | | | | | | | | | | | | | |
| 1952 | 13.0 | 17.0 | 19.4 | 23.1 | 24.6 | 21.2 | 18.4 | | | | | | | | | | | | | |
| 1953 | 11.2 | 14.2 | 15.7 | 17.9 | 17.6 | 13.3 | 8.3 | -1.0 | | | | | | | | | | | | |
| 1954 | 15.1 | 18.4 | 20.4 | 23.0 | 23.9 | 22.0 | 21.4 | 22.9 | 52.6 | | | | | | | | | | | |
| 1955 | 16.7 | 19.8 | 21.7 | 24.2 | 25.2 | 23.9 | 23.9 | 25.7 | 41.7 | 31.6 | | | | | | | | | | |
| 1956 | 15.7 | 18.4 | 19.9 | 21.9 | 22.3 | 20.8 | 20.2 | 20.6 | 28.9 | 18.4 | 6.6 | | | | | | | | | |
| 1957 | 13.2 | 15.4 | 16.4 | 17.7 | 17.6 | 15.7 | 14.4 | 13.6 | 17.5 | 7.7 | -2.5 | -10.8 | | | | | | | | |
| 1958 | 15.3 | 17.5 | 18.7 | 20.1 | 20.2 | 18.8 | 18.1 | 18.1 | 22.3 | 15.7 | 10.9 | 13.1 | 43.4 | | | | | | | |
| 1959 | 15.1 | 17.1 | 18.1 | 19.3 | 19.4 | 18.1 | 17.3 | 17.2 | 20.5 | 15.0 | 11.1 | 12.7 | 26.7 | 12.0 | | | | | | |
| 1960 | 14.0 | 15.8 | 16.6 | 17.6 | 17.5 | 16.2 | 15.3 | 14.9 | 17.4 | 12.4 | 8.9 | 9.5 | 17.3 | 6.1 | 0.5 | | | | | |
| 1961 | 14.8 | 16.5 | 17.3 | 18.3 | 18.3 | 17.1 | 16.4 | 16.2 | 18.6 | 14.4 | 11.7 | 12.8 | 19.6 | 12.9 | 12.6 | 26.9 | | | | |
| 1962 | 13.3 | 14.8 | 15.4 | 16.1 | 15.9 | 14.7 | 13.9 | 13.4 | 15.2 | 11.2 | 8.5 | 8.9 | 13.3 | 6.8 | 5.2 | 7.6 | -8.7 | | | |
| 1963 | 13.8 | 15.2 | 15.8 | 16.6 | 16.4 | 15.3 | 14.6 | 14.3 | 15.9 | 12.4 | 10.2 | 10.8 | 14.8 | 9.9 | 9.3 | 12.5 | 5.9 | 22.8 | | |
| 1964 | 13.9 | 15.3 | 15.9 | 16.6 | 16.4 | 15.4 | 14.7 | 14.4 | 16.0 | 12.8 | 10.9 | 11.5 | 15.1 | 10.9 | 10.7 | 13.5 | 9.3 | 19.6 | 16.5 | |
| 1965 | 13.8 | 15.1 | 15.7 | 16.3 | 16.2 | 15.2 | 14.6 | 14.3 | 15.7 | 12.8 | 11.1 | 11.6 | 14.7 | 11.1 | 11.0 | 13.2 | 10.1 | 17.2 | 14.4 | 12.5 |
| 1966 | 12.6 | 13.7 | 14.2 | 14.7 | 14.4 | 13.4 | 12.7 | 12.4 | 13.4 | 10.7 | 9.0 | 9.2 | 11.7 | 8.2 | 7.7 | 9.0 | 5.7 | 9.7 | 5.6 | 0.6 |
| 1967 | 13.1 | 14.2 | 14.6 | 15.1 | 14.9 | 14.0 | 13.4 | 13.1 | 14.2 | 11.6 | 10.1 | 10.5 | 12.8 | 9.9 | 9.6 | 11.0 | 8.6 | 12.4 | 9.9 | 7.8 |
| 1968 | 13.0 | 14.0 | 14.5 | 14.9 | 14.7 | 13.8 | 13.3 | 13.0 | 14.0 | 11.6 | 10.2 | 10.5 | 12.7 | 10.0 | 9.8 | 11.0 | 8.9 | 12.2 | 10.2 | 8.6 |
| 1969 | 12.0 | 13.0 | 13.3 | 13.7 | 13.4 | 12.5 | 11.9 | 11.6 | 12.4 | 10.1 | 8.7 | 8.9 | 10.7 | 8.2 | 7.8 | 8.7 | 6.6 | 9.0 | 6.8 | 5.0 |
| 1970 | 11.7 | 12.6 | 12.9 | 13.2 | 13.0 | 12.1 | 11.5 | 11.1 | 11.9 | 9.7 | 8.4 | 8.6 | 10.2 | 7.8 | 7.4 | 8.2 | 6.3 | 8.3 | 6.4 | 4.8 |

## Appendix C-1

Large-Capitalization Stocks: Percent per annum total returns for all historical periods

From 1926 to 2016

| End Date | Start Date 1946 | 1947 | 1948 | 1949 | 1950 | 1951 | 1952 | 1953 | 1954 | 1955 | 1956 | 1957 | 1958 | 1959 | 1960 | 1961 | 1962 | 1963 | 1964 | 1965 |
|---|---|---|---|---|---|---|---|---|---|---|---|---|---|---|---|---|---|---|---|---|
| 1971 | 11.8 | 12.6 | 12.9 | 13.3 | 13.0 | 12.2 | 11.6 | 11.3 | 12.0 | 10.0 | 8.8 | 8.9 | 10.5 | 8.3 | 8.0 | 8.7 | 7.0 | 9.0 | 7.3 | 6.1 |
| 1972 | 12.0 | 12.9 | 13.2 | 13.5 | 13.3 | 12.5 | 12.0 | 11.7 | 12.4 | 10.5 | 9.4 | 9.5 | 11.0 | 9.0 | 8.8 | 9.5 | 8.1 | 9.9 | 8.6 | 7.6 |
| 1973 | 10.9 | 11.7 | 11.9 | 12.2 | 11.9 | 11.2 | 10.6 | 10.2 | 10.8 | 9.0 | 7.9 | 7.9 | 9.2 | 7.3 | 6.9 | 7.4 | 6.0 | 7.4 | 6.0 | 4.9 |
| 1974 | 9.4 | 10.0 | 10.2 | 10.4 | 10.1 | 9.3 | 8.7 | 8.2 | 8.7 | 6.9 | 5.7 | 5.7 | 6.7 | 4.8 | 4.3 | 4.6 | 3.0 | 4.1 | 2.5 | 1.2 |
| 1975 | 10.2 | 10.9 | 11.1 | 11.3 | 11.0 | 10.3 | 9.7 | 9.4 | 9.9 | 8.1 | 7.1 | 7.1 | 8.2 | 6.4 | 6.1 | 6.5 | 5.2 | 6.3 | 5.0 | 4.1 |
| 1976 | 10.6 | 11.3 | 11.5 | 11.7 | 11.5 | 10.8 | 10.3 | 9.9 | 10.4 | 8.8 | 7.8 | 7.9 | 9.0 | 7.3 | 7.1 | 7.5 | 6.3 | 7.5 | 6.4 | 5.6 |
| 1977 | 10.0 | 10.7 | 10.8 | 11.0 | 10.7 | 10.0 | 9.5 | 9.2 | 9.6 | 8.1 | 7.1 | 7.1 | 8.1 | 6.5 | 6.2 | 6.6 | 5.4 | 6.4 | 5.4 | 4.5 |
| 1978 | 9.9 | 10.5 | 10.7 | 10.9 | 10.6 | 9.9 | 9.4 | 9.1 | 9.5 | 8.0 | 7.1 | 7.1 | 8.0 | 6.5 | 6.2 | 6.6 | 5.5 | 6.4 | 5.4 | 4.7 |
| 1979 | 10.2 | 10.8 | 10.9 | 11.1 | 10.9 | 10.2 | 9.7 | 9.4 | 9.8 | 8.4 | 7.5 | 7.6 | 8.5 | 7.1 | 6.8 | 7.2 | 6.2 | 7.1 | 6.2 | 5.6 |
| 1980 | 10.7 | 11.3 | 11.5 | 11.7 | 11.5 | 10.9 | 10.4 | 10.2 | 10.6 | 9.2 | 8.4 | 8.5 | 9.4 | 8.1 | 7.9 | 8.3 | 7.4 | 8.4 | 7.6 | 7.1 |
| 1981 | 10.3 | 10.8 | 11.0 | 11.2 | 10.9 | 10.3 | 9.9 | 9.6 | 10.0 | 8.7 | 7.9 | 7.9 | 8.8 | 7.5 | 7.3 | 7.7 | 6.8 | 7.7 | 6.9 | 6.3 |
| 1982 | 10.6 | 11.1 | 11.3 | 11.5 | 11.2 | 10.7 | 10.3 | 10.0 | 10.4 | 9.1 | 8.4 | 8.4 | 9.3 | 8.1 | 7.9 | 8.2 | 7.4 | 8.3 | 7.6 | 7.1 |
| 1983 | 10.9 | 11.4 | 11.6 | 11.8 | 11.6 | 11.0 | 10.6 | 10.4 | 10.8 | 9.6 | 8.8 | 8.9 | 9.8 | 8.6 | 8.5 | 8.8 | 8.1 | 8.9 | 8.3 | 7.9 |
| 1984 | 10.7 | 11.3 | 11.4 | 11.6 | 11.4 | 10.9 | 10.5 | 10.2 | 10.6 | 9.5 | 8.8 | 8.8 | 9.6 | 8.5 | 8.4 | 8.7 | 8.0 | 8.8 | 8.2 | 7.8 |
| 1985 | 11.2 | 11.8 | 11.9 | 12.1 | 11.9 | 11.4 | 11.1 | 10.8 | 11.2 | 10.1 | 9.5 | 9.6 | 10.4 | 9.3 | 9.2 | 9.6 | 8.9 | 9.7 | 9.2 | 8.8 |
| 1986 | 11.4 | 11.9 | 12.1 | 12.3 | 12.1 | 11.6 | 11.3 | 11.1 | 11.5 | 10.4 | 9.7 | 9.8 | 10.6 | 9.6 | 9.5 | 9.9 | 9.3 | 10.1 | 9.6 | 9.3 |
| 1987 | 11.2 | 11.8 | 11.9 | 12.1 | 11.9 | 11.4 | 11.1 | 10.9 | 11.3 | 10.2 | 9.6 | 9.7 | 10.5 | 9.5 | 9.4 | 9.7 | 9.1 | 9.9 | 9.4 | 9.1 |
| 1988 | 11.4 | 11.9 | 12.0 | 12.2 | 12.0 | 11.6 | 11.2 | 11.1 | 11.4 | 10.4 | 9.8 | 9.9 | 10.6 | 9.7 | 9.6 | 10.0 | 9.4 | 10.1 | 9.7 | 9.4 |
| 1989 | 11.8 | 12.3 | 12.5 | 12.6 | 12.5 | 12.0 | 11.7 | 11.6 | 11.9 | 10.9 | 10.4 | 10.5 | 11.3 | 10.3 | 10.3 | 10.6 | 10.1 | 10.9 | 10.4 | 10.2 |
| 1990 | 11.4 | 11.9 | 12.1 | 12.2 | 12.1 | 11.6 | 11.3 | 11.2 | 11.5 | 10.5 | 10.0 | 10.1 | 10.8 | 9.9 | 9.8 | 10.2 | 9.6 | 10.3 | 9.9 | 9.7 |
| 1991 | 11.8 | 12.3 | 12.5 | 12.6 | 12.5 | 12.1 | 11.8 | 11.6 | 12.0 | 11.0 | 10.5 | 10.6 | 11.3 | 10.5 | 10.4 | 10.8 | 10.3 | 11.0 | 10.6 | 10.4 |
| 1992 | 11.7 | 12.2 | 12.4 | 12.5 | 12.4 | 11.9 | 11.7 | 11.5 | 11.8 | 10.9 | 10.4 | 10.5 | 11.2 | 10.4 | 10.3 | 10.7 | 10.2 | 10.9 | 10.5 | 10.3 |
| 1993 | 11.7 | 12.2 | 12.3 | 12.5 | 12.3 | 11.9 | 11.6 | 11.5 | 11.8 | 10.9 | 10.4 | 10.5 | 11.2 | 10.4 | 10.3 | 10.6 | 10.2 | 10.8 | 10.5 | 10.3 |
| 1994 | 11.5 | 11.9 | 12.1 | 12.2 | 12.1 | 11.7 | 11.4 | 11.2 | 11.5 | 10.7 | 10.2 | 10.3 | 10.9 | 10.1 | 10.1 | 10.4 | 9.9 | 10.5 | 10.2 | 10.0 |
| 1995 | 11.9 | 12.4 | 12.5 | 12.7 | 12.6 | 12.2 | 11.9 | 11.8 | 12.1 | 11.3 | 10.8 | 10.9 | 11.5 | 10.8 | 10.7 | 11.1 | 10.6 | 11.3 | 10.9 | 10.8 |
| 1996 | 12.1 | 12.6 | 12.7 | 12.9 | 12.8 | 12.4 | 12.1 | 12.0 | 12.3 | 11.5 | 11.1 | 11.2 | 11.8 | 11.1 | 11.1 | 11.4 | 11.0 | 11.6 | 11.3 | 11.1 |
| 1997 | 12.5 | 13.0 | 13.1 | 13.3 | 13.2 | 12.8 | 12.6 | 12.4 | 12.8 | 12.0 | 11.6 | 11.7 | 12.3 | 11.6 | 11.6 | 11.9 | 11.5 | 12.2 | 11.9 | 11.7 |
| 1998 | 12.8 | 13.3 | 13.4 | 13.6 | 13.5 | 13.1 | 12.9 | 12.8 | 13.1 | 12.3 | 11.9 | 12.1 | 12.7 | 12.0 | 12.0 | 12.3 | 12.0 | 12.6 | 12.3 | 12.2 |
| 1999 | 13.0 | 13.4 | 13.5 | 13.7 | 13.6 | 13.3 | 13.1 | 12.9 | 13.3 | 12.5 | 12.1 | 12.3 | 12.9 | 12.2 | 12.2 | 12.5 | 12.2 | 12.8 | 12.5 | 12.4 |
| 2000 | 12.5 | 12.9 | 13.1 | 13.2 | 13.1 | 12.8 | 12.6 | 12.4 | 12.7 | 12.0 | 11.6 | 11.7 | 12.3 | 11.7 | 11.6 | 11.9 | 11.6 | 12.2 | 11.9 | 11.8 |
| 2001 | 12.0 | 12.4 | 12.6 | 12.7 | 12.6 | 12.2 | 12.0 | 11.9 | 12.2 | 11.4 | 11.0 | 11.1 | 11.7 | 11.0 | 11.0 | 11.3 | 10.9 | 11.5 | 11.2 | 11.1 |
| 2002 | 11.3 | 11.7 | 11.8 | 11.9 | 11.8 | 11.4 | 11.2 | 11.1 | 11.3 | 10.6 | 10.2 | 10.3 | 10.8 | 10.1 | 10.1 | 10.3 | 10.0 | 10.5 | 10.2 | 10.0 |
| 2003 | 11.6 | 12.0 | 12.1 | 12.2 | 12.1 | 11.7 | 11.5 | 11.4 | 11.7 | 10.9 | 10.6 | 10.6 | 11.2 | 10.5 | 10.5 | 10.7 | 10.4 | 10.9 | 10.6 | 10.5 |
| 2004 | 11.6 | 11.9 | 12.1 | 12.2 | 12.1 | 11.7 | 11.5 | 11.4 | 11.6 | 10.9 | 10.6 | 10.6 | 11.2 | 10.5 | 10.4 | 10.7 | 10.4 | 10.9 | 10.6 | 10.5 |
| 2005 | 11.5 | 11.8 | 11.9 | 12.0 | 11.9 | 11.6 | 11.4 | 11.3 | 11.5 | 10.8 | 10.4 | 10.5 | 11.0 | 10.4 | 10.4 | 10.6 | 10.3 | 10.8 | 10.5 | 10.3 |
| 2006 | 11.5 | 11.9 | 12.0 | 12.1 | 12.0 | 11.7 | 11.5 | 11.3 | 11.6 | 10.9 | 10.5 | 10.6 | 11.1 | 10.5 | 10.5 | 10.7 | 10.4 | 10.9 | 10.6 | 10.5 |
| 2007 | 11.4 | 11.8 | 11.9 | 12.0 | 11.9 | 11.6 | 11.4 | 11.2 | 11.5 | 10.8 | 10.4 | 10.5 | 11.0 | 10.4 | 10.4 | 10.6 | 10.3 | 10.7 | 10.5 | 10.3 |
| 2008 | 10.4 | 10.8 | 10.8 | 10.9 | 10.8 | 10.5 | 10.2 | 10.1 | 10.3 | 9.7 | 9.3 | 9.3 | 9.8 | 9.2 | 9.1 | 9.3 | 9.0 | 9.4 | 9.1 | 9.0 |
| 2009 | 10.7 | 11.0 | 11.1 | 11.2 | 11.0 | 10.7 | 10.5 | 10.4 | 10.6 | 9.9 | 9.6 | 9.6 | 10.1 | 9.5 | 9.5 | 9.6 | 9.3 | 9.7 | 9.5 | 9.3 |
| 2010 | 10.7 | 11.0 | 11.1 | 11.2 | 11.1 | 10.8 | 10.6 | 10.5 | 10.7 | 10.0 | 9.7 | 9.7 | 10.2 | 9.6 | 9.6 | 9.8 | 9.4 | 9.8 | 9.6 | 9.4 |
| 2011 | 10.6 | 10.9 | 11.0 | 11.1 | 11.0 | 10.6 | 10.4 | 10.3 | 10.5 | 9.9 | 9.5 | 9.6 | 10.0 | 9.5 | 9.4 | 9.6 | 9.3 | 9.7 | 9.4 | 9.3 |
| 2012 | 10.7 | 11.0 | 11.1 | 11.2 | 11.0 | 10.7 | 10.5 | 10.4 | 10.6 | 10.0 | 9.6 | 9.7 | 10.1 | 9.6 | 9.5 | 9.7 | 9.4 | 9.8 | 9.5 | 9.4 |
| 2013 | 11.0 | 11.3 | 11.4 | 11.5 | 11.3 | 11.0 | 10.8 | 10.7 | 10.9 | 10.3 | 10.0 | 10.1 | 10.5 | 10.0 | 9.9 | 10.1 | 9.8 | 10.2 | 10.0 | 9.8 |
| 2014 | 11.0 | 11.3 | 11.4 | 11.5 | 11.4 | 11.1 | 10.9 | 10.8 | 11.0 | 10.4 | 10.1 | 10.1 | 10.5 | 10.0 | 10.0 | 10.2 | 9.9 | 10.3 | 10.0 | 9.9 |
| 2015 | 10.9 | 11.2 | 11.2 | 11.3 | 11.2 | 10.9 | 10.7 | 10.6 | 10.8 | 10.2 | 9.9 | 10.0 | 10.4 | 9.9 | 9.8 | 10.0 | 9.7 | 10.1 | 9.9 | 9.7 |
| 2016 | 10.9 | 11.2 | 11.3 | 11.3 | 11.2 | 10.9 | 10.8 | 10.6 | 10.8 | 10.3 | 9.9 | 10.0 | 10.4 | 9.9 | 9.9 | 10.0 | 9.8 | 10.1 | 9.9 | 9.8 |

**Appendix C-1**

Large-Capitalization Stocks: Percent per annum total returns for all historical periods

From 1926 to 2016

| End Date | Start Date 1966 | 1967 | 1968 | 1969 | 1970 |
|---|---|---|---|---|---|
| 1966 | -10.1 | | | | |
| 1967 | 5.6 | 24.0 | | | |
| 1968 | 7.4 | 17.3 | 11.1 | | |
| 1969 | 3.2 | 8.0 | 0.8 | -8.5 | |
| 1970 | 3.3 | 7.0 | 1.8 | -2.5 | 3.9 |

Large-Capitalization Stocks: Percent per annum total returns for all historical periods

From 1926 to 2016

| End Date | \| Start Date 1966 | 1967 | 1968 | 1969 | 1970 | 1971 | 1972 | 1973 | 1974 | 1975 | 1976 | 1977 | 1978 | 1979 | 1980 | 1981 | 1982 | 1983 | 1984 | 1985 |
|---|---|---|---|---|---|---|---|---|---|---|---|---|---|---|---|---|---|---|---|---|
| 1971 | 5.1 | 8.4 | 4.8 | 2.8 | 9.0 | 14.3 | | | | | | | | | | | | | | |
| 1972 | 6.9 | 10.1 | 7.5 | 6.6 | 12.2 | 16.6 | 19.0 | | | | | | | | | | | | | |
| 1973 | 4.0 | 6.1 | 3.4 | 2.0 | 4.8 | 5.1 | 0.8 | -14.7 | | | | | | | | | | | | |
| 1974 | 0.0 | 1.4 | -1.5 | -3.4 | -2.4 | -3.9 | -9.3 | -20.8 | -26.5 | | | | | | | | | | | |
| 1975 | 3.3 | 4.9 | 2.7 | 1.5 | 3.3 | 3.2 | 0.6 | -4.9 | 0.5 | 37.2 | | | | | | | | | | |
| 1976 | 5.0 | 6.6 | 4.8 | 4.1 | 6.0 | 6.4 | 4.9 | 1.6 | 7.7 | 30.4 | 23.9 | | | | | | | | | |
| 1977 | 3.9 | 5.3 | 3.6 | 2.8 | 4.3 | 4.3 | 2.8 | -0.2 | 3.8 | 16.4 | 7.3 | -7.2 | | | | | | | | |
| 1978 | 4.1 | 5.4 | 3.8 | 3.2 | 4.5 | 4.6 | 3.3 | 0.9 | 4.4 | 13.9 | 7.0 | -0.5 | 6.6 | | | | | | | |
| 1979 | 5.1 | 6.4 | 5.0 | 4.5 | 5.9 | 6.1 | 5.1 | 3.3 | 6.6 | 14.8 | 9.8 | 5.5 | 12.4 | 18.6 | | | | | | |
| 1980 | 6.7 | 8.0 | 6.9 | 6.6 | 8.0 | 8.5 | 7.8 | 6.5 | 10.0 | 17.6 | 14.0 | 11.7 | 18.8 | 25.4 | 32.5 | | | | | |
| 1981 | 6.0 | 7.1 | 6.0 | 5.6 | 6.9 | 7.2 | 6.5 | 5.2 | 8.0 | 14.1 | 10.6 | 8.1 | 12.3 | 14.3 | 12.2 | -4.9 | | | | |
| 1982 | 6.8 | 8.0 | 7.0 | 6.7 | 8.0 | 8.3 | 7.8 | 6.7 | 9.4 | 15.0 | 12.1 | 10.3 | 14.1 | 16.1 | 15.3 | 7.5 | 21.5 | | | |
| 1983 | 7.6 | 8.8 | 7.9 | 7.7 | 8.9 | 9.3 | 8.9 | 8.1 | 10.7 | 15.8 | 13.4 | 11.9 | 15.5 | 17.4 | 17.0 | 12.3 | 22.0 | 22.6 | | |
| 1984 | 7.6 | 8.6 | 7.8 | 7.6 | 8.8 | 9.1 | 8.7 | 7.9 | 10.3 | 14.8 | 12.6 | 11.2 | 14.1 | 15.4 | 14.8 | 10.8 | 16.5 | 14.1 | 6.3 | |
| 1985 | 8.7 | 9.7 | 9.0 | 8.9 | 10.1 | 10.5 | 10.2 | 9.6 | 11.9 | 16.3 | 14.3 | 13.3 | 16.2 | 17.6 | 17.5 | 14.7 | 20.2 | 19.7 | 18.3 | 31.7 |
| 1986 | 9.1 | 10.2 | 9.5 | 9.4 | 10.6 | 11.0 | 10.8 | 10.2 | 12.4 | 16.5 | 14.7 | 13.8 | 16.5 | 17.8 | 17.6 | 15.3 | 19.9 | 19.5 | 18.4 | 25.0 |
| 1987 | 8.9 | 9.9 | 9.3 | 9.2 | 10.3 | 10.7 | 10.4 | 9.9 | 11.9 | 15.6 | 13.9 | 13.0 | 15.3 | 16.3 | 16.0 | 13.8 | 17.3 | 16.5 | 15.0 | 18.1 |
| 1988 | 9.3 | 10.2 | 9.6 | 9.5 | 10.6 | 11.0 | 10.8 | 10.3 | 12.2 | 15.6 | 14.1 | 13.3 | 15.4 | 16.3 | 16.1 | 14.2 | 17.2 | 16.5 | 15.3 | 17.7 |
| 1989 | 10.1 | 11.1 | 10.5 | 10.5 | 11.6 | 12.0 | 11.8 | 11.4 | 13.3 | 16.6 | 15.3 | 14.6 | 16.7 | 17.6 | 17.6 | 16.0 | 18.9 | 18.5 | 17.9 | 20.4 |
| 1990 | 9.6 | 10.5 | 9.9 | 9.9 | 10.8 | 11.2 | 11.0 | 10.6 | 12.3 | 15.3 | 14.0 | 13.3 | 15.0 | 15.8 | 15.5 | 13.9 | 16.2 | 15.6 | 14.6 | 16.1 |
| 1991 | 10.3 | 11.2 | 10.7 | 10.7 | 11.6 | 12.0 | 11.9 | 11.5 | 13.2 | 16.1 | 14.9 | 14.4 | 16.1 | 16.8 | 16.7 | 15.3 | 17.6 | 17.2 | 16.5 | 18.0 |
| 1992 | 10.2 | 11.1 | 10.6 | 10.5 | 11.5 | 11.8 | 11.7 | 11.3 | 12.9 | 15.6 | 14.5 | 13.9 | 15.5 | 16.1 | 16.0 | 14.7 | 16.6 | 16.2 | 15.5 | 16.7 |
| 1993 | 10.2 | 11.0 | 10.5 | 10.5 | 11.4 | 11.7 | 11.6 | 11.3 | 12.8 | 15.3 | 14.2 | 13.7 | 15.1 | 15.7 | 15.5 | 14.3 | 16.1 | 15.6 | 14.9 | 15.9 |
| 1994 | 9.9 | 10.7 | 10.2 | 10.2 | 11.0 | 11.3 | 11.2 | 10.8 | 12.2 | 14.8 | 13.5 | 13.0 | 14.3 | 14.8 | 14.5 | 13.3 | 14.9 | 14.3 | 13.6 | 14.4 |
| 1995 | 10.7 | 11.5 | 11.1 | 11.1 | 11.9 | 12.2 | 12.1 | 11.9 | 13.2 | 15.6 | 14.6 | 14.1 | 15.5 | 16.0 | 15.8 | 14.8 | 16.4 | 16.0 | 15.4 | 16.3 |
| 1996 | 11.1 | 11.9 | 11.5 | 11.5 | 12.3 | 12.6 | 12.6 | 12.3 | 13.7 | 15.9 | 15.0 | 14.6 | 15.8 | 16.4 | 16.3 | 15.3 | 16.8 | 16.5 | 16.0 | 16.9 |
| 1997 | 11.7 | 12.5 | 12.1 | 12.2 | 13.0 | 13.3 | 13.3 | 13.1 | 14.4 | 16.6 | 15.8 | 15.4 | 16.7 | 17.2 | 17.1 | 16.3 | 17.8 | 17.5 | 17.2 | 18.1 |
| 1998 | 12.2 | 13.0 | 12.6 | 12.7 | 13.5 | 13.8 | 13.8 | 13.6 | 14.9 | 17.1 | 16.3 | 16.0 | 17.2 | 17.8 | 17.7 | 16.9 | 18.4 | 18.2 | 17.9 | 18.8 |
| 1999 | 12.4 | 13.2 | 12.9 | 12.9 | 13.7 | 14.1 | 14.1 | 13.9 | 15.2 | 17.3 | 16.5 | 16.2 | 17.4 | 17.9 | 17.9 | 17.2 | 18.5 | 18.3 | 18.1 | 18.9 |
| 2000 | 11.8 | 12.5 | 12.1 | 12.2 | 12.9 | 13.2 | 13.2 | 13.0 | 14.2 | 16.1 | 15.3 | 15.0 | 16.1 | 16.5 | 16.4 | 15.7 | 16.9 | 16.6 | 16.3 | 16.9 |
| 2001 | 11.0 | 11.7 | 11.3 | 11.4 | 12.0 | 12.3 | 12.2 | 12.0 | 13.1 | 14.9 | 14.2 | 13.8 | 14.8 | 15.1 | 15.0 | 14.2 | 15.2 | 14.9 | 14.5 | 15.0 |
| 2002 | 10.0 | 10.6 | 10.2 | 10.2 | 10.8 | 11.0 | 10.9 | 10.7 | 11.7 | 13.4 | 12.6 | 12.1 | 13.0 | 13.3 | 13.0 | 12.2 | 13.1 | 12.7 | 12.2 | 12.5 |
| 2003 | 10.4 | 11.0 | 10.7 | 10.7 | 11.3 | 11.5 | 11.5 | 11.2 | 12.2 | 13.8 | 13.1 | 12.7 | 13.6 | 13.7 | 13.6 | 12.9 | 13.8 | 13.4 | 13.0 | 13.3 |
| 2004 | 10.4 | 11.0 | 10.7 | 10.7 | 11.3 | 11.5 | 11.4 | 11.2 | 12.2 | 13.7 | 13.0 | 12.6 | 13.5 | 13.7 | 13.5 | 12.8 | 13.6 | 13.3 | 12.9 | 13.2 |
| 2005 | 10.3 | 10.9 | 10.5 | 10.5 | 11.1 | 11.3 | 11.2 | 11.0 | 11.9 | 13.5 | 12.7 | 12.4 | 13.1 | 13.4 | 13.2 | 12.5 | 13.3 | 12.9 | 12.5 | 12.8 |
| 2006 | 10.4 | 11.0 | 10.7 | 10.7 | 11.2 | 11.4 | 11.4 | 11.1 | 12.0 | 13.5 | 12.8 | 12.5 | 13.2 | 13.5 | 13.3 | 12.6 | 13.4 | 13.0 | 12.6 | 12.9 |
| 2007 | 10.3 | 10.8 | 10.5 | 10.5 | 11.1 | 11.3 | 11.2 | 11.0 | 11.8 | 13.3 | 12.6 | 12.2 | 13.0 | 13.2 | 13.0 | 12.3 | 13.1 | 12.7 | 12.3 | 12.6 |
| 2008 | 8.9 | 9.4 | 9.0 | 9.0 | 9.5 | 9.6 | 9.5 | 9.2 | 10.0 | 11.3 | 10.6 | 10.2 | 10.9 | 11.0 | 10.7 | 10.0 | 10.6 | 10.2 | 9.8 | 9.9 |
| 2009 | 9.2 | 9.7 | 9.4 | 9.4 | 9.9 | 10.0 | 9.9 | 9.7 | 10.5 | 11.7 | 11.1 | 10.7 | 11.3 | 11.5 | 11.2 | 10.6 | 11.2 | 10.8 | 10.4 | 10.5 |
| 2010 | 9.4 | 9.9 | 9.5 | 9.5 | 10.0 | 10.2 | 10.0 | 9.8 | 10.6 | 11.8 | 11.2 | 10.8 | 11.4 | 11.6 | 11.4 | 10.7 | 11.3 | 10.9 | 10.5 | 10.7 |
| 2011 | 9.2 | 9.7 | 9.4 | 9.3 | 9.8 | 9.9 | 9.8 | 9.6 | 10.3 | 11.6 | 10.9 | 10.6 | 11.1 | 11.3 | 11.1 | 10.4 | 11.0 | 10.6 | 10.2 | 10.4 |
| 2012 | 9.3 | 9.8 | 9.5 | 9.5 | 9.9 | 10.1 | 10.0 | 9.8 | 10.5 | 11.7 | 11.1 | 10.7 | 11.4 | 11.4 | 11.2 | 10.6 | 11.1 | 10.8 | 10.4 | 10.6 |
| 2013 | 9.8 | 10.2 | 10.0 | 9.9 | 10.4 | 10.6 | 10.5 | 10.3 | 11.0 | 12.2 | 11.6 | 11.3 | 11.8 | 12.0 | 11.8 | 11.2 | 11.7 | 11.4 | 11.1 | 11.3 |
| 2014 | 9.9 | 10.3 | 10.0 | 10.0 | 10.5 | 10.6 | 10.5 | 10.4 | 11.0 | 12.2 | 11.6 | 11.3 | 11.9 | 12.0 | 11.8 | 11.3 | 11.8 | 11.5 | 11.2 | 11.3 |
| 2015 | 9.7 | 10.1 | 9.9 | 9.8 | 10.3 | 10.4 | 10.3 | 10.1 | 10.8 | 11.9 | 11.4 | 11.0 | 11.6 | 11.7 | 11.5 | 11.0 | 11.5 | 11.2 | 10.9 | 11.0 |
| 2016 | 9.7 | 10.2 | 9.9 | 9.9 | 10.3 | 10.5 | 10.4 | 10.2 | 10.8 | 11.9 | 11.4 | 11.1 | 11.6 | 11.7 | 11.5 | 11.0 | 11.5 | 11.2 | 10.9 | 11.0 |

**Appendix C-1**

Large-Capitalization Stocks: Percent per annum total returns for all historical periods

From 1926 to 2016

| End Date | 1986 | 1987 | 1988 | 1989 | 1990 | 1991 | 1992 | 1993 | 1994 | 1995 | 1996 | 1997 | 1998 | 1999 | 2000 | 2001 | 2002 | 2003 | 2004 | 2005 |
|---|---|---|---|---|---|---|---|---|---|---|---|---|---|---|---|---|---|---|---|---|
| 1971 | | | | | | | | | | | | | | | | | | | | |
| 1972 | | | | | | | | | | | | | | | | | | | | |
| 1973 | | | | | | | | | | | | | | | | | | | | |
| 1974 | | | | | | | | | | | | | | | | | | | | |
| 1975 | | | | | | | | | | | | | | | | | | | | |
| 1976 | | | | | | | | | | | | | | | | | | | | |
| 1977 | | | | | | | | | | | | | | | | | | | | |
| 1978 | | | | | | | | | | | | | | | | | | | | |
| 1979 | | | | | | | | | | | | | | | | | | | | |
| 1980 | | | | | | | | | | | | | | | | | | | | |
| 1981 | | | | | | | | | | | | | | | | | | | | |
| 1982 | | | | | | | | | | | | | | | | | | | | |
| 1983 | | | | | | | | | | | | | | | | | | | | |
| 1984 | | | | | | | | | | | | | | | | | | | | |
| 1985 | | | | | | | | | | | | | | | | | | | | |
| 1986 | 18.7 | | | | | | | | | | | | | | | | | | | |
| 1987 | 11.8 | 5.3 | | | | | | | | | | | | | | | | | | |
| 1988 | 13.4 | 10.8 | 16.6 | | | | | | | | | | | | | | | | | |
| 1989 | 17.7 | 17.4 | 23.9 | 31.7 | | | | | | | | | | | | | | | | |
| 1990 | 13.2 | 11.9 | 14.2 | 13.0 | -3.1 | | | | | | | | | | | | | | | |
| 1991 | 15.9 | 15.4 | 18.0 | 18.5 | 12.4 | 30.5 | | | | | | | | | | | | | | |
| 1992 | 14.7 | 14.0 | 15.9 | 15.7 | 10.8 | 18.5 | 7.6 | | | | | | | | | | | | | |
| 1993 | 14.1 | 13.5 | 14.9 | 14.5 | 10.6 | 15.6 | 8.8 | 10.1 | | | | | | | | | | | | |
| 1994 | 12.6 | 11.9 | 12.8 | 12.2 | 8.7 | 11.9 | 6.3 | 5.6 | 1.3 | | | | | | | | | | | |
| 1995 | 14.9 | 14.5 | 15.7 | 15.5 | 13.1 | 16.6 | 13.4 | 15.3 | 18.1 | 37.6 | | | | | | | | | | |
| 1996 | 15.6 | 15.3 | 16.5 | 16.4 | 14.4 | 17.6 | 15.2 | 17.2 | 19.7 | 30.1 | 23.0 | | | | | | | | | |
| 1997 | 17.0 | 16.8 | 18.1 | 18.2 | 16.6 | 19.8 | 18.1 | 20.3 | 23.0 | 31.2 | 28.1 | 33.4 | | | | | | | | |
| 1998 | 17.8 | 17.8 | 19.0 | 19.2 | 17.9 | 20.8 | 19.5 | 21.6 | 24.1 | 30.5 | 28.2 | 30.9 | 28.6 | | | | | | | |
| 1999 | 18.1 | 18.0 | 19.1 | 19.4 | 18.2 | 20.9 | 19.7 | 21.5 | 23.6 | 28.6 | 26.4 | 27.6 | 24.8 | 21.0 | | | | | | |
| 2000 | 16.0 | 15.8 | 16.7 | 16.7 | 15.4 | 17.5 | 16.1 | 17.2 | 18.3 | 21.3 | 18.3 | 17.2 | 12.3 | 4.9 | -9.1 | | | | | |
| 2001 | 14.0 | 13.7 | 14.4 | 14.2 | 12.9 | 14.4 | 12.9 | 14.0 | 14.0 | 15.9 | 12.7 | 10.7 | 5.7 | -1.0 | -10.5 | -11.9 | | | | |
| 2002 | 11.5 | 11.1 | 11.5 | 11.1 | 9.7 | 10.8 | 9.3 | 9.3 | 9.3 | 10.3 | 6.9 | 4.4 | -0.6 | -6.8 | -14.6 | -17.2 | -22.1 | | | |
| 2003 | 12.4 | 12.0 | 12.5 | 12.2 | 10.9 | 12.1 | 11.0 | 11.1 | 11.1 | 12.2 | 9.4 | 7.6 | 3.8 | -0.6 | -5.3 | -4.1 | 0.1 | 28.7 | | |
| 2004 | 12.3 | 12.0 | 12.4 | 12.1 | 10.9 | 12.0 | 10.7 | 11.0 | 11.0 | 12.1 | 9.5 | 8.0 | 4.8 | 1.3 | -2.3 | -0.5 | 3.6 | 19.5 | 10.9 | |
| 2005 | 11.9 | 11.6 | 12.0 | 11.7 | 10.5 | 11.5 | 10.3 | 10.5 | 10.5 | 11.4 | 9.1 | 7.6 | 4.8 | 1.8 | -1.1 | 0.5 | 3.9 | 14.4 | 7.9 | 4.9 |
| 2006 | 12.1 | 11.8 | 12.2 | 11.9 | 10.9 | 11.8 | 10.6 | 10.9 | 10.9 | 11.8 | 9.7 | 8.4 | 6.0 | 3.4 | 1.1 | 2.9 | 6.2 | 14.7 | 10.4 | 10.2 |
| 2007 | 11.8 | 11.5 | 11.8 | 11.6 | 10.5 | 11.4 | 10.3 | 10.5 | 10.5 | 11.3 | 9.3 | 8.2 | 5.9 | 3.7 | 1.7 | 3.3 | 6.1 | 12.8 | 9.2 | 8.6 |
| 2008 | 9.1 | 8.6 | 8.8 | 8.4 | 7.3 | 7.9 | 6.7 | 6.5 | 6.5 | 6.8 | 4.8 | 3.4 | 1.0 | -1.4 | -3.6 | -2.9 | -1.5 | 2.4 | -2.2 | -5.2 |
| 2009 | 9.7 | 9.4 | 9.5 | 9.2 | 8.2 | 8.8 | 7.7 | 7.8 | 7.6 | 8.0 | 6.2 | 5.0 | 2.9 | 0.9 | -0.9 | 0.0 | 1.6 | 5.5 | 2.1 | 0.4 |
| 2010 | 9.9 | 9.6 | 9.8 | 9.5 | 8.5 | 9.1 | 8.1 | 8.1 | 8.0 | 8.5 | 6.8 | 5.7 | 3.8 | 2.0 | 0.4 | 1.4 | 3.0 | 6.7 | 3.9 | 2.7 |
| 2011 | 9.6 | 9.3 | 9.5 | 9.2 | 8.2 | 8.8 | 7.8 | 7.8 | 7.7 | 8.1 | 6.5 | 5.5 | 3.7 | 2.0 | 0.6 | 1.5 | 2.9 | 6.2 | 3.6 | 2.6 |
| 2012 | 9.9 | 9.5 | 9.7 | 9.4 | 8.6 | 9.1 | 8.2 | 8.2 | 8.1 | 8.5 | 7.0 | 6.1 | 4.5 | 2.9 | 1.7 | 2.6 | 4.0 | 7.1 | 4.9 | 4.2 |
| 2013 | 10.6 | 10.3 | 10.5 | 10.3 | 9.5 | 10.0 | 9.2 | 9.3 | 9.2 | 9.7 | 8.3 | 7.5 | 6.0 | 4.7 | 3.6 | 4.6 | 6.2 | 9.2 | 7.4 | 7.0 |
| 2014 | 10.7 | 10.4 | 10.6 | 10.4 | 9.6 | 10.2 | 9.4 | 9.5 | 9.4 | 9.9 | 8.6 | 7.8 | 6.5 | 5.2 | 4.2 | 5.3 | 6.7 | 9.6 | 8.0 | 7.7 |
| 2015 | 10.4 | 10.1 | 10.3 | 10.0 | 9.3 | 9.8 | 9.0 | 9.1 | 9.0 | 9.4 | 8.2 | 7.5 | 6.2 | 5.0 | 4.1 | 5.0 | 6.3 | 8.9 | 7.4 | 7.1 |
| 2016 | 10.4 | 10.2 | 10.3 | 10.1 | 9.4 | 9.9 | 9.1 | 9.2 | 9.2 | 9.5 | 8.4 | 7.7 | 6.5 | 5.4 | 4.5 | 5.4 | 6.7 | 9.1 | 7.7 | 7.5 |

Start Date (column headers above) / End Date (row labels)

## Appendix C-1

Large-Capitalization Stocks: Percent per annum total returns for all historical periods

From 1926 to 2016

| End Date | Start Date 2006 | 2007 | 2008 | 2009 | 2010 | 2011 | 2012 | 2013 | 2014 | 2015 | 2016 |
|---|---|---|---|---|---|---|---|---|---|---|---|
| 1971 | | | | | | | | | | | |
| 1972 | | | | | | | | | | | |
| 1973 | | | | | | | | | | | |
| 1974 | | | | | | | | | | | |
| 1975 | | | | | | | | | | | |
| 1976 | | | | | | | | | | | |
| 1977 | | | | | | | | | | | |
| 1978 | | | | | | | | | | | |
| 1979 | | | | | | | | | | | |
| 1980 | | | | | | | | | | | |
| 1981 | | | | | | | | | | | |
| 1982 | | | | | | | | | | | |
| 1983 | | | | | | | | | | | |
| 1984 | | | | | | | | | | | |
| 1985 | | | | | | | | | | | |
| 1986 | | | | | | | | | | | |
| 1987 | | | | | | | | | | | |
| 1988 | | | | | | | | | | | |
| 1989 | | | | | | | | | | | |
| 1990 | | | | | | | | | | | |
| 1991 | | | | | | | | | | | |
| 1992 | | | | | | | | | | | |
| 1993 | | | | | | | | | | | |
| 1994 | | | | | | | | | | | |
| 1995 | | | | | | | | | | | |
| 1996 | | | | | | | | | | | |
| 1997 | | | | | | | | | | | |
| 1998 | | | | | | | | | | | |
| 1999 | | | | | | | | | | | |
| 2000 | | | | | | | | | | | |
| 2001 | | | | | | | | | | | |
| 2002 | | | | | | | | | | | |
| 2003 | | | | | | | | | | | |
| 2004 | | | | | | | | | | | |
| 2005 | | | | | | | | | | | |
| 2006 | 15.8 | | | | | | | | | | |
| 2007 | 10.5 | 5.5 | | | | | | | | | |
| 2008 | -8.4 | -18.5 | -37.0 | | | | | | | | |
| 2009 | -0.7 | -5.6 | -10.7 | 26.5 | | | | | | | |
| 2010 | 2.3 | -0.8 | -2.9 | 20.6 | 15.1 | | | | | | |
| 2011 | 2.3 | -0.2 | -1.6 | 14.1 | 8.4 | 2.1 | | | | | |
| 2012 | 4.1 | 2.3 | 1.7 | 14.6 | 10.9 | 8.8 | 16.0 | | | | |
| 2013 | 7.3 | 6.1 | 6.2 | 17.9 | 15.9 | 16.2 | 23.9 | 32.4 | | | |
| 2014 | 8.0 | 7.0 | 7.3 | 17.2 | 15.5 | 15.6 | 20.4 | 22.7 | 13.7 | | |
| 2015 | 7.3 | 6.4 | 6.5 | 14.8 | 13.0 | 12.6 | 15.3 | 15.1 | 7.4 | 1.4 | |
| 2016 | 7.7 | 6.9 | 7.1 | 14.5 | 12.8 | 12.5 | 14.7 | 14.3 | 8.9 | 6.5 | 12.0 |

## Appendix C-2

Small-Capitalization Stocks: Percent per annum total returns for all historical periods

From 1926 to 2016

| End Date | Start Date 1926 | 1927 | 1928 | 1929 | 1930 | 1931 | 1932 | 1933 | 1934 | 1935 | 1936 | 1937 | 1938 | 1939 | 1940 | 1941 | 1942 | 1943 | 1944 | 1945 |
|---|---|---|---|---|---|---|---|---|---|---|---|---|---|---|---|---|---|---|---|---|
| 1926 | 0.3 | | | | | | | | | | | | | | | | | | | |
| 1927 | 10.7 | 22.1 | | | | | | | | | | | | | | | | | | |
| 1928 | 19.6 | 30.6 | 39.7 | | | | | | | | | | | | | | | | | |
| 1929 | -4.5 | -6.0 | -17.6 | -51.4 | | | | | | | | | | | | | | | | |
| 1930 | -12.4 | -15.4 | -25.1 | -45.1 | -38.1 | | | | | | | | | | | | | | | |
| 1931 | -20.2 | -23.7 | -32.2 | -46.7 | -44.3 | -49.8 | | | | | | | | | | | | | | |
| 1932 | -18.2 | -21.0 | -27.5 | -38.5 | -33.5 | -31.1 | -5.4 | | | | | | | | | | | | | |
| 1933 | -6.3 | -7.2 | -11.4 | -19.1 | -8.1 | 4.9 | 51.6 | 142.9 | | | | | | | | | | | | |
| 1934 | -3.3 | -3.8 | -7.0 | -13.1 | -2.4 | 9.4 | 41.9 | 73.7 | 24.2 | | | | | | | | | | | |
| 1935 | 0.3 | 0.3 | -2.1 | -6.9 | 3.7 | 15.0 | 41.4 | 61.7 | 32.0 | 40.2 | | | | | | | | | | |
| 1936 | 5.0 | 5.5 | 3.7 | 0.0 | 10.8 | 22.1 | 45.8 | 62.5 | 42.1 | 52.0 | 64.8 | | | | | | | | | |
| 1937 | -2.7 | -3.0 | -5.2 | -9.2 | -1.9 | 4.8 | 18.5 | 24.0 | 4.8 | -1.0 | -16.8 | -58.0 | | | | | | | | |
| 1938 | -0.4 | -0.4 | -2.3 | -5.7 | 1.5 | 8.0 | 20.4 | 25.4 | 9.9 | 6.5 | -2.8 | -25.3 | 32.8 | | | | | | | |
| 1939 | -0.3 | -0.4 | -2.1 | -5.2 | 1.4 | 7.1 | 17.7 | 21.5 | 8.2 | 5.3 | -2.0 | -17.6 | 15.4 | 0.3 | | | | | | |
| 1940 | -0.7 | -0.7 | -2.3 | -5.2 | 0.8 | 5.8 | 14.9 | 17.8 | 6.2 | 3.5 | -2.6 | -14.6 | 8.1 | -2.4 | -5.2 | | | | | |
| 1941 | -1.2 | -1.3 | -2.8 | -5.5 | -0.1 | 4.4 | 12.3 | 14.4 | 4.2 | 1.6 | -3.7 | -13.5 | 3.6 | -4.7 | -7.1 | -9.0 | | | | |
| 1942 | 1.0 | 1.1 | -0.2 | -2.6 | 2.8 | 7.2 | 14.9 | 17.1 | 8.0 | 6.2 | 2.0 | -5.8 | 10.7 | 5.8 | 7.6 | 14.7 | 44.5 | | | |
| 1943 | 4.6 | 4.8 | 3.9 | 1.8 | 7.3 | 12.0 | 19.7 | 22.3 | 14.2 | 13.1 | 10.1 | 4.0 | 21.0 | 18.7 | 23.8 | 35.3 | 65.0 | 88.4 | | |
| 1944 | 6.7 | 7.1 | 6.3 | 4.5 | 9.9 | 14.5 | 22.0 | 24.7 | 17.3 | 16.7 | 14.3 | 9.2 | 25.2 | 23.9 | 29.3 | 39.7 | 61.1 | 70.2 | 53.7 | |
| 1945 | 9.4 | 9.9 | 9.2 | 7.6 | 13.1 | 17.8 | 25.2 | 27.9 | 21.2 | 21.0 | 19.2 | 15.0 | 30.4 | 30.1 | 35.8 | 45.9 | 64.2 | 71.3 | 63.4 | 73.6 |
| 1946 | 8.3 | 8.7 | 8.0 | 6.5 | 11.5 | 15.7 | 22.3 | 24.5 | 18.3 | 17.8 | 16.0 | 12.0 | 24.9 | 23.9 | 27.7 | 34.2 | 45.2 | 45.0 | 33.1 | 23.9 |
| 1947 | 7.9 | 8.3 | 7.6 | 6.2 | 10.9 | 14.7 | 20.8 | 22.8 | 17.0 | 16.4 | 14.6 | 10.9 | 22.2 | 21.1 | 24.0 | 28.8 | 36.5 | 35.0 | 24.2 | 15.7 |
| 1948 | 7.5 | 7.8 | 7.2 | 5.7 | 10.2 | 13.7 | 19.3 | 21.1 | 15.6 | 15.0 | 13.3 | 9.8 | 19.8 | 18.6 | 20.8 | 24.5 | 30.2 | 28.0 | 18.4 | 11.0 |
| 1949 | 7.9 | 8.3 | 7.7 | 6.4 | 10.6 | 14.0 | 19.4 | 21.0 | 15.8 | 15.3 | 13.7 | 10.5 | 19.8 | 18.7 | 20.7 | 24.0 | 28.8 | 26.7 | 18.6 | 12.7 |
| 1950 | 9.0 | 9.4 | 8.9 | 7.7 | 11.8 | 15.2 | 20.3 | 21.9 | 17.1 | 16.7 | 15.2 | 12.3 | 21.2 | 20.2 | 22.2 | 25.4 | 29.9 | 28.2 | 21.3 | 16.6 |
| 1951 | 9.0 | 9.3 | 8.8 | 7.7 | 11.6 | 14.8 | 19.7 | 21.1 | 16.5 | 16.1 | 14.8 | 12.0 | 20.1 | 19.2 | 21.0 | 23.7 | 27.5 | 25.7 | 19.6 | 15.3 |
| 1952 | 8.8 | 9.1 | 8.6 | 7.5 | 11.2 | 14.2 | 18.8 | 20.2 | 15.8 | 15.3 | 14.0 | 11.4 | 18.9 | 18.0 | 19.5 | 21.8 | 25.1 | 23.3 | 17.6 | 13.7 |
| 1953 | 8.2 | 8.5 | 8.0 | 6.9 | 10.4 | 13.3 | 17.5 | 18.7 | 14.6 | 14.1 | 12.8 | 10.3 | 17.2 | 16.2 | 17.4 | 19.3 | 22.1 | 20.2 | 14.9 | 11.3 |
| 1954 | 9.7 | 10.0 | 9.6 | 8.6 | 12.1 | 14.9 | 19.1 | 20.4 | 16.4 | 16.0 | 14.9 | 12.6 | 19.3 | 18.6 | 19.9 | 21.9 | 24.7 | 23.1 | 18.5 | 15.4 |
| 1955 | 10.0 | 10.3 | 9.9 | 9.0 | 12.4 | 15.1 | 19.2 | 20.4 | 16.6 | 16.3 | 15.2 | 13.0 | 19.4 | 18.7 | 19.9 | 21.8 | 24.4 | 22.9 | 18.6 | 15.9 |
| 1956 | 9.8 | 10.1 | 9.7 | 8.8 | 12.1 | 14.7 | 18.5 | 19.7 | 16.0 | 15.7 | 14.6 | 12.6 | 18.6 | 17.8 | 18.9 | 20.6 | 22.9 | 21.5 | 17.5 | 14.9 |
| 1957 | 8.9 | 9.2 | 8.8 | 7.9 | 11.0 | 13.4 | 17.1 | 18.1 | 14.6 | 14.2 | 13.1 | 11.1 | 16.6 | 15.8 | 16.8 | 18.2 | 20.1 | 18.7 | 14.8 | 12.3 |
| 1958 | 10.3 | 10.7 | 10.3 | 9.4 | 12.5 | 15.0 | 18.6 | 19.6 | 16.2 | 15.9 | 15.0 | 13.1 | 18.6 | 17.9 | 18.9 | 20.4 | 22.4 | 21.1 | 17.6 | 15.4 |
| 1959 | 10.5 | 10.8 | 10.5 | 9.7 | 12.7 | 15.0 | 18.5 | 19.5 | 16.3 | 15.9 | 15.0 | 13.2 | 18.5 | 17.8 | 18.8 | 20.2 | 22.1 | 20.9 | 17.6 | 15.5 |
| 1960 | 10.1 | 10.4 | 10.0 | 9.2 | 12.1 | 14.4 | 17.7 | 18.6 | 15.5 | 15.1 | 14.2 | 12.5 | 17.4 | 16.8 | 17.6 | 18.9 | 20.6 | 19.4 | 16.2 | 14.2 |
| 1961 | 10.6 | 10.9 | 10.6 | 9.9 | 12.7 | 14.9 | 18.1 | 19.0 | 16.0 | 15.7 | 14.9 | 13.2 | 18.0 | 17.4 | 18.2 | 19.5 | 21.1 | 20.0 | 17.0 | 15.2 |
| 1962 | 10.0 | 10.2 | 9.9 | 9.1 | 11.9 | 13.9 | 17.0 | 17.8 | 14.9 | 14.6 | 13.8 | 12.1 | 16.6 | 16.0 | 16.7 | 17.8 | 19.3 | 18.2 | 15.3 | 13.5 |
| 1963 | 10.3 | 10.6 | 10.3 | 9.5 | 12.2 | 14.2 | 17.2 | 18.0 | 15.2 | 14.9 | 14.1 | 12.5 | 16.9 | 16.3 | 17.0 | 18.1 | 19.5 | 18.4 | 15.7 | 14.0 |
| 1964 | 10.6 | 10.9 | 10.6 | 9.9 | 12.5 | 14.5 | 17.4 | 18.2 | 15.5 | 15.2 | 14.4 | 12.9 | 17.1 | 16.6 | 17.3 | 18.3 | 19.7 | 18.6 | 16.1 | 14.4 |
| 1965 | 11.3 | 11.6 | 11.3 | 10.7 | 13.2 | 15.2 | 18.0 | 18.8 | 16.2 | 16.0 | 15.2 | 13.8 | 17.9 | 17.4 | 18.1 | 19.2 | 20.5 | 19.6 | 17.1 | 15.6 |
| 1966 | 10.8 | 11.1 | 10.8 | 10.2 | 12.6 | 14.5 | 17.2 | 18.0 | 15.4 | 15.2 | 14.4 | 13.0 | 17.0 | 16.4 | 17.1 | 18.0 | 19.3 | 18.3 | 16.0 | 14.5 |
| 1967 | 12.2 | 12.5 | 12.2 | 11.6 | 14.1 | 16.0 | 18.7 | 19.5 | 17.0 | 16.8 | 16.1 | 14.8 | 18.7 | 18.3 | 19.0 | 20.0 | 21.3 | 20.4 | 18.2 | 16.9 |
| 1968 | 12.7 | 13.0 | 12.8 | 12.2 | 14.6 | 16.5 | 19.1 | 19.9 | 17.5 | 17.3 | 16.7 | 15.4 | 19.3 | 18.8 | 19.5 | 20.5 | 21.8 | 21.0 | 18.9 | 17.6 |
| 1969 | 11.6 | 11.9 | 11.7 | 11.1 | 13.4 | 15.2 | 17.7 | 18.4 | 16.1 | 15.8 | 15.2 | 13.9 | 17.5 | 17.1 | 17.7 | 18.6 | 19.7 | 18.9 | 16.8 | 15.5 |
| 1970 | 10.9 | 11.1 | 10.9 | 10.3 | 12.5 | 14.2 | 16.6 | 17.3 | 15.0 | 14.7 | 14.1 | 12.9 | 16.3 | 15.8 | 16.3 | 17.1 | 18.2 | 17.3 | 15.3 | 14.0 |

# Appendix C-2

Small-Capitalization Stocks: Percent per annum total returns for all historical periods

From 1926 to 2016

| End Date | Start Date 1926 | 1927 | 1928 | 1929 | 1930 | 1931 | 1932 | 1933 | 1934 | 1935 | 1936 | 1937 | 1938 | 1939 | 1940 | 1941 | 1942 | 1943 | 1944 | 1945 |
|---|---|---|---|---|---|---|---|---|---|---|---|---|---|---|---|---|---|---|---|---|
| 1971 | 11.0 | 11.2 | 11.0 | 10.4 | 12.6 | 14.3 | 16.6 | 17.3 | 15.0 | 14.8 | 14.2 | 13.0 | 16.3 | 15.8 | 16.4 | 17.1 | 18.1 | 17.3 | 15.3 | 14.1 |
| 1972 | 10.9 | 11.1 | 10.9 | 10.3 | 12.4 | 14.0 | 16.3 | 16.9 | 14.7 | 14.5 | 13.9 | 12.7 | 15.9 | 15.5 | 16.0 | 16.7 | 17.6 | 16.8 | 14.9 | 13.7 |
| 1973 | 9.8 | 10.0 | 9.7 | 9.1 | 11.2 | 12.7 | 14.9 | 15.4 | 13.3 | 13.0 | 12.4 | 11.2 | 14.3 | 13.8 | 14.2 | 14.9 | 15.7 | 13.6 | 13.0 | 11.8 |
| 1974 | 9.1 | 9.3 | 9.0 | 8.4 | 10.4 | 11.8 | 13.9 | 14.4 | 12.3 | 12.1 | 11.4 | 10.3 | 13.2 | 12.7 | 13.1 | 13.7 | 14.4 | 13.6 | 11.7 | 10.6 |
| 1975 | 9.8 | 10.0 | 9.8 | 9.2 | 11.1 | 12.6 | 14.7 | 15.2 | 13.2 | 12.9 | 12.3 | 11.2 | 14.1 | 13.6 | 14.0 | 14.6 | 15.4 | 14.6 | 12.8 | 11.7 |
| 1976 | 10.6 | 10.8 | 10.6 | 10.0 | 12.0 | 13.4 | 15.5 | 16.0 | 14.0 | 13.8 | 13.2 | 12.2 | 15.0 | 14.6 | 15.0 | 15.6 | 16.4 | 15.7 | 14.0 | 12.9 |
| 1977 | 10.8 | 11.1 | 10.9 | 10.3 | 12.2 | 13.7 | 15.7 | 16.2 | 14.3 | 14.1 | 13.5 | 12.5 | 15.3 | 14.9 | 15.3 | 15.9 | 16.7 | 16.0 | 14.3 | 13.3 |
| 1978 | 11.1 | 11.3 | 11.1 | 10.6 | 12.4 | 13.9 | 15.9 | 16.4 | 14.5 | 14.3 | 13.7 | 12.7 | 15.5 | 15.1 | 15.5 | 16.1 | 16.8 | 16.2 | 14.6 | 13.6 |
| 1979 | 11.6 | 11.8 | 11.6 | 11.1 | 13.0 | 14.4 | 16.4 | 16.9 | 15.0 | 14.8 | 14.3 | 13.4 | 16.1 | 15.7 | 16.1 | 16.7 | 17.5 | 16.8 | 15.3 | 14.3 |
| 1980 | 12.1 | 12.3 | 12.1 | 11.6 | 13.5 | 14.9 | 16.8 | 17.3 | 15.5 | 15.3 | 14.8 | 13.9 | 16.6 | 16.2 | 16.6 | 17.2 | 18.0 | 17.4 | 15.9 | 15.0 |
| 1981 | 12.1 | 12.3 | 12.1 | 11.7 | 13.5 | 14.8 | 16.8 | 17.3 | 15.5 | 15.3 | 14.8 | 13.9 | 16.5 | 16.2 | 16.6 | 17.2 | 17.9 | 17.3 | 15.8 | 14.9 |
| 1982 | 12.4 | 12.6 | 12.4 | 12.0 | 13.7 | 15.1 | 17.0 | 17.5 | 15.7 | 15.6 | 15.1 | 14.2 | 16.8 | 16.4 | 16.8 | 17.4 | 18.1 | 17.5 | 16.1 | 15.3 |
| 1983 | 12.8 | 13.0 | 12.9 | 12.4 | 14.2 | 15.5 | 17.4 | 17.9 | 16.2 | 16.0 | 15.6 | 14.7 | 17.2 | 16.9 | 17.3 | 17.9 | 18.6 | 18.0 | 16.7 | 15.8 |
| 1984 | 12.4 | 12.6 | 12.5 | 12.0 | 13.8 | 15.0 | 16.9 | 17.3 | 15.7 | 15.5 | 15.0 | 14.2 | 16.6 | 16.3 | 16.7 | 17.3 | 17.9 | 17.4 | 16.0 | 15.2 |
| 1985 | 12.6 | 12.8 | 12.7 | 12.3 | 13.9 | 15.2 | 17.0 | 17.5 | 15.8 | 15.7 | 15.2 | 14.4 | 16.8 | 16.5 | 16.9 | 17.4 | 18.1 | 17.5 | 16.2 | 15.4 |
| 1986 | 12.5 | 12.7 | 12.6 | 12.2 | 13.8 | 15.1 | 16.8 | 17.3 | 15.7 | 15.5 | 15.1 | 14.2 | 16.6 | 16.3 | 16.6 | 17.2 | 17.8 | 17.3 | 16.0 | 15.2 |
| 1987 | 12.1 | 12.3 | 12.2 | 11.8 | 13.4 | 14.6 | 16.3 | 16.7 | 15.1 | 15.0 | 14.5 | 13.7 | 16.0 | 15.7 | 16.0 | 16.5 | 17.2 | 16.6 | 15.4 | 14.6 |
| 1988 | 12.3 | 12.5 | 12.3 | 11.9 | 13.5 | 14.7 | 16.4 | 16.8 | 15.3 | 15.1 | 14.7 | 13.9 | 16.1 | 15.8 | 16.2 | 16.7 | 17.3 | 16.8 | 15.5 | 14.8 |
| 1989 | 12.2 | 12.5 | 12.3 | 11.9 | 13.5 | 14.6 | 16.3 | 16.7 | 15.2 | 15.0 | 14.6 | 13.8 | 16.0 | 15.7 | 16.0 | 16.5 | 17.1 | 16.6 | 15.4 | 14.7 |
| 1990 | 11.6 | 11.8 | 11.7 | 11.3 | 12.8 | 13.9 | 15.5 | 15.9 | 14.4 | 14.2 | 13.8 | 13.0 | 15.2 | 14.9 | 15.2 | 15.6 | 16.2 | 15.6 | 14.5 | 13.7 |
| 1991 | 12.1 | 12.3 | 12.1 | 11.7 | 13.2 | 14.4 | 15.9 | 16.3 | 14.9 | 14.7 | 14.3 | 13.5 | 15.7 | 15.4 | 15.7 | 16.1 | 16.7 | 16.2 | 15.0 | 14.3 |
| 1992 | 12.2 | 12.4 | 12.3 | 11.9 | 13.4 | 14.5 | 16.1 | 16.5 | 15.0 | 14.9 | 14.5 | 13.7 | 15.8 | 15.5 | 15.8 | 16.3 | 16.8 | 16.3 | 15.2 | 14.5 |
| 1993 | 12.4 | 12.5 | 12.4 | 12.0 | 13.5 | 14.6 | 16.1 | 16.5 | 15.1 | 15.0 | 14.6 | 13.8 | 15.9 | 15.6 | 15.9 | 16.3 | 16.9 | 16.4 | 15.3 | 14.6 |
| 1994 | 12.2 | 12.4 | 12.3 | 11.9 | 13.3 | 14.4 | 15.9 | 16.3 | 14.9 | 14.8 | 14.4 | 13.6 | 15.6 | 15.4 | 15.7 | 16.1 | 16.6 | 16.1 | 15.0 | 14.4 |
| 1995 | 12.5 | 12.7 | 12.6 | 12.2 | 13.6 | 14.7 | 16.2 | 16.6 | 15.2 | 15.1 | 14.7 | 14.0 | 15.9 | 15.7 | 16.0 | 16.4 | 16.9 | 16.5 | 15.4 | 14.7 |
| 1996 | 12.6 | 12.8 | 12.6 | 12.3 | 13.7 | 14.7 | 16.2 | 16.6 | 15.2 | 15.1 | 14.7 | 14.0 | 16.0 | 15.7 | 16.1 | 16.4 | 16.9 | 16.5 | 15.4 | 14.8 |
| 1997 | 12.7 | 12.9 | 12.8 | 12.4 | 13.8 | 14.9 | 16.3 | 16.7 | 15.3 | 15.2 | 14.8 | 14.2 | 16.1 | 15.8 | 16.1 | 16.5 | 17.0 | 16.6 | 15.6 | 14.9 |
| 1998 | 12.4 | 12.6 | 12.5 | 12.1 | 13.5 | 14.5 | 15.9 | 16.3 | 15.0 | 14.8 | 14.5 | 13.8 | 15.7 | 15.4 | 15.7 | 16.1 | 16.6 | 16.1 | 15.1 | 14.5 |
| 1999 | 12.6 | 12.8 | 12.7 | 12.3 | 13.7 | 14.7 | 16.1 | 16.5 | 15.2 | 15.0 | 14.7 | 14.0 | 15.9 | 15.6 | 15.9 | 16.3 | 16.8 | 16.3 | 15.3 | 14.7 |
| 2000 | 12.4 | 12.6 | 12.4 | 12.1 | 13.4 | 14.4 | 15.8 | 16.1 | 14.9 | 14.7 | 14.4 | 13.7 | 15.5 | 15.3 | 15.5 | 15.9 | 16.4 | 16.0 | 15.0 | 14.4 |
| 2001 | 12.5 | 12.7 | 12.6 | 12.2 | 13.6 | 14.5 | 15.9 | 16.2 | 14.9 | 14.8 | 14.5 | 13.9 | 15.6 | 15.4 | 15.7 | 16.0 | 16.5 | 16.1 | 15.1 | 14.5 |
| 2002 | 12.1 | 12.3 | 12.2 | 11.9 | 13.1 | 14.1 | 15.4 | 15.7 | 14.5 | 14.4 | 14.0 | 13.4 | 15.1 | 14.9 | 15.1 | 15.5 | 15.9 | 15.5 | 14.6 | 14.0 |
| 2003 | 12.7 | 12.8 | 12.7 | 12.4 | 13.7 | 14.6 | 15.9 | 16.3 | 15.1 | 14.9 | 14.6 | 14.0 | 15.7 | 15.5 | 15.7 | 16.1 | 16.6 | 16.1 | 15.2 | 14.6 |
| 2004 | 12.7 | 12.9 | 12.8 | 12.5 | 13.7 | 14.7 | 16.0 | 16.3 | 15.1 | 15.0 | 14.7 | 14.0 | 15.8 | 15.5 | 15.8 | 16.1 | 16.6 | 16.2 | 15.3 | 14.7 |
| 2005 | 12.6 | 12.8 | 12.7 | 12.4 | 13.6 | 14.6 | 15.8 | 16.2 | 15.0 | 14.8 | 14.5 | 13.9 | 15.6 | 15.4 | 15.6 | 16.0 | 16.4 | 16.0 | 15.1 | 14.6 |
| 2006 | 12.7 | 12.9 | 12.7 | 12.4 | 13.7 | 14.6 | 15.8 | 16.2 | 15.0 | 14.9 | 14.5 | 14.0 | 15.6 | 15.4 | 15.6 | 16.0 | 16.4 | 16.0 | 15.1 | 14.6 |
| 2007 | 12.5 | 12.6 | 12.5 | 12.2 | 13.4 | 14.3 | 15.5 | 15.8 | 14.7 | 14.6 | 14.2 | 13.7 | 15.3 | 15.0 | 15.3 | 15.6 | 16.0 | 15.6 | 14.8 | 14.2 |
| 2008 | 11.7 | 11.8 | 11.7 | 11.4 | 12.6 | 13.4 | 14.6 | 14.9 | 13.8 | 13.6 | 13.3 | 12.7 | 14.3 | 14.1 | 14.3 | 14.6 | 15.0 | 14.6 | 13.7 | 13.2 |
| 2009 | 11.9 | 12.0 | 11.9 | 11.6 | 12.7 | 13.6 | 14.8 | 15.1 | 14.0 | 13.8 | 13.5 | 12.9 | 14.5 | 14.3 | 14.5 | 14.8 | 15.2 | 14.8 | 13.9 | 13.4 |
| 2010 | 12.1 | 12.2 | 12.1 | 11.8 | 13.0 | 13.8 | 15.0 | 15.3 | 14.2 | 14.0 | 13.7 | 13.2 | 14.7 | 14.5 | 14.7 | 15.0 | 15.4 | 15.0 | 14.2 | 13.7 |
| 2011 | 11.9 | 12.0 | 11.9 | 11.6 | 12.7 | 13.6 | 14.7 | 15.0 | 13.9 | 13.8 | 13.5 | 12.9 | 14.4 | 14.2 | 14.4 | 14.7 | 15.1 | 14.7 | 13.9 | 13.4 |
| 2012 | 11.9 | 12.1 | 12.0 | 11.7 | 12.8 | 13.6 | 14.8 | 15.1 | 14.0 | 13.9 | 13.5 | 13.0 | 14.5 | 14.3 | 14.5 | 14.8 | 15.1 | 14.8 | 14.0 | 13.4 |
| 2013 | 12.3 | 12.4 | 12.3 | 12.0 | 13.1 | 14.0 | 15.1 | 15.4 | 14.3 | 14.2 | 13.9 | 13.4 | 14.9 | 14.6 | 14.8 | 15.1 | 15.5 | 15.2 | 14.3 | 13.9 |
| 2014 | 12.2 | 12.3 | 12.2 | 11.9 | 13.0 | 13.8 | 15.0 | 15.2 | 14.2 | 14.1 | 13.8 | 13.2 | 14.7 | 14.5 | 14.7 | 15.0 | 15.3 | 15.0 | 14.2 | 13.7 |
| 2015 | 12.0 | 12.1 | 12.0 | 11.7 | 12.8 | 13.6 | 14.7 | 15.0 | 13.9 | 13.8 | 13.5 | 13.0 | 14.4 | 14.2 | 14.4 | 14.7 | 15.1 | 14.7 | 13.9 | 13.4 |
| 2016 | 12.1 | 12.3 | 12.2 | 11.9 | 13.0 | 13.7 | 14.8 | 15.1 | 14.1 | 14.0 | 13.7 | 13.1 | 14.6 | 14.4 | 14.5 | 14.8 | 15.2 | 14.8 | 14.1 | 13.6 |

## Appendix C-2

Small-Capitalization Stocks: Percent per annum total returns for all historical periods

From 1926 to 2016

| End Date | Start Date 1946 | 1947 | 1948 | 1949 | 1950 | 1951 | 1952 | 1953 | 1954 | 1955 | 1956 | 1957 | 1958 | 1959 | 1960 | 1961 | 1962 | 1963 | 1964 | 1965 |
|---|---|---|---|---|---|---|---|---|---|---|---|---|---|---|---|---|---|---|---|---|
| 1926 | | | | | | | | | | | | | | | | | | | | |
| 1927 | | | | | | | | | | | | | | | | | | | | |
| 1928 | | | | | | | | | | | | | | | | | | | | |
| 1929 | | | | | | | | | | | | | | | | | | | | |
| 1930 | | | | | | | | | | | | | | | | | | | | |
| 1931 | | | | | | | | | | | | | | | | | | | | |
| 1932 | | | | | | | | | | | | | | | | | | | | |
| 1933 | | | | | | | | | | | | | | | | | | | | |
| 1934 | | | | | | | | | | | | | | | | | | | | |
| 1935 | | | | | | | | | | | | | | | | | | | | |
| 1936 | | | | | | | | | | | | | | | | | | | | |
| 1937 | | | | | | | | | | | | | | | | | | | | |
| 1938 | | | | | | | | | | | | | | | | | | | | |
| 1939 | | | | | | | | | | | | | | | | | | | | |
| 1940 | | | | | | | | | | | | | | | | | | | | |
| 1941 | | | | | | | | | | | | | | | | | | | | |
| 1942 | | | | | | | | | | | | | | | | | | | | |
| 1943 | | | | | | | | | | | | | | | | | | | | |
| 1944 | | | | | | | | | | | | | | | | | | | | |
| 1945 | | | | | | | | | | | | | | | | | | | | |
| 1946 | -11.6 | | | | | | | | | | | | | | | | | | | |
| 1947 | -5.6 | 0.9 | | | | | | | | | | | | | | | | | | |
| 1948 | -4.4 | -0.6 | -2.1 | | | | | | | | | | | | | | | | | |
| 1949 | 1.1 | 5.8 | 8.3 | 19.7 | | | | | | | | | | | | | | | | |
| 1950 | 7.7 | 13.2 | 17.6 | 28.9 | 38.7 | | | | | | | | | | | | | | | |
| 1951 | 7.7 | 12.1 | 15.1 | 21.4 | 22.3 | 7.8 | | | | | | | | | | | | | | |
| 1952 | 7.0 | 10.5 | 12.6 | 16.6 | 15.5 | 5.4 | 3.0 | | | | | | | | | | | | | |
| 1953 | 5.3 | 7.9 | 9.1 | 11.5 | 9.6 | 1.3 | -1.8 | -6.5 | | | | | | | | | | | | |
| 1954 | 10.3 | 13.4 | 15.3 | 18.5 | 18.3 | 13.6 | 15.7 | 22.5 | 60.6 | | | | | | | | | | | |
| 1955 | 11.3 | 14.2 | 15.9 | 18.8 | 18.6 | 15.0 | 16.8 | 21.8 | 39.1 | 20.4 | | | | | | | | | | |
| 1956 | 10.6 | 13.1 | 14.6 | 16.9 | 16.5 | 13.1 | 14.2 | 17.2 | 26.3 | 12.1 | 4.3 | | | | | | | | | |
| 1957 | 8.3 | 10.3 | 11.3 | 12.9 | 12.0 | 8.7 | 8.8 | 10.0 | 14.6 | 2.4 | -5.6 | -14.6 | | | | | | | | |
| 1958 | 11.8 | 14.0 | 15.3 | 17.2 | 17.0 | 14.5 | 15.5 | 17.7 | 23.2 | 15.3 | 13.7 | 18.7 | 64.9 | | | | | | | |
| 1959 | 12.2 | 14.2 | 15.4 | 17.2 | 16.9 | 14.7 | 15.6 | 17.5 | 22.1 | 15.5 | 14.4 | 17.9 | 38.5 | 16.4 | | | | | | |
| 1960 | 11.1 | 12.9 | 13.9 | 15.3 | 14.9 | 12.8 | 13.3 | 14.7 | 18.1 | 12.2 | 10.6 | 12.2 | 22.9 | 6.1 | -3.3 | | | | | |
| 1961 | 12.3 | 14.1 | 15.1 | 16.5 | 16.2 | 14.4 | 15.1 | 16.5 | 19.7 | 14.8 | 13.9 | 15.9 | 25.1 | 14.1 | 13.0 | 32.1 | | | | |
| 1962 | 10.7 | 12.2 | 13.0 | 14.2 | 13.8 | 11.9 | 12.3 | 13.3 | 15.7 | 11.1 | 9.8 | 10.7 | 16.6 | 7.0 | 4.0 | 7.9 | -11.9 | | | |
| 1963 | 11.4 | 12.9 | 13.7 | 14.8 | 14.5 | 12.8 | 13.2 | 14.2 | 16.5 | 12.4 | 11.4 | 12.5 | 17.8 | 10.1 | 8.6 | 12.9 | 4.3 | 23.6 | | |
| 1964 | 12.0 | 13.4 | 14.2 | 15.3 | 15.0 | 13.5 | 14.0 | 14.9 | 17.1 | 13.5 | 12.7 | 13.8 | 18.6 | 12.2 | 11.4 | 15.4 | 10.4 | 23.5 | 23.5 | |
| 1965 | 13.3 | 14.8 | 15.6 | 16.7 | 16.6 | 15.2 | 15.8 | 16.8 | 19.0 | 15.8 | 15.3 | 16.6 | 21.3 | 16.0 | 16.0 | 20.3 | 17.5 | 29.3 | 32.3 | 41.8 |
| 1966 | 12.2 | 13.6 | 14.3 | 15.3 | 15.0 | 13.7 | 14.1 | 14.9 | 16.7 | 13.7 | 13.1 | 14.0 | 17.7 | 12.9 | 12.4 | 15.2 | 12.1 | 19.1 | 17.6 | 14.8 |
| 1967 | 14.8 | 16.2 | 17.0 | 18.1 | 18.0 | 16.9 | 17.5 | 18.6 | 20.6 | 18.0 | 17.8 | 19.1 | 23.1 | 19.1 | 19.5 | 23.2 | 21.7 | 29.9 | 31.5 | 34.3 |
| 1968 | 15.6 | 17.0 | 17.9 | 19.0 | 18.9 | 17.9 | 18.5 | 19.6 | 21.6 | 19.2 | 19.1 | 20.4 | 24.2 | 20.7 | 21.2 | 24.7 | 23.7 | 30.9 | 32.4 | 34.7 |
| 1969 | 13.5 | 14.8 | 15.5 | 16.4 | 16.2 | 15.1 | 15.6 | 16.3 | 17.9 | 15.5 | 15.2 | 16.1 | 19.1 | 15.6 | 15.5 | 17.8 | 16.2 | 20.8 | 20.4 | 19.8 |
| 1970 | 12.1 | 13.2 | 13.8 | 14.6 | 14.3 | 13.2 | 13.5 | 14.1 | 15.5 | 13.1 | 12.7 | 13.3 | 15.8 | 12.4 | 12.1 | 13.7 | 11.8 | 15.2 | 14.1 | 12.6 |

Small-Capitalization Stocks: Percent per annum total returns for all historical periods

From 1926 to 2016

| End Date | Start Date 1946 | 1947 | 1948 | 1949 | 1950 | 1951 | 1952 | 1953 | 1954 | 1955 | 1956 | 1957 | 1958 | 1959 | 1960 | 1961 | 1962 | 1963 | 1964 | 1965 |
|---|---|---|---|---|---|---|---|---|---|---|---|---|---|---|---|---|---|---|---|---|
| 1971 | 12.3 | 13.4 | 13.9 | 14.7 | 14.4 | 13.4 | 13.7 | 14.3 | 15.5 | 13.3 | 12.9 | 13.5 | 15.8 | 12.7 | 12.4 | 14.0 | 12.3 | 15.4 | 14.4 | 13.1 |
| 1972 | 12.0 | 13.0 | 13.5 | 14.2 | 14.0 | 13.0 | 13.2 | 13.8 | 14.9 | 12.8 | 12.4 | 12.9 | 15.0 | 12.1 | 11.8 | 13.1 | 11.6 | 14.2 | 13.2 | 12.0 |
| 1973 | 10.1 | 11.0 | 11.4 | 11.9 | 11.6 | 10.6 | 10.7 | 11.1 | 12.0 | 9.9 | 9.4 | 9.7 | 11.4 | 8.5 | 8.0 | 8.9 | 7.2 | 9.1 | 7.8 | 6.2 |
| 1974 | 8.9 | 9.7 | 10.0 | 10.5 | 10.2 | 9.1 | 9.2 | 9.4 | 10.3 | 8.2 | 7.6 | 7.8 | 9.3 | 6.5 | 5.9 | 6.6 | 4.8 | 6.3 | 4.9 | 3.2 |
| 1975 | 10.1 | 10.9 | 11.3 | 11.8 | 11.5 | 10.6 | 10.7 | 11.0 | 11.9 | 10.0 | 9.5 | 9.8 | 11.3 | 8.8 | 8.3 | 9.2 | 7.7 | 9.3 | 8.2 | 6.9 |
| 1976 | 11.4 | 12.2 | 12.6 | 13.2 | 13.0 | 12.1 | 12.3 | 12.7 | 13.6 | 11.8 | 11.4 | 11.8 | 13.4 | 11.0 | 10.7 | 11.7 | 10.4 | 12.2 | 11.4 | 10.4 |
| 1977 | 11.8 | 12.6 | 13.1 | 13.6 | 13.4 | 12.6 | 12.7 | 13.1 | 14.1 | 12.4 | 12.0 | 12.4 | 13.9 | 11.8 | 11.5 | 12.4 | 11.3 | 13.1 | 12.3 | 11.5 |
| 1978 | 12.1 | 13.0 | 13.4 | 13.9 | 13.7 | 12.9 | 13.1 | 13.5 | 14.4 | 12.8 | 12.5 | 12.9 | 14.4 | 12.3 | 12.1 | 13.0 | 12.0 | 13.7 | 13.1 | 12.3 |
| 1979 | 12.9 | 13.8 | 14.2 | 14.8 | 14.6 | 13.9 | 14.1 | 14.5 | 15.4 | 13.9 | 13.6 | 14.1 | 15.6 | 13.6 | 13.5 | 14.5 | 13.5 | 15.3 | 14.8 | 14.2 |
| 1980 | 13.6 | 14.5 | 14.9 | 15.5 | 15.4 | 14.6 | 14.9 | 15.3 | 16.2 | 14.8 | 14.6 | 15.0 | 16.5 | 14.7 | 14.6 | 15.6 | 14.8 | 16.5 | 16.1 | 15.6 |
| 1981 | 13.6 | 14.5 | 14.9 | 15.4 | 15.3 | 14.6 | 14.9 | 15.3 | 16.2 | 14.8 | 14.6 | 15.0 | 16.4 | 14.7 | 14.6 | 15.5 | 14.8 | 16.4 | 16.0 | 15.5 |
| 1982 | 14.0 | 14.8 | 15.2 | 15.8 | 15.7 | 15.0 | 15.3 | 15.7 | 16.5 | 15.2 | 15.0 | 15.5 | 16.9 | 15.2 | 15.1 | 16.1 | 15.4 | 16.9 | 16.6 | 16.2 |
| 1983 | 14.6 | 15.4 | 15.9 | 16.4 | 16.3 | 15.7 | 16.0 | 16.4 | 17.2 | 16.0 | 15.8 | 16.3 | 17.7 | 16.1 | 16.1 | 17.0 | 16.4 | 17.9 | 17.6 | 17.3 |
| 1984 | 14.0 | 14.8 | 15.2 | 15.7 | 15.6 | 15.0 | 15.2 | 15.6 | 16.4 | 15.1 | 15.0 | 15.4 | 16.7 | 15.1 | 15.1 | 15.9 | 15.2 | 16.7 | 16.3 | 16.0 |
| 1985 | 14.3 | 15.0 | 15.4 | 15.9 | 15.8 | 15.2 | 15.5 | 15.9 | 16.6 | 15.4 | 15.3 | 15.7 | 16.9 | 15.5 | 15.4 | 16.2 | 15.6 | 17.0 | 16.7 | 16.4 |
| 1986 | 14.1 | 14.8 | 15.2 | 15.7 | 15.6 | 15.0 | 15.2 | 15.6 | 16.3 | 15.2 | 15.0 | 15.4 | 16.6 | 15.1 | 15.1 | 15.9 | 15.3 | 16.6 | 16.3 | 15.9 |
| 1987 | 13.5 | 14.2 | 14.6 | 15.0 | 14.8 | 14.3 | 14.4 | 14.8 | 15.5 | 14.3 | 14.1 | 14.5 | 15.6 | 14.2 | 14.1 | 14.8 | 14.2 | 15.4 | 15.1 | 14.7 |
| 1988 | 13.7 | 14.4 | 14.7 | 15.2 | 15.0 | 14.5 | 14.7 | 15.0 | 15.7 | 14.6 | 14.4 | 14.7 | 15.8 | 14.5 | 14.4 | 15.1 | 14.5 | 15.7 | 15.4 | 15.0 |
| 1989 | 13.6 | 14.3 | 14.6 | 15.0 | 14.9 | 14.4 | 14.5 | 14.9 | 15.5 | 14.4 | 14.3 | 14.6 | 15.7 | 14.3 | 14.3 | 14.9 | 14.4 | 15.5 | 15.2 | 14.8 |
| 1990 | 12.7 | 13.3 | 13.6 | 14.0 | 13.9 | 13.3 | 13.4 | 13.7 | 14.3 | 13.3 | 13.1 | 13.3 | 14.3 | 13.0 | 12.9 | 13.5 | 12.9 | 13.9 | 13.5 | 13.2 |
| 1991 | 13.3 | 13.9 | 14.2 | 14.6 | 14.5 | 14.0 | 14.1 | 14.4 | 15.0 | 14.0 | 13.8 | 14.1 | 15.1 | 13.8 | 13.8 | 14.4 | 13.8 | 14.8 | 14.5 | 14.2 |
| 1992 | 13.5 | 14.1 | 14.4 | 14.8 | 14.7 | 14.2 | 14.3 | 14.6 | 15.2 | 14.2 | 14.1 | 14.4 | 15.3 | 14.1 | 14.0 | 14.6 | 14.1 | 15.1 | 14.8 | 14.5 |
| 1993 | 13.6 | 14.2 | 14.5 | 14.9 | 14.8 | 14.3 | 14.5 | 14.8 | 15.4 | 14.4 | 14.3 | 14.5 | 15.5 | 14.3 | 14.2 | 14.8 | 14.3 | 15.3 | 15.0 | 14.7 |
| 1994 | 13.4 | 14.0 | 14.3 | 14.7 | 14.6 | 14.1 | 14.2 | 14.5 | 15.1 | 14.1 | 14.0 | 14.2 | 15.1 | 14.0 | 13.9 | 14.5 | 14.0 | 14.9 | 14.6 | 14.3 |
| 1995 | 13.8 | 14.4 | 14.7 | 15.1 | 15.0 | 14.5 | 14.6 | 14.9 | 15.5 | 14.6 | 14.4 | 14.7 | 15.6 | 14.5 | 14.4 | 15.0 | 14.5 | 15.4 | 15.2 | 14.9 |
| 1996 | 13.9 | 14.4 | 14.7 | 15.1 | 15.0 | 14.6 | 14.7 | 15.0 | 15.6 | 14.6 | 14.5 | 14.8 | 15.6 | 14.6 | 14.5 | 15.1 | 14.6 | 15.5 | 15.3 | 15.0 |
| 1997 | 14.0 | 14.6 | 14.9 | 15.3 | 15.2 | 14.7 | 14.9 | 15.2 | 15.7 | 14.8 | 14.7 | 15.0 | 15.8 | 14.8 | 14.7 | 15.3 | 14.8 | 15.7 | 15.5 | 15.2 |
| 1998 | 13.6 | 14.1 | 14.4 | 14.8 | 14.7 | 14.2 | 14.4 | 14.6 | 15.1 | 14.3 | 14.1 | 14.4 | 15.2 | 14.2 | 14.1 | 14.6 | 14.2 | 15.0 | 14.8 | 14.5 |
| 1999 | 13.9 | 14.4 | 14.7 | 15.0 | 15.0 | 14.5 | 14.7 | 14.9 | 15.4 | 14.6 | 14.5 | 14.7 | 15.5 | 14.5 | 14.5 | 15.0 | 14.5 | 15.4 | 15.1 | 14.9 |
| 2000 | 13.5 | 14.0 | 14.3 | 14.7 | 14.6 | 14.1 | 14.3 | 14.5 | 15.0 | 14.2 | 14.0 | 14.3 | 15.0 | 14.1 | 14.0 | 14.5 | 14.0 | 14.8 | 14.6 | 14.4 |
| 2001 | 13.7 | 14.2 | 14.5 | 14.8 | 14.7 | 14.3 | 14.4 | 14.7 | 15.1 | 14.3 | 14.2 | 14.4 | 15.2 | 14.2 | 14.2 | 14.7 | 14.3 | 15.0 | 14.8 | 14.6 |
| 2002 | 13.1 | 13.6 | 13.9 | 14.2 | 14.1 | 13.7 | 13.8 | 14.0 | 14.5 | 13.7 | 13.5 | 13.8 | 14.5 | 13.5 | 13.5 | 13.9 | 13.5 | 14.2 | 14.0 | 13.7 |
| 2003 | 13.8 | 14.3 | 14.6 | 14.9 | 14.8 | 14.4 | 14.6 | 14.8 | 15.3 | 14.5 | 14.4 | 14.6 | 15.3 | 14.4 | 14.4 | 14.8 | 14.4 | 15.2 | 15.0 | 14.8 |
| 2004 | 13.9 | 14.4 | 14.7 | 15.0 | 14.9 | 14.5 | 14.6 | 14.9 | 15.3 | 14.6 | 14.4 | 14.7 | 15.4 | 14.5 | 14.5 | 14.9 | 14.5 | 15.2 | 15.0 | 14.8 |
| 2005 | 13.8 | 14.3 | 14.5 | 14.8 | 14.7 | 14.3 | 14.5 | 14.7 | 15.1 | 14.3 | 14.3 | 14.5 | 15.2 | 14.3 | 14.3 | 14.7 | 14.3 | 15.0 | 14.8 | 14.6 |
| 2006 | 13.8 | 14.3 | 14.5 | 14.8 | 14.7 | 14.4 | 14.5 | 14.7 | 15.2 | 14.4 | 14.3 | 14.5 | 15.2 | 14.3 | 14.3 | 14.7 | 14.4 | 15.0 | 14.8 | 14.6 |
| 2007 | 13.5 | 13.9 | 14.2 | 14.5 | 14.4 | 14.0 | 14.1 | 14.3 | 14.7 | 14.0 | 13.9 | 14.1 | 14.7 | 13.9 | 13.9 | 14.2 | 13.9 | 14.5 | 14.3 | 14.1 |
| 2008 | 12.4 | 12.9 | 13.1 | 13.3 | 13.2 | 12.8 | 12.9 | 13.1 | 13.5 | 12.8 | 12.6 | 12.8 | 13.4 | 12.6 | 12.5 | 12.9 | 12.5 | 13.1 | 12.8 | 12.6 |
| 2009 | 12.6 | 13.1 | 13.3 | 13.6 | 13.5 | 13.1 | 13.2 | 13.4 | 13.7 | 13.0 | 12.9 | 13.1 | 13.7 | 12.9 | 12.8 | 13.1 | 12.8 | 13.4 | 13.2 | 12.9 |
| 2010 | 12.9 | 13.3 | 13.6 | 13.8 | 13.7 | 13.4 | 13.5 | 13.6 | 14.0 | 13.3 | 13.2 | 13.4 | 14.0 | 13.2 | 13.1 | 13.5 | 13.1 | 13.7 | 13.5 | 13.3 |
| 2011 | 12.7 | 13.1 | 13.3 | 13.5 | 13.4 | 13.1 | 13.2 | 13.3 | 13.7 | 13.0 | 12.9 | 13.1 | 13.6 | 12.9 | 12.8 | 13.1 | 12.8 | 13.3 | 13.1 | 12.9 |
| 2012 | 12.7 | 13.1 | 13.3 | 13.6 | 13.5 | 13.1 | 13.2 | 13.4 | 13.8 | 13.1 | 13.0 | 13.1 | 13.7 | 12.9 | 12.9 | 13.2 | 12.9 | 13.4 | 13.2 | 13.0 |
| 2013 | 13.2 | 13.6 | 13.8 | 14.0 | 13.9 | 13.6 | 13.7 | 13.9 | 14.2 | 13.6 | 13.5 | 13.6 | 14.2 | 13.5 | 13.4 | 13.8 | 13.4 | 14.0 | 13.8 | 13.6 |
| 2014 | 13.0 | 13.4 | 13.6 | 13.9 | 13.8 | 13.4 | 13.5 | 13.7 | 14.1 | 13.4 | 13.3 | 13.4 | 14.0 | 13.3 | 13.2 | 13.5 | 13.2 | 13.8 | 13.6 | 13.4 |
| 2015 | 12.7 | 13.1 | 13.3 | 13.6 | 13.5 | 13.1 | 13.2 | 13.4 | 13.7 | 13.1 | 13.0 | 13.1 | 13.7 | 12.9 | 12.9 | 13.2 | 12.9 | 13.4 | 13.2 | 13.0 |
| 2016 | 12.9 | 13.3 | 13.5 | 13.7 | 13.7 | 13.3 | 13.4 | 13.6 | 13.9 | 13.3 | 13.2 | 13.3 | 13.9 | 13.2 | 13.1 | 13.4 | 13.1 | 13.6 | 13.4 | 13.3 |

## Appendix C-2

Small-Capitalization Stocks: Percent per annum total returns for all historical periods

From 1926 to 2016

# Appendix C-2

Small-Capitalization Stocks: Percent per annum total returns for all historical periods

From 1926 to 2016

| End Date | Start Date 1966 | 1967 | 1968 | 1969 | 1970 | 1971 | 1972 | 1973 | 1974 | 1975 | 1976 | 1977 | 1978 | 1979 | 1980 | 1981 | 1982 | 1983 | 1984 | 1985 |
|---|---|---|---|---|---|---|---|---|---|---|---|---|---|---|---|---|---|---|---|---|
| 1971 | 9.0 | 12.5 | -0.5 | -10.3 | -1.9 | 16.5 | | | | | | | | | | | | | | |
| 1972 | 8.3 | 11.1 | 0.5 | -6.9 | 0.2 | 10.3 | 4.4 | | | | | | | | | | | | | |
| 1973 | 2.4 | 3.8 | -5.6 | -12.3 | -8.7 | -5.6 | -15.1 | -30.9 | | | | | | | | | | | | |
| 1974 | -0.4 | 0.5 | -7.8 | -13.6 | -11.1 | -9.4 | -16.7 | -25.6 | -19.9 | | | | | | | | | | | |
| 1975 | 4.0 | 5.3 | -1.8 | -6.3 | -2.7 | 0.6 | -3.1 | -5.4 | 10.6 | 52.8 | | | | | | | | | | |
| 1976 | 8.0 | 9.6 | 3.5 | 0.0 | 4.2 | 8.4 | 6.8 | 7.4 | 24.4 | 55.1 | 57.4 | | | | | | | | | |
| 1977 | 9.3 | 10.9 | 5.5 | 2.6 | 6.7 | 10.6 | 9.7 | 10.8 | 24.6 | 44.5 | 40.5 | 25.4 | | | | | | | | |
| 1978 | 10.4 | 11.9 | 7.0 | 4.5 | 8.4 | 12.2 | 11.6 | 12.8 | 24.4 | 38.9 | 34.6 | 24.4 | 23.5 | | | | | | | |
| 1979 | 12.4 | 14.1 | 9.7 | 7.5 | 11.5 | 15.3 | 15.1 | 16.7 | 27.4 | 39.8 | 36.7 | 30.5 | 33.1 | 43.5 | | | | | | |
| 1980 | 14.1 | 15.8 | 11.7 | 9.9 | 13.8 | 17.5 | 17.6 | 19.4 | 29.1 | 39.8 | 37.4 | 32.8 | 35.3 | 41.7 | 39.9 | | | | | |
| 1981 | 14.1 | 15.6 | 11.9 | 10.2 | 13.8 | 17.2 | 17.3 | 18.8 | 27.1 | 35.8 | 33.1 | 28.7 | 29.6 | 31.7 | 26.2 | 13.9 | | | | |
| 1982 | 14.9 | 16.4 | 12.9 | 11.4 | 14.9 | 18.1 | 18.2 | 19.7 | 27.2 | 34.8 | 32.4 | 28.6 | 29.3 | 30.8 | 26.8 | 20.7 | 28.0 | | | |
| 1983 | 16.1 | 17.6 | 14.4 | 13.1 | 16.5 | 19.6 | 19.9 | 21.4 | 28.4 | 35.3 | 33.3 | 30.1 | 31.0 | 32.5 | 29.9 | 26.7 | 33.7 | 39.7 | | |
| 1984 | 14.8 | 16.1 | 13.0 | 11.7 | 14.8 | 17.5 | 17.6 | 18.7 | 24.7 | 30.4 | 28.1 | 24.8 | 24.8 | 25.0 | 21.6 | 17.4 | 18.6 | 14.2 | -6.7 | |
| 1985 | 15.3 | 16.6 | 13.7 | 12.5 | 15.4 | 18.0 | 18.1 | 19.2 | 24.7 | 29.9 | 27.8 | 24.8 | 24.8 | 24.9 | 22.1 | 18.8 | 20.1 | 17.6 | 7.9 | 24.7 |
| 1986 | 14.8 | 16.1 | 13.3 | 12.1 | 14.8 | 17.2 | 17.3 | 18.3 | 23.2 | 27.8 | 25.7 | 22.9 | 22.6 | 22.5 | 19.8 | 16.7 | 17.3 | 14.8 | 7.5 | 15.4 |
| 1987 | 13.6 | 14.7 | 12.0 | 10.9 | 13.3 | 15.5 | 15.4 | 16.2 | 20.6 | 24.4 | 22.3 | 19.6 | 19.0 | 18.5 | 15.7 | 12.6 | 12.4 | 9.5 | 3.0 | 6.5 |
| 1988 | 14.0 | 15.1 | 12.5 | 11.5 | 13.8 | 15.9 | 15.8 | 16.6 | 20.7 | 24.3 | 22.4 | 19.8 | 19.3 | 18.9 | 16.5 | 13.8 | 13.8 | 11.6 | 6.7 | 10.4 |
| 1989 | 13.8 | 14.8 | 12.4 | 11.4 | 13.6 | 15.6 | 15.5 | 16.2 | 20.0 | 23.3 | 21.5 | 19.1 | 18.5 | 18.1 | 15.8 | 13.4 | 13.4 | 11.4 | 7.3 | 10.3 |
| 1990 | 12.2 | 13.0 | 10.7 | 9.6 | 11.7 | 13.3 | 13.2 | 13.7 | 17.1 | 19.9 | 18.0 | 15.6 | 14.8 | 14.1 | 11.8 | 9.3 | 8.8 | 6.6 | 2.6 | 4.2 |
| 1991 | 13.3 | 14.2 | 11.9 | 11.0 | 13.0 | 14.7 | 14.6 | 15.1 | 18.5 | 21.2 | 19.5 | 17.3 | 16.7 | 16.2 | 14.2 | 12.1 | 12.0 | 10.3 | 7.1 | 9.2 |
| 1992 | 13.6 | 14.5 | 12.4 | 11.5 | 13.4 | 15.1 | 15.0 | 15.5 | 18.7 | 21.3 | 19.7 | 17.7 | 17.2 | 16.7 | 14.9 | 13.0 | 13.0 | 11.6 | 8.8 | 10.9 |
| 1993 | 13.9 | 14.7 | 12.7 | 11.8 | 13.7 | 15.3 | 15.3 | 15.8 | 18.8 | 21.3 | 19.8 | 17.9 | 17.4 | 17.0 | 15.3 | 13.6 | 13.6 | 12.4 | 10.0 | 12.0 |
| 1994 | 13.5 | 14.3 | 12.3 | 11.5 | 13.3 | 14.8 | 14.7 | 15.2 | 18.0 | 20.3 | 18.8 | 17.0 | 16.5 | 16.1 | 14.5 | 12.8 | 12.8 | 11.6 | 9.3 | 11.1 |
| 1995 | 14.1 | 14.9 | 13.0 | 12.3 | 14.0 | 15.5 | 15.5 | 16.0 | 18.7 | 21.0 | 19.6 | 17.8 | 17.4 | 17.1 | 15.6 | 14.2 | 14.2 | 13.2 | 11.2 | 13.0 |
| 1996 | 14.2 | 15.0 | 13.2 | 12.4 | 14.1 | 15.6 | 15.5 | 16.0 | 18.7 | 20.8 | 19.5 | 17.8 | 17.5 | 17.1 | 15.7 | 14.4 | 14.4 | 13.5 | 11.7 | 13.4 |
| 1997 | 14.5 | 15.3 | 13.5 | 12.8 | 14.4 | 15.8 | 15.8 | 16.3 | 18.8 | 20.9 | 19.6 | 18.1 | 17.7 | 17.4 | 16.1 | 14.9 | 14.9 | 14.1 | 12.5 | 14.1 |
| 1998 | 13.8 | 14.5 | 12.8 | 12.1 | 13.6 | 14.9 | 14.9 | 15.3 | 17.7 | 19.6 | 18.3 | 16.8 | 16.4 | 16.0 | 14.8 | 13.5 | 13.5 | 12.6 | 11.0 | 12.4 |
| 1999 | 14.2 | 14.9 | 13.3 | 12.6 | 14.1 | 15.4 | 15.4 | 15.8 | 18.1 | 20.0 | 18.8 | 17.3 | 17.0 | 16.7 | 15.5 | 14.3 | 14.3 | 13.6 | 12.1 | 13.5 |
| 2000 | 13.7 | 14.3 | 12.7 | 12.0 | 13.5 | 14.7 | 14.7 | 15.0 | 17.2 | 19.0 | 17.8 | 16.4 | 16.0 | 15.7 | 14.5 | 13.3 | 13.3 | 12.5 | 11.1 | 12.3 |
| 2001 | 13.9 | 14.6 | 13.0 | 12.4 | 13.8 | 15.0 | 14.9 | 15.3 | 17.4 | 19.1 | 18.0 | 16.6 | 16.3 | 16.0 | 14.8 | 13.8 | 13.8 | 13.1 | 11.7 | 12.9 |
| 2002 | 13.1 | 13.7 | 12.1 | 11.5 | 12.8 | 14.0 | 13.9 | 14.2 | 16.2 | 17.8 | 16.6 | 15.3 | 14.9 | 14.6 | 13.4 | 12.4 | 12.3 | 11.6 | 10.3 | 11.3 |
| 2003 | 14.1 | 14.7 | 13.1 | 12.7 | 14.0 | 15.1 | 15.1 | 15.5 | 17.5 | 19.0 | 18.0 | 16.7 | 16.4 | 16.1 | 15.1 | 14.1 | 14.1 | 13.5 | 12.4 | 13.5 |
| 2004 | 14.2 | 14.8 | 13.4 | 12.8 | 14.2 | 15.2 | 15.2 | 15.6 | 17.5 | 19.0 | 18.0 | 16.8 | 16.5 | 16.2 | 15.2 | 14.3 | 14.3 | 13.7 | 12.6 | 13.7 |
| 2005 | 14.0 | 14.6 | 13.2 | 12.6 | 13.9 | 15.0 | 14.9 | 15.2 | 17.1 | 18.5 | 17.6 | 16.4 | 16.1 | 15.8 | 14.8 | 13.9 | 13.9 | 13.4 | 12.3 | 13.3 |
| 2006 | 14.1 | 14.6 | 13.3 | 12.7 | 14.0 | 15.0 | 14.9 | 15.3 | 17.1 | 18.5 | 17.5 | 16.4 | 16.1 | 15.8 | 14.9 | 14.0 | 14.0 | 13.5 | 12.5 | 13.4 |
| 2007 | 13.6 | 14.1 | 12.8 | 12.2 | 13.4 | 14.4 | 14.3 | 14.6 | 16.4 | 17.7 | 16.7 | 15.6 | 15.3 | 15.0 | 14.1 | 13.3 | 13.2 | 12.7 | 11.7 | 12.5 |
| 2008 | 12.0 | 12.5 | 11.2 | 10.6 | 11.7 | 12.6 | 12.5 | 12.8 | 14.3 | 15.5 | 14.6 | 13.4 | 13.1 | 12.7 | 11.8 | 10.9 | 10.8 | 10.2 | 9.2 | 9.9 |
| 2009 | 12.4 | 12.9 | 11.6 | 11.0 | 12.1 | 13.0 | 12.9 | 13.1 | 14.7 | 15.9 | 15.0 | 13.9 | 13.5 | 13.2 | 12.3 | 11.5 | 11.4 | 10.8 | 9.8 | 10.6 |
| 2010 | 12.7 | 13.2 | 12.0 | 11.5 | 12.5 | 13.4 | 13.3 | 13.6 | 15.1 | 16.3 | 15.4 | 14.3 | 14.0 | 13.7 | 12.9 | 12.1 | 12.0 | 11.5 | 10.6 | 11.3 |
| 2011 | 12.4 | 12.8 | 11.6 | 11.1 | 12.1 | 13.0 | 12.9 | 13.1 | 14.6 | 15.7 | 14.8 | 13.8 | 13.5 | 13.2 | 12.3 | 11.6 | 11.5 | 10.9 | 10.0 | 10.7 |
| 2012 | 12.5 | 13.0 | 11.7 | 11.3 | 12.3 | 13.1 | 13.0 | 13.2 | 14.7 | 15.8 | 14.9 | 13.9 | 13.6 | 13.3 | 12.5 | 11.8 | 11.7 | 11.2 | 10.3 | 11.0 |
| 2013 | 13.1 | 13.6 | 12.4 | 11.9 | 12.9 | 13.8 | 13.7 | 13.9 | 15.4 | 16.5 | 15.6 | 14.7 | 14.4 | 14.1 | 13.4 | 12.6 | 12.6 | 12.1 | 11.3 | 12.0 |
| 2014 | 12.9 | 13.3 | 12.2 | 11.7 | 12.7 | 13.5 | 13.4 | 13.7 | 15.0 | 16.1 | 15.3 | 14.3 | 14.1 | 13.8 | 13.1 | 12.3 | 12.3 | 11.8 | 11.0 | 11.7 |
| 2015 | 12.5 | 13.0 | 11.8 | 11.4 | 12.3 | 13.1 | 13.0 | 13.2 | 14.6 | 15.6 | 14.8 | 13.8 | 13.5 | 13.3 | 12.6 | 11.9 | 11.8 | 11.3 | 10.6 | 11.2 |
| 2016 | 12.8 | 13.2 | 12.1 | 11.6 | 12.6 | 13.3 | 13.3 | 13.5 | 14.8 | 15.8 | 15.0 | 14.1 | 13.8 | 13.6 | 12.9 | 12.2 | 12.2 | 11.7 | 11.0 | 11.6 |

## Appendix C-2

Small-Capitalization Stocks: Percent per annum total returns for all historical periods

From 1926 to 2016

| End Date | Start Date 1986 | 1987 | 1988 | 1989 | 1990 | 1991 | 1992 | 1993 | 1994 | 1995 | 1996 | 1997 | 1998 | 1999 | 2000 | 2001 | 2002 | 2003 | 2004 | 2005 |
|---|---|---|---|---|---|---|---|---|---|---|---|---|---|---|---|---|---|---|---|---|
| 1971 | | | | | | | | | | | | | | | | | | | | |
| 1972 | | | | | | | | | | | | | | | | | | | | |
| 1973 | | | | | | | | | | | | | | | | | | | | |
| 1974 | | | | | | | | | | | | | | | | | | | | |
| 1975 | | | | | | | | | | | | | | | | | | | | |
| 1976 | | | | | | | | | | | | | | | | | | | | |
| 1977 | | | | | | | | | | | | | | | | | | | | |
| 1978 | | | | | | | | | | | | | | | | | | | | |
| 1979 | | | | | | | | | | | | | | | | | | | | |
| 1980 | | | | | | | | | | | | | | | | | | | | |
| 1981 | | | | | | | | | | | | | | | | | | | | |
| 1982 | | | | | | | | | | | | | | | | | | | | |
| 1983 | | | | | | | | | | | | | | | | | | | | |
| 1984 | | | | | | | | | | | | | | | | | | | | |
| 1985 | | | | | | | | | | | | | | | | | | | | |
| 1986 | 6.9 | | | | | | | | | | | | | | | | | | | |
| 1987 | -1.6 | -9.3 | | | | | | | | | | | | | | | | | | |
| 1988 | 6.0 | 5.6 | 22.9 | | | | | | | | | | | | | | | | | |
| 1989 | 7.0 | 7.1 | 16.4 | 10.2 | | | | | | | | | | | | | | | | |
| 1990 | 0.6 | -0.9 | 2.0 | -7.0 | -21.6 | | | | | | | | | | | | | | | |
| 1991 | 6.9 | 6.9 | 11.3 | 7.7 | 6.5 | 44.6 | | | | | | | | | | | | | | |
| 1992 | 9.1 | 9.4 | 13.6 | 11.4 | 11.9 | 33.6 | 23.3 | | | | | | | | | | | | | |
| 1993 | 10.5 | 11.0 | 14.8 | 13.3 | 14.1 | 29.2 | 22.2 | 21.0 | | | | | | | | | | | | |
| 1994 | 9.6 | 10.0 | 13.1 | 11.5 | 11.8 | 22.1 | 15.4 | 11.7 | 3.1 | | | | | | | | | | | |
| 1995 | 11.9 | 12.5 | 15.5 | 14.5 | 15.3 | 24.5 | 19.9 | 18.8 | 17.7 | 34.5 | | | | | | | | | | |
| 1996 | 12.4 | 13.0 | 15.8 | 14.9 | 15.6 | 23.3 | 19.5 | 18.5 | 17.7 | 25.8 | 17.6 | | | | | | | | | |
| 1997 | 13.2 | 13.8 | 16.5 | 15.8 | 16.5 | 23.3 | 20.0 | 19.4 | 19.0 | 24.8 | 20.2 | 22.8 | | | | | | | | |
| 1998 | 11.5 | 11.9 | 14.1 | 13.2 | 13.6 | 18.9 | 15.7 | 14.4 | 13.2 | 15.8 | 10.2 | 6.7 | -7.3 | | | | | | | |
| 1999 | 12.7 | 13.2 | 15.3 | 14.6 | 15.1 | 20.1 | 17.3 | 16.5 | 15.8 | 18.5 | 14.8 | 13.9 | 9.7 | 29.8 | | | | | | |
| 2000 | 11.6 | 11.9 | 13.7 | 13.0 | 13.3 | 17.5 | 14.8 | 13.8 | 12.8 | 14.5 | 10.9 | 9.2 | 5.1 | 11.9 | -3.6 | | | | | |
| 2001 | 12.2 | 12.6 | 14.3 | 13.7 | 14.0 | 18.0 | 15.6 | 14.7 | 14.0 | 15.6 | 12.8 | 11.8 | 9.2 | 15.4 | 8.8 | 22.8 | | | | |
| 2002 | 10.5 | 10.8 | 12.3 | 11.5 | 11.6 | 15.0 | 12.6 | 11.6 | 10.6 | 11.6 | 8.6 | 7.2 | 4.3 | 7.4 | 0.9 | 3.2 | -13.3 | | | |
| 2003 | 12.9 | 13.2 | 14.8 | 14.3 | 14.6 | 18.0 | 16.0 | 15.3 | 14.8 | 16.2 | 14.1 | 13.6 | 12.1 | 16.4 | 13.3 | 19.6 | 18.1 | 60.7 | | |
| 2004 | 13.1 | 13.5 | 15.0 | 14.5 | 14.8 | 18.0 | 16.2 | 15.6 | 15.1 | 16.4 | 14.5 | 14.2 | 13.0 | 16.8 | 14.3 | 19.3 | 18.2 | 37.9 | 18.4 | |
| 2005 | 12.8 | 13.1 | 14.5 | 14.0 | 14.2 | 17.1 | 15.4 | 14.8 | 14.3 | 15.4 | 13.6 | 13.2 | 12.0 | 15.1 | 12.8 | 16.4 | 14.9 | 26.2 | 11.9 | 5.7 |
| 2006 | 12.9 | 13.2 | 14.6 | 14.1 | 14.4 | 17.1 | 15.4 | 14.9 | 14.4 | 15.4 | 13.9 | 13.5 | 12.5 | 15.2 | 13.3 | 16.4 | 15.2 | 23.6 | 13.3 | 10.8 |
| 2007 | 12.0 | 12.3 | 13.5 | 13.0 | 13.2 | 15.6 | 14.0 | 13.4 | 12.9 | 13.7 | 12.1 | 11.6 | 10.6 | 12.8 | 10.8 | 13.0 | 11.5 | 17.2 | 8.3 | 5.2 |
| 2008 | 9.3 | 9.4 | 10.4 | 9.8 | 9.8 | 11.8 | 10.1 | 9.4 | 8.6 | 9.0 | 7.3 | 6.5 | 5.1 | 6.4 | 4.1 | 5.1 | 2.8 | 5.8 | -2.7 | -7.4 |
| 2009 | 10.0 | 10.1 | 11.1 | 10.6 | 10.6 | 12.6 | 11.1 | 10.4 | 9.8 | 10.2 | 8.7 | 8.0 | 6.9 | 8.2 | 6.3 | 7.5 | 5.7 | 8.7 | 1.9 | -1.2 |
| 2010 | 10.8 | 10.9 | 11.9 | 11.5 | 11.5 | 13.5 | 12.1 | 11.5 | 10.9 | 11.4 | 10.0 | 9.5 | 8.6 | 10.0 | 8.4 | 9.6 | 8.3 | 11.3 | 5.6 | 3.6 |
| 2011 | 10.2 | 10.3 | 11.2 | 10.8 | 10.8 | 12.6 | 11.2 | 10.6 | 10.1 | 10.5 | 9.2 | 8.6 | 7.7 | 8.9 | 7.3 | 8.4 | 7.0 | 9.6 | 4.5 | 2.6 |
| 2012 | 10.5 | 10.6 | 11.5 | 11.1 | 11.1 | 12.9 | 11.6 | 11.0 | 10.5 | 10.9 | 9.7 | 9.2 | 8.3 | 9.6 | 8.1 | 9.2 | 8.0 | 10.4 | 5.9 | 4.4 |
| 2013 | 11.6 | 11.8 | 12.7 | 12.3 | 12.3 | 14.1 | 12.9 | 12.4 | 12.0 | 12.5 | 11.4 | 11.0 | 10.3 | 11.6 | 10.4 | 11.6 | 10.7 | 13.2 | 9.3 | 8.3 |
| 2014 | 11.3 | 11.4 | 12.3 | 11.9 | 12.0 | 13.6 | 12.4 | 12.0 | 11.6 | 12.0 | 10.9 | 10.6 | 9.9 | 11.1 | 9.9 | 10.9 | 10.1 | 12.3 | 8.7 | 7.8 |
| 2015 | 10.7 | 10.9 | 11.7 | 11.3 | 11.3 | 12.9 | 11.7 | 11.2 | 10.8 | 11.2 | 10.2 | 9.8 | 9.1 | 10.1 | 9.0 | 9.9 | 9.0 | 11.0 | 7.6 | 6.7 |
| 2016 | 11.2 | 11.3 | 12.1 | 11.8 | 11.8 | 13.3 | 12.3 | 11.8 | 11.4 | 11.8 | 10.8 | 10.5 | 9.9 | 11.0 | 9.9 | 10.8 | 10.1 | 12.0 | 8.9 | 8.2 |

## Appendix C-2

Small-Capitalization Stocks: Percent per annum total returns for all historical periods

From 1926 to 2016

| End Date | Start Date 2006 | 2007 | 2008 | 2009 | 2010 | 2011 | 2012 | 2013 | 2014 | 2015 | 2016 |
|---|---|---|---|---|---|---|---|---|---|---|---|
| 1971 | | | | | | | | | | | |
| 1972 | | | | | | | | | | | |
| 1973 | | | | | | | | | | | |
| 1974 | | | | | | | | | | | |
| 1975 | | | | | | | | | | | |
| 1976 | | | | | | | | | | | |
| 1977 | | | | | | | | | | | |
| 1978 | | | | | | | | | | | |
| 1979 | | | | | | | | | | | |
| 1980 | | | | | | | | | | | |
| 1981 | | | | | | | | | | | |
| 1982 | | | | | | | | | | | |
| 1983 | | | | | | | | | | | |
| 1984 | | | | | | | | | | | |
| 1985 | | | | | | | | | | | |
| 1986 | | | | | | | | | | | |
| 1987 | | | | | | | | | | | |
| 1988 | | | | | | | | | | | |
| 1989 | | | | | | | | | | | |
| 1990 | | | | | | | | | | | |
| 1991 | | | | | | | | | | | |
| 1992 | | | | | | | | | | | |
| 1993 | | | | | | | | | | | |
| 1994 | | | | | | | | | | | |
| 1995 | | | | | | | | | | | |
| 1996 | | | | | | | | | | | |
| 1997 | | | | | | | | | | | |
| 1998 | | | | | | | | | | | |
| 1999 | | | | | | | | | | | |
| 2000 | | | | | | | | | | | |
| 2001 | | | | | | | | | | | |
| 2002 | | | | | | | | | | | |
| 2003 | | | | | | | | | | | |
| 2004 | | | | | | | | | | | |
| 2005 | | | | | | | | | | | |
| 2006 | 16.2 | | | | | | | | | | |
| 2007 | 4.9 | -5.2 | | | | | | | | | |
| 2008 | -11.3 | -22.6 | -36.7 | | | | | | | | |
| 2009 | -2.8 | -8.4 | -10.0 | 28.1 | | | | | | | |
| 2010 | 3.2 | 0.2 | 2.1 | 29.7 | 31.3 | | | | | | |
| 2011 | 2.1 | -0.5 | 0.7 | 17.6 | 12.7 | -3.3 | | | | | |
| 2012 | 4.3 | 2.4 | 4.0 | 17.8 | 14.5 | 7.0 | 18.2 | | | | |
| 2013 | 8.7 | 7.6 | 9.9 | 22.8 | 21.5 | 18.4 | 31.0 | 45.1 | | | |
| 2014 | 8.0 | 7.0 | 8.9 | 19.2 | 17.5 | 14.3 | 20.9 | 22.2 | 2.9 | | |
| 2015 | 6.8 | 5.8 | 7.3 | 15.7 | 13.7 | 10.5 | 14.2 | 12.9 | -0.4 | -3.6 | |
| 2016 | 8.4 | 7.6 | 9.2 | 16.9 | 15.3 | 12.9 | 16.4 | 16.0 | 7.6 | 10.1 | 25.6 |

## Appendix C-3

Long-term Corporate Bonds: Percent per annum total returns for all historical periods

From 1926 to 2016

| End Date | Start Date 1926 | 1927 | 1928 | 1929 | 1930 | 1931 | 1932 | 1933 | 1934 | 1935 | 1936 | 1937 | 1938 | 1939 | 1940 | 1941 | 1942 | 1943 | 1944 | 1945 |
|---|---|---|---|---|---|---|---|---|---|---|---|---|---|---|---|---|---|---|---|---|
| 1926 | 7.4 | | | | | | | | | | | | | | | | | | | |
| 1927 | 7.4 | 7.4 | | | | | | | | | | | | | | | | | | |
| 1928 | 5.9 | 5.1 | 2.8 | | | | | | | | | | | | | | | | | |
| 1929 | 5.2 | 4.5 | 3.1 | 3.3 | | | | | | | | | | | | | | | | |
| 1930 | 5.8 | 5.4 | 4.7 | 5.6 | 8.0 | | | | | | | | | | | | | | | |
| 1931 | 4.4 | 3.9 | 3.0 | 3.1 | 2.9 | -1.9 | | | | | | | | | | | | | | |
| 1932 | 5.3 | 5.0 | 4.5 | 4.9 | 5.5 | 4.3 | 10.8 | | | | | | | | | | | | | |
| 1933 | 6.0 | 5.8 | 5.5 | 6.0 | 6.7 | 6.3 | 10.6 | 10.4 | | | | | | | | | | | | |
| 1934 | 6.8 | 6.7 | 6.6 | 7.3 | 8.1 | 8.1 | 11.7 | 12.1 | 13.8 | | | | | | | | | | | |
| 1935 | 7.1 | 7.0 | 7.0 | 7.6 | 8.3 | 8.4 | 11.2 | 11.3 | 11.7 | 9.6 | | | | | | | | | | |
| 1936 | 7.1 | 7.0 | 7.0 | 7.5 | 8.1 | 8.1 | 10.3 | 10.1 | 10.0 | 8.2 | 6.7 | | | | | | | | | |
| 1937 | 6.7 | 6.6 | 6.5 | 7.0 | 7.4 | 7.4 | 9.0 | 8.6 | 8.2 | 6.3 | 4.7 | 2.7 | | | | | | | | |
| 1938 | 6.6 | 6.6 | 6.5 | 6.9 | 7.3 | 7.2 | 8.6 | 8.2 | 7.8 | 6.3 | 5.2 | 4.4 | 6.1 | | | | | | | |
| 1939 | 6.4 | 6.4 | 6.3 | 6.6 | 6.9 | 6.8 | 8.0 | 7.6 | 7.1 | 5.8 | 4.9 | 4.3 | 5.0 | 4.0 | | | | | | |
| 1940 | 6.2 | 6.2 | 6.1 | 6.3 | 6.6 | 6.5 | 7.5 | 7.0 | 6.6 | 5.4 | 4.6 | 4.1 | 4.5 | 3.7 | 3.4 | | | | | |
| 1941 | 6.0 | 5.9 | 5.8 | 6.1 | 6.3 | 6.1 | 7.0 | 6.6 | 6.1 | 5.0 | 4.0 | 3.8 | 4.0 | 3.4 | 3.1 | 2.7 | | | | |
| 1942 | 5.8 | 5.7 | 5.6 | 5.8 | 6.0 | 5.8 | 6.6 | 6.2 | 5.7 | 4.7 | 4.0 | 3.6 | 3.8 | 3.2 | 2.9 | 2.7 | 2.6 | | | |
| 1943 | 5.6 | 5.5 | 5.4 | 5.6 | 5.8 | 5.6 | 6.3 | 5.8 | 5.4 | 4.5 | 3.9 | 3.5 | 3.6 | 3.1 | 2.9 | 2.7 | 2.7 | 2.8 | | |
| 1944 | 5.6 | 5.5 | 5.4 | 5.5 | 5.7 | 5.5 | 6.1 | 5.8 | 5.3 | 4.5 | 4.0 | 3.6 | 3.8 | 3.4 | 3.3 | 3.2 | 3.4 | 3.8 | 4.7 | |
| 1945 | 5.5 | 5.4 | 5.3 | 5.5 | 5.6 | 5.4 | 6.0 | 5.6 | 5.2 | 4.5 | 4.0 | 3.7 | 3.8 | 3.5 | 3.4 | 3.4 | 3.6 | 3.9 | 4.4 | 4.1 |
| 1946 | 5.3 | 5.2 | 5.1 | 5.3 | 5.4 | 5.2 | 5.7 | 5.3 | 5.0 | 4.3 | 3.8 | 3.5 | 3.6 | 3.3 | 3.2 | 3.1 | 3.2 | 3.3 | 3.5 | 2.9 |
| 1947 | 5.0 | 4.9 | 4.7 | 4.8 | 4.9 | 4.7 | 5.2 | 4.8 | 4.4 | 3.7 | 3.3 | 2.9 | 3.0 | 2.6 | 2.4 | 2.3 | 2.2 | 2.2 | 2.0 | 1.1 |
| 1948 | 4.9 | 4.8 | 4.7 | 4.8 | 4.9 | 4.7 | 5.1 | 4.8 | 4.4 | 3.8 | 3.3 | 3.0 | 3.1 | 2.8 | 2.6 | 2.5 | 2.5 | 2.5 | 2.4 | 1.9 |
| 1949 | 4.9 | 4.8 | 4.6 | 4.7 | 4.8 | 4.6 | 5.0 | 4.7 | 4.3 | 3.7 | 3.3 | 3.1 | 3.1 | 2.8 | 2.7 | 2.6 | 2.6 | 2.6 | 2.6 | 2.2 |
| 1950 | 4.8 | 4.7 | 4.5 | 4.6 | 4.7 | 4.5 | 4.9 | 4.5 | 4.2 | 3.6 | 3.2 | 3.0 | 3.0 | 2.8 | 2.6 | 2.6 | 2.6 | 2.6 | 2.5 | 2.1 |
| 1951 | 4.5 | 4.3 | 4.2 | 4.3 | 4.3 | 4.2 | 4.5 | 4.1 | 3.8 | 3.2 | 2.9 | 2.6 | 2.6 | 2.3 | 2.2 | 2.1 | 2.0 | 2.0 | 1.8 | 1.4 |
| 1952 | 4.4 | 4.3 | 4.2 | 4.2 | 4.3 | 4.1 | 4.4 | 4.1 | 3.8 | 3.3 | 2.9 | 2.7 | 2.7 | 2.4 | 2.3 | 2.2 | 2.2 | 2.1 | 2.0 | 1.7 |
| 1953 | 4.4 | 4.3 | 4.2 | 4.2 | 4.3 | 4.1 | 4.4 | 4.1 | 3.8 | 3.3 | 2.9 | 2.7 | 2.7 | 2.5 | 2.4 | 2.3 | 2.3 | 2.2 | 2.2 | 1.9 |
| 1954 | 4.4 | 4.3 | 4.2 | 4.3 | 4.3 | 4.2 | 4.4 | 4.1 | 3.8 | 3.4 | 3.1 | 2.9 | 2.9 | 2.7 | 2.6 | 2.5 | 2.5 | 2.5 | 2.5 | 2.2 |
| 1955 | 4.3 | 4.2 | 4.1 | 4.1 | 4.2 | 4.0 | 4.3 | 4.0 | 3.7 | 3.2 | 2.9 | 2.7 | 2.7 | 2.5 | 2.4 | 2.4 | 2.4 | 2.3 | 2.3 | 2.1 |
| 1956 | 3.9 | 3.8 | 3.7 | 3.7 | 3.7 | 3.6 | 3.8 | 3.5 | 3.2 | 2.8 | 2.4 | 2.2 | 2.2 | 2.0 | 1.9 | 1.8 | 1.7 | 1.6 | 1.6 | 1.3 |
| 1957 | 4.1 | 4.0 | 3.8 | 3.9 | 3.9 | 3.7 | 4.0 | 3.7 | 3.4 | 3.0 | 2.7 | 2.5 | 2.5 | 2.3 | 2.2 | 2.2 | 2.1 | 2.1 | 2.1 | 1.9 |
| 1958 | 3.9 | 3.8 | 3.6 | 3.7 | 3.7 | 3.5 | 3.7 | 3.5 | 3.2 | 2.8 | 2.5 | 2.3 | 2.3 | 2.1 | 2.0 | 1.9 | 1.9 | 1.8 | 1.8 | 1.6 |
| 1959 | 3.7 | 3.6 | 3.5 | 3.5 | 3.5 | 3.4 | 3.6 | 3.3 | 3.0 | 2.6 | 2.3 | 2.2 | 2.1 | 1.9 | 1.8 | 1.8 | 1.7 | 1.7 | 1.6 | 1.4 |
| 1960 | 3.9 | 3.8 | 3.7 | 3.7 | 3.7 | 3.6 | 3.7 | 3.5 | 3.3 | 2.9 | 2.6 | 2.4 | 2.4 | 2.3 | 2.2 | 2.1 | 2.1 | 2.1 | 2.0 | 1.8 |
| 1961 | 3.9 | 3.8 | 3.7 | 3.7 | 3.7 | 3.6 | 3.8 | 3.5 | 3.3 | 2.9 | 2.7 | 2.5 | 2.5 | 2.4 | 2.3 | 2.2 | 2.2 | 2.2 | 2.2 | 2.0 |
| 1962 | 4.0 | 3.9 | 3.8 | 3.8 | 3.9 | 3.7 | 3.9 | 3.7 | 3.5 | 3.1 | 2.9 | 2.7 | 2.7 | 2.6 | 2.5 | 2.5 | 2.5 | 2.5 | 2.5 | 2.3 |
| 1963 | 4.0 | 3.9 | 3.8 | 3.8 | 3.8 | 3.7 | 3.9 | 3.6 | 3.4 | 3.1 | 2.9 | 2.7 | 2.7 | 2.6 | 2.5 | 2.5 | 2.5 | 2.5 | 2.5 | 2.3 |
| 1964 | 4.0 | 3.9 | 3.8 | 3.8 | 3.8 | 3.7 | 3.9 | 3.7 | 3.5 | 3.1 | 2.9 | 2.8 | 2.8 | 2.7 | 2.6 | 2.6 | 2.6 | 2.6 | 2.6 | 2.5 |
| 1965 | 3.9 | 3.8 | 3.7 | 3.7 | 3.6 | 3.6 | 3.8 | 3.6 | 3.3 | 3.0 | 2.8 | 2.7 | 2.7 | 2.5 | 2.5 | 2.5 | 2.4 | 2.4 | 2.4 | 2.3 |
| 1966 | 3.8 | 3.7 | 3.6 | 3.6 | 3.6 | 3.5 | 3.7 | 3.5 | 3.2 | 2.9 | 2.7 | 2.6 | 2.6 | 2.5 | 2.4 | 2.4 | 2.4 | 2.3 | 2.3 | 2.2 |
| 1967 | 3.6 | 3.5 | 3.4 | 3.4 | 3.4 | 3.3 | 3.4 | 3.2 | 3.0 | 2.7 | 2.5 | 2.3 | 2.3 | 2.2 | 2.1 | 2.1 | 2.1 | 2.0 | 2.0 | 1.9 |
| 1968 | 3.5 | 3.4 | 3.3 | 3.4 | 3.4 | 3.2 | 3.4 | 3.2 | 3.0 | 2.7 | 2.5 | 2.3 | 2.3 | 2.2 | 2.2 | 2.1 | 2.1 | 2.1 | 2.0 | 1.9 |
| 1969 | 3.3 | 3.2 | 3.1 | 3.1 | 3.1 | 2.9 | 3.1 | 2.9 | 2.7 | 2.4 | 2.2 | 2.0 | 2.0 | 1.9 | 1.8 | 1.7 | 1.7 | 1.7 | 1.6 | 1.5 |
| 1970 | 3.6 | 3.5 | 3.4 | 3.4 | 3.4 | 3.3 | 3.4 | 3.2 | 3.1 | 2.8 | 2.6 | 2.5 | 2.5 | 2.3 | 2.3 | 2.3 | 2.2 | 2.2 | 2.2 | 2.1 |

## Appendix C-3

Long-term Corporate Bonds: Percent per annum total returns for all historical periods

From 1926 to 2016

| End Date | Start Date 1926 | 1927 | 1928 | 1929 | 1930 | 1931 | 1932 | 1933 | 1934 | 1935 | 1936 | 1937 | 1938 | 1939 | 1940 | 1941 | 1942 | 1943 | 1944 | 1945 |
|---|---|---|---|---|---|---|---|---|---|---|---|---|---|---|---|---|---|---|---|---|
| 1971 | 3.7 | 3.6 | 3.6 | 3.6 | 3.6 | 3.5 | 3.6 | 3.4 | 3.3 | 3.0 | 2.8 | 2.7 | 2.7 | 2.6 | 2.6 | 2.5 | 2.5 | 2.5 | 2.5 | 2.4 |
| 1972 | 3.8 | 3.7 | 3.6 | 3.7 | 3.7 | 3.6 | 3.7 | 3.5 | 3.4 | 3.1 | 2.9 | 2.8 | 2.8 | 2.7 | 2.7 | 2.7 | 2.7 | 2.7 | 2.7 | 2.6 |
| 1973 | 3.7 | 3.7 | 3.6 | 3.6 | 3.6 | 3.5 | 3.6 | 3.5 | 3.3 | 3.0 | 2.9 | 2.8 | 2.8 | 2.7 | 2.6 | 2.6 | 2.6 | 2.6 | 2.6 | 2.5 |
| 1974 | 3.6 | 3.5 | 3.4 | 3.4 | 3.5 | 3.4 | 3.5 | 3.1 | 3.1 | 2.9 | 2.7 | 2.6 | 2.6 | 2.5 | 2.5 | 2.4 | 2.4 | 2.4 | 2.4 | 2.3 |
| 1975 | 3.8 | 3.7 | 3.7 | 3.7 | 3.7 | 3.6 | 3.7 | 3.6 | 3.4 | 3.2 | 3.0 | 2.9 | 2.9 | 2.8 | 2.8 | 2.8 | 2.8 | 2.8 | 2.8 | 2.7 |
| 1976 | 4.1 | 4.0 | 3.9 | 4.0 | 4.0 | 3.9 | 4.0 | 3.9 | 3.7 | 3.5 | 3.4 | 3.3 | 3.3 | 3.2 | 3.2 | 3.2 | 3.2 | 3.2 | 3.2 | 3.2 |
| 1977 | 4.0 | 4.0 | 3.9 | 3.9 | 3.9 | 3.9 | 4.0 | 3.8 | 3.7 | 3.5 | 3.3 | 3.2 | 3.2 | 3.2 | 3.2 | 3.1 | 3.2 | 3.2 | 3.2 | 3.1 |
| 1978 | 4.0 | 3.9 | 3.8 | 3.8 | 3.9 | 3.8 | 3.9 | 3.7 | 3.6 | 3.4 | 3.2 | 3.2 | 3.2 | 3.1 | 3.1 | 3.1 | 3.1 | 3.1 | 3.1 | 3.0 |
| 1979 | 3.8 | 3.7 | 3.7 | 3.7 | 3.7 | 3.6 | 3.7 | 3.6 | 3.4 | 3.2 | 3.1 | 3.0 | 3.0 | 2.9 | 2.9 | 2.9 | 2.9 | 2.9 | 2.9 | 2.8 |
| 1980 | 3.7 | 3.6 | 3.5 | 3.5 | 3.6 | 3.5 | 3.6 | 3.4 | 3.3 | 3.1 | 2.9 | 2.8 | 2.8 | 2.8 | 2.7 | 2.7 | 2.7 | 2.7 | 2.7 | 2.7 |
| 1981 | 3.6 | 3.5 | 3.4 | 3.5 | 3.5 | 3.4 | 3.5 | 3.3 | 3.2 | 3.0 | 2.8 | 2.8 | 2.8 | 2.7 | 2.6 | 2.6 | 2.6 | 2.6 | 2.6 | 2.6 |
| 1982 | 4.2 | 4.1 | 4.1 | 4.1 | 4.1 | 4.0 | 4.1 | 4.0 | 3.9 | 3.7 | 3.6 | 3.5 | 3.5 | 3.4 | 3.4 | 3.4 | 3.5 | 3.5 | 3.5 | 3.5 |
| 1983 | 4.2 | 4.1 | 4.1 | 4.1 | 4.1 | 4.1 | 4.2 | 4.0 | 3.9 | 3.7 | 3.6 | 3.5 | 3.6 | 3.5 | 3.5 | 3.5 | 3.5 | 3.5 | 3.6 | 3.5 |
| 1984 | 4.4 | 4.4 | 4.3 | 4.3 | 4.3 | 4.3 | 4.4 | 4.3 | 4.2 | 4.0 | 3.9 | 3.8 | 3.8 | 3.8 | 3.8 | 3.8 | 3.8 | 3.8 | 3.9 | 3.8 |
| 1985 | 4.8 | 4.7 | 4.7 | 4.7 | 4.8 | 4.7 | 4.8 | 4.6 | 4.6 | 4.4 | 4.3 | 4.3 | 4.3 | 4.3 | 4.3 | 4.3 | 4.3 | 4.4 | 4.4 | 4.4 |
| 1986 | 5.0 | 5.0 | 4.9 | 5.0 | 5.0 | 5.0 | 5.1 | 4.9 | 4.9 | 4.7 | 4.6 | 4.5 | 4.5 | 4.5 | 4.6 | 4.6 | 4.7 | 4.7 | 4.8 | 4.8 |
| 1987 | 4.9 | 4.9 | 4.8 | 4.9 | 4.9 | 4.9 | 5.0 | 4.8 | 4.8 | 4.6 | 4.5 | 4.5 | 4.5 | 4.5 | 4.5 | 4.5 | 4.6 | 4.6 | 4.6 | 4.6 |
| 1988 | 5.0 | 5.0 | 4.9 | 5.0 | 5.0 | 5.0 | 5.1 | 4.9 | 4.9 | 4.7 | 4.6 | 4.6 | 4.6 | 4.6 | 4.6 | 4.6 | 4.7 | 4.7 | 4.8 | 4.8 |
| 1989 | 5.2 | 5.2 | 5.1 | 5.2 | 5.2 | 5.1 | 5.3 | 5.1 | 5.1 | 4.9 | 4.8 | 4.8 | 4.8 | 4.8 | 4.8 | 4.9 | 4.9 | 5.0 | 5.0 | 5.0 |
| 1990 | 5.2 | 5.2 | 5.1 | 5.2 | 5.2 | 5.2 | 5.3 | 5.1 | 5.1 | 5.0 | 4.9 | 4.8 | 4.9 | 4.9 | 4.9 | 4.9 | 4.9 | 5.0 | 5.0 | 5.1 |
| 1991 | 5.4 | 5.4 | 5.4 | 5.4 | 5.4 | 5.4 | 5.5 | 5.3 | 5.3 | 5.2 | 5.1 | 5.1 | 5.1 | 5.1 | 5.1 | 5.2 | 5.2 | 5.3 | 5.3 | 5.3 |
| 1992 | 5.5 | 5.4 | 5.4 | 5.5 | 5.5 | 5.5 | 5.6 | 5.5 | 5.4 | 5.3 | 5.2 | 5.2 | 5.2 | 5.2 | 5.2 | 5.3 | 5.3 | 5.4 | 5.4 | 5.4 |
| 1993 | 5.6 | 5.6 | 5.5 | 5.6 | 5.6 | 5.6 | 5.7 | 5.6 | 5.5 | 5.4 | 5.3 | 5.3 | 5.4 | 5.3 | 5.4 | 5.4 | 5.5 | 5.5 | 5.6 | 5.6 |
| 1994 | 5.4 | 5.4 | 5.4 | 5.4 | 5.4 | 5.4 | 5.5 | 5.4 | 5.3 | 5.2 | 5.1 | 5.1 | 5.1 | 5.1 | 5.2 | 5.2 | 5.2 | 5.3 | 5.3 | 5.3 |
| 1995 | 5.7 | 5.7 | 5.6 | 5.7 | 5.7 | 5.7 | 5.8 | 5.7 | 5.7 | 5.5 | 5.5 | 5.4 | 5.5 | 5.5 | 5.5 | 5.5 | 5.6 | 5.7 | 5.7 | 5.7 |
| 1996 | 5.6 | 5.6 | 5.6 | 5.6 | 5.7 | 5.6 | 5.7 | 5.6 | 5.6 | 5.5 | 5.5 | 5.4 | 5.4 | 5.4 | 5.4 | 5.5 | 5.5 | 5.6 | 5.6 | 5.6 |
| 1997 | 5.7 | 5.7 | 5.7 | 5.7 | 5.7 | 5.7 | 5.7 | 5.7 | 5.7 | 5.6 | 5.5 | 5.5 | 5.5 | 5.5 | 5.6 | 5.6 | 5.7 | 5.7 | 5.8 | 5.8 |
| 1998 | 5.8 | 5.8 | 5.8 | 5.8 | 5.8 | 5.8 | 5.9 | 5.8 | 5.8 | 5.7 | 5.6 | 5.6 | 5.6 | 5.6 | 5.6 | 5.7 | 5.7 | 5.8 | 5.9 | 5.9 |
| 1999 | 5.6 | 5.6 | 5.6 | 5.6 | 5.6 | 5.6 | 5.7 | 5.6 | 5.6 | 5.4 | 5.4 | 5.4 | 5.4 | 5.4 | 5.4 | 5.4 | 5.5 | 5.5 | 5.7 | 5.6 |
| 2000 | 5.7 | 5.7 | 5.7 | 5.7 | 5.7 | 5.7 | 5.8 | 5.7 | 5.7 | 5.6 | 5.5 | 5.5 | 5.5 | 5.5 | 5.6 | 5.6 | 5.6 | 5.7 | 5.7 | 5.7 |
| 2001 | 5.8 | 5.7 | 5.7 | 5.8 | 5.8 | 5.8 | 5.9 | 5.8 | 5.7 | 5.6 | 5.6 | 5.6 | 5.6 | 5.6 | 5.6 | 5.7 | 5.7 | 5.8 | 5.8 | 5.8 |
| 2002 | 5.9 | 5.9 | 5.9 | 5.9 | 5.9 | 5.9 | 6.0 | 5.9 | 5.9 | 5.8 | 5.7 | 5.7 | 5.8 | 5.7 | 5.8 | 5.8 | 5.9 | 5.9 | 6.0 | 6.0 |
| 2003 | 5.9 | 5.9 | 5.9 | 5.9 | 5.9 | 5.9 | 6.0 | 5.9 | 5.9 | 5.8 | 5.7 | 5.7 | 5.7 | 5.8 | 5.8 | 5.9 | 5.9 | 6.0 | 6.0 | 6.0 |
| 2004 | 5.9 | 5.9 | 5.9 | 6.0 | 5.9 | 5.9 | 6.0 | 5.9 | 5.9 | 5.8 | 5.8 | 5.8 | 5.8 | 5.8 | 5.8 | 5.9 | 5.9 | 6.0 | 6.0 | 6.0 |
| 2005 | 5.9 | 5.9 | 5.9 | 5.9 | 5.9 | 5.9 | 6.0 | 5.9 | 5.9 | 5.8 | 5.8 | 5.7 | 5.8 | 5.8 | 5.8 | 5.9 | 5.9 | 6.0 | 6.0 | 6.0 |
| 2006 | 5.9 | 5.8 | 5.9 | 5.9 | 5.9 | 5.9 | 6.0 | 5.9 | 5.9 | 5.8 | 5.7 | 5.7 | 5.8 | 5.7 | 5.8 | 5.8 | 5.9 | 5.9 | 6.0 | 6.0 |
| 2007 | 5.9 | 5.8 | 5.8 | 5.8 | 5.9 | 5.9 | 6.0 | 5.8 | 5.8 | 5.7 | 5.7 | 5.7 | 5.7 | 5.7 | 5.7 | 5.8 | 5.8 | 5.9 | 5.9 | 5.9 |
| 2008 | 5.9 | 5.9 | 5.8 | 5.9 | 5.9 | 5.9 | 6.0 | 5.9 | 5.9 | 5.8 | 5.7 | 5.8 | 5.8 | 5.7 | 5.8 | 5.8 | 5.9 | 5.9 | 6.0 | 6.0 |
| 2009 | 5.9 | 5.8 | 5.8 | 5.8 | 5.9 | 5.9 | 6.0 | 5.9 | 5.8 | 5.7 | 5.7 | 5.7 | 5.7 | 5.7 | 5.7 | 5.8 | 5.8 | 5.9 | 5.9 | 5.9 |
| 2010 | 5.9 | 5.9 | 5.9 | 6.0 | 5.9 | 5.9 | 6.0 | 6.0 | 5.9 | 5.8 | 5.8 | 5.7 | 5.8 | 5.8 | 5.8 | 5.9 | 5.9 | 6.0 | 6.0 | 6.0 |
| 2011 | 6.1 | 6.0 | 6.0 | 6.1 | 6.1 | 6.1 | 6.2 | 6.1 | 6.1 | 6.0 | 5.9 | 5.9 | 6.0 | 6.0 | 6.0 | 6.0 | 6.1 | 6.1 | 6.2 | 6.2 |
| 2012 | 6.1 | 6.1 | 6.1 | 6.1 | 6.1 | 6.1 | 6.2 | 6.1 | 6.1 | 6.0 | 6.0 | 6.0 | 6.0 | 6.0 | 6.0 | 6.1 | 6.1 | 6.2 | 6.2 | 6.3 |
| 2013 | 6.0 | 5.9 | 5.9 | 6.0 | 6.0 | 6.0 | 6.1 | 5.9 | 5.9 | 5.9 | 5.8 | 5.8 | 5.8 | 5.8 | 5.9 | 5.9 | 5.9 | 6.0 | 6.0 | 6.0 |
| 2014 | 6.1 | 6.1 | 6.0 | 6.1 | 6.1 | 6.1 | 6.2 | 6.1 | 6.1 | 6.0 | 5.9 | 5.9 | 6.0 | 5.9 | 6.0 | 6.0 | 6.1 | 6.1 | 6.2 | 6.2 |
| 2015 | 6.0 | 6.0 | 6.0 | 6.0 | 6.0 | 6.0 | 6.1 | 6.0 | 6.0 | 5.9 | 5.9 | 5.9 | 5.9 | 5.9 | 5.9 | 5.9 | 6.0 | 6.0 | 6.1 | 6.1 |
| 2016 | 6.0 | 6.0 | 6.0 | 6.0 | 6.0 | 6.0 | 6.1 | 6.1 | 6.0 | 5.9 | 5.9 | 5.9 | 5.9 | 5.9 | 5.9 | 5.9 | 6.0 | 6.0 | 6.1 | 6.1 |

## Appendix C-3

Long-term Corporate Bonds: Percent per annum total returns for all historical periods

From 1926 to 2016

| End Date | Start Date | | | | | | | | | | | | | | | | | | | |
|---|---|---|---|---|---|---|---|---|---|---|---|---|---|---|---|---|---|---|---|---|
| | 1946 | 1947 | 1948 | 1949 | 1950 | 1951 | 1952 | 1953 | 1954 | 1955 | 1956 | 1957 | 1958 | 1959 | 1960 | 1961 | 1962 | 1963 | 1964 | 1965 |
| 1926 | | | | | | | | | | | | | | | | | | | | |
| 1927 | | | | | | | | | | | | | | | | | | | | |
| 1928 | | | | | | | | | | | | | | | | | | | | |
| 1929 | | | | | | | | | | | | | | | | | | | | |
| 1930 | | | | | | | | | | | | | | | | | | | | |
| 1931 | | | | | | | | | | | | | | | | | | | | |
| 1932 | | | | | | | | | | | | | | | | | | | | |
| 1933 | | | | | | | | | | | | | | | | | | | | |
| 1934 | | | | | | | | | | | | | | | | | | | | |
| 1935 | | | | | | | | | | | | | | | | | | | | |
| 1936 | | | | | | | | | | | | | | | | | | | | |
| 1937 | | | | | | | | | | | | | | | | | | | | |
| 1938 | | | | | | | | | | | | | | | | | | | | |
| 1939 | | | | | | | | | | | | | | | | | | | | |
| 1940 | | | | | | | | | | | | | | | | | | | | |
| 1941 | | | | | | | | | | | | | | | | | | | | |
| 1942 | | | | | | | | | | | | | | | | | | | | |
| 1943 | | | | | | | | | | | | | | | | | | | | |
| 1944 | | | | | | | | | | | | | | | | | | | | |
| 1945 | | | | | | | | | | | | | | | | | | | | |
| 1946 | 1.7 | | | | | | | | | | | | | | | | | | | |
| 1947 | -0.3 | -2.3 | | | | | | | | | | | | | | | | | | |
| 1948 | 1.1 | 0.8 | 4.1 | | | | | | | | | | | | | | | | | |
| 1949 | 1.7 | 1.7 | 3.7 | 3.3 | | | | | | | | | | | | | | | | |
| 1950 | 1.8 | 1.8 | 3.2 | 2.7 | 2.1 | | | | | | | | | | | | | | | |
| 1951 | 1.0 | 0.9 | 1.7 | 0.9 | -0.3 | -2.7 | | | | | | | | | | | | | | |
| 1952 | 1.4 | 1.3 | 2.0 | 1.5 | 0.9 | 0.4 | 3.5 | | | | | | | | | | | | | |
| 1953 | 1.6 | 1.6 | 2.3 | 1.9 | 1.6 | 1.4 | 3.5 | 3.4 | | | | | | | | | | | | |
| 1954 | 2.0 | 2.1 | 2.7 | 2.5 | 2.3 | 2.4 | 4.1 | 4.4 | 5.4 | | | | | | | | | | | |
| 1955 | 1.9 | 1.9 | 2.4 | 2.2 | 2.0 | 2.0 | 3.2 | 3.1 | 2.9 | 0.5 | | | | | | | | | | |
| 1956 | 1.1 | 1.0 | 1.4 | 1.0 | 0.7 | 0.5 | 1.1 | 0.5 | -0.4 | -3.2 | -6.8 | | | | | | | | | |
| 1957 | 1.7 | 1.7 | 2.1 | 1.8 | 1.7 | 1.6 | 2.3 | 2.1 | 1.8 | 0.6 | 0.7 | 8.7 | | | | | | | | |
| 1958 | 1.4 | 1.3 | 1.7 | 1.4 | 1.2 | 1.1 | 1.7 | 1.4 | 1.0 | -0.1 | -0.3 | 3.1 | -2.2 | | | | | | | |
| 1959 | 1.2 | 1.2 | 1.5 | 1.2 | 1.0 | 0.9 | 1.3 | 1.0 | 0.6 | -0.3 | -0.5 | 1.7 | -1.6 | -1.0 | | | | | | |
| 1960 | 1.7 | 1.7 | 2.0 | 1.8 | 1.7 | 1.7 | 2.2 | 2.0 | 1.8 | 1.2 | 1.4 | 3.5 | 1.8 | 3.9 | 9.1 | | | | | |
| 1961 | 1.9 | 1.9 | 2.2 | 2.1 | 2.0 | 2.0 | 2.4 | 2.3 | 2.2 | 1.7 | 1.9 | 3.8 | 2.6 | 4.2 | 6.9 | 4.8 | | | | |
| 1962 | 2.2 | 2.3 | 2.6 | 2.5 | 2.4 | 2.4 | 2.9 | 2.9 | 2.8 | 2.5 | 2.8 | 4.5 | 3.6 | 5.1 | 7.3 | 6.4 | 7.9 | | | |
| 1963 | 2.2 | 2.3 | 2.6 | 2.5 | 2.4 | 2.4 | 2.9 | 2.8 | 2.7 | 2.4 | 2.7 | 4.1 | 3.4 | 4.5 | 6.0 | 5.0 | 5.0 | 2.2 | | |
| 1964 | 2.4 | 2.4 | 2.7 | 2.6 | 2.6 | 2.6 | 3.0 | 3.0 | 2.9 | 2.7 | 2.9 | 4.2 | 3.6 | 4.6 | 5.7 | 4.9 | 4.9 | 3.5 | 4.8 | |
| 1965 | 2.2 | 2.3 | 2.5 | 2.4 | 2.4 | 2.4 | 2.8 | 2.7 | 2.6 | 2.4 | 2.6 | 3.7 | 3.1 | 3.8 | 4.7 | 3.8 | 3.6 | 2.1 | 2.1 | -0.5 |
| 1966 | 2.1 | 2.1 | 2.4 | 2.3 | 2.2 | 2.2 | 2.6 | 2.5 | 2.4 | 2.2 | 2.4 | 3.3 | 2.7 | 3.4 | 4.0 | 3.2 | 2.9 | 1.7 | 1.5 | -0.1 |
| 1967 | 1.8 | 1.8 | 2.0 | 1.9 | 1.8 | 1.8 | 2.1 | 2.0 | 1.9 | 1.6 | 1.7 | 2.5 | 1.9 | 2.4 | 2.9 | 2.0 | 1.5 | 0.3 | -0.2 | -1.8 |
| 1968 | 1.8 | 1.8 | 2.0 | 1.9 | 1.9 | 1.8 | 2.1 | 2.0 | 1.9 | 1.7 | 1.8 | 2.5 | 2.0 | 2.4 | 2.8 | 2.1 | 1.7 | 0.7 | 0.4 | -0.7 |
| 1969 | 1.4 | 1.4 | 1.6 | 1.4 | 1.3 | 1.3 | 1.5 | 1.4 | 1.3 | 1.0 | 1.1 | 1.7 | 1.1 | 1.4 | 1.7 | 0.9 | 0.4 | -0.6 | -1.1 | -2.2 |
| 1970 | 2.0 | 2.0 | 2.2 | 2.1 | 2.1 | 2.1 | 2.3 | 2.3 | 2.2 | 2.0 | 2.1 | 2.8 | 2.4 | 2.7 | 3.1 | 2.5 | 2.3 | 1.6 | 1.5 | 0.9 |

# Appendix C-3

Long-term Corporate Bonds: Percent per annum total returns for all historical periods

From 1926 to 2016

| End Date | Start Date 1946 | 1947 | 1948 | 1949 | 1950 | 1951 | 1952 | 1953 | 1954 | 1955 | 1956 | 1957 | 1958 | 1959 | 1960 | 1961 | 1962 | 1963 | 1964 | 1965 |
|---|---|---|---|---|---|---|---|---|---|---|---|---|---|---|---|---|---|---|---|---|
| 1971 | 2.4 | 2.4 | 2.6 | 2.5 | 2.5 | 2.5 | 2.8 | 2.7 | 2.7 | 2.5 | 2.7 | 3.3 | 3.0 | 3.4 | 3.7 | 3.3 | 3.1 | 2.6 | 2.6 | 2.3 |
| 1972 | 2.5 | 2.6 | 2.8 | 2.7 | 2.7 | 2.7 | 3.0 | 2.9 | 2.9 | 2.8 | 2.9 | 3.6 | 3.2 | 3.6 | 4.0 | 3.6 | 3.5 | 3.0 | 3.1 | 2.9 |
| 1973 | 2.5 | 2.5 | 2.7 | 2.6 | 2.6 | 2.6 | 2.9 | 2.9 | 2.8 | 2.7 | 2.8 | 3.4 | 3.1 | 3.5 | 3.8 | 3.4 | 3.3 | 2.9 | 2.9 | 2.7 |
| 1974 | 2.3 | 2.3 | 2.5 | 2.4 | 2.4 | 2.4 | 2.6 | 2.6 | 2.5 | 2.4 | 2.5 | 3.1 | 2.7 | 3.0 | 3.3 | 2.9 | 2.8 | 2.4 | 2.4 | 2.1 |
| 1975 | 2.7 | 2.7 | 2.9 | 2.9 | 2.8 | 2.9 | 3.1 | 3.1 | 3.1 | 3.0 | 3.1 | 3.6 | 3.4 | 3.7 | 4.0 | 3.7 | 3.6 | 3.3 | 3.3 | 3.2 |
| 1976 | 3.2 | 3.2 | 3.4 | 3.4 | 3.4 | 3.4 | 3.7 | 3.7 | 3.7 | 3.6 | 3.8 | 4.3 | 4.1 | 4.5 | 4.8 | 4.5 | 4.5 | 4.3 | 4.4 | 4.4 |
| 1977 | 3.1 | 3.2 | 3.3 | 3.3 | 3.3 | 3.4 | 3.6 | 3.6 | 3.6 | 3.5 | 3.7 | 4.2 | 4.0 | 4.3 | 4.6 | 4.4 | 4.3 | 4.1 | 4.2 | 4.2 |
| 1978 | 3.0 | 3.1 | 3.2 | 3.2 | 3.2 | 3.2 | 3.5 | 3.5 | 3.5 | 3.4 | 3.5 | 4.0 | 3.8 | 4.1 | 4.4 | 4.1 | 4.1 | 3.8 | 4.0 | 3.9 |
| 1979 | 2.8 | 2.8 | 3.0 | 3.0 | 2.9 | 3.0 | 3.2 | 3.2 | 3.2 | 3.1 | 3.2 | 3.6 | 3.4 | 3.7 | 3.9 | 3.7 | 3.6 | 3.4 | 3.4 | 3.3 |
| 1980 | 2.6 | 2.7 | 2.8 | 2.8 | 2.8 | 2.8 | 3.0 | 3.0 | 2.9 | 2.8 | 2.9 | 3.4 | 3.1 | 3.4 | 3.6 | 3.3 | 3.3 | 3.0 | 3.1 | 2.9 |
| 1981 | 2.5 | 2.5 | 2.7 | 2.6 | 2.6 | 2.6 | 2.8 | 2.8 | 2.8 | 2.7 | 2.8 | 3.2 | 3.0 | 3.2 | 3.4 | 3.1 | 3.0 | 2.8 | 2.8 | 2.7 |
| 1982 | 3.4 | 3.5 | 3.7 | 3.6 | 3.7 | 3.7 | 3.9 | 3.9 | 3.9 | 3.9 | 4.0 | 4.5 | 4.3 | 4.6 | 4.8 | 4.6 | 4.6 | 4.5 | 4.6 | 4.6 |
| 1983 | 3.5 | 3.6 | 3.7 | 3.7 | 3.7 | 3.8 | 4.0 | 4.0 | 4.0 | 4.0 | 4.1 | 4.5 | 4.4 | 4.6 | 4.9 | 4.7 | 4.7 | 4.6 | 4.7 | 4.7 |
| 1984 | 3.8 | 3.9 | 4.1 | 4.1 | 4.1 | 4.1 | 4.4 | 4.4 | 4.4 | 4.4 | 4.5 | 5.0 | 4.8 | 5.1 | 5.3 | 5.2 | 5.2 | 5.1 | 5.2 | 5.2 |
| 1985 | 4.4 | 4.5 | 4.7 | 4.7 | 4.7 | 4.8 | 5.0 | 5.1 | 5.1 | 5.1 | 5.3 | 5.7 | 5.6 | 5.9 | 6.2 | 6.1 | 6.1 | 6.1 | 6.2 | 6.3 |
| 1986 | 4.8 | 4.9 | 5.0 | 5.1 | 5.1 | 5.2 | 5.4 | 5.5 | 5.6 | 5.6 | 5.7 | 6.2 | 6.1 | 6.4 | 6.7 | 6.6 | 6.7 | 6.6 | 6.8 | 6.9 |
| 1987 | 4.7 | 4.7 | 4.9 | 4.9 | 5.0 | 5.0 | 5.3 | 5.3 | 5.4 | 5.4 | 5.5 | 6.0 | 5.9 | 6.2 | 6.4 | 6.3 | 6.4 | 6.3 | 6.5 | 6.6 |
| 1988 | 4.8 | 4.9 | 5.0 | 5.1 | 5.1 | 5.2 | 5.4 | 5.5 | 5.5 | 5.5 | 5.7 | 6.1 | 6.0 | 6.3 | 6.6 | 6.5 | 6.5 | 6.5 | 6.7 | 6.7 |
| 1989 | 5.0 | 5.1 | 5.3 | 5.3 | 5.4 | 5.5 | 5.7 | 5.7 | 5.8 | 5.8 | 6.0 | 6.4 | 6.3 | 6.6 | 6.9 | 6.8 | 6.9 | 6.8 | 7.0 | 7.1 |
| 1990 | 5.1 | 5.2 | 5.3 | 5.4 | 5.4 | 5.5 | 5.7 | 5.8 | 5.8 | 5.8 | 6.0 | 6.4 | 6.3 | 6.6 | 6.9 | 6.8 | 6.9 | 6.8 | 7.0 | 7.1 |
| 1991 | 5.4 | 5.5 | 5.6 | 5.7 | 5.7 | 5.8 | 6.0 | 6.1 | 6.2 | 6.2 | 6.4 | 6.8 | 6.7 | 7.0 | 7.3 | 7.2 | 7.3 | 7.3 | 7.4 | 7.5 |
| 1992 | 5.5 | 5.5 | 5.7 | 5.7 | 5.8 | 5.9 | 6.1 | 6.2 | 6.3 | 6.3 | 6.5 | 6.8 | 6.8 | 7.1 | 7.3 | 7.3 | 7.3 | 7.3 | 7.5 | 7.6 |
| 1993 | 5.6 | 5.7 | 5.9 | 5.9 | 6.0 | 6.1 | 6.3 | 6.4 | 6.4 | 6.5 | 6.6 | 7.0 | 7.0 | 7.2 | 7.5 | 7.4 | 7.5 | 7.5 | 7.7 | 7.8 |
| 1994 | 5.4 | 5.4 | 5.6 | 5.7 | 5.7 | 5.8 | 6.0 | 6.1 | 6.1 | 6.1 | 6.3 | 6.7 | 6.6 | 6.9 | 7.1 | 7.0 | 7.1 | 7.1 | 7.2 | 7.3 |
| 1995 | 5.8 | 5.9 | 6.0 | 6.1 | 6.1 | 6.2 | 6.4 | 6.5 | 6.6 | 6.6 | 6.8 | 7.1 | 7.1 | 7.4 | 7.6 | 7.6 | 7.6 | 7.6 | 7.8 | 7.9 |
| 1996 | 5.7 | 5.8 | 5.9 | 6.0 | 6.0 | 6.1 | 6.3 | 6.4 | 6.5 | 6.5 | 6.6 | 7.0 | 6.9 | 7.2 | 7.4 | 7.4 | 7.5 | 7.4 | 7.6 | 7.7 |
| 1997 | 5.8 | 5.9 | 6.1 | 6.1 | 6.2 | 6.3 | 6.5 | 6.5 | 6.6 | 6.6 | 6.8 | 7.1 | 7.1 | 7.3 | 7.6 | 7.5 | 7.6 | 7.6 | 7.8 | 7.9 |
| 1998 | 5.9 | 6.0 | 6.2 | 6.2 | 6.3 | 6.3 | 6.5 | 6.6 | 6.7 | 6.7 | 6.9 | 7.2 | 7.2 | 7.4 | 7.7 | 7.6 | 7.7 | 7.7 | 7.8 | 7.9 |
| 1999 | 5.6 | 5.7 | 5.9 | 5.9 | 6.0 | 6.0 | 6.2 | 6.3 | 6.4 | 6.4 | 6.5 | 6.9 | 6.8 | 7.0 | 7.2 | 7.2 | 7.3 | 7.2 | 7.4 | 7.5 |
| 2000 | 5.8 | 5.8 | 6.0 | 6.0 | 6.1 | 6.2 | 6.4 | 6.4 | 6.5 | 6.5 | 6.7 | 7.0 | 6.9 | 7.2 | 7.4 | 7.3 | 7.4 | 7.4 | 7.5 | 7.6 |
| 2001 | 5.9 | 5.9 | 6.1 | 6.1 | 6.2 | 6.3 | 6.5 | 6.5 | 6.6 | 6.6 | 6.7 | 7.1 | 7.0 | 7.3 | 7.5 | 7.4 | 7.5 | 7.5 | 7.6 | 7.7 |
| 2002 | 6.0 | 6.1 | 6.3 | 6.3 | 6.4 | 6.4 | 6.6 | 6.7 | 6.8 | 6.8 | 6.9 | 7.3 | 7.2 | 7.4 | 7.7 | 7.6 | 7.7 | 7.7 | 7.8 | 7.9 |
| 2003 | 6.0 | 6.1 | 6.3 | 6.3 | 6.3 | 6.4 | 6.6 | 6.7 | 6.7 | 6.8 | 6.9 | 7.2 | 7.2 | 7.4 | 7.6 | 7.6 | 7.6 | 7.6 | 7.8 | 7.8 |
| 2004 | 6.1 | 6.1 | 6.3 | 6.3 | 6.4 | 6.5 | 6.7 | 6.6 | 6.7 | 6.8 | 6.9 | 7.2 | 7.2 | 7.4 | 7.6 | 7.6 | 7.7 | 7.6 | 7.8 | 7.9 |
| 2005 | 6.1 | 6.1 | 6.3 | 6.3 | 6.4 | 6.5 | 6.6 | 6.7 | 6.8 | 6.8 | 6.9 | 7.2 | 7.2 | 7.4 | 7.6 | 7.6 | 7.6 | 7.6 | 7.7 | 7.8 |
| 2006 | 6.0 | 6.1 | 6.2 | 6.3 | 6.3 | 6.4 | 6.6 | 6.6 | 6.7 | 6.7 | 6.8 | 7.1 | 7.1 | 7.3 | 7.5 | 7.5 | 7.5 | 7.5 | 7.6 | 7.7 |
| 2007 | 6.0 | 6.0 | 6.2 | 6.2 | 6.3 | 6.3 | 6.5 | 6.6 | 6.6 | 6.6 | 6.8 | 7.0 | 7.0 | 7.2 | 7.4 | 7.4 | 7.4 | 7.4 | 7.5 | 7.6 |
| 2008 | 6.0 | 6.1 | 6.2 | 6.2 | 6.3 | 6.4 | 6.5 | 6.6 | 6.7 | 6.7 | 6.8 | 7.1 | 7.0 | 7.2 | 7.4 | 7.4 | 7.4 | 7.4 | 7.6 | 7.6 |
| 2009 | 6.0 | 6.0 | 6.2 | 6.2 | 6.2 | 6.3 | 6.5 | 6.5 | 6.6 | 6.6 | 6.7 | 7.0 | 7.0 | 7.2 | 7.3 | 7.3 | 7.3 | 7.3 | 7.4 | 7.5 |
| 2010 | 6.1 | 6.1 | 6.3 | 6.3 | 6.3 | 6.4 | 6.6 | 6.6 | 6.7 | 6.7 | 6.8 | 7.1 | 7.1 | 7.3 | 7.4 | 7.4 | 7.4 | 7.4 | 7.5 | 7.6 |
| 2011 | 6.2 | 6.3 | 6.4 | 6.5 | 6.5 | 6.6 | 6.8 | 6.8 | 6.9 | 6.9 | 7.0 | 7.3 | 7.3 | 7.4 | 7.6 | 7.6 | 7.6 | 7.6 | 7.8 | 7.8 |
| 2012 | 6.3 | 6.4 | 6.5 | 6.5 | 6.6 | 6.7 | 6.8 | 6.9 | 6.9 | 7.0 | 7.1 | 7.3 | 7.3 | 7.5 | 7.7 | 7.6 | 7.7 | 7.7 | 7.8 | 7.9 |
| 2013 | 6.1 | 6.1 | 6.3 | 6.3 | 6.4 | 6.4 | 6.6 | 6.6 | 6.7 | 6.7 | 6.8 | 7.1 | 7.0 | 7.2 | 7.4 | 7.3 | 7.4 | 7.4 | 7.5 | 7.5 |
| 2014 | 6.2 | 6.3 | 6.4 | 6.5 | 6.5 | 6.6 | 6.7 | 6.8 | 6.9 | 6.9 | 7.0 | 7.2 | 7.2 | 7.4 | 7.6 | 7.5 | 7.6 | 7.6 | 7.7 | 7.7 |
| 2015 | 6.1 | 6.2 | 6.3 | 6.4 | 6.4 | 6.5 | 6.6 | 6.7 | 6.7 | 6.7 | 6.8 | 7.1 | 7.1 | 7.2 | 7.4 | 7.4 | 7.4 | 7.4 | 7.5 | 7.6 |
| 2016 | 6.1 | 6.2 | 6.3 | 6.4 | 6.4 | 6.5 | 6.6 | 6.7 | 6.7 | 6.7 | 6.8 | 7.1 | 7.1 | 7.2 | 7.4 | 7.4 | 7.4 | 7.4 | 7.5 | 7.5 |

## Appendix C-3

Long-term Corporate Bonds: Percent per annum total returns for all historical periods

From 1926 to 2016

| End Date | Start Date 1966 | 1967 | 1968 | 1969 | 1970 |
|---|---|---|---|---|---|
| 1966 | 0.2 | | | | |
| 1967 | -2.4 | -5.0 | | | |
| 1968 | -0.8 | -1.3 | 2.6 | | |
| 1969 | -2.7 | -3.6 | -2.9 | -8.1 | |
| 1970 | 1.2 | 1.5 | 3.7 | 4.3 | 18.4 |

# Appendix C-3

Long-term Corporate Bonds: Percent per annum total returns for all historical periods

From 1926 to 2016

| End Date | Start Date 1966 | 1967 | 1968 | 1969 | 1970 | 1971 | 1972 | 1973 | 1974 | 1975 | 1976 | 1977 | 1978 | 1979 | 1980 | 1981 | 1982 | 1983 | 1984 | 1985 |
|---|---|---|---|---|---|---|---|---|---|---|---|---|---|---|---|---|---|---|---|---|
| 1971 | 2.8 | 3.3 | 5.5 | 6.5 | 14.6 | 11.0 | | | | | | | | | | | | | | |
| 1972 | 3.4 | 4.0 | 5.8 | 6.7 | 12.1 | 9.1 | 7.3 | | | | | | | | | | | | | |
| 1973 | 3.1 | 3.6 | 5.0 | 5.6 | 9.3 | 6.4 | 4.2 | 1.1 | | | | | | | | | | | | |
| 1974 | 2.4 | 2.7 | 3.9 | 4.1 | 6.7 | 3.9 | 1.7 | -1.0 | -3.1 | | | | | | | | | | | |
| 1975 | 3.6 | 4.0 | 5.1 | 5.5 | 8.0 | 6.0 | 4.8 | 4.0 | 5.4 | 14.6 | | | | | | | | | | |
| 1976 | 4.9 | 5.4 | 6.6 | 7.1 | 9.4 | 8.0 | 7.4 | 7.5 | 9.7 | 16.6 | 18.6 | | | | | | | | | |
| 1977 | 4.6 | 5.0 | 6.1 | 6.5 | 8.4 | 7.1 | 6.4 | 6.3 | 7.6 | 11.4 | 9.9 | 1.7 | | | | | | | | |
| 1978 | 4.2 | 4.6 | 5.5 | 5.8 | 7.5 | 6.2 | 5.5 | 5.2 | 6.0 | 8.4 | 6.4 | 0.8 | -0.1 | | | | | | | |
| 1979 | 3.6 | 3.9 | 4.7 | 4.8 | 6.2 | 5.0 | 4.2 | 3.8 | 4.3 | 5.8 | 3.7 | -0.9 | -2.1 | -4.2 | | | | | | |
| 1980 | 3.2 | 3.4 | 4.1 | 4.2 | 5.4 | 4.2 | 3.4 | 3.0 | 3.2 | 4.3 | 2.4 | -1.4 | -2.4 | -3.5 | -2.8 | | | | | |
| 1981 | 2.9 | 3.1 | 3.7 | 3.8 | 4.8 | 3.7 | 3.0 | 2.5 | 2.7 | 3.5 | 1.8 | -1.3 | -2.1 | -2.7 | -2.0 | -1.2 | | | | |
| 1982 | 4.9 | 5.2 | 5.9 | 6.1 | 7.3 | 6.5 | 6.0 | 5.9 | 6.5 | 7.7 | 6.8 | 4.9 | 5.6 | 7.0 | 11.0 | 18.7 | 42.6 | | | |
| 1983 | 5.0 | 5.2 | 5.9 | 6.1 | 7.2 | 6.4 | 6.1 | 6.0 | 6.4 | 7.6 | 6.7 | 5.1 | 5.7 | 6.9 | 9.8 | 14.4 | 23.1 | 6.3 | | |
| 1984 | 5.6 | 5.9 | 6.5 | 6.8 | 7.9 | 7.1 | 6.9 | 6.8 | 7.4 | 8.5 | 7.8 | 6.5 | 7.2 | 8.5 | 11.2 | 15.0 | 21.0 | 11.4 | 16.9 | |
| 1985 | 6.7 | 7.0 | 7.7 | 8.0 | 9.1 | 8.5 | 8.4 | 8.5 | 9.1 | 10.3 | 9.8 | 8.9 | 9.8 | 11.3 | 14.1 | 17.9 | 23.2 | 17.3 | 23.3 | 30.1 |
| 1986 | 7.3 | 7.6 | 8.3 | 8.7 | 9.7 | 9.2 | 9.1 | 9.2 | 9.9 | 11.0 | 10.7 | 9.9 | 10.9 | 12.4 | 14.9 | 18.2 | 22.5 | 18.0 | 22.1 | 24.9 |
| 1987 | 6.9 | 7.2 | 7.9 | 8.2 | 9.2 | 8.6 | 8.5 | 8.6 | 9.1 | 10.1 | 9.8 | 9.0 | 9.7 | 10.9 | 12.9 | 15.4 | 18.4 | 14.1 | 16.1 | 15.9 |
| 1988 | 7.1 | 7.4 | 8.0 | 8.3 | 9.2 | 8.7 | 8.6 | 8.7 | 9.2 | 10.2 | 9.8 | 9.1 | 9.8 | 10.9 | 12.7 | 14.8 | 17.3 | 13.5 | 15.0 | 14.5 |
| 1989 | 7.4 | 7.8 | 8.4 | 8.7 | 9.6 | 9.1 | 9.0 | 9.1 | 9.7 | 10.6 | 10.3 | 9.7 | 10.3 | 11.3 | 13.0 | 14.9 | 17.1 | 13.9 | 15.2 | 14.9 |
| 1990 | 7.4 | 7.7 | 8.3 | 8.6 | 9.4 | 9.0 | 8.9 | 9.0 | 9.5 | 10.3 | 10.0 | 9.4 | 10.1 | 11.0 | 12.4 | 14.1 | 15.9 | 13.0 | 14.0 | 13.5 |
| 1991 | 7.9 | 8.2 | 8.8 | 9.0 | 9.9 | 9.5 | 9.4 | 9.5 | 10.0 | 10.9 | 10.6 | 10.1 | 10.7 | 11.6 | 13.0 | 14.6 | 16.3 | 13.7 | 14.7 | 14.4 |
| 1992 | 7.9 | 8.2 | 8.8 | 9.1 | 9.9 | 9.5 | 9.4 | 9.5 | 10.0 | 10.8 | 10.6 | 10.1 | 10.6 | 11.5 | 12.8 | 14.2 | 15.7 | 13.3 | 14.1 | 13.7 |
| 1993 | 8.1 | 8.4 | 9.0 | 9.2 | 10.0 | 9.7 | 9.6 | 9.7 | 10.2 | 10.9 | 10.7 | 10.2 | 10.8 | 11.6 | 12.8 | 14.1 | 15.5 | 13.3 | 14.0 | 13.7 |
| 1994 | 7.6 | 7.9 | 8.4 | 8.6 | 9.3 | 9.0 | 8.9 | 8.8 | 9.3 | 10.0 | 9.8 | 9.3 | 9.8 | 10.4 | 11.4 | 12.5 | 13.7 | 11.5 | 12.0 | 11.6 |
| 1995 | 8.2 | 8.5 | 9.0 | 9.2 | 10.0 | 9.6 | 9.6 | 9.7 | 10.1 | 10.8 | 10.6 | 10.2 | 10.7 | 11.3 | 12.4 | 13.5 | 14.6 | 12.7 | 13.2 | 12.9 |
| 1996 | 8.0 | 8.2 | 8.7 | 9.0 | 9.6 | 9.3 | 9.2 | 9.3 | 9.7 | 10.3 | 10.1 | 9.7 | 10.1 | 10.7 | 11.7 | 12.7 | 13.7 | 11.8 | 12.3 | 11.9 |
| 1997 | 8.1 | 8.4 | 8.9 | 9.1 | 9.8 | 9.4 | 9.4 | 9.5 | 9.8 | 10.4 | 10.2 | 9.9 | 10.3 | 10.9 | 11.8 | 12.7 | 13.6 | 11.9 | 12.3 | 12.0 |
| 1998 | 8.2 | 8.5 | 8.9 | 9.1 | 9.8 | 9.5 | 9.4 | 9.5 | 9.9 | 10.4 | 10.3 | 9.9 | 10.3 | 10.9 | 11.7 | 12.6 | 13.4 | 11.8 | 12.2 | 11.9 |
| 1999 | 7.7 | 7.9 | 8.4 | 8.6 | 9.2 | 8.9 | 8.8 | 8.8 | 9.2 | 9.7 | 9.5 | 9.1 | 9.4 | 10.0 | 10.7 | 11.4 | 12.2 | 10.6 | 10.9 | 10.5 |
| 2000 | 7.8 | 8.1 | 8.5 | 8.7 | 9.3 | 9.0 | 8.9 | 9.0 | 9.3 | 9.8 | 9.6 | 9.2 | 9.6 | 10.0 | 10.8 | 11.5 | 12.2 | 10.7 | 11.0 | 10.6 |
| 2001 | 7.9 | 8.2 | 8.6 | 8.8 | 9.3 | 9.0 | 9.0 | 9.0 | 9.3 | 9.8 | 9.6 | 9.3 | 9.6 | 10.1 | 10.8 | 11.5 | 12.1 | 10.7 | 11.0 | 10.6 |
| 2002 | 8.1 | 8.4 | 8.8 | 9.0 | 9.5 | 9.3 | 9.2 | 9.3 | 9.6 | 10.1 | 9.9 | 9.6 | 9.9 | 10.3 | 11.0 | 11.7 | 12.3 | 11.0 | 11.2 | 10.9 |
| 2003 | 8.1 | 8.3 | 8.7 | 8.9 | 9.4 | 9.1 | 9.1 | 9.1 | 9.4 | 9.9 | 9.7 | 9.4 | 9.7 | 10.1 | 10.8 | 11.4 | 12.0 | 10.7 | 10.9 | 10.6 |
| 2004 | 8.1 | 8.3 | 8.7 | 8.9 | 9.4 | 9.1 | 9.1 | 9.1 | 9.4 | 9.8 | 9.7 | 9.4 | 9.7 | 10.1 | 10.7 | 11.3 | 11.8 | 10.6 | 10.8 | 10.5 |
| 2005 | 8.0 | 8.2 | 8.6 | 8.8 | 9.3 | 9.0 | 9.0 | 9.0 | 9.3 | 9.7 | 9.6 | 9.3 | 9.5 | 9.9 | 10.5 | 11.0 | 11.6 | 10.4 | 10.6 | 10.3 |
| 2006 | 7.9 | 8.1 | 8.5 | 8.6 | 9.1 | 8.9 | 8.8 | 8.9 | 9.1 | 9.5 | 9.3 | 9.0 | 9.3 | 9.7 | 10.2 | 10.7 | 11.2 | 10.1 | 10.3 | 10.0 |
| 2007 | 7.8 | 8.0 | 8.3 | 8.5 | 8.9 | 8.7 | 8.6 | 8.7 | 8.9 | 9.3 | 9.1 | 8.8 | 9.1 | 9.4 | 9.9 | 10.4 | 10.9 | 9.8 | 9.9 | 9.7 |
| 2008 | 7.8 | 8.0 | 8.3 | 8.5 | 8.9 | 8.7 | 8.6 | 8.7 | 8.9 | 9.3 | 9.1 | 8.8 | 9.1 | 9.4 | 9.9 | 10.4 | 10.8 | 9.8 | 9.9 | 9.6 |
| 2009 | 7.7 | 7.9 | 8.2 | 8.3 | 8.8 | 8.6 | 8.5 | 8.5 | 8.7 | 9.1 | 8.9 | 8.6 | 8.9 | 9.2 | 9.6 | 10.1 | 10.5 | 9.5 | 9.6 | 9.3 |
| 2010 | 7.8 | 8.0 | 8.3 | 8.4 | 8.9 | 8.6 | 8.6 | 8.6 | 8.8 | 9.2 | 9.0 | 8.8 | 9.0 | 9.3 | 9.7 | 10.2 | 10.6 | 9.6 | 9.7 | 9.5 |
| 2011 | 8.0 | 8.2 | 8.5 | 8.6 | 9.1 | 8.9 | 8.8 | 8.9 | 9.1 | 9.4 | 9.3 | 9.0 | 9.2 | 9.5 | 10.0 | 10.4 | 10.8 | 9.9 | 10.0 | 9.8 |
| 2012 | 8.1 | 8.2 | 8.6 | 8.7 | 9.1 | 8.9 | 8.9 | 8.9 | 9.1 | 9.4 | 9.3 | 9.1 | 9.3 | 9.6 | 10.0 | 10.4 | 10.8 | 9.9 | 10.0 | 9.8 |
| 2013 | 7.7 | 7.9 | 8.2 | 8.3 | 8.7 | 8.5 | 8.4 | 8.5 | 8.7 | 9.0 | 8.8 | 8.6 | 8.8 | 9.0 | 9.5 | 9.9 | 10.2 | 9.3 | 9.4 | 9.2 |
| 2014 | 7.9 | 8.1 | 8.4 | 8.5 | 8.9 | 8.7 | 8.6 | 8.7 | 8.9 | 9.2 | 9.0 | 8.8 | 9.0 | 9.3 | 9.7 | 10.1 | 10.4 | 9.6 | 9.7 | 9.4 |
| 2015 | 7.7 | 7.9 | 8.2 | 8.3 | 8.7 | 8.5 | 8.4 | 8.4 | 8.6 | 8.9 | 8.8 | 8.5 | 8.7 | 9.0 | 9.4 | 9.7 | 10.1 | 9.2 | 9.3 | 9.1 |
| 2016 | 7.7 | 7.9 | 8.1 | 8.3 | 8.6 | 8.4 | 8.4 | 8.4 | 8.6 | 8.9 | 8.7 | 8.5 | 8.7 | 8.9 | 9.3 | 9.6 | 10.0 | 9.1 | 9.2 | 9.0 |

## Appendix C-3

Long-term Corporate Bonds: Percent per annum total returns for all historical periods

From 1926 to 2016

| End Date | Start Date 1986 | 1987 | 1988 | 1989 | 1990 | 1991 | 1992 | 1993 | 1994 | 1995 | 1996 | 1997 | 1998 | 1999 | 2000 | 2001 | 2002 | 2003 | 2004 | 2005 |
|---|---|---|---|---|---|---|---|---|---|---|---|---|---|---|---|---|---|---|---|---|
| 1971 | | | | | | | | | | | | | | | | | | | | |
| 1972 | | | | | | | | | | | | | | | | | | | | |
| 1973 | | | | | | | | | | | | | | | | | | | | |
| 1974 | | | | | | | | | | | | | | | | | | | | |
| 1975 | | | | | | | | | | | | | | | | | | | | |
| 1976 | | | | | | | | | | | | | | | | | | | | |
| 1977 | | | | | | | | | | | | | | | | | | | | |
| 1978 | | | | | | | | | | | | | | | | | | | | |
| 1979 | | | | | | | | | | | | | | | | | | | | |
| 1980 | | | | | | | | | | | | | | | | | | | | |
| 1981 | | | | | | | | | | | | | | | | | | | | |
| 1982 | | | | | | | | | | | | | | | | | | | | |
| 1983 | | | | | | | | | | | | | | | | | | | | |
| 1984 | | | | | | | | | | | | | | | | | | | | |
| 1985 | | | | | | | | | | | | | | | | | | | | |
| 1986 | 19.8 | | | | | | | | | | | | | | | | | | | |
| 1987 | 9.3 | -0.3 | | | | | | | | | | | | | | | | | | |
| 1988 | 9.8 | 5.1 | 10.7 | | | | | | | | | | | | | | | | | |
| 1989 | 11.4 | 8.7 | 13.4 | 16.2 | | | | | | | | | | | | | | | | |
| 1990 | 10.4 | 8.2 | 11.2 | 11.4 | 6.8 | | | | | | | | | | | | | | | |
| 1991 | 12.0 | 10.4 | 13.3 | 14.2 | 13.1 | 19.9 | | | | | | | | | | | | | | |
| 1992 | 11.6 | 10.3 | 12.5 | 13.0 | 11.9 | 14.5 | 9.4 | | | | | | | | | | | | | |
| 1993 | 11.8 | 10.7 | 12.6 | 13.0 | 12.2 | 14.1 | 11.3 | 13.2 | | | | | | | | | | | | |
| 1994 | 9.7 | 8.5 | 9.8 | 9.6 | 8.4 | 8.8 | 5.3 | 3.3 | -5.8 | | | | | | | | | | | |
| 1995 | 11.3 | 10.4 | 11.8 | 12.0 | 11.3 | 12.2 | 10.4 | 10.7 | 9.5 | 27.2 | | | | | | | | | | |
| 1996 | 10.4 | 9.5 | 10.6 | 10.6 | 9.8 | 10.3 | 8.5 | 8.3 | 6.7 | 13.6 | 1.4 | | | | | | | | | |
| 1997 | 10.6 | 9.8 | 10.8 | 10.9 | 10.2 | 10.7 | 9.2 | 9.2 | 8.2 | 13.4 | 7.0 | 12.9 | | | | | | | | |
| 1998 | 10.6 | 9.9 | 10.8 | 10.9 | 10.3 | 10.7 | 9.5 | 9.5 | 8.7 | 12.7 | 8.3 | 11.8 | 10.8 | | | | | | | |
| 1999 | 9.2 | 8.4 | 9.2 | 9.0 | 8.4 | 8.5 | 7.2 | 6.9 | 5.9 | 8.4 | 4.1 | 5.0 | 1.2 | -7.4 | | | | | | |
| 2000 | 9.4 | 8.7 | 9.5 | 9.4 | 8.8 | 9.0 | 7.8 | 7.6 | 6.8 | 9.1 | 5.8 | 6.9 | 5.0 | 2.2 | 12.9 | | | | | |
| 2001 | 9.5 | 8.9 | 9.5 | 9.5 | 8.9 | 9.1 | 8.1 | 7.9 | 7.3 | 9.3 | 6.6 | 7.7 | 6.4 | 4.9 | 11.8 | 10.6 | | | | |
| 2002 | 9.9 | 9.3 | 10.0 | 9.9 | 9.5 | 9.7 | 8.8 | 8.8 | 8.3 | 10.2 | 7.9 | 9.1 | 8.3 | 7.7 | 13.3 | 13.5 | 16.3 | | | |
| 2003 | 9.6 | 9.1 | 9.7 | 9.6 | 9.2 | 9.3 | 8.5 | 8.4 | 8.0 | 9.6 | 7.6 | 8.5 | 7.8 | 7.2 | 11.2 | 10.7 | 10.7 | 5.3 | | |
| 2004 | 9.6 | 9.1 | 9.6 | 9.6 | 9.1 | 9.3 | 8.5 | 8.5 | 8.0 | 9.5 | 7.7 | 8.5 | 7.9 | 7.4 | 10.7 | 10.2 | 10.0 | 7.0 | 8.7 | |
| 2005 | 9.4 | 8.9 | 9.4 | 9.3 | 8.9 | 9.1 | 8.3 | 8.3 | 7.9 | 9.2 | 7.5 | 8.2 | 7.7 | 7.2 | 9.9 | 9.3 | 9.0 | 6.6 | 7.3 | 5.9 |
| 2006 | 9.1 | 8.6 | 9.1 | 9.0 | 8.6 | 8.7 | 8.0 | 7.9 | 7.5 | 8.7 | 7.1 | 7.7 | 7.2 | 6.7 | 8.9 | 8.3 | 7.8 | 5.8 | 5.9 | 4.5 |
| 2007 | 8.8 | 8.3 | 8.7 | 8.6 | 8.2 | 8.3 | 7.6 | 7.5 | 7.1 | 8.2 | 6.7 | 7.2 | 6.7 | 6.3 | 8.1 | 7.4 | 6.9 | 5.1 | 5.1 | 3.9 |
| 2008 | 8.8 | 8.3 | 8.8 | 8.7 | 8.3 | 8.4 | 7.7 | 7.6 | 7.2 | 8.2 | 6.9 | 7.4 | 6.9 | 6.5 | 8.2 | 7.6 | 7.2 | 5.7 | 5.8 | 5.1 |
| 2009 | 8.6 | 8.1 | 8.5 | 8.4 | 8.0 | 8.1 | 7.4 | 7.3 | 7.0 | 7.9 | 6.6 | 7.0 | 6.6 | 6.2 | 7.6 | 7.1 | 6.6 | 5.3 | 5.3 | 4.7 |
| 2010 | 8.7 | 8.3 | 8.7 | 8.6 | 8.2 | 8.3 | 7.7 | 7.6 | 7.3 | 8.2 | 7.0 | 7.4 | 7.0 | 6.7 | 8.1 | 7.6 | 7.3 | 6.2 | 6.3 | 5.9 |
| 2011 | 9.0 | 8.6 | 9.0 | 9.0 | 8.6 | 8.7 | 8.2 | 8.1 | 7.9 | 8.7 | 7.7 | 8.1 | 7.7 | 7.5 | 8.9 | 8.5 | 8.3 | 7.4 | 7.7 | 7.6 |
| 2012 | 9.1 | 8.7 | 9.1 | 9.0 | 8.7 | 8.8 | 8.3 | 8.3 | 8.0 | 8.8 | 7.8 | 8.2 | 7.9 | 7.7 | 9.0 | 8.7 | 8.5 | 7.8 | 8.0 | 8.0 |
| 2013 | 8.5 | 8.1 | 8.4 | 8.3 | 8.0 | 8.1 | 7.5 | 7.5 | 7.2 | 7.9 | 6.9 | 7.3 | 6.9 | 6.7 | 7.8 | 7.4 | 7.1 | 6.3 | 6.4 | 6.2 |
| 2014 | 8.8 | 8.4 | 8.7 | 8.7 | 8.4 | 8.4 | 8.0 | 7.9 | 7.7 | 8.4 | 7.5 | 7.8 | 7.5 | 7.3 | 8.4 | 8.1 | 7.9 | 7.2 | 7.4 | 7.2 |
| 2015 | 8.4 | 8.1 | 8.4 | 8.3 | 8.0 | 8.0 | 7.6 | 7.5 | 7.2 | 7.9 | 7.0 | 7.3 | 7.0 | 6.8 | 7.8 | 7.4 | 7.2 | 6.5 | 6.6 | 6.5 |
| 2016 | 8.4 | 8.0 | 8.3 | 8.2 | 7.9 | 8.0 | 7.5 | 7.5 | 7.2 | 7.8 | 7.0 | 7.3 | 7.0 | 6.8 | 7.7 | 7.4 | 7.2 | 6.5 | 6.6 | 6.5 |

# Appendix C-3

Long-term Corporate Bonds: Percent per annum total returns for all historical periods
From 1926 to 2016

|          | Start Date |      |      |      |      |      |      |      |      |      |      |
|----------|------|------|------|------|------|------|------|------|------|------|------|
| End Date | 2006 | 2007 | 2008 | 2009 | 2010 | 2011 | 2012 | 2013 | 2014 | 2015 | 2016 |
| 1971 |  |  |  |  |  |  |  |  |  |  |  |
| 1972 |  |  |  |  |  |  |  |  |  |  |  |
| 1973 |  |  |  |  |  |  |  |  |  |  |  |
| 1974 |  |  |  |  |  |  |  |  |  |  |  |
| 1975 |  |  |  |  |  |  |  |  |  |  |  |
| 1976 |  |  |  |  |  |  |  |  |  |  |  |
| 1977 |  |  |  |  |  |  |  |  |  |  |  |
| 1978 |  |  |  |  |  |  |  |  |  |  |  |
| 1979 |  |  |  |  |  |  |  |  |  |  |  |
| 1980 |  |  |  |  |  |  |  |  |  |  |  |
| 1981 |  |  |  |  |  |  |  |  |  |  |  |
| 1982 |  |  |  |  |  |  |  |  |  |  |  |
| 1983 |  |  |  |  |  |  |  |  |  |  |  |
| 1984 |  |  |  |  |  |  |  |  |  |  |  |
| 1985 |  |  |  |  |  |  |  |  |  |  |  |
| 1986 |  |  |  |  |  |  |  |  |  |  |  |
| 1987 |  |  |  |  |  |  |  |  |  |  |  |
| 1988 |  |  |  |  |  |  |  |  |  |  |  |
| 1989 |  |  |  |  |  |  |  |  |  |  |  |
| 1990 |  |  |  |  |  |  |  |  |  |  |  |
| 1991 |  |  |  |  |  |  |  |  |  |  |  |
| 1992 |  |  |  |  |  |  |  |  |  |  |  |
| 1993 |  |  |  |  |  |  |  |  |  |  |  |
| 1994 |  |  |  |  |  |  |  |  |  |  |  |
| 1995 |  |  |  |  |  |  |  |  |  |  |  |
| 1996 |  |  |  |  |  |  |  |  |  |  |  |
| 1997 |  |  |  |  |  |  |  |  |  |  |  |
| 1998 |  |  |  |  |  |  |  |  |  |  |  |
| 1999 |  |  |  |  |  |  |  |  |  |  |  |
| 2000 |  |  |  |  |  |  |  |  |  |  |  |
| 2001 |  |  |  |  |  |  |  |  |  |  |  |
| 2002 |  |  |  |  |  |  |  |  |  |  |  |
| 2003 |  |  |  |  |  |  |  |  |  |  |  |
| 2004 |  |  |  |  |  |  |  |  |  |  |  |
| 2005 |  |  |  |  |  |  |  |  |  |  |  |
| 2006 | 3.2 |  |  |  |  |  |  |  |  |  |  |
| 2007 | 2.9 | 2.6 |  |  |  |  |  |  |  |  |  |
| 2008 | 4.8 | 5.6 | 8.8 |  |  |  |  |  |  |  |  |
| 2009 | 4.4 | 4.8 | 5.9 | 3.0 |  |  |  |  |  |  |  |
| 2010 | 5.9 | 6.6 | 8.0 | 7.6 | 12.4 |  |  |  |  |  |  |
| 2011 | 7.9 | 8.8 | 10.4 | 11.0 | 15.2 | 17.9 |  |  |  |  |  |
| 2012 | 8.3 | 9.1 | 10.5 | 10.9 | 13.6 | 14.3 | 10.7 |  |  |  |  |
| 2013 | 6.2 | 6.6 | 7.3 | 7.0 | 8.1 | 6.6 | 1.4 | -7.1 |  |  |  |
| 2014 | 7.4 | 7.9 | 8.7 | 8.7 | 9.9 | 9.2 | 6.4 | 4.4 | 17.3 |  |  |
| 2015 | 6.5 | 6.9 | 7.4 | 7.2 | 8.0 | 7.1 | 4.5 | 2.6 | 7.7 | -1.0 |  |
| 2016 | 6.5 | 6.9 | 7.3 | 7.2 | 7.8 | 7.0 | 5.0 | 3.6 | 7.4 | 2.8 | 6.7 |

## Appendix C-4

Long-term Government Bonds: Percent per annum total returns for all historical periods

From 1926 to 2016

| End Date | Start Date 1926 | 1927 | 1928 | 1929 | 1930 | 1931 | 1932 | 1933 | 1934 | 1935 | 1936 | 1937 | 1938 | 1939 | 1940 | 1941 | 1942 | 1943 | 1944 | 1945 |
|---|---|---|---|---|---|---|---|---|---|---|---|---|---|---|---|---|---|---|---|---|
| 1926 | 7.8 | | | | | | | | | | | | | | | | | | | |
| 1927 | 8.3 | 8.9 | | | | | | | | | | | | | | | | | | |
| 1928 | 5.5 | 4.4 | 0.1 | | | | | | | | | | | | | | | | | |
| 1929 | 5.0 | 4.1 | 1.7 | 3.4 | | | | | | | | | | | | | | | | |
| 1930 | 4.9 | 4.2 | 2.7 | 4.0 | 4.7 | | | | | | | | | | | | | | | |
| 1931 | 3.1 | 2.2 | 0.6 | 0.8 | -0.5 | -5.3 | | | | | | | | | | | | | | |
| 1932 | 5.0 | 4.5 | 3.7 | 4.6 | 5.0 | 5.2 | 16.8 | | | | | | | | | | | | | |
| 1933 | 4.4 | 3.9 | 3.1 | 3.7 | 3.7 | 3.4 | 8.1 | -0.1 | | | | | | | | | | | | |
| 1934 | 5.0 | 4.6 | 4.0 | 4.7 | 4.9 | 5.0 | 8.7 | 4.9 | 10.0 | | | | | | | | | | | |
| 1935 | 5.0 | 4.7 | 4.1 | 4.7 | 5.0 | 5.0 | 7.8 | 4.9 | 7.5 | 5.0 | | | | | | | | | | |
| 1936 | 5.2 | 4.9 | 4.5 | 5.1 | 5.3 | 5.4 | 7.7 | 5.5 | 7.5 | 6.2 | 7.5 | | | | | | | | | |
| 1937 | 4.8 | 4.5 | 4.1 | 4.5 | 4.7 | 4.7 | 6.4 | 4.5 | 5.6 | 4.2 | 3.8 | 0.2 | | | | | | | | |
| 1938 | 4.8 | 4.6 | 4.2 | 4.6 | 4.8 | 4.8 | 6.3 | 4.6 | 5.6 | 4.5 | 4.4 | 2.8 | 5.5 | | | | | | | |
| 1939 | 4.9 | 4.7 | 4.4 | 4.7 | 4.9 | 4.9 | 6.3 | 4.8 | 5.7 | 4.8 | 4.8 | 3.9 | 5.7 | 5.9 | | | | | | |
| 1940 | 5.0 | 4.8 | 4.5 | 4.9 | 5.0 | 5.0 | 6.2 | 5.0 | 5.7 | 5.0 | 5.0 | 4.4 | 5.9 | 6.0 | 6.1 | | | | | |
| 1941 | 4.7 | 4.5 | 4.2 | 4.5 | 4.6 | 4.6 | 5.7 | 4.5 | 5.1 | 4.4 | 4.3 | 3.7 | 4.6 | 4.3 | 3.5 | 0.9 | | | | |
| 1942 | 4.6 | 4.5 | 4.2 | 4.5 | 4.5 | 4.5 | 5.5 | 4.4 | 4.9 | 4.3 | 4.2 | 3.6 | 4.3 | 4.0 | 3.4 | 2.1 | 3.2 | | | |
| 1943 | 4.5 | 4.3 | 4.0 | 4.3 | 4.4 | 4.3 | 5.2 | 4.1 | 4.6 | 4.0 | 3.9 | 3.4 | 3.9 | 3.6 | 3.1 | 2.1 | 2.6 | 2.1 | | |
| 1944 | 4.4 | 4.2 | 4.0 | 4.2 | 4.3 | 4.2 | 5.0 | 4.1 | 4.5 | 3.9 | 3.8 | 3.3 | 3.8 | 3.5 | 3.0 | 2.3 | 2.7 | 2.4 | 2.8 | |
| 1945 | 4.7 | 4.6 | 4.3 | 4.6 | 4.6 | 4.6 | 5.4 | 4.6 | 5.0 | 4.5 | 4.5 | 4.1 | 4.6 | 4.5 | 4.3 | 3.9 | 4.7 | 5.1 | 6.7 | 10.7 |
| 1946 | 4.5 | 4.3 | 4.1 | 4.3 | 4.4 | 4.3 | 5.0 | 4.2 | 4.6 | 4.1 | 4.0 | 3.7 | 4.1 | 3.9 | 3.6 | 3.2 | 3.7 | 3.8 | 4.4 | 5.2 |
| 1947 | 4.1 | 4.0 | 3.7 | 3.9 | 4.0 | 3.9 | 4.5 | 3.8 | 4.0 | 3.6 | 3.5 | 3.1 | 3.4 | 3.2 | 2.8 | 2.4 | 2.6 | 2.5 | 2.6 | 2.5 |
| 1948 | 4.1 | 4.0 | 3.7 | 3.9 | 3.9 | 3.9 | 4.5 | 3.7 | 4.0 | 3.6 | 3.5 | 3.1 | 3.4 | 3.2 | 2.9 | 2.5 | 2.7 | 2.6 | 2.7 | 2.7 |
| 1949 | 4.2 | 4.1 | 3.8 | 4.0 | 4.1 | 4.0 | 4.6 | 3.9 | 4.1 | 3.8 | 3.7 | 3.4 | 3.7 | 3.5 | 3.2 | 2.9 | 3.2 | 3.2 | 3.4 | 3.5 |
| 1950 | 4.0 | 3.9 | 3.7 | 3.8 | 3.9 | 3.8 | 4.3 | 3.7 | 3.9 | 3.5 | 3.4 | 3.1 | 3.4 | 3.2 | 2.9 | 2.6 | 2.8 | 2.8 | 2.9 | 2.9 |
| 1951 | 3.7 | 3.6 | 3.3 | 3.5 | 3.5 | 3.4 | 3.9 | 3.3 | 3.4 | 3.1 | 3.0 | 2.7 | 2.8 | 2.6 | 2.4 | 2.0 | 2.1 | 2.0 | 2.0 | 1.9 |
| 1952 | 3.6 | 3.5 | 3.3 | 3.4 | 3.4 | 3.3 | 3.8 | 3.2 | 3.3 | 3.0 | 2.8 | 2.6 | 2.7 | 2.5 | 2.3 | 1.9 | 2.0 | 1.9 | 1.9 | 1.8 |
| 1953 | 3.6 | 3.5 | 3.3 | 3.4 | 3.4 | 3.3 | 3.8 | 3.2 | 3.3 | 3.0 | 2.9 | 2.6 | 2.8 | 2.6 | 2.4 | 2.1 | 2.2 | 2.1 | 2.1 | 2.0 |
| 1954 | 3.7 | 3.6 | 3.4 | 3.5 | 3.6 | 3.5 | 3.9 | 3.4 | 3.5 | 3.2 | 3.1 | 2.9 | 3.0 | 2.9 | 2.7 | 2.4 | 2.6 | 2.5 | 2.5 | 2.5 |
| 1955 | 3.6 | 3.4 | 3.2 | 3.4 | 3.4 | 3.3 | 3.7 | 3.1 | 3.3 | 3.0 | 2.9 | 2.6 | 2.8 | 2.6 | 2.4 | 2.2 | 2.3 | 2.2 | 2.2 | 2.2 |
| 1956 | 3.3 | 3.1 | 2.9 | 3.0 | 3.0 | 3.0 | 3.3 | 2.8 | 2.9 | 2.6 | 2.5 | 2.2 | 2.3 | 2.2 | 1.9 | 1.7 | 1.7 | 1.6 | 1.6 | 1.5 |
| 1957 | 3.4 | 3.3 | 3.1 | 3.2 | 3.2 | 3.1 | 3.5 | 3.0 | 3.1 | 2.8 | 2.7 | 2.5 | 2.6 | 2.4 | 2.2 | 2.0 | 2.1 | 2.0 | 2.0 | 1.9 |
| 1958 | 3.1 | 3.0 | 2.8 | 2.9 | 2.8 | 2.8 | 3.1 | 2.6 | 2.7 | 2.4 | 2.3 | 2.1 | 2.1 | 2.0 | 1.8 | 1.5 | 1.6 | 1.5 | 1.4 | 1.3 |
| 1959 | 2.9 | 2.8 | 2.6 | 2.7 | 2.7 | 2.6 | 2.9 | 2.4 | 2.5 | 2.2 | 2.1 | 1.9 | 1.9 | 1.8 | 1.6 | 1.3 | 1.4 | 1.3 | 1.2 | 1.1 |
| 1960 | 3.2 | 3.1 | 2.9 | 3.0 | 3.0 | 2.9 | 3.2 | 2.8 | 2.9 | 2.6 | 2.5 | 2.3 | 2.4 | 2.3 | 2.1 | 1.9 | 2.0 | 1.9 | 1.9 | 1.8 |
| 1961 | 3.2 | 3.0 | 2.9 | 3.0 | 2.9 | 2.9 | 3.2 | 2.7 | 2.8 | 2.6 | 2.5 | 2.3 | 2.4 | 2.2 | 2.1 | 1.9 | 1.9 | 1.9 | 1.8 | 1.8 |
| 1962 | 3.3 | 3.1 | 3.0 | 3.1 | 3.1 | 3.0 | 3.3 | 2.9 | 3.0 | 2.7 | 2.6 | 2.5 | 2.5 | 2.4 | 2.3 | 2.1 | 2.2 | 2.1 | 2.1 | 2.1 |
| 1963 | 3.2 | 3.1 | 2.9 | 3.0 | 3.0 | 3.0 | 3.2 | 2.8 | 2.9 | 2.7 | 2.6 | 2.4 | 2.5 | 2.4 | 2.2 | 2.1 | 2.1 | 2.1 | 2.1 | 2.0 |
| 1964 | 3.2 | 3.1 | 2.9 | 3.0 | 3.0 | 3.0 | 3.2 | 2.8 | 2.9 | 2.7 | 2.6 | 2.4 | 2.5 | 2.4 | 2.3 | 2.1 | 2.1 | 2.1 | 2.1 | 2.1 |
| 1965 | 3.2 | 3.0 | 2.9 | 3.0 | 3.0 | 2.9 | 3.2 | 2.8 | 2.9 | 2.6 | 2.6 | 2.4 | 2.5 | 2.4 | 2.2 | 2.1 | 2.1 | 2.1 | 2.1 | 2.0 |
| 1966 | 3.2 | 3.1 | 2.9 | 3.0 | 3.0 | 2.9 | 3.2 | 2.8 | 2.9 | 2.7 | 2.6 | 2.4 | 2.5 | 2.4 | 2.3 | 2.1 | 2.2 | 2.1 | 2.1 | 2.1 |
| 1967 | 2.9 | 2.7 | 2.6 | 2.7 | 2.6 | 2.6 | 2.8 | 2.4 | 2.5 | 2.3 | 2.2 | 2.0 | 2.1 | 2.0 | 1.8 | 1.7 | 1.7 | 1.7 | 1.6 | 1.6 |
| 1968 | 2.8 | 2.7 | 2.5 | 2.6 | 2.6 | 2.5 | 2.7 | 2.4 | 2.4 | 2.2 | 2.1 | 2.0 | 2.0 | 1.9 | 1.8 | 1.6 | 1.6 | 1.6 | 1.6 | 1.5 |
| 1969 | 2.6 | 2.5 | 2.3 | 2.4 | 2.4 | 2.3 | 2.5 | 2.1 | 2.2 | 2.0 | 1.9 | 1.7 | 1.8 | 1.7 | 1.5 | 1.4 | 1.4 | 1.3 | 1.3 | 1.2 |
| 1970 | 2.8 | 2.7 | 2.5 | 2.6 | 2.6 | 2.5 | 2.7 | 2.4 | 2.5 | 2.3 | 2.2 | 2.0 | 2.1 | 2.0 | 1.9 | 1.7 | 1.7 | 1.7 | 1.7 | 1.6 |

# Appendix C-4

Long-term Government Bonds: Percent per annum total returns for all historical periods
From 1926 to 2016

| End Date | Start Date 1926 | 1927 | 1928 | 1929 | 1930 | 1931 | 1932 | 1933 | 1934 | 1935 | 1936 | 1937 | 1938 | 1939 | 1940 | 1941 | 1942 | 1943 | 1944 | 1945 |
|---|---|---|---|---|---|---|---|---|---|---|---|---|---|---|---|---|---|---|---|---|
| 1971 | 3.0 | 2.9 | 2.8 | 2.8 | 2.8 | 2.8 | 3.0 | 2.7 | 2.7 | 2.5 | 2.5 | 2.3 | 2.4 | 2.3 | 2.2 | 2.1 | 2.1 | 2.1 | 2.1 | 2.0 |
| 1972 | 3.1 | 3.0 | 2.8 | 2.9 | 2.9 | 2.8 | 3.1 | 2.7 | 2.8 | 2.6 | 2.6 | 2.4 | 2.5 | 2.4 | 2.3 | 2.2 | 2.2 | 2.2 | 2.2 | 2.2 |
| 1973 | 3.0 | 2.9 | 2.8 | 2.8 | 2.8 | 2.8 | 3.0 | 2.6 | 2.7 | 2.5 | 2.5 | 2.3 | 2.4 | 2.3 | 2.2 | 2.1 | 2.1 | 2.1 | 2.1 | 2.1 |
| 1974 | 3.0 | 2.9 | 2.8 | 2.8 | 2.8 | 2.8 | 3.0 | 2.7 | 2.7 | 2.6 | 2.5 | 2.4 | 2.4 | 2.4 | 2.3 | 2.1 | 2.1 | 2.2 | 2.2 | 2.1 |
| 1975 | 3.1 | 3.0 | 2.9 | 3.0 | 3.0 | 2.9 | 3.1 | 2.8 | 2.9 | 2.7 | 2.7 | 2.6 | 2.6 | 2.5 | 2.4 | 2.3 | 2.4 | 2.4 | 2.4 | 2.4 |
| 1976 | 3.4 | 3.3 | 3.2 | 3.2 | 3.2 | 3.2 | 3.4 | 3.1 | 3.2 | 3.0 | 3.0 | 2.9 | 3.0 | 2.9 | 2.8 | 2.7 | 2.8 | 2.8 | 2.8 | 2.8 |
| 1977 | 3.3 | 3.2 | 3.1 | 3.2 | 3.2 | 3.1 | 3.3 | 3.0 | 3.1 | 3.0 | 2.9 | 2.8 | 2.9 | 2.8 | 2.7 | 2.6 | 2.7 | 2.7 | 2.7 | 2.7 |
| 1978 | 3.2 | 3.1 | 3.0 | 3.1 | 3.1 | 3.0 | 3.2 | 2.9 | 3.0 | 2.9 | 2.8 | 2.7 | 2.8 | 2.7 | 2.6 | 2.5 | 2.6 | 2.5 | 2.6 | 2.6 |
| 1979 | 3.1 | 3.0 | 2.9 | 3.0 | 3.0 | 2.9 | 3.1 | 2.9 | 2.9 | 2.8 | 2.7 | 2.6 | 2.7 | 2.6 | 2.5 | 2.4 | 2.5 | 2.5 | 2.5 | 2.4 |
| 1980 | 3.0 | 2.9 | 2.8 | 2.9 | 2.8 | 2.8 | 3.0 | 2.7 | 2.8 | 2.6 | 2.6 | 2.5 | 2.5 | 2.4 | 2.3 | 2.3 | 2.3 | 2.3 | 2.3 | 2.3 |
| 1981 | 3.0 | 2.9 | 2.8 | 2.8 | 2.8 | 2.8 | 3.0 | 2.7 | 2.7 | 2.6 | 2.5 | 2.4 | 2.5 | 2.4 | 2.3 | 2.2 | 2.3 | 2.3 | 2.3 | 2.2 |
| 1982 | 3.5 | 3.5 | 3.4 | 3.4 | 3.4 | 3.4 | 3.6 | 3.3 | 3.4 | 3.3 | 3.2 | 3.1 | 3.2 | 3.2 | 3.1 | 3.0 | 3.1 | 3.1 | 3.1 | 3.1 |
| 1983 | 3.5 | 3.4 | 3.3 | 3.4 | 3.4 | 3.4 | 3.5 | 3.3 | 3.3 | 3.2 | 3.2 | 3.1 | 3.2 | 3.1 | 3.0 | 3.0 | 3.0 | 3.0 | 3.1 | 3.0 |
| 1984 | 3.7 | 3.6 | 3.5 | 3.6 | 3.6 | 3.6 | 3.7 | 3.5 | 3.6 | 3.4 | 3.4 | 3.3 | 3.4 | 3.4 | 3.3 | 3.2 | 3.3 | 3.3 | 3.3 | 3.3 |
| 1985 | 4.1 | 4.0 | 3.9 | 4.0 | 4.0 | 4.0 | 4.2 | 4.0 | 4.0 | 3.9 | 3.9 | 3.8 | 3.9 | 3.9 | 3.8 | 3.8 | 3.8 | 3.9 | 3.9 | 3.9 |
| 1986 | 4.4 | 4.3 | 4.3 | 4.3 | 4.3 | 4.3 | 4.5 | 4.3 | 4.4 | 4.3 | 4.3 | 4.2 | 4.3 | 4.3 | 4.2 | 4.2 | 4.3 | 4.3 | 4.3 | 4.4 |
| 1987 | 4.3 | 4.2 | 4.1 | 4.3 | 4.2 | 4.2 | 4.4 | 4.2 | 4.3 | 4.2 | 4.1 | 4.1 | 4.2 | 4.1 | 4.1 | 4.0 | 4.1 | 4.1 | 4.2 | 4.2 |
| 1988 | 4.4 | 4.3 | 4.2 | 4.3 | 4.3 | 4.3 | 4.5 | 4.3 | 4.4 | 4.2 | 4.2 | 4.2 | 4.3 | 4.2 | 4.2 | 4.2 | 4.2 | 4.2 | 4.3 | 4.3 |
| 1989 | 4.6 | 4.5 | 4.4 | 4.5 | 4.5 | 4.5 | 4.7 | 4.5 | 4.6 | 4.5 | 4.5 | 4.4 | 4.5 | 4.5 | 4.5 | 4.4 | 4.5 | 4.5 | 4.6 | 4.6 |
| 1990 | 4.6 | 4.5 | 4.5 | 4.5 | 4.6 | 4.6 | 4.7 | 4.5 | 4.6 | 4.5 | 4.5 | 4.5 | 4.5 | 4.5 | 4.5 | 4.5 | 4.5 | 4.6 | 4.6 | 4.7 |
| 1991 | 4.8 | 4.7 | 4.7 | 4.8 | 4.8 | 4.8 | 5.0 | 4.8 | 4.9 | 4.8 | 4.8 | 4.7 | 4.8 | 4.8 | 4.8 | 4.7 | 4.8 | 4.8 | 4.9 | 4.9 |
| 1992 | 4.8 | 4.8 | 4.7 | 4.8 | 4.8 | 4.8 | 5.0 | 4.8 | 4.9 | 4.8 | 4.8 | 4.8 | 4.9 | 4.8 | 4.8 | 4.8 | 4.9 | 4.9 | 5.0 | 5.0 |
| 1993 | 5.0 | 5.0 | 4.9 | 5.0 | 5.0 | 5.0 | 5.2 | 5.0 | 5.1 | 5.0 | 5.0 | 5.0 | 5.1 | 5.1 | 5.1 | 5.0 | 5.1 | 5.2 | 5.2 | 5.3 |
| 1994 | 4.8 | 4.8 | 4.7 | 4.8 | 4.8 | 4.8 | 5.0 | 4.8 | 4.9 | 4.8 | 4.8 | 4.8 | 4.8 | 4.8 | 4.8 | 4.8 | 4.9 | 4.9 | 4.9 | 5.0 |
| 1995 | 5.2 | 5.1 | 5.1 | 5.2 | 5.2 | 5.2 | 5.4 | 5.2 | 5.3 | 5.2 | 5.2 | 5.2 | 5.3 | 5.2 | 5.2 | 5.2 | 5.3 | 5.3 | 5.4 | 5.5 |
| 1996 | 5.1 | 5.0 | 5.0 | 5.1 | 5.1 | 5.1 | 5.3 | 5.1 | 5.2 | 5.1 | 5.1 | 5.1 | 5.1 | 5.1 | 5.1 | 5.1 | 5.2 | 5.2 | 5.3 | 5.3 |
| 1997 | 5.2 | 5.2 | 5.1 | 5.2 | 5.2 | 5.2 | 5.4 | 5.2 | 5.3 | 5.3 | 5.3 | 5.2 | 5.3 | 5.3 | 5.3 | 5.3 | 5.4 | 5.4 | 5.5 | 5.5 |
| 1998 | 5.3 | 5.3 | 5.2 | 5.3 | 5.3 | 5.4 | 5.5 | 5.4 | 5.4 | 5.4 | 5.4 | 5.3 | 5.4 | 5.4 | 5.4 | 5.4 | 5.5 | 5.5 | 5.6 | 5.7 |
| 1999 | 5.1 | 5.1 | 5.0 | 5.1 | 5.1 | 5.1 | 5.3 | 5.1 | 5.2 | 5.1 | 5.1 | 5.1 | 5.2 | 5.2 | 5.2 | 5.2 | 5.2 | 5.3 | 5.3 | 5.4 |
| 2000 | 5.3 | 5.3 | 5.2 | 5.3 | 5.3 | 5.4 | 5.5 | 5.4 | 5.4 | 5.4 | 5.4 | 5.3 | 5.4 | 5.4 | 5.4 | 5.4 | 5.5 | 5.5 | 5.6 | 5.6 |
| 2001 | 5.3 | 5.3 | 5.2 | 5.3 | 5.3 | 5.3 | 5.5 | 5.3 | 5.4 | 5.3 | 5.4 | 5.3 | 5.4 | 5.4 | 5.4 | 5.4 | 5.5 | 5.5 | 5.6 | 5.6 |
| 2002 | 5.5 | 5.4 | 5.4 | 5.5 | 5.5 | 5.5 | 5.7 | 5.5 | 5.6 | 5.5 | 5.5 | 5.5 | 5.6 | 5.6 | 5.6 | 5.6 | 5.5 | 5.7 | 5.7 | 5.8 |
| 2003 | 5.4 | 5.4 | 5.3 | 5.4 | 5.4 | 5.4 | 5.6 | 5.4 | 5.5 | 5.4 | 5.5 | 5.4 | 5.5 | 5.5 | 5.5 | 5.5 | 5.6 | 5.6 | 5.7 | 5.7 |
| 2004 | 5.4 | 5.4 | 5.4 | 5.5 | 5.5 | 5.5 | 5.6 | 5.5 | 5.6 | 5.5 | 5.5 | 5.5 | 5.5 | 5.5 | 5.5 | 5.5 | 5.6 | 5.6 | 5.7 | 5.7 |
| 2005 | 5.5 | 5.4 | 5.4 | 5.5 | 5.5 | 5.5 | 5.7 | 5.5 | 5.6 | 5.5 | 5.5 | 5.5 | 5.6 | 5.6 | 5.6 | 5.6 | 5.7 | 5.7 | 5.7 | 5.8 |
| 2006 | 5.4 | 5.4 | 5.3 | 5.4 | 5.4 | 5.4 | 5.6 | 5.5 | 5.5 | 5.5 | 5.5 | 5.5 | 5.5 | 5.5 | 5.5 | 5.5 | 5.6 | 5.6 | 5.7 | 5.7 |
| 2007 | 5.5 | 5.4 | 5.4 | 5.5 | 5.5 | 5.5 | 5.7 | 5.5 | 5.6 | 5.5 | 5.5 | 5.5 | 5.6 | 5.6 | 5.6 | 5.6 | 5.6 | 5.7 | 5.7 | 5.8 |
| 2008 | 5.7 | 5.7 | 5.6 | 5.7 | 5.7 | 5.7 | 5.9 | 5.8 | 5.8 | 5.8 | 5.8 | 5.8 | 5.9 | 5.9 | 5.9 | 5.9 | 5.9 | 6.0 | 6.0 | 6.1 |
| 2009 | 5.4 | 5.4 | 5.4 | 5.4 | 5.4 | 5.5 | 5.6 | 5.5 | 5.5 | 5.5 | 5.5 | 5.5 | 5.5 | 5.5 | 5.5 | 5.5 | 5.6 | 5.6 | 5.7 | 5.7 |
| 2010 | 5.5 | 5.4 | 5.4 | 5.5 | 5.5 | 5.5 | 5.7 | 5.5 | 5.6 | 5.5 | 5.5 | 5.5 | 5.6 | 5.6 | 5.6 | 5.6 | 5.6 | 5.7 | 5.7 | 5.8 |
| 2011 | 5.7 | 5.7 | 5.6 | 5.7 | 5.8 | 5.8 | 5.9 | 5.8 | 5.8 | 5.8 | 5.8 | 5.8 | 5.9 | 5.9 | 5.9 | 5.8 | 5.9 | 5.9 | 6.0 | 6.0 |
| 2012 | 5.7 | 5.7 | 5.6 | 5.7 | 5.7 | 5.7 | 5.9 | 5.7 | 5.8 | 5.8 | 5.8 | 5.7 | 5.8 | 5.8 | 5.8 | 5.8 | 5.9 | 6.0 | 6.0 | 6.1 |
| 2013 | 5.4 | 5.4 | 5.4 | 5.4 | 5.5 | 5.5 | 5.6 | 5.5 | 5.6 | 5.5 | 5.5 | 5.5 | 5.6 | 5.6 | 5.6 | 5.5 | 5.6 | 5.6 | 5.7 | 5.7 |
| 2014 | 5.6 | 5.6 | 5.5 | 5.6 | 5.7 | 5.7 | 5.8 | 5.7 | 5.8 | 5.7 | 5.7 | 5.7 | 5.8 | 5.8 | 5.8 | 5.8 | 5.8 | 5.9 | 5.9 | 6.0 |
| 2015 | 5.6 | 5.6 | 5.5 | 5.6 | 5.6 | 5.6 | 5.8 | 5.6 | 5.8 | 5.7 | 5.7 | 5.7 | 5.8 | 5.7 | 5.8 | 5.8 | 5.8 | 5.8 | 5.8 | 5.9 |
| 2016 | 5.5 | 5.5 | 5.5 | 5.6 | 5.6 | 5.6 | 5.7 | 5.6 | 5.6 | 5.6 | 5.6 | 5.6 | 5.6 | 5.6 | 5.6 | 5.6 | 5.7 | 5.7 | 5.8 | 5.8 |

## Appendix C-4

Long-term Government Bonds: Percent per annum total returns for all historical periods
From 1926 to 2016

| End Date | Start Date 1946 | 1947 | 1948 | 1949 | 1950 | 1951 | 1952 | 1953 | 1954 | 1955 | 1956 | 1957 | 1958 | 1959 | 1960 | 1961 | 1962 | 1963 | 1964 | 1965 |
|---|---|---|---|---|---|---|---|---|---|---|---|---|---|---|---|---|---|---|---|---|
| 1926 | | | | | | | | | | | | | | | | | | | | |
| 1927 | | | | | | | | | | | | | | | | | | | | |
| 1928 | | | | | | | | | | | | | | | | | | | | |
| 1929 | | | | | | | | | | | | | | | | | | | | |
| 1930 | | | | | | | | | | | | | | | | | | | | |
| 1931 | | | | | | | | | | | | | | | | | | | | |
| 1932 | | | | | | | | | | | | | | | | | | | | |
| 1933 | | | | | | | | | | | | | | | | | | | | |
| 1934 | | | | | | | | | | | | | | | | | | | | |
| 1935 | | | | | | | | | | | | | | | | | | | | |
| 1936 | | | | | | | | | | | | | | | | | | | | |
| 1937 | | | | | | | | | | | | | | | | | | | | |
| 1938 | | | | | | | | | | | | | | | | | | | | |
| 1939 | | | | | | | | | | | | | | | | | | | | |
| 1940 | | | | | | | | | | | | | | | | | | | | |
| 1941 | | | | | | | | | | | | | | | | | | | | |
| 1942 | | | | | | | | | | | | | | | | | | | | |
| 1943 | | | | | | | | | | | | | | | | | | | | |
| 1944 | | | | | | | | | | | | | | | | | | | | |
| 1945 | | | | | | | | | | | | | | | | | | | | |
| 1946 | -0.1 | | | | | | | | | | | | | | | | | | | |
| 1947 | -1.4 | -2.6 | | | | | | | | | | | | | | | | | | |
| 1948 | 0.2 | 0.3 | 3.4 | | | | | | | | | | | | | | | | | |
| 1949 | 1.7 | 2.3 | 4.9 | 6.4 | | | | | | | | | | | | | | | | |
| 1950 | 1.4 | 1.8 | 3.3 | 3.2 | 0.1 | | | | | | | | | | | | | | | |
| 1951 | 0.5 | 0.6 | 1.4 | 0.8 | -2.0 | -3.9 | | | | | | | | | | | | | | |
| 1952 | 0.6 | 0.7 | 1.4 | 0.9 | -0.9 | -1.4 | 1.2 | | | | | | | | | | | | | |
| 1953 | 1.0 | 1.1 | 1.7 | 1.4 | 0.2 | 0.2 | 2.4 | 3.6 | | | | | | | | | | | | |
| 1954 | 1.6 | 1.8 | 2.5 | 2.4 | 1.6 | 1.9 | 4.0 | 5.4 | 7.2 | | | | | | | | | | | |
| 1955 | 1.3 | 1.5 | 2.0 | 1.8 | 1.1 | 1.3 | 2.6 | 3.1 | 2.9 | -1.3 | | | | | | | | | | |
| 1956 | 0.7 | 0.8 | 1.1 | 0.9 | 0.1 | 0.1 | 0.9 | 0.9 | 0.0 | -3.5 | -5.6 | | | | | | | | | |
| 1957 | 1.2 | 1.4 | 1.8 | 1.6 | 1.0 | 1.1 | 2.0 | 2.2 | 1.8 | 0.0 | 0.7 | 7.5 | | | | | | | | |
| 1958 | 0.6 | 0.7 | 1.0 | 0.8 | 0.2 | 0.2 | 0.8 | 0.7 | 0.2 | -1.5 | -1.6 | 0.5 | -6.1 | | | | | | | |
| 1959 | 0.4 | 0.5 | 0.7 | 0.5 | -0.1 | -0.1 | 0.4 | 0.3 | -0.2 | -1.7 | -1.8 | -0.5 | -4.2 | -2.3 | | | | | | |
| 1960 | 1.3 | 1.4 | 1.7 | 1.5 | 1.1 | 1.2 | 1.8 | 1.9 | 1.6 | 0.7 | 1.2 | 2.9 | 1.5 | 5.5 | 13.8 | | | | | |
| 1961 | 1.3 | 1.3 | 1.6 | 1.5 | 1.1 | 1.2 | 1.7 | 1.8 | 1.6 | 0.8 | 1.1 | 2.5 | 1.3 | 3.9 | 7.2 | 1.0 | | | | |
| 1962 | 1.6 | 1.7 | 1.9 | 1.8 | 1.5 | 1.7 | 2.2 | 2.3 | 2.1 | 1.5 | 1.9 | 3.2 | 2.4 | 4.7 | 7.1 | 3.9 | 6.9 | | | |
| 1963 | 1.6 | 1.7 | 1.9 | 1.8 | 1.6 | 1.6 | 2.1 | 2.2 | 2.0 | 1.5 | 1.8 | 3.0 | 2.2 | 4.0 | 5.6 | 3.0 | 4.0 | 1.2 | | |
| 1964 | 1.7 | 1.8 | 2.0 | 1.9 | 1.6 | 1.8 | 2.2 | 2.3 | 2.2 | 1.7 | 2.0 | 3.0 | 2.4 | 3.9 | 5.2 | 3.1 | 3.8 | 2.4 | 3.5 | |
| 1965 | 1.6 | 1.7 | 2.0 | 1.9 | 1.6 | 1.7 | 2.1 | 2.2 | 2.1 | 1.6 | 1.9 | 2.8 | 2.2 | 3.4 | 4.4 | 2.6 | 3.1 | 1.8 | 2.1 | 0.7 |
| 1966 | 1.7 | 1.8 | 2.0 | 2.0 | 1.7 | 1.8 | 2.2 | 2.3 | 2.2 | 1.8 | 2.1 | 2.9 | 2.4 | 3.5 | 4.3 | 2.8 | 3.2 | 2.3 | 2.6 | 2.2 |
| 1967 | 1.2 | 1.2 | 1.4 | 1.3 | 1.1 | 1.1 | 1.5 | 1.5 | 1.3 | 0.9 | 1.1 | 1.7 | 1.1 | 2.0 | 2.5 | 1.0 | 1.0 | -0.1 | -0.5 | -1.8 |
| 1968 | 1.1 | 1.2 | 1.4 | 1.3 | 1.0 | 1.1 | 1.4 | 1.4 | 1.2 | 0.8 | 1.0 | 1.5 | 1.0 | 1.7 | 2.2 | 0.8 | 0.8 | -0.2 | -0.4 | -1.4 |
| 1969 | 0.9 | 0.9 | 1.1 | 1.0 | 0.7 | 0.7 | 1.0 | 1.0 | 0.8 | 0.4 | 0.5 | 1.0 | 0.5 | 1.1 | 1.4 | 0.2 | 0.1 | -0.9 | -1.2 | -2.1 |
| 1970 | 1.3 | 1.3 | 1.5 | 1.4 | 1.2 | 1.3 | 1.5 | 1.6 | 1.4 | 1.1 | 1.3 | 1.8 | 1.3 | 2.0 | 2.4 | 1.3 | 1.3 | 0.7 | 0.6 | 0.1 |

# Appendix C-4

Long-term Government Bonds: Percent per annum total returns for all historical periods

From 1926 to 2016

| End Date | Start Date 1946 | 1947 | 1948 | 1949 | 1950 | 1951 | 1952 | 1953 | 1954 | 1955 | 1956 | 1957 | 1958 | 1959 | 1960 | 1961 | 1962 | 1963 | 1964 | 1965 |
|---|---|---|---|---|---|---|---|---|---|---|---|---|---|---|---|---|---|---|---|---|
| 1971 | 1.7 | 1.8 | 2.0 | 1.9 | 1.7 | 1.8 | 2.1 | 2.1 | 2.1 | 1.8 | 2.0 | 2.5 | 2.1 | 2.8 | 3.2 | 2.3 | 2.5 | 2.0 | 2.1 | 1.9 |
| 1972 | 1.9 | 1.9 | 2.1 | 2.1 | 1.9 | 2.0 | 2.3 | 2.3 | 2.3 | 2.0 | 2.2 | 2.7 | 2.4 | 3.0 | 3.4 | 2.6 | 2.8 | 2.4 | 2.5 | 2.3 |
| 1973 | 1.8 | 1.8 | 2.0 | 1.9 | 1.8 | 1.8 | 2.1 | 2.2 | 2.1 | 1.8 | 2.0 | 2.5 | 2.2 | 2.7 | 3.1 | 2.3 | 2.4 | 2.0 | 2.1 | 2.0 |
| 1974 | 1.8 | 1.9 | 2.1 | 2.0 | 1.9 | 1.9 | 2.2 | 2.3 | 2.2 | 1.9 | 2.1 | 2.6 | 2.3 | 2.8 | 3.2 | 2.5 | 2.6 | 2.2 | 2.3 | 2.2 |
| 1975 | 2.1 | 2.2 | 2.3 | 2.3 | 2.1 | 2.2 | 2.5 | 2.5 | 2.5 | 2.3 | 2.5 | 2.9 | 2.7 | 3.2 | 3.5 | 2.9 | 3.0 | 2.7 | 2.9 | 2.8 |
| 1976 | 2.5 | 2.6 | 2.8 | 2.8 | 2.6 | 2.7 | 3.0 | 3.1 | 3.1 | 2.9 | 3.1 | 3.6 | 3.4 | 3.9 | 4.3 | 3.7 | 3.9 | 3.7 | 3.9 | 3.9 |
| 1977 | 2.4 | 2.5 | 2.7 | 2.7 | 2.5 | 2.6 | 2.9 | 2.9 | 2.9 | 2.7 | 2.9 | 3.3 | 3.1 | 3.7 | 4.0 | 3.4 | 3.6 | 3.4 | 3.5 | 3.5 |
| 1978 | 2.3 | 2.4 | 2.6 | 2.5 | 2.4 | 2.5 | 2.7 | 2.8 | 2.8 | 2.6 | 2.7 | 3.1 | 2.9 | 3.4 | 3.7 | 3.2 | 3.3 | 3.1 | 3.2 | 3.2 |
| 1979 | 2.2 | 2.3 | 2.4 | 2.4 | 2.3 | 2.3 | 2.6 | 2.6 | 2.6 | 2.4 | 2.6 | 2.9 | 2.7 | 3.2 | 3.5 | 2.9 | 3.1 | 2.8 | 2.9 | 2.9 |
| 1980 | 2.0 | 2.1 | 2.2 | 2.2 | 2.1 | 2.1 | 2.3 | 2.4 | 2.3 | 2.2 | 2.3 | 2.6 | 2.4 | 2.8 | 3.1 | 2.6 | 2.7 | 2.4 | 2.5 | 2.5 |
| 1981 | 2.0 | 2.1 | 2.2 | 2.2 | 2.1 | 2.1 | 2.3 | 2.4 | 2.3 | 2.2 | 2.3 | 2.6 | 2.4 | 2.8 | 3.0 | 2.6 | 2.6 | 2.4 | 2.5 | 2.4 |
| 1982 | 2.9 | 3.0 | 3.2 | 3.1 | 3.0 | 3.1 | 3.4 | 3.5 | 3.4 | 3.3 | 3.5 | 3.9 | 3.7 | 4.1 | 4.4 | 4.0 | 4.2 | 4.0 | 4.2 | 4.2 |
| 1983 | 2.8 | 2.9 | 3.1 | 3.1 | 3.0 | 3.1 | 3.3 | 3.4 | 3.4 | 3.2 | 3.4 | 3.7 | 3.6 | 4.0 | 4.3 | 3.9 | 4.0 | 3.9 | 4.0 | 4.0 |
| 1984 | 3.2 | 3.2 | 3.4 | 3.4 | 3.3 | 3.4 | 3.6 | 3.7 | 3.7 | 3.6 | 3.8 | 4.1 | 4.0 | 4.4 | 4.7 | 4.3 | 4.5 | 4.4 | 4.5 | 4.6 |
| 1985 | 3.8 | 3.9 | 4.0 | 4.1 | 4.0 | 4.1 | 4.4 | 4.5 | 4.5 | 4.4 | 4.6 | 5.0 | 4.9 | 5.3 | 5.6 | 5.3 | 5.5 | 5.4 | 5.6 | 5.7 |
| 1986 | 4.2 | 4.3 | 4.5 | 4.6 | 4.5 | 4.6 | 4.9 | 5.0 | 5.0 | 5.0 | 5.2 | 5.6 | 5.5 | 5.9 | 6.3 | 6.0 | 6.2 | 6.1 | 6.4 | 6.5 |
| 1987 | 4.1 | 4.2 | 4.3 | 4.4 | 4.3 | 4.4 | 4.7 | 4.8 | 4.8 | 4.7 | 4.9 | 5.3 | 5.2 | 5.6 | 5.9 | 5.6 | 5.8 | 5.8 | 6.0 | 6.1 |
| 1988 | 4.2 | 4.3 | 4.5 | 4.5 | 4.4 | 4.6 | 4.8 | 4.9 | 4.9 | 4.9 | 5.1 | 5.4 | 5.4 | 5.8 | 6.0 | 5.8 | 6.0 | 5.9 | 6.1 | 6.2 |
| 1989 | 4.5 | 4.6 | 4.8 | 4.8 | 4.8 | 4.9 | 5.1 | 5.2 | 5.3 | 5.2 | 5.4 | 5.8 | 5.7 | 6.1 | 6.4 | 6.2 | 6.4 | 6.4 | 6.6 | 6.7 |
| 1990 | 4.5 | 4.6 | 4.8 | 4.8 | 4.8 | 4.9 | 5.2 | 5.3 | 5.3 | 5.3 | 5.5 | 5.8 | 5.7 | 6.1 | 6.4 | 6.2 | 6.4 | 6.3 | 6.5 | 6.7 |
| 1991 | 4.8 | 4.9 | 5.1 | 5.2 | 5.1 | 5.2 | 5.5 | 5.6 | 5.7 | 5.6 | 5.8 | 6.2 | 6.1 | 6.5 | 6.8 | 6.6 | 6.8 | 6.8 | 7.0 | 7.1 |
| 1992 | 4.9 | 5.0 | 5.2 | 5.2 | 5.2 | 5.3 | 5.6 | 5.7 | 5.7 | 5.7 | 5.9 | 6.2 | 6.2 | 6.6 | 6.8 | 6.6 | 6.8 | 6.8 | 7.0 | 7.1 |
| 1993 | 5.2 | 5.3 | 5.4 | 5.5 | 5.5 | 5.6 | 5.8 | 6.0 | 6.0 | 6.0 | 6.2 | 6.5 | 6.5 | 6.9 | 7.2 | 7.0 | 7.2 | 7.2 | 7.4 | 7.5 |
| 1994 | 4.9 | 5.0 | 5.1 | 5.2 | 5.2 | 5.3 | 5.5 | 5.6 | 5.7 | 5.6 | 5.8 | 6.1 | 6.1 | 6.4 | 6.7 | 6.5 | 6.7 | 6.7 | 6.8 | 7.0 |
| 1995 | 5.3 | 5.5 | 5.6 | 5.7 | 5.7 | 5.8 | 6.0 | 6.1 | 6.2 | 6.2 | 6.4 | 6.7 | 6.7 | 7.1 | 7.3 | 7.1 | 7.3 | 7.3 | 7.5 | 7.7 |
| 1996 | 5.2 | 5.3 | 5.5 | 5.5 | 5.5 | 5.6 | 5.9 | 6.0 | 6.0 | 6.0 | 6.2 | 6.5 | 6.5 | 6.8 | 7.1 | 6.9 | 7.1 | 7.1 | 7.3 | 7.4 |
| 1997 | 5.4 | 5.5 | 5.7 | 5.7 | 5.7 | 5.9 | 6.1 | 6.2 | 6.3 | 6.2 | 6.4 | 6.7 | 6.7 | 7.1 | 7.3 | 7.1 | 7.3 | 7.3 | 7.5 | 7.6 |
| 1998 | 5.6 | 5.7 | 5.8 | 5.9 | 5.9 | 6.0 | 6.2 | 6.3 | 6.4 | 6.4 | 6.6 | 6.9 | 6.9 | 7.2 | 7.5 | 7.3 | 7.5 | 7.5 | 7.7 | 7.8 |
| 1999 | 5.3 | 5.4 | 5.5 | 5.6 | 5.6 | 5.7 | 5.9 | 6.0 | 6.0 | 6.0 | 6.2 | 6.5 | 6.5 | 6.8 | 7.0 | 6.8 | 7.0 | 7.0 | 7.2 | 7.3 |
| 2000 | 5.5 | 5.7 | 5.8 | 5.9 | 5.8 | 6.0 | 6.2 | 6.3 | 6.3 | 6.3 | 6.5 | 6.8 | 6.8 | 7.1 | 7.3 | 7.2 | 7.4 | 7.4 | 7.5 | 7.7 |
| 2001 | 5.5 | 5.6 | 5.8 | 5.8 | 5.8 | 5.9 | 6.1 | 6.2 | 6.3 | 6.3 | 6.4 | 6.7 | 6.7 | 7.0 | 7.3 | 7.1 | 7.3 | 7.3 | 7.4 | 7.5 |
| 2002 | 5.7 | 5.8 | 6.0 | 6.0 | 6.0 | 6.1 | 6.3 | 6.5 | 6.5 | 6.5 | 6.7 | 7.0 | 6.9 | 7.3 | 7.5 | 7.3 | 7.5 | 7.5 | 7.7 | 7.8 |
| 2003 | 5.6 | 5.7 | 5.9 | 5.9 | 5.9 | 6.0 | 6.3 | 6.4 | 6.4 | 6.4 | 6.6 | 6.8 | 6.8 | 7.1 | 7.4 | 7.2 | 7.4 | 7.4 | 7.5 | 7.6 |
| 2004 | 5.7 | 5.8 | 5.9 | 6.0 | 6.0 | 6.1 | 6.3 | 6.4 | 6.4 | 6.4 | 6.6 | 6.9 | 6.9 | 7.2 | 7.4 | 7.2 | 7.4 | 7.4 | 7.6 | 7.7 |
| 2005 | 5.7 | 5.8 | 6.0 | 6.0 | 6.0 | 6.1 | 6.3 | 6.4 | 6.5 | 6.5 | 6.6 | 6.9 | 6.9 | 7.2 | 7.4 | 7.2 | 7.4 | 7.4 | 7.6 | 7.7 |
| 2006 | 5.6 | 5.7 | 5.9 | 5.9 | 5.9 | 6.0 | 6.2 | 6.3 | 6.4 | 6.4 | 6.5 | 6.8 | 6.8 | 7.0 | 7.2 | 7.1 | 7.3 | 7.3 | 7.4 | 7.5 |
| 2007 | 5.7 | 5.8 | 6.0 | 6.0 | 6.0 | 6.1 | 6.3 | 6.4 | 6.4 | 6.4 | 6.6 | 6.8 | 6.8 | 7.1 | 7.3 | 7.2 | 7.3 | 7.3 | 7.5 | 7.6 |
| 2008 | 6.0 | 6.1 | 6.3 | 6.3 | 6.3 | 6.4 | 6.6 | 6.7 | 6.8 | 6.8 | 6.9 | 7.2 | 7.2 | 7.4 | 7.7 | 7.5 | 7.7 | 7.7 | 7.8 | 7.9 |
| 2009 | 5.6 | 5.7 | 5.9 | 5.9 | 5.9 | 6.0 | 6.2 | 6.3 | 6.3 | 6.3 | 6.5 | 6.7 | 6.7 | 7.0 | 7.1 | 7.0 | 7.1 | 7.2 | 7.3 | 7.4 |
| 2010 | 5.7 | 5.8 | 5.9 | 6.0 | 6.0 | 6.1 | 6.3 | 6.3 | 6.4 | 6.4 | 6.5 | 6.8 | 6.8 | 7.0 | 7.2 | 7.1 | 7.2 | 7.2 | 7.3 | 7.4 |
| 2011 | 6.0 | 6.1 | 6.2 | 6.3 | 6.3 | 6.4 | 6.6 | 6.7 | 6.7 | 6.7 | 6.9 | 7.1 | 7.1 | 7.4 | 7.6 | 7.4 | 7.6 | 7.6 | 7.7 | 7.8 |
| 2012 | 6.0 | 6.1 | 6.2 | 6.2 | 6.2 | 6.3 | 6.5 | 6.6 | 6.7 | 6.7 | 6.8 | 7.0 | 7.0 | 7.3 | 7.5 | 7.3 | 7.5 | 7.5 | 7.6 | 7.7 |
| 2013 | 5.7 | 5.8 | 5.9 | 5.9 | 5.9 | 6.0 | 6.2 | 6.3 | 6.3 | 6.3 | 6.4 | 6.7 | 6.6 | 6.9 | 7.1 | 6.9 | 7.1 | 7.1 | 7.2 | 7.3 |
| 2014 | 5.9 | 6.0 | 6.1 | 6.2 | 6.2 | 6.3 | 6.5 | 6.5 | 6.6 | 6.6 | 6.7 | 6.9 | 6.9 | 7.2 | 7.4 | 7.2 | 7.4 | 7.4 | 7.5 | 7.6 |
| 2015 | 5.8 | 5.9 | 6.0 | 6.1 | 6.1 | 6.2 | 6.3 | 6.4 | 6.5 | 6.5 | 6.6 | 6.8 | 6.8 | 7.0 | 7.2 | 7.1 | 7.2 | 7.2 | 7.3 | 7.4 |
| 2016 | 5.8 | 5.8 | 6.0 | 6.0 | 6.0 | 6.1 | 6.3 | 6.3 | 6.4 | 6.4 | 6.5 | 6.7 | 6.7 | 6.9 | 7.1 | 7.0 | 7.1 | 7.1 | 7.2 | 7.3 |

## Appendix C-4

Long-term Government Bonds: Percent per annum total returns for all historical periods

From 1926 to 2016

# Appendix C-4

Long-term Government Bonds: Percent per annum total returns for all historical periods

From 1926 to 2016

| End Date | Start Date 1966 | 1967 | 1968 | 1969 | 1970 | 1971 | 1972 | 1973 | 1974 | 1975 | 1976 | 1977 | 1978 | 1979 | 1980 | 1981 | 1982 | 1983 | 1984 | 1985 |
|---|---|---|---|---|---|---|---|---|---|---|---|---|---|---|---|---|---|---|---|---|
| 1971 | 2.1 | 1.8 | 4.7 | 6.4 | 12.7 | 13.2 | | | | | | | | | | | | | | |
| 1972 | 2.6 | 2.4 | 4.9 | 6.2 | 10.3 | 9.4 | 5.7 | | | | | | | | | | | | | |
| 1973 | 2.1 | 1.9 | 3.9 | 4.7 | 5.8 | 5.8 | 2.2 | -1.1 | | | | | | | | | | | | |
| 1974 | 2.4 | 2.2 | 3.9 | 4.7 | 6.7 | 5.4 | 2.9 | 1.6 | 4.4 | | | | | | | | | | | |
| 1975 | 3.0 | 3.0 | 4.6 | 5.3 | 7.1 | 6.2 | 4.5 | 4.1 | 6.7 | 9.2 | | | | | | | | | | |
| 1976 | 4.2 | 4.3 | 5.9 | 6.7 | 8.5 | 7.9 | 6.8 | 7.1 | 10.0 | 12.9 | 16.8 | | | | | | | | | |
| 1977 | 3.8 | 3.8 | 5.2 | 5.8 | 7.3 | 6.6 | 5.5 | 5.5 | 7.2 | 8.2 | 7.7 | -0.7 | | | | | | | | |
| 1978 | 3.4 | 3.4 | 4.6 | 5.1 | 6.3 | 5.6 | 4.5 | 4.4 | 5.5 | 5.8 | 4.6 | -0.9 | -1.2 | | | | | | | |
| 1979 | 3.1 | 3.0 | 4.1 | 4.5 | 5.6 | 4.8 | 3.8 | 3.5 | 4.3 | 4.3 | 3.1 | -1.0 | -1.2 | -1.2 | | | | | | |
| 1980 | 2.6 | 2.5 | 3.5 | 3.8 | 4.6 | 3.9 | 2.9 | 2.6 | 3.1 | 2.9 | 1.7 | -1.8 | -2.1 | -2.6 | -3.9 | | | | | |
| 1981 | 2.5 | 2.5 | 3.3 | 3.6 | 4.4 | 3.7 | 2.8 | 2.5 | 2.9 | 2.7 | 1.7 | -1.1 | -1.1 | -1.1 | -1.1 | 1.9 | | | | |
| 1982 | 4.4 | 4.5 | 5.5 | 5.9 | 6.8 | 6.4 | 5.8 | 5.8 | 6.6 | 6.8 | 6.5 | 4.9 | 6.0 | 7.9 | 11.2 | 19.6 | 40.4 | | | |
| 1983 | 4.2 | 4.3 | 5.2 | 5.5 | 6.3 | 5.9 | 5.3 | 5.3 | 6.0 | 6.1 | 5.8 | 4.3 | 5.1 | 6.4 | 8.4 | 12.9 | 18.9 | 0.7 | | |
| 1984 | 4.8 | 4.9 | 5.7 | 6.1 | 6.9 | 6.6 | 6.1 | 6.1 | 6.8 | 7.0 | 6.8 | 5.6 | 6.5 | 7.9 | 9.8 | 13.5 | 17.7 | 7.8 | 15.5 | |
| 1985 | 6.0 | 6.1 | 7.0 | 7.5 | 8.3 | 8.0 | 7.7 | 7.8 | 8.6 | 9.0 | 9.0 | 8.2 | 9.3 | 10.9 | 13.1 | 16.8 | 20.9 | 15.0 | 23.0 | 31.0 |
| 1986 | 6.8 | 6.9 | 7.9 | 8.3 | 9.2 | 9.0 | 8.7 | 8.9 | 9.8 | 10.2 | 10.3 | 9.7 | 10.9 | 12.5 | 14.6 | 18.1 | 21.6 | 17.3 | 23.5 | 27.7 |
| 1987 | 6.3 | 6.5 | 7.3 | 7.7 | 8.5 | 8.3 | 8.0 | 8.1 | 8.8 | 9.2 | 9.2 | 8.5 | 9.5 | 10.7 | 12.3 | 14.9 | 17.2 | 13.0 | 16.3 | 16.6 |
| 1988 | 6.5 | 6.6 | 7.4 | 7.8 | 8.5 | 8.4 | 8.1 | 8.2 | 8.9 | 9.2 | 9.2 | 8.6 | 9.5 | 10.6 | 12.0 | 14.2 | 16.1 | 12.5 | 15.0 | 14.9 |
| 1989 | 6.9 | 7.1 | 7.9 | 8.3 | 9.0 | 8.8 | 8.6 | 8.8 | 9.4 | 9.8 | 9.8 | 9.3 | 10.2 | 11.3 | 12.6 | 14.6 | 16.3 | 13.2 | 15.5 | 15.5 |
| 1990 | 6.9 | 7.0 | 7.8 | 8.2 | 8.9 | 8.7 | 8.5 | 8.6 | 9.2 | 9.6 | 9.6 | 9.1 | 9.9 | 10.8 | 12.0 | 13.7 | 15.2 | 12.3 | 14.1 | 13.9 |
| 1991 | 7.4 | 7.5 | 8.3 | 8.7 | 9.3 | 9.2 | 9.0 | 9.2 | 9.8 | 10.1 | 10.2 | 9.7 | 10.5 | 11.5 | 12.6 | 14.2 | 15.6 | 13.1 | 14.8 | 14.6 |
| 1992 | 7.4 | 7.5 | 8.3 | 8.6 | 9.3 | 9.1 | 9.0 | 9.1 | 9.7 | 10.0 | 10.0 | 9.6 | 10.4 | 11.2 | 12.2 | 13.7 | 14.9 | 12.6 | 14.0 | 13.8 |
| 1993 | 7.8 | 7.9 | 8.6 | 9.0 | 9.6 | 9.5 | 9.4 | 9.5 | 10.1 | 10.4 | 10.5 | 10.1 | 10.8 | 11.7 | 12.7 | 14.1 | 15.1 | 13.1 | 14.4 | 14.3 |
| 1994 | 7.2 | 7.3 | 8.0 | 8.3 | 8.9 | 8.7 | 8.6 | 8.7 | 9.2 | 9.4 | 9.4 | 9.0 | 9.6 | 10.4 | 11.2 | 12.3 | 13.2 | 11.2 | 12.2 | 11.9 |
| 1995 | 7.9 | 8.1 | 8.7 | 9.1 | 9.7 | 9.6 | 9.4 | 9.6 | 10.1 | 10.4 | 10.4 | 10.1 | 10.8 | 11.5 | 12.4 | 13.5 | 14.4 | 12.6 | 13.7 | 13.5 |
| 1996 | 7.6 | 7.8 | 8.4 | 8.7 | 9.3 | 9.2 | 9.0 | 9.1 | 9.6 | 9.8 | 9.9 | 9.5 | 10.1 | 10.8 | 11.5 | 12.6 | 13.3 | 11.6 | 12.5 | 12.3 |
| 1997 | 7.9 | 8.0 | 8.6 | 9.0 | 9.5 | 9.4 | 9.2 | 9.4 | 9.9 | 10.1 | 10.1 | 9.8 | 10.4 | 11.0 | 11.8 | 12.8 | 13.5 | 11.9 | 12.7 | 12.5 |
| 1998 | 8.0 | 8.2 | 8.8 | 9.1 | 9.6 | 9.5 | 9.4 | 9.5 | 10.0 | 10.2 | 10.3 | 10.0 | 10.5 | 11.1 | 11.8 | 12.8 | 13.5 | 12.0 | 12.8 | 12.6 |
| 1999 | 7.5 | 7.6 | 8.2 | 8.5 | 8.9 | 8.8 | 8.7 | 8.8 | 9.2 | 9.4 | 9.4 | 9.1 | 9.5 | 10.1 | 10.7 | 11.5 | 12.1 | 10.6 | 11.3 | 11.0 |
| 2000 | 7.9 | 8.0 | 8.5 | 8.8 | 9.3 | 9.2 | 9.1 | 9.2 | 9.6 | 9.8 | 9.9 | 9.6 | 10.0 | 10.6 | 11.2 | 12.0 | 12.6 | 11.2 | 11.8 | 11.6 |
| 2001 | 7.7 | 7.9 | 8.4 | 8.7 | 9.1 | 9.0 | 8.9 | 9.0 | 9.4 | 9.6 | 9.6 | 9.3 | 9.8 | 10.3 | 10.8 | 11.6 | 12.1 | 10.8 | 11.4 | 11.1 |
| 2002 | 8.0 | 8.1 | 8.7 | 8.9 | 9.4 | 9.3 | 9.2 | 9.3 | 9.7 | 9.9 | 9.9 | 9.6 | 10.1 | 10.6 | 11.1 | 11.9 | 12.4 | 11.1 | 11.7 | 11.5 |
| 2003 | 7.8 | 7.9 | 8.5 | 8.7 | 9.2 | 9.1 | 8.9 | 9.0 | 9.4 | 9.6 | 9.6 | 9.3 | 9.7 | 10.2 | 10.7 | 11.4 | 11.8 | 10.6 | 11.2 | 10.9 |
| 2004 | 7.8 | 8.0 | 8.5 | 8.7 | 9.1 | 9.0 | 8.9 | 9.0 | 9.4 | 9.5 | 9.6 | 9.3 | 9.7 | 10.1 | 10.6 | 11.3 | 11.7 | 10.5 | 11.0 | 10.8 |
| 2005 | 7.8 | 7.9 | 8.4 | 8.7 | 9.1 | 9.1 | 8.9 | 9.0 | 9.3 | 9.5 | 9.5 | 9.2 | 9.6 | 10.0 | 10.5 | 11.1 | 11.5 | 10.4 | 10.9 | 10.7 |
| 2006 | 7.7 | 7.8 | 8.2 | 8.5 | 8.9 | 8.8 | 8.7 | 8.7 | 9.1 | 9.2 | 9.2 | 9.0 | 9.3 | 9.7 | 10.1 | 10.7 | 11.1 | 10.0 | 10.4 | 10.2 |
| 2007 | 7.7 | 7.8 | 8.3 | 8.5 | 8.9 | 8.8 | 8.7 | 8.8 | 9.1 | 9.2 | 9.2 | 9.0 | 9.3 | 9.7 | 10.1 | 10.7 | 11.1 | 10.0 | 10.4 | 10.2 |
| 2008 | 8.1 | 8.2 | 8.7 | 8.9 | 9.3 | 9.2 | 9.1 | 9.2 | 9.5 | 9.7 | 9.7 | 9.5 | 9.8 | 10.2 | 10.6 | 11.2 | 11.6 | 10.6 | 11.0 | 10.8 |
| 2009 | 7.5 | 7.6 | 8.1 | 8.3 | 8.6 | 8.5 | 8.4 | 8.5 | 8.8 | 8.9 | 8.9 | 8.7 | 9.0 | 9.3 | 9.7 | 10.2 | 10.5 | 9.5 | 9.9 | 9.7 |
| 2010 | 7.6 | 7.7 | 8.1 | 8.3 | 8.7 | 8.6 | 8.5 | 8.5 | 8.8 | 8.9 | 9.0 | 8.7 | 9.0 | 9.3 | 9.7 | 10.2 | 10.5 | 9.5 | 9.9 | 9.7 |
| 2011 | 8.0 | 8.1 | 8.5 | 8.7 | 9.1 | 9.0 | 8.9 | 9.0 | 9.3 | 9.4 | 9.4 | 9.2 | 9.5 | 9.8 | 10.2 | 10.7 | 11.0 | 10.1 | 10.5 | 10.3 |
| 2012 | 7.9 | 8.0 | 8.4 | 8.6 | 8.9 | 8.9 | 8.8 | 8.8 | 9.1 | 9.2 | 9.2 | 9.0 | 9.3 | 9.6 | 10.0 | 10.5 | 10.7 | 9.9 | 10.2 | 10.0 |
| 2013 | 7.4 | 7.5 | 7.9 | 8.1 | 8.4 | 8.3 | 8.2 | 8.2 | 8.5 | 8.6 | 8.6 | 8.4 | 8.6 | 8.9 | 9.2 | 9.7 | 9.9 | 9.1 | 9.3 | 9.1 |
| 2014 | 7.7 | 7.8 | 8.2 | 8.4 | 8.7 | 8.6 | 8.5 | 8.6 | 8.9 | 9.0 | 9.0 | 8.8 | 9.0 | 9.3 | 9.7 | 10.1 | 10.3 | 9.5 | 9.8 | 9.6 |
| 2015 | 7.6 | 7.6 | 8.0 | 8.2 | 8.5 | 8.4 | 8.3 | 8.4 | 8.6 | 8.7 | 8.7 | 8.5 | 8.8 | 9.1 | 9.4 | 9.8 | 10.0 | 9.2 | 9.5 | 9.3 |
| 2016 | 7.4 | 7.5 | 7.9 | 8.1 | 8.4 | 8.3 | 8.2 | 8.2 | 8.5 | 8.6 | 8.5 | 8.3 | 8.6 | 8.9 | 9.1 | 9.5 | 9.8 | 9.0 | 9.2 | 9.0 |

## Appendix C-4

Long-term Government Bonds: Percent per annum total returns for all historical periods

From 1926 to 2016

| End Date | Start Date 1986 | 1987 | 1988 | 1989 | 1990 | 1991 | 1992 | 1993 | 1994 | 1995 | 1996 | 1997 | 1998 | 1999 | 2000 | 2001 | 2002 | 2003 | 2004 | 2005 |
|---|---|---|---|---|---|---|---|---|---|---|---|---|---|---|---|---|---|---|---|---|
| 1971 | | | | | | | | | | | | | | | | | | | | |
| 1972 | | | | | | | | | | | | | | | | | | | | |
| 1973 | | | | | | | | | | | | | | | | | | | | |
| 1974 | | | | | | | | | | | | | | | | | | | | |
| 1975 | | | | | | | | | | | | | | | | | | | | |
| 1976 | | | | | | | | | | | | | | | | | | | | |
| 1977 | | | | | | | | | | | | | | | | | | | | |
| 1978 | | | | | | | | | | | | | | | | | | | | |
| 1979 | | | | | | | | | | | | | | | | | | | | |
| 1980 | | | | | | | | | | | | | | | | | | | | |
| 1981 | | | | | | | | | | | | | | | | | | | | |
| 1982 | | | | | | | | | | | | | | | | | | | | |
| 1983 | | | | | | | | | | | | | | | | | | | | |
| 1984 | | | | | | | | | | | | | | | | | | | | |
| 1985 | | | | | | | | | | | | | | | | | | | | |
| 1986 | 24.5 | | | | | | | | | | | | | | | | | | | |
| 1987 | 10.1 | -2.7 | | | | | | | | | | | | | | | | | | |
| 1988 | 9.9 | 3.3 | 9.7 | | | | | | | | | | | | | | | | | |
| 1989 | 11.9 | 8.0 | 13.8 | 18.1 | | | | | | | | | | | | | | | | |
| 1990 | 10.8 | 7.6 | 11.2 | 12.0 | 6.2 | | | | | | | | | | | | | | | |
| 1991 | 12.1 | 9.8 | 13.2 | 14.4 | 12.6 | 19.3 | | | | | | | | | | | | | | |
| 1992 | 11.5 | 9.5 | 12.1 | 12.8 | 11.0 | 13.5 | 8.1 | | | | | | | | | | | | | |
| 1993 | 12.4 | 10.7 | 13.1 | 13.8 | 12.8 | 15.1 | 13.0 | 18.2 | | | | | | | | | | | | |
| 1994 | 9.9 | 8.2 | 9.9 | 9.9 | 8.3 | 8.9 | 5.6 | 4.4 | -7.8 | | | | | | | | | | | |
| 1995 | 11.9 | 10.6 | 12.4 | 12.8 | 11.9 | 13.1 | 11.6 | 12.8 | 10.2 | 31.7 | | | | | | | | | | |
| 1996 | 10.7 | 9.4 | 10.8 | 11.0 | 10.0 | 10.6 | 9.0 | 9.2 | 6.4 | 14.2 | -0.9 | | | | | | | | | |
| 1997 | 11.1 | 10.0 | 11.3 | 11.5 | 10.7 | 11.4 | 10.1 | 10.5 | 8.7 | 14.8 | 7.1 | 15.9 | | | | | | | | |
| 1998 | 11.3 | 10.2 | 11.5 | 11.7 | 11.0 | 11.6 | 10.5 | 10.9 | 9.5 | 14.3 | 9.1 | 14.4 | 13.1 | | | | | | | |
| 1999 | 9.7 | 8.6 | 9.6 | 9.6 | 8.8 | 9.1 | 7.9 | 7.8 | 6.2 | 9.2 | 4.3 | 6.0 | 1.5 | -9.0 | | | | | | |
| 2000 | 10.4 | 9.5 | 10.5 | 10.5 | 9.9 | 10.3 | 9.3 | 9.5 | 8.3 | 11.2 | 7.5 | 9.7 | 7.7 | 5.2 | 21.5 | | | | | |
| 2001 | 10.0 | 9.1 | 10.0 | 10.0 | 9.4 | 9.6 | 8.7 | 8.8 | 7.7 | 10.1 | 6.8 | 8.5 | 6.7 | 4.7 | 12.2 | 3.7 | | | | |
| 2002 | 10.4 | 9.6 | 10.5 | 10.5 | 10.0 | 10.3 | 9.5 | 9.7 | 8.8 | 11.0 | 8.4 | 10.0 | 8.8 | 7.8 | 14.1 | 10.5 | 17.8 | | | |
| 2003 | 9.9 | 9.1 | 9.9 | 9.9 | 9.4 | 9.6 | 8.8 | 8.9 | 8.0 | 9.9 | 7.5 | 8.7 | 7.6 | 6.5 | 10.8 | 7.4 | 9.3 | 1.4 | | |
| 2004 | 9.8 | 9.1 | 9.8 | 9.8 | 9.3 | 9.5 | 8.8 | 8.9 | 8.1 | 9.8 | 7.6 | 8.7 | 7.7 | 6.8 | 10.3 | 7.7 | 9.1 | 4.9 | 8.5 | |
| 2005 | 9.7 | 9.0 | 9.7 | 9.7 | 9.2 | 9.4 | 8.7 | 8.8 | 8.0 | 9.6 | 7.6 | 8.6 | 7.7 | 7.0 | 9.9 | 7.7 | 8.7 | 5.9 | 8.2 | 7.8 |
| 2006 | 9.3 | 8.6 | 9.2 | 9.2 | 8.7 | 8.9 | 8.2 | 8.2 | 7.5 | 8.9 | 7.0 | 7.8 | 7.0 | 6.2 | 8.6 | 6.6 | 7.2 | 4.7 | 5.8 | 4.4 |
| 2007 | 9.3 | 8.7 | 9.3 | 9.3 | 8.8 | 8.9 | 8.3 | 8.3 | 7.7 | 8.9 | 7.2 | 8.0 | 7.3 | 6.6 | 8.8 | 7.1 | 7.6 | 5.7 | 6.8 | 6.2 |
| 2008 | 10.0 | 9.4 | 10.0 | 10.0 | 9.6 | 9.8 | 9.3 | 9.4 | 8.8 | 10.1 | 8.6 | 9.4 | 8.8 | 8.4 | 10.5 | 9.3 | 10.1 | 8.8 | 10.4 | 10.8 |
| 2009 | 8.8 | 8.2 | 8.7 | 8.7 | 8.3 | 8.3 | 7.8 | 7.8 | 7.1 | 8.2 | 6.7 | 7.3 | 6.6 | 6.1 | 7.7 | 6.3 | 6.6 | 5.1 | 5.7 | 5.1 |
| 2010 | 8.9 | 8.3 | 8.8 | 8.8 | 8.3 | 8.4 | 7.9 | 7.9 | 7.3 | 8.3 | 6.9 | 7.5 | 6.9 | 6.4 | 7.9 | 6.6 | 7.0 | 5.7 | 6.3 | 5.9 |
| 2011 | 9.5 | 9.0 | 9.5 | 9.5 | 9.1 | 9.3 | 8.8 | 8.8 | 8.3 | 9.3 | 8.1 | 8.7 | 8.2 | 7.9 | 9.4 | 8.4 | 8.8 | 7.9 | 8.7 | 8.7 |
| 2012 | 9.3 | 8.8 | 9.3 | 9.2 | 8.9 | 9.0 | 8.5 | 8.5 | 8.1 | 9.0 | 7.8 | 8.4 | 7.9 | 7.5 | 8.9 | 7.9 | 8.3 | 7.4 | 8.1 | 8.1 |
| 2013 | 8.4 | 7.9 | 8.3 | 8.3 | 7.9 | 7.9 | 7.4 | 7.4 | 6.9 | 7.7 | 6.5 | 7.0 | 6.5 | 6.0 | 7.2 | 6.2 | 6.4 | 5.4 | 5.8 | 5.5 |
| 2014 | 9.0 | 8.4 | 8.9 | 8.8 | 8.5 | 8.6 | 8.1 | 8.2 | 7.7 | 8.5 | 7.4 | 7.9 | 7.5 | 7.1 | 8.3 | 7.4 | 7.7 | 6.9 | 7.4 | 7.3 |
| 2015 | 8.6 | 8.1 | 8.5 | 8.5 | 8.1 | 8.2 | 7.8 | 7.8 | 7.3 | 8.1 | 7.0 | 7.4 | 7.0 | 6.7 | 7.7 | 6.9 | 7.1 | 6.3 | 6.7 | 6.5 |
| 2016 | 8.4 | 7.9 | 8.3 | 8.2 | 7.9 | 7.9 | 7.5 | 7.5 | 7.1 | 7.8 | 6.8 | 7.2 | 6.7 | 6.4 | 7.4 | 6.5 | 6.7 | 6.0 | 6.3 | 6.1 |

## Appendix C-4

Long-term Government Bonds: Percent per annum total returns for all historical periods

From 1926 to 2016

| End Date | Start Date 2006 | 2007 | 2008 | 2009 | 2010 | 2011 | 2012 | 2013 | 2014 | 2015 | 2016 |
|---|---|---|---|---|---|---|---|---|---|---|---|
| 1971 | | | | | | | | | | | |
| 1972 | | | | | | | | | | | |
| 1973 | | | | | | | | | | | |
| 1974 | | | | | | | | | | | |
| 1975 | | | | | | | | | | | |
| 1976 | | | | | | | | | | | |
| 1977 | | | | | | | | | | | |
| 1978 | | | | | | | | | | | |
| 1979 | | | | | | | | | | | |
| 1980 | | | | | | | | | | | |
| 1981 | | | | | | | | | | | |
| 1982 | | | | | | | | | | | |
| 1983 | | | | | | | | | | | |
| 1984 | | | | | | | | | | | |
| 1985 | | | | | | | | | | | |
| 1986 | | | | | | | | | | | |
| 1987 | | | | | | | | | | | |
| 1988 | | | | | | | | | | | |
| 1989 | | | | | | | | | | | |
| 1990 | | | | | | | | | | | |
| 1991 | | | | | | | | | | | |
| 1992 | | | | | | | | | | | |
| 1993 | | | | | | | | | | | |
| 1994 | | | | | | | | | | | |
| 1995 | | | | | | | | | | | |
| 1996 | | | | | | | | | | | |
| 1997 | | | | | | | | | | | |
| 1998 | | | | | | | | | | | |
| 1999 | | | | | | | | | | | |
| 2000 | | | | | | | | | | | |
| 2001 | | | | | | | | | | | |
| 2002 | | | | | | | | | | | |
| 2003 | | | | | | | | | | | |
| 2004 | | | | | | | | | | | |
| 2005 | | | | | | | | | | | |
| 2006 | 1.2 | | | | | | | | | | |
| 2007 | 5.4 | 9.9 | | | | | | | | | |
| 2008 | 11.9 | 17.6 | 25.9 | | | | | | | | |
| 2009 | 4.5 | 5.6 | 3.5 | -14.9 | | | | | | | |
| 2010 | 5.6 | 6.7 | 5.7 | -3.2 | 10.1 | | | | | | |
| 2011 | 8.9 | 10.5 | 10.7 | 6.0 | 18.3 | 27.1 | | | | | |
| 2012 | 8.1 | 9.3 | 9.2 | 5.4 | 13.1 | 14.7 | 3.4 | | | | |
| 2013 | 5.2 | 5.8 | 5.2 | 1.5 | 6.0 | 4.7 | -5.0 | -12.8 | | | |
| 2014 | 7.2 | 8.0 | 7.8 | 5.0 | 9.5 | 9.4 | 4.0 | 4.3 | 24.7 | | |
| 2015 | 6.4 | 7.0 | 6.7 | 4.2 | 7.7 | 7.3 | 2.8 | 2.6 | 11.3 | -0.7 | |
| 2016 | 6.0 | 6.5 | 6.1 | 3.9 | 6.9 | 6.3 | 2.6 | 2.4 | 8.0 | 0.5 | 1.8 |

# Appendix C-5

Intermediate-term Government Bonds: Percent per annum total returns for all historical periods

From 1926 to 2016

| End Date | Start Date 1926 | 1927 | 1928 | 1929 | 1930 | 1931 | 1932 | 1933 | 1934 | 1935 | 1936 | 1937 | 1938 | 1939 | 1940 | 1941 | 1942 | 1943 | 1944 | 1945 |
|---|---|---|---|---|---|---|---|---|---|---|---|---|---|---|---|---|---|---|---|---|
| 1926 | 5.4 | | | | | | | | | | | | | | | | | | | |
| 1927 | 4.9 | 4.5 | | | | | | | | | | | | | | | | | | |
| 1928 | 3.6 | 2.7 | 0.9 | | | | | | | | | | | | | | | | | |
| 1929 | 4.2 | 3.8 | 3.4 | 6.0 | | | | | | | | | | | | | | | | |
| 1930 | 4.7 | 4.5 | 4.5 | 6.4 | 6.7 | | | | | | | | | | | | | | | |
| 1931 | 3.5 | 3.1 | 2.8 | 3.4 | 2.1 | -2.3 | | | | | | | | | | | | | | |
| 1932 | 4.2 | 4.0 | 3.9 | 4.7 | 4.3 | 3.1 | 8.8 | | | | | | | | | | | | | |
| 1933 | 3.9 | 3.7 | 3.6 | 4.1 | 3.7 | 2.7 | 5.3 | 1.8 | | | | | | | | | | | | |
| 1934 | 4.5 | 4.4 | 4.3 | 4.9 | 4.7 | 4.2 | 6.5 | 5.4 | 9.0 | | | | | | | | | | | |
| 1935 | 4.7 | 4.7 | 4.7 | 5.2 | 5.1 | 4.8 | 6.6 | 5.9 | 8.0 | 7.0 | | | | | | | | | | |
| 1936 | 4.6 | 4.5 | 4.5 | 4.9 | 4.8 | 4.5 | 5.9 | 5.2 | 6.3 | 5.0 | 3.1 | | | | | | | | | |
| 1937 | 4.3 | 4.2 | 4.2 | 4.6 | 4.4 | 4.1 | 5.2 | 4.4 | 5.1 | 3.8 | 2.3 | 1.6 | | | | | | | | |
| 1938 | 4.5 | 4.4 | 4.4 | 4.7 | 4.6 | 4.3 | 5.3 | 4.7 | 5.3 | 4.4 | 3.6 | 3.9 | 6.2 | | | | | | | |
| 1939 | 4.5 | 4.4 | 4.4 | 4.7 | 4.6 | 4.3 | 5.2 | 4.7 | 5.3 | 4.5 | 3.8 | 4.1 | 5.4 | 4.5 | | | | | | |
| 1940 | 4.4 | 4.3 | 4.3 | 4.6 | 4.4 | 4.2 | 5.0 | 4.5 | 4.9 | 4.2 | 3.7 | 3.8 | 4.6 | 3.7 | 3.0 | | | | | |
| 1941 | 4.1 | 4.0 | 4.0 | 4.2 | 4.1 | 3.9 | 4.5 | 4.0 | 4.3 | 3.7 | 3.1 | 3.1 | 3.5 | 2.6 | 1.7 | 0.5 | | | | |
| 1942 | 4.0 | 3.9 | 3.9 | 4.1 | 3.9 | 3.7 | 4.3 | 3.8 | 4.1 | 3.4 | 3.0 | 2.9 | 3.2 | 2.5 | 1.8 | 1.2 | 1.9 | | | |
| 1943 | 3.9 | 3.8 | 3.8 | 4.0 | 3.9 | 3.6 | 4.1 | 3.7 | 3.9 | 3.4 | 2.9 | 2.9 | 3.1 | 2.5 | 2.0 | 1.7 | 2.4 | 2.8 | | |
| 1944 | 3.8 | 3.7 | 3.7 | 3.9 | 3.7 | 3.5 | 4.0 | 3.6 | 3.7 | 3.2 | 2.8 | 2.8 | 2.9 | 2.4 | 2.0 | 1.8 | 2.2 | 2.3 | 1.8 | |
| 1945 | 3.7 | 3.6 | 3.6 | 3.8 | 3.6 | 3.4 | 3.8 | 3.5 | 3.6 | 3.1 | 2.7 | 2.7 | 2.9 | 2.4 | 2.0 | 1.8 | 2.2 | 2.3 | 2.0 | 2.2 |
| 1946 | 3.6 | 3.5 | 3.5 | 3.6 | 3.5 | 3.3 | 3.6 | 3.3 | 3.4 | 2.9 | 2.6 | 2.5 | 2.7 | 2.2 | 1.9 | 1.7 | 2.0 | 2.0 | 1.7 | 1.6 |
| 1947 | 3.5 | 3.4 | 3.3 | 3.5 | 3.3 | 3.1 | 3.5 | 3.1 | 3.2 | 2.8 | 2.4 | 2.4 | 2.5 | 2.1 | 1.8 | 1.6 | 1.8 | 1.7 | 1.5 | 1.4 |
| 1948 | 3.4 | 3.3 | 3.3 | 3.4 | 3.2 | 3.1 | 3.4 | 3.0 | 3.1 | 2.7 | 2.4 | 2.3 | 2.4 | 2.0 | 1.8 | 1.6 | 1.8 | 1.8 | 1.6 | 1.5 |
| 1949 | 3.4 | 3.3 | 3.2 | 3.3 | 3.2 | 3.0 | 3.3 | 3.0 | 3.1 | 2.7 | 2.4 | 2.3 | 2.4 | 2.1 | 1.8 | 1.7 | 1.9 | 1.8 | 1.7 | 1.7 |
| 1950 | 3.3 | 3.2 | 3.1 | 3.2 | 3.1 | 2.9 | 3.2 | 2.9 | 2.9 | 2.6 | 2.3 | 2.2 | 2.3 | 2.0 | 1.7 | 1.6 | 1.7 | 1.7 | 1.5 | 1.5 |
| 1951 | 3.1 | 3.1 | 3.0 | 3.1 | 3.0 | 2.8 | 3.0 | 2.7 | 2.8 | 2.4 | 2.2 | 2.1 | 2.1 | 1.8 | 1.6 | 1.5 | 1.6 | 1.5 | 1.4 | 1.3 |
| 1952 | 3.1 | 3.0 | 3.0 | 3.1 | 2.9 | 2.7 | 3.0 | 2.7 | 2.7 | 2.4 | 2.1 | 2.1 | 2.1 | 1.8 | 1.6 | 1.5 | 1.6 | 1.6 | 1.4 | 1.4 |
| 1953 | 3.1 | 3.0 | 2.9 | 3.0 | 2.9 | 2.7 | 3.0 | 2.7 | 2.8 | 2.4 | 2.2 | 2.1 | 2.2 | 1.9 | 1.7 | 1.6 | 1.7 | 1.7 | 1.6 | 1.6 |
| 1954 | 3.1 | 3.0 | 2.9 | 3.0 | 2.8 | 2.7 | 3.0 | 2.7 | 2.8 | 2.5 | 2.2 | 2.2 | 2.2 | 2.0 | 1.8 | 1.7 | 1.8 | 1.8 | 1.7 | 1.7 |
| 1955 | 2.9 | 2.9 | 2.8 | 2.9 | 2.8 | 2.6 | 2.8 | 2.6 | 2.6 | 2.3 | 2.1 | 2.0 | 2.0 | 1.8 | 1.6 | 1.5 | 1.6 | 1.6 | 1.5 | 1.5 |
| 1956 | 2.8 | 2.8 | 2.7 | 2.8 | 2.6 | 2.5 | 2.7 | 2.4 | 2.5 | 2.2 | 2.0 | 1.9 | 1.9 | 1.7 | 1.5 | 1.4 | 1.5 | 1.5 | 1.4 | 1.3 |
| 1957 | 3.0 | 2.9 | 2.9 | 2.9 | 2.8 | 2.7 | 2.9 | 2.6 | 2.7 | 2.4 | 2.2 | 2.2 | 2.2 | 2.0 | 1.9 | 1.8 | 1.9 | 1.9 | 1.8 | 1.8 |
| 1958 | 2.9 | 2.8 | 2.7 | 2.8 | 2.7 | 2.5 | 2.7 | 2.5 | 2.5 | 2.3 | 2.1 | 2.0 | 2.0 | 1.8 | 1.7 | 1.6 | 1.7 | 1.7 | 1.6 | 1.6 |
| 1959 | 2.8 | 2.7 | 2.6 | 2.7 | 2.6 | 2.4 | 2.6 | 2.4 | 2.4 | 2.2 | 2.0 | 1.9 | 1.9 | 1.7 | 1.6 | 1.5 | 1.6 | 1.5 | 1.5 | 1.4 |
| 1960 | 3.0 | 2.9 | 2.9 | 3.0 | 2.9 | 2.7 | 2.9 | 2.7 | 2.7 | 2.5 | 2.3 | 2.3 | 2.3 | 2.2 | 2.0 | 2.0 | 2.1 | 2.1 | 2.0 | 2.1 |
| 1961 | 3.0 | 3.0 | 2.9 | 2.9 | 2.8 | 2.7 | 2.9 | 2.7 | 2.7 | 2.5 | 2.3 | 2.3 | 2.3 | 2.1 | 2.0 | 2.0 | 2.1 | 2.1 | 2.0 | 2.0 |
| 1962 | 3.0 | 3.0 | 2.9 | 3.0 | 2.9 | 2.8 | 3.0 | 2.8 | 2.8 | 2.6 | 2.4 | 2.4 | 2.3 | 2.3 | 2.2 | 2.2 | 2.2 | 2.1 | 2.2 | 2.2 |
| 1963 | 3.0 | 2.9 | 2.9 | 2.9 | 2.8 | 2.8 | 2.9 | 2.8 | 2.8 | 2.6 | 2.4 | 2.4 | 2.4 | 2.3 | 2.2 | 2.1 | 2.3 | 2.2 | 2.2 | 2.2 |
| 1964 | 3.0 | 3.0 | 2.9 | 3.0 | 2.9 | 2.8 | 3.0 | 2.8 | 2.8 | 2.6 | 2.5 | 2.4 | 2.5 | 2.4 | 2.2 | 2.2 | 2.3 | 2.3 | 2.3 | 2.3 |
| 1965 | 3.0 | 2.9 | 2.9 | 2.9 | 2.8 | 2.7 | 2.9 | 2.7 | 2.7 | 2.6 | 2.4 | 2.4 | 2.4 | 2.3 | 2.2 | 2.2 | 2.2 | 2.2 | 2.2 | 2.2 |
| 1966 | 3.0 | 3.0 | 2.9 | 3.0 | 2.9 | 2.8 | 2.9 | 2.8 | 2.8 | 2.6 | 2.5 | 2.5 | 2.5 | 2.4 | 2.2 | 2.3 | 2.3 | 2.3 | 2.3 | 2.3 |
| 1967 | 3.0 | 2.9 | 2.9 | 2.9 | 2.8 | 2.7 | 2.9 | 2.7 | 2.8 | 2.6 | 2.4 | 2.4 | 2.4 | 2.3 | 2.2 | 2.2 | 2.3 | 2.3 | 2.3 | 2.3 |
| 1968 | 3.0 | 3.0 | 2.9 | 3.0 | 2.9 | 2.8 | 2.9 | 2.8 | 2.8 | 2.6 | 2.5 | 2.5 | 2.5 | 2.4 | 2.3 | 2.3 | 2.4 | 2.4 | 2.4 | 2.4 |
| 1969 | 2.9 | 2.9 | 2.8 | 2.9 | 2.8 | 2.7 | 2.8 | 2.7 | 2.7 | 2.5 | 2.4 | 2.4 | 2.4 | 2.3 | 2.2 | 2.2 | 2.2 | 2.3 | 2.2 | 2.3 |
| 1970 | 3.2 | 3.2 | 3.1 | 3.2 | 3.1 | 3.0 | 3.2 | 3.0 | 3.1 | 2.9 | 2.8 | 2.8 | 2.8 | 2.7 | 2.7 | 2.6 | 2.7 | 2.7 | 2.7 | 2.8 |

Intermediate-term Government Bonds: Percent per annum total returns for all historical periods

From 1926 to 2016

| End Date | Start Date 1926 | 1927 | 1928 | 1929 | 1930 | 1931 | 1932 | 1933 | 1934 | 1935 | 1936 | 1937 | 1938 | 1939 | 1940 | 1941 | 1942 | 1943 | 1944 | 1945 |
|---|---|---|---|---|---|---|---|---|---|---|---|---|---|---|---|---|---|---|---|---|
| 1971 | 3.3 | 3.3 | 3.3 | 3.3 | 3.3 | 3.2 | 3.3 | 3.2 | 3.2 | 3.1 | 2.9 | 2.9 | 3.0 | 2.9 | 2.8 | 2.8 | 2.9 | 2.9 | 3.0 | 3.0 |
| 1972 | 3.4 | 3.3 | 3.3 | 3.4 | 3.3 | 3.2 | 3.4 | 3.2 | 3.3 | 3.1 | 3.0 | 3.0 | 3.0 | 3.0 | 2.9 | 2.9 | 3.0 | 3.0 | 3.0 | 3.1 |
| 1973 | 3.4 | 3.4 | 3.3 | 3.4 | 3.3 | 3.2 | 3.4 | 3.3 | 3.3 | 3.1 | 3.0 | 3.0 | 3.1 | 3.1 | 3.0 | 3.0 | 3.0 | 3.1 | 3.1 | 3.1 |
| 1974 | 3.4 | 3.4 | 3.4 | 3.4 | 3.4 | 3.3 | 3.4 | 3.3 | 3.3 | 3.2 | 3.1 | 3.1 | 3.2 | 3.1 | 3.0 | 3.0 | 3.1 | 3.2 | 3.2 | 3.2 |
| 1975 | 3.5 | 3.5 | 3.5 | 3.5 | 3.5 | 3.4 | 3.5 | 3.4 | 3.5 | 3.3 | 3.2 | 3.2 | 3.3 | 3.2 | 3.2 | 3.2 | 3.3 | 3.3 | 3.3 | 3.4 |
| 1976 | 3.7 | 3.7 | 3.7 | 3.7 | 3.7 | 3.6 | 3.7 | 3.6 | 3.7 | 3.5 | 3.5 | 3.5 | 3.5 | 3.4 | 3.4 | 3.4 | 3.5 | 3.6 | 3.6 | 3.6 |
| 1977 | 3.7 | 3.6 | 3.6 | 3.7 | 3.6 | 3.6 | 3.7 | 3.6 | 3.6 | 3.5 | 3.4 | 3.4 | 3.5 | 3.4 | 3.4 | 3.4 | 3.5 | 3.5 | 3.5 | 3.6 |
| 1978 | 3.7 | 3.6 | 3.6 | 3.7 | 3.6 | 3.6 | 3.7 | 3.6 | 3.6 | 3.5 | 3.4 | 3.4 | 3.5 | 3.4 | 3.4 | 3.4 | 3.5 | 3.5 | 3.5 | 3.6 |
| 1979 | 3.7 | 3.6 | 3.6 | 3.7 | 3.6 | 3.6 | 3.7 | 3.6 | 3.6 | 3.5 | 3.4 | 3.4 | 3.5 | 3.4 | 3.4 | 3.4 | 3.5 | 3.5 | 3.5 | 3.6 |
| 1980 | 3.7 | 3.6 | 3.6 | 3.7 | 3.6 | 3.6 | 3.7 | 3.6 | 3.6 | 3.5 | 3.4 | 3.4 | 3.5 | 3.4 | 3.4 | 3.4 | 3.5 | 3.5 | 3.5 | 3.6 |
| 1981 | 3.8 | 3.7 | 3.7 | 3.8 | 3.7 | 3.7 | 3.8 | 3.7 | 3.7 | 3.6 | 3.6 | 3.6 | 3.6 | 3.6 | 3.5 | 3.6 | 3.6 | 3.7 | 3.7 | 3.7 |
| 1982 | 4.2 | 4.1 | 4.1 | 4.2 | 4.2 | 4.1 | 4.2 | 4.2 | 4.2 | 4.1 | 4.0 | 4.1 | 4.1 | 4.1 | 4.1 | 4.1 | 4.2 | 4.2 | 4.3 | 4.3 |
| 1983 | 4.2 | 4.2 | 4.2 | 4.2 | 4.2 | 4.2 | 4.3 | 4.2 | 4.3 | 4.2 | 4.1 | 4.1 | 4.2 | 4.2 | 4.1 | 4.2 | 4.3 | 4.3 | 4.4 | 4.4 |
| 1984 | 4.4 | 4.4 | 4.4 | 4.4 | 4.4 | 4.4 | 4.5 | 4.4 | 4.5 | 4.4 | 4.3 | 4.3 | 4.4 | 4.4 | 4.4 | 4.4 | 4.5 | 4.5 | 4.6 | 4.7 |
| 1985 | 4.6 | 4.6 | 4.6 | 4.7 | 4.7 | 4.6 | 4.8 | 4.7 | 4.7 | 4.7 | 4.6 | 4.6 | 4.7 | 4.7 | 4.7 | 4.7 | 4.8 | 4.9 | 4.9 | 5.0 |
| 1986 | 4.8 | 4.8 | 4.8 | 4.9 | 4.8 | 4.8 | 4.9 | 4.9 | 4.9 | 4.8 | 4.8 | 4.8 | 4.9 | 4.9 | 4.9 | 4.9 | 5.0 | 5.1 | 5.2 | 5.2 |
| 1987 | 4.8 | 4.8 | 4.8 | 4.9 | 4.8 | 4.8 | 4.9 | 4.8 | 4.9 | 4.8 | 4.8 | 4.8 | 4.9 | 4.8 | 4.8 | 4.9 | 5.0 | 5.1 | 5.1 | 5.2 |
| 1988 | 4.8 | 4.8 | 4.8 | 4.8 | 4.8 | 4.8 | 4.9 | 4.9 | 4.9 | 4.8 | 4.8 | 4.8 | 4.9 | 4.9 | 4.9 | 4.9 | 5.0 | 5.1 | 5.1 | 5.2 |
| 1989 | 4.9 | 4.9 | 4.9 | 5.0 | 5.0 | 4.9 | 5.1 | 5.0 | 5.1 | 5.0 | 4.9 | 5.0 | 5.0 | 5.0 | 5.0 | 5.1 | 5.2 | 5.2 | 5.3 | 5.4 |
| 1990 | 5.0 | 5.0 | 5.0 | 5.1 | 5.0 | 5.0 | 5.1 | 5.1 | 5.1 | 5.1 | 5.0 | 5.1 | 5.1 | 5.1 | 5.1 | 5.2 | 5.3 | 5.3 | 5.4 | 5.5 |
| 1991 | 5.1 | 5.1 | 5.1 | 5.2 | 5.2 | 5.2 | 5.3 | 5.2 | 5.3 | 5.2 | 5.2 | 5.2 | 5.3 | 5.3 | 5.3 | 5.4 | 5.5 | 5.5 | 5.6 | 5.7 |
| 1992 | 5.2 | 5.2 | 5.2 | 5.2 | 5.2 | 5.2 | 5.3 | 5.3 | 5.3 | 5.3 | 5.2 | 5.3 | 5.4 | 5.3 | 5.4 | 5.4 | 5.5 | 5.6 | 5.6 | 5.7 |
| 1993 | 5.3 | 5.3 | 5.3 | 5.3 | 5.3 | 5.3 | 5.4 | 5.4 | 5.4 | 5.4 | 5.3 | 5.4 | 5.5 | 5.4 | 5.5 | 5.5 | 5.6 | 5.7 | 5.7 | 5.8 |
| 1994 | 5.1 | 5.1 | 5.1 | 5.2 | 5.2 | 5.1 | 5.2 | 5.2 | 5.2 | 5.2 | 5.2 | 5.2 | 5.3 | 5.2 | 5.3 | 5.3 | 5.4 | 5.5 | 5.5 | 5.6 |
| 1995 | 5.3 | 5.3 | 5.3 | 5.3 | 5.3 | 5.3 | 5.4 | 5.4 | 5.4 | 5.4 | 5.3 | 5.4 | 5.4 | 5.4 | 5.5 | 5.5 | 5.6 | 5.7 | 5.7 | 5.8 |
| 1996 | 5.2 | 5.2 | 5.2 | 5.3 | 5.3 | 5.2 | 5.4 | 5.3 | 5.4 | 5.3 | 5.3 | 5.3 | 5.4 | 5.4 | 5.4 | 5.4 | 5.5 | 5.6 | 5.6 | 5.7 |
| 1997 | 5.3 | 5.3 | 5.3 | 5.3 | 5.3 | 5.3 | 5.4 | 5.4 | 5.5 | 5.4 | 5.3 | 5.4 | 5.5 | 5.4 | 5.4 | 5.5 | 5.6 | 5.6 | 5.7 | 5.8 |
| 1998 | 5.3 | 5.3 | 5.4 | 5.4 | 5.4 | 5.4 | 5.5 | 5.4 | 5.6 | 5.5 | 5.4 | 5.5 | 5.5 | 5.5 | 5.5 | 5.6 | 5.7 | 5.7 | 5.8 | 5.9 |
| 1999 | 5.2 | 5.2 | 5.3 | 5.3 | 5.3 | 5.3 | 5.5 | 5.3 | 5.4 | 5.3 | 5.3 | 5.3 | 5.4 | 5.4 | 5.4 | 5.4 | 5.5 | 5.6 | 5.6 | 5.7 |
| 2000 | 5.3 | 5.3 | 5.3 | 5.4 | 5.4 | 5.4 | 5.5 | 5.4 | 5.5 | 5.4 | 5.4 | 5.4 | 5.5 | 5.5 | 5.5 | 5.6 | 5.6 | 5.7 | 5.8 | 5.8 |
| 2001 | 5.3 | 5.3 | 5.4 | 5.4 | 5.4 | 5.4 | 5.5 | 5.5 | 5.5 | 5.5 | 5.4 | 5.5 | 5.5 | 5.5 | 5.5 | 5.6 | 5.7 | 5.7 | 5.8 | 5.9 |
| 2002 | 5.4 | 5.4 | 5.5 | 5.5 | 5.5 | 5.5 | 5.6 | 5.6 | 5.6 | 5.6 | 5.5 | 5.6 | 5.6 | 5.6 | 5.7 | 5.7 | 5.8 | 5.9 | 5.9 | 6.0 |
| 2003 | 5.4 | 5.4 | 5.4 | 5.5 | 5.5 | 5.4 | 5.6 | 5.5 | 5.6 | 5.5 | 5.5 | 5.5 | 5.6 | 5.6 | 5.6 | 5.6 | 5.7 | 5.8 | 5.8 | 5.9 |
| 2004 | 5.4 | 5.4 | 5.4 | 5.4 | 5.4 | 5.4 | 5.5 | 5.5 | 5.5 | 5.5 | 5.4 | 5.5 | 5.5 | 5.5 | 5.6 | 5.6 | 5.7 | 5.7 | 5.8 | 5.9 |
| 2005 | 5.3 | 5.3 | 5.3 | 5.4 | 5.4 | 5.3 | 5.5 | 5.4 | 5.5 | 5.4 | 5.4 | 5.4 | 5.5 | 5.5 | 5.5 | 5.5 | 5.6 | 5.7 | 5.7 | 5.8 |
| 2006 | 5.3 | 5.3 | 5.3 | 5.3 | 5.3 | 5.3 | 5.4 | 5.4 | 5.4 | 5.4 | 5.4 | 5.4 | 5.4 | 5.4 | 5.4 | 5.4 | 5.6 | 5.6 | 5.6 | 5.7 |
| 2007 | 5.3 | 5.3 | 5.3 | 5.4 | 5.4 | 5.4 | 5.5 | 5.4 | 5.5 | 5.4 | 5.4 | 5.5 | 5.5 | 5.5 | 5.5 | 5.5 | 5.6 | 5.7 | 5.7 | 5.8 |
| 2008 | 5.4 | 5.4 | 5.4 | 5.5 | 5.5 | 5.5 | 5.6 | 5.5 | 5.6 | 5.5 | 5.5 | 5.6 | 5.6 | 5.6 | 5.6 | 5.7 | 5.7 | 5.8 | 5.8 | 5.9 |
| 2009 | 5.3 | 5.3 | 5.3 | 5.4 | 5.4 | 5.4 | 5.5 | 5.4 | 5.5 | 5.4 | 5.4 | 5.4 | 5.5 | 5.5 | 5.5 | 5.5 | 5.6 | 5.7 | 5.7 | 5.8 |
| 2010 | 5.4 | 5.4 | 5.4 | 5.4 | 5.4 | 5.4 | 5.5 | 5.5 | 5.5 | 5.5 | 5.4 | 5.5 | 5.5 | 5.5 | 5.5 | 5.6 | 5.6 | 5.7 | 5.7 | 5.8 |
| 2011 | 5.4 | 5.4 | 5.4 | 5.5 | 5.5 | 5.4 | 5.5 | 5.5 | 5.5 | 5.5 | 5.5 | 5.5 | 5.6 | 5.6 | 5.6 | 5.6 | 5.7 | 5.7 | 5.8 | 5.8 |
| 2012 | 5.3 | 5.3 | 5.3 | 5.4 | 5.4 | 5.4 | 5.5 | 5.4 | 5.4 | 5.4 | 5.4 | 5.5 | 5.5 | 5.5 | 5.5 | 5.6 | 5.6 | 5.7 | 5.7 | 5.8 |
| 2013 | 5.2 | 5.2 | 5.2 | 5.3 | 5.3 | 5.3 | 5.4 | 5.3 | 5.4 | 5.3 | 5.3 | 5.3 | 5.4 | 5.4 | 5.4 | 5.4 | 5.5 | 5.5 | 5.6 | 5.6 |
| 2014 | 5.2 | 5.2 | 5.2 | 5.3 | 5.3 | 5.2 | 5.3 | 5.3 | 5.3 | 5.3 | 5.3 | 5.3 | 5.4 | 5.3 | 5.4 | 5.4 | 5.5 | 5.5 | 5.5 | 5.6 |
| 2015 | 5.2 | 5.2 | 5.2 | 5.2 | 5.2 | 5.2 | 5.3 | 5.3 | 5.3 | 5.3 | 5.2 | 5.3 | 5.3 | 5.3 | 5.3 | 5.3 | 5.4 | 5.5 | 5.5 | 5.5 |
| 2016 | 5.1 | 5.1 | 5.1 | 5.2 | 5.2 | 5.2 | 5.3 | 5.2 | 5.3 | 5.2 | 5.2 | 5.2 | 5.3 | 5.3 | 5.3 | 5.3 | 5.4 | 5.4 | 5.4 | 5.5 |

## Appendix C-5

Intermediate-term Government Bonds: Percent per annum total returns for all historical periods

From 1926 to 2016

| End Date | Start Date 1946 | 1947 | 1948 | 1949 | 1950 | 1951 | 1952 | 1953 | 1954 | 1955 | 1956 | 1957 | 1958 | 1959 | 1960 | 1961 | 1962 | 1963 | 1964 | 1965 |
|---|---|---|---|---|---|---|---|---|---|---|---|---|---|---|---|---|---|---|---|---|
| 1926 | | | | | | | | | | | | | | | | | | | | |
| 1927 | | | | | | | | | | | | | | | | | | | | |
| 1928 | | | | | | | | | | | | | | | | | | | | |
| 1929 | | | | | | | | | | | | | | | | | | | | |
| 1930 | | | | | | | | | | | | | | | | | | | | |
| 1931 | | | | | | | | | | | | | | | | | | | | |
| 1932 | | | | | | | | | | | | | | | | | | | | |
| 1933 | | | | | | | | | | | | | | | | | | | | |
| 1934 | | | | | | | | | | | | | | | | | | | | |
| 1935 | | | | | | | | | | | | | | | | | | | | |
| 1936 | | | | | | | | | | | | | | | | | | | | |
| 1937 | | | | | | | | | | | | | | | | | | | | |
| 1938 | | | | | | | | | | | | | | | | | | | | |
| 1939 | | | | | | | | | | | | | | | | | | | | |
| 1940 | | | | | | | | | | | | | | | | | | | | |
| 1941 | | | | | | | | | | | | | | | | | | | | |
| 1942 | | | | | | | | | | | | | | | | | | | | |
| 1943 | | | | | | | | | | | | | | | | | | | | |
| 1944 | | | | | | | | | | | | | | | | | | | | |
| 1945 | | | | | | | | | | | | | | | | | | | | |
| 1946 | 1.0 | | | | | | | | | | | | | | | | | | | |
| 1947 | 1.0 | 0.9 | | | | | | | | | | | | | | | | | | |
| 1948 | 1.3 | 1.4 | 1.8 | | | | | | | | | | | | | | | | | |
| 1949 | 1.5 | 1.7 | 2.1 | 2.3 | | | | | | | | | | | | | | | | |
| 1950 | 1.4 | 1.4 | 1.6 | 1.5 | 0.7 | | | | | | | | | | | | | | | |
| 1951 | 1.2 | 1.2 | 1.3 | 1.1 | 0.5 | 0.4 | | | | | | | | | | | | | | |
| 1952 | 1.3 | 1.3 | 1.4 | 1.3 | 0.9 | 1.0 | 1.6 | | | | | | | | | | | | | |
| 1953 | 1.5 | 1.6 | 1.7 | 1.6 | 1.5 | 1.7 | 2.4 | 3.2 | | | | | | | | | | | | |
| 1954 | 1.6 | 1.7 | 1.8 | 1.8 | 1.7 | 2.0 | 2.5 | 3.0 | 2.7 | | | | | | | | | | | |
| 1955 | 1.4 | 1.4 | 1.5 | 1.5 | 1.3 | 1.4 | 1.7 | 1.7 | 1.0 | -0.7 | | | | | | | | | | |
| 1956 | 1.2 | 1.3 | 1.3 | 1.2 | 1.1 | 1.1 | 1.3 | 1.2 | 0.5 | -0.5 | -0.4 | | | | | | | | | |
| 1957 | 1.8 | 1.8 | 1.9 | 1.9 | 1.9 | 2.1 | 2.3 | 2.5 | 2.3 | 2.2 | 3.6 | 7.8 | | | | | | | | |
| 1958 | 1.5 | 1.6 | 1.6 | 1.6 | 1.5 | 1.6 | 1.8 | 1.9 | 1.6 | 1.3 | 2.0 | 3.2 | -1.3 | | | | | | | |
| 1959 | 1.4 | 1.4 | 1.5 | 1.4 | 1.3 | 1.4 | 1.5 | 1.5 | 1.2 | 1.0 | 1.4 | 2.0 | -0.8 | -0.4 | | | | | | |
| 1960 | 2.1 | 2.1 | 2.2 | 2.3 | 2.2 | 2.4 | 2.6 | 2.8 | 2.7 | 2.7 | 3.4 | 4.3 | 3.2 | 5.5 | 11.8 | | | | | |
| 1961 | 2.0 | 2.1 | 2.2 | 2.2 | 2.2 | 2.3 | 2.5 | 2.7 | 2.6 | 2.6 | 3.1 | 3.8 | 2.9 | 4.3 | 6.7 | 1.8 | | | | |
| 1962 | 2.2 | 2.3 | 2.4 | 2.5 | 2.5 | 2.6 | 2.8 | 2.9 | 2.9 | 2.9 | 3.5 | 4.1 | 3.4 | 4.6 | 6.3 | 3.7 | 5.6 | | | |
| 1963 | 2.2 | 2.3 | 2.4 | 2.4 | 2.4 | 2.5 | 2.7 | 2.8 | 2.8 | 2.8 | 3.2 | 3.8 | 3.1 | 4.0 | 5.1 | 3.0 | 3.6 | 1.6 | | |
| 1964 | 2.3 | 2.4 | 2.5 | 2.5 | 2.5 | 2.6 | 2.8 | 2.9 | 2.9 | 2.9 | 3.3 | 3.8 | 3.2 | 4.0 | 4.9 | 3.3 | 3.7 | 2.8 | 4.0 | |
| 1965 | 2.2 | 2.3 | 2.4 | 2.4 | 2.4 | 2.5 | 2.7 | 2.7 | 2.7 | 2.7 | 3.1 | 3.5 | 3.0 | 3.6 | 4.2 | 2.8 | 3.1 | 2.8 | 2.5 | 1.0 |
| 1966 | 2.4 | 2.4 | 2.5 | 2.5 | 2.6 | 2.7 | 2.8 | 2.9 | 2.9 | 2.9 | 3.2 | 3.6 | 3.1 | 3.7 | 4.3 | 3.1 | 3.4 | 2.8 | 3.2 | 2.8 |
| 1967 | 2.3 | 2.4 | 2.4 | 2.5 | 2.5 | 2.6 | 2.7 | 2.8 | 2.8 | 2.8 | 3.0 | 3.4 | 2.9 | 3.4 | 3.9 | 2.8 | 3.0 | 2.5 | 2.7 | 2.2 |
| 1968 | 2.4 | 2.5 | 2.5 | 2.6 | 2.6 | 2.7 | 2.8 | 2.9 | 2.9 | 2.9 | 3.2 | 3.5 | 3.1 | 3.5 | 4.0 | 3.0 | 3.2 | 2.8 | 3.0 | 2.8 |
| 1969 | 2.3 | 2.3 | 2.4 | 2.4 | 2.4 | 2.5 | 2.6 | 2.7 | 2.6 | 2.6 | 2.9 | 3.1 | 2.8 | 3.1 | 3.5 | 2.6 | 2.7 | 2.3 | 2.4 | 2.1 |
| 1970 | 2.8 | 2.9 | 3.0 | 3.0 | 3.1 | 3.2 | 3.3 | 3.4 | 3.4 | 3.5 | 3.8 | 4.1 | 3.8 | 4.2 | 4.6 | 3.9 | 4.2 | 4.0 | 4.4 | 4.4 |

**Appendix C-5**

Intermediate-term Government Bonds: Percent per annum total returns for all historical periods

From 1926 to 2016

| End Date | Start Date 1946 | 1947 | 1948 | 1949 | 1950 | 1951 | 1952 | 1953 | 1954 | 1955 | 1956 | 1957 | 1958 | 1959 | 1960 | 1961 | 1962 | 1963 | 1964 | 1965 |
|---|---|---|---|---|---|---|---|---|---|---|---|---|---|---|---|---|---|---|---|---|
| 1971 | 3.0 | 3.1 | 3.2 | 3.3 | 3.3 | 3.4 | 3.6 | 3.7 | 3.7 | 3.8 | 4.1 | 4.4 | 4.1 | 4.5 | 5.0 | 4.4 | 4.6 | 4.5 | 4.9 | 5.0 |
| 1972 | 3.1 | 3.2 | 3.3 | 3.3 | 3.4 | 3.5 | 3.7 | 3.8 | 3.8 | 3.9 | 4.1 | 4.4 | 4.2 | 4.6 | 5.0 | 4.4 | 4.7 | 4.6 | 4.9 | 5.0 |
| 1973 | 3.2 | 3.2 | 3.3 | 3.4 | 3.4 | 3.6 | 3.7 | 3.8 | 3.8 | 3.9 | 4.1 | 4.4 | 4.2 | 4.6 | 5.0 | 4.5 | 4.7 | 4.6 | 4.9 | 5.0 |
| 1974 | 3.2 | 3.3 | 3.4 | 3.5 | 3.5 | 3.6 | 3.8 | 3.9 | 3.9 | 4.0 | 4.2 | 4.5 | 4.3 | 4.7 | 5.0 | 4.5 | 4.7 | 4.7 | 5.0 | 5.1 |
| 1975 | 3.4 | 3.5 | 3.6 | 3.6 | 3.7 | 3.8 | 4.0 | 4.1 | 4.1 | 4.2 | 4.4 | 4.7 | 4.5 | 4.8 | 5.2 | 4.8 | 5.0 | 4.9 | 5.2 | 5.3 |
| 1976 | 3.7 | 3.8 | 3.9 | 4.0 | 4.0 | 4.1 | 4.3 | 4.4 | 4.5 | 4.5 | 4.8 | 5.1 | 4.9 | 5.3 | 5.6 | 5.2 | 5.5 | 5.5 | 5.8 | 5.9 |
| 1977 | 3.6 | 3.7 | 3.8 | 3.9 | 3.9 | 4.0 | 4.2 | 4.3 | 4.3 | 4.5 | 4.6 | 4.9 | 4.7 | 5.1 | 5.4 | 5.0 | 5.2 | 5.2 | 5.5 | 5.6 |
| 1978 | 3.6 | 3.7 | 3.8 | 3.8 | 3.9 | 4.0 | 4.2 | 4.3 | 4.3 | 4.4 | 4.6 | 4.8 | 4.7 | 5.0 | 5.3 | 4.9 | 5.1 | 5.1 | 5.3 | 5.4 |
| 1979 | 3.6 | 3.7 | 3.8 | 3.9 | 3.9 | 4.0 | 4.2 | 4.2 | 4.3 | 4.4 | 4.6 | 4.8 | 4.7 | 4.9 | 5.2 | 4.9 | 5.1 | 5.0 | 5.2 | 5.3 |
| 1980 | 3.6 | 3.7 | 3.8 | 3.9 | 3.9 | 4.0 | 4.1 | 4.2 | 4.3 | 4.3 | 4.5 | 4.8 | 4.6 | 4.9 | 5.2 | 4.8 | 5.0 | 5.0 | 5.2 | 5.2 |
| 1981 | 3.8 | 3.9 | 4.0 | 4.0 | 4.1 | 4.2 | 4.3 | 4.4 | 4.5 | 4.5 | 4.7 | 4.9 | 4.8 | 5.1 | 5.3 | 5.1 | 5.2 | 5.2 | 5.4 | 5.5 |
| 1982 | 4.4 | 4.5 | 4.6 | 4.7 | 4.8 | 4.9 | 5.0 | 5.2 | 5.2 | 5.3 | 5.5 | 5.8 | 5.7 | 6.0 | 6.3 | 6.0 | 6.2 | 6.3 | 6.5 | 6.7 |
| 1983 | 4.5 | 4.6 | 4.7 | 4.8 | 4.8 | 5.0 | 5.1 | 5.2 | 5.3 | 5.4 | 5.6 | 5.8 | 5.8 | 6.1 | 6.3 | 6.1 | 6.3 | 6.3 | 6.6 | 6.7 |
| 1984 | 4.7 | 4.8 | 4.9 | 5.0 | 5.1 | 5.2 | 5.4 | 5.5 | 5.6 | 5.7 | 5.9 | 6.1 | 6.1 | 6.3 | 6.6 | 6.4 | 6.6 | 6.7 | 6.9 | 7.1 |
| 1985 | 5.1 | 5.2 | 5.3 | 5.4 | 5.5 | 5.6 | 5.8 | 5.9 | 6.0 | 6.1 | 6.3 | 6.6 | 6.5 | 6.8 | 7.1 | 6.9 | 7.2 | 7.2 | 7.5 | 7.7 |
| 1986 | 5.3 | 5.4 | 5.5 | 5.6 | 5.7 | 5.9 | 6.0 | 6.2 | 6.3 | 6.4 | 6.6 | 6.9 | 6.8 | 7.1 | 7.4 | 7.2 | 7.5 | 7.5 | 7.8 | 8.0 |
| 1987 | 5.3 | 5.4 | 5.5 | 5.6 | 5.7 | 5.9 | 6.0 | 6.1 | 6.2 | 6.3 | 6.5 | 6.7 | 6.7 | 7.0 | 7.2 | 7.1 | 7.3 | 7.4 | 7.6 | 7.7 |
| 1988 | 5.3 | 5.4 | 5.5 | 5.6 | 5.7 | 5.8 | 6.0 | 6.1 | 6.2 | 6.3 | 6.5 | 6.7 | 6.7 | 6.9 | 7.2 | 7.0 | 7.2 | 7.3 | 7.5 | 7.7 |
| 1989 | 5.5 | 5.6 | 5.7 | 5.8 | 5.9 | 6.0 | 6.1 | 6.3 | 6.4 | 6.5 | 6.7 | 6.9 | 6.9 | 7.1 | 7.4 | 7.3 | 7.5 | 7.5 | 7.8 | 7.9 |
| 1990 | 5.5 | 5.7 | 5.8 | 5.9 | 5.9 | 6.1 | 6.2 | 6.4 | 6.4 | 6.5 | 6.8 | 7.0 | 7.0 | 7.2 | 7.5 | 7.3 | 7.5 | 7.6 | 7.8 | 8.0 |
| 1991 | 5.8 | 5.9 | 6.0 | 6.1 | 6.2 | 6.3 | 6.5 | 6.6 | 6.7 | 6.8 | 7.0 | 7.2 | 7.2 | 7.5 | 7.7 | 7.6 | 7.8 | 7.9 | 8.1 | 8.2 |
| 1992 | 5.8 | 5.9 | 6.0 | 6.1 | 6.2 | 6.3 | 6.5 | 6.6 | 6.7 | 6.8 | 7.0 | 7.2 | 7.2 | 7.5 | 7.7 | 7.6 | 7.7 | 7.8 | 8.1 | 8.2 |
| 1993 | 5.9 | 6.0 | 6.1 | 6.2 | 6.3 | 6.4 | 6.6 | 6.7 | 6.8 | 6.9 | 7.1 | 7.3 | 7.3 | 7.6 | 7.8 | 7.7 | 7.9 | 8.0 | 8.2 | 8.3 |
| 1994 | 5.7 | 5.8 | 5.9 | 5.9 | 6.0 | 6.2 | 6.3 | 6.4 | 6.5 | 6.6 | 6.8 | 7.0 | 6.9 | 7.2 | 7.4 | 7.3 | 7.5 | 7.5 | 7.7 | 7.8 |
| 1995 | 5.9 | 6.0 | 6.1 | 6.2 | 6.3 | 6.4 | 6.5 | 6.6 | 6.7 | 6.8 | 7.0 | 7.2 | 7.1 | 7.4 | 7.7 | 7.5 | 7.7 | 7.8 | 8.0 | 8.1 |
| 1996 | 5.8 | 5.9 | 6.0 | 6.1 | 6.2 | 6.3 | 6.4 | 6.5 | 6.6 | 6.7 | 6.9 | 7.1 | 7.1 | 7.3 | 7.5 | 7.4 | 7.6 | 7.6 | 7.8 | 7.9 |
| 1997 | 5.8 | 5.9 | 6.0 | 6.1 | 6.2 | 6.3 | 6.5 | 6.6 | 6.7 | 6.7 | 6.9 | 7.1 | 7.1 | 7.3 | 7.5 | 7.4 | 7.6 | 7.6 | 7.8 | 7.9 |
| 1998 | 5.9 | 6.0 | 6.1 | 6.2 | 6.3 | 6.4 | 6.5 | 6.7 | 6.7 | 6.8 | 7.0 | 7.2 | 7.2 | 7.4 | 7.6 | 7.5 | 7.6 | 7.7 | 7.9 | 8.0 |
| 1999 | 5.8 | 5.9 | 6.0 | 6.1 | 6.1 | 6.2 | 6.4 | 6.5 | 6.5 | 6.6 | 6.8 | 7.0 | 6.9 | 7.2 | 7.4 | 7.2 | 7.4 | 7.4 | 7.6 | 7.7 |
| 2000 | 5.9 | 6.0 | 6.0 | 6.1 | 6.2 | 6.4 | 6.5 | 6.6 | 6.7 | 6.8 | 6.9 | 7.1 | 7.1 | 7.3 | 7.5 | 7.4 | 7.5 | 7.6 | 7.7 | 7.8 |
| 2001 | 5.9 | 6.0 | 6.1 | 6.2 | 6.3 | 6.4 | 6.5 | 6.6 | 6.7 | 6.8 | 6.9 | 7.1 | 7.1 | 7.3 | 7.5 | 7.4 | 7.5 | 7.6 | 7.7 | 7.8 |
| 2002 | 6.0 | 6.1 | 6.2 | 6.3 | 6.4 | 6.5 | 6.6 | 6.7 | 6.8 | 6.9 | 7.1 | 7.2 | 7.2 | 7.4 | 7.6 | 7.5 | 7.7 | 7.7 | 7.9 | 8.0 |
| 2003 | 5.9 | 6.0 | 6.1 | 6.2 | 6.3 | 6.4 | 6.5 | 6.6 | 6.7 | 6.8 | 7.0 | 7.1 | 7.1 | 7.3 | 7.5 | 7.4 | 7.5 | 7.6 | 7.7 | 7.8 |
| 2004 | 5.9 | 6.0 | 6.1 | 6.2 | 6.2 | 6.3 | 6.5 | 6.6 | 6.6 | 6.7 | 6.9 | 7.0 | 7.0 | 7.2 | 7.4 | 7.3 | 7.4 | 7.4 | 7.6 | 7.7 |
| 2005 | 5.8 | 5.9 | 6.0 | 6.1 | 6.2 | 6.3 | 6.4 | 6.5 | 6.5 | 6.6 | 6.7 | 6.9 | 6.9 | 7.1 | 7.2 | 7.1 | 7.3 | 7.3 | 7.4 | 7.5 |
| 2006 | 5.8 | 5.9 | 6.0 | 6.0 | 6.1 | 6.2 | 6.3 | 6.4 | 6.5 | 6.5 | 6.7 | 6.8 | 6.8 | 7.0 | 7.1 | 7.0 | 7.2 | 7.2 | 7.3 | 7.4 |
| 2007 | 5.9 | 5.9 | 6.0 | 6.1 | 6.2 | 6.3 | 6.4 | 6.5 | 6.5 | 6.6 | 6.7 | 6.9 | 6.9 | 7.0 | 7.2 | 7.1 | 7.2 | 7.3 | 7.4 | 7.5 |
| 2008 | 6.0 | 6.1 | 6.1 | 6.2 | 6.3 | 6.4 | 6.5 | 6.6 | 6.6 | 6.7 | 6.9 | 7.0 | 7.0 | 7.2 | 7.3 | 7.2 | 7.3 | 7.4 | 7.5 | 7.6 |
| 2009 | 5.8 | 5.9 | 6.0 | 6.1 | 6.1 | 6.2 | 6.3 | 6.4 | 6.5 | 6.5 | 6.7 | 6.8 | 6.8 | 7.0 | 7.1 | 7.0 | 7.1 | 7.2 | 7.3 | 7.4 |
| 2010 | 5.9 | 5.9 | 6.0 | 6.1 | 6.1 | 6.2 | 6.3 | 6.4 | 6.5 | 6.6 | 6.7 | 6.8 | 6.8 | 7.0 | 7.1 | 7.0 | 7.1 | 7.2 | 7.3 | 7.4 |
| 2011 | 5.8 | 5.9 | 6.1 | 6.1 | 6.2 | 6.3 | 6.4 | 6.5 | 6.5 | 6.6 | 6.7 | 6.8 | 6.8 | 7.0 | 7.1 | 7.1 | 7.2 | 7.2 | 7.3 | 7.4 |
| 2012 | 5.8 | 5.9 | 6.0 | 6.1 | 6.1 | 6.2 | 6.3 | 6.4 | 6.4 | 6.5 | 6.6 | 6.7 | 6.7 | 6.9 | 7.0 | 7.0 | 7.1 | 7.1 | 7.2 | 7.3 |
| 2013 | 5.7 | 5.8 | 5.8 | 5.9 | 6.0 | 6.0 | 6.1 | 6.2 | 6.3 | 6.3 | 6.4 | 6.5 | 6.5 | 6.7 | 6.8 | 6.8 | 6.9 | 6.9 | 7.0 | 7.0 |
| 2014 | 5.6 | 5.7 | 5.8 | 5.9 | 5.9 | 6.0 | 6.1 | 6.2 | 6.2 | 6.3 | 6.4 | 6.5 | 6.5 | 6.6 | 6.8 | 6.7 | 6.8 | 6.9 | 7.0 | 7.0 |
| 2015 | 5.6 | 5.7 | 5.7 | 5.8 | 5.8 | 5.9 | 6.0 | 6.1 | 6.1 | 6.2 | 6.3 | 6.4 | 6.4 | 6.5 | 6.7 | 6.6 | 6.7 | 6.8 | 6.9 | 6.9 |
| 2016 | 5.5 | 5.6 | 5.7 | 5.7 | 5.8 | 5.9 | 6.0 | 6.0 | 6.1 | 6.1 | 6.2 | 6.4 | 6.3 | 6.5 | 6.6 | 6.5 | 6.6 | 6.6 | 6.7 | 6.7 |

**Appendix C-5**

Intermediate-term Government Bonds: Percent per annum total returns for all historical periods

From 1926 to 2016

# Appendix C-5

Intermediate-term Government Bonds: Percent per annum total returns for all historical periods

From 1926 to 2016

| End Date | Start Date 1966 | 1967 | 1968 | 1969 | 1970 | 1971 | 1972 | 1973 | 1974 | 1975 | 1976 | 1977 | 1978 | 1979 | 1980 | 1981 | 1982 | 1983 | 1984 | 1985 |
|---|---|---|---|---|---|---|---|---|---|---|---|---|---|---|---|---|---|---|---|---|
| 1971 | 5.7 | 5.9 | 7.2 | 8.0 | 12.7 | 8.7 | | | | | | | | | | | | | | |
| 1972 | 5.6 | 5.8 | 6.8 | 7.3 | 10.1 | 6.9 | 5.2 | | | | | | | | | | | | | |
| 1973 | 5.5 | 5.6 | 6.4 | 6.8 | 8.7 | 6.1 | 4.9 | 4.6 | | | | | | | | | | | | |
| 1974 | 5.5 | 5.6 | 6.3 | 6.6 | 8.1 | 6.0 | 5.2 | 5.1 | 5.7 | | | | | | | | | | | |
| 1975 | 5.7 | 5.9 | 6.5 | 6.8 | 8.1 | 6.4 | 5.8 | 6.0 | 6.8 | 7.8 | | | | | | | | | | |
| 1976 | 6.4 | 6.5 | 7.2 | 7.5 | 8.7 | 7.4 | 7.2 | 7.7 | 8.8 | 10.3 | 12.9 | | | | | | | | | |
| 1977 | 5.9 | 6.1 | 6.6 | 6.8 | 7.8 | 6.6 | 6.2 | 6.4 | 6.9 | 7.3 | 7.0 | 1.4 | | | | | | | | |
| 1978 | 5.8 | 5.8 | 6.3 | 6.5 | 7.3 | 6.2 | 5.8 | 5.9 | 6.2 | 6.3 | 5.8 | 2.4 | 3.5 | | | | | | | |
| 1979 | 5.6 | 5.7 | 6.1 | 6.3 | 7.0 | 5.9 | 5.6 | 5.7 | 5.8 | 5.9 | 5.4 | 3.0 | 3.8 | 4.1 | | | | | | |
| 1980 | 5.5 | 5.6 | 5.9 | 6.1 | 6.7 | 5.7 | 5.4 | 5.4 | 5.6 | 5.5 | 5.1 | 3.2 | 3.8 | 4.0 | 3.9 | | | | | |
| 1981 | 5.8 | 5.8 | 6.2 | 6.3 | 6.9 | 6.1 | 5.8 | 5.9 | 6.0 | 6.1 | 5.8 | 4.4 | 5.2 | 5.8 | 6.6 | 9.5 | | | | |
| 1982 | 7.0 | 7.2 | 7.6 | 7.8 | 8.5 | 7.8 | 7.7 | 8.0 | 8.4 | 8.7 | 8.8 | 8.2 | 9.6 | 11.2 | 13.7 | 18.9 | 29.1 | | | |
| 1983 | 7.0 | 7.2 | 7.6 | 7.8 | 8.4 | 7.8 | 7.7 | 7.9 | 8.3 | 8.6 | 8.7 | 8.1 | 9.2 | 10.4 | 12.1 | 14.9 | 17.8 | 7.4 | | |
| 1984 | 7.4 | 7.5 | 7.9 | 8.2 | 8.8 | 8.2 | 8.2 | 8.4 | 8.8 | 9.1 | 9.2 | 8.8 | 9.9 | 11.0 | 12.5 | 14.7 | 16.5 | 10.7 | 14.0 | |
| 1985 | 8.0 | 8.2 | 8.6 | 8.8 | 9.5 | 9.0 | 9.0 | 9.3 | 9.7 | 10.1 | 10.3 | 10.0 | 11.2 | 12.3 | 13.7 | 15.8 | 17.4 | 13.8 | 17.1 | 20.3 |
| 1986 | 8.3 | 8.5 | 8.9 | 9.2 | 9.8 | 9.4 | 9.4 | 9.7 | 10.1 | 10.5 | 10.7 | 10.5 | 11.6 | 12.6 | 13.9 | 15.7 | 17.0 | 14.1 | 16.5 | 17.7 |
| 1987 | 8.1 | 8.2 | 8.6 | 8.8 | 9.4 | 9.0 | 9.0 | 9.2 | 9.6 | 9.9 | 10.1 | 9.8 | 10.7 | 11.5 | 12.5 | 13.8 | 14.5 | 11.8 | 12.9 | 12.5 |
| 1988 | 8.0 | 8.1 | 8.5 | 8.7 | 9.2 | 8.8 | 8.8 | 9.0 | 9.4 | 9.6 | 9.8 | 9.5 | 10.3 | 11.0 | 11.8 | 12.8 | 13.3 | 10.8 | 11.5 | 10.9 |
| 1989 | 8.2 | 8.4 | 8.7 | 8.9 | 9.4 | 9.0 | 9.1 | 9.3 | 9.6 | 9.9 | 10.0 | 9.8 | 10.5 | 11.2 | 11.9 | 12.8 | 13.3 | 11.2 | 11.8 | 11.4 |
| 1990 | 8.3 | 8.4 | 8.8 | 8.9 | 9.4 | 9.1 | 9.1 | 9.3 | 9.6 | 9.8 | 10.0 | 9.8 | 10.5 | 11.1 | 11.7 | 12.5 | 12.9 | 11.0 | 11.5 | 11.1 |
| 1991 | 8.5 | 8.7 | 9.0 | 9.2 | 9.7 | 9.4 | 9.4 | 9.6 | 9.9 | 10.2 | 10.3 | 10.2 | 10.8 | 11.4 | 12.0 | 12.8 | 13.1 | 11.5 | 12.0 | 11.7 |
| 1992 | 8.5 | 8.6 | 9.0 | 9.1 | 9.6 | 9.3 | 9.3 | 9.5 | 9.8 | 10.0 | 10.1 | 10.0 | 10.6 | 11.1 | 11.6 | 12.3 | 12.6 | 11.0 | 11.5 | 11.1 |
| 1993 | 8.6 | 8.7 | 9.0 | 9.2 | 9.7 | 9.4 | 9.4 | 9.6 | 9.8 | 10.1 | 10.2 | 10.0 | 10.6 | 11.1 | 11.6 | 12.2 | 12.5 | 11.1 | 11.4 | 11.1 |
| 1994 | 8.1 | 8.2 | 8.5 | 8.6 | 9.0 | 8.7 | 8.7 | 8.9 | 9.1 | 9.3 | 9.3 | 9.1 | 9.6 | 10.0 | 10.4 | 10.9 | 11.0 | 9.6 | 9.8 | 9.4 |
| 1995 | 8.4 | 8.5 | 8.8 | 8.9 | 9.3 | 9.0 | 9.0 | 9.2 | 9.4 | 9.6 | 9.7 | 9.5 | 10.0 | 10.4 | 10.8 | 11.3 | 11.4 | 10.1 | 10.4 | 10.1 |
| 1996 | 8.2 | 8.3 | 8.5 | 8.7 | 9.0 | 8.7 | 8.7 | 8.9 | 9.1 | 9.2 | 9.3 | 9.1 | 9.6 | 9.9 | 10.3 | 10.7 | 10.8 | 9.6 | 9.7 | 9.4 |
| 1997 | 8.2 | 8.3 | 8.5 | 8.7 | 9.0 | 8.7 | 8.7 | 8.9 | 9.1 | 9.2 | 9.3 | 9.1 | 9.5 | 9.8 | 10.2 | 10.5 | 10.6 | 9.5 | 9.6 | 9.3 |
| 1998 | 8.2 | 8.3 | 8.6 | 8.7 | 9.1 | 8.8 | 8.8 | 8.9 | 9.1 | 9.3 | 9.3 | 9.2 | 9.5 | 9.9 | 10.2 | 10.5 | 10.6 | 9.5 | 9.7 | 9.4 |
| 1999 | 7.9 | 8.0 | 8.2 | 8.4 | 8.7 | 8.4 | 8.4 | 8.5 | 8.7 | 8.8 | 8.8 | 8.7 | 9.0 | 9.3 | 9.5 | 9.8 | 9.9 | 8.8 | 8.9 | 8.6 |
| 2000 | 8.0 | 8.1 | 8.4 | 8.5 | 8.8 | 8.5 | 8.5 | 8.7 | 8.8 | 8.9 | 9.0 | 8.8 | 9.2 | 9.4 | 9.7 | 10.0 | 10.0 | 9.0 | 9.1 | 8.8 |
| 2001 | 8.0 | 8.1 | 8.3 | 8.5 | 8.8 | 8.5 | 8.5 | 8.6 | 8.8 | 8.9 | 8.9 | 8.8 | 9.1 | 9.3 | 9.6 | 9.9 | 9.9 | 9.0 | 9.0 | 8.8 |
| 2002 | 8.2 | 8.3 | 8.5 | 8.6 | 8.9 | 8.6 | 8.6 | 8.8 | 8.9 | 9.0 | 9.1 | 8.9 | 9.2 | 9.5 | 9.7 | 10.0 | 10.0 | 9.1 | 9.2 | 9.0 |
| 2003 | 8.0 | 8.1 | 8.3 | 8.4 | 8.7 | 8.5 | 8.4 | 8.6 | 8.7 | 8.8 | 8.8 | 8.7 | 9.0 | 9.2 | 9.4 | 9.7 | 9.7 | 8.8 | 8.9 | 8.6 |
| 2004 | 7.9 | 7.9 | 8.1 | 8.2 | 8.5 | 8.3 | 8.3 | 8.3 | 8.5 | 8.6 | 8.6 | 8.4 | 8.7 | 8.9 | 9.1 | 9.3 | 9.3 | 8.5 | 8.6 | 8.3 |
| 2005 | 7.7 | 7.8 | 7.9 | 8.0 | 8.3 | 8.1 | 8.0 | 8.1 | 8.2 | 8.3 | 8.3 | 8.2 | 8.4 | 8.6 | 8.8 | 9.0 | 9.0 | 8.2 | 8.2 | 8.0 |
| 2006 | 7.6 | 7.6 | 7.8 | 7.9 | 8.2 | 7.9 | 7.9 | 8.0 | 8.1 | 8.2 | 8.2 | 8.0 | 8.3 | 8.4 | 8.6 | 8.8 | 8.7 | 8.0 | 8.0 | 7.7 |
| 2007 | 7.6 | 7.7 | 7.9 | 8.0 | 8.2 | 8.0 | 8.0 | 8.0 | 8.1 | 8.2 | 8.2 | 8.1 | 8.3 | 8.5 | 8.6 | 8.8 | 8.8 | 8.1 | 8.1 | 7.8 |
| 2008 | 7.8 | 7.8 | 8.0 | 8.1 | 8.3 | 8.1 | 8.1 | 8.2 | 8.3 | 8.4 | 8.4 | 8.2 | 8.5 | 8.6 | 8.8 | 9.0 | 9.0 | 8.2 | 8.3 | 8.0 |
| 2009 | 7.5 | 7.6 | 7.7 | 7.8 | 8.0 | 7.8 | 7.8 | 7.9 | 8.0 | 8.0 | 8.0 | 7.9 | 8.1 | 8.3 | 8.4 | 8.6 | 8.5 | 7.8 | 7.8 | 7.6 |
| 2010 | 7.5 | 7.6 | 7.7 | 7.8 | 8.0 | 7.8 | 7.8 | 7.9 | 7.9 | 8.0 | 8.0 | 7.9 | 8.1 | 8.2 | 8.4 | 8.5 | 8.5 | 7.8 | 7.8 | 7.6 |
| 2011 | 7.5 | 7.6 | 7.8 | 7.8 | 8.0 | 7.8 | 7.8 | 8.0 | 8.0 | 8.0 | 8.0 | 7.9 | 8.1 | 8.2 | 8.4 | 8.5 | 8.5 | 7.8 | 7.9 | 7.6 |
| 2012 | 7.4 | 7.5 | 7.6 | 7.7 | 7.9 | 7.7 | 7.7 | 7.8 | 7.8 | 7.9 | 7.9 | 7.7 | 7.9 | 8.0 | 8.2 | 8.3 | 8.3 | 7.6 | 7.6 | 7.4 |
| 2013 | 7.2 | 7.2 | 7.4 | 7.4 | 7.6 | 7.4 | 7.4 | 7.5 | 7.5 | 7.5 | 7.5 | 7.4 | 7.6 | 7.7 | 7.8 | 7.9 | 7.9 | 7.2 | 7.2 | 7.0 |
| 2014 | 7.1 | 7.1 | 7.3 | 7.3 | 7.5 | 7.3 | 7.3 | 7.4 | 7.4 | 7.4 | 7.4 | 7.3 | 7.4 | 7.6 | 7.7 | 7.8 | 7.7 | 7.1 | 7.1 | 6.9 |
| 2015 | 7.0 | 7.0 | 7.1 | 7.2 | 7.4 | 7.2 | 7.1 | 7.2 | 7.2 | 7.3 | 7.3 | 7.1 | 7.3 | 7.4 | 7.5 | 7.6 | 7.5 | 6.9 | 6.9 | 6.7 |
| 2016 | 6.9 | 6.9 | 7.0 | 7.1 | 7.3 | 7.1 | 7.0 | 7.1 | 7.1 | 7.2 | 7.1 | 7.0 | 7.1 | 7.2 | 7.3 | 7.4 | 7.4 | 6.8 | 6.8 | 6.6 |

## Appendix C-5

Intermediate-term Government Bonds: Percent per annum total returns for all historical periods

From 1926 to 2016

| End Date | Start Date 1986 | 1987 | 1988 | 1989 | 1990 | 1991 | 1992 | 1993 | 1994 | 1995 | 1996 | 1997 | 1998 | 1999 | 2000 | 2001 | 2002 | 2003 | 2004 | 2005 |
|---|---|---|---|---|---|---|---|---|---|---|---|---|---|---|---|---|---|---|---|---|
| 1971 | | | | | | | | | | | | | | | | | | | | |
| 1972 | | | | | | | | | | | | | | | | | | | | |
| 1973 | | | | | | | | | | | | | | | | | | | | |
| 1974 | | | | | | | | | | | | | | | | | | | | |
| 1975 | | | | | | | | | | | | | | | | | | | | |
| 1976 | | | | | | | | | | | | | | | | | | | | |
| 1977 | | | | | | | | | | | | | | | | | | | | |
| 1978 | | | | | | | | | | | | | | | | | | | | |
| 1979 | | | | | | | | | | | | | | | | | | | | |
| 1980 | | | | | | | | | | | | | | | | | | | | |
| 1981 | | | | | | | | | | | | | | | | | | | | |
| 1982 | | | | | | | | | | | | | | | | | | | | |
| 1983 | | | | | | | | | | | | | | | | | | | | |
| 1984 | | | | | | | | | | | | | | | | | | | | |
| 1985 | | | | | | | | | | | | | | | | | | | | |
| 1986 | 15.1 | | | | | | | | | | | | | | | | | | | |
| 1987 | 8.8 | 2.9 | | | | | | | | | | | | | | | | | | |
| 1988 | 7.9 | 4.5 | 6.1 | | | | | | | | | | | | | | | | | |
| 1989 | 9.2 | 7.3 | 9.6 | 13.3 | | | | | | | | | | | | | | | | |
| 1990 | 9.3 | 7.9 | 9.7 | 11.5 | 9.7 | | | | | | | | | | | | | | | |
| 1991 | 10.3 | 9.4 | 11.1 | 12.8 | 12.6 | 15.5 | | | | | | | | | | | | | | |
| 1992 | 9.9 | 9.0 | 10.3 | 11.4 | 10.7 | 11.2 | 7.2 | | | | | | | | | | | | | |
| 1993 | 10.1 | 9.3 | 10.5 | 11.3 | 10.9 | 11.2 | 9.2 | 11.2 | | | | | | | | | | | | |
| 1994 | 8.2 | 7.4 | 8.1 | 8.4 | 7.5 | 6.9 | 4.2 | 2.7 | -5.1 | | | | | | | | | | | |
| 1995 | 9.1 | 8.4 | 9.1 | 9.6 | 9.0 | 8.8 | 7.2 | 7.2 | 5.3 | 16.8 | | | | | | | | | | |
| 1996 | 8.4 | 7.8 | 8.3 | 8.6 | 8.0 | 7.7 | 6.2 | 5.9 | 4.2 | 9.2 | 2.1 | | | | | | | | | |
| 1997 | 8.4 | 7.8 | 8.3 | 8.6 | 8.0 | 7.8 | 6.5 | 6.4 | 5.2 | 8.9 | 5.2 | 8.4 | | | | | | | | |
| 1998 | 8.6 | 8.0 | 8.5 | 8.7 | 8.3 | 8.1 | 7.1 | 7.0 | 6.2 | 9.2 | 6.8 | 9.3 | 10.2 | | | | | | | |
| 1999 | 7.8 | 7.2 | 7.6 | 7.7 | 7.2 | 6.9 | 5.9 | 5.7 | 4.8 | 6.9 | 4.6 | 5.5 | 4.0 | -1.8 | | | | | | |
| 2000 | 8.1 | 7.6 | 8.0 | 8.1 | 7.7 | 7.5 | 6.6 | 6.6 | 5.9 | 7.9 | 6.2 | 7.2 | 6.8 | 5.2 | 12.6 | | | | | |
| 2001 | 8.1 | 7.6 | 8.0 | 8.1 | 7.7 | 7.5 | 6.7 | 6.7 | 6.1 | 7.8 | 6.4 | 7.3 | 7.0 | 6.0 | 10.1 | 7.6 | | | | |
| 2002 | 8.3 | 7.9 | 8.3 | 8.4 | 8.1 | 7.9 | 7.3 | 7.3 | 6.9 | 8.5 | 7.3 | 8.2 | 8.2 | 7.7 | 11.0 | 10.2 | 12.9 | | | |
| 2003 | 8.0 | 7.6 | 7.9 | 8.0 | 7.7 | 7.5 | 6.9 | 6.8 | 6.4 | 7.8 | 6.7 | 7.4 | 7.2 | 6.6 | 8.8 | 7.6 | 7.5 | 2.4 | | |
| 2004 | 7.7 | 7.3 | 7.6 | 7.7 | 7.3 | 7.1 | 6.5 | 6.4 | 6.0 | 7.2 | 6.2 | 6.7 | 6.5 | 5.9 | 7.5 | 6.2 | 5.7 | 2.3 | 2.3 | |
| 2005 | 7.4 | 7.0 | 7.2 | 7.3 | 6.9 | 6.7 | 6.1 | 6.0 | 5.6 | 6.7 | 5.7 | 6.1 | 5.8 | 5.2 | 6.4 | 5.2 | 4.6 | 2.3 | 1.8 | 1.4 |
| 2006 | 7.2 | 6.8 | 7.0 | 7.0 | 6.7 | 6.5 | 5.9 | 5.8 | 5.4 | 6.4 | 5.5 | 5.8 | 5.5 | 4.9 | 5.9 | 4.9 | 4.3 | 2.3 | 2.3 | 2.2 |
| 2007 | 7.3 | 6.9 | 7.1 | 7.2 | 6.9 | 6.7 | 6.1 | 6.2 | 5.8 | 6.6 | 5.8 | 6.2 | 6.0 | 5.5 | 6.4 | 5.6 | 5.3 | 3.8 | 4.1 | 4.8 |
| 2008 | 7.5 | 7.2 | 7.4 | 7.5 | 7.2 | 7.0 | 6.6 | 6.5 | 6.2 | 7.1 | 6.4 | 6.7 | 6.6 | 6.2 | 7.2 | 6.5 | 6.4 | 5.3 | 5.9 | 6.8 |
| 2009 | 7.1 | 6.8 | 7.0 | 7.0 | 6.7 | 6.5 | 6.1 | 6.0 | 5.7 | 6.4 | 5.7 | 6.0 | 5.8 | 5.4 | 6.2 | 5.5 | 5.2 | 4.2 | 4.5 | 4.9 |
| 2010 | 7.1 | 6.8 | 7.0 | 7.0 | 6.7 | 6.6 | 6.1 | 6.0 | 5.8 | 6.5 | 5.8 | 6.1 | 5.9 | 5.6 | 6.3 | 5.6 | 5.4 | 4.5 | 4.8 | 5.3 |
| 2011 | 7.2 | 6.9 | 7.1 | 7.1 | 6.8 | 6.7 | 6.2 | 6.2 | 5.9 | 6.6 | 6.0 | 6.3 | 6.1 | 5.8 | 6.5 | 5.9 | 5.8 | 5.0 | 5.3 | 5.8 |
| 2012 | 7.0 | 6.7 | 6.8 | 6.8 | 6.6 | 6.4 | 6.0 | 6.0 | 5.7 | 6.3 | 5.7 | 6.0 | 5.8 | 5.5 | 6.1 | 5.6 | 5.4 | 4.7 | 4.9 | 5.2 |
| 2013 | 6.6 | 6.3 | 6.4 | 6.4 | 6.1 | 6.0 | 5.6 | 5.5 | 5.2 | 5.8 | 5.2 | 5.4 | 5.2 | 4.9 | 5.4 | 4.8 | 4.6 | 3.9 | 4.0 | 4.2 |
| 2014 | 6.4 | 6.1 | 6.3 | 6.3 | 6.0 | 5.8 | 5.4 | 5.4 | 5.1 | 5.6 | 5.1 | 5.2 | 5.1 | 4.8 | 5.2 | 4.7 | 4.5 | 3.8 | 3.9 | 4.1 |
| 2015 | 6.3 | 6.0 | 6.1 | 6.1 | 5.8 | 5.7 | 5.3 | 5.2 | 4.9 | 5.4 | 4.9 | 5.1 | 4.9 | 4.6 | 5.0 | 4.5 | 4.3 | 3.6 | 3.7 | 3.9 |
| 2016 | 6.1 | 5.8 | 6.0 | 5.9 | 5.7 | 5.5 | 5.2 | 5.1 | 4.8 | 5.3 | 4.8 | 4.9 | 4.7 | 4.4 | 4.8 | 4.3 | 4.1 | 3.5 | 3.6 | 3.7 |

## Appendix C-5

Intermediate-term Government Bonds: Percent per annum total returns for all historical periods

From 1926 to 2016

| End Date | Start Date 2006 | 2007 | 2008 | 2009 | 2010 | 2011 | 2012 | 2013 | 2014 | 2015 | 2016 |
|---|---|---|---|---|---|---|---|---|---|---|---|
| 1971 | | | | | | | | | | | |
| 1972 | | | | | | | | | | | |
| 1973 | | | | | | | | | | | |
| 1974 | | | | | | | | | | | |
| 1975 | | | | | | | | | | | |
| 1976 | | | | | | | | | | | |
| 1977 | | | | | | | | | | | |
| 1978 | | | | | | | | | | | |
| 1979 | | | | | | | | | | | |
| 1980 | | | | | | | | | | | |
| 1981 | | | | | | | | | | | |
| 1982 | | | | | | | | | | | |
| 1983 | | | | | | | | | | | |
| 1984 | | | | | | | | | | | |
| 1985 | | | | | | | | | | | |
| 1986 | | | | | | | | | | | |
| 1987 | | | | | | | | | | | |
| 1988 | | | | | | | | | | | |
| 1989 | | | | | | | | | | | |
| 1990 | | | | | | | | | | | |
| 1991 | | | | | | | | | | | |
| 1992 | | | | | | | | | | | |
| 1993 | | | | | | | | | | | |
| 1994 | | | | | | | | | | | |
| 1995 | | | | | | | | | | | |
| 1996 | | | | | | | | | | | |
| 1997 | | | | | | | | | | | |
| 1998 | | | | | | | | | | | |
| 1999 | | | | | | | | | | | |
| 2000 | | | | | | | | | | | |
| 2001 | | | | | | | | | | | |
| 2002 | | | | | | | | | | | |
| 2003 | | | | | | | | | | | |
| 2004 | | | | | | | | | | | |
| 2005 | | | | | | | | | | | |
| 2006 | 3.1 | | | | | | | | | | |
| 2007 | 6.5 | 10.1 | | | | | | | | | |
| 2008 | 8.7 | 11.6 | 13.1 | | | | | | | | |
| 2009 | 5.8 | 6.7 | 5.1 | -2.4 | | | | | | | |
| 2010 | 6.1 | 6.8 | 5.7 | 2.2 | 7.1 | | | | | | |
| 2011 | 6.5 | 7.2 | 6.5 | 4.4 | 8.0 | 8.8 | | | | | |
| 2012 | 5.8 | 6.3 | 5.5 | 3.7 | 5.8 | 5.2 | 1.7 | | | | |
| 2013 | 4.6 | 4.8 | 3.9 | 2.2 | 3.4 | 2.1 | -1.0 | -3.7 | | | |
| 2014 | 4.4 | 4.6 | 3.8 | 2.3 | 3.3 | 2.4 | 0.3 | -0.4 | 3.0 | | |
| 2015 | 4.1 | 4.2 | 3.5 | 2.2 | 3.0 | 2.2 | 0.7 | 0.3 | 2.4 | 1.8 | |
| 2016 | 3.9 | 4.0 | 3.4 | 2.2 | 2.9 | 2.2 | 0.9 | 0.7 | 2.2 | 1.9 | 1.9 |

# Appendix C-6

U.S. Treasury Bills: Percent per annum total returns for all historical periods

From 1926 to 2016

| End Date | Start Date 1926 | 1927 | 1928 | 1929 | 1930 | 1931 | 1932 | 1933 | 1934 | 1935 | 1936 | 1937 | 1938 | 1939 | 1940 | 1941 | 1942 | 1943 | 1944 | 1945 |
|---|---|---|---|---|---|---|---|---|---|---|---|---|---|---|---|---|---|---|---|---|
| 1926 | 3.3 | | | | | | | | | | | | | | | | | | | |
| 1927 | 3.2 | 3.1 | | | | | | | | | | | | | | | | | | |
| 1928 | 3.3 | 3.3 | 3.6 | | | | | | | | | | | | | | | | | |
| 1929 | 3.7 | 3.8 | 3.8 | 4.7 | | | | | | | | | | | | | | | | |
| 1930 | 3.4 | 3.5 | 3.6 | 3.6 | 2.4 | | | | | | | | | | | | | | | |
| 1931 | 3.0 | 3.0 | 2.9 | 2.7 | 1.7 | 1.1 | | | | | | | | | | | | | | |
| 1932 | 2.7 | 2.6 | 2.5 | 2.3 | 1.5 | 1.0 | 1.0 | | | | | | | | | | | | | |
| 1933 | 2.4 | 2.3 | 2.2 | 1.9 | 1.2 | 0.8 | 0.6 | 0.3 | | | | | | | | | | | | |
| 1934 | 2.2 | 2.0 | 1.9 | 1.6 | 1.0 | 0.6 | 0.5 | 0.2 | 0.2 | | | | | | | | | | | |
| 1935 | 2.0 | 1.8 | 1.7 | 1.4 | 0.8 | 0.5 | 0.4 | 0.2 | 0.2 | 0.2 | | | | | | | | | | |
| 1936 | 1.8 | 1.7 | 1.5 | 1.2 | 0.7 | 0.5 | 0.4 | 0.2 | 0.2 | 0.2 | 0.2 | | | | | | | | | |
| 1937 | 1.7 | 1.5 | 1.4 | 1.1 | 0.7 | 0.4 | 0.3 | 0.2 | 0.2 | 0.2 | 0.2 | 0.3 | | | | | | | | |
| 1938 | 1.5 | 1.4 | 1.2 | 1.0 | 0.6 | 0.4 | 0.3 | 0.2 | 0.2 | 0.2 | 0.2 | 0.1 | 0.0 | | | | | | | |
| 1939 | 1.4 | 1.3 | 1.1 | 0.9 | 0.5 | 0.3 | 0.3 | 0.2 | 0.1 | 0.1 | 0.1 | 0.1 | 0.0 | 0.0 | | | | | | |
| 1940 | 1.3 | 1.2 | 1.1 | 0.8 | 0.5 | 0.3 | 0.2 | 0.2 | 0.1 | 0.1 | 0.1 | 0.1 | 0.0 | 0.0 | 0.0 | | | | | |
| 1941 | 1.2 | 1.1 | 1.0 | 0.8 | 0.5 | 0.3 | 0.2 | 0.2 | 0.1 | 0.1 | 0.2 | 0.1 | 0.1 | 0.1 | 0.1 | 0.1 | | | | |
| 1942 | 1.2 | 1.1 | 0.9 | 0.7 | 0.5 | 0.3 | 0.2 | 0.2 | 0.1 | 0.1 | 0.2 | 0.2 | 0.1 | 0.1 | 0.1 | 0.3 | 0.3 | | | |
| 1943 | 1.1 | 1.0 | 0.9 | 0.7 | 0.4 | 0.3 | 0.2 | 0.2 | 0.1 | 0.1 | 0.2 | 0.2 | 0.1 | 0.1 | 0.1 | 0.3 | 0.3 | 0.3 | | |
| 1944 | 1.1 | 1.0 | 0.9 | 0.7 | 0.4 | 0.3 | 0.2 | 0.2 | 0.1 | 0.1 | 0.2 | 0.2 | 0.2 | 0.1 | 0.2 | 0.3 | 0.3 | 0.3 | 0.3 | |
| 1945 | 1.1 | 1.0 | 0.8 | 0.7 | 0.4 | 0.3 | 0.2 | 0.2 | 0.1 | 0.1 | 0.2 | 0.2 | 0.2 | 0.2 | 0.2 | 0.3 | 0.3 | 0.3 | 0.4 | 0.3 |
| 1946 | 1.0 | 0.9 | 0.8 | 0.7 | 0.4 | 0.3 | 0.3 | 0.2 | 0.2 | 0.2 | 0.2 | 0.2 | 0.2 | 0.2 | 0.2 | 0.3 | 0.3 | 0.3 | 0.4 | 0.3 |
| 1947 | 1.0 | 0.9 | 0.8 | 0.7 | 0.4 | 0.3 | 0.3 | 0.2 | 0.2 | 0.2 | 0.2 | 0.2 | 0.2 | 0.2 | 0.3 | 0.3 | 0.4 | 0.4 | 0.5 | 0.4 |
| 1948 | 1.0 | 0.9 | 0.8 | 0.7 | 0.4 | 0.3 | 0.3 | 0.3 | 0.2 | 0.3 | 0.3 | 0.3 | 0.3 | 0.3 | 0.3 | 0.4 | 0.4 | 0.4 | 0.5 | 0.5 |
| 1949 | 1.0 | 0.9 | 0.8 | 0.7 | 0.5 | 0.4 | 0.3 | 0.3 | 0.3 | 0.3 | 0.3 | 0.3 | 0.3 | 0.4 | 0.4 | 0.5 | 0.5 | 0.5 | 0.6 | 0.6 |
| 1950 | 1.0 | 0.9 | 0.8 | 0.7 | 0.5 | 0.4 | 0.4 | 0.4 | 0.3 | 0.4 | 0.4 | 0.4 | 0.4 | 0.4 | 0.5 | 0.5 | 0.6 | 0.6 | 0.7 | 0.7 |
| 1951 | 1.0 | 0.9 | 0.9 | 0.7 | 0.6 | 0.5 | 0.4 | 0.4 | 0.4 | 0.4 | 0.5 | 0.5 | 0.5 | 0.5 | 0.6 | 0.6 | 0.7 | 0.7 | 0.8 | 0.8 |
| 1952 | 1.1 | 1.0 | 0.9 | 0.8 | 0.6 | 0.5 | 0.5 | 0.5 | 0.5 | 0.5 | 0.5 | 0.5 | 0.6 | 0.6 | 0.6 | 0.7 | 0.7 | 0.8 | 0.8 | 0.9 |
| 1953 | 1.1 | 1.0 | 0.9 | 0.8 | 0.7 | 0.6 | 0.6 | 0.5 | 0.5 | 0.5 | 0.6 | 0.6 | 0.6 | 0.6 | 0.7 | 0.7 | 0.8 | 0.8 | 0.9 | 1.0 |
| 1954 | 1.1 | 1.0 | 0.9 | 0.8 | 0.7 | 0.6 | 0.6 | 0.6 | 0.6 | 0.6 | 0.6 | 0.6 | 0.6 | 0.7 | 0.7 | 0.8 | 0.8 | 0.9 | 0.9 | 1.0 |
| 1955 | 1.1 | 1.0 | 0.9 | 0.8 | 0.7 | 0.6 | 0.6 | 0.6 | 0.6 | 0.6 | 0.7 | 0.7 | 0.7 | 0.7 | 0.8 | 0.8 | 0.9 | 1.0 | 1.0 | 1.1 |
| 1956 | 1.1 | 1.1 | 1.0 | 0.9 | 0.8 | 0.7 | 0.7 | 0.7 | 0.7 | 0.7 | 0.7 | 0.8 | 0.8 | 0.8 | 0.9 | 0.9 | 1.0 | 1.1 | 1.1 | 1.2 |
| 1957 | 1.2 | 1.1 | 1.1 | 1.0 | 0.8 | 0.8 | 0.8 | 0.8 | 0.8 | 0.8 | 0.9 | 0.9 | 0.9 | 1.0 | 1.0 | 1.1 | 1.1 | 1.2 | 1.3 | 1.3 |
| 1958 | 1.2 | 1.1 | 1.1 | 1.0 | 0.9 | 0.8 | 0.8 | 0.8 | 0.8 | 0.9 | 0.9 | 0.9 | 0.9 | 1.0 | 1.0 | 1.1 | 1.2 | 1.2 | 1.3 | 1.3 |
| 1959 | 1.3 | 1.2 | 1.1 | 1.1 | 0.9 | 0.9 | 0.9 | 0.9 | 0.9 | 0.9 | 1.0 | 1.0 | 1.0 | 1.1 | 1.1 | 1.2 | 1.3 | 1.3 | 1.4 | 1.4 |
| 1960 | 1.3 | 1.2 | 1.2 | 1.1 | 1.0 | 1.0 | 0.9 | 0.9 | 1.0 | 1.0 | 1.0 | 1.1 | 1.1 | 1.1 | 1.2 | 1.3 | 1.3 | 1.4 | 1.5 | 1.5 |
| 1961 | 1.3 | 1.3 | 1.2 | 1.1 | 1.0 | 1.0 | 1.0 | 1.0 | 1.0 | 1.0 | 1.1 | 1.1 | 1.1 | 1.2 | 1.3 | 1.4 | 1.4 | 1.5 | 1.5 | 1.6 |
| 1962 | 1.4 | 1.3 | 1.3 | 1.2 | 1.1 | 1.0 | 1.0 | 1.0 | 1.1 | 1.1 | 1.1 | 1.2 | 1.2 | 1.3 | 1.3 | 1.4 | 1.4 | 1.5 | 1.6 | 1.6 |
| 1963 | 1.4 | 1.4 | 1.3 | 1.2 | 1.1 | 1.1 | 1.1 | 1.1 | 1.1 | 1.2 | 1.2 | 1.2 | 1.3 | 1.3 | 1.4 | 1.5 | 1.5 | 1.6 | 1.6 | 1.7 |
| 1964 | 1.5 | 1.4 | 1.4 | 1.3 | 1.2 | 1.1 | 1.1 | 1.1 | 1.2 | 1.2 | 1.3 | 1.3 | 1.3 | 1.4 | 1.5 | 1.6 | 1.6 | 1.7 | 1.7 | 1.8 |
| 1965 | 1.5 | 1.5 | 1.4 | 1.4 | 1.3 | 1.2 | 1.2 | 1.2 | 1.3 | 1.3 | 1.4 | 1.4 | 1.5 | 1.5 | 1.6 | 1.7 | 1.7 | 1.8 | 1.8 | 1.9 |
| 1966 | 1.6 | 1.6 | 1.5 | 1.5 | 1.4 | 1.3 | 1.3 | 1.4 | 1.4 | 1.4 | 1.5 | 1.5 | 1.6 | 1.6 | 1.7 | 1.7 | 1.8 | 1.9 | 1.9 | 2.0 |
| 1967 | 1.7 | 1.6 | 1.6 | 1.5 | 1.5 | 1.4 | 1.4 | 1.4 | 1.5 | 1.5 | 1.6 | 1.6 | 1.7 | 1.7 | 1.8 | 1.8 | 1.9 | 2.0 | 2.0 | 2.1 |
| 1968 | 1.7 | 1.7 | 1.7 | 1.6 | 1.5 | 1.5 | 1.4 | 1.6 | 1.6 | 1.6 | 1.7 | 1.7 | 1.8 | 1.8 | 1.9 | 2.0 | 2.0 | 2.1 | 2.2 | 2.2 |
| 1969 | 1.8 | 1.8 | 1.8 | 1.7 | 1.7 | 1.6 | 1.5 | 1.7 | 1.7 | 1.8 | 1.8 | 1.9 | 1.9 | 2.0 | 2.0 | 2.1 | 2.2 | 2.3 | 2.3 | 2.4 |
| 1970 | 2.0 | 1.9 | 1.9 | 1.9 | 1.8 | 1.8 | 1.8 | 1.8 | 1.8 | 1.9 | 1.9 | 2.0 | 2.1 | 2.1 | 2.2 | 2.3 | 2.3 | 2.4 | 2.5 | 2.6 |

# Appendix C-6

U.S. Treasury Bills: Percent per annum total returns for all historical periods

From 1926 to 2016

| End Date | Start Date 1926 | 1927 | 1928 | 1929 | 1930 | 1931 | 1932 | 1933 | 1934 | 1935 | 1936 | 1937 | 1938 | 1939 | 1940 | 1941 | 1942 | 1943 | 1944 | 1945 |
|---|---|---|---|---|---|---|---|---|---|---|---|---|---|---|---|---|---|---|---|---|
| 1971 | 2.0 | 2.0 | 1.9 | 1.9 | 1.8 | 1.8 | 1.9 | 1.9 | 1.9 | 2.0 | 2.0 | 2.1 | 2.1 | 2.2 | 2.3 | 2.3 | 2.4 | 2.5 | 2.6 | 2.6 |
| 1972 | 2.0 | 2.0 | 2.0 | 2.0 | 1.9 | 1.9 | 1.9 | 1.9 | 2.0 | 2.0 | 2.1 | 2.1 | 2.2 | 2.2 | 2.3 | 2.4 | 2.4 | 2.5 | 2.6 | 2.7 |
| 1973 | 2.1 | 2.1 | 2.1 | 2.1 | 2.0 | 2.0 | 2.0 | 2.0 | 2.1 | 2.1 | 2.2 | 2.2 | 2.3 | 2.4 | 2.4 | 2.5 | 2.6 | 2.7 | 2.7 | 2.8 |
| 1974 | 2.3 | 2.2 | 2.2 | 2.2 | 2.1 | 2.1 | 2.2 | 2.2 | 2.2 | 2.3 | 2.3 | 2.4 | 2.4 | 2.5 | 2.6 | 2.7 | 2.7 | 2.8 | 2.9 | 3.0 |
| 1975 | 2.3 | 2.3 | 2.3 | 2.3 | 2.2 | 2.2 | 2.2 | 2.3 | 2.3 | 2.4 | 2.4 | 2.5 | 2.5 | 2.6 | 2.7 | 2.8 | 2.8 | 2.9 | 3.0 | 3.1 |
| 1976 | 2.4 | 2.4 | 2.3 | 2.3 | 2.3 | 2.3 | 2.3 | 2.3 | 2.4 | 2.4 | 2.5 | 2.5 | 2.6 | 2.7 | 2.7 | 2.8 | 2.9 | 3.0 | 3.1 | 3.1 |
| 1977 | 2.4 | 2.4 | 2.4 | 2.4 | 2.3 | 2.3 | 2.4 | 2.4 | 2.4 | 2.5 | 2.5 | 2.6 | 2.7 | 2.7 | 2.8 | 2.9 | 3.0 | 3.0 | 3.1 | 3.2 |
| 1978 | 2.5 | 2.5 | 2.5 | 2.5 | 2.4 | 2.4 | 2.5 | 2.5 | 2.5 | 2.6 | 2.6 | 2.7 | 2.8 | 2.8 | 2.9 | 3.0 | 3.1 | 3.1 | 3.2 | 3.3 |
| 1979 | 2.7 | 2.6 | 2.6 | 2.6 | 2.6 | 2.6 | 2.6 | 2.7 | 2.7 | 2.8 | 2.8 | 2.9 | 2.9 | 3.0 | 3.1 | 3.2 | 3.3 | 3.3 | 3.4 | 3.5 |
| 1980 | 2.8 | 2.8 | 2.8 | 2.8 | 2.7 | 2.7 | 2.8 | 2.8 | 2.9 | 2.9 | 3.0 | 3.1 | 3.1 | 3.2 | 3.3 | 3.4 | 3.5 | 3.5 | 3.6 | 3.7 |
| 1981 | 3.0 | 3.0 | 3.0 | 3.0 | 3.0 | 3.0 | 3.0 | 3.1 | 3.1 | 3.2 | 3.2 | 3.3 | 3.4 | 3.5 | 3.5 | 3.6 | 3.7 | 3.8 | 3.9 | 4.0 |
| 1982 | 3.1 | 3.1 | 3.1 | 3.1 | 3.1 | 3.1 | 3.2 | 3.2 | 3.3 | 3.3 | 3.4 | 3.5 | 3.5 | 3.6 | 3.7 | 3.8 | 3.9 | 4.0 | 4.1 | 4.2 |
| 1983 | 3.2 | 3.2 | 3.2 | 3.2 | 3.2 | 3.2 | 3.3 | 3.3 | 3.4 | 3.4 | 3.5 | 3.6 | 3.6 | 3.7 | 3.8 | 3.9 | 4.0 | 4.1 | 4.2 | 4.3 |
| 1984 | 3.3 | 3.3 | 3.3 | 3.3 | 3.3 | 3.3 | 3.4 | 3.4 | 3.5 | 3.6 | 3.6 | 3.7 | 3.8 | 3.9 | 3.9 | 4.0 | 4.1 | 4.2 | 4.3 | 4.4 |
| 1985 | 3.4 | 3.4 | 3.4 | 3.4 | 3.4 | 3.4 | 3.5 | 3.5 | 3.6 | 3.6 | 3.7 | 3.8 | 3.9 | 3.9 | 4.0 | 4.1 | 4.2 | 4.3 | 4.4 | 4.5 |
| 1986 | 3.5 | 3.5 | 3.5 | 3.5 | 3.4 | 3.5 | 3.5 | 3.6 | 3.6 | 3.7 | 3.8 | 3.8 | 3.9 | 4.0 | 4.1 | 4.2 | 4.3 | 4.3 | 4.4 | 4.5 |
| 1987 | 3.5 | 3.5 | 3.5 | 3.5 | 3.5 | 3.5 | 3.5 | 3.6 | 3.7 | 3.7 | 3.8 | 3.9 | 3.9 | 4.0 | 4.1 | 4.2 | 4.3 | 4.4 | 4.5 | 4.6 |
| 1988 | 3.5 | 3.5 | 3.5 | 3.5 | 3.5 | 3.5 | 3.6 | 3.6 | 3.7 | 3.8 | 3.8 | 3.9 | 4.0 | 4.1 | 4.1 | 4.2 | 4.3 | 4.4 | 4.5 | 4.6 |
| 1989 | 3.6 | 3.6 | 3.6 | 3.6 | 3.6 | 3.6 | 3.7 | 3.7 | 3.8 | 3.8 | 3.9 | 4.0 | 4.1 | 4.1 | 4.2 | 4.3 | 4.4 | 4.5 | 4.6 | 4.7 |
| 1990 | 3.7 | 3.7 | 3.7 | 3.7 | 3.7 | 3.7 | 3.7 | 3.8 | 3.8 | 3.9 | 4.0 | 4.1 | 4.1 | 4.2 | 4.3 | 4.4 | 4.5 | 4.6 | 4.7 | 4.8 |
| 1991 | 3.7 | 3.7 | 3.7 | 3.7 | 3.7 | 3.7 | 3.8 | 3.8 | 3.9 | 3.9 | 4.0 | 4.1 | 4.2 | 4.2 | 4.3 | 4.4 | 4.5 | 4.6 | 4.7 | 4.8 |
| 1992 | 3.7 | 3.7 | 3.7 | 3.7 | 3.7 | 3.7 | 3.8 | 3.8 | 3.9 | 3.9 | 4.0 | 4.1 | 4.1 | 4.2 | 4.3 | 4.4 | 4.4 | 4.5 | 4.6 | 4.7 |
| 1993 | 3.7 | 3.7 | 3.7 | 3.7 | 3.7 | 3.7 | 3.8 | 3.8 | 3.9 | 3.9 | 4.0 | 4.1 | 4.1 | 4.2 | 4.3 | 4.4 | 4.4 | 4.5 | 4.6 | 4.7 |
| 1994 | 3.7 | 3.7 | 3.7 | 3.7 | 3.7 | 3.7 | 3.8 | 3.8 | 3.9 | 3.9 | 4.0 | 4.1 | 4.1 | 4.2 | 4.3 | 4.4 | 4.4 | 4.5 | 4.6 | 4.7 |
| 1995 | 3.7 | 3.7 | 3.7 | 3.7 | 3.7 | 3.7 | 3.8 | 3.8 | 3.9 | 3.9 | 4.0 | 4.0 | 4.1 | 4.2 | 4.3 | 4.4 | 4.5 | 4.5 | 4.6 | 4.7 |
| 1996 | 3.7 | 3.7 | 3.8 | 3.7 | 3.7 | 3.8 | 3.8 | 3.8 | 3.9 | 4.0 | 4.0 | 4.1 | 4.2 | 4.2 | 4.3 | 4.4 | 4.5 | 4.5 | 4.6 | 4.7 |
| 1997 | 3.7 | 3.7 | 3.7 | 3.8 | 3.8 | 3.8 | 3.8 | 3.9 | 3.9 | 4.0 | 4.0 | 4.1 | 4.1 | 4.2 | 4.3 | 4.3 | 4.4 | 4.5 | 4.6 | 4.7 |
| 1998 | 3.8 | 3.8 | 3.8 | 3.8 | 3.8 | 3.8 | 3.8 | 3.9 | 3.9 | 3.9 | 4.1 | 4.1 | 4.2 | 4.3 | 4.3 | 4.4 | 4.5 | 4.6 | 4.6 | 4.7 |
| 1999 | 3.8 | 3.8 | 3.8 | 3.8 | 3.8 | 3.8 | 3.9 | 3.9 | 4.0 | 4.0 | 4.1 | 4.1 | 4.2 | 4.3 | 4.3 | 4.4 | 4.5 | 4.6 | 4.6 | 4.7 |
| 2000 | 3.8 | 3.8 | 3.8 | 3.8 | 3.8 | 3.8 | 3.9 | 3.9 | 4.0 | 4.0 | 4.1 | 4.2 | 4.2 | 4.3 | 4.4 | 4.4 | 4.5 | 4.6 | 4.7 | 4.7 |
| 2001 | 3.8 | 3.8 | 3.8 | 3.8 | 3.8 | 3.8 | 3.9 | 3.9 | 4.0 | 4.0 | 4.1 | 4.2 | 4.2 | 4.3 | 4.4 | 4.4 | 4.5 | 4.5 | 4.6 | 4.7 |
| 2002 | 3.7 | 3.8 | 3.8 | 3.8 | 3.8 | 3.8 | 3.9 | 3.9 | 3.9 | 4.0 | 4.1 | 4.1 | 4.2 | 4.2 | 4.3 | 4.4 | 4.5 | 4.5 | 4.5 | 4.6 |
| 2003 | 3.7 | 3.7 | 3.8 | 3.7 | 3.7 | 3.8 | 3.8 | 3.9 | 3.9 | 4.0 | 4.0 | 4.1 | 4.1 | 4.2 | 4.3 | 4.3 | 4.4 | 4.5 | 4.5 | 4.6 |
| 2004 | 3.7 | 3.7 | 3.7 | 3.7 | 3.7 | 3.7 | 3.8 | 3.8 | 3.9 | 3.9 | 4.0 | 4.0 | 4.1 | 4.2 | 4.2 | 4.3 | 4.4 | 4.4 | 4.5 | 4.6 |
| 2005 | 3.7 | 3.7 | 3.7 | 3.7 | 3.7 | 3.7 | 3.8 | 3.8 | 3.9 | 3.9 | 4.0 | 4.0 | 4.1 | 4.1 | 4.2 | 4.3 | 4.3 | 4.4 | 4.5 | 4.5 |
| 2006 | 3.7 | 3.7 | 3.7 | 3.7 | 3.7 | 3.7 | 3.8 | 3.8 | 3.9 | 3.9 | 4.0 | 4.0 | 4.1 | 4.1 | 4.2 | 4.3 | 4.3 | 4.4 | 4.5 | 4.5 |
| 2007 | 3.7 | 3.7 | 3.7 | 3.7 | 3.7 | 3.8 | 3.8 | 3.8 | 3.9 | 3.9 | 4.0 | 4.0 | 4.1 | 4.2 | 4.2 | 4.3 | 4.3 | 4.4 | 4.5 | 4.5 |
| 2008 | 3.7 | 3.7 | 3.7 | 3.7 | 3.7 | 3.7 | 3.8 | 3.8 | 3.8 | 3.9 | 3.9 | 4.0 | 4.1 | 4.1 | 4.2 | 4.2 | 4.3 | 4.4 | 4.4 | 4.5 |
| 2009 | 3.6 | 3.6 | 3.6 | 3.6 | 3.6 | 3.6 | 3.7 | 3.7 | 3.8 | 3.8 | 3.9 | 3.9 | 4.0 | 4.1 | 4.1 | 4.2 | 4.2 | 4.3 | 4.4 | 4.4 |
| 2010 | 3.6 | 3.6 | 3.6 | 3.6 | 3.6 | 3.6 | 3.7 | 3.7 | 3.7 | 3.8 | 3.8 | 3.9 | 3.9 | 4.0 | 4.1 | 4.1 | 4.2 | 4.2 | 4.3 | 4.4 |
| 2011 | 3.6 | 3.6 | 3.6 | 3.6 | 3.6 | 3.6 | 3.7 | 3.7 | 3.7 | 3.7 | 3.8 | 3.8 | 3.9 | 3.9 | 4.0 | 4.1 | 4.1 | 4.2 | 4.2 | 4.3 |
| 2012 | 3.5 | 3.5 | 3.5 | 3.5 | 3.5 | 3.5 | 3.6 | 3.6 | 3.7 | 3.7 | 3.7 | 3.8 | 3.8 | 3.9 | 3.9 | 4.0 | 4.1 | 4.1 | 4.2 | 4.2 |
| 2013 | 3.5 | 3.5 | 3.5 | 3.5 | 3.5 | 3.5 | 3.5 | 3.6 | 3.6 | 3.6 | 3.7 | 3.7 | 3.8 | 3.8 | 3.9 | 3.9 | 4.0 | 4.1 | 4.1 | 4.2 |
| 2014 | 3.5 | 3.4 | 3.4 | 3.4 | 3.4 | 3.5 | 3.5 | 3.6 | 3.6 | 3.6 | 3.6 | 3.7 | 3.7 | 3.8 | 3.8 | 3.9 | 3.9 | 4.0 | 4.0 | 4.1 |
| 2015 | 3.4 | 3.4 | 3.4 | 3.4 | 3.4 | 3.4 | 3.4 | 3.5 | 3.5 | 3.6 | 3.6 | 3.6 | 3.7 | 3.7 | 3.8 | 3.8 | 3.9 | 3.9 | 4.0 | 4.0 |
| 2016 | 3.4 | 3.4 | 3.4 | 3.4 | 3.4 | 3.4 | 3.4 | 3.4 | 3.5 | 3.5 | 3.6 | 3.6 | 3.6 | 3.7 | 3.7 | 3.8 | 3.8 | 3.9 | 3.9 | 4.0 |

## Appendix C-6

U.S. Treasury Bills: Percent per annum total returns for all historical periods
From 1926 to 2016

| End Date | Start Date 1946 | 1947 | 1948 | 1949 | 1950 | 1951 | 1952 | 1953 | 1954 | 1955 | 1956 | 1957 | 1958 | 1959 | 1960 | 1961 | 1962 | 1963 | 1964 | 1965 |
|---|---|---|---|---|---|---|---|---|---|---|---|---|---|---|---|---|---|---|---|---|
| 1926 | | | | | | | | | | | | | | | | | | | | |
| 1927 | | | | | | | | | | | | | | | | | | | | |
| 1928 | | | | | | | | | | | | | | | | | | | | |
| 1929 | | | | | | | | | | | | | | | | | | | | |
| 1930 | | | | | | | | | | | | | | | | | | | | |
| 1931 | | | | | | | | | | | | | | | | | | | | |
| 1932 | | | | | | | | | | | | | | | | | | | | |
| 1933 | | | | | | | | | | | | | | | | | | | | |
| 1934 | | | | | | | | | | | | | | | | | | | | |
| 1935 | | | | | | | | | | | | | | | | | | | | |
| 1936 | | | | | | | | | | | | | | | | | | | | |
| 1937 | | | | | | | | | | | | | | | | | | | | |
| 1938 | | | | | | | | | | | | | | | | | | | | |
| 1939 | | | | | | | | | | | | | | | | | | | | |
| 1940 | | | | | | | | | | | | | | | | | | | | |
| 1941 | | | | | | | | | | | | | | | | | | | | |
| 1942 | | | | | | | | | | | | | | | | | | | | |
| 1943 | | | | | | | | | | | | | | | | | | | | |
| 1944 | | | | | | | | | | | | | | | | | | | | |
| 1945 | | | | | | | | | | | | | | | | | | | | |
| 1946 | 0.4 | | | | | | | | | | | | | | | | | | | |
| 1947 | 0.4 | 0.5 | | | | | | | | | | | | | | | | | | |
| 1948 | 0.6 | 0.7 | 0.8 | | | | | | | | | | | | | | | | | |
| 1949 | 0.7 | 0.8 | 1.0 | 1.1 | | | | | | | | | | | | | | | | |
| 1950 | 0.8 | 0.9 | 1.0 | 1.1 | 1.2 | | | | | | | | | | | | | | | |
| 1951 | 0.9 | 1.0 | 1.2 | 1.3 | 1.3 | 1.5 | | | | | | | | | | | | | | |
| 1952 | 1.0 | 1.1 | 1.3 | 1.4 | 1.4 | 1.6 | 1.7 | | | | | | | | | | | | | |
| 1953 | 1.1 | 1.2 | 1.3 | 1.5 | 1.5 | 1.7 | 1.7 | 1.8 | | | | | | | | | | | | |
| 1954 | 1.1 | 1.2 | 1.3 | 1.4 | 1.4 | 1.5 | 1.4 | 1.3 | 0.9 | | | | | | | | | | | |
| 1955 | 1.1 | 1.2 | 1.3 | 1.4 | 1.4 | 1.5 | 1.5 | 1.4 | 1.2 | 1.6 | | | | | | | | | | |
| 1956 | 1.3 | 1.3 | 1.4 | 1.5 | 1.6 | 1.6 | 1.7 | 1.7 | 1.6 | 2.0 | 2.5 | | | | | | | | | |
| 1957 | 1.4 | 1.5 | 1.6 | 1.7 | 1.8 | 1.9 | 1.9 | 2.0 | 2.0 | 2.4 | 2.8 | 3.1 | | | | | | | | |
| 1958 | 1.4 | 1.5 | 1.6 | 1.7 | 1.7 | 1.8 | 1.9 | 1.9 | 1.9 | 2.2 | 2.4 | 2.3 | 1.5 | | | | | | | |
| 1959 | 1.5 | 1.6 | 1.7 | 1.8 | 1.9 | 1.9 | 2.0 | 2.0 | 2.1 | 2.3 | 2.5 | 2.5 | 2.2 | 3.0 | | | | | | |
| 1960 | 1.6 | 1.7 | 1.8 | 1.9 | 1.9 | 2.0 | 2.1 | 2.1 | 2.2 | 2.4 | 2.5 | 2.6 | 2.4 | 2.8 | 2.7 | | | | | |
| 1961 | 1.6 | 1.7 | 1.8 | 1.9 | 2.0 | 2.0 | 2.1 | 2.1 | 2.2 | 2.3 | 2.5 | 2.5 | 2.3 | 2.6 | 2.4 | 2.1 | | | | |
| 1962 | 1.7 | 1.8 | 1.9 | 2.0 | 2.1 | 2.1 | 2.1 | 2.2 | 2.2 | 2.4 | 2.5 | 2.5 | 2.4 | 2.6 | 2.5 | 2.4 | 2.7 | | | |
| 1963 | 1.8 | 1.9 | 2.0 | 2.1 | 2.2 | 2.2 | 2.2 | 2.3 | 2.3 | 2.5 | 2.6 | 2.6 | 2.5 | 2.7 | 2.7 | 2.7 | 2.9 | 3.1 | | |
| 1964 | 1.9 | 2.0 | 2.0 | 2.2 | 2.3 | 2.3 | 2.3 | 2.4 | 2.4 | 2.6 | 2.7 | 2.7 | 2.7 | 2.8 | 2.8 | 2.9 | 3.1 | 3.3 | 3.5 | |
| 1965 | 2.0 | 2.1 | 2.1 | 2.3 | 2.4 | 2.4 | 2.4 | 2.5 | 2.5 | 2.7 | 2.8 | 2.9 | 2.8 | 3.0 | 3.0 | 3.1 | 3.3 | 3.5 | 3.7 | 3.9 |
| 1966 | 2.1 | 2.2 | 2.3 | 2.4 | 2.5 | 2.5 | 2.6 | 2.7 | 2.7 | 2.9 | 3.0 | 3.0 | 3.0 | 3.2 | 3.3 | 3.4 | 3.6 | 3.8 | 4.1 | 4.3 |
| 1967 | 2.2 | 2.3 | 2.4 | 2.5 | 2.6 | 2.7 | 2.8 | 2.8 | 2.8 | 3.0 | 3.1 | 3.2 | 3.2 | 3.3 | 3.4 | 3.5 | 3.7 | 3.9 | 4.1 | 4.3 |
| 1968 | 2.3 | 2.4 | 2.5 | 2.6 | 2.8 | 2.8 | 2.9 | 2.9 | 3.0 | 3.1 | 3.3 | 3.3 | 3.3 | 3.5 | 3.6 | 3.7 | 3.9 | 4.1 | 4.3 | 4.5 |
| 1969 | 2.5 | 2.6 | 2.7 | 2.8 | 2.9 | 3.0 | 3.0 | 3.1 | 3.2 | 3.4 | 3.5 | 3.6 | 3.6 | 3.8 | 3.9 | 4.0 | 4.3 | 4.5 | 4.7 | 4.9 |
| 1970 | 2.7 | 2.8 | 2.9 | 3.0 | 3.1 | 3.2 | 3.3 | 3.3 | 3.4 | 3.6 | 3.7 | 3.8 | 3.8 | 4.0 | 4.1 | 4.3 | 4.5 | 4.7 | 5.0 | 5.2 |

# Appendix C-6

U.S. Treasury Bills: Percent per annum total returns for all historical periods
From 1926 to 2016

| End Date \ Start Date | 1946 | 1947 | 1948 | 1949 | 1950 | 1951 | 1952 | 1953 | 1954 | 1955 | 1956 | 1957 | 1958 | 1959 | 1960 | 1961 | 1962 | 1963 | 1964 | 1965 |
|---|---|---|---|---|---|---|---|---|---|---|---|---|---|---|---|---|---|---|---|---|
| 1971 | 2.7 | 2.8 | 2.9 | 3.0 | 3.1 | 3.2 | 3.3 | 3.4 | 3.4 | 3.6 | 3.7 | 3.8 | 3.9 | 4.0 | 4.1 | 4.3 | 4.5 | 4.7 | 4.9 | 5.1 |
| 1972 | 2.8 | 2.9 | 3.0 | 3.0 | 3.1 | 3.2 | 3.3 | 3.4 | 3.5 | 3.6 | 3.7 | 3.8 | 3.9 | 4.0 | 4.1 | 4.2 | 4.4 | 4.6 | 4.8 | 4.9 |
| 1973 | 2.9 | 3.0 | 3.1 | 3.2 | 3.3 | 3.4 | 3.5 | 3.6 | 3.6 | 3.8 | 3.9 | 4.0 | 4.1 | 4.2 | 4.3 | 4.4 | 4.6 | 4.8 | 5.0 | 5.1 |
| 1974 | 3.1 | 3.2 | 3.3 | 3.4 | 3.5 | 3.6 | 3.7 | 3.8 | 3.8 | 4.0 | 4.1 | 4.2 | 4.3 | 4.5 | 4.6 | 4.7 | 4.9 | 5.1 | 5.3 | 5.4 |
| 1975 | 3.2 | 3.3 | 3.4 | 3.5 | 3.6 | 3.7 | 3.7 | 3.8 | 3.9 | 4.1 | 4.2 | 4.3 | 4.4 | 4.5 | 4.6 | 4.8 | 5.0 | 5.1 | 5.3 | 5.5 |
| 1976 | 3.2 | 3.3 | 3.4 | 3.5 | 3.6 | 3.7 | 3.8 | 3.9 | 4.0 | 4.1 | 4.2 | 4.3 | 4.4 | 4.6 | 4.7 | 4.8 | 5.0 | 5.1 | 5.3 | 5.4 |
| 1977 | 3.3 | 3.4 | 3.5 | 3.6 | 3.7 | 3.8 | 3.9 | 3.9 | 4.0 | 4.2 | 4.3 | 4.4 | 4.4 | 4.6 | 4.7 | 4.8 | 5.0 | 5.1 | 5.3 | 5.4 |
| 1978 | 3.4 | 3.5 | 3.6 | 3.7 | 3.8 | 3.9 | 4.0 | 4.1 | 4.2 | 4.3 | 4.4 | 4.5 | 4.6 | 4.7 | 4.8 | 4.9 | 5.1 | 5.3 | 5.4 | 5.5 |
| 1979 | 3.6 | 3.7 | 3.8 | 3.9 | 4.0 | 4.1 | 4.2 | 4.3 | 4.4 | 4.5 | 4.7 | 4.8 | 4.8 | 5.0 | 5.1 | 5.2 | 5.4 | 5.5 | 5.7 | 5.8 |
| 1980 | 3.8 | 3.9 | 4.0 | 4.1 | 4.2 | 4.3 | 4.4 | 4.5 | 4.6 | 4.8 | 4.9 | 5.0 | 5.1 | 5.3 | 5.4 | 5.5 | 5.7 | 5.9 | 6.0 | 6.2 |
| 1981 | 4.1 | 4.2 | 4.3 | 4.4 | 4.5 | 4.7 | 4.8 | 4.9 | 5.0 | 5.1 | 5.3 | 5.4 | 5.5 | 5.7 | 5.8 | 5.9 | 6.1 | 6.3 | 6.5 | 6.7 |
| 1982 | 4.3 | 4.4 | 4.5 | 4.6 | 4.7 | 4.8 | 4.9 | 5.1 | 5.2 | 5.3 | 5.5 | 5.6 | 5.7 | 5.9 | 6.0 | 6.1 | 6.3 | 6.5 | 6.7 | 6.9 |
| 1983 | 4.4 | 4.5 | 4.6 | 4.7 | 4.8 | 4.9 | 5.1 | 5.2 | 5.3 | 5.4 | 5.6 | 5.7 | 5.8 | 6.0 | 6.1 | 6.2 | 6.4 | 6.6 | 6.8 | 7.0 |
| 1984 | 4.5 | 4.6 | 4.8 | 4.9 | 5.0 | 5.1 | 5.2 | 5.3 | 5.4 | 5.6 | 5.7 | 5.8 | 5.9 | 6.1 | 6.2 | 6.4 | 6.6 | 6.8 | 6.9 | 7.1 |
| 1985 | 4.6 | 4.7 | 4.8 | 4.9 | 5.1 | 5.2 | 5.3 | 5.4 | 5.5 | 5.7 | 5.8 | 5.9 | 6.0 | 6.2 | 6.3 | 6.4 | 6.6 | 6.8 | 7.0 | 7.1 |
| 1986 | 4.6 | 4.8 | 4.9 | 5.0 | 5.1 | 5.2 | 5.3 | 5.4 | 5.5 | 5.7 | 5.8 | 5.9 | 6.0 | 6.2 | 6.3 | 6.4 | 6.6 | 6.8 | 6.9 | 7.1 |
| 1987 | 4.7 | 4.8 | 4.9 | 5.0 | 5.1 | 5.2 | 5.3 | 5.4 | 5.5 | 5.7 | 5.8 | 5.9 | 6.0 | 6.2 | 6.3 | 6.4 | 6.6 | 6.7 | 6.9 | 7.0 |
| 1988 | 4.7 | 4.8 | 4.9 | 5.0 | 5.1 | 5.2 | 5.3 | 5.4 | 5.5 | 5.7 | 5.8 | 5.9 | 6.0 | 6.2 | 6.3 | 6.4 | 6.6 | 6.7 | 6.9 | 7.0 |
| 1989 | 4.8 | 4.9 | 5.0 | 5.1 | 5.2 | 5.3 | 5.4 | 5.5 | 5.6 | 5.8 | 5.9 | 6.0 | 6.1 | 6.2 | 6.3 | 6.5 | 6.6 | 6.8 | 6.9 | 7.1 |
| 1990 | 4.9 | 5.0 | 5.1 | 5.2 | 5.3 | 5.4 | 5.5 | 5.6 | 5.7 | 5.8 | 5.9 | 6.0 | 6.1 | 6.3 | 6.4 | 6.5 | 6.7 | 6.8 | 6.9 | 7.0 |
| 1991 | 4.9 | 5.0 | 5.1 | 5.2 | 5.3 | 5.4 | 5.5 | 5.6 | 5.7 | 5.8 | 5.9 | 6.0 | 6.1 | 6.3 | 6.4 | 6.5 | 6.6 | 6.7 | 6.9 | 7.0 |
| 1992 | 4.8 | 4.9 | 5.0 | 5.1 | 5.2 | 5.3 | 5.4 | 5.5 | 5.6 | 5.7 | 5.9 | 6.0 | 6.0 | 6.2 | 6.3 | 6.4 | 6.5 | 6.7 | 6.8 | 6.9 |
| 1993 | 4.8 | 4.8 | 5.0 | 5.1 | 5.2 | 5.3 | 5.4 | 5.5 | 5.5 | 5.7 | 5.8 | 5.9 | 6.0 | 6.1 | 6.2 | 6.3 | 6.5 | 6.5 | 6.7 | 6.8 |
| 1994 | 4.8 | 4.9 | 5.0 | 5.1 | 5.2 | 5.2 | 5.3 | 5.4 | 5.5 | 5.6 | 5.7 | 5.8 | 5.9 | 6.0 | 6.1 | 6.2 | 6.3 | 6.5 | 6.6 | 6.7 |
| 1995 | 4.8 | 4.9 | 5.0 | 5.1 | 5.2 | 5.2 | 5.3 | 5.4 | 5.5 | 5.6 | 5.7 | 5.8 | 5.9 | 6.0 | 6.1 | 6.2 | 6.3 | 6.4 | 6.5 | 6.6 |
| 1996 | 4.8 | 4.9 | 5.0 | 5.1 | 5.2 | 5.2 | 5.3 | 5.4 | 5.5 | 5.6 | 5.7 | 5.8 | 5.9 | 6.0 | 6.1 | 6.2 | 6.3 | 6.4 | 6.5 | 6.6 |
| 1997 | 4.8 | 4.9 | 5.0 | 5.1 | 5.2 | 5.2 | 5.3 | 5.4 | 5.5 | 5.6 | 5.7 | 5.8 | 5.9 | 6.0 | 6.0 | 6.1 | 6.3 | 6.4 | 6.5 | 6.5 |
| 1998 | 4.8 | 4.9 | 5.0 | 5.1 | 5.1 | 5.2 | 5.3 | 5.4 | 5.5 | 5.6 | 5.7 | 5.8 | 5.8 | 5.9 | 6.0 | 6.1 | 6.2 | 6.3 | 6.4 | 6.5 |
| 1999 | 4.8 | 4.9 | 5.0 | 5.1 | 5.2 | 5.2 | 5.3 | 5.4 | 5.5 | 5.6 | 5.7 | 5.7 | 5.8 | 5.9 | 6.0 | 6.1 | 6.2 | 6.3 | 6.4 | 6.4 |
| 2000 | 4.8 | 4.9 | 5.0 | 5.1 | 5.2 | 5.2 | 5.3 | 5.4 | 5.5 | 5.6 | 5.7 | 5.7 | 5.8 | 5.9 | 6.0 | 6.1 | 6.2 | 6.3 | 6.3 | 6.4 |
| 2001 | 4.8 | 4.9 | 5.0 | 5.1 | 5.2 | 5.2 | 5.3 | 5.4 | 5.4 | 5.5 | 5.6 | 5.7 | 5.7 | 5.9 | 6.0 | 6.0 | 6.1 | 6.2 | 6.3 | 6.4 |
| 2002 | 4.8 | 4.8 | 5.0 | 5.1 | 5.1 | 5.2 | 5.2 | 5.3 | 5.4 | 5.5 | 5.5 | 5.6 | 5.7 | 5.8 | 5.8 | 5.9 | 6.0 | 6.1 | 6.2 | 6.2 |
| 2003 | 4.7 | 4.8 | 5.0 | 5.1 | 5.1 | 5.1 | 5.2 | 5.2 | 5.3 | 5.4 | 5.4 | 5.5 | 5.6 | 5.7 | 5.7 | 5.8 | 5.9 | 6.0 | 6.0 | 6.1 |
| 2004 | 4.6 | 4.7 | 4.8 | 4.9 | 5.0 | 5.0 | 5.1 | 5.1 | 5.2 | 5.3 | 5.4 | 5.4 | 5.5 | 5.6 | 5.6 | 5.7 | 5.8 | 5.8 | 5.9 | 6.0 |
| 2005 | 4.6 | 4.7 | 4.8 | 4.9 | 4.9 | 5.0 | 5.0 | 5.1 | 5.1 | 5.2 | 5.3 | 5.4 | 5.4 | 5.5 | 5.6 | 5.6 | 5.7 | 5.8 | 5.8 | 5.9 |
| 2006 | 4.6 | 4.7 | 4.8 | 4.8 | 4.9 | 5.0 | 5.0 | 5.1 | 5.1 | 5.2 | 5.3 | 5.4 | 5.4 | 5.5 | 5.5 | 5.6 | 5.7 | 5.7 | 5.8 | 5.9 |
| 2007 | 4.6 | 4.7 | 4.7 | 4.8 | 4.9 | 4.9 | 5.0 | 5.1 | 5.1 | 5.2 | 5.3 | 5.3 | 5.4 | 5.5 | 5.5 | 5.6 | 5.6 | 5.7 | 5.8 | 5.8 |
| 2008 | 4.6 | 4.6 | 4.7 | 4.8 | 4.8 | 4.9 | 4.9 | 5.0 | 5.1 | 5.1 | 5.2 | 5.3 | 5.3 | 5.4 | 5.4 | 5.5 | 5.6 | 5.6 | 5.7 | 5.7 |
| 2009 | 4.5 | 4.6 | 4.6 | 4.7 | 4.7 | 4.8 | 4.9 | 4.9 | 5.0 | 5.1 | 5.1 | 5.2 | 5.2 | 5.3 | 5.3 | 5.4 | 5.5 | 5.5 | 5.6 | 5.6 |
| 2010 | 4.4 | 4.5 | 4.5 | 4.6 | 4.7 | 4.7 | 4.8 | 4.8 | 4.9 | 5.0 | 5.0 | 5.1 | 5.1 | 5.2 | 5.2 | 5.3 | 5.3 | 5.4 | 5.4 | 5.5 |
| 2011 | 4.4 | 4.4 | 4.5 | 4.5 | 4.6 | 4.6 | 4.7 | 4.8 | 4.8 | 4.9 | 4.9 | 5.0 | 5.0 | 5.1 | 5.1 | 5.2 | 5.2 | 5.3 | 5.3 | 5.4 |
| 2012 | 4.3 | 4.3 | 4.4 | 4.5 | 4.5 | 4.6 | 4.6 | 4.7 | 4.7 | 4.8 | 4.8 | 4.9 | 4.9 | 5.0 | 5.0 | 5.1 | 5.1 | 5.2 | 5.2 | 5.3 |
| 2013 | 4.2 | 4.3 | 4.3 | 4.4 | 4.4 | 4.5 | 4.5 | 4.6 | 4.6 | 4.7 | 4.8 | 4.8 | 4.8 | 4.9 | 4.9 | 5.0 | 5.0 | 5.1 | 5.1 | 5.1 |
| 2014 | 4.2 | 4.2 | 4.3 | 4.3 | 4.4 | 4.4 | 4.5 | 4.5 | 4.6 | 4.6 | 4.7 | 4.7 | 4.7 | 4.8 | 4.8 | 4.9 | 4.9 | 5.0 | 5.0 | 5.0 |
| 2015 | 4.1 | 4.2 | 4.2 | 4.3 | 4.3 | 4.4 | 4.5 | 4.4 | 4.5 | 4.6 | 4.6 | 4.6 | 4.7 | 4.7 | 4.8 | 4.8 | 4.8 | 4.9 | 4.9 | 4.9 |
| 2016 | 4.0 | 4.1 | 4.1 | 4.2 | 4.2 | 4.3 | 4.3 | 4.4 | 4.4 | 4.5 | 4.5 | 4.6 | 4.6 | 4.6 | 4.7 | 4.7 | 4.8 | 4.8 | 4.8 | 4.8 |

**Appendix C-6**

U.S. Treasury Bills: Percent per annum total returns for all historical periods

From 1926 to 2016

## Appendix C-6

U.S. Treasury Bills: Percent per annum total returns for all historical periods

From 1926 to 2016

| End Date | Start Date 1966 | 1967 | 1968 | 1969 | 1970 | 1971 | 1972 | 1973 | 1974 | 1975 | 1976 | 1977 | 1978 | 1979 | 1980 | 1981 | 1982 | 1983 | 1984 | 1985 |
|---|---|---|---|---|---|---|---|---|---|---|---|---|---|---|---|---|---|---|---|---|
| 1971 | 5.3 | 5.4 | 5.7 | 5.8 | 5.5 | 4.4 | | | | | | | | | | | | | | |
| 1972 | 5.1 | 5.1 | 5.3 | 5.3 | 4.9 | 4.1 | 3.8 | | | | | | | | | | | | | |
| 1973 | 5.3 | 5.4 | 5.6 | 5.3 | 5.4 | 5.0 | 5.4 | 6.9 | | | | | | | | | | | | |
| 1974 | 5.6 | 5.7 | 5.9 | 5.6 | 5.9 | 5.8 | 6.2 | 7.5 | 8.0 | | | | | | | | | | | |
| 1975 | 5.6 | 5.7 | 5.9 | 6.0 | 5.9 | 5.8 | 6.1 | 6.9 | 6.9 | 5.8 | | | | | | | | | | |
| 1976 | 5.6 | 5.6 | 5.8 | 5.9 | 5.8 | 5.7 | 5.9 | 6.4 | 6.3 | 5.4 | 5.1 | | | | | | | | | |
| 1977 | 5.5 | 5.6 | 5.7 | 5.8 | 5.7 | 5.6 | 5.8 | 6.2 | 6.0 | 5.3 | 5.1 | 5.1 | | | | | | | | |
| 1978 | 5.7 | 5.7 | 5.9 | 5.9 | 5.9 | 5.8 | 6.0 | 6.3 | 6.2 | 5.8 | 5.8 | 6.1 | 7.2 | | | | | | | |
| 1979 | 6.0 | 6.1 | 6.2 | 6.3 | 6.3 | 6.3 | 6.5 | 6.9 | 6.9 | 6.7 | 6.9 | 7.5 | 8.8 | 10.4 | | | | | | |
| 1980 | 6.3 | 6.4 | 6.6 | 6.7 | 6.7 | 6.8 | 7.0 | 7.4 | 7.5 | 7.4 | 7.8 | 8.5 | 9.6 | 10.8 | 11.2 | | | | | |
| 1981 | 6.8 | 7.0 | 7.2 | 7.3 | 7.4 | 7.5 | 7.8 | 8.2 | 8.4 | 8.4 | 8.9 | 9.7 | 10.8 | 12.1 | 13.0 | 14.7 | | | | |
| 1982 | 7.0 | 7.2 | 7.4 | 7.6 | 7.6 | 7.7 | 8.0 | 8.5 | 8.6 | 8.7 | 9.1 | 9.8 | 10.8 | 11.7 | 12.1 | 12.6 | 10.5 | | | |
| 1983 | 7.1 | 7.3 | 7.5 | 7.6 | 7.7 | 7.8 | 8.1 | 8.5 | 8.6 | 8.7 | 9.1 | 9.7 | 10.4 | 11.1 | 11.3 | 11.3 | 9.7 | 8.8 | | |
| 1984 | 7.3 | 7.4 | 7.6 | 7.8 | 7.9 | 7.9 | 8.2 | 8.6 | 8.8 | 8.8 | 9.2 | 9.7 | 10.4 | 10.9 | 11.0 | 11.0 | 9.7 | 9.3 | 9.8 | |
| 1985 | 7.3 | 7.4 | 7.6 | 7.8 | 7.8 | 7.9 | 8.2 | 8.5 | 8.7 | 8.7 | 9.0 | 9.5 | 10.0 | 10.4 | 10.5 | 10.3 | 9.2 | 8.8 | 8.8 | 7.7 |
| 1986 | 7.3 | 7.4 | 7.5 | 7.7 | 7.7 | 7.8 | 8.1 | 8.4 | 8.5 | 8.5 | 8.8 | 9.1 | 9.6 | 9.9 | 9.8 | 9.6 | 8.6 | 8.1 | 7.9 | 6.9 |
| 1987 | 7.2 | 7.3 | 7.4 | 7.6 | 7.6 | 7.7 | 7.9 | 8.2 | 8.3 | 8.3 | 8.5 | 8.8 | 9.2 | 9.4 | 9.3 | 9.0 | 8.1 | 7.6 | 7.3 | 6.4 |
| 1988 | 7.1 | 7.2 | 7.4 | 7.5 | 7.6 | 7.6 | 7.8 | 8.1 | 8.1 | 8.1 | 8.3 | 8.6 | 8.9 | 9.1 | 8.9 | 8.7 | 7.8 | 7.4 | 7.1 | 6.4 |
| 1989 | 7.2 | 7.3 | 7.4 | 7.6 | 7.6 | 7.6 | 7.8 | 8.1 | 8.1 | 8.2 | 8.3 | 8.6 | 9.0 | 9.1 | 8.9 | 8.6 | 7.9 | 7.5 | 7.3 | 6.8 |
| 1990 | 7.2 | 7.3 | 7.5 | 7.6 | 7.6 | 7.7 | 7.8 | 8.1 | 8.1 | 8.1 | 8.3 | 8.5 | 8.8 | 8.9 | 8.8 | 8.5 | 7.9 | 7.6 | 7.4 | 7.0 |
| 1991 | 7.1 | 7.2 | 7.4 | 7.5 | 7.5 | 7.6 | 7.7 | 8.0 | 8.0 | 8.0 | 8.1 | 8.3 | 8.6 | 8.7 | 8.5 | 8.3 | 7.7 | 7.3 | 7.2 | 6.8 |
| 1992 | 7.0 | 7.1 | 7.2 | 7.3 | 7.3 | 7.4 | 7.5 | 7.7 | 7.7 | 7.7 | 7.8 | 8.0 | 8.2 | 8.3 | 8.1 | 7.9 | 7.3 | 6.9 | 6.7 | 6.4 |
| 1993 | 6.9 | 6.9 | 7.0 | 7.1 | 7.1 | 7.2 | 7.3 | 7.5 | 7.5 | 7.5 | 7.6 | 7.7 | 7.9 | 7.9 | 7.7 | 7.5 | 6.9 | 6.6 | 6.4 | 6.0 |
| 1994 | 6.8 | 6.8 | 6.9 | 7.0 | 7.1 | 7.2 | 7.3 | 7.3 | 7.3 | 7.5 | 7.4 | 7.5 | 7.6 | 7.7 | 7.5 | 7.2 | 6.7 | 6.3 | 6.1 | 5.8 |
| 1995 | 6.7 | 6.8 | 6.9 | 6.9 | 7.0 | 7.0 | 7.1 | 7.2 | 7.2 | 7.2 | 7.3 | 7.4 | 7.5 | 7.5 | 7.4 | 7.1 | 6.6 | 6.3 | 6.1 | 5.7 |
| 1996 | 6.7 | 6.7 | 6.8 | 6.9 | 6.9 | 6.9 | 7.0 | 7.1 | 7.2 | 7.1 | 7.2 | 7.3 | 7.4 | 7.4 | 7.2 | 7.0 | 6.5 | 6.2 | 6.0 | 5.7 |
| 1997 | 6.6 | 6.7 | 6.8 | 6.8 | 6.8 | 6.8 | 6.9 | 7.1 | 7.1 | 7.0 | 7.1 | 7.2 | 7.3 | 7.3 | 7.1 | 6.9 | 6.4 | 6.1 | 6.0 | 5.7 |
| 1998 | 6.6 | 6.6 | 6.7 | 6.7 | 6.8 | 6.8 | 6.9 | 7.0 | 7.0 | 6.9 | 7.0 | 7.1 | 7.1 | 7.2 | 7.0 | 6.8 | 6.3 | 6.1 | 5.9 | 5.6 |
| 1999 | 6.5 | 6.6 | 6.6 | 6.7 | 6.7 | 6.7 | 6.8 | 6.9 | 6.9 | 6.8 | 6.9 | 7.0 | 7.1 | 7.1 | 6.9 | 6.7 | 6.2 | 6.0 | 5.8 | 5.5 |
| 2000 | 6.5 | 6.5 | 6.6 | 6.7 | 6.7 | 6.7 | 6.8 | 6.9 | 6.9 | 6.8 | 6.9 | 6.9 | 7.0 | 7.0 | 6.8 | 6.6 | 6.2 | 6.0 | 5.8 | 5.6 |
| 2001 | 6.4 | 6.5 | 6.5 | 6.6 | 6.6 | 6.6 | 6.7 | 6.7 | 6.7 | 6.7 | 6.7 | 6.8 | 6.9 | 6.9 | 6.7 | 6.5 | 6.1 | 5.9 | 5.7 | 5.5 |
| 2002 | 6.3 | 6.3 | 6.4 | 6.4 | 6.4 | 6.4 | 6.5 | 6.6 | 6.6 | 6.5 | 6.5 | 6.6 | 6.7 | 6.6 | 6.5 | 6.3 | 5.9 | 5.7 | 5.5 | 5.3 |
| 2003 | 6.1 | 6.2 | 6.2 | 6.3 | 6.3 | 6.3 | 6.3 | 6.4 | 6.4 | 6.3 | 6.3 | 6.4 | 6.4 | 6.4 | 6.2 | 6.0 | 5.7 | 5.4 | 5.3 | 5.0 |
| 2004 | 6.0 | 6.1 | 6.1 | 6.1 | 6.1 | 6.1 | 6.2 | 6.2 | 6.2 | 6.1 | 6.2 | 6.2 | 6.2 | 6.2 | 6.0 | 5.8 | 5.5 | 5.2 | 5.1 | 4.8 |
| 2005 | 5.9 | 6.0 | 6.0 | 6.0 | 6.0 | 6.0 | 6.1 | 6.1 | 6.1 | 6.0 | 6.1 | 6.1 | 6.1 | 6.1 | 5.9 | 5.7 | 5.4 | 5.1 | 5.0 | 4.7 |
| 2006 | 5.9 | 5.9 | 6.0 | 6.0 | 6.0 | 6.0 | 6.0 | 6.1 | 6.1 | 6.0 | 6.0 | 6.0 | 6.1 | 6.0 | 5.9 | 5.7 | 5.3 | 5.1 | 5.0 | 4.7 |
| 2007 | 5.9 | 5.9 | 6.0 | 6.0 | 6.0 | 6.0 | 6.0 | 6.0 | 6.0 | 6.0 | 6.0 | 6.0 | 6.0 | 6.0 | 5.8 | 5.6 | 5.3 | 5.1 | 4.9 | 4.7 |
| 2008 | 5.8 | 5.8 | 5.8 | 5.9 | 5.8 | 5.8 | 5.9 | 5.9 | 5.9 | 5.8 | 5.8 | 5.9 | 5.9 | 5.8 | 5.7 | 5.5 | 5.2 | 5.0 | 4.8 | 4.6 |
| 2009 | 5.6 | 5.7 | 5.7 | 5.7 | 5.7 | 5.7 | 5.7 | 5.7 | 5.7 | 5.7 | 5.7 | 5.7 | 5.7 | 5.6 | 5.5 | 5.3 | 5.0 | 4.8 | 4.6 | 4.4 |
| 2010 | 5.5 | 5.5 | 5.6 | 5.6 | 5.6 | 5.5 | 5.6 | 5.6 | 5.6 | 5.5 | 5.5 | 5.5 | 5.5 | 5.5 | 5.3 | 5.1 | 4.8 | 4.6 | 4.5 | 4.3 |
| 2011 | 5.4 | 5.4 | 5.4 | 5.4 | 5.4 | 5.4 | 5.4 | 5.4 | 5.4 | 5.4 | 5.3 | 5.4 | 5.4 | 5.3 | 5.1 | 5.0 | 4.6 | 4.4 | 4.3 | 4.1 |
| 2012 | 5.3 | 5.3 | 5.3 | 5.3 | 5.3 | 5.3 | 5.3 | 5.3 | 5.3 | 5.2 | 5.2 | 5.2 | 5.2 | 5.1 | 5.0 | 4.8 | 4.5 | 4.3 | 4.1 | 3.9 |
| 2013 | 5.2 | 5.2 | 5.2 | 5.2 | 5.2 | 5.1 | 5.2 | 5.1 | 5.1 | 5.1 | 5.1 | 5.1 | 5.1 | 5.0 | 4.8 | 4.7 | 4.4 | 4.2 | 4.0 | 3.8 |
| 2014 | 5.1 | 5.1 | 5.1 | 5.1 | 5.1 | 5.0 | 5.0 | 5.0 | 5.0 | 4.9 | 4.9 | 4.9 | 4.9 | 4.9 | 4.7 | 4.5 | 4.2 | 4.0 | 3.9 | 3.7 |
| 2015 | 5.0 | 5.0 | 5.0 | 5.0 | 4.9 | 4.9 | 4.9 | 4.9 | 4.9 | 4.8 | 4.8 | 4.8 | 4.8 | 4.7 | 4.6 | 4.4 | 4.1 | 3.9 | 3.8 | 3.6 |
| 2016 | 4.9 | 4.9 | 4.9 | 4.9 | 4.8 | 4.8 | 4.8 | 4.8 | 4.8 | 4.7 | 4.7 | 4.7 | 4.7 | 4.6 | 4.4 | 4.3 | 4.0 | 3.8 | 3.6 | 3.5 |

# Appendix C-6

U.S. Treasury Bills: Percent per annum total returns for all historical periods

From 1926 to 2016

| End Date | Start Date 1986 | 1987 | 1988 | 1989 | 1990 | 1991 | 1992 | 1993 | 1994 | 1995 | 1996 | 1997 | 1998 | 1999 | 2000 | 2001 | 2002 | 2003 | 2004 | 2005 |
|---|---|---|---|---|---|---|---|---|---|---|---|---|---|---|---|---|---|---|---|---|
| 1971 | | | | | | | | | | | | | | | | | | | | |
| 1972 | | | | | | | | | | | | | | | | | | | | |
| 1973 | | | | | | | | | | | | | | | | | | | | |
| 1974 | | | | | | | | | | | | | | | | | | | | |
| 1975 | | | | | | | | | | | | | | | | | | | | |
| 1976 | | | | | | | | | | | | | | | | | | | | |
| 1977 | | | | | | | | | | | | | | | | | | | | |
| 1978 | | | | | | | | | | | | | | | | | | | | |
| 1979 | | | | | | | | | | | | | | | | | | | | |
| 1980 | | | | | | | | | | | | | | | | | | | | |
| 1981 | | | | | | | | | | | | | | | | | | | | |
| 1982 | | | | | | | | | | | | | | | | | | | | |
| 1983 | | | | | | | | | | | | | | | | | | | | |
| 1984 | | | | | | | | | | | | | | | | | | | | |
| 1985 | | | | | | | | | | | | | | | | | | | | |
| 1986 | 6.2 | | | | | | | | | | | | | | | | | | | |
| 1987 | 5.8 | 5.5 | | | | | | | | | | | | | | | | | | |
| 1988 | 6.0 | 5.9 | 6.3 | | | | | | | | | | | | | | | | | |
| 1989 | 6.6 | 6.7 | 7.4 | 8.4 | | | | | | | | | | | | | | | | |
| 1990 | 6.8 | 7.0 | 7.5 | 8.1 | 7.8 | | | | | | | | | | | | | | | |
| 1991 | 6.6 | 6.7 | 7.0 | 7.3 | 6.7 | 5.6 | | | | | | | | | | | | | | |
| 1992 | 6.2 | 6.2 | 6.3 | 6.3 | 5.6 | 4.5 | 3.5 | | | | | | | | | | | | | |
| 1993 | 5.8 | 5.7 | 5.7 | 5.6 | 4.9 | 4.0 | 3.2 | 2.9 | | | | | | | | | | | | |
| 1994 | 5.5 | 5.5 | 5.5 | 5.3 | 4.7 | 4.0 | 3.4 | 3.4 | 3.9 | | | | | | | | | | | |
| 1995 | 5.6 | 5.5 | 5.5 | 5.4 | 4.9 | 4.3 | 4.0 | 4.1 | 4.7 | 5.6 | | | | | | | | | | |
| 1996 | 5.5 | 5.5 | 5.5 | 5.3 | 4.9 | 4.4 | 4.2 | 4.4 | 4.9 | 5.4 | 5.2 | | | | | | | | | |
| 1997 | 5.5 | 5.4 | 5.4 | 5.3 | 5.0 | 4.6 | 4.4 | 4.6 | 5.0 | 5.4 | 5.2 | 5.3 | | | | | | | | |
| 1998 | 5.4 | 5.4 | 5.4 | 5.3 | 5.0 | 4.6 | 4.5 | 4.6 | 5.0 | 5.2 | 5.1 | 5.1 | 4.9 | | | | | | | |
| 1999 | 5.4 | 5.3 | 5.3 | 5.2 | 4.9 | 4.6 | 4.5 | 4.6 | 4.9 | 5.1 | 5.0 | 4.9 | 4.8 | 4.7 | | | | | | |
| 2000 | 5.4 | 5.4 | 5.3 | 5.3 | 5.0 | 4.7 | 4.6 | 4.8 | 5.1 | 5.2 | 5.2 | 5.2 | 5.1 | 5.3 | 5.9 | | | | | |
| 2001 | 5.3 | 5.3 | 5.2 | 5.2 | 4.9 | 4.7 | 4.6 | 4.7 | 4.9 | 5.0 | 5.0 | 4.9 | 4.8 | 4.8 | 4.9 | 3.8 | | | | |
| 2002 | 5.1 | 5.0 | 5.0 | 4.9 | 4.7 | 4.4 | 4.3 | 4.4 | 4.6 | 4.5 | 4.5 | 4.4 | 4.2 | 4.0 | 3.8 | 2.7 | 1.6 | | | |
| 2003 | 4.9 | 4.8 | 4.8 | 4.7 | 4.4 | 4.1 | 4.0 | 4.1 | 4.2 | 4.0 | 4.0 | 3.9 | 3.6 | 3.4 | 3.1 | 2.2 | 1.3 | 1.0 | | |
| 2004 | 4.7 | 4.6 | 4.5 | 4.4 | 4.2 | 3.9 | 3.8 | 3.8 | 3.9 | 3.7 | 3.7 | 3.5 | 3.3 | 3.0 | 2.7 | 1.9 | 1.3 | 1.1 | 1.2 | |
| 2005 | 4.6 | 4.5 | 4.5 | 4.3 | 4.1 | 3.9 | 3.7 | 3.8 | 3.8 | 3.6 | 3.6 | 3.5 | 3.2 | 3.0 | 2.7 | 2.1 | 1.7 | 1.7 | 2.1 | 3.0 |
| 2006 | 4.6 | 4.5 | 4.5 | 4.4 | 4.1 | 3.9 | 3.8 | 3.8 | 3.9 | 3.7 | 3.7 | 3.6 | 3.4 | 3.2 | 3.0 | 2.6 | 2.3 | 2.5 | 3.0 | 3.9 |
| 2007 | 4.6 | 4.5 | 4.5 | 4.4 | 4.2 | 4.0 | 3.9 | 3.9 | 4.0 | 3.8 | 3.8 | 3.7 | 3.5 | 3.4 | 3.2 | 2.9 | 2.7 | 2.9 | 3.4 | 4.1 |
| 2008 | 4.5 | 4.4 | 4.3 | 4.2 | 4.0 | 3.8 | 3.7 | 3.7 | 3.8 | 3.7 | 3.7 | 3.5 | 3.4 | 3.2 | 3.1 | 2.7 | 2.5 | 2.7 | 3.0 | 3.5 |
| 2009 | 4.3 | 4.2 | 4.1 | 4.0 | 3.8 | 3.6 | 3.5 | 3.5 | 3.6 | 3.4 | 3.4 | 3.3 | 3.1 | 2.9 | 2.8 | 2.4 | 2.2 | 2.3 | 2.5 | 2.8 |
| 2010 | 4.1 | 4.0 | 4.0 | 3.9 | 3.7 | 3.5 | 3.3 | 3.3 | 3.3 | 3.2 | 3.2 | 3.0 | 2.9 | 2.7 | 2.5 | 2.2 | 2.0 | 2.0 | 2.2 | 2.4 |
| 2011 | 4.0 | 3.9 | 3.8 | 3.7 | 3.5 | 3.3 | 3.2 | 3.2 | 3.1 | 3.0 | 3.0 | 2.8 | 2.7 | 2.5 | 2.3 | 2.0 | 1.8 | 1.8 | 1.9 | 2.0 |
| 2012 | 3.8 | 3.7 | 3.7 | 3.5 | 3.3 | 3.1 | 3.0 | 3.0 | 3.0 | 2.8 | 2.8 | 2.7 | 2.5 | 2.3 | 2.1 | 1.8 | 1.6 | 1.6 | 1.7 | 1.8 |
| 2013 | 3.7 | 3.6 | 3.5 | 3.4 | 3.2 | 3.0 | 2.9 | 2.9 | 2.9 | 2.6 | 2.6 | 2.5 | 2.3 | 2.2 | 2.0 | 1.7 | 1.5 | 1.5 | 1.5 | 1.6 |
| 2014 | 3.5 | 3.5 | 3.4 | 3.3 | 3.1 | 2.9 | 2.8 | 2.7 | 2.7 | 2.5 | 2.5 | 2.4 | 2.2 | 2.0 | 1.8 | 1.6 | 1.4 | 1.4 | 1.4 | 1.4 |
| 2015 | 3.4 | 3.3 | 3.3 | 3.1 | 2.9 | 2.8 | 2.6 | 2.6 | 2.6 | 2.4 | 2.4 | 2.2 | 2.1 | 1.9 | 1.7 | 1.5 | 1.3 | 1.3 | 1.3 | 1.3 |
| 2016 | 3.3 | 3.2 | 3.1 | 3.0 | 2.8 | 2.7 | 2.5 | 2.5 | 2.5 | 2.3 | 2.3 | 2.1 | 2.0 | 1.8 | 1.6 | 1.4 | 1.2 | 1.2 | 1.2 | 1.2 |

# Appendix C-6

U.S. Treasury Bills: Percent per annum total returns for all historical periods

From 1926 to 2016

## Appendix C-7

Inflation: Percent per annum total returns for all historical periods

From 1926 to 2016

| End Date | Start Date 1926 | 1927 | 1928 | 1929 | 1930 | 1931 | 1932 | 1933 | 1934 | 1935 | 1936 | 1937 | 1938 | 1939 | 1940 | 1941 | 1942 | 1943 | 1944 | 1945 |
|---|---|---|---|---|---|---|---|---|---|---|---|---|---|---|---|---|---|---|---|---|
| 1926 | -1.5 | | | | | | | | | | | | | | | | | | | |
| 1927 | -1.8 | -2.1 | | | | | | | | | | | | | | | | | | |
| 1928 | -1.5 | -1.5 | -1.0 | | | | | | | | | | | | | | | | | |
| 1929 | -1.1 | -1.0 | -0.4 | 0.2 | | | | | | | | | | | | | | | | |
| 1930 | -2.1 | -2.2 | -2.3 | -3.0 | -6.0 | | | | | | | | | | | | | | | |
| 1931 | -3.4 | -3.7 | -4.2 | -5.2 | -7.8 | -9.5 | | | | | | | | | | | | | | |
| 1932 | -4.4 | -4.9 | -5.4 | -6.5 | -8.6 | -9.9 | -10.3 | | | | | | | | | | | | | |
| 1933 | -3.8 | -4.1 | -4.5 | -5.1 | -6.4 | -6.6 | -5.0 | 0.5 | | | | | | | | | | | | |
| 1934 | -3.2 | -3.4 | -3.6 | -4.0 | -4.8 | -4.5 | -2.7 | 1.3 | 2.0 | | | | | | | | | | | |
| 1935 | -2.6 | -2.7 | -2.8 | -3.0 | -3.5 | -3.0 | -1.3 | 1.8 | 2.5 | 3.0 | | | | | | | | | | |
| 1936 | -2.2 | -2.3 | -2.3 | -2.5 | -2.9 | -2.3 | -0.8 | 1.7 | 2.1 | 2.1 | 1.2 | | | | | | | | | |
| 1937 | -1.8 | -1.9 | -1.8 | -1.9 | -2.1 | -1.6 | -0.2 | 2.0 | 2.3 | 2.4 | 2.2 | 3.1 | | | | | | | | |
| 1938 | -1.9 | -1.9 | -1.9 | -2.0 | -2.2 | -1.7 | -0.6 | 1.2 | 1.3 | 1.1 | 0.5 | 0.1 | -2.8 | | | | | | | |
| 1939 | -1.8 | -1.8 | -1.8 | -1.8 | -2.0 | -1.6 | -0.6 | 0.9 | 1.0 | 0.8 | 0.2 | -0.1 | -1.6 | -0.5 | | | | | | |
| 1940 | -1.6 | -1.6 | -1.6 | -1.6 | -1.8 | -1.3 | -0.4 | 0.9 | 1.0 | 0.8 | 0.4 | 0.2 | -0.8 | 0.2 | 1.0 | | | | | |
| 1941 | -0.9 | -0.9 | -0.8 | -0.8 | -0.9 | -0.4 | 0.6 | 1.9 | 2.0 | 2.0 | 1.9 | 2.0 | 1.7 | 3.3 | 5.2 | 9.7 | | | | |
| 1942 | -0.3 | -0.3 | -0.2 | -0.1 | -0.1 | 0.4 | 1.3 | 2.6 | 2.8 | 2.9 | 2.9 | 3.2 | 3.2 | 4.8 | 6.6 | 9.5 | 9.3 | | | |
| 1943 | -0.2 | -0.1 | 0.0 | 0.1 | 0.1 | 0.6 | 1.5 | 2.6 | 2.9 | 2.9 | 2.9 | 3.2 | 3.2 | 4.4 | 5.7 | 7.3 | 6.2 | 3.2 | | |
| 1944 | 0.0 | 0.0 | 0.2 | 0.2 | 0.2 | 0.7 | 1.5 | 2.6 | 2.8 | 2.9 | 2.8 | 3.1 | 3.0 | 4.1 | 5.0 | 6.0 | 4.8 | 2.6 | 2.1 | |
| 1945 | 0.1 | 0.2 | 0.3 | 0.4 | 0.4 | 0.8 | 1.6 | 2.6 | 2.7 | 2.8 | 2.8 | 3.0 | 2.9 | 3.8 | 4.5 | 5.2 | 4.2 | 2.5 | 2.2 | 2.3 |
| 1946 | 0.9 | 1.0 | 1.2 | 1.3 | 1.3 | 1.8 | 2.6 | 3.6 | 3.9 | 4.0 | 4.1 | 4.4 | 4.5 | 5.5 | 6.4 | 7.3 | 6.8 | 6.2 | 7.3 | 9.9 |
| 1947 | 1.2 | 1.4 | 1.5 | 1.7 | 1.7 | 2.2 | 3.0 | 4.0 | 4.2 | 4.4 | 4.5 | 4.8 | 5.0 | 5.9 | 6.7 | 7.5 | 7.2 | 6.8 | 7.7 | 9.6 |
| 1948 | 1.3 | 1.4 | 1.6 | 1.7 | 1.8 | 2.3 | 3.0 | 3.9 | 4.1 | 4.3 | 4.4 | 4.6 | 4.8 | 5.6 | 6.2 | 6.9 | 6.5 | 6.1 | 6.7 | 7.8 |
| 1949 | 1.2 | 1.3 | 1.4 | 1.5 | 1.6 | 2.0 | 2.7 | 3.5 | 3.7 | 3.8 | 3.9 | 4.1 | 4.2 | 4.9 | 5.4 | 5.9 | 5.5 | 4.9 | 5.2 | 5.8 |
| 1950 | 1.3 | 1.5 | 1.6 | 1.7 | 1.8 | 2.2 | 2.9 | 3.7 | 3.9 | 4.0 | 4.0 | 4.2 | 4.3 | 4.9 | 5.4 | 5.9 | 5.5 | 5.0 | 5.3 | 5.8 |
| 1951 | 1.5 | 1.6 | 1.8 | 1.9 | 2.0 | 2.4 | 3.0 | 3.8 | 4.0 | 4.1 | 4.1 | 4.3 | 4.4 | 5.0 | 5.5 | 5.9 | 5.5 | 5.1 | 5.4 | 5.8 |
| 1952 | 1.5 | 1.6 | 1.8 | 1.9 | 1.9 | 2.3 | 2.9 | 3.6 | 3.8 | 3.9 | 4.0 | 4.1 | 4.2 | 4.7 | 5.1 | 5.5 | 5.1 | 4.7 | 4.9 | 5.2 |
| 1953 | 1.5 | 1.6 | 1.7 | 1.8 | 1.9 | 2.2 | 2.8 | 3.5 | 3.6 | 3.7 | 3.8 | 3.9 | 4.0 | 4.4 | 4.8 | 5.1 | 4.7 | 4.3 | 4.4 | 4.7 |
| 1954 | 1.4 | 1.5 | 1.6 | 1.7 | 1.8 | 2.1 | 2.7 | 3.3 | 3.4 | 3.5 | 3.5 | 3.7 | 3.7 | 4.1 | 4.4 | 4.7 | 4.3 | 3.9 | 4.0 | 4.2 |
| 1955 | 1.4 | 1.5 | 1.6 | 1.7 | 1.7 | 2.1 | 2.6 | 3.2 | 3.3 | 3.4 | 3.4 | 3.5 | 3.5 | 3.9 | 4.2 | 4.4 | 4.0 | 3.6 | 3.7 | 3.8 |
| 1956 | 1.4 | 1.5 | 1.6 | 1.7 | 1.8 | 2.1 | 2.6 | 3.2 | 3.3 | 3.3 | 3.3 | 3.5 | 3.5 | 3.8 | 4.1 | 4.3 | 3.9 | 3.6 | 3.6 | 3.7 |
| 1957 | 1.5 | 1.5 | 1.7 | 1.8 | 1.8 | 2.1 | 2.6 | 3.2 | 3.3 | 3.3 | 3.3 | 3.4 | 3.5 | 3.8 | 4.0 | 4.2 | 3.9 | 3.5 | 3.6 | 3.7 |
| 1958 | 1.5 | 1.6 | 1.7 | 1.8 | 1.8 | 2.1 | 2.6 | 3.1 | 3.2 | 3.3 | 3.3 | 3.4 | 3.4 | 3.7 | 3.9 | 4.1 | 3.8 | 3.4 | 3.4 | 3.5 |
| 1959 | 1.5 | 1.6 | 1.7 | 1.8 | 1.8 | 2.1 | 2.5 | 3.0 | 3.1 | 3.2 | 3.2 | 3.3 | 3.3 | 3.6 | 3.8 | 3.9 | 3.6 | 3.3 | 3.3 | 3.4 |
| 1960 | 1.5 | 1.6 | 1.7 | 1.8 | 1.8 | 2.1 | 2.5 | 3.0 | 3.1 | 3.1 | 3.1 | 3.2 | 3.2 | 3.5 | 3.7 | 3.8 | 3.5 | 3.2 | 3.2 | 3.3 |
| 1961 | 1.4 | 1.5 | 1.6 | 1.7 | 1.8 | 2.0 | 2.4 | 2.9 | 3.0 | 3.0 | 3.0 | 3.1 | 3.1 | 3.4 | 3.5 | 3.7 | 3.4 | 3.1 | 3.1 | 3.1 |
| 1962 | 1.4 | 1.5 | 1.6 | 1.7 | 1.7 | 2.0 | 2.4 | 2.8 | 2.9 | 3.0 | 3.0 | 3.0 | 3.0 | 3.3 | 3.4 | 3.6 | 3.3 | 3.0 | 3.0 | 3.0 |
| 1963 | 1.4 | 1.5 | 1.6 | 1.7 | 1.7 | 2.0 | 2.4 | 2.8 | 2.9 | 2.9 | 2.9 | 3.0 | 2.9 | 3.2 | 3.4 | 3.5 | 3.2 | 2.9 | 2.9 | 2.9 |
| 1964 | 1.4 | 1.5 | 1.6 | 1.7 | 1.7 | 2.0 | 2.3 | 2.8 | 2.8 | 2.9 | 2.9 | 2.9 | 2.9 | 3.1 | 3.3 | 3.4 | 3.1 | 2.8 | 2.8 | 2.8 |
| 1965 | 1.4 | 1.5 | 1.6 | 1.7 | 1.7 | 2.0 | 2.3 | 2.7 | 2.8 | 2.8 | 2.8 | 2.9 | 2.9 | 3.1 | 3.2 | 3.3 | 3.1 | 2.8 | 2.8 | 2.8 |
| 1966 | 1.5 | 1.6 | 1.7 | 1.7 | 1.8 | 2.0 | 2.4 | 2.8 | 2.8 | 2.8 | 2.8 | 2.9 | 2.9 | 3.1 | 3.2 | 3.3 | 3.1 | 2.8 | 2.8 | 2.8 |
| 1967 | 1.5 | 1.6 | 1.7 | 1.8 | 1.8 | 2.0 | 2.4 | 2.8 | 2.8 | 2.8 | 2.8 | 2.9 | 2.9 | 3.1 | 3.2 | 3.3 | 3.1 | 2.8 | 2.8 | 2.8 |
| 1968 | 1.6 | 1.7 | 1.8 | 1.8 | 1.9 | 2.1 | 2.4 | 2.8 | 2.9 | 2.9 | 2.9 | 3.0 | 3.0 | 3.1 | 3.3 | 3.4 | 3.2 | 2.9 | 2.9 | 2.9 |
| 1969 | 1.7 | 1.8 | 1.9 | 1.9 | 2.0 | 2.2 | 2.5 | 2.9 | 3.0 | 3.0 | 3.0 | 3.0 | 3.0 | 3.2 | 3.4 | 3.5 | 3.2 | 3.0 | 3.0 | 3.0 |
| 1970 | 1.8 | 1.9 | 2.0 | 2.0 | 2.1 | 2.3 | 2.6 | 3.0 | 3.0 | 3.1 | 3.1 | 3.1 | 3.1 | 3.3 | 3.4 | 3.5 | 3.3 | 3.1 | 3.1 | 3.1 |

# Appendix C-7

Inflation: Percent per annum total returns for all historical periods

From 1926 to 2016

| End Date | Start Date 1926 | 1927 | 1928 | 1929 | 1930 | 1931 | 1932 | 1933 | 1934 | 1935 | 1936 | 1937 | 1938 | 1939 | 1940 | 1941 | 1942 | 1943 | 1944 | 1945 |
|---|---|---|---|---|---|---|---|---|---|---|---|---|---|---|---|---|---|---|---|---|
| 1971 | 1.8 | 1.9 | 2.0 | 2.1 | 2.1 | 2.3 | 2.6 | 3.0 | 3.0 | 3.1 | 3.1 | 3.1 | 3.1 | 3.3 | 3.4 | 3.5 | 3.3 | 3.1 | 3.1 | 3.1 |
| 1972 | 1.9 | 1.9 | 2.0 | 2.1 | 2.1 | 2.3 | 2.6 | 3.0 | 3.1 | 3.1 | 3.1 | 3.1 | 3.1 | 3.3 | 3.4 | 3.5 | 3.3 | 3.1 | 3.1 | 3.2 |
| 1973 | 2.0 | 2.1 | 2.2 | 2.2 | 2.3 | 2.5 | 2.8 | 3.1 | 3.2 | 3.2 | 3.2 | 3.3 | 3.3 | 3.5 | 3.6 | 3.7 | 3.5 | 3.3 | 3.3 | 3.3 |
| 1974 | 2.2 | 2.3 | 2.4 | 2.4 | 2.5 | 2.7 | 3.0 | 3.3 | 3.4 | 3.4 | 3.4 | 3.5 | 3.5 | 3.7 | 3.8 | 3.9 | 3.7 | 3.6 | 3.6 | 3.6 |
| 1975 | 2.3 | 2.4 | 2.5 | 2.5 | 2.6 | 2.8 | 3.1 | 3.4 | 3.5 | 3.5 | 3.5 | 3.6 | 3.6 | 3.8 | 3.9 | 4.0 | 3.8 | 3.7 | 3.7 | 3.7 |
| 1976 | 2.3 | 2.4 | 2.5 | 2.6 | 2.6 | 2.8 | 3.1 | 3.4 | 3.5 | 3.6 | 3.6 | 3.6 | 3.6 | 3.8 | 3.9 | 4.0 | 3.9 | 3.7 | 3.7 | 3.8 |
| 1977 | 2.4 | 2.5 | 2.6 | 2.7 | 2.7 | 2.9 | 3.2 | 3.5 | 3.6 | 3.6 | 3.6 | 3.7 | 3.7 | 3.9 | 4.0 | 4.1 | 3.9 | 3.8 | 3.8 | 3.9 |
| 1978 | 2.5 | 2.6 | 2.7 | 2.8 | 2.8 | 3.0 | 3.3 | 3.6 | 3.7 | 3.7 | 3.8 | 3.8 | 3.8 | 4.0 | 4.1 | 4.2 | 4.1 | 3.9 | 4.0 | 4.0 |
| 1979 | 2.7 | 2.8 | 2.9 | 3.0 | 3.0 | 3.2 | 3.5 | 3.8 | 3.9 | 4.0 | 4.0 | 4.0 | 4.1 | 4.2 | 4.4 | 4.4 | 4.3 | 4.2 | 4.2 | 4.3 |
| 1980 | 2.9 | 3.0 | 3.1 | 3.2 | 3.2 | 3.4 | 3.7 | 4.0 | 4.1 | 4.1 | 4.2 | 4.2 | 4.2 | 4.4 | 4.5 | 4.6 | 4.5 | 4.4 | 4.4 | 4.5 |
| 1981 | 3.0 | 3.1 | 3.2 | 3.3 | 3.3 | 3.5 | 3.8 | 4.1 | 4.2 | 4.2 | 4.3 | 4.3 | 4.4 | 4.5 | 4.6 | 4.7 | 4.6 | 4.5 | 4.5 | 4.6 |
| 1982 | 3.0 | 3.1 | 3.2 | 3.3 | 3.3 | 3.5 | 3.8 | 4.1 | 4.2 | 4.2 | 4.2 | 4.3 | 4.3 | 4.5 | 4.6 | 4.7 | 4.6 | 4.5 | 4.5 | 4.6 |
| 1983 | 3.0 | 3.1 | 3.2 | 3.3 | 3.3 | 3.5 | 3.8 | 4.1 | 4.2 | 4.2 | 4.2 | 4.3 | 4.3 | 4.5 | 4.6 | 4.7 | 4.6 | 4.5 | 4.5 | 4.6 |
| 1984 | 3.0 | 3.1 | 3.2 | 3.3 | 3.4 | 3.5 | 3.8 | 4.1 | 4.2 | 4.2 | 4.2 | 4.3 | 4.3 | 4.5 | 4.6 | 4.7 | 4.6 | 4.4 | 4.5 | 4.5 |
| 1985 | 3.1 | 3.1 | 3.2 | 3.3 | 3.4 | 3.5 | 3.8 | 4.1 | 4.2 | 4.2 | 4.2 | 4.3 | 4.3 | 4.5 | 4.6 | 4.7 | 4.5 | 4.4 | 4.5 | 4.5 |
| 1986 | 3.0 | 3.1 | 3.2 | 3.3 | 3.3 | 3.5 | 3.8 | 4.0 | 4.1 | 4.1 | 4.2 | 4.2 | 4.2 | 4.4 | 4.5 | 4.6 | 4.5 | 4.4 | 4.4 | 4.4 |
| 1987 | 3.0 | 3.1 | 3.2 | 3.3 | 3.3 | 3.5 | 3.8 | 4.0 | 4.1 | 4.1 | 4.2 | 4.2 | 4.2 | 4.4 | 4.5 | 4.6 | 4.5 | 4.4 | 4.4 | 4.4 |
| 1988 | 3.1 | 3.1 | 3.2 | 3.3 | 3.4 | 3.5 | 3.8 | 4.0 | 4.1 | 4.1 | 4.2 | 4.2 | 4.3 | 4.4 | 4.5 | 4.6 | 4.5 | 4.4 | 4.4 | 4.4 |
| 1989 | 3.1 | 3.2 | 3.3 | 3.3 | 3.4 | 3.5 | 3.8 | 4.1 | 4.1 | 4.2 | 4.2 | 4.2 | 4.3 | 4.4 | 4.5 | 4.6 | 4.5 | 4.4 | 4.4 | 4.5 |
| 1990 | 3.1 | 3.2 | 3.3 | 3.4 | 3.4 | 3.6 | 3.8 | 4.1 | 4.2 | 4.2 | 4.2 | 4.3 | 4.3 | 4.4 | 4.5 | 4.6 | 4.5 | 4.4 | 4.4 | 4.5 |
| 1991 | 3.1 | 3.2 | 3.3 | 3.4 | 3.4 | 3.6 | 3.8 | 4.1 | 4.1 | 4.2 | 4.2 | 4.2 | 4.3 | 4.4 | 4.5 | 4.6 | 4.5 | 4.4 | 4.4 | 4.4 |
| 1992 | 3.1 | 3.2 | 3.3 | 3.4 | 3.4 | 3.6 | 3.8 | 4.1 | 4.1 | 4.1 | 4.1 | 4.2 | 4.2 | 4.4 | 4.5 | 4.5 | 4.4 | 4.3 | 4.4 | 4.4 |
| 1993 | 3.1 | 3.2 | 3.3 | 3.3 | 3.4 | 3.6 | 3.8 | 4.0 | 4.1 | 4.1 | 4.1 | 4.2 | 4.2 | 4.3 | 4.4 | 4.5 | 4.4 | 4.3 | 4.3 | 4.4 |
| 1994 | 3.1 | 3.2 | 3.3 | 3.3 | 3.4 | 3.5 | 3.8 | 4.0 | 4.1 | 4.1 | 4.1 | 4.2 | 4.2 | 4.3 | 4.4 | 4.5 | 4.4 | 4.3 | 4.3 | 4.4 |
| 1995 | 3.1 | 3.2 | 3.3 | 3.3 | 3.4 | 3.5 | 3.7 | 4.0 | 4.0 | 4.1 | 4.1 | 4.1 | 4.2 | 4.3 | 4.4 | 4.4 | 4.3 | 4.3 | 4.3 | 4.3 |
| 1996 | 3.1 | 3.2 | 3.3 | 3.3 | 3.4 | 3.5 | 3.7 | 4.0 | 4.0 | 4.1 | 4.1 | 4.1 | 4.1 | 4.3 | 4.4 | 4.4 | 4.3 | 4.2 | 4.3 | 4.3 |
| 1997 | 3.1 | 3.2 | 3.2 | 3.3 | 3.4 | 3.5 | 3.7 | 3.9 | 4.0 | 4.1 | 4.0 | 4.1 | 4.1 | 4.2 | 4.3 | 4.4 | 4.3 | 4.2 | 4.2 | 4.2 |
| 1998 | 3.1 | 3.1 | 3.2 | 3.3 | 3.3 | 3.5 | 3.7 | 3.9 | 4.0 | 4.0 | 4.0 | 4.0 | 4.1 | 4.2 | 4.3 | 4.3 | 4.2 | 4.1 | 4.2 | 4.2 |
| 1999 | 3.1 | 3.1 | 3.2 | 3.3 | 3.3 | 3.5 | 3.7 | 3.9 | 3.9 | 4.0 | 4.0 | 4.0 | 4.0 | 4.1 | 4.2 | 4.3 | 4.2 | 4.1 | 4.1 | 4.2 |
| 2000 | 3.1 | 3.1 | 3.2 | 3.3 | 3.3 | 3.4 | 3.7 | 3.9 | 3.9 | 4.0 | 4.0 | 4.0 | 4.0 | 4.1 | 4.2 | 4.3 | 4.1 | 4.1 | 4.1 | 4.1 |
| 2001 | 3.1 | 3.1 | 3.2 | 3.2 | 3.3 | 3.4 | 3.6 | 3.9 | 3.9 | 3.9 | 3.9 | 4.0 | 4.0 | 4.1 | 4.2 | 4.2 | 4.1 | 4.0 | 4.0 | 4.1 |
| 2002 | 3.0 | 3.1 | 3.2 | 3.2 | 3.3 | 3.4 | 3.6 | 3.8 | 3.9 | 3.9 | 3.9 | 4.0 | 4.0 | 4.1 | 4.2 | 4.2 | 4.1 | 4.0 | 4.0 | 4.0 |
| 2003 | 3.0 | 3.1 | 3.2 | 3.2 | 3.3 | 3.4 | 3.6 | 3.8 | 3.8 | 3.9 | 3.9 | 3.9 | 3.9 | 4.0 | 4.1 | 4.2 | 4.0 | 4.0 | 4.0 | 4.0 |
| 2004 | 3.0 | 3.1 | 3.2 | 3.2 | 3.3 | 3.4 | 3.6 | 3.8 | 3.8 | 3.9 | 3.9 | 3.9 | 3.9 | 4.0 | 4.1 | 4.2 | 4.1 | 4.0 | 4.0 | 4.0 |
| 2005 | 3.0 | 3.1 | 3.2 | 3.2 | 3.3 | 3.4 | 3.6 | 3.8 | 3.8 | 3.9 | 3.9 | 3.9 | 3.9 | 4.0 | 4.1 | 4.1 | 4.0 | 4.0 | 4.0 | 4.0 |
| 2006 | 3.0 | 3.1 | 3.2 | 3.2 | 3.3 | 3.4 | 3.6 | 3.8 | 3.8 | 3.8 | 3.9 | 3.9 | 3.9 | 4.0 | 4.1 | 4.1 | 4.0 | 4.0 | 4.0 | 4.0 |
| 2007 | 3.0 | 3.1 | 3.2 | 3.2 | 3.3 | 3.4 | 3.6 | 3.8 | 3.8 | 3.8 | 3.9 | 3.9 | 3.9 | 4.0 | 4.1 | 4.1 | 4.0 | 4.0 | 4.0 | 4.0 |
| 2008 | 3.0 | 3.1 | 3.1 | 3.2 | 3.2 | 3.3 | 3.5 | 3.7 | 3.8 | 3.8 | 3.8 | 3.8 | 3.8 | 3.9 | 4.0 | 4.1 | 4.0 | 3.9 | 3.9 | 3.9 |
| 2009 | 3.0 | 3.1 | 3.1 | 3.2 | 3.2 | 3.3 | 3.5 | 3.7 | 3.7 | 3.8 | 3.8 | 3.8 | 3.8 | 3.9 | 4.0 | 4.0 | 4.0 | 3.9 | 3.9 | 3.9 |
| 2010 | 3.0 | 3.0 | 3.1 | 3.2 | 3.2 | 3.3 | 3.5 | 3.7 | 3.7 | 3.7 | 3.8 | 3.8 | 3.8 | 3.9 | 4.0 | 4.0 | 3.9 | 3.8 | 3.9 | 3.9 |
| 2011 | 3.0 | 3.0 | 3.1 | 3.2 | 3.2 | 3.3 | 3.5 | 3.7 | 3.7 | 3.7 | 3.7 | 3.8 | 3.8 | 3.9 | 3.9 | 4.0 | 3.9 | 3.8 | 3.8 | 3.9 |
| 2012 | 3.0 | 3.0 | 3.1 | 3.1 | 3.2 | 3.3 | 3.5 | 3.6 | 3.7 | 3.7 | 3.7 | 3.8 | 3.8 | 3.9 | 3.9 | 4.0 | 3.9 | 3.8 | 3.8 | 3.8 |
| 2013 | 3.0 | 3.0 | 3.1 | 3.1 | 3.2 | 3.3 | 3.4 | 3.6 | 3.7 | 3.7 | 3.7 | 3.7 | 3.7 | 3.8 | 3.9 | 3.9 | 3.8 | 3.7 | 3.7 | 3.8 |
| 2014 | 2.9 | 3.0 | 3.0 | 3.1 | 3.1 | 3.2 | 3.4 | 3.6 | 3.6 | 3.6 | 3.7 | 3.7 | 3.7 | 3.8 | 3.8 | 3.9 | 3.8 | 3.7 | 3.7 | 3.7 |
| 2015 | 2.9 | 3.0 | 3.0 | 3.1 | 3.1 | 3.2 | 3.4 | 3.5 | 3.6 | 3.6 | 3.6 | 3.6 | 3.7 | 3.7 | 3.8 | 3.8 | 3.8 | 3.7 | 3.7 | 3.7 |
| 2016 | 2.9 | 2.9 | 3.0 | 3.1 | 3.1 | 3.2 | 3.4 | 3.5 | 3.6 | 3.6 | 3.6 | 3.6 | 3.6 | 3.7 | 3.8 | 3.8 | 3.7 | 3.7 | 3.7 | 3.7 |

## Appendix C-7

Inflation: Percent per annum total returns for all historical periods

From 1926 to 2016

| End Date | Start Date 1946 | 1947 | 1948 | 1949 | 1950 | 1951 | 1952 | 1953 | 1954 | 1955 | 1956 | 1957 | 1958 | 1959 | 1960 | 1961 | 1962 | 1963 | 1964 | 1965 |
|---|---|---|---|---|---|---|---|---|---|---|---|---|---|---|---|---|---|---|---|---|
| 1926 | | | | | | | | | | | | | | | | | | | | |
| 1927 | | | | | | | | | | | | | | | | | | | | |
| 1928 | | | | | | | | | | | | | | | | | | | | |
| 1929 | | | | | | | | | | | | | | | | | | | | |
| 1930 | | | | | | | | | | | | | | | | | | | | |
| 1931 | | | | | | | | | | | | | | | | | | | | |
| 1932 | | | | | | | | | | | | | | | | | | | | |
| 1933 | | | | | | | | | | | | | | | | | | | | |
| 1934 | | | | | | | | | | | | | | | | | | | | |
| 1935 | | | | | | | | | | | | | | | | | | | | |
| 1936 | | | | | | | | | | | | | | | | | | | | |
| 1937 | | | | | | | | | | | | | | | | | | | | |
| 1938 | | | | | | | | | | | | | | | | | | | | |
| 1939 | | | | | | | | | | | | | | | | | | | | |
| 1940 | | | | | | | | | | | | | | | | | | | | |
| 1941 | | | | | | | | | | | | | | | | | | | | |
| 1942 | | | | | | | | | | | | | | | | | | | | |
| 1943 | | | | | | | | | | | | | | | | | | | | |
| 1944 | | | | | | | | | | | | | | | | | | | | |
| 1945 | | | | | | | | | | | | | | | | | | | | |
| 1946 | 18.2 | | | | | | | | | | | | | | | | | | | |
| 1947 | 13.5 | 9.0 | | | | | | | | | | | | | | | | | | |
| 1948 | 9.8 | 5.8 | 2.7 | | | | | | | | | | | | | | | | | |
| 1949 | 6.8 | 3.2 | 0.4 | -1.8 | | | | | | | | | | | | | | | | |
| 1950 | 6.6 | 3.8 | 2.2 | 1.9 | 5.8 | | | | | | | | | | | | | | | |
| 1951 | 6.5 | 4.3 | 3.1 | 3.2 | 5.8 | 5.9 | | | | | | | | | | | | | | |
| 1952 | 5.6 | 3.7 | 2.6 | 2.6 | 4.2 | 3.3 | 0.9 | | | | | | | | | | | | | |
| 1953 | 5.0 | 3.2 | 2.3 | 2.2 | 3.3 | 2.4 | 0.8 | 0.6 | | | | | | | | | | | | |
| 1954 | 4.4 | 2.8 | 1.9 | 1.8 | 2.5 | 1.7 | 0.3 | 0.1 | -0.5 | | | | | | | | | | | |
| 1955 | 4.0 | 2.5 | 1.7 | 1.6 | 2.1 | 1.4 | 0.3 | 0.2 | -0.1 | 0.4 | | | | | | | | | | |
| 1956 | 3.9 | 2.5 | 1.8 | 1.7 | 2.2 | 1.7 | 0.8 | 0.8 | 0.9 | 1.6 | 2.9 | | | | | | | | | |
| 1957 | 3.8 | 2.6 | 2.0 | 1.9 | 2.3 | 1.9 | 1.2 | 1.3 | 1.4 | 2.1 | 2.9 | 3.0 | | | | | | | | |
| 1958 | 3.6 | 2.5 | 1.9 | 1.9 | 2.3 | 1.8 | 1.3 | 1.3 | 1.5 | 2.0 | 2.5 | 2.4 | 1.8 | | | | | | | |
| 1959 | 3.5 | 2.4 | 1.9 | 1.8 | 2.2 | 1.8 | 1.3 | 1.4 | 1.5 | 1.9 | 2.3 | 2.1 | 1.6 | 1.5 | | | | | | |
| 1960 | 3.3 | 2.4 | 1.9 | 1.8 | 2.1 | 1.8 | 1.3 | 1.4 | 1.5 | 1.8 | 2.1 | 1.9 | 1.6 | 1.5 | 1.5 | | | | | |
| 1961 | 3.2 | 2.2 | 1.8 | 1.7 | 2.0 | 1.7 | 1.3 | 1.3 | 1.4 | 1.7 | 1.9 | 1.7 | 1.4 | 1.2 | 1.1 | 0.7 | | | | |
| 1962 | 3.1 | 2.2 | 1.7 | 1.7 | 1.9 | 1.6 | 1.3 | 1.3 | 1.4 | 1.6 | 1.8 | 1.6 | 1.3 | 1.2 | 1.1 | 0.9 | 1.2 | | | |
| 1963 | 3.0 | 2.2 | 1.7 | 1.7 | 1.9 | 1.6 | 1.3 | 1.3 | 1.4 | 1.6 | 1.8 | 1.6 | 1.4 | 1.3 | 1.3 | 1.2 | 1.4 | 1.6 | | |
| 1964 | 2.9 | 2.1 | 1.7 | 1.6 | 1.9 | 1.6 | 1.3 | 1.3 | 1.4 | 1.6 | 1.7 | 1.6 | 1.4 | 1.3 | 1.2 | 1.2 | 1.4 | 1.4 | 1.2 | |
| 1965 | 2.8 | 2.1 | 1.7 | 1.7 | 1.9 | 1.6 | 1.3 | 1.4 | 1.4 | 1.6 | 1.7 | 1.6 | 1.4 | 1.4 | 1.4 | 1.3 | 1.5 | 1.6 | 1.6 | 1.9 |
| 1966 | 2.9 | 2.2 | 1.8 | 1.8 | 2.0 | 1.7 | 1.5 | 1.5 | 1.6 | 1.7 | 1.9 | 1.8 | 1.6 | 1.6 | 1.6 | 1.7 | 1.9 | 2.0 | 2.2 | 2.6 |
| 1967 | 2.9 | 2.2 | 1.9 | 1.8 | 2.0 | 1.8 | 1.6 | 1.6 | 1.7 | 1.8 | 2.0 | 1.9 | 1.8 | 1.8 | 1.8 | 1.9 | 2.1 | 2.2 | 2.4 | 2.8 |
| 1968 | 3.0 | 2.3 | 2.0 | 2.0 | 2.2 | 2.0 | 1.7 | 1.8 | 1.9 | 2.0 | 2.2 | 2.1 | 2.0 | 2.1 | 2.1 | 2.2 | 2.4 | 2.6 | 2.8 | 3.3 |
| 1969 | 3.1 | 2.5 | 2.2 | 2.2 | 2.4 | 2.2 | 2.0 | 2.0 | 2.1 | 2.3 | 2.5 | 2.4 | 2.4 | 2.4 | 2.5 | 2.6 | 2.9 | 3.1 | 3.4 | 3.8 |
| 1970 | 3.2 | 2.6 | 2.3 | 2.3 | 2.5 | 2.3 | 2.2 | 2.2 | 2.3 | 2.5 | 2.7 | 2.6 | 2.6 | 2.7 | 2.8 | 2.9 | 3.2 | 3.4 | 3.7 | 4.1 |

## Appendix C-7

Inflation: Percent per annum total returns for all historical periods

From 1926 to 2016

| End Date | Start Date 1946 | 1947 | 1948 | 1949 | 1950 | 1951 | 1952 | 1953 | 1954 | 1955 | 1956 | 1957 | 1958 | 1959 | 1960 | 1961 | 1962 | 1963 | 1964 | 1965 |
|---|---|---|---|---|---|---|---|---|---|---|---|---|---|---|---|---|---|---|---|---|
| 1971 | 3.2 | 2.6 | 2.4 | 2.4 | 2.5 | 2.4 | 2.2 | 2.3 | 2.4 | 2.6 | 2.7 | 2.7 | 2.7 | 2.7 | 2.8 | 3.0 | 3.2 | 3.4 | 3.6 | 4.0 |
| 1972 | 3.2 | 2.7 | 2.4 | 2.4 | 2.6 | 2.4 | 2.3 | 2.3 | 2.4 | 2.6 | 2.7 | 2.7 | 2.7 | 2.8 | 2.9 | 3.0 | 3.2 | 3.4 | 3.6 | 3.9 |
| 1973 | 3.4 | 2.9 | 2.6 | 2.6 | 2.8 | 2.7 | 2.6 | 2.6 | 2.8 | 2.9 | 3.1 | 3.1 | 3.1 | 3.2 | 3.3 | 3.4 | 3.7 | 3.9 | 4.1 | 4.4 |
| 1974 | 3.7 | 3.2 | 3.0 | 3.0 | 3.2 | 3.1 | 3.0 | 3.1 | 3.2 | 3.4 | 3.5 | 3.6 | 3.6 | 3.7 | 3.9 | 4.0 | 4.3 | 4.6 | 4.8 | 5.2 |
| 1975 | 3.8 | 3.3 | 3.1 | 3.1 | 3.3 | 3.2 | 3.1 | 3.2 | 3.4 | 3.5 | 3.7 | 3.7 | 3.8 | 3.9 | 4.1 | 4.2 | 4.5 | 4.7 | 5.0 | 5.4 |
| 1976 | 3.8 | 3.4 | 3.2 | 3.2 | 3.4 | 3.3 | 3.2 | 3.3 | 3.4 | 3.6 | 3.8 | 3.8 | 3.8 | 4.0 | 4.1 | 4.3 | 4.5 | 4.8 | 5.0 | 5.3 |
| 1977 | 3.9 | 3.5 | 3.3 | 3.3 | 3.5 | 3.4 | 3.3 | 3.4 | 3.6 | 3.7 | 3.9 | 3.9 | 4.0 | 4.1 | 4.2 | 4.4 | 4.7 | 4.9 | 5.1 | 5.4 |
| 1978 | 4.1 | 3.7 | 3.5 | 3.5 | 3.7 | 3.6 | 3.5 | 3.6 | 3.8 | 3.9 | 4.1 | 4.2 | 4.2 | 4.3 | 4.5 | 4.7 | 4.9 | 5.1 | 5.4 | 5.7 |
| 1979 | 4.3 | 3.9 | 3.8 | 3.8 | 4.0 | 3.9 | 3.9 | 4.0 | 4.1 | 4.3 | 4.5 | 4.5 | 4.6 | 4.8 | 4.9 | 5.1 | 5.4 | 5.6 | 5.9 | 6.2 |
| 1980 | 4.5 | 4.2 | 4.0 | 4.1 | 4.3 | 4.2 | 4.2 | 4.3 | 4.4 | 4.6 | 4.8 | 4.9 | 4.9 | 5.1 | 5.3 | 5.5 | 5.7 | 6.0 | 6.2 | 6.6 |
| 1981 | 4.7 | 4.3 | 4.2 | 4.2 | 4.4 | 4.4 | 4.3 | 4.4 | 4.6 | 4.8 | 4.9 | 5.0 | 5.1 | 5.3 | 5.4 | 5.6 | 5.9 | 6.1 | 6.4 | 6.7 |
| 1982 | 4.6 | 4.3 | 4.2 | 4.2 | 4.4 | 4.3 | 4.3 | 4.4 | 4.5 | 4.7 | 4.9 | 5.0 | 5.1 | 5.2 | 5.4 | 5.5 | 5.8 | 6.0 | 6.2 | 6.5 |
| 1983 | 4.6 | 4.3 | 4.2 | 4.2 | 4.4 | 4.3 | 4.3 | 4.4 | 4.5 | 4.7 | 4.9 | 4.9 | 5.0 | 5.1 | 5.3 | 5.5 | 5.7 | 5.9 | 6.1 | 6.4 |
| 1984 | 4.6 | 4.3 | 4.1 | 4.2 | 4.4 | 4.3 | 4.3 | 4.4 | 4.5 | 4.7 | 4.8 | 4.9 | 5.0 | 5.1 | 5.2 | 5.4 | 5.6 | 5.8 | 6.0 | 6.3 |
| 1985 | 4.6 | 4.3 | 4.2 | 4.2 | 4.3 | 4.3 | 4.3 | 4.4 | 4.5 | 4.6 | 4.8 | 4.9 | 4.9 | 5.0 | 5.2 | 5.3 | 5.5 | 5.7 | 5.9 | 6.1 |
| 1986 | 4.5 | 4.2 | 4.1 | 4.1 | 4.3 | 4.2 | 4.2 | 4.3 | 4.4 | 4.5 | 4.7 | 4.7 | 4.8 | 4.9 | 5.0 | 5.2 | 5.4 | 5.5 | 5.7 | 5.9 |
| 1987 | 4.5 | 4.2 | 4.1 | 4.1 | 4.3 | 4.2 | 4.2 | 4.3 | 4.4 | 4.5 | 4.7 | 4.7 | 4.8 | 4.9 | 5.0 | 5.1 | 5.3 | 5.5 | 5.6 | 5.8 |
| 1988 | 4.5 | 4.2 | 4.1 | 4.1 | 4.3 | 4.2 | 4.2 | 4.3 | 4.4 | 4.5 | 4.7 | 4.7 | 4.8 | 4.9 | 5.0 | 5.1 | 5.3 | 5.4 | 5.6 | 5.8 |
| 1989 | 4.5 | 4.2 | 4.1 | 4.1 | 4.3 | 4.2 | 4.2 | 4.3 | 4.4 | 4.5 | 4.7 | 4.7 | 4.8 | 4.9 | 5.0 | 5.1 | 5.3 | 5.4 | 5.6 | 5.7 |
| 1990 | 4.5 | 4.2 | 4.1 | 4.2 | 4.3 | 4.3 | 4.2 | 4.3 | 4.4 | 4.6 | 4.7 | 4.8 | 4.8 | 4.9 | 5.0 | 5.1 | 5.3 | 5.4 | 5.6 | 5.8 |
| 1991 | 4.5 | 4.2 | 4.1 | 4.1 | 4.3 | 4.3 | 4.2 | 4.3 | 4.4 | 4.5 | 4.7 | 4.7 | 4.8 | 4.8 | 5.0 | 5.1 | 5.2 | 5.4 | 5.5 | 5.7 |
| 1992 | 4.5 | 4.2 | 4.1 | 4.1 | 4.3 | 4.2 | 4.2 | 4.3 | 4.4 | 4.5 | 4.6 | 4.7 | 4.7 | 4.8 | 4.9 | 5.0 | 5.1 | 5.3 | 5.4 | 5.6 |
| 1993 | 4.4 | 4.2 | 4.1 | 4.1 | 4.2 | 4.2 | 4.1 | 4.2 | 4.3 | 4.4 | 4.6 | 4.6 | 4.6 | 4.7 | 4.8 | 4.9 | 5.1 | 5.2 | 5.3 | 5.5 |
| 1994 | 4.4 | 4.1 | 4.0 | 4.1 | 4.2 | 4.2 | 4.1 | 4.2 | 4.3 | 4.4 | 4.5 | 4.5 | 4.6 | 4.7 | 4.8 | 4.9 | 5.0 | 5.1 | 5.2 | 5.4 |
| 1995 | 4.4 | 4.1 | 4.0 | 4.0 | 4.2 | 4.1 | 4.1 | 4.2 | 4.2 | 4.4 | 4.5 | 4.5 | 4.5 | 4.6 | 4.7 | 4.8 | 4.9 | 5.0 | 5.1 | 5.3 |
| 1996 | 4.3 | 4.1 | 4.0 | 4.0 | 4.1 | 4.1 | 4.1 | 4.1 | 4.2 | 4.3 | 4.4 | 4.5 | 4.5 | 4.6 | 4.7 | 4.8 | 4.9 | 5.0 | 5.1 | 5.2 |
| 1997 | 4.3 | 4.0 | 3.9 | 4.0 | 4.1 | 4.0 | 4.0 | 4.1 | 4.2 | 4.3 | 4.4 | 4.4 | 4.4 | 4.5 | 4.6 | 4.7 | 4.8 | 4.9 | 5.0 | 5.1 |
| 1998 | 4.2 | 4.0 | 3.9 | 3.9 | 4.0 | 4.0 | 4.0 | 4.0 | 4.1 | 4.2 | 4.3 | 4.3 | 4.4 | 4.4 | 4.5 | 4.6 | 4.7 | 4.8 | 4.9 | 5.0 |
| 1999 | 4.2 | 4.0 | 3.9 | 3.9 | 4.0 | 4.0 | 3.9 | 4.0 | 4.1 | 4.2 | 4.3 | 4.3 | 4.3 | 4.4 | 4.5 | 4.5 | 4.6 | 4.7 | 4.8 | 4.9 |
| 2000 | 4.2 | 3.9 | 3.9 | 3.9 | 4.0 | 4.0 | 3.9 | 4.0 | 4.1 | 4.2 | 4.2 | 4.3 | 4.3 | 4.4 | 4.4 | 4.5 | 4.6 | 4.7 | 4.8 | 4.9 |
| 2001 | 4.1 | 3.9 | 3.8 | 3.8 | 3.9 | 3.9 | 3.9 | 3.9 | 4.0 | 4.1 | 4.2 | 4.2 | 4.2 | 4.3 | 4.4 | 4.4 | 4.5 | 4.6 | 4.7 | 4.8 |
| 2002 | 4.1 | 3.9 | 3.8 | 3.8 | 3.9 | 3.9 | 3.8 | 3.9 | 4.0 | 4.1 | 4.1 | 4.2 | 4.2 | 4.3 | 4.3 | 4.4 | 4.5 | 4.6 | 4.6 | 4.7 |
| 2003 | 4.1 | 3.8 | 3.8 | 3.8 | 3.9 | 3.8 | 3.8 | 3.9 | 3.9 | 4.0 | 4.1 | 4.1 | 4.1 | 4.2 | 4.3 | 4.3 | 4.4 | 4.5 | 4.6 | 4.7 |
| 2004 | 4.1 | 3.8 | 3.7 | 3.8 | 3.9 | 3.8 | 3.8 | 3.8 | 3.9 | 4.0 | 4.1 | 4.1 | 4.1 | 4.2 | 4.2 | 4.3 | 4.4 | 4.5 | 4.6 | 4.6 |
| 2005 | 4.0 | 3.8 | 3.7 | 3.8 | 3.9 | 3.8 | 3.8 | 3.8 | 3.9 | 4.0 | 4.1 | 4.1 | 4.1 | 4.2 | 4.2 | 4.3 | 4.4 | 4.4 | 4.5 | 4.6 |
| 2006 | 4.0 | 3.8 | 3.7 | 3.7 | 3.8 | 3.8 | 3.8 | 3.8 | 3.9 | 4.0 | 4.0 | 4.1 | 4.1 | 4.1 | 4.2 | 4.2 | 4.3 | 4.4 | 4.5 | 4.5 |
| 2007 | 4.0 | 3.8 | 3.7 | 3.7 | 3.8 | 3.8 | 3.8 | 3.8 | 3.9 | 4.0 | 4.0 | 4.1 | 4.1 | 4.1 | 4.2 | 4.2 | 4.3 | 4.4 | 4.5 | 4.5 |
| 2008 | 4.0 | 3.7 | 3.7 | 3.7 | 3.8 | 3.7 | 3.7 | 3.8 | 3.8 | 3.9 | 4.0 | 4.0 | 4.0 | 4.0 | 4.1 | 4.2 | 4.2 | 4.3 | 4.4 | 4.4 |
| 2009 | 3.9 | 3.7 | 3.6 | 3.7 | 3.8 | 3.7 | 3.7 | 3.7 | 3.8 | 3.9 | 3.9 | 4.0 | 4.0 | 4.0 | 4.1 | 4.1 | 4.2 | 4.3 | 4.3 | 4.4 |
| 2010 | 3.9 | 3.7 | 3.6 | 3.6 | 3.7 | 3.7 | 3.6 | 3.7 | 3.8 | 3.8 | 3.9 | 3.9 | 3.9 | 4.0 | 4.0 | 4.1 | 4.1 | 4.2 | 4.3 | 4.3 |
| 2011 | 3.9 | 3.7 | 3.6 | 3.6 | 3.7 | 3.7 | 3.6 | 3.7 | 3.7 | 3.8 | 3.9 | 3.9 | 3.9 | 4.0 | 4.0 | 4.0 | 4.1 | 4.2 | 4.2 | 4.3 |
| 2012 | 3.9 | 3.7 | 3.6 | 3.6 | 3.7 | 3.6 | 3.6 | 3.7 | 3.7 | 3.8 | 3.8 | 3.9 | 3.9 | 3.9 | 4.0 | 4.0 | 4.1 | 4.1 | 4.2 | 4.2 |
| 2013 | 3.8 | 3.6 | 3.5 | 3.6 | 3.6 | 3.6 | 3.6 | 3.6 | 3.7 | 3.7 | 3.8 | 3.8 | 3.8 | 3.9 | 3.9 | 4.0 | 4.0 | 4.1 | 4.1 | 4.2 |
| 2014 | 3.8 | 3.6 | 3.5 | 3.5 | 3.6 | 3.6 | 3.5 | 3.6 | 3.6 | 3.7 | 3.8 | 3.8 | 3.8 | 3.8 | 3.9 | 4.0 | 4.0 | 4.1 | 4.1 | 4.1 |
| 2015 | 3.7 | 3.5 | 3.5 | 3.5 | 3.6 | 3.5 | 3.5 | 3.5 | 3.6 | 3.6 | 3.7 | 3.7 | 3.7 | 3.8 | 3.8 | 3.8 | 3.9 | 3.9 | 4.0 | 4.0 |
| 2016 | 3.7 | 3.5 | 3.4 | 3.4 | 3.5 | 3.5 | 3.5 | 3.5 | 3.5 | 3.6 | 3.7 | 3.7 | 3.7 | 3.7 | 3.8 | 3.8 | 3.9 | 3.9 | 4.0 | 4.0 |

**Appendix C-7**

Inflation: Percent per annum total returns for all historical periods
From 1926 to 2016

| Start Date | 1966 | 1967 | 1968 | 1969 | 1970 |
|---|---|---|---|---|---|
| End Date | | | | | |
| 1966 | 3.4 | | | | |
| 1967 | 3.2 | 3.0 | | | |
| 1968 | 3.7 | 3.9 | 4.7 | | |
| 1969 | 4.3 | 4.6 | 5.4 | 6.1 | |
| 1970 | 4.5 | 4.8 | 5.4 | 5.8 | 5.5 |

# Appendix C-7

Inflation: Percent per annum total returns for all historical periods

From 1926 to 2016

| End Date | Start Date 1966 | 1967 | 1968 | 1969 | 1970 | 1971 | 1972 | 1973 | 1974 | 1975 | 1976 | 1977 | 1978 | 1979 | 1980 | 1981 | 1982 | 1983 | 1984 | 1985 |
|---|---|---|---|---|---|---|---|---|---|---|---|---|---|---|---|---|---|---|---|---|
| 1971 | 4.3 | 4.5 | 4.9 | 5.0 | 4.4 | 3.4 | | | | | | | | | | | | | | |
| 1972 | 4.2 | 4.3 | 4.6 | 4.6 | 4.1 | 3.4 | 3.4 | | | | | | | | | | | | | |
| 1973 | 4.8 | 5.0 | 5.3 | 5.4 | 5.2 | 5.2 | 6.1 | 8.8 | | | | | | | | | | | | |
| 1974 | 5.6 | 5.9 | 6.3 | 6.5 | 6.6 | 6.9 | 8.1 | 10.5 | 12.2 | | | | | | | | | | | |
| 1975 | 5.7 | 6.0 | 6.4 | 6.6 | 6.7 | 6.9 | 7.8 | 9.3 | 9.6 | 7.0 | | | | | | | | | | |
| 1976 | 5.6 | 5.9 | 6.2 | 6.4 | 6.4 | 6.6 | 7.2 | 8.2 | 8.0 | 5.9 | 4.8 | | | | | | | | | |
| 1977 | 5.7 | 5.9 | 6.2 | 6.4 | 6.4 | 6.6 | 7.1 | 7.9 | 7.7 | 6.2 | 5.8 | 6.8 | | | | | | | | |
| 1978 | 6.0 | 6.2 | 6.5 | 6.7 | 6.7 | 6.9 | 7.4 | 8.1 | 7.9 | 6.9 | 6.9 | 7.9 | 9.0 | | | | | | | |
| 1979 | 6.5 | 6.7 | 7.0 | 7.3 | 7.4 | 7.6 | 8.1 | 8.8 | 8.8 | 8.1 | 8.4 | 9.7 | 11.1 | 13.3 | | | | | | |
| 1980 | 6.9 | 7.1 | 7.4 | 7.7 | 7.8 | 8.1 | 8.6 | 9.3 | 9.3 | 8.8 | 9.2 | 10.3 | 11.6 | 12.9 | 12.4 | | | | | |
| 1981 | 7.0 | 7.2 | 7.6 | 7.8 | 7.9 | 8.1 | 8.6 | 9.2 | 9.3 | 8.9 | 9.2 | 10.1 | 10.9 | 11.5 | 10.7 | 8.9 | | | | |
| 1982 | 6.8 | 7.0 | 7.3 | 7.5 | 7.6 | 7.8 | 8.2 | 8.7 | 8.2 | 8.2 | 8.4 | 9.0 | 9.5 | 9.6 | 8.3 | 6.4 | 3.9 | | | |
| 1983 | 6.6 | 6.8 | 7.1 | 7.2 | 7.3 | 7.5 | 7.8 | 8.2 | 8.2 | 7.7 | 7.8 | 8.2 | 8.5 | 8.4 | 7.2 | 5.5 | 3.8 | 3.8 | | |
| 1984 | 6.5 | 6.7 | 6.9 | 7.0 | 7.1 | 7.2 | 7.5 | 7.9 | 7.8 | 7.3 | 7.4 | 7.7 | 7.8 | 7.6 | 6.5 | 5.1 | 3.9 | 3.9 | 4.0 | |
| 1985 | 6.4 | 6.5 | 6.7 | 6.8 | 6.9 | 7.0 | 7.2 | 7.5 | 7.4 | 7.0 | 7.0 | 7.3 | 7.3 | 7.1 | 6.1 | 4.8 | 3.8 | 3.8 | 3.9 | 3.8 |
| 1986 | 6.1 | 6.2 | 6.4 | 6.5 | 6.5 | 6.6 | 6.8 | 7.1 | 6.9 | 6.5 | 6.5 | 6.6 | 6.6 | 6.3 | 5.3 | 4.2 | 3.3 | 3.2 | 2.9 | 2.4 |
| 1987 | 6.0 | 6.2 | 6.3 | 6.4 | 6.4 | 6.5 | 6.7 | 6.9 | 6.8 | 6.3 | 6.3 | 6.4 | 6.4 | 6.1 | 5.2 | 4.2 | 3.4 | 3.4 | 3.3 | 3.1 |
| 1988 | 6.0 | 6.1 | 6.2 | 6.3 | 6.3 | 6.4 | 6.5 | 6.7 | 6.6 | 6.2 | 6.1 | 6.3 | 6.2 | 5.9 | 5.1 | 4.1 | 3.6 | 3.6 | 3.5 | 3.4 |
| 1989 | 5.9 | 6.0 | 6.2 | 6.2 | 6.2 | 6.3 | 6.4 | 6.6 | 6.5 | 6.1 | 6.0 | 6.1 | 6.1 | 5.8 | 5.1 | 4.3 | 3.7 | 3.7 | 3.7 | 3.7 |
| 1990 | 5.9 | 6.0 | 6.1 | 6.2 | 6.2 | 6.3 | 6.4 | 6.6 | 6.5 | 6.1 | 6.0 | 6.1 | 6.1 | 5.8 | 5.2 | 4.5 | 4.0 | 4.0 | 4.1 | 3.9 |
| 1991 | 5.8 | 5.9 | 6.0 | 6.1 | 6.1 | 6.1 | 6.2 | 6.4 | 6.3 | 5.9 | 5.9 | 5.9 | 5.9 | 5.6 | 5.0 | 4.4 | 3.8 | 3.9 | 3.9 | 3.9 |
| 1992 | 5.7 | 5.8 | 5.9 | 5.9 | 5.9 | 6.0 | 6.1 | 6.2 | 6.1 | 5.7 | 5.7 | 5.7 | 5.7 | 5.4 | 4.8 | 4.2 | 3.7 | 3.8 | 3.8 | 3.8 |
| 1993 | 5.6 | 5.7 | 5.8 | 5.8 | 5.8 | 5.8 | 6.0 | 6.0 | 5.9 | 5.6 | 5.5 | 5.6 | 5.5 | 5.2 | 4.7 | 4.1 | 3.6 | 3.7 | 3.7 | 3.7 |
| 1994 | 5.5 | 5.6 | 5.7 | 5.7 | 5.7 | 5.7 | 5.8 | 5.9 | 5.8 | 5.4 | 5.4 | 5.4 | 5.3 | 5.1 | 4.6 | 4.0 | 3.6 | 3.6 | 3.6 | 3.6 |
| 1995 | 5.4 | 5.5 | 5.5 | 5.6 | 5.5 | 5.6 | 5.6 | 5.7 | 5.6 | 5.3 | 5.2 | 5.2 | 5.2 | 4.9 | 4.4 | 3.9 | 3.6 | 3.5 | 3.5 | 3.5 |
| 1996 | 5.3 | 5.4 | 5.5 | 5.5 | 5.5 | 5.5 | 5.6 | 5.6 | 5.5 | 5.2 | 5.1 | 5.1 | 5.1 | 4.8 | 4.4 | 3.9 | 3.6 | 3.5 | 3.5 | 3.5 |
| 1997 | 5.2 | 5.3 | 5.3 | 5.4 | 5.3 | 5.3 | 5.4 | 5.5 | 5.3 | 5.1 | 5.0 | 5.0 | 4.9 | 4.7 | 4.2 | 3.8 | 3.4 | 3.4 | 3.4 | 3.3 |
| 1998 | 5.1 | 5.1 | 5.2 | 5.2 | 5.2 | 5.2 | 5.3 | 5.3 | 5.2 | 5.0 | 4.8 | 4.8 | 4.7 | 4.5 | 4.1 | 3.6 | 3.3 | 3.3 | 3.3 | 3.2 |
| 1999 | 5.0 | 5.1 | 5.1 | 5.1 | 5.1 | 5.1 | 5.2 | 5.2 | 5.1 | 4.8 | 4.7 | 4.7 | 4.6 | 4.4 | 4.0 | 3.6 | 3.3 | 3.3 | 3.2 | 3.2 |
| 2000 | 5.0 | 5.0 | 5.1 | 5.1 | 5.1 | 5.0 | 5.1 | 5.2 | 5.0 | 4.8 | 4.7 | 4.7 | 4.5 | 4.4 | 4.0 | 3.6 | 3.2 | 3.2 | 3.1 | 3.1 |
| 2001 | 4.9 | 4.9 | 5.0 | 5.0 | 4.9 | 4.9 | 5.0 | 5.0 | 4.9 | 4.6 | 4.6 | 4.5 | 4.4 | 4.3 | 3.9 | 3.5 | 3.2 | 3.1 | 3.1 | 3.1 |
| 2002 | 4.8 | 4.8 | 4.9 | 4.9 | 4.9 | 4.8 | 4.9 | 4.9 | 4.8 | 4.6 | 4.5 | 4.5 | 4.4 | 4.2 | 3.8 | 3.4 | 3.2 | 3.1 | 3.0 | 3.0 |
| 2003 | 4.7 | 4.8 | 4.8 | 4.8 | 4.8 | 4.8 | 4.8 | 4.8 | 4.7 | 4.5 | 4.4 | 4.4 | 4.3 | 4.1 | 3.7 | 3.4 | 3.1 | 3.1 | 3.1 | 3.0 |
| 2004 | 4.7 | 4.7 | 4.8 | 4.8 | 4.7 | 4.7 | 4.8 | 4.8 | 4.7 | 4.4 | 4.3 | 4.3 | 4.2 | 4.0 | 3.7 | 3.4 | 3.1 | 3.1 | 3.1 | 3.0 |
| 2005 | 4.6 | 4.7 | 4.7 | 4.7 | 4.6 | 4.7 | 4.7 | 4.7 | 4.6 | 4.4 | 4.3 | 4.3 | 4.2 | 4.0 | 3.7 | 3.3 | 3.1 | 3.1 | 3.1 | 3.0 |
| 2006 | 4.6 | 4.6 | 4.7 | 4.7 | 4.6 | 4.6 | 4.7 | 4.7 | 4.6 | 4.3 | 4.3 | 4.2 | 4.1 | 4.0 | 3.6 | 3.3 | 3.1 | 3.1 | 3.0 | 3.0 |
| 2007 | 4.5 | 4.6 | 4.7 | 4.7 | 4.6 | 4.6 | 4.6 | 4.7 | 4.4 | 4.3 | 4.3 | 4.2 | 4.1 | 3.8 | 3.7 | 3.4 | 3.1 | 3.1 | 3.1 | 3.0 |
| 2008 | 4.4 | 4.5 | 4.6 | 4.5 | 4.5 | 4.5 | 4.5 | 4.5 | 4.4 | 4.2 | 4.1 | 4.1 | 4.0 | 3.8 | 3.5 | 3.2 | 3.0 | 3.0 | 3.0 | 2.9 |
| 2009 | 4.4 | 4.5 | 4.5 | 4.5 | 4.5 | 4.4 | 4.5 | 4.5 | 4.4 | 4.2 | 4.1 | 4.1 | 4.0 | 3.8 | 3.5 | 3.2 | 3.0 | 3.0 | 3.0 | 2.9 |
| 2010 | 4.3 | 4.4 | 4.4 | 4.4 | 4.4 | 4.4 | 4.4 | 4.4 | 4.3 | 4.1 | 4.0 | 4.0 | 3.9 | 3.7 | 3.4 | 3.2 | 3.0 | 2.9 | 2.9 | 2.9 |
| 2011 | 4.3 | 4.4 | 4.4 | 4.4 | 4.4 | 4.3 | 4.4 | 4.4 | 4.3 | 4.1 | 4.0 | 3.9 | 3.9 | 3.7 | 3.4 | 3.2 | 3.0 | 2.9 | 2.9 | 2.9 |
| 2012 | 4.2 | 4.3 | 4.3 | 4.3 | 4.3 | 4.3 | 4.3 | 4.3 | 4.2 | 4.0 | 3.9 | 3.9 | 3.8 | 3.7 | 3.4 | 3.1 | 2.9 | 2.9 | 2.9 | 2.8 |
| 2013 | 4.2 | 4.3 | 4.3 | 4.3 | 4.2 | 4.2 | 4.2 | 4.2 | 4.1 | 3.9 | 3.8 | 3.8 | 3.7 | 3.6 | 3.3 | 3.1 | 2.9 | 2.9 | 2.8 | 2.8 |
| 2014 | 4.1 | 4.2 | 4.2 | 4.2 | 4.1 | 4.1 | 4.1 | 4.2 | 4.0 | 3.8 | 3.8 | 3.7 | 3.7 | 3.5 | 3.2 | 3.0 | 2.8 | 2.8 | 2.7 | 2.7 |
| 2015 | 4.1 | 4.1 | 4.1 | 4.1 | 4.1 | 4.0 | 4.1 | 4.1 | 4.0 | 3.8 | 3.7 | 3.7 | 3.6 | 3.4 | 3.2 | 2.9 | 2.8 | 2.7 | 2.7 | 2.6 |
| 2016 | 4.1 | 4.1 | 4.1 | 4.1 | 4.0 | 4.0 | 4.0 | 4.0 | 3.9 | 3.7 | 3.7 | 3.6 | 3.5 | 3.4 | 3.1 | 2.9 | 2.7 | 2.7 | 2.7 | 2.6 |

## Appendix C-7

Inflation: Percent per annum total returns for all historical periods
From 1926 to 2016

| End Date | Start Date 1986 | 1987 | 1988 | 1989 | 1990 | 1991 | 1992 | 1993 | 1994 | 1995 | 1996 | 1997 | 1998 | 1999 | 2000 | 2001 | 2002 | 2003 | 2004 | 2005 |
|---|---|---|---|---|---|---|---|---|---|---|---|---|---|---|---|---|---|---|---|---|
| 1971 | | | | | | | | | | | | | | | | | | | | |
| 1972 | | | | | | | | | | | | | | | | | | | | |
| 1973 | | | | | | | | | | | | | | | | | | | | |
| 1974 | | | | | | | | | | | | | | | | | | | | |
| 1975 | | | | | | | | | | | | | | | | | | | | |
| 1976 | | | | | | | | | | | | | | | | | | | | |
| 1977 | | | | | | | | | | | | | | | | | | | | |
| 1978 | | | | | | | | | | | | | | | | | | | | |
| 1979 | | | | | | | | | | | | | | | | | | | | |
| 1980 | | | | | | | | | | | | | | | | | | | | |
| 1981 | | | | | | | | | | | | | | | | | | | | |
| 1982 | | | | | | | | | | | | | | | | | | | | |
| 1983 | | | | | | | | | | | | | | | | | | | | |
| 1984 | | | | | | | | | | | | | | | | | | | | |
| 1985 | | | | | | | | | | | | | | | | | | | | |
| 1986 | 1.1 | | | | | | | | | | | | | | | | | | | |
| 1987 | 2.8 | 4.4 | | | | | | | | | | | | | | | | | | |
| 1988 | 3.3 | 4.4 | 4.4 | | | | | | | | | | | | | | | | | |
| 1989 | 3.6 | 4.5 | 4.5 | 4.6 | | | | | | | | | | | | | | | | |
| 1990 | 4.1 | 4.9 | 5.1 | 5.4 | 6.1 | | | | | | | | | | | | | | | |
| 1991 | 4.0 | 4.5 | 4.6 | 4.6 | 4.6 | 3.1 | | | | | | | | | | | | | | |
| 1992 | 3.8 | 4.3 | 4.2 | 4.2 | 4.0 | 3.0 | 2.9 | | | | | | | | | | | | | |
| 1993 | 3.7 | 4.0 | 4.0 | 3.9 | 3.7 | 2.9 | 2.8 | 2.7 | | | | | | | | | | | | |
| 1994 | 3.6 | 3.9 | 3.8 | 3.7 | 3.5 | 2.8 | 2.8 | 2.7 | 2.7 | | | | | | | | | | | |
| 1995 | 3.5 | 3.7 | 3.6 | 3.5 | 3.3 | 2.8 | 2.7 | 2.7 | 2.6 | 2.5 | | | | | | | | | | |
| 1996 | 3.4 | 3.7 | 3.6 | 3.5 | 3.3 | 2.9 | 2.8 | 2.8 | 2.8 | 2.9 | 3.3 | | | | | | | | | |
| 1997 | 3.3 | 3.5 | 3.4 | 3.3 | 3.1 | 2.7 | 2.6 | 2.6 | 2.6 | 2.5 | 2.5 | 1.7 | | | | | | | | |
| 1998 | 3.2 | 3.3 | 3.2 | 3.1 | 3.0 | 2.6 | 2.5 | 2.4 | 2.4 | 2.3 | 2.2 | 1.7 | 1.6 | | | | | | | |
| 1999 | 3.1 | 3.3 | 3.2 | 3.1 | 2.9 | 2.6 | 2.5 | 2.5 | 2.4 | 2.4 | 2.3 | 2.0 | 2.1 | 2.7 | | | | | | |
| 2000 | 3.1 | 3.3 | 3.2 | 3.1 | 3.0 | 2.7 | 2.6 | 2.6 | 2.6 | 2.5 | 2.5 | 2.3 | 2.6 | 3.0 | 3.4 | | | | | |
| 2001 | 3.0 | 3.2 | 3.1 | 3.0 | 2.9 | 2.6 | 2.5 | 2.5 | 2.4 | 2.4 | 2.4 | 2.2 | 2.3 | 2.5 | 2.5 | 1.6 | | | | |
| 2002 | 3.0 | 3.1 | 3.0 | 2.9 | 2.8 | 2.5 | 2.5 | 2.4 | 2.4 | 2.4 | 2.4 | 2.2 | 2.3 | 2.5 | 2.4 | 2.0 | 2.4 | | | |
| 2003 | 2.9 | 3.1 | 3.0 | 2.9 | 2.7 | 2.5 | 2.4 | 2.4 | 2.3 | 2.3 | 2.3 | 2.2 | 2.2 | 2.4 | 2.3 | 1.9 | 2.1 | 1.9 | | |
| 2004 | 3.0 | 3.1 | 3.0 | 2.9 | 2.8 | 2.5 | 2.5 | 2.5 | 2.4 | 2.4 | 2.4 | 2.3 | 2.4 | 2.5 | 2.5 | 2.3 | 2.5 | 2.6 | 3.3 | |
| 2005 | 3.0 | 3.1 | 3.0 | 2.9 | 2.8 | 2.6 | 2.5 | 2.5 | 2.5 | 2.5 | 2.5 | 2.4 | 2.5 | 2.6 | 2.6 | 2.5 | 2.7 | 2.8 | 3.3 | 3.4 |
| 2006 | 3.0 | 3.1 | 3.0 | 2.9 | 2.8 | 2.6 | 2.5 | 2.5 | 2.5 | 2.5 | 2.5 | 2.4 | 2.5 | 2.6 | 2.6 | 2.5 | 2.7 | 2.8 | 3.1 | 3.0 |
| 2007 | 3.0 | 3.1 | 3.0 | 3.0 | 2.9 | 2.7 | 2.6 | 2.6 | 2.6 | 2.6 | 2.6 | 2.6 | 2.7 | 2.8 | 2.8 | 2.7 | 2.9 | 3.0 | 3.3 | 3.3 |
| 2008 | 2.9 | 3.0 | 2.9 | 2.8 | 2.7 | 2.5 | 2.5 | 2.5 | 2.5 | 2.5 | 2.4 | 2.4 | 2.4 | 2.5 | 2.5 | 2.4 | 2.5 | 2.5 | 2.7 | 2.5 |
| 2009 | 2.9 | 3.0 | 2.9 | 2.8 | 2.7 | 2.6 | 2.5 | 2.5 | 2.5 | 2.5 | 2.5 | 2.5 | 2.5 | 2.5 | 2.5 | 2.4 | 2.5 | 2.6 | 2.7 | 2.6 |
| 2010 | 2.8 | 2.9 | 2.8 | 2.8 | 2.7 | 2.5 | 2.4 | 2.4 | 2.4 | 2.4 | 2.4 | 2.4 | 2.4 | 2.5 | 2.4 | 2.3 | 2.4 | 2.4 | 2.5 | 2.4 |
| 2011 | 2.8 | 2.9 | 2.8 | 2.8 | 2.7 | 2.5 | 2.5 | 2.5 | 2.5 | 2.4 | 2.4 | 2.4 | 2.4 | 2.5 | 2.5 | 2.4 | 2.5 | 2.5 | 2.6 | 2.5 |
| 2012 | 2.8 | 2.9 | 2.8 | 2.7 | 2.6 | 2.5 | 2.5 | 2.4 | 2.4 | 2.4 | 2.4 | 2.3 | 2.4 | 2.4 | 2.4 | 2.3 | 2.4 | 2.4 | 2.5 | 2.5 |
| 2013 | 2.7 | 2.8 | 2.7 | 2.7 | 2.6 | 2.4 | 2.4 | 2.4 | 2.4 | 2.4 | 2.3 | 2.3 | 2.3 | 2.4 | 2.4 | 2.3 | 2.3 | 2.3 | 2.4 | 2.3 |
| 2014 | 2.7 | 2.7 | 2.7 | 2.6 | 2.6 | 2.4 | 2.3 | 2.3 | 2.3 | 2.3 | 2.3 | 2.3 | 2.2 | 2.4 | 2.4 | 2.2 | 2.3 | 2.2 | 2.2 | 2.1 |
| 2015 | 2.6 | 2.7 | 2.6 | 2.5 | 2.4 | 2.3 | 2.3 | 2.2 | 2.3 | 2.2 | 2.2 | 2.1 | 2.1 | 2.3 | 2.2 | 2.1 | 2.2 | 2.1 | 2.1 | 2.0 |
| 2016 | 2.6 | 2.6 | 2.6 | 2.5 | 2.4 | 2.3 | 2.3 | 2.2 | 2.2 | 2.2 | 2.2 | 2.1 | 2.1 | 2.2 | 2.1 | 2.1 | 2.1 | 2.1 | 2.1 | 2.0 |

# Appendix C-7

Inflation: Percent per annum total returns for all historical periods

From 1926 to 2016

| End Date | Start Date 2006 | 2007 | 2008 | 2009 | 2010 | 2011 | 2012 | 2013 | 2014 | 2015 | 2016 |
|---|---|---|---|---|---|---|---|---|---|---|---|
| 2006 | 2.5 | | | | | | | | | | |
| 2007 | 3.3 | 4.1 | | | | | | | | | |
| 2008 | 2.2 | 2.1 | 0.1 | | | | | | | | |
| 2009 | 2.3 | 2.3 | 1.4 | 2.7 | | | | | | | |
| 2010 | 2.2 | 2.1 | 1.4 | 2.1 | 1.5 | | | | | | |
| 2011 | 2.3 | 2.3 | 1.8 | 2.4 | 2.2 | 3.0 | | | | | |
| 2012 | 2.2 | 2.2 | 1.8 | 2.2 | 2.1 | 2.3 | 1.7 | | | | |
| 2013 | 2.1 | 2.1 | 1.7 | 2.1 | 1.9 | 1.7 | 1.6 | 1.5 | | | |
| 2014 | 2.0 | 1.9 | 1.6 | 1.9 | 1.7 | 1.5 | 1.3 | 1.1 | 0.8 | | |
| 2015 | 1.9 | 1.8 | 1.5 | 1.7 | 1.5 | 1.2 | 1.0 | 0.7 | 0.7 | 0.7 | |
| 2016 | 1.9 | 1.8 | 1.6 | 1.7 | 1.6 | 1.6 | 1.4 | 1.3 | 1.2 | 1.4 | 2.1 |